The Hidden Hand

The Hidden Hand

Britain, America, and

Cold War Secret Intelligence

RICHARD J. ALDRICH

THE OVERLOOK PRESS
Woodstock & New York

First published in the United States in 2002 by
The Overlook Press, Peter Mayer Publishers, Inc.
Woodstock & New York

WOODSTOCK:
One Overlook Drive
Woodstock, NY 12498
www.overlookpress.com
[for individual orders, bulk and special sales, contact our Woodstock office]

NEW YORK:
141 Wooster Street
New York, NY 10012

∞ The paper used in this book meets the requirements for paper
permanence as described in the ANSI Z39.48-1992 standard.

Library of Congress Cataloging-in-Publication Data
Aldrich, Richard J.
The hidden hand : Britain, America, and Cold War secret intelligence / Richard J. Aldrich
p. cm.
Originally published: London : John Murray, 2001.
Includes bibliographical references and index.
1. Intelligence service—History—20th century. 2. United States. Central Intelligence
Agency. 3. Great Britain. Secret Intelligence Service. 4. Cold War. I. Title
JF1525.I6 A436 2002   327.1241'009'045—dc21   2002020648

Printed in the United States of America
ISBN 1-58567-274-2
FIRST EDITION
1 3 5 7 9 8 6 4 2

For Libby
(the real informative information)

Contents

Illustrations

The author and publishers would like to thank the following for permission to reproduce illustrations: Plates 1 and 2, Liddell Hart Centre for Military Archives, King's College, London; 3 and 28, National Portrait Gallery, London; 4, 5, 8, 10, 13, 14, 15, 16, 17, 20, 27, 31 and 32, United States National Archives; 6, 11, 12, 18, 19, 21, 22, 25, 26, 29 and 30, Imperial War Museum; 7, Mrs Katy Lethbridge; 9, Public Record Office; 23 and 24, Australian War Memorial. The cartoons that appear on pp. 130 and 395 are reproduced courtesy of the Public Records Office.

Abbreviations

A-2	US Air Force Intelligence
ABN	Anti-Bolshevik Nations
ACAS(I)	Assistant Chief of the Air Staff (Intelligence)
ACEN	Assembly of Captive European Nations
ACUE	American Committee for United Europe
AFCN	American Friends of the Captive Nations
AFL-CIO	American Federation of Labor-Congress of Industrial Organisations
AFO	Anti-Fascist Organisations [Burmese]
AFPFL	Anti-Fascist People's Freedom League [Burmese]
AFSA	Armed Forces Security Agency [American]
AFSS	Air Force Security Service [American]
AKEL	Greek Cypriot Communist Party
ASA	Army Security Agency [American]
ASIO	Australian Security Intelligence Organisation
ASIS	Australian Secret Intelligence Service
AVH	Hungarian Security Service
BfV	West German Security Service
BJ	Blue Jacket file for signals intelligence
BNA	Burmese National Army
BRIAM	British Advisory Mission Vietnam
BRUSA	Anglo-American signals intelligence agreement, 1943
BSCF	British Society for Cultural Freedom
'C'	Chief of the British Secret Intelligence Service (MI6)
CAB	Cabinet [British]
CAS	Chief of the Air Staff [British]
CAS (B)	Civil Affairs Service [Burmese]
CAT	Civil Air Transport [American]
CCF	Congress for Cultural Freedom
CCRAK	Combined Command, Reconnaissance Activities, Korea
CD	Chief of the Special Operations Executive [British]
CEP	Captured Enemy Personnel
CGT	French Trade Unions Council
CIA	Central Intelligence Agency [American]

CIC	Counter Intelligence Corps [American]
CID	Criminal Investigation Department or Division
CIG	Central Intelligence Group [American]
CIGS	Chief of the Imperial General Staff [British]
C in C	Commander in Chief
CIOS	Combined Intelligence Objectives Sub-committee
CNO	Chief of Naval Operations [American]
CNS	Chief of the Naval Staff [British]
COCOM	Western controls on trade with the Eastern bloc
comint	communications intelligence
comsec	communications security
COS	Chiefs of Staff [British]
Cosmic	a high level of NATO security clearance
CPGB	Communist Party of Great Britain
CRD	Cultural Relations Department of the Foreign Office
CRE	Central Reconnaissance Establishment [British]
CT	Communist Terrorist [Malayan]
CX	prefix for a report originating with SIS
DCI	Director of Central Intelligence, the head of the CIA
DFP	Directorate of Forward Plans [British]
DMI	Director of Military Intelligence
DNI	Director of Naval Intelligence
DoD	Department of Defence [American]
DP	Displaced Person
DSI	Director of Scientific Intelligence
DSO	Defence Security Officer (MI5)
EDC	European Defence Community
EEC	European Economic Community
elint	electronic intelligence
EOKA	Greek Cypriot guerrilla organisation
ESD 44	Economic Survey Detachment 44 [American]
EUCOM	European Command
EUSAK	Eighth US Army in Korea
FBI	Federal Bureau of Investigation [American]
FECOM	Far Eastern Command [American]
FLN	Front Libération National [Algerian]
FOIA	Freedom of Information Act [American]
Force 136	SOE in the Far East [British]
FORD	Foreign Office Research Department
FTUC	Free Trades Unions Committee
G-2	US Army Intelligence
GC&CS	Government Code and Cipher School
GCHQ	Government Communications Headquarters [British]
GLADIO	Western stay-behind organisation
GPU	Soviet secret service, 1917–26
GRU	Soviet Military Intelligence

GX	captured German aerial photography of the Soviet Union
HF/DF	High Frequency/Direction Finding
HMG	Her Majesty's Government
IB	Intelligence Bureau [Indian]
ICBM	intercontinental ballistic missile
IDC	Imperial Defence College
ID/CCG	Intelligence Division of Control Commission, Germany [British]
IFF	Identification Friend or Foe
IRD	Information Research Department of the Foreign Office
ISLD	SIS in the wartime Middle East and Far East [British]
JARIC	Joint Air Reconnaissance Intelligence Centre [British]
JCC	Joint Concealment Centre [British]
JCS	Joint Chiefs of Staff [American]
JIB	Joint Intelligence Bureau [British]
JIC	Joint Intelligence Committee
JIC/FE	Joint Intelligence Committee, Far East [British]
JIC/ME	Joint Intelligence Committee, Middle East [British]
JSM	Joint Services Mission, Washington [British]
JS/TIC	Joint Scientific and Technical Intelligence Committees [British]
KGB	Soviet secret service, 1954–91
KLO	Korean Labor Organisation
KMAG	Korean Military Advisory Group [American]
KMT	Kuomintang, Chinese nationalist party
KPD	German Communist Party
LCESA	London Communications–Electronics Security Agency [British]
LCS	London Controlling Section [British]
LIO	Labor Information Officer [American]
LRDG	Long Range Desert Group [British]
LSIB	London Signals Intelligence Board [British]
LSIC	London Signals Intelligence Committee [British]
MCP	Malayan Communist Party
MGB	Soviet secret service, 1946–53
MI5	Security Service [British]
MI6	Secret Intelligence Service (also SIS) [British]
MiG	Mikoyan – Soviet fighter aircraft
MLO	Military Liaison Officer, Malaya [British]
MNLA	Malayan National Liberation Army
MoD	Ministry of Defence
MoMA	Museum of Modern Art in New York
MPAJA	Malayan People's Anti-Japanese Army
MRBM	medium-range ballistic missile
MSS	Malayan Security Service
MVD	Soviet secret service, 1953–4
NATO	North Atlantic Treaty Organisation

NEABS	Near Eastern Broadcasting Station
NID	Naval Intelligence Division [British]
NIE	National Intelligence Estimate [American]
NKGB	Soviet secret service, 1943–6
NKVD	Soviet secret service, 1934–43
NSA	National Security Agency [American]
NSC	National Security Council [American]
NSG	Naval Security Group [American]
NUS	National Union of Students [British]
NVDA	National Volunteer Defence Army [Tibetan]
OAS	Organisation Armée Secrète, the anti-Gaullist rebels in Algeria
OB	order of battle
OCB	Operation Co-ordination Board [American]
OEEC	Organisation for European Economic Co-operation
OGPU	Soviet secret service, 1926–34
ONI	Office of Naval Intelligence [American]
OPC	Office of Policy Co-ordination [American]
OPS	Overseas Planning Section, part of PUSD [British]
OSO	Office of Special Operations of the CIA [American]
OSO–DoD	Office of Special Operations, Department of Defense [American]
OSS	Office of Strategic Services [American]
OUN	Ukrainian nationalist organisation
PFIAB	President's Foreign Intelligence Advisory Board [American]
PHP	Post Hostilities Planners [British]
PKI	Indonesian Communist Party
PLA	People's Liberation Army [Chinese]
PPS	Policy Planning Staff [American]
PRC	People's Republic of China
PRU	Photographic Reconnaissance Unit
PSB	Psychological Strategy Board
PUSC	Permanent Under-Secretary's Committee [British]
PUSD	Permanent Under-Secretary's Department [British]
PV	positive vetting
PWE	Political Warfare Executive [British]
R5	Requirements 5 section of SIS dealing with the Soviet Union
RAAF	Royal Australian Air Force
RCMP	Royal Canadian Mounted Police
RFE	Radio Free Europe
ROK	Republic of Korea
RS	Requirements Section of SIS [British]
SAM	surface-to-air missile
SAS	Special Air Service [British]
Savak	Iranian Security Service
SB	Special Branch [British]
SCAP	Supreme Commander Allied Powers [MacArthur]

SCIU	Special Counter Intelligence Unit [Allied]
SD	State Department [American]
SDECE	French intelligence service
SEAC	South East Asia Command [Allied]
SEATO	South East Asia Treaty Organisation
SEP	surrendered enemy personnel
SHAEF	Supreme Headquarters Allied Expeditionary Force
SHAPE	Supreme Headquarters Allied Powers Europe
SI	Secret Intelligence
SIB	Security Intelligence Bureau proposed for South Vietnam
SIFE	Security Intelligence Far East (MI5) [British]
sigint	signals intelligence
SIME	Security Intelligence Middle East (MI5/SI) [British]
SIS	Secret Intelligence Service (also MI6) [British]
SOE	Special Operations Executive [British]
SSU	Strategic Services Unit, residue of OSS [American]
STIB	Scientific and Technical Intelligence Bureau of ID/CCG
SWPA	South West Pacific Area [Allied]
T	Treasury [British]
TCS	SIS section for scientific intelligence
T Force	scientific and technical intelligence unit in Germany
TICOM	Target Intelligence Committee dealing with signals intelligence
TRIC	Technical Radio Interception Committee [British]
Typex	British rotor cryptograph
UB	Polish security service
UKUSA	UK–USA signals intelligence agreements, 1948
Ultra	British classification for signals intelligence
UPA	Ukrainian nationalist guerrilla organisation
USCIB	US Communications Intelligence Board
USIS	US Information Service
V-2	German ballistic missile
VHB	very heavy bomber
VISTRE	Visual Inter-Service Training and Research Establishment [British]
VOA	Voice of America
WAY	World Assembly of Youth
WFDY	World Federation of Democratic Youth
WIN	Polish resistance organisation
W/T	wireless telegraphy
X-2	Counter-intelligence branch of OSS
Y	wireless interception, usually low-level

Historians of Secret Service
and their Enemies

It is imperative that the fact that such intelligence was available should NEVER be disclosed.

British Chiefs of Staff, 31 July 1945[1]

The story of modern secret service offers us a clear warning. Governments are not only adept at hiding substantial secrets, they are quick to offer their own carefully packaged versions of the past. The end of the Second World War was quickly followed by a litany of secret service stories, often concerning the Special Operations Executive or SOE, Britain's wartime sabotage organisation, which suggested that now that the war was over its stories of clandestine activity could be told. Innumerable figures who had worked with SOE or its American sister service, the Office of Strategic Services, sat down to write their memoirs. This was misleading since some of the most important aspects of the conflict with Germany remained hidden. Only in the early 1970s, three decades after the end of the war, did the story of Ultra and Bletchley Park – the effort which defeated the German Enigma cipher machine – burst upon a surprised world. Thereafter much of the strategic history of the Second World War had to be rewritten. One of its most important aspects, the fact that the intentions of the Axis had been largely transparent to the Allies, had been methodically airbrushed from thirty years of historical writing.

This was a carefully orchestrated process. Before the end of the war, Britain's most senior intelligence official, Victor Cavendish-Bentinck, cousin of the Duke of Portland and Chairman of the Joint Intelligence Committee or JIC, turned his mind to the problem of the management of the past. British records were certainly not a threat. Many would be burned at the end of the war and others could remain under lock and key for decades. But unfortunately, in the summer of 1944, with the invasion of France under way, Italian, Japanese and German records were spilling out into the open from embassies and headquarters in the chaos of Axis retreat. Initially this haemorrhage of enemy secret papers did not seem to worry him:

> I expect that all we will need do will be to send half a dozen people out to see that the right archives are being sealed and placed under guard and that proper security measures are taken, after which it will probably be necessary to have one person keeping an eye on this business who could go round from time to time and see that the proper security measures are being taken and that our interests are being looked after until the research students and historians get to work on a job that will probably occupy the rest of their lives or the period until the next war, whichever may be the shortest.[2]

But his complacency was short lived. Gradually, it dawned on the authorities that some of the most hidden aspects of the war were now in danger of seeping into the public domain. If Allied and Axis materials were compared side by side, then some of the innermost secrets of the war – the successes of Ultra and the remarkable efforts of secret deception teams that helped to mask the D-Day invasion – might soon be revealed.

GCHQ, the new post-war name given to the organisation based at Bletchley Park, was foremost in pressing for the tightest secrecy. The breaking of enemy codes and ciphers, known as signals intelligence or sigint, was, in its view, best hidden for ever. The mysteries of sigint had to be carefully protected for use against 'future enemies', who were already massing on the horizon in 1945. There were also potential problems with the German acceptance of defeat. GCHQ argued that, if it became known that the Allies had been using Ultra to read Hitler's Enigma communications, the Germans were likely to use it as an excuse to say that they were 'not well and fairly beaten'. The dangerous but attractive myths of 'defeat by betrayal' that had circulated in Germany after 1918 might surface once more.[3]

By July 1945 the London Signals Intelligence Board, Britain's highest sigint authority, had convened a special committee to examine the problem of how to handle history and historians. They were the first to suggest what became the standard Whitehall remedy. Simply to lock these secrets up was not enough and positive information-control was probably required. The public would soon demand a detailed and authoritative narrative of the war and something substantial had to be put in place. First, official historians should be recruited and indoctrinated into Ultra and then ordered not to 'betray' it in their writings. Secondly, a further body had to be created to review their work and also to sanitise the memoirs of senior figures.[4]

Strategic deception was also a hot subject which the secret services wished to see hidden for ever. Sir David Petrie, the head of MI5, kept various Allied neutrals who knew too much, including Spaniards and Swedes, in detention and incommunicado from their embassies beyond the end of the war in Europe. This was to gain time to figure out how MI5 could seal the secret of the Allied manipulation of the German secret service, the Abwehr, as a conduit for British deception.[5] A detailed history of deception was written by Roger Hesketh, an experienced deception planner, but this was for in-house consultation by those who were tasked to keep the art of strategic deception alive for future contingencies. No mention of deception and the turning of German agents by MI5 was permitted in the public history that emerged prior to 1972.[6]

By the end of July 1945 the leading lights of British intelligence were increasingly worried about the complexity of the history problem. They were beginning to recognise the scale of the project before them. Large areas of the past would have to be controlled if important secret methods were to be protected and embarrassments avoided. It would need a concerted programme for the management of history equivalent to a wartime deception operation itself. The problem was passed to the Joint Intelligence Committee. On the last day of July 1945 the JIC considered the problem of 'The Use of Special Intelligence by Historians' and warned the Chiefs of Staff that these things 'should NEVER be disclosed'. But sealing this subject, even for a few years, seemed almost impossible. As GCHQ had already realised, when intelligent historians got busy, 'the comparing of the German and British documents is bound to arouse suspicion in their minds that we succeeded in reading the enemy ciphers'. What would tip them off was the speed of Allied reactions to Axis moves. London and Washington had based most of their strategy and operations upon masses of information that 'could not have been received from agents or other means slower than Special Intelligence'.

There was nothing for it but to 'indoctrinate' some historians into the secret and ask them to work with the authorities on official accounts in order to disguise it. The tens of thousands who worked on Ultra and deception would also have to be bound by an iron code of secrecy. Retiring Ministers, generals and diplomats would have to be exhorted to remove all mention of these things from their memoirs. Meanwhile the official history programme would become the last deception operation of the Second World War, with the objective of covering the tracks of sigint and of deception itself. These measures were quickly co-ordinated with the Americans.[7]

In March 1946 Colonel Wingate of the London Controlling Section, the main wartime deception centre, had achieved agreement with the Americans over the redrafting of Eisenhower's final report on the D-Day operation and the invasion of Europe in 1944 to avoid any reference to deception. London was appalled to see that deception had appeared in the first draft and the Chiefs of Staff were asked to make representations at a high level 'to stop the rot spreading any further'. The same group also had to get to work on the memoirs of Eisenhower's aide, Captain Harry Butcher, who eventually published *My Three Years with Eisenhower* in 1946, dealing with the General's time as Commander in Chief in Europe, but only after it had been toned down to suggest that deception was a minor matter at the tactical level, while all references to strategic deception were removed. London Controlling Section and its successors were requesting press restrictions in the 1950s and the 1960s to prevent any public mention of its wartime activities.[8]

Britain's top intelligence officials were pessimistic, believing that this elaborate scheme would not long survive sustained scrutiny. Any intelligent comparison of say, Field Marshal Erwin Rommel's moves in the Western Desert, with the response of his opponents, General Bernard Montgomery and the Eighth Army, would give the game away, pointing to a break in Axis communications traffic. But the JIC underestimated the power of positive information control. Official history, in many magisterial team-written volumes, together with authoritative memoirs and voluminous histories produced by leading figures such as Winston Churchill, constrained the conceptual horizons of an entire generation. The spell was not broken until 1972 when J. C. Masterman published his memoir *The Doublecross System*. Masterman was an Oxford don who had run the committee which controlled wartime deception operations. He managed to persuade Whitehall to relent on its secrecy partly because many of its inhabitants, and indeed the then Foreign Secretary Sir Alec Douglas-Home, had been taught by him at Oxford. The decision to allow publication was resisted by many in intelligence, including Sir Dick White, long-time head first of MI5 and then of SIS, but others in government felt that this was a necessary counterblast to the damage done to the reputation of secret service by figures such as Kim Philby. The *Doublecross* memoir was soon followed by Frederick Winterbotham's *Ultra Secret*, which began to tell the story of the codebreakers at Bletchley Park. In the event the historians had not detected these secret things and instead had been informed by the practitioners.[9]

Not everyone had been taken in. Six years after the war, Sir Herbert Butterfield issued a strident warning about official history. Well connected, but ultimately denied an opportunity to join the privileged ranks of the insiders who were writing the official histories of the war, Butterfield probably knew about the Ultra secret. Seemingly tipped off about what was afoot he said as much as he dared and warned, 'I must say that I do not personally believe that there is a government in Europe which wants the public to know the truth.' He then explained how the mechanisms of secrecy and government claims of 'openness' worked in tandem. 'Firstly, that governments try to press upon the historian the key to all the drawers but one, and are very anxious to spread the belief that this single one contains no secret of importance: secondly, that if the historian can only find out the thing which the government does not want him to know, he will lay his hands on something that is likely to be significant.' This exhortation echoes down the years as if written yesterday. It stands as a salutary warning to scholars working in the immediate wake of any major conflict who feed only upon material available in official archives. Government files that are allowed into the public domain are placed there by the authorities as the result of deliberate decisions. The danger is that those who work only on this controlled material may become something close to official historians, albeit once removed. There is a potential cost involved in researching in government-managed archives where the collection of primary material is quick and convenient. Ultimately there is no historical free lunch.[10]

The Cold War dominated the international scene for half a century and it was against this backdrop that other aspects of world politics were played out. This prolonged conflict was pervasive, shaping all our lives and sublimating itself in unexpected places. Secret service is fundamental to any understanding of the Cold War. At the highest levels it was intelligence, especially very secret intelligence, that underpinned, even legitimated, so many policies launched in the conflict's name. At the lower levels it was the secret services that formed the front line. Cold War fighting, and a growing conviction that the Cold War could be won through special operations or covert action, was critical in determining the character of this struggle. By the early 1950s, operations to influence the world by unseen methods – the hidden hand – became ubiquitous and seemed to transform even everyday aspects of society into an extension of this battleground. The Cold War was fought, above all, by the intelligence services. Now that this conflict is over, a struggle is being waged to understand the role of the hidden hand and its work behind the scenes. This latter struggle has been an uneven one since the single historian, armed with a pencil, is pitted in adversarial contest against the efforts of the authorities.

At the end of the Cold War, as at the end of the Second World War, new and more sophisticated modes of control were required. Public commitment to openness moved in parallel with a range of activities which remained sensitive. Well-packaged programmes of document release have allowed governments to move beyond an old-fashioned 'stonewalling' approach to protecting government secrets into a new era in which the authorities set the agenda for archive-based researchers of secret service. The new openness that has been announced in London,

Washington and Moscow thus has an ambiguous quality. On the one hand, undeniably, it has brought forth many thousands of new documents, some of them fascinating and all previously classified. On the other hand, this often serves to cloak a more elaborate programme of information-management.[11] In Britain, for example, when fewer than a hundred files relating to MI5 activities during the First World War were released – all that seems to survive from the security activities of that period – the public reaction was not dismay but delight. Newspaper headlines claimed, 'MI5 thrills historians with secret service archives'. The climate of restriction in the 1980s had been so severe that these limited and tardy revelations generated excitement. The authorities were sensitive to this and put archival releases on secret service activities at the forefront of their claims to be embarking on a new era of openness.[12]

The scale of twentieth-century archives often overwhelms contemporary historians. The problem is particularly marked in the British and American national archives, which delineate the boundary between the private working files of Whitehall or Washington and what the authorities deem fit for public inspection. In London, for example, the authorities select about 2 per cent of Whitehall's records for permanent preservation and the rest are destroyed. But individual historians struggle even to examine the slivers that have been chosen for preservation. This problem of scale distracts us from the wider problems of the selection and destruction of records. Historians do contest with government over secrecy, but mostly these are tactical skirmishes. Arguments usually take place over the closure of individual documents located within the thin slice of material selected for preservation. Meanwhile the bulk of contemporary history heads towards the incinerators unseen and largely uncontested. Most historians are remarkably untroubled by this and some have come to think of the selected materials in the Public Record Office as an analogue of reality.

Contemporary historians who explore the state are quite unique. Nowhere else is the researcher confronted with evidence precisely managed by their subject. From astronomy to agriculture, from botany to the built environment, no investigator confronts information so deliberately preselected. Historians are what they eat and the convenient but unwholesome diet of processed food on offer in national archives has resulted in a flabby historical posture. Of course, the huge proportion of records not selected for preservation by officials are fairly unimportant and include materials such as the routine forms processed by social security offices. But within this vast programme of selection, declassification and destruction there is ample scope to massage the representation of the more secretive aspects of government.

The new openness is double edged and in some ways has served only to increase this problem. In April 1995 President Bill Clinton issued Executive Order 12958 requiring government agencies to release materials that were more than twenty-five years old, with few exceptions. Some parts of government had been tardy in this area and the US Army set out to discover exactly what archives of this vintage were still closed within its domain and now needed to be released. A dismayed survey team eventually reported that there were 296 million pages of documents awaiting declassification. The process was begun with the archivists and record managers dubbing this the 'assault on the mountain' in deliberate parody of the famous battle for Hamburger Hill during the Vietnam War, an event which was itself reinterpreted through the release of these new archives. So far 160 million pages of new US Army material have been released. The US Army is only one of many agencies involved in this process. The CIA has developed a high-tech Declassification Factory using digital technology to deal with its backlog, but with 93 million pages of documents exempted from Clinton's Executive Order, it has a mere 66 million pages to process. Alongside this laudable exercise in openness we also have to consider what may be hidden beneath these mountains of paper. There can be no doubt that some authorities have a curious view of accelerated declassification. In 1998 officials prepared a report on the 'Operations Security Impact on Declassification Management within the Department of Defense', for the US Assistant Secretary of Defense. They warned that 'Declassification decisions primarily need to be assessed in terms of value to adversarial organizations [rather than] public disclosure for the sake of openness.' It also suggested that 'interesting declassified material' such as information about the assassination of John F. Kennedy could be released and even posted on the Internet, as a 'diversion'. Newly released archives on such high-profile subjects could be used to 'reduce the unrestrained public appetite for "secrets" by providing good faith distraction material'. If investigative journalists and contemporary historians were absorbed with the vexatious, but rather tired, debates over the grassy knoll, they would not be busy probing into areas where they were unwelcome.[13]

Accordingly, a central contention of this book is that we do not yet know the full story of the Cold War, indeed we may never know. Substantial Cold War secret service archives have been released, but much more remains closed, while further material has disappeared in a whirl of organised destruction. In some respects this is quite proper. Secret services are worthless if they do not keep themselves hidden. Without a track record of intense secrecy, future agents will not dare to work for them. Secret services are defence forces fighting with information rather than weapons and a reputation for extreme secrecy is the most potent instrument in their armoury. Stripped of this, they become ineffective and their self-esteem plummets. There are few things more useless than a second-rate and demoralised secret service. Yet many researchers feel impelled to work to uncover these secrets. In countries such as Britain and the United States (but not France), secret services worked closely with the core executive during the Cold War. The nerve centres of government, such as the National Security Council and the Cabinet Office, were not only the focus of policy and planning, but were also intimately involved in the direction of the hidden hand. Therefore properly to understand the inner thoughts and purposes of those at the highest level, it is essential to consider the work of secret services. Historians of government are bound to find these things compelling and see it as one of their primary duties to uncover them. Accordingly, secret services will always enjoy an adversarial relationship with those on the outside who wish to study government

Efforts to manage historians have been at their least subtle in Moscow. Following the advent of *glasnost* in the East, visitors from the West have accessed Soviet materials with only limited success. There has been no general opening of the critical areas of KGB archives or Stalin's Secretariat. Moscow's archives policy has been highly manipulative. Only specific batches of documents have been released, often ripped from their archival context, and only selected historians have been given access to this material. Sometimes payments are demanded and sometimes a KGB co-author is imposed. Much more has been achieved by those who have worked with KGB officers who fled to the West, taking their memories with them and sometimes, quite remarkably, taking their archives as well.[14]

Glasnost in the West has been rather different and the management of secret service archives practised by government has been quite sophisticated. The declassification of documents has been both substantial and selective. Millions of pages of hitherto highly secret files have made their way to the archives, yet there has been a clear preference for certain types of material. The image that the authorities have been keen to project is of an 'enemy-led' activity. Ultimately, secret service activity appears more justifiable when directed against the totalitarian regimes of Nazi Germany or Stalin's Soviet Union during a period of total war or while confronted with the threat of total war. It seems more questionable when the hidden hand is directed towards Third World states, neutrals, allies or the citizens of one's own country.

The prevailing distortion is the result of omission. This follows the precedent of the hiding of Ultra and deception techniques after the Second World War. While archives, memoirs and most books offer us a reassuring 'enemy-led' view of secret services initiated to vanquish distasteful and illiberal foreign foes, the reality was different. The Western intelligence community – a network of co-operation between the secret services of developed states – began in the first decades of the twentieth century to trade surveillance material on agitators, subversives, labour activists, pacifists and anti-colonial nationalists. In many cases these were the troublesome elements among their own citizenry. Foreign intelligence, outside the context of active war, was a more difficult area of co-operation. Developed states have spent a great deal of time watching neutral and friendly states, even each other, rendering the process of co-operation more awkward. Many still held true to the familiar dictum that 'There are no friendly secret services, only the secret services of friendly states.'[15]

There can be no question but that the Anglo-American intelligence relationship has been uniquely close. More than half of the intelligence circulated in Western capitals during the twentieth century was gathered by a process of exchange with allied services, something of which even their political masters were not always aware. Yet a strand of deep ambiguity was injected by the uniquely 'global' experience of both Britain and the United States in the twentieth century. These two countries were closest because they alone shared the experience of managing a system of world power, albeit one in decline and one in the ascendant. Both came to understand that a global intelligence system was synonymous with successful management of empire, formal or informal. It was therefore entirely natural that, in mid-century, Britain encouraged the development of the American intelligence community, with a view to countering Germany, Japan and then the Soviet Union. Intelligence served to vanquish aggressive challengers to the Anglo-American pattern of dominance. Many who served in the CIA during the 1950s had been trained in secret service by instructors loaned by British organisations such as SOE and SIS and spoke of these organisations with some reverence.[16]

But intelligence has also served to increase tension among the Western powers. One facet of Anglo-American co-operation in the wider world was what Churchill called the 'changing of the guard', an orderly process in which British and American differences were put aside in pursuit of loftier objectives and the maintenance of world order. The second facet offers a picture of American intelligence as assisting a corporate foreign policy in the displacement of Britain in the wider world. These transatlantic tensions over business and empire were present throughout the twentieth century. But in the 1950s they were joined by anxieties of a new kind. British officials began to describe the American Cold War apparatus as a Frankenstein's monster which might precipitate some major crisis, often forgetting that it was London that had done so much to encourage the creation of this American apparatus only a decade earlier. Both these facets – co-operation and conflict – have their counterpart in reality. But official history and official archives tend to emphasise the first. The purpose of this study is to redress the balance and so here emphasis is placed upon the second.[17]

The hidden hand of secret service manifested itself everywhere in the first two decades of the Cold War and this book cannot hope to capture all its aspects. On one level it sets out to offer a different view of the clandestine Cold War that was waged by the West against the East. It seeks to escape the well-explored world of moles and mole-hunters, which has received so much emphasis, and instead to look at the regular work of British and American secret service officers engaged in other fascinating but neglected areas of the struggle against world communism. The Cold War involved a great deal of fighting by those who were frustrated by the straitjacket imposed by nuclear deterrence, rendering this conflict more dangerous than we have hitherto realised. This Cold War fighting began controversially in Central and Eastern Europe and then spread gradually to most areas of the underdeveloped world by the 1960s.[18]

Western secret services were also engaged in an awkward struggle of ally against ally. Britain's secret services were certainly less engaged with the Cold War than those of the United States. Instead they were busy containing a more elusive enemy, the decline of Britain as a world power. Set in these wider terms, neutral countries – even allies like the United States – could look threatening and sometimes received the attentions of Whitehall's hidden hand. Secret service organisations and covert propaganda agencies that were set up in 1947 as anti-Soviet did not remain solely anti-Soviet for very long. Instead they soon mutated to serve a much expanded purpose. 'Anti-anti-British' was their own compelling definition of this broader tasking. In other words, the new secret agencies of the post-war period were turned against all those who offered a potential threat to what remained of Britain's position in the world.[19] But the Cold War introduced a new sense of threat. The United States was now more than just an economic rival and political competitor. By the late 1940s it seemed to pose a military danger to Britain's continued existence. The US, together with a minority element in Britain, was showing signs of wishing to 'win' the Cold War before the Soviet Union achieved strategic parity with the West. By contrast most policy-makers in London sought a less challenging solution and were prepared to work for coexistence with Moscow. In December 1950 Sir Bill Slim, the Chief of the Imperial General Staff, returned from a visit to Washington and warned his fellow service chiefs that:

> The United States were convinced that war was inevitable, and that it was almost certain to take place within the next eighteen months; whereas we did not hold this view, and were still hopeful that war could be avoided. This attitude of the United States was dangerous because there was the possibility that

they might think that because war was inevitable, the sooner we got it over with the better, and we might as a result be dragged unnecessarily into World War III.[20]

Throughout the 1950s, Washington wished to press on with a forward policy, often by covert means, while London wished to apply the brakes. In April 1954, President Eisenhower eloquently expressed the American view of this intense controversy. The British, he complained, 'have a morbid obsession that any positive move on the part of the free world may bring upon us World War III'.[21]

Initially, Washington had been slower than London to engage with the Cold War, but by the 1950s it was making up for lost time. The urge to 'do something' about communism expressed itself through a programme of radio propaganda and 'liberation' activities. Between 1948 and 1950 these expanded rapidly, partly in response to pressure from the influential director of the Policy Planning Staff at the State Department, George Kennan. On 6 January 1949, Kennan wrote to Frank Wisner, who superintended American covert action, complaining that the operations he had planned for 1949–50 met only the minimum requirement. 'As the international situation develops, every day makes more evident the importance of the role which will have to be played by covert operations if our national interests are to be adequately protected.' London saw this as provocative and dangerous. By 1951, some believed that this was part of an American decision to set a target date for war, hoping to fight a preventative war while the United States still enjoyed military superiority. This resulted in a mercurial change in the nature of British thinking about threat assessment. American acceptance of the likelihood of war had become the main enemy, while the Soviets were seen as unpleasant yet comparatively cautious and predictable. After the outbreak of the Korean War in the summer of 1950 the British increasingly focused on containing the possibility of war, more than on containing communism. In practice that meant containing Washington and secret service was often at the forefront of this most awkward struggle.[22]

Washington shared London's ambiguous vision of its allies as troublesome, unpredictable and deserving of constant vigilance. The British and the French in Europe, the Israelis in the Middle East and the Nationalist Chinese in Taiwan often seemed duplicitous and vexatious associates. They were content to draw vast resources from the United States through generous assistance schemes, yet seemed to apply themselves only erratically to the main business of dealing with the Soviet Union. Washington did not hesitate to deploy its secret services to address this problem. London's determination to look to the past, to Empire and Commonwealth, rather than to look to a potential future as an integral part of Europe, was especially frustrating. George Kennan visited

London in 1949 and compared Britain in Europe to the place of New England in early America, inevitably submerging its political identity in a wider United States. Some leading American figures were infuriated by Britain's hesitant attitude towards European unity. The United States had poured billions into reconstruction and the encouragement of a strong and unified Western Europe through the Marshall Plan, the programme of American aid for European economic recovery, while Britain had agreed to support what was an explicitly federalist European scheme. Britain was alarmed when it realised that the United States sought a federal United States of Europe constructed in its own image. It led the resistance against the federalist Europe which Washington envisaged as the ideal bulwark against Soviet communism. In Britain, Labour and Conservative administrations alike truculently refused to move forward with ideas such as a European army, which the United States saw as critical to plans for German rearmament and the security of the West.

One of the most elaborate post-war CIA operations in Western Europe sought directly to undermine British foreign policy in this area. The CIA rescued the European Movement from bankruptcy, encouraged replacements for the anti-federalist British leadership and then financed a massive popular campaign to encourage support for unity among European youth. The CIA also covertly funded British groups, even Labour MPs, who would oppose British foreign policy on federalism. Hidden American funds were secretly offered to ardent British federalists who worked with the *Economist* in a campaign of influence designed to persuade key opinion-formers that a more positive line on Europe would pay dividends to British business.

This sort of activity was not an exception. Around the world Britain was perceived as old fashioned in its attempts to manage the Third World through a system of suggestible princes and pashas. By contrast the CIA actively promoted younger nationalist elements in areas like the Middle East, often middle-ranking military officers with political ambitions, who seemed to be both anti-communist and anti-British. Colonel Gamal Abdel Nasser, the Egyptian leader during the Suez Crisis, was a CIA protégé of the early 1950s. Nevertheless, British and American secret services were equally comfortable teaming up together against other allies, such as the French and the Belgians, or against mutually troublesome Third World neutrals. Secret service in this turbulent period often seemed an anarchic struggle of 'all against all'.

Lurking beneath the internecine struggle between the Western Allies was a further conflict that was no less awkward. Each 'national' intelligence community in the West was regularly convulsed by rancorous quarrels. This was most visible in the United States where, ironically, repeated attempts at centralisation only created further separate fiefdoms that fought bitterly over policy and resources. Responsibility for the direction of US covert operations before 1950 was vague. Immediately after the war such activities were carried out by a curious array of private bodies and also military organisations that had absorbed some remnants of the wartime OSS. After June 1948, however, the National Security Council decreed that such activities were superintended by Frank Wisner's Office of Policy Co-ordination (OPC), which was to carry out covert operations of the sort that 'if uncovered the United States Government can plausibly disclaim any responsibility for'. Curiously, Wisner received his orders from not one but three separate authorities. Although OPC came under the administrative umbrella of the CIA, it took its orders from the State Department and the National Security Council, which insisted that they would 'maintain a firm guiding hand'.[23] Here was a perfect recipe for infighting and confusion. As one OPC official remarked at the time, 'Divided or part authority never works. No person or agency can at the same time serve God (NSC), Mammon (State) and an Administrative and Financial Overlord (only), which the Director of CIA now is.' In 1950, the new Director of the CIA, Walter Bedell Smith, insisted that OPC be fully subordinated to the CIA, but such were the animosities that this uncomfortable process took years to complete. Moreover, this was the wrong decision and instead of taking covert action away from the State Department and placing it with a separate CIA, all of the CIA should have been placed under the State Department. The decisions reached at this time served only to decentralise the Washington system further.[24] In the 1950s American signals intelligence was similarly a byword for bitter division and pointless duplication. The 1960s American government spawned yet new intelligence agencies such as the Defense Intelligence Agency. Stupefied British officials in Vietnam remarked that there were more than a dozen American intelligence services camped out around the outskirts of Saigon and their competition was hard fought and bitter.[25]

British poverty prevented the lavish duplication and labyrinthine rivalries of the American intelligence system. But London's secret service struggles were sometimes more vicious precisely because the stakes were smaller. For a decade after 1945, Whitehall was locked in a prolonged struggle between hawks and doves over secret service approaches to the Soviets. Top military figures often sided with the Americans in wishing to accelerate the clandestine Cold War and indulge in Cold War fighting. Lord Tedder, Chief of the Air Staff, declared that he looked forward to the collapse of the Soviet Union within five years under the weight of these secret pressures. Field Marshal Bernard Montgomery, the first post-war Chief of the Imperial General Staff, called for 'an all out offensive by every available agency', while Air Marshal Sir John

Slessor advocated the use of every secret weapon and technique short of assassination.

Britain's Foreign Secretaries urged the diplomats to resist what they described as the 'fascist' tendencies of the military. Nor did they believe that the hidden hand of subversive warfare against Moscow would pay dividends. A bitter struggle developed between the diplomats and the military, first over how the Soviets should be viewed, and later over how far they should be deliberately subverted. The legacy of these internal battles was significant. We can trace the central architecture of the current British foreign policy-making machine to a struggle by the diplomats to prevent 'wild' military elements from taking over the direction of Britain's secret Cold War and to stop the creation of independent agencies capable of launching covert operations. For this reason all aspects of the British Secret Intelligence Service stayed very firmly under the control of the Foreign Office in a manner that was quite different to the position of the CIA in the United States.

These sorts of struggles – one Whitehall corridor against another – required the tightest secrecy of all. In 1946 Montgomery vented his fury in his private diary about the problems of communicating secretly with his fellow commanders in these matters. He wished to send extremely sensitive information, including 'red hot personal views on personalities', to senior officers in the Middle East. He had marked his telegrams 'very private' but to his 'great shock' he discovered that senior officials in Whitehall had the power to order the cipher branch to hand the messages over to senior officials and had done so. To his intense dismay some of his 'extremely outspoken and inflammatory material' had been doing the rounds. What were the options for really secure communications? If he committed it to SIS for transmission, what Montgomery called 'C's secret channel', it was certain that 'hot signals' would be shown privately to the Foreign Secretary 'which would be even worse'. He had wondered about some secure Cabinet Office channel, but this had to be 'written off' because it 'might well be open to the Prime Minister'. Ultimately the only safe conduit was 'by hand of officer' who had to be flown personally to the recipient in Middle East with the letter buttoned in his jacket pocket.[26]

These three vistas of secret service – East versus West, West versus West, and each Western state bitterly divided against itself – must somehow be reconciled. How, or indeed why, could the special intelligence relationship between Britain, the United States and other close Allies continue, indeed develop and grow, alongside these multiple acrimonies? A central purpose of this book is to explain the curious coexistence of these complex and seemingly contradictory struggles. The intense fragmentation of secret service into myriad compartments in all countries offers us some answers. The 'Western intelligence community' is a useful shorthand term, but it is often misleading. Most intelligence co-operation in the West took place in specific functional areas. The result was many separate Western intelligence communities specialising in subjects such as human intelligence, signals intelligence, photographic interpretation, domestic security and covert action. Many areas were extremely arcane and obscure, such as atomic intelligence-gathering from seismic sensing or intelligence derived from the undersea acoustic monitoring of submarine engines. Specialisation and fragmentation were increased by the rigid compartments and 'need to know' rules required for reasons of security. The result was loose federations of many groups, a myriad of patterns, rather than any coherent Western intelligence community.

These complex patterns rendered many aspects of Western intelligence co-operation peculiarly resilient. Co-operative links would often survive high-level disagreements over Cold War policy, or the revelations about the dramatic security failures and moles of the 1950s and 1960s. Thus the Suez Crisis of 1956 fractured some relationships, but other kinds of intelligence co-operation continued quite undisturbed. The notorious Kim Philby affair destroyed some aspects of the Anglo-American intelligence relationship, but other aspects continued quite untroubled by these dramatic revelations. The fissiparous nature of secret service, each component with its own concerns and networks, makes any generalisation about the overall mosaic of Western intelligence co-operation more difficult.

What follows is an attempt to begin to piece together some of this mosaic, but it is not an easy pattern to trace. The hidden hand assisted British and American policy in every area of the world and so the story must necessarily be fragmentary and uneven, requiring some diversions from the main throughfares of the Cold War narrative and some re-tracing of steps. The central purpose of this study, which arises out of more than ten years in the archives, is to 'say it with documents'. It seeks to provide the first well-documented and reliable account of post-war British secret service and its relations with its important American partners, from the moment of Hitler's breathtaking assault on the Soviet Union in June 1941 to the near-simultaneous departure of Macmillan and Kennedy at the end of 1963. The limitations of constructing such a story from archives controlled by the subject that one is studying, or their successors, are self-evident. Notwithstanding this, there are remarkable fragments of the story which have lain undiscovered in improbable places for more than fifty years. Since the end of the Cold War we have heard much about the historical treasures that have been released from the archives of Moscow and Beijing, and the new light that they have thrown upon the Cold War. But the greatest secrets may still remain locked within Western archives, and we do not yet know the real shape of British or American policy during the dramatic early post-war years. Here too new archives on a tremendous scale await us and new revelations are only just around the corner. Our best hope of completing this complex mosaic, and understanding how the West fought the Cold War, are aggressive and inquisitive historians who believe that there are no real secrets, only lazy researchers. When the vast pattern of Western Cold War is finally reconstructed, and when we can stand back and gaze upon it as a whole, at its very centre we are likely to find the hidden hand.[27]

PART I

From World War to Cold War
1941–1945

1

Fighting with the Russians

The habits of the Red Army are particularly worthy of mention ... Faeces were
everywhere. From baths to lift shafts to cupboards; from the Flying Control
Tower to the chairs in the Officers' Mess; and the Russians, both Officers and
men, were working and feeding in these surroundings. Lavatory pans were
filled, the seats put down and the seats themselves piled high. The Officers'
Mess in particular seemed to come in for especially liberal treatment ... Bugs
too were everywhere. And in places four or five D.D.T.ings were needed ...
Wing Commander George Keat, Austria, 1 October 1945

Wing Commander George Keat of the RAF encountered Soviets
forces for the first time in Austria on 1 October 1945. Germany
and Austria had been partitioned among the Allies and his task was to
take over control of Schwechat Airfield from the Red Army Air Force,
and report on what he found there. His first encounter with the front-
line reality of Soviet military power, the force that had crushed Hitler's
Reich, made a deep impression. He was simultaneously struck by its raw
power and by its filth and squalor. This was, he confessed, 'one of the
most disgusting experiences of my life'.

Face-to-face encounters of this very physical kind, often at quite a low
level, were critically important in shaping the outlook of Western intelligence upon the Soviet Union during the war. This was especially true for
secret service officers and for the military liaison staffs who enjoyed
extended contact with their Soviet counterparts, and even for diplomats,
incarcerated in their embassies. Physical experience filled a vacuum.
Lacking coherent evidence about the future pattern of Soviet behaviour
in world affairs – indeed confronted with a complete absence of serious
information about high-level Soviet thinking – they chose to report the
microcosm of their personal experiences on the ground. There was
large-scale intelligence exchange between East and West during the war
against the Axis, leading to some notable successes. Nevertheless, British
and American intelligence officers in Moscow, by and large, did not get
on well with their Soviet counterparts. The texture of this relationship

was characterised by abrasiveness and deep suspicion. This fed directly into secret service views of future Soviet behaviour in world affairs.

The views of Wing Commander Keat in Austria are symptomatic. The thoughts that welled up as a result of his experiences then flowed out into his prescriptions for how the Soviets should be treated. His recommendations capture a tidal wave of physical revulsion and deep suspicion that fed into Western thinking, particularly Western military thinking, after 1942. Recounting his Austrian exploits to London, he moved seamlessly from expositions on the backwardness of Soviet troops to generalisations about Soviet peoples and their barbaric character. Prescriptions about the need for steely toughness in any dealings with them followed naturally. Forces that lacked an efficient latrine system were more 'foreign' than the tidy Germans. Keat developed the idea of the Soviet soldier who was not only 'filthy' and 'scruffy' but also characterised by 'a dullness and stupidity of expression that is quite remarkable'. These were not urbane Europeans and so they required a quite different sort of treatment: 'They are peasants and should be regarded as such.'

Prescription quickly followed and Keat explained that 'if a firm hand is taken they respect it'. Indeed, he insisted that he had used this approach and had achieved results. If a robust demand is made, 'respectful acquiescence almost inevitably follows.' By contrast, he warned, the idea of building up a friendly relationship and developing a partnership based on amicability and deliberate bonhomie, which inspired some new Anglo-American wartime initiatives towards Moscow, was fruitless. Any attempt to ingratiate oneself with the Soviets, he said, 'is met with a contemptuous refusal'. The way to deal with this sort of organism was to draw a line in the sand – in a word, containment. Britain, he continued, should give the Soviets full credit for their supreme achievements in war, but should not condone 'their general filth and stupidity'. There should be 'no mincing of words'. 'Treat them', he exhorted, 'with the stern justice they themselves know and understand. This is no time, I have found, for appeasement.'[1]

Keat's missive was unexceptional. A vast wartime influx of sombre reports by intelligence and military liaison officers shaped a mental construct of the Soviet Union developing in London and Washington. On exactly the same day, 1 October 1945, the British Military Attaché in Poland was penning his thoughts on the new Soviet occupation and reflecting on the 'widespread murder, rape and loot by Russian troops so familiar to us here'. Again, high policy directed by Moscow was read from face-to-face encounters with barbaric acts perpetrated by what he called 'a primitive and largely Asiatic race'. Racial stereotypes suffused his thinking. Even making 'every allowance for semi-Orientals in a generally lower state', he confessed himself shocked by the 'dirty, ill-disciplined and lawless Russian soldiery'. The Soviets alarmed British representatives on the ground, not so much through the extent of newly established Soviet rule in Europe as through their barbaric behaviour.

The idea of containment arose naturally in response to the image of dangerous barbarians at the gates of a civilised Europe. But it also reflected a sense that it was a realistic objective. The Soviet forces were immense, but in 1945 they were in an 'extreme state of military exhaustion' and were also perceived as technologically inferior. These ground-level views percolated upwards and eventually distilled themselves as controversial intelligence reports circulating at Cabinet level in London and Washington. Among the military they reinforced hostile attitudes that had been established as early as 1918, when the West had supported the Whites against the Bolsheviks in the Russian civil war. Indeed, not a few of those compiling the reports were British and American veterans of the White Campaign. Others, like Captain Clanchy, wartime head of the Russian Section of Britain's Naval Intelligence – NID 16 – had witnessed the purges while an attaché in the 1930s and confessed himself already 'deeply disillusioned' by his previous experiences in Russia.[2]

More broadly, the massive wartime increase in co-operation and contact was critical in shaping views of the Soviet Union and how it should be dealt with. It was the military who enjoyed the majority of workaday contacts. These wartime experiences resulted in military views that were starkly different from those of the diplomats based in London and Washington, many of whom felt that the war had lowered the profile of communism and the Communist Party within the Soviet Union and rendered it a more 'normal' country. By contrast the diplomats saw cause for optimism and they believed this transition would continue after the war.

Cold War conceptions of the Soviets and of containment, eventually popularised by diplomats like George Kennan and Frank Roberts from late 1945 – who had also enjoyed prolonged personal contact with the Soviets – were already firmly accepted by the Western military as early as 1943, but less so by the diplomats. Thereafter controversy raged over the future behaviour of Stalin and his acolytes. During 1945 Stalin himself settled the dispute through palpable demonstrations of unpleasant behaviour in Eastern Europe, especially in the Soviet Zone of Germany. But, although a stern interpretation of Soviet ambitions was more widely accepted by the end of 1945, the division between diplomatic and military minds continued. Well into the 1950s, various camps in Whitehall and Washington fought their own Cold War for control of a conflict that was neither strictly military nor strictly political. The new bone of contention was whether to stop at containment or to try to roll back Soviet domination in Eastern Europe by all means short of open warfare, including a programme of resistance, subversion and psychological warfare. Some maverick individuals in the remnants of wartime secret services had already begun the first unauthorised steps in this enterprise by 1946.

The hostility of the military mind towards the Soviets was not new, and bad wartime experiences overlaid an already hostile predisposition. The West had been engaged in a low-level Cold War with the Soviets since 1917. Military officers and colonial policemen had played a leading role in a global struggle against Bolshevism and the work of the Comintern (the Soviet-controlled Communist International) which stretched through the inter-war period and was barely interrupted by the Second World War. It was accompanied by vitriolic propaganda and large-scale programmes of espionage and subversion by both sides. Indeed, both London and Washington were slow to recognise the rise of the Axis powers during the 1930s in part because their intelligence services were obsessed with the Bolshevik threat. In late 1941, British intelligence chiefs in India complained that they still could not get their subordinates to turn their eyes eastward to focus on the growing Japanese menace. They remained stubbornly fixated upon the North West Frontier and the 'old enemy' of Russia that threatened to set the Empire ablaze. Moscow represented double jeopardy. The 'odious' nature of Bolshevism, with its desire to subvert the social and political fabric of Empire, did not detract from suspicions of the Soviet Union as a rival imperial power.[3]

Moscow directed a highly organised campaign through the Comintern to seek control of communist and socialist organisations outside the Soviet Union, and to subvert those that eluded it. The still-controversial affair of the Zinoviev letter of 1924 – which tried to claim subversive links between Moscow and the British Labour Party – stood as testimony to fears of Moscow's attempt to manipulate the British left. More important was the highly effective campaign run by Willi Münzenberg to mobilise Western intellectuals and leading cultural figures in favour of Soviet objectives. Twenty years ahead of their opponents in the West, the Soviets recognised that the struggle between communism and capitalism would be more than a traditional conflict between states. Instead it would be a struggle between ideas, societies and ways of life, played out as much in the fields of trade unionism, literature and music as in the world inhabited by diplomats and the military. In this respect the Soviets invented the concept of the Cold War and were adept practitioners by the 1930s. However, the majority of the Soviet Union's secret service operations beyond its frontiers during the inter-war period were of a security policing variety. White Russian émigré communities across the world were penetrated and networks of anti-Soviet activity disrupted, often by bloody assassination.

The role of the British secret service was dictated by the accident of

Empire. The Soviet Union was effectively contained from the outset by a curtain of British colonies, or by states under strong British influence. From the Baltic states to the Balkans, from Turkey to India, areas of traditional intrigue with Czarist Russia now formed the front line in an espionage war which raged through the 1920s and 1930s. From remote areas such as Persia, local British intelligence officers cast their lines deep inside the Eurasian hinterland. In the early 1930s figures such as Leo Steveni, the British Military Attaché at Meshed, ran agents into Central Asian territories and interrogated refugees escaping from Stalin's southern rimlands. These efforts to monitor activities inside the Soviet Union were remarkably similar to those conducted from the British and American embassies in Teheran after 1945. Leo Steveni, who finished his career as regional head of the Secret Intelligence Service in Asia, was well equipped for these duties, for he had served with the Whites and acted as a liaison with Admiral Kolchak during the Russian civil war.[4]

MI5 and Special Branch units watched the work of communists in the colonies and their work was effective. Meticulous letter interception of coded communist communications in the Far East eventually led to the collapse of the Comintern in the Far East. In 1931 its entire archive was seized in the international settlement of Shanghai and key figures were arrested. Even Ho Chi Minh, leader of the Indochinese Communist Party, found himself imprisoned by the British in Hong Kong and only narrowly escaped extradition to the French, who wished to execute him. When the Comintern attempted the gradual revival of its networks within the colonies of Asia, the agent it chose for this work was himself in the employ of the British Special Branch. By the 1930s, even the Secretary General of the Malayan Communist Party, Lai Tek, was working for the British. Lai Tek had been deliberately inserted more than a decade before and his career advanced through the ranks of the MCP by the judicious arrest of his superiors.[5]

American officials were equally committed to the Cold War of the 1920s and the 1930s. Several red scares swept the United States in the early 1920s. Government intelligence and private detective agencies employed by industry worked together to try and negate Bolshevik influence within labour movements, while the nascent FBI took a strong interest. As in Britain, Army and Navy Intelligence adopted a leading role in the interwar surveillance of communists, collecting a vast amount of what they called 'negative intelligence', a euphemism for domestic political surveillance. In the late 1920s, the FBI and the American military strengthened links with a pre-existing network of Empire–Commonwealth security policing to form the first coherent 'Western intelligence community'. Surveillance records generated by Britain's MI5 and the Special Branch on suspected Soviet agents, fellow travellers and colonial agitators that no longer exist in Britain can nevertheless be read in US archives. This material underlines the origins of the Western intelligence community which lie, not so much in the exchange of intelligence on enemy states, as in swapping security information on their own citizens.[6]

This low-level inter-war conflict with the Soviets conditioned the attitudes of military, intelligence and police officials in the West. Limited and uncertain moves towards co-operation with the Soviets against the Axis during the mid-1930s were overshadowed by the Stalinist purges, which undermined faith in the Soviet armed forces. The purges alarmed even those well disposed towards Moscow, while in the Soviet Union they eliminated many interested in building bridges with the capitalist states. Even a hint of foreign associations could trigger denunciation, arrest and worse. Unsurprisingly, in the summer and early autumn of 1939, with war with Germany imminent, London and Paris still took their time about seeking an alliance with Moscow.[7] Indeed, between 1939 and 1941 London and Washington considered the Soviet Union to be effectively an ally of Germany. In Berlin, Joachim von Ribbentrop, Hitler's Foreign Minister, ardently pursued the idea of a four-power bloc, consisting of Germany, Italy, Japan and the Soviet Union, which would carve up the world between them. Ribbentrop, although not overly bright, was a practical man and believed in the idea of the 1939 Nazi–Soviet Pact, a common-sense network of military and economic agreements that also gave Stalin Eastern Poland and the Baltic states. However, Stalin did not share Ribbentrop's geo-strategic vision, any more than Hitler did, and both signed it to buy time. Like Chamberlain's Munich Agreement of the previous year, it was underpinned by a sense of unpreparedness for war and set against the background of a frantic race to rearm.[8]

Ribbentrop's four-power geo-political scheme struck fear into the hearts of British strategists, confronting them with the prospect of an unholy alliance dividing up the world between four revisionist powers. But for intelligence and security officers the near-enemy status accorded the Soviet Union was not an unwelcome development. It confirmed their suspicions, nurtured during the inter-war years, that the Soviets were the real enemy. Simultaneously the Nazi–Soviet Pact came close to causing the collapse of many Western communist parties. In the 1930s communist parties had launched broad anti-fascist fronts and had enjoyed bumper recruitment as a reward. But the new line from Moscow was all but inexplicable and the communist membership deserted in droves. MI5 and Special Branch found it easy to recruit disillusioned members willing to shed light on the bitter internal arguments developing within the Communist Party of Great Britain. Meanwhile, Soviet humiliation in the Winter War with Finland in 1940 ensured that there was a universally low regard for Soviet military power.[9]

By 1940 London was planning covert intervention against Moscow. Forerunners of the sabotage organisation in London, the Special Operations Executive or SOE, prepared for the sabotage of Soviet oil production. Meanwhile an elite group from the Coldstream Guards was undertaking ski training in the French Alps. Its members belonged to a secretive fifth battalion of the famous regiment, formed from volunteers specifically for despatch to fight as an 'International Brigade' in Finland. This move was halted only by the surprise Russo-Finnish armistice of March 1940. However, the Special Operations Executive continued to prepare exotic anti-Soviet schemes while British Military Intelligence looked at fomenting uprisings in Transcaucasia. Remarkably, in preparation, during March–April 1940 Britain undertook secret reconnaissance flights inside the Soviet Union to obtain intelligence on important targets. Britain came far closer to war with the Soviet Union than is commonly realised and it is the Anglo-Soviet alliance of 1942 that represents the aberration, not the onset of post-war anti-Soviet hostility.[10]

April 1941 brought dramatic change. Signals intelligence from the growing British effort against German high-grade ciphers based at Bletchley Park – known as Ultra – began to show something quite unexpected. German troops had begun to move away from the West to the borders of the Soviet Union. SIS had been receiving agent reports as early as April the previous year indicating that Germany was preparing to attack the Soviet Union but it was not believed in London. The idea that Hitler would fail to finish off his weak British opponents in the West and instead plunge into the Soviet hinterland seemed so implausible that even the firm evidence from Ultra was hard to believe. It was not until May 1941 that London fully accepted that Hitler intended an all out attack on Stalin, rather than merely presenting him with an ultimatum demanding more territory in Central Europe. Even on 31 May, the Permanent Under-Secretary at the Foreign Office Sir Alexander Cadogan still found it almost beyond belief. Although Stalin also refused to accept that a German attack was imminent, not everyone in Moscow suffered from myopia. On 18 June, four days before Hitler's Operation Barbarossa crashed down on the Soviet frontier, Sir Stafford Cripps, the British Ambassador, who had returned to Britain on a brief visit, and Ivan Maisky, the Soviet Ambassador to London, had a very frank and private talk about the future over lunch. Both of them knew what was coming. Cripps told Eden, 'He tried to persuade himself and me that they could hold the Germans, I don't think he succeeded in convincing himself, and he did nothing to convince me.'[11]

Stalin was not an ideal figure in the world of leaders as intelligence consumers. But there had been other problems. The Soviet agent networks in Germany had been badly damaged by the purges and those who had survived this process had been mercilessly hunted down by Hitler's security elements. Indeed some had endured a German concentration camp before being handed to the Soviets and placed in the Gulag as a result of the brief period of the Nazi–Soviet Pact which encouraged a trading of desired political prisoners. Moreover it is likely that German Enigma messages and also the German one-time pad system remained beyond the capabilities of the cipher specialists in the NKVD, the Soviet secret service.[12]

Hitler's impending Operation Barbarossa brought with it the difficult issue of intelligence co-operation with new allies in Moscow. Churchill's decision to pass Ultra-derived information about Hitler's plans to the Soviets required him to disguise its source. When he instructed Cripps to hand over intelligence about German armoured formations redeployed to the East, it was described as having come from a human spy. Unfortunately, this ruse also fooled Cripps, who did not appreciate the critical importance of the information. He decided not to bother Stalin personally and handed it a Soviet junior minister. If the message ever reached Stalin, no response was forthcoming. Churchill was furious with Cripps. But Stalin would certainly have regarded any warning from London with suspicion. Logically, London had everything to gain and nothing to lose by trying to draw the Soviets into a war with Germany, so Stalin suspected a plot. Matters were not helped by Stalin's intense personal distrust of Churchill.[13]

Stalin was equally stubborn in refusing to believe strident warnings about the impending attack from neutral and communist sources. More than eighty separate warnings were rejected. Some of these pointers were quite unambiguous. Heinkel bombers, converted for photo-reconnaissance, had recently crashed well inside the Soviet Union with huge mapping cameras in their bomb-bays. They had been busy charting the future course of Hitler's Panzer armies in the East. But Stalin dismissed this as a German effort to give substance to what he thought would be a mere ultimatum. So rigid was his thinking that, when Soviet border troops relayed the news of the German invasion on 22 June 1941, he ordered them not to open fire. He was convinced that this must be some mistake by an over-eager local unit. When the true nature of the German assault became clear, he suffered mental paralysis, and retreated to his country dacha for seven days of complete isolation.[14]

London and Washington did not expect the Soviet Union to last long. In London, the highest intelligence authority, the Joint Intelligence Committee or JIC, predicted that the Soviet Union, weakened by Stalin's recent purges, would hold out for only eight to ten weeks against Hitler's crack units. Henry Stimson, the American Secretary of War, insisted that the Soviets would capitulate immediately. Nevertheless, it was decided to send a unit called 30 Military Mission to offer the Soviets every assistance, even if this contribution could serve only to make the presumed German victory in the East a little more costly. No secret service element joined 30 Military Mission, as London concluded that the only efficient part of Stalin's regime – the NKVD – would soon smell out any clandestine activity. The British Military Attaché in Moscow was instructed to begin handing over intelligence on the order of battle of the German forces. But its source – Ultra decrypts of German communications from Bletchley Park – continued to remain hidden, as it would do throughout the war.[15]

Hitler's attack on the Soviet Union in the summer of 1941 transformed what was essentially a European war into a world war, a process completed by Japan's surprise attack at Pearl Harbor later that year. A global war required global strategic intelligence, providing military forces with operational information at record speed. Expansion followed for the two kinds of intelligence-gathering that could provide intelligence quickly: signals intelligence and photo-reconnaissance. By the end of the war an estimated 30,000 people were involved in the highly secret business of Allied signals intelligence. This was the 'industrial revolution' in intelligence-gathering – hitherto a cottage industry – and this revolution would continue to gather pace into the 1950s and 1960s.

Wartime Axis communications were never completely penetrated by the West. But by 1941 the successful American attack upon Japanese diplomatic communications – known as Magic – and the British penetration by Ultra into growing amounts of German Enigma traffic transformed the nature of the war. In the West, the clearest window into the thinking of Adolf Hitler was provided not by Ultra but by the messages that 'Hitler's Japanese Confidant', the Japanese Ambassador in Berlin, sent back to Tokyo. The speed of this process was remarkable. At times these Axis telegrams could arrive on Churchill's or Roosevelt's desks before they reached their intended recipient. In a war of mobility, this was of critical importance. This kind of work was demanding and of the highest technical difficulty. Vast numbers of personnel were required. And so Britain and the United States were compelled to look more sympathetically at the idea of intelligence-sharing with allies, even in this super-sensitive area. In 1942 the British and the Americans signed the Holden Agreement, the first milestone in signals intelligence co-operation, heralding further treaties in 1943 and 1944, and the emergence of an elaborate new 'diplomacy of intelligence'. Britain signed these agreements on behalf of the Empire–Commonwealth, while other agreements and understandings had been reached with European Allies and neutral states.[16]

The important questions surrounding Western secret service and the

Soviet Union during wartime concern signals intelligence rather than human agents. For much of the inter-war period, Britain's codebreakers at the Government Code and Cypher School (GC&CS), SIS and MI5 had been more interested in the Soviet Union than in Germany or Japan. How did GC&CS, which ran Bletchley Park, guardian of Britain's most important wartime secrets, react to its new Soviet ally? The British official history of intelligence has declared that Britain stopped breaking Soviet communications traffic on 22 June 1941. But this is no more plausible than the contention that the British ceased work on American communications traffic after Pearl Harbor on 8 December 1941. Britain continued to intercept and break a certain amount of Soviet and American traffic during the war. In July 1941, sigint personnel in India were still working on Soviet material and showed no signs of winding down their activities. In London, the Soviet material under attack consisted mostly of Comintern traffic between agents in Eastern and Central Europe and their controllers in Moscow. This work was based not at Bletchley Park but in a secret central London location on the top floors of Berkeley Street. This was GC&CS's London diplomatic communications annexe, of which we still know remarkably little. Here, for the duration of the war, those on the top floors rubbed shoulders only with a select band of personnel working on the traffic of neutrals and Allies, including the American, Spanish and Free French.[17]

Despite Britain's continued efforts against some Soviet communications, Moscow's new Allied status introduced a different set of calculations. Now that the Soviets were joined in battle with Hitler's legions, it was in Britain's interest to see secure Soviet communications. Indeed this was imperative if London and Washington were going to give Moscow precious battle-winning intelligence derived from Ultra. They dared not allow this material to leak back to the Germans. Accordingly, on the very day that the Germans attacked, Britain sent a stark warning to Moscow about the insecurity of its military communications. Co-operation between GC&CS and the Finnish codebreakers during the Russo-Finnish Winter War had shown the ease with which Soviet messages were being broken. Such warnings to allies were not uncommon, and British and American signals intelligence chiefs were also struggling with the extreme insecurity of Chiang Kai-shek's armed forces in China. But this effort proved hopeless and their Chinese allies were soon taken 'out of the loop' for any sensitive Allied intelligence.[18]

By the autumn of 1941, London and Moscow were exchanging detailed estimates of the German order of battle. Each service intelligence branch in London was busy drawing up detailed information for its Soviet opposite numbers. But the guiding principle was only to provide information that was already in the hands of the Germans. This order was driven directly by what the British Director of Military Intelligence (DMI) called 'the insecurity of Russian ciphers'. Within days of Barbarossa, Churchill had held detailed consultations with the Chief of SIS, Sir Stewart Menzies, who was also responsible for Ultra distribution. Improbably, each individual item of Ultra given to the Soviets was to be personally approved by Churchill. Menzies set up a direct wireless link between SIS headquarters in Broadway Buildings, London and the SIS station in the British Embassy in Moscow. As early as 17 July 1941, Churchill and Menzies found themselves arguing over whether they should warn Moscow that the Fourth Panzer Army was about to surround large Soviet forces at Smolensk. Menzies was adamant they should not.[19]

Improvement in Soviet cipher security was essential if Moscow was to be offered more of the priceless dividends of Ultra, even in a disguised form. The main vehicle for this 'improvement' was the British 30 Military Mission in Moscow, which had begun to arrive by air within days of the German attack. In all but name, 30 Mission was a large intelligence station. The staff had been chosen for their deep knowledge of the Soviet Union and language skills which, perversely, meant many had served with the Whites during the civil war, or as attachés during the prickly 1920s. Some were from White émigré families, guaranteeing their impeccably anti-communist credentials. The Mission's chief, General Noel Mason-MacFarlane, had been head of intelligence for the British Expeditionary Force in France in 1939–40. 'Mason-Mac', as he was known, wondered what the perennially suspicious NKVD would make of such an improbable team. But in the event his robust character and love of amateur dramatics made him an ideal choice. He was well suited to the inexplicable delays, punctuated by acrimonious insults, that typified wartime intelligence relations with Moscow.[20]

Mason-Mac need not have worried about cutting an improbable figure in Moscow. Instead this role fell to the head of a parallel British SOE mission, intended to liaise with the NKVD on resistance and sabotage. The rotund and boisterous Brigadier George Hill was an extraordinary choice as leader. Not only had Hill been an active practitioner of clandestine activities against the Bolsheviks in the inter-war period, he had chosen to publicise his role in a well-known memoir. His deputy, Major Turkouski, was a Pole who hated Russians with a passion and loathed communism. Hill's twin saving graces were his ability to speak fluent Russian and his tremendous capacity to absorb alcohol.

Why had Hugh Dalton, the Minister responsible for SOE, chosen such a person? There were two reasons. First, although Dalton had an infinite range of sympathetic figures from the British left to choose from, it was already clear that such credentials cut no ice with the Soviets. Sir

Stafford Cripps had been picked on this basis, only to discover that the Soviets hated him all the more for being of the far left while not being strictly communist. Cripps represented the competition. At least with a good safe vigorous anti-Bolshevik like George Hill, SOE seemed to feel, everyone knew where they were. Moreover, Hill had the right personal attributes, he treated his hosts with unfailing courtesy and he had the stamina to deal with the incessant drinking bouts.[21]

Second, and more importantly, the activities of both Mason-Mac's 30 Mission and Hill's SOE Mission were determined by a shared belief in imminent Soviet collapse. In November 1941, London showed its hand and frankly told Moscow of its fears that the Soviet oilfields at Baku were about to fall into German hands. SOE even offered assistance in oilfield demolition and, remarkably, on 22 November, Stalin accepted. His lieutenant, Andrei Vyshinsky, allowed a British team, including members of SOE's 16(GR) subversion and sabotage group from the Middle East, to contact the NKVD at Baku and to make joint preparations to blow up the oilfields.[22]

This SOE group, eventually styled Mission 131, was warmly welcomed there by Merkulov, the deputy head of the NKVD, who had a fearsome reputation and had played a key role in the Katyn Wood massacre of 10,000 Polish officers in 1940. But, here in Baku, Merkulov proved an excellent host. The Mission's handbook on oilwell demolition was translated into Russian and a great deal of hospitality exchanged. By December 1941 the German advance had slowed, so demolition was postponed and some equipment was moved to safer areas. In London, Victor Cavendish-Bentinck, head of the JIC, complained about the British mania for offering the Soviets advice in areas in which they were already competent. But it could not be denied that SOE had scored a notable success with the Soviets where others had failed.[23]

SIS and SOE were also engaged in a degree of carcase-picking. In the short term, the Soviets, under severe pressure, seemed willing to receive material assistance from unexpected quarters. In the medium term, both SOE and SIS had extraordinary ambitions to inherit valuable NKVD agent networks on a global basis, once Moscow was overrun. SOE missions in far-flung places were told to prepare for this expected windfall. London ordered the SIS and SOE Mission at Singapore to develop closer relations with the NKVD, which had been supplying London with valuable intelligence on Axis schemes in Central Asia since the summer of 1941. Then, in September 1941, London asked the local heads of SOE and SIS at Singapore to receive jointly an NKVD liaison mission of five officers. By December 1941 the final details were under discussion at Kuibyshev, east of a besieged Moscow. London explained to Singapore that in the 'event of a collapse of the present regime in Russia there would be sufficient senior NKVD officials at key points in British territory who could continue to control and direct, for our purposes, NKVD agents in various parts of the world'. Ironically, it was Singapore that was soon to fall, while Moscow repelled its besiegers. On 25 December, the NKVD liaison mission was redirected to Rangoon, but this too was soon overrun.[24]

George Hill, head of the SOE Mission in Moscow, continued to be a hit with the Soviets beyond the convivial, but eventually abortive, Baku Mission. Fat, bald and garrulous, he was a great raconteur and played the game. After he had signed an agreement with the NKVD that offered assurance that they would not conduct active operations in each other's countries without clearance they began to co-operate. Hill secured permission from Menzies for NKVD agents to travel to England by sea for parachute insertion into Western Europe. This was not undertaken lightly, but after some animated discussion with Churchill it was agreed that these individuals would be brought to London and dropped by RAF Special Duties Squadrons. Churchill was probably swayed by the contents of the Iscott sigint traffic taken from the Comintern radio network which showed that Soviet undercover networks were genuinely working hard against the Axis all over Europe. Agents were dropped into the Balkans, Italy and France despite the protests of the French government in exile.

Hill's sense of duty knew few bounds. He further cemented his relationship with the Soviets by taking up with a girl from the NKVD. Who secured more information from whom as the result of this domestic alliance is a vexed question. Such amatory arrangements had been *de rigueur* for heads of SIS stations in Eastern Europe between the wars. Indeed, a string of such mistresses were kept on the books as 'agents' – by way of a back-door pension – and some were still being paid for past services rendered in the 1950s. However, Hill reportedly pushed back the boundaries of achievement for a British head of station in this field when he managed to persuade the Foreign Office to send him £20,000 worth of diamonds from Hatton Garden in order to persuade his mistress of the benefits of leaning towards the British camp. Understandably, Anthony Eden was uncomfortable about the possibility of having to account for this deployment of government funds.[25]

Hill was not an uncritical collaborator. Although he dutifully threw himself into the new alliance with gusto, privately he pressed caution on his superiors. In 1942 he warned that Colonel Ossipov, his NKVD partner, wanted to work with SOE in Turkey, Persia, the Balkans and Central Europe. 'Such co-operation', he warned, 'is full of dangers and at best would be very tricky.' SOE in London, he observed, was 'right in being sceptical' about its practicality, and 'right in instructing me to stall for the time being'. The green light awaited Anglo-Soviet talks on other issues. The Soviets had a clear long-term plan for Europe once Hitler was defeated, 'which our Government has certainly not'. He continued, 'What they ... want is, with our help, to infiltrate their agents into Central Europe, the Balkans, and in fact where ever they have difficulties ... to create Communist cells in order to establish Communist domination when the time becomes ripe. We must steer clear of such a trap. This is not going to be easy, as we have already agreed in principle to drop Soviet agents into enemy territory ...' Like his counterparts in 30 Military Mission, Hill actively disliked the Bolsheviks, but was clever enough to cultivate a relationship as required by London. He was also capable of standing back and taking the long-term view. None of the Allies, he conceded, was really fighting for the same aims in this war: 'Not even we and the United States'. Accordingly, even if SOE facilitated Soviet agent-insertion, the NKVD should not be allowed to get inside SOE. London, he advised, should at all costs avoid working with the NKVD on a deep 'inter-organisational basis'. However, officers working in SOE's Russian section using captured members of General Vlasov's Russian fascists nevertheless were suspicious of his close relations with Moscow.[26]

SOE in London needed no urging from Hill to obstruct the scope and scale of NKVD operations launched from England. Although a number of agents were despatched to Germany, Italy and France, perhaps a dozen, the programme was plagued by deliberate hesitation on both sides. The Soviets often sent poor-quality agents, seeming not to wish to trust their best people to the British conduit. London unearthed all sorts of communications and transport problems which caused delay and arguments. Some of the agents were not overly endowed with intelligence, and the codename for these agents, Pickaxes, may have been chosen intentionally to imply manual labourers. In 1944 SOE and the NKVD found themselves in a further dispute over London's plans to subvert Soviet citizens serving the Wehrmacht. This seemed a good idea on the face of it since by now one in eight soldiers fighting for Hitler was a former Soviet citizen. It was during the early phases of D-Day that SOE secured the surrender of thousands of Russians in German uniform in France, and forty were recruited into the SOE Russian section. But Moscow recoiled. On 15 May 1944 the SOE station in Moscow advised London that no more Pickaxes would be sent for despatch, and limited co-operation began to peter out.[27]

Hill's Army colleagues in 30 Military Mission were less creative in the area of Anglo-Soviet relations. Presuming that the Soviet Union would soon fall to German conquest they did not trouble to disguise their disdain for what they saw. The titanic clash between Hitler's experienced divisions and the poorly organised but determined Soviet defenders offered an extraordinary spectacle for these officers. The Soviets suffered astronomical casualties and lost vast territories. But by late 1941 critical German mistakes had revealed themselves that would eventually cost Hitler the war. The offensive had begun too late in 1941, because of problems in the Balkans that had diverted key German forces. The size of the Red Army had been greatly underestimated by Berlin. Finally, Hitler had decided to sweep south towards the oilfields of the Caucasus and the gateway to India, rather than seeking a decisive blow against Moscow. Even by August 1941 the previous predictions of the JIC in London that the Soviets would be an eight-week pushover were clearly quite wrong. By September, rain and mud were already slowing the German advance.[28]

The survival of the Soviet regime, albeit in a temporary location at Kuibyshev, slowed intelligence co-operation. By 1942 the Soviets were less desperate, and formal procedure began to reassert itself. Russian officials at Kuibyshev, and also the Russian Liaison Group under General Golikov that had arrived in London, were creatures of the purges. Obsessively secretive, they would do nothing without going through the wearisome formula of obtaining authority from a high level in Moscow. In London, Golikov did business with the British Army's 'Soviet specialists', which meant the hardened anti-communists in the War Office. The only exception was the Royal Navy, which commanded the respect of its Soviet equivalent and developed successful channels for exchanging detailed information on northern waters. Captain Alafuzov, a liaison officer to Britain's Admiral Miles in Moscow, regularly handed over intelligence on the Japanese and tried to help in battles with Soviet diplomats for visas for more British staff to be sent to Moscow. On one occasion in 1942 he greeted Miles with the words, 'Good morning, Admiral, I have to announce this morning a decisive victory over our common enemy ... [the] Soviet Ministry of Foreign Affairs.' But Alafuzov was careless with his comments and in May 1948 was arrested and tried for his pains. Worries about Ultra security continued to impede the flow from Britain. Mason-Mac was a gloomy commander for 30 Mission in Moscow. Increasingly beset by black moods, he was given to condemning his Soviet opposite numbers for being crooked, stupid and obstructive, and characterising them as 'terribly oriental and parochial'. Even his naval colleague and successor as head of the Mission, Admiral Miles, who enjoyed better personal relations, privately complained of having to deal with 'men of peasant stock disguised as officers'.[29]

Order of battle intelligence remained the highlight of co-operation. Intelligence items supplied by the British had proved crucial, including detailed information on German armoured formations during the battle for Moscow in late 1941. Away from the 'concentration camp' atmosphere that prevailed in Moscow, things were better. In early 1942, the

Royal Navy built on its convoy operation to Archangel in northern Russia and gained permission to open a station for intercepting low-grade wireless traffic known as 'Y' interception, and allocated it the comically transparent cover-name of Wye Cottage. The Soviets tolerated this sigint establishment because of their deep mutual concern for convoy protection. But despite British suspicions that Soviet naval cryptanalysts might also be reading high-grade German naval signals, the issue of Ultra could not be raised by British officers. Simultaneously, in Moscow, Edward Crankshaw, a British sigint expert from Bletchley Park, was reaching agreements with his Soviet opposite number, Major Tulbovitch, on Army and Air Force 'Y', and received a variety of German Army signals materials. Crankshaw, encouraged by these exchanges on 'Y', asked London whether he could move on to talk to the Soviets about Ultra, but the reply was a firm negative.[30]

American relations with the Soviets developed more slowly. Despite the best intentions of President Franklin D. Roosevelt and his special representative, the frail but animated Harry Hopkins, a familiar pattern could be detected. Colonel Ivan Yeaton, the American Military Attaché in Moscow, shared the anti-Bolshevik mentality of his British counterparts. He sent a continual stream of doom-laden messages, and evaded orders from American Military Intelligence in Washington (G-2), to exchange real information with the Soviets. His reports were full of upbeat news on the activities of the pro-German fifth column in the Ukraine, Georgia and the Baltic states. He was summarily removed in October 1941. American supplies were already beginning to flow, but an American military mission would not appear until 1943.[31]

The United States was increasingly conscious of being left behind, even by the modest standards of Anglo-Soviet intelligence exchanges. It was unaware of the limited discussions over 'Y' interception and also over subjects such as bacteriological warfare. But during the summer of 1942 Anglo-American 'turf' negotiations between OSS, SIS and SOE made it very clear that London wished to monopolise relations with the NKVD, and indeed over many other interesting areas, although eventually William J. Donovan, the head of OSS, would insist on sending his own mission to Moscow.[32] By 1943, as American–Soviet exchanges were growing as a result of Lend-Lease – Washington's programme of military supply assistance – American officials on the ground in Moscow began to express similar sentiments to their British counterparts, regarding unequal exchange, obstruction and 'stupidity'. But the US position was different. As the key volume manufacturer of military technology in the West, its hand was stronger. Both the American military and the State Department increasingly recommended that the United States should move towards a system of exchange that was based on *quid pro quo*.[33]

Mason-Mac's anti-Soviet activities were directly encouraged by Field Marshal Sir Alan Brooke, Chief of the Imperial General Staff, in London. In April 1942 the Foreign Office complained that Brooke 'is pressing General MacFarlane to be as inquisitive as possible'. This, it noted, was 'the exact opposite' of what Anthony Eden wanted. As early as September 1942 the diplomats had concluded that with the British military 'their main interest in supplies to the USSR is as a means of getting information'.[34] During 1942, the gloomy Mason-Mac was replaced by Admiral Miles, who in 1943 was in turn succeeded by General Sir Giffard Martel. Indeed there was a 'sweep out' of many of the senior officers in 30 Mission. Cripps, the British Ambassador, had tired of Martel's complaints and asked London to send veterans of the current war with combat experience. But experienced officers were not to be had and instead he was sent staff officers with inflated egos. Unfortunately 30 Mission remained consistently hostile to its hosts and Giffard Martel led the way. Like his predecessors, he viewed the Soviets as incomprehensible 'Asiatics'.[35]

Matters were made worse by problems with the limited Ultra that London offered the Soviets in a disguised form. Ultra had enabled London to detect Hitler's plans for a massive offensive planned for May 1943 on the eastern front. But British warnings were rendered ineffective by delays in the German schedule. New weapons had not yet arrived for what turned out to be the Führer's scheme to strike at Kursk in Operation Zitadelle, the largest tank battle of the Second World War. Only when new armour had arrived in early July did Hitler give the final order to attack. Some historians have suggested that Churchill decided not to pass full information to Moscow due to growing hostility. But this is not the case. Instead the failure of the Germans to keep to their own schedule drove British intelligence predictions off course and prompted the Soviets to complain about being given bad information.[36]

Late 1943 saw important changes in American military relations with the Soviets. An American military mission at last arrived in Moscow. This was led by Major-General John Deane, assisted by General Hoyt Vandenberg, the post-war commander of Central Intelligence Group, an organisation that preceded the CIA in 1946–7. This was a more benign American military presence, and at a higher level, than Moscow had previously seen. However, those with the most intense dislike of the Soviet Union, the former Military Attachés, now assumed prominence in Washington. General J. A. Michela had been assigned to the G-2 section dealing with the Soviet Union, while his predecessor Colonel Yeaton had taken over the section dealing with exchanges of technical information. At the top, General Clayton Bissell replaced General George Strong as head of G-2 in Washington. Bissell immediately began to stress the importance of gathering intelligence on the Soviet Army. All these figures, together with General Edwin Sibert, the US Army intelligence chief in Europe, embodied an attitude that was years ahead of other departments in Washington in identifying the Soviet Union as a future opponent. This attitude connected comfortably with military thinking in London.

All these streams now began to merge. Hitherto Britain and the United States had had separate patterns of intelligence-gathering in Moscow. In early February 1944, long-term Soviet experts in British and American Military Intelligence met in London for a remarkable two-week conference to compare their pictures of the Soviet Air Force and Soviet Army. These two groups even prepared a joint Anglo-American version of the Soviet order of battle. They also concluded a formal agreement to continue exchanging intelligence gathered on the Soviet armed forces and their progress on the eastern front. This agreement was drafted by the leading American and British exponents on the Soviet order of battle, Randolph Zander and Nicholas Ignatieff respectively. The principal source of information underpinning this agreement was material from Ultra decrypts of German radio traffic on the eastern front. This agreement of February 1944 was nothing short of a landmark treaty. It was not only the first Anglo-American 'Cold War' intelligence treaty, it also underlined the critical importance of Military Intelligence officers in marking the Soviets as the next enemy, to the dismay of the diplomats.

The diplomats were not supine in the face of growing military hostility. In early 1944, Anthony Eden finally tired of General Martel's tirades against the Soviets. Martel was recalled and yet another head of Britain's 30 Military Mission was despatched in the form of Eden's old friend Lieutenant-General 'Branco' Burrows. However, Burrows was another Soviet 'expert' who spoke fluent Russian and insisted on wearing his campaign medals from his service with the Whites in 1919 to the reception where he was presented to Joseph Stalin. Burrows chose to work closely with the new high-powered American co-operative Military Mission, which was now overtaking the British in terms of the intelligence it charmed from the Soviets. Unsurprisingly, by the summer of 1944 Stalin was already working for the removal of Burrows.[37]

In London and Washington, Military Intelligence figures returning from Moscow were hailed as 'experts' on the Soviet question. The evicted Giffard Martel was invited to air his views on the Soviets at British Chiefs of Staff meetings and urged a 'firm line'. His expositions only reinforced Brooke's intense suspicions about the Soviets. Diplomats had met with his successor, Burrows, before his departure and urged him to be generous, arguing that 'a policy of reprisals for its own sake would not pay', but Brooke and the DMI decided to ask the the JIC to look at the issue of 'reciprocity as regards information'. A struggle for control of the JIC view of the Soviets had already commenced. Cavendish-Bentinck observed, 'I have tried without success to impress upon my colleagues that the trouble lies mainly in the personalities of the Service representatives we have sent to Russia. This is one of the few cases where I feel sympathy with the Russian attitude. If I had had to deal with most of the Service representatives we have sent to Russia I should have difficulty in resisting an inclination to be obstructive and tiresome.'[38] Stalin took the same line. In late September 1944 he met with Sir Archibald Clark-Kerr and Averell Harriman, the British and American Ambassadors respectively. Stalin and his Foreign Minister Molotov both politely requested that Burrows, the new head of 30 Mission, be removed on the ground that he looked upon Soviet officers 'as savages and this hurt them'. Clark-Kerr, obviously embarrassed, suggested there had been a misunderstanding, but the Soviets were persistent: 'Here Stalin begged me to believe him for he was telling the truth.' A few days later Burrows was recalled and not replaced, for the diplomats were anxious to avoid further military representation of any kind in Moscow.[39]

Stalin and Molotov had hit upon a rich seam. Cultural and racial stereotypes served to distort Western intelligence on Soviet capabilities and intentions throughout the war and for many years thereafter. This idea of Russians as semi-oriental barbarian hordes reached its height during the last stages of the war, especially in Germany and Poland. A substantial proportion of the German population in the east committed suicide, rather than face the wrath of the Soviet forces as they made their way towards Berlin in early 1945. However, racial assumptions did not only apply to the Soviets and were endemic in the intelligence machines of wartime Whitehall and Washington. The extent to which this skewed both British and American intelligence about Japan in the 1930s and the 1940s is now extremely well documented. Ideas about the limited potential of 'orientals' were not the sole preserve of middle-ranking Army officers. Sir Alexander Cadogan, the senior official at the Foreign Office, described the Japanese in his diary as 'little yellow dwarf slaves'. During the war Roosevelt ordered a programme of research at the Smithsonian Institute which encouraged his own belief that the characteristics of races, such as intelligence or aggression, were determined by physiological features, especially skull shapes.[40]

Therefore, discussion about the Russians as 'semi-orientals' was important. Some asserted that Russian Europeanness was a mere façade behind which lurked 'oriental' characteristics, which were more peasant-like, ranging from a low cunning to extreme violence. There were attempts to typify the Slav as slow-thinking and dull. Slavs were often described as resistant to sustained activity, naturally disorganised and technologically incompetent – therefore quite the opposite of their German opponents. More importantly, it has been argued that the supposedly truculent nature of the Slav peasant was often employed to excuse Stalin's extreme methods in mobilising the Soviet population. The Gulag was repulsive, but arbitrary terror was thought necessary by some in the West to turn the war effort around in this very different land, marked out above all by human intractability.[41]

At some point during late 1943 or early 1944, Western signals intelligence priorities shifted dramatically, giving the Soviets much greater emphasis. Hitherto, London had been anxious to press the Soviets to improve their cipher security at every opportunity. But in April 1944 it suddenly decided not to tell the Soviets about the good results that the German Luftwaffe sigint organisation was achieving against the Soviet Air Force.[42] For some time Bletchley Park had been reading the Ultra key used by the Luftwaffe sigint organisation to send its material back to Berlin. Thus, for the rest of the war, its entire 'take' was also enjoyed by London. One result was superbly detailed and accurate intelligence reports on Soviet air power. 'Scooping' German sigint on the Soviets was a growing activity. By late 1944 the Royal Navy was also receiving top-secret Ultra material that gave it German Naval Intercept Service reports of Soviet units in northern waters.[43] Bletchley Park had been happily collecting Luftwaffe sigint traffic on the Soviet Union since the summer of 1942, if not before. By the end of the war the haul was vast and British Air Intelligence brought it all together at the end of 1945 in a survey called 'Soviet Air Force' and then produced a review of German intelligence work on the Russian Air Force order of battle, the latter running to more than 200 pages.[44]

Bletchley Park's successful effort to scoop German sigint on the Soviet Union had a direct effect on its own relations with Soviet sigint agencies. In 1945 it explained that 'the decision for co-operation on the part of the British authorities waxed and waned perpetually owing to the insecurity of Russian ciphers and the careless way in which their low grade ciphers were used for high grade secrets. Of this there was abundant evidence in the German Air Force Enigma traffic originated by the German Y service as studied by Hut 3 (3G).' Sigint exchange was increasingly hampered by different negotiating styles. The Soviets clearly enjoyed haggling over individual documents and bartered like rug-merchants, but the British found this tiresome. Bletchley Park complained that the Soviets' attitude was 'precisely that of a horse-dealer who enjoys the poste and riposte of a bargain' and their whole concept of intelligence exchange was 'on an eye for an eye basis'. GC&CS had hoped to open a range of intercept stations across the Soviet Union on the basis of swapping low-level

Luftwaffe codes. But in the event it only managed to open the one naval intercept station – Wye Cottage – developed at Polyarnoe.[45]

By early 1945, vast quantities of intelligence were available to the West on the Soviet armed forces. Sigint intercepts were now augmented by German prisoners who had previously fought on the eastern front. The British depended more heavily than ever upon their enemies for intelligence about their allies. By 29 June 1945, MI3c, the Military Intelligence section responsible for the Soviet Union, declared that almost all of its information on the Soviets had come from captured German documents, POWs and the German sigint effort. By contrast its allies in Moscow had given it almost nothing.[46] From the summer of 1944, other kinds of radio monitoring were in progress. Britain's propaganda agency, and sister organisation to SOE, the Political Warfare Executive, was busy compiling detailed reports on Soviet radio propaganda in Europe.[47]

The Soviets were known to be reading substantial quantities of British material. In 1941 the Foreign Office held an animated discussion about how to pass information to the Soviets by sleight of hand. One way was to send information to the Moscow Embassy in a British cipher that it knew the Soviets to be reading. But life was made more complex by the fact that the Soviets were aware that the British knew that this channel was being read, and so still might suspect that the information was being foisted upon them.[48] The various British missions also provided the Soviets with opportunities. In June 1944 the British needed to send eight new Typex enciphering machines to the senior British naval liaison officer, because the old ones were worn out. Typex was the main British high-grade cipher machine and the equivalent of the German Enigma machine. Moscow insisted that these Typex machines would 'have to be examined by the Soviet Customs Authorities', and this provided plenty of opportunity for detailed inspection by Soviet cryptographic experts. In addition, John Cairncross, who spent much of the war at Bletchley Park, was regularly handing material to the Soviets.[49]

In September 1944, despite a deteriorating climate in East–West relations, dramatic exchanges of secret intelligence were still possible. A notable example was co-operation against the key German secret weapon, the V-2 ballistic missile which threatened south-east England. Churchill specifically pressed Stalin for intelligence co-operation against the V-2. Stalin gave this immediate clearance and an Anglo-American missile intelligence team headed out to Moscow to join its Soviet counterparts. Together they visited the V-2 test site at Blizna in occupied Poland and then returned to Moscow. All this occurred before the first V-2 had landed in England. Despite a German scorched-earth policy, they had been able to identify the type of fuels being used and the peculiar launching mechanisms. The leaders of the British and American teams confessed themselves to be very pleased and the exchange of missile data continued into the autumn.[50]

The American OSS organisation, the remnants of which would become the CIA in 1947, developed only limited relations with the NKVD. The British, as we have seen, tried to monopolise such dealings at the outset. However, by the autumn of 1944 OSS launched a wave of operations into Central and South-eastern Europe just as the Soviet Army moved into these areas. These operations, authorised by the US Joint Chiefs of Staff, were designed not only to gather intelligence, but also to carry out political operations against the fading Nazi regimes in countries from Rumania to Hungary. Rounded up quickly by NKVD teams advancing with Soviet forces, they did nothing to reduce Soviet suspicions about OSS. Indeed a number of OSS and SOE missions into areas such as Poland and Rumania at the end of the war appear to have done little other than to alarm the local Soviet forces and enmesh local friendly elements in pointless trouble.[51]

Authoritative figures, such as General Marshall, the US Army Chief of Staff, made bold attempts to sustain co-operation. In 1945 the Soviets were given raw Magic decrypts of Japanese communications for the first time and were told of their source. This had a definite impact upon the Soviet leadership, who already knew a lot about Western signals intelligence achievements through the use of human agents. However, Marshall could not single-handedly reverse the decline in East–West confidence. By the end of 1944 almost all exchanges on the German order of battle, the main area of intelligence co-operation, had ceased. In April 1945, both Eden and Churchill confirmed that the military missions should adopt tough bartering tactics when dealing with the Soviets, and British and American intelligence officers inside the Soviet Union now had little liaison to do. Their attentions were now directed almost entirely to gathering information on the cities, airbases and ports around them. Unmistakably, this was target data for planning future air attacks. At the end of the war the JIC in London defined a new policy of exchange based on 'hard bargaining and reciprocity'.[52]

The hostile attitudes of intelligence in the West were partly fuelled by events in their own countries. British and American intelligence had not, in all cases, been required to travel to Moscow to meet up with their Soviet counterparts. Security services in Britain and the United States could not help but be aware that communist parties and the NKVD were busy in their own countries. Surveillance of the Communist Party of Great Britain continued from the inter-war period into the twilight period of the Nazi–Soviet Pact and the Phoney War. The most startling cases of Soviet espionage were uncovered during this period between 1939 and 1941. A Soviet spy was uncovered in the Cipher Department of the Foreign Office. John Herbert King had been suborned by NKVD agents of Dutch nationality and had handed over large quantities of telegraphic traffic and ciphers to the Soviets for money. This included conversations between Hitler and Sir Nevile Henderson, the British Ambassador in Berlin. It allowed Moscow detailed insight into the European developments at a critical moment. Careful comparison of the material that King had access to and the course of Moscow's foreign policy has shown how this directly improved the performance of Soviet diplomats in negotiations with London. Caught in 1939, King eventually received ten years' imprisonment. His case underlined the vulnerability of the British government to espionage conducted without the assistance of overt members of the Communist Party or even regular contact with the NKVD.

But these lessons were not learned. Instead, the focus continued to be upon what was seen as the classic pattern of activity based around obvious subversives. Welcome confirmation of this classic pattern was received by MI5 in 1943 in the form of the Douglas Frank Springhall case. Springhall was National Organiser of the Communist Party and used this position to recruit communist clerical staff, and even an Army officer, Captain Ormond Uren, to spy for the Soviets. Springhall and Uren both received long prison sentences. More importantly MI5 activity increasingly concentrated on Communist Party networks. The Springhall case was also welcomed by those in MI5 who had argued for a continued high level of surveillance against communists beyond June 1941, when the Soviets had become allies. This had been an awkward position to maintain at a time when the service's resources had been stretched by Axis activities and the need to supply MI5 officers to bolster Army security in a dozen locations around the world.[53] MI5 took a trenchantly anti-Soviet line throughout the war, maintaining heavy surveillance of Bolsheviks and repeatedly warning the Foreign Office that the Marxist–Leninist leopard had not 'changed its spots'. In 1942 Sir David Petrie, head of MI5, wrote to Cadogan and several other key figures about the dangers of the Anglo-Soviet Treaty of 1942. He enclosed an analysis by Roger Hollis, 'Head of the Division that Deals with Communism', setting out the case for a Soviet reversion to type once the war with Germany was safely moving towards victory.[54]

Sir Archibald Clark-Kerr, the ebullient British Ambassador who replaced Cripps, testified to this when recounting his first impressions in December 1942. In Moscow, he ventured, he felt he lived 'in a cage'. The NKVD helped to confirm this by providing a level of surveillance which was tangible. Only very occasionally did any individual dare to accept an invitation to meet him, and contacts were limited to rare meetings with senior Soviet officials. Clark-Kerr took his impossibly lively Airedale terrier on walkabouts in Moscow to break the ice, but though the citizenry loved the dog, they gave the Ambassador and his obvious NKVD entourage a wide berth. The difficulty in meeting ordinary individuals, or fathoming what they were really thinking, was 'largely due to the very thorough activities of the Moscow Secret Police'.[55] But Clark-Kerr could still make light of his predicament. In 1943 he compared his NKVD entourage with that of the Japanese Ambassador: 'Whereas I have to content myself with a meagre band of four guards, M. Sato gets eight.'[56]

2

A Cold War in Whitehall

This is very bad.

Anthony Eden, 23 August 1944[1]

Extended contact with the Soviets on the ground shaped the impressions of intelligence. This nurtured a pre-existing stereotype of Russian barbarians whose boorish behaviour was intolerable and with whom it was impossible to conduct sensible bargaining. Intelligence officers and military staffs in Moscow, like Mason-MacFarlane and Martel, denied much real information about wider Soviet foreign policy, drew conclusions from the microcosm of their own day-to-day experiences. These experiences were mostly bad and they filtered upwards into high-level strategic appreciations and intelligence estimates circulating among the military in London and in Washington.

But the military is ultimately a hierarchical organisation and impressions travel downwards more easily than they travel up. The tone was set at the top by senior service officers, who had sustained an anti-Soviet attitude for twenty years before the advent of prickly wartime contacts with individual Soviets. Field Marshal Sir Alan Brooke, the British wartime Chief of the Imperial General Staff, led this anti-Soviet tendency. He loathed what he called 'this semi-Asiatic race with innate bargaining instincts'. By 1943 he had concluded that the Soviets were bound to be the next enemy. At the time he blithely reassured the diplomats that any anti-Soviet thinking was merely routine contingency planning. But that same year he confided his real thoughts in his diary. The Soviet Union, he insisted, 'cannot fail to become the main threat in fifteen years from now. Therefore, foster Germany, gradually build her up and bring her into the Federation of Western Europe. Unfortunately all this must be done under the cloak of a holy alliance between England, Russia and America. Not an easy policy ...'[2] By 1944 Brooke's true feelings were an open secret in the War Office. Victor Cavendish-Bentinck, Chairman of the JIC, astutely observed that this had a profound effect on those around him. In the Army these negative attitudes trickled down the chain of command: 'If the upper hierarchy of the War Office are anti-Guatemalan, then gradually the humblest subaltern on Salisbury Plain will be convinced that the Guatemalans are the lowest of twirps.'[3]

British diplomats, especially those serving outside Moscow, developed an entirely different view of where the Soviets were going. Although negotiations with the Soviets were frequently awkward, many felt that there was a strong possibility of change. Some even forecast the long-term continuation of the decline of communism which had been seen within the Soviet Union during the war, and the prospect that it was gradually becoming a 'normal' country. By 1944 a bitter battle, focused on the JIC, was raging in Whitehall between the diplomats and the military over intelligence estimates that forecast future Soviet behaviour. This was provoked by intelligence questions about the 'basic assumptions' for post-war planning. Who, the planners asked, would be the next enemy? Radically different intelligence predictions about how the Soviets would behave after the war reflected divergent roles as well as different circumstances. British diplomats recognised that, ultimately, it was their task to maintain good relations with the Soviets. The bottom line for the military was to be ready to deal with matters should diplomatic relations ever break down, and breakdown, sooner or later, was what they expected.

The Whitehall battle over intelligence on the Soviets was long and bitter. It reflected not only different roles and responsibilities, but also the problems of shifting power. Whitehall had responded to the war by replicating itself. The Foreign Office itself had moved from having no more than a dozen cosy departments to having twenty-seven. All over London, new ministries and departments sprang into existence, dealing with things that government had hitherto left alone: food rationing, transport, propaganda, coalmining were all mobilised and regulated. Many of these new ministries had roles that impinged on British foreign policy and the diplomats were anxious not to lose control to the 'planners' of information, civil affairs, economic warfare and other strange activities. In a fierce conflict marked by resignations and recriminations, the diplomats hung on to core aspects of foreign policy by a whisker. This Cold War in Whitehall did not end with the arrival of the Japanese surrender in August 1945. Instead the tensions between military and diplomatic mindsets ran on for more than a decade. Intelligence and special operations were at the heart of this protracted struggle and, ultimately, this determined the very architecture of the British Cold War machine itself.

London diplomats had become accustomed to viewing Moscow as neither good nor bad, but as an irrelevance. During the inter-war period the Soviet Union had enjoyed a reputation for surly isolation. Although notably uncooperative it was also viewed as unproblematic. Intelligence agreed that the Red Army was weak from self-inflicted injuries – the drastic purges – carried out in the 1930s. Victims included many experienced middle-ranking Army officers who had been murdered in their hundreds. Accordingly the Soviets were thought incapable of harbouring anything more than defensive aims, perhaps erecting a security cordon that would allow them to protect socialism from German ambitions. In 1940, Sir Alexander Cadogan captured the mood, observing, 'I personally attach no importance whatever to Russia.' Moscow could do Britain little immediate harm or good.[4]

Accordingly, the Soviets could only represent a problem as part of an unholy alliance with the Axis powers. Between 1939 and 1941 there was indeed the possibility that the world would be divided between four snarling revisionists: Germany, Italy, Japan and the Soviet Union. This course of action – an unholy alliance – made geo-strategic sense and Ribbentrop, Hitler's Foreign Minister, pressed this idea on an unreceptive Führer throughout 1939 and 1940. In this period the Soviets were viewed as *de facto* allies of the Germans and, at a high level in the War Office, reams of strategic planning for a war against Russia were completed. Understandably, London's tentative search for an alliance with the Soviets before June 1941 lacked sincerity and suggested that any such deal would be a flimsy expedient.[5]

Operation Barbarossa, Hitler's attack on the Soviet Union, launched on 22 June 1941, changed everything. Transforming a series of regional conflicts into a genuine world war, this attack could be considered the fulcrum of the twentieth century. Initially it was not recognised as such. Senior figures in Whitehall and Washington suggested that the Soviets would only hold out for a matter of weeks. But, once it appeared that the Soviet Union would survive, British diplomats moved with surprising speed to embrace the idea that the Soviets would be important, benign and co-operative after the war.[6] This favourable view seemed to follow naturally from the unimaginable destruction inflicted by Germany on the Soviets. It seemed self-evident that Moscow would need a long period of post-war reconstruction, perhaps with Western assistance. A continued Grand Alliance – Britain, the United States and the Soviet Union – focused upon a proposed United Nations organisation, seemed the obvious way of securing a much needed breathing space for recovery. Even as late as 1944, Anthony Eden still seemed committed to this ideal of a co-operative Soviet Union. Post-war co-operation with Moscow, he stressed, would be the key to the long-term suppression of Germany.

The war also revised the image of Stalin. In the public mind he was mystically transformed by the newsreels from a malevolent creature into 'Good Old Uncle Joe'. The Red Army was shown triumphing in a hundred nameless battles on the eastern front and by 1944 a public atmosphere was created 'where criticism of the Soviet Union was tantamount to treason'. British diplomats were sensitive to the change in public mood. Even those who were not swept up by enthusiasm for the Soviet war effort believed that a genuine change had overtaken the Soviet leadership. Religion and nationalism had been allowed to revive. The Red Army had asserted itself as a force quite independent of the Party. Some British diplomats even talked airily about the Soviet abandonment of communism.[7]

The leading light among the British 'co-operators' was Christopher Warner. Warner took over the Northern Department of the Foreign Office in May 1941, a month before the launch of Operation Barbarossa. He knew nothing of the Soviet Union and had certainly never been there. He could not have formed a greater contrast to the cynical old Russia hands, the Military Intelligence veterans and Indian Army planners that now thronged the service departments and SIS. Warner was genuinely moved by the scale of the sacrifice by Russian forces that were now carrying on the fight against Hitler alone and he suspected that the Western Allies would not return to the continent for a long time. Meanwhile Churchill and Roosevelt had agreed on a Mediterranean sideshow, a decision that Stalin greeted with open disgust. Warner recognised the depth of distrust generated in Moscow by this Second Front issue. Early in December 1942 he warned his colleagues:

> You have here, I fear, constant fuel for the Soviet suspicion that we and the Americans in reality wish to see the Russians and the Germans bleed each other to the maximum and to shut the U.S.S.R. out of the post-war settlement as much as possible.
> This is clearly a serious matter ...[8]

This captured the Soviets' fears well; they had good reason to be anxious about attitudes in London and in Washington.

When Germany had first invaded the Soviet Union in June 1941, the United States was still not at war. At this moment an enterprising journalist had stopped an obscure senator from Independence, Missouri called Harry S. Truman on the steps of Capitol Hill and asked him how the United States should react to this new development in world politics. Truman responded with customary Mid-Western directness. Both regimes were nasty, he said, and so this new development represented an opportunity. The United States should help the weaker side, whichever it was, but only with a view to sustaining the conflict as long as possible. Ideally Hitler's Germany and Stalin's Soviet Union would grind each other to pieces. There were many among the British and American military who shared this cast of mind.[9]

By mid-1943, with no Second Front in sight, this was precisely how

Moscow saw Western thinking. There were plenty of indicators of growing Soviet hostility. In July 1943, Ivan Maisky, the Soviet Ambassador in London, was recalled and replaced by a relatively junior official, Feodor Gusev, previously Soviet Ambassador in Canada. Since he was only 38 years of age and had only one year of foreign service, this was a deliberate snub to London. During 1938–40 Gusev had been an underling in the part of the Soviet Foreign Ministry dealing with Britain and became its head when his former boss 'disappeared' in the purges. 'He then knew little English, took no initiative and had the appearance of having come from a collective farm after a short course of GPU training.' Gusev had indeed previously served in the GPU, the pre-war Soviet secret service. Cadogan dismissed him as 'stupid and inarticulate' and complained that his conversation was limited to saying 'How are you?' in a voice of thunder. Even Christopher Warner, a remorseless optimist, had to concede that all this looked 'rather sinister'. Orme Sargent, a Deputy Under-Secretary, thought it an alarming indication that the Soviets had 'made up their mind to plough a lonely furrow'. Anthony Eden also found it 'disquietening' but thought it would be unwise to refuse the appointment. Their determination to press on with 'co-operation' reflected fears that the Soviets would detach themselves from the united war effort.[10]

This dogged determination of the diplomats to cling to forecasts of post-war 'co-operation' with the Soviets has caused puzzlement in many quarters. How could any intelligent person remain so optimistic in the face of a mixture of calculated insults and deliberate barbarities on the part of the Soviets? How could anyone fail to notice the revealing shadow cast by their pre-war record of nefarious activities? Inevitably, perhaps, some have sought to explain optimism in terms of a semi-conspiracy, pointing to an influx into government of left-leaning intellectuals, such as Stafford Cripps, the first wartime Ambassador to Moscow. Naive efforts to secure a better relationship, they argue, were exploited by others who ranged from independently minded fellow travellers to full-blown Soviet agents. As we shall see, there can be no question that Cripps was exploited in this way.[11]

But the diplomats were not without evidence for a changing Soviet Union. Stalin had mobilised all of Soviet society, forcing him to reawaken ideas that had hitherto been unpalatable and appeal to a wider audience. This meant invoking pre-revolutionary Russian heroes and reviving religion. Great publicity was given to encouraging messages from the Patriarch of the Orthodox Church and even from Muslim religious leaders. A Council to assist 'Religious Cults' was suddenly set up, albeit 'largely drawn from the NKVD', which began to arrange for things such as the heating of churches in winter. Some saw this as the thawing of Soviet communism.[12] In any case, important wartime business remained to be conducted and negotiating complex post-war settlements seemed almost unthinkable without striving for a fairly friendly Moscow. Moreover, the diplomats had a trump card. They rightly identified the possibility that pessimism would serve as a self-fulfilling prophecy. Everyone accepted that the Soviets were over-sensitive and looked for slights. Anything other than open-handed co-operation was likely to result in disaster. Anti-Soviet intelligence estimates were bound to leak and aggravate the very problem they predicted. Optimism and efforts to broaden the dialogue on practical matters at least offered some hope of escape from the trap of perpetual confrontation.[13] Cadogan caught the attitude of most British diplomats at an early stage in the war: 'It is essential to treat the Russians as though we thought they were reasonable human beings. But as they are not in fact reasonable human beings, but dominated by an almost insane suspicion we have to combine this treatment with an infinite patience.'[14]

Standing like a rock against a tide of diplomatic optimism and patience was the owlish and bespectacled figure of Sir Alan Brooke, Chief of the Imperial General Staff. 'Brookie', as he was known to his contemporaries, epitomised military hostility to the Soviet Union. Bad personal relations between 30 Mission in Moscow and the Soviets ultimately darkened the picture, but Brooke already carried a gloomy vision from 1917. His deputy, Lieutenant-General Henry Pownall, also viewed his new Soviet allies with distaste. Indeed, on 29 June 1941, a week after the German attack, Pownall noted in his diary that he could not bring himself to refer to the Soviets as allies. They were, he said, 'a dirty lot of murdering thieves' and 'double-crossers of the deepest dye'. Like Harry S. Truman in Washington, he rejoiced to see Stalin and Hitler, 'the two biggest cutthroats in Europe', going for each other with vigour. The brigadiers and colonels in the War Office Directorates of Military Intelligence and Operations took their cue from Brooke and Pownall.[15]

In late 1941, when the fate of the Soviet Union hung in the balance, Christopher Warner visited a new Military Intelligence section dealing with the Soviet Union known as MI3c. He was appalled by what he found, declaring that this section was so 'anti-Russian as to be dangerous'. Warner was not alone. Cavendish-Bentinck also paid MI3c a visit. As head of the Foreign Office department that stayed in touch with the military – the Service Liaison Department – he liked his service colleagues. Nevertheless he found MI3c to be a very odd place: 'Whenever the Russians achieve some success or even succeed in stemming the German advance, these officers become plunged in gloom. A Russian defeat fills them with joy.' This was all the more alarming because the officers of MI3c were, in his opinion, moderately bright, which he considered uncharacteristic of British Military Intelligence.[16]

Brooke's deep-rooted hostility to the Soviet Union reached out beyond the service departments and affected the redirection of Britain's Secret Intelligence Service. It was no secret that the wartime head of SIS, Sir Stewart Menzies, a long-serving officer who had assumed command in 1939, was regarded as a dud. His main talent was bureaucratic manoeuvre and he used this to resist the wholesale reform of SIS throughout the war, a treatment that in fact it cried out for. Cadogan, the senior official in the Foreign Office, gave full rein to his dismay about Menzies in the early years of the war, complaining that he 'babbles and wanders' and needed to be replaced. Instead Foreign Office minders were attached to SIS to keep an eye on his lack of progress.[17]

Brooke also took a dim view of Menzies. In 1943 he tried to make SIS more responsive to service demands. This involved imposing yet more minders – three senior officers from the services – upon SIS as deputy directors. They would serve in SIS but their brief was to watch over service interests. These figures were little more effective than the SIS organisation they were benchmarking, but they allowed Brooke to feed his priorities into SIS. Brigadier E. H. L. Beddington was Brooke's choice as Army representative and both were clear that they loathed Menzies. Although moving from the Army to SIS, Beddington had his new terms of reference drafted to ensure he was not solely answerable to Menzies. Shortly after the arrival of this new military middle management in SIS, Menzies began to turn SIS attention away from the Axis powers to the Soviet Union. This deliberate shift was marked by the setting up of a new anti-Soviet section. After all, signals intelligence was providing the vast bulk of the war-winning operational intelligence against the Axis, so Menzies had spare capacity.[18]

By the end of the war the head of the new SIS anti-Soviet section was the rising star of SIS, Kim Philby, a long-term Soviet agent. His memoirs, although highly selective, are, like the best propaganda, largely accurate. Philby rightly observed that, for many veteran SIS officers, this new shift was a welcome return to the familiar enemy of the inter-war years: 'When the defeat of the Axis was in sight, SIS thinking reverted to its old and congenial channels; and a modest start was made by setting up a small section, known as Section IX, to study past records of Soviet and Communist activity.' As a stopgap an officer named Sam Curries, approaching retiring age, was imported from MI5 to get the section going. This seemingly unusual choice was not as strange as it first appeared. SIS and MI5 had worked with increasing closeness during the war. Moreover, MI5 had quietly kept up a steady stream of work on communists. Philby had spent the war in SIS counter-intelligence work and was a natural choice as his permanent successor.[19]

The main focus of sensitive work against the Soviets in Whitehall was

not SIS or MI5. Its heartland was the world of the future military planners. Whitehall had never liked planning, regarding it as 'crystal-ball
gazing', and Cadogan had successfully fought the creation of planning
bodies in the Foreign Office. Churchill was even more opposed.
Although in private he worried ceaselessly about post-war issues, and
especially about the Soviets, his approach was to put off such matters
until he judged the moment right. When, in 1942, he discovered that
some diplomats had been sounding out the Soviets on plans for the
future of Eastern Europe without consulting him, he was reported to
have 'emitted several vicious screams of rage'.[20]

But future strategic planning was unavoidable. With it came a clear
need for long-range intelligence on the Soviets, indeed on the shape of
the post-war world generally. Planners needed 'basic assumptions' to
work with. The trigger came as early as 1942 when an offer of post-war
bases from the Norwegian government in exile prompted the creation of
a small future planning body. Good staff were needed for wartime operational activities and so the members of this small group were variously
described as 'hopeless' or 'charming but rather deaf' or 'entirely out of
touch'. Cavendish-Bentinck saw them as nothing more than 'a figure of
fun'. He had no idea of the furores they and their successors would
unleash.[21]

By 1943 the bigger post-war issues were emerging and more dynamic
individuals were drafted in. The diplomats were keen to retain a grip on
this growth area. The 'sternest voice, and certainly the guiding hand',
they insisted, should be a diplomat. By late 1943 this group had been
remoulded as the Post Hostilities Planning Committee – or PHP – a
group of military officers chaired by a diplomat. Cavendish-Bentinck had
made no bones about his purpose, demanding the 'infiltration' of this
future-look committee. It was no accident that the diplomat Gladwyn
Jebb was chosen for the job. For the previous two years Jebb had been on
loan to the Special Operations Executive – the new sabotage and secret
army organisation – as its senior official. SOE was another odd body
with foreign policy pretensions that made the diplomats suspicious. Jebb
was no stranger to controversy, but even so he was surprised by the volatile nature of his new job.[22]

What these planners needed to get going were intelligence forecasts
on future Soviet policy. The JIC had little to go on, so instead it was given
vague and optimistic Foreign Office background briefs about the continuation of the Grand Alliance between the four main Allies, Britain, the
United States, China and the Soviet Union, together with the creation of
the United Nations and free and independent federations in Eastern
Europe. By the end of 1943 the military and the diplomats had begun to
get out of step on these basic intelligence assumptions. The Chiefs of

Staff, and Brooke in particular, told this committee privately that the idea of a future UN – the continuation of the wartime Grand Alliance – together running an international police force was a farce.

The Chiefs of Staff had already developed their own private intelligence appreciation of the post-war world. This was a fixed idea, unlikely to be shaken by any JIC appreciation, still less by the words of the diplomats. Gladwyn Jebb returned from prolonged and anxious discussion with Brooke and his circle to report what this idea was: 'It was pretty clear that the COS for their part did not accept the Four Power Thesis. They argued that what in practice was likely to happen was that the [Anglo-American] Combined Chiefs of Staff would continue in being; that the Russians would ... have their own security organisation; and that China was anyhow rather a joke.' These were prophetic words. They revealed the military not only as anti-Bolshevik but also as anti-idealist. In their eyes, the bedrock of world politics would always be the threat of military power or the use of force.[23]

The struggle in Whitehall over forecasting Soviet intentions was complex. The military enjoyed support among a few diplomats who had, like Washington's George Kennan, boasted detailed personal knowledge of real Soviet behaviour. Foremost was Sir Owen O'Malley, who had been British Minister in Budapest and was now British Ambassador to the Polish government in exile in London. O'Malley was dismissive of diplomatic colleagues who forecast that the Soviets would allow a free Central–Eastern European confederation after the war, deriding it as 'Alice in Wonderland'. He accused them of deliberately ignoring the 'sinister side' of Soviet policy. He was also disturbed by those who happily accepted the idea of Soviet predominance in some areas, predicting that it would bring untold misery rather than stability. As early as April 1943 he went on the offensive.

O'Malley saw this partly as a moral question, and he did not mince his words. 'At what cost in human values would not the sovietization of central and south-eastern Europe be achieved?' How could London contemplate 'the surrender to the cruel and heathenish tyranny of the Soviets of a large part of the heritage of Roman and Byzantine civilisation'? But his Foreign Office colleagues felt that to spotlight the embarrassing difficulties that lay ahead was merely unhelpful. O'Malley's intervention, although generating one of the first sustained debates about how assessments of future Soviet intentions might be made, was too hot to handle and it was not allowed to circulate around Whitehall.

O'Malley's critics were stung into action and were quick to develop a counter-charge. The military school of thinking about the Soviets, they replied, was rooted in racism. Gladwyn Jebb, who sat with the military planners on PHP, complained that stereotyped views could be found 'running through the whole passage'. O'Malley, he complained, saw the Russians as 'sub-human, Asiatic barbarians', while feeling that the Germans, 'though our enemies now, may at some future point become our allies ... Presumably we just sit down and prepare for a war with Russia.' On 10 May 1943, Jebb denounced the idea that the Soviets would take over Eastern Europe as quite implausible. Indulging in some stereotypes himself, he continued, 'Personally I don't believe the Russians have either the capacity or the inclination to absorb 110 million tempestuous sub-humans.'[24]

This clash between diplomatic and military mindsets was revealing. Those who took a pessimistic view tended to be those who had seen Soviet practices at first hand. Although such individuals could claim a realistic understanding of the texture of Soviet behaviour, this told them only how they would rule. It told them nothing about the extent of Soviet territorial ambitions. Yet diplomatic optimists could claim no greater knowledge of Soviet intentions and, like Jebb, were reduced to arguing that Soviet appetites would be limited by what they were practically capable of absorbing. In 1943 there was no solid intelligence on Stalin's intentions and both camps were arguing from profound ignorance.

In late 1943, the main future planning vehicle, the PHP, struggled to find consensus. Its members continued to talk of a co-operative Soviet Union, whose appetite would be limited by weakness and the need for ten years of rehabilitation.[25] But on 20 March 1944 this compromise was blown apart by the JIC in a forecast entitled 'Soviet Policy after the War'. The JIC removed the weak linchpin of consensus – long post-war recovery times – by arguing that the strategic heartland of the Soviet Union, now located safely behind the Urals, would not need rehabilitation. Reconstruction problems would apply only to those areas occupied by Germany, offering the prospect of a strong and confident Soviet Union.[26] The JIC had sounded the klaxon about Soviet capabilities, and trouble now loomed. Moreover, by May 1944 the military figures on PHP had again been upgraded. With new status and seeming backing from the JIC, it opted for a worst-case future scenario. The committee pointed out that the Soviets would be the most powerful force on the continent by 1945 while the Americans would be on their way home. It pretended that there was no political agenda to this estimate and that this reflected 'natural prudence' and a wish to cover all eventualities. But underneath lurked a clear presumption that any sound intelligence estimate would finger the post-war Soviet Union as hostile and dangerous.[27]

The PHP controversy finally exploded in late May 1944. Although the explosive material was intelligence estimates about hostile Soviet behaviour, the issue that lit the blue touchpaper was Germany. The controversy began quietly, with the PHP calling for updated forecasts from the diplomats. Jebb and Cavendish-Bentinck were initially inclined to be tolerant. They knew that the military needed some sort of paper opponent to plan their own force scales. This reflected the fact that the 'main enemy' for the military was not the Germans nor even the Soviets but the British Treasury, bent on post-war retrenchment. The military had to find a plausible post-war adversary if they were to have any hope of avoiding radical cuts in their forces. Jebb also accepted that extreme optimists – like Warner – were 'adopting an ostrich like policy'. The Soviets might well misbehave when the war was over.[28]

Cavendish-Bentinck, Whitehall's intelligence co-ordinator, was also half sympathetic. He knew that the workaday business of swapping intelligence with the Soviets was hard going and that some anti-Soviet feeling arose not out of prejudice but out of justified annoyance: 'I have seen it said ... that the Service Departments are violently anti-Russian. I do not think that is quite correct. They are peeved with the Russians because the latter have been on the whole frustrating.' But, although he and Jebb counselled a middle way, they were beginning to feel like the jam in the sandwich. Moreover, the state of denial in the Foreign Office regarding German ambitions in the 1930s cast a long shadow, giving the diplomats an 'ostrich like' reputation.[29]

Their advice to seek a middle way went unheeded. Senior diplomats sought to block the military by any means possible. Cavendish-Bentinck was dismayed to learn that they looked to him and the JIC, the source of high-level intelligence estimates, to provide a roadblock. If JIC forecasts were to be more benign, then the military would be undermined. Cavendish-Bentinck pleaded that this 'was not easy' and in any case the JIC was overworked with wartime operational business. But his pleas were ignored and he was required to come up with a more sympathetic portrait of Moscow's intentions, even while Soviet misbehaviour over Polish governments in exile was becoming apparent by early 1944.[30]

All pretence at Whitehall consensus was abandoned on 20 July 1944. The military had fired the first shots by effectively calling for the rearmament of Germany against the Soviets. The PHP, invigorated with younger officers, was now closer to the Chiefs of Staff. The military chiefs insisted that any Western association in Europe and what remained of a dismembered Germany should be specifically for use against a hostile Soviet Union. Jebb was quickly withdrawn as chair of PHP, which ceased to be a joint diplomatic–military committee.[31] Christopher Warner was outraged. He was determined to blunt the military incursion into the realm of British foreign policy. Military thinking, he insisted, however speculative, was now dangerous: 'The distance to the next step – "we had better start building up Germany pretty soon and so we had better not knock her down too completely" – is a very short one, particularly for the military mind and for those who suffer from the anti-Bolshevik complex.' Recriminations developed within the Foreign Office. Warner accused Cavendish-Bentinck of selling out to the military.[32]

Jebb tried to convince the military that active and open anti-Soviet precautions would amount to a self-fulfilling prophecy by destroying any prospect of a continued Grand Alliance. The policy of building up enemies in order to be ready to defeat allies, he complained, seemed 'to derive from some kind of suicidal mania'.[33] Sargent saw the military line as a 'most disastrous heresy' and others warned of 'almost fascist assumptions'. Warner counselled complete separation, suggesting that the PHP should be given 'all the rope they want to hang themselves'. Anthony Eden was briefed on the widening schism and he agreed that PHP's thinking was dangerous. All this, he ordered, should 'be avoided like the plague'.[34]

The diplomats tried to comfort themselves with the thought that PHP was only a temporary outfit. It had been entrusted with future strategy only because the regular Joint Planners were busy with wartime military operations. As soon as the fighting in Europe ceased, the regular military planners would take over, so PHP was doomed. The only way it could prolong its life was to get into preparatory work for the Allied Control Commissions that would look after occupied territories, but this work was dull and PHP had been trying to 'shuffle out of control work'. '[We] need not regret', noted the diplomats, 'these gentlemen committing hari-kiri'.[35] But the diplomats were wrong. By August 1944 it was becoming clear that the members of PHP were not renegades, but instead were mere symptoms of a deeply entrenched military mentality.

In mid-August 1944 British diplomats steeled themselves for an 'assault on the wild talk' of the PHP.[36] Eden was warned that the Chiefs of Staff and their subordinates 'are thinking and talking of the Soviet Union as being enemy number one and even of securing German assistance against her ... these, I fear, are their real thoughts.' He was urged to find a way of 'putting a stop to this kind of thinking and speaking'. Eden was shocked. 'This is very bad', he wrote, and shot off to talk to General 'Pug' Ismay, Secretary to the Chiefs of Staff. Ismay proved to be slippery and misleading. He politely assured Eden that the Chiefs of Staff had 'given no thought to the issue' and insisted that the controversy was the work of a few eccentric and misguided staff officers in PHP. This was quite untrue.[37] Back in the Foreign Office, Jebb and Cavendish-Bentinck knew where these ideas really emanated from and that the dynamic force behind them was Brooke.[38]

A subterranean struggle was also developing over JIC intelligence appreciations. Cavendish-Bentinck had been told to use the JIC to apply the brakes to the military and his efforts were partly successful. In late

August 1944 everyone eagerly awaited a new JIC forecast on 'Russian Capabilities in Relations to the Strategic Interests of the British Commonwealth'. Cavendish-Bentinck delivered a masterly performance and steered JIC's political forecasts back towards a reaffirmation of the idea of 'co-operation' and benign Soviet intentions. Capability was less easy to fudge because the Soviets now looked strong. The JIC predicted a rapid Soviet recovery and great post-war military strength. War with Britain, it conceded, was a real option for the Soviets within ten years. The diplomats regarded the contents of the paper as 'explosive'. But in reality Cavendish-Bentinck had done his job. The military had hoped that nasty Soviet behaviour in Poland would be regarded as a vindication of their views. Instead the sober words of the JIC had a dampening effect upon them. Staff colonels recorded that the latest views of the JIC were 'rather a setback for the would be drinkers of Russian blood', adding that the 'proposed world wide appreciation of our war against Russia is to be dropped'.[39]

The struggle for control of JIC assessments of the Soviets continued into September 1944. The military now dismissed diplomatic forecasts of Soviet policy as 'the usual story, but this time even more foolishly worded'. Instead they demanded a full-scale secret study of the options open to an aggressive Moscow. They proposed that 'a special inter-Service team should undertake a study of the courses of action open to an aggressive Russia', setting their findings out in detail. This was an amazing proposal – the setting up of nothing less than a shadow Politburo consisting of British intelligence officers, who would second-guess Stalin's post-war moves. The scheme harked back to an earlier bold experiment in British strategic intelligence at the start of the war. In 1940 a sub-group of the JIC, called the Future Operations (Enemy) Section, had tried to anticipate Hitler's thinking in exactly the same way. When Cavendish-Bentinck chaired a JIC meeting on 18 September 1944, these new proposals were 'suddenly produced' by the military. But the JIC concluded that it did not have the information to run such a shadow exercise. If it ever did, it would not want to commit it to paper. By October, a new agreement between Eden and the Chiefs of Staff over tight security for talks about the Soviets 'shot down the proposals' and no more was heard of them.[40]

Tight security was the big issue emerging from this confrontation in the autumn of 1944. The military had clearly decided to finger Moscow as the next enemy and the diplomats could do little about this. But Christopher Warner's main worry was that they were talking about it too openly. When General Sir Giffard Martel had returned from 30 Mission in May 1944 the diplomats wanted him to be ordered not to 'speak about his experience in Russia at all'. On 30 August Eden was warned that high-placed military officers were talking 'freely' of the Soviet menace in front of foreigners. A few days later it was clear that well-informed journalists were on to the military idea of using Germany against the Soviets. Moscow had its sources and the news would soon reach the Soviet Embassy, the diplomats said, if it 'was not perfectly well known there already'.[41]

At the end of September 1944 PHP produced plans for a West European bloc which was 'even more hostile to Russia' than before. It was now obvious to all that this 'must represent the real thoughts of the Chiefs of Staff'. The diplomats had their confidential sources in the War Office – liberal-minded officers, who tended to be those on temporary wartime duty. These 'sources' had spoken frankly to the Foreign Office of their 'anxiety about the attitude towards Russia of their superiors and asked whether something could not be done to stop it'. The advent of Control Commissions for Axis territory meant that military contacts with the Soviets were growing. 'If drastic action is not taken at the top' there would be confrontations that might be 'fatal'. Eden was called in once again. Senior diplomats warned him that this matter was 'of such importance' and the dangers were 'so great' that he should act immediately. Some sort of counter-directive had to be issued, and indeed deliberately leaked to the Soviets. Only the sternest action could prevent the situation 'from getting completely out of hand'. Eden decided it was now time to speak to Churchill.[42]

Eden had another 'showdown' with the Chiefs of Staff on 4 October. They could not agree on forecasts of future Soviet intentions. The military conjured up the ultimate nightmare of a future Soviet–German alliance, arguing that if the West did not join up with Germany then the Soviets would. Once more Eden pointed to the paranoid nature of Soviet foreign policy – something on which they were all agreed – and warned of self-fulfilling prophecies. This was a strong argument and he used it effectively to extract promises of the severest security clampdown on talk of the Soviets as an enemy. Current papers were withdrawn. In future all such dangerous talk would be placed in special confidential annexes that would be given super-tight circulation and 'restricted to the narrowest possible limits'. Meanwhile the main papers – merely top secret – would refer to the Soviets using 'brief and anodyne phrases'.

The results were surreal since no one could be sure who had seen the real paper. The privileged few who were part of this inner circle joked that any papers across which 'the shadow of the bear' might fall were to be labelled 'Burn before reading'. Eventually any thoughts on this sensitive subject 'would be recorded in cypher on a one time pad' and made available only to the eyes of the Cabinet Secretary. In short, Eden had ensured that there were to be 'no more games of Russian scandal'. But there were also practical problems here. What were they to do, military officials asked, 'when the conclusions of a secret annexe contradict the conclusions of the main paper'? These were strange times in Whitehall, with relations between the diplomats and the military at an all-time low.[43]

But the damage had already been done. Much of the earlier work had already fallen into the hands of the Soviets. In Washington, the figure in charge of the Chancellery – indeed of all British Embassy security – was the Soviet spy Donald Maclean. PHP papers routinely went there and it seems likely that he had seen most of them. In the government departments in Canberra and Ottawa too, copies of PHP papers made their way into the hands of Soviet agents in 1944 and 1945. In 1999 Oleg Tsarev, a senior retired KGB officer, reviewed the seminal material obtained by Soviet intelligence in the mid-1940s and spirited out to Moscow. The work of the PHP on rearming Germany against the Soviets was a prize exhibit.[44]

Whitehall feared leaks to Washington as well as to Moscow. Roosevelt, of all Allied leaders, seemed most committed to the ideal of a continued Grand Alliance. Thinking always in groups of four, he envisaged a post-war world secured by Four World Policemen. The United States, the Soviet Union, Britain and China would develop the UN as the mainstay of his liberal internationalist vision. British diplomats were anxious to prevent the leakage of anti-Soviet planning, fearing that Roosevelt would be infuriated by such talk. But at the military level at least there was a growing private Anglo-American consensus on the 'Russia problem'. In June 1944, Major-General Colin Gubbins, the head of SOE, visited General MacArthur at his South West Pacific Area headquarters. MacArthur launched into a tirade lasting one and a half hours against Russia. Not much later another senior British intelligence officer visited the Americans and accidentally came across 'super-secret' appreciations of the Soviet Union as the next enemy that were circulating in Washington.[45]

By the end of 1944 the diplomats had at least regained full control of the JIC. One of Cavendish-Bentinck's subordinates, Sir Arthur Noble, was set the task of ensuring that the Soviets were portrayed as defensive in their behaviour. The title of his new paper said it all: 'Russia's Strategic Interests and Intentions from the Point of View of her Security'. But by early 1945 events in Europe undermined its assertions and, while the turmoil in Central and Eastern Europe lasted, the JIC was notably silent on the big question of Soviet policy. In May 1945 the committee recommended that matters such as intelligence exchange be handled on a *quid pro quo* basis but specifically emphasised that 'we exclude any discussion of matter of high policy'. Only in January 1946 did the JIC feel safe to revisit this explosive issue.[46]

In May 1945, within days of Germany's defeat, Churchill ordered plans for war with the Soviets to be drawn up. During 1944 the Whitehall Cold War had focused on intelligence forecasts, but now the talk was of action. Churchill's stated objective was the 'elimination of Russia'. This plan was codenamed Operation Unthinkable and was only declassified in 1999. It called for hundreds of thousands of British and American troops, supported by 100,000 rearmed German soldiers, to unleash a surprise attack upon their war-weary Eastern ally. Meanwhile the RAF would attack Soviet cities from bases in Northern Europe.[47]

Operation Unthinkable was an 'independent staff study' conducted for Churchill under the direct control of Pug Ismay, the Secretary to the Chiefs of Staff. It was Ismay who had assured Eden a few months before that anti-Soviet thinking was a problem restricted to eccentric medium-level staff officers only. But, although Churchill's requests were executed with thoroughness, there was no enthusiasm. The military planners were not optimistic, noting Hitler's failure to conquer the Soviet Union even with more than a hundred divisions. Rearmed German forces, they argued, would be quickly demoralised, having been defeated once already and knowing full well the terrible nature of war on the eastern front. There was now plenty of intelligence on the Red Army and knowledge of its strengths and weaknesses. On the one hand, 'The Army is exceedingly tough, lives and moves on a lighter scale of maintenance than any Western Army and employs bold tactics based largely on disregard for losses in attaining a set objective. Security and deception are of the highest quality at all levels. Equipment has improved throughout the war and is now good . . .' On the other hand, the Red Army was suffering from war-weariness and had taken heavy casualties. It was short of staff officers and talented mid-level commanders. Above all discipline had collapsed with the end of fighting and all across Eastern Europe there was now an orgy of barely controlled 'looting and drunkenness'. Moscow might find such a rabble difficult to form up for another battle. Britain's best option seemed to be a drive to the East for the line around Danzig–Breslau and then to try and hold it. But the planners were 'extremely doubtful' that it could pulled off in the face of 'very heavy odds'.[48]

The Chiefs of Staff – Brooke, Cunningham and Tedder – were horrified by Churchill's idea. They knew of the scheme from the outset, but were invited to comment only once the study was completed. Although they shared Churchill's distaste for the Soviets, they enjoyed a stronger sense of reality and knew that this was a war the West could not win. On 24 May they met to talk about 'the possibility of taking on Russia should trouble arise in our future discussions'. Brooke believed that the whole idea was 'fantastic' and 'the chances of success quite impossible'. They met again to discuss it on 31 May, only to become even more certain that the whole thing was indeed 'unthinkable'. At very best they would get no further than the Germans had got, and then what would follow? The Chiefs of Staff argued that instead they should turn attention to how Britain could be defended against a Soviet occupation of France and the Low Countries. Churchill agreed and ordered Ismay to set military planners upon this new defensive study.

All this only hints at what was really at the back of Churchill's mind. Why did he think that the West might be able to take on the Soviets in the summer of 1945? The answer was clearly the advent of nuclear weapons. The impending test of the atomic bomb – carried out on 16 July 1945 – might shift the balance of power between East and West. The possibility of chemical and biological warfare might also have been in Churchill's mind. These sorts of thoughts and discussions are not ordinarily recorded in formal minutes. But Brooke captured the reality of these intensely secret and private conversations in his diary. Churchill, he wrote, now saw 'himself as the sole possessor of the bombs and capable of dumping them where he wished, thus all-powerful and capable of dictating to Stalin'.[49]

The possibility of atomic power may have prompted Churchill to go beyond mere staff studies. On the ground in Europe secret plans had been drawn up as early as November 1944 for the seizure of Berlin using airborne troops in the event of a German capitulation in the west. Airborne forces had been practising for this eventuality for several months. Detailed logistical planning was undertaken by airborne commanders as late as March 1945. They were not told that it was effectively a contingency plan to thwart the Soviets. There were parallel plans to seize the naval base at Kiel, while individual Allied commanders also offered schemes for a dash to Berlin.[50]

Churchill only spoke of these issues much later. 'Nothing', he complained, 'would convince the Americans of the Russian danger.' He had 'wanted [US General] Patton to take Prague', followed by a battle conference between himself, Stalin and Truman (who became president on Roosevelt's death in April 1945) where the armies met. Churchill also asserted that he 'wanted German arms to be kept handy in case they were required'. But this proposal 'was entirely unacceptable to the Americans'. In April Churchill had urged Roosevelt that Western troops should stay put, up to 150 miles into Soviet-designated areas, and withdraw only when they were satisfied that Moscow was keeping its agreements on Eastern Europe. But Roosevelt was close to death and in no condition to consider a resolute stand.[51]

In the spring and summer of 1945 the Soviets settled a long debate. Western intelligence estimates regarding the Soviet Union's ambitions became progressively grimmer, reflecting its real conduct in Eastern Europe and its demeanour at the conference table. Ultimately, it was not the extent, but the nature, of Soviet rule in Poland and Eastern Germany that was decisive. Logically, this revealed little about the long-term ambitions of Soviet foreign policy. But who would attempt to argue that Moscow was benign in the face of startling reports of a tide of bestial behaviour that was moving west? Reports of Soviet brutality were not new, they were merely closer to home. As early as December 1942 diplomats had reluctantly conceded that it was 'the universal opinion of all countries bordering on Russia and having the experience of Russian rule that the German jackboot, however horrible, is the lesser evil compared with the kindly dominion of Mother Russia'.[52]

Poland was the raw issue for Eden and Churchill. Churchill would often engage his circle in anxious conversations about what they could do to prevent more Poles being murdered by the Soviets. Although Eden and Churchill were progressively infuriated by the excessive expectations of the London Poles during the war, they were also alarmed by growing knowledge of what awaited them. At the Foreign Ministers Conference in Moscow in October 1943, Britain had originally intended to tell the Soviets in detail about the glorious campaign of sabotage and guerrilla activity which the Polish resistance was waging, supported by SOE. But then the British changed their minds, realising that any resistance leaders identified would soon be liquidated. By the end of 1944 it was quite clear that the rival Soviet-backed Polish government in exile, the Lublin Poles, depended largely on the NKVD.[53]

The Warsaw Rising of August 1944, when the Soviets deliberately left the Polish resistance to be crushed at the hands of the Germans before moving forward, was not, as some have suggested, the turning point for British perceptions. Cavendish-Bentinck of the JIC insisted that in fact tough German defences had 'annihilated a Russian armoured force which was advancing' on Warsaw. The Lord Privy Seal and prominent Labour MP Arthur Greenwood went further, asserting that the Soviets were quite justified in holding back. He told Eden that 'the present controversy would be paralleled if the Germans had occupied Dublin and an uprising by the I.R.A. interfering with our plans for recapturing the city became the subject for similar controversy with Moscow'. He went on to complain about the Poles as a running sore in Anglo-Soviet relations, partly because they expressed 'anti-Semitism in a virulent form'.[54]

Instead, it was the nature of everyday Soviet rule on the ground that incensed British officials. On 22 May 1945 Sir Owen O'Malley lamented that 'the Russians had been leading us up the garden path' on Poland and had never had any intention of delivering on their undertakings about political freedoms. Soviet policy was unfolding in Central and Eastern Europe with mechanical precision and consisted of 'purges, arrests and executions' together with the progressive destruction of tradition and of educated classes. The West had tolerated Soviet lies because of the need for a united front against Germany, but O'Malley now urged a reversal of this line. He warned that the policy of trying to win the Soviets over by concessions was 'quicksand' and 'will engulf us'.

He wanted open confrontation. The Soviets were now militarily exhausted and behind in 'scientific strength'. It was time 'to take the gloves off'. Britain should give a lead and make 'plain to all the evidence that the Soviet system is utterly antagonistic to our way of life, as cruel and ambitious as the Nazi system, and potentially more dangerous to the security of the United Kingdom'. O'Malley wanted his exhortation to be handed to Churchill. It did not get that far and instead fell into the hands of Christopher Warner, who handled the response. Warner still clung uneasily to the old policies of consensus, but could not challenge all the facts of O'Malley's account. He therefore chose his line carefully, arguing that O'Malley's message 'contained nothing particularly new' and that the British Embassy in Moscow had already moved independently to a harder policy.[55]

It was ironic that O'Malley's missive was sent on 22 May 1945. On the same day the Joint Planning Staff completed their unenthusiastic survey of Churchill's Operation Unthinkable. Both O'Malley and Warner were most likely unaware of these activities. Yet the diplomats continued to try and use the JIC as a brake on military thinking. Even as Unthinkable was being drafted, the JIC explicitly cautioned that the Germans would exploit their value in the East–West struggle to the maximum as a way of 'fooling the Allies' into reconstructing Germany as a major power.[56] Warner was quite wrong in asserting that O'Malley's warnings about Soviet behaviour contained nothing new. O'Malley was the first British official to call for Cold War – a declaration of ideological incompatibility, combined with a considered programme of information warfare directed at the systematic exposure of nefarious communist deeds. This was the position that the Foreign Office, and indeed Warner himself, would eventually convert to in twelve months' time.[57]

The Potsdam Conference in Berlin during July 1945 provided many with their first physical encounter with the Soviets. A large British delegation toured the obvious landmarks, including the Reichstag and Hitler's bunker. Churchill viewed the bunker by flashlight in the company of Russian soldiers 'but didn't make much comment'. Outside he joked with the Soviet soldiers whom he had considered taking on only two months before and sat on Hitler's chair, which had been brought outside. Sir Alexander Cadogan, Eden's Permanent Under-Secretary, also visited the Führer's 'dugout' and purchased an Iron Cross from a Soviet sentry for the price of three cigarettes.

But the most memorable sight at Potsdam was the intense security that surrounded Stalin. All those who met Stalin's entourage regarded this as quite formidable. When he arrived at the conference on 16 July 1945, he was accompanied by thousands of NKVD security troops. Their sullen omnipresence was felt by all. Even Cadogan, a veteran of such meetings, was forcibly struck by this vast manifestation of Uncle Joe's paranoia. On Sunday 22 July, when the British diplomat left an evening session of the conference and was halfway out of the park of the Cecilien Hof Palace where the conference was taking place, he was held up by Russian sentries at a crossroads:

> From the road on the left emerged a platoon of Russian tommy-gunners in skirmishing order, then a number of guards and units of the N.K.V.D. army. Finally appeared another screen of skirmishers. The enormous officer who always sits behind Uncle at meetings was apparently in charge of operations, and was running about, directing tommy-gunners to cover all the alleys in the Park giving access to the main road. All this because Uncle wanted 5 minutes exercise and fresh air, and walked out to pick up his car 500 yards from the Palace!

Cadogan noted sarcastically that this was all the more curious given that the whole park was already ringed with other sentries.[58]

The experience was repeated endlessly. Two days later some American staff officers were making their way to their car during a break in the conference proceedings. The facilities in the Palace were inadequate for the numbers there and a British officer came up behind them and, in obvious discomfort, said, 'I'm looking for a bush to pee behind but I am afraid of being shot.' The rubble-strewn area around the conference building was 'swarming with Russian guards' and there seemed literally to be a tommy-gunner behind every bush and rock. The British officer proved to be none other than Brooke. Brooke returned after a long perambulation and 'complained bitterly to General Marshall that he had not been able to find a bush without a Russian behind it'.[59]

Efforts to forecast Soviet policy were ultimately bound up with efforts to fathom the nature of a single personality. In the summer of 1945 public opinion still viewed Stalin as good old Uncle Joe, hero of the eastern front, an image that all in Whitehall had effectively abandoned. Stalin clearly enjoyed attempting to manipulate and distort the manner in which he was perceived by the West, and in a climate where information was scarce this was not difficult. Moreover, it was not clear how much he was in complete control, nor how much he was swayed by faction-fighting in Moscow.[60]

How did Churchill, who was receiving a range of 'Special Intelligence' on the Soviet Union – including decrypted Comintern messages – to which few were privy, reconcile these diverse factors? He had a personal input which hardly anyone else could claim, namely some experience of dealing with Stalin directly. Although Stalin did not travel outside territories under Soviet control, he relished contact with foreign leaders. He often charmed them and surprised them with his warmth, intelligence and rationality, albeit underpinned by a firm realism and a clear sense of his own demands. Eden explained the puzzling business of dealing with the urbane Stalin when he recounted to Hugh Dalton, the Minister of Economic Warfare, his prolonged meeting with the Soviet leader in early 1942. Stalin had struck him as surprisingly small, with physical movements 'rather like those of a cat'. Eden confessed that he knew full well what horrors Stalin was guilty of and so 'tried hard to think of him as dripping with the blood of his opponents and rivals, but somehow the picture wouldn't fit'.[61]

Benign and productive encounters between Churchill and Stalin were the most critical intelligence input. Churchill treasured the famous 'percentages deal' of October 1944 in which they had divided South-eastern Europe on the basis of a crude but effective agreement, without telling Washington. Just like the intelligence officers below him, the Prime Minister was inclined to generalise from his own personal experience, rather than reading the analysis of others or trying to attempt rigorous analytical thought. Private meetings reinforced his view of Stalin, which always had a tinge of 'Good King – Evil Counsellors' about it. Churchill often asserted to Eden that the Marshal had to watch out for the hard line element in the Politburo. When Churchill returned to office in November 1951, he was adamant that, if he could only make personal contact with Stalin, much of the poison could be dispelled. Ultimately, Churchill, like Eden, was perplexed by the dichotomy of a charming and urbane figure whom he knew to be a monster. Through 1944 and 1945 his views about Moscow swung wildly, alternately buoyed up by good personal exchanges with Stalin and angered by Soviet behaviour over Warsaw.[62] But Stalin's 'warmth' was arguably a misleading impression created by a rigid Soviet system. He compared well as a human figure with other prominent Soviet personalities because he alone could make concessions. By contrast, his Foreign Minister, Molotov, was known to Western diplomats as 'stone-bottom', because if you tried to kick him into compliance, all you got was a broken toe. This reflected not only Molotov's limited personality, but also the extent to which no individual dare make a concession without the personal approval of Stalin.[63]

3

Secret Service at the War's End: SIS and the CIA

I am concerned at the general drift that the F.O. should take over these fantastic things. We aren't a Department Store.

Sir Alexander Cadogan, 24 November 1944[1]

The bitter battles over intelligence assessment in Whitehall during 1944 and 1945 underlined the fact that the international landscape confronting Britain's secret services had been made anew. Germany and Japan had vanished as military powers, while the United States and the Soviet Union – both military weaklings in 1939 – were now dominant. The war had accelerated the struggle for liberation from colonial rule in what would become the Third World from which dozens of newly independent states would emerge by the 1960s. No less important were the radical scientific changes that brought forward new methods and weapons of war. Atomic weapons, electronics, jet propulsion, radar, biological and chemical warfare, proximity fuses and a dozen other developments had prompted a revolution in strategic affairs.

Secret service was not immune from this revolution for the war had greatly changed the practice of intelligence-gathering. The traditional spy-craft of human agents and double agents had played its role, especially in areas such as deception. But these hand-crafted operations had been overshadowed by the gathering and processing of signals intelligence on an industrial scale and by aerial photography. Monitoring of more accessible sources, from the enemy press to civilian mail, provided a mountain of information which initially no one knew how to control. Intelligence, therefore, was not only becoming industrial in scale, it was also becoming managerial, developing structures, boards and bureaucracies to deal with enormous flows of secret material. The cottage-industry approach of the inter-war years was finished.

There were also new activities, since special operations and subversion had benefited from new opportunities. The Second World War had witnessed the first large-scale efforts to create secret armies that were supplied by air and co-ordinated by wireless. More importantly, radio propaganda had emerged, permitting subversion to serve as a truly mass weapon. Radio was the critical element linking all these developments in a broad information revolution. Thus, in 1945, those in London and Washington who set out to redesign secret service for the future confronted a formidable task.[2]

In July 1945, Britain's new Prime Minister, Clement Attlee, elected with a landslide Labour majority, flew to join Churchill at the Potsdam Conference where the 'Big Three' – Britain, the United States and the Soviet Union – were arguing over a devastated Europe. Attlee, a radical in foreign affairs, was deeply committed to the United Nations and the idea of international co-operation. He accepted that Stalin might feel the need for a security belt of territories in Eastern Europe and access to the Mediterranean. But the abrasive style of Soviet diplomacy, together with the brutal texture of Soviet rule, was already removing any hope of true co-operation. Attlee also saw Truman as a problem. London was beset by contradictory fears of abandonment and entrapment. On the one hand, some feared that the United States was acquiring overseas bases, not to support its allies, but to create what Attlee called 'a glacis plate' behind which it could retreat into a renewed isolationism, abandoning its allies. On the other hand, others feared America's new interventionists. It was not the Soviets, they insisted, but the Americans, the 'go-getters' of Wall Street, who promised to speed the end of Britain's place in the wider world. It was commercial rivalry that prompted America abruptly to end Lend-Lease support in August 1945, plunging Britain into economic crisis. Capitol Hill feared that Lend–Lease would smooth Britain's transition to peacetime manufacture for export. Those who saw the United States as dangerously expansionist also feared a collision between the Americans and the Soviets, which might entrap Britain in war. As early as 12 February 1945, senior British diplomats were complaining that 'ham-fisted' Americans might well find themselves in a 'head-on collision with Russia'. 'We do not want to be dragged into a collision with Russia by the United States.'[3]

'Intelligence is regarded as a Cinderella service,' remarked one British intelligence chief. 'War', he added, is 'the Fairy Godmother who changes Cinderella into the Princess'.[4] The Second World War imposed this transformation upon British intelligence. Between 1939 and 1945, Winston Churchill played a central role. Although his own activities as a consumer of intelligence could be bumbling and erratic, he nevertheless gave intelligence the highest priority, as he had done throughout his life. He was also anxious to promote strong mechanisms for its superior direction and centralised control. But in the summer of 1945, with the war almost over, Churchill had gone. Many presumed British intelligence would revert from riches to rags and resume a lowly inter-war status, characterised by neglect and chronic underfunding. Some prescient individuals even sought to plan their post-war future in 1944 with the declared objective of getting proposals approved by Churchill, before the uncertainty of a general election interposed itself.[5]

The feared deep cuts in intelligence never came. The experience of the over-hasty dismantling of the intelligence services after the First World War was too fresh in the collective memory of Whitehall and Westminster. Awkward post-war tasks, in Germany, Greece, Palestine and South-east Asia, ensured that even those who wished to dismantle much of the secret service found they could not. By 1947 the onset of a new war – the Cold War – was clear to all, marked by new propaganda agencies such as the Soviet Cominform, and new secret services such as the American CIA. Money in the British system was always excruciatingly tight, but by 1948 British intelligence was slowly expanding once more. Wartime subversive organisations like SOE and the Political Warfare Executive found themselves being revived even before they finished disbanding. Some attempts were made to preserve specialist knowledge – typically in deception work – but elsewhere secret tradecraft survived in the reservoir of individual memory alone.

The alarming nature of future war was the main threat that British intelligence focused on after 1945. Whitehall feared that any future war would open with what officials termed a devastating 'nuclear Pearl Harbor'. In November 1944 the British Chiefs of Staff had instructed Sir Henry Tizard, President of Magdalen College, Oxford and a distinguished government scientist, to look into the revolutionary scientific developments of the last few years. His task was to forecast 'future weapons and methods of war'. Tizard's report was an 'exceptionally secret matter', submitted for the eyes of the Chiefs of Staff alone in the summer of 1945, and revised again after the atomic attacks on Hiroshima and Nagasaki. It made for hair-raising reading. Reviewing the extraordinary progress made in dangerous technologies, from bacteriological warfare to guided missiles, it was evident that extreme vigilance by active intelligence was more important than ever. It was also evident that the key intelligence target would be strategic weapons and particularly 'weapons of mass destruction'.[6]

Air Marshal Sir John Slessor, a senior RAF officer, was one of the most forward thinking in this area. His lively mind seized upon the key issue which would preoccupy the British military for the next ten years. On 16 July 1945, well before the atomic attack on Hiroshima and Nagasaki, he warned, 'The one thing – or combination of things – that seems to me likely really to revolutionise warfare and to render obsolete all hitherto known methods of waging it ... is the rocket-propelled atomic bomb. Whether this will render warfare itself as obsolete as the duel without first destroying civilisation, is clearly the most vital question in the world today and one which we in this country must solve satisfactorily or perish.' This, in turn, led him to emphasise 'the vital importance of our maintaining a really efficient Secret Intelligence Service and developing long-range stratospheric Photo Recce aircraft'. In one bound, Slessor's aggressive and probing intelligence had already begun to anticipate the vexed territory of the CIA's high-flying U-2 spy-plane together with the 'bomber gap' and 'missile gap' issues that would arrive in the 1950s.[7]

Above all, the threat of a 'nuclear Pearl Harbor' ensured that there was no possibility of the rapid contraction of intelligence services. As early as September 1945, Victor Cavendish-Bentinck, Chairman of the JIC, was able to extract a firm promise that a substantial intelligence structure would remain intact. He warned that, before the war, intelligence had been 'starved of resources' and 'lacked an adequate machine' for collating and controlling. Rapid expansion after 1939 had led to an 'improvised' system that was too complicated. 'We now have an opportunity to set our house in order.' Although numbers would fall gradually with the end of wartime tasks, the secret services suffered less under post-war austerity than any other aspect of defence. By May 1947, as Britain's economic crisis began to bite, the special status of intelligence was enshrined in the landmark statement on 'Future Defence Policy' by the Cabinet Defence Committee. Cabinet recognised that within the Soviet Union:

> The high standard of security achieved renders our collection of intelligence difficult and makes it all the more likely that Russia will have the advantage of surprise at the outset ...
>
> It is of the greatest importance that our intelligence organisation should be able to provide us with adequate and timely warning. The smaller the armed forces the greater the need for developing our intelligence services in peace to enable them to fulfil this responsibility.

But, as we shall see, principle was one thing and practice quite another. The intelligence budget needed constant work to defend it and expand it.[8]

Throughout the Second World War, Anthony Eden had suffered bureaucratic torture at the hands of the secret services. Alexander Cadogan, his senior official, struggled in vain to impose some order, but eventually found the numbers of proliferating secret and semi-secret bodies beyond him. One of the underlying sources of trouble was SIS – often known as MI6 – and its Chief, Sir Stewart Menzies. Deep uncertainty about the effectiveness of SIS ensured that new clandestine requirements in the area of intelligence, deception, sabotage, subversion and propaganda were met by forming new bodies outside SIS. SOE, the wartime sabotage organisation, was an obvious example. This ensured that they were dynamic and vigorous, but it also resulted in myriad secret services fighting among themselves. SIS should have been the hub of the wheel, but it was not judged strong or effective enough.

Cadogan had taken an instant dislike to Menzies even before his appointment in 1939. Menzies, he insisted, was putting up smokescreens to cover the deficiencies of SIS, which had been underfunded for two decades. Ultimately, SIS was under Foreign Office control and this had allowed Cadogan in 1942 to post a diplomat, Patrick Reilly, ostensibly as personal assistant to Menzies but really to act as a minder. At the end of 1943, Reilly was relieved by Robert Cecil. Reilly resumed his awkward task in 1946 and was still there in 1950, by which time SIS was often referred to in the Foreign Office as 'Mr Reilly's friends', a phrase that neatly captured the semi-detached status of SIS. Brooke had also insisted on appointing his representatives to SIS in 1943 and, by the end of war, SIS headquarters at Broadway Buildings was awash with senior representatives and co-ordinators.[9] The continued survival of Menzies, someone who combined modest intellectual capabilities with arcane pre-war administrative practices, is one of the mysteries of this period. As late as 1951 he continued to conduct much of his business over club lunches in Pall Mall. Those who dealt with him learned whether their stock was rising or falling with SIS on the basis of the venue. If their standing was high, the lunchtime destination would be White's; if it was low, it was lunch elsewhere.[10]

Patrick Reilly was horrified by what he saw in the SIS headquarters in Broadway Buildings. His first job was to try and do something about the 'deplorable' state of relations between SIS and the new sabotage service, SOE, but this proved to be beyond salvation. Next, he was ordered to 'impose some sort of order on Menzies' private office'. Reilly recalled that well into the war there were still 'a lot of old hands' from the pre-war days, 'a very varied body of men' but broadly characterised by low intelligence, reflecting the fact that Menzies' predecessor had been 'much against university graduates'. The start of the war was marked by a 'great scramble' for people of first-class ability, but SIS was not even in the race and so 'was rather left behind'. The level of brainpower, and indeed intellectual honesty, was 'not very high'. Reilly was dismayed by SIS files coming up to Menzies which contained 'prejudices', 'misrepresentations' and even 'downright falsehoods'. Even in the early 1950s, diplomats and military staff officers, when meeting together, enjoyed referring to SIS officers as 'the failed BAs'. But the area in which intellectual capacity was most obviously lacking was at the top. Even the kindest described Menzies as someone with experience and integrity 'but not a man of great intellectual ability'.

Menzies' private office was run by devoted staff, but the system operated on an amateur basis. During the war there was no regular system for presenting papers for Menzies, which were brought in by the officers handling cases – often in disorder. Everything had the feel of a small family business rather than a government department. Reilly remembered:

> There was a system whereby outside Menzies' door there were two little lights, red and green, and when he was busy the red light was on and when he was free the green light went on, and there would usually be a little queue in the corridor of people waiting to see him. They would go in with their files and very often they were complicated files. Menzies would ask them to leave them and it might be a long time before he dealt with them.

Reilly's job was to try and reform the system, but reform went slowly. The flow of paperwork gradually became a little more orderly, but the general pattern of business was the same and the eccentric system of lights remained outside Menzies' door.[11]

Despite these obvious defects, SIS enjoyed a good war. Menzies controlled the flow of Ultra material to Churchill and basked in its reflected glory. More importantly, signals intelligence had accelerated the work of SIS against its Axis enemies such as Hitler's secret service, the Abwehr. It is often forgotten that SIS was also responsible for counter-espionage if it was outside British territory. Counter-espionage was now big business for SIS, and its specialist department for this, Section V, under Colonel Felix Cowgill, expanded from a mere handful of staff at the start of the war to a complement of over 250 by 1945. This expansion, like all expansions of secret service activity, resulted in friction, particularly with MI5. Kim Philby was the most energetic figure in Cowgill's successful section.[12]

As we have seen, the volatile debate developing in Whitehall as to whether the Soviet Union should be considered benign or malignant had its impact on SIS. Menzies had pulled in many military officers to fill the expanding ranks of SIS during the war, some literally rounded up in the bars of Pall Mall clubs. By 1943 the three service assistant directors imposed by the Chiefs of Staff were firmly embedded. And in any case SIS had a strong pre-war tradition of anti-Soviet and anti-Comintern activity. Unsurprisingly, then, long before the end of the war with Germany senior officers in SIS began to turn their thoughts towards the next enemy. The first stage was the development of Section IX, to study past records of Soviet and communist activity. Sam Curries was imported from MI5 to get the section going. But this appointment was 'a stop-gap one'; as soon as the reduction of wartime work allowed, he would be replaced by a regular SIS officer.[13]

Curries' temporary unit eventually became a post-war section called

Requirements 5 – or R5 – which boasted new staff, including Robert Carew Hunt, who later became a renowned academic expert on the Soviet Union. Valentine Vivian, deputy head of SIS, and Felix Cowgill were strongly interested in this section and it was Kim Philby who was designated to take command. Robert Cecil was the personal assistant to Menzies at the time. He recalled that in February or early March 1944 there arrived on his desk the draft charter for the new anti-Soviet section. Its staffing scale was considerable, with a lot of posts in overseas SIS stations. Cecil embodied the optimism of the diplomats and suggested that all this anti-Soviet provision was excessive. 'Within hours Vivian and Philby had descended on me, upholding their requirements and insisting that these be transmitted to the Foreign Office ... I gave way.' In retrospect Cecil thought it amusing that Philby demanded a large British Cold War apparatus, when he could have settled for a small one.[14]

The final shape of post-war SIS was determined by a Reorganisation Committee set up on 19 September 1945. This consisted of a senior SIS officer, Philby, and a representative from GC&CS, now renamed Government Communications Headquarters (GCHQ). The question was whether SIS should be organised to deal with geographical regions like the Middle East or thematic subjects such as scientific intelligence. The outcome was a compromise. The 'Production' part of SIS that ran agents was organised on geographical lines with regional controllers. The 'Requirements' part responsible for collating and distributing intelligence was organised thematically. Philby's section therefore owned not only the Soviet Union, but also communism worldwide, the plum job in post-war SIS. Other support sections dealt with the administration, finance, training and development. Further small units were concerned with war planning or with 'Special Political Action', the SIS term for covert interventions and peacetime special operations.[15]

SIS was superficially rearranged rather than thoroughly reformed at the end of the war. Like so many wartime organisations, the young and talented could not wait to leave, while less promising, often superannuated figures wished to cling on. Figures who had been a joke even in the 1930s, such as Harold Steptoe, the eccentric SIS man in Shanghai, stayed on: Steptoe went out to run the important Teheran station after the war. In 1948, Malcolm Muggeridge, who had spent the war as an SIS officer in Algiers and Paris, was continuing to meet up with old friends who were still in SIS to swap gossip about the 'office'. He was amazed to learn 'that all the worst dead-beats were still firmly entrenched'. Reviewing the line-up of the more senior figures, he despaired. 'It would be difficult to find any organization, private or public, directed by four so essentially incompetent people.' Given that SIS was bound to be the leading edge in the developing Cold War, he found it 'grotesque'.[16]

The one area that received concerted attention was relations between SIS and its customers. The British secret services have often been portrayed as working in obscure isolation, but by 1944 this was rarely the case. Wartime pressures had forced even backward organisations such as SIS to develop elaborate systems for liaising with their customers across Whitehall and for receiving feedback on the value of their efforts, and on changing requirements. SIS held routine monthly meetings with the sub-sections of Military Intelligence which consumed their product, each section having specific responsibilities. Some of these sections were geographical – MI2b was China – while some were thematic – MI10b was radar technology. There were conventions for tasking SIS with enquiries, through 'Standing Questionnaires', which defined subjects of permanent interest, and 'MI6 Special Question' forms, which were used by customers for issues of more transient interest. The latter forms also had attached cancellation slips for use when a request had been met. SIS was continually coaching its customers to be better consumers. It pressed for specific questions and for some background information on why the question was being asked instead of enquiries offered 'point blank'. SIS was usually dealing with about 300 Special Questions worldwide at any one time in the late 1940s. It also tried to educate its customers on how intelligence was graded, using the terms 'Casual', 'Occasional' and 'Reliable' to describe how it rated their informants.[17]

Inevitably Germany was the source of some of the best SIS dividends. In September 1947, Major Dixon, an Army technical intelligence officer, praised an unusual present, a 'Russian anti-tank shell delivered to his office by M.I.6'. He was keen to receive further surprises of this sort.[18] But SIS, MI5 and GCHQ all shared the problem of surges in work which occurred whenever there was an international crisis. Things would be quiet for weeks and then they would be confronted by a wave of requests. In July 1948 the Berlin blockade, Stalin's attempt to lay siege to the Western sectors of this city located deep within the Soviet Zone of Germany, began to bite. Dick White of MI5 complained that 'an enormous number of appreciations were being urgently requested ... the turn-out of paper was going up by leaps and bounds'.[19]

Although the military had encouraged SIS to give early attention to the Soviet Union, it was never wholly focused upon the Cold War. Among its central duties was the support for British influence in far-flung territories. For this reason the main SIS station in the Middle East was soon plucked from the General Headquarters in Palestine and buried within the diplomatic accommodation of the British Middle East Office in the Shariah Talumbat Compound. In South-east Asia, SIS shifted from Lord Mountbatten's end-of-war headquarters at Singapore, where he had accepted the surrender of Japanese troops in Malaya, to

the expanding offices of Britain's Special Commissioner for South East
Asia.

SIS had a strong local identity in the regional Middle East. Indeed, on
19 August 1945, the regional Middle East Defence Committee called for
the creation of an entirely separate and specialist Middle East secret
service. The American OSS had recently toyed with a similar super-secret
intelligence service run under the cover of archaeologists and anthropol-
ogists working out of Harvard University and dealing with issues such as
airbases, oil and markets in Islamic areas. It claimed to be inspired by a
comparable scheme that was being developed by SIS at its wartime base
in Palestine. All this reflected the fact that SIS was largely concerned with
the politics of Britain's informal empire in the Middle East – a curious
part of the world where Britain appeared still to predominate – yet only
owned Cyprus and Kenya by 1948. Secret service was especially colonial
in the Persian Gulf, a region which had been superintended from India.
Each British outpost enjoyed a 'secret service grant' to subsidise local
clandestine activity. In the end no separate Middle Eastern service was
created, but London recognised that out there SIS would be busy with
'local intelligence requirements'.[20]

By contrast, Britain's temporary wartime sabotage organisation, SOE,
was everything that SIS was not. Churchill had decided that the task of
sabotage and subversion should be given to a new and vibrant organisation. Hence SOE had been created from embryonic sabotage units that
were being set up by SIS and Military Intelligence in 1938–9. SIS and the
military both resented losing control of this area. Bitter wrangles followed. The first Minister to control SOE, Hugh Dalton, scribbled
despairingly in November 1941: 'This is a slow war of attrition, and
slowest of all in Whitehall.'[21]

SIS projected itself as run by established professionals, but it was in
fact a bastion of the British amateur tradition. By contrast SOE, dis-
dained by its sister organisation as 'amateur', drew in fresh and talented
people from business, universities, indeed from every conceivable walk
of life. This produced some failures, but the broad outcome was a
modern and effective service. More importantly, because of its claims to
be damaging the enemy, it had swelled to an enormous size. In Asia,
where fighting against Japan did not cease until August 1945, SOE personnel outnumbered their SIS counterparts by more than ten to one. SIS
chiefs were alarmed by the rise of SOE and in private they fully confessed its superiority. 'Little Bill' Stephenson, the senior SIS officer in the
United States who ran the vast British Security Co-ordination outfit in
New York, predicted in 1944 that SIS would be rolled up at the end of
the war, while SOE would be allowed to continue. SOE, he insisted, was
vigorous and innovative while SIS was past it. In fact, as we shall see,

exactly the reverse occurred at the end of the war. SIS continued in its dotage while SOE was broken up and subjected to a 'hostile takeover' in which most SOE expertise and its more dynamic personnel were lost.[22]

The Second World War had unleashed SOE and more than a dozen similar parvenus into the world of clandestine activity, ranging from the Special Air Service (SAS) to propaganda organisations like the Political Warfare Executive. But these newcomers were as politically clumsy and naive as they were energetic. Whitehall had its fixed boundaries and SIS considered itself to own the world of secret service, the Foreign Office saw itself as the centre of British overseas policy, while the three services claimed all military activity. The new clandestine services trampled all these boundaries underfoot in a headlong rush to get going. The result was a series of bitter bureaucratic struggles, and by the end of the war many established Whitehall figures could not wait to rid themselves of what they called the 'funnies'.

It was not only the Whitehall bureaucrats who hated SOE. Many regular service officers regarded all special forces as crooks and skivers. Early in the war, senior RAF staff officers told SOE they did not wish to associate their service with the dishonourable business of parachuting agents in civilian clothes for the purpose of attempting to kill members of the opposing forces. Eventually the RAF was compelled to assist. Others just regarded special operations units as a soft option for those who wished to slide away from the rigours of front line infantry soldiering. One general asserted that these special units 'contributed nothing to Allied victory. All they did was to offer a too-easy, because romanticised, form of gallantry to a few anti-social irresponsible individualists, who sought a more personal satisfaction from the war than of standing their chance, like proper soldiers, of being bayoneted in a slit trench or burnt alive in a tank.' This was a sentiment expressed repeatedly by senior officers. Admiral Somerville found Mountbatten's wartime South East Asia Command teeming with curious irregular units 'kicking their heels', claiming special privileges, but obviously without much to do.[23]

The diplomats nursed an intense hatred of SOE, and indeed of its sister propaganda service, the PWE. In order to enthuse resistance movements, both organisations had found themselves compelled to make incursions into the realm of politics, often addressing the sensitive issue of post-war settlements. In Europe, the Middle East and as far as China, diplomats continually accused SOE of developing its own separate foreign policy. SOE and PWE were often found engaged in volatile activities in sensitive neutral countries such as Spain, Switzerland and Turkey. Anthony Eden wanted to deal with SOE, PWE and areas like economic warfare by taking them over. But his experienced right-hand man, Alexander Cadogan, hated them dearly, and wanted them banished far from his domain. Cadogan was horrified by Eden's suggestion that the Foreign Office should develop sections full of these murky undiplomatic characters who spent their time undertaking 'fantastic things'. 'We aren't a Department Store,' he complained in his diary, insisting that the diplomats should stick to their core business. But Eden got his way. Cadogan was appalled: 'We are taking over the remnants of M. of I., M.E.W. [respectively Ministries of Information and of Economic Warfare], S.O.E. Are we competent to do it? We can't do it.'[24]

Few things were more important for the long-term future of British secret service than this argument between Eden and Cadogan, for they represented the two alternate possible futures for British secret intelligence and special operations. It was fortunate for Britain that Eden eventually won the argument. In late 1945 the Foreign Office achieved a formal veto over any future special operations, while SIS, which was under Foreign Office control, absorbed SOE. Soon, propaganda also came within the bounds of Cadogan's beloved Foreign Office, turning it into a 'department store' whose business went far beyond straight diplomacy. The post-war pattern of British special operations and propaganda was tied directly into the core of British foreign policy-making. In Washington, as we shall see, these activities escaped diplomatic control and the CIA became a rival centre of American foreign policy which even its own officers feared had become a state within a state.

Eden had found wartime special operations annoying, but he also saw them as valuable. Indeed during 1944, when the control of SOE continued to be a live issue, he seems to have used SOE operations moving to and from Poland to influence the composition of the unstable Polish government in exile in London. His hope was to render it less viciously anti-Soviet and therefore to open the way to brokering some sort of deal with Moscow to secure its future. Eventually this proved to be an empty hope.[25]

On 23 November 1944 Eden saw an opportunity to extend diplomatic control. Lord Selborne, SOE's Minister, was about to resign and leave government. Eden immediately wrote to Churchill asking that SOE be placed under him as a tidy short-term measure. But it was clear that the Foreign Secretary was already looking ahead. He argued that, in the future, 'in liberated territories and in neutral countries there may from time to time be useful scope for a covert organisation to further [British] policy ... and I should therefore be sorry to see the abandonment of all the machinery for "special operations" even when the war is over'. Although he couched this in gentle terms – it was only to be a temporary arrangement – he also knew that possession would be nine-tenths of the law when the war was over. It was 'too soon' to consider post-war machinery; however, he added, 'of one thing I am sure': in the future SIS and special operations had to be under the same controlling chief. Without this rationalisation, which would prevent further feuding between special operations and secret intelligence, 'nothing but chaos can ensue'. To pave the way for this proposed merger of SIS and SOE, Eden argued, he should now take over as the Minister responsible for SOE. After all, as Foreign Secretary, he was already the responsible Minister for SIS and for the policy of the Political Warfare Executive. He went on, 'I am also in my personal capacity the minister for MI5.' For Eden to acquire SOE as well would simply be 'a step in the right direction'.[26] Churchill, like Eden and Cadogan, was heartily sick of the feuding between SOE and SIS and the endless struggles for control of policy towards areas that had significant resistance movements. But equally he thought it too late in the war to attempt a major upheaval in the architecture of secret service. The Chiefs of Staff were suspicious of Eden, so instead Churchill pressed his close friend 'Top' Selborne to stay on until the end of the war.

Meanwhile, some in SOE clearly had their eye on an emerging Cold War in Europe as a likely avenue for perpetuating their organisation's existence as a separate entity. In January 1945, Colin Gubbins, the head of SOE, wrote to Cadogan explaining that he wanted to drop one of his officers, Captain John Coates, into Budapest. The diplomats gave Gubbins a firm no, citing the 'unfortunate experiences' with the Soviets that had resulted from recent SOE missions in Rumania and Bulgaria. SOE dropped a few agents into Prague in May 1945, but these were NKVD agents inserted on Moscow's behalf, the last remnants of the fairly solid co-operative relationship developed by George Hill, the SOE man in Moscow.[27]

By June 1945, Victor Cavendish-Bentinck was less busy with the JIC and the bitter arguments over post-hostilities planning. So he was free to chair a temporary committee on which parts of SOE would be required in the near future and should be allowed to live on, and which parts should be scrapped. One of the first areas to consider was the Middle East, where fighting had long since ended. He was not looking forward to this job and expected to be faced with 'all sorts of suggestions from SOE for grandiose activities' accompanied by allegations that these schemes were 'absolutely necessary in those countries'. He was extremely pleased to get a long letter from Lord Killearn, the British Ambassador in Cairo, that gave him the ammunition to deflate SOE post-war schemes. For Killearn, the critical matter was not the emerging Cold War. He conceded that the Soviets were 'very active' in the region, but he was not prepared 'to swallow the Bolshevist Bogie hook line and sinker'. Some sleeper organisation might eventually be useful to counter Bolshevist propaganda, but in any case he did not think SOE was very good at this sort of work.

Much more important were SOE's local functions. Throughout the war SOE had been preoccupied with 'other activities' in the Middle East, 'in other words the payment of baksheesh' for the purpose of smoothing general British influence in the region. This had been crucial in an area where Arab nationalism was growing fast among intellectuals and middle-ranking Army officers, inclining them to side with anyone who would rid the Middle East of the remains of the European colonial presence. This was the tendency that needed to be countered with extensive bribery. SOE's political 'baksheesh' programme had been operating in Egypt since early 1942, when it had been set up by Major Carver and a Mr Masterson from SOE, together with the Embassy. They had managed 'the bribery of certain officials, to enlist their support in looking after British interests'. All were 'agreed that certain monies would be paid monthly to certain individuals'. In 1945 Killearn reviewed SOE's plans for post-war Egypt: 'If I understand correctly S.O.E.'s summary of their activities, they propose to spend approximately £10,000 a year on oral dissemination of pro-British views: £9,000 a year on the paying of patronage to selected politicians and Government officials; and a further sum of approximately £12,000 per annum on special secret payments in this country "at the request of His Majesty's Representatives".' Killearn wanted control of this programme and felt that all this could be done by the SIS officers in Cairo. 'As you know we already have our S.S. [Secret Service] arrangements here which work well.' He confessed, 'I shouldn't in the least break my heart if S.O.E. were totally wound up in Egypt.' Few SOE staff stayed on in the Middle East. One was Dr Robin Zaehner, who remained at the Embassy in Teheran until 1947 and 'whose chief function is that of bribing the Persian press'. He returned in 1951 ahead of the Anglo-American overthrow of the Mossadegh government in 1953. Against the wishes of London, Mountbatten retained over 500 SOE staff in South-east Asia to help deal with the difficult situations in Indochina and Indonesia.[28]

SOE was also well established under the Twenty-first Army Group in occupied Germany and Austria. The Chiefs of Staff had more influence in areas of occupation and had been persuaded by Harry Sporborg, Gubbins' deputy, that with Europe in its present unsettled state it would be 'unwise' to lose 'valuable SOE contacts' in Austria, some of whom were high ranking. On 24 September 1945, twenty-four SOE personnel were still at large in Austria working on their 'long-term role'.[29] The diplomats were soon on to this. Robin Hankey, a diplomat who was about to take over the Northern Department from Christopher Warner, claimed that SOE 'were endeavouring to prolong their lives unnecessarily'. He continued, 'I was assured that the Chiefs of Staff attached importance to their duties, but what these duties were nobody knew.' He feared offending the Soviets with 'activities of the cloak and dagger variety'. Hankey was anxious to speak to Cadogan's successor, Orme Sargent, about the related issue of SOE activities in Germany, 'which seem to me to be of a somewhat dangerous political character'. But in the end the military insisted on retaining their services in Germany. By December 1945 the SIS station in Austria had absorbed the eight remaining SOE staff and their high-level contacts.[30]

SOE in Germany was employed in an operation to acquire some files from the East which were considered 'most valuable' by the Director of Military Intelligence in London. This was an operation that involved the covert removal of an entire archive, and the limited surviving record of this episode speaks unambiguously of 'the "lifting" of the material from the Russian Zone' of Germany. This operation was successful and remained covert, but a no less successful American operation a few months later was blown and became embarrassingly public. This involved a similar 'intelligence foray into Czechoslovakia' and was self-confessedly a 'raid' to secure intelligence materials, archives and other gems including:

> a. German counter-intelligence correspondence relating to Bohemia-Moravia, papers belonging to Himmler, Von Ribbentrop, Frank and Funk ...
> b. Gestapo and German intelligence papers relating to Bohemia-Moravia,
> c. President Benes files from 1918 to 1938,
> d. Locations of treasures spotted in caves in Czechoslovakia.

Although the material was bagged, the operation was noisy and the *Herald Tribune* obtained 'the complete story'. Czech retaliation, including the closing of borders to all American travellers, made control of the press impossible. The State Department had no choice but to admit involvement and sent a message to the American Embassy in Prague authorising the Ambassador to apologise for the affair. This sort of event made diplomats in London and Washington nervous.

Elsewhere in Germany, the main SOE unit called ME 42 still had thirty-four staff in operation on 15 January 1946, who were gradually being merged with SIS stations. Their role was not only to retain agents as intelligence contacts but also to establish stay-behind parties for resistance work. ME 42 was identifying agents in each major town 'selected from among the people now being used as informers for political intelligence' to undertake sabotage in the event of a Soviet push westward. The unit sought about ten stay-behind agents in each major town chosen from categories such as the police, local government, bankers, industrialists, railways, trade unions, professions, teachers and clergy.[31]

SOE was clinging on successfully by making itself useful to regional commands facing awkward problems, but its main obstacle to survival lay in London. Sir Colin Gubbins and his deputy Harry Sporborg were painfully aware that SOE had made few allies in Whitehall during the war. At the end of April 1945, Sporborg was probing figures like Christopher Warner about the value of some sort of SOE–NKVD treaty that would take co-operation into the post-war period. But, while the diplomats allowed SOE to go on a 'fishing expedition' in Moscow, they saw this for what it was. Sporborg was one of a number trying every ruse to get some high-level commitment to a prolonged life for SOE.[32]

Gubbins knew he had more support among the military and in May he persuaded the Chiefs of Staff to set up their own SOE Evaluation Committee which would contact regional commanders and obtain 'an unbiased opinion of the SOE organisation'. But although many regional commanders had valued SOE, and produced long papers setting out their triumphs, like Cavendish-Bentinck's temporary committee, every-one called for tighter co-ordination and centralised control. This pointed fatefully towards one single secret service. Even with central control, not all were enthusiastic. The commanders in the Middle East were keen to point out that a lot of SOE equipment delivered to the guerrillas in Greece had subsequently been used against the British. 'British casualties during the post-war occupation troubles in that country amounted to one thousand.' Some were keen to lay these at SOE's door. More broadly they thought that SOE's forecasts of its diversionary capability were 'optimistic': 'Whilst subversive activities in Greece were a constant source of irritation and hindrance to the enemy, yet he reacted much more to our overall deception plans and as far as can be seen the strate-gic effect of SOE operations was negligible.'[33] Some reports were more upbeat, but all were mixed, and this was not the sort of commentary that Gubbins and Sporborg had hoped for.

Senior commanders from the major theatres of war were contacted and advice poured in from all sides. John Slessor, who had been Deputy Commander of the Allied Air Forces in the Mediterranean, was the first to reply. 'The intelligence set-up in Cairo is a mess,' he announced. Multiplicity was the root of the problem. There were 'far too many different agencies and organisations, all with direct access to the great, too often crossing each others wires and cutting each others throats ... Of course, the real answer, I am sure to all this is drastic re-organisation at the top.' He wanted all the secret and semi-secret services, including propaganda and deception, rolled into one service 'under a single head' who would be an associate member of the Chiefs of Staff Committee – almost a fourth armed service.[34]

Mountbatten also offered his views as a veteran of secret service man-agement and someone who nurtured a boyish enthusiasm for special operations. In South East Asia Command he had presided over more than a dozen secret services which enjoyed internecine rivalry more than anything else. He had developed a sophisticated system, called P Division, which accorded the different secret services priorities for their activities. But he found that they could work together only when SOE had battered the local SIS station into submission. In August 1945 Mountbatten told the Chiefs of Staff that he preferred the American Office of Strategic Services. Although OSS had not been joined 'at the roots' to the higher direction of war in Washington, nevertheless he insisted that it was very good because it covered the full range of secret intelligence, special operations and political warfare and other 'nefarious objects'. He felt that this holistic approach was the way ahead and had made OSS 'a very good organisation'.[35]

The outcome was increasingly obvious. By 14 August 1945 Cavendish-Bentinck's committee had finished its work. The Chiefs of Staff postponed any formal decision because the whole question of post-war defence organisation was up in the air. The only new factor was the arrival of a Labour government. Clement Attlee decided to send the question on to the Cabinet Defence Committee. But his mind was already made up. Selborne had written to the new Prime Minister adver-tising SOE's special services and underlining their usefulness in the trou-bled post-war era. But Attlee was hard to convince and associated these things with the underhand approach of Bolsheviks. He replied frankly that his government would have no need of a 'Comintern'-type organisa-tion.[36]

If Attlee was going to permit any post-war special operations capabil-ity then it was going to be small. He therefore took the advice offered him by his new Foreign Secretary, Ernest Bevin. Bevin followed Eden's line and urged Attlee to put the remnants of SOE within SIS and 'definitely under "C", as a section of his organisation'. Cabinet Office officials around Attlee were more forthright, having been plagued, like Cadogan, with wartime SOE troubles. T. L. Rowan in the Prime Minister's Office explained that his extreme sufferings over the last few years had inclined him 'very strongly to the view' that SIS should take over everything. All this mirrored Eden's vision set out in 1944. As M. R. D. Foot has recorded, Ernest Bevin 'himself signed SOE's death warrant on lines laid down by Eden'.[37]

Eden was thus the architect of the post-war system for controlling special operations, and so the diplomats came out on top. The two enquiries conducted by Cavendish-Bentinck and by the Chiefs of Staff had little material bearing on the outcome. In mid-January, a series of Chiefs of Staff meetings confirmed the SIS takeover.[38] Harold Caccia, who was now Chairman of the JIC, took the opportunity to emphasise diplomatic control. He drew attention to the directive on the future of special operations: 'That directive gave the Foreign Office the right of veto throughout ... it would be seen that they wished to use that veto rather drastically ...' He expanded on his own experience in Greece. The recruitment of agents in any country for this kind of thing in peacetime, whether they were conscious and unconscious agents, would be 'politically dangerous'.

Menzies told the Chiefs of Staff that SIS would concentrate on a special operations organisation 'capable of rapid expansion in an emergency'. This would be a sleeper unit based in London 'trained in the operational side', for which he would need about twenty officers well versed in special operations methods, but nothing would be done abroad. Menzies argued that the fact that his secret intelligence officers, who were nevertheless given some training in special operations, 'were in foreign countries and employing agents, would considerably reduce the time required to build up a resistance movement if and when required'. An additional benefit was economy, for the compromise approach in which special operations were kept asleep would involve SIS in an extra expenditure of only £40,000 a year.[39]

On the ground the effect was quickly apparent. One senior SOE officer, who had commanded the most effective sabotage network in France, was one of the few who transferred to the SIS sleeper unit at the end of the war. Supervising six staff in the Department of Training and Development, his task was to pool and protect SOE expertise. The experience was dispiriting. After enduring years of sneering by SIS about the 'amateurs of SOE' he found the true situation to be exactly the reverse. When he asked about the SIS photography department he discovered that, unlike SOE, SIS had no such facility, but he was reassured that a few SIS officers dabbled in photography as a hobby. This experience was repeated all along the line.[40]

By 1948, on paper at least, the Foreign Office – working together with the Colonial Office – had authority over all the activities of SIS, and indeed MI5 overseas. When London drafted an intelligence charter governing the Far East it set out these rights and permissions explicitly. 'Before any intelligence or counter-intelligence activities are carried on in any territory of any foreign government or in British or British protected territory, the Senior British Diplomatic representative, or the principal British Authority must be informed and his approval assured.' This exhortation about approval for operations was sometimes observed in the breach, but it showed how embedded the Eden legacy had become. Eden himself remained a lifelong adherent of tight political control of secret service, and would reaffirm this when he returned as Prime Minister in the 1950s.[41]

One of the best-kept secrets of most intelligence services is that about half the material they circulate to their masters is not their own. Liaison with friends and allies was a critical consideration for SIS. Relations with American secret services, notably William J. Donovan's OSS, were complex and sometimes difficult. By 1945 open rivalry had developed in the remoter areas of the world where London and Washington had considered themselves to be in competition. The decision to keep this relationship going was based on carefully calculated realism rather than mawkish sentiment. The history of the Anglo-American special intelligence relationship abounds with hagiography. But the real relationship between the British and American secret services in 1945 was often prickly, as can be seen from the memoirs and private diaries of the time.

Graham Greene served under Kim Philby in the SIS counter-intelligence wing, Section V. Greene recalled that his wartime unit had occupied one floor of a large Edwardian house in Ryder Street, close to St James's. (These premises were later sold and taken over, not inappropriately, by the *Economist,* which boasted its own Intelligence Unit.) The floor above the SIS Section V at Ryder Street was given over to the counter-intelligence department of the OSS station in London, known as X-2. Greene recalled, 'Security was a game we played less against the enemy than against the allies on the floor above,' and he described the mutual torments they inflicted on one another in the name of fun. But this curious patchwork of rivalry and co-operation was nevertheless regulated. OSS, SIS and SOE had been busy signing treaties with each other since 1942 and all were anxious to preserve this treaty system beyond the end of the war. This was made difficult by Harry Truman's decision to abolish OSS. On 20 September 1945 the President had passed Executive Order 9621 ensuring that OSS was disbanded with almost immediate effect, from 1 October. He was influenced by the Park Report, a collected survey of OSS misdemeanours during the war. He was also confronted with an economising Republican Congress that required deep cuts in defence budgets. Wisely, he gave top priority to signals intelligence and was determined to keep that going above all else.[42]

American special operations, or 'covert action' as it was becoming known in Washington, launched its own determined publicity campaign. A bitter battle over the fate of OSS in 1945 had prompted Donovan and his enemies to engage in a public quarrel in which each side leaked extensive details of OSS wartime exploits. This gathered momentum in 1946 and 1947 with a wave of memoirs, sensational magazine articles and films. Although OSS was abolished, its adherents replied with a barrage of Hollywood films. One, simply entitled *OSS,* starred Alan Ladd, Paramount Studios' resident tough guy, hammering the Germans in France before D-Day. Other Hollywood OSS epics starred Gary Cooper and James Cagney and offered a remorselessly upbeat version of secret service. The message was that an America who engaged in the wider world needed these things; but the message had not convinced Truman.[43]

American OSS, like SOE, was a new organisation which had grown quickly and which had made too many enemies. Instead of being preserved, elements of OSS were broken up and then secreted away, under Army or Foreign Service cover, to await what the more astute knew would be the rapid post-war revival of American agent-based secret service. The wait was longer than many had expected. Harry S. Truman did not create the Central Intelligence Agency until July 1947, and a semi-detached unit for covert action only came along a year later in 1948. American secret service did not come to a halt during this interregnum, but the temporary conduits through which it was carried out led to problems, not least in terms of co-operation with London.

In the professional world of intelligence there was an abiding recognition that the United States would not return to pre-war isolationism and that an organisation like OSS would soon be essential. Pressure for revival was apparent even before OSS had been abolished. On 29 August 1945, J. Edgar Hoover, Director of the FBI – no friend of William Donovan or the OSS – nevertheless wrote to the US Attorney General declaring that 'the future welfare of the United States necessitates and demands the operation of an efficient, world-wide intelligence service'. Hoover then added a warning note: 'It is well-known that the British and Russian Governments, while ostensibly discontinuing their intelligence services or even denying the existence of such organisations in individual countries, are actually intensifying their coverage.' But the British model – which had helped OSS get going in 1940 and 1941 – was now a source of negative feelings. Although some in OSS and in the Army were urging the British model upon the White House, others regarded OSS as a victim of its over-close relations with London during the early years of the war. The FBI observed sourly that the British model had been touted by those who had 'something to sell'. Hoover wanted a post-war American overseas secret service that ran agents – some sort of a CIA – but did not want it modelled on London. The British system, he observed shrewdly, had spent the war 'basking in the self-generated light of its own brilliance'.[44]

By October 1945, the emerging Cold War was focusing minds in Washington. Jimmy Byrnes, the new American Secretary of State, got together to discuss the issue with the Secretaries of the Army and Navy. They all agreed there was a crying need for a centralised intelligence service, and indeed all liked William Donovan's plan for American post-war intelligence. The main problems were the 'Gestapo' tag given to it by the wartime enemies of OSS, together with the awkward issue of who should own it. The British model continued to ride high. Byrnes was influenced by his recent visit to see Eisenhower's headquarters in Paris. Eisenhower had lavished praise upon his British intelligence chief, General Kenneth Strong, and the US Army Air Corps had held forth on the superior quality of the British intelligence system over its American counterpart. All those at the meeting 'felt that the British Intelligence Service was the best in the business'. They were troubled that Congress had refused to fund American expansion because American intelligence was thought to be poor, for this would only guarantee that it would remain poor.[45]

Despite the persecution of its enemies, and a parsimonious Congress, small pieces of OSS had survived. In London, elements of the service were discreetly preserved and liaison with the British continued. London had been a large wartime OSS station, acting as a stepping stone for the continent and offering connections with the many European governments in exile dotted around the second-class hotels of Kensington. London would soon become host to a large CIA station. Although the OSS Secret Intelligence branch was winding down, its core activities were protected. In November 1945 American intelligence officers in London noted the 'establishment of a permanent unit ... separated organizationally and geographically from the liquidating unit'. This new element, commanded by John A. Bross, now called the Strategic Services Unit – London, or SSU London, and sheltering under Army cover, kept links going with SIS in the nearby Broadway Buildings.

'Intelligence reports from Broadway increased almost 100% in volume, particularly reports on Russian activities,' SSU reported in November 1945. SSU undertook to supply Jimmy Byrnes with reports of special interest during his visit to the London Conference of Foreign Ministers in the same month. Most intelligence exchanged with SIS concerned the developing Cold War in Germany and Austria together with Soviet Army order of battle material, which detailed the size and location of its units. SSU in London boasted seventy-three personnel on 7 December 1945, including ten local British employees. This was an embryonic CIA station in waiting, commanded by someone who would become one of the CIA's leading lights in the post-war era.[46]

In December 1945, the overall head of SSU in Washington, General Quinn, was still a major point of contact for the SIS station in Washington. As SSU attempted to prolong its limited existence, access to SIS material allowed Quinn to increase the unit's importance. Typically, he was able to write to the US Air Force Intelligence Chief, General Quesada, presenting himself as the gatekeeper of British SIS material:

Certain British Intelligence Service reports of special interest are currently received by us. In general, these reports deal with political problems of importance in Europe. Those of recent date have been of immediate interest in reporting on Germany and Austria; they discuss the political forces current in that area. Reports on that area as well as on others seem to me to be of considerable importance, not only because of their content but because of their source.

SIS material, he wrote, was received by SSU 'under special conditions', but he was willing to supply some 'significant reports' to the US Air Force 'by some special arrangement' from the British for highly restricted use.[47]

Liaison with the secret service of a friendly state is always ambiguous. Both parties view the process as a form of legitimised spying upon each other, as much as upon common enemies. Thus the SIS intelligence given to John Bross and SSU in 1945–6 was partly valuable for what it told Washington about the views of London. SIS was producing a lot of good intelligence on Spain in a series of reports codenamed 'Coventry' which also went to Bross. SSU noted that the British Foreign Office was guided 'to a considerable extent' by these reports in making policy, especially on Gibraltar. Thus SIS material aided Washington in dealing with its British counterparts over Spain. 'We are thus afforded an opportunity of making it possible for the two key American agencies in the U.K. engaged in Anglo-American discussions on Spain to read the mind as it were of their British opposites before sitting down at the Conference table.'[48] SSU also boasted an X-2 unit which dealt with counter-intelligence under Lieutenant-Commander Winston M. Scott. Scott had worked closely during the war with SIS Section V and with MI5. In 1946 it was still the familiar figures from former Section V, including Kim Philby, who were his regular contacts, freely exchanging material on British and American persons who were thought to be suspicious.[49]

Initially the flow of traffic was uneven. Exchange between SSU on the one hand and SIS and MI5 on the other continued without interruption. But this was not true of the higher-level material produced by the JIC. This reflected uncertainty about continued intelligence exchange among some service intelligence chiefs in Washington. Admiral Inglis, the American Director of Naval Intelligence, was opposed to further work with the British. London intelligence chiefs played the game skilfully. They continued to send large numbers of JIC reports to the Americans via Britain's JIC Washington, located at the Embassy, hinting meanwhile at British hopes of reciprocation. By contrast the flow of American JIC reports to Britain had ceased abruptly in August 1945. But the British tactic of sustained generosity, continuing to bombard Washington with JIC material, eventually paid dividends. On 25 September 1946 the American JIC concluded:

If it is desired to continue to receive the British JIC intelligence estimates it is submitted that it must be done on an exchange basis, otherwise the source will dry up. Since there are many areas, particularly in parts of Europe, the Near East and the Middle East, where the British sources of information are superior to those of the United States, it is believed desirable that the United States J.I.C. continue to receive such estimates. This view is reinforced when the world situation is considered.

What the committee wanted was a continued supply of British JIC papers and it suggested that exchange now proceed on a 'quid pro quo basis'. London delegates to major post-war Anglo-American conferences always departed for Washington armed with plenty of new JIC material.[50]

This revived exchange of top-level JIC material was not always what it seemed. Many of the more substantial JIC reports – typically London's large annual survey of Soviet intentions and capabilities, running to seventy pages – were sent verbatim to Washington.[51] However, the Americans were often given modified material produced by the 'British Joint Intelligence Committee in Washington'. On 12 July 1946 the Americans received twenty-two copies of such a paper on Soviet interests and intentions in the Middle East. Recipients were also carefully selected, and these went to the US Joint Chiefs of Staff and their subordinates, including their JIC, to American service intelligence chiefs, to the head of SSU, but not always to the State Department. The same was true of British JIC material on Palestine sent to Washington in 1948 which played up the dangers of Soviet interest in the area.[52] Similarly, Washington produced dry-cleaned versions of American papers for London. In 1949 US officials discussed 'a sanitized version of J.I.C. 286/2 for processing and release to the British', a paper which dealt with 'Communist penetration in the United States'.[53]

Despite this mild 'doctoring' of material by both sides, Washington service intelligence chiefs remained uncomfortable about the JIC exchange. The American JIC was very different to its British counterpart, being more subordinated to the military. Some in Washington felt the gentle but unremitting British pressure to exchange papers and for comments on British papers exposed an institutional inadequacy in the American system. The bottom line was that Washington still did not have proper centralised intelligence. In 1949 General Charles Cabell, the head of USAF intelligence, warned that the British request for comments on their papers was 'merely a device to increase the flow of U.S. intelligence material to the British' and provided London with a window on its policy which it would not otherwise have.[54]

Anglo-American intelligence co-operation should have been smoothed by the creation of the Central Intelligence Agency in 1947.

Certainly one of the first British priorities was to conclude a CIA–SIS treaty, not dissimilar to the agreements that had defined relations between OSS, SIS and SOE during the war. But the CIA that Truman approved in 1947 was an odd creature, very different from the CIA that its principal founder, William J. Donovan, had envisaged. Donovan had recommended an all-embracing organisation that combined secret intelligence, special operations, counter-intelligence and substantial propaganda activities. When London decided in the autumn of 1945 to roll up SOE and place it under SIS, this move not only reflected a desire to restore central direction, it was also the result of seeing Donovan's superior wartime system at close hand.[55]

Ironically, just as London moved towards the Donovan approach, putting everything into one organisation, Washington abandoned it. The new CIA handled only intelligence; meanwhile Washington developed a different organisation for 'covert action'. This was the Office of Policy Co-ordination (OPC) under Frank Wisner, a seasoned former OSS officer who had waited out the interregnum in Germany. OPC took its orders from George Kennan at the State Department and from the National Security Council, which was created in 1947 to co-ordinate high-level military and diplomatic policy, and it was connected to the CIA only for purposes of administrative support and 'rations'. Designed for 'stirring up trouble' in Eastern Europe, it was intensely disliked by those in the new CIA responsible for quietly collecting intelligence. This was the old SOE–SIS dichotomy, but with a difference. In the post-war Washington system, it was special operations that had the upper hand. Many key figures in the post-war Washington elite, including Allen Welsh Dulles, George Kennan, Paul Hoffman, John McCloy and Paul Nitze, were adherents and urged Wisner on to yet grander schemes.

The unhappy place of Wisner's OPC in the American chain of secret service command was recognised from the start. In 1947 the US National Security Council had appointed a Survey Group of high-level consultants, including Allen Dulles, to look at the CIA. One of the most awkward problems they wrestled with was the relationship between intelligence and covert action. In May 1948, in an interim verdict, they stressed that the two were interdependent, with resistance groups providing a highly important source of information and timely intelligence being critical in guiding covert action. The two, they thought, should be brought together. Dulles and his group had been watching opposite developments in London and the irony was not lost on them: 'The Allied experience in the carrying out of secret operations and secret intelligence during the last war has pointed up the close relationship of the two activities. The British, for example, who had separate systems during the war, have now come round to the view that secret intelligence and secret operations should be carried out under a single operational head and have reorganized their services accordingly'.[56] But George Kennan resisted the integration of OPC into the CIA. While accepting that Allen Dulles' Survey Group 'hits the organisational problem head on', Kennan insisted that the merger 'should not be done at this time'. Covert action was simply too critical to his emerging vision of containment to allow the CIA greater control. The current pattern in which his Policy Planning Staff were writing many of Wisner's briefs suited him best.[57] Exactly twenty years later, in January 1968, senior CIA officers such as Richard Bissell and Robert Amory would look back at this experimental period of OPC separation from CIA and condemn it as organisationally disastrous with a legacy that stretched out over decades.[58]

In the late 1940s, Wisner, Kennan and the Navy Secretary James Forrestal, backed by the National Security Council, comprised a formidable axis and expanded covert action at an astonishing pace. The Director of the CIA, Admiral Hillenkoetter, disliked this but was painfully aware that if he interfered 'there would have been a call from the State Department'. Forrestal and Kennan in particular would not tolerate CIA interference in OPC; and, in the words of a CIA officer who observed their relations closely at the time, with this high-powered backing Wisner could 'have run right over Hillenkoetter'. By the time OPC was finally merged with CIA in 1950, Wisner presided over a staff of close to 2,000 personnel with forty-seven stations around the world and a budget approaching $200 million.[59]

The National Security Council approved the Dulles Report in August 1949 and moves were supposed to be set in train for the merger of OPC and the secret intelligence wing of the CIA. But matters were complicated by personalities. Hillenkoetter wanted Colonel Robert Schow, a senior CIA intelligence man with experience in Germany, to take over the new combined office. But Hillenkoetter did not know how to push. Meanwhile Kennan and the State Department backed Wisner and told him to stay in place for the duration of the tussle. The State Department conceded, 'The situation has the makings of a jumble, because it is obviously impossible to get a man big enough to be over Wisner and small enough to be under Hilly.'[60]

Early 1950 brought some sort of solution. A fiery new figure, General Walter Bedell Smith, accepted the Directorship of the CIA and immediately insisted that he enjoy complete direction over all these activities. Washington had finally found a man 'big enough' to command Frank Wisner, although it took Bedell Smith years to integrate the intelligence and covert action wings of the CIA. Thereafter, the culture of covert action developed a firm grip on the American system and continued to dominate the CIA into the 1960s. Moreover, while the CIA now looked outwardly more like SIS, being an integrated package handling all secret service activities with human agents, it had escaped from higher control. The trajectory of American developments thus remained very different from those in Britain. The State Department, the Joint Chiefs of Staff and the National Security Council had competed for ownership of the CIA, but now it was slipping away from all of them, to become a rival policy-maker in its own right. This would have a profound effect, not only on the nature of the Cold War, but also on the conduct of Anglo-American relations.

PART II

The Cold War Gets Going
1945–1949

4

MI5: Defectors, Spy-trials and Subversion

This issue of Australian security is a real teaser. Since we spoke of the matter last Tuesday morning, I have heard of still a further incident which reveals a pretty serious state of affairs. It looks as if they have been penetrated at all possible levels.

General Leslie Hollis to Sir Henry Tizard, 19 February 1948[1]

Intelligence in the early Cold War contains numerous paradoxes. SIS, despite its lacklustre performance in the conflict with the Axis, had had a 'good war'. Basking in the reflected glory of Bletchley Park, it emerged to seize control of its most dangerous rival, SOE. Britain's Security Service, MI5, despite remarkable triumphs such as the Doublecross System that turned Hitler's agents for deception purposes, did not have a 'good war'. MI5 was associated with the temporary surrender of civil liberties and with claustrophobic security measures such as mail censorship, things that all now wanted swept away. For political reasons, the new Prime Minister, Clement Attlee, was especially anxious to keep security on a tight leash. Yet major challenges confronted Britain in the realm of subversion and counter-espionage during the Attlee years. An under-resourced MI5, together with other security elements, struggled to handle a deluge of unpopular security work that few wished to admit was in progress.

At the top the severity of the security problem was understood from the outset. Cadogan, Menzies, Montgomery and others were aware of the penetration of Whitehall by Soviet agents and remarked on it during the war and soon after. As early as 1943, Menzies warned Cadogan about the penetration of SIS, telling him frankly that he had 'communists in his organization'. What action they took, if any, remains unknown. But on 14 April 1944 Churchill recorded, 'We are purging all our secret establishments of communists because we know they owe no allegiance to us or our cause and will always betray our secrets to the Soviets even while we are working together ...' In Britain, Canada and Australia examples of Soviet espionage and subversion came to light in the period before the onset of the Berlin Crisis in 1948. The story of work against Soviet espionage in the West is now dominated by something called Venona, Western efforts to break into the enciphered wireless traffic of Soviet intelligence, which began to produce dividends in early 1948. But, as we shall see, this effort to read Soviet communications has tended to distract from an intriguing story that precedes it.[2]

MI5 had maintained strong surveillance of the Communist Party of Great Britain – known as the CPGB – throughout the war. The Cabinet, including Labour's Herbert Morrison, the Home Secretary, encouraged this and ensured that resulting MI5 reports were disseminated at a high level. Ernest Bevin, Minister of Labour and a powerful figure in the Cabinet, was also intensely suspicious of CPGB. In March 1943 Morrison circulated a detailed MI5 briefing on CPGB to Cabinet, explaining that he was doing so because it was 'reliable and of such interest'. He thought it essential to circulate it to the War Cabinet because it showed that, despite the wartime united front against Hitler, the higher echelons of CPGB had abandoned none of their long-term revolutionary objectives. MI5 and the Special Branch were also keeping a close eye on the Trotskyist movement in Britain led by James Heston. But Morrison asserted that there was 'no evidence of external funding' from the Soviet Union. With a total membership below 1,000 and an impact upon industry that was at best 'slight', they were not considered a threat.[3]

Despite a consensus in the wartime coalition government about the need for surveillance of CPGB, MI5 emerged from the war under a political cloud. Clement Attlee decided on a new director of MI5 from outside the service who had strong democratic values. No serious reorganisation of MI5 was undertaken until the 1950s and the substantial section responsible for Soviet activities was being run down even in December 1945. Attlee resisted pressure, from those more conscious of Soviet activities, to introduce active security investigations into the background of those with access to government secrets, known as positive vetting. MI5 was not only a demoralised service, it was also overstretched by twin demands made on it by the struggle against communist infiltration of areas such as defence science and by a vast pattern of unrest spreading across the Empire in the Middle East, Africa and Asia. MI5, overworked but unloved, could not keep up with its routine duties and had little incentive to carry through innovative searches for high-level Soviet penetration in the inner circles of the British establishment.

The private diaries of Britain's elite betray a surprising disquiet regarding the future of MI5 at the end of the war. At its broadest, this was no more than an understandable reaction to the suffocating blanket of security that been thrown over southern England in preparations for D-Day. But there were also more precise concerns. There were several incidents in which MPs in Westminster appear to have been kept under surveillance with microphones or phone taps in pursuit of possible security leaks about operational plans. Information gained from postal censorship had been used for overt political purposes. All were thoroughly conscious of the potential abuses to which surveillance could be put.[4]

Part of the disquiet arose not from MI5 but from the work of Allies. European governments in exile were billeted across London, and some, like the Polish and the French, had large security elements which seemed to operate freely. In the summer of 1944, the MP Tom Driberg was pursuing the issue of the mistreatment of Jewish soldiers within the Polish Home Army. He complained to Eden that he had learned 'from an extremely reliable source' that the Polish secret service 'have my phone tapped'. 'This', he conceded, 'seems quite fantastic, but my informant is, as I say, a reliable one.' Eden agreed to look into it.[5] The Allied secret services of the European continent were embedded in the wartime governments in exile, which had been billeted in an odd assortment of buildings in west London. The Free French secret service in London, to name but one, had behaved in a vicious and arbitrary way. French nationals in London were often picked up and taken to its Duke Street HQ for interrogation. As a result there were cases before the courts. In February 1944, Eden had warned Churchill that members of the French secret service were 'behaving as if they were beyond the law'. Eden had insisted on a new agreement between the French and MI5, whereby the British would carry out any arrests and MI5 would be present at subsequent interrogations.[6]

But there were also anxieties about MI5 itself. Field Marshal Sir Alan Brooke, the Chief of the Imperial General Staff, was clearly worried. On 19 November 1944, he noted:

> Long talk with P J Grigg [Minister for War] on future of MI5 and the dangers attending the future should it fall into the wrong hands ...
>
> Finally Lennox who controls [War Office liaison with] MI5 to discuss the future of this organisation and the grave danger of it falling into the clutches of unscrupulous political hands of which there are too many at present.

Alexander Cadogan was aware that some sort of subterranean enquiry was being conducted into MI5 in 1944. MI5 was anxious to stay away from Churchill's immediate political entourage during this process. Whatever the nature of these manoeuvrings, the general disquiet about security activities throughout the country was detected even by junior officers. They recall 'a strong current of prejudice against MI5 in many prominent circles' at the end of the war.[7]

During the general election campaign of June 1945 these private concerns erupted into remarkable public controversy. Churchill chose a major election broadcast on the BBC to warn the public of what a future Labour government might have in store in the field of public security. In a wild moment, he claimed that in order to enforce its will Labour would:

> have to fall back on some form of Gestapo, no doubt very humanely administered in the first instance. And this would nip opinion in the bud; it would stop criticism as it reared its head, and it would gather all the power to the supreme party and the party leaders ... and where would the ordinary simple folk – the common people as they like to call them in America – where would they be, once this mighty organism had got them in their grip?

In case anyone had failed to get the message about the dangers of this 'formidable machine', Churchill added, 'Socialism is inseparately interwoven with Totalitarianism.' Clement Attlee was incensed and vigorous protests ensured that the offending remarks were eventually withdrawn. This ill-advised intervention by a war-weary Churchill was wide of the mark. Labour harboured long-standing suspicions of the secret services, dating back to the Zinoviev letter which had been unearthed by the secret services and which had contributed to the collapse of the Labour government in the 1920s. But Churchill's claims redoubled Attlee's pre-existing determination to keep MI5 small and under firm ministerial control.[8]

In this highly charged political atmosphere there was never any prospect of an internal candidate taking the vacant post of director of MI5. Instead a wide variety of trusted wartime figures were considered. The shortlist included Pug Ismay, who ran the Chiefs of Staff Secretariat; Kenneth Strong, Eisenhower's popular intelligence chief, and Mountbatten's intelligence chief, William Penney. On the day, Percy Sillitoe, Chief Constable of Kent, was appointed director of MI5 on a salary of £3,000 a year.[9] But this was not only a political decision by Attlee that reflected general consensus in Whitehall. Sillitoe simply outperformed the other candidates. On the night of 19 November 1945 Cadogan helped to interview Penney and Strong 'but didn't much plump for either of them'. A week later the same group met in the Cabinet Secretary's Office: 'we were unanimous in choosing Sillitoe, Chief Constable. I thought he certainly seemed good.' Guy Liddell, MI5's inside candidate, had to content himself with being deputy, while the appointment of an outsider was regarded within the service as a vote of no confidence.[10]

Many individuals in government have recalled with approval Sillitoe's 'trenchant views on the dangers of police states and the importance of restrictions on police power'. However, Sillitoe performed better at interview than on the job. The lack of long-term professional experience in the area of security intelligence soon showed and he himself recorded, 'The prospect suddenly before me caused me qualms that would not have been occasioned by the offer of any straightforward police work.' He continued, 'I had no way of gauging my potential ability to direct the Security Service. In common with the vast majority of the public, I knew very little about the work of MI5, and virtually nothing about the duties of its chief.'[11] He exaggerated his ignorance of security matters. As Chief Constable of Kent during the D-Day preparations, security had preoccupied him considerably and required him to work closely with the authorities in London. The main problem was that, with the general trend towards university-educated officers in the higher echelons of the secret services, some regarded Sillitoe with a combination of professional and intellectual contempt. Even his sympathetic biographer could not bring himself to describe the appointment as a success.[12]

MI5 was not reorganised or reinvigorated. Under Sillitoe it retained its old pattern of organisation with six divisions mostly based at its Curzon Street headquarters in Mayfair. The cream of MI5 was widely regarded to be B Division, which until recently had been headed by Guy Liddell, whose B1(b) section had been involved in the Doublecross deception effort against Germany. It also contained a small but elite and highly secretive B5(b) section under Maxwell Knight, which kept a wartime watch on CPGB. Sillitoe reportedly disliked the extreme secrecy and relative autonomy of Knight's small crack unit based in Dolphin Square. It was soon broken up and transferred back to Curzon Street. Accordingly, Yves Tangye recalled, 'there were only two or three people in the Russian section of MI5 by the end of the war'. This was in sharp contrast to SIS, which, as we have seen, had begun to create a new Soviet section in 1944. The shift to peacetime also brought the loss of MI5's valuable wartime powers, including blanket postal censorship and the ability to intern people almost at will.[13]

By contrast MI5's responsibilities in 1945 were uniquely vast. Although it was responsible for security and counter-intelligence only in British territory, British territory had expanded remarkably in the last days of the war. British occupation troops were spread all over Europe and Asia. On 9 June 1945, one of the last acts of Sillitoe's predecessor as director of MI5, Sir David Petrie, was to set out on an expedition across Europe to speak to his officers in Eisenhower's SHAEF HQ in Germany and 'elsewhere on the Continent' for he knew that MI5 was stretched to the limit.[14] Although security in Germany and Austria was, in theory, the responsibility of the British Military Government, MI5 was asked to advise on the growing security problems. By 19 July 1946 one British official lamented that 'The number of low grade agents of Russian allegiance who have recently arrived in our Zone [of Germany] is so large as to make it burdensome to keep a tally of them.' Soviet efforts to recruit any Germans working for the British Control Commission had 'increased markedly'. But as yet there was no attempt to repeat the spectacular success of the wartime Doublecross operations by recruiting Soviet agents.[15]

How did Britain and the United States respond to would-be Soviet defectors in the awkward period between 1944 and 1946? In this twilight period between world war and Cold War, many had identified the Soviet Union as the 'next target', but active intelligence-gathering activities were risky and the façade of the wartime Grand Alliance remained important. The story of the first defectors indicates that, while the antennae of the secret services were being retuned, this was an uneven process and was certainly not yet publicly admissible. Some elements, typically in SIS or in US Army Intelligence in Europe, had begun to refocus on the Soviets in 1944. But diplomats in London and Washington regarded defectors as an unwelcome embarrassment and wished to return them to their home country, regardless of their fate.

In April 1944, Victor Kravchenko, a Soviet diplomat stationed in Washington, decided to defect. British and American officials regarded this as horribly embarrassing and a threat to good relations with the Soviets. Charles Bohlen, a rising star in the State Department, confessed that he 'attached no great importance to the incident' but hoped Kravchenko could be persuaded to return to the Soviet Union. London diplomats expressed regret that the Russian could not be expelled and indeed was legally permitted to apply for residency. They added hopefully: 'It is of course quite possible that the GPU may solve the difficulty for the immigration authorities by bumping him off themselves.' (The GPU had in fact become the NKVD in 1934, but many still used the old-fashioned term.) Victor Kravchenko's case prompted London to review its general line on Soviet defectors at this late stage in the war, taking into account what it knew of other cases, including those of Walter Krivitsky and Grigory Bessedovsky, two other high-profile wartime defectors. It did not believe Kravchenko's assertions of political dissidence and took a cynical view of all Soviet officials trying to jump ship:

> The alternatives are (1) that he really believes what he said in his statement: (it seems a bit odd however that it should take him 22 years to come to this conclusion, the last seven months of which he spent in the United States); (2) he may have been recalled and just decided it was nicer here; (3) the hostages held against his name back home (the GPU usually keeps an eye on the relatives of Soviet officials abroad) may have died, or he may have just decided that he does not really care what happens to them; (4) he may have been caught with his wrists in the till and decided to take the breeze; (5) he may have a girlfriend here of whom his superiors disapprove.

The general consensus was to hope that the whole business would 'soon be forgotten'.[16] Miraculously, Kravchenko managed to avoid repatriation and by the late 1940s was being treated as a valuable exhibit by the State Department.

Disdain was a fairly uniform wartime attitude and saved diplomatic embarrassment, but it entailed a high cost. In Istanbul in 1944, the US Military Attaché was approached by Major Akhmed, the Assistant Military Attaché in the Soviet Embassy. Akhmed faced a dilemma. He had been recalled to Moscow and did not know the reason. The purpose might be quite innocent, a routine reassignment perhaps. But he feared that he had been implicated in some ongoing purge trials and recognised that his fate was at least uncertain. He contacted the US Military Attaché and explained that he wished to defect, bringing with him important information on Soviet intelligence operations within the United States, including espionage within the atomic programme. But the US Military Attaché considered this behaviour improper and followed correct procedure. He informed Akhmed's superior, the Soviet Military Attaché. Sensing that something was wrong Akhmed fled just in time and successfully turned himself over to the Turkish Security Service, which was less well disposed to the Soviets, offering it what he knew of Soviet operations inside Turkey. Only in 1947, with the advent of the Truman Doctrine, the formal proclamation of American containment, did the Turkish Security Service feel the climate had changed sufficiently for it to offer Akhmed safely to the American authorities for debriefing. But by then much of what he had to tell was out of date.[17]

Alexander Rado, the famous chief of the Soviet GRU military intelligence network in wartime Switzerland – the linchpin of the so-called Red Orchestra, the large GRU spy network in Nazi-occupied Europe – presents an especially fascinating case. Rado had run a large and successful intelligence network operating into Switzerland which had been broken up by the Swiss police in 1943. At this point Rado had asked Moscow about the possibility of taking refuge at the British Embassy by approaching the British intelligence service, SIS, but permission was denied. Instead Rado made his way to Paris. There he linked up with his radio operator, a British communist called Alexander Foote. While in liberated Paris, Rado, Foote and their distinguished colleague Leopold Trepper, who ran other Red Orchestra networks in wartime Europe, were all persuaded to return voluntarily to Moscow in January 1945 to submit a final report on their wartime activities. The offer had been made by the Soviet Military Mission which had arrived in Paris in November 1944 to join the growing army of intelligence outfits that were establishing themselves in the newly liberated capital.

But Rado's journey was erratic. His colleague Leopold Trepper recalled that, while travelling to Moscow via the Middle East, Rado attempted to defect to MI5 in Cairo. Trepper noted that at the time 'Rado's disappearance obsessed me', and he praised Rado's 'realism as a man of learning' who had the sense to realise that 'nothing had changed in the Kingdom of the GPU'. But, Trepper added, Rado's flight was to no avail. MI5 at Cairo returned him to the Soviets in the interests of 'good Anglo-Soviet relations'. Why was Rado, a significant intelligence catch by any standards, deliberately handed back to the Soviets in July 1945 at a time when the British secret services were already refocusing on their new target? Trepper blames Rado's fate on the malignant influence of Kim Philby, while others have suggested that this bizarre episode was the result of unholy collaboration between three of Stalin's Englishmen, Philby, Donald Maclean and James Klugmann.[18]

The real story is quite different. MI5 documents reveal a great deal about the outlying stations of British intelligence and about defection during the early Cold War. In fact, Rado did not trust British intelligence and chose not to attempt a full defection. Instead of trading on his high status to obtain sanctuary from the Gulag that he felt increasingly sure awaited him, he played an independent game and presented himself as a lower-grade Soviet agent of Hungarian origin who had worked for the Soviets and wished to return to France. Neither the local MI5 organisation in Cairo nor Alex Kellar, a senior MI5 officer in London who saw his case, recognised his importance. However, once he had been discarded by MI5 as a lowly Soviet agent he was designated a mere Displaced Person (DP), swept into the repatriation programme and forced to return to the Soviet Union. Months later Rado's true espionage status, and his surprisingly high-level personal contacts in London with socialist figures such as Harold Laski, became clear. At this point the Foreign Office, which had helped to determine his fate, decided it was best to keep silent about his six-month stay with the authorities in Cairo and the manner of his forcible transfer into Soviet custody.

Alexander Rado, Leopold Trepper and Alexander Foote, the three Red Orchestra veterans, left Paris on a Russian aircraft on 8 January 1945 with five other passengers bound for Moscow. Heavy fighting was still in progress in Northern and Central Europe. Their short-range aircraft was forced to take a long detour, stopping at Marseilles, Tripolitania, Cairo, Palestine and Teheran. The flight was supposedly for 'Russian PoWs', and they all travelled under false names, but in reality it was a VIP flight, including leading Soviet political exiles from the 1920s invited to return to Moscow by Molotov. Rado fell into conversation with them and explained that his network had been uncovered and rolled up by the Swiss counter-espionage service. One of the passengers expressed surprise that Rado was coming home of his own accord, explaining to him 'that failures were harshly dealt with in Russia and that once there he was not likely to be able to return to Paris'. Rado had agreed to travel because he was a professional geographer and thought the trip would be interesting. But at this point 'Rado's fears were aroused'. Once they arrived in Egypt, further conversations with Foote and Trepper increased his anxiety. He suspected that he would not be able to return to his wife Helen and his young family, still in Paris. The travellers were not under any restraint in Cairo and on 11 January he fled from the hotel where he was staying and presented himself at the British Embassy.

There Rado appealed for asylum. He gave officials his real name and explained that he was really a Hungarian who had worked as an agent for the Soviets in Paris and Geneva and that he was travelling under a false identity. He played up his background as an academic geographer with an eminent academic reputation but said nothing of the Red Orchestra. He explained that he now believed 'that he would be shot on arrival in the Soviet Union' and claimed British protection, asking to be sent to Paris or London. But he was told that as a non-British national he could not be assisted by the Embassy. This might have been the end of the matter, but his presence had been routinely reported to Britain's Security Intelligence Middle East or SIME, which took an interest in his case.

David Muire, a talented officer working on deception in the Middle East, once offered an irreverent definition of SIME as 'MI5 behaving rather like MI6 [SIS] but doing it rather better'. SIME was the Middle Eastern manifestation of MI5 and worked with a number of local bodies including the counter-espionage wing of SIS, Section V. Since the summer of 1944, it had been run by Brigadier Douglas Roberts and was still based in the Grey Pillars building of the military HQ in Cairo. Rado was interrogated by two MI5 officers, Captains Bidmead and Dunkerly, on 12 January 1945. The NKVD was now combing Cairo looking for him and Rado was dependent on SIME for protection. Yet he was terse and disingenuous with his captors. They noted that for 'a man of such training and education he is extremely vague when telling his story and gives the briefest details on each point of it'. Instead of attempting to sell himself to MI5 as a Soviet intelligence chief, he behaved like any Comintern agent of the 1930s, pretending to be inconsequential and hoping to slip through the net of British imperial security. He presented himself as a lowly sub-agent of his own Swiss network and instead chose to play up his time in the resistance in France in 1944. He explained that he had held the rank of lieutenant with the Maquis in Villiers for a year from late 1943 to late 1944 and had interrogated German prisoners. He said nothing about his Comintern background, or indeed about his previous time in Moscow, where he had married Lenin's secretary, then Helen Jansen, in 1931.

Two hours after his interrogation Rado made a suicide attempt. By 17 January, after a further attempt on his own life, he was in a Cairo hospital. The Soviets had now tracked him down and were requesting his return. Successful in slipping through his MI5 interrogation as a low-level agent, his case would now be treated as one of a mere Displaced Person. But Killearn, the British Ambassador in Cairo, seemed to sense that he was more than just a faceless refugee and asked London what should be done with him. London was surprised that Killearn should take an interest when Europe was awash with refugees. It suggested that he be handed over to the Cairo police, who, as it knew, would hand him over to the Russians unless the British told them to do otherwise.

In 1945, local security in Cairo was still largely in the hands of the British. Although nominally independent, King Farouk of Egypt had agreed that, for the duration of the war, matters such as policing would be run by London. The Cairo police were thus still a force under British control and the many British officers in the Egyptian police fell into three categories: the 'Nine', the commandants and senior officers retained by the Egyptians at London's request; the 'Indispensables', the officers retained at the Egyptians' own request; and the European Liaison Officers, paid for by the British authorities. On 5 February Rado was handed over to the Egyptian police and kept in Zeitoun detention camp. On 30 July he was surrendered to the Soviets and left in an aircraft for Moscow. Killearn noted that his departure was watched by the Cairo police and that Rado 'showed considerable reluctance to board the aircraft but was eventually persuaded to do so'.

British officials were free of the Rado case for only a few weeks. The Embassy in Cairo soon received a letter from Rado's sister-in-law, Mrs Jansen, writing on behalf of his wife Helen, who was ill, enquiring about his whereabouts. The Red Cross had informed Rado's family, tactfully, that he had been injured in an 'air accident' but had not mentioned his repeated suicide attempts, adding that he was interned in Zeitoun camp at Cairo. British officials were alarmed by the high-level contacts in London that the Rado family now conjured up. As a renowned geographer and well-connected European socialist, Rado had important friends, including the Minister of Education, Ellen Wilkinson, and the publisher Victor Gollancz. They all wanted to know what they had to do to secure Rado's release from the Zeitoun camp in Cairo.

British officials in Cairo said as little as possible. They explained that Rado had left by air for Moscow 'under escort'. A further letter was soon received at the British Embassy in Cairo asking 'by what authority was he handed over?' Killearn was disturbed. But, since Rado had been handed over to the Cairo police and thence to the Soviets on instructions from London, he considered it a London problem. On 15 November 1945 he wrote to Ernest Bevin 'regarding the disposal of Alexander Rado', explaining that SIME had handed him over to the Egyptian police, 'in accordance with the instructions in your telegram'. Killearn added tartly, 'In the circumstances I have the honour to request that you will reply direct to Mrs Jansen.'

The Foreign Office knew it was in a tight corner. Initially, Rado had appeared to be a lowly DP and Soviet agent to whom Killearn had shown too much solicitude. Inundated with DPs in Europe its approach was to send them eastward with all despatch. But now it was uncertain how to respond. Thomas Brimelow, a senior official in the Foreign Office Northern Department who had special responsibility for DP issues, noted that more information could be obtained by making further enquiries of the Embassy in Cairo. Then he added, 'but I do not want to ask, as my chief anxiety is to steer clear of this case'. With the approval of Ernest Bevin and the Legal Department, an evasive reply was despatched to Mrs Jansen suggesting that 'you address your enquiries to the Soviet Embassy in Cairo'. Rado's family knew that the Foreign Office was hiding something and were persistent. Further letters followed and by the autumn of 1947 they had persuaded Professor Harold Laski of the London School of Economics, who had just been elected chairman of the Labour Party, to write to Bevin on their behalf. Laski asked Bevin if 'as an act of great humanity' he could give Mrs Helen Rado any further information about her husband's disappearance, particularly, 'if he is dead, the grounds on which he was executed'.

Laski's intervention only made the diplomats more reticent. Thomas Brimelow reflected that, although it had given Rado to the Egyptians in February 1945, the British Embassy had also seen him three days before his departure in July. It had decided to grant a transit visa for his unwilling excursion via Palestine and Teheran to Moscow. By now Rado's full background was becoming clearer. By 1946, the Foreign Office had identified him as the 'Head of Soviet Espionage in Switzerland': 'He appears to have worked, not too successfully, as a Soviet agent ... To judge by the story he told the Embassy in Cairo, and by his attempted suicide there, he was in terror of the Russians, and it is quite possible that he was shot on arrival in the U.S.S.R. But we do not really know what the Russians had against him, not do we know what happened to him after he left Egypt'. Brimelow urged his colleagues to 'keep silent on this score'. Bevin's reply to Laski was polite but brief and uninformative. In common with previous missives, it failed to mention that Rado had been in the hands of SIME, the local MI5, or that London had decided to pass him on to the British-run Egyptian police in the sure knowledge that he would then be handed into Soviet custody for despatch to Moscow.

Alexander Rado is probably the most famous Soviet agent of the

Second World War. But his intriguing sojourn in the hands of British security has been misunderstood. Some have claimed that he tried to defect but was rejected by the British, while others have even suggested that he was hunted down on the streets of Cairo by British security and handed over to the Soviets. Instead, Rado, caught in the hiatus between conflicts, played an independent, and ultimately unsuccessful, game hoping to make his own way back to Paris or London. He sought to make himself sufficiently interesting to the British at Cairo to avoid being handed over to the Soviets, who he believed would kill him, but sufficiently dull to avoid the prolonged attention of the MI5 officers at SIME. But he was unaware of the prevailing British policy towards DPs and POWs sought by the Soviets, the final details of which were being agreed at the Yalta Conference even while he was in Cairo. How SIME would have treated him had he announced himself to be the GRU Chief in Switzerland, on the run from his masters, is a question that must remain unanswered. Instead he passed virtually unnoticed through one of the largest MI5 stations outside London. British security did not know who Rado was in early 1945 and his fate was determined by mischance and ignorance.

Amusingly, if we are to believe the autobiographies of Rado's colleagues in the Red Orchestra, Trepper and Foote, both the British and the Soviets mistakenly came to suspect each other of 'liquidating' Rado in 1945. Alexander Foote, who stayed with the main NKVD party flying from Paris to Cairo in January 1945 and arrived in Moscow, knew that Rado's disappearance in Cairo would place him under extreme suspicion. As a British national and a senior member of the same GRU network in Switzerland, on his arrival in Moscow he was accused of working for the British as a double agent. He simply presumed that Rado had defected to the British in Cairo. But Moscow placed a more arcane interpretation on Rado's disappearance, suggesting that MI5 had 'liquidated' him in Cairo to prevent him from travelling to Moscow and revealing Foote's position as a double agent working for British intelligence. Foote was not in fact a double agent but a loyal wartime servant of Moscow. Accordingly, although Foote loathed Rado, it was nevertheless fortunate for him that the Soviets reclaimed Rado in the summer of 1945. Once Rado had been transported to Moscow, it was the turn of London to conclude that Rado had probably been shot by the Soviet authorities for failing in his mission for the GRU. In fact Rado endured ten years of prison, before being released at the same time as Leopold Trepper, following the death of Stalin.[19]

Igor Gouzenkou began his hazardous journey from humble Soviet Embassy cipher clerk to Cold War icon in September 1945. Enjoying the genuine obscurity that Rado had feigned in Cairo, his fate was very nearly the same. When he attempted to defect to the authorities in Canada, where he was stationed, the first instinct of many in authority was to return him to the Soviets like an inconvenient piece of lost property. But crucially his efforts to evade return to the Soviet Union occurred just a little later than the endgame of the Rado case. The period between his defection in September 1945 and the public disclosure of his decision in March 1946 reveals a great deal about the changing Western attitudes towards the Soviet Union and Soviet defectors.

Although Igor Gouzenkou initially found his reception no more enthusiastic than that afforded to Rado, his defection had a transformative effect on the landscape for others. In the six months between his uneasy defection and public revelations about his case, defectors moved from being an unwelcome ·burden to being a desirable commodity. Commonwealth security then emerged as a major issue among Western states, with elaborate investigations being launched in Canberra and Ottawa as a direct result. Meanwhile, defectors and the espionage threat became indelibly associated with atomic weapons and strategic technology. The United States Congress had already implemented the McMahon Act in early 1946, making the passing of atomic information to any other power a criminal offence, when the Gouzenkou story broke. Unaware of wartime Anglo-American–Canadian co-operation in this field, Congress sought only to secure national control over the valuable commercial applications of atomic energy. But, once the act was passed, the Gouzenkou case ensured that the American resumption of atomic co-operation with Britain and the Commonwealth would be withheld pending the construction of a suitably heavyweight security apparatus.

Igor Gouzenkou was a lieutenant in the Soviet Army posted as a cipher clerk to the Soviet Embassy in Ottawa in 1943. In the autumn of 1945, when his tour was over, he concluded that life was better in the West. Unlike Rado, he did not expect a free passage. To secure his future he seized a bundle of files on Soviet espionage in North America in the hope of trading this for secure asylum. This included some of the most sensitive recent atomic intelligence traffic to and from Moscow. Gouzenkou fled the Soviet Embassy, with his wife and child in tow, on the evening of 5 September 1945. His first port of call was the offices of the *Ottawa Journal*, but an editor turned him away, unable to comprehend his story. He was directed to the Royal Canadian Mounted Police (RCMP), which had MI5-type responsibilities, but instead he decided to head for the Department of Justice. It was evening however, and this was closed. The next morning, after further fruitless visits to the Department of Justice and the press, where he showed off his collection of purloined espionage documents, he headed home with threats of committing suicide. The Soviets were already looking for him.

Unknown to Gouzenkou, his activities were already causing panic in high places. On the same morning, 6 September, his wish to defect with a cargo of espionage materials was made known to Canada's Premier, Mackenzie King, and his immediate circle. King was loath to risk an 'incident' with the Soviets on the eve of a major three-power Conference of Foreign Ministers in London, which he hoped would calm worsening relations between East and West. He was briefed by Norman Robertson, the senior diplomat in charge of Canadian intelligence, including its signals intelligence effort. Reportedly the Gouzenko material showed clearly that Soviet intelligence was busy in the United States and Canada and had penetrated the State Department and the Manhattan Project that had built the atomic bomb. Gouzenkou also offered important Soviet intelligence cable traffic, which Western cryptanalysts had so far found quite unbreakable. To Norman Robertson, who was attempting to secure Canada's place in an expanding network of post-war Western intelligence alliances, the would-be defector's material looked like valuable collateral and so he urged his chief to seize the opportunity. Robertson knew that the evidence was priceless and they contacted 'Little Bill' Stephenson, a prominent Canadian who, as we have seen, had headed the wartime SIS station in New York, British Security Co-ordination. Stephenson, like Robertson, advised giving Gouzenkou asylum, but they were overruled by King.

Mackenzie King saw things quite differently. 'It was like a bomb on top of everything,' he lamented to his diary, and it seemingly threatened all sorts of dangerous or damaging possibilities. He was not prepared to upset the Soviets just because an eccentric individual was trying to improve his own circumstances. Thus Gouzenkou was refused asylum and returned to his apartment; like Rado, he threatened suicide to avoid the fate awaiting him on return to the Soviet Union. Nevertheless, King ordered that a watch be kept on his premises to see if the Soviets collected him. If he did commit suicide, his cache of documents could then be quickly seized with less chance of an incident. Robertson was dismayed and argued that this meant that the government would be a party either to suicide or murder. But King, who was prone to remarkable outbursts of sentimentality when the mood took him, remained unmoved.[20]

By the evening of the same day, 6 September, the Soviets had settled the issue. A tough four-man Soviet security unit arrived at the Gouzenkous' flat, broke down the door and began to turn it upside down. The RCMP surveillance team then arrived and the Soviets retreated into the night, refusing to be held and claiming diplomatic immunity. Wisely, Gouzenkou and his family had been hiding with a neighbour. Only at this point, after dangling in the wind for some thirty hours, were they taken into protective custody and given asylum. They were whisked away to Camp X, a large wartime secret service facility in Canada superintended by Stephenson. A joint team provided by the RCMP, the American FBI and British intelligence now began to pick over the treasure trove of materials that Gouzenkou had brought from the Soviet Embassy. This team included Peter Dwyer, the SIS head of station in Washington, and Roger Hollis from MI5 in London. Sir Stewart Menzies later arrived on the scene in person. Immediately it was clear that they were looking at an elaborate network of espionage which included Canadian civil servants, scientists and politicians together with British citizens and the likely compromise of important cipher systems.[21]

Gouzenkou's revelations about the scale of Soviet espionage in North America were inseparable from atomic issues. First, his material revealed the espionage of Allan Nunn May, a British atomic scientist working on the Manhattan Project who returned to London in October 1945. Secondly, it strongly influenced the thinking of Attlee, King and Truman as they considered the possibility of international control for the atomic bomb. Even as the London Conference of Foreign Ministers broke up in disagreement, MI5 was preparing to arrest Nunn May while Truman, Byrnes, Attlee and King were in constant communication over what they considered to be a dangerous issue. King and Robertson had abandoned their routine business and travelled to London for extended discussions with officials and Ministers.

MI5 and SIS wanted to arrest Nunn May at once, and even the usually cautious Attlee acceded, calling for a 'show-down'. Truman and King were more wary, anxious that public opinion might be affected and that the possibilities of agreement on troublesome atomic issues might thereby be impeded. Attlee was willing to accommodate Truman and King, but Ernest Bevin, who had been briefed by King over dinner on 10 September and was keen to see action, weighed in with the words 'I think we are being too tender.' So Nunn May was arrested. By this stage Dr John Cockroft from the British atomic programme had reviewed the exact nature of Nunn May's espionage. He guessed, correctly, that although he could have handed over some samples of uranium, he knew little real detail about the technical process of making the bomb, which was the most demanding aspect of attaining such a capability.[22]

On 19 February 1946 the Gouzenkou story burst on an unsuspecting public. The United States was rocked by press revelations which focused on Soviet espionage within the Manhattan programme undertaken by Nunn May. A garbled version of the story was leaked in Washington to the remorseless political columnist Drew Pearson. Pearson presented these events as clear evidence of the Soviet Union's plans for world domination, well outside its current probings into areas such as Turkey and Iran. King was horrified, but now the material was out he chose to ride the wave and announced a Canadian Royal Commission to investigate Soviet espionage in Canada and produce a public report. Thirteen persons identified by Gouzenko's documents were already being held by the RCMP without access to lawyers and were threatened with punishment if they did not speak. Most chose to co-operate and the result was an increasingly detailed picture of Soviet clandestine activities.[23]

General Leslie R. Groves, head of the American atomic programme, was a key figure in prompting the Gouzenkou enquiry. Since 1944, Groves had become increasingly aware of widespread Soviet espionage in the Anglo-American–Canadian atomic programme, but had been reluctant to be the first to lift the lid. Some of the sources of his information remain mysterious. But now the Gouzenkou case conveniently allowed London and Ottawa to take the heat, while providing a welcome counter to State Department officials who still favoured seeking improved relations with the Soviets. Drew Pearson now penned further press stories suggesting that Gouzenkou had revealed networks of 1,700 spies across the United States and Canada. Anti-communist activists on Capitol Hill, who had hitherto been obscure figures running a small pre-McCarthyite House Un-American Activities Committee, now announced that they were chasing these Soviet spies. An embryonic China Lobby was already emerging. General Patrick Hurley, Washington's former Ambassador in China, returned from his wartime confrontations with the Chinese communists to confirm that Washington had already known that the Soviets had been busy stealing atomic secrets. By March 1946 the Gouzenkou episode was indelibly associated in the public mind with the problem of managing atomic power and retaining the American nuclear monopoly. In mid-1946, some 11,900 copies of the Gouzenkou Report, known as the Blue Book, were issued and the US Army bought a further 13,000 copies of a shortened version commissioned from an American journalist. Sir Alexander Clutterbuck, the British High Commissioner in Ottawa, offered London some wise observations. The report, he conceded, was a brilliant work of investigation and, moreover, unlike most government reports, was a racy read. But he was disturbed by the disregard for civil liberties displayed by the Commission in obtaining evidence and saw this as pointing to future trouble.[24]

Bevin was quick to recognise the value of the Gouzenkou case. He gave discreet instructions to his private secretary, Pierson Dixon, that it was to be plugged for all it was worth, but without the Foreign Office being seen to take a hand. Bevin wanted 4,000 copies of the report ordered from Canada and persuaded Mackenzie King to promise that they would be printed quickly. He also wanted the Blue Book circulated to various trade unions in Britain and had got King to promise to supply sufficient numbers. The addresses of the union secretaries were to be obtained from Labour Party headquarters at Transport House, and officials would then 'send the books out in "a plain sealed wrapper" from the Foreign Office. i.e. there should be no indication that they have come from the Foreign Office'. Bevin also wanted to see Kravchenko's book *I Chose Freedom* circulated. Robert Hale had bought the UK rights but were slow in publishing it. The Foreign Office, which wished to buy 200 copies for discreet distribution, persuaded a number of people, including Robert Bruce Lockhart, the wartime propaganda co-ordinator, to push Hale privately to publish faster.[25] The Soviets felt compelled to respond to this level of publicity. They insisted that the Commission had propagated 'vulgar slander, stupid invention, unpardonable lies, the exposition of the bubbling slanderous fabrications and generally unpardonable ravings of Igor Gouzenkou, a traitor to his Motherland'.[26]

In Britain, the trial of Allan Nunn May provoked diverse reactions. Some scientists considered Nunn May to be the 'first martyr of the atomic age'. Popular opinion was less sympathetic and the *News Chronicle* carried letters that suggested such an individual should be 'shot as a traitor or shut up as a dangerous lunatic'. Scientific communities everywhere, bastions of liberal and free thought, were now under extreme scrutiny for political loyalty. The Canadian High Commissioner in Canberra presciently forecast that this would soon reverberate in Australia, where communist influence in scientific and intellectual circles was considerable. At the University of Sydney, 300 scientific workers had held a meeting on the issue and the gathering, he insisted, had been 'stiff with Communists'. Liberal-minded scientists concerned about the impact of new weapons and methods of warfare were now routinely suspect.[27]

By mid-1946 the Gouzenkou and Nunn May revelations were a *cause célèbre*. They had arrived during critical discussions in Britain about the possibility of a more offensive policy towards the Soviet Union. Action now seemed imperative. The Foreign Office concluded that it was essential to deal with 'infiltration of crypto-communists' into Western organisations, societies and overseas delegations; 'this means using Special Branch, CID and/or MI5,' it asserted. But it was also in the public realm that measures were required. Robin Hankey, the new head of the Northern Department, argued that the real lesson of the Gouzenkou affair was the dangerous distance between benign public impressions of the Soviets and the nasty reality that had been revealed in Canada: 'This makes it more than ever necessary to quish our own public opinion into a correct view of Russian aims and activities.'[28] Events in Canada also dominated the view of Soviet intelligence services taken by SIS, for so much of its other information was, by its own admission, of wartime or pre-war vintage.[29]

Gouzenkou also had an impact at the top. After reading the Canadian Blue Book, Herbert Morrison, who had been the wartime Home Secretary and was now Lord President of the Council, wrote to Attlee urging the importance of the case as showing the vast extent of the communist fifth column in the West. He was anxious that the Soviet Union had discouraged 'certain selected sympathizers' from openly joining the Communist Party so that they could do clandestine work and seemingly 'was secretly preparing for a Third World War'. It was he said, 'quite a thriller with plenty of human interest'. The revelations were also a turning point for opinion in the Foreign Office, which itself bought 400 copies of the report for distribution to officials in government in order to 'alert' them to the extent of Soviet spy activities. By the end of 1946, the JIC had turned its attention to the role of communists in Whitehall, especially in the key area of atomic power and defence science. Positive vetting and the first British Cold War security purge were not far off.[30]

Whitehall and Washington were now very jumpy about Soviet espionage. In the summer of 1946 the British Chiefs of Staff set up a 'special' contingency war plans body called the Future Planning Section, staffed with the brightest officers. Shortly afterwards they were approached by the US Joint Chiefs of Staff, who asked if they wished to get together for joint emergency war planning on what they thought would soon be a war against the Soviets in Germany. This was just what the British wanted – a chance to sustain the Anglo-American military alliance – and to tie it into the defence of a weak and vulnerable Europe. Yet as Montgomery, the new Chief of the Imperial General Staff, recorded, he vetoed any such discussions as too dangerous. 'It was a sure bet', he noted, 'that the Russians would hear about it within a matter of days if not hours.' He was sensitive to the extent of Soviet penetration of Whitehall and Washington, even of very sensitive military planning bodies. The US Joint Chiefs of Staff made another approach on 1 August 1946 and again Montgomery was very anxious that this overture 'of the greatest importance' should not leak. He now decided that the talks should go ahead, but only amid the tightest security. They were kept extremely secret and were conducted on a need-to-know basis. The US Joint Chiefs of Staff were equally anxious about penetration and had 'so far kept the whole matter secret from the State Department and the President'.[31] London also knew that Washington now took a dim view of security throughout the British Commonwealth. Severe measures were ordered by the Royal Commission in Ottawa. There was close co-operation between the RCMP, MI5 and the FBI, which led to the formation of the Canadian Internal Security Panel. Vigorous vetting of government employees was carried out by the RCMP from 1946, which had 'recently re-organised its Special Branch'. This restored American confidence in the Canadians. But Washington's suspicions now turned from Canada to Australia.[32]

Soviet espionage in Australia had been known to an inner core of Western officials since 1944. It became clear from decrypted Japanese codes that Tokyo was somehow obtaining very sensitive American documents about the war effort in General MacArthur's South-West Pacific Area command by tapping into a Soviet espionage net, and it appeared that they were being obtained at source by Soviet agents in Canberra. Exactly how the Japanese were raking off the proceeds of this Soviet espionage is still not clear, but the facts were unmistakable.[33]

In 1946 information from Gouzenkou also pointed to espionage in Australia. Again espionage was focusing on major strategic developments relating to science and future warfare, not least in atomic weapons, biological and chemical weapons, guided missiles and counter-measures such as radar. Vast uninhabited spaces were required to develop some of the more noxious weapons on this list and so in July 1946 the British had held the Informal Commonwealth Conference on Defence Science in London to agree a global programme for weapons development with their Commonwealth affiliates. Australia's wide open spaces seemed critical to British plans to develop guided missiles, pilotless aircraft and atomic weapons. Meanwhile Suffield in Canada and Proserpine in Australia became main sites for developing biological and chemical weapons.[34]

Percy Sillitoe, the Director of MI5, saw the connection immediately and intervened in Commonwealth discussions on defence science as early as the end of 1946. If these plans were to go ahead, he argued, 'it is of vital importance that Australian security arrangements ... should be of the highest order'. MI5 had already been to Australia to look over the secret policing arrangements provided by Canberra's Commonwealth Investigation Service. MI5 had found that this local organism was 'neither organised at H.Q, nor adequately staffed, nor has it sufficient powers ... nor is it capable of conducting adequate vetting enquiries'. In other words Australia was a security intelligence weakling. On 11 January 1947, Sillitoe warned the JIC bluntly that 'serious leakages might take place'. Now was the time for action and a beefed-up Australian organisation was required. With a proper security service capable of conducting organised vetting of staff, good security on the testing ranges would be easy to achieve, although security for longer-term basic research in laboratories, where communism was rife, looked more difficult. Sillitoe had already identified the nub of the matter, the dire threat to military scientific co-operation with the United States. He warned, 'If there were to be leakages of U.S. information in Australia the responsibility will no doubt be brought home to the U.K.'[35]

In July 1947 Montgomery had a meeting with General J. F. Evetts, Senior Military Adviser to the British Ministry of Supply, about joint weapons development in Australia. The Commonwealth Investigation Service had been strengthened, but was not yet working in an integrated way with MI5 on the security of the new missile projects. Montgomery was anxious that if equipment went missing MI5 would be thought responsible. He noted that 'good security precautions are very necessary' because of the 'rapid appearance in Australia of a spy who is known to have been connected with the Canadian espionage trials last year'. But Sillitoe and Montgomery were now moving to lock an open stable door after the horse had bolted. At the end of the same year, in November and December 1947, new signals intelligence showed the British and the Americans that sensitive documents had in fact been leaking from Canberra to Soviet intelligence since 1943.[36]

The Americans had first informed the British about the efforts of American Army codebreakers to decipher Soviet communications, including intelligence traffic, in 1945. Soviet cryptographic systems were of high quality, but weaknesses had been introduced by poor procedure, notably using so-called 'one-time' cipher pads for processing messages more than once. This provided the Western cryptanalysts with a way in. Limited progress had been made by the end of 1946, and in early 1947 a British cryptanalyst joined the American team based at Arlington Hall, Virginia, just outside Washington. At the end of 1947, breaks into Soviet secret service traffic showed the presence of an active Soviet agent inside the Australian government. This Commonwealth dimension prompted GCHQ to devote more effort to this programme, which was given the American codename Venona and the British codename Bride. Venona eventually pointed to the presence of important Soviet spies such as the atomic scientist Klaus Fuchs, in 1950, and the diplomat Donald Maclean, in 1951. Although Venona was betrayed to the Soviets by an American defector in 1948, Moscow could do nothing about the masses of previously recorded Soviet radio traffic. Patient work on this material continued and provided clues about Soviet espionage as late as 1980.[37]

Venona revelations about Australia soon resonated at the highest level. On 27 January 1948, Admiral Hillenkoetter, Director of the CIA, warned President Truman, 'Indications have appeared that there is a leak in high government circles in Australia, to Russia. This may, in magnitude, approach that of the Canadian spy case exposé of last year insofar as high Australian government officials are concerned. The British government is now engaged in expensive undercover investigations to determine just where, in Australian government, the leak is.' Venona revealed that, since 1943, highly sensitive material had been passed to Soviet intelligence from the Canberra Department of External Affairs.

Australian officials had handed over what the Soviets considered to be spectacular stuff, including copies of the 'explosive' work of the British Post Hostilities Planners. This was the volatile material that had caused a rupture between the military and the diplomats in Whitehall in 1944. Eden had secured an end to its circulation abroad in late 1944, but by then it was too late. PHP had made its way via Canberra to Moscow.[38]

London did not regard the Australians as competent enough to handle this crisis. In April 1946, Lord Alanbrooke (as Sir Alan Brooke had become) had endured prolonged defence discussions at the Dominions Prime Ministers' Conference. He confided in his diary that the Dominion Premiers were equipped 'with mentalities limited to the normal horizon of a Whitehall charwoman'. He reserved special derision for Australia's Minister for External Affairs, Dr Evatt, from whose department the material proved to be leaking. This posed a direct threat to Anglo-American relations. Until the security crisis was resolved, Britain and its Commonwealth partners were likely to be regarded as insanitary and the flow of information from Washington would probably be meagre.[39]

A top team was required for this task and in February 1948 Sir Percy Sillitoe was dispatched to Australia. With him came Roger Hollis, head of MI5's C Division, concerned with protective security and background checks (later himself to be wrongly accused of working for the Soviets), and Roger Hemblys-Scales. They joined Courtney Young, MI5's resident Security Liaison Officer in Australia. Venona information about leaks had persuaded the Australian Prime Minister, Joseph Chifley, and Defence Minister, Sir Frederick Shedden, to permit their investigations. In July 1948, following discussions in London between Attlee, Sillitoe and Chifley, Canberra accepted British proposals for the establishment of a new and comprehensive Australian Security Intelligence Organisation (ASIO). This would be designed by London and its staff given British guidance. In addition, large numbers of scientific and technical secret projects were transferred into government departments to bring them under 'full security control'.[40]

Sillitoe returned to London, but Hollis and Hemblys-Scales remained in Australia to set up ASIO and work on the list of Venona suspects. ASIO was almost entirely focused on this task, which was known as the 'Case'. Tracing contact with sensitive British PHP documents pointed to likely suspects, including a typist, Frances Bernie, who helped to run a communist youth league and who worked personally for Dr Evatt, the Minister for External Affairs. It also pointed to two Australian diplomats with communist leanings, Ian Milner and Jim Hill. On 8 February 1949, Chifley, Evatt, Shedden and the Australian Solicitor General had a tense meeting with the three MI5 officers, Hollis, Hemblys-Scales and Young.

They reviewed plans for the development of ASIO. Courtney Young was the more influential as MI5's long-standing representative in Australia and had endeared himself to his Australian hosts by his hard drinking, something which helped to offset his preference for wearing a monocle. Young also knew a great deal about Soviet espionage tradecraft, having distinguished himself in his previous posting by ghost-writing the semi-confessional autobiography of Rado's radio operator Alexander Foote, *Handbook for Spies*. Foote had finally tired of working for the Soviets and took the opportunity to jump ship when visiting Berlin in March 1947. There he presented himself to British intelligence and offered to tell all he knew in return for a safe passage home. By March 1947 such defectors were no longer turned away and instead welcomed with open arms.[41]

Venona had provided MI5 with a list of twelve names of possible Soviet agents operating in Australia. Hollis and Courtney Young did not tell the Australians that the names came from intercepts, but the nature of the material led some of the more experienced ASIO hands to suspect this. Twelve names seemed a short list and was much the same number of people identified by the Gouzenkou defection in Canada. But the Venona material was tricky because many of these were codenames rather than real names and their identities could be deduced only by careful circumstantial guesswork; so the trail was long. Even with unenciphered material from Gouzenkou, mistakes had been made and clumsy translation had led to the dogged pursuit of harmless individuals who had never been near Soviet intelligence. By 1950, Ian Milner and Jim Hill, the two External Affairs officers, had been identified positively, but they had refused to 'come over'. Jim Skardon, MI5's most experienced interrogator, had made a soft approach to Hill when he visited London in 1950, trying to persuade him to 'be sensible' and 'make a clean breast of it'. This was a confidence trick designed to extract a confession. MI5 and ASIO did not have evidence that they were willing to present in court. But the recent sentencing of the atom bomb spy Klaus Fuchs to fourteen years in a British jail was not an incentive. Hill faced MI5's best interrogator down and stolidly denied everything. This was the great weakness of Venona material, since – even when the messages pointed unambiguously to the identity of a Soviet agent – additional evidence such as a confession was required, and without this the agent could not be convicted.

The exhausting investigation of the Venona-derived list kept ASIO's staff of somewhere under 200 busy well into the 1950s. Each new suspect opened a world of further associates and contacts who required separate examination. The task was difficult, since the Communist Party of Australia had long expected to be banned and had built up a substantial underground organisation. Not unlike the Communist Party of India, seasoned by years of close attention from colonial security, it had

achieved some infiltration of the police, and even the penetration of
ASIO seemed a possibility. In 1949, one operation alone, the bugging
and surveillance of a suspect Soviet diplomat's flat in Canberra, kept
large numbers of ASIO staff busy round the clock. Each visitor to the flat
was suspicious and had to be tailed and investigated. ASIO staff were
learning the hardest lesson of counter-subversion. Attending to security
cases diligently only manufactured more leads and opened more cases.[42]

Despite this hard work, the United States remained sceptical. On 19
April 1949, a month after the formation of ASIO, Sir Frederick Shedden,
the Australian Defence Minister, visited Washington to assert that
Australia was now secure. Attlee was no less concerned to secure
Australia's rehabilitation and wrote a supporting letter to Truman pleading the Australian case. 'I am most anxious for you to know', he began,
'that I have received most reassuring reports of the creation of ASIO.' He
continued, 'It will henceforth be possible for highly confidential and delicate investigations to be undertaken … throughout the past four
months officers of the British Security Service have been aiding and
advising the Australians towards this end and it is from these reports to
me that I have felt able to send you this encouraging account'.[43] But
Truman chose to reserve judgement and did not move to re-establish
defence science links with Australia.

Britain continued to chip away at the problem. In September 1949
Shedden sat down in London with the Chiefs of Staff to review progress
after a recent visit to Washington. He had been forced to 'devote much
time' there to the question of classified information and he had 'done his
best to impress the Americans by sending them a considerable amount of
paper indicating the present position in Australia of Communism, the
Trade Unions etc.', but he was not sure how much good this had done.
For the time being the Americans had decided to maintain their
embargo. The issue of the embargo bothered Shedden because he
believed that in a future war Australia would be in an American
command area and this would raise all sorts of awkward problems. What
the British Chiefs of Staff wanted to know was how to play the awkward
triangular relationship between London, Washington and Canberra.
They asked, 'did the Australian Government wish His Majesty's
Government to continue to act rather as "agents" in this matter or would
they prefer to deal direct with the Americans'? Shedden responded that
he wanted the British as 'support' rather than 'agents'.[44]

Australia was only part of the problem. The whole Commonwealth,
both old and new, presented London with a range of security headaches.
One official wrote in late 1948, 'Whatever the position may be in theory,
there are, in practice, two categories of American information. One category consists of what may be termed "super-secret" information which

is only disclosed to a very few people in the UK and the USA. The second category is of a top secret nature, but has a wider distribution.' But to talk of two categories of top secret was an understatement. To deal with security headaches, Whitehall had gradually been introducing a bewildering range of additional security levels that were effectively above mere top secret. A key purpose was sleight of hand. Those who were not getting the very top stuff were not to be told that they were not 'in the know'. The PHP fiasco had seen the arrival of 'limited circulation' and 'specially restricted circulation', which were in practice higher levels of top secret. The growing use of the 'confidential annexe' to a main paper could hide the existence of these appendices from the uninitiated. Some very secret military documents had only a few copies typed up and were kept in the Standard File, an impressive bright-red binder belonging to the Secretary of the Chiefs of Staff.[45]

The transfer of power in South Asia and new states entering the Commonwealth in 1947 and 1948 had required further refinements. In India a great deal of material was destroyed before government was handed over in 1947. By September of that year security conditions in Indian government offices had deteriorated to the point where London was passing the 'lowest minimum' of secret and top-secret material to Delhi, and British officials were told that if any questions were asked they should 'feign ignorance'. London noted that, to avoid disclosing this policy, 'steps are being taken to see that [the Indians] receive intelligence summaries which are, apparently, Top Secret, and similar to those which go to other Commonwealth countries'.[46]

On 14 July 1949, Colonel Martin Furnival-Jones of MI5 explained to the JIC why caution was necessary. His main worry was 'the situation in the Office of the High Commissioner for India, in London. Krishna Menon, the Indian High Commissioner, 'had tendencies towards the extreme left' and there was 'no question whatever that there were six members of the Communist Party on his staff'. They were consorting with others in Britain with similar views and had access in Whitehall, although they were not receiving secret material. MI5 was busy and its liaison officers had held bilateral discussions with Delhi. As a result 'purge measures were being taken', but there was no knowing how far this situation was replicated in India. These were not matters that London wished Washington to hear of, and the scale of the Commonwealth security headache was only too clear.[47]

By 1949 London was faced with an awkward dilemma. The JIC saw the retention of the confidence and co-operation of both Commonwealth countries and the United States as vital. But to 'retain both will not be easy in view of known American opinion on certain members of the Commonwealth'. Reluctantly MI5 was asked to rank the security of the Commonwealth countries based partly on information that had emerged at a recent Commonwealth Security Conference it had hosted in London. Only Canada made the top category. Australia, New Zealand and South Africa were in a medium-security category, while India, Pakistan and Ceylon formed a lowly underclass.[48]

Clement Attlee was a tough-minded individual. Despite the scares provided by these cases he was determined to avoid an American-style 'security purge'. He was repelled by the sort of inquisition that had already begun under the notorious House Un-American Activities Committee in Washington. Indeed, he instinctively set his face against all clandestine activities and ignored calls from right-wing MPs for some sort of British version of the enquiries gathering pace in Washington in the late 1940s. He had also been sensitised to potential controversy over domestic security by Churchill's ill-advised Gestapo speech of 1945. But by the end of 1946 Gouzenkou and Nunn May, together with hints of what was to come in Australia, were reverberating around Whitehall and Westminster. The looming threat to Anglo-American defence co-operation fed into discussions on every subject. Bevin was particularly anxious to reverse the McMahon Act which had cut Britain off from atomic co-operation with Washington. This showed itself during Anglo-American discussions on developing American airbases on British territory. Attlee was uncomfortable with the possibility of hosting American aircraft. He warned Bevin that US bases did not necessarily increase security and that, once these were established, Britain 'would find it difficult not ... to follow the US lead in any further crisis with the Soviet Union'. He added that 'in return for this little real protection would have been afforded'. Bevin's underlying rationale was revealing, for he hoped that an offer of British bases might facilitate 'our getting much desired assistance from the Americans in atomic and other fields', although he conceded that this argument 'might come as something of a shock to public opinion'.[49]

By January 1947 action could not be delayed. The JIC had completed a long investigation into the acquisition of secret technical information by Soviet agents in Britain. This was presented to a surprised Cabinet Defence Committee. While London worried about Canberra and Ottawa, vast numbers of Soviet diplomats were in Britain hoovering up information. The Soviet Embassy had 126 staff, including the Military Attaché with a staff of no fewer than twenty-three and the Naval Attaché with a staff of sixteen. There were a further 124 individuals under the Soviet Trade Delegation. Although Bevin had decided that the attaché staff would have to live under the same draconian travel restrictions as their British equivalents in Moscow, all this was circumvented by the Trade Delegation staff, who were not restricted. By using 'semi-overt methods' in an open country they could obtain much of what they wanted. Meanwhile, British exports to the Soviet Union remained suspiciously small. The Soviets simply bought samples of the most up-to-date equipment they could obtain, and then reverse-engineered the product to manufacture it themselves. This was the case with the latest jet engines recently procured from Rolls-Royce. The many British communists employed in UK armaments firms only increased the wider problem of 'legitimate espionage' by Soviet trade officials in Britain.[50]

Attlee chaired a special meeting in March 1947 of the Cabinet Defence Committee on Soviet scientific espionage. There was talk of cutting the 'inflated' staffs of Soviet trade delegations which provided a happy home for numerous intelligence officers. But Attlee warned that this, together with the removal of known communists from secret work, would not itself be effective 'since some of those who were or might become important Soviet agents were probably not open members of the Communist Party'. Regrettably, more intrusive investigations would be required.[51]

Attlee's response was very traditional – a new Cabinet committee was created. This was the highly secret Cabinet Committee on Subversive Activities, known as GEN 183. Its working party began its investigations in May 1947 and within a year had produced recommendations for a low-key approach to the problem of Soviet espionage in government. This meant checking names against existing MI5 files and was known as 'negative vetting', which was welcomed by Attlee as suitably restrained and inoffensive. The working party consisted of Sillitoe, Sir Edward Bridges, Permanent Secretary at the Treasury, and A. J. D. Winnifrith from the Treasury establishments section. Roger Hollis, who ran MI5's C Division, responsible for personnel security, also assisted in the months before he was despatched to Australia. The presence of Hollis reflected the fact that a small-scale purge was already under way. At the end of the war, MI5 had been working to arrange the discreet transfer of key civil servants suspected of communism away from secret work. But this was a small programme and the working party realised that it faced a challenge of a different order. Moreover, anything on a scale sufficient to meet the new challenge would have to be a publicly avowed procedure, which would probably provoke an outcry.

Groups of the extreme right and left 'which might provide breeding grounds for subversive activity' were reviewed by this working party. Its members decided that fascists and revolutionary communists could be excluded as 'intolerable to public opinion and common sense'. But the 'principal danger' was seen as the Communist Party of Great Britain, identified as the only group working for a foreign power. Reviewing communist espionage in Britain over two decades, including the infamous John Herbert King and Springhall cases, they also found some alarming loose ends. Moscow, they noted, had enjoyed access to important classified documents from a British Embassy for 'a considerable period before the last war' but its channels had never been uncovered. The Gouzenkou case was uppermost in their minds. All were struck by the way in which the Communist Party had been the key organisational framework for Soviet intelligence officers in Canada. By the technique of encouraging secret membership, selected sympathisers had risen unnoticed to positions in government. The working party was astounded at the numbers of people who had been recruited over the years, without any individual revealing this network to the authorities. The conviction of Allan Nunn May, it insisted, pointed strongly to the likelihood that the same system was operating in Britain.[52]

Attlee's working party observed uncomfortably that a series of telegrams between Soviet intelligence in Ottawa and Moscow made 'elaborate arrangements for a further meeting with "our man in London"' ready for when Nunn May returned from Canada to Britain. All fields of government were clearly vulnerable, but first and foremost were military secrets: atomic research, radar and industrial intelligence. Checking employees engaged on work of 'a particularly secret character' against existing Security Service records would not pick up secret members of the Communist Party, or indeed those who had been members of juvenile groups such as the Young Communist League. The system, the working party concluded, had to be 'tightened up'.

Henceforth, Whitehall would be divided into 'safe' and 'unsafe' departments. The latter would include all those regularly engaged on secret work such as the Cabinet Office and the Ministry of Defence. Anyone to whom suspicions were attached would be quietly moved out of these places and 'offered safe alternative employment'. But the working party was the first to concede that this system was defective. Many scientific specialists were fit only for a narrow spectrum of work, while crypto-communists thronged the corridors of universities and scientific research institutes. MI5 would have to vet non-government employees engaged on secret contract work by specialised firms.

MI5, small and overburdened, was very reluctant to expand into this potentially limitless field of enquiry. It feared that it might 'swamp the more positive security work of the Service', namely following up real leads on real spies. There were also political problems. Even this low-key system was bound to be exposed sooner or later. Civil service representatives had already smelt a rat and were pressing for assurances that employment would not be refused on grounds of membership of a political party. So far Whitehall had artfully evaded offering any reply to such enquiries. In March 1948 Attlee decided to face the music and described the system in outline to the House of Commons. The far left gave him a hot reception, accusing him of 'grovelling to the Tories and the big dollar boys of America'. Although he gave robust replies he was also misleading. When asked about the BBC he insisted this was a matter for the Governors of the BBC and not for the state. But in reality the state was pushing a clandestine purge of the BBC, especially the overseas services, to the dismay of the Director-General, who then had to placate the angry unions.[53]

The Gouzenkou case was therefore a mixed blessing. It turned attention back to Soviet espionage and accelerated the Venona programme. For MI5 and for stalwart anti-communists such as Ernest Bevin and Herbert Morrison, all this was a bonus. But it was also distorting. It produced a picture of Soviet espionage that seemed largely focused on national communist parties and espionage directed narrowly at 'secret weapons'. The arrest of Douglas Springhall, National Organiser of the Communist Party, and his sentencing to seven years' imprisonment seemed to confirm this. The spotlight was now upon CPGB and its membership; those without obvious links to CPGB were unintended beneficiaries of this approach and remained hidden.[54]

In May 1948, MI5 submitted a major report to Attlee on the extent to which CPGB had penetrated British society. MI5 considered the civil service to be relatively risk-free. There were perhaps no more than twenty persons at the policy-making administrative grade who were members of CPGB or who could 'be regarded as virtually committed to it'. None was higher than assistant secretary. There were perhaps 200 such persons among the clerical and secretarial grades. But what worried MI5 was the 'zeal, pertinacity and cohesion' of CPGB when it came to seizing control of trade unions, 'powerfully assisted by the apathy of its opponents'. The Security Service observed that, although the number of communists in the civil service was minute, they were 'at present in control of the Civil Service Clerical Association, the most important Civil Service Trade Union'.[55]

The Whitehall purge had to be small scale because the security apparatus could not cope with anything else. Sillitoe was especially concerned that the number of names submitted to MI5 should be kept to 'an absolute minimum'. There were over 1,000,000 civil service posts and the negative vetting of even those engaged on 'secret duties' in 'unsafe departments' was a mammoth task. In early 1949 Attlee revealed to the Commons that fewer than twenty people had been identified by the negative vetting procedure. To the delight of the authorities, one of those uncovered was not a communist, but instead a fascist found lurking in the War Office. This lent the whole process a welcome air of even-handedness.[56]

Almost certainly one of those gently sidelined from sensitive government work at an early stage was P. M. S. Blackett, Professor of Physics at

Manchester University and the wartime Naval Scientific Adviser who had drawn up the blueprint for Britain's post-war scientific intelligence system in mid-1945 on behalf of the JIC. American officials were quick to finger him as a risk. US Naval Intelligence warned in September 1949 that communist parties around the world had 'spark-plugged a vast number of new associations of "atomic" and other scientists'. It insisted that 'the International Communists have also achieved an International Subversion Network, the components of which interlock through such well-known figures as Harlow SHAPLEY of Harvard, French atomic scientists JOLIOT-CURIE and British Professor PMS BLACKETT'. There was no evidence against Blackett, but in the prevailing climate he was bound to be purged.[57] Ironically, freeing Blackett from official duties had unpredictable consequences. His overseas links were not to Moscow but to Delhi, where he admired Nehru's vibrant post-colonial state. Blackett became a military scientific adviser to India, visiting a dozen times up to 1971. Knowledgeable and well connected in the world of defence science he was now a free agent. One of the fields to which he made a substantial contribution was the Indian atomic bomb programme.[58]

The months of January and February 1947 had been a turning point, not just in the Cold War but also in domestic affairs. A very bad winter, replete with labour troubles, put new doubts in Attlee's mind. He became more certain about the need to resist the Soviets, while the Czech coup which brought the communists to power in Prague in the spring of 1948 followed by the Berlin blockade in the following autumn had a profound effect on public opinion. At this point the Labour leadership chose to expel several MPs for continually supporting the communist position against Bevin's foreign policy. Attlee's suspicions of communists at home and abroad were growing. By 1950, against the background of a long and acrimonious dock strike, Attlee, Bevin and the Cabinet were content to blame a growing proportion of the widespread domestic unrest on the hidden hand of communism and subversion.[59]

Security, in the decade following the war, was a miserable business for the denizens of Whitehall, but there remained one crumb of comfort. If Britain was regarded as somewhat insecure, and the Commonwealth states as rather worse, then – in the eyes of Washington – the continental European was regarded as beyond the pale. Whitehall did everything possible to increase the suspicions of continentals during this period, in the hope of benefiting by comparison, and its prize exhibit was the French.

As late as 1945, Roosevelt had regarded de Gaulle and his government in exile as closet fascists bent on establishing a right-wing police state after the war. Considerable work had to be undertaken, notably by OSS, to disabuse him of this notion. By 1946, the wheel had turned full circle and Washington considered Paris to be riddled with communists. The British Chiefs of Staff deployed this stereotype to reinforce London's position as Washington's 'special' partner. In March 1948, as negotiations began to shape what would become the NATO treaty, the British expressly warned the Americans off any substantial security talks with the French. This was because of 'extensive penetration of the political system by Communists, a natural garrulous tendency in the French character, a certain decline of moral standards in Europe, a French lack of security consciousness, and the possibility that present ministers may be replaced by less reliable persons ...'. Staff talks with the French, they insisted, could be considered secure only if information was issued for the personal use of each French officer concerned. This in turn, they suggested, should be delivered orally by them only to their immediate superiors, and 'provided it can be guaranteed those superiors are not Communist or fellow travellers'. London had effectively gazetted the French a nation of traitors. It enjoyed ranking the three French services in order of dubiousness: 'The Navy is estimated most secure, the Army less secure, and the Air Force, being most heavily infiltrated, least secure.' London took a more benign view of the Low Countries, whose military were, in any case, more inclined to follow a British lead. 'Communist penetration in Holland, Belgium and Luxembourg is negligible,' it noted, and 'security arrangements within those Governments and Armed Forces are reasonably satisfactory'. Accordingly, early NATO talks were held in Washington between Britain, Canada and the United States only.[60]

American officials made no effort to hide their own suspicions. In August 1948, the US Military Attaché in Paris, General Taite, decided to let his feelings be known. France, he insisted, had received billions in aid from the Marshall Plan and from military programmes such as the Mutual Security Programme, but the results seemed to him disappointing. Rounding on the French General Staff he lectured them firmly, 'We are not going to re-arm you, for you are unwilling to fight. You will never be a great military nation again. We will not rearm you, but we will rearm the Germans.'

This prompted 'discussions' in Washington. French military leaders admitted that the outburst was not altogether unjustified. They accepted the presence of substantial 'corrupt elements' that had 'penetrated French public life since liberation'. The French General Staff conceded that 1,000 billion francs had been spent on the reconstruction of the armed forces, but as yet there was no Air Force, while the Army had innumerable bands and musicians to parade on 14 July on the Champs Elysées. Much of this was mere incompetence, but they chose to ascribe

it to 'a deliberate Communist plan to spread confusion' and to 'demoralise the spirit of the Army'. They called for the outlawing of the
Communist Party in France 'and the elimination of Communist agents
and fellow travellers from the armed force and from the administration'.
Security agencies in London and Washington were already preparing to
assist, and were about to move from passive security to active counter-
subversion, and from the defensive to the offensive.[61]

5

The Counter-Offensive: From CRD to IRD

The more I study this the less I like it ...
Ernest Bevin commenting on the counter-offensive, May 1946[1]

Not all the wartime diplomats in the Foreign Office were determined to turn a blind eye to the activities of the Soviets in pursuit of 'co-operation'. In 1943 the Foreign Office had created an obscure outfit called the Cultural Relations Department or CRD, to manage the growing business of intellectual, cultural, societal and artistic contacts, often of an organised sort, with a view to promoting Allied goodwill. Very quickly this new department realised that this was a huge area of Soviet manipulation and many seemingly 'international' organisations, which claimed to be representative of world opinion, were in fact fronts that took their orders from Moscow. Even as the war was ending, CRD had become the front-line unit in a clandestine struggle to prevent Moscow's domination of the world of international movements, federations and festivals. By November 1945, Sir Archibald Clark-Kerr, the British Ambassador in Moscow, was urging London to take more action to stem the Soviet practice of obtaining control of international labour, youth, women's and other organisations 'for the purpose of using them as instruments of Soviet foreign policy'. He expected 'similar attacks' on students' organisations, as well as on those with humanitarian and cultural objectives, and wanted counter-measures stepped up. Clark-Kerr wrote again on 15 December warning about the Soviet search for an 'instrument for influencing international youth'. CRD in London was already hard at work on this problem.[2]

The principal battleground was the struggle for the mind of European youth. CRD was particularly irked by the fact that the new Prime Minister, Clement Attlee, had permitted a communist-organised World Youth Congress to take place in London in November 1945. This had concluded its business by setting up the World Federation of Democratic Youth (WFDY), one of the leading Soviet-owned international organisations of the post-war period. CRD and the Home Office had come round to the view that it was a communist front and wanted a general ban, but found that the State Department was 'actively supporting the preparatory work' for the Congress, partly because WFDY had the blessing of an unsuspecting Eleanor Roosevelt. Ernest Bevin smelt a rat and although invited to address the main rally at the Albert Hall thought it safer to decline.[3]

The Cabinet had decided to allow the Congress to go ahead despite warnings about the strong communist elements behind it. Cabinet argued that 'the more foreigners were allowed to visit this country and breathe the air of intellectual freedom in which we live the better' and that this would contrast well with the Soviet policy of 'black out' already visible in Eastern Europe. But this proved to be naive. Instead, the considerable facilities afforded them allowed the Congress to give the impression it had received official British blessing, and many British organisations attended and only discovered later on that 'effective control of the proceedings was already in Communist hands'. A 'vast' delegation of Soviet youth, with an average age of forty, had arrived a month before the conference to make preparations. By controlling the agendas, framing the motions and 'shouting the others down' they had 'swept the board'. Motions had been passed asserting that conditions in Belsen were nothing compared to those in colonial West Africa and that monstrous British colonialists 'cut off the thumbs of Bombay cotton-workers to avoid Indian competition' with British home cotton production. To add insult to injury, two of the three Balkan delegations proved to be armed with briefcases full of counterfeit sterling currency. Needless to say CRD knew it had been outsmarted and was angry. It was determined to prevent a repetition and if possible pay the Soviets back in the same coin. Non-communist youth organisations in Britain were now keen to resist obvious communist encroachment, and CRD was eager to give them every encouragement.[4]

William Montagu-Pollock, head of CRD, was the leading figure in this counter-campaign. Shocked by the reverse represented by the London Congress in November 1945 he was determined to fight back. In March 1946 he warned that the communist grip on the British section of the WFDY was 'so strong' that it was past saving. What CRD needed to do was 'to set up a rival political organisation' so that it could intervene substantially in this important field.[5]

CRD teamed up with incensed members of non-communist British youth groups. The key figure was Elizabeth Welton, the Secretary of the Standing Conference of National Voluntary Youth Organisations. She offered to help set up a secret group that would work against the communists. She was also in close touch with similar-minded groups in Belgium, France, the Netherlands and the USA, and reported that other private anti-communist groups were being set up in Denmark, Sweden and Switzerland. In the late spring of 1946 she prepared to depart on a tour of Holland, Belgium and France to cement relations with these groups, especially the Union Patriotique des Organisations de la Jeunnesse in Paris. But she confessed to being filled with trepidation. Her European collaborators had warned her that life was dangerous for the opponents of organised communism on the continent. Recently there had been 'two cases of sudden death by poisoning and a mysterious disappearance of anti-communist organisers' in Europe, and everyone was on their guard. Welton was not exaggerating, for by 1948 fifteen individuals involved in youth work in Denmark had been 'liquidated' by their communist opponents.[6] CRD noted that Welton's connection with the authorities was to be 'kept dark', but she would be given some training and preparation before departing. 'Mr Hollis of M.I.5. is expected to brief her,' it recorded, in order to give her the benefit of Whitehall's intelligence on European youth movements and the issue of 'who is a Communist and who is not'.[7]

Whitehall was interested in student politics as well as youth affairs and was especially anxious about communist inroads into the National Union of Students in Britain. CRD teamed up with MI5 and SIS to observe these activities. At a remarkably early stage in the Cold War it decided to take measures, again by creating its own counter-groups. The National Union of Students played into the hands of CRD because it was short of money. Hoping to attend a student festival in Prague in August in 1946 the NUS approached the Foreign Office in May to request a government grant to cover the costs of travel. Privately, CRD was incensed and stated that it was not going to 'finance this clandestine agency of communism', but it encouraged further meetings with student leaders to track their activities.[8]

CRD was worried that this student festival would result in the setting up of an International Students Federation 'in which the communists will hold all the strings', a repeat of what had happened with youth organisations and the WFDY in London the previous year. So its first aim was to 'discourage the NUS' from taking part, but it knew this would be difficult as the students' union had 'three near-Communists' on its Executive Committee and had been effectively communist controlled since 1940. The decision was made to warn the NUS off, but if the 'worst comes to the worst' and the NUS attended the conference, CRD resolved to 'take fairly rigorous action'. It would have to get clearance at a high level from Ministers, but in the worsening international climate of May 1946 it had 'no doubt that it would be forthcoming'.[9]

Together with MI5, CRD busied itself checking the background of the NUS delegation members. MI5 alleged that a number of them, including Carmel Brickman, were members of the Communist Party and that A. T. James, the President of the NUS, 'had a record of close association with Communist activities'.[10] By July 1946 CRD had built up what it saw as a detailed profile of the links between the NUS and other political groups. Founded in 1922, the NUS had what CRD called 'an innocent record' up to 1940, when it had come under growing communist influence. CRD claimed that lurking beneath the NUS was in fact another body – the University Labour Federation – an organisation that seemed to be confirmed in its crypto-communism by the fact that it had been forcibly disaffiliated from the Labour Party on the ground of communist infiltration in 1940. It was also communists on the NUS Executive who had set up the World Youth Congress in London in November 1945, leading to the creation of WFDY.[11]

SIS took over from MI5 the business of monitoring youthful British communists once they reached the continent. In the summer of 1946, the new R5 Requirements section of SIS, which dealt with world communism, tracked the efforts of British communists who had been denied visas by the Foreign Office to reach a meeting of the WFDY in Vienna. Special attention was paid to Kutty Hookham, Joint Secretary of the World Youth Federation, and one of the few British nationals to elude Foreign Office restrictions. SIS explained that she had achieved this by first visiting the headquarters of the new WFDY in Paris, then going on to Moscow, and then travelling from Moscow to Vienna. She was due back in Paris for another WFDY meeting. The Soviets were able to watch British efforts to impede the progress of British delegates with some clarity, for the SIS officer liaising with CRD was none other than Kim Philby, head of R5.[12]

By July 1946, CRD was ready for action on three fronts. First, to try and create an element more resistant to communism within the NUS; second, to try and prevent a British delegation going to the International Student Congress in Prague; and third, to try and set up rival conferences, even rival non-communist youth and student organisations. These CRD-sponsored groups would constitute 'a standing perpetual challenge to gang-rule wherever it becomes manifest – whether by Nazi parties or Soviet parties, or by Zionist movements'. CRD urged that if it mobilised properly it could arrange a great deal of open criticism in the meeting and 'we should show these Communist tricksters what world opinion ... thinks of them'.

But there was much secret work to be done. In the summer of 1946 the developed political warfare apparatus that CRD needed for countering organised communism at the international level was not there. This was the fault of those who had hastily dismantled Britain's propaganda machinery after the war. Rather unfairly CRD rounded on the overt information services that remained, namely the British Council: 'What has it ever done to vindicate the true principles animating the political organisation of this country and to proclaim them to the world? ... How much more worth doing at this critical epoch than so many of the Council's current frivolities with ballet girls and second-rate painters.' In July 1946, CRD was the loudest voice in Whitehall urging action 'at a high level' on political warfare against Moscow. Propaganda had to be 'overhauled' and 'strengthened'.[13]

In tackling the NUS, CRD was initially baffled by the lack of a way in. Its objective was 'the creation of a body of opinion to balance the extremists' within the NUS. It hoped to find a sympathetic individual on the Executive who disliked the communist element. Once this person had been identified, 'could we not work on him to make his opinions known?' But in reality CRD did not know where to begin. Eventually, contacts were developed with the Secretary of the NUS, Margaret Richards, through a former member of the NUS office who now worked in the British Council.[14] At the end of July 1946 CRD reported, 'Enquiries are on foot about the management of the N.U.S.: whether ... there exists a governing body, and whether any of this personnel might be induced to work for the creation of a body of opinion within the Union of the delegation to balance the extremists.'[15]

Sir Patrick Nichols, the British Ambassador in Prague, was watching preparations for the Student Congress there. Nichols thought it would be difficult to block communist students attending, so instead the tactic should be somehow to get more non-communist students on to the British delegation. 'In other words,' he said, 'we have to choose between infiltration and boycott.' He favoured infiltration. Nichols also warned that the British delegates selected for Prague included the familiar Kutty Hookham, 'an ardent communist'.[16]

By January 1947, CRD's longer-term project, a rival youth conference, was under way. George Haynes, Secretary of the National Council of Social Service, an umbrella organisation of British youth groups, was leading the effort. CRD had held informal discussion with similar elements in the USA, France, Belgium and Holland who 'very much hoped' that Britain would take the lead in this struggle. But these individuals needed a 'special' grant to help finance the operation. CRD took the point but was worried that Labour backbenchers would be suspicious and realise that it was 'an open attack on W.F.D.Y.'. It was important to disguise the 'international aspect of British youth work' and it warned that the grant application would have to be 'more carefully wrapped up'.[17]

At this point, Hector McNeil, a Foreign Office Minister, thought it might be wise to seek greater support among senior Cabinet Ministers for the growing campaign against WFDY. On 19 February 1947 he met with Chuter Ede, the Home Secretary, and Stafford Cripps, the Chancellor. 'I had a very bad time,' he reported; 'neither of them are prepared to accept the evidence of MI5.' Cripps was especially hostile as he was closely involved in the activities of both WFDY and the NUS. Gladwyn Jebb, who was now responsible for the large-scale negotiations ongoing in Europe, was outraged at the treatment meted out to his own Minister: 'To anyone who does not wilfully blind himself, it must be obvious that WFDY is inspired and controlled by Moscow . . . It seems to me grotesque that this bogus body, whose meetings appear to be dominated by elderly Russian Major-Generals, should pose as the only representative of "democratic youth" everywhere.'[18] Cripps was still adamant that these organisations were free and independent. In July 1948 the redoubtable Kutty Hookham wrote to thank him for intervening to secure visas for the latest travels of the International Youth Trust.[19]

By January 1948, CRD's project for an International Youth Congress was tottering forward, but it was a sickly patient compared to the well-resourced and well-organised events supported by Moscow. CRD staff attended the meetings of the Congress's parent body, the National Council of Social Service, which was being funded with small grants from the Ministry of Education, but they were dismayed by the indecisiveness of the worthy individuals who staffed it. They came away 'depressed and despairing', for these figures were 'so afraid' of doing anything that might provoke an attack by the better-organised WFDY. It was clear that genuinely independent bodies were not going to lead the way of their own accord, so CRD would have to step in and get things going. 'It is essential that we act quickly and boldly now,' it urged. There were further meetings between Montagu-Pollock and Elizabeth Welton, the most reliable individual on the inside. Officials now began to approach youth organisations privately and 'indirectly' to persuade them to quit WFDY and to join the CRD-sponsored rival.[20]

When it finally took place, the International Youth Congress proved a triumph. CRD measured its success by the extent to which it was attacked in the Soviet press. The experience also confirmed CRD in its tactics of creating new rival bodies rather than attempting to steer existing groups away from WFDY. Recent confrontations between various youth organisations in Europe seemed to show that 'any kind of "Trojan Horse" tactics are useless' and that competing bodies built afresh were more promising. Although the NUS had broken away from communist control by mid-1948 and left the WFDY later that year, nevertheless the approach of building anew was CRD's chosen forward path. The

International Youth Congress, held at London University in January 1948, gave birth to the World Assembly of Youth or WAY, Britain's first covertly orchestrated international organisation. By January 1948 Britain could also boast a proper covert political warfare section, the Information Research Department or IRD, founded at the same time. But for the last two critical years it had been CRD and Montagu-Pollock – one of Britain's least-known but most effective Cold War warriors – who filled the gap.[21]

SOE and its sister wartime propaganda service, the Political Warfare Executive or PWE, had been reduced to almost nothing in 1945. It was only in May the following year that senior British diplomats began to think about reviving shadow warfare. Indeed it was only in early January of that year that the JIC felt safe to return to the vexed issue of forecasting Soviet intentions. Its mammoth report now landed on the desk of several individuals including Frank Roberts, an influential British diplomat serving in Moscow. Roberts was a clear-minded individual who punched above his weight and, like George Kennan in the US context, his despatches from Moscow were important in forming British policy in the first year after the war. Roberts stressed the global nature of Soviet policy, connected by the ubiquitous activities of the communist parties 'directed, if not controlled in detail from Moscow'. This, Roberts remarked, required an equally co-ordinated response. The result was the creation of the Foreign Office Russia Committee, which then oversaw the gradual revival of a department of British covert political warfare.[22]

But the creation of the Russia Committee was also a symptom of the continuing Cold War within Whitehall. During bitter arguments about future Soviet intentions, diplomats had used the JIC as a brake on the work of the military planners. But diplomatic control over the JIC could not be guaranteed. Creating the Russia Committee provided a key co-ordinating centre that was controlled by diplomats rather than the Cabinet Office or the Chiefs of Staff. This explains its strange remit, which included the work of high-level intelligence appreciation.[23]

The Russia Committee also marked a new style of British foreign policy. Cadogan had nurtured an extreme aversion to planning, but the new Permanent Under-Secretary, Orme Sargent, felt that in the current climate 'it would be valuable to have a joint planning committee of this kind'. The model was clearly borrowed from the Chiefs of Staff. William Hayter, who now chaired the JIC, also pressed for a planning committee, precisely because he was impressed by the military system. It was imperative to get organised since the military were now the Foreign Office's rivals for control of Britain's Cold War.[24]

By 1946 there were no more arguments about 'co-operation' with the Soviets. The arguments were now about how far to go in responding to

Soviet hostility and a more militant tendency was emerging in the Foreign Office. Ironically, these militants included Christopher Warner, still head of the Northern Department. Throughout the war, Warner had stuck doggedly to 'co-operation', but now, like a lover scorned, he was full of bitterness and had come to hate the Soviets. On 2 April 1946, he chaired the first meeting of the Russia Committee, which looked at the Soviet 'offensive against Great Britain as leader of social democracy in the world'. Warner offered an unabashed comparison with Hitler's Germany, arguing, 'We should be very unwise not to take the Russians at their word just as we should have taken Mein Kampf at its face value.' A week later Bevin wrote to Attlee employing exactly those words.[25]

Warner was joined on the Russia Committee by Ivone Kirkpatrick, a peppery Ulsterman. Kirkpatrick was ordered to draw up a detailed programme for a covert propaganda offensive that would involve the BBC, the Royal Institute for International Affairs and the press. Bringing in the BBC increased the importance of having its workers vetted by MI5. Kirkpatrick went to his task with a will, drawing on his own wartime experience of working with SOE and PWE, when he had looked after the propaganda beamed out over Europe. He was not only convinced of the supreme value of subversive activities, he was certain that properly organised it could be done even better. He enthused, 'The V sign was emblazoned all over the world. But at the same time we acted. We parachuted men, money and arms into occupied territory. We were not inhibited by fear that the Germans would find out what we were doing, or that they might react or that we might be criticised. Propaganda on a larger scale was co-ordinated with our policy. The result was a success.' Britain's response to the Soviet occupation of Eastern Europe, and to the apparent threat to Western Europe, was to be the same as that to Hitler's occupation of France. Kirkpatrick offered the first glimmerings of an offensive strategy that would, by 1948, be termed 'liberation'. Orme Sargent liked these ideas, but Bevin most definitely did not and was persuaded to approve this policy only in Iran, where the confrontation with the Soviets was becoming intense. Instead Bevin, the Foreign Secretary, called for something that would 'put over the positive results of British attitudes', rather than negative attacks on Moscow.[26]

Between mid-1946, when officials decided that covert propaganda was required, and mid-1947, when Bevin gave his final approval, a great deal of slippage took place. Sargent, together with junior Ministers Hector McNeil and Christopher Mayhew, had clearly decided just to carry on with what they could get away with, but this meant things were done on an amateur basis. By the end of 1946, Denis Healey, in charge of the International Department of the Labour Party, was working with figures such as Mayhew in the Foreign Office against the Soviet policy in Eastern

Soviet propaganda, which attacked Ernest Bevin for taking a Churchillian line and for accepting Marshall Plan subsidies, prompted the formation of the Information Research Department in early 1948

Europe and in aiding persecuted social democrat parties in countries like Rumania.[27]

Bevin's change of policy on British use of the hidden hand was justified by the setting up of the Soviet Cominform, a propaganda organisation and the successor to the inter-war Comintern, in 1947. Bevin was a man who thought about things in deeply personal terms – Britain's foreign policy was termed 'my foreign policy' – and the creation of IRD was triggered by his extreme hatred of his Soviet opposite number, Molotov. Molotov was an impassive follower of Stalin's instructions at the wearisome post-war Foreign Ministers Conferences. Argument was useless and Bevin found him an increasingly frustrating opponent. Bevin enjoyed contrasting his own proletarian origins and workman's hands with Molotov's very different background. But the Briton's temper could get the better of him and, according to one account, he had to be restrained from physically attacking Molotov at one session of the Paris

Peace Conference in 1946. Despite his slavish devotion to Stalin, Molotov was eventually sacked and his Jewish wife arrested during the purges of 1949. Continuing to slide into disfavour in the early 1950s, he was probably saved from execution only by Stalin's own death in 1953.[28]

So bitter personal exchanges between Bevin and Molotov speeded the revival of a British covert political warfare department. In 1947 Bevin was publicly taunted by Molotov at the United Nations in New York. The Soviet propaganda material was well prepared and Bevin got the worst of it. He smarted at the public embarrassment and regretted Britain's lack of negative material on the Soviets with which to reply. Christopher Mayhew, who favoured the reinvigoration of wartime covert propaganda, seized the opportunity. Returning with Bevin on the *Queen Mary*, he advocated a new Foreign Office department to conduct covert or 'black' propaganda. Within months this would emerge as the Information Research Department. Mayhew was the ideal advocate for this in Westminster for he was close to Attlee, sharing his Haileybury background and love of cricket. But the Soviets were also useful allies. The formation of the Soviet Cominform in late 1947 helped underline the case that there were no fewer than three members of the Politburo assigned to aggressive propaganda.[29]

In 1948 Bevin warned a meeting of the Commonwealth Prime Ministers that the Soviets had hitherto employed the UN as 'a sort of Trojan Horse by means of which they could smuggle in their propaganda to the embarrassment of freedom-loving nations'. But now IRD was ready for them and so the Soviets were currently 'being defeated' in the present Foreign Ministers' meeting in Paris. 'It was now the turn of the Soviet Government to be publicly arraigned, and doubtless they would soon learn that their misuse of the organisations would not pay.' Bevin could not hide his satisfaction at having paid Molotov back by resorting to similar tactics.[30]

IRD differed from the diverse bodies dealing with wartime propaganda in that it was entirely under Foreign Office control. The importance of IRD is difficult to overestimate. Before 1950, when defence programmes were being cut and the secret services were pleased to hold their programmes steady, it was expanding rapidly. By the early 1950s, IRD, working closely with SIS, constituted the largest department of the Foreign Office. It received £150,000 a year from the Foreign Office budget, boosted by a further £100,000 from the secret service vote, the budget for clandestine activities.[31]

British diplomats were itching to respond to nasty activities by the Soviets and their proxies in Eastern Europe. In 1945 and 1946 widespread arrests and dirty tricks during so-called 'elections' had become so blatant that many called for a tough response. In Rumania in 1946 both the British and the Americans had uncovered clear evidence of a bungled Soviet plot to assassinate the King. But the Soviet Colonel in charge of the plot had been too talkative and had blabbed details to his Rumanian girlfriend; as a result, the King had narrowly escaped death. The Soviets then thought it expedient to eliminate the incautious Soviet Colonel, and his car was mysteriously showered with hand-grenades in January 1947. No attempt was made to catch the perpetrators.

Events in Rumania paled beside what British diplomats described as the 'bestial' goings-on in Bulgaria. Here the leading non-communist, Petkov, was arrested and sentenced to death on charges of working for Anglo-American imperialism. Western protests on his behalf were useless and he was executed in September 1947. The Bulgarian communist leader seemed to enjoy telling Western diplomats that Petkov would have been spared but for their protests, which, he insisted, constituted an intolerable interference in Bulgaria's internal affairs. Such provocations were hard to take and communist behaviour in Eastern Europe seemed actively to invite a propaganda campaign. After all, the real details were so lurid that they required no embellishment. IRD's favourite subject was the Stalinist forced labour camps such as the terrible Arctic mining outpost at Kolyma. This allowed IRD to reply in kind to the accusations of forced labour in the British colonies and also suggested comparison between Nazi Germany and Stalin's Soviet Union.[32]

IRD's work was made easier by natural contact with the press through those who had worked in SOE, SIS or PWE during the war and had now moved into journalism. Malcolm Muggeridge was one example. Having served with SIS in Africa early in the war he ended up as SIS liaison to French military security in liberated Paris in 1944. He found post-war employment with the *Daily Telegraph* and was soon writing leaders on the international situation. His social contacts with the secret world remained strong and included figures such as Robert Bruce Lockhart and Dick White. Initially he was visited by old acquaintances, but later on SIS officers whom he had not previously met drifted in when they wanted him to 'do a job' for them. Although personally unknown to him, they were, he claimed, instantly recognisable by their manner.

Muggeridge found this work at once troubling and tedious. Though the tasks were undemanding, he feared that his secret links might be exposed. 'But it is easy money,' he reflected, 'and the great thing is not to worry about it.' Periodically, he came back to work for SIS full time on information work. In July 1949 he noted in his diary, 'Final discussion on MI6 project. Practically decided to take it on ... Usual set-up – improvised office, gang of uniformed porters downstairs self-consciously doing nothing, pass to get in which had to be counter-signed.' Many operations to influence the press run by SIS and IRD required armies of temporary staff contracted for such specific projects. Muggeridge was soon back in regular journalism and by the outbreak of the Korean War he was Acting Editor of the *Daily Telegraph*. In the 1950s he would help to run one of the larger CIA-backed efforts to influence intellectual opinion in Britain.[33]

Muggeridge usefully spanned the worlds of intelligence and the intelligentsia, with constant contact in the fields of journalism, literature, culture and religion. He moved in a circle of writers, including George Orwell, who had been involved in wartime propaganda work, and were now being used by IRD. Muggeridge and Orwell were both fierce anti-communists, though for markedly different reasons, and Muggeridge found it 'interesting how we disagreed about our agreement'. Orwell, like Graham Greene, J. B. Priestley and many other luminaries of the literary scene, had spent the war engaged in propaganda activities, so work for IRD was only a continuation of past practice.[34]

However, to the surprise of many, Orwell not only offered his literary services but also handed his contacts a blacklist of thirty-five communists and fellow travellers. When this information was released in 1998 it was greeted with surprise by the British left. But they had forgotten that Orwell had spent a long time in the Burmese police before becoming a wartime propaganda broadcaster. The go-between for IRD and Orwell was Celia Kirwan, a pre-war debutante who went to work for IRD in 1949. She had been close to Orwell since 1946 and was also the sister-in-law of Arthur Koestler, another active left-wing anti-communist who had written the influential *Darkness at Noon*. Kirwan repeatedly visited Orwell at his sanatorium when his health was failing in 1949. Orwell's books, especially *Animal Farm* and *1984*, were far more valuable than the work of intellectuals like Koestler. First, the books were more accessible. Secondly, they were strongly anti-totalitarian but no more anti-communist than they were anti-fascist. Thirdly, Orwell had fine left-wing credentials including service during the Spanish civil war in the International Brigades.[35]

IRD were soon busy propagating Orwell's work with vigour. Foreign rights were bought up and then offered to foreign publishers free of charge and some of the expensive work of translation was also undertaken on their behalf. By 1955 rights to Orwell's *1984* had been bought in Burmese, Chinese, Italian, Finnish, French, Swedish, Dutch, Danish, German, Spanish, Norwegian, Latvian, Indonesian, Polish, Ukrainian, Portuguese, Persian, Telegu, Japanese, Korean, Hebrew, Bengali and Gujarati. IRD's John Rayner in Singapore was working on a special illustrated version in Chinese. At the request of the Colonial Office, IRD purchased the right to circulate a strip cartoon of *Animal Farm* in Cyprus, Tanganyika, Kenya, Uganda, North and South Rhodesia, Nyasaland, Sierra Leone, the Gold Coast, Nigeria, Trinidad, Jamaica, Fiji, British

Guiana and British Honduras. John Rennie, who had become head of IRD, identified Indochina as the top-priority location to which to send prints of the film of *Animal Farm* which they had just acquired.[36]

Orwell was also of great interest to the Americans. By June 1951 Dean Acheson, the Secretary of State, had ordered the US Embassy in London 'to assist foreign publishers' in bringing out further translations of *Animal Farm*. Acheson urged, 'Offer $100 PORT[uguese] book and serial rights; $50 VIET[namese] book rights. Publication RIO and Saigon. Use contingency funds, Reply soonest.'[37] Orwell would doubtless have made an international impact of his own accord, but it is hard to escape the conclusion that the work of IRD and its American partners did much to lift his profile.

The rise of IRD denoted a British acceptance that struggles between states were becoming struggles to the death between societies, involving new areas of propaganda such as religion, another subject in which Muggeridge took an interest. On both sides of the Atlantic no stone was being left unturned in the new propaganda war. Harry Truman attempted to construct a remarkable religious anti-communist front against an atheistic Kremlin. But although he established close bilateral co-operation with specific religious leaders, such as Pope Pius XII, his efforts to form a broad religious united front, including the Dalai Lama in Tibet, came to naught.[38] Religious propaganda found favour with London, where Ernest Bevin was anxious to give IRD's propaganda a positive spin, emphasising Western civilisation, rather than engaging in a slanging match about the evils of communism. The Archbishop of Canterbury was invited to join the Russia Committee. In 1946, Kenneth Grubb, wartime Controller of Overseas Propaganda at the British Ministry of Information, became chairman of the World Council of Churches' influential Commission of the Churches on International Affairs and continued to work closely with Whitehall.[39]

IRD received formal approval in late 1947 and came on stream in 1948. Soon the new department discovered that it was playing catch-up with obscure sections of Whitehall that were ahead in authorising counter-measures against the Soviets, as were some British regional administrators in the Empire. The Americans too had been busy, often using the substantial number of wartime secret services officers who had ostensibly returned to their pre-war occupations. Iran, a cause of immediate post-war abrasion between London and Moscow, was a natural setting for the rapid and extemporised revival of British secret activities. Lord Killearn in Cairo, who had been hostile to the survival of SOE, was nevertheless willing to countenance the continued presence of a few SOE and PWE staff in this critical area. Wartime Iran had been jointly occupied by Britain and the Soviet Union to keep the Germans away from the oil and to ensure a free flow of Lend–Lease supplies to the Soviets. But in 1945 the Soviets revealed a marked reluctance to withdraw from the country, which then became the scene of the Azerbaijan Crisis of late 1945 and early 1946. A radical pro-Soviet element, the Tudeh Party, seized power in Iran's northern province and set up an autonomous government. Under these diverse pressures, the weak central government in Teheran appeared to be on the brink of permitting this large region to break away to join the Soviet Union.

Iran was critical for the balance of payments of the ailing post-war British economy. Iran's southern oilfields, owned by the Anglo-Iranian Oil Company or AIOC, in which Britain had a controlling interest, represented the most important of Britain's many areas of informal empire; indeed they were its biggest external asset. The Soviets were aware of this and since 1944 had directed a relentless stream of propaganda against the exploitative British imperial presence. Soviet propaganda attacks upon the British were, in a way, ironic. Moscow perceived Britain as being the architect behind Iranian resistance to its demands for territorial concessions in northern Iran. In fact Britain initially chose not to encourage Iranian resistance to the Soviets for fear of prejudicing its own claims in the south where the oilfields lay. Instead it was the United States which sought to block the Soviets, with Britain only joining wholeheartedly as strikes spread to the southern oilfields in 1946.[40]

During the struggle for the control of Iran in 1946, Britain was unable to resist using the remnants of its subversive apparatus to defend its vast interests. Confronted with the possibility of Soviet-backed secession in the north, or even the possibility of the pro-Soviet Tudeh Party coming to power, British officials together with key figures in AIOC began to develop their own plans. Their answer was to develop a counter-secession by encouraging rebellion by the pro-British tribes in south-west Iran, centring on the friendly Khuzistan Arabs and the Bakhtiari and Qashqai tribes. If the worst came to the worst, a pro-British south-west Iran, together with its invaluable oil reserves, could break away and declare for London.

In London, Orme Sargent, a quiet enthusiast for covert schemes, directed that it was 'desirable to investigate the possibility of encouraging any demand from the people of South West Persia for provincial autonomy'. Bevin, who was of an opposite persuasion when it came to the use of the hidden hand, was horrified. He countermanded Sargent's instructions and insisted that Britain should not develop the secessionist movement, adding that this would be 'doing what the Russians do'. But the stakes were too high and Bevin's orders were simply ignored by officials below him and by the informal network of British influence in the region.[41]

Colonel Underwood was the key to the British scheme. Underwood was a strange figure who had been at Abadan throughout the war, 'paid by SOE'. He was one of a handful of SOE staff that London was anxious to keep in place in the region at the end of the war, beyond the time when SOE itself was rolled up. During the war he had been SOE's Field Commander in Persia 'with cover as Political Adviser in Khuzistan area (S. Persia)'. SOE noted that this was 'an extremely important area. The work being done there has been undertaken at the request of the Minister and AIOC'. Underwood stayed on after 1945 in the dual guise of British military attaché and 'political adviser' to the AIOC. His role was ambiguous, since he was both the employee of a private company and a British official with diplomatic immunity.[42]

Local Americans captured the nature of his role more precisely, describing him as the 'godfather' of the local tribal union. This latterday Lawrence of Arabia had already organised the Khuzistan Arabs to strike a blow at Tudeh-based communist power in the region. It was no coincidence that Underwood was in Cairo when the tribal union decided to appeal to the Arab League in that city. The British Embassy denied that it was involved in the uprisings of the southern tribes, but there were clearly secret meetings between the tribal leaders and British consuls in the area. Bevin rightly suspected that 'our people right down there' were not taking any notice of his directives.

Although the uprising was not of long duration, it achieved its objectives. It was a shot across the bows that threatened the break-up of Iran and brought the volatile Quvam government in Teheran back on to a middle course. As the British Embassy reported, 'strong pressure has been maintained on the [Iranian] Prime Minister to suppress subversive activities'. The tribal uprising, although now quiescent, underlined what would happen if he did not take a hard line with the Tudeh Party. Meanwhile, with an election approaching, British propaganda officials had been active with the press. They reported that their 'publicity has aimed at influencing Persian public opinion in such a way that the full support of the Prime Minister could not be given to the Tudeh party'. In the short term, British interests in southern Iran had been secured. London was getting itself into gear. Iranians who were receiving sponsored training were to 'go on the air with the BBC'. There was also a scheme mooted for 'providing receiving sets for the tribes in Persia to enable them to hear BBC broadcasts.'[43]

The ensuing propaganda battle with the Soviets in Iran was crucial. It constituted an early lesson in the critical role of this activity in the coming struggle with the Soviet Union, not only in areas like Germany, but throughout the Third World. More significantly it underlined the importance of such propaganda alongside growing information activity by the

United States. The Soviet threat was the more immediate, but in the long term the Americans would prove the more formidable rival in the lucrative Gulf region.[44] In December 1948, Washington considered its contingency plans for a Soviet invasion of Iran. Again the Qashqai tribes to the south, in the Shiraz–Bushire area, were immediately identified as the most likely prospects for long-term resistance: 'they would fight any invader – especially the Russians' and offered an ideal base for 'clandestine operations'. The tribes were mercurial and, while they would fight against anyone, who they would fight *for* was 'debatable' – their decision would probably be 'influenced by gold and other material things'. What they really needed was their own version of Underwood. The US Military Mission called for people 'who speak the language fluently and who know the country and the tribes – i.e., Lawrence of Arabia type'. One possibility they identified was 'Young Archie Roosevelt (nephew of young Teddy)'; they also wanted 'qualified CIA radio operators'.[45] Surviving oddments of SOE and PWE undertook many strange duties in the transitional period between the end of the war and the arrival of IRD. In remote regions, where commercial interests were strong and governments were weak, the needs of local ambassadors were often unusual.

As early as 1947, personnel from OSS and its sister wartime propaganda service, the Office of War Information, were also finding new roles within a new informal American programme of covert action designed to support the Marshall Plan in Western Europe. The initial aim of early American covert action was undermining communism in Greece, Italy, Germany, and, especially France. Like British efforts in Iran, this first wave of American covert actions was often launched alongside the corporatist framework of labour organisations like the American Federation of Labor (AFL), or through Marshall Plan agencies like the Economic Co-operation Administration that were close to industry and labour.

France and Italy were also of great interest to London. In 1946, British diplomats at the Paris Embassy had suggested covertly supplying arms to bolster the right against the growing strength of the communists. But after reflection London and Washington chose less direct methods, including the provision of large sums of money to buy off communist strikers and to subsidise non-communist newspapers. British and American secret service intervention in Italy and France followed in the wake of American private networks. The lead elements here were the links between American, British, French and Italian labour organisations. In 1945 and 1946, AFL was already giving $200,000 to anti-communist groups in Italy and indeed, rather than being encouraged, was urged by Washington not to go too far.[46] The main weapon against communism in France and Italy was an overt one, the Marshall Plan. But, as communist fortunes began to decline under its impact, attempted leftist coups were expected by both British and American officials. By the end of 1947 the American Ambassador in Italy, James Dunn, predicted that an election early in 1948 would result in a communist defeat. He continued, 'It is the belief of the Italian intelligence services that as a result of this trend the Communists have abandoned hope of a legitimate electoral victory and are now preparing for action by force. The series of strategically planned strikes and civil disturbances which they have already carried out and are expected to continue are the preliminary skirmishes leading to the attempt to overthrow the government.' The $600 million of aid author-ised by the Marshall Plan to Italy and France was supplemented by $10 million of 'unvouchered funds' fed by the CIA and other covert methods to pay for anti-communist propaganda and for bribes to aid the Christian Democrats and other non-communist parties. This programme was suc-cessful, but was seen as the beginning rather than the end of a broad anti-communist programme in Europe.[47]

France was viewed as a critical battleground where even the armed forces were considered to be riddled with secret communists. Again, ini-tially the lead element in American intervention in France, as in Italy, was the labour leader Irving Brown and the AFL. As early as May 1947 Pierre Le Brun, the leader of the French Trade Union Council, the CGT, com-plained to American diplomats of American private influence in France and the extension to Europe of the Monroe Doctrine, which declared South America the backyard to the US. During a wave of strikes Brown urged that the government should not on any account meet the strikers' demands for fear of lending greater authority to the communist-controlled CGT. He was also adamant that there should be concerted action to break up the pro-Soviet organisation, the World Federation of Trade Unions, which was based in Paris, in order to reduce the commu-nist hold on French and Italian unions. Brown was clearly driving American policy on organised labour in Europe. In November 1947, when he left Paris for a conference with the British TUC and Ernest Bevin in London, American diplomats there were ordered to give him all possible assistance.[48]

In May 1948, Paul Devinat, a French official, wrote to William Donovan, the former OSS chief, urging American subsidies for the French non-communist press. 'Now that the Italian elections are over and that we can concern ourselves about the situation in other European countries', Devinat suggested, the 'most urgent task' was to 'fight the influence of the communist party in France through the press'. Thanks to the cost of scarce newsprint, independent newspaper publishers could not make ends meet and, in the resulting vacuum, subsidised communist material was making real headway. This, he said, could be dealt with by discreetly supplying new printing machinery, newsprint and even indirect subsidy:

> It is easy to imagine that an agency could be set up in France for the distribution of the advertising of a certain number of American firms who are directly or indirectly interested in the products or manufactured articles imported under the Marshall Plan. Such advertising could be given to a certain number of judiciously selected newspapers. The income which these papers would thus receive would allow them to balance their budget, which usually shows a deficit.

Donovan was impressed and passed Devinat's letter on to the US Joint Chiefs of Staff in Washington. He added that Devinat had been talking to General Revers about the possibility of reassembling parts of 'the underground organization' to fight the communists.[49]

Encouraged by the French themselves, Paris became a testing ground for all sorts of Anglo-American psychological operations, including 'blip-verts', short subliminal messages inserted into film material supplied under the auspices of the Marshall Plan. It was also a testing ground for some of the first CIA-sponsored defector literature. In 1949 London secured a success with Alexander Foote's *Handbook for Spies*, written (as we have seen) largely by his MI5 debriefer Courtney Young. The CIA and the State Department also had a huge success when they sponsored a translated version of the memoirs of Victor Kravchenko, the Soviet official who defected in Washington in 1944.

When Kravchenko had first defected, the authorities had reacted with indifference or even active hostility. But by 1949 such figures were prized assets. *I Chose Freedom*, Kravchenko's extensively rewritten account, sold 400,000 copies worldwide and caused a storm among European communists. It was highly effective in France where communists were an influential part of mainstream intellectual and political life. It reinforced the impact of *Darkness at Noon*, written by Arthur Koestler, who was now working with the CIA-sponsored Congress for Cultural Freedom, and of George Orwell's *1984*. Kravchenko made high-profile public appearances in France and a bitter legal battle broke out when the communists claimed that the book was a fabrication. During the subsequent court case the American authorities trawled France and Germany to find supporting witnesses and funded his legal representation.[50]

By 1949 London had found that IRD propaganda had proved 'surprisingly popular' among Western European governments as anti-communist source material. Thus the French government, though not actively involved, 'tacitly permits quiet circulation of material to French Government officials and key individuals in France'.[51] British and American support galvanised the French authorities. In the autumn of 1950 a fresh wave of anti-communist activity was carried out, much of it petty harassment. Between 7 and 9 September the French arrested and expelled 288 foreign communists, most of whom formed part of the 'para-military apparatus' of the French Communist Party. They expelled the exile base of the Spanish Communist Party from France and its journal *Mundo Obrere*. They set up an anti-communist propaganda organisation Paix et Liberté, with semi-official sponsorship, and considerable assistance from IRD and the CIA. Most importantly, in September 1950 there was a major reorganisation of the French internal security system with a view to providing 'a means for dealing with the Communist fifth column in the event of an emergency'. Especially satisfactory was a decree banning the Paris-based headquarters of various Soviet front organisations including the World Federation of Trade Unions, the International Democratic Federation of Women and the World Federation of Democratic Youth.[52]

As Soviet front organisations were evicted from Paris, IRD and the CIA moved quickly to fill the vacuum. Britain's most successful front organisation, the rival non-communist youth movement, World Assembly of Youth, now set up its Paris headquarters. In November 1950 the CIA's Frank Wisner helped to create the International Federation of War Veterans' Organisations, representing ten million non-communist veterans across Western Europe and North America, with headquarters at 16 Rue des Apennines. The theme of its founding conference was 'peace with freedom', and resolutions passed by the conference 'named the USSR as an aggressor, endorsed European collective security, asked the USSR to take a lead in disarmament' and also approved American economic assistance to Europe. 'Pope Pius XII gave us his blessing,' enthused Wisner, and 'good wishes were also received from Trygvie Lie', the UN Secretary General.[53]

By the early 1950s Western covert propaganda was taking on more diverse qualities. No longer purely anti-communist, it had broadened out to become an instrument that could be deployed against anything hostile to British or American policy. In September 1952 Walter Bedell Smith, Director of the CIA, wrote to General Gruenther at SHAPE, the Supreme Headquarters Allied Powers Europe, asking for his help in a campaign to 'hit hard' at figures and publications that had been running damaging and misleading 'intelligence items' on the United States in papers such as France's *Le Monde*. Bedell Smith considered that some of these items had used documents which were forgeries and he was clearly angry. 'We have asked both the French and British to assist in sustaining an increasing campaign of attack, exposure and ridicule against "Le Monde" and Beuve-Méry.' Beuve-Méry was the editor of *Le Monde*, and Bedell Smith was determined to ensure that he was sacked, stressing that he hoped that 'a permanent sawing off job can be done'. Achieving this, he thought, would require 'additional pressure ... beyond that which has already taken place'. A campaign against a leading French newspaper and its editor was a sensitive matter and these messages between Bedell Smith and Gruenther were carried between Washington and SHAPE by safe hand of trusted officers rather than being sent by cable.[54]

In February 1947, Iceland – because of its strategic value in the North Atlantic – was one of the first targets for British anti-communist propaganda. The British Ambassador, Sir G. Shepherd, asked for 'anti-communist material which could be passed to newspapers which are in sympathy with our views'. By October 1949, IRD was supplying the Icelandic government with quantities of anti-communist material to be used in 'the forthcoming election campaign'.[55] In mid-1949, contingency planning was developed for a possible counter-coup in Iceland, where the Communist Party was electorally strong, holding up to a third of the seats in parliament. By 1950 the Commander-in-Chief Atlantic had developed four separate plans 'to land forces in Iceland against possible opposition in order to restore the democratic government of Iceland'.[56] In June 1949 George Kennan, the main architect of the American containment doctrine, and the NSC staff also gave more attention to 'the preventative aspects of the problem' in Iceland. Nevertheless, plans for the worst eventuality were drawn up. By August 1949, Western planning envisaged a counter-coup using a rapid reaction force. Plan Torchwood would use a select airborne unit from Fort Bragg, North Carolina, home of the developing American Special Forces, to be flown to Iceland via Goose Bay and Greenland and supported by a Marine fighter squadron and a fast carrier group. The problem was that the forces from Fort Bragg would not arrive until four days after the communists had seized power and the carrier group six days. The answer was that 'this operation should became a British commitment', given that the distance from the UK was only 800 miles instead of 2,400. But at present there were 'no British airborne forces available in the U.K. which could undertake operations to insure the security of Iceland'. London had decided to pull the 16th Parachute Brigade Group back from Germany by September 1949, thus providing 'adequate forces in the U.K. to undertake the contemplated operation'.[57] All this denoted a hardening of attitudes and a shift from propaganda towards special operations.

6

The Fifth Column of Freedom:
Britain Embraces Liberation

We are already at war with Russia, but the Kremlin is using a weapon – the
religion of Communism – that we are doing nothing to counter, as we could,
and should, with our corresponding weapon, the religion of Freedom – a
fifth column based on the Atlantic Charter.

Air Marshal John Slessor, 6 September 1947[1]

On 30 December 1946 the American Naval Attaché at Odessa, the
principal Soviet naval base on the Black Sea, reported some remarkable events to Washington. They did not concern the Red Fleet, the
ostensible reason for his presence there, but instead something much
more sensitive: an extraordinary guerrilla war raging in the Soviet hinterland. Odessa was situated in the Ukraine, a region which had fought on
Hitler's side during the Second World War. Here Germany had been able
to raise the most formidable of several Waffen SS units composed of
Soviet citizens: the Galicia Division. Although the war was now over, elements of the Ukrainian Galicia Division were still fighting on against
Moscow in the name of Ukrainian independence. Similar guerrilla
conflicts flickered on inside the Soviet empire into the early 1950s, in
Poland and the Baltic states, but the struggle in the Ukraine, situated
within the Soviet Union itself, was especially fascinating to Western intelligence.

Unsurprisingly, the key opponent for the 25,000 Ukrainian guerrillas
operating in this area was the Soviet secret service, now called the MGB.
Although the damage that the guerrillas inflicted on the locality was considerable – they had recently attacked a train near Tarnopol killing over
180 people – it was their anti-MGB operations that must have reverberated most strongly at the centre in Moscow. On 8 December 1946 they
had assassinated the MGB chief in Odessa, General Gorodevich, in a
brazen attack on one of the city's main streets. The perpetrators fired a

deadly volley from a second-floor window near the General's headquarters and then made a clean escape. MGB officers were a favourite target for the guerrillas. They would vanish by night and their bodies would be found the next morning in a prominent public place. In accordance with local custom they were despatched and had their eyes cut out. These corpses were often decorated with provocative placards declaring 'Long Live America and England'.[2]

Western secret service operations linked to the myriad Ukrainian exile groups were well under way by 1946. In October of that year, the successor to the wartime OSS, known as SSU, looked carefully at these groups. What officials called the 'development of operations involving the use of Ukrainian Nationalist organisations for the purpose of collecting secret information on Eastern Europe and the USSR' had prompted a thorough investigation. The scene was confused. Many Western secret services were making use of a bewildering range of groups and individuals. SSU conceded that it was going to be hard to avoid 'duplication of effort' and that 'security hazards' were inevitable. These shadowy émigré and guerrilla groups were difficult to assess. The Ukrainians, it complained, were good at pretending that 'their past record is a clean one' and that they have 'excellent intelligence services leading directly into the USSR', but many of these factions were complete unknowns. Experience had taught SSU that the only certainty was these outfits were full of con-artists and were 'the most highly opportunistic groups in Europe ... adroit political intriguers and past masters in the art of propaganda'. The US Counter Intelligence Corps or CIC had been running some hair-raising operations with them in Germany. They reported that some exile groups in that country, including the Ukrainian Student Organisation, had been 'set up to present a fly trap for RIS [Russian Intelligence Service] penetration', while others were genuinely penetrated by the Soviets. There were rumours of brusque treatment meted out to Soviet agents identified by this means in Germany. The intelligence war in Germany was already well advanced. As a result of this wave of counter-operations, SSU reported that 'ABN is expected to be liquidated by CIC' with the consent of the Ukrainians and, having been cleansed, its more valuable intelligence activities were to be transferred and 'resumed under a different cover'.[3]

But in the aftermath of the Second World War it was Britain's SIS that had primary responsibility for managing Ukrainian exile groups in Western Europe. SIS looked after them until 1953 when, deciding they were a busted flush, it handed them over, with some relief, to the large CIA station outside Munich. As late as 1957, a still unspecified number of operations were conducted by the CIA, with arms, money and agents being air-dropped close to Ukrainian cities such as Lvov. Moscow could not allow these activities to go unpunished. In 1959, when Soviet agents murdered Stephan Bandera, the leader of the Ukrainian nationalists in exile based in Germany, SIS took extraordinary steps to publicise this atrocity, even to the extent of having its sister organisation, IRD, produce a ghost-written book on the subject. The guerrilla war had petered out by 1953, and terrorist attacks had ceased by the late 1950s. But subsequent events show that this campaign was not forgotten by the Ukrainian nationalists or by the KGB. With the final achievement of Ukrainian independence in 1991, a vast stone memorial to the SS Galicia Division was erected. If this was a calculated affront to Moscow then it was successful, for in 1993 the monument was completely destroyed by a huge bomb.[4]

How did this extraordinary situation – London's clandestine sponsorship of a remote war in the Soviet hinterland – come about? After all, as we have seen, in 1945, Eden, the Foreign Office and SIS had co-operated to terminate Britain's special operations tradition with unseemly haste. Ernest Bevin, the new Foreign Secretary, was a confirmed opponent of special activities, as was Clement Attlee.[5] If Whitehall had set its face so decisively against post-war special operations and secret armies in 1945, how did Britain's SIS find itself embroiled in a clandestine war in the Ukraine, and indeed elsewhere on the periphery of the Soviet empire?

A glorious multitude of special operations units – often referred to as 'private armies' or 'funnies' – had been formed on an *ad hoc* basis during the Second World War. Some, like the SAS and SOE, scored notable victories. However, as we have seen, while they surprised their enemies in the field, they lost the battle against a more dangerous foe, Ministers and civil servants in Whitehall. Special units had become a byword for distasteful ministerial squabbling and administrative mayhem. By early 1946, SAS, SOE and PWE had been dissolved and their expertise largely dispersed. On 10 November 1945, the Foreign Office won a right of veto over all future British special operations.[6] Yet by May 1946, with London infuriated by Soviet activities in Canada, Australia and, especially, Germany, underground warfare was being revived. 'Black propaganda', the specialism of PWE, was the vanguard. Several diplomats, including Ivone Kirkpatrick, who had worked with SOE and PWE during the war, were increasingly convinced that these were the weapons of choice in prosecuting the Cold War. The new Permanent Under-Secretary at the Foreign Office, Sir Orme Sargent, agreed that limited covert propaganda activities should be revived in 1946, paving the way for the creation of IRD.[7]

The struggle to revive British special operations was more acrimonious, and here the balance was tipped decisively by Britain's military leaders. Senior special operations chiefs, including Sir Colin Gubbins and

Fitzroy Maclean, were pressing for revival even at the end of the war. In retirement they took their own private steps to ensure that those with 'special skills' could be recalled at short notice. The formation of the Special Forces Club, a few streets away from Harrods in Knightsbridge, was no mere social exercise. Its membership was a roster of available figures with unique skills and experience. By 1946, some of its members had already found themselves recalled to fight in unpleasant insurgencies in the colonies. Small-scale units, often created unofficially, carried out reprisals and other unattributable activities.

But placing a revived SOE at the centre of Britain's new Cold War strategy was a different matter. Decisive action by the military in 1947 turned the tables. Pressed by energetic figures such as Montgomery and Tedder, Britain moved on from the idea of modest propaganda counter-offensive and cultural warfare against communist student groups to commit itself to an aggressive campaign of special operations which aimed to liberate satellites in the Eastern bloc. The central figure was Air Marshal John Slessor, Tedder's irascible understudy as Assistant Chief of the Air Staff. His experience as a senior RAF commander in the wartime Middle East had convinced him of the enormous potential of secret service, if organised properly. For Slessor, Soviet Cold War tactics, such as subversion and espionage, were quite simply a direct act of war against the West, albeit at the clandestine level. They were a sneak attack and deserved a reply in kind. Slessor, a volatile and outspoken figure who did not believe in half-measures, in 1947 outlined a plan for special operations to achieve victory for the West in the Cold War.

Senior figures wishing to pursue radical strategic schemes faced an obvious first step. This was to thrash out the new ideas with Britain's remarkable one-man military think-tank, Basil Liddell Hart. Writing to him in September 1947, Slessor argued that Britain needed to respond to the Soviets with 'a fifth column of freedom', controlled by a centralised Cold War planning staff. He called for a revival of SOE and also for 'a first-class Political Warfare Service to get busy within Russia and all her satellite states at once in peacetime'. Liddell Hart replied giving his approval. 'You go to the root of the matter in emphasising the vital necessity of the psychological counter-offensive, based on a "religion of freedom".'[8] Less than three years later, Liddell Hart had a change of heart and turned decisively against SOE-type operations and the promotion of resistance movements. But in 1947 there was no inkling of these future doubts.[9]

Slessor also wrote to William J. Donovan on the same theme of how to counter the 'dangerous fifth column'. Slessor, now encouraged by both Liddell Hart and Donovan, elaborated on his ideas: 'The way to avert a hot war is to win the cold one. We should have a first class PWE working full out in conjunction with the Americans and using every known weapon from bribery to kidnapping – anything short of assassination.' He confessed that he had been 'dismayed' by the speed with which SOE and PWE networks had been dismantled at the end of the war.[10]

Slessor had been busy selling these ideas to his immediate superiors, the Chiefs of Staff. Convinced of the wisdom of reviving special operations, at the end of 1947 they opened discussions with Sargent at the Foreign Office. But Slessor could not wait. Anxious to press ahead, he went straight to 'C', Sir Stewart Menzies. Meeting over a clubland lunch – Menzies' favourite vehicle for Whitehall business – Slessor was disheartened by the limited scale of psychological warfare and SOE-type operations that Menzies thought they might undertake against the Soviets. Menzies was defensive and emphasised that everything depended on cash, since special operations were expensive. The issue, he said, was whether the government 'would cough up the money required to enable him to operate effectively – it might be a formidable addition to the Secret Service vote'.

The secret service vote was the sum that Parliament allocated annually for clandestine activities, and traditionally no questions were asked about its purpose. Slessor was thinking of an allocation in 'the order of at least £10 million a year' for the new wave of clandestine warfare, which seemed to him 'the minimum sort of scale on which our secret operations to win the Cold War should be considered'. But he was appalled to find that 'C' was thinking in terms of £½ million, which seemed to him pathetically inadequate. 'I wonder what the enemy are spending!' he exclaimed. He went on to argue that although there would have to be 'a very substantial covert expenditure' it would be worth it. Parliament should be asked for £10 million for the secret service vote and SIS should not hesitate to say 'frankly what it was for'.[11]

By 1948, Slessor had become the Commandant of the Imperial Defence College, where Britain's most senior officers from the three services came together to be given advanced training. There were no prizes for guessing what formed the centrepiece of the curriculum during 1948 and 1949 – the Cold War, and how to win it. Holding private seminars with wartime experts on subversion, including Robert Bruce Lockhart of PWE, Slessor was now developing the theme of winning the Cold War as an explicit critique of Ernest Bevin and current British foreign policy, for in his view, Bevin and the diplomats were losing the Cold War.

Slessor, Montgomery and Tedder changed the whole direction of the clandestine offensive. Prior to 1947, young energetic middle-ranking officials such as Ivone Kirkpatrick had accepted the need for renewed propaganda. But now paramilitary operations were in the ascendant. The

Cominform, the Czech coup in March 1948 and then the Berlin Crisis through the summer of 1948 convinced Montgomery that Bevin's approach to the Cold War lacked teeth. Montgomery was, if possible, more outspoken than Slessor. He was also hugely self-important. Having won a confrontation with Attlee over Middle East strategy in the summer of 1947 by threatening the mass resignation of the three Chiefs of Staff, he had no fear of Cabinet Ministers. The key issue was speed and intensity. Although Bevin had moved some way along the road towards a counter-offensive near the end of 1947, the military deemed it too little too late, and extreme tensions developed. In September 1948 the Chiefs of Staff told Cabinet Ministers that Britain should seek 'to weaken the Russian hold' over the areas the Soviet Union dominated and that 'all possible means short of war must be taken'.[12]

In Washington, similar fears about 'losing the Cold War' stirred the same sort of response. American informal covert actions were under way even before the creation of the CIA in the summer of 1947, but as yet there seemed to be no organised focus. Again the impetus was military. On 12 February 1948, shortly after the communist coup in Czechoslovakia, James Forrestal, Secretary of Defense at the newly formed Pentagon, held a meeting with Admiral Hillenkoetter, Director of the CIA, about stemming the floodtide of communism in Europe. The CIA's mandate contained no direct reference to covert actions, only some deliberately vague 'catch-all' clauses. But Forrestal and Hillenkoetter, with legal advice from the CIA's General Counsel, Larry Houston, decided that as long as the President or the National Security Council approved and Congress kept giving funds 'you've got no problem': 'Who is there left to object?' There followed a vast and rapid expansion of American covert activity whose cost grew from $2 million in 1948 to nearly $200 million by 1952.[13]

On 2 March 1948, Hillenkoetter created the Special Procedures Group within the CIA. This burgeoned quickly into Frank Wisner's semi-detached Office of Policy Co-ordination or OPC. OPC reflected a welter of conflicting claims and tensions over covert action. NSC direction was essential to give its covert actions some sort of authorisation. Direction by Policy Planning Staff figures in the State Department reflected their chief George Kennan's intense interest in this area and his determination to tie these activities into his core strategy. But Kennan knew that the State Department, like the British Foreign Office, harboured a deep aversion to such matters. George Marshall, Secretary of State, was adamantly opposed to anything that might sully the State Department's reputation.[14]

All this was embodied in the infamously vague National Security Council directive 10/2. The question of where ultimate responsibility lay for covert action and psychological warfare remained open for two and a half years. Allen Dulles, then acting as a high-level outside consultant on United States intelligence organisations, and privately hoping to succeed Hillenkoetter as DCI, identified this problem as early as 1 January 1949. Dulles wanted OPC fully embedded in the CIA. But this happened only when Walter Bedell Smith took over as DCI in October 1950.[15]

The American impetus for covert action was driven, above all, by a belief that war in Europe was very near. In March 1948, General Lucius Clay, the US Military Governor in Germany, notified Washington of a changing Soviet attitude and warned that war might come suddenly. In the first week of April, Montgomery visited Clay in Germany and immediately realised that the Americans were on a hair trigger: 'In this electrical atmosphere of suspicion and mistrust there are many varying opinions. General Clay considers that World War III will begin in six months time: indeed he might well bring it on himself by shooting his way up the autobahn if the Russians become difficult about things, he is a real "He-man" ...' British forces were almost as twitchy, with several alerts and semi-mobilisations during early 1948. The French seemed more relaxed. Montgomery noted that the French Military Governor in Germany, General Koenig, 'thinks World War III will begin in about two years time or perhaps a little sooner ... and spends a good deal of time on the Riviera'.[16]

By August 1948, with the onset of the Berlin Crisis, Forrestal called for an overall policy towards the Soviets. Kennan's Policy Planning Staff were ready with a roster of new covert actions and psychological warfare, which was endorsed by the National Security Council on 18 August as directive 20/1. The satellite states were to split away from the Soviet Union. This reflected the optimism that flowed from the recent Tito–Stalin split (Yugoslavia had with impunity broken away from the Eastern bloc that June). But Kennan had already moved beyond this concept of liberating the satellites, advocating not only the gradual rescue of Eastern Europe but also attempts to split away minority national groups within the Soviet Union itself. The United States would strive to 'modify' Soviet borders, especially in the Baltic area.[17]

Like Montgomery and Slessor, Kennan sought to win the Cold War by all means short of war. It was, he stressed, 'not our primary aim in time of peace to set the stage for a war regarded as inevitable'. But equally this was a deliberate and dangerous policy of brinkmanship: 'Admittedly we are aiming at the creation of circumstances and situations which would be difficult for the present Soviet leaders to stomach, and which they would not like. It is possible ... that they would not be able to retain their power in Russia.' War, especially a limited conventional war, was a real possibility and, accordingly, his detailed plans ran smoothly from crisis assessment to a lengthy final component entitled 'Basic Objectives in Time of War'. This included sections on the 'Choice of a New Ruling Group' in the Soviet Union and on 'The Problem of De-Communization'. These remarkable documents were breathtaking in their ambition; it was not for nothing that Kennan had been put in charge of long-range planning.[18]

Kennan and the CIA were careful to co-ordinate some of these ideas with London, especially with the British Chiefs of Staff. In the middle of the busy summer of 1948, Hillenkoetter took the time to visit London. He was especially impressed by Britain's efforts with IRD and, although he took home with him only one copy of the outline British plan for covert operations, this outline made the rounds and was examined with great interest by George Kennan and others on his return to Washington. British thinking among the military at least was proceeding along almost identical lines.[19] The creation of IRD, and its precursors like CRD, had given London a temporary edge in dealing with Washington. In 1949 and even 1950, American officials still considered the British to be ahead in aspects of black propaganda.[20]

In London the showdown over special operations came in August and September 1948. Tensions were building over the Berlin Crisis and American B-29 bombers had already arrived in Britain from the United States on 15 July. By September many observers had resigned themselves to war. On the 22nd of that month, Malcolm Muggeridge was rung up by an SIS contact who asked if he could lecture on communism on a crash intelligence course the service had put on for intelligence officers at Worcester College, Oxford. Conversing with various Whitehall denizens, including Donald Maclean, he gained the sense 'that an atomic war with Russia is almost a certainty'. Amid an air of general mobilisation, he drove down to Oxford with Dick White of MI5, who 'also seemed certain war could more or less be taken for granted'.[21]

The military were in a combative mood. In August the British Chiefs asked Bevin for a high-level forecast of Russian moves as an essential precursor to planning 'a proper "cold war" organisation'. But this forecast was not to their liking and instead they gave preference to their own 'in-house' study by the three directors of service intelligence. The directors set about the task 'in no uncertain way'. The keystone of Soviet policy, they argued, was the 'inevitability of a struggle in order to establish Communism throughout the earth'. Moscow was, in their view, not defensively minded but bent on a programme designed for world domination. Their response was no less radical: 'the only method of preventing the Russian threat is by utterly defeating Russian directed Communism'. The new doctrine of 'winning the Cold War' was being born.

The idea of a 'Cold War' was relatively new, but it was irresistible, and an ideal metaphor. For the first time in history, the directors argued, a totalitarian organisation of states was attempting to impose its will on the rest of the world by means other than armed conflict, which could be 'conveniently' described as Cold War. Montgomery noted approvingly, 'We couldn't win the "cold war" unless we carried our offensive inside Russia and the satellite states. In fact what was required was a world-wide offensive by every available agency. To date we had failed to unify our forces to oppose the Soviet "cold war" aggression. At present we are in danger of losing the "cold war".' Montgomery and the directors of intelligence of the three services were dissatisfied not just with the lack of a British response to the Soviet clandestine programme, but with the whole British approach to the Cold War. 'We have *not* integrated with our Allies, we have *not* selected our strategic aim, we have *not* got a high-level integrated plan, we have *not* allocated our world resources, and we have *not* designated our "cold war" forces.' Now they demanded an organisation that could exercise the higher direction of this all-out Cold War offensive and control all executive action under someone of ministerial rank.

This was political dynamite and Montgomery knew it. It was more than a deliberate and personal attack on the Foreign Secretary, Ernest Bevin. The military were proposing nothing less than the removal of the direction of the Cold War, by now the central concern of British foreign policy, from Bevin's grasp. Their alternative concept of a new ministerial supremo in charge of fighting the Cold War was left deliberately vague. But it could not help but recall the early days of SOE and its ministerial chief, the forceful and irascible Hugh Dalton, who inflicted so much misery and alarm upon Eden.

On 9 September 1948, Montgomery led the Chiefs of Staff into a staff conference with the Minister of Defence, the mild-mannered A. V. Alexander. Arthur Tedder, the most articulate and intellectual of the three Chiefs, put their case, stating plainly that the present efforts to prevent the spread of communist domination were completely inadequate. The Cold War, he argued, now required the employment of 'all our resources, short of actual shooting'. He tried to reassure Alexander that this was not an attempt to undermine Bevin, but the facts were inescapable. Montgomery enjoyed watching Alexander in an undisguised state of panic, recording that the Minister of Defence 'again lost his nerve' and wished to water down their recommendations. But the Chiefs were adamant that their volatile proposal should go to Bevin 'in its original state' so that their views should be 'absolutely clear'. The next day their démarche was handed to Bevin.

Bevin responded on 29 September by sending Ivone Kirkpatrick to discuss the Cold War.[22] This was a clever move. Kirkpatrick was probably closer to the views of the military than any other senior diplomat, and was keen to disabuse them of the view that the Foreign Office had been doing nothing. He conceded that it was time to improve the Cold War 'machinery', but insisted that the Chiefs were 'incorrect' when they claimed that the newly formed IRD was the only body prosecuting the Cold War. He explained that the task of planning 'all the other measures' was the responsibility of the weekly Russia Committee, which brought together all the senior policy-makers of the Foreign Office concerned with Russia and called on experts as required. This was, in fact, 'the Cold War Planning Staff'.

This was a remarkable revelation. The Russia Committee, the central brain set up to manage Cold War issues in May 1946, was still completely unknown to the Chiefs of Staff more than two years later. As Kirkpatrick himself confessed, Sir Ian Jacob, the head of the European Service of the BBC, was a regular member. But all this time later the Chiefs were not only uninvited, they were unaware of its existence. Although at first sight this seems bizarre, the explanation was quite straightforward. There had been rising tensions between the diplomats and the military over how to handle the Soviet Union since 1942. One of the central purposes of the Russia Committee was to reassert Foreign Office control. Nevertheless, as Kirkpatrick now agreed, it was high time one of the three Chiefs joined it.

Kirkpatrick had some good defensive points to make. It was difficult, he said, for the West to wage an all-out subversive Cold War since 'some of the tactics open to the Russians were not open to ourselves'. Nor was it easy to co-ordinate measures 'with our Allies', some of whom were not yet up to speed or were thoroughly disorganised. But he then blurted out the main issue that had retarded Britain's own Cold War counter-offensive: 'The Foreign Secretary was inclined to the view that covert activities would not pay a dividend.'[23]

Bevin's approach was anti-communist, but in a different style. He had eventually backed the creation of IRD and half a dozen associated bodies – funded through the secret service vote in the same manner as SIS – in early January 1948. He urged his Cabinet colleagues to take a firmer approach to ideological competition with the Soviet Union, by pushing British social democracy and the values of Western civilisation. Cabinet gave its approval for a small IRD organisation, but under Bevin it became big, expanding faster than any other section of Britain's overseas policy machine. Bevin wanted IRD's work to be largely 'positive', projecting British achievements instead of turning the Soviets into bogeymen. In his view this approach 'could be expected to relax rather than raise international tension'. More importantly, as someone who took all criticism personally, he resented the encroachment of the military into 'his' foreign policy.[24]

Bevin dealt with the military skilfully. Kirkpatrick played a sympathetic tune for them, but gave little away. The Chief of the Air Staff, Arthur Tedder, now joined the Russia Committee, but Britain's 'Cold War Planning Staff' remained under Bevin's control. The Foreign Office also agreed to a 'review' of intelligence on Russia, involving the Chiefs of Staff, the JIC and 'C', but this seems to have produced no real results.[25] Instead, the scene now shifted to the new-style Foreign Office Russia Committee, which was briefed to examine Montgomery's desire for an 'all out offensive' by every available agency, with Tedder in attendance. Before the committee met the military were offered a Whitehall-wide platform to vent their views about the 'present so-called peace' at the meeting of Commonwealth Prime Ministers in London. The Chiefs attended for security discussions on 20 October 1948 and Tedder was, if anything, in a fiercer mood than Monty. He argued that the present situation was not open war in the military sense but equally it 'is not peace': 'we do most earnestly urge that it be fully recognised that we, the whole democratic world, are faced now by the stark reality of a cold-blooded, utterly unprincipled, ruthless and world-wide war, directed from, and closely controlled by, the Kremlin. A war which is waged like a human disease which searches out the weak spot in every individual.' Tedder went on: 'You may say this is politics. What has this to do with the military?' He countered by arguing that in France the Cold War had undermined the government to the point where the defence of Europe was imperilled and by asserting that attempts to sabotage the Marshall Plan had potential economic consequences.[26]

A month later, on 25 November, Tedder finally had his chance when the newly expanded Russia Committee met. Major figures from Britain's Cold War were there to offer their opinion on the value of 'special operations'. Kirkpatrick introduced the central question: should they begin stirring up trouble in the Eastern bloc? He stressed that the idea was to emulate the sort of costly civil war that the West had confronted in Greece. Equally prominent in everyone's mind was the ongoing Berlin Crisis and the surprise breakaway of Tito's Yugoslavia from the Eastern bloc the previous June. Both events strongly influenced the discussion. Kirkpatrick was cautious, proposing that Britain should 'start any kind of offensive operations in a small area', partly for reasons of financial stringency, and he suggested Albania.

Albania was vulnerable by reason of being physically cut off from the Eastern bloc by Yugoslavia and Greece. Overturning Enver Hoxha's communist government would be a boost to those fighting the civil war in Greece, where the communist guerrillas were receiving aid and sanctuary from across the border. Most of the Foreign Office officials were negative. Gladwyn Jebb, senior wartime SOE official, pointed out that

United Nations observers in Greece would get to hear of any British operation, with 'unpleasant consequences'. Frank Roberts noted that it was easy for the Russians to do such things unattributably, since they worked through the local communist parties, but for Britain it would be more difficult. Esler Dening, formerly Mountbatten's wartime political adviser in South-east Asia, and a man with great experience of wartime SOE troubles, stressed the dangers of using part of the Albanian population against the rest: 'It meant that you became beholden to the people on whom you depended.' Roger Makins, who had been serving in the Washington Embassy, argued that the value of underground movements was doubtful, insisting that, in the last war, 'if the effort expended on underground operations had been put into straight military operations the results would have paid us better'.

In short, the diplomats moved in the shadow of their own painful wartime SOE experiences, and few were uncritical. Even Tedder, representing the military's new hard line, had well-grounded reservations. Although anxious to set up a specialist planning staff to look at the various instruments available, he stated clearly that he was 'sceptical of the value of SOE unless followed up by military action. He likened these operations to a barrage laid down before an attack by troops; if it was laid down too far ahead your friends were simply annihilated.' In other words, it was all quite pointless unless Britain intended, at some future point, to support these groups with *overt* military force and to risk open war. There could be no more prescient forecast of the fate of those who were to rise against the Soviets in East Berlin in 1953 and in Hungary in 1956. Yet, despite this scepticism, the Russia Committee sanctioned the operation against Albania. Albania was probably the price that Bevin had to pay to prevent a full showdown with the Chiefs of Staff. The Russia Committee was required only to work out the framework. It declared 'that our aim should certainly be to liberate the countries within the Soviet orbit by any means short of war'. Certain essentials were agreed: the importance of working with the Americans; of getting clear Cabinet approval; and of having the requisite planning organisation. All were agreed to move forward with special operations and a degree of Cold War fighting using a revived SOE.

Why had this decision been taken, when the practical problems of encouraging resistance inside the secret police states of the Eastern bloc had been so clearly identified at the outset? The answer was the pressure exerted by the recent Czech coup and the continuing Berlin Crisis, together with worries about France, Italy and Greece, resulting in a fear of being nibbled to death. The Chiefs of Staff warned that the West was being gradually pushed into a corner by Soviet Cold War methods and that by the time a hot war erupted it would be too weak to resist. Tedder spoke frankly, stating 'that unless we reformed our present machinery for conducting the "cold war", we might lose it in which case the Services would have to conduct a hot war, which was the last thing they wanted to do'.

During these crucial discussions on 25 November, the familiar military–diplomatic division re-emerged. Tedder declared that 'we should aim at winning the "cold war" (by which he meant the overthrow of the Soviet regime) in five years time'. Frank Roberts, recently returned from Britain's Moscow Embassy, was amazed and shot back that this was 'an impossible task'. However, the course was now set and 'a small permanent team' was set up to look at Albania and to 'consider plans which would subsequently be executed by ourselves and the Americans'.[27] In 1948 and 1949, officials in Washington, also heartened by events in Tito's Yugoslavia, adopted a similar, but wider-ranging, programme of covert action, designed to hasten what they presumed to be the gradual disintegration of the Eastern bloc, and qualified enthusiasm for this idea was incorporated in mainstream policy towards the Soviet Union.[28]

At the end of 1948 the Chiefs of Staff seemed to have won. The Russia Committee confirmed a sea-change in Britain's Cold War tactics that embraced liberation and all methods short of war. But in fact they had lost, for they were now confronted by two immovable obstacles. The first was that of resource. Britain had broken up its special operations assets in 1945 to the point where they could not quickly be reassembled. The limited capabilities of the small numbers of special operations personnel in SIS were now subject to conflicting demands. Required to begin liberation, they were also busy with contingency preparations for a hot war which some thought might be only months away and which most believed would begin in the Middle East. The SIS cupboard for either contingency was almost bare.

Planning for a hot war had been under way for a while. In 1947 and early 1948, Kim Philby found himself SIS station commander in Turkey. One of his principal duties was to roam about in a Land Rover conducting detailed survey work for SIS wartime contingency plans, involving for example the demolition of roads and railways in case the Soviets advanced. By mid-1948 these plans were beginning to take shape and London staffs were prepared to set out 'the scale of M.I.6 effort that can be made available in the event of war breaking out with RUSSIA with little warning'. On the face of it an impressive menu of SIS activities was set out:

(a) The supply of information – tactical and strategical, military, political, economic and scientific.

(b) Covert Propaganda (spreading rumours, false information, 'black broadcasts', etc).

(c) The organisation of bases, areas and Safe Houses.

(d) The marking of targets.

(e) The organisation of escape routes.

(f) The infiltration and exfiltration of personnel and stores to and from enemy occupied countries by air and sea.

(g) Industrial and other sabotage, including organising strikes, etc.

(h) The stimulation of indigenous resistance.

(i) Cooperation with S.A.S. and L.R.D.G. [Long Range Desert Group] type units.

(j) 'Coup de main' operations to attack special targets or carry out demolitions.

But the devil was in the detail. SIS conceded that in the first *three months* of such a war it could do little of this. This was primarily because hitherto there had been plans but no physical preparation. 'At present there is a Foreign Office ban on carrying out any preparatory measures for Special Operations. This is unlikely to be lifted, unless war appears inevitable.' The Foreign Office had imposed its veto, insisting that any preparations meant informing other governments that war might be imminent, creating 'alarm and despondency'; there would 'probably be a leakage of plans'. It added that special personnel would have to be infiltrated ahead of time and if left in countries for a long time would become suspect. All these arguments had force, but the end result was that SIS was left working up wartime operations from scratch.

SIS accepted that in the first three months it could only conduct intelligence work, broadcast some propaganda and offer 'very limited assistance in marking of vital targets'. It might be able to conduct some 'coup de main' operations, but only if these were planned and if the necessary personnel, equipment and so on were provided well ahead of time by the military. This was a tacit admission that SIS had almost no in-house special operations capacity of its own. Arguments flared among the SIS War Plans section as to whether it should draft in ex-SOE or alternatively ex-SAS personnel and which were likely to be the most manageable and the most security-minded. Moreover, SIS feared that the populations of many countries of the Middle East 'may be actively hostile to us, in which case Special Operations would not succeed in the early stages of the war'. Activities might have to be restricted to Greece and Turkey only. This was the natural consequence of the diplomatic emasculation of Britain's special operations capabilities in 1945, but in 1948 it was not what the Chiefs wished to hear.[29]

Even at the end of 1949 there was little more capacity. The Turks were also setting a great deal of store by special operations and had developed three large units whose sole purpose was to prepare for wartime guerrilla operations. British plans were not to offer support via the secret services but instead to para-drop two battalions of sappers into strategic areas to demolish roads, communications and anything else of value. Britain's

Middle East Land Forces HQ was reorganising an Engineer Regiment 'to carry out special demolition tasks in Persia and Iraq'. It had considered the introduction of sleeper agents in peacetime but concluded that this was 'not practicable'. Targets included the Iranian railways and the oil-production facilities at Iran, Iraq and Qatar.[30]

Although the diplomats had the strongest objections to sleeper agents in foreign countries, they were willing to work with overseas officials whom they trusted. With regard to Austria, the Permanent Under-Secretary's Department agreed to 'send an MI6 technical adviser to advise the Austrian authorities' on how to conduct strategic demolitions in the event of a Soviet attack.[31] Special operations enthusiasts existed within SIS, but Menzies knew his limitations and joined with the Foreign Office in attempting to block military pressure for anything ambitious. A further obstacle obstructing the paths of the Chiefs of Staff was the considerable figure of Ernest Bevin himself. Although plagued by increasing ill-health, Bevin was a robust individual schooled by a decade of tough inter-war trade union politics. He was not about to surrender the higher direction of the Cold War to the military, or indeed to compromise the role of the Foreign Office as the key co-ordinator for Britain's overseas policy. Nor was the démarche by the Chiefs of Staff in the autumn of 1948 an isolated incident. It was the culmination of five years of diplomatic–military wrangling over the Soviet Union. Montgomery had forced concessions from Bevin by bullying – ironically much the same method that Bevin and the military had used together to extract concessions from Attlee on the Middle East a year before.

Bevin's concessions were only tactical. Within the Foreign Office the message had gone out that references to Cold War fighting, and even the use of the term 'Cold War', were to be discouraged. This met with opposition. Whatever the internal wrangling within Whitehall, many senior diplomats now believed that a twilight struggle was under way, and 'Cold War' captured its essence. The diplomats thus reconciled themselves to some 'planning' and to some 'Cold War fighting'. Sterndale Bennett, who superintended Far Eastern matters at the Foreign Office, was attending the course run by Slessor at the Imperial Defence College, where predictably 'Cold War' was flavour of the month. Returning from one of these sessions he explained his ambivalence to a colleague in March 1949: 'I know that the term "Cold War" is much disliked in the Foreign Office as tending to misleading analogies, in the matter of methods and machinery, with a military war. But it is so commonly used nowadays, even officially ... and in any case it is very expressive of a state of affairs which undoubtedly exists.' Indeed, as Slessor had pointed out to senior officers, the term was being used by Ministers all the time, not only by Ernest Bevin but also by left-wing members of the Cabinet. Bevin had used the term repeatedly in his exchanges with the Soviets at the Paris Conference in September 1948. On 1 November that year even Stafford Cripps accused the Soviets of practising Cold War by use of 'fifth column agents' and covert aggression. Like it or not, the idea of fighting a Cold War had come to stay. The outcome of the IDC discussions was that a reluctant A. V. Alexander was compelled by the Chiefs of Staff to write to Attlee stressing 'the need for further developing the United Kingdom organisation for conducting the Cold War', adding that 'something should be done to stiffen the Russia Committee'. Alexander asked for a 'Staff Conference' with Attlee, Bevin and the Chiefs of Staff, but there is no indication that Attlee or Bevin complied.[32]

Bevin beat Montgomery and the Chiefs of Staff by sleight of hand. In early 1949, after the military ultimatum, there followed a complete re-ordering of the central machine of British foreign policy. Bevin created the Permanent Under-Secretary's Department (PUSD) with its own committee (PUSC) and an elaborate system of sub-committees. This secretive super-department absorbed all the most sensitive elements of the Foreign Office, including the Services Liaison Department, whose head controlled the Joint Intelligence Committee. PUSD was given extensive responsibility for intelligence and special operations. The term PUSD itself was considered secret and was often used as a cover-name for SIS.

Accordingly, almost as soon as the Chiefs of Staff had placed Arthur Tedder on the Russia Committee, its much vaunted role as the key 'Cold War Planning Staff' began to be sidelined. The small sub-committee that it set up to look at special operations against Albania was quietly moved to PUSD, and eventually became the Overseas Planning Section (OPS). Here, the military were allowed very limited representation within PUSD, at the lowly rank of colonel. This was no threat to the authority of the Foreign Office. PUSD was an effective block on the ambitions of the military to run Britain's clandestine operations.

PUSD also handled 'planning'. This represented a deliberate emulation of the American State Department, where George Kennan and Robert Joyce presided over the Policy Planning Staff. Common machinery at the top seemed essential if policies in London and Washington were going to be properly co-ordinated. Moreover, planning and special operations always seemed to be connected in some indefinable way. Certainly, those who had always hated special operations, like Cadogan, also hated 'planning'. Those more sympathetic to special operations, such as Kirkpatrick, once nicknamed 'King Planner', were keen. But there was also a general agreement that, while the Chiefs of Staff might be a menace, their planning machinery, with its neatly numbered papers, gave a splendid outward impression of efficiency and orderliness.

Preparations for PUSC and PUSD began in late 1948 and these bodies formally began operations on 1 February the following year. William Hayter, Secretary of the JIC, was initially responsible for the operations of the Secretariat. In April, he told the Americans that this PUSD had arisen partly in emulation of 'George Kennan's outfit in the State Department' and he expressed 'a lively interest' in the workings of the Policy Planning Staff. He added that Gladwyn Jebb was touring the States and was 'looking forward to an opportunity to compare notes with Mr Kennan' with a view to improving the workings of PUSD. As with other mechanisms, the British hoped that a mirror would become a window – if they copied the American system they would achieve closer consultation on its activities.[33]

PUSD certainly defeated Montgomery and the Chiefs of Staff. As early as March 1949 Christopher Warner admitted that 'special liaison arrangements' between the military and IRD were 'a complete failure'. On 17 June diplomats met with the Chiefs of Staff to discuss co-operation on Cold War propaganda. They all agreed that the present set-up was not working well, but they could not agree why. They decided to seek 'an individual who understood the mysteries of propaganda' on an 'ad hoc basis' but no one seemed sure where to look.[34] Malcolm Muggeridge went to see Montgomery that month as the Field Marshal relinquished his role as Chief of the Imperial General Staff and moved to SHAPE in Paris. Muggeridge found him 'got up in his usual fancy dress ... eyes are glazed over and mad-looking'. He worried that the strain of his immense fame 'might have cracked his wits a bit'. Montgomery spent most of the hour expounding his own view, which his listener considered to be a 'clear case of advanced megalomania'. Montgomery was still completely preoccupied with the Cold War fighting theme that had gripped him a year before, asserting loudly to Muggeridge that they were now 'at war with Communism'. Although he felt that they could win a shooting war, he said this would be no use unless they 'defeated Communism'. He then gave Muggeridge the line about the urgent need for 'a co-ordinated command in the cold war, someone responsible for conducting it'. At present there was 'No plan, no plan at all'. With Montgomery's departure for Paris, Bevin's most dangerous and irascible enemy was gone from Whitehall.[35]

By September 1949, a year after gaining access to the Russia Committee, the Chiefs of Staff realised they had been completely side-tracked. Bevin had agreed to liberation, but the only significant outcome was a small unsuccessful operation by SIS and the CIA against Albania. Everything else was effectively snarled up in sub-committees and red tape. The Chiefs' frustrations were gauged by Captain Hillgarth, the go-between for Churchill (then in opposition) and the military. Hillgarth told Churchill that the Chiefs of Staff were angry and bitterly disappointed. A special committee, which included the Vice Chief of the Imperial General Staff, had been appointed by Bevin to look at all aspects of fighting the Cold War. Although 'it started off energetically enough and took a lot of evidence', no recommendations had appeared and the report was months overdue. Another committee, set up by Bevin to look at the interface between intelligence and propaganda, had reported two months before that a specialist should be appointed to carry out 'a definite plan'. Although it had settled on Donald Maclachlan, Foreign Editor of the *Economist*, as the ideal person, he had not yet been approached: 'Meanwhile the Russia Committee of the Foreign Office (with one representative of the Chiefs of Staff present at its meetings) remains the only body concerned with the Cold War. It meets once a fortnight but does nothing, and the Service member can't get it to do anything.'[36]

Skilful Foreign Office heel-dragging had taken effect by the summer of 1949. Events over the next twelve months, the explosion of a Soviet atomic bomb and the outbreak of the Korean War, would serve only to increase its determination to apply the diplomatic brakes. But the British military, and more importantly the Americans, had secured the green light to conduct operations in Albania, Poland and even within the Soviet Union itself in the volatile Ukraine. For the British military their best hope of escaping diplomatic encirclement was to join up with the Americans in an all-out effort to win the Cold War.

7

Liberation or Provocation?
Special Operations in the Eastern Bloc

The propensity of the revolution to devour its own, the suspicions of the Kremlin regarding its agents and the institutions of denunciation, purge and liquidation are grave defects in the Soviet system which have never been adequately exploited.

NSC 58, 'US Policy towards the Soviet Satellite States in Eastern Europe',
14 September 1949[1]

More than any other aspect of liberation in the late 1940s, Operation Valuable, the SIS and CIA attempt to liberate Albania, was British owned. This was rooted in complex wartime struggles between OSS and SOE in the Balkans. SOE belligerently insisted on dominance in the Balkans, provoking William J. Donovan to launch his own independent activities in the region. SOE had the dubious honour of arming and training Enver Hoxha, a wartime communist resistance leader and by far the most effective killer of Germans. By 1946 he had secured power in Albania, declaring himself the new president and establishing close links with Moscow.

London had reasons to hate the post-war Hoxha regime in Albania. Britain was embroiled in a vicious civil war in neighbouring Greece, supporting the government against the communists. Stalin largely respected the Balkan 'percentages deal' which he had concluded in Moscow with Churchill in October 1944, and so did not send aid to the communist guerrillas in Greece. Instead they received it from the Albanian communists and, prior to 1948, from the bellicose Tito. British commitments in the Mediterranean, from Greece through to Palestine, were placing London under unbearable strain, eventually prompting American military aid in the form of the Truman Doctrine in March 1947. More pointedly, in 1946, the Hoxha regime, which was paranoid about its security, had begun firing on British warships sailing in the Adriatic. Two British destroyers sank in the three-mile-wide Corfu Channel after hitting

Albanian mines. The International Court of Justice found Hoxha guilty, but he had refused to accept responsibility.[2]

Aside from the 'grudge factor', Albania was an attractive target because of its geographical seclusion from the Eastern bloc. After the Tito–Stalin split in the summer of 1948 there was simply no land-route that would allow Soviet forces to intervene to help Hoxha suppress a rebellion. Tito, who counted himself lucky to have drifted away from Soviet control without suffering intervention himself, could not be persuaded to intervene in Albania, for fear of Soviet reprisals. Nevertheless, his benign neutrality consigned Albania to vulnerable isolation. This was a key factor for SIS, whose resources for this sort of operation were self-confessedly limited. The uprising in Albania was the work of the Special Political Action section of SIS. This was very small, no more than a few officers staffing a planning unit. Menzies deliberately avoided creating a real special operations section, instead requiring all new SIS officers to do a little basic training in special operations. The main 'outdoor' training centre for SIS was at Gosport in a curious and remote fort dating back to the Napoleonic era. Here operational exercises included covert landings on the Dorset coast, but these amateur affairs had a supreme air of unreality.[3]

Operation Valuable was therefore run by former SOE personnel recalled specifically for the purpose. Leadership fell to Colonel David Smiley, a tough and highly experienced SOE officer. Smiley had spent a long period in wartime Albania training guerrillas together with Julian Amery, who was also recalled for the operation. Striding about with a tommy gun and his 'favourite corduroy trousers' Smiley had been a distinctive figure and survived for two years in wartime Albania close to the neighbouring German garrison. He had then joined SOE in the Far East. Embroiled in the struggle for control over Indochina in late 1945 he had survived a shoot-out with OSS-backed guerrillas in Laos. But his closest call had been at the hands of an SOE device. A thermite briefcase, designed to incinerate its top-secret contents in an emergency, had accidentally detonated prematurely, inflicting severe burns. By 1947, Smiley was serving as part of the British occupation in Germany when he was recalled to secret service by SIS for the operation against Albania.[4]

The limited nature of SIS resources prompted early discussions with Frank Wisner and his deputy Franklin Lindsay in 1948. The American case officer at the planning stage was James Macarger. But the most active supporter of the proposal in Washington was Robert Joyce of the Policy Planning Staff, who hoped that the successful liberation of Albania would send shock waves right across the Eastern bloc. Albania also seemed an ideal laboratory in which to refine and develop techniques, and the first wave of activities in 1948–9 constituted a probing operation, rather than an all-out attempt to unseat Hoxha.[5]

Nineteen-forty-eight was a year of preparations. SIS provided most of the Albanian operatives, known to their training officers as 'Pixies'. It ransacked the Displaced Persons camps of Germany and Italy for likely agents. The result was a motley crew of over 200 volunteers, mostly in a poor state of health, a proportion of whom were almost certainly working for Albanian state security. Smiley trained his Pixie teams on Malta during the summer of 1949 and planned to deliver them to the Albanian coast by boat. Meanwhile the Americans trained their Albanians in southern Germany and prepared them to be dropped by parachute from C-47 Dakota aircraft.

Political preparations for a new regime had also begun. An Albanian National Committee was created to provide a semblance of government in exile. As Washington noted politely, the Albanian émigrés 'are too heterogeneous to be placed in any definite political and social classification'. Predictably, no single figure could be found who would command universal support inside and outside Albania. The committee was an uneasy coalition between the supporters of tribal warlord King Zog, who had reigned in the late 1920s, and the Balli Kombetar group, which had run a National Front in Athens and Rome, and several smaller groups. King Zog had been exceedingly unpopular outside his own tribal district before the war. Only now that the Hoxha government 'requisitions everything' did he glow by comparison. Everyone from peasants to traders to shopkeepers supported him over Hoxha, with the exception of the young progressive intellectuals who did not like the idea of a return to stultifying monarchism. Above politics and unsullied by personal collaboration with the Axis, Zog was 'the only Albanian who could unify most of the elements in exile'.

The Americans preferred the intellectual group Balli Kombetar, led by former judge Hasan Dosti, which had begun as an anti-Axis resistance movement and had 'organised a plot to assassinate leading Italian and Albanian fascists' in the late 1930s. But it was weak and had ignominiously collaborated for a while to shelter from attacks by the vigorous communists before fleeing to Italy in 1943. The British preferred the Legalitati group, formed in 1943 by Major Abas Kupi, who sought to restore the Zog monarchy. But, like Dosti's intellectuals, he had resorted to collaborating with the Axis regime in Tirana to protect himself from the communists. In October 1944, SOE evacuated him together with his two sons and close followers. There were at least four other groups with adherents in Italy, Egypt, Greece, the United States and even Australia. The CIA-sponsored Free Europe Committee, the umbrella organisation co-ordinating the radio warfare against the Eastern bloc and the exile group activities, did what it could to lend this uneasy federation of groups some political respectability.[6]

The first move in Operation Valuable took place in October 1949. A flotilla of SIS-chartered boats ferried a group of twenty-six Pixies to the Albanian coast. They were ambushed soon after landing and suffered four casualties. The remainder fled. Most were fortunate to escape over the mountains into neighbouring Greece, where the local authorities took them to be communist guerrillas. SIS had to undertake tactful work to persuade the Greeks to release them. Although there was clearly a substantial potential partisan movement on the ground in Albania it could not be energised. Each attempt to insert agents was met by the Albanian security forces. Hot receptions were a constant factor whether the Pixies were inserted by sea or by parachute.[7] Anglo-American frictions plagued operations at all levels. Things had got off to a bad start in early 1949 when the British and French had uncovered an amateur and undeclared US operation to overthrow Tito in neighbouring Yugoslavia, of which they knew nothing. Wisner's OPC had begun to infiltrate right-wing exiles into Yugoslavia, mostly Serb Chetniks. Bizarrely they were clothed in US Air Force uniforms and they were quickly rounded up by the security police. For a while they were herded about on Belgrade's main railway station. Charles Bateman, the senior British diplomat overseeing policy in this part of the world, exclaimed that this was 'inconceivably stupid' and demanded action against 'this idiotic American behaviour'. Bevin teamed up with the US Ambassador to London, Cavendish Cannon, to convince Washington that there was no alternative to Tito and that to try and unseat him was unrealistic and 'would be playing straight into the Soviet hand'.[8]

Bevin also argued over Albania. American planners favoured youthful Albanian nationalists who sought to develop a non-communist republic and leaned towards the United States. Bevin explained that 'the British had followed a policy of unrelenting hostility to the Hoxha Government', but he was openly scathing of the CIA-funded Free Albania Committee. At a meeting with Acheson he asked, 'Are there any Kings around that could be put in? ... a person we could handle was needed.' He captured much of the essence of the British approach to perpetuating influence in dependent areas in the mid-twentieth century. During the war similar tensions had arisen between OSS, which favoured young nationalists, often middle-ranking officers in the armed forces, and the British, who had preferred to sponsor the traditional, golf-playing sultans and rajahs.[9] Bevin himself had come to the Foreign Office in 1945 determined to change this aspect of British policy, convinced that it was storing up trouble. In November that year, he lectured Lord Halifax, Britain's Ambassador in Washington, on the subject, insisting that this was why Britain had never achieved a genuine partnership with the peoples of the Mediterranean and the Middle East. Instead, 'our

foreign policy has rested on too narrow a footing mainly on the personalities of kings, princes or pashas'. But in no time at all Bevin fell back on
traditional policies, typified by his support for King Abdullah in Jordan,
unkindly referred to in the Foreign Office as 'Mr Bevin's Little King'.[10]

SIS backed away from liberation after similar disappointments during
the 1950 operational 'season'. Indeed, although Bevin had agreed to
Operation Valuable, it was against his better judgement and was forced
on him by pressure from Tedder and Montgomery. Away from
Whitehall, Bevin now worked secretly to oppose it. In mid-September
1949 he had met his opposite numbers Acheson and Schuman for talks
in Washington. The Americans had wanted 'to make more trouble for
the Albanian regime'. But Bevin had asserted that 'there is no substitute
for the present Hoxha regime and that the Free Albania Committee is
not a hopeful prospect'. He was already backing away from Operation
Valuable only months after Smiley's first wave of Pixies had landed on
Albania's hostile shores.[11]

By 1951 Albania was a purely CIA operation. The CIA persevered and
changed tactics. The situation in Greece had now stabilised, so attempts
were made to infiltrate groups by land over the border, but the result was
depressingly familiar. The CIA was encouraged by a single surviving
group equipped with a W/T transmitter that seemed to be well established. But the balance of opinion is that this one operational station set
up inside Albania had been 'turned' by state security and was being used
to lure in more unsuspecting groups.[12]

Public knowledge of Operation Valuable was initiated by the appearance of Kim Philby's provocative but stylish memoirs in 1968. This led
many down the years to leap to the conclusion that his role in its planning
resulted in its demise. But this is improbable. In September 1949, as the
first waves went ashore, Philby had only just arrived in Washington and
was still waiting to take over from Peter Dwyer as head of station desig-
nate. Day-to-day planning was in the hands of working groups attended
by Earl Jellicoe, a wartime SAS officer. Landings and drops were decided
more locally. Instead Operation Valuable fell foul of the danger that
awaits all large-scale covert paramilitary operations, namely that they
require forces on a scale that makes them impossible to screen.
Penetration by low-level agents of Hoxha's security forces was inevitable.
Moreover, the degree of fear achieved by Hoxha's regime was extremely
effective, since few villagers would risk retribution by not denouncing
agents landing in their locality.[13]

The operation against isolated and vulnerable Albania was an obvious
move, so much so that the Soviets had been expecting it for three years.
Britain already had former SOE officers in the area, advising the Greek
forces against communist guerrillas. On 20 December 1946 Moscow

Radio accused the Tsaldaris government in Greece of 'forming in secrecy a corps of Hitlerite mercenaries and traitors'. These bands were not just for counter-insurgency, they were also intended for 'sabotage in Yugoslavia and Albania with a view to destroying the peaceful work of the peoples of those countries'. Moscow insisted that 'This criminal activity is being carried out under the guidance of British officers. Experienced collaborators of British espionage, of the Intelligence Service, are working at various points in Greece with groups of traitors who sought shelter in Greece from the neighbouring countries ... These are facts that Tsaldaris and his kind prefer to keep hidden.'[14]

Philby was not inactive, but he was engaged at a higher level of activity – dealing with strategic questions – rather than the grubby business of field officers. As the Pixies were fighting their way ashore in the autumn of 1949, he was attending meetings that were concerned with more elevated matters. On 16 November he and Peter Dwyer met with the Americans to discuss the establishment of a new communications centre for the CIA in Britain carrying much of the US traffic from Europe. The CIA group was led by the Director, Admiral Hillenkoetter, together with his intelligence operations chief, Colonel Robert Schow, and Franklin Lindsay, Deputy Chief of OPC. Commander Johnson, a senior CIA communications officer, accompanied them to offer technical advice. The US Air Force was represented by Major-General Anderson and the RAF by its Chief Signals Officer, Air Vice Marshal Edward Barker Addison. Addison was present because of the nature of the radio communications centre proposed by the CIA. The US party explained that the 'station is to be established, operated, financed, and manned by CIA personnel, logged as an RAF radio station, and the U.S. Air Force in the United Kingdom to be used as security cover for this operation'. All parties proved to be in agreement and the plan went forward. By 1954 this British-based channel was carrying more CIA radio traffic than any other in the world.[15] The Soviets were not about to risk the cover of an agent at this level in order to catch a few ragged groups of Albanian émigrés.

Western operations against the Soviets in Poland seemed better conceived than those into Albania. The Second World War had shown that there were two routes to effective covert paramilitary operations. First, short-term raids, often conducted by groups like the SAS, which caused mayhem behind enemy lines in wartime and required little in the way of indigenous networks on the ground. Secondly, long-term complex 'secret army' type operations that attempted to harness the local populations into extensive guerrilla forces. In Poland, the Baltic states and the Ukraine, extensive anti-Soviet resistance groups had certainly been present on the ground in 1945. On the face of it the prospects for resistance in these countries seemed good. But the timing was bad. By 1948, when SIS and OPC/CIA began to make serious efforts to exploit them, they had been badly depleted or penetrated.

In 1944, the Soviets decided to halt their advance on Warsaw to allow the Germans space to crush the main non-communist resistance forces, the Polish Home Army, before continuing their advance. This was one of the most controversial episodes of the war. Thereafter, as we have seen, Poland was brutally but effectively run by Soviet security. What remained of the Home Army went to ground and dared not resurface. The elements that did so were those which were controlled by the Soviets. Why then did both SIS and the CIA choose to encourage resistance here, in an area where Soviet rule was at its most brutal, in the late 1940s? Poland held out to SIS and the CIA the possibility of higher risks but also larger rewards. Unlike Albania, Poland was one of the Red Army's strategic highroads to Western Europe in any future war. The recruitment of resistance networks here, even if they remained 'asleep' in peacetime, was potentially valuable. The US Army was pressing Frank Wisner's OPC hard to proceed with this sort of work, believing that hot war might be no more than six months away. Moreover, there were vast numbers of Polish exiles in the West, especially in Britain, the Commonwealth and the Empire. These were not the starving and the ragged of the Displaced Persons camps, like those Albanians who had thronged to Operation Valuable, but regular military units that had proved themselves in main-force engagements during the last war. Indeed some were still serving within the British Army's Pioneer Corps.

The central figure was General Wladyslaw Anders, wartime Commander of the Polish Forces. Unsullied by factional political allegiance he was probably the most prestigious East European exiled in the West in the late 1940s. Throughout those years SIS attempted to persuade him to stay in London and to run operations into Poland for intelligence-gathering purposes. But Anders became increasingly disillusioned with the small scale of the British operations and increasingly enamoured of American plans for a Volunteer Freedom Corps, a sort of foreign legion made up of Eastern bloc exiles. In June 1950 he left London for Washington to discuss plans for the emigration of 38,000 Polish Army veterans from the UK to the US to join the planned Corps.[16]

However, Western intelligence services were not the only ones to recognise the potential of this immense reservoir of effective Polish military personnel outside Poland. The Soviet MGB made active and effective efforts to control it. It is likely that the MGB itself was responsible for the initiation of liberation operations targeted on Poland. In 1947 Joseph Sienko, a member of the Home Army, which had now renamed itself the Freedom and Independence Movement, with the acronym WIN, 'escaped' from Poland and travelled to London. Here Sienko convinced the remnants of the wartime Polish government in exile that a substantial resistance movement remained, with perhaps as many as 20,000 members. General Anders was persuaded to contact SIS and the CIA to seek support. However, in reality, Sienko and all that remained of WIN were controlled by the UB, the Polish communist security police operating under the tutelage of the MGB.[17]

By 1950 a huge programme of material support, consisting largely of airdrops of arms, money (in gold bullion) and radios was in progress, supervised from the CIA's large stations in southern Germany. WIN, with its headquarters in London, claimed 500 active members, 20,000 part-timers and 100,000 resistance fighters on call awaiting the rising against the communists. But the UB collected this material because many of the WIN operatives were unaware that at a higher level they were controlled by the security police, which lent their activities greater credibility. Most of the effort was put in by the CIA. The leading CIA officers were veterans of the OSS wartime Yugoslavia campaign, Franklin Lindsay and John Bross. They had entertained some doubts in 1951 when WIN had requested that the CIA parachute in experienced American military officers to supervise training. Bross recalled that the idea of 'an American general, hanging from a parachute, descending into a Communist country, gave us some pause for thought'. Although there had been concerns about the security of WIN, reality only dawned in December 1952 when Polish official media chose to reveal the nature and extent of the operation.[18]

Depressing experiences across Eastern Europe, capped by Poland, triggered Lindsay's decision to quit the CIA at the end of 1952. He had come to the conclusion that the chances of such networks being penetrated were very high. Allen Dulles asked Lindsay, a very experienced officer, to prepare a retiring report. When the first draft was uncompromisingly negative he called Lindsay to a private meeting at his home and pressed him to rewrite it. However, events elsewhere in Eastern Europe were confirming the accuracy of all that Lindsay had said.[19]

Matters were different again in the Baltic states and the Ukraine. Here both the CIA and SIS were active, but with different objectives. As in Poland, these areas were not sympathetic to Soviet rule and they had enjoyed greater success in impeding the Red Army during and after the war. Resistance groups managed to perpetuate insurgencies in the Baltic states and the Ukraine into the 1950s. But they had achieved this remarkable longevity in the face of MGB security operations only by limiting their activities. Beyond 1948 these insurgencies were in a downward spiral and had lost the initiative.

Neither the CIA nor SIS in Germany had any serious intention of attempting to reverse this spiral. Certainly the idea of detaching these areas from Soviet rule was recognised by most field officers as ludicrous. As early as 1945, London had taken a long look at Stephan Bandera's OUN Ukrainian nationalist organisation and concluded that they would never be more than a 'nuisance' to the Soviets. However, a nucleus of potential resistance continued to hold out attractive prospects in the event of a future war, especially as its locations were so deep inside the Soviet Union. Moreover, there was the prospect of intelligence, always a scarce commodity within the borders of the Soviet Union, and experience during the last war had shown that resistance networks were an excellent means of collecting it. However, utilising these groups required something of a double game on the part of the CIA and SIS. No Ukrainian guerrilla would be anxious to risk his neck in order to provide better-quality intelligence for monthly bulletins to be circulated around the desks of London or Washington. In order to gain co-operation from resistance networks in the Baltic states and the Ukraine, the West had at least to talk the language of liberation. However, the number of missions and quantities of supplies sent to these areas were paltry compared to the secret army efforts of the Second World War. In the Baltic states, SIS had been working to establish links with guerrilla groups since 1944. Contrary to some suggestions, it had never entertained serious hopes of prising away those countries from Soviet control. Although smaller, and thus theoretically less vulnerable than CIA operations into Poland, these met the same fate and found themselves controlled by the MGB.[20]

Only the guerrilla war in the Ukraine appears to have resisted the insidious penetration of security forces. Perhaps more than anywhere, what remained of the population of the Ukraine had to develop an extraordinarily tough mentality merely to survive. Anxiety to escape Soviet rule here was deep rooted. Having endured massive executions during Stalin's purges in the 1930s, the region suffered further persecutions designed to eliminate traitors as the Germans had advanced on it in 1941. The NKVD was reliably reported to have executed more than 10,000 political prisoners and suspects in Lvov alone, rather than transport them east in the muddy autumn of that year. By November it was busy killing industrial workers who had protested against the starvation rations, soldiers who had complained about the lack of munitions, German POWs and even Red Army wounded who could not be evacuated. Many had little to lose by welcoming the invading enemy, hoping that under the Germans they might live a little longer.

The Germans set about removing the ethnic Russians and the Jews, actively assisted by the Ukrainians. Many went to terrible deaths, some processed in mobile gas vans, others poisoned, before being disposed of down mine-shafts. Thousands were shot, some not fatally, only to be buried alive in the mile upon mile of defensive ditches that stretched around each town. German rule over the much depleted population was no more benign, with many despatched to Germany as forced labour. Even those who had found a place in the new German structure of authority, for example as ancillary police, were unsafe, because the NKVD had left behind substantial numbers of agents. Communist infiltrators had orders to seek to provoke the Germans into unpleasant reprisals against the population, thus generating more support for pro-Soviet partisans.[21]

Ukrainian nationalism, and the utopian vision of independent Ukraine free from Soviet or German rule, became a sort of mental refuge. Fragmented guerrilla groups, including the OUN Ukrainian nationalist organisations that followed Stephan Bandera, and the UPA – the so-called Ukrainian Insurgent Army – emerged amid the chaos. Initially, as we have seen, the Ukrainian nationalists had attempted to collaborate with the Germans, who recruited a division of the Waffen SS, the Galicia Division, in the Ukraine. But by 1943 the nationalist guerrillas were fighting a two-front war against all foreign occupiers. Their main obstacle was the diversity of the vast Ukrainian territory. Bandera's followers, speaking the Galician dialect, could barely make themselves understood in areas like the Donbas, which were more heavily Russified.[22] Nevertheless there were plenty of recruits in 1945 and 1946. The war had transformed the Ukraine and utterly changed people's outlook. Few choices were made freely and all of them had involved extreme danger. It created a vast outlaw class of those who had been tainted by some contact with the Germans, for initially the returning Soviet authorities permitted no middle ground. Even those who had been forcibly taken off to labour camps in Germany often found themselves incarcerated for decades. Better to join OUN or UPA and enjoy a free life in the mountains.[23]

Only in the Ukraine were the tables turned on Soviet security. Elsewhere, the MGB infiltrated guerrilla groups and their émigré supporters in the West. But in the Ukraine the guerrilla effort was run by an MGB officer – Babenko – who had defected to the nationalists. MGB security troops wore the Ukrainians down only gradually, forcing the guerrillas into a marginal existence in mountainous areas of the Carpathians. It was ironic that the toughest guerrilla elements to be backed by SIS and the CIA were situated in areas extremely unsuited to detachment from Soviet control. As an MGB officer Babenko had been serving against Germany. For an unknown reason he had been sentenced to ten years' imprisonment but had soon escaped. He came to Odessa and led a group of UPA underground fighters from 'the many catacombs that underlie the city'. His raids on MGB and military officials were 'quite frequent' and the population in Odessa regarded him as a 'local Robin

Hood'. No Soviet officer could feel safe while this figure was at large. On 12 July 1946 one of the MGB majors stationed in Odessa was swimming at the local Arcadia beach when a team of guerrillas 'poured five shots into his body and escaped'. Under a 'great cloud of secrecy' a wide search was mounted for the assassins while the newspapers reported that he had died due to a 'tragic accident'. Later that year a large industrial plant near Kharkov was blown up and there was a revolt of major proportions in the Donbas coalmine area. Many government officials were killed but the revolt was gradually suppressed.[24] At one time the numbers of guerrillas were estimated to be 10,000 around Lvov and 15,000 in the Carpathian Mountains. But at the end of 1946 American officers reported that 'many have been killed or hanged' in continual raids by MGB troops, and for every fifteen people who went to serve with the guerrillas 'only one remains alive today'.[25]

Western efforts to employ the Ukrainians faced another type of problem. 'Ukrainian' operations by SIS and CIA increasingly focused on the support of exile groups in the West. In a dozen Western capitals the Ukrainian émigrés revealed their fragmented nature. Obscure struggles developed within the various groups for control that were no less bitter than those against the Soviets. These problems were multiplied for the CIA-supported free radio stations, with their troupes of conspiratorially minded exiles from several dozen 'captive nations' safely billeted in Washington, London and Munich. The scope for vicious infighting was limitless.

The Ukrainians fought on into the mid-1950s and were clearly regarded by Moscow as the most dangerous of the nationalist opponents. It was for this reason that they singled out Western-based Ukrainian exile leaders for special treatment, sending an unsuccessful assassin to eliminate Ukrainian émigré leaders in Berlin in 1950 and a more successful agent, Karl Anders, to murder Stephan Bandera in 1959. Several groups of SIS agents had been dropped into the Ukraine by mid-1951. Insertion was achieved by RAF aircraft from airfields in the Mediterranean, usually Malta or Crete. The RAF were confident that these 'special duties' flights would go undetected by Soviet air defences, because RAF and USAF electronic intelligence flights had found large holes in the Soviet air defence system and radar networks. The first SIS effort to drop in Ukrainians was Operation Project 1, under Colonel Harold Gibson, an old hand in SIS who had been in charge of the station in Prague in 1939. Anthony Cavendish, an SIS officer who worked on these operations, recalled their despatch:

> At suitable phases of the moon, teams of two or three highly trained agents were dropped into the Ukraine or Byelorussia. I knew that PROJECTS II, III, and IV went ahead and after arrival the dropped agents made radio contact

with their base station in Western Germany. However, several of the agents were captured, tried – some in show trials – and then shot. Today I still wonder whether those who did continue in radio contact did so under KGB control.

SIS was using the Ukrainians mostly for intelligence by this stage and held out little hope of liberation. Yet most of the intelligence coming out of the Soviet Union via émigré organisations was considered suspect for two basic reasons, and all reports from émigré sources were labelled 'Mauve'. The main reason for suspicion was that the émigré organisations were political bodies for lobbying on behalf of their countries in the West, and were not primarily set up as intelligence-gathering units. Always anxious to recruit more members, they were insecure and often penetrated by the Soviets. SIS also complained that the Ukrainians who worked for it were over-anxious to please and could never resist exaggerating their achievements and embellishing the intelligence they had obtained.[26]

It seems puzzling that these operations continued for some years in the face of obvious failure. But we should not be surprised. These activities were mounted using doctrines and personnel developed during the Second World War. The success of OSS, SOE and SAS against occupation by a German totalitarian regime that was outwardly similar to Soviet occupation in the Eastern bloc encouraged many to think that success was only just around the corner. Moreover, the clandestine war against the Germans in Europe had suffered its reverses. In any large-scale war of resistance, some penetration was inevitable and seemed only to be a test of resolve. But this idea of resolve was exacerbated by the American 'project'-based system for evaluating its officers. By 1949 Frank Wisner's OPC was under tremendous pressure to expand its activities. Promotion was expansion driven, depending upon the number of 'projects' initiated and continuing, not on any deeper criteria of success or failure. This ensured an in-built bias against closing operations even if they were stalling and their dividends were small. In the 1970s when Congress began to probe covert operations, it identified this kind of benchmark for special operations as a major deficiency.[27]

How far the CIA was committed to physical assistance to the Ukrainians is clouded by the problem of simultaneous planning for both a cold war and a hot war. Although many exotic plans for the use of Ukrainian resistance groups were developed by the West, including attacks on divisional MGB headquarters, most of these related to military planning for a future war. Washington was hugely enamoured of Hitler's successful attempts to recruit Soviet citizens into the German Wehrmacht. As early as 1948 the US Air Force had decided to remove all Ukrainian cities from their priority target list and instead 'request

Psychological Warfare Division to take the necessary action to ... capitalize on this'. In other words the Ukraine areas would be relied upon to rebel and would not need to bombed in a future war. But this was not a Cold War liberation programme; instead it was a contingency plan for guerrilla warfare in a possible Third World War.[28]

What was the value of liberation as practised by SIS and the CIA? Former operatives have been markedly unenthusiastic. Harry Rositzke, a senior retired CIA officer with responsibilities for the Eastern bloc, condemned the record as 'one of almost uniform failure'.[29] Others have shared this view. But few have appreciated the full complexities and it is probable that not all those working in the field were aware of the arcane strategic discussion about the multiple possibilities that liberation offered. Western efforts in this area, at first glance, appear strategically ill-conceived, and operationally shoddy. The concept, as Tedder had identified during discussion in the Russia Committee as early as November 1948, was flawed, unless one intended to follow up a rising of resistance forces with a full invasion. There were also operational weaknesses. SIS had retained little special operations capability and the DP camps where it sought its material were swarming with low-grade agents of every hue. OPC operations reflected a hastily expanded American apparatus asked to do too much too quickly. George Kennan has something to answer for, demanding that his Policy Planning Staff and the National Security Council should retain control of OPC, while the CIA remained mere functionaries for Wisner's semi-detached organisation. That control was used to urge upon OPC an even greater scale of activity than the eager Wisner was contemplating. In early January 1949 he sent Kennan an outline of OPC operational and budgetary plans for the year 1949–50. Kennan wanted more: 'In my opinion, this presentation contains the minimum of what is required from the foreign policy standpoint in the way of covert operations during the coming year ... As the international situation develops, every day makes more evident the importance of the role which will have to be played by covert operations if our national interests are to be adequately protected.' In all of the State Department, those having 'full knowledge' of OPC operations were restricted to just three: Kennan, Maynard Barnes and John Davies. These three were later joined by Robert Joyce. Kennan wanted a special team of four or five within PPS 'designated to guide Wisner's operations'. He was clear that 'while this Department should take no responsibility for his operations, we should nevertheless maintain a firm guiding hand'. But he could not get more staff for the co-ordination of OPC operations, because the 'stubborn' personnel section of the State Department was not cleared to know, so OPC needs could not be explained to them![30]

Extreme secrecy would later allow Kennan to deny everything. He argued there had been no attempt at the construction of a vast edifice of Cold War fighting. Testifying before the Church Committee which investigated the CIA in 1975, he insisted that when recommending the development of a covert action capability in 1948 the State Department had wanted only 'a small contingency force' that could operate 'on a limited basis'. Diplomats did not 'plan to develop large scale continuing operations. Instead, they hoped to establish a small capability that could be activated at their discretion.' Nothing could have been further from the truth.[31] Yet an underlying logic underpinned Kennan's desire to expand covert operations. Liberation had little chance of liberating the 'captive nations' of the East. But for many in Washington this was not the central goal. For Kennan, the individual success of particular covert actions was relatively unimportant and what mattered was to maintain the pressure on the communists. This ensured that the Soviets would be kept off balance, and so less likely to pursue probing activities in the West's own 'sore spots': Italy, France, Greece, the Middle East. It also placed the Soviets under the kind of psychological strain that was likely to aggravate the fundamental contradictions that he frequently pointed to in the communist system. These contradictions, Kennan hoped, would eventually cause the communist monolith to shake itself to pieces.

Kennan's demand for expanded covert action was partly a reaction to attacks on him by the American right in 1947 following the publication of his infamous 'Mr X' article in the journal *Foreign Affairs*. After outlining the essentials of containment, in rather loose and journalistic language, Kennan was charged by his critics with allocating a burdensome role to American forces, more precisely the United States Treasury, imposing the weight of global militarised containment though it seemed to offer only stalemate. The right-wing economising Congress, seeking post-war drawdown, was not in the mood for new burdens. Stung by this criticism, Kennan put forward OPC, with its radio stations and its covert paramilitary operations, as the answer to the problem of eternal stalemate. Moreover, as he realised, for purposes of morale and self-credibility, the West had to seen to be doing something to respond to what was undoubtedly a major Soviet campaign of subversion and espionage in the West.[32]

For others in Washington, especially the military, liberation was not only a way of keeping the Soviets off balance, it was also a pathfinding activity for the larger-scale covert action that would be carried out during a conventional war with the Soviet Union, which many believed firmly was at best only a few years away. The outbreak of the Korean War in the summer of 1950 only increased the pressure for such preparations. As Christopher Simpson has shown, large numbers of East Europeans were held in various obscure 'holding tanks' by the military, often Labour Service battalions, with a view to using them in the East in a future conflict. Lending a sense of urgency to all these activities was a general view that, however flawed, the concept of liberation allowed the West to 'do something'. Liberation, which had a strong radio-warfare content alongside its paramilitary aspects, provided the ultimate vehicle for an ideological expression of the American position on the Cold War.[33]

Did the liberation activities of the West achieve Kennan's strategic objective of increasing general pressure on Stalin? The answer is inescapably yes. Stalin's paranoid vision quickly multiplied the limited range of Western activities into something much larger. Moscow saw these covert operations as merely the tip of a vast subversive iceberg. It is clear that the Soviets were from the outset aware of many Western contacts with dissident national groups inside and outside the Eastern bloc. It is equally clear that it would not have taken much clandestine activity of this sort to ring alarm bells for Stalin, whose paranoia had assumed fantastic proportions. His daughter recalled her shock at learning that he no longer trusted his own MGB chief, Lavrenti Beria, while later Khrushchev famously claimed to have overheard him muttering, 'Finished. I trust no one, not even myself.' Stalin's agents in the West were well enough placed to know about the broad scale of Western liberation activities and it was not in his nature to rest until all the networks had been discovered. Western efforts at subversion prompted him to take a harder line in his external policy and indeed helped to propel him towards participation in the Korean War.[34]

But the most important question regarding liberation centres upon the remarkable and bloody wave of purges that swept Eastern bloc communist parties between late 1948 and 1953. The Tito heresy of 1948 – with Yugoslavia splitting from the Soviet bloc to confront Stalin with anti-Soviet communism – triggered a wave of bloody repression across that bloc that surprised everyone. Senior Communist Party leaders, seemingly hitherto faithful adherents to Moscow, were accused of treacherous dealings with agents of the British, the Americans and the Yugoslavs. The first major trials began in Albania on 12 May 1949. László Rajk, the Hungarian Foreign Secretary, was arrested and tried in the autumn of 1949, quickly followed by Traicho Kostov, the Bulgarian Deputy Premier. Both were quickly executed, and many others followed. Curiously, the linking element in many of the trials in Eastern Europe was contact between the accused and Noel Field. Field was an American who had taken a PhD in political science at Harvard, joined the State Department and then worked with relief organisations in Europe since the Spanish civil war. Field was also a friend of Allen Dulles.[35]

The Czech purges were complex but offer a good example of the manner in which external contacts served as a trigger. The Czech authorities had begun by targeting intellectuals who had spent the war in Britain and who were 'suspected of involvement with Western intelligence services', together with Slovak nationalists. These episodes went through transformations as each wave of victims denounced others, and by 1952 the purges had changed direction and developed an increasingly anti-semitic quality, although this theme was always present. By the major trials of late 1952, eleven of the fourteen defendants were Jews, and 'Zionism' had been added to the usual standard heresies. This also represented a search for scapegoats for Czechoslovakia's economic difficulties of the early 1950s, brought on by stiff increases in production demands by the Soviets. But fear of foreign influence also played its part.

In 1949, when the Czech purges got going, the main victims were hundreds of officials from the Ministries of Foreign Trade, Foreign Affairs and Information. 'It was significant that these were the ministries that maintained contact with foreigners and foreign states as part of their normal duties.' Five of the six most prominent figures arrested in Czechoslovakia in 1949 had spent some of the war in London and three had enjoyed contact with a relief organisation run by Herman Field – the brother of Noel – which was based in Krackow in 1939. Herman Field was still visiting some of these figures in Czechoslovakia as late as 1947, and this formed the basis of the charge of working 'as an agent of the Western imperialists' and their 'espionage services'. Noel Field himself had 'disappeared' in Prague in May 1949, and was followed by his brother Herman, who vanished in Warsaw in August the same year. During subsequent trials references to their statements showed that they had been arrested and interrogated.

A further wave of arrests followed across Eastern Europe in 1950, and these included Otto Sling of the Central Committee of the Communist Party in Czechoslovakia. After his trial the Czech authorities explained, 'Otto Sling received instructions from his Anglo-American imperialist masters to develop in Czechoslovakia a subversive action similar to that of Rajk's gang in Hungary and Traicho Kostov's gang in Bulgaria ... Within the framework of their dark plans, they had considered removing Klement Gottwald, the President of the Republic, by assassination.' Washington noted that the 'charges against Sling of involvement with Noel Field are identical with those made against Laszlo Rajk during his trial in Budapest in September 1949'. The other issue was internment in French camps after service in the International Brigades in Spain. Because Noel Field had been secretary of a League of Nations committee formed to extend assistance to foreign volunteers who had fought for the Spanish Republic, all this was suspect. The Czech government announced that its detainees had been recruited as spies while in the French camps. They were 'the object of blackmail first of the French and American and then of German and other intelligence services'. For good measure the

Czechs added that the SS archives had now fallen into the hands of the British and American secret services, so they were making use of all the agents the Nazis had infiltrated into the communist parties of Europe. This latter charge, at least, was not entirely without foundation.

By 1951 the purges in Czechoslovakia were turning upon the purgers. In February 1951 there was 'a major blow' against intelligence and security officials when the two Deputy Ministers of National Security were arrested, including Karel Svab who headed the Secret Intelligence and Counter-Intelligence Division of the Security Ministry. In his wake went his two lieutenants, the head of counter-espionage and the head of foreign (offensive) intelligence. By 1953 when the purges ended, thirty of the ninety-seven party members elected in May 1949 were either arrested, executed or in disgrace.[36]

The purges in Eastern Europe were vigorous and far-reaching, so much so that they even damaged the German Communist Party – the KPD – in the Western Zones. In 1949, General Serov, the MGB chief in the Soviet Zone, required the East German security elements known as the Stasi to investigate all German communists who might have had contacts with Noel Field. Thereafter KPD officials from the West were often arrested while visiting the Soviet Zone and then subjected to torture. Remarkably this included Kurt Müller, the deputy head of the KPD, who was arrested by Stasi officers pretending to be Soviet security. Müller's treatment was supervised throughout by the Soviets and the evidence collected included forced confessions of collaboration with the usual Western intelligence agencies. He endured three years of interrogation before being sent to Siberia, initially for twenty-five years. However, in 1955 he and several other KPD officials were set free with one of the last batches of German POWs released from Siberia and allowed to return to the West. The purges were relentless. Müller's successor as deputy chairman, Fritz Sperling, visited the East in February 1951 and endured a similar fate. The hanging of Slansky, former Secretary General of the Czech Communist Party, and his ten 'accomplices' in Prague was greeted enthusiastically in East Germany in 1953 and a similar show trial there was probably halted only by the East Berlin rising and the fall from power of Beria, Stalin's MGB chief, in June 1953.[37]

There is no doubt that CIA and SIS operations added to Stalin's paranoia and encouraged, if they needed encouragement, his fears of a vast conspiracy. But the question that remains unanswered is the extent to which the West deliberately *attempted to encourage* the purges to bring down more destruction upon the communist cadres of the Eastern bloc. Were the purges free-standing extensions of Stalin's paranoia over events in Yugoslavia, or was there some deliberate external provocation? In 1972 a book entitled *Splinter Factor* by Stuart Steven argued that the purges were

1. Berlin, June 1945: Winston Churchill sits in Hitler's chair and jests with Soviet soldiers a month after he has ordered a feasibility study of a war with Moscow codenamed Operation Unthinkable

2. Anthony Eden and Alexander Cadogan together in the garden of the British Embassy in Teheran. They had different answers to the problem of secret service control. Eden won the argument

3. Major-General Sir Stewart Menzies, Chief of the Secret Intelligence Service or 'C', 1939–52

4. On the right Major-General Sir John Sinclair with General Mark Clark. Sinclair was wartime Director of Military Intelligence, then deputy to Menzies, and became 'C' in the summer of 1952

5. A captured soldier of the Wehrmacht, but not German. By 1945, one in eight of Hitler's soldiers was a citizen of the USSR. Some of these units were retained by the West after the war

6. Air Marshal Sir John Slessor (*left*) and Marshal of the RAF Sir Arthur Tedder (*right*) were architects of British plans for the liberation of the Eastern bloc through special operations in 1948

7. Major-General John S. Lethbridge the first head of Britain's Intelligence Division in Germany, 1945–7

8. Former German POWs and captured German scientists who had worked inside the Soviet Union were a key intelligence source. Pictured here is the last major Soviet release of German POWs to the West in 1955

9. A rare photograph of the inside of Britain's early
electronic intelligence 'ferret' aircraft in 1945

10. Commander Edward Travis, Director of
Government Communications Headquarters,
1944–52

11. Intelligence failure in Palestine – the bombing of the King David Hotel, 1946

12. 'Boy Scout' – the Shah of Iran – with his family. He was restored to power by means of a joint CIA-SIS *coup d'état* in 1953. The CIA reported that the Shah was petrified by the 'hidden hand' of British secret service

13. Forward posts in Korea often had thermite incendiary grenades handy to destroy sensitive signals intelligence material if they were in danger of being overrun

14. British Commandos attached to CCRAK plant demolition charges on a railway behind enemy lines eight miles south of Songjun in Korea in April 1951

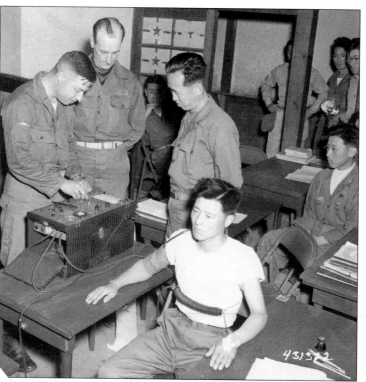

15. Political prisoners suffered terribly on both sides during the Korean War. These civilians were forced into caves and deliberately killed by suffocation in October 1950

16. Training Korean internal security personnel in interrogation

made far worse because of a deliberate and successful attempt by the Western secret services to encourage a self-inflicted injury – to persuade the Soviets to attack their own creatures, the Eastern bloc communist parties. Inevitably, the key figure in this story is Noel Field. Some have claimed that Field was used to place individuals sympathetic to the West in Central European communist parties. He was certainly still in Prague in the spring of 1949, when he was seized by the Hungarian security police, held and interrogated repeatedly until 1954. His brother was held in Poland. Were Field and his contacts part of a deliberate plot to smear the communist parties of Eastern Europe with a suspicious taint of Western contact?[38]

Allen Dulles reportedly claimed that provoking the purges was his 'biggest ever success'. Dulles had been one of the forerunners of American post-war covert operations in Western Europe, and had helped to run SSU in Germany in 1946, taking an interest in anti-communist operations in Italy from 1947. He was the main consultant to the CIA on covert operations in 1949 and joined the agency in a formal role to superintend all covert action in 1951. He served as DCI from February 1953 to November 1961. Allen Dulles was perhaps in a better position than anyone else to fathom the extent of connections between liberation and the purges.[39] But expert commentators on the history of the Eastern bloc remain perplexed and divided by Steven's idea of a 'Splinter Factor'. Bennett Kovrig regards the book as quite persuasive and asserts that the arguments rest on 'corroborated evidence'. Votjech Mastny considers the same book to be 'scurrilous' and based on 'hearsay' but nevertheless thinks the 'basic idea is credible'. Most writers on SIS are unconvinced, for the claims of Allen Dulles are easily dismissed as an attempt to take credit for an unexpected windfall, offsetting an otherwise lamentable episode of reverses and failures.[40]

New material lends support to the claims of Dulles, suggesting that at the very least, as the purges developed, the CIA and SIS sought to increase their ferocity as an additional objective for liberation. Sceptics have pointed out that the purges began before the West gave the official green light for liberation in late 1948. But new accounts reveal American liberation efforts as being stronger and beginning sooner than previously thought. SIS was running exploratory operations in the Baltic as early as 1944. Support for anti-communist groups was ongoing in Rumania and Bulgaria through the remnants of OSS and American Army Intelligence as early as 1946. In October of that year SSU was having to exfiltrate resistance leaders from Rumania with whom it had maintained contact as the security police closed in on them. British diplomats complained about this vigorously. Bits and pieces of Western destabilisation had begun as early as 1946. Therefore, while the first wave of purges in Eastern Europe occurred even before the Stalin–Tito split, they coincided with these initial post-war secret service excursions into the Eastern bloc.[41]

Provoking purges and other internal trouble was very much in the spirit of the later conclusions of the Russia Committee in November and December 1948. The military and diplomats like Ivone Kirkpatrick were in a minority in thinking that substantial headway could be made with what they called 'loosening the Soviet hold on the orbit countries and ultimately enabling them to regain their independence'. But the majority of the Russia Committee thought it was quite unrealistic and instead wished to proceed with a more limited short-term policy of just stirring up trouble inside the Eastern bloc to keep the Soviets on the defensive. Stirring up trouble meant 'promoting civil discontent, internal confusion and possibly strife in the satellite countries'. This was known as 'Option B' and its intention was to make the Eastern bloc 'not a source of strength but a source of weakness' and to ensure that if there was a war it would need 'armies of occupation to hold it down'. Gladwyn Jebb disliked even this and warned that if the West intensified the Cold War it might bring real war nearer, and in any case he did not think the West had the resources for widespread special operations and wanted to 'postpone any more offensive action'. But at the other extreme the Chiefs of Staff wished to press on and were 'anxious to see the matter taken in hand'. Option B – just stirring up trouble without trying to liberate – offered a convenient middle way on which most could agree.[42]

Kennan certainly *intended* to turn the gigantic Eastern bloc security apparatus in on itself and explicitly said so in the plans he helped to draft. By September 1949 the National Security Council was approving papers that set out a policy to 'attack the weaknesses in the Stalinist penetration of satellite governments and mass organisations' and by this means to 'reduce and eventually eliminate their power'. These documents remain heavily sanitised more than half a century after they were approved. However, their meaning is unambiguous: 'The propensity of the revolution to devour its own, the suspicions of the Kremlin regarding its agents and the institutions of denunciation, purge and liquidation are grave defects in the Soviet system which have never been adequately exploited.' This was going to be taken up and it was now American policy to 'exploit Moscow's tendency to purge its own amid the Soviet Satellite States in Eastern Europe'.[43]

Deception planners in London actively pressed the same ideas. In 1949 they argued that senior Soviet officials under Stalin and indeed throughout the Eastern bloc were highly susceptible to this sort of disinformation and a small amount of resistance might cause a great deal of destabilisation. 'Their mutual mistrusts, their anxiety for personal survival and their cynical disloyalty towards their colleagues make them vulnerable to "planted" as well as real suspicions concerning each other,' the planners argued. They advocated special operations that were specifically designed to link top communist officials with opposition movements 'and thereby provoke in due course such purges and oppressive measures in the Soviet Union as might lead to the complete disruption of the Soviet government and system'. Some even hoped that the resulting stresses and strains might eventually instigate 'an anti-Stalinist counter-revolution'. By July 1950 John Drew was advocating 'framing' or 'smearing' operations that would be 'directed against individuals in positions of authority'. The following month, after talks with the Americans, operations to 'plant' material on Moscow began.[44]

The British deliberately sought to push the CIA towards more of these kinds of activities. By 1950, as we shall see, London was becoming convinced that CIA paramilitary efforts to prise away another country from the Eastern bloc were over-ambitious and bound to fail. Britain's Permanent Under-Secretary's Committee set to work on a counter-plan for future special operations against the Eastern bloc for submission to Washington. As an alternative London set out areas in which special operations against the Eastern bloc were likely to be more productive, and one of these target areas was quite explicitly identified as 'specialist operations designed ... to poison relations between the satellite Governments and the Soviet Union'.[45]

Stalin's fantastic paranoia was the central factor in the extraordinary wave of arrests and executions that swept over the Eastern bloc between 1948 and 1953. But the purges had more than one cause and Western intelligence played its part – after 1949 quite intentionally – sanctioned by both the National Security Council and the Permanent Under-Secretary's Department. Finding even a few deviationists with links to the Western secret services was bound to accelerate powerfully the search for others. A number of the show trials were ludicrous, but some of the Western equipment produced as evidence had more than a hint of authenticity. In 1955, when Noel Field was finally released from prison along with dozens of other prisoners who found their freedom after the death of Stalin, IRD took the opportunity to play up the theme of his work in the East. However, his personal role is still a mystery. George Hodos, one of the victims of the show trials, asked, 'What role did Noel Field play – he whose ghostlike figure propelled the wave of purges from Budapest through Prague and Warsaw to East Berlin?' The question remains unanswered. What is now clear is that the purges, far from resulting in weakness and disorder, resulted in a consolidation of the Eastern bloc.[46] The front line in the conflict with this increasingly resilient Soviet empire was Germany and Austria.

8

The Front Line: Intelligence in Germany and Austria

[V]ery good intelligence was coming from places where it was easy to get and
none at all from the places where it was difficult to get.

Dick White, 18 July 1948[1]

On the ground in Europe, the nasty business of Cold War fighting
began before the German surrender on Lüneburg Heath in May
1945. Many units seemed to march out of the Second World War into the
Cold War without breaking step. One such was the Nazi Werwolf movement, which organised stay-behind forces designed to slow the Allied
advance. Most were quickly exterminated. But in the ethnic German
regions of Poland and Czechoslovakia some survived, and here MGB
detachments initially found themselves outgunned by large elements of
the Polish and German counter-revolutionary undergrounds. Through
the autumn of 1945 MGB troops launched raids against Werwolf strongholds and the core was soon eradicated, but some cells survived until
early 1947. Other Germans surrendering in both the East and the West
were busy trading in what assets they had.

By 1946, the MGB was claiming that Werwolf units were being
employed by the West, not only to gather intelligence in the Eastern
Zone, but also to terrorise Soviet troops. British intelligence officers in
Germany were certainly thinking along these lines. When an anti-Soviet
resistance leader came their way offering his services in late 1947, they
debated his usefulness against the Soviets. In the event they sidestepped
the issue and handed him over to the Americans, whose work in this area
they thought more aggressive and advanced. The MGB was not tardy in
this area itself and had already recruited SS men as spies and saboteurs.
The question of which side first recruited former Nazis is largely academic. This was not the first or the last conflict in which secret service
personnel quickly found re-employment. However, the scale on which

this was done, and the assets which former Nazis had at their disposal, made this factor very significant.[2]

No one's hands were clean when it came to ex-SS personnel. The French would later complain bitterly about the American failure to hand over the notorious SS 'Butcher of Lyon' – Klaus Barbie – who was wanted for war crimes against the resistance. Instead he was spirited away by American counter-intelligence to be deployed against the German Communist Party in Bavaria. Yet the French were also active in recruiting into the French Foreign Legion to serve in Indochina entire units of specialist SS Partisanjägers trained to hunt guerrillas. On 14 March 1946, Admiral Lord Louis Mountbatten, Supreme Allied Commander South East Asia, arrived in Saigon on a tour of inspection. The French mounted an honour guard of their Foreign Legion 'consisting entirely of German ex-SS guards'. When Mountbatten's officers protested, the French replied that they were proud of their SS men, who 'were by far their smartest legionaries'.[3]

At the end of the war many British SOE officers looked forward to speedy demobilisation. But, for those who wished to prolong their careers in secret service, new opportunities were opening. On 15 September 1944, the JIC began to consider an intelligence organisation for the British occupation of Germany. The JIC Chairman, Victor Cavendish-Bentinck, identified watching clandestine Nazi networks such as the Werwolf and 'an underground nucleus of the Army' as a vast requirement. Menzies, Chief of SIS, declared that there were at least 275,000 Germans to be arrested, some of whom would be tough customers. He pointed out the need for some 'Executive Arm' to do this work, adding that elements of SOE, Commando battalions and other special forces would be ideal. The JIC considered whether they should be pooled 'to form a "Black and Tan" Force', but decided that this would give too high a profile to 'repression'. Nevertheless, many 'suitable personnel' from SOE were kept busy in Germany beyond 1945.

Skilled specialists were essential to the creation of what became the Intelligence Division of the British Control Commission Germany, known simply as ID. Even in 1944 the JIC envisaged a staff of no fewer than 1,200 British intelligence officers for ID. There were only 240 intelligence officers to be found in all of the British forces currently in France, but by the end of 1945 ID had outgrown this projection and was larger than either SIS or MI5. Because of the paramilitary nature of much of its work Menzies asserted that 'there could be no question of a civilian at the head, at least at first', and wanted one clear leader in absolute control when dealing with the Germans, the Americans and the Russians. The redoubtable Major-General John S. 'Tubby' Lethbridge was placed in direct command of the huge ID organisation, which included substantial numbers 'attached' from MI5 and SIS. But the main body of ID files has been completely destroyed and the files of its main American collaborator, the Deputy Director of Intelligence at EUCOM HQ, the command centre for US forces in Europe, are 'missing'. Piecing together the history of this large organisation is not easy and what follows can only be a partial glimpse.[4]

ID began as a military organisation because of the Werwolf movement. Werwolf was a guerrilla organisation which aimed to create stay-behind forces to plague the Allies as they moved in on Hitler's Germany, and to keep the ideological torch of Nazism burning. British and American military chiefs came to expect an enormous Nazi resistance movement, not dissimilar to the Allied effort in France. The idea of a formidable mountain citadel in which Hitler would make his last stand had assumed legendary proportions in Allied intelligence circles by the spring of 1945. Eisenhower and Montgomery believed in its existence and on 21 April 1945 General Walter Bedell Smith, Eisenhower's Chief of Staff, explained to the press that the reason that Allied forces were not advancing on Berlin quickly was because of expectations of a Nazi last stand among the crags of Bavaria.[5]

The Werwolf organisation did not live up to expectations for it inherited all the personal feuds and rivalries of the Reich's multiple party and secret police systems. Moreover, to recruit, arm and train properly implied an admission of coming defeat which, although obvious to military minds, was still inadmissible. Created in 1944 by the SS and led by police chief Hans Prützmann, the movement drew some inspiration from Allied resistance efforts. A special SS study unit was formed and its staff, accompanied by Abwehr and Gestapo experts, were sent to observe the Warsaw Rising in 1944. But only in February 1945 did Martin Bormann and Joseph Goebbels offer serious support to Werwolf. Goebbels was the most fanatical, employing radio propaganda to draw recruits from the SS and the Hitler Youth. Radio Werwolf, which began broadcasting on 1 April, urged the German population to resist to the last.

Werwolf was a significant short-term problem. Its forces attacked supply lines, inflicted casualties by terrorist methods including poison, and assassinated those who collaborated with the new occupying powers, including Allied-appointed mayors in Westphalia. Perhaps the most important operation, orchestrated by Prützmann, was a volunteer special unit that dropped into the Netherlands and then moved across the border into Western Germany to assassinate Franz Oppenhoff, *Oberbürgermeister* of the ancient imperial capital of Aachen. Disguised as downed Luftwaffe pilots, the members of the unit entered his home but discovered he was at a neighbour's house. Oppenhoff was summoned to assist the 'German fliers', but when he arrived he was immediately shot at close range through the temple with a pistol. General N. E. Brazzin, the first Soviet commandant of Berlin, died in an ambush on 16 June attributed to a Werwolf unit.

But without external support the Nazi underground was no more than an escape route out of Germany, and never offered real resistance. The fading struggle by the Werwolf was a pathetic episode. Most of its human material was drawn from members of the Hitler Youth and were teenagers, even children, and on both the eastern and western fronts they could face speedy execution. Moreover, its leader, Prützmann, did not die gloriously in a final Alpine struggle. Instead he was incarcerated by the British, along with 80,000 other political prisoners, and committed suicide by drowning himself in a latrine. During the winter of 1945–6, British and American intelligence organisations ran a large-scale counter-insurgency operation called Operation Nursery. The name of the operation reflected that the knowledge that most of its targets were former Hitler Youth. In a series of raids and sporadic gun-battles the main leaders and some 800 adherents were netted, along with supplies and large quantities of currency still wrapped in Reichsbank cellophane. Operation Nursery effectively destroyed Werwolf as a coherent organisation in the British Zone.

Werwolf had two important legacies. First, it lent a military complexion to Allied intelligence in post-war Germany and delayed an initial impulse to focus on the Soviets from the outset. Secondly, as the occupation got into its stride, Werwolf changed from being a real problem to being a subject of political convenience. The high level of publicity given to work against Nazi stay-behind groups raises some interesting questions. Operation Selection Board, which was accompanied by lurid press stories, seems to carry the stamp of deliberate exaggeration. British intelligence gave a great deal of publicity to the operation. The British press responded enthusiastically with elaborate and somewhat far-fetched stories. Most prominent was the theme of a new biological weapon being developed by underground Nazi groups which the SS guerrillas were planning to unleash against the Allies, if their terms and conditions were not met. On 24 February 1947 the *Daily Mail* announced the existence of a 'Nazi Germ Warfare Threat'. There were also assertions about the plot possibly being directed by Martin Bormann, who was suspected of being alive and in hiding in the vicinity. There is no evidence of a real biological warfare threat and it is quite possible that the Western Allies were playing up Selection Board to counter extensive claims by the Soviets that ex-Nazis were being harboured by British and American intelligence.[6]

How far did ID recruit former Nazis in Germany? Despite great attention to this subject the answers remain unclear. Specific examples have been identified and well documented, but whether these were aberrations or part of a wider pattern is unknown. The most spectacular episode is probably the absorption of an entire SS Division of Ukrainians who temporarily retained their weapons and were hidden by the British Army. They were obviously meant for some special forces purpose in the event that hostilities with the Soviets erupted at an early date. Eventually 10,000 of these Ukrainians were brought to Britain on the grounds that they were from an area under Polish rather than Soviet authority and were joined by a similar number of Balts with military backgrounds.[7]

For the most part the British approach to war criminals was unenthusiastic, incompetent and lacklustre rather than conspiratorial. Discussing the matter in the summer of 1944, Cavendish-Bentinck, Britain's top intelligence co-ordinator, said he thought that the Allies were unlikely to catch more than a proportion of people on their blacklist and that key figures like Himmler would get away. Others in the Foreign Office felt that the whole business was an embarrassing nuisance and, perhaps inspired by the fate of Mussolini, counselled 'we should do better to give the German people time to bump them off themselves'.[8] Thus by 1947 considerable numbers with an unpleasant past were at large and available for hire, instead of facing imprisonment or worse, which was surely their due. Even among the forty-four defendants tried at the Belsen concentration camp in November 1945, only eleven received the death penalty, prompting an outcry in both East and West. The French were incensed that none of their witnesses had even been allowed to give evidence and as a result guilty individuals had been acquitted. In May 1946 former SS men found guilty of murdering eight SAS soldiers captured in uniform were given sentences as short as two years, prompting outrage in Britain. In some cases where witnesses had almost all perished proof was thin. Meanwhile the British Judge Advocate General's department confessed to being short of experienced lawyers and in some cases to be operating without experience or guidelines. Patrick Dean, a diplomat with German responsibilities, was especially indignant: 'numbers of concentration camp guards and others who must have known and taken part in the horrible crimes committed in these camps escape justice in consequence ... It is quite fantastic to go to all the trouble to try and to convict these Germans (many of whom are the worst form of SS thug) and then to impose sentences of imprisonment which in some cases run down to periods of a few months only.' Dean warned starkly that 'these terrible murderers' would soon be released into the new Germany at a time when Allied control had begun to relax. There were certainly those ready to offer them new employment as they emerged from prison in 1947 and 1948.[9]

It is ironic that, while laxity was the order of the day with the prosecution of German war criminals, punctiliousness extended to the vexed question of repatriating Cossacks and other Soviet citizens from the British Zone. In early July, Ivone Kirpatrick informed London that British authorities were now holding senior officers of the Vlasov Army, Hitler's corps of Anti-Soviet Russian Fascists. They had also senior members of General Schilenkov's Free Russia Committee 'under house arrest in Tyrol', although the whereabouts of Vlasov and Schilenkov themselves was not known. They asked for guidance. They were told that the Secretary of State had ruled that they 'must be repatriated to the USSR regardless of their own wishes in the matter'.[10]

London regarded all these Soviet citizens, prominent or otherwise, as an expensive nuisance and was anxious to see them repatriated as soon as possible. The alternative – resettling over two million people at a time when Europe was destitute – was not welcomed by Eden or by his successor Bevin. They were despatched eastwards as fast as hard-pressed transport would allow, and by November 1945 more than half of the 19,500 Soviet nationals in Britain had been repatriated. However, the issues were complex and London aroused Moscow's fury by insisting that persons from the Baltic states and Poland were not Soviet citizens.

London officials were quite aware that the many Soviets who had fought for the Germans would receive harsh treatment if returned home. Remarkably, at the end of the war, one in eight soldiers serving in the German Army was a Soviet citizen. Under one reading of the Geneva Convention, a reading employed by the Americans, these troops were entitled to be treated as German POWs and could not be forcibly repatriated. But London read Geneva differently, and in any case the Soviet Union had not bothered to sign the Geneva Convention. What mattered to the British was the Yalta Agreement, in which Britain had agreed to return these people to the Soviet Union. London saw Yalta as a good deal, with Stalin promising to keep out of France and Italy and allowing communism to be crushed in Greece.[11] It is quite clear that the British government at the time was uncomfortable about the whole business and took steps to keep the programme of forcible return secret. In many ways it represented the last hurrah of the diplomatic policy of co-operation with the Soviets. The Soviets were given something they wanted badly, which did not impinge in any way upon British interests. Perhaps for this reason, London continually pressed the Americans not to backslide in the work of repatriation.[12]

Further muddying the waters was the problem of bandits. In Austria, the British Army's Field Security units found their greatest challenge was the banditry practised by gangs of refugees who had previously been members of non-German units of the SS or who had been in Yugoslav partisan organisations, and who had cut loose as freebooters at the end of the war. These were large well-armed groups that raided both sides of the Austrian and Yugoslav border at will. For fear of these roving bands, HQs were forced to mount a level of security guard that was unheard of during the war. One group was rounded up in late 1947 after prolonged surveillance in a joint Anglo-Yugoslav security operation.[13]

Germany and Austria formed the front line in the emerging Cold War with the Eastern bloc. But the front line was complex and riven with confusions and multiple animosities. Western intelligence was simultaneously seeking several objectives. First, it was preparing itself for an arduous struggle against what it presumed to be a vast and fanatical Nazi resistance movement, linked to Hitler's expected last stand in some Wagnerian 'Alpine redoubt'. But the Werwolf threat, consisting mostly of hastily recruited children and teenagers, proved to be shadow rather than substance. Secondly, intelligence was also centrally involved in the business of processing prisoners and information for war crimes. This was soon overshadowed by a third task, finding intelligence and security personnel, together with their archives and agents, who would be of use against the Soviets. The detailed military intelligence that the Germans had gathered against the Soviets in battle was invaluable. The shift from adversary to ally was accelerated by the sheer impossibility of screening the very large numbers of POWs and Displaced Persons, most of whom were without papers. All but the most extensive war crimes tended to be overlooked. While the Allies competed for German intelligence assets, their attitudes were different. By late 1945 the British had developed cold feet about some of the nasty characters they had encountered, regarding them as either too alarming or too expensive to look after. Some of these were handed to Washington as an act of 'goodwill'.

The search for 'intelligence assets' overlapped with a fourth, much wider activity which was only intelligence in its widest sense – the quest for booty. As early as 1943, British military chiefs had begun to recognise the massive revolution in the nature of warfare brought about by science and technology. Germany was patently ahead in many fields such as rocket technology and chemical warfare. The race was on to acquire this material. By 1944 this competition had broadened to encompass commercial, technological and scientific 'booty' of every sort. Moscow was accused by the West of sweeping the Soviet Zone of Germany clean of every transportable item of worth. But this was a widespread practice resisted vainly by Allied personnel tasked with 'German reconstruction'. General Lucius D. Clay, the American Military Governor in Germany, commented that much of this activity was 'squarely in the commercial field' and that 'we are perhaps doing the same thing that Russia is doing'. Government and private organisations alike from British, France, United States and the Soviet Union descended on Germany removing what some estimated to be $5 billion of material in patents and other industrial secrets alone.[14]

Only in the 1990s has the scale of these 'hidden reparations' – mostly scientific and technological booty – become clear. The need to begin physical reconstruction, together with fears of a propaganda own-goal, eventually brought the locust-like activities to a halt. But the unseen exploitation of German science and technology was colossal. Intelligence agencies were responsible for a vast cataloguing of technical and scientific documents, ideas and patents by means of systematic microfilming. They were transferred to businesses and academic institutions in Britain, France and the United States. There was also a huge programme of on-site inspection of plants and research facilities, and prototypes were swiftly removed for 'evaluation'. The scale remains hard to quantify but some historians have described this as the 'biggest transfer of mass intelligence ever made from one country to another'.

The struggle for German assets was complex. Allied officials concerned with reconstruction wished to create a prosperous environment upon which to build democratic foundations. They were determined to resist 'piracy' by those working for British ministries ranging from the Air Ministry to the Board of Trade. The 'pirates' were anxious to remove the best material unofficially before it became entangled in the vexed inter-Allied politics of formal reparations. In this sense, all four administrating powers were competing against themselves and against each other. The Americans hesitated over full civilian exploitation until informed by the British that without agreement from Washington they would 'go ahead unilaterally'. Meanwhile the powers combined to resist parity for minor Allies, who sensed – correctly – that they would receive no more than the crumbs from under the intelligence table.[15]

In 1944, Eisenhower's SHAEF headquarters set up a joint Allied group to exploit captured material in the ongoing war against Germany, called the Combined Intelligence Objectives Sub-committee. At an early stage one of its units captured Dr Werner Osenberg, the head of the planning office of the National Research Council, together with his records of the names and specialisms of 15,000 of the top German scientists. But once Germany had been occupied SHAEF ceased to exist. CIOS was replaced by competing agencies in each zone. The British developed the British Intelligence Objectives Sub-committee, with its field collectors known as T-Force. The American boasted their equivalent Field Intelligence Agency, Technical. Even more valuable than scientific artefacts were the German scientists themselves. In the Soviet-occupied areas everything moveable seemed to be placed on railway cars and shipped east, including machinery, cattle and even bathtubs and radiators.[16]

By 1946 the accelerating Cold War introduced a new motivation, the cause of 'denial'. Stern efforts were made to prevent the key scientists from migrating to the Soviet Zone even if they were not of value to the

West. This widened the field of intelligence interest to lesser figures who were initially too numerous to track. In March that year, when asked about a range of mid-level German scientists from laboratories at Pelzerhaken, some of whom had knowledge of signals intelligence, the British Director of Naval Intelligence was resigned to losing them. It was thought that there was 'no practicable possibility of stopping their migration'. But there was also the possibility of eventual recompense. These second-order German scientists, if treated well, might return to 'provide useful information later about Russian activities'. Thus the names and destinations of scientists moving into the Soviet Zone were all recorded.[17]

However, in August 1946 the JIC reviewed policy on the Soviet recruitment of German scientists. Hitherto it had interested itself only in those 'required by us'. Many who had been released by British intelligence were being swept up by the Soviets. There was growing pressure to shift attention to those who would be 'a potential source of strength to the Russians', a policy of denial. But in practice only the Americans had the resource to do this on a large scale. The Americans had just decided to move 1,000 German experts and their families to the USA 'expressly to deny them to a potentially hostile power'.[18] The Joint Scientific and Technical Intelligence Committees in London ran a joint working party on what they called the problem of the 'enticement' of German scientists. In September 1946 they heard, 'One recently engaged scientist is said to have been offered a villa, complete with domestic staff, a very liberal allowance of food and cigarettes, a car, and even clothing and footwear.' Those who had services to sell could command a good price.[19]

The new 'denial' programme, which eventually encompassed over 3,000 scientists and technicians, was codenamed Operation Matchbox. Over 18,000 people were being tracked by the same programme. In practice it focused on scientists in the 'specially dangerous' areas known as 'Category A'. These included nuclear physics, radar, guided missiles, homing torpedoes, codes, ciphers, deception, radio direction-finding, biological warfare, chemical warfare including the new Sarin nerve gas and the rather grisly details of 'German physiological trials' with these gases. There was also intense interest in one or two fantastic projects such as 'methods of causing temporary blindness by using ultra-violet rays'. Individuals who worked in these areas found themselves traded like commodities and moved from one holding-tank to another. Key German scientists ended up in a compound with the appropriate code-name Dustbin. This was the main interrogation centre which, from June 1945, was located at Schloss Kransberg, close to Frankfurt.

Trading in exotic species of German scientist was one of the main pastimes for the intelligence services of all four occupying powers. The

French were often catalysts for such exchanges, enjoying reasonable relations with all parties, but trusted by none. Colonel P. M. Wilson, a British intelligence officer with the Enemy Personnel Exploitation Section, explained, 'We ... require the French to do a great deal for us in regard to finding Germans' and also giving 'clearances for their evacuation from the French zone to U.K.'. Thus if any obvious restrictions were placed on French intelligence officers entering his HQ this would have 'unfavourable effects on our relations with them'. The upshot was that Colonel Wilson had to maintain a front office, which looked like his main centre of activities, and meanwhile create a 'special office' in the rear of which the French were unaware, and to which he transferred his own 'Top Secret activities'. He was also worried that others, including the Americans, might obtain 'information of a highly secret nature regarding French activities, and their connection with similar Russian activities'.[20]

Generally, Ernest Bevin took a dim view of secret service activities. But, since he was a former stevedore, these reservations were outweighed by the very high priority he gave to commerce and trade. Almost from the moment he assumed office in the summer of 1945 he was calling for detailed intelligence on the fate of German aviation science. He was not disappointed. By the end of that year Operation Medico had secured large quantities of equipment for the new RAF College at Cranwell and Operation Surgeon had acquired the entire Focke-Wolfe experimental laboratory at Detmold. Advanced wind-tunnel designs were of particular interest. T-Force was also busy acquiring civilian machine prototypes, which it described as coming 'under the heading of booty'. It met with increasing opposition from those in the Control Commission who were now trying to re-establish some sort of German industrial base. Nevertheless, in September 1947, the British Rayon Federation wrote to thank the Board of Trade for the valuable materials acquired from the giant chemical combine IG Farben Industrie at Dormagen, and other textile manufacturers benefited widely.[21]

Defence-related intelligence was the hottest property in post-war Germany. Technical intelligence teams from the Royal Navy were keen to acquire the latest German U-boats, and even more anxious to deny them to the Soviets. Fortunately for the British the surviving examples were located at a port under British control. The Royal Navy repeatedly assured the Soviets that three extant submarines of the newest class had been badly damaged and then sunk in deep water by the Germans. In fact they were undergoing detailed examination by the Admiralty, and the Soviets failed to press their claim for a sizeable portion of the U-boat fleet.[22]

The intelligence-exploitation programme did not go unnoticed by the British public. In the summer of 1947 there was public outcry in London when the V-2 rocket experts, General Walter Dornberger and Dr Wernher von Braun were transferred to the United States with the agreement of British intelligence. Braun's programme had made extensive use of slave labour drawn from the Soviet Union and he had hidden his Nazi Party membership. Lowrie, the American correspondent of the *Daily Express*, suspected that their backgrounds were less than clean and was an active campaigner on the recycling of those he regarded as Nazis. American intelligence officers in Washington regarded such journalists as a problem: 'Lt Col. Montie F. Cone, Intelligence Division, Exploitation Section says that Lowrie is a Communist and that he was responsible for the stories that appeared in the London press a month ago to the effect that the United States Army had brought outstanding German criminals to this country – specifically mentioning Wernher von Braun at Fort Bliss – and mollycoddling them.' This had resulted in a wave of letter-writing to the newspapers in London 'by the sort of person who was glad of an opportunity of criticising the United States', and the US intelligence officers feared 'another Lowrie campaign against the exploitation program'. The issue of the extent to which denazification programmes were evaded and war criminals provided with safe havens is too broad to be dealt with in this book. However, persistent researchers have demonstrated that it was substantial.[23]

Exploitation of German weaponry seems to have helped Britain to fill the mass-destruction weapons gap in the period before the production of its first successful atomic bomb in 1952. The British took a particular interest in German chemical warfare specialists and chemical weapons stocks. In December 1949 the CIA produced a highly detailed report on British mass-destruction capabilities that was sent to the White House. 'The UK possesses the capability of conducting large-scale, sustained chemical warfare, employing standard World War II equipment with improvement ... including the use of captured German "G" nerve gases.' In part this reflected the view of some senior British officers, including Montgomery, that gas was a more humane weapon insofar as it did not leave the problem of a devastated country once a war was terminated.[24]

Scientific and technical intelligence was the most prized item of military value in post-war Germany. But London and Washington were also aware that the Germans had been fighting the Soviets for four long years, so opportunities to collect military intelligence on the Soviet armed forces abounded. In late May 1945 British security captured 'a group of 30 German Air Force Officers who are intelligence experts on the Russian Air Force'. General Kenneth Strong, Eisenhower's British Intelligence Chief, asked the JIC in London what to do with them, adding that they were likely to be the first batch of many similar groups. Strong had no hesitation in suggesting that they should be sent to Britain and put through detailed interrogation to be squeezed of every drop of information. Then, he went on, they should be sent 'to Post Office Box 1142 at Alexander, Virginia, USA for final disposal'. This was a discreet reference to a secret American programme set up for the same purpose. In London there was much sucking of teeth for fear that the Germans would enjoy using an opportunity of 'making mischief between London and Moscow'. But the JIC conceded that the Soviets would already be interrogating German prisoners in the East about the capabilities of the RAF and so permission was given to proceed. As a result Britain and the United States produced extremely detailed intelligence on the Soviet Air Force in 1945 and 1946.[25]

What was the fate of individuals arriving at 'Post Office Box 1142' in Alexander, Virginia? Many Germans went quickly to work for intelligence in Washington and soon acquired US citizenship. One example was General Ernst Shultes, who had been Chief of Staff of an army corps on the Elbe in 1945. In 1948 he was commissioned by Lieutenant-General Al Wedemeyer of the US Army to write 'an extensive study' concerning the re-establishment of the German armed forces for the defence of Western Europe against Soviet attack. In 1952 he was given US citizenship and was employed by the Eurasian Branch of US Army Intelligence (G-2) in Washington. In 1955, General Trudeau, the head of US Army Intelligence in Washington, asserted that since 1950 Shultes had made a 'major contribution' by heading up the effort to exploit captured German General Staff records. Trudeau conceded that, even ten years after the war, the 'material pertaining to German combat experience in Eastern Europe and the Soviet Union is the basis for much of our current thinking on the present tactics, organization and logistics of the Soviet ground forces'.[26]

Germany was the critical intelligence window upon the Soviet Union, and this window was opened much wider by the stream of defectors and refugees from the East. Other sources tended to be barren, for signals intelligence now made little headway against largely secure Soviet communications, human agents enjoyed only a short life in Stalin's secure state, and risky aerial spy-flights were only rarely attempted. By contrast the vast numbers of people exiting the Soviet bloc were an inexhaustible supply of material. Moreover, their information allowed more secret instruments – such as spy-flights – to be targeted on the top Soviet installations. In many areas, such as submarines and rocket engines, the Germans were the world leaders in 1945. What German material and scientists the Soviets had captured offered a benchmark of Soviet capacity in these areas about which little was otherwise known. But in other areas where the Germans were not ahead this information could also be misleading.[27]

The sense of urgency that underpinned this search for intelligence is often overlooked. In 1948 many in SIS and MI5 believed that a war, focused on Germany and the Middle East, was perhaps only weeks away. During the many moments of tension, demands for intelligence went up exponentially. The pressure to locate these useful Germans was intense. Officials in London were anxious that some might get the impression that in Germany 'the British condone unlimited non-selective and competitive body snatching'.[28] Germany was an ideal window on the Soviets for several reasons. First, the Soviets had attempted to suck Germany dry of scientists and technicians. By the late 1940s they had finished with many of these individuals, who were returning from the Soviet Union to the Soviet Zone of Germany with rich tales of places that were otherwise impenetrable to Western intelligence. Secondly, moving agents from the West into the East was easier in Germany than anywhere else. Thirdly, the cost of the British intelligence effort against the Soviets launched from Germany was borne by the Germans and not by Britain. At a time of economic stringency in London this was immensely important. Thus recovered statehood in Germany, Austria and Japan, which ended these occupation subsidies in the 1950s, was especially problematic for Britain. All four powers bemoaned the loss of their elaborate administrations, which helped to hide bloated intelligence staffs.

Operation Dragon Return, under way by 1949, underlines the valuable technical intelligence that Britain was obtaining on the Soviet military machine through Germany. This involved re-recruiting German scientists formerly employed inside the Soviet Union. The key to recruiting these individuals was the offer of scientific employment away from the drab conditions of Germany. British intelligence efforts were thus dependent on other Whitehall departments, such as the Ministry of Labour, which were exhorted to find attractive destinations for them. Dragon Return was controlled by the Director of the Scientific and Technical Intelligence Bureau (STIB), a key section of Britain's ID, which employed many German, as well as British, personnel. Most of these operations were straightforward defections. More rarely, individuals were persuaded to stay 'in place' for some time, on the promise of future scientific work in the West. This work was painstaking and dangerous. By September 1950, Dragon Return had expanded to focus on a large group of German scientists and technicians who had been working in three main locations deep inside the Soviet Union:

(i)   CHIMKI – Guided missile research and development
(ii) KUIBYCHEV – Aircraft research and development
(iii) PODBERESJE – Aircraft research and development

Contact had been made, under carefully controlled conditions, with a cross-section of German scientists and technicians who had returned to

Germany. British intelligence dared not show its hand by letting the Russians realise just how valuable to the West this security leak was. Dragon Return provided superb intelligence on guided-missile research and development. All this fed directly into the JIC's Inter-Services Guided Missile Intelligence Working Party in London and an Anglo-American Working Party on Guided Missiles.

One of Dragon Return's greatest feats occurred over the weekend 2/3 December 1950. After preparations 'over several years', technicians were brought out of Berlin, debriefed and sent back to their Soviet programmes using RAF transport. This exploited high-grade Germans who 'are not allowed to move out of the Russian Zone where they have their jobs and accommodation found for them'. British intelligence was in touch with the circle of friends of one of the returnees over a period and was able to arrange for him to be contacted by a friend from his home city who worked for the British STIB. Offers of an academic post in Western Germany were discussed and a plan was conceived to enable him, without compromising himself, to visit the West and discuss his academic future with an officer of STIB who also knew his former university professor.

Legitimate business was arranged for him in the Russian Sector of Berlin over the weekend, and the RAF sent a special aircraft to pick him up. The returnee then spent the night in the British Zone in company with a former colleague and STIB officers, returning to Berlin by an RAF aircraft the following day so that he was able to resume his work without disclosing his connection with British intelligence. The idea was to extricate him and return him repeatedly.[29] One Soviet defector alone, Dr Tokaev, a Soviet aerospace engineer, provided remarkable details on aviation research and guided-missile developments inside the Soviet bloc.[30]

Money was always a problem for the British, despite the subsidy of occupation costs. This caused bitter arguments over the handling of Soviet defectors and refugees. Defectors represented one of the best sources of intelligence on Soviet-controlled areas, but they also posed an alarming security problem. They might be kidnapped by Soviet teams or might themselves have been planted by Soviet intelligence, and could then reveal much about Western defector handling. It had taken London until the end of 1949 for the JIC to set out a general policy on this matter, which was still being refined in 1950. The most difficult issue was the cost of the defectors' disposal (or resettlement) after interrogation, which no intelligence service wished to bear. American efforts were dogged not by money but by inter-service rivalry and by the slow handover of defector activities from American service intelligence to an expanding CIA. US intelligence in Vienna was no less busy than in Berlin or Munich. Here, in 1950, an American Foreign Service officer called

Horace G. Torbert found himself appointed co-ordinator of intelligence for the American Zone of occupation in Austria. A co-ordinator was increasingly essential because there were so many intelligence activities in Vienna. 'I worked very hard at trying to get a handle on this whole problem,' he recalled. 'I identified about thirty more or less autonomous U.S. intelligence units operating in or through Austria.' Working together with the local CIA chief, John Richardson, and later Laughlin Campbell, he discovered that American psychological warfare was almost as large and diverse as intelligence.[31]

In 1950 General Shortt, the British Director of Military Intelligence, decided to try and get a grip on the defector problem. He complained that many defectors and deserters were just being dumped in DP camps, which were obvious targets and far from secure. They were in danger of being kidnapped, or even of being bamboozled by the visiting Russian Repatriation Commission to return to Soviet-held territory. This held two further dangers. Lengthy Soviet interrogation and the circumstances of detention in the Western Zones would provide the Russians with intelligence about British methods. Any such returning deserter might be 'persuaded' to make wild allegations about his treatment to discourage others from deserting to the British or Americans. There was pressure for money to be earmarked for defectors from the secret service vote, as British Military Intelligence could not find the £100 to £200 a head needed for 'disposal of an individual'. What British intelligence in Germany and Austria wanted was money for the payment of fares, 'e.g. to Australia', which it regarded as small beer compared with the propaganda value of demonstrating the benefits of defecting. But arguments over the funding of defector programmes dragged on into the 1950s, and in the meantime many deserters and defectors received a raw deal when they arrived in the British Zone of Germany.[32]

The Americans encountered different problems developing a coherent defector policy. In 1949 Washington was pleased to secure two defecting non-commissioned officers from the Red Army in Vienna. They were hurriedly flown over to the United States and, as one official recalled, 'treated just the wrong way': 'They were given a sort of hero's welcome and taken, as I remember, on guided tours of Skyline Drive and all sorts of things. The next thing somebody knew, they said they wanted to go back. So they were taken back to Vienna and ceremoniously handed back to the Russian commander there. It was then decided that we had better have a better method of dealing with defectors.' But the development of better methods was impeded by the continuing struggle for control between the intelligence sections of the three armed services and the CIA. Eventually an Inter-Agency Defector Committee was established in Washington together with elaborate CIA field facilities at Wiesbaden, but this did not prevent 'many strong disputes' over access to key defectors, and the many American intelligence services continued to play 'catch as catch can'.[33]

Although Robert Schow, who ran the CIA's secret intelligence arm, identified a string of 'unfortunate incidents involving the handling of defectors' as early as August 1949, prompting a National Security Council Intelligence Directive on the subject, matters did not improve quickly.[34] Poor handling continued to lead to casualties. Left to their own devices and disorientated by the experience of living in the West, a substantial number decided to redefect. Typical was the case of a Soviet Army colonel codenamed Icarus who had been in charge of uranium shipments from the Soviet Zone of Germany to the Soviet Union. In June 1950 he defected, leaving behind his German mistress. He was extensively debriefed but then became increasingly depressed. He eventually opted to return to the Soviet Zone with predictable results. He was speedily executed and his mistress was incarcerated.[35]

Despite these mishaps, defectors and returnees were the key currency in a Europe with large numbers of persons on the move. In Berlin the SIS station spent eight months on an elaborate double operation designed to recruit an important KGB source. Despite 'great skill and persistence' the end result of that operation was information that filled only half a page. By contrast, routine low-level work proved much more productive. In the meantime through a series of carefully encouraged low-level defections (interpreters and secretaries) the same officer who was running the double operation had paved the way for 'interrogations covering in great detail all the principal Russian Intelligence headquarters in Berlin and the Soviet sector, with names and descriptions of hundreds of staff and agent personnel'. For SIS, CIA and every other intelligence outfit, interrogating defectors, returnees and refugees proved more productive than the high-wire business of recruiting double agents.[36]

A great deal of the Western intelligence activity based in Germany was directed at Germany and Germans, rather than at the Soviet threat. This was accompanied by considerable competition between the Western powers for influence, especially with the nascent German secret services. These issues remain more obscure. Donald Cameron Watt, who served in a Field Security section with British Military Intelligence in Austria, vividly recalled his time there. Although a military unit, by 1947 about 95 per cent of its energies were devoted to civilian security intelligence matters. And a substantial part of those energies were absorbed with watching political activities among the tens of thousands of Yugoslav and Hungarian refugees, who included people 'from every range of pre-war and war-time political organisations in those two countries'. No less active were smaller numbers of refugees from Rumania, Greece, Bulgaria and Poland. 'There was even a single Chinese, who must have kept every intelligence agency in Austria, official or unofficial, busy trying to discover exactly what he was doing as he travelled around the western zones of Austria.'[37]

In Germany, ID gathered material on almost every aspect of life in post-war Germany. This inter-service organisation, which also hid SIS and MI5 personnel, employed thousands of staff. It began life, as we have noted, under Major-General John S. 'Tubby' Lethbridge, but was gradually civilianised, not least through the recruitment of many Germans. Initially, it was preoccupied with post-war Nazi underground organisations which were targeted in Operation Nursery and later Operation Selection Board. By 1950 it had developed a wider remit.[38] ID always maintained a large section which was tasked with specifically German matters. This was:

> responsible for political, social and industrial Intelligence. It deals with political trends, the study of political parties, and the chief personalities of each party. It evaluates reactions of the German population to the correct [current?] situation and the effect on general morale of measures taken by the occupying powers. It is also responsible for the vetting of important industrialists, and aspirants for high level posts in the German administration. It follows the course of German Youth Movements, Universities, Churches and Trade Unions, always with the intention of discovering or counteracting undesirable trends ...

Further sections were responsible for 'combating and studying all subversive activities of movements'. The most valuable instrument was a vast card system known as the Central Personality Index which contained the records of thousands of 'subversive elements'. The British intelligence apparatus had considerable powers, not only of arrest but also of interception. A key branch of ID was the semi-independent Censorship Branch. This had a separate headquarters in Herford and had three censorship stations, at Hamburg, Peine and Bonn. It censored a proportion of civilian, POW and DP inter-zonal and international mail, and a small percentage of intra-zonal mail. 'In addition monitoring of telecommunications is done at static units and by mobile vans spread throughout the zone.'[39]

One of the targets of this apparatus was the German Communist Party or KPD. The British and the Americans were intensely interested in all political developments within their respective areas and the KPD most of all. The United States took a harder line on this party than the British. As early as 1948, General Clay sternly warned Washington that he had evidence of communist sympathisers 'infecting' his HQ and had begun to call for the elimination of communism from Western Germany, starting with the barring of communists from public office. American personnel denounced as fellow travellers were personally investigated by the FBI on their return to the United States.[40] This bears a remarkable similarity to MacArthur's regime in Japan, where over 60 per cent of the intelligence effort by the US military was directed against internal subversion and domestic communism.[41]

By 1948 US Army Counter Intelligence Corps (CIC) units were clearly using ex-Gestapo personnel to investigate communism. Britain's ID worked with the Americans on Operation Apple Pie to recruit members of Section VI of the Reichssicherheitshauptamt or Chief Reich Security Office, including Walter Schellenberg. Eugene Fischer, the head of Munich's Gestapo section tasked with wartime anti-communism, was quickly employed by the local CIC to work against the Bavarian KPD. Because the best German anti-communist experts had been recruited by the Americans, and also because London regarded some of these ex-Nazis as too hot to handle, when the British came to set up the new German security service it was dominated by security amateurs. Konrad Adenauer, the first West German post-war Chancellor, considered it to be penetrated by the KPD and refused to use it.[42]

American fears about KPD activity were probably exaggerated and the propaganda war unleashed upon it from 1948 unjustified. During the late 1940s both the CIC and Britain's ID continued to search for a KPD paramilitary shadow organisation, but no evidence of it was found. Some radical members advocated direct action, but the KPD suspected that many of its radical members were 'plants' by the American CIC. London authorised a more limited anti-communism, including the quiet purging of local police forces. In February 1948, ID together with the Public Safety Division of the British Control Commission was busy scrutinising the Hamburg police and then moved on from force to force trying to prevent KPD penetration. Inevitably, the Korean War accelerated the pace. On 19 September 1950, Britain's Public Safety Division searched the recently completed KPD national Party headquarters in Düsseldorf and a week later decided to requisition the building for use as a British barracks. This was transparent harassment, and implementation of this decision meant overcoming a cordon of 2,000 demonstrators.[43]

By the early 1950s the British and American security agencies had parted company on how to deal with the KPD. British intelligence feared that excessive suppression would drive it completely underground and make it hard to maintain surveillance. It accused German police organisations of acting with excessive zeal and employing barely legal measures, and later they conceded that they had indeed adopted a heavy-handed approach. On 10 August 1954 the American High Commissioner's Office reported to the State Department that the KPD was 'riddled with agents' of Western security:

> The KPD is under the observation of more hostile agencies probably than any other political party in the world. Much of the mail of its members is surreptitiously examined by Western officials, and many of their home calls are tapped. Although it has not gone underground, the repeated harassments by the governments in the form of arrests and long detentions of important leaders . . . confiscations and attacks by anti-communist refugees, etc. on communist meetings have brought the party to a position where to all intents and purposes it is operating as an underground party.

The civil rights of KPD members were seriously infringed, not least their being denied compensation open to other citizens for persecution under the Nazis. Remarkably, KPD officials from the West were also being arrested by the security authorities when they visited the Soviet Zone, thereby extending the anti-Tito purges which had begun in the Eastern bloc in late 1948. The life of senior KPD members was extremely uncomfortable by 1950. In 1956, the Party was finally banned by the West German courts as unconstitutional, but the ban did not make much difference because it had been harassed, its papers closed down and its vehicles impounded, often through the abuse of petty legislation, for more than five years.[44]

The best-known example of a Nazi security chief who escaped justice and found comfortable re-employment in Allied secret service was the Gestapo officer Klaus Barbie. Barbie committed terrible crimes against the civilians of Lyon, including women and children. He was also crushingly effective against the resistance, capturing key figures such as General Delestraint, commander of the Armée Secrète, and Jean Moulin, head of the resistance. After an attack by the resistance in which five German soldiers died he descended on the small villages of St Claude and Larrivoire in the Jura Mountains. Many of the inhabitants were killed on the spot, the villages systematically burned and 300 men deported to the concentration camp of Buchenwald. After the liberation of France he was actively sought by the French government for his crimes. US Army intelligence, which had recruited him, actively protected him for some thirty years before French persistence brought him to trial in the 1980s. This frustration of justice was an organised campaign by elements in the US Army. Allan R. Ryan, who conducted a belated enquiry for the US Attorney General's Office, concluded that it could not be dismissed as 'merely the unfortunate action of renegade officers'. He added that 'the United States Government cannot disclaim responsibility for their actions'.[45] But Barbie's post-war career began not with the Americans but with the British and owed much to imperfect liaison between the Allies.

Early British attempts to penetrate Nazi groups often involved German deserters who had worked for Britain's PWE, broadcasting to Germany at the end of the war. They were given positions on local town councils but asked privately to collect intelligence on 'the activities of Communists and subversive personalities' and also to 'recruit sub-agents'. In 1946 another former broadcaster who was being cultivated by British intelligence was Christof Hoffman, a wartime German diplomat who had been in charge of the British propaganda station Radio Bratislava at the end of the war. He was soon working for a 'Major Kruk' in British intelligence at Bad Godesberg near Bonn, and it was through Hoffman that the British seemed to have tried to recruit Klaus Barbie in late 1946 and early 1947.

Hoffman's net was not producing enough intelligence, and the British came to believe that Barbie, who was active in Nazi self-help and escape groups, was the answer: 'Maj[or] Kruk was very interested in obtaining Barbie's services.' But Barbie, who was still roaming free, was suspicious and would meet Kruk only in the American Zone. His anxiety that this was some sort of setpiece trap was increased when Hoffman was himself arrested in April 1947. Although initially Barbie had been 'very eager to contact the British Intelligence Service', he now smelt a rat. He was not convinced that the British wished to re-employ him, rather than to place him on trial, and concluded that he was safer approaching the Americans.[46]

There were several British near-misses. From late 1945, British and American intelligence were watching a group of former SS officers who had formed a sophisticated resistance organisation in occupied Germany. These men hoped to achieve some rapprochement with the Allies and offer a cadre of experienced post-war leaders while Germany was rebuilt as a bulwark against communism. Their ideas were based on the example of the Freikorps groups that had appeared at the end of the First World War. The security elements of both the British ID and American CIC were aware that one of the leading figures was Klaus Barbie, and watched this group for some time. By May 1946 they had inserted an American CIC agent, who could pass comfortably for a Swiss German. They also encouraged them to develop contacts with a British officer 'who pretended to be a British Fascist and a secret sympathiser who promised them benign contacts with the British Foreign Office'.[47]

But Barbie was too smooth to be caught by this operation, and by early 1947 he had already escaped from the British and Americans three times. In August 1946 he had been picked up by the American CIC but leapt from the jeep in which he was being taken to prison. The startled American driver crashed. Barbie was pursued and lightly wounded by gunfire, but made his escape. He also claimed that he was arrested by the British on the railway station in Hamburg. Initially beaten, he was locked in the coal cellar of an old house, the makeshift prison cells of the local Field Security Unit, together with two other SS men. After three days the soldier on guard apologised that there would be no exercise that day, explaining that he was the only person in the building. The soldier then moved to a room above and began practising the flute. The SS men broke out of the cellar using a piece of iron pipe and crept away, leaving the soldier to his musical endeavours.[48]

In early 1947 ID and CIC felt they knew enough to make what was hoped to be a final swoop on Nazi groups. This was Operation Selection Board, launched on a rainy night in February in the Stuttgart and Marburg areas and directed at fifty-seven named targets, including Barbie. Barbie eluded capture by leaping from the bathroom window at the back of one of the target houses as it was being raided. The CIC officer in charge of this operation was Captain Robert Frazier.[49] The British ran a further snatch in June, codenamed Operation Dry Martini, to pick up some of the last remnants they had missed in the British Zone.[50]

Seventy people were caught in these dragnets, but Barbie, who had fled to the Munich area, was not among them. He was recruited in Munich by an entirely separate American CIC unit that had not been involved in Operation Selection Board and was used by it against the KPD, the Soviets and, remarkably, the French. The main CIC headquarters at the United States Forces Europe HQ became aware of this awkward state of affairs only in April 1947. By then the CIC Region IV at Munich was determined to protect Barbie as one of its most effective agents. It argued, 'It is felt that his value as an informant infinitely outweighs any use he may have in prison.' After he had been employed as an agent for six months he was finally arrested in October that year and sent for detailed interrogation at the European Command Intelligence Center near Frankfurt. But curiously he was interrogated only about his contacts with Nazis and subversives in Germany in 1945–6 and not about his years in wartime France. This is peculiar because it was precisely upon his French expertise that his CIC operations were drawing.[51]

Barbie was valuable to the US because of his wartime work in France. He knew many other German intelligence and Gestapo officers who had worked in France and who were now hiding in the French Zone of Germany. The long border shared by the American and the French Zones, together with the fact that Heidelberg, the US Forces Europe headquarters, was a few miles from the French Zone, was the key to Barbie's desirability. The US CIC was anxious about communist penetration of the French secret services, even to the extent that some considered them close to being hostile services. CIC told Barbie that one of his key tasks would be to gather intelligence on this French apparatus. It wanted:

1. Information pertaining to the degree of collaboration between the Soviet and the French Intelligence Services.
2. Degree of Communist penetration of the French Intelligence Service.
3. Activities of the Communist party of France in the French Zone of Germany and of the KPD in that Zone.
4. Any information concerning the activities of French Intelligence for the Soviets in the US Zone.[52]

Barbie was also tasked with penetrating the KPD in cities such as Munich, where the Party was reported to run a clandestine radio station.[53]

Barbie succeeded in penetrating the Bavarian branches of the KPD and was soon obtaining the minutes of meetings in major centres such as Frankfurt. Working with US Army CIC officers, some of whom were expatriate Germans, he commanded great professional respect. They saw him as a superb counter-intelligence officer who had an instinctive talent for manipulating human beings. One officer recalled a case where he was convinced that a suspect was a communist agent but had made no progress in proving it. 'Barbie told me I was wrong. Of course I accepted his judgement. He always said use guile not duress ... except where a bit of duress is needed.'[54]

The Americans could not now place Barbie in internment for fear that the British or the French would claim him. His security from arrest was assured by inter-Allied tensions. His knowledge about 'CIC, its agents, subagents, funds, etc. is too great', they concluded, to risk handing him over. Barbie was now spinning a story about having had a wartime career in the Waffen SS, a military unit. One technical intelligence specialist at US Army CIC HQ recalled that when Barbie was released from European Command Intelligence Center in early 1948 it was deemed advisable to continue using him as an informant in Region IV:

> because of his detailed knowledge of CIC modus operandi and because of the apprehension of [CIC] headquarters that Barbie, if not employed, would continue his overtures to the British to work for them as an informant. If Barbie had been allowed to make these overtures the British would have found out that the reason CIC had not turned Barbie in or reported him in connection with Selection Board was based on the fact that he was employed by CIC as an informant.

Although Barbie's situation had initially come about through simple confusion between different CIC units which had not been communicating with each other, the Americans felt that it would now look suspicious to the British if they admitted to having recruited him and that it would cause an 'embarrassing situation'.[55]

It was intelligence operations against the French by Barbie, and also by his colleague Kurt Merk, that imperilled French efforts to obtain Barbie from 1950. CIC explained that its agents were producing valuable material: 'These men have worked their way into intelligence positions in the French Zone, where they have access to classified material of counter intelligence interest.' This material included not only French Communist Party documents but also documents on 'French Intelligence Activities from LINDAU into the US Zone'.[56] In 1950, the French, who were now aware that the Americans had Barbie, pressed for his extradition. US Army CIC was increasingly aware of the nature of his wartime past, but it concluded that the real reason the French security wanted to get hold of him was because French communist sympathisers in its ranks wanted to discover more about the extent of American penetration of the KPD. It decided to arrange his escape down a 'Rat Line' to resettlement in Bolivia, rather than hand him over to the French. The Rat Line was an operation used to move valuable contacts out of Europe and resettle them elsewhere, often in South America. It ran through Italy, where visas, documents and the co-operation of local officials could be purchased with ease. In 1966, when the US State Department queried US Army Intelligence about Barbie it replied that 'BARBIE's performance for US Army Intelligence was outstanding and he was considered to be one of the most valuable assets targeted against Soviet intelligence operations and the subversive communist elements in southern Germany'. It added that he could not be exposed to French interrogation because of the 'high level operations and operational procedures which would have been compromised'. This, in turn, reflected the fact that during the 1950s and 1960s Washington continued to regard the French intelligence services as badly penetrated by the Soviets.[57]

The Klaus Barbie episode underlines the wider point that relations between British, French and American intelligence in Germany were rather awkward. Intelligence co-operation or 'liaison' usually contains a fundamental duality. As we have seen, liaison simultaneously seeks close co-operation against an enemy and also affords a window into the activities of an allied secret service. It is thus a classic secret service problem and has inspired equally time-honoured solutions. During the Cold War, this involved compartmentalisation, ensuring that secret services with ambiguous relations could maintain both friendly and distant relations simultaneously. This was the solution preferred by early post-war American intelligence in Germany as it was in the process of evolving from OSS into SSU and finally into CIA. During these changes the possible merger of American sections with distinctly different relations with the British prompted some fascinating discussions that illuminate the problems of intelligence and allies.[58]

On 2 and 3 February 1946, Brigadier Robin Brooke of SIS paid a visit to the SSU Mission HQ in Germany. Brooke had some far-reaching and sensitive proposals for an Anglo-American exchange of cover and documentation (C&D) materials for agents moving backwards and forwards into the Soviet Zone and for general exchanges of other expertise. He even offered access to the full SIS range of London C&D facilities. He was fulsome and encouraging, giving the American SSU the impression that 'if we wanted to do so, we could establish a joint British–American C&D in London'. But there were problems. SIS had a long and irritating wartime history of using 'co-operation and co-ordination', together with the advantages of a London base, to extend a degree of control over American espionage activities in Europe. Brooke's offer was thus examined with justifiable caution. A week later General Sibert, the head of US Army Intelligence in Germany, offered his opinion on the proposed extension of co-operation with SIS. He was worried about the 'political implications of some of our operations'.

Wider issues were also arising as the result of a proposal to merge the American SSU counter-intelligence (X-2) element and the SSU secret intelligence (SI) element in Germany. First came the issue of security. X-2 had especially strict security measures, including a refusal to employ anyone who was not of American nationality. It was 'largely as the result of their strict security requirements that the British have been prepared to share their information so fully and extensively'. In practice the material shared derived from signals intelligence. X-2 had also worked closely with the SIS offensive counter-intelligence component – Section V – to exploit this material during the war, and it wanted to 'continue their current very close liaison with the British' and to gain access to such British material. So at the very least quite a few foreign members of SI units would have to be weeded out during the merger. But there was also a greater structural problem in combining X-2 and SI:

> The X-2 representatives are also concerned on the ground that whereas they have no secrets from the British, the SI Branch has been engaged in certain activities which if known to the British would not be approved of by them. This, in turn, would make it necessary to decide whether the X-2 collaboration with the British could be continued and whether this collaboration could be extended to SI as well, at least within Germany.
>
> There is a division of opinion on this point, some believing that much more valuable intelligence can be obtained on the British Zone (and elsewhere in Germany) through close cooperation with the British, than would be possible through our continuing to operate on our present independent basis and through our own agents in the British Zone. This school of thought cites the expressed desire of the British to co-operate with us more closely on the positive [SIS] side; the fact that our major target in Germany is the Germans and what they are doing, and not what the British are doing in Germany; and the

fact that the best positive intelligence which we have yet received from the British Zone has come from agents which we originally operated but turned over to the British for their operation.

The other school argues that the British would not cooperate fully and would continue to maintain their own secret sources in the American Zone; and that we would never receive from the British any significant information regarding their plans and policies and activities which they would not like to have us Americans know.

Either way, and whatever Washington decided, it seemed to SSU high time to tidy up its act in the area of liaison. It conceded that it was 'essential for us to revise our present method of operation in the British Zone for the reason that it is not sufficiently secure'. There was 'some indication' that the British had become aware of 'the nature of certain of our activities'. The general issue of how to handle liaison was all the more pressing because in early 1946 Allen Dulles had been discussing the need 'for the closest possible collaboration with the Swedish, the Danish and the Norwegian Intelligence Services', especially in penetrating Germany. The Swedes had recently doubled their intelligence budget and Washington knew there were liaison dividends to be had.[59]

In the event the well-worn solution of a structural division, or liaison firewall, had to be resurrected to deal with the problem. On the Cold War's new front line and indeed eventually all around the world, CIA stations would be divided into two sections: officers conducting joint operations with the host country; and officers conducting independent American operations, hopefully unknown to the host. On 3 May 1946, Colonel R. Dodderidge, who commanded the SSU station in Paris, argued strongly for just such a firewall between joint operations with the French and his more sensitive independent activities. SSU in Paris, he complained, was carrying out its own clandestine intelligence operations, semi-overt work with a range of informants, liaison with the French secret services and investigative security work for the American Embassy, all from the same location. At present all SSU officers were 'known to the French Security Services' and this was bad. 'To combine, thus, overt and clandestine functions under one central office in a foreign country is, I believe, a violation of the fundamental principles of intelligence work.' Dodderidge rightly presumed that the French had already uncovered something of SSU's 'clandestine intelligence work'. If this activity was going to continue with any measure of success it 'should be kept separate and distinct from the liaison work with French Intelligence'. Nevertheless, he insisted, all these undertakings, although carefully separated, should be controlled by a single head of station in Paris.[60]

Liaison between what became the CIA in June 1947 and foreign services was increasingly sophisticated and broadly well managed. By contrast liaison between the myriad rival American secret services remained problematic. At its most basic there were real financial costs to competition. At the end of 1950, Robert Murphy, the American Ambassador in Belgium – a man with extensive experience of wartime intelligence – surveyed the European scene. He warned that as regards US Army Intelligence, CIA and many other American organisations the problem was that 'in the field they go pretty well their independent ways'. He went on:

> The net result from our government's point of view is an expensive one because the professional informers with whom we deal abroad deliberately shop among the several American intelligence agencies often selling the same bill of goods more than once and getting the agencies to bid against each other. At one time this was particularly true in Germany and the foreign informers with whom our agencies dealt literally had a field day selling the same report more than once.[61]

The problems extended well beyond that of wasted resources. The same report, however spurious and fantastic, if entering the system through several different channels tended to receive seemingly independent confirmation from several agencies and was thus accorded a high degree of plausibility in Washington. In Germany and Austria this problem became so widespread that eventually a rather imperfect listing of more seasoned freelance intelligence merchants who were 'suspected double dealers or near criminals' was circulated among the numerous American and Allied secret services. This was particularly necessary in centres such as Berlin and Vienna where by 1949 the black market had begun to decline as a source of income for the residents and where, as one practitioner recalled, in the absence of other gainful occupations, 'intelligence was certainly the major industry'.[62] Nevertheless, both London and Washington knew there were priceless intelligence commodities to be had in the ruins of the Third Reich, if only they knew where to look.

9

Operation Dick Tracy:
Air Intelligence in London
and Washington

DICK TRACY is the largest collection of all, and was also the first to be found; at Hitler's mountain retreat in Berchtesgaden.
David A. Paine (JARIC), 'Berchtesgaden to Brampton', November 1960[1]

British and American Air Intelligence enjoyed a very close partner-ship. This was, in part, a product of enmities elsewhere between the different American services. Service rivalry is a ubiquitous aspect of most national defence establishments. But senior British figures were still shocked by the openly expressed hatred of one American armed service for another, which exceeded the bounds of normal rivalry. The result was beneficial to Anglo-American relations. Leo Amery, the wartime Secretary for India, once noted in his diary that although all the American services were 'jealous' of the British they 'will always fraternise with their sister service on our side against their enemy service'. General Pug Ismay, the Secretary to the Chiefs of Staff, had apparently asked American sailors in the Mediterranean about their mechanisms for co-operating with the US Army. The sailors were amazed at the idea that they might have dealings with the Army, responding, 'Do you think we would have that bunch of rattlesnakes on board?'[2]

American inter-service enmity helped to create a merger of Anglo-American Air Intelligence effort against the Soviet Union in which the main business was 'target intelligence'. This enmity was accentuated in 1947 as Washington separated the US Army Air Force from the Army and created, for the first time, a US Air Force as an independent third service. In the words of General Charles Cabell, the new USAF was 'struggling mightily' to achieve a co-equal existence with the Army and Navy. Moreover, prior to 1947 it had been allowed only limited intelligence functions, and even these were of recent creation. Air Intelligence seemed neglected and this was one of the factors that had made the creation of a separate USAF necessary. Thereafter the embryonic USAF intelligence set-up looked instinctively to the RAF for support.[3]

This Anglo-American collaboration also reflected wider strategic and operational developments. In 1946 Major-General Carl Spaatz, the head of what was then the US Army Air Force, met with Air Chief Marshal Lord Arthur Tedder, Chief of the Air Staff in London, to negotiate the Spaatz–Tedder agreement. This provided for the preparation of four or five East Anglian airbases for use by American bombers in time of crisis. Such joint operational planning inevitably pointed towards joint intelligence. In the period before Britain acquired nuclear weapons, real estate constituted its strongest bargaining chip. Although Curtis LeMay, the head of US Strategic Air Command, was reluctant to embark on a strategy that left him dependent on other countries, in the short term he had little choice. American long-range bombers such as the B-36, with a range of 4,000 nautical miles, only began to make their appearance in 1951, leaving the US desperate in the short term for airbases close to the Soviet Union. Using bases in Japan, North Africa and the UK, the US Joint Chiefs of Staff believed that they could bring 80 per cent of Soviet industry within range of air attack. When the Korean War broke out, American contingency plans for a hot war required over half the American air strike on the Soviet Union to be launched from Britain, rendering it an 'unsinkable Aircraft Carrier'.[4]

Close Anglo-American co-operation on target intelligence for air strikes was also the result of a remarkable scoop. Air intelligence benefited from fantastic treasures rescued from a collapsing Germany at the end of the war. As we have seen, Bletchley Park was already eavesdropping on the Luftwaffe signals intelligence service and its work on the Soviet Air Force as early as 1943. But in May 1945 British and American intelligence teams had overrun Luftwaffe intelligence centres with vast stocks of priceless mapping photography and aerial target traces for the Soviet Union that had been gathered by Heinkel photo-reconnaissance aircraft throughout the campaign on the eastern front. The recovery operation was fraught, but by June 1945 most of this material was in London. This invaluable – but hitherto unknown – intelligence programme provided the strategic target intelligence for the USAF and the RAF for the next two decades. Because it provided target traces some waggish individual (whose wit got the better of his spelling) codenamed the key phase Operation Dick Tracy. As further phases developed the mass of material was given the generic designation 'GX'. The story of its rescue and exploitation was dramatic, fascinating and complex. Those who worked on this endeavour exclaimed that it was all 'too horrible to be put down on paper', but nevertheless they penned an internal classified history of their efforts.

GX material was hidden at several strategic locations across Germany. Some material was 'saved only by a matter of hours from a fiery end in burning canal barges' as the Germans tried to destroy it. Other material was 'removed from under the very noses of the Russian Army' in the first heady days of German surrender. The best material came from Hitler's mountain retreat at the Berchtesgaden in Bavaria and was codenamed Dick Tracy. An American team secured this only by a matter of hours. It had 'just moved this material under cover when the Russians, who knew of its existence and were looking for it, arrived on the scene'. Dick Tracy was supplemented by other collections from places as far afield as Vienna codenamed Orwell, from Oslo codenamed Monthly and from Berlin codenamed Tenant. There were nine different collections in all. In mid-June the material was flown to Britain, arriving at the US 8th Army Air Force Headquarters and then moved to the Anglo-American Central Interpretation Unit at Pinetree in Essex. Here joint Anglo-American exploitation was begun.[5]

There were special reasons why London became the centre for Operation Dick Tracy. In August 1945 General Sibert, head of US Army Intelligence in Germany, rather belatedly asked Washington 'about the permissibility of joint conduct with the British of Intelligence research activities on Russia'. In fact he had been pursuing these for some months. Within a day the US Chief of Staff General George Marshall refused permission and extended this refusal to a general injunction that intelligence activities should 'not involve joint research work on Russia with any Allied nationals' because of the sensitivity involved. However, Major-General Quesada, the US Army Intelligence chief in Washington, realised that this would outlaw joint work on Dick Tracy and other projects. Experienced staff officers redrafted the injunction so that it focused on continental Europe only. This edict remained in place until 1946.[6]

One participant remembered the crates arriving in London. Hapless airmen carried a seemingly endless supply of heavy boxes from the aircraft. As one batch was brought off the plane, a box crashed to the floor and split open. It was found to contain not photo materials but smuggled Swiss watches. Lurking under GX were also some private enterprise operations conducted by individuals. The contents of this particular box were quickly 'tidied away' before officers arrived. The crates mostly contained prints that were twelve inches by twelve, together with some original film. There was also a mass of plots, target traces, maps and other valuable documents providing air intelligence cover of the whole of the Soviet Union as far as Siberia. There were also a lot of scrapbooks and fascinating personal effects belonging to German crews who had flown over the Soviet Union. The latter were irresistible to the airmen who came upon them and, in their own carefully chosen words, were 'all "mislaid" within 24 hours, and never found', constituting prize souvenirs of the air war on the eastern front.

Exploiting this mammoth haul was a daunting task. After a number of false starts a complex system was finally developed to classify all GX material. The idea was originally to copy all of it, but in the event there was so much that the RAF was 'selective' and kept the product of only 8,000 sorties that had generated between 800,000 and 1,000,000 prints. The copying process for even this portion of GX was vast and initially required the services of some 200 officers. In October 1945 the project was moved to Medmenham in Berkshire and the main work on copying the excellent Dick Tracy material was completed by a target date of March 1946. Further material, captured from the burning river barges by Montgomery's Twenty-first Army, arrived that March. In May the following year the whole operation was still going and, together with the Central Interpretation Unit, was moved to Nuneham Park, about three miles from Huntingdon in Cambridgeshire. Medmenham was handed over to the reformed 90 Group as the new RAF signals headquarters which was gearing up for an electronic intelligence effort against the Soviet Union, of which we will hear more in the next chapter.[7]

GX was so enormous that even the preliminary sorting work on the more obscure collections went on until January 1949. In Montgomery's captured materials in particular there were some extraordinary finds that did not fit comfortably into an air intelligence programme. Among this collection were several large mahogany cases of beautifully arranged 35mm photographic prints, some 15,000 of them, showing the complete pictorial story of the German 1936 expedition to Borneo and Africa. (These were given to the Royal Geographical Society in London.) Secretive entrepreneurial activities ensured that the GX collection continually expanded. In 1954 it acquired more material in the form of annotated target prints of vital areas of which the RAF and USAF did not yet have cover. They were obtained for an undisclosed sum from 'two gentleman of Europe' and proved to be of 'great intelligence value'. Even in 1958 new areas of the collection were still being discovered by analysts, including 3,200 mosaics of Finland. The key material representing areas that were a high priority for bombing in any future strike against the Soviet Union went to Air Intelligence in Whitehall, while the main stock was kept at the Joint Air Reconnaissance Intelligence Centre or JARIC located at Nuneham Park. Here GX was stored in a huge new building characterised by miles of shelves and 'acres of brown linoleum'.

GX was always on the move. In May 1957 JARIC and its GX collection moved to Brampton, also in Cambridgeshire. Here the prints were stored separately from the 30,000 volatile negatives and film, which were kept in the 'notorious K Bay'. The alarming nature of K Bay derived from the fact that much of its stock was nitrate film – a material which develops its own oxygen when burning, thus flaring like magnesium. In September 1960 a long-feared fire finally broke out in K Bay which was contained only with difficulty. The most valuable material was 22,000 target plots and traces filed in brown envelopes, Britain's key targets in any future war, which were stamped with a sortie number and placed in ranks of grey filing cabinets. In the early 1960s efforts were still being made to reconcile gaps between British and American batches of records, but the physical task of managing and sorting and preserving this colossal body of decaying material seemed endless.[8]

What was the value of Dick Tracy? This intelligence scoop provided mass photography on a scale unimaginable before the advent of widespread satellite reconnaissance in the mid-1960s and remained a key intelligence resource for more than two decades. It also boosted the confidence of the RAF Bomber Command and US Strategic Air Command. On 3 November 1948, during the latter phase of the Berlin Crisis, James Forrestal, the US Defense Secretary, had one of his famous dinner parties which – as usual – degenerated into an informal business meeting. Curtis LeMay was there and talk soon turned to war with Russia. The assembled company interrogated LeMay 'on our ability to drive home attacks on targets in Russia'. LeMay replied that 'the Germans had obtained excellent air photographs of all important targets in Russia up to the Ural Mountains and that we are in possession of all of the German material descriptive of these Russian targets'. The audience was impressed. But privately LeMay knew that, even with the best intelligence, the nascent Strategic Air Command had a long way to go in finding targets over a large landmass. GX remained of critical importance as late as 1960. Even then much of the RAF and USAF target data consisted of predicted radar pictures of targets which were derived from this ageing German photo cover. Although the British and Americans would make a number of clandestine flights over the Soviet Union in the 1950s the coverage obtained was small and GX was replaced only with the arrival of satellite photography in the 1960s.[9]

Exploiting GX cemented the existing Anglo-American air intelligence relationship. In May 1945, several large US Army Air Force intelligence teams were already working with the British. A four-man team was based at the Air Ministry dealing with – sometimes prickly – signals intelligence issues, headed by Kingman Douglas, who would later become deputy director of the CIA. Others, like Lieutenant-Colonel Lewis Powell, were at Bletchley Park. Powell had participated in the American swoop on Hitler's Berchtesgaden. Human treasures were also collected there which called for joint exploitation in London. Having learned that the Germans had moved most of their General Staff down to the Berchtesgaden, Powell joined General George McDonald, the US Army Air Force Intelligence chief, to investigate even before the formal surrender. The 101st Airborne Division had occupied the area and the RAF had 'just blitzed the chalets of Hitler and the senior officers'. They had found the intelligence staff who specialised on the Soviet Air Force billeted in a school halfway up a mountain. McDonald wanted the German experts as well as the GX material. In the event, the German intelligence officers 'were happy to go to England, as we asked them to do. They were afraid of what the Russians might do to them.' The deal was that they would share all the intelligence they had on the Soviet Air Force, and the Allies would release them within a year. 'It was fascinating to work with these German intelligence officers. We put them up in house outside London.' Powell remained as the American Air Intelligence liaison chief in London.[10] Partly as a result of his presence there some German specialists on the Soviet Air Force travelled on to Washington rather than returning to Germany in late 1945.[11]

German military advisers of the sort depicted in Stanley Kubrick's nuclear strategic comedy *Dr Strangelove* were in fact ubiquitous. By 1946 the US Joint Chiefs of Staff had asked none other than General Alfred Jodl, who had commanded the planning staff of OKW, Hitler's High Command, to set out his ideas for the most effective Western attack against the Soviet Union. In his typically thorough report Jodl urged air attack against the southern Soviet Union:

> The vital key-points for the entire Soviet war machine are in the oil areas of Ploesti, Baku and Maikop, with the Grosny refineries, and about eight (8) to ten (10) large power plants which deliver practically all the energy (power) required by the Russian armament industry. The German Air Force studied this question precisely and had models made of all the plants in question. These models were brought to the area south of Flensburg at the end of April 1945 and, under my orders, stored. I assume that nowadays they are in the possession of the British.

General McDonald wasted no time in asking his opposite number, the newly appointed Air Vice Marshal Lawrie Pendred, to search the models out.[12]

Anxiety to continue air intelligence co-operation grew rather than diminished in the years immediately after the war. A vast array of scientific and technical materials of air interest, especially missiles, continued to be extracted. In April 1947, a specialist from Wright Field, the US Air Technical Intelligence Center, contacted Washington regarding Project Abstract: 'This project has been carried out in the Theater with the assistance of the British. To date 3 Boxes of vitally important documents and cylinders containing the locations of alleged burials of other documents and guided missiles equipment have been found in the British Zone.' The American concluded that further British co-operation was 'essential in the operation'. American officers in Germany strongly recommended 'furtherance of joint operation' and pressed Washington for authority to pursue the project 'on joint British–US basis'.[13] Predictably the answer was yes. London formed an ideal forward base for exploitation, and much of the material was spread across the two Zones, demanding that it be pieced together. By the summer of 1945 British and American Air Intelligence each had half of this invaluable picture. Mutual exchange and assistance was self-evidently desirable.

By the end of 1945 the first wave of exploitation was finished. British Air Intelligence had consolidated its haul into two reports, one entitled 'The Soviet Air Force' and the other surveying German intelligence work on the Soviet Air Force order of battle. Digesting the German intelligence had been tough work. London and Washington soon discovered they had swallowed two battling German factions which 'violently disagreed' with each other. The high-level Berlin-based Ic Section of OKL, the Luftwaffe High Command in Berlin, was feuding with the theatre command level Auswertestelle Ost. By late 1945 the sixteen senior Luftwaffe intelligence officers who had been captured were drawn evenly from the two factions. Ic claimed to be the higher-echelon organisation, but Ost was able to produce more evidence. Their main bone of contention was over the rate of Soviet aircraft production, something which offered an eerie foretaste of the 'bomber gap' and the 'missile gap' arguments that would preoccupy Western intelligence in the 1950s.

What could not be disputed was that signals intelligence had been Germany's key source and gave all its work a broad authority. It was by far the most voluminous and also the fastest source and covered the whole of the eastern front. It was 'excellently supplemented in the north by the Finnish monitoring service'. The sigint take was better when the front was mobile, forcing Soviet units to use wireless transmission, while static periods resulted in proliferation of secure land-lines that could not be intercepted. Radio silence and deception caused the Germans 'considerable difficulties'. After sigint, captured POWs were the best source and allowed them some insight into what was going on behind the front lines.[14]

Perversely, London and Washington sometimes had to hide their co-operation from their mutual friends. In the summer of 1946 Swedish intelligence requested British help in investigating mysterious reports of missiles flying over Sweden. Initially they were dismissed as meteorites, but later pieces of missiles began to be found in remote areas of Sweden. Assistance with tracing radar was given and missile fragments were brought back to the UK for analysis. The source was thought to be Soviet missile-testing stations inherited from the Germans in the Baltic. Understandably the Swedes were irked to find that their country was being used as a free missile testing range, but they were also twitchy about the possibility of compromising their neutrality. A British offer of a flight of specially equipped aircraft to track the missiles was eventually declined. The Chief of the Swedish Combined Intelligence Board urged the 'extreme delicacy' of co-operation, asking the British 'to take all possible measures to prevent the Americans finding out about Swedish full co-operation with us in investigating the mysterious missiles'.[15] The British gave the Swedes assurances vis-à-vis the Americans and promptly dishonoured them. Air Vice Marshal Elmhirst, the head of Air Intelligence in London, at once gave everything to George McDonald in Washington. But he warned McDonald that the Swedes were developing 'cold feet' and they agreed to maintain the fiction of their non-cooperation in this area.[16]

Air power was the cutting edge of post-war strategy and it was appropriate that Anglo-American air intelligence was in turn the cutting edge of Western intelligence co-operation. In early 1946, two years ahead of the famous UKUSA agreement on sigint, McDonald and Elmhirst had concluded a formal deal on 'world-wide exchange of photographic cover of every description on an entirely world-wide basis' and 'without financial compensation'. This was soon extended to include microfilming of the voluminous Luftwaffe intelligence reports on the Soviet Air Force. It represented the first of many Anglo-American post-war intelligence treaties.[17]

London and Washington not only exchanged sensitive target materials, they integrated their target intelligence staffs. In June 1947 the British Joint Intelligence Bureau produced an especially hard-nosed study, 'The Characteristics of Russian Towns as Targets for Air Attack'. It gave attention 'particularly to incendiary attack' and was essentially an analysis of how well Soviet towns would burn and whether their incineration would take industrial plant with it. The news for the planners was not good. Gorki, for example, covered only eight square miles as a town, but the related industrial areas spread for another hundred square miles around. A high proportion of Soviet living accommodation was made of wood and might burn well. 'The centres of Russian towns generally provided compact and inflammable targets for incendiary attack,' but, the Bureau noted, the industrial areas were dispersed and would be hard to bomb. Only six copies of this report made their way outside the JIB. But Washington received one of the first copies because Major Daniel T. Selko of the US Air Force was part of the JIB team which wrote it. Soon further copies of this 'extremely useful' survey made their way to Washington.[18] This close co-operation on the really detailed problems of target intelligence continued into the later 1940s and early 1950s. A series of conferences were held between JIB and the US Air Force Target Analysis Division to consider how fast Soviet railways could recover from bombing. Discussions centred around a detailed study written by two experts from the Southern Region of Britain's railways, S. W. Smart, the Superintendent of Operations, and A. H. Cantrell, the Assistant Chief Engineer. They had been set 'sample recuperation problems' for restoring railway services after various degrees of bombing.[19]

On 23 June 1948, the McDonald–Elmhirst agreement was replaced by a full USAF–RAF Joint Agreement on Target Intelligence, which was ratified by their successors, Lawrie Pendred and Charles Cabell, in the autumn of that year. Pendred wrote to Cabell in affable terms taking evident pleasure in what he called 'our intelligence offensive'.[20] This treaty had its opponents. Rear Admiral Tom Inglis, the US Navy Intelligence chief, was 'violently opposed' to the US Air Force as a separate service and 'resented its existence'. He disliked the close relationship with Air Intelligence in London even more and 'threatened to cut off the flow of U.S. Navy acquired intelligence to us so long as we had a British officer in our shop'. Cabell recalled, 'I refused to accede to his demand and he soon dropped it.'[21]

Tom Inglis had serious reasons for why the Americans should avoid the embraces of London's senior intelligence officials which he set out before James Forrestal during October 1947. He conceded that the British had made all their intelligence available to the United States 'with practically no restrictions', including 'very valuable material', but parallel efforts by British officers to access American long-range research and development were also 'more and more persistent'. This problem had to be handled with 'some finesse'. 'The British have been very inquisitive and acquisitive and missed very little information which we have. Also the British have been restive and impatient with our control machinery and have frequently compared the free and casual access which our representatives have to their information with the channelling and red tape which their representatives suffer.' Inglis also feared that much of what was handed over was going to the Commonwealth or 'into commercial channels where it could be used in competition with American products'. He stressed that it 'must also be remembered that British Government is British Business'. Moreover, he argued that general British decline combined with a tendency to 'pull the rug out from under the US in countries like Greece and Iran' made Britain look 'less of an asset and more of a liability'. He was also alarmed by the strongly socialist credentials of figures such as Stafford Cripps. By early 1948 alarms about British Commonwealth security gave the warnings offered by Inglis a rather prescient air.[22]

Despite these anxieties, by late 1948 the tide of Western intelligence agreements had become irresistible. October 1948 even saw the completion of an Anglo-American naval intelligence treaty between Inglis and his opposite number, Vice Admiral Longley-Cook, the Director of Naval Intelligence in London.[23] However, the scope and texture of naval intelligence co-operation between London and Washington was always less than that relating to air intelligence. In the early 1950s the US Office of Naval Intelligence was finding that the process of getting certain material out of London was proving 'very difficult' and 'long delayed'.[24]

Air intelligence co-operation was a close Allied partnership, but not everything recovered in Germany was exchanged. In February 1946, US Air Technical Intelligence teams were making their way through the massive archives of Göring's Luftwaffe headquarters in Berlin. They happened upon a most interesting collection of documents on the British, including papers giving details of the mission by Major Christie of SIS to Holland in November 1939 to explore peace terms with Prince Hohenlohe-Langenberg, who was close to Göring. The archives also disclosed a range of embarrassing pro-German activities by prominent British personalities and evidence of large-scale leaks from Ambassador Henderson's British Embassy in Berlin before the war. These documents did the rounds in Washington 'by safe hand of officer' before disappearing into the State Department.[25]

Surprising news about British activities accelerated Washington's accession to the new Anglo-American Target Intelligence Treaty in 1948. The Americans suddenly discovered that the British had been running risky photo-reconnaissance flights inside the Soviet Union: the US Navy found by accident that 'the British were taking photography of the southern shoreline of the Caspian Sea'. Knowledge of the operation, run from a remote airfield on Crete and aimed at Soviet missile-development complexes, was kept within a small circle. This material was irresistibly attractive to Washington for one simple reason. The State Department had banned similar spy-flights by American aircraft as too provocative.[26] The RAF certainly had the capability for such flights. In November 1947 it had reformed two strategic photo-reconnaissance squadrons at RAF Benson – No. 541 with Spitfire XIXs and No. 540 with the special Mosquito PR34. The latter was an aircraft of remarkable speed and range, capable of 2,500 miles with its under-wing drop tanks and extra tanks in the bomb bay. It was probably this aircraft that began to probe the Soviet Union in 1948 from bases in Iraq, Crete and Cyprus.[27]

Britain was not the only country undertaking risky overflights into the Soviet Union in the late 1940s. Perhaps prompted by being used as an ersatz missile-testing range, and encouraged by the British, the Swedes tried their hand about the same time. In November 1948 a special

Swedish photo-recce unit equipped with high-flying aircraft reported that 'while over-flying Soviet-controlled territory in Finland at 38,000 feet' its plane had been intercepted by fighters and came under accurate radar-controlled anti-aircraft fire. Although it was undamaged, the pilot reported that 'flak bursts beneath him shook his plane'.[28] London tried to persuade other European countries to share the risk. When Attlee was asked about photo-reconnaissance of the Soviet Navy in the Spitzbergen area, he replied that it would be good to get the Danes to do it rather than the RAF. However, despite this forward attitude, British target intelligence interest did not give first priority to Moscow, nor indeed to other targets deep inside the Soviet Union. Although the RAF had a long-range programme that aimed at covering all of the Soviet bloc, its short-term 'crash' targets in 1948 were, in fact, in Western Europe, focused on Germany west of the Elbe river. If war broke out soon a vital task would be the destruction of certain key bridges and other installations that would impede the progress of the Russians towards the Channel coast, together with airfields that might be used by Soviet bombers to attack Britain. Thus, in the short term, target traces of Germany and France were as valuable as anything else.[29]

In late 1948, the Berlin Crisis was in progress and Foreign Secretary Ernest Bevin was pressing for a tough line, having just negotiated the arrival of US atomic-capable bombers in East Anglia, although as yet without atomic weapons. (American atomic weapons would not arrive in Britain until July 1950, prompted by the outbreak of the Korean War.) Against this dramatic background, US Air Force Intelligence officers in London were impressed – but also alarmed – by the first RAF overflights over the Soviet Union. Some saw them as excessively risky ventures and began to speculate about what they might imply in relation to wider British strategic intentions. They were struck by the 'reported relaxing of the Foreign Office attitude toward covert aerial reconnaissance over the USSR' in contrast to the line taken by the State Department which was 'adamant concerning our observance of a respectful limit from the coastline'. Was it, they asked, the first signs of desperation by a country gripped by 'economic poverty and extreme vulnerability' and which had lost its judgement?

It was conceivable, American officers argued, that the British might be considering provoking a war with the Soviet Union. Although the idea seemed at first glance fanciful, the possibility remained and the thesis was, they insisted, entirely logical. Not only was the British economy seemingly in terminal decline, but Britain was faced with a Soviet Union that would be increasingly capable of waging a successful global war. The eventual result of the Soviet atomic programme, which most intelligence estimates assumed would produce its first bomb in the early 1950s, would be that the 'UK will become untenable' – in other words, completely destroyed in the early stages of a future war. If, as many came to believe, a hot war with the Soviet Union was very likely in the next ten years, then by far the most acceptable time-frame for this event, from the British point of view, was now, in the late 1940s. This stemmed from the fact that for the next two or three years the United States would have a nuclear monopoly. Only by provoking a war soon, they argued, could the UK avoid atomic destruction. This train of thought was as alarming as it was logical: 'It must be assumed that there is a possibility that the British government might consider provoking a war in the immediate future if faced with probable victory now with Western help, over a USSR unprepared for a global war as against almost certain annihilation in such a war a few years hence.'

These officers had little evidence that Britain was looking for a preventative war other than the RAF intelligence overflights. They accepted that everything else in their report was speculation and that 'a lot of exception will be taken to it', but they felt strongly that the possibility was worth considering. In late 1948, in the midst of the Berlin Crisis, British and American chiefs were beginning to turn their minds to these atomic problems in the knowledge that the eventual arrival of the Soviet bomb would change the situation irrevocably. However, none of them had guessed that that event was only months away – a spectacular intelligence failure. Once the Soviets exploded their first atomic bomb on 29 August 1949, the situation was reversed. Britain then became very vulnerable and anxious to avoid war, while Washington faced a limited period of relative invulnerability. From late 1949, the boot would be on the other foot, and it would be the turn of British intelligence officers to worry about American partiality to the idea of preventative war.[30]

10

The Failure of Atomic Intelligence

[T]he intelligence services are at war with Russia and we are losing heavily in
the field in which I am engaged.

Commander Eric Welsh, head of Atomic Intelligence, June 1952[1]

In 1948, Britain's GCHQ was directed to make Soviet atomic weapons
its absolute top priority target. Also in this category were other
weapons of mass destruction, chemical and biological weapons, together
with the strategic means of delivery such as bombers and missiles. But
the task was hopeless for most Soviet ciphers could not be broken; moreover deep inside the Soviet Union communications used secure land-
lines rather than radios. SIS fared no better as it did not have agents deep
inside the Soviet Union, and in any case did not know where to send
them. In March 1948 London conceded that it 'is not yet known where
the Russians are developing their atomic plants'. Its best guess that year
was that the Soviets might explode their first atomic bomb in early 1954.
American intelligence broadly agreed, suggesting 1953. This guess was
wide of the mark by somewhere between four and five years.

Moscow's surprise test on 29 August 1949 dealt the West a shattering
psychological blow. This explosion, followed by Allied encounters with
the superior MiG fighter in Korea the following year – secretly piloted by
Soviet crews – banished any thoughts of the Soviets as technically inferior. The British JIC and its subordinates had sneered at the Soviet
approach to science, which involved having many of its experts in con-
centration-camp laboratories run by the MGB. The rest were harassed by
the police, and the whole atomic bomb project was in the hands of
Lavrenti Beria and the MGB. Defecting scientists painted a grim picture
of this environment and suggested that this factor reduced their
effectiveness by 50 per cent. Dr Tokaev, the star aeronautics defector of
1948, reinforced this gloomy picture. In June 1949, only two months
before the Soviet bomb, the British Joint Scientific and Technical
Intelligence Committees had concluded 'It seems certain ... that the

scientific potential of the USSR, though immense in numbers, is in fact less formidable than it appears. It is perhaps a reasonable deduction that, while much competent and original work is being done and will continue to be done, Soviet scientists are unlikely to rise to the greatest heights of scientific thought and imagination, from which the major advances in human knowledge proceed.' Here ideological insights, about the necessity of freedom to great intellectual achievement, multiplied pre-existing racial stereotypes about the backwardness of the Russians. This was further multiplied by the German prism through which the Soviet effort was viewed. The West knew about Soviet science that the Germans had learned of, but not much more. This resulted in insights into some fields and mistakes in others, such as Soviet rocket science, where progress was underestimated.[2]

Consequently the shock of the Soviet atomic bomb test in August 1949 was intense. President Truman reacted quickly, ordering work to begin on the American H-bomb. More importantly, the Soviet bomb fundamentally recast Anglo-American relations. From this point London would fear any forward activity in the Cold War, knowing that it risked obliteration. Washington, by contrast, sought to quicken the pace, knowing that within a decade it too would become vulnerable to attack and thereafter would be compelled towards an increasingly inert position.[3]

Second-guessing the Soviet atomic bomb programme – together with the even more obscure Soviet efforts in chemical and biological warfare – was undeniably a tall order. But it was made yet more difficult by the calamitous disorder within British scientific intelligence after the war. This situation was puzzling given the outstanding achievements of figures like Professor R. V. Jones, the Scientific Intelligence Adviser to the Air Ministry. Jones understood scientific intelligence and at the height of the war he and his team had identified the new radio guidance system that was enabling the Luftwaffe to bomb London accurately. His team had persuaded an incredulous Churchill of the existence of this system and then went on to devise instruments to investigate it, creating counter-measures within weeks. Jones was in many senses the father of a new field of electronic intelligence and radio counter-measures. Moreover, in 1945 London had given exceedingly high priority to scientific and technical matters and to their impact on warfare. Henry Tizard's special report on this subject, revised after Hiroshima and Nagasaki, ensured that the revolutionary developments of the previous five years were absorbed into British strategic thinking. The JIC was also on the ball. As early as the spring of 1945 it gave Professor P. M. S. Blackett of Naval Intelligence control of an *ad hoc* committee set up to review the future of scientific and technical intelligence. On 19 May 1945 it submitted its plan to the JIC.[4]

The Director of Military Intelligence immediately detected the central flaw in Professor Blackett's plan. Instead of concentrating the scientific intelligence effort of the services in one organisation, they were to be spread across Whitehall. Each service intelligence department was to have a penny packet of scientific intelligence staff headed by a scientific intelligence adviser. Technical matters were separated and dispersed in the same way. They would get together on occasion in joint committees. Yet the targets of this sort of work – radar or missiles – were shared problems with greater scope for economy of effort and inter-service collaboration than almost any other area of intelligence. R. V. Jones had fought Blackett in committee. He had set out an alternative option of a more centralised scientific intelligence service with a single director closely linked to SIS. But Blackett's curious arrangement pandered to the political desire of each service to maintain a separate identity and so it won the day. The legacy was an incredible two decades of inter-service squabbling.[5]

Blackett's new organism sat next to neither the producers nor the consumers of intelligence. The scientific and technical elements of service intelligence were located together in rented buildings in Bryanston Square, together with Kenneth Strong's new Joint Intelligence Bureau. Bryanston Square was not only a shabby building noted for its rotting linoleum, but was also situated too far from Whitehall. Scientific intelligence had 'been … exiled north of Marble Arch' and so the service was looked upon as 'a dustbin for misfits'. In March 1947, even Sir Stewart Menzies, not known for his interest in modernisation, was expressing deep concern to the Chiefs of Staff about the weakness of Britain's scientific and technical intelligence. In 1948 Francis Crick, who had a background in scientific intelligence for the Navy, tried to reform it but without success. Despairing, he departed for pure research work in Cambridge which would eventually lead to a Nobel Prize. There were further failed efforts in 1949. In November 1952, Churchill returned for a second term as Prime Minister and found things still in disarray. He was obliged to recall Jones in the hope of a major overhaul of the entire system. But this was not achieved until 1964.[6]

Disorganisation and dispersal was completed in 1945 by the mishandling of atomic intelligence. This was completely separated from the rest of Britain's scientific intelligence effort, even though many of its scientific processes were related to other fields. In 1945, Sir John Anderson, the Director of the British component of what had become the Manhattan Project, moved British atomic intelligence to the Foreign Office and the Ministry of Supply, in an attempt to mirror the American system and thus to perpetuate future co-operation. Although this was an odd place to put atomic intelligence, Menzies had been especially keen to avoid disturbing existing Anglo-American wartime atomic machinery. However the abrupt termination of Anglo-American atomic co-operation in 1946 rendered this a useless ploy. As atomic intelligence co-operation was gradually restored the British discovered that the Americans were doing things differently. Meanwhile the crucial area of British atomic intelligence languished at the Ministry of Supply in the 'secure cages' at the Shell Mex buildings, far removed from any other intelligence centre in Whitehall.[7]

But Blackett's nemesis was not, as some have suggested, R. V. Jones, Churchill's brilliant architect of the wartime 'Wizard War'. Instead it was General Sir Kenneth Strong, who had served as Eisenhower's intelligence chief for the D-Day landings. In 1945 Strong had volunteered to set up a body called the Joint Intelligence Bureau, which would bring together areas of activity that could easily be pooled by the services, such as economic and geographical intelligence. But his messianic obsession with centralised inter-service intelligence seemed politically dangerous, and for the time being he was able to capture only bits and pieces of the intelligence system that no one wanted. Typically, its topographical intelligence archives inherited the thousands of holiday snaps of French beaches donated in response to a public appeal prior to the invasion of Europe in 1944.

Yet Strong, starting out with this improbable collection of 'beach intelligence', was the wave of the future. For almost twenty years he waged an unremitting campaign as JIB chief for 'jointery' and centralisation, while periodic rounds of economies also worked in his favour. He was a natural empire-builder and he had already identified a key role for JIB in target intelligence – tying it at an early stage to the business end of atomic weapons, the hot issue of the day. Helped by excellent personal relations with figures like Eisenhower, his star was rising. In the mid-1950s, JIB would take over atomic intelligence. Finally, in 1964, Strong would become the first head of the Defence Intelligence Staff under a newly centralised Ministry of Defence (MoD) in which Army, Navy and Air Intelligence components were subsumed.[8]

Britain's atomic intelligence programme itself was run from the outset by Commander Eric Welsh. Welsh was a short, owlish and somewhat rotund former Naval Intelligence officer who had joined the Royal Navy in the First World War as an ordinary seaman. Formidably intelligent and courageous, he was soon commissioned at sea for gallantry in action and then taken into Naval Intelligence. During the inter-war period he left the service, but maintained his intelligence contacts. As technical manager of a company called International Paints and Compositions he specialised in maritime chemical developments for the hulls of naval vessels and worked all around the Baltic. By the late 1930s he was assisting with the now famous Norsk Hydro plant at Vermork in Norway which was soon producing heavy water required for atomic engineering. When the Germans arrived in 1940 he departed quickly for Britain, leaving his Norwegian family in place, who then served as agents during future expeditions.[9]

Welsh began the war by running agents against German naval activities in the Baltic, which was a haven for the development and testing of revolutionary new weapons. Moving from Naval Intelligence into SIS, he was increasingly involved in scientific intelligence, including the collection of data on the V-2 testing site at Peenemünde. He was also involved in the Oslo Report, a startling document produced by the agent Paul Rosbaud, which offered R. V. Jones critical details of a range of German scientific developments at an early stage of the war. Thereafter, a chance meeting with Menzies led to Welsh being given responsibility for atomic intelligence in SIS. Neither Welsh nor Menzies really knew much about atomic weapons and it was a typically spur-of-the-moment appointment by 'C'. Welsh was then closely involved with the famous SOE operation against the heavy-water plant in Norway, later celebrated in the film *The Heroes of Telemark*.

The raid on the heavy-water plant was launched from SOE's Special Training School No. 61, known as Farm Hall, a remarkable building which served as a menagerie for all sorts of different wartime agents moving in and out of Britain *en route* to the continent. For this reason it was comprehensively wired for sound. In 1945 it provided Welsh with the ideal location to debrief ten captured German atomic scientists about their wartime activities. Listening in to their conversations, British monitors held their breath when they heard the Germans discuss the question of whether their accommodation was bugged, only to dismiss the possibility on the ground that the British were not sophisticated enough to try such a trick. Although the German atomic scientists enjoyed sumptuous food and accommodation, Welsh was not soft on them and often told them that his personal preference would be to have them shot. He always appeared before them in full-dress naval uniform with medals – earning himself the nickname 'Goldfasan', or the Golden Pheasant.[10]

By 1946 German atomic scientists who had returned from Farm Hall to Germany had become a liability. These were a special category of person whom the West least desired to lose to the Soviets. They remained under constant 'special surveillance' under an Anglo-American covert scheme called Operation Scrum Half. This was co-ordinated by Commander Welsh, who sat on the Anglo-American Atomic Energy Intelligence Committee and was a regular visitor to Broadway Buildings. SIS in Germany was very interested, but security on the ground was provided by ID, and by US Army Intelligence in the American Zone.[11] By April 1948 Welsh and his boss, Dr Michael Perrin, the Director of

Atomic Energy at the Ministry of Supply, had become more anxious about the 'kidnapping or murder' of selected German scientists in the atomic field. There had been an unconfirmed attempt to kidnap the famous Professor Werner Heisenberg, leader of the German wartime atomic effort, in late 1947 and this had probably focused their minds. They made a special visit to Germany to set up more elaborate counter-measures, including 'a special covert joint Anglo/US Intelligence Security Surveillance Board' and a range of other contingency plans collectively called Operation Dinner Party.[12]

Dr Bertie Blount had responsibility for creating a list of vulnerable atomic scientists, which had now grown to approximately thirty. Blount was hidden in a special atomic section of the British Control Commission known as the Research Branch of the Office of the Economic Adviser. He took a practical line and advised General Haydon, the new chief of ID in Germany, that they should worry only about 'kidnapping and not murder, since the latter merely denies the scientists to both sides'. He also suggested that the scheme be extended to cover the eventuality of a Soviet invasion as well as an outbreak of kidnapping. Haydon conceded that 'murder may be a lesser evil than kidnapping' but added dryly that it would be quite good to try and prevent either eventuality. Operation Dinner Party had two phases, 'red warning' and 'scramble warning', depending on the level of threat.[13] Seasoned intelligence officers who knew their business regarded both these variants of the operation as unrealistic. If the Soviets tried to snatch these figures they would probably get them. Robert Schow, Deputy Director of Intelligence at EUCOM, who would soon become chief of CIA secret intelligence in Washington, also had little time for this special security surveillance. As far as he was concerned there were only two solutions, incarceration or permanent evacuation to the United States or Britain, and he recommended the latter. The Military Governor General Clay also declared it was absurd to have such vital people living freely in Germany but under massive surveillance, the cost of which was 'prohibitive'. That senior German atomic scientists were living openly in Germany in 1948 cannot help but prompt the thought that there was more to their presence than meets the eye and that some atomic deception operations against the Soviets may have been afoot.[14]

Germany and Germans continued to be a critical source of the limited intelligence on Soviet strategic programmes. German scientists and technicians seemed to offer tangential access to an otherwise inaccessible target. Personnel working for an organisation set up to mine and process uranium in the Soviet Zone of Germany were recruited by both the British and the Americans, as were technicians providing other components for the immensely complex process of refining uranium. Both also developed sources within the huge industrial combine IG Farben, which had factories across the Soviet Zone. Information about rail shipments to the Soviet Union was also being sent by radio and this was intercepted in the West. During 1948 two Germans who passed through Britain's interrogation camp at Friedland brought tantalising news of the first Soviet plutonium-producing reactor – Cheliabinsk-40 – which was situated near Kyshtym east of the Urals and close to two large lakes used for cooling. This plant was central to the Soviet weapons programme. All this allowed some guestimates of Soviet uranium production and some export control measures, but was not a substitute for agents at the heart of the Soviet nuclear programme.[15]

At the other end of the world, intelligence teams were exploiting a parallel source – Japanese POWs. Over a million had fallen into Soviet hands at the end of the war and had endured harsh conditions in central Siberia and the Urals, where many had been used for labour. In the late 1940s they were allowed to return. Lieutenant-Colonel W. K. Benson of the CIA, who chaired the Joint Atomic Energy Intelligence Committee in Washington, set considerable store by this. But although they were able to supply first-hand accounts of the intense efforts the Soviets were putting into new uranium mining, in some cases within the Arctic circle, it did not tell them much about Soviet atomic bombs.[16]

Allied exchange of this material was complicated. Initially, Horace Calvert headed the London Office of the Manhattan Project's Foreign Intelligence Section, whose main duty was to liaise with Eric Welsh. Welsh posted a series of SIS officers, the first of whom was William Mann, to sit in the equivalent office in Washington, which was being absorbed into what would become the CIA. But this set-up was eliminated by the McMahon Act of 1946, which made it a criminal offence for any American citizen to pass atomic information to a foreigner. An SIS officer with atomic responsibility continued to be sent to Washington, but he hung around in Washington rather than achieving liaison with the right office.[17]

German scientists continued to provide tantalising glimpses of Soviet work on the bomb. In February 1947 Western intelligence interrogated Frafft Ehricke, who had been the assistant chief of rocket engine development at Peenemünde. In April 1946 he had been invited to Leipzig to join a group of German scientists who were travelling to Moscow under a Professor Pose to work on the Soviet atomic bomb project. They had already spent two months in Moscow discussing the details of how to advance the project with Professor Peter Kapitza, a leading Soviet atomic scientist. They had then returned to Germany to collect a team of seventy German scientists and technicians to take back to Moscow. The Germans were to undertake much of the ancillary research in related fields in which they were expert, 'whereas the development of the bomb was to be left entirely in the hands of Russian scientists'.[18]

Signals intelligence had told the West very little about Soviet bomb production but its efforts were not completely barren. On 20 April 1949, Admiral Hillenkoetter, the American Director of Central Intelligence, surveyed intelligence efforts on the Soviet atomic programme. The CIA had been holding discussions with USAF, which wanted intelligence that would support 'the counter offensive bombing of the Soviet atomic installations', and this was now receiving a very high priority. The Agency had decided that it was now 'essential that every means be utilized to ... fix the precise location of the major atomic installations in the USSR'. Production facilities were a key question, so that Soviet capabilities to produce a stockpile could be gauged in peace and also attacked in a future war. 'The most productive in the past and the most promising method, and hence the one most deserving of priority, is Special Intelligence', Hillenkoetter observed. Special Intelligence was a euphemism for signals intelligence. Signals intelligence, he explained, had offered material on the way in which the Soviet programme was organised and administered, providing the 'basic framework' into which all the other intelligence was fitted. This other material came from interrogating returning German scientists, POWs and escapees, from human agents and from combing published Soviet scientific literature. Seismic detectors were also under development. These different approaches were mutually supportive. Material from the open literature had been of 'great value' in offering context for the sigint work. Despite heading the CIA, in the atomic field Hillenkoetter put his money on the signals intelligence experts, urging that 'an expansion of the COMINT effort is required'. American signals intelligence resources were already over-committed, and more atomic intelligence would mean more spending in this area.[19]

What sorts of predictions had this intelligence effort generated in the first years of the Cold War? The best guesses were made early on. Perversely the more effort that was applied thereafter, the worse they became. In November 1946 the JIC surveyed the future scale of air attack against Britain and made its only lucky guess, predicting that if the Soviets acquired atomic weapons before 1951 they would have acquired a number unlikely to exceed five.[20] This was spot on, but it was also a fluke that was not repeated. Exactly a year later, Whitehall conceded that 'intelligence about Soviet development of atomic weapons is very scanty', but, on the basis of what they had, officials thought it unlikely that the Soviets would have a sufficient stock of bombs to give a 'decisive result' in war before 1957. They also suspected that the Soviets would 'devote special attention to the rapid development of biological weapons', perhaps allowing them to attack earlier.[21]

Such forecasts were now forming the very foundations of British defence policy. With Britain's military leaders pinning their hopes on the prospect of no war before 1957, the re-equipping of British armed forces was postponed, while resources were ploughed into the exploitation of new developments in defence science, in the hope of skipping a whole generation of designs and types. In other words, the Chiefs of Staff decided to play the game long. This made the JIC uneasy. It accepted that it knew very little about Soviet atomic bombs and its tentative forecasts were qualified by protestations of ignorance. But its projections were still taken as gospel by service planners working out the architecture of British post-war defence. The Admiralty, when thinking about the future target date for the major re-equipment of the fleet, asserted in March 1948 that 'HMG [His Majesty's Government] have accepted the assumption that no probable enemy will be able to use weapons of mass destruction, (viz. V.2, atomic and biological weapons) before 1954, and possibly 1957.' Increasingly, 1957 became the fixed date of Soviet atomic sufficiency employed in British military planning and research.'[22]

In July 1948 the JIC completed its annual review of intelligence on Soviet intentions and capabilities, a document running to more than seventy pages. Soviet atomic weapons were the most important subject and the JIC based much of its guesswork on Soviet supplies of uranium, which it considered to be 'the limiting factor'. Given what it took as the Soviet start date, and given the extreme technical difficulties, the JIC thought it just possible that the Soviets might 'produce their first atomic bomb by January 1951, and that their subsequent stockpile of bombs in January 1953 may be of the order to 6 to 22'.

But as we have seen the JIC then cast doubt on its own worst-case analysis, dismissing this projection as the maximum possible assuming that Soviet work would progress as rapidly as the British and American work had done in wartime. Allowances for the slower progress of the Soviets 'will almost certainly retard the first bomb by some three years'. London had never credited the Soviets with particular scientific prowess, so the JIC's very best guess for the first Soviet atom bomb was early 1954.[23] Washington was broadly in line. Although US Air Force Intelligence expected the Soviets to produce a bomb more quickly, the Navy view had prevailed. On 29 March 1948 the American JIC stated, 'The probable date by which the Soviets will have exploded their first test bomb is 1953.' Again, this gave a projected operational date for a Soviet nuclear force of about 1956/7.[24]

Because 1953/4 was a long way off, London and Washington had strong suspicions that Moscow would be giving a lot of priority to biological and chemical weapons, stimulated by knowledge of German nerve-gas developments which had revolutionised this field. Western intelligence was, if possible, even more ignorant about Soviet biological and chemical warfare projects than it was about atomic developments. In November 1946 the JIC thought that the Soviets would have manufactured considerable stocks of the 'three new German nerve gases' including Tabun by 1951.[25] The problems of collection were similar to atomic intelligence. SIS confessed that its intelligence on Soviet chemical warfare was hopeless. Alan Lang-Brown, head of the SIS scientific section, known as the Technical Collection Service, confessed, 'In the case of C.W ... we are at present up against something like a blank wall.' The problem was that this research was going on 'in inaccessible regions in central Russia' and not in countries 'such as Sweden or Switzerland where secret intelligence is relatively easily gathered'. Even defectors, who had proved to be the best hope of progress in this and other fields, were mostly chance windfalls, and there was little chance of actively encouraging other defectors from the right target groups.[26]

London considered that only the Americans were making any headway in the trickier field of bacteriological warfare. During the war the Americans had developed a full-scale production plant for anthrax which could produce enough bombs for a substantial attack over six major cities in a period of nine months. The Americans were focused on a virus called Brucella which was a superior agent, being easier to produce and presenting no problem of long-term contamination. But they wondered what the Soviets had captured when they overran a large Japanese bacteriological weapons establishment at Harbin in Manchuria.[27] All their information was derived from increasingly stale German or Japanese intelligence, or from knowledge of what German facilities had been captured in 1945. Reviewing what it knew in December 1948, the American Joint Intelligence Group was confident that the Soviets did not have enough biological capacity to exploit it in an intensive military fashion and instead could conduct only small-scale operations, 'particularly of a covert nature'. German intelligence reports dating from 1940 identified the key centre as the remote Vozrozhdeniya Island in the Aral Sea. In 1936 the entire population had been evacuated at six hours' notice and the area handed over to the Biotechnical Institute. Now no one was allowed to approach within eighty kilometres. As early as 1937 experiments were being conducted with the plague virus. Continuous work had been conducted at the site since that time, and British biological warfare intelligence had since identified another site closer to Moscow. In 1945 the Soviets had captured about 6,000 tons of German nerve gas – a state-of-the-art weapon against which there was little defence. They had also seized intact a full-scale manufacturing plant at Dyernfurth near Breslau, which was presumably still in operation. But these were little more than rumours and there was simply no hard intelligence available on these issues.[28]

Intelligence on Soviet chemical and biological capability probably spurred on Britain's intense interest in this area in the 1950s. The British chemical programme was well advanced by the late 1940s and possessed new nerve agents, some captured from the Germans, but they were thought too nasty for testing in Britain. In 1947 Dr Perren from Porton Down went out to visit the Benin area in Nigeria to identify a new testing ground for 'new chemical warfare agents now being developed in this country', a reference to nerve gas. One of the requirements of any testing site in Nigeria was a good supply of pigs and goats, the unfortunate subjects of this expanded testing programme. Successful tests led to the construction of a nerve-gas production plant at Nancekuke in Cornwall in the early 1950s.[29]

The first secret Long Range Detection Flights, which sought to pick up samples of radioactivity in the air, were flown over Germany in the autumn of 1944. They were required by General Groves, head of the Manhattan Project, who feared that the Germans might make dirty conventional bombs by adding radioactive material, even though they could not make proper atomic weapons. B-26 medium bombers of the US Army Air Force were used, flying out of Britain for what were considered to be 'suicidally' low runs over certain industrial areas. Their missions were so secret that the intelligence officers from the Manhattan Engineering District would not tell the crews what they were collecting. Detecting atomic explosions after the fact was a relatively safe business compared with these perilous missions.[30]

The collection of radioactive samples of air and water, together with seismology, was established as early as 1947 as the key remote technique for detecting atomic explosions. A month after assuming the job of Director of Central Intelligence, Hillenkoetter was making extensive recommendations, not least for special flights by 'suitably equipped planes' to carry out air sampling around the perimeter of the Soviet Union. This could be done quickly, while a chain of seismic monitoring stations 'feeding data in Central Control' would take longer. Admiral Lewis Strauss, who had replaced Groves as head of the US atomic weapons programme, repeated this call in April 1948 and action was soon under way employing a fleet of USAF B-29s. The battle for control of US atomic intelligence was already emerging, with General Curtis LeMay insisting that this area should be a US Air Force Intelligence programme and not a CIA one.[31]

Strauss strongly resisted the participation of the British in atomic intelligence, as he was adamant that they were 'very lax about security'. On 7 January 1948 he expressed grave doubts about working with the British and the Canadians on long-range detection. Yet those running the American programme knew they had geographic gaps which only the

British could cover. Against Strauss' wishes the British were somehow told of American atomic tests in the spring of 1948 and were able to try out their embryonic British system against the American tests. Strauss was incensed when he discovered this unauthorised leak to the British. In September that year a British delegation visited Washington to attend the first discussions on operational Long Range Detection Flights. Again Strauss opposed this meeting, and after it had happened he was unable to discover by whom clearance had been given.

Thereafter the RAF routinely carried out two atomic detection patterns. The first were Operation Bismuth flights from Northern Ireland and the second were Operation Nocturnal flights from Gibraltar. These used modified gasmask filters to collect samples – protected from hail by a wire grid – which could later be tested with a Geiger counter. When American detection flights over the Pacific picked up the first Soviet bomb in August 1949 there was some discussion as to whether the McMahon Act would allow the US to inform London. Finally, forewarned by the Americans on 10 September that a radioactive airmass was likely to appear soon, the RAF was able to lay on extra flights. By 22 September, Harwell – the site of Britain's first atomic pile – had carried out its own tests and was able to confirm the American results.[32]

Scrambling to launch extra 'special air monitoring flights' became a regular part of RAF duties. In October 1951 Freddie Morgan, the new British Controller of Atomic Energy, wrote to congratulate Slessor, who had become Chief of the Air Staff, on 'extremely valuable' results. Part of the urgency arose from the need to demonstrate Britain's ability to 'fill certain gaps' with information that was not available to the Americans, with the hope of underlining the value of more joint operations. But Slessor's pleasure was short lived, for he was soon horrified to see the 'full story' of these top-secret flights in the *Daily Express*, and a leak enquiry was launched to find the culprit. However, the much more secret British programme of seismic detection remained undisclosed.[33]

These indirect means of gathering atomic intelligence on the Soviet Union had failed to give any advance warning of Moscow's first test. From the outset the indirect approach to intelligence-gathering had its stern critics. Charles Turney, the leading naval scientific intelligence specialist, observed in 1947 that, daunted by the difficulties of penetrating central Siberia, the British had tried 'semi-overt means' such as chatting to Eastern bloc nuclear physicists at scientific conferences. This was, he said, simply dodging the hard work that lay ahead. 'The long-term problem is to effect a penetration of Russia itself (no other country matters by comparison), and this has barely been started.'[34] Immediately after the explosion of the Soviet bomb, Turney felt both depressed and vindicated. The indirect approach was 'widely adrift', he lamented. 'We should have got far better information from a messenger or labourer in the right place than from any number of Professors of Physics swanning round Europe.' The lessons were clear: the British needed to do more clandestine work. It was now 'vital to take every opportunity of pressing for authority to carry out active intelligence operations against Russia. Whether they are in fact practicable ... is a matter for M.I.6.'[35]

Expanded SIS operations with agents against the Soviet atomic programme were not practicable. In the wake of the first Soviet test, atomic intelligence was expanded but did not improve. Matters were not helped by the fact that Eric Welsh suffered a heart attack in early 1949 and spent a long period in the King Edward VII Memorial Hospital for Officers. Thereafter he was plagued with further heart attacks and died in November 1954.[36] During June 1952, by then a very ill man, Welsh, who was still head of Atomic Intelligence, reviewed Britain's batting average in this field. The scores 'made depressing reading'. He confessed that whenever he had information to report it was always 'in the nature of a post mortem over Russian achievements'. To be fair, he added, to gain the information that the British had secured about Soviet tests at a great distance, for example through atmospheric sampling, was a 'remarkable feat'. They had followed with some success the first test in August 1949 and the second in September 1951 and a third some weeks later in September of the same year.

Welsh was quite clear about the failings of Atomic Intelligence. In his view the role of intelligence was not to track past events but to give forecasts. In the atomic intelligence field they needed to be able to give the Chiefs of Staff warning about future Soviet intentions and capabilities. He conceded, 'we are making a very poor stab of it in the field of Atomic Energy Intelligence. Long distance detection techniques supply History *not* News. Nothing is as stale as yesterday's newspaper. What the J.I.C. want and what the J.I.C. demand is preknowledge of what are the enemies' intentions for tomorrow.' In other words the questions that they could not yet answer were the critical ones. When would the Soviets have a stockpile of atomic bombs which in their opinion would justify the risk of open warfare? What kinds of fissionable material were they making and what was their present stockpile of bombs? What was their current rate of production? These were the questions to which the policy-makers and the planners in Whitehall and Washington really wanted answers.[37]

Efforts to answer these questions eventually led them into vast, complex and ultimately highly inaccurate intelligence programmes to estimate ore production inside the Soviet bloc and to track ore shipments outside it. Refugees from the uranium mine at Erzgebirge in the Soviet Zone of Germany were always of interest. The mine was run by the

MGB as a punishment operation, and twenty miners died on average each day due to the lack of even elementary safety. Interviewing those who had managed to flee from this horrible place told the West a great deal about the mine, but gauging how much uranium it was producing was remarkably difficult.[38] The elaborate Music programme, which attempted to deduce uranium production by measuring gas in the atmosphere, was, by London's own admission, even more inaccurate. Later it would try to guess the throughput of Soviet uranium production factories by simply measuring the dimensions of various buildings. A lot of time was also spent mulling over Stalin's statements in *Pravda* and trying to deduce something from his changing intonations when asked questions by journalists on international control of atomic weapons. The West came to believe, wrongly, that the Soviets were short of uranium, while in fact the MGB had conducted an exhaustive and productive search inside the Soviet Union and there was no shortage. These programmes were ultimately useless substitutes for what the West really needed – an agent on the inside of the Soviet strategic weapons programme. This they did not have, and would not have until such an individual volunteered himself in the late 1950s.[39]

The Soviet atomic bomb in 1949 had a profound impact on Anglo-American relations. The arrival of Soviet atomic power that could reach anywhere in Europe showed that Britain might bear the brunt of any nuclear retaliation. This would become an issue of immense sensitivity and one that would increasingly dominate the British approach to the Cold War. Washington had anticipated this dramatic change in Britain's strategic situation, although it did not expect it to occur until the 1950s. In December 1948, at a conference attended by the top American war planners the key question had been asked with admirable clarity by General S. E. Anderson: 'What is the possibility of our being denied England as a base?' Major-General Charles Cabell, the US Air Force Intelligence chief, expanded on the question, adding, 'what would happen in the event that the British were convinced that the Russians had an atomic bomb? Of course, he added, 'the world believes that Russia has no atomic bomb at the present time'.

Cabell revealed to his colleagues that he had already, very discreetly, gone to 'a little means' to try and uncover the answer to this question. So far as he could determine, the British would 'grit their teeth and continue to accept American deployments in Britain'. General Lauris Norstad added that, 'without raising it bluntly', he had also pursued this question with Arthur Tedder and with the British Secretary of State for Air. Although the British all realised that when the Soviets acquired atomic weapons an entirely new era would follow, 'I was very agreeably surprised that the general feeling seemed to be . . . that we still have to go on with the operations.' But nagging doubts now began to surface about American access to strategic bases throughout the Empire–Commonwealth. The Americans conceded that the Karachi aerodrome in Pakistan, which was essential for hitting central Soviet Union, might have to be taken and held by force. The same was true in Egypt where – bizarrely – they looked to the overstretched British to hold key airfield facilities for long enough against their reluctant Egyptian hosts to enable them to use the airfields for the purpose of atomic attack on the Soviet Union.[40]

Washington understood the importance of this change very well. Britain's position as a world power was ebbing and clearly it was 'unusually difficult' for a 'proud people' to accept their new position as 'the weakest of the Three Great Powers'. But the geo-strategic changes brought on by the new weapons and methods of war had effected a transformation in Britain that was arguably more fundamental than the gradual slipping of imperial power, and this new development had affected the attitude of the population at large: 'World War II has given the British people a deep realisation of personal danger and of their vulnerability as a nation. For four years little more than the 22-mile wide English Channel stood between them and the Wehrmacht. The Luftwaffe and the V-Bombs made the war a personal matter to tens of millions.'[41] By September 1949, news of the Soviet atomic bomb had increased this sense of threat and had created what might be called a 'vulnerability gap' between the British and the Americans. In any future war, London would almost certainly be vaporised, while Washington was not within range of Soviet bombers and missiles and would probably not suffer the same fate. In June 1950, the outbreak of the Korean War turned this 'vulnerability gap' into an abyss. Suddenly Whitehall felt the urge to apply the brakes, and in this frightening environment getting accurate intelligence became ever more important.

11

GCHQ:
Signals Intelligence Looks East

[A]n organisation which will compel the respect of the Services and take its
proper place as the unchallenged headquarters of all signals intelligence.
'A Note on the Future of G.C.&C.S. [GCHQ]', 17 September 1944[1]

Two immediate observations can be made about the place of GCHQ
in the early Cold War. First, almost nothing has been written about
this organisation.[2] Second, by any measurement, whether volume of
product, size of budget or numbers of personnel, GCHQ was the most
important service. Personnel is the easiest aspect to track. In 1966,
GCHQ and its attendant supporting collection arms commanded about
11,500 staff. This was not only more than SIS and MI5 combined. It was
also larger than the entire Diplomatic Service, including the Foreign
Office in London and all its overseas embassies and consulates. Yet we
know almost nothing of this vast army of technicians and codebreakers
who spied on the airwaves.[3]

This curious disparity is not difficult to account for. And those who
prefer a conspiratorial approach can identify a deliberate element in the
improbably low profile of GCHQ. As we have seen, in the summer of
1945, the JIC deemed signals intelligence, together with deception, to be
the two areas that were absolutely beyond the pale in terms of the writing
of the history of the Second World War. Both the JIC and the London
Signals Intelligence Board devoted much time to airbrushing these
matters out of history. Bletchley Park and signals intelligence, or sigint,
during the European War remained secret until the 1970s. By contrast,
books about the role of SOE in the Second World War began to appear
in the late 1940s. Indeed, by the 1950s the multiplying accounts of
Churchill's increasingly 'unsecret army' provided a convenient historical
distraction.[4]

Yet historians needed no help from the authorities to go badly off track. The arcane matters of modern code- and cipher-breaking – or cryptanalysis – are not an immediately attractive subject for historical writing. The work of special operations or secret agents, dependent on human beings for their progress, has seemed more accessible and more comprehensible. Market forces have also played their part. Since the 1960s British popular culture has developed a strong appetite for revelations about Soviet agents in high places, especially 'molemania', with its rich tapestry of governmental embarrassment and tales of nefarious doings. In 1963 the Profumo Scandal confirmed the ever expanding public appetite for such subjects. Thereafter, in both East and West, secret services themselves capitalised on public tastes, sponsoring more semi-official accounts of defecting agents, of which Kim Philby's *My Silent War* must surely count as one of the most successful.

The critical change at GCHQ towards the end of the war concerned not targets, but attitude. Led by an aggressive managerial figure, Sir Edward Travis, and having brought in highly intelligent university-educated staff who enjoyed free thinking and free speaking, GCHQ saw an atmosphere of constructive self-criticism develop. In 1945, all of Britain's established secret services were still somewhat antiquated in their approach to operations, reflecting the inter-war years of moribund leadership and underfunding. But GCHQ had the keenest appreciation of this fact and was the most active in seeking to transform itself.

The pre-war Government Code and Cypher School, the predecessor to GCHQ, had not been a real intelligence service, but rather a code- and cipher-breaking centre. It had also been something of an underdog, working in the shadow of Menzies, without even the limited organisational intelligence structures of SIS and MI5. Wartime expansion, the construction of Bletchley Park, active university recruitment and contact with the Americans had opened the eyes of GCHQ to what was possible. Now a core of determined individuals were eager to promote change. In 1944 they began the long-range planning that would turn wartime Bletchley Park – with its chess-players and crossword puzzlers – into GCHQ, Britain's premier post-war secret service, with a strong sense of identity, a substantial budget and predatory designs on other bodies. Three key figures were instrumental in this change. First, Gordon Welchman, the man behind Bletchley Park's Hut Six, which focused on the breaking of the German Enigma. Second, Harry Hinsley, who would serve as the 'sherpa' for important Anglo-American Commonwealth sigint summits immediately after the war. Third, Edward Crankshaw, who had handled wartime sigint discussions with the Soviets.

On 15 September 1944, only weeks after the liberation of Paris, GCHQ established a committee to study its post-war future. These three influential GCHQ officers set out their future vision for Travis. They surveyed the entire British intelligence scene, calling for a more central-ised 'Foreign Intelligence Office' as part of a coherent British national intelligence organisation. Led by Gordon Welchman, they pressed for a comprehensive body dealing with all forms of sigint, and also with a modern signals security organisation with the latest communications engineering. This would become a truly modern Intelligence Centre gov-erning all types of interception activities.

The pre-war Government Code and Cypher School, they conceded, had been 'little more than a cryptographic centre' with no ability to sift, collect or interpret material. There was little appreciation of the coming importance of electronic engineering. There was no conception of the imminent requirement for large-scale planning to cope with the exploita-tion of intelligence produced on an industrial scale. University-based recruiting in wartime had saved them. This had brought in some natural leaders who, together with the few pre-war figures of wide outlook on the permanent staff, had made 'a passable show in this war'. The war against Japan, with its need for major organisations overseas, would con-tinue for some time, probably into 1946 – or so they thought. Japanese traffic presented complicated problems to which they felt they could not make major contributions. The Americans were ahead on Japanese systems and they should be left to it. Sigint for figures such as Mountbatten and Slim fighting in Burma was not considered a high man-agerial priority.

Instead Welchman's group made a hard-nosed proposal. There were few people in GCHQ with real ability in general planning and strategic co-ordination. Indeed, they said, 'it would be difficult to count as many as a dozen'. They should not be wasted on the Japanese War. So, they insisted, 'as soon as the German war is over, as many as possible of the few potential planners should be set to work in the direction of our three immediate objectives, instead of devoting more of their time to Japanese problems'. GCHQ should not lose touch with developments in the field of Japanese sigint problems, since there were things worth learning in this sphere. But they sought to extract technical benefits from the Japanese War, not to expend resources upon it. For British commanders in Burma the tag of the 'Forgotten Army' was wholly appropriate.[5]

GCHQ moved quickly. Time was against it, so it was 'imperative to make an approach to the present Prime Minister at the earliest possible moment'. No successor to Churchill, they feared, however sympathetic, could have a real appreciation of 'the fruits of intelligence in this war' or his keen understanding of the importance of tight security. In Churchill, they had a heavyweight advocate and they wanted to strike while the iron was hot. They dreaded a return to the pre-war situation of under-recognition of what sigint could achieve. Extreme secrecy was its own

worst enemy, for even now the true scale of their wartime output was
known to a 'very few' in 'high places'. Moreover, the really talented sigint
planners were newcomers, and soon they would be lured back to their
pre-war occupations, unless positive action was taken to retain them.
Quite simply this came down to cash. GCHQ had to have high status to
secure 'a sufficiently liberal supply of money to enable it to attract men of
first rate ability'. The Welchman group were thinking particularly of engineers and electronics experts; even now GCHQ had to subsist with
'amateurish engineering groups'. They were also sensitive to the shift to
peacetime intelligence, arguing that, in the post-war period, Bletchley
would have to give equal weight to 'all types of intelligence about foreign
countries, including scientific, commercial and economic matters'. This
was a tacit reference to the targeting of neutral and friendly states.[6]

These ambitions shaped the progress of GCHQ as it moved from its
wartime site at Bletchley Park to new accommodation at Eastcote in
Uxbridge on the suburban fringes of north-west London. By 1946, it had
escaped the formal control of Menzies, the Chief of SIS, to become more
of a separate intelligence service in its own right. It quickly achieved a
managerial role in the new field of electronic intelligence, the monitoring
of non-communication electronic signals from radars and missiles,
known as elint, and hitherto dominated by the three services. GCHQ's
incursion into this field began in 1948 and was completed in 1952. But
there were further battles ahead. It was 1969 before its wish to control all
aspects of signals work, including communications security, or comsec,
was realised.[7]

In 1945 GCHQ continued to advocate a centralised Foreign
Intelligence Office, tied closely to the Prime Minister and the Cabinet
Office. William F. Clarke, who had served continuously from 1916, now
applied his long experience to GCHQ in the post-war world. He warned
that the 'enormous power wielded by the Treasury' might be brought to
bear against it. As in 1919, work on military ciphers might cease in favour
of concentration on diplomatic material only. This, he said, might be 'disastrous' and the resulting damage to ongoing cryptographic research
might mean that, in a future conflict, enemy military traffic would prove
inaccessible. It was also essential, he counselled, to build up the prestige
of GCHQ. Many in government did not know of its true value. There
was, too, the 'potential danger' of a Labour government coming to
power, recalling the inter-war Labour government and its aversion to
things secretive. Clarke paused to consider Roosevelt's emerging United
Nations, observing that if the new international organisation took the
step of abolishing all code and cipher communications this action 'would
contribute more to a permanent peace than any other'. 'This however',
he predicted, 'is probably the counsel of perfection' and would not

happen. Instead codemaking and codebreaking would be even bigger business in the post-war world.[8]

When did GCHQ begin to work on Soviet codes and ciphers? Although the official history of British intelligence insists that Churchill ordered this to stop when Moscow became an ally in June 1941, it is now clear that it never stopped completely. John Croft, who worked at Britain's wartime diplomatic codebreaking centre, at Berkeley Street in London, was one of those who soldiered on. Croft did not mix with the majority of specialists working on Axis communications but was one of those rarer types working on the communications traffic of neutrals and allies on Berkeley Street's upper floors. He was engaged on wartime Comintern traffic in Europe, codenamed Iscott. Although circulated to only a very select group of individuals within Whitehall, this material revealed little more than a dutiful struggle against their shared enemy, Nazi Germany. There is no indication whether this material was exchanged with Washington or not. Despite the lack of any known Anglo-American treaty covering diplomatic traffic, material was exchanged on many countries, including the Free French, Portugal, Spain and Switzerland. GCHQ was reluctant to give the Americans material on territories close to Britain, for example Egypt, while the US Army felt it unwise to offer the British Latin American systems. Whether some of this very limited Soviet product was exchanged remains unknown.[9]

In practice it is all but impossible to draw a distinction between GCHQ's work on wartime Germany and its growing work on the Soviet Union in the 1940s. Knowledge of Germany required the tracking of events on the eastern front and involved learning as much as possible about the Soviet effort. British intelligence began to value the Germans for their knowledge of the Soviet Union as soon as Ultra came on stream. The Luftwaffe had an especially efficient sigint system and was busy listening into Soviet traffic. German messages used to send sigint summaries back to Berlin were, in turn, intercepted. This 'second-hand' sigint proved to be London's best source on the performance of the Soviet forces. As early as 1943 the JIC was able to produce detailed and accurate reports on the capabilities and characteristics of the Soviet Air Force in battle, based on Luftwaffe sigint material.[10]

In July 1944 Britain and the United States were gearing up for piratical raids on the archives and laboratories of a collapsing Germany, and sigint material was one treasure that was actively sought. The Combined Intelligence Priorities Committee began consulting at Bletchley Park about what material it wished to scoop from an occupied Germany. Suitably briefed, by early 1945 Intelligence Assault Units were moving into Germany with the forward elements of Allied formations, looking for all kinds of German documents, experimental weapons and atomic plant. Combined Anglo-American Target Intelligence Committee (TICOM) teams were despatched from Bletchley Park to Germany to seek out cryptographic equipment and sigint personnel. They were not disappointed. At Hitler's Berchtesgaden, they joined Air Intelligence groups in turning over the spoils. These include a Luftwaffe communications centre and a large amount of communications equipment. Eventually German POWs were persuaded to lead them to a vast haul of signals materials buried nearby and four large German lorries were loaded to capacity with contents that were then unearthed. The teams returned to Bletchley Park with their haul on 6 June 1945.[11]

The Allies wanted bodies as well as documents. On 19 May 1945 the British caught Generalmajor Klemme, the Senior Commander of Radio Intelligence for the Luftwaffe at the Husum-Milstedt intercept station, and he was then taken to Neumünster Prison. He was quickly moved to Neumünster camp for civilian prisoners and then to Adeilheide. He worked with the British in Germany until 10 March 1948, when he was considered to have been drained of all he knew about Soviet communications. Other key staff, including Major Oeljeschaeger and Major Beulmann from the Cryptographic Centre, which had been based in a stable block of the Marstall-Neues Palais at Potsdam commanding Branch 3 (responsible for planning), set off for Hitler's Alpine HQ at the Berchtesgaden on 1 May. A few days later, with the Allies closing in, they stopped at Viehoff to burn all the records of Branch 3 and fell into Allied hands on 22 May near Munich. They were flown to Britain on 5 July, where they were placed in a 'special camp' and were surprised to be met by their Branch Chief, Lieutenant-Colonel Friedrich, who had arrived before them. By June 1945 the British and Americans had scooped most of the senior Luftwaffe sigint officers.[12]

By 22 July, the US Army European Theatre Interrogation Center had completed a dossier on the 'German G-2 Service in the Russian campaign' running to over 220 pages. This gave considerable attention to the role of the Wehrmacht's Signal Intelligence Liaison Officers, 'the most important man' in the circle of intelligence sources for each major headquarters in the East, who delivered the fruits of German Signal Reconnaissance Regiments tasked with wireless interception on the battlefront. Soviet radio discipline, the Center concluded, was very good, and much depended on the interpretation of radio silence or knowing the transmission habits of particular operators. The United States was soon seeking to reconstruct this German service if only to ensure the security of the communications of the nascent German administration. In 1947, Dr Erich Hutenhain laid the foundations of a new German crypto service based at Camp King, Oberursel, co-located with the early Gehlen Organisation, a revived German wartime body that had dealt with Army intelligence on the eastern front. Inevitably, this unit had to be treated to a surprise briefing on Ultra and the inadequacy of wartime German Enigma machines.[13]

The Soviets were also swooping on German cryptographic assets. Bletchley Park discovered to its surprise that the Soviets had taken over some German Enigma-based communications nets and were using them for their own purposes. But initial hopes of a post-war dividend from the breaking of Enigma were quickly dashed. Roy Jenkins, who was then working at Bletchley, recalled:

> When the Russians got to Berlin they took over the Fish machines in the War Ministry, somewhat changed the settings, and proceeded to use them for sending signals traffic to Belgrade and other capitals in their new empire. We continued to do the intercepts and played around with trying to break the messages. We never succeeded. I think it was a combination of the new settings being more secure (which raises the question of how much the Russians had found out about our previous success) and the edge of tension having gone off our effort.

Elsewhere Allied recovery teams overran a German sigint operation that was still chattering away, producing decrypts of mid-level Soviet Army Group traffic. The Germans offered to stop the offending machinery at once, but they were urged not to disturb the precious flow and so this unit kept working.[14]

GCHQ's corporate takeover of the Axis sigint effort was not limited to Germany. In September 1945, British Field Security Units located a valuable prize, capturing Admiral Chudoh, the Japanese Chief Signals Intelligence Officer for the southern armies, in Saigon. There were even greater dividends in post-war Italy. These derived partly from the fortuitous coincidence that the deputy chief of the SIS station in Rome from 1944, Sheridan Russell, had previously worked at Bletchley Park and was sensitive to the fact that the Italians were talented cryptanalysts and was scooping them up where he could. Russell was an extraordinary figure. Originally a classical musician and fluent in French, Italian and Russian, he nevertheless encountered real difficulty in finding useful employment during the early stages of the war.

In 1941 Russell was censoring POW mail in a singularly unattractive location near Liverpool. It was only a chance encounter at a railway station with a friend who was working at Bletchley Park that resulted in his transfer to more interesting work. Soon he was engaged in the translation of naval intelligence, twelve hours at a shift, in the small Italian section in Hut Five of Bletchley Park. He worked in the 'Watch', which dealt with items of immediate interest, and his task was to translate 'at break-neck speed' long strips of messages produced by a machine that had been captured from an Italian naval vessel. Russell was of a somewhat conservative turn of mind and disapproved of what he considered to be the racy lifestyle of some of his female colleagues. On being allocated to his billet at Bletchley Park he discovered a woman's shoes and stockings under his predecessor's bed and reacted with great moral indignation. In May 1943 he joined a small party of cryptanalysts who were despatched to Algiers in support of the invasion of Sicily, moving to Malta as the Allies advanced. This was one of Bletchley Park's primitive out-stations and Russell, who often took the night-shift, chose to break codes in light silk pyjamas for coolness combined with knee-length hiking socks sprinkled with Dettol and flit for protection against the voracious insects. He was eccentric but also fantastically able and at the surrender of the Italian fleet in 1943 he dealt with the takeover of Italian Naval Intelligence.[15]

Russell then joined SIS. In 1944 he was responsible for recruiting and training Italian agents at two stations that were set up in the countryside outside Bari, who were then sent into northern Italy. Ex-Italian Air Force personnel, who were already familiar with the operation of radio transmitters, were a favourite source of recruits. Russell affectionately referred to his agents as 'thugs' and later several of them became prominent in post-war Italian governments. Soon he was second in command of the SIS station in Rome under his namesake, Brian Ashford Russell, which was billeted in style in a lavish apartment that had belonged to a mistress of a former high-ranking fascist government official. Local SIS transport was a super-charged four-seated Italian sports car which he drove very slowly, mostly to take SIS staff on tours of the classical sights. The whole post-surrender scene in Italy was chaotic, with the possibility of the Yugoslavs fighting the Allies near Trieste, and a poverty-stricken local population was struggling against the devalued lira.[16]

Others were bidding in the same market for talented cryptanalysts. After the Italian surrender in 1943 a substantial remnant of eighty Italian sigint staff under Major Barbieri continued to work for the Germans at a station near Brescia until April 1945. When this latter group were finally interrogated in Rome in mid-1945 they proved to have a large quantity of material, including photostatic copies of the codebooks of Turkey, Rumania, Ecuador and Bolivia. They had reconstructed codebooks from France, Switzerland and the Vatican. They also had smaller amounts of British and American traffic. By 1945 Barbieri's unit had been concentrating on French diplomatic traffic, 'a large number being messages to Paris either from BONNET [French Ambassador] in NEW YORK or from CATROUX [French Ambassador] in Moscow'. This traffic offered insights into subjects as diverse as Soviet–Yugoslav relations, Soviet policy in Germany, French economic negotiations with the United States and French plans for exploiting the Saar coalmines in Germany.[17]

Under new British management, this precocious Italian unit worked on without a break into the post-war period and without deviating from its French target. Berkeley Street in London was already doing extensive work on Free French communications, but more help was always welcome. Britain monitored the traffic of most of its allies throughout the war and felt justified in continuing to do so, for it regarded many of its partners as either insecure or untrustworthy or both. Much of this stemmed from a sense of indignation at their behaviour in 1939 and 1940. In November 1944 Churchill wrote to Eden, 'The Belgians are extremely weak, and their behaviour before the war was shocking. The Dutch were entirely selfish and fought only when attacked, and then for a few hours ...' The Free French, as other historians have shown, came in for especially close attention during the war and this continued afterwards. In the course of the major diplomatic conferences of 1945–6, Jimmy Byrnes, the new American Secretary of State, was apparently more eager to see decrypted French material than anything else, concerned that Paris was likely to be double-dealing with Moscow.[18]

French traffic from Moscow was of great interest to London, permitting a precise measure of an uncertain Cold War ally. In March 1944, the former French Air Minister, Pierre Cot, began a special diplomatic mission to Moscow to examine the possibility of reviving traditional Franco-Soviet co-operation against Germany in post-war Europe. This was a fascinating subject. In Moscow, in particular, French wartime diplomacy was wild and troublesome. The first Free French Ambassador, Roger Garreau, had proved to be a 'preposterous person' for whom diplomacy was 'a really savage business'. Alarmed British diplomats complained that Garreau threw into his work all of his 'immense self-importance ... his loud voice, his reckless indiscretions, his heavy breathing, his pop eyes and all the fury that dwells in his bantam body'. One day he would attack his prime enemies, the Nazis and the traitors of Vichy France, but the next he would turn to attack his ally, the United States, which he loudly denounced as 'a land of Jews and Negroes'. In 1945 Garreau was finally replaced by General Georges Catroux, a man of more sober habits, but French traffic from Moscow or Washington would always be worth watching.[19]

Major Barbieri's sigint unit was an Italian Army Intelligence element within 808 Communication Service Battalion. Barbieri was proud of his efforts against the French, but pressed for more staff. So many of the best cryptographers, he complained, had been captured by the French in Africa, and he added, 'the FRENCH are now employing them in their own service!' Nevertheless, the British concluded that the Italians were 'doing remarkably well with the limited reserves at their disposal'.[20] By mid-1946 the British were giving their Italians new tasks, including Soviet Taper five-figure traffic. British liaison officers with the Italians were working closely with GCHQ in Britain on the identification of new 'Taper groups'. Remarkably, some of the Italian operators did 'not know that they are intercepting Taper traffic' because the British were telling the Italian interception staff as little as possible about the traffic they were working on. Occasionally an operator, after intercepting several typical Taper messages, would note that 'the procedure signal … is often used by the Russians'. It was obvious that senior Italian sigint officers knew that Taper traffic 'which had been taken with so much depth and continuity for the past month' was Soviet intelligence traffic. The process was productive yet precarious. British sigint officers handled Barbieri's organisation carefully lest they do something that might 'lead to them asking what is done with traffic they are passing' and then refusing to co-operate further.[21]

Despite taking on these freelancers, GCHQ shrank at the end of 1945. The pressure to demobilise, combined with the end of the need for operational sigint, affected even the most privileged ranks of signals intelligence. British Army sigint collection units went from 4,000 personnel in December 1945 to about 1,000 by the following March.[22] Reorganisation was facilitated by relocation, for some of its equipment was constructed at the laboratories of the Post Office Research Department at Dollis Hill in north London and it was no coincidence that Travis chose to move his organisation to Eastcote near Uxbridge in north-west London, only a few miles from Dollis Hill. Here it remained until 1952 when his successors chose to relocate to Cheltenham, influenced – it was rumoured – by an affection for the turf.[23]

In the late 1940s, as we have seen, the key target for GCHQ was the Soviet bomb. The British Chiefs of Staff were fascinated by the problem of Britain's relative vulnerability to attack by weapons of mass destruction and wanted forecasts on this crucial issue. The JIC exhorted Britain's codebreakers to focus their efforts upon this, together with other strategic weapons systems such as chemical and biological programmes, ballistic rockets and air defence. Although the JIC placed these subjects in a special high-priority category, it was to no avail. The Soviet bomb took the Western Allies by complete surprise on 29 August 1949. Other Soviet activities, including espionage and diplomatic initiatives, constituted second and third priorities, but here too there were thin pickings. Many Soviet messages employed one-time pads, a secure system which, if correctly used, could not be broken. The extent to which Britain was surprised by the Tito–Stalin split in 1948 underlines the limited success enjoyed against its diplomatic targets. Secure Soviet communications were only part of the problem. Moscow and its satellites used land-lines, which could not be easily intercepted, instead of wireless transmissions. It was these problems that prompted the British to follow the Soviets down the path of more extensive physical bugging in the mid-1950s.[24]

High-priority targets aside, GCHQ was nevertheless providing Whitehall with large quantities of material in the late 1940s, albeit of a secondary and tertiary order. Some medium-level Soviet systems were vulnerable, especially military systems. GCHQ also continued to attack the communications of many states with vulnerable cipher systems. Some were persuaded by the British and Americans to adopt Hägelin-type machines previously used by the Axis, in the belief that these provided a secure means of communication. This was a belief that GCHQ did nothing to undermine. The JIC also asked GCHQ to look at subjects such as Arab nationalism, the relations of Arab states with the UK and USA, and the attitude of the Soviet Union, France, Italy and the Arab states towards the future of the ex-Italian colonies, especially Libya. GCHQ was also urged to focus on the Zionist movement, including its intelligence services. These subjects proved more accessible. In 1946 Alan Stripp, a codebreaker who had spent the war in India working on Japanese codes, suddenly found himself redeployed to the Iranian border, and throughout the Azerbaijan Crisis of 1946 he worked on Iranian and Afghan communications.[25]

Much GCHQ activity was hidden by the use of the signals units of the armed services for interception. Each of the three services operated half a dozen sites in Britain. GCHQ also had a number of civilian out-stations including a sigint-processing centre at 10 Chesterfield Street in London, a listening post covering London at Ivy Farm, Knockholt in Kent and a Post Office listening post at Gilnahirk in Northern Ireland. GCHQ had overseas stations hidden within embassies and high commissions in countries such as Turkey and Canada. There were also service outposts. In the Middle East, the base of Ayios Nikolaos, just outside Famagusta on Cyprus, became a critical intelligence centre, receiving Army and RAF sigint units as they gradually departed from Palestine, Iraq and Egypt. Further east, the Navy maintained its intercept site at HMS Anderson near Colombo on Ceylon, and the Army began reconstruction of its pre-war sigint site at Singapore. But the main British sigint centre in Asia after 1945 was Hong Kong, initially staffed by RAF personnel. Here, with help from Australia's budding sigint organisation, which was effectively under GCHQ management, Chinese and Soviet radio traffic was captured.[26]

London decided to give GCHQ the lion's share of British intelligence resources. On 22 January 1952, the Chiefs of Staff had met together with Ivone Kirkpatrick, by then Permanent Under-Secretary at the Foreign Office, to review plans for improving British intelligence. GCHQ came out on top. Its cutting-edge programmes, mostly in the area of computers and 'high speed analytical equipment' for communications intelligence, were given 'highest priority', and government research and supply elements were instructed accordingly. The Admiralty was beginning a new programme to build better receivers for ground-based and seaborne Technical Search Operations. Elint was no less critical and so new airborne radio search receivers for the Central Signals Establishment were also given 'all possible priority'. The Chiefs of Staff continually stressed the 'very great importance' of speeding up development and construction in these 'very sensitive' areas.[27]

By November 1952 a fuller review of British intelligence was under way. The process was prolonged by the primitive nature of available managerial instruments. Patrick Reilly, who liaised between SIS and the Foreign Office, confessed that no one really knew what Britain spent on intelligence. Now 'for the first time' Sir Edward Bridges from the Treasury and a committee of permanent secretaries were assembling some figures so they could review intelligence costs in the context of the overall defence budget. The Chiefs of Staff wanted 'increased expenditure on intelligence' within the general programme of rearmament, but were unsure of the figures or how much detail to give to ministers. All were crystal clear that in the short term the emphasis should be 'for Sigint'. The Director of GCHQ reported that he was busy filling the 300 extra staff posts recently authorised and proposed a further increment for an extra 366 staff to follow. In the late 1940s and early 1950s GCHQ was moving from strength to strength.[28]

As early as 1945, most English-speaking countries had committed themselves to the idea of post-war signals intelligence co-operation. Policy-makers at the highest level had come to expect a world in which a global sigint alliance rendered enemy intentions almost transparent. They were not about to relinquish that privilege willingly. In the autumn of 1945, when Truman was publicly winding up OSS, he was also secretly giving permission for American sigint activity to continue and approved negotiations on continued Allied co-operation. All desired the maximum option. On 19 November, Andrew Cunningham, the First Sea Lord, attended a critical meeting of the British Chiefs of Staff. There was 'much discussion about 100 per cent cooperation with the USA about Sigint,' he recorded, adding that they had 'decided that less than 100 percent was not worth having'. In Ottawa, George Glazebrook recommended to the Canadian JIC that Canada enhance its independent sigint effort in order to stake a claim in this secretive and emerging co-operative system. 'It is paramount,' he said, 'that Canada should make an adequate contribution to the general pool.'[29]

In the latter stages of the war, Travis together with the British services had fought hard to maintain British dominance in the field of Ultra and other forms of sigint in the West. This had made a deep impression on the intelligence officers of the American armed forces fighting in Europe who felt an unpleasant sense of dependency. In early February 1945 the US Army Air Force held a conference of all senior intelligence officers (A-2s) across Europe. There 'every A-2 expressed his disappointment at our utter dependence on the R.A.F.' in sigint matters. The US Ninth Air Force had deployed some tactical listening or Y units, but the British had controlled the flow of strategic sigint. The lesson was clear. Colonel Robert D. Hughes, Director of Intelligence for the US Ninth Air Force, warned Washington that the US Army Air Force needed its own air sigint units with control over sigint policy and sigint research: 'We feel that you should demand, and organize under your control, for peace as well as war, an organization similar to that of the R.A.F. ... Unlike other highly technical forms of intelligence, in which our American Air Forces have shared, we have continued to depend entirely on the R.A.F for this level of work in "Y".' The experience of wartime co-operation was thus ambiguous. There had been close collaboration. But this integration allowed the Americans to sense that the terms and conditions of sharing were important, schooling them in the meaning of intelligence power. Many American officials were now determined that the post-war agreements should allow the United States a more global capability.[30]

In March 1946, William Friedman of the Army Security Agency, and one of America's most senior codebreakers, travelled to London to complete details of, and sign, a revised version of the wartime BRUSA agreement on signals intelligence between Britain and the United States. Key aspects of the post-war relationship were already beginning to fall into place, with the Americans opening a Special US Liaison Office (SUSLO) in London and the British opening an equivalent British Liaison Office under Douglas Nicoll at Arlington Hall in Virginia. Yet the way ahead was strewn with obstacles. The complex package of agreements, letters and memoranda of understanding, often referred to as the 'UKUSA treaty' that sealed a vast Western sigint alliance, was not completed until 1948.[31]

As UKUSA emerged, Britain derived considerable benefit from its dominance over its Empire–Commonwealth partners. The semi-feudal relationship which London enjoyed is no better illustrated than in Australia, where sigint operations were controlled by London. Only in 1940 did Australia establish its own separate organisation. When this became the Australian Defence Signals Bureau, formed at Albert Park Barracks in Melbourne on 12 November 1947, it remained in the shadow of GCHQ. Four Australian applicants for the directorship were rejected in favour of Britain's Commander Teddy Poulden, who filled the senior posts with twenty GCHQ staff and communicated with GCHQ in his own special cipher. During the winter of 1946–7, a Commonwealth sigint conference was held in London, chaired by Edward Travis, during which each country was accorded designated spheres of activity.[32]

Canada's sigint organisation, under the long-serving Lieutenant-Colonel Ed Drake, suffered similar treatment. On 13 April 1946 the Canadian Prime Minster, Mackenzie King, authorised the consolidation of a number of wartime organisations into a small post-war unit of about 100 staff known as the Communications Branch of the National Research Council (CBNRC). Again, the senior posts were filled by staff seconded by GCHQ, prompting them to say that CBNRC stood for 'Communications Branch – No Room for Canadians', and by the late 1940s Drake had resolved to offset this by developing better relations with the US Army Security Agency.[33] However, the Americans were also inclined to give Canada second-class treatment. During the 1948 discussions on the UKUSA agreements it became clear that the US Communications Intelligence Board was equally anxious to prevent an information free-for-all among its signatories. It preferred to hand material to the Canadians 'on a "need to know" basis' and was keen to prevent a proliferation of liaison officers.[34]

UKUSA also touched on codemaking as well as codebreaking. Weak Commonwealth security had a huge bearing on cryptographic sharing within UKUSA. By early 1949 London was willing to offer Australia details of the cryptographic principles and also 'research aimed to improve current U.K. cypher systems', but details from combined US-UK systems could be handed over only on approval from Washington. There was a distinct hierarchy and the new Commonwealth was out in the cold. India, Pakistan and Ceylon were not permitted anything over and above what they were in possession of in August 1947. Perhaps worried by the Commonwealth factor, the US Joint Chiefs of Staff decided to keep a separate set of cipher systems that were for American communications only. In October 1949 London proposed a full and complete interchange of cryptographic principles, but the idea was rejected by Washington.[35]

Lurking beneath this was the suspicion that Britain and the United States might attack each other's communications. Extensive work on the French and the Dutch naturally inspired such fears. Moreover, there was historical precedent. In the period up until December 1941 British codebreakers had certainly been busy working on American diplomatic systems such as Grey. American intelligence liaison staff in London, who were beginning to put together the early stages of co-operation against the Axis, were amused, rather than alarmed, by the complications that this generated. Some were convinced that, once joined together in a war against the Axis, London would have more interest in the total security of all American systems. But in practice British anxiety to ensure American cipher security extended only to those systems carrying Ultra and Magic. There are some indications that the British continued to undertake limited wartime work on medium-grade American communications. John Croft recalled some work ongoing on American systems at Berkeley Street during the war. Predictably, clear traffic from American oil companies was also being intercepted in 1944 as they began to look for new markets in Europe.[36]

Counter-measures had to be taken. In 1948 and 1949 Whitehall regularly received instructions on the use of the word 'Guard', a term used on documents 'which must never, so far as can be foreseen, be disclosed to the Americans'. Washington used a similar term 'Control' for the same purpose, a term later replaced by 'Noforn' or no foreign eyes. The general purpose was to prevent 'embarrassment of relations' between London and Washington and also 'to preserve certain sources of intelligence'. Subjects for the use of Guard included discussion of senior US personalities or matters 'affecting British trade interests, in which the Americans might be our rivals'. Interestingly, these telegrams required 'special cypher precautions'. Moreover, any details of communication security including 'instructions on British cypher systems' were also to be given the Guard treatment. London thought it probable that the United States would try and read British communications if it could. The whole business had a surreal quality because the existence of the word Guard itself had to be 'guarded'. When sending such material by post 'two envelopes must always be used' and 'the inner envelope only must be marked "GUARD"'.[37] The use of Guard and Control soon became widely known to officials on both sides of the Atlantic. Nevertheless, leaving the word Guard off documents could have disastrous consequences. One of Churchill's wartime telegrams about controversial activities in Greece was sent without Guard and made its way quickly round an inter-Allied HQ and thence into the hands of American journalists like Drew Pearson, who made much of it. Perhaps for this reason, even in his second administration Churchill 'had a phobia about the procedures surrounding the use of Guard'.[38]

Although GCHQ representatives were often overawed by the scale of American sigint resources, matters looked quite different from Washington. Here there were several types of trouble. With the war over, and an economising Republican Congress controlling the federal purse strings, resources for American comint – or communications intelligence – interception activities were remarkably tight before 1950. This led to a state of parlous under-preparedness prior to the Korean War. It also prevented the European expansion that American sigint had hoped for. In 1949, Army Security Agency interception units in Europe were still passing their product to GCHQ rather than back to Washington for analysis. GCHQ retained primary responsibility for areas such as Eastern Europe, the Near East and Africa.[39]

Yet financial stringency did not prevent the two American armed services responsible for sigint from continuing their notorious wartime rivalry. In 1947, they were joined by a newly independent US Air Force. The creation of a US Air Force sigint outfit prompted James Forrestal, the Secretary of Defense, to launch an enquiry into sigint in August 1948, chaired by Admiral Earl E. Stone. Composed of officers from the three services the board was hopelessly split from the outset. Only the Army took a rational position, urging a unified cryptological service, contrasting Britain's co-ordinated GCHQ with what it called the 'hydra headed German wartime COMINT effort'. The Stone Board produced a divided report and Forrestal buried it. It was unearthed by his successor, Louis Johnson, in March 1949. Under more pressure from Congress for budget savings the Army plan for consolidation looked good and was now recommended to Truman. Truman urged, 'So be it. Go back and fix up the orders.' In the words of an American internal history: 'Then the screaming started.' The Air Force and, in particular, the Navy had no wish to be relieved of their most precious intelligence assets. So while a centralised Armed Forces Security Agency (AFSA) was set up on 20 May 1949 it was a weakling, undermined by jealous service chiefs and by the Congressional budget cuts which had caused it to be created. Perversely, AFSA became an unwanted fourth service, ineffectually trying to co-ordinate, but not commanding, fragmented American sigint. For GCHQ, the task of liaising with this multiple entity was becoming more difficult.[40]

Allied exchange of comint was of several types. A narrow range of comint-producing agencies exchanged all manner of material, both raw and processed. A much wider range of bodies circulated the finished product. The key instrument was the 'comintsum' – a digest of the latest 'hot' material – which made its way around comint-cleared centres. London would send twenty copies of this document to Washington on a regular basis, with two copies going to Air Force Intelligence, two to Army Intelligence and so forth.[41] The UKUSA agreements of 1948 simply codified and smoothed out what was clearly a pre-existing practice. As early as 28 April 1948, General Charles P. Cabell, the new chief of USAF Intelligence, reviewed the comint arrangements in support of the atomic strike plan Halfmoon. 'At the present time,' he noted with satisfaction, 'there is complete interchange of communications intelligence information between the cognisant United States and British agencies. It is not believed that the present arrangements … could be improved.'[42]

More mysterious is British and American co-operation with obscure 'third parties'. The recovery of a range of sigint files from the Baltic states at the end of the war – codenamed Stella Polaris – was a fascinating aspect of this issue. In May 1946, American naval codebreakers received reports that the Stella Polaris files originally contained a range of American State Department and military codes obtained from the American Embassy in Sofia and elsewhere. Reports varied as to where these came from, perhaps the Russians, the Japanese or the Hungarians, but the consensus was that they had been obtained by bribery. Stella Polaris was also reported to have obtained a great many other codes from the head of the Hungarian sigint unit, General Petrikovicz. It was widely believed that much of the Stella Polaris material had now been transferred from Stockholm to a new French sigint centre based at 9 Avenue du Maréchal Maunouroy in Paris.[43]

Stella Polaris material, together with other fragments of Soviet codebooks, was fed into the most important Anglo-American sigint programme codenamed Venona, which, as we have seen, would be producing the names of Soviet spies in the West by 1948. This was an attempt to exploit weak operational practice in Soviet intelligence traffic. Periodically short of fresh enciphering materials the Soviets had abused their theoretically very secure one-time pad system and re-used materials that were safe only if used once. Occasionally, there were periodic leaps forward for those working on an otherwise mind-numbing difficult task that offered only partial breaks into a small percentage of MGB messages. Gouzenkou – a cipher clerk – brought over material which allowed the decrypting of other messages that he did not have copies of, but which had been recorded by the West before his defection. The same was true of the Australian cases. Here the controversial and speculative PHP papers from 1944 and 1945, which had caused so much trouble in Whitehall, for the first time proved really useful, though perhaps not in a manner which the authors had intended. Makarov, the MGB chief in Australia, considered his purloining of PHP papers to be such an important coup that he asked Moscow for permission to send them by cipher rather than courier. Moscow intelligence chiefs had indeed been delighted by this material. But two long PHP papers, 'Security in the Western Mediterranean and the Eastern Atlantic' and 'Security of India and the Indian Ocean', provided the West with a vast word-for-word crib to get into much other Soviet traffic from Australia for that period. The Australian dimension of Venona, together with the need for copies of sensitive British wartime documents to attack it, speeded up Anglo-American co-operation in this area.[44]

Although the British and the Americans had been working on MGB traffic continuously from 1945, they began to collaborate on Venona only in late 1947. The breaks were now sufficient to show that during the war agents with access to British and American secrets had compromised an immense quantity of material. In early 1948 Venona offered its first tantalising clues to the possibility of spies within the British Foreign Office and in various Commonwealth governments. It was not until three years later, in the spring of 1951, that their precise identities were uncovered. Yet Philby, Burgess and Maclean eluded the authorities. On Friday, 25 May, Donald Maclean and Guy Burgess headed for the continent, tipped off that the net was closing in on them. Remarkably, Kim Philby, suspected of involvement, remained and bluffed it out. This denied Venona the fruits of more than three years of Anglo-American cryptanalytical struggle.

But it was another Friday, three years earlier, that had marked the greatest disaster for British and American sigint. On Friday, 29 October 1948, just as Venona really began to produce some dividends, the Soviets implemented a massive change in all their communications security procedures. All radio nets, including military systems, moved over to one-time pads, which henceforth were not re-used. Much of the procedural material that had been sent 'in clear' between operators running medium-grade Army, Navy, Air Force and police systems in the Soviet bloc was now encrypted for the first time. Operator chatter was banned. Over a period of twenty-four hours, almost every Soviet system from which the East was deriving intelligence was lost. This included new Venona messages. The wipeout was almost total. In 1955 when the CIA and SIS began their famous operation to tunnel under East Berlin to tap into Soviet telephone communications, one of the motives was to try and claw back some of the ground lost. The CIA remarked that this new operation 'provided the United States and the British with a unique source of intelligence on the Soviet orbit of a kind and quality which had not been available since 1948'. Accordingly American cryptographers referred to the fateful events of Friday, 29 October 1948 as 'Black Friday'.[45]

The instigator of 'Black Friday' had been William Weisband, a US Army Security Agency cipher clerk. Weisband had been recruited by the Soviets as an agent in 1947, but his espionage was not discovered until 1950. Although the evidence against him was complete and compelling, he was not prosecuted for fear of advertising the work of signals intelligence to other countries which might take similar steps to upgrade their communications.[46] Weisband is little known, yet the wider impact of his espionage, perhaps some of the most damaging Soviet agent activity of the early Cold War, offers some important insights into signals intelligence. Like Tyler Kent, the valuable agent the Soviets had recruited in London in the early 1930s, he was a lowly functionary in a cipher unit, not a high-level agent. Now, clearly, checking the reliability only of senior officials was no longer enough and, as the Cold War organisms expanded remorselessly, the problem of vetting and clearing all staff in their teeming thousands became an insurmountable problem for the West. Weisband also probably helped to trigger a rethink on Western approaches to busting Soviet communications. Hitherto Britain and the United States gained most of their successes against Soviet communications by the sweat of cryptanalysis. By contrast the Soviets broke into some high-level traffic because their agents repeatedly obtained the solutions, and because the Soviets were very good at bugging diplomatic premises, including the code-rooms of embassies. It is likely that the most damaging work of high-level Soviet agents in the West was when they served as facilitators of Soviet sigint, opening back doors to the interception of thousands of sensitive messages. By the 1950s the West was trying to move down the same track.[47]

The closest Anglo-American signals intelligence relationship during the immediate post-war period was that developed between the RAF and the US Air Force. General Charles Cabell, chief of US Air Force Intelligence in 1948, found RAF Intelligence under the convivial Lawrie Pendred to be an ideal partner for his newly independent service. This growing friendship also reflected the fact that GCHQ had identified air power as a critical area for sigint, especially those arcane forms of sigint associated with strategic bombing. Sigint in the air was one of the major growth areas of the early intelligence Cold War. Air Intelligence was keen to develop elint or electronic intelligence. This involved the interception of electronic signals that did not carry messages, but instead offered information about subjects such as radar sites and air defences. Such information was invaluable for the operational planning of air attack against the Soviet Union. It was equally invaluable to anyone planning peacetime spy-flights in Soviet airspace and looking for gaps in Soviet radar cover. Thus, in this area, air intelligence collectors were also consumers, not least to protect the security of their own sensitive and dangerous overflight missions. Elint was developed by Professor R. V. Jones in the face of radio-guided German air raids during the Second World War and was later sited at the Central Signals Establishment at RAF Watton in Norfolk.[48] Towards the end of the war it was refined against Japan. An elaborate elint unit was set up under Mountbatten's South East Asia Command (SEAC) under the improbable cover-name of the Noise Investigation Bureau, and early elint-equipped listening aircraft known as Ferrets patrolled the night skies over Rangoon and then Singapore listening to Japanese radars in the spring and summer of 1945. Ferrets were odd aircraft with a myriad of domes, bulges and aerials on the outside, while inside they looked like a primitive flying laboratory, cluttered with oscilloscopes and every conceivable type of electronic apparatus.[49]

The Anglo-American elint exchange began early. General Curtis LeMay had been given permission to begin trading elint with the British on an informal basis at the end of 1947, but it is likely that co-operation began even earlier. By 1948 elint-sharing was being brought within the growing body of Western signals intelligence agreements. At this time GCHQ was attempting to extend its control over elint activity by the armed services and approached Washington with a proposal to 'extend the present British–U.S. Comint collaboration to include countermeasures, intercept activities and intelligence' in the field of elint. This was put forward by Colonel Marr-Johnston, the GCHQ Liaison Officer in Washington, who then negotiated with Captain J. Wenger, a senior US naval cryptanalyst. He suggested co-ordinated patterns of ferret flights with the resulting intelligence being swapped 'via Comint channels'. By 1952 GCHQ had achieved complete control over elint in the UK and was managing relations with the Americans in this field.[50]

Initially, the RAF was ahead of the US Air Force in elint. Britain's wartime elint work had largely been carried out by 100 Group. This was run down immediately after the war, but by September 1946 things were undergoing a revival and the remaining expertise was pooled into a new 90 Group together with a Radio Warfare Establishment co-located with the Central Signals Establishment at RAF Watton, with a satellite station at Shepherds Grove.[51] By 1947 a fleet of specially equipped Lancaster and Lincoln aircraft was patrolling the East German border, complemented by the monitoring of basic low-level Soviet voice traffic by ground stations at locations such as RAF Gatow in Berlin. British ferrets began their first forays into the Baltic in June 1948 and into the Black Sea in September 1948. Other flights operated out of RAF Habbaniya in Iraq.[52] In 1948 they began to be supplemented by new American ferret variants of the B-29 flying missions from Scotland to the Spitzbergen area. From 1950 B-29 ferrets were also supplied to the RAF and renamed Washingtons under the Mutual Assistance Act.[53] Much of the perimeter of the Soviet Union was covered by a British undercover team operating in northern Iran monitoring Soviet radar in the Caucasus, as well as Soviet missile tests at Kapustin Yar on the edge of the Caspian Sea. The team conducting this activity were posing as archaeologists, a favourite British cover for all sorts of intelligence-gathering, including atomic intelligence work ongoing in India at the same time. This information was useful for RAF crews flying aerial reconnaissance of this area from bases in Crete from 1948.[54] Their US partners had not been inactive. In July 1946 the first post-war American elint operations with ferret aircraft were launched from Thule airbase in Greenland. The early flights were designed to test new airborne equipment with a view to beginning to map emissions in the polar region, where gaps in Soviet radar cover were suspected. This activity – appropriately codenamed Project Nanook – was run jointly by the Army Security Agency and Strategic Air

Command. But it would be 1947 before the US Air Force came into being with its own sigint unit, the Air Force Security Service (AFSS).[55]

Early Western elint efforts in the air were spurred on by the knowledge that the Soviets had launched their own ferret programme. In April 1948 an American radar station in Germany reported that it was being probed by ferret aircraft, and in November 1948 a Soviet aircraft circled a US radar station at Hokkaido in Japan for an hour and then escaped without interception due to bad weather. Defectors also brought teasing snippets. In May 1948, Václav Cukr, General Secretary of the Czech Air Force Association, escaped to the West with information about a group of Dakota-like aircraft at Zote airfield outside Prague. These mysterious aircraft were kept under constant guard in 'special hangars' and had 'several special antennae on the outside of the plane'.[56]

At sea an even more sensitive signals-collection programme was under way. Much of what London and Washington knew about the Soviet Navy had been derived from captured German material, or from what the British had gleaned from their uncommonly good relations with the Soviet Navy during the war. But by 1948 this information was becoming outdated. The US Navy decided to send two submarines into the Barents Sea to test the possibility of intercepting Soviet signals off the major Arctic ports. In August 1949 it sent two further boats, modified with the latest snorkels, to see if they could monitor missile tests in the same area. The specialist equipment was installed in the USS *Cochino* (Spanish for pig) by the British at Portsmouth, but was operated by US Naval Security Group personnel. In August 1949 the USS *Cochino*, escorted by three other submarines, headed for Arctic waters. However, water poured in through a malfunctioning snorkel and a serious battery fire developed and burned for fifteen hours. Despite a rescue by the USS *Tusk* in the stormy seas off the Norwegian coast, seven crew were lost and the *Cochino* sank in 950 feet of water. These were the first casualties in one of the most secretive and dangerous areas of Cold War signals intelligence activity. But London and Washington were not deterred by these inauspicious beginnings, and by the early 1950s the British and American sigint submarines were regular visitors to the headquarters of the Soviet Atlantic and Pacific fleets.[57]

The Royal Navy also conducted surface operations around the Soviet northern periphery. In October and November 1949, the cruiser HMS *Superb* undertook a month-long elint investigation of the Kola Peninsula and the naval base of Murmansk. The Royal Navy also maintained a chain of fixed stations in the UK and a forward listening station at Kiel on the Baltic.[58] The destruction of US Navy elint aircraft off the coast of Latvia in April 1950 while they were trying to identify new Soviet missile bases seemed to indicate that aerial collection in these areas was more hazardous than ship-based or submarine-based work. Further missions were postponed, but the outbreak of the Korean War resulted in enhanced demand for intelligence, and operations resumed. From 1952 onwards much of this work was carried out by American RB-50Gs operating out of Lakenheath in Suffolk.[59]

Elint in northern areas was a multinational activity. During the war, Bletchley Park had worked with the Norwegians and, as we have seen, by 1946 the RAF was assisting the Swedish Air Force in investigating what were thought to be Soviet rocket tests that had intruded into Swedish airspace. Washington took responsibility for co-operation with the Norwegians and encouraged reconnaissance in the area of Murmansk and Novaya Zemlya. By January 1949, detailed material on Soviet radars from Swedish intelligence was making its way to Washington via British representatives who had taken responsibility for co-operation with Sweden. There was particular interest in the possibility that the Soviets might be attempting the further development of German stealth technology, such as radar-absorbent coverings for submarine periscopes and snorkels.[60]

The Korean War prompted a major expansion of bomber command communications and navigation which in return demanded a greater elint and comint input. Some elint could be monitored from sites in Britain, and these were expanded. The 47th Radio Squadron of the US AFSS opened a station at Kirknewton airbase in Scotland listening to activity around the Kola Peninsula. But a great deal of traffic was short range, requiring collection by ships and aircraft. Elint had become so large that liaison arrangements had to be expanded and London proposed the appointment of an additional officer, Squadron Leader J. R. Mitchell, as 'liaison officer for GCHQ' specialising in elint. Washington agreed and appointed William Trites and Forrest G. Hogg to equivalent roles in Britain.[61]

The comint and elint effort against the Soviet Air Force and associated nuclear strategic systems was one of GCHQ's key achievements in the first post-war decade. Although the imminent arrival of the first Soviet atomic bomb went undetected, the deployment of an atomic-armed Soviet strategic air force certainly did not. During the late 1940s and early 1950s the JIB in London and the USAF target intelligence staffs had been busy exchanging sensitive data on 'the mission of blunting the Soviet atomic offensive'. This involved the early counter-force targeting of Soviet nuclear forces in the hope of destroying them on the ground before they could be used. This was politically sensitive because it raised the issue of the use of nuclear weapons at an early stage in any future conflict. Nevertheless, senior RAF officers in London gave particular attention to this matter because of the vulnerability of the UK.

Washington was impressed by the 'considerable progress that London had made on the counter atomic problem'. Here GCHQ and the RAF had amassed 'a significant amount of evaluated intelligence, particularly in the special intelligence field, which would be of the greatest value'. Most of the airfields and the operational procedures for Soviet strategic air forces in the European theatre had been mapped by 1952.[62] Indeed, during the immediate post-war years there were substantial sigint successes in the area of the Soviet order of battle on the ground and at sea, as well as in the air. The full Anglo-American intelligence exchange in the atomic counter-targeting field was somewhat ironic given the different views held in London and Washington on nuclear strategic issues by 1949, views which continued to diverge thereafter. However, full intelligence exchange on targets carried on regardless. Although Soviet atomic weapons and strategic delivery systems remained GCHQ's top targets, it worked on a most diverse range of subjects. In the late 1940s it was also engaged in Britain's end-of-Empire struggles, including the vicious guerrilla war in progress in Palestine.

12

Defeat in Palestine

The Stern Group is a gang of desperadoes 300 to 500 strong: its speciality is assassination.

Joint Intelligence Committee, 9 September 1947[1]

GCHQ was not only busy with the Cold War, it was engaged in Britain's hot wars of decolonisation across the Empire. Between 1945 and the outbreak of the Korean War in 1950, Britain's sigint specialists were busy on a remarkable range of tasks around the world. In Palestine, Malaya and other remote locations, GCHQ – together with the remnants of Britain's very secret wartime deception organisation – was brought out to engage some unlikely enemies. Britain's wartime deception had been run by London Controlling Section, the main centre for orchestrating the complex deception operations by MI5, SIS, Bletchley Park and others that had masked Eisenhower's successful assault on the Normandy beaches in 1944. At the end of the war it had been preserved on a care-and-maintenance basis. A small number of staff kept the techniques of strategic deception alive, compiled dossiers on the deception lessons of the last war and drew up strategic deception plans for the next. But by July 1947, with Britain under extreme pressure from a mounting guerrilla war with the Jewish underground in Palestine, London Controlling Section, now renamed the Hollis Committee, considered a more active role.

London Controlling Section drafted plans to frustrate the ships carrying illegal immigrants from Europe to Palestine. Immigrants were placing a strain on the authorities, and the experienced fighters among them were being quickly absorbed into the underground. The British plan was to try to misdirect ships by the use of false radio messages, causing them to be intercepted by the Royal Navy. Eventually the idea was rejected as fraught with all sorts of political dangers. Equally worrying was the likelihood that this sort of trick would soon be exposed for what it was. The result would probably be that the Jewish organisations would 'change their frequencies and codes' to prevent radio monitoring 'with a consequent loss of Signals intelligence to ourselves'. The London Signals Intelligence Committee was unwilling to 'blow' its capabilities in this area unless ordered by a higher authority. Together with aerial reconnaissance, it was already allowing many ships to be caught and turned back.[2]

Despite the attentions of GCHQ, London Controlling Section, aerial reconnaissance and other arcane organisations, Palestine was the intelligence war that Britain lost. The British security forces outnumbered their adversaries by more than twenty to one, a better ratio than Britain enjoyed later in its successful campaign against the guerrillas in Malaya (seventeen to one). In 1948 the Army blamed its numbing defeat on restrictions imposed by London and by the civil authorities in Palestine which tied its hands and obstructed a 'get tough' policy. But this was not the case. In reality, getting tough had never paid dividends; instead it was intelligence failure that played a large part in explaining the débâcle.[3] Not only was British intelligence poor, but the JIC had to concede by September 1947 that the Irgun, the main underground opposition, could deploy between 5,000 and 6,000 fighters who were 'well trained in street-fighting and sabotage'. Moreover, the Irgun's own intelligence organisation contained many who had cut their operational teeth in the European War and were, the JIC lamented, 'excellent'. Indeed some of those serving with both the official Haganah and the Irgun had previously worked for SIS or SOE.[4]

Trouble had begun in 1919 when Britain was mandated Palestine by the League of Nations and opened the territory up to Jewish immigration. The shifting balance of the population and contradictory agreements resulted in unrest and violent riots. There followed the creation of underground Jewish military organisations such as the Irgun that rejected the moderate Jewish line and demanded the immediate creation of a Jewish state. By 1939 the Irgun had already begun to turn its violence from the rival Arabs on to the British, but the advent of the Second World War highlighted their common cause against Germany and a temporary ceasefire followed. The Irgun was fragmented, however, and its ceasefire was not observed by all. One of its leaders, Colonel Abraham Stern, led a breakaway group determined to continue the fight against the British. Stern's group was initially known as the Lehi group and only later as the Stern Gang. These groups were small, numbering no more than 4,500, and they did not enjoy the support of the majority of the Jewish population. Meanwhile, the official Jewish Agency trained its own legally established armed forces, the Haganah and the more elite Palmach, for war against the Axis. The underground Irgun also limited itself to secret arming and training during the early years of the war.

The British eliminated Abraham Stern in 1942. The public story was that Stern had been shot while trying to escape capture. Privately the British told American officers of OSS serving in the Middle East the full story. The British had in fact 'discovered Stern's hiding place and he was surrounded and caught unarmed. He raised his arms to surrender, but was drilled through and through by the police. Their explanation (unofficially) is that they could take no chances with such a dangerous character ... therefore, they liquidated him on the spot.'[5] The Stern Gang apart, during the war the Army had pursued a relaxed policy towards most armed Zionist groups, which was a legacy from an alliance against the Arab revolt in Palestine during the late 1930s and so a *de facto* truce was in operation. But by 1944, with the German threat banished from the Middle East, the Irgun was free to resume its anti-British position. After years of quiet re-arming its ranks were bolstered by new refugees, including Menachem Begin, who had arrived from Poland to become the Irgun commander in 1943. In February 1944 the informal truce was broken dramatically with well-organised attacks on police and tax offices which revealed good guerrilla intelligence and excellent organisation. Matters were made worse by the manner in which different groups competed against each other, prompting the selection of high-profile targets.[6]

Even in 1944, the policing and intelligence system in Palestine, last revised in 1938 by Sir David Petrie, who was soon to become wartime director of MI5, was focused on the rural Arabs not on the urban Jewish population. This meant that the police spoke Arabic rather than the bewildering range of languages spoken by the Jewish immigrants. The police CID – the main intelligence-gathering force – had successes. It infiltrated the Haganah and the Palmach and always had the minutes of the Jewish Agency executive within hours of its meetings. Its messages to the World Zionist Organisation in London were also intercepted. But the cell structure of the Irgun and Lehi frustrated it, and this was reflected in the JIC's inflated estimates of their numbers – three times their real size.[7]

On 8 August 1944 the High Commissioner for Palestine, Sir Ronald MacMichael, narrowly escaped death at the hands of Lehi gunmen during an attack on his motorcade. Undeterred, the Lehi turned its attention to a bigger target, the British Minister of State for the Middle East, Lord Moyne. On 6 November 1944, two members of the Lehi murdered Moyne in Cairo as he arrived to keep a luncheon engagement. Many in Cairo, including Moyne's successor, Lord Killearn, pressed for a tough response. Although his killers were executed, Churchill ordered restraint, knowing that sweeping and systematic searches would drive more in to the arms of the guerrillas. Counter-terrorism remained a matter for the police, while the Army was to be used as mobile columns to support them in emergencies. Fighting now subsided until the end of the Second

World War. After the murder of Lord Moyne in Cairo, Egyptian security, which was heavily supervised by the British, tried to turn one of Moyne's assassins, Eliahu Beth-Tsouri. But he replied that he could not help even if he had wanted to. Everyone in his group had false addresses and false names and no one really knew who they were working with. Tom Wilkin, the only British policeman who was sufficiently integrated into Jewish society to make any inroads in infiltrating the Lehi, was assassinated by them in September 1944.[8]

Indeed, the British intelligence system, as other historians have discovered, although rumoured to be omnipresent in the Middle East, lived off its reputation and was in fact very weak. What should have been the cutting edge, the Political Section of CID – effectively the Special Branch – was very small and had almost no Hebrew or Yiddish speakers. There was also a local MI5 office – the Defence Security Office – but this was staffed not by well-trained regular MI5 staff, who were already over-stretched elsewhere, but by enterprising amateurs who were seconded to the unit. There were a myriad of Army intelligence outfits including General Staff Intelligence and Field Security Units. Not for the first time, Army and police did not co-operate in an ideal fashion, a problem that would resurface in Malaya by 1948. Their tendency to work alone was reinforced by enemy penetration. As the security intelligence well knew, government offices themselves contained agents of the underground, and classified material was making its way to their opponents.

But this was only half the problem. Their adversaries were small but of high quality. Although the British had interrogation centres for processing prisoners, little information was extracted and, crucially, almost no one was turned. Some in the Jewish Agency warned the British of violent attacks of which they did not approve, but this was rare. In contrast to the fighting in Ireland in the 1920s and in Malaya and Kenya in the 1950s, it was impossible to get members of the Irgun or the Stern Gang to offer information or to broadcast propaganda, still less to become members of counter-gangs or pseudo-gangs. In Kenya, for example, the ability to get terrorists to become active counter-terrorists was a 'critical aspect' of success. For this reason, the undercover work attempted in Palestine was often as directionless as the overt sweep and search, blundering about in the hope of a contact.[9]

The end of the war in 1945 had brought the Labour government of Clement Attlee to power. Although Attlee was committed to dispersing the Empire as quickly as possible – especially Palestine – he was blocked by Bevin and Montgomery. Although these latter figures did not see eye to eye, for different reasons they both wanted Britain to hang on to footholds in the Middle East. Montgomery was the most fervent. In early 1947 he threatened Attlee with the mass resignation of the Chiefs of Staff over Middle East defence issues – which might have brought the precarious Attlee government down – and so got his way.[10] But Zionist groups were now determined to evict the British. The end of the war saw the underground groups more anxious to force the British government to a decision on Palestine, and violence escalated once more. Already well armed, their stocks were supplemented by easy raids on service depots. SIME, the MI5 umbrella organisation in the Middle East, suspected them of being responsible for a raid on an RAF station on the night of 25 November 1945 when they helped themselves to eight Vickers machine guns and sixty-one Sten guns. SIME reckoned that the armoury of one of the guerrilla organisations, the Irgun, ran to run to 2,000 rifles, 270 sub-machine guns and 300 pistols.[11]

Montgomery sent the tough British 6th Airborne Division to Palestine. But the Army tactics were still those used during the Arab rebellion of the 1930s. This rebellion had been largely rural, had involved obvious military formations and had been supported by most of the Arab population. Opponents, both military and civilian, had been easy to identify and punish. But the Jewish underground chose an urban strategy and constituted only a small proportion of the population. Matters were made worse by changes at the top. There had been friction between the military command and the civilian administration. The Colonial Office chose a new police chief from the ranks of the military, selecting Colonel Nicol Gray, a former Royal Marine who had seen much front-line action in Europe. Gray was a man of action and had little time for subtle intelligence work.[12]

Action certainly followed and between April and July 1946 an accelerating cycle of incident and reprisal developed. In March 1946 the Irgun raided one of the largest military bases in the Middle East at Sarafand, held up a quartermaster and walked off with the contents of one of the armouries. On 23 April an attack on a police station left three dead. Two days later six soldiers from the 6th Airborne Division were killed in their tented encampment. Pressure for arbitrary retaliation was building within the ranks of the British forces. In mid-June a wave of attacks destroyed five trains and ten of the eleven bridges connecting Palestine to neighbouring states. Then on 18 June, when two captured Irgun members were sentenced, six British officers were seized in retaliation. On 29 June, known as 'Black Saturday', London's restraint broke down. Widespread raids netted 2,700 of the overt leaders and members of the Jewish Agency, but no Irgun leaders nor the missing British officers.

The British arrests came as the various underground groups were planning a bomb attack on government offices at the King David Hotel in Jerusalem. Many were anxious to hold off, but Menachem Begin was keen to go ahead. The importance of reprisal against British action was critical, he argued. Begin was also worried about documents captured in earlier raids and now held in government offices located in the King David Hotel, which would reveal the links between political figures such as David Ben-Gurion and the underground groups. He wanted them destroyed before the British could make them public. Most importantly he feared that the operation would be blown unless it went ahead soon. On 22 July 1946, six young members of the Irgun entered the basement of the hotel. They appeared to be delivering churns of milk, but these were packed with 500lb of explosive. At 12.37 p.m. an explosion sheared off all of the south wing, causing ninety-one deaths and forty-five further casualties. Several sections of the Palestine government were completely destroyed. The King David Hotel was also the nerve centre of the British anti-terrorist effort and this attack marked a devastating blow. Large-scale cordon and search operations began in Tel Aviv. But all these operations left the key underground organisations more or less untouched.[13]

General Cunningham, the Army commander, told London in November that he opposed general reprisals against the population, having seen 'the examples in Ireland and even the Arab Rebellion'. Instead he had obtained the advice of 'an expert' with a view to improving the chances of hunting the individuals concerned and 'catching them on the job'. Cunningham wanted to get advance warning of attacks and then eliminate the perpetrators – he insisted that 'I have always been clear that the best method of dealing with terrorists is to kill them.' But all this depended on excellent advance intelligence warning of specific attacks, which he did not have.[14]

From late 1946 through until March 1947 terrorist attacks continued against the background of an intense argument in London. The military led by Montgomery argued for a tougher policy, while the Colonial Office argued that such an approach would generate recruits for the terrorists. Montgomery obtained his wish on 2 March 1947, when martial law was declared in Tel Aviv and in the Jewish quarter of Jerusalem. By bringing economic life to a halt, the Army hoped to pressurise the majority of the Jewish population to expose the committed terrorists in the underground. But the principal result of this approach was to end all Jewish co-operation against the attacks. The underground seemed doubly anxious to prove that martial law was a failure, and the volume of attacks increased.

On 11 July 1947 the Irgun captured two British sergeants from Army Intelligence in Natanya, Cliff Martin and Mervyn Paice, who had been working for Field Security. The Irgun used them as hostages against three of their members awaiting execution after being convicted of terrorism. On 19 July the three Irgun members were executed, and two days later the bodies of the two sergeants were found hanging in an orange grove. Booby-traps had been planted on the bodies and an officer was badly injured while recovering them. Passions now boiled over and policemen in Tel Aviv went on the rampage. Rioting developed and before order was restored five Jews had been killed and sixteen injured, and many Jewish shops had been burned down. An armoured car was driven through a funeral procession and the police fired on a bus, a taxi and a crowded café. However, the underground had won, for there were no more executions of terrorists. This was probably the turning point in the campaign and the British press now began calling for withdrawal from a campaign which, they concluded, could not be won by military means.[15]

Not all British revenge attacks were spontaneous. The particular problems of insurgency and terrorism promoted a demand in some quarters for special units to take the war to the enemy. As would prove repeatedly to be the case, this call came not only from the regular military but from the locally raised units and police forces, who often felt the regular military were not up to the job, or from ex-members of the special forces who felt that a fresh approach was needed. In February 1947, Brigadier Bernard Fergusson, a senior officer in the Palestine Police who had served with General Orde Wingate and the Chindits behind enemy lines in Burma, explained to the Colonial Office that a special paramilitary police unit was being formed. Wartime SOE and SAS officers made up its core: 'There is in the Army a small number of Officers who have both the technical and physical knowledge of terrorism, having themselves been engaged in similar operations on what may be termed the terrorist side in countries occupied by the enemy in the late war.' He explained that there had been frequent occasions recently when the scale of terrorist action had been very substantial, 'necessitating special measures for which normal resources and organisations are inadequate'. Fergusson himself was a special forces enthusiast and would soon move on to look after these issues at SHAPE HQ, and would superintend political warfare during the Suez Campaign.[16] Roy Farran was a leader of one of these special police squads. He recalled his exhilaration as he was given his orders:

> In Jerusalem Police Headquarters the brief was explained to us. We would each have full power to operate as we pleased within our specific areas. We were to advise on defence against terror and to take an active part in hunting the dissidents ... It was to all intents and purposes a carte blanche and the original conception of our part filled me with excitement. A free hand for us against terror when all others were so closely hobbled![17]

The squads operated for some weeks. They dressed up as members of the Jewish population and roamed about in delivery vans planning ambushes and meeting with some success.

But soon they were embroiled in the Rubowitz Case. In May 1947, Alexander Rubowitz, a sixteen-year-old-member of the Lehi, was abducted in a taxi and did not resurface. Accusations were made and the squads were stood down. Meanwhile Farran was suspected of involvement and fled abroad to Syria. Offered immunity from arrest by Fergusson, he returned only to be arrested. London was told nothing for three weeks, to the eventual fury of Arthur Creech Jones, the Colonial Secretary. A farcical court-martial followed at which Fergusson refused to give evidence and Farran's written version of events, penned in his cell, was ruled inadmissible. After his inevitable acquittal, he was required to resign his commission. As a grand finale, Fergusson flew the senior police officers out over the Mediterranean and threw Farran's 'confessions' into the sea.[18] Other curious activities had been going on for some time. In October 1946 allegations surfaced of substantial illegal arms sales by Army officers to the Arabs. When enquiries were made the two officers named were on the staff of the local MI5 chief, the Defence Security Officer. No action was taken as they were both mysteriously 'on leave' and their return date was unknown.[19]

One of the least enviable tasks for British intelligence was attempting to prevent illegal immigrants passing from Europe to Palestine. They were thought to be swelling the numbers of a population that British forces were already failing to control and providing the guerrillas with further experienced fighters. Yet many of these illegal immigrants were refugees who had endured the full weight of Hitler's assault on the Jews in Europe and were hoping to find sanctuary in a new Jewish state. Turning their ships back was a sorry task, but one increasingly demanded by the British administration in Jerusalem, buckling under the burden of the insurgency being fought on the ground. The main thrust of the intelligence effort against the illegal refugees was provided by sigint together with RAF aerial photo-reconnaissance aircraft. No fewer than four reconnaissance squadrons were moved to Palestine during the campaign. In 1946 this led to the interception of seventeen ships by the Royal Navy, which turned them back to their ports of origin. The Irgun retaliated with attacks on RAF bases in Palestine. Even when the ships were intercepted the situation was not ideal. Some of them could not make it back to their point of departure, and the refugees were then held in unpleasant camps on Cyprus prompting headlines in New York.[20]

Attlee was foremost in demanding action to stop illegal immigration into Palestine, ideally at source. On 31 March 1947, Hector McNeil, Minister of State at the Foreign Office, explained to him that there had been a special meeting to discuss 'ways and means' of stopping the immigration traffic. MI5, SIS, New Scotland Yard, the Colonial Office, the Foreign Office and the Admiralty got together to develop a joint strategy.

McNeil said that they had identified the flow of immigrants from the south of France as a 'running sore' and they had decided to make this location 'the forefront of our attack'. Measures were to be taken in co-operation with the French and liaison was to 'be carried out by the representatives of M.I.6 [SIS] in Paris'.

Attlee was in the mood for action. He wanted the 'utmost pressure' put on the Italians, Greeks and French to stop the departure of ships carrying the immigrants. But he also recognised that mere 'general protests' to these government were likely to be ineffective. 'It is essential that we should take all possible steps to stop this traffic at source,' he insisted. He urged officials to 'think out what practical measures might be taken in each country to prevent the departure of illegal immigrants'. London, he went on, 'should send experts from this country' to assist in devising 'enforcing measures'. By 30 July, British representatives on the spot in Marseilles were trying to induce the French 'to co-operate in some use of force' against the would-be transportees.[21]

Although the language was vague, pressure from the top for direct action was intense. It is difficult to avoid the conclusion that these exhortations from Attlee to 'take all possible steps' – only declassified in 1999 – sit congruently with accounts from several sources that direct action was authorised. Former SOE officers were employed by SIS to attach limpet mines to some of the ships leaving Europe for Israel. The scheme was reportedly devised by Colonel Harold Perkins and implemented by Frederick Vanden Heuvel, who had been the long-serving SIS head of station in Berne. SIS had already felt the heat of the Palestine struggle. It suffered its only post-war active service casualty in Tel Aviv when the underground assassinated Major Desmond Doran – the former head of station in Bucharest – on his balcony with a hand grenade on 9 September 1946. The chance to respond was doubtless welcomed.[22]

Yet against the background of demobilisation and the UK economic crisis of 1947 and an accelerating Cold War in Europe in 1948, the Attlee government could not take the strain. Faced with a choice of increasing troop levels to impose martial law, which would create a furore in the US and at the UN, or withdrawal, it chose the latter. All military personnel were to be gone by May 1948. The Irgun seized its opportunity and carried out a series of massacres against Arab villages in their departing wake.

Even as the British retreated from Palestine, MI5 was looking for ulterior explanations for events there. In September 1948, at a meeting at the Colonial Office, MI5 officers offered their views on 'relations between the Stern Gang and Moscow'. They stressed that Moscow was willing to support the Stern Gang and, 'although not necessarily communist at heart', they would 'gladly accept this support'. But the evidence for such explanations was lacking and they had to concede that there was 'little concrete evidence to show that the Stern Gang received actual material assistance from Russia'. They fell back on vague statements about the Gang's propaganda following the communist line on the subject of Anglo-American imperialism.[23]

American pressure for withdrawal from Palestine had pushed Anglo-American relations to breaking point. Washington refused to act against newspaper advertisements collecting funds to support terrorist groups working against the British. However, the FBI was effective against arms-trafficking. In January 1948 it seized 56 tonnes of explosives *en route* to Tel Aviv. Three months later two men were arrested in New York for attempting to supply some 600 weapons to the Irgun.[24] Meanwhile in Europe the CIA was also aware of illegal air-traffic in arms moving between Prague and customers in Palestine using American crews and American C-54s. They would land in Prague and in one instance the pro-tests of air-traffic controllers were overruled by the 'senior secret police officer who stated that the flight was a government operation'. Some thirty-five heavy crates were loaded on board.[25]

The ordeal suffered by British forces on the ground in Palestine ended on 30 June 1948. The UN decreed that Palestine should be partitioned, resulting in the creation of the State of Israel. A team of UN observers and mediators – UNSCOB – was now responsible for preserving the set-tlement. But tensions with the Israelis remained high, for London had treaty obligations to defend both Egypt and Transjordan. As a result the RAF mounted heavy photo-reconnaissance against Israel throughout this period. In May 1948, a month before the formal birth of the State of Israel, clandestine high-level overflights were ordered by the RAF Commander in the region without reference to London. This reflected rumours about the development of an embryonic Israeli Air Force. The RAF mounted 'P.R. cover every 48 hours Tel Aviv–Jaffa area and Jewish held airfields'. These flights continued into December with the results being passed to the Foreign Office and to the UN Mediator, 'both of whom were glad to have them'. John Slessor, the Chief of the Air Staff, was aware that they were in progress but no Minister was notified.

But in the week before Christmas these flights came to the attention of A. V. Alexander, the Minister of Defence. He was surprised that 'Ministerial authority was never obtained for these flights' and took the matter up with Attlee. Alexander nevertheless argued that they should continue because of Plan Barter, the British secret military scheme to defend Transjordan against attack by Israel. If Britain had to defend Transjordan without these flights it would be forced to 'go into action blindfold'. 'It seems to me that if we refrained from sending our recon-naissance aircraft over this area in the circumstances we should get no thanks from anyone and merely deprive ourselves of important intelligence which may, in certain eventualities, be vital to us … It is my view that we should accept what risk there may be.' Clement Attlee agreed. He accepted their advice, but added two important warnings. He felt it was 'quite wrong to expose unarmed aircraft to the risk of attack' and wanted fighter escorts for all types of reconnaissance work. He also wanted government Ministers to stop calling these sorts of activities 'training flights' when they referred to them in the House of Commons. Clearly, this was a deliberately misleading practice and the real purpose of such flights was 'obvious'.[26]

Alexander responded that armed escorts were not always provided. The high-altitude reconnaissance work was being done by Mosquito aircraft 'which rely on speed and altitude to avoid detection' and to provide escorts would slow them down and attract 'undesirable attention'. He suggested that these high-level flights by Mosquitoes over Israel should continue, but he pointed out that low-level tactical reconnaissance was also 'now taking place over the Egyptian frontier' to map detailed disposition of Israeli land forces and this was done by appropriate fighter aircraft, which could defend themselves. Alexander, Bevin and the Secretary of State for Air, Arthur Henderson, discussed these low-level flights again and agreed they 'should continue until further notice'.[27]

RAF photo-reconnaissance squadrons based in Egypt – also a troubled location – were being used mostly to conduct detailed reconnaissance of the border between Israel and Egypt, which was the focus for a growing number of incidents. The photographic 'take' was made available to multiple customers: the US State Department and also to the UN in New York, as well as to London and to the British Commanders in the Middle East. It was valued by many, but Attlee was nevertheless right to identify this work as hazardous. Disaster followed only a week after Attlee's exhortations. On 7 January 1949, four RAF Spitfires of 208 Squadron were sent out to reconnoitre and photograph an incursion of some twenty miles into Egypt by an Israeli force. Two Spitfires conducted the low-level tactical photography while the others flew above providing a defensive 'cap'. One Spitfire was immediately hit by ground fire. His fellow pilots 'saw him climb up steeply and bale out from his aircraft which was on fire'. Meanwhile the remaining three RAF Spitfires were attacked by Spitfires of the Israeli Air Force, which employed the same camouflage colours and the same distinctive red propeller bosses. They dived on the RAF Spitfires from higher altitude and all were shot down. Of the four pilots on this mission, one was killed, two were captured by the Israelis and one managed to return to Egypt.

At the same time a Mosquito had been carrying out a high-level photo-reconnaissance of the same area, but was escorted by four

Tempest fighters, as Attlee had suggested. This passed off without incident. But later that day a force of thirteen RAF aircraft, searching for the missing Spitfires, was attacked by the Israelis and another RAF aircraft – a Tempest – was lost and the pilot killed. Three other Tempests were hit and damaged in the engagement, but managed to return to base.[28]

This engagement – resulting from intelligence overflights – remains Britain's greatest loss of operational aircraft on a single day since 1945. Unlike the Americans, who lost many reconnaissance aircraft destroyed around the periphery of the Soviet Union, Britain felt the heat in an end-of-Empire conflict. Indeed the overflights took place because of fears of an impending war between Israeli and Transjordan in which Britain and the United States might find themselves supporting opposite sides. This is instructive in terms of the direction of Britain's post-war intelligence effort as a whole. Empire issues were looming larger by 1948 as trouble flared not only in the Middle East but also in Asia.

PART III

The Cold War Turns Hot
1950–1956

13

The Korean War

A war against China, however started, with the express purpose of getting the
Communists out of the saddle, and thus compressing the Soviet orbit, is what
Mr Dulles and Co. appear to be advocating . . .
Foreign Office comments on PUSD 'Sore Spots' review, 22 February 1952[1]

The Korean War erupted early on the morning of Sunday, 25 June
1950 with the surprise invasion of South Korea by North Korea.
Like the detonation of the first Soviet atomic bomb almost a year before,
it took the West completely by surprise. But the deeper resonance came
not from the menacing events of August 1949 but from an earlier surprise attack. It recalled another bitter Sunday morning almost a decade
earlier – the attack on Pearl Harbor. Because there was no warning in
1950 the substantial sums disbursed on secret service did not seem to be
paying dividends and, as with Pearl Harbor, Congress wanted to know
why. Initially the finger of blame was pointed squarely at the CIA. This
reflected its designated centralising and co-ordinating role. It also
reflected deliberate scapegoating during off-the-record briefings by
senior figures such as the Secretary of State, Dean Acheson. Surprise
attack does not always mean intelligence failure and in the Korean case
the small CIA station established in Seoul in 1949 had managed to insert
several dozen agents into North Korea during the pre-existing semi-civil
war. A few agents had survived and returned across the 38th parallel
which divided North from South Korea to report on increased troop
movements and armoured build-ups. This had not led to a direct prediction of the invasion. But it had allowed the CIA to circulate warnings on
20 June about the North Korean mobilisation to members of President
Truman's Cabinet, including Acheson.

Admiral Hillenkoetter, Director of the CIA, knew all about the Sunday-
morning surprise attacks. He had been literally blown out of the water
while serving on the battleship USS *West Virginia* at Pearl Harbor in
December 1941. He now headed for Capitol Hill with 'a stack of

documents' and 'a good story to tell'. With Truman's approval, he was extremely direct in providing Congress with evidence of the prior circulation of these documents. He was eventually able to convince Congress that the CIA had performed adequately, if not with distinction, in Korea. That one Senator initially accused Hillenkoetter of forging the receipt slips for some of these documents testifies to the 'hot' political climate in which intelligence chiefs operated and the constant danger of being selected as a scapegoat in any crisis.[2]

The recriminations of the summer of 1950 obscured the real reasons for intelligence failure. First, although American intelligence had begun to be revived in 1947 following a period of post-war retrenchment, this revival was largely focused on the Marshall Plan and the Berlin blockade, while Asia remained starved of intelligence resources. Secondly, the CIA was in fact the minor player in Asia, battling to re-establish itself after its ejection from its base in mainland China in 1949, but regarded as an alien presence by the immensely jealous and proprietorial General MacArthur, Supreme Commander Allied Powers (SCAP) in Japan. Thirdly, intelligence resources were fragmented and lacked co-ordination.

There had been other intelligence failures in 1950. In early that year, at Truman's request, the CIA had sent out Jay Vanderpool to resolve a dispute between the British and MacArthur's HQ over estimates of the size of the North Korean forces. British intelligence claimed that there were only 36,000 troops, while MacArthur's intelligence claimed 136,000. Vanderpool endorsed the British, but MacArthur was much nearer the true figure.[3] Later, on 6 October, the Chinese Communist Party's Politburo held an emergency session and decided to despatch 'volunteers' to Korea. This was a subtle strategy which involved the introduction of regular Chinese People's Liberation Army (PLA) units wearing their normal uniforms, while preserving the fiction that the war was limited to Korea. But, as late as the 12 October, Truman and Acheson were strongly influenced in their thinking by CIA suggestions that Beijing's threats to intervene were a bluff and that 'there are no convincing indications of an actual Chinese Communist intention to resort to full scale intervention in Korea'. The British JIC in London fared no better in forecasting these matters.[4] All this reflected the fact that the very limited resources in Asia had been largely directed at the Soviets. Little intelligence effort had been directed at China, and effectively none at North Korea.

In the late 1940s a degree of confusion and fragmentation had prevailed in the American post-war intelligence community. Signals intelligence was not centralised, the CIA was still trying to gain control of covert operations from its semi-detached sister organisation OPC, and meanwhile psychological warfare was developing in half a dozen unrelated locations. Most importantly, the three armed services remained the most energetic players in all these fields, ensuring that most activities were duplicated or worse. The bitter experience of the Korean War would eventually enforce a degree of rationalisation.

In Asia the CIA, and its partner OPC, laboured under special handicaps. Working closely with George Kennan's Policy Planning Staff, OPC had focused its efforts on Europe and the Mediterranean, resisting communist encroachment in countries like Italy and France under the auspices of the Marshall Plan, and then embracing ideas of liberation current in London and Washington in 1949. With the exception of Ed Lansdale's successful campaign in the Philippines, OPC had made little impression in Asia. Real obstacles confronted it on that continent. The CIA's predecessor, OSS, had established itself widely in Chiang Kai-shek's Nationalist China by 1945, to the dismay of Chiang's own xenophobic security service. But these OSS stations, which soon became the first CIA stations in Asia, were gradually squeezed as Chinese Nationalist fortunes declined in the ensuing civil war with the communists. The first major CIA station in Asia was codenamed Economic Survey Detachment 44. Commanded by Colonel Amos Moscrip, it was co-located with the US Army's military headquarters at Shanghai, and was eventually ejected in October 1948. Its satellite stations, like the one run by Major John K. Singlaub at Mukden, eventually fled under fire, and only narrowly avoided capture.

But the main CIA problem in Asia was its narrow focus on the Soviets. On 11 December 1947, the improbably named Lloyd George, who superintended the CIA's Far Eastern Division, explained the hierarchy of targets for ESD 44. 'Mr George said that ESD had two fundamental directives, (1) to observe and report on Soviet activities in China and (2) to follow closely Soviet penetration in northern Korea, and one secondary objective, to observe Chinese Communist activities.' In other words Chinese and North Korean activities were of little interest in themselves.[5]

As China fell, it would have been natural for the CIA and OPC to fall back upon American-occupied Japan. But Japan was a feudal kingdom dominated by General MacArthur, SCAP. Here MacArthur enjoyed a fearsome reputation for intolerance towards entities that he did not control. During the Second World War he had frequently boasted that he had not allowed William Donovan's OSS to enter his theatre. He was no less 'jealous' of the CIA, which he 'despised'. During the unhappy period of transition of OSS to CIA, their China stations had been supported by the US Navy Seventh Fleet, rather than the Army, adding an additional layer of revulsion for the partisan MacArthur. The General allowed no more than a handful of CIA to enter Japan. Meanwhile:

MacArthur informed Truman that FECOM's [Far Eastern Command's] own organic intelligence organisation under his trusted aide, Major General Charles Willoughby, was more than sufficient to meet American requirements. He considered the Agency's officers rank amateurs in Asia and let it be known that he and Willoughby combined decades of Far Eastern experience. Any political or military intelligence President Truman might need, they could supply.

MacArthur's ability to truncate the clear global remit of Hillenkoetter's CIA, and Truman's tolerance of his extraordinary arrogance, bore testimony to the formidable unseen political power of wartime combat leaders who were associated in the public mind with victory over the Axis. Even premiers were political pygmies alongside these wartime giants. MacArthur would not permit any substantial CIA presence in Japan. Unbeknown to him, however, the CIA opened an undeclared network of clandestine safe houses in Japan by sending officers like Tom McAnn to Tokyo 'on leave'. But the majority of experienced CIA personnel evacuated in late 1948 were dispersed from China.[6]

Yet MacArthur's own intelligence system was not up to the job. He himself was weak on intelligence and his subordinate, the aristocratic Prussian Willoughby, sarcastically known as 'Sir Charles', was worse. Willoughby was valued by MacArthur for his extreme loyalty, even sycophancy, while his other deficiencies were overlooked. But they were widely known. Even in 1945, British intelligence chiefs had expressed wonderment at his curious attitudes, in particular his complete lack of interest in all but tactical intelligence and his active disregard for anything happening outside his own immediate vicinity. The same phenomenon occurred in 1950, with Korea being regarded by Willoughby as barely on the fringe of his responsibilities.

Willoughby's attentions were directed elsewhere. Dangerously right-wing and an open admirer of Franco, he was obsessed with the problem of domestic communist subversion. This was reflected in the intelligence arrangements at the Dai-Ichi Building in Tokyo. Willoughby lavished attention on the G-2 Intelligence Staff of SCAP which worked on counter-intelligence and domestic security in Japan. By contrast the G-2 Intelligence Staff of FECOM, which had a foreign intelligence role throughout the region, was a Cinderella service, suffering further cutbacks even as the Korean War broke out in 1950. MacArthur had once described Willoughby as 'my lovable fascist'. This was on target, for Willoughby saw communist and Jewish conspiracies everywhere, even in Washington and in the ranks of the SCAP administration itself.[7]

Willoughby's obsession with communist subversion was the source of the distorted situation in Japan. Everything was focused on domestic security, and foreign intelligence languished. The US Army CIC and SCAP G-2 served as apologists for dubious pre-war police figures whom they regarded as 'effective'. They faced down objections from Americans in the civil sections who were anxious to carry forward the project of democratisation and who considered the police guilty of 'outrageous violations' of fundamental human rights. Colonel H. E. Pulliam, head of the G-2 Civil Intelligence Section, offered an uncompromising response: 'Genghis Khan, Cesare Borgia and Charles V had each relied upon a centralized police, Japan should do likewise.' Anti-communism was the key criterion and, he insisted, 'mawkish sentimentality over the individual rights of man' could not sit easily alongside practical considerations in a world of external conflict.[8]

Most intelligence coming to FECOM from the Asian mainland was historical or 'dead' intelligence, obtained from former prisoners, deserters or refugees. This information was often very detailed but it was also out of date. The main sources were Japanese POWs returning from Soviet captivity to Japan, or Chinese refugees fleeing to areas like Hong Kong. Increasingly sophisticated efforts were made to screen this vast human detritus for information. MacArthur's FECOM organisation also hosted a small unit for running human spies called Joint Special Operations Branch, as did the US Air Force. But, like the programmes for processing refugees, their main focus was on Soviet military activity, not on events in China or Korea.[9]

Although Willoughby was not doing much intelligence-gathering outside Japan, he fought others who might. Quite simply, he saw the CIA issue as a continuation of his old feud with William Donovan's OSS. Privately, in a letter to General Al Wedemeyer, a fellow veteran of the war against Japan, he let rip with his old prejudices. CIA officers were either 'complete newcomers … working under various thin covers' who had 'not been in the business long enough', or worse, they were 'left-overs from OSS'. OSS, he insisted 'is obviously the intellectual parent of CIA'. He continued, 'They are out here in our area. I have given them moral support and urge co-operative joint operations; we are of course years ahead of the game. I did not need OSS during the War and expect to operate without the CIA. They have nothing to offer in the past or at this time.' At once dismissive but also fearful, Willoughby warned Wedemeyer that the CIA was making 'preposterous claims' about a superior capacity, adding that his Army Intelligence was now being 'smeared' by the newcomers.[10]

Willoughby battled with all those who might rival Army dominance of intelligence in Japan. General Charles Cabell, the US Air Force Director of Intelligence, described MacArthur's intelligence set-up as a 'closed corporation', unhealthily obsessed with internal subversion and with little time for the international scene outside Japan. Willoughby had declared himself 'too busy' even to meet with Cabell when he came out to inspect USAF intelligence elements in the Far East. 'Instead he sent a bottle of whisky to my hotel room.' Cabell was finally able to force a meeting only because Willoughby's permanent quarters proved to be in the same hotel. Willoughby finally showed up in a bathrobe to a short and unproductive meeting. This did not augur well for Western intelligence on the brink of a major war.[11]

Britain was an almost invisible partner alongside the towering presence of MacArthur and the SCAP organisation. There had been bitter arguments about the intelligence dividend from captured Japanese atomic materials in the SCAP area, and so relations with the small British intelligence component in Tokyo were already awkward. MacArthur's intelligence staff in Tokyo only liaised with the British 'unofficially'. Britain enjoyed very little independent capability, and its intelligence specialists conceded that without information from MacArthur they would 'know little more than appears in the Press'. This was exacerbated by the wider problem of Anglo-American antagonism over the British recognition of communist China in 1949, which reflected London's policy of recognising whoever was *de facto* in power. Washington tied its flag instead to the mast of Chiang Kai-shek's beleaguered Nationalist regime in Taiwan (Formosa).[12]

The surprise invasion of 1950 wiped out Britain's very limited intelligence capacity in Korea itself. This took the form of a newly opened SIS station in Seoul run by a middle-ranking SIS officer called George Blake. In 1948 he was withdrawn from Germany and retrained to reinforce SIS operations from China into the Soviet Union. With China now in turmoil, SIS instead sent him to Seoul to open the first SIS station in Korea, based at the British Embassy. But Blake's main target was still the Soviet Union, not East Asia. Although they were investigating the increased troop movements in June 1950, Blake and his colleagues were also taken by surprise. More importantly, because London and Washington were not yet committed to the war, much of the Western diplomatic corps decided to remain in Seoul as neutrals, and became captives of the North Korean troops. Accordingly, the new SIS station was overrun within days. Its staff occupied themselves with burning their codes and ciphers in a quiet corner of the Embassy garden, hoping not to attract the attention of North Korean troops.[13] Soon George Blake and his compatriots from the British Embassy were all captives in the North.

At the outset Anglo-American intelligence co-operation was bad. On 11 July 1950 the Directors of Intelligence in London told the Chiefs of Staff that their opposite numbers in Washington considered that Korea and Formosa were 'not covered' by agreements on intelligence exchange 'in view of the political difference between us over China'. As a result 'no intelligence had been received from the Americans on either of these countries'.[14]

Denied much in the way of their own sources at the operational level in Korea, London continued to doubt American intelligence when it became available. In April 1951, exactly a year after it had been proved wrong about North Korean troop numbers, British Military Intelligence was still refusing to accept American estimates, arguing that they were infected with 'MacArthuritis'. The fact that American Military Intelligence from Washington was 'based almost entirely on Far Eastern Command and there is no independent check' rendered it highly suspect. Meanwhile Washington was withholding from London its top intelligence on the Chinese order of battle, derived from signals intelligence. London had repeatedly asked for it but General Omar Bradley, Chair of the US Joint Chiefs of Staff, had confessed to his colleagues in April 1951 that 'this scares us on security grounds'. Exactly what Bradley had in mind is not clear. But Donald Maclean, the Soviet agent who had been in the British Embassy in Washington and was now head of the Foreign Office North American Department in London, was under MI5 surveillance from March 1951 and slipped through the tightening net to freedom on 25 May that year. Bradley was clearly vindicated in restricting sigint at this time.[15]

However, sigint material was especially thin because the Soviets had trained the North Koreans well and material of value was usually sent by the safe hand of an officer. Moreover, communications between the North Korean capital, P'Yongyang, and Moscow were routed through the Soviet Embassy in P'Yongyang and made use of one-time pads. This effectively shut off high-level dividends from sigint. When the Chinese entered the war they did the same. The situation was made worse by the extensive use of land-lines and undersea cables, which prevented radio interception.[16] Whatever the quantity of signals traffic available before the outbreak of the Korean War, the British and the Americans were not well disposed to intercept it. American signals intelligence had been in a state of disarray since the end of the Second World War, split between the feuding armed services – a state of affairs made worse by the creation of a weak Armed Forces Security Agency.

The largest American sigint operation in the region was the Army Security Agency, with its headquarters at the Tokyo First Arsenal, an eighteen-acre facility seven miles outside Tokyo, but this boasted only forty-seven officers and about 200 staff. Across the region it disposed of only four listening stations, which operated a nine-to-five day as a result of personnel shortages. Moreover, morale was low and the nature of sigint-collection during peacetime intrinsically tedious. The conscripts that constituted the rank and file of these sigint units had a high turnover.

They were short of the necessary skills but long on disciplinary problems, alcoholism and rampant venereal disease.[17] Prior to the summer of 1950 the limited American sigint facilities in Asia were mostly targeted on the Soviet military, with some residual Chinese coverage. Sigint was almost the only form of intelligence-gathering not subject to MacArthur's cramping orders. But its performance was still hampered by the fact that MacArthur and his staff were poor consumers of the material. Few of his officers had the security clearance to see sigint and still fewer knew how to use it, employing it exclusively to build up a picture of the enemy order of battle.[18]

What of intelligence on the ground in Korea before June 1950? All American troops, who had been present since the end of the Second World War, had been withdrawn from Korea by 1 July 1949 and defence had become the responsibility of the government of South Korea (ROK). (In 1950, the brief withdrawal of the Soviets from the UN Security Council allowed the reinforcements to be designated a UN force, though they were mostly American.) Various remits had required MacArthur to maintain an intelligence watch on this area, but there was a justifiable sense that this was no longer a priority concern for him. All of the three ROK service intelligence organisations were running agents in North Korea, together with their secret service – the Higher Intelligence Department. Although the casualty rates were very high, taken together with prisoners captured during the ongoing guerrilla war between North and South a detailed picture of the North Korean military had been constructed by 1950. However, Seoul's priorities were very similar to those of MacArthur. Domestic security and internal secret policing were very high on the agenda. Foreign intelligence was secondary and concentrated on order of battle rather than attack warning. Although a great deal was passed to the Americans, in common with intelligence provided by Taiwan it was regarded as politically skewed and therefore untrustworthy. Moreover, experienced US military attachés responsible for sifting and forwarding South Korean material were withdrawn immediately prior to the invasion, leaving intelligence liaison in the hands of a small advisory group with only four intelligence officers.[19]

US signals intelligence activity had ceased in Korea with the departure of American forces in 1949. As Matthew Aid has shown in his brilliant study, US sigint conceded in 1951 that 'Prior to the attack there was virtually no COMINT covering North Korea; what little North Korea radio traffic was intercepted was not being analysed.' In the summer of 1950 it was gradually dawning on intelligence managers that Korea was an emerging hotspot, but a slumbering bureaucracy had not yet issued directives for an expanded intelligence effort there. Even if this had been implemented it is unlikely that the invasion would have been detected by this or other means. The North Korean Army observed scrupulous radio silence, and much of its traffic was sent by land-line. Soviet radio security advisers in Korea were fully aware of the potential of techniques such as traffic analysis and direction finding, which allowed intelligence to be squeezed even from traffic that had not been broken.[20] Successful sigint began to develop only in the latter part of the war, when the front line became stable. Both Britain and the United States built up substantial operations to intercept tactical radio traffic. Special operations were launched in an attempt to capture both radio equipment and ciphers and quite a lot of this material was recovered. Elaborate precautions were taken for fear that Western crypto centres might be overrun, and at forward outposts filing cabinets and safes were ostentatiously topped by thermite grenades, ready to torch crypto material at short notice.[21]

One of the most successful sigint coups during the Korean War was carried out by the CIA and was designed to disrupt cable networks. Having learned from Korean seamen that some sort of cable stretched between the Shantung Peninsula in mainland China and Dairen in Manchuria, it was realised that this must be the marine telegraph cable carrying much of the traffic between Chinese forces in Korea and Beijing. The Yellow Sea is generally quite shallow and a converted armed junk, normally employed on coastal raids, and commanded by a former Air Force master sergeant, was used to search for it: 'Early one May morning, his trailing grapples fetched up the thick, weedy cable. While barnacles popped from the cable to crunch beneath his boots on the swaying deck, the sergeant wielded a fire axe, whacking out a three foot length of cable. He then ran to the wheelhouse, called for maximum speed, and hightailed it back across the Yellow Sea.' Those working on signals intelligence were delighted. The Chinese were now forced to use an improvised radio teletype. For the duration of the conflict and also during the protracted ceasefire negotiations, this provided a rich source of intelligence.[22]

The CIA's fortunes were only marginally improved by the onset of the Korean War. On the one hand the war at last allowed it a real foothold in Japan and a rationale for expansion. On the other hand, it was now expected to launch extensive operations from a very low base. Surprised by this new war, and forced to work in the shadow of MacArthur and FECOM, CIA operations chiefs searched for a radical approach to accelerate their operations in Asia. Their answer was Hans Tofte, a Dane who had lived for many years in Manchuria and the United States and who had previously served with both OSS and British Security Co-ordination in Washington during 1941–5. Tofte was placed in command and charged with the overnight generation of CIA activities – for which he made use of US Air Force cover organisations. The tiny CIA station was moved from a laughable temporary location in a Tokyo hotel to a giant new complex at Atsugi Air Force Base, hiding there as 6006 Air Squadron. Within weeks of his arrival it boasted over 1,000 personnel. He was joined by a unit from the semi-detached OPC organisation, headed by George Aurell, who would become CIA station chief in Bangkok in the 1960s. In the early stages they were largely dependent on Chinese Nationalist organisations for their intelligence.[23]

Attempts to conjure up large-scale secret service operations overnight are rarely successful. When they are undertaken in the face of opposition from secure police states the result is bound to be grim. Life was alarmingly short for the majority of CIA human agents employed in the Korean War. The main source of personnel was the Korean Labor Organisation (KLO), a manual labour pool that consisted mostly of North Korean students, deserters and refugees. The CIA gradually took over the management of the KLO, while workaday administration was carried out by the refugees themselves. Discipline was extremely harsh and alarming rumours circulated of unauthorised trials of suspected communist infiltrators who then disappeared. Despite draconian measures adopted to prevent communist infiltration of training camps, the large volume of human material consumed by such operations made some communist penetration inevitable.[24]

At least 2,000 agents were inserted into North Korea during the Korean War, but few survived. Agents were given the usual wartime OSS/SOE-type paramilitary training including parachuting, radio procedure, escape and evasion, demolition and use of firearms. But such training was of little avail in an environment as sterile as North Korea. Even if they reached a locality where they could depend on friends and family, intense fear on the part of the local population normally resulted in denunciation to the authorities. The effectiveness of Tofte's operations remains hotly contested. However, suspicions were raised when he provided Washington with implausible 'film footage' of his agents conducting unopposed 'covert operations' in broad daylight in decidedly unKorean-looking surroundings. At the end of the Korean War he was removed and disciplined for falsifying many of the claims made by his organisation.[25]

Once Seoul had been recaptured in late 1950, the main CIA station was located in the newly renovated Traymore Hotel, using the cover-name Joint Armistice Commission, Korea (JACK). It also maintained a large operational base on the island of Chodo on the west coast of Korea. Operations were professionally superintended by Ben Vandervoort, a CIA officer who had been a colonel in the US 82nd Airborne Division. The problems were formidable. Most committed anti-communists had retreated south with UN forces at the start of the war, denuding the North of any potential support networks for agents. Substantial numbers of parachute drops and coastal insertions resulted in 'a few successful small teams' reporting on troop movements, but hopes for a large-scale resistance network of the sort achieved in wartime France never materialised.[26]

The CIA was required to 'co-ordinate' its operations with MacArthur's huge intelligence and special operations entity called Combined Command for Reconnaissance Activities, Korea, or CCRAK. The Army background of CIA figures such as Vandervoort certainly helped and efforts were made to join up the various operations, notably by making Vandervoort simultaneously deputy head of CCRAK. But secret services rarely co-operate well on the ground unless separated geographically. The system under CCRAK offered the worst of all possible worlds, for it created heavy competition for everything from agents to parachutes to transport. Anxiety to protect sources led to absurd secrecy even within individual services. In May 1952 this confusion culminated in a US Air Force strike on a US Air Force Intelligence unit operating from a disguised junk in the Yellow Sea. 'Every service was intent on running its own intelligence network,' recalled one officer. The biggest turf battles were fought in Washington and Tokyo, but 'the differences filtered down and the result was we all worked independently'.[27] The struggles between the CIA and MacArthur in Korea had ignited wider issues between the CIA and the military. Should the armed services be allowed to conduct intelligence-gathering by use of secret agents in parallel to the CIA? In October 1952, negotiations on 'the conditions, type and extent to which the Services may conduct espionage operations' were 'progressing' but no agreement had been possible. In April 1953 this issue was still live, and the best compromise was to appoint military staff to head the CIA within FECOM. Similar arguments over the rights and permissions of the CIA with regard to military operations were going on simultaneously in European headquarters at SHAPE, EUCOM and NATO.[28]

The military flinched at deploying a major asset – the large American 10th Special Forces Group at Fort Bragg – until late in the war. Remarkably, senior American officers feared that units would be captured and subjected to communist 'brainwashing techniques' which had claimed the headlines in the early 1950s. They envisaged entire American units being persuaded to fight for the communists, or to indulge in dastardly acts of sabotage or assassination, to the vast propaganda advantage of the East. Accordingly they were forbidden to serve behind the lines in Korea as organised units. Anxieties about communist success with brainwashing in Korea led to a series of scientific experiments in the same field in the United States which stretched on into the 1960s.[29]

MacArthur soon asked for British forces to join CCRAK in raids behind the North Korean lines. London looked on invitations for British participation in CCRAK as a mixed blessing and the issue was relayed to Attlee. Few details of Britain's part in this brutal undercover war have surfaced. In the early 1950s its small special operations capability resided mostly in the SAS and the Royal Marines. More than two years into the Korean War, Whitehall's Inter-Service Committee on Raiding Operations reported that this area was moribund and that there had been no production of new special operations equipment since 1945.[30] The SAS was busy in Malaya, so in Korea the British CCRAK contribution consisted largely of a Royal Navy Volunteer Group and 41 Independent Commando, Royal Marines, an all-volunteer outfit of ten officers and 240 other ranks. Commanded by Lieutenant-Colonel Drysdale, they joined with 320 volunteers from the US Army and Navy and 300 South Koreans to form Special Activities Group. They carried out sixty days of intensive training at Camp McGill on Tokyo Bay and employed a submarine, USS *Perch*, converted for special operations. Once the US Navy had fought off a hostile takeover-bid from the US Army, outdoor fighting could begin. In September 1950 these forces were used in diversionary raids launched at Kusan from the frigate HMS *Whitesand Bay*, as part of a deception plan to cover the major amphibious landings at Inchon. They then attempted to capture the Kimpo airfield outside Seoul and were used to 'destroy key enemy installations and pers[onnel] in Seoul prior to the capture of that city'.[31] In October they launched successful raids to destroy railway lines and tunnels in North Korea before fighting their way back to the coast. But at the end of the year, as the possibilities for raids diminished, 41 Commando reverted to more conventional operations. This was something of a relief for the British, who confessed that co-ordination between the many 'funny parties' had been a nightmare, while 'clandestine organisations continued to multiply and spread as a law unto themselves', raising the spectre of serious friendly-fire incidents.[32]

Washington also hoped for an SAS battalion for land-based special operations. The SAS only had one operational squadron and a territorial unit. While they were *en route* to Korea, London got cold feet about attaching them to CCRAK and diverted them to Malaya. By the second year of the war there were no specifically British or American special units operating behind the lines and the Koreans were left to bear the brunt of this dangerous work. A few individual British ex-SOE and ex-SAS officers were given to CCRAK. Major Ellery Anderson, a former SAS officer and veteran of resistance operations in France, led a mixed British, American and Korean CCRAK unit conducting guerrilla-training operations. His controversial account of the clandestine war in Korea presents itself as constrained 'by loyalties which sometimes over-ride conscience', with much 'left unsaid'. Nevertheless, the dangers and torments of CCRAK operations are starkly revealed.[33]

Optimism informed the first British-led efforts. Anderson and his colleagues were enthused by their wartime experiences in France, Yugoslavia and Albania. The poor road communications and mountainous country of Korea suggested immediate parallels with the Balkans. This prompted CCRAK operations designed to cause long-term rail disruption, which met with some success. In 1951, Anderson led para-dropped teams to destroy North Korean trains deep inside mountain tunnels, rendering the wreckage almost impossibly difficult to clear. His contemporaneous plans to capture Russian staff officers advising the North Korean forces were vetoed at a high level as too provocative. Sabotage operations met with a modicum of success and teams inserted by air often reported at least one bridge destroyed before they went off the air.[34]

But later in 1951 there were failed attempts to branch out from straightforward railway sabotage into the more complex business of constructing permanent resistance forces inside North Korea. The organisation made elementary mistakes, including making parachute supply drops by day, matters that the North Korean Security Police could hardly fail to notice. Their distinctive green police uniforms with red piping were soon in evidence everywhere and the embryonic guerrilla groups were destroyed or led away for interrogation. The problems of surviving for any length of time within a country with an active security police were underestimated. One experienced American officer recalled that the simple act of moving from one village to another required different documents, the nature or colour of which changed on an irregular basis. By the end of the war, confronted with large numbers of line-crossing agents, the North Koreans devised an ingenious system of small pinholes in documents. Only the security police would have the right key and would check travel documents by holding them up to the light: 'If the pinholes were not in the right configuration the individual carrying the documents was subject to arrest, torture and death.'

'Radios were captured, stolen or abandoned with their codes, and false information was sent back.' Both Army Intelligence operations and the CIA ran into 'frequent problems with captured radios and false radio transmissions'. But wider problems were encountered that probably dogged Western operations in all rural areas of communist countries:

> There was a certain ethnocentricity at work here ... We generally assumed that any North Korean sent back to his homeland could quickly and easily fit back in, no matter what part of the country he was sent to. To us a North Korean was a North Korean was a North Korean. But such was not the case. If a stranger showed up in a village he was immediately suspected of being either an infiltrator or a deserter and the local police were notified.

It was the same story as Eastern Europe, and North Koreans were alert to the possibility of *agents provocateurs* planted by the security police to test the loyalty of the local population. This technique had been used most famously by the NKVD, which dropped 'German' parachutists among suspect Soviet minorities such as the Volga Germans to test their loyalty in 1941. Those who had welcomed them were led away and summarily shot.[35]

Undeterred by initial reverses, and anxious to exploit the brief summer campaigning season, senior CCRAK officers ordered Anderson to develop a new and hasty programme. In future British and American officers would rarely be allowed to venture behind enemy lines on airborne penetration missions. Large-scale shallow penetration of the enemy front was to be attempted using individual Korean para-dropped agents. Inserted fifty miles behind the lines and armed only with a pistol, they were expected to make their way back to their own lines, gathering military information *en route*. Senior officers conceded that only about a third of those inserted would return, but they expected 'some really good information'. Anderson, who had direct experience of North Korea, was less sanguine. Scepticism turned to dismay when he learned that those selected for insertion were fresh recruits and would have seven days to prepare for their mission. It was clear that these agents were regarded as expendable in the extreme.

When the 'fifteen specially selected Koreans' he had been promised arrived at Anderson's facility for training, he could scarcely believe his eyes. Pathetic and malnourished, they were mostly shy rustic youths in their teens, some as young as fifteen. A week was enough for them to master the use of basic firearms, but they 'had only the haziest idea of the parachute drill'. Accompanying his 'agents' as far as their dropping zones triggered a sense of black depression:

> Never before had I taken unprepared men into battle and now I was about to do something far worse. I was sending untrained men into the most frightening and lonely of battles ... the cold night air rushed in through the open jump door. The tense queue of men waited to jump. Red light, green light, and the first man stumbled out into the night, then the next, then the next. The fourth hesitated and was pushed by those behind, and so the procession of fear went on until the fuselage was empty but for myself ... For one wild moment I longed to jump after them and, like the ancient mariner, felt that I 'had done a hellish thing'.

In 1952 the emphasis changed again. Line-crossing had proved ineffective and there were attempts to build up guerrilla groups on northern coastal islands near the mouth of the Yalu river. With CCRAK's own Special Air Mission to conduct supply flights, pre-existing groups of separatists, bandits and smugglers were built up. Descending towards one makeshift island runway Anderson was overcome by a sense of the outpost's fragility: 'I felt it could be easily smashed and its little garrison annihilated like a beetle trodden underfoot.' His words were prophetic and many island guerrilla groups were soon eradicated by North Korean security troops. Later he learned that one of his British CCRAK colleagues, Lieutenant Leo Samuel Acton-Adams, had been captured after calling down artillery fire on his own command bunker as it was overrun. He was later shot during his third escape attempt, only two days before the armistice brought an effective end to combat in Korea.

Assessing the effectiveness of guerrilla-type operations is problematic. Guerrillas rarely hold ground and their impact should be measured primarily in terms of the logistical drain on enemy forces and the psychological impact on the population. Anderson observed that it was 'impossible to judge the effect of our very presence behind the lines'. If battalions had been diverted to look for his parties, and if strategic installations across North Korea had been more heavily guarded as a result of raiding, then he could claim success. But the net effect, he conceded, was unfathomable. Meanwhile the war as a whole he judged to be a tragedy.[36]

The line-crossing operations have produced personal accounts which often contradict each other over details. But all sing with one voice about their unease at the nature of such intelligence missions. Remarkably, American CCRAK officers recalled that for many agents 'their first jump was on a combat mission behind the enemy lines'. In early 1953 it was common to insert groups of ten almost on a weekly basis and hear nothing from them at all. 'These airdrops were virtual suicide missions for all involved.' Yet the CCRAK picture reported to Washington by its officers in Tokyo was unremittingly optimistic, claiming that in the first ten months of 1952 CCRAK guerrillas accounted for 19,000 communists killed or wounded. Agent operations had reached 1,400 and the hope was to hit 2,000 by March 1953. General Mark Clark, who succeeded Matthew Ridgway as the Commander of UN forces in Korea, urged additional funding for CCRAK, adding that Eisenhower, the President-elect, was 'very interested' in extending this kind of operation.[37]

But the deepest reservations about the secret war in Korea held by British and American personnel concerned not intelligence and special operations, but counter-intelligence and internal security. The improbably named Ivor Pink, a British diplomat in Tokyo, warned London about the severity of the anti-communist witch-hunt that MacArthur had allowed his intelligence chief to launch in Japan. Those with liberal or Jewish associations, often seen as essentially the same thing, were removed from posts. The US Army CIC was used to mount extensive surveillance on journalists and trade union leaders, and wild conspiracy stories circulated. Perversely, MacArthur's own plans for the regeneration of Japan contained strong socialist elements.[38]

Matters were far worse in Korea. Western security co-operation with South Korea was handled by Colonel Donald Nichols of the US 6004 Air Intelligence Service Squadron. Nichols was an eccentric figure and as late as 1945 he had been a sergeant superintending a motor transport pool at an airbase in Guam. But by 1946 he had transferred to a US Army CIC unit in Korea and, having found his calling, was rising fast. By 1948 he was responsible for all Air Force security throughout Korea and also for training the counter-intelligence services of the South Korean Premier, Syngman Rhee. Nichols developed a close relationship with Rhee and was watching many of his political opponents, including the South Korean Labour Party. In a remarkably frank memoir he wrote of the various unpleasant methods used by both American and South Korean personnel under his control.

However, Nichols' characteristic iron self-control had buckled during July 1950 in the chaotic first weeks of the North Korean invasion. As South Korean security elements prepared to flee their facilities in Seoul at very short notice they were confronted with the problem of what to do with 1,800 political prisoners in the vicinity, some of whom were communists, some Rhee's rivals. Nichols remembered:

> I stood by helplessly, witnessing the entire affair. Two big bull-dozers worked constantly. One made a ditch-type grave. Trucks loaded with the condemned arrived. Their hands were already tied behind them. They were hastily pushed into line along the edge of the newly opened grave. They were quickly shot in the head and pushed into the grave … I tried to stop this from happening, however, I gave up when I saw I was wasting my time.

Publicly, the affair was attributed to the invading North Koreans. But privately even the hardened Nichols was troubled by 'terrible nightmares' in the decades that followed. Remaining in command of the 6004 Air Intelligence Service Squadron after the Korean War, his principal mission continued to be support for Rhee's security agencies. In 1957 certain 'irregularities' resulted in him being relieved of his command and taken back to the United States for investigation, but the nature of these activities had long been known among those who served in Korea.[39]

Some senior officers found the harsh nature of the South Korean security system convenient when dealing with infiltrators. During an operations conference at EUSAK (US Eighth Army in Korea) on 8 January 1951 the issue of what to do with 'Enemy in Civilian Clothing' came up for discussion. This proved to be an annoying subject for there were many suspected North Korean low-grade agents drifting around in front-line areas and the consensus was that 'We cannot execute them, although they can be shot before they become prisoners.' Senior officers in the US Army IX Corps dismissed the problem as none too difficult, stating that in their command area 'We just turn them over to the ROK's and they take care of them.' The 'ROKs' were the South Korean armed forces and the manner in which they took care of any enemy caught in civilian clothing was hardly a secret. The existence of agents working for either side was clearly nasty, brutish and short.[40]

The unpleasant police state existing in South Korea quickly revealed itself to British personnel there. On 29 October 1950, when the Chinese entered the war and the communist forces swept south for a second time, there was further panic and another great spree of executions as political enemies were massacred rather than evacuated from their camps. But this time there was a complicating factor. British officials and troops were often in the vicinity when this was happening. On 15 December British troops witnessed a particularly nasty massacre by Rhee's security police. Alec Adams, a British diplomat in Seoul and later British Ambassador to Bangkok, gave London a graphic account of the reaction of British soldiers:

> As I understand it, considerable feeling was aroused among British troops both because of the callous way in which the executions were carried out and because they mistook two of those shot for boys (they were in fact women wearing trousers). Fearing that there would be an incident if British troops were again subjected to the spectacle of mass executions in their vicinity, I represented to the United States Embassy yesterday the urgent need to dissuade the Korean authorities from running any risks.

Another mass execution occurred only two days later, but this time Allied troops were kept away. However, journalists had got wind of what was going on and London told Adams that the press were giving 'a lot of trouble'. Australian, American and British journalists all learned of executions of groups of up to sixty prisoners, often civilians thought to be guerrillas. James Cameron of the *Picture Post* reported on Rhee's concentration camps and described them as 'worse than Belsen', which he had also witnessed personally. But his story was never printed, causing a furore among the magazine staff.[41] Only fringe-left papers such as the communist *Daily Worker* carried extensive stories about atrocities by the South Korean government. Attlee's Cabinet panicked and rummaged in the cupboard to try and find legislation that prevented publication of such material. The only instrument they could find was a charge of treason which carried a mandatory death penalty, so the issue was allowed to lapse. Informal pressure was applied to editors, and IRD was brought into play to contradict the massacre stories which London knew to be correct.[42] It is likely that George Blake, the SIS officer in Korea

captured when Seoul was overrun in the summer of 1950 and supposedly later turned by a Soviet interrogator in a North Korean camp, found
his existing disillusionment with the West greatly reinforced by his experiences in Korea during the period before his capture. An extended guerrilla war had been fought across the South since 1948, with Rhee clinging
on to control in rural areas by fearsome police tactics. By day the police
tortured suspects for information and at night retreated to their block-
houses. There were few regimes less worthy of Western support and
Blake would have been strange if this had not given him pause for
thought.[43]

Intelligence improved in the course of the conflict. Aerial reconnaissance quickly filled some of the gaps left by other forms of intelligence
and was critical in informing the day-to-day operations and especially the
punishing air bombardment of the North Korean forces, but intelligence
for ground forces was neglected. Anxious about the possibility of Soviet
intervention, American sigint facilities in the region had remained
focused on Soviet targets for weeks beyond the initial invasion, while
North Korean targets were neglected. Once the belated shift to Korean
targets began, an impossible shortage of Korean linguists was discovered
and there followed extraordinary episodes in bribery as competing units
tried to secure some of the few competent civilian hirelings available.[44]

Incredibly, even under pressure of war, neither Washington nor
FECOM in Japan was willing to surrender any sigint units to support
General Walker's EUSAK on the ground and most were in any case static
rather than mobile units. General Willoughby gave explicit orders that
any such transfer should be blocked. Walker was resourceful and created
his own sigint unit from scratch, known as Group M. Using a motley collection of South Korean Army and Air Force signals personnel together
with US Air Force advisers, they learned the sigint trade on the job and
made a vital contribution during the bitter fighting to defend the Pusan
perimeter in late 1950. When a small comint detachment from outside
the theatre finally arrived, EUSAK requisitioned its equipment for M,
but sent the personnel packing. The result was a furore.[45]

Bombing paved the way for some sigint success at the operational
level and within a few months of the outbreak of war the North Korean
communications system was collapsing under the strain of American
bombing. Radios and electronic spare parts were in increasingly short
supply. Mounting casualties also affected radio security discipline. As a
result most North Korean Peoples' Army codes at the operational level
were being solved within hours by South Koreans in EUSAK's sigint
team. EUSAK had several days' vital warning of the offensive against the
Pusan perimeter at the end of August 1950, together with detailed information about the plan of attack. The perimeter held by only the narrow-

est of margins and without sigint the result would probably have been very different. In September, sigint offered General Ned Almond, commander of the Inchon landings, which outflanked the communist forces near Seoul, detailed information of what his opponents knew of his amphibious attack. Nevertheless, sigint operations both in Korea and in the FECOM area remained *ad hoc*, with only limited co-operation between the three American cryptanalytical services, which all strove to ignore the new Armed Forces Security Agency. On the ground South Korean operators and later Nationalist Chinese from Taiwan proved critical in the supply of sigint. Their final triumph was highly effective work against the Chinese Air Force at the end of the war, contributing substantially to heavy communist losses. But Washington still refused to update their equipment for fear of compromising American sigint secrets.[46]

The whole Korean War was characterised by a fog of uncertainty on all sides. Western signals intelligence and human espionage alike delivered thin pickings. For much of the war POW interrogation and air reconnaissance fed the planners at both operational and strategic levels. Moreover, Washington did not trust its Asian collaborators in the field of intelligence, while London was dubious of material emanating from Washington. Equally, despite their well-placed agents, Chinese and Soviet appreciations of Western thinking were probably poor. Both Moscow and Beijing took a great deal of time to come to the conclusion that there was little to be gained from pursuing the war. By the time they had reached this conclusion it had dragged on for more than four years.

The wider impact of the Korean War cannot be overestimated. It sped up the militarisation of the Cold War and extended it from a largely European–Mediterranean conflict to a global confrontation. More than any event prior to the Cuban Missile Crisis it threatened to turn the Cold War into a hot war. Korea also accelerated an alarming divergence between Britain and Washington which had been apparent since the surprise testing of the Soviet atomic bomb in August 1949. Lurking under this political divergence was a strategic 'vulnerability gap'. Britain was now very vulnerable to Soviet atomic weapons, while the United States was likely to remain out of range until the late 1950s. The Korean War ensured that this problem could not be ignored. Moreover, it brought with it a heightened profile for the China Lobby together with MacArthur abroad and McCarthyism at home. As late as 1948 London had pressed Washington to take a tougher line over the Cold War, but by 1950 it was applying the brakes. It now identified choices: to search for peaceful mutual coexistence or to drive forward in the hope of winning the Cold War. For Attlee, and for his successor Churchill, this was no choice at all and both were willing to accept Soviet gains in Eastern Europe in return for a more stable version of the Cold War.

Days after the Korean War broke out the British Ambassador in Moscow held 'certain conversations' with Andrei Gromyko, the Soviet Deputy Foreign Minister, about how to 'put a stop to present hostilities in Korea'. A deal seemed possible in which the Soviets might 'put some pressure on North Korea to end hostilities'. The Russians' 'price' seemed to be an American cancellation of the commitment to defend Taiwan (Formosa) if attacked by the Chinese, an option that was also very attractive to Beijing. Pierson Dixon from PUSD discussed this with the Chiefs of Staff on 12 July 1950. There was a widespread view in Whitehall that American commitment to Taiwan 'might well lead to a world war'. This was doubly alarming given that the 'latest intelligence appreciation was that the Chinese Communists might attack Formosa in the very near future – possibly by the 15th July'. If the attack came, the Chiefs of Staff believed the Americans would hold Taiwan, but Britain would lose Hong Kong. More importantly, 'there was a most serious risk we would provoke a world war'. They continued, 'We were in no position to fight at the moment. If war broke out now, it was highly probable that both Western Europe and the Middle East would be overrun. We must leave the Americans in no doubt as to our unpreparedness ... Everything possible therefore should be done to get the Americans to agree not to use their forces for the defence of Formosa in the event of a Communist attack.' For the time being London was at pains to avoid revealing to Washington just how far apart their positions were. But it soon became clear. The gap continued to widen.[47]

In July 1950 Whitehall was beginning to peer into the nuclear abyss. Convinced that total war might be only days away, the British Chiefs of Staff now began to consider the practical issues of what would actually happen at 'H Hour'. They had to face the fact that the systems for command and control of American nuclear forces in Britain, and the mechanism for joint decision, were shaky. Given that Britain was 'the main base for the offensive', this was worrying. The Chiefs of Staff asked Tedder, who was now head of the British Joint Services Mission in Washington, to start to firm up a very flabby system for joint consultation. On 28 July, Tedder received a message from London that is so revealing about the developing British predicament vis-à-vis the United States that it is worth reproducing at length:

Strictly private for Lord Tedder from Chiefs of Staff.
1. You are of course aware of the existence of an American plan in the event of a major war to initiate immediately an atomic attack on Russia from bases in this country: you also know that a substantial U.S. bomber force is already in this country.
2. We emphasised in our defence policy review the importance of the Allies being prepared to use, and if necessary initiate the use of, the atomic bomb in

the event of Russian aggression. And this policy has general acceptance here. On the other hand it has always been stressed here that the decision as to the initiation of such an offensive must be taken by Governments if and when the time comes.

3. While accepting that this decision may not be possible in advance, we feel it to be of the utmost importance that the policy and all its implications should be clearly thought out and understood in advance by all concerned, not least by Ministers who will have to take the decision. At the moment this is a very loose end which we feel must be tied up now firmly and formally.

4. The fact is that all we, the Chiefs of Staff, know about this plan is (a) that it exists, (b) certain broad details which our planners were able to glean during their last visit to America last year and (c) that there may be considerable difference of opinion about it not only between Strategic Air Command and the Air Staff in the Pentagon but also, judging from certain discussions at Horatius [a recent conference], between the airmen and the soldiers in America in relation to the employment of Strategic Air Forces in the defence of Western Europe.

5. This is clearly no longer an acceptable position. We cannot possibly afford to risk misunderstandings and last moment divergences of policy on a matter of such vital importance to us all. At present it is not unduly fanciful to imagine a situation in which Vandenburg [chief of the USAF] or LeMay [chief of Strategic Air Command] sends Johnson [the USAF Commander in Britain] an order to initiate the offensive while we have to resist any action pending consideration by the Prime Minister and Government to Government discussions.

Although they respected General Leon Johnson, the senior USAF Commander in Britain, the Chiefs of Staff felt the 'problems are getting too big for him'. He was a first-class operational commander but had no real awareness of wider policy issues. They were made more nervous by the fact that he 'appears to be the mouth piece of General LeMay', whose default setting was certainly not restraint or lengthy deliberation before action.[48]

These tensions boiled over repeatedly during the Korean War. London increasingly feared that many in Washington actively wanted a wider war, with China if not with the Soviet Union, in which Britain would be in the front line. In November 1952, the Foreign Secretary Anthony Eden and his Minister of State, Selwyn Lloyd, were in Washington to discuss Korea. The Indian delegation at the UN had recently put up a proposal for peace negotiations which the Americans had hated. There followed a two-hour confrontation with Dean Acheson which Eden described as 'one of the most disagreeable he has ever encountered'. Acheson had previously been at a cocktail reception and was in a mood to give full vent to his feelings: 'Dean assailed Selwyn Lloyd in a manner that was only half-jocular, accusing him of not having dealt honourably with the Americans.' He added that 'if Britain could not make up her mind that she was with the United States on this matter it would be the end of Anglo-American co-operation, there would be no more NATO, etcetera'. He then rounded on various Commonwealth leaders who were pressing for a peaceful solution to the Korean War, speaking of the Indian leaders in 'contemptuous terms' and deriding Mike Pearson, the Canadian Foreign Minister, as 'an empty glass of water'.[49]

This growing divide between London and Washington also extended to policy on the Soviet Union. Throughout his second period of office (1951–5) Churchill sought some kind of deal on mutual coexistence with Moscow, both before and after Stalin's death in 1953. The Geneva Conference of 1954, which Washington had fought hard to avoid, was as close as London got. Here Eden and the Soviet Foreign Minister Molotov co-operated to drag a reluctant John Foster Dulles, the US Secretary of State, towards a general settlement which was not of his choosing. Eden and Dulles had begun to articulate their differences very freely. John Talhoudin, a junior British diplomat in attendance, recalled one memorable exchange: 'Eden and Dulles were waiting for the lift in the hotel at Geneva and it was evident that Eden was annoyed with Dulles and I heard him say "The trouble with you is that you want World War III".' Geneva was a triumph for Eden, steering Korea towards armistice and Indochina towards a brief period of quiescence. China was persuaded to accept an agreement despite moving towards victory in the Indochina conflict. But Dulles was furious at this search for a compromise and briefed the press against Eden in its closing stages.[50]

Secret service went to the heart of this looming crisis in Anglo-American relations in a paradoxical way. On the one hand, close intelligence co-operation allowed London its best window into American military planning and showed how close Washington was to all-out war. On the other hand, the developing activities of American psychological warfare and covert action all around the perimeter of the Soviet Union and China, which were mostly carried out by the secret services, looked increasingly dangerous. In the early 1950s the British JIC concluded that one of the most likely causes of war would be a Western attempt to detach one of the Soviet satellite nations. All this raised the question of how close intelligence co-operation should be handled in a decade when Britain moved from containing the Soviet Union to containing the threat of war more generally. Increasingly it began to dawn on officials in London that containing the general threat of war meant in practice that they would be 'containing America'.[51] This was a task that extended right across Asia and beyond.

14

Cold War Fighting in Asia

The U.K. ... fears that we have a secret policy in the Far East – namely, to
overthrow Peiping.
Paul Nitze addressing the US Joint Chiefs of Staff, 4 April 1951[1]

Although Britain steadily withdrew its visible military forces from Asia
and the Middle East after 1945, the hidden hand of secret service
remained in the region. Intelligence-collection in particular lent a new
utility to the remnants of an old Empire that was situated in an area of
growing interest to the United States. Intelligence-collection assets, unlike
defence forces, enjoyed a low profile that could survive the withdrawal of
Empire. Prolonged through Commonwealth connections, discreet leasing
arrangements and so-called 'communication facilities' on remote islands,
Britain's intelligence power in the wider world survived the turning points
of 1956 and 1968, much beloved of the historians of the 'End of Empire'.
What Washington termed the 'strategic value of residual Empire' lasted into
the 1970s. It was finally eroded, not by imperial retreat, but by the arrival of
satellite platforms and also by President Nixon's rapprochement with
China. Even then, Hong Kong remained an intelligence centre of outstanding importance which signed off only with the hand-over to China in 1997.[2]

The intelligence dimension of Britain's residual Empire is of immense
importance. It helped to maintain Britain as an intelligence power and a
valued partner for the United States. In Asia, the United States was at
war, or on the brink of war, almost continually from 1950 to 1974. Four
of the five crises in which American Presidents seriously considered the
use of nuclear weapons occurred in Asia. Here, more than anywhere else,
intelligence counted in a dramatic and immediate way. On the other
hand, the Asian dimension of secret service also brought with it extraordinary hazards. Asia had always been an area of 'unspecial' relations
between London and Washington. The theme of economic rivalry had
always been strong and their strategic outlooks differed. From 1950 their
policies were sharply divergent.[3]

The 'loss of China' to the communists in 1949 was a traumatic event for the United States, compounded by communist China's intervention in Korea a year later. The American public had been taught to idealise their relationship with China as a 'sister republic' that was expected to become a reflection of the United States. What became known as the 'China Lobby' in Washington was determined that communist rule in China should not be allowed to establish itself on the mainland untroubled. Even before the Korean War, Frank Wisner's OPC had begun a small programme to keep resistance alive in mainland China. These efforts gained momentum from the wars in Korea and Indochina, represented as operations to hit Chinese supply lines to these areas. This was the strategy sketched out by Colonel Bill Depuy and Richard Stilwell, the CIA officers superintending Asia from Washington in 1951.

These operations underlined the CIA's general inclination towards covert action rather than intelligence-gathering. More specifically, it underlined a preference for paramilitary-style covert action. OPC, both before and after it was fully absorbed into the CIA, contained many colonels and majors on secondment from Army units and they carried a military culture with them. As in Europe, CIA operations in Asia represented more a means of venting frustration against the general intractability of Cold War problems, and a means of finding ideological expression, rather than realistic plans to overturn communist rule. Yet these programmes were remarkable in their scale, and by 1951 'Cold War fighting' would be in progress around much of the perimeter of China.[4]

Clement Attlee was horrified by these activities and did not hesitate to say so at an early stage. In December 1950, following the surprise Chinese intervention in Korea, he travelled hurriedly to Washington to speak to Truman amid fears that American forces might be compelled to use nuclear weapons. Attlee took a high-powered delegation, including the Chief of the Imperial General Staff, Field Marshal Sir William Slim. Truman was accompanied at the talks by Acheson, the Secretary of State, and Marshall, the Secretary of Defense, together with the Chairman of the US Joint Chiefs of Staff, Omar Bradley. Attlee was exceedingly blunt, stating that he 'did not want to become involved in a major war with China'. He was also uncomfortable about supporting a government in South Korea which was 'very corrupt and inefficient'. He was willing to hold out in Korea in the short term, but only so 'a cease-fire may be secured; then we could begin to talk. It was very important that this be regarded as a primary point.'

Attlee was bothered by the insidious spread of war. There was, he insisted, a growing trend in American policy towards a covert war all around China's borders which seemed pointless and certainly would not draw China towards the peace table:

The Prime Minister said, very frankly, that this had not appealed to him very much. He wondered what could be done in the way of economic warfare or subversive activity or through other actions which amounted merely to pin-pricks which could really lead eventually to the settlement. Our cards were not good enough to lead to that effect. The policy suggested was for a kind of limited war and this did not appeal to the British people or to the bulk of the United Nations. They feared that, if we began on a limited war, this might become a full war ... the Government of the United Kingdom does not approve of limited warfare against the Chinese if this were not directed to the immediate terrain of Korea but became a kind of war around the perimeter of China.

Attlee wanted to get the Chinese communists seated in the UN and to get talking with them. Truman understood where Attlee was going but replied that it was not practical politics on Capitol Hill and that what Attlee was suggesting 'was political dynamite in the United States'. Acheson's further comments only reinforced Attlee's fears that a general war was looming. The leader of East Germany, Acheson said, had just sent a letter to Adenauer, the West German leader, which 'had a danger-ous similarity to the letter which the North Koreans had written to the Government of Korea just before they attacked'. Andrei Vyshinsky, the Soviet Foreign Minister from 1949 to 1953, had been making speeches in the United Nations arguing that American actions in Korea were 'the first step to the Third World War'. Acheson added, 'One had to ask how near we are to war.' If things were, regrettably, 'gathering speed', the last thing he wanted to do was to try to 'buy off the aggressor just before the crash came'. The veiled reference to 1938 and 1939 was hard to miss. Attlee sensed that Washington believed that all-out war was now quite close.[5]

A month after Attlee's visit, senior officials in Washington sat down to review their policy towards resistance groups in mainland China and on the extent to which they should be stimulated from Taiwan. They set out with a basic premise that 'The United States desires the overthrow of the Chinese Communist regime' but conceded that Washington would 'not have the support of friendly countries in its efforts'. They were in the meantime unsure whether they wished to 'take the initiative in creating a new, permanent leadership' in China or merely pursue a policy that 'creates a state of chaos on the mainland'. At this point the communists were admitting to 400,000 guerrillas still active on the mainland, of whom the United States had high hopes, although they knew the military value of Chiang Kai-shek's forces on Taiwan to be low.[6]

Wherever the West could gain access to the perimeter of China the pinprick war was accelerated. Pakistan, India, Burma, Thailand, Laos, Taiwan, Hong Kong, Japan and Korea all served as springboards for insurgency against Beijing. These attacks were supported by the CIA, but were pressed home with even more vigour by Taiwan's secret agencies, still smarting from their defeats on the mainland. Thus the Chinese civil war did not end in 1949 and no armistice was signed. Taiwan felt at liberty to back guerrillas against Beijing's Anti-Revolutionary Suppression Campaign led by the Ministry of State Security. In 1952, it claimed that its 'Free China seaborne guerrillas' had fought no fewer than 609 separate engagements. Several thousand casualties had been inflicted in what were, in some cases, battalion-sized engagements which looked like a limited war.[7] In October 1952, Taiwan carried out a large 'raid' on Nan-jih that involved 4,000 regulars and 1,000 special forces, returning with 720 prisoners. These arrived just in time to participate in Chiang Kai-shek's birthday parade. The CIA's task was to train and upgrade this effort. However, when these parties made the mistake of advancing inland they were usually surrounded and destroyed. Early attempts to rouse the mainland population to rebellion by moving through inland rural areas were gradually abandoned in favour of large-scale coastal hit-and-run raids or propaganda leaflet-dropping.[8]

The CIA on Taiwan conducted its activities through cover organisations: Western Enterprises Inc. and the airline Civil Air Transport (CAT), which together dropped teams of Nationalists on to the mainland. Some agents were Chinese POWs from the Korean War who had chosen to be repatriated to Taiwan rather than China. These operations were of two main kinds. Resistance missions sought to build up a long-term resistance movement in remote areas, while commando raids using small boats sought to 'destroy key installations'. The CIA and the Taiwan Secret Service had different objectives, with the former wishing to keep some of these activities secret while the latter preferred to trumpet them. The CIA's worries about boasting were confirmed in November 1952 when two of its officers were captured on a mission over the mainland. The CIA had decided that it wanted to collect an agent for extensive debriefing, but the original infiltration team had been captured and 'doubled' and was now working for Chinese security. The low-flying C-47 aircraft conveying the new team was damaged and crashed before it reached the collection point. The two CAT pilots were killed but the two young CIA case officers, Richard G. Fecteau and John T. Downey, who had recently joined the CIA, survived and were incarcerated on spying charges for almost two decades in Chinese jails, until Richard Nixon secured their release. Nevertheless, with the Korean War in full swing the pressure from Washington was to increase the pace. In July 1952, even the US Ambassador in Taipei, the capital of Taiwan, was ordered to get busy 'expanding and developing resistance in China to the Peiping regime's control, particularly in South China'.[9]

The inner meaning of Cold War fighting has often been misunderstood. This is not surprising since, even at the time, its general purpose was not agreed. Only a minority believed that real liberation could be achieved and individual countries be prised away. Some saw it as a form of ideological aggression, the only honest expression of America as a freedom-loving nation. It helped relieve the frustration of the frozen front in which real conflict was increasingly prohibited by nuclear deterrence. Yet others saw it as a way of keeping the enemy off balance. If Stalin and Mao could be kept busy worrying about their own backyards they would not intrude into the Western spheres.

William Donovan, one of America's longest-serving practitioners of covert warfare, took the latter view that Cold War fighting was really about keeping the communists off balance, not about real liberation. Having undertaken a range of 'privateer' covert activities in Europe in the late 1940s, Donovan turned his attention to Asia in the 1950s. In 1953 he was sent out to Bangkok to beef up covert warfare on that continent. He was a clear-minded individual and in May that year he returned briefly to the US and spoke to the Naval War College at Rhode Island about his objectives. With the recent death of Stalin and with attention focused on some of the failed risings in Poland and Berlin, he took the opportunity to expound on the nature and purpose of continued Cold War fighting.

'Whether it is fought on the battlefield of Korea or in the ballot boxes of Italy, it remains a war which involves the survival of the kind of life we want to live.' The era of a big shooting war, he thought, was over, while war by conspiracy and subversion remained. East Asia would be its main battleground, and Donovan was optimistic about what could be done from Taiwan, arousing resistance movements on the mainland using radios, pamphlets and leaflets together with covert operations. Taiwan was being well supplied with modern arms and equipment, and 'Chinese guerrilla forces are active on the mainland.' Operational nuclei were being organised, he claimed, with small well-trained and well-screened cadres to activate a resistance force in the countryside. Donovan knew China well and insisted there were 'many regions of China which offer ideal areas for resistance organization due to their topography, tradition and the independence of their people. For instance, last year in Kansu Province in Northwest China 20,000 peasants rose in open rebellion against their Communist leaders.' But he was equally clear that he was not advocating liberation, only making trouble for the communists. He warned that 'China will not fall into our hands like a ripe pear.' Americans should 'harbor no hopes' of rolling back either the Soviet Union or communist China. Instead, the aim was to halt 'Mao's expansionism'. Their task was to delay the consolidation of communist power, to bring 'constant headaches to Red authority' and to 'breed chaos and confusion'. But Donovan also knew the limits and warned his listeners 'not to arouse the population to premature and futile revolt when they have no weapons, but to foment unrest and discontent, and sustain hope'. Not every policy-maker enjoyed such clarity of thought in this area.[10]

By March 1954, Asia was thought more promising than Europe, and the Cold War fighting programme there was still expanding. The CIA and the Department of Defense came to an agreement on the joint development of an 'aggressive' clandestine raiding effort from Taiwan. These raids were intended to keep the Chinese communists off balance, to destroy communications and vital installations and to present 'an increased threat to the mainland'. They were also designed to destroy China's coastal trade.[11]

Away from Taiwan, Cold War fighting was now the order of the day all around the 3,000-mile perimeter of China's southern and eastern borders. In Burma, the CIA gave extensive support to the Chinese Nationalist warlord General Li Mi from Yunnan Province, whose Nationalist Kuomintang (KMT) forces loyal to Chiang Kai-shek had retreated into northern Burma at the end of the Chinese civil war. The idea had originated with the Pentagon during the early stages of the Korean War and was intended to distract Chinese forces from Korea. The plan was presented at a high level to Harry Truman and the National Security Council. Lloyd George, head of the CIA's Far Eastern Division, recalled Truman's orders clearly: 'Don't tell the American Ambassador in Rangoon what the hell is going on.' Accordingly Ambassador David McKendree was told nothing about this operation.[12] Once established in the remote Shan States of northern Burma, Li Mi ran a semi-independent kingdom based on banditry supplied by both Western Enterprises Inc. from Taiwan and the CIA's Sea Supply Company in Thailand. In 1951 several thousand of his troops attempted an invasion of Yunnan province in southern China, but the local population failed to rise in support. Li Mi was reinforced and in 1952 repeated his operation with an estimated 10,000 troops. Although he penetrated sixty miles into China he was eventually repelled with heavy losses. Thereafter his troops settled down in northern Burma and diversified into a more comfortable existence based on opium cultivation, smuggling and banditry.[13]

London and Paris took special exception to these operations launched from Burma. Not only did they threaten to provoke the communist Chinese into piecemeal retaliation, perhaps against Hong Kong or Indochina, but they also aggravated the already dangerous domestic instability in Burma. General Jean de Lattre de Tassigny, who was both the French High Commissioner and Commander in Chief in Indochina, told British and American intelligence that he was fed up with these trou-blemakers and 'was imprisoning every Chinese nationalist he could get his hands on'. The British feared that Burma would descend into chaos, perhaps turning communist and ending Britain's cherished hopes of drawing the country back within the Commonwealth. At an intelligence conference in 1952, British officers openly confronted their American counterparts over these operations, insisting that 'Their military value and offensive action against the Communist Armies is nil but they are a very serious political threat both to the Burmese Government and to *world peace*: – to the Burmese government from the stand point of inter-nal security; to world peace because the presence of KMT forces close to China and based on foreign soil might be well used as a provocation or excuse for an attack.' However, American representatives at this confer-ence flatly refused to discuss these operations, although later the United States agreed to keep Britain better informed of operations using KMT rebels.[14]

British officials had other reasons for trying to avoid trouble in Burma. They had visited the State Department in July 1951 to complain that Rangoon was having to deal with Li Mi's KMT troops by taking its forces away from the business of guarding 'certain oil installations which the British Government wished protected by Burmese troops' from ban-ditry. They could see a time when the Burmese would join with Beijing to deal with Li Mi. They offered to ignore Washington's previous transpar-ently dishonest assurances that the US was not involved if, they said, 'British and American undercover agents "get together" on this matter in Burma to the end that common action to solve this problem be taken'. State Department officials realised that London and Rangoon were now 'convinced' that the CIA was behind the provision of supplies to the guerrillas. However, American diplomats insisted that neither they nor Taipei had any control. There was no meeting of minds here and the Americans simply informed London that there had been more fighting with the Chinese in Yunnan and hoped that the British would 'share our pleasure upon learning that the Kuomintang troops were successful in causing the Communist troops trouble'.[15]

Co-ordination and control across the whole field were certainly poor. Washington was still attempting to make the fusion of Wisner's OPC and the CIA's intelligence-gathering arm a reality in the field. In Bangkok in particular, the main CIA centre in South-east Asia, the covert action arm of the CIA tended to exceed its authority and undertake wild activities, to the dismay of the intelligence-gathering arm. In the spring of 1952 a dispute broke out between the two wings of the CIA station in Bangkok when the OPC element tried to steal an agent from the intelligence section who was a senior official working in the Thai government. OPC then kidnapped the station's radio operator to try and prevent Washington from finding out what was going on. The CIA's Inspector General Lyman Kirkpatrick together with its Director of Policy and Plans, Colonel Pat Johnson, had to be sent out to Bangkok to prevent them from 'shooting live bullets at each other'.[16]

By 1954 some pretence was made at shifting KMT forces out of Burma. Small numbers of troops were moved and 'unserviceable weapons' were being surrendered. But the main forces of KMT were defiant and declared 'that they had no intention of quitting Burma until the mainland of China had been regained by Chiang Kai-shek'. The Karens, with whom the British had enjoyed a long-term, if uneven, relationship, were now having open discussions with the KMT about co-operating against the Rangoon government. London maintained a sneaking admiration for the rebel Karen tribes. It noted that the Karen chiefs had recently invited forty Burmese communist rebels from the White Flag faction to dinner and then murdered them, an exercise in diplomacy that was 'quite unique'.[17]

American diplomats on the ground were the last to know the full extent of what the CIA was doing. William Sebald was a senior Foreign Service officer in the US Embassy in Rangoon in the early 1950s and gradually realised that, in Washington, it was the CIA and the China Lobby backing the KMT that were in the driving seat. Sebald and his colleagues sympathised with the Rangoon government and with the British position, but by January 1953 they were afraid that if they expressed these views they would find themselves 'on the wrong side of Washington opinion', a dangerous place to be in the early 1950s. There was the possibility that the China Lobby and the McCarthyites would 'spread distorted stories' asserting that 'the KMTs would be able and willing to defeat Red China were it not for the "Red" Government of Burma'. Sebald believed that the Burmese Army should have been fighting communist rebels in Burma instead of Li Mi's KMT forces, he also feared a punitive raid into Burma by Beijing. American press articles by leading journalists such as Joseph Alsop were now alleging CIA support for Li Mi, and eventually Sebald understood that this was a joint CIA-Taiwan operation that was out of control. In November 1953 the full truth began to dawn:

> The jungle generals sent a message to Li Mi in Taipei strongly hinting that unless the United States favored them and stopped its pressures, they would be forced to tell the world of the former relations between the United States and themselves. This ... suggests a not too subtle form of blackmail in which the Chinese Government [in Taiwan] seems to be involved. It also lent credence to the recurrent reports that our C.I.A. had originally given covert support to the KMTs. We asked the Department for advance guidance in the event this story should break ...

As usual, the ordinary Foreign Service officers were left to clear up the mess on the ground once covert action policies had gone astray.[18]

By the end of 1953 the CIA were using their own airline, Civil Air Transport, to begin to move some of Li Mi's guerrillas out of Burma. The operation was run from the somewhat volatile CIA station in Thailand. A Joint Evacuation Committee was set up to negotiate the process which included Colonel Raymond Palmer from the US Embassy and Colonel Chatichai Choonhavan from the Thai Army, together with Willis Bird and Saul G. Marias from CAT. On 21 October 1953 Al Cox, who was described as the 'President' of CAT, flew into Bangkok to seal the arrangements, agreed a price of $123 per evacuee, and confirmed an offer of four 'special C-46s' to fly them out, hopefully rising later to six aircraft. But they were clearly envisaging removing no more than 2,500 of the estimated 15,000 KMT troops in Burma. Cox was in fact a senior member of the CIA Far East Division and by 1960 was running the paramilitary branch of the CIA covert action staff.[19] In March 1954 the Burmese Prime Minister complained directly to President Eisenhower. The much touted withdrawal, he said, was partial, with no arms being surrendered. The few troops that were leaving were doing so with 'bad grace' and were handing their arms to the Karen rebels. He deplored the fact that Taiwan was 'permitted to commit this aggression in this country under the guise, so blatantly false, that they are crusaders against the menace of communism in the East'. He demanded that Eisenhower place 'the utmost pressure' on Taipei.[20]

In fact it was only in 1958 that the CIA chief on Taipei, Ray Cline, began real efforts to repatriate KMT fighters to Taiwan. CIA support for the KMT in Burma during the 1950s came into the category of 'implausible denial', a noisy activity that was hardly covert at all and certainly fooled no one in Burma. As one American diplomat put it, 'we'd been caught red-handed supplying KMT guerrillas in the Shan state and contributing to the disruption in the Shan state, making efforts to make trouble for the Communists in Yunnan Province next door at Burma's expense'. The winding down of CIA support after 1958 marked an end to a 'chilly period' in US-Burmese relations.[21]

The confusion caused by Western Cold War fighting in Asia is underlined by the manner in which, despite adding to Burma's internal security problems during this period, Washington was simultaneously contracting to help Rangoon improve its internal security. In September 1953 the State Department and a delegation from the Burmese Embassy in Washington met at the offices of Inpolco in Washington, a private company that specialised in providing expertise in police methods at a training school in Vienna in Virginia, and which also supplied 'certain pieces of equipment'. The Burmese delegation was acting on behalf of

Inspector General U Pe Than, head of the Rangoon Special Branch. They examined a range of interesting artefacts – from bullet-proof vests to a James Bond-style 'miniature tape recorder with wristwatch microphone' priced at $390 – and were then invited to inspect the curriculum of the security training school at Vienna. Later the State Department asked if Inpolco would let it know of 'any extra-curricular purchases of equipment', adding that the head of the Burmese delegation loved the wristwatch 'and obviously yearns for one'.[22]

India too was a natural launch-pad for Cold War fighting against communist China. Rivalry between Czarist Russia, British India, China, and the tribes of smaller states for suzerainty in Central Asia had constituted the famous 'Great Game' of the late nineteenth century. More recently, the wartime British authorities in India had co-operated with Donovan's OSS in supporting Tibet, to the intense anger of the wartime Chinese government. The arrival of new governments in Delhi in 1947, and in Beijing in 1949, seemed to point to warmer Sino-Indian relations. The Indian Prime Minister Pandit Nehru was especially anxious to cultivate Mao and remained publicly sceptical of the Western line during the Korean War. But privately his line began to change in October 1950, when the Chinese communist PLA defeated the small Tibetan Army and marched into Lhasa, expelling the local Indian diplomatic mission.

London was restrained in its criticism of China, stressing that it recognised Chinese suzerainty in Tibet but not sovereignty. Since Britain had devolved its interests in that part of the world to Delhi, the Foreign Office concluded that 'any attempt to intervene in Tibet would be impractical and unwise' and limited itself to supporting India. The American line was different. As early as 24 July 1950, following the outbreak of the Korean War, the United States informed the British that it was willing to help the Tibetans with 'their desire for arms' and, if allowed transit through India, it would help 'with procurement and financing of the Tibetan purchases'. Nevertheless Washington moved cautiously, adding that 'any project had best be undertaken by the Tibetans themselves rather than initiated by us'. Assistance remained low key because of British opposition and Indian uncertainty. American officials from Delhi worked with the Tibetans by visiting the border town of Kalimpong as 'tourists', although their activities were known to the local Indian Security Service, known as IB, that watched all movements intently. It was the CIA that financed the move of one of the Dalai Lama's elder brothers, Thupten Norbu, to the United States in 1950.[23]

India's attitude was also changing. Overtly, it remained critical of the American Cold War effort in Asia, but privately it now joined in. Brutal Chinese PLA action in Tibet eroded any fraternal feelings that Nehru had entertained for the Beijing regime. The CIA had been assisting

Tibetan resistance groups since the summer of 1950, probably with tacit Indian approval. Washington now approached Nehru and offered to help India 'in every possible way' to support the Khampa and Amdoan resistance groups in Tibet.[24] The Indian IB opened bigger offices in northern India at Kalimpong, Darjeeling and Gangtok, to counter communist infiltration and to help forge resistance groups into a unified force now called the National Volunteer Defence Army or NVDA. A low-level border war now began. Detailed arrangements were finalised by Nehru's sister, Vijaylakshmi Nehru, the Indian Ambassador in Washington, and in March 1951 a secret Indo-American agreement was signed relating to military aid and secret service co-operation. London wished to see Tibetan resistance stiffened but was anxious to act through proxies so as not to provoke the Chinese directly or jeopardise Hong Kong. 'We are not supplying arms to Tibet,' the Foreign Office asserted, but only 'selling to India certain arms to replace some of the arms she may supply to Tibet from her own stocks'. Krishna Menon, who had moved from being the Indian High Commissioner in London to become India's Foreign Secretary, complained that Britain was 'passing the buck'.[25]

For the United States, these developments had a dual purpose. Although the situation in Tibet was not materially changed, Delhi was now embroiled in the Cold War and had learned a salutary lesson in the perils of non-alignment. An agreement between Tibet and Beijing signed in May 1951, offering some local autonomy, resulted only in a temporary lull in the fighting. By 1953, Chinese efforts to extend the revolution into Tibet's outlying province of Kham led to intensified fighting. One of Tibet's two co-Prime Ministers fled to Kalimpong to encourage the resistance. Meanwhile 12,000 KMT soldiers, who had been hiding in the mountains near Tibet since the end of the Chinese civil war, joined the NVDA guerrillas. The fighting spread, and the CIA and the Taiwan secret service accelerated air-drops from both India and Thailand. A Chinese crackdown only accelerated the cycle of covert action and reaction.

But in late 1953 Delhi got wind of American plans to draw Pakistan into the South East Asian Treaty Organisation (SEATO) and of an American security agreement with Pakistan. This had a neuralgic effect upon Nehru which no amount of reassurance from Eisenhower could counteract. Nehru now began talks with China to defuse tensions over Tibet. When the United States confirmed its ties with Pakistan through the Baghdad Pact in 1955, Nehru responded by visiting Moscow. Joint US–Taiwan–Indian assistance to the Tibetan rebels was now brought shuddering to a halt by the cross-cutting local rivalries over areas like Kashmir. Meanwhile the PLA took the opportunity to launch new operations against the NVDA, forcing the Dalai Lama to reach an accommodation with Beijing. The CIA admitted temporary defeat and suspended its operations in Tibet in 1955.[26]

Most liberation operations against China had a KMT input. But Taiwan did not enjoy a monopoly and Chiang Kai-shek was not viewed by the CIA as an ideal partner. Even in late 1948, some of Chiang Kai-shek's most experienced warlords had recognised that the corrupt nature of the KMT regime was the largest impediment to full American support. They had approached the CIA with the idea of creating a 'Third Force', a democratic and anti-communist alternative to Chiang's corrupt Nationalist KMT. Most experienced CIA 'China hands' recognised that this was a more realistic way to resist communist consolidation in China. When the CIA's proposal to work with Third Force adherents reached Washington it sent diplomats in the Far Eastern Division 'into shock'. But at a higher level these ideas were thought attractive. Acheson privately told Sir Oliver Franks, the British Ambassador in Washington, that while the Americans would use Taiwan as a base for operations against the mainland, Assistant Secretary Dean Rusk was leading a team of military, CIA and Nationalist KMT Army representatives who would push forward with plans to depose Chiang and perhaps place Taiwan directly under MacArthur's military control. In the mid-1950s, the CIA was still pursuing the Third Force option quite vigorously.[27]

Pursuit of the Third Force option reflected deep disillusionment with Chiang Kai-shek. Washington thought claims for the numbers of his armed forces 'deceptive' and believed that their presumed loyalty would evaporate under an attack. Co-ordination between the various branches of the armed forces was 'non-existent' with Chiang practising divide and rule. He did not want an efficient modern command system, 'which he cannot manipulate as of yore'. Backing him was no longer attractive since the idea that Washington wanted 'to place the KMT back in the saddle on the mainland again' would alienate waverers on the mainland and also allies who disliked Chiang. The Chinese communists would have a 'beautiful ready-made propaganda line created for their use'.

In 1951 Washington considered altering the Nationalist government on Taiwan, if necessary using a *'coup d'état* following preliminary measures to assure suitable conditions'. This was obviously risky, but it felt that 'with the right propaganda line, the job could be done with the minimum of repercussions'. There were obvious problems with this solution since other equally corrupt allied regimes in other countries would fear similar house-cleaning measures. Moreover, even if successful, 'the United States would have the problem of how to dispose of the deposed'. Instead, after due reflection, Washington opted for a twin-track policy of gently trying to alter the government on Taiwan through Chiang's son and heir Chiang Ching-kuo, while backing Third Force groups outside

Taiwan, from Hong Kong and Hanoi. However, it accepted that these were in the hands of disapproving allies and that 'these spots will doubtless be denied to us'. So they fell back on operations launched from the Japanese island of Okinawa.[28]

The widespread Cold War fighting across Asia in the early 1950s confronted Britain's SIS with a perplexing dilemma. Although it disapproved of many American policies, one of Britain's most highly valued contributions to American security was its intelligence on China and Vietnam. Not only did Britain enjoy elaborate signals intelligence facilities in Hong Kong and a long-established network of agents and contacts, often established through commercial conduits, it also had staff with a lifetime of experience interpreting events in Asia. Indeed, as the Vietnam War escalated in the 1960s, experienced British intelligence officers retiring from Asia found themselves in demand in Washington as analysts. Hong Kong was invaluable as a watchtower on China and also as a launch-pad for operations. As Frank Wisner had once observed to Kim Philby, 'whenever there is somewhere we want to destabilize, the British have an island nearby'. But provoking communist China through Cold War fighting was the last thing that London wanted. Thus Hong Kong was one British island where secret service co-operation was anything but straightforward, and indeed it was often hidden-hand activity that created the flashpoints.[29]

Joseph Buckholder Smith, a CIA officer who worked closely with SIS officers in Asia for many years, recalled 'it was our Hong Kong station, with its guy lines trailing across the Straits of Formosa, that really set their teeth on edge'. Britain was anxious to preserve its commercial interests and to protect Hong Kong, which was ultimately dependent on Beijing's goodwill. By contrast, Washington, already pursuing a rigid economic embargo of China, and without an embassy in Beijing, had little to lose. Menzies, the SIS Chief, insisted that his staff and the CIA in Hong Kong keep 'at arm's length' in this 'sensitive spot', even to the extent that for a while intelligence material on China was only exchanged in Singapore, where the CIA maintained a much smaller station.[30]

This was an argument over practical interests rather than the nature of the Beijing regime. London had no illusions about Mao as a mere socialist 'agrarian reformer'. SIS had had excellent relations with the Chinese communists throughout the Second World War and knew that Mao Tsetung was a real communist. The wartime head of station in Chungking, Colonel Harmon, had enjoyed a close friendship with Chou En-lai, Mao's Foreign Minister, and had seconded a British academic, Michael Lindsay, to the communists to manage their radio network. This picture was confirmed for the British Cabinet in March 1949. Ernest Bevin explained to his fellow Ministers that the Special Branch in Hong Kong had just conducted a surprise raid on a leading Chinese communist and the diaries and documentation that were seized painted 'a revealing picture of the ruthless fervour, efficiency and cynicism of the Chinese Communists and provide abundant evidence that, far from the Chinese Communist Party being moderated by any special "Chinese" factors, it is strictly orthodox, confident, mature, and at the highest level very well organized. There is no trace of Titoism.'[31] London drew greater distinctions between Beijing and Moscow. But it did not resist American policies of Cold War fighting in Asia because of some prescient anticipation of a Sino-Soviet split that was still ten years away. Instead it dragged its heels because it saw CIA activities as unrealistic and dangerously adverse to its own imperial interests in Asia, especially the survival of Hong Kong, which could be overrun by communist Chinese forces almost at will.

Violent Western disagreements over policy towards communist China did not lessen the insatiable demand for intelligence on China during the 1950s and 1960s. With the closure of American diplomatic premises in mainland China even the British Embassy in Beijing offered the United States an important window on communist China. More importantly, the American Consulate General in Hong Kong grew to become the largest 'consulate' in the world – indeed bigger than most embassies – with forty-two vice consuls and hundreds of staff. This 'consulate' absorbed many of the American Foreign Service's more experienced Sinologists now ejected from China. The CIA station in Hong Kong, commanded by Al Cox in the mid-1950s, also expanded rapidly, rivalling even the huge CIA station on Taiwan at Taipei. William Colby, who later rose to become director of the CIA, recalled that at this time 'The great challenges to secret intelligence gathering were ... in Berlin, Vienna and Hong Kong.'[32]

British military commanders in Hong Kong were the most sympathetic to American intelligence. In June 1952, General Terence Airey, the British Commander, was fighting British regional intelligence chiefs in Singapore for permission for an Anglo-American Intelligence Committee in Hong Kong to specialise in military aspects of communist China, which was a 'favourite project of his'. Airey had previously worked at Eisenhower's SHAPE HQ in Paris and was quick to reassure the Americans that the French would not be told of this group. He sought escape from 'the academic and unreasonable restrictions imposed by Singapore ... mil[itary] and civil auth[orities] on exchange of Far East infor[mation] anywhere except Singapore' and wanted the power to overrule the Governor of Hong Kong to give 'sensitive, though vital information to US'. Meanwhile he was pressing the Director of Military Intelligence in London, General Shortt, about his plan 'to greatly increase Brit covert agent org[anisation] on mainland China'. Shortt wanted 'much stronger and riskier measures' to improve intelligence. One of the key intelligence targets in China was atomic developments. Agents were continually despatched towards the uranium gaseous diffusion plant under construction at Lanchow and the plutonium plant at Pao Tou, both in north-central China. But there was little success, and hard information on the Chinese atomic programme had to await the advent of satellite photography in the 1960s.[33]

As in Germany and Austria, the key American intelligence operation at Hong Kong used refugees rather than agents. The vast 'China-watching group' was a mirror-image of 'Project Wringer', which debriefed refugees from the Eastern bloc entering Austria. It involved the in-depth interrogation of knowledgeable refugees and defectors, many from academia, the military or business, escaping from communist China. This developed into more elaborate operations, based on Chinese families in Hong Kong who had influential relatives in Communist China, which were shared with British organisations. This watchtower on China offered not only the usual forms of political, economic and military intelligence, but also an excellent window on Chinese society. This was vital to CIA officers trying to assess the impact of their efforts to destabilise China. Much intelligence work was designed to service what Colby called the 'paramilitary and political action culture' which had 'unquestionably become dominant in the CIA'.[34]

CIA support for guerrilla activity was increasingly focused on southeast China, where it was hoped it might reduce Chinese assistance to Ho Chi Minh, the communist leader in Indochina. This was reinforced by a propaganda campaign using radio and air-dropped leaflets.[35] The large numbers of refugees passing through Hong Kong allowed the CIA to measure the level of dissent. In March 1950 it reported on the impact of an air-dropped propaganda campaign against the towns of the southern province of Kwantung. Consistent with the traditions of covert action, this operation had its element of farce: 'Upon these leaflet raids there was always a certain amount of humour. The natives dare not pick them up off the streets for fear of Communist retaliation. However, practically half the town would head for every scalable roof and with impunity get the leaflets there.'[36] A key part of the CIA's work on destabilisation was its attempts to assess the effectiveness of the communist secret police run by the Ministry of State Security, with which resistance groups had to contend. Its interest extended not only to current Chinese dissident groups, but also to the more ambitious programme of operations by 'retardation groups' that would begin work only in the event of all-out war with China, which often seemed imminent. In 1951 Taiwan's secret service claimed that it controlled 1,600,000 guerrilla troops, but

American officials believed that resisters numbered more like 300,000 and that Taipei's actual control over them was 'almost non-existent'. Nevertheless, the CIA believed that at the very least in a war they could 'tie down very large numbers' of communist troops. As late as 1969, the CIA reports on the Chinese secret police were still based primarily on Hong Kong interrogation material.[37]

CIA reports from Hong Kong regularly found their way on to the President's desk. In 1950, Admiral Hillenkoetter, the Director of the CIA, sent Harry Truman an urgent message on China, prefacing it with the remark: 'A trusted informant from Hong Kong has provided the following information.' A decade later in June 1960 the National Security Council declared Hong Kong to be simply 'the most important source of hard economic, political and military information on Communist China'. This situation prevailed throughout the 1960s and Hong Kong's value as the American watchtower on China grew with the extent of American military involvement in Asia. Edwin Martin, the US Consul General in Hong Kong in the late 1960s, recalled this period – the height of Mao Tse-tung's Cultural Revolution – as the most productive because of the huge flow of refugees: 'There was a lot of faction fighting among the Red Guards and other communist groups who delighted in exposing what they would consider past crimes of the Party. They published their own little papers, they published documents.' As a result there was 'a real explosion of information' about what was going on in China.[38]

President Lyndon Johnson received similar Hong Kong material on subjects as diverse as Soviet military assistance to China and contacts between the Chinese and Latin American communist parties in 1964. In the late 1960s attention turned to Vietnam. Indeed, as late as 1970, intelligence from an agent recruited in Hong Kong was at the centre of a high-level controversy over Nixon's decision to extend the war into Cambodia. However, the most important intelligence product from Hong Kong came from the large sigint station run jointly by the British, Americans and Australians at Little Sai Wan. Like the British SIS, the CIA also used Hong Kong for its black-market exchange service to provide currency for operations throughout Asia. Decline only came in the 1970s, with Nixon's extraction of the United States from the Vietnam War and his surprise rapprochement with communist China, heralding the beginning of joint Sino-American intelligence operations focused on the Soviet Union, including Soviet missile development.[39]

The most awkward flare-ups happened inside Hong Kong itself and were caused by either covert action or subversion rather than by intelligence-gathering operations. An obvious area of confrontation was economic warfare, which paralleled the subversion war. The main instrument here was COCOM restrictions, an agreed programme of

Western economic blockade that tried to prevent useful Western products from reaching communist countries and indeed to prevent the East exporting profitably to the West. In the abstract these measures seemed sensible, but in practice in Hong Kong, a centre of entrepôt trade, they could quickly become ludicrous. Chickens could not be imported from communist China's neighbouring Kwantung Province into Hong Kong, this much was clear. But if a live communist chicken laid an egg while illegally in Hong Kong, was the egg also a communist product? These matters were a regular cause of friction between British and American officials in Hong Kong. Even during the Korean War, Britain resisted these restrictions. A key role for numerous American vice consuls was to make discreet enquiries to ensure that the Hong Kong authorities were policing these issues properly. Eventually they rode along with British patrols intercepting junks in Hong Kong waters that were smuggling steel plate or rubber tyres.

One of the many American vice consuls in Hong Kong, Richard E. Johnson, remembered that, during the Korean War, he received an urgent request from Washington to investigate the possible re-export to China of Western condoms:

And the question was: What are Hong Kong's requirements for prophylactic rubbers? And I had to go all around Hong Kong, talking to importers of prophylactic rubbers and asking: How many do you think Hong Kong uses? And how many are reexported to China? And I wrote about a ten- or twelve-page airgram, which received commendations from Washington. Then I got a further communication saying, 'Please update this carefully. We have heard that the Chinese Communists are using prophylactic rubbers to protect the muzzles of their guns from moisture.'

Just as this unusual military function for condoms was confirmed by intelligence reports from Korea, he received another telegram from the Pentagon that said: 'Forget all about it.' The Pentagon's experts had discovered that if you try to protect your gun muzzles in this way, they would simply rust and pit out the muzzles because the moisture would collect with no air circulating in the muzzle. 'So any prophylactic rubbers that want to go to Communist China, okay.' Although it was easy to ridicule trade restrictions with mainland China these measures did hurt Beijing. The CIA identified the quasi-illicit gold trade between Hong Kong and Macao, the neighbouring Portuguese colony, as a key source of hard currency that Beijing used for buying essential technologies throughout the world.[40]

Alongside battles over COCOM controls, overt and covert psywar activity from Hong Kong was growing fast even before the outbreak of the Korean War. In Washington, staffers working on NSC document 48/2 – a key American blueprint for future Cold War fighting – noted that the US Information Service office in Hong Kong 'has greatly expanded its activities in recent months. It is now mailing approximately 80,000 items of printed matter monthly to about 9,000 addresses within Communist China. Some distribution is also being conducted through underground channels with the co-operation of Nationalist groups and commercial smugglers.' The use of covert channels was essential as the Chinese communist censors were catching most of the overt mailshots. US Information Service admitted to the British that it was used by what it referred to quaintly as 'the other Agency' for covert activities. In December 1951, Adam Watson, London's psywar liaison officer in Washington, was asked to look into US Information Service links 'with covert activities'. USIS tried to 'smooth over British suspicions' by suggesting that this was either unauthorised use of the US Information Service label by 'Taiwan supported anti-communist groups' or else Beijing making fraudulent claims. But Watson now knew that USIS had broken agreements on activity into China based in Hong Kong and was used for CIA activity.[41]

American operations continued to grow. The overt activities alone of USIS in Hong Kong ran to $3.2 million for the years 1958–61. It sought not only to destabilise the Chinese communist regime, but also to destroy any sympathy between the Chinese overseas population and the mainland, and thus targeted audiences right across Asia. One of its most successful ventures was a seemingly independent magazine in Mandarin Chinese called *World Today* which enjoyed a huge circulation in Taiwan and South-east Asia. Its popular mixture of current affairs together with 'quite a bit of stuff on movie stars' competed on the newsstands with straight magazines, and the fact that it was not free added enormously to its credibility.[42] The Beijing authorities devoted considerable energy to exposing CIA and USIS propaganda activities in Hong Kong. In November 1958 they issued a long and detailed press story entitled 'US spy ring seeks to control education, culture in Hong Kong'. It asserted that 'the United States espionage organisations have been exerting every effort to control schools, film enterprises, publishing houses and cultural organisations in Hong Kong by deception, bribery and to use them as tools to poison the minds of the Hong Kong compatriots and carry out criminal activities against China.' They correctly identified the attempts of the Asia Foundation, the Ford Foundation and the Mercius Foundation to draw in local schools with offers of grants. American teachers in schools, they insisted, had been recruiting graduating students as agents with a view to sending them into mainland China. Plenty of American front organisations in Hong Kong were identified, including the Asian Film Company, established in 1954, used 'to shoot reactionary films', along with publishing houses such as the Asia Press and the Union Press. The American Consulate General also watched any bookstores or film companies that were distributing material sympathetic to communism.[43]

Sir Alexander Graham, Hong Kong's Governor, took the toughest line on the CIA. When aircraft from the CIA's own private airline, Civil Air Transport, evacuated from mainland China to Hong Kong in 1949, he impounded them prior to handing them over to the communists. William J. Donovan, the wartime head of OSS, together with Richard Heppner, head of his wartime China station, arrived to act as lawyers on CAT's behalf. Graham was warned that they would make it 'hot for him' in London unless he relented, which he eventually did. The CIA believed that Beijing had developed an extensive communist underground organisation in Hong Kong by infiltrating labour groups, which Graham appeared to tolerate. By contrast, he seemed intolerant of Taiwan's secret organisations using the colony as a springboard for operations into mainland China. While the CIA was financing Taiwan's anti-communist groups in Hong Kong, the British were cracking down on them and arresting their leaders. By August 1951 eight undercover operatives from Taiwan were in custody. Graham later recalled his fury at 'extremely ham handed' CIA activities and taking 'a very strong line to stop them being so stupid'.[44]

Matters reached a crisis point on 11 April 1955, towards the end of the First Taiwan Straits Crisis. Against the background of growing artillery barrages between Taiwan and mainland China, Taiwan's secret service arranged the bombing of an Air India airliner, The Kashmir Princess, carrying Chinese communist journalists to the neutralist Bandung Conference of Asian leaders in Indonesia. The bomb was planted when the plane refuelled at Hong Kong and the plane exploded and plunged into the sea as it approached the Indonesian coast. All passengers and crew were killed. Beijing claimed that it had warned the security authorities in Hong Kong that Taiwan's secret service would attempt to sabotage the plane. Chou En-lai, the Chinese Foreign Minister, had intended to travel on this aircraft, but wisely changed his mind at the last minute. Graham told London that security teams from communist China, Hong Kong and India were collaborating closely in an attempt to catch the perpetrators. But relations were prickly and the Indians had to serve as a buffer between the British and the communist Chinese security organisations. Nevertheless, by May 1955 a team consisting of Inspector Kaon of the Indian IB, MI5, the Hong Kong Special Branch and three representatives of the Chinese secret service were in Hong Kong and were busy on the case.

The Chinese secret service claimed to have had heard rumours of planned attacks on Chinese delegations as they passed through Hong

Kong on their way to Bandung as early as March 1955. But on the day before the bombing all it knew was that Taiwan's secret service was 'actively making preparations'. Shortly after the attack the Beijing authorities had secured very detailed intelligence on the perpetrators from one of their agents. This identified the chief saboteur as one Chou Chu, alias Chow Tse Ming, a member of the ground crew at Kai Tak airfield. They asserted that the device was a small time bomb supplied by the United States and that it was part of a batch of bombs shipped from Keelung to Hong Kong on 5 April on the SS *Szechuan*, a merchant vessel owned by Butterfield and Swire; they also knew the identities of the individuals who had transported the bombs. Taiwan's secret service in Hong Kong, they added, had arranged for Chou Chu to receive training in bombing airliners that emphasised placing the device 'close to a fuel tank in one of the wings'.

Chou Chu was still calmly going to work at Kai Tak on 18 May, a week after the bombing, but by the time a raid was made on his home that night 'he had bolted'. Raids were then made on the homes of the many other individuals named by Beijing. These produced further evidence. 'Other raids followed throughout the night on information gained as a result.' Chou Chu escaped to Taiwan on an aircraft owned by CAT at 10.00 a.m. on 18 May. CAT claimed that he had 'stowed away' and confirmed that the escapee's name was Chou Chu, alias Chow Tse Ming. The Hong Kong authorities tried to secure his return by pretending that he was wanted for a low-grade smuggling offence, but it knew the game was up. The Hong Kong Special Branch blamed Beijing for passing on the intelligence tardily and only through the Indian IB. 'If the Chinese had made their information available to us earlier we could have put him under surveillance and probably prevented his escape,' they claimed. Although seven suspects were held for detailed questioning, the agent-based evidence could not be revealed in court, so they were merely deported.[45]

Beijing was furious. In August 1955 it complained that, despite the provision of detailed intelligence, including a list of the names of thirty-nine secret agents connected with the case, among them Chao Pin-cheng, Taiwan's secret service chief in Hong Kong, no prosecutions had been secured. Beijing insisted that the raids provided evidence that Chou Chu had received his training in explosives from Taiwan and had 'escaped ... under cover and aid of the United States'. It blamed the failures on the fact that there were 'lurking within the Hong Kong Government's political department' numbers of 'Kuomintang secret agents'.[46]

How true were Beijing's accusations? Files declassified in 1999 show that the Prime Minister, Anthony Eden, was told in October 1955 that the Hong Kong Special Branch was in no doubt that evidence it had procured independently proved that Chou Chu had indeed been recruited by Taiwan's secret service. After the crash he had boasted of his actions to four separate witnesses, proclaiming that he had sabotaged the aircraft using 'a small time bomb which made a slight ticking noise' and he had been 'praised' and given 'a reward of 600,000 Hong Kong dollars'. Shortly before fleeing to Taiwan he spent a sum well beyond his normal means. Extradition was obviously impossible. All Eden could do was order a vigorous purge of Taiwan's secret service in Hong Kong. Thirty-six people were deported and eight incarcerated. Eden was furious that the real culprit could not be brought to book and scrawled the single word 'Bad' on his brief.[47]

The CIA head of station in Hong Kong in the early 1960s, Peer de Silva, confirmed that Taiwan's secret service remained a perennial source of trouble. China, like other divided states – Germany, Vietnam and Korea – abounded with double agents and Hong Kong was the obvious conduit. Because the Special Branch in Hong Kong knew that de Silva worked with Taiwan's secret service, it came to him with complaints about their activities, which he bore philosophically. Agents were deported to Kwantung on the mainland or to Taiwan on a weekly basis depending on their allegiance. 'Altogether', recalled de Silva, 'it was never ending burlesque, except that people did die performing it.'[48]

China, not the Soviet Union, was the 'driver' in American policy during the second half of the twentieth century. Although confronting the Soviet Union in a Cold War, the United States was close to hot war with the communists in China. Thus it was China that electrified Anglo-American differences. China went to the very heart of disagreements about how a Cold War that was turning hotter should be managed. Attlee, then Churchill and Eden, also worried that the United States would become embroiled in the 'wrong war', a vast conflict in Asia which would absorb its strength, leaving Europe exposed. More precisely, they feared the numerous flashpoints that might lead to conventional war followed by the use of atomic weapons. The extensive Cold War fighting around the periphery of communist China clearly had this potential.[49] The Straits crises over the offshore islands of Quemoy and Matsu in 1954–5, and again in 1958 were the natural outcome of the persistent and dangerous policy of Cold War fighting. London saw Chiang Kai-shek as a 'palooka' who needed to be restrained because any kind of war would result in the loss of Hong Kong. But Chiang understood the domestic politics of Washington. Throughout the Straits crises, American senators demanded that the US equip him for an improbable all-out attack on the 'soft belly' of the mainland.[50]

Was John Foster Dulles really seeking an all-out hot war with Beijing as London feared? It appears not, for during periods of high tension senior figures in Washington seem to have been trying to slow the pace of activities. On 18 February 1955, during the first of the recurrent Straits crises Dulles contacted his brother Allen Dulles and Frank Wisner to make sure that leafleting operations over mainland China had been suspended, but Wisner said that they were considering resumption. John Foster Dulles was 'reluctant to see action of a provocative nature taken at this time unless it is of real value'. But Wisner was adamant that his staff had gone a long way in helping the Chinese Nationalists to improve the quality of their covert activities and now that 'things are being accomplished' he did not want to lose momentum. He added, 'the Chinats are doing it anyway. We can't stop it.'[51]

The answer was that John Foster Dulles wanted neither a hot war with China, nor did he want restraint. Instead he desired something just short of a hot war that kept up intense psychological pressure and was designed to serve as part of a broader project against the entire communist bloc. On 10 February 1955 he outlined his conviction that 'The whole Communist domain was˜over-extended', and that it was therefore essential to keep the communist regimes under pressure, which in turn would 'lead to disintegration'. Cold War fighting and other hidden-hand activities were also an arena in which the ideological dimension of American foreign policy, which was large, could find expression. All this went to the heart of the question of what the Cold War should be. Should it be primarily 'Cold', as London clearly wished, or should it be something just short of 'War', as Dulles preferred? The latter strategy required greater risks, but held out the prospect of some sort of 'victory' even if liberation was itself improbable. The nature of those risks was also becoming clear as a struggle developed over a parallel programme of Cold War fighting in Europe.[52]

15

The Struggle to Contain Liberation

It is doubtful whether, in a year's time, the US will be able to control the Frankenstein monster which they are creating.
Vice Admiral Eric Longley-Cook, Director of Naval Intelligence, 6 July 1951[1]

Covert action was expanding very fast in the early 1950s. The 'loss' of China in 1949 followed by the outbreak of the Korean War in 1950 seemed to demand a vigorous reaction. Accordingly, in the four years between 1949 and 1952, Frank Wisner's Office of Policy Co-ordination grew from 302 personnel to 2,812, with 3,142 additional overseas contract employees. Its budget increased from $4.7 million to $82 million per year. American covert action staff had been stationed in only seven countries in 1949 but by 1952 they were present in forty-seven.[2] Korea also accelerated British anxieties about American approaches to the Cold War. On 6 July 1950, Malcolm Muggeridge, a former SIS officer, met with serving SIS officers to talk about the new war in Korea. Dick White of MI5 was also there and offered the opinion that younger diplomats in the Foreign Office were 'all anti-American and against Korean intervention'. They mused on how 'leftism' seemed to be 'finding its last foothold in Eton, The Times and the diplomatic service'. But anti-American sentiments were not the monopoly of young diplomats in Whitehall and now welled up across the political spectrum. In December 1950, Muggeridge met Montgomery, who was about to become deputy commander of SHAPE and who was certainly committed to an aggressive Cold War stance. Nevertheless he was unashamedly 'gleeful over MacArthur's reverses' in recent battles in Korea. Anxiety about an American taste for Cold War fighting moved in the context of a broad, unfocused but growing anti-Americanism in Britain.[3]

In both Europe and Asia, the Foreign Office and SIS were now trying to reduce liberation operations. On the surface, their arguments appeared to concentrate on the practical possibilities of Cold War fighting and what they might achieve, against the background of the

disastrous Anglo-American operations against Albania. But more fundamentally these arguments were about the shadow of nuclear power. The
detonation of a Soviet A-bomb in August 1949, followed by the communist victory in China in October 1949 and finally the Korean War in June
1950, influenced Western thinking profoundly. The Foreign Office, SIS
and even some military figures in Britain now regarded a strategy of liberation as much too provocative. Increasingly, Britain's purpose, they
declared, was to opt for stable containment. Not everyone in London
favoured Churchill's idea of a summit with Stalin, but all were anxious
that the Cold War should stay cold. The Foreign Office had never been
comfortable with the paramilitary aspects of liberation. Indeed, the
whole architecture of Britain's secret Cold War apparatus can be understood partly in terms of a struggle by diplomats to control aberrant
figures like Montgomery and Slessor, Chief of the Air Staff. This had
largely been achieved, but there remained the larger problem of the
Americans.

The multiple shocks of 1949 and 1950 had a very different effect in
Washington. Although the US was appalled by the surprise advent of
Soviet atomic power, American cities remained largely invulnerable.
There were still no Soviet bombers or missiles within plausible range of
the United States, but American planners knew this would not always be
the case. At some point in the late 1950s the Soviets would clearly acquire
inter-continental ballistic missiles or ICBMs and the era of real American
superiority would be over. Beyond the late 1950s, there would be a period
of mutual assured destruction and relatively stable deterrence.
Meanwhile, between 1949 and the late 1950s, there appeared to be a 'vulnerability gap' that favoured the Americans and allowed them to 'do
something'. Some Americans saw this gap as a window of opportunity
and wanted to jump through it before it closed.

Patrick Reilly, whose task was day-to-day liaison between the Foreign
Office and SIS, was the first to notice the enhanced British aversion to
confrontation. When the Russia Committee met in February 1950, he
raised a puzzling instruction he had received to eliminate the term 'Cold
War' from a planning paper the committee was preparing for the
Permanent Under-Secretary's Committee or PUSC. His superiors had
simply told him not to use the phrase 'Cold War' at all, explaining that
this term had 'given rise to some loose talk about winning or losing the
Cold War'. The whole concept of Cold War had led to 'too much emphasis upon offensive aspects' at the expense of what diplomats preferred,
namely 'the need for constructive action by the non-Communist Powers
in their own territory'. Air Vice Marshal Sir Arthur Sanders, the military
representative on the committee, was dismayed, and said that he found
the term 'very convenient'. But Christopher Warner, the senior diplomat

present, asserted that any reference to winning or losing the Cold War 'should be forbidden in the Foreign Office'.[4]

Stern disapproval could also be detected at the operational level. By July 1950, even the Russia Committee had concluded that liberation was impossible and that in the foreseeable future, nothing short of a hot war could shake the Soviet grip on the Eastern bloc. 'The best we can hope to do', it suggested, was to keep alive 'some sort of moral resistance' by means of propaganda. But propaganda was also off the menu, for in the same month the Foreign Office decided to halt BBC overseas broadcasts in Baltic languages, fearing that it 'might further stimulate the unrest that already exists in these regions'. Meanwhile, it observed, clandestine resources were best directed towards the quiet gathering of intelligence rather than stirring up trouble.[5]

By contrast the military in Washington had incorporated liberation into its long-term thinking, and their answer to its inherent dangers was military superiority at all levels. Superiority would offer an umbrella of deterrence under which more provocative Cold War fighting could be conducted, without much danger of retaliation or escalation to a hot war. If Moscow perceived itself as militarily weaker, it would have to tolerate these provocations, perhaps even the rolling back of the Eastern bloc, and would not dare to respond violently. This idea lay at the heart of the American blueprint for global containment drawn up in 1949 and 1950 and known as NSC 68 which set out targets for substantial Western rearmament. It has long been recognised that the advent of the Korean War offered timely validation for efforts by the US Joint Chiefs of Staff to militarise the Cold War. But the crucial links between high-level strategic superiority and the low-level business of subverting the Eastern bloc have not been fully recognised. A careful reading of this famous Cold War blueprint which was finalised in April 1950 makes these connections between overt nuclear superiority and covert warfare very clear. NSC 68 argued that 'Without supreme aggregate military strength, in being and readily mobilizable, a policy of containment – which is in effect a policy of calculated and gradual coercion – is no more than a policy of bluff'; it added, 'it is clear that a substantial and rapid building up of strength in the free world is necessary to support a firm policy intended to check and to roll back the Kremlin's drive for world domination'. Military superiority, especially in the nuclear field, was central to any prospect of carrying the Allies with them in the enterprise of liberation. It was evident that without an extension of the umbrella of nuclear and conventional deterrence to America's allies in a convincing way, the alliance commitment to winning the Cold War would begin to unravel. NSC 68 stated that 'unless our combined strength is rapidly increased, our allies will tend to become increasingly reluctant to support a firm foreign policy on our part and increasingly anxious to seek other solutions, even though they are agreed that appeasement means defeat'.[6]

In early 1950 the military in London were busy developing their fabled 'Global Strategy' paper, Britain's own version of NSC 68. The Americans called it the 'Slessor paper', reflecting its intellectual paternity. In June 1951, this paper was given one of its regular updates prior to its presentation to Commonwealth Defence Ministers. Its arguments are remarkable and stand as a firm testament, not only to the continued commitment of the British Chiefs of Staff to the idea of Cold War fighting, which put them out of step with the rest of Whitehall and Westminster, but also to the inseparability of this and the drive for nuclear superiority. Like the United States they believed that military superiority was an essential precursor to liberation. They asserted that 'our ability to win the cold war' was 'rightly our first defence priority', and added:

> ... It is essential to our ability to win the cold war, which we cannot do without an increasing assumption of the offensive in the political and economic fields, that Allied foreign policy should not be cramped by the fear that if we go too far we could not defend ourselves against armed attack. In this respect Western superiority in atomic power and the security of the UK against air attack are vital factors. Cold war policy must therefore be related to military strength ... *The Aim in the Cold War* ... first a stabilisation of the anti-Communist front in the present free world and then, as the Western powers become militarily less weak, the intensification of 'cold' offensive measures aimed at weakening the Russian grip on the satellite states and ultimately achieving their complete independence of Russian control ... We should not be unduly anxious about provoking the Russians. If it suited them to embark on armed aggression they would do so without waiting for provocation ...
>
> ... even now the Allies could afford to adopt a more forward strategy in the cold war, and should be making all possible plans and preparations to be more and more offensive as their military strength grows.[7]

More than a year after the concept of winning the Cold War had been outlawed in the higher reaches of the Foreign Office, the British military were still anxious to increase the pace.

But in reality the British military had no capacity for Cold War fighting. The Army itself had eliminated regular SAS units in 1945 – an extraordinary self-inflicted wound – and resurrected elements were already at full stretch in Malaya. Meanwhile SIS capabilities together with propaganda and psychological warfare remained securely under the control of the Foreign Office. Following Eden's wartime prescription, the management of British special operations policy was now controlled by diplomats located in PUSD's shadowy Overseas Planning Section, run by Paul Falla. Situated in rooms adjacent to the Permanent Under-

Secretary's office, Falla had to try and keep SIS and the military in line. Although SIS Chief Stewart Menzies was as anxious as anyone to resist liberation, there were gung-ho junior SIS officers about. Falla worked with James Fulton of SIS and Colonel Douglas Darling, an ex-SAS officer from the MoD. Meanwhile the Russia Committee, with its high-level military representation, had been sidelined. In November 1951, Sir William Strang, the Permanent Under-Secretary, was told of complaints by Slessor that under the new Whitehall committee structure he never had direct contact with the Foreign Secretary. But this was exactly what the diplomats intended. The Russia Committee was gradually stripped of some of its original functions and was reorganised in November 1952. Direct military input on Cold War operations had been reduced to a minimum.[8]

The same applied to propaganda and political warfare. In June 1951 the Chiefs of Staff invited Sir Pierson Dixon and Christopher Warner to discuss this subject and the diplomats sat patiently through complaints from the Chiefs about matters well outside the military province, including the fact that 'a number of teachers in our schools had Communist leanings'. Dixon was patently dishonest and informed the military that in the satellite states the Foreign Office was still trying to 'foster the spirit of revolt'. For their part the military continued to complain about the 'clutter of Committees all dabbling in the problem' of Cold War and stressed that there was 'an urgent need now for one Minister and one Civil Servant' to have control of the whole effort. But Dixon and Warner replied that the new Cabinet committees on communism, which had military representation, were adequate and had Attlee's sanction.[9] Simultaneously, the three armed services continued to press for expansion in military psywar, adding that the United States was directing 'considerable money and resources' at this and that Britain should follow suit. A Whitehall inter-departmental working party on psywar was set up, chaired by the RAF. In the chairman's view 'the requirement of a psychological warfare organisation exists primarily in cold war' and also to a lesser degree in limited war, but not in total war. But this met with 'vigorous opposition' from the diplomats, who believed that the armed services were 'attempting an incursion into the Foreign Office's spheres of influence'. Despite the protests of the military, the diplomats had their foot firmly on the brake pedal.[10]

By 1951 the desire of the British military to do something about winning the Cold War was being effectively contained, but diplomats in London recognised that it was the Americans who had the real capacity to do things that looked dangerous. The Foreign Office's anxieties in this area represented a strange turn of events, for as late as 1948 it had been trying to encourage greater American commitment to the Cold War, fearing that Britain might be abandoned in the face of Soviet power. But now it felt entrapped by American military figures who seemed over-zealous, to the point where they were likely to spark a war in which Britain would be destroyed.[11] At first glance, the worries of Whitehall appear somewhat exaggerated and paranoid. Conventional accounts emphasise that Truman had never committed himself to a real liberation effort, and that some so-called liberation escapades represented conces-sions to Washington lobby groups or permitted his successor, Eisenhower, some political posturing on the electoral hustings. Indeed, the approach of Truman, and then Eisenhower, to liberation has often been characterised as more talk than action. The most substantial ele-ments of liberation certainly consisted of talk. The large-scale activity was the radios, including Voice of America, Radio Free Europe, Radio Liberation (later Liberty) and also Radio in the American Sector, which were engaged in a battle consisting of ever more powerful Western broadcasting and Eastern jamming. By 1952 Truman could accurately claim that the weight of these broadcasts directed at communist coun-tries was greater than all the domestic radio output of the United States combined. The scale of resources deployed was quite fantastic – some-thing which NSC 68 addressed in an annexe declassified only in 1999, which describes what Washington called 'The Ring Plan'.[12]

'The Ring Plan' was simply a scheme to surround the Eastern bloc with enormously powerful transmitters to overcome jamming. Radio warfare officials such as Chester Opal worked with physicists like Jerome Wiesner, later President of the Massachusetts Institute of Technology (MIT), and scientific advisers from the White House. Edward Barrett, who superintended the programme at the State Department, used to joke, 'Listen, we get this thing working, we're going to be able to turn on the lights in Moscow and anybody with a metal filling in his mouth is going to be able to pick up the Voice of America.' Joking apart, this seemed a realistic way of combining American technological and ideo-logical power in the peaceful penetration of the Eastern bloc. Chester Opal saw himself as creating an 'incendiary potential', adding that 'The Ukraine was top of our list. Number two on our list was Poland, Number three on our list was Hungary.' 'If you have enough power you can pick it up in your bed springs. This was the intention.' Opal said that this all activity had 'flowed out of NSC 68'.[13]

The highly sensitive annexes of NSC 68 now underline the centrality of psychological warfare to mainstream American Cold War strategy. They asserted that the penetration of the Iron Curtain presented 'a special problem' to which great energy should be devoted. 'A group of social and natural scientists have already been engaged to investigate every possible method of getting information into the Soviet world.' This investigation was going to include every scheme thus far put forward, 'no matter how unlikely or unprofitable it may appear to be'. Others commented that the scale of resources devoted might soon be equivalent to that devoted to the wartime Manhattan Project.[14] The rate of expansion on the ground was tremendous. In 1949 Voice of America had been broadcasting only in Russian and Ukrainian. In 1950 the CIA loaned one of its officers, Archie Roosevelt, to preside over expansion into Armenian, Azerbaijani, Georgian, Tatar and Uzbeck. Broadcasters with the right accent were acquired from eastern Iran and the signal was enhanced by a ship-based booster transmitter on a ship operating out of Rhodes, disguised as a coastguard cutter, in an effort to beat the jamming. Initial VOA broadcasts were 'very aggressive' with 'a lot of name-calling ... hasty words like "jackals" and "wolves"', but by 1952 aggressive broadcasting had been handed over to Radio Liberty, allowing Voice to cultivate a more civilised image.[15]

British responses oscillated between derision and fear. In July 1951 PUSD noted that the Americans were 'setting up an array of very powerful transmitters all around the Soviet periphery ... breaking through Soviet jamming'. It doubted that it would be successful, but, if it was, it worried that the Soviets 'might feel compelled to take counter-action'. All this was part of what it saw as an alarming American policy of 'dislodging' the Soviets from Eastern Europe, and it went on to add that any 'move towards compression may have the most far reaching consequences for the whole free world'.[16] Paul Falla, head of Overseas Planning Section, thought the American schemes all very improbable. This vast programme, he argued, was all predicated on a questionable American notion that the Soviet monolith might actually be quite brittle, and hopefully would not need too much encouragement to shake itself to pieces. He remarked that 'some, at any rate, expect the walls of Jericho to fall down after the first half dozen blasts or so on the "Coherent Transmitter Array" or whatever their latest engine of psychological warfare is called'.[17]

Both Truman and Eisenhower certainly exaggerated liberation to placate the American right. On Capitol Hill, McCarthyites, the China Lobby, Captive Nation campaigners, the Catholic Church and many others, although separate, tended to hunt as a pack. Their targets were officials in Truman's Democratic administration whom they regarded as liberal and 'soft on communism'. No one was safe and by 1952 even quite senior CIA officers, such as Cord Meyer, were being dragged before their boards of enquiry. Ironically it was Meyer, now head of the CIA's International Organisations Division, who superintended the Agency's radio programme. Truman, and then Eisenhower, used liberation to counter these charges and to assume an ideological position of non-acceptance of the Eastern bloc. For the White House these supposedly 'secret' programmes were frequently paraded publicly to suggest progress in a struggle which the more astute recognised as essentially static, if not stagnant.[18]

But while Truman and Eisenhower approached liberation with caution, at the operational level matters were different. Rapid expansion resulted in an enormous programme of activity for its own sake, but without clear purpose. Many in Washington believed, like William Donovan, that the Eastern bloc might easily crumble if pressurised. Moreover, limited liberation might keep the Soviets on the defensive, and less likely to launch probing initiatives against the West. But how much activity and of what sort? This ambivalence is encapsulated in Eisenhower's Volunteer Freedom Corps, a 'Foreign Legion' of Eastern bloc exiles, defectors and escapees. The establishment of this Corps was approved by Congress and progressed as far as the recruitment and training of several thousand Eastern bloc exiles by the US Army. But it was stalled by protests from alarmed European allies. Truman and Eisenhower went some way with liberation, but stopped short of giving the clandestine agencies the green light. Liberation was stuck on amber.[19]

An amber light was enough for some of those leading the American Cold War fighting apparatus in the 1950s. Frank Wisner, C. D. Jackson and Allen Dulles interpreted these guidelines generously. The dominant culture of the CIA already leaned towards special operations rather than intelligence, a trend that accelerated when Dulles became director in 1953. Moreover, at the operational level matters were often confused. Dissident groups inside the Eastern bloc were good sources of intelligence, but, as even the cautious British SIS had discovered, they were unlikely to co-operate unless the West held out some hope of rescue. Matters were also blurred by 'retardation operations' intended for a future hot war. This involved the construction of sleeper groups with arms caches, in both Eastern and Western Europe, which would awake only in a hot war, to collect intelligence and to create mayhem in the Soviet Army's rear areas. These were favoured by the growing special warfare departments of the American armed services, which had been deeply impressed by what the Germans had achieved by recruiting legions of anti-communist Soviet citizens.[20]

The special operations and psychological warfare divisions of the US Army were keen on the idea of recruiting Soviet citizens. The wartime Vlasov Russian Army of Liberation was a subject of perpetual fascination and dozens of studies were completed on this subject. They focused on the Prague Manifesto of 14 November 1944, in which General Andrei Vlasov appealed to a range of minorities to join the Russians in overthrowing the Bolsheviks. Although many volunteers wished to join

Vlasov's wartime Russian Army of Liberation, the idea filled Hitler and Himmler with distaste. Vlasov had never been forgiven for his disparaging remarks about the Wehrmacht or for his observation that 'it takes a Russian to lick the Russians'. Vlasov was in the last analysis a Russian nationalist. He was handed over to the Soviets by the US Army in 1945 and hanged in Moscow in 1946 'for active espionage-sabotage and terrorist activity'. But now the US Army called for a revival of Vlasov's legions and the reissue of the Prague Manifesto as the 'Washington Manifesto'. There were lessons to be learned from the German 'mishandling' of anti-Soviet Russians.[21]

There were also organisational reasons for continued covert action in the 1950s. When Walter Bedell Smith became the new Director of Central Intelligence in 1950, he thought he was taking over an intelligence organisation, but he now found that the CIA was a diverse entity engaged in a lot of secret Cold War fighting, and indeed even open Cold War fighting. The Agency acquired its own radio stations, newspapers, airlines, even small private armies. This activity brought huge resources and by 1951, after it had absorbed Frank Wisner's OPC, Bedell Smith decided to allow it to continue to grow. In October that year he chaired a staff meeting at CIA headquarters at which this issue was considered. Covert action had 'assumed such a very large size in comparison to our intelligence function that we have almost arrived at the stage where it is necessary to decide whether the CIA will remain an intelligence agency or become a "cold war department"'. But no decision was taken and instead Bedell Smith allowed these activities to roll on under their own momentum.[22]

For London the breakpoint with the Americans over covert action also came in late 1951. British and American secret services now found themselves increasingly at odds on the ground, and SIS had begun discreet efforts to hamper CIA activities which it thought particularly ill advised. Robert Joyce of the Policy Planning Staff told the US Joint Chiefs of Staff that SIS and the CIA had begun 'to foul each other up in some of their covert operations'. Consequently, in December 1951, Joyce led a team to London for an emergency meeting with SIS on liberation:

> I outlined to the British as best I could the NSC-68 policies and indicated why Bedell Smith desired to beef up his covert operations ... I tried to obtain their approval for our point of view and to obtain their agreement that they would not foul up our operations. I must say that in December I got a very negative reaction. The British were strongly inclined to accept the status quo ... The pitch is that the U.K. wants a voice in decisions on these matters. They are worried that the Americans will go too far too fast. They repeatedly emphasised that they are only 25 miles away from the Continent and that this is much too close for comfort.

SIS said that its line was that it was only 'interested in intelligence gathering, not in subversion'. The more two sides talked, the further apart they appeared to be. Joyce had tried to reassure SIS by explaining that much of the expanded CIA activity consisted of 'retardation operations' rather than liberation. What the CIA wanted to do was create nucleus groups that would form the basis of partisan activity in the event of a future open conflict; this required time and could not be done at short notice. All of this, he protested, was designed not to accelerate the Cold War, but to plan prudently in case of a hot war. But references to hot war were not well calculated to calm British nerves.[23]

Alarmed by Joyce's presentation, the British now sprang into action. PUSD, the new Foreign Office control centre, had already begun a review of liberation activities and its task was to find a way to slow the Americans down. Originating with the small Overseas Planning Section and Pierson Dixon, its ideas then went to the ten-person C Committee, which formed the main interface between senior SIS officers and PUSD. These ideas were finally endorsed by the Permanent Under-Secretary's Committee in January 1952 and emerged as 'Future Policy towards Soviet Russia', which set out a new gradualist approach to liberation that might be called 'general softening'.[24] PUSD argued that the West should abandon the idea of promoting mass insurrections and revolts completely. Instead it should aim at reaching peaceful coexistence with the Eastern bloc by negotiating a number of local settlements that 'might be expected to lead cumulatively to a general stabilisation'. While PUSD accepted that the impact of the Tito–Stalin split of 1948 was highly favourable for the West, it could not see it being repeated and concluded that 'operations designed to liberate the satellites are impracticable and would involve unacceptable risks'.

Instead PUSD mapped out a more general programme of covert operations designed to hasten broad changes right across the Soviet system. This meant viewing the Soviet system as a whole, and regarding subversion as part of a longer-term psychological attack on the political structure of the whole Soviet empire, including the Soviet Union itself. Instead of risings and revolts PUSD preferred 'a series of specialist operations against specific targets' within the communist governments, economies and armies to reduce their effectiveness and to 'poison' their mutual relations. After all, Eastern Europe was undergoing a series of vicious purges, which blatantly advertised the possibilities for encouraging more self-inflicted damage.

In reality this new approach to liberation was directed at the Americans rather than the Soviets. Broader covert measures aimed at a 'general softening' were only proposed by the British as an attempt to divert the United States into activities that they considered to be less dangerous. In reality London wanted SIS and the CIA to do nothing beyond intelligence-gathering. CIA activities seemed not only provocative, but also ill directed and rudderless, with all the implicit possibilities of unintentional collision. London asserted that the Americans:

> are already engaged in attempts to weaken the structure of the Soviet empire by various means including broadcasting, refugee organisations working from outside and covert activities and propaganda behind the Iron Curtain; and there are some indications that they rate the possibility of detaching the satellites by subversion and revolt a good deal higher than we do. As their strength grows, they will no doubt be impatient . . .

What concerned PUSD most was not the direction of US policy but that there did not seem to be one. What was it all for and where was it going? The long-term aims of United States policy, it complained, 'are not clear' and instead its covert apparatus appeared 'more concerned with means than ends'.

The dismal fate of risings in East Berlin in 1953, and Hungary in 1956, was clearly forecast by PUSD. The end result of liberation, it predicted, was that the anti-Soviet elements that were being built up in the satellites would 'get out of control' and rise up of their own accord: 'We might then be faced with a choice between supporting the revolutionary movement by force of arms or abandoning the revolutionaries to their fate'. The West, it continued, would then reluctantly choose the latter and they would be crushed. This would 'inevitably lead to a strengthening of the Soviet hold over the whole of the Soviet empire and the liquidation of all potential supporters of the West.' Moreover the West's limited intelligence networks would then be wiped out. Whether it led to a war, or a renewed Soviet crackdown, it added uncomfortably, 'it is clearly on the European nations rather than on the United States that the first repercussions would fall'. But Washington was already far down the road on Cold War fighting. London knew that Washington would not pay heed to criticisms which seemed 'only obstructive and negative'. However, it argued, they 'might be more ready to listen' if the British proposed 'a more forward policy aimed not at fomenting revolt in the satellites but at weakening the whole fabric of the Soviet Empire'. London wanted to be 'in a position to put forward suggestions and criticisms as a partner from the inside'. This course would clearly involve SIS in going some way with the Americans towards a more forward policy. In other words, London was getting on the American bus, but only to apply the handbrake.[25]

All this was presented to Washington by Sir Oliver Franks, the British Ambassador, and by Air Chief Marshal Sir William Elliott, the new head of the British Joint Services Mission. Predictably the Americans saw right through it and were less than delighted. On 12 March 1952, key American figures, including Paul Nitze and Robert Joyce from the State Department, met together with General Omar Bradley and the rest of the US Joint Chiefs of Staff at the Pentagon to consider the 'British paper on covert operations'. Bradley thought it all 'very timid' and encapsulated the mood: 'What worries me is that this paper has an appeasement ring to it.' Superficially much of the problem seemed to be different views on how brittle the Eastern bloc might be in the face of radio psychological warfare and other pressures. London had sent the Americans a pessimistic JIC paper on the subject. There was also clear divergence on atomic matters. The Americans thought the West was relatively as strong as it would ever be and the Soviets were catching up, suggesting that 'we have got to do some things now to keep even'. But the British believed that the West would be stronger in five years time and wanted to wait. Nitze suggested that the answer was to put the British through an 'educational process' to help them understand current American strategic thinking, but he added that this should be done gently, as 'we do not want to scare the British to death'.

More fundamentally, the issue was not Soviet vulnerability. It was instead different British and American appreciations of *their own* national vulnerability, in other words a 'vulnerability gap' between the two allies. British views were determined by their desire to avoid a war in Europe. If conventional, it would bring the Soviets to the Channel ports, and if nuclear, it would eradicate Britain. Joyce put it succinctly: the British 'want to influence us a little and perhaps even control us a little. This is the guts of the matter.'[26]

Although these British anxieties related to covert action or special operations, NSC 68 and the 'Global Strategy' paper had already underlined that they could not be separated from questions of nuclear strategy. Moreover, close Anglo-American co-operation on the intelligence side also served to intensify worries about open war. High-level intelligence contact was providing the British with simultaneous insights into American thinking about a possible first strike or 'preventative war'. During late 1951 and early 1952 liberation had come together with fears of preventative war to create an atmosphere of near panic in Whitehall. These matters were so sensitive that many were reluctant to commit them to paper, so they are not easy to uncover. American thinking was increasingly fascinated by the idea that Soviet strength was growing and that Moscow was becoming more, not less, dangerous. By the late 1950s the Soviets would be able to threaten the United States with missiles; they would also be more confident. Far better, some senior planners thought, to confront the problem now. At the end of 1951, just as Robert Joyce was preparing to travel to London to talk to SIS, and just as Attlee was preparing to hand over the reins of government to Churchill's second administration, these issues burst on the Whitehall scene.

In the summer of 1951, the Director of Naval Intelligence, Vice Admiral Eric Longley-Cook, was preparing to retire. Liberated from the constraints of office he now felt free to speak his mind, at least to a select group at the highest level. In a remarkable presentation entitled 'Where are we going?' he argued that, although the Soviets were paranoid, they were also conservative and defensive. Cautious by nature, they were going nowhere and presented Britain with little real threat. If anything the stolid Russians were a force for stability in the world system. They would try to move their objectives forward by means of psychological or economic means but 'not by a general military offensive'. The main threat to strategic stability and indeed to the survival of the United Kingdom, he suggested, came from America:

> (vi) Many people in America have made up their minds that war with Russia is inevitable and there is a strong tendency in military circles to 'fix' the zero date for war.
>
> (vii) It is doubtful whether, in a year's time, the US will be able to control the Frankenstein monster which they are creating.
>
> (viii) There is a definite danger of the U.S.A. becoming involved in a preventative war against Russia, however firmly their N.A.T.O. allies object.

Longley-Cook had reached these conclusions after a number of visits to the United States to meet with senior American intelligence chiefs and planners. His view also reflected prolonged immersion in the work of Britain's highest-level intelligence committee, the JIC. In October 1950 the British JIC and its American counterpart had come together for a major conference in Washington. Here, the British JIC team confronted a 'deep-seated conviction' on the part of the American military that 'all out war against the Soviet Union was not only inevitable but imminent'. The British JIC exerted super-human efforts to convince its American partners to endorse a combined appreciation of the Soviet threat based on what it called 'factual intelligence'. However, Longley-Cook continued, the Americans were quick to alter this to fit 'their own pre-conceived ideas' as soon as the British JIC team had departed Washington. 'United States intelligence studies tend to fit in with the prejudged conclusion that a shooting war with the Soviet Union at some time is inevitable.' The Americans, he warned, 'have accordingly gone ahead to prepare for an inevitable clash of arms with the Soviet Union, "fixed" for mid or late 1952'. Longley-Cook argued that, at the very least, the British should tell the United States that it 'cannot expect to use our territory for a war against Russia or to have our support'.

Longley-Cook claimed that the American fascination with the idea of preventative war had moved beyond the Pentagon and had joined up with extremist sentiments that abounded in American public life, characterised by McCarthyism and the 'present witch hunt against President Roosevelt's former political advisers' who had concluded the Yalta accords. Some, he said, were eager for war because the United States had never known real war and the devastation that it could bring. Others were eager for war because they could see what might be coming their way. This was 'very apparent among the dwellers of the larger American cities, who visualise in their own concentrated home towns the ruins of Hamburg and Berlin'. He added, 'These, and other Americans, say – "We have the bomb; let us use it now while the balance is in our favour. Since war with Russia is inevitable, let's get it over with *now*".'

> Finally, I have been impressed and concerned by my conversations with many responsible and influential Americans who are obviously convinced that war with Russia is inevitable and who have no clear idea what their policy is going to be once they reach a position of strength. Some talk of an 'ultimatum from strength', but many more believe in the necessity for 'smashing the Russians' at the earliest possible moment.[27]

Only six copies of Longley-Cook's extraordinary exposition were produced for the 'eyes only' purview of Whitehall's innermost circle. What most made of this report we will never know. Almost immediately, they were 'ordered to be destroyed'. One copy only survived in the Prime Minister's Office, sent to Clement Attlee in the last weeks of his administration. He had been 'very interested' but had been swept out of office. Churchill, who now began his second administration, was given this document on 21 December 1951 and read it in early January 1952 when beginning a visit to the United States. He was initially dismissive of it, even wondering if Longley-Cook was some kind of communist and ordering that 'a sharp eye should be kept on the writer'. But after several encounters with his American hosts Churchill found his own cherished ideas for a summit with the Soviets abruptly rubbished by Truman. He also detected an increasingly bellicose atmosphere in Washington and returned to London in a state of dejection. In April 1952 he wrote to his Private Secretary, 'I want to see the Secret report prepared by the late Director of Naval Intelligence and sent me by the First Lord when I was in America. Let me have it back again.'[28]

During his time in Washington Churchill had sought greater reassurance from the Americans about the circumstances in which the bomb might be used and greater detail on American target plans for a future war. He managed to extract a briefing on the main American emergency war plan from the US Secretary of Defense and promises of further atomic intelligence exchange despite its contravention of the McMahon

Act of 1946. Although the record of these conversations is very obscure on the point, Churchill clearly pressed for some sort of veto on the use of American airpower from British bases and was rebuffed. Instead the meetings came up with the formula that the use of such airpower would be 'a matter for joint decision', in the circumstances prevailing at the time, a vague formulation which was open to interpretation. This formulation became the orthodox wisdom on the matter of US airpower in Britain and was repeated by British premiers from Churchill down to Margaret Thatcher in the 1980s.[29]

To what extent was Longley-Cook exaggerating the level of threat? John Slessor, the Chief of the Air Staff, also saw the paper and responded that there 'is to my mind, a lot in what Longley Cook says'. But he also thought that the temptation of the United States to rush into a preventative war had been produced by a fear of the Soviets overtaking it in the arms race and that this fear was now waning in Washington.[30] Longley-Cook's warning was not only on target, it was also one of several such warnings which had circulated in Whitehall. Air Chief Marshal Sir Guy Garrod had been moved to write privately to Tedder and Slessor warning about preventative war after lecturing at the US Air Warfare College in 1948. The issue had come up during his lecture and Garrod had argued that it was 'not a practicable proposition for democratic countries' because it was an act of wanton aggression. But the prevailing attitude that revealed itself in discussions afterwards 'was more extreme' than he had expected. After the students had dispersed, senior officers talked frankly with Garrod. General Orville Anderson, the Commandant, had argued that the Cold War was just as much a war of aggression as a shooting war and that the Soviets were trading on an 'artificial distinction'. This gave the West the moral right to counter-attack by armed force. Moreover, the arrival of the atom bomb had made the time factor 'critical' and it was dangerous to wait for an armed attack before launching an armed counter-attack:

> [General Anderson] admitted that the use of atomic weapons might create a wilderness in the country attacked and that this would result in a post-war problem similar to our present problem of rehabilitating Germany but on a vaster scale. The view was put forward that if we waited until Russia was able to develop and launch atomic weapons this wilderness might be created in Western Europe or even the United States and the result might be the end of Western civilisation. We can afford, however, to create a wilderness in Russia without serious repercussion on Western civilisation ... we have a moral obligation to stop Russia's aggression now by force, if necessary, rather than face the consequences of delay.

This, warned Garrod, was 'General Anderson's thesis in bold outline'. Slessor and Major-General Bill Williams were scheduled to lecture at the

US Air War College and he felt that they should know what 'sort of atmosphere' awaited them.[31]

On 19 April 1950, General George C. Kenney at the US Air Force Headquarters at Maxwell Air Force Base, Alabama wrote to Hoyt Vandenberg, who had moved from being head of the Central Intelligence Group to be chief of staff of the US Air Force. Kenney was reflecting on a recent Commanders Conference and wanted to highlight some critical issues that had emerged. The Soviet atomic stockpile, he feared, was expanding much faster than Charles Cabell, their Director of Intelligence, believed. Moreover, he said, current planning for a response to a Soviet attack – such as Plan Offtackle – was hopelessly over-optimistic. 'The one conclusion that almost everyone seemed to reach was that if we waited until Russia hit us, Europe, very probably including the United Kingdom, would be lost to us.' Once this had happened the possibility of gaining air superiority in order to repeat something like the Normandy beachhead, and then to push back into an occupied Europe, would be 'almost inconceivable'. The Soviets would never be dislodged from Europe. Equally, the current idea of holding a Soviet push at the River Elbe 'does not appear feasible' given the level of forces in Europe. The United States might win, but if many Soviet bombers got through 'civilisation as we now know it would be a thing of the past'. Given this gloomy outlook for both Europe and America, and with the situation getting worse by the day, there was only one answer. Kenney wrote:

> I believe that we have got to do something about the conception that we must wait until Russia hits us before we can start shooting. I realize that this is a matter beyond your control, but perhaps something can be done about educating the public or at least preventing them from becoming too apathetic about the situation, which in the final analysis is a question of survival. If we ignore the warnings ... continually made by Communists all over the world and allow a new and far greater Pearl Harbor to overtake us, there is a good probability that we will lose the hot war as well as the cold war. I believe that something can be done to bring it home to the people of this country and to their representatives in Congress that we are now actually at war. By all previous definitions, we are now in a state of war with Russia. Whether we call it a cold war or apply any other term, we are not winning. We are not seriously mobilizing to start winning or to undertake the offensive between now and mid-summer 1952. When a state of war exists, it is not necessary to tell our opponent what our next move is going to be. It seems to me that almost any analysis of the situation shows that the only way that we can be certain of winning is to take the offensive as soon as possible and hit Russia hard enough to a least prevent her from taking over Europe. If we plan and execute the operation properly, the weight of our attack in the early stages may be sufficient to compel Russia to accept our terms for a real peace.

> It would not be a preventative war, because we are already at war.[32]

This was not an outburst by one belligerent Air Force general. Instead, Kenney's views were, as he rightly stressed, symptomatic of a dominant mindset among senior USAF commanders in the early 1950s. It was a frightening argument because it was underpinned by a compelling, if amoral, rationale. Kenney's allusion to Pearl Harbor was especially poignant. It was just such an argument by senior Japanese figures in late 1941, proclaiming that Japan's situation was bad but likely to get worse, that propelled it from a 'Cold War' of semi-blockade into what it saw as a preventative war on 7 December 1941. Like Kenney, the Japanese had envisaged an effective first strike, followed by a favourable armistice.

The British JIC team had detected this problem in 1950. A rift between the British and American JICs over the likelihood of war and its possible date had been developing since 1949 and was already apparent at a troubled conference between the British, American and Canadian JIC teams held at the Pentagon soon after the outbreak of the Korean War in August 1950. The conference had been extended into September but still ended in barely concealed disagreement.[33] On 7 August 1950, slightly less than a year after the explosion of the Soviet atomic bomb, Major-General T. H. Landon, the US Air Force Director of Plans, recounted a recent gathering of British and American intelligence chiefs on the 'Present World Situation'. They had been poles apart and there had been fierce arguments. London insisted that the Soviets would not be ready for general war before 1955 but the Americans expected war in 1952 'or even earlier'. He was worried about 'divergence on this most important question' and suggested that a British JIC team be invited to Washington again to try and iron the difficulties out. A month later, in September 1950, General Orville Anderson was sacked from the US Air Force when he promoted ideas of preventative war publicly and gained front-page newspaper headlines. The following year the regular summer Anglo-American JIC conference was characterised by stand-up rows. The divergences were becoming ever wider and pointed to future trouble.[34]

Remarkably, we now know that preventative-war thinking was a dominant strain within the US Air Force from 1948 until at least 1953. This is confirmed by the unpublished memoirs of General Charles P. Cabell. Cabell served as the US Air Force Intelligence chief at this time and then became deputy director of the CIA under Kennedy. He recalled:

> During this general period and lasting for several years, there were many advocates of a 'preemptive' or 'preventative' war with the Soviet Union. The theory was that the Soviet Union was determined upon attaining world domination and that somewhere along the line a general war between East and West was inevitable. So – went the theory – if war was to come anyhow, it behooved the United States to ensure the winning of that war by launching it herself at a time of her choosing, before the Russians were ready – and that meant soon.

Cabell recalled that the theory was 'simple, logical and attractive to men of action' and there were many proponents in the USAF. 'Some of my honored friends and advisers pressed me hard to climb on that bandwagon.' But Cabell resisted, believing that there were other courses open and that preventative war would be an 'act of immorality and despair'.[35]

Fears of a possible preventative war, perhaps initiated by a confrontation over a rebellion in Eastern Europe, were the main cause of rapidly cooling Anglo-American relations in the early 1950s. By 1952, London had the two issues somewhat tangled up. During the PUSD discussions in early 1952 on covert action, SIS had been notably determined to stamp out any British support for American ideas. But support for Washington had come from an unexpected quarter. In early 1952 the bookish staff of the Foreign Office Research Department – known as FORD – had simultaneously circulated their own paper on the 'Internal Stability of the Soviet Regime'. Although it did not call for more action against the Soviets, its views supported those who did. It argued that the Soviet system was getting stronger and more stable all the time and, as it did so, it would become 'nastier' and more troublesome, unless short-term measures were taken to keep it off balance. In a fit of absence of mind, senior officials had allowed the FORD paper wide circulation.[36]

SIS officers were apoplectic when they read it. They declared that 'the result of the FORD paper is to present an argument for preventative war'.[37] The Foreign Office argued that SIS – referred to as 'Mr Reilly's friends' – was over-sensitive and that there was 'no serious discrepancy' between FORD and the mainstream policy of damping things down. But it was clearly embarrassed and wanted to keep the issue 'out of court' and 'deal with M.I.6 by direct discussion'.[38] The eventual response of Paul Falla's Overseas Planning Section to the complaints of SIS, given in July 1952, was disarmingly candid. Falla conceded that 'It is true that in some circles the situation is so regarded. In fact, if war were an instrument of policy that Western Governments could readily contemplate using, there would be very strong arguments for it. We cannot obscure those arguments, at least in official circles. It is just fortunate that most of our minds do not work in such a way as to accept them.' Exactly where these 'circles' were remains unclear, but the general impact of ideas of preventative war upon Anglo-American relations was highly corrosive.[39]

In 1952 General Omar Bradley warned senior American diplomatic and military chiefs that Anglo-American relations were now deteriorating fast. 'There have been so many irritants in our relationships with the British in recent months that I think we may have a showdown with them sometime in the near future.' Some of these matters were very sensitive and he did not think they should be addressed at an official meeting;

instead he thought the Americans should just sit down with some key British figures 'and call each other names for a while' and try to get the mutual bad feeling out of their system. Admiral Sherman, US Chief of the Naval Staff, volunteered that 'the explanation of these difficulties' had been conveyed to him very confidentially by Mountbatten: 'He told me that the British are increasingly apprehensive regarding the effects upon them if the development of US policy leads to the involvement of the UK in a war ... the UK would suffer devastation.' But Sherman wanted everyone to be 'very careful' in order 'to protect the security' of his source, believing that Mountbatten, then Fourth Sea Lord, would be carpeted for speaking to Washington with candour.[40]

Meanwhile, at a lower level, liberation efforts on the ground were not going well. As we have seen, by the end of the operational season of 1950 the idea of liberation had already been badly dented by the failed SIS–CIA Operation Valuable in Albania. SIS now gave up on Albania and Colonel David Smiley pulled his Pixies out, although the CIA continued a faltering programme into that country long after. In the summer of 1951 General Bradley asked his colleagues about progress in Albania: 'What is the chance of getting a free government there?'. H. Freeman Matthews from the State Department knew the score and replied, 'None, now.' But his colleague, Frederick Reinhardt interjected, 'You might want to try getting one forcefully ... The Greeks and Yugoslavs would split it up for you.' After all, he added, the covert programme of military assistance to the Yugoslavs was growing and they were getting more confident all the time. London and Washington had already opened discussions on an overt invasion of Albania. But matters were made complicated by the fact that 'the British have a split position', with the Foreign Office wishing to do nothing and to preserve an independent communist Albania while 'in some places in the British Government they are thinking of a split Albania'. London's diplomats did not want to stir up trouble, but the British military remained interested in more aggressive measures.[41]

Unsurprisingly, it was only in military surroundings that British Army officers offered their views freely. On 22 August 1952, Bradley's opposite number, Field Marshal William Slim, Chief of the Imperial General Staff, addressed Allied commanders at General Eisenhower's SHAPE Headquarters in Paris. Here he had no qualms about calling for a crusade against the East. Slim could not fail to be aware of how directly he cut across British policy at the highest level, since he had accompanied Churchill on his visit to the United States earlier that year, the key purpose of which was to sell Truman the idea of a summit with the Soviets. But his presentation at SHAPE HQ made no concessions to Churchill's search for mutual coexistence, and instead called for victory:

> To end this cold war, we ought to be very much more aggressive. We, the British especially I think, are too much on the defensive. And as our strength grows, so should our aggression in the cold war. We should aim first of all at separating the satellites from Russia. It is not an impossible objective, especially in a country like Czechoslovakia, where the people can still remember freedom. Or in Poland, where they can still remember freedom. In Russia they can't ... the idea of separating a national movement from Russia, as has happened in Yugoslavia, is not all that impossible and we should aim at doing it.

Slim was profoundly influenced in his thinking by the Tito model. He urged officers 'not to bother too much' whether separatist states splitting away from Stalin remained communist or not. It followed from this that the Western propaganda effort should not be so much against communism in the satellite countries: 'It should be against Russia, the domination of Russia. It should be nationalist propaganda.' This, he suggested, had been the critical mistake in Western liberation efforts so far, not to exploit the potential separation between Russia and communism.

Slim stressed that he was pressing not for hot war, just for a markedly more aggressive Cold War. Again, drawing on the Yugoslav example, he argued that as long as the states leaving the Soviet orbit stayed communist this could be done without all-out confrontation. 'Russia won't go to war for that reason,' he maintained. He contrasted this with overt military encroachments, which he regarded as dangerous: 'if you go and put a big American airbase in Finland' which touched on the historic and continuing national interests of Russia 'then you are taking a risk'. Slim's position was cogent, but it was now far removed from that of SIS, of the Foreign Office and indeed of the British Prime Minister.[42]

Slim's position on Czechoslovakia, however artfully presented, could not survive the experiences of failed risings in Poland, Czechoslovakia and East Berlin in the summer of 1953, prompted by Stalin's death in the spring of that year. As PUSD had predicted, the West decided that it could not risk overt assistance to the rebels, and therefore sat on its hands while pro-Western elements were rounded up.[43] There were plenty of elements who wished to intervene. Senior commanders in the US Army pressed for assistance to the guerrillas and moved the 10th Special Forces Group from their base at Fort Bragg to Bad Tölz in Germany. 'Everybody wanted to go,' recalled their commander, and 'get a taste of the action'. British intelligence reported that the repression in Berlin in 1953 was relatively mild, but when the same thing occurred in Hungary in 1956 the results were brutal.[44] The CIA was not entirely disappointed with the outcome of the Berlin riots. On the one hand it thought it unlikely that overt resistance would spread to other satellite states. On the other hand the riots were likely to result in self-inflicted injuries. The CIA looked forward to 'a purge of the newly installed hierarchy in Germany' and the prospect that the repercussions would have a bad effect on the delicate post-Stalin power balance in the Kremlin. Provoking further purges was looked on by some as a welcome bonus.[45]

President Eisenhower was gradually retreating from liberation-type activities and harassment even before Berlin. The death of Stalin in February 1953 seemed to open up a range of new possibilities. At the National Security Council's 'Solarium Exercise' a month later, Eisenhower listened to three competing prescriptions for future policy towards the Eastern bloc. Robert Bowie, then head of the Policy Planning Staff, remembered, 'I think part of his purpose was to make sure that everyone understood that the basic policy was containment and not roll-back.' This reflected an acceptance that Soviet control of the satellites looked firm and difficult to disrupt. The Berlin riots in June 1953 only underscored this. Bowie went on, 'realistically the conclusion was that if you tried to intervene you risked a Third World War'. Washington accepted that prising away a satellite was improbable, but was still keen to create troublesome problems in the East.[46]

By September 1953, even George Kennan, perhaps the key architect of expanded covert action against the Eastern bloc, had begun to get cold feet. Kennan was enjoying a sabbatical at Princeton University when a perplexed C. D. Jackson asked him for his views on current strategy towards 'minorities behind the iron curtain'. Kennan now urged the 'greatest caution', especially with regard to exile groups like the Ukrainians. Such groups, he warned, 'have sometimes been able to swing government policy to an amazing degree'. They had 'flirted very heavily with the Nazis in the late Thirties'. He now saw them for what they were and 'honesty compels me to face the fact that they are probably selling the U.S. Government a dangerous bill of goods'. This was a complete U-turn on Kennan's thinking in 1949.[47] In the same month, US Ambassadors across Europe came together at Luxembourg and discussed the 'concept and ideas for psychological warfare in Europe'. They were having to deal with the diplomatic fall-out of liberation and warned that Western Europeans were 'distrustful' of American strategy towards Eastern Europe:

> Pronouncements by important American officials about the 'liberation' of Eastern Europe cause fear and anxiety in Western European capitals. It is generally believed that American impatience and implacable hostility to Communism might result in hasty and ill-considered action and that American political warfare and covert operations directed against Eastern Europe might set up a chain reaction leading to military conflict, which Western Europe desires to avoid under almost any circumstances.

'How hot should be the cold war?' asked America's leading Ambassadors in Europe. Western Europe would go along with keeping the Eastern

European pot 'lukewarm' or 'even simmering', but they feared that American political warfare was inclined to 'keep the pot at constant boiling point'. They warned Washington that this was divisive and 'dangerous'. Ironically, far from breaking up Eastern Europe instead it 'serves the Kremlin's objective to break the Western Alliance'. Premature revolts, they said, would retard any tendency of the Soviets to lower their troop levels. A revolt would only destroy the healthiest resistance elements within the satellite countries. They added that resistance elements, historically, had proven effective 'only on the eve of liberation by military force', like the resistance in France just before and after the Normandy landings. 'During the occupation of France thousands of persons who attempted active resistance were shot, deported or imprisoned.' The resistance elements who survived were the quiet organisers and the pamphleteers. In the light of events in Hungary in 1956 this was a prescient warning. The Ambassadors advised soft propaganda that would build such groups rather than expose them to danger, including activities such as cultural exchange. Western policy was already shifting towards the policy of gradualised liberation and roll-back by stealth that would emerge as a consensus in the late 1950s.[48]

In December 1953 when Churchill met Eisenhower again at Bermuda he continued to press the idea of a meeting with the Soviets to exploit post-Stalin opportunities. But Eisenhower counselled that this would be seen by the Soviets as a sign of weakness. Churchill did not directly blame the seemingly easygoing President for what he increasingly saw as American warmongering, but blamed instead his Secretary of State, John Foster Dulles. The Prime Minister was increasingly angry and complained later to his doctor, who accompanied him to the conference, 'I am bewildered. It seems that everything is left to Dulles. It appears that the President is no more than a ventriloquist's doll.' He added that Dulles preached 'like a Methodist Minister' and his 'bloody text is always the same', namely that 'nothing but evil' could come out of a summit meeting with the Soviets. Churchill had begun to feel his years and confessed that ten years before he could have 'dealt with him' but now he did not have the energy, adding that 'I have not been defeated by this bastard but by my own decay.' He felt this to be a personal failure and became tearful. But he was wrong on two counts. He had thought Eisenhower 'weak and stupid' but in fact the President chose to protect his friendship with him by blaming Dulles. Second, even the Foreign Office staff accompanying Churchill knew that the chances of a genuine summit were slim.[49]

Churchill's interest in nuclear power continued to grow and by early 1954, he was obsessed by the possibility of war. The United States exploded its first hydrogen bomb in March that year and the Soviets matched this in September. Churchill was fixated by the extraordinary power and danger of these new weapons. His views now began to parallel those of the Longley-Cook report of which he had initially been so dismissive. Aware that America was as yet relatively invulnerable to atomic attack because of the Soviets' limited delivery systems, he saw the dreadful attraction of preventative war. The idea of a showdown before the Soviets could respond contained an obvious military logic and he conceded, 'If I were American I'd do this.'[50]

Although Eisenhower had abandoned liberation, during 1954 and 1955 he remained committed to keeping the temperature at boiling point. In 1954 he was still enamoured of the Volunteer Freedom Corps. This would serve as an ideological beacon and also form a useful corps of individuals with intimate knowledge of Eastern Europe for any future confrontation. Eisenhower stressed the British wartime example of fifteen foreign battalions in the Pioneer Corps. But these plans were put on hold for fear of upsetting sensitive negotiations over a European Defence Community (EDC), which sought to mask German rearmament by creating a European army. Instead, the US Army in Germany continued to use its Labor Service Organisation as a holding tank for 10,600 Eastern Europeans and about 15,900 Germans. In August 1955 the President tried again to go ahead with the Volunteer Freedom Corps to 'provide a cadre of trained personnel to form and control to U.S. advantage any large numbers of defected Soviet Orbit personnel in the event of war'. But he needed the co-operation of the West German government, which was not forthcoming.[51]

Although talks between the CIA and SIS had reached agreement on winding down much of the liberation effort as early as the spring of 1956, the failed Hungarian Revolution of that October sounded the real death knell of these ill-advised activities. The pathetic efforts of the Hungarian underground against the invading Soviet forces also exposed the stupidity of any marginal policy of stirring up trouble somewhere short of liberation. All the cracks and inconsistencies were now on public view. Privately both Eisenhower and John Foster Dulles had been inconsistent, sometimes emphasising caution and sometimes becoming excited about the prospect of Titoism. Their lieutenants had pursued additional medium-term objectives in the general area of 'harassment' and 'pressure', but these were never clear and now, when Washington was presented with something that was far beyond its expectations, the result was paralysis and inaction.[52] The CIA had had ample warning of Soviet intentions to crush the rebels. During the early stages, it established close contacts with employees of the Hungarian state railway system and gained access to all the information which passed across a telegraph net that ran from one railway switching point to another, right across

Hungary. Messages passed through the metal of the rail track itself, recording the movement of rolling stock. It became clear that numbers of carriages were being assembled on the border between Hungary and the Soviet Ukraine. The Soviets were preparing to move in and use force. The CIA chief in Vienna recalled that these 'were very sad days' – 'we sat powerless on the sidelines watching the Soviets preparing to crush the revolution'.[53]

How close British special forces came to participation in supporting the uprising remains a mystery. SIS had employed former Royal Marines in training a few Hungarians on the border in the early 1950s, but only for stay-behind purposes in the event of a Soviet invasion of the West. When the fighting broke out in Hungary, Major Ellery Anderson, veteran of CCRAK operations in Korea, pressed his superiors for permission to lead volunteers to assist the Hungarians. He managed to get as far as Vienna 'with hundreds of others' before being restrained. The futility of resistance operations against police states was now beyond any doubt: 'When I returned home after the Hungarian frontier had been closed and the trains had dragged their truckloads of prisoners back to Russia, and an uneasy, bloody repression had settled upon yet another country, I was forced to face reality.'[54]

Soviet troops had begun to advance on Budapest just before dawn on 4 November 1956. On the same day, Imre Nagy, leader of the disgraced government, sought and was given political asylum in the Yugoslav Embassy. In order to extract him from the Embassy he was lured on to a 'Yugoslav' bus by the KGB, which proved to have a Russian driver and several Russian passengers. He was then taken to Rumania, where the Securitate held him for interrogation in an operation overseen by the KGB, and was eventually shot. The Rumanian Securitate also helped to rebuild the Hungarian security service, the AVH, which was in a bad way. During the uprising the demonstrators had focused particular attention on the AVH and hundreds of its officers had been shot. The Securitate assisted with training the new officers and with reorganisation.[55]

Hungary caused a great deal of heart-searching within the community of American Cold War practitioners. Jim Hoofnagel, a senior USIS officer responsible for much Voice of America output, addressed the US War College shortly afterwards. He spoke openly of his fears that the uprising had been encouraged by 'our intemperate language and by our calling for a rising in eastern Europe'. This sparked a lively debate and others involved in the broadcast programme insisted that the revolt was a purely internal episode, driven by years of frustration at Soviet rule: 'You mean to tell me that Dulles' clamor caused a poor guy who was at the end of the street in Budapest to march right into the mouth of the Russian cannon because he thought that the United States would liberate him ... This is silly. These people had simply had it up to here.' There were lengthy arguments about the lack of American intervention. In Washington the division was largely one of levels. Those near the top, who had 'to meet the future in history', were more moderate and 'had hundred of reasons why no action was taken in Budapest'. But 'the second rung and third rung people were all for it' and clearly felt 'we had let down the Hungarians'. Either way, many were privately satisfied to see the first limited war behind the Iron Curtain regardless of the outcome.[56]

The multiplicity of radio stations has made it hard to find out what had actually gone out on the airwaves. The White House was anxious about the role of the CIA's radios and ordered Allen Dulles to discover quickly what was broadcast by Radio Free Europe (RFE) before the uprising. Dulles' reply was a qualified one. He told the White House that as far as he could determine from 'scripts currently available' it appeared that 'no RFE broadcast to Hungary before the revolution could be considered as inciting to armed revolt'. He added, 'No RFE broadcast to Hungary implied promises of American military intervention.' However, he conceded that once the revolution was under way RFE 'occasionally went beyond the authorized' and there was clear evidence of 'attempts by RFE to provide tactical advice' to those on the ground. In fact RFE had been confused, initally regarding the Nagy government as a communist stooge, then later rebroadcasting some newspaper reports that seem to imply that tangible Western assistance would arrive.[57] Predictably, the new Soviet-imposed Hungarian government claimed much more. In a detailed report to the Secretary General of the UN it alleged that the 'counter-revolution' was 'organised from the West'. CIA groups had operated under the guise of hospital and Red Cross personnel, it stated, and Radio Free Europe had urged the Hungarians to violate the ceasefire. It also announced the capture of agents who had worked for the Americans and for General Gehlen, the resurrected German wartime intelligence expert on the Soviet Union, now based near Munich. But after the ludicrous 'confessions' during the purge trials of the late 1940s and early 1950s, these statements had no credibility.[58]

Almost any retrospective examination of Western activity directed towards Hungary was bound to be tinged by anxiety to avoid or cast blame. Fortunately, a month before the rising, the Free Europe Committee hired a consultant to look into its parallel leaflet, press and mailing campaigns in Eastern Europe. It commissioned Professor Hugh Seton-Watson of London University, 'a warm friend of Free Europe Committee' and 'the most respected scholar in the field of East European (and Soviet) affairs'. He also worked for SIS and so was very much on the inside. Completing his sixteen-page report in October 1956, Seton-Watson acknowledged that in each country the problems of how to accelerate the 'thaw' in Soviet domination in the East were complex, but by and large 'I still feel inclined to urge that even greater efforts be made in this direction.' Specifically on Hungary he thought more Free Europe Committee work would 'help rather than hinder political evolution'. He added, 'I have discovered no evidence of the frequently heard assertions that Free Europe activities are run by emigres who, themselves comfortably established abroad, give their compatriots orders which would recklessly expose them to danger.' Free Europe received this verdict on 6 November. Detailed and thoughtful, it probably stands as the most objective evidence of fairly clean hands in the Hungarian affair.[59]

Even though largely unprovoked by the West, Hungary was a body blow to the architects of liberation. In 1956 Frank Wisner was still a leading exponent of liberation, deeply committed to freeing the peoples of Eastern Europe. Like Ellery Anderson, he had rushed to the Hungarian border to observe the miserable spectacle of freedom fighters and refugees fleeing to the West. It was too much for him to bear and by the time he reached the CIA station in Rome he was beginning a mental breakdown. He was taken into Bethesda Naval Hospital near Washington for treatment. Six months later, after several periods of electro-convulsive therapy, he was able to return to duty, but suffered a relapse. Wisner was eventually made nominal head of the CIA's London station, in the hope that in a relatively relaxed post he would recuperate. But he remained unwell and tragically committed suicide in 1963.[60]

Not all exponents of covert warfare saw Hungary as a disaster. The backwash of the Soviet repression of that satellite was the eventual trial and execution of five Hungarian leaders including Imre Nagy. The public reaction in the West was one of horror, but privately some officials were not entirely displeased. C. D. Jackson discussed the matter with Cord Meyer and then wrote to Allen Dulles, suggesting that 'we have been handed a silver-platter opportunity through the murder of these five Hungarians', adding, 'Let's not muff it this time.' Jackson wanted to exploit the mood of international outrage over these executions and to press the UN to deny accreditation to the new Hungarian delegation sent by the hardline government in Budapest to the UN. A campaign of non-recognition and of breaking off diplomatic relations with the new Hungarian government would also mean the US would have to close its Embassy in Budapest. This, in turn, raised the tricky question of the fate of Cardinal Mindszenty, the leader of the Catholic Church in Hungary who was now a refugee inside the US Embassy in Budapest. What if the Embassy was closed and the Cardinal could not leave Hungary? The world had already witnessed the fate that had befallen Nagy when he was enticed out of the Yugoslav Embassy in Budapest. Jackson told Allen

Dulles, 'I am going to be shockingly cold-blooded' and explained that his staff had been in private discussion with the Vatican about repression in Eastern Europe. Cardinal Tardini of the Vatican had been 'curt' and clearly disapproved of Mindszenty's decision to seek asylum in the Embassy, observing, 'Cardinal Mindszenty used to be a martyr. Today, he is simply a refugee.' Jackson argued that to remove Mindszenty's sanctuary would 'pose a very interesting problem for the Communists', and predicted that 'if, at the end of the line, Mindszenty were to become a martyr again I think the Kremlin case would receive a tremendous setback'. The non-survival of anti-communist elements in Hungary would be balanced by further embarrassments for the Soviets on the world stage. It is hard to resist the conclusion that events in Hungary not only confirmed the bankruptcy of liberation as a strategy, but also underlined the manner in which many Cold Warriors in the West had already shifted away from a simple strategy of liberation. They were not primarily interested in the fate of individual Eastern bloc countries and instead regarded resistance movements in the East as mere footsoldiers in a wider campaign of pressure and counter-pressure that extended across all of Europe.[61]

16

The CIA's Federalist Operation: ACUE and the European Movement

OCB Special Staff to develop an outline of a special project for dealing with the *London Economist* staff through personal contact.

Action: Taquey and Hirsch.

Morning conference of OCB Special Staff to review 'Action Items'
chaired by C. D. Jackson, 19 October 1953[1]

Covert operations are central to any understanding of events in post-war Western Europe. No less than the Eastern bloc, Western Europe was also a battleground, although the hidden-hand techniques deployed here were softer and more subliminal than those associated with Cold War fighting. Thomas W. Braden, the outspoken head of the CIA's International Organisations Division in the early 1950s, has asserted candidly that 'newspapers, radio stations, magazines, airlines, ships, businesses, and voluntary organizations had been bought, subsidized, penetrated or invented as assets for the cold war'.[2]

In the late 1940s a great variety of Western organisations, not just intelligence agencies, drew up clandestine programmes designed both to undermine communist influence in Western Europe and to ensure a welcome for the Marshall Plan. The examples are legion, from electoral politics and organised labour to science and cultural affairs. American officials, trying to stabilise post-war Europe in the face of growing communist parties in France and Italy, assumed that this required rapid unification, perhaps leading to a United States of Europe. President Truman's Marshall Plan was designed to encourage a federal Europe and this was even more strongly emphasised under his successor, Eisenhower. European unification also offered a way to solve the tricky problem of German rearmament, by absorbing Germany into a wider unit.[3] The creation of a federalist United States of Europe was therefore a holy grail for Washington. Extensive covert operations for the specific promotion of European unity were launched by the CIA's greatest luminaries – William J. Donovan, Allen Dulles, Walter Bedell Smith, Tom Braden and Frank Wisner – and they continued for over a decade. However, they had to overcome substantial obstacles, the biggest of which was London, which under both Labour and Conservative administrations staunchly resisted the idea of a federal Europe.

The most remarkable US covert operation was vast secret funding of the European Movement. By the early 1950s promoting European unity was the largest CIA operation in Western Europe. The European Movement was an umbrella group which led a prestigious, if disparate, set of organisations urging rapid unification in Europe, focusing its efforts upon the Council of Europe. The European Movement counted Winston Churchill, Paul-Henri Spaak, Konrad Adenauer, Léon Blum and Alcide De Gasperi as its five Presidents of Honour. In 1948, its main handicap was scarcity of funds; indeed it was bankrupt and close to collapse. The discreet injection of approximately $4 million by the CIA between 1949 and 1960 was central to efforts to drum up mass support for the Marshall Plan, the Schuman Plan (for integrating European coal, iron and steel production), the European Defence Community and a European Assembly with sovereign powers. This covert contribution never formed less than half the European Movement's budget and, after 1952, it was probably two-thirds. Simultaneously this programme sought to undermine the staunch resistance of the British Labour government, and then of the Conservatives, to federalist ideas.[4]

The conduit for American assistance was the American Committee on United Europe (ACUE), directed by senior figures from the American intelligence community. ACUE was set up in the early summer of 1948 by Allen Dulles, then heading a committee reviewing the organisation of the CIA on behalf of the National Security Council, and also by William J. Donovan, founder of OSS. They were responding to separate requests for assistance from Winston Churchill and from Count Richard Coudenhove-Kalergi, a veteran pan-European campaigner from Austria. ACUE worked closely with US government officials involved with the Marshall Plan, particularly those in the Economic Co-operation Administration (ECA). But ACUE also had a fascinating East European dimension, which tied it into liberation and the volatile exile groups working with the CIA and Radio Free Europe.

The full story of this covert operation is only now emerging as the complete records of ACUE have come to light. In addition we can also draw on one of the strangest doctoral dissertations ever completed by a research student in Britain. The contents of this thesis on the early European Movement, written by F. X. Rebattet at the University of Oxford in 1962, were so sensitive that it was closed to readers in the

Bodleian Library for three decades. It was opened to public inspection only in the early 1990s. F. X. Rebattet was the son of George Rebattet, Secretary General (1952–5) of the European Movement. His study was conducted with full access to the internal papers of the European Movement and with the co-operation of its senior figures. It is astonishing for its frankness on the issue of covert American funding and on how the matter was concealed.[5]

The CIA funding operation through ACUE tells us a lot about the nature of American intervention in Western Europe. The origins of this programme lay less in the formal provisions of National Security Council directives, which CIA historians have studied *ad nauseam*, and more in an informal and personal transatlantic network. This was a pattern of human friendships created by members of the intelligence and resistance community during the Second World War. Until 1950, much US aid to non-communist groups in Europe was sent through unofficial channels, although with government approval and support.[6] ACUE typifies the liberal philosophy underpinning many such CIA covert operations. It made little attempt to manipulate organisations or individuals. Instead it sought genuinely independent vehicles that seemed complementary to American policy, and tried to speed them up. This is far away from the stereotypical image of the CIA 'puppet-master'. Instead, the early history of ACUE shows us prominent European politicians in search of discreet American assistance, rather than the CIA in search of proxies. Indeed many Europeans in receipt of covert funding belonged to the non-communist left, confirming Peter Coleman's adept characterisation of these CIA activities in Europe as a 'liberal conspiracy'.[7]

Many Americans working for the CIA through ACUE were either themselves liberals, idealists or determined federalists, often with a strong belief in the United Nations. Others simply viewed American federalism as an ideal political model which should be exported. ACUE certainly believed that the United States had a wealth of experience to offer in the field of assimilation. It exemplified what Christopher Thorne called America as an 'idea nation', anxious to export its values and political culture. Strikingly, the same small band of senior officials, many of them from the Western intelligence community, were central in supporting the three most important 'insider' groups emerging in the 1950s: the European Movement, the Bilderberg Group and Jean Monnet's Action Committee for a United States of Europe. At a time when some British anti-federalists saw a continued 'special relationship' with the United States as an obvious antidote to European federalism, it is ironic that European federalism should have been sustained by the CIA. Quite simply, the most enthusiastic federalist power in post-war Europe was the United States.[8]

CIA and ACUE must be understood in the context of all US covert operations in Europe. Between 1948 and 1950 these expanded rapidly, partly in response to pressure from senior State Department officials such as George Kennan. Only a small number of State Department officials were ever told about covert operations. Matters were further confused by the semi-detached nature of the CIA's covert action arm – Frank Wisner's OPC – and its tendency to collaborate with American private networks. Despite this early confusion, the broad objectives of American operations in post-war Europe are now clear. The CIA – as we have already seen – were using bases in Western Europe, especially at Munich, to provoke dissonance inside Central-Eastern Europe and were creating stay-behind or GLADIO networks against the possibility of a Soviet incursion into Western Europe.[9] West European political parties, often of the non-communist left and centre, were subsidised. Famously, during the Italian election of 1948, various political groups were paid millions of dollars which helped to revitalise the hitherto listless campaign of the future Prime Minister, De Gasperi.[10] The CIA helped American and European trade unionists to undermine the Soviet-controlled World Federation of Trade Unions in Paris. Staunchly anti-communist members of the American Federation of Labor, led by David Dubinsky, Jay Lovestone and Irving Brown, were often more zealous than government agencies thought wise.[11] The United States also attempted to influence cultural and intellectual trends in Europe, funding a variety of groups, conferences and publications. This developed into a 'battle of the festivals' featuring the Congress for Cultural Freedom and the magazine *Encounter*, to which famous figures such as Raymond Aron, Stephen Spender and Arthur Koestler contributed.

The CIA's growing international cultural and labour activities triggered a crucial change in early 1951. Much of this work was now placed under a new department of the Agency, the International Organisations Division.[12] The use of private networks and organisations had been gathering pace since 1947, encouraged by Allen Dulles, an enthusiast for covert operation. He had also used his position as chairman of the Council of Foreign Relations to seek the help of US charitable foundations. However, by late 1950, when Dulles exchanged his informal role as a consultant on covert action for a senior post within the CIA, these fuzzy operations with youth groups, trade unions and cultural organisations lacked coherence, being dispersed untidily across geographically organised sections. In the words of one CIA officer, this area was an 'operational junk heap'. Thomas W. Braden, who was Dulles' innovative special assistant, proposed a new International Organisations Division to superintend all such work. Braden then headed this exciting new CIA division until replaced by Cord Meyer in 1954. Crucially, the work done by Braden, Dulles and Bedell Smith as founders and directors of ACUE in 1948–50 set out the path for this controversial new division. The activities of Braden's International Organisations Division, while brilliant, were also dangerous and pointed to future trouble.[13]

The origins of CIA covert funding for European federalists may be traced back to the little-known figure of Count Coudenhove-Kalergi. Like other prominent pan-Europeanists of the inter-war period his ideas owed much to disillusionment caused by the First World War. Exiled to the United States in 1943, by the eve of the first Marshall Plan discussions in March 1947 he was successfully lobbying US Senator J. W. Fulbright for Congressional support for the idea of European unity and succeeded in having motions passed in favour of a 'United States of Europe' on Capitol Hill. Allen Dulles and William J. Donovan, who helped Coudenhove-Kalergi in 1947, now came together to create the short-lived Committee for a Free and United Europe designed to support such federalist groups in Europe.[14]

In the summer of 1948 a rival group, the more prestigious International Executive of the European Movement, closely associated with Winston Churchill, arrived in New York to urge the formation of an American committee to support its own efforts for unification. This mission was led by Churchill's son-in-law and President of the European Movement, Duncan Sandys. It also included the European Movement's Secretary General, Joseph H. Retinger, and its finance chief, Major Edward Beddington-Behrens.[15] Two American committees supporting two rival groups would have been embarrassing, so Coudenhove-Kalergi, who was a prickly and awkward character, was dropped amid much recrimination. A new body, the American Committee on United Europe (ACUE), was formed to support Churchill and the European Movement. Although Churchill was now Leader of the Opposition in Britain, he remained the most prestigious of European statesmen.[16] Moreover, he was effectively the founder of the European Movement. As early as 21 March 1943, in a broadcast speech, he offered his vision of a United Europe, with a High Court 'to adjust disputes and prevent future wars'.[17]

The European Movement tried, somewhat uncertainly, to focus and co-ordinate the efforts of pro-unity groups throughout Europe. It pinned its hopes on the European Assembly at Strasbourg. In late October 1948 Britain, France and the Benelux countries had decided to establish a Council of Europe, consisting of a Council of Ministers and an advisory European Assembly which, in practice, served as an irregular conference of national delegations. In August the following year the Assembly of the Council of Europe held its first session at Strasbourg.[18]

ACUE and its short-lived predecessor were only two of many 'American' and 'Free' committees established during 1948 and 1949 which were all closely linked by common funding and complementary objectives. Senior figures from the US intelligence community provided the leadership of ACUE during its first three years. The Chairman was William J. Donovan who, despite the demise of OSS, was not in retirement, and continued to work for the CIA as late as 1955.[19] The Vice Chairman was Allen Dulles, while day-to-day ACUE administration was controlled by Thomas W. Braden, the Executive Director, who had also served in OSS. Braden formally joined the CIA as special assistant to Allen Dulles in late 1950. Donovan and Dulles were well-known espionage chiefs, which was likely to prompt awkward questions about the nature of ACUE. Accordingly, in turn, during the early 1950s, Dulles, Braden and finally Donovan were succeeded by less well-known figures.[20]

ACUE's Board of Directors, set up in 1949, was drawn from prestigious groups. It contained senior figures from government, such as Lucius Clay, Bedell Smith, the Secretary for War Robert T. Paterson and the Director of the Budget James E. Webb. It recruited Marshall Plan (ECA) personnel and other officials responsible for formulating US policy in Europe, including the chief ECA Administrator Paul Hoffman and his deputies Howard Bruce and William C. Foster, together with the US Representative on the North Atlantic Council Charles M. Spofford. Prominent politicians, financiers and lawyers were members, including Herbert H. Lehman, Charles R. Hook and Conrad N. Hilton. Finally, it included AFL-CIO figures already involved in the politics of labour movements, notably Arthur Goldberg, now Chief Counsel for the CIO who had run the wartime OSS Labor Desk, together with the prominent unionists David Dubinsky and Jay Lovestone.[21]

The ACUE's primary role was to fund European unity groups. Many originated with wartime resistance groups with which Donovan and Dulles had worked previously. Strict criteria were set out for the receipt of secret subsidies: the groups supported had to believe in a rapid rather than a gradual approach to Western European integration, including giving the Council of Europe more authority, and to back the early realisation of the aims of the Marshall Plan and of NATO (which was founded in 1949). Programmes receiving support also had to favour the inclusion of Western Germany within a unified Europe. The ACUE's secondary objectives, entirely overt, included publicising European unity within the United States, lobbying Congress on European issues and sponsoring scholarly research on federalism. This overt work allowed ACUE to maintain a public 'front' existence with offices in New York.[22]

Despite this well-organised US apparatus, it was competing groups of Europeans actively seeking discreet American support who set most of its agenda. The European Movement had told ACUE in no uncertain terms that it wanted 'moral support and money'. In March 1949 Winston Churchill visited New York to discuss final details with Donovan and Dulles and also to attend the formal launch of ACUE at a public lunch in his honour. He followed this up by writing on 4 June to ask what short-term funds ACUE could provide.[23] In practice, control of the flow of American money soon passed to the European Movement's President, Duncan Sandys. On 24 June, Sandys wrote to Donovan confidentially setting out his requirements. The European Movement, he revealed, was nearly bankrupt and needed £80,000 to survive the next six months.

Cord Meyer, who joined Braden's International Organisations Division in 1951, recalled that the 'European political and cultural leaders who solicited our aid ... made it a condition that there be no publicity, since the Communist propaganda machine could exploit any overt evidence of official American support as proof that they were puppets of the American imperialists.' This was certainly the case with the European Movement. While Sandys pleaded for 'a really large contribution from America', at the same time he confessed to being 'very anxious that American financial support for the European Movement should not be known', even to the International Council of the Movement. He was worried about charges of 'American intervention'.[24] Both Sandys and ACUE knew that if Moscow, or indeed even the French, uncovered this link they would have a field day, presenting it as US capitalist imperialism in Europe.

At this early stage, Churchill was the most vital link between ACUE and the European Movement. He enjoyed unrivalled personal contacts with American and European leaders; his fascination with intelligence and subversion kept him in touch with practitioners on both sides of the Atlantic; and he shared the view of Allen Dulles and Donovan that the promotion of European unity through ACUE was the 'unofficial counterpart' to the Marshall Plan.[25] More importantly, as late as 1949 (but no later), Churchill also subscribed to the wider objectives of ACUE's various sister committees promoting liberation for Eastern Europe. ACUE and the European Movement, he insisted, should join hands with the Free Europe Committee because complete European unity implied nothing less than the liberation of all of Eastern Europe. At the formal launch of ACUE in New York on 29 March 1949, he declared, 'There can be no permanent peace while ten capitals of Eastern Europe are in the hands of the Soviet Communist Government. We have our relations with these nations behind the iron curtain. They send their delegates to our meetings and we know their feelings and how gladly they would be incorporated in the new United Europe ... We therefore take as our aim and ideal, nothing less than the union of Europe as a whole.'[26] The delegates to whom Churchill referred were primarily from the Assembly of

Captive European Nations (ACEN). His views were widely shared in Washington. During a conversation in 1949 with William Hayter, the Chairman of the British JIC in London, George Kennan stated that in the long term Europe could only move towards federalism, or unification 'Phase Two', once an over-extended Soviet Union had withdrawn to its own borders.[27] However, Churchill's support for both liberation and the European Movement was now about to evaporate.

The CIA had its greatest impact on the European Movement in 1949 and 1950. Funds channelled through ACUE saved the European Movement from financial collapse during the first meetings of the Consultative Assembly of the Council of Europe at Strasbourg. Despite the substantial financial aid given by ACUE in 1949, Tom Braden returned from Europe in early 1950 to report that, once again, 'the Movement is very low on funds'. ACUE had supported conferences held at Brussels in February 1949 and at Westminster in April the same year which had laid the foundations for the Council of Europe, and was paying part of the costs of the European Movement's secretariat and administration. More money was forthcoming, but this strained ACUE's resources.[28]

In 1950 ACUE also helped to resolve awkward leadership problems in Europe. In the early summer, following talks with leaders of the European Movement – including Paul-Henri Spaak and the Belgian Foreign Minister Paul van Zeeland – Tom Braden and William J. Donovan concluded, rather prematurely, that Europe was on the brink of federation. If those who were taking the lead received substantial support immediately, they argued, enormous progress would be made during the next year. At the same time, they perceived a seemingly immovable obstacle, the growing resistance of the British to a federal Europe. Attlee's Labour government, while not anti-Europe, preferred distant co-operation by independent states and fiercely resisted any diminution of sovereignty through federalism. The Foreign Secretary Ernest Bevin had already played a key role in emasculating the Council of Europe at Strasbourg.[29] The Conservatives were also deeply uneasy when faced with federalism. In late 1949 and early 1950 the President of the European Movement itself, Duncan Sandys, working closely with Churchill, feared that his organisation was moving too quickly. Although Sandys had himself indulged in outbursts of federalist rhetoric, they now realised the full implications. The Sandys leadership began to drag its feet. Churchill was also backing away fast. The resulting bitter disputes inside the European Movement had material effects, dissuading prominent Swiss industrialists like Nestlé from providing further funding. By early 1950 the European Movement, always a somewhat fragmented body, was close to disintegration, with the influential

French-based European Union of Federalists withdrawing from its International Executive in protest.[30]

Senior CIA officers were now turning their attention to the problem. Frank Wisner was especially enthusiastic about speeding European unification. He was a frequent visitor to the Paris Embassy and was intimate with the Ambassador, David Bruce, and also with Averell Harriman, who was running ECA. In February 1950, Wisner wrote to Harriman to explain that 'we are presently working on an over-all project that will seek to promote Western European political integration' and that he wanted ECA support. But Wisner was worried about the current turbulence in the European Movement. He feared that the Movement was 'presently dominated ... by those, including some prominent Britains', who advocate a 'slow and step-by-step' approach to unity.

'In short', continued Wisner, 'we seem to be faced with this dilemma.' If the CIA backed the European Movement as it stood, and led by Sandys, would it not be supporting those 'advocating a slow approach to the problem'? He added, 'would we not thereby deny our support to just those Continentals and some British who are today among the most active and effective workers on behalf of just that type of unity we most hope to see achieved?' He said he was thinking of energetic people like the British Labour MP and ardent federalist Richard Mackay, who 'had made such a valuable contribution on behalf of European Unity during last Summer's Strasbourg meeting'. Wisner advocated a diversified approach that would allow a range of support to the real activists while bypassing the foot-draggers in the main European Movement. He wanted to extend support directly to groups such as the European Union of Federalists, the Economic League for European Co-operation, the French Council for United Europe, the Nouvelles Equipes Internationales and the Socialist Movement for a United States of Europe. But this diversification could only be a palliative, for the European Movement was the high-profile organisation and needed sorting out.[31]

In April 1950 ACUE spelt out its 'Program for the Future'. The top item on the agenda was to secure the speedy resolution of the leadership problem in the European Movement 'and if possible the transfer of leadership to the Continent, with particular regard for France'.[32] Strife in the European Movement was so bad by May that year that ACUE abruptly refused to continue funding. In June it sent Donovan and Braden back to Europe on a troubleshooting mission.[33] Braden confirmed that the European Movement was torn between its British and continental leadership: increasingly anti-federalist statements by the Attlee government had forced the hand of Spaak, who led the continental federalists. Spaak confided to Braden that he had been reluctant to pursue rapid continental federalism in the absence of British support on account of the special relationship between London and Washington. But if the US would back him he promised to press ahead without Britain, knowing that 'Britain will be forced sooner or later and in a greater or lesser degree to come along'. Braden liked Spaak's direct approach. He warned the Directors of ACUE that unless they backed the continental federalists against London then inevitably 'leadership on the continent will go to British Labour' with dire consequences for unification. Meanwhile, if offered really substantial ACUE support by Braden, Spaak was willing to launch a takeover bid for the leadership of the European Movement, removing it from Duncan Sandys and the British.[34]

In the event, Sandys required only a light push and offered little resistance. During late 1949 and early 1950 he had struggled in vain to find a compromise formula that would embrace both the reticence of the British and Scandinavian elements and the radical federalist position taken by the likes of Henri Frenay, Chairman of the European Union of Federalists. Matters had reached stalemate as early as 16 December 1949. The Secretary General of the European Movement, Joseph Retinger, put the case for his departure frankly: 'The various Movements composing the European Movement are looking with increasing suspicion on your activities; our American friends do not agree with your tactics.' In July 1950, largely as a result of the Braden–Donovan mission, Sandys departed and Spaak's federalist element took control.[35]

Financial matters had added to the private confrontation among leaders of the European Movement. The whole financial structure under Sandys was 'very unorthodox'. Throughout 1949 strong attacks were made on him over curious expenses incurred and 'a certain squandering of funds'. In 1950 'a very bad financial situation' was bequeathed to Spaak and arguments developed about the distribution of new tranches of secret funding that were beginning to arrive from the United States.[36] ACUE now played a significant role in smoothing the transition to a new era. With American support, Spaak had the resources to move the International Secretariat of the European Movement from London and Paris to Brussels. Subsequently, Braden told Walter Bedell Smith that during early 1950 'Sandys attempted to disband the European Movement.' He added that 'Spaak and Retinger together have handled the Sandys situation ... and kept the whole fracas from reaching the public.'[37]

The Americans were very keen on Spaak and had already made an unsuccessful bid to install him as director general of the Organisation of European Economic Co-operation (OEEC). In the words of one historian, the 'American choice for "Mr Europe" was ... Paul-Henri Spaak', but British 'foot-dragging' and hostility prevented his appointment.[38] Nevertheless, Spaak now got busy transforming the European

Movement. An 'efficient' secretariat was set up in Brussels, with experienced national representatives, including George Rebattet, former secretary of the French Maquis, and Léon Radfoux, Spaak's former *chef de cabinet*. The primary objective of this new secretariat was to generate a popular groundswell of support for federalism through the 'initiation of major propaganda campaigns in all countries', including a United Europe Week. Tom Braden reported that the goals were a free-trade area with a single currency and free movement of labour, together with more power for the Assembly of the Council of Europe at Strasbourg.[39]

How closely did the CIA and ACUE follow mainstream American policy during the period 1949–51? Washington was divided over how much pressure to apply on European issues. Some parts of the Truman administration were closer to ACUE than others. ACUE followed American policy most closely in tying European unity to the cause of East European exile groups and to political warfare against the Eastern bloc. In May 1950, during the London Foreign Ministers Conference, the United States persuaded Britain and France to give the exile groups associate membership of the Council of Europe. A year later the White House endorsed State Department plans to accelerate these efforts. Outlining its proposals in a Special Guidance paper entitled 'The Concept of Europe', it admitted its concern that the current propaganda effort in Eastern Europe lacked the 'positive qualities which are necessary to arouse nations'. Several studies had been made in an attempt to find a positive concept that would stir the populations of Eastern Europe, and it concluded that the themes of 'European Unity' and 'Return to Europe' would succeed. Its 'solely European' nature ensured that it could not be 'dismissed as another manoeuvre of American imperialism'. Nor could the Soviets appropriate the European ideal in the way they had shamelessly used themes such as 'freedom', 'democracy' and 'peace'. As the Council of Europe had recently adopted a Charter of Human Rights, this offered a particularly choice instrument with which to highlight the more unpleasant aspects of Soviet rule. The White House hoped this would encourage Eastern bloc populations to stiffen their resistance – 'retard the Sovietization of their minds, especially the minds of their youth'. George M. Elsey, a member of Truman's staff, noted on 16 May 1951 that all this was 'going in the right direction ... a good contribution toward the goal we were discussing at noon, namely, a subverting of Iron Curtain countries'.[40]

American policy was more divided over unification pressure in Western Europe. Senior State Department figures worried about alienating an anti-federalist Britain and the Commonwealth, with which the United States sought to collaborate in other areas of the world. Kennan was anxious to reassure British officials, speaking instead of a long period characterised by some kind of loose 'Atlantic Community'. He added that British objections to any merger of sovereignty with Western Europe 'were of such strength that they must be accepted', and that Washington ought not to push Britain further than it wished to go. Looking to the long term, however, even Kennan was firmly in favour of a federal Europe that would totally absorb Britain, drawing his inspiration for a future Europe from the American federal model. It 'was clear that eventual union was in his mind', wrote one wary British official. Kennan pointed to the painful economic adjustments which Britain would have to make, comparing them to those which New England underwent during the expansion of the United States. Nevertheless, he returned from visits to Europe with a fuller appreciation of the complex problems of the Commonwealth and of sterling, and the reluctance of Britain to submerge its identity in a federal Europe.[41]

Averell Harriman and his ECA officials, together with Spaak and Bruce, were less sensitive. They constantly urged Washington to apply greater pressure on Ernest Bevin to change his mind about an integrated Western Europe. On 19 January 1950, Spaak complained bitterly to Kennan and the Secretary of State, Dean Acheson, of what he saw as Britain's attempts to obstruct both OEEC and the Council of Europe. When Kennan, Paul Nitze of the PPS and Charles Bohlen from the Paris Embassy met a few days later, Nitze summed up the dilemma: although Britain's Commonwealth ties and its fears over sovereignty inclined it against federalism, would a continental federation be strong enough without Britain? They agreed that Bevin had been 'back-sliding' over commitments to OEEC and that this now required action. Bohlen, representing frustrated American officials based in Paris, including ECA, complained that the United States was shy of applying real pressure in London, as it habitually did in Paris, because of the close wartime relationship. The Empire–Commonwealth should be broken up, he argued, allowing Britain to merge with a federal Europe. However, Kennan replied that the Commonwealth was valuable, and the United States should do no more than try gently to persuade Britain to move towards Europe.[42]

Initially Donovan was not only an advocate of covert pressure, he was an opponent of overt pressure. In March 1950 he worked hard to impress upon key Congressional figures that tough measures would be counter-productive. He was especially anxious that crude conditions should not be attached to the renewal of Marshall Plan aid. In a presentation before the House of Representatives Committee on Foreign Affairs he warned that if you say, 'Here is the rule we are going to put in. You are going to have unification, or else,' then this would 'destroy the very thing you want to accomplish'. It would not only alienate

Europeans, it would also be 'exploited propagandawise' by the Soviet Union. Congress was concerned that Europe would take the money and just 'go through the motions'. Donovan came very close to outlining the secret business of ACUE. His patient explanations persuaded Congress that it was better backing the active European federalists, or as he put it 'giving Spaak an instrument'.[43] However, by the autumn of 1950, his patience was becoming exhausted and he joined attempts to persuade Acheson to push Britain into joining the Schuman Plan relating to coal, iron and steel manufacture in Europe.[44]

Acheson's approach dismayed both ACUE and American officials in Europe who had the task of carrying out the agreements on European economic co-operation. They found Britain exasperating and wanted some bullying done. David Bruce, Averell Harriman and the Ambassador in London, Lewis Douglas, all agreed that Britain was their 'big problem'. They wanted action. Harriman was the most vociferous, and meeting with Bruce and John J. McCloy, the US High Commissioner in Germany, in January 1950, he explained that he had had enough of Bevin and of the Chancellor of the Exchequer, Sir Stafford Cripps, whom he found 'petulant and arrogant'. 'Harriman was extremely perturbed,' saying that hitherto he 'had been a firm believer in U.S. attitude of persuasion against coercion'. But now he 'felt the US should no longer tolerate interference and sabotage of Western European integration by the United Kingdom ... the Marshall Plan is breaking down because of British opposition'. He warned that if the British Labour Party won the forthcoming general election of 1950, as seemed likely, it would 'be even more cocky'. 'The U.S. would not stand for this much longer.' In March 1950, senior American officials in Europe called for a study of the degree and timing of pressure to brought to bear on Britain. Nevertheless, Douglas warned against acting during the British election, noting that Labour might derive advantage from posing as a defender of the Commonwealth against American pressure.[45]

CIA activity through ACUE did not challenge Acheson's policy of avoiding open pressure on Britain over federalism. Nevertheless, Donovan and Braden preferred the leadership of ECA in Paris, including Harriman and Milton Katz, the ECA's counsel. Personal connections were important here, as Katz had previously served as a senior officer in the secret intelligence branch of OSS, overseeing operations in wartime Europe, while Bruce, the OSS chief of station in wartime London, had been head of ECA in Paris before becoming ambassador.[46] The ECA, delighted to learn of Spaak's impending leadership of the European Movement, offered its own discreet assistance to the European Movement, which had been 'previously withheld because of concern over the leadership', until then in British hands.[47]

The Braden–Donovan mission of June 1950 also helped to confirm ACUE's view of Britain's Labour Party as the big enemy of European federalism.[48] They witnessed the remarkable attack that the British delegation launched on the French federalists at Strasbourg that summer.[49] Labour leaders had been hostile to European federalism from the outset. Some had seen it as a stalking horse for Churchill. Others saw it more simply as a Conservative device to sow dissension and confusion in the ranks of the Labour Party. Either way, as early as January 1947, the Labour Party National Executive was advising members to withhold support. Calls from some Party members for a decidedly socialist vision of a united Europe were studiously ignored. By 1949 Bevin had developed a particular hatred of both Spaak and Harriman, reflecting his tendency to see things in personal terms.[50]

ACUE was not a mere passive observer of British anti-federalism. It sought to undermine it by supporting leading pro-European federalist dissenters within the British Labour Party such as the Member of Parliament for Hull North West, Richard W. Mackay, who had devised a compromise route to federalism which became known as the 'Mackay Plan', and who was admired, as we have seen, by Wisner. These activities were resented by the Labour leadership.[51] Richard Mackay was undoubtedly something of a zealot. On his first trip to New York in February 1949 he was already urging American political intervention on the federalist issue and warned, 'If the United States does nothing but give money to Europe without insisting on Europe creating for itself a real Union of Europe, it is throwing money down the drain, and that is what is happening at the present time.' Mackay exhorted ACUE to push the Europeans into federalism 'so that trade and population in Europe can move as freely as they do in the USA'. He also identified London as the main problem. Britain's obsession with remaining a first-class power, rather than a mere state of Europe, was the key issue. He said that 'the obstacle at the present time is the British Government, and the only question is how to overcome this obstacle ... Someone has got to give the British a push.'[52]

The CIA's Frank Wisner was immensely impressed by Mackay. Thomas Braden called him 'a most energetic worker for unity'. Letters between Mackay, Braden and Allen Dulles over money show how closely this group was working together. During the crisis period of March 1950, Mackay visited the United States again and held extended conversations with ACUE. He stressed that 'the creation of a common currency and the abolition of currency and custom barriers are the urgent tasks of Western Europe'. He also set out ideas for an inner committee of dedicated European federalists who would prepare the detail of such proposals for further meetings of the next Assembly at Strasbourg.[53] This inner committee, he continued, would be composed of people from five or six European countries: he suggested Maurice Schumann (a close associate of de Gaulle) from France, F. Jacobson from Denmark, von Natters from Holland. ACUE decided that he needed £10,000 to cover the expenses of this sort of work, £5,000 coming from ACUE and £1,000 payable immediately. In return ACUE would have the right to appoint a 'liaison officer' to his committee, and Mackay would also agree that one or two members might be drawn from the International Federation of Trade Unions.[54]

But, as fast as Wisner and Braden tried to build Mackay up, the Labour Party was cutting him down. He was demoted from Labour Party Representative at the General Affairs Committee of the Assembly in Strasbourg to a mere delegate to the Assembly.[55] Although Hugh Dalton, who was now Chancellor of the Duchy of Lancaster and a member of the Cabinet, liked Mackay personally, he warned Attlee in March 1950 that he was 'a lone wolf', adding that 'we shall have to keep an eye on him.'[56] From January 1950 much of Mackay's activity was dependent on ACUE funding, assisting him in developing his plan and his inner committee. However, in 1951, the British and Scandinavians vetoed the presentation of the Mackay Plan to the full Strasbourg Assembly.[57] As Braden had cautioned, 'The British were suspicious of the Assembly' – they 'will only go ahead step by step and ... fear, above all, to be forced to give up any point of their national sovereignty, no matter how slight'.[58]

This was dangerous stuff. The CIA was now engaged in a covert subsidy of dissident British elements in the hope of undermining a key area of British foreign policy. How far were the authorities in Britain aware of the work of the CIA and ACUE by 1950? It appears the British Foreign Office had noticed only ACUE's overt publicity campaign in the USA, which had caused some irritation in London. In early February 1950 Joseph Retinger, Secretary General of the European Movement, asked if Attlee and Bevin would state publicly their support for European unification. Donovan desired these statements from all European leaders, intending to publish them together as part of an attempt to persuade Congress to continue Marshall Plan aid. As most of the statesmen of Western Europe had complied, Bevin was told he would have to say something. But Bevin's message of 'support' was so unenthusiastic that ACUE asked the Foreign Office whether there had been some mistake, only to be told that Bevin had personally insisted upon the insertion of the more offensive sentences.[59] ACUE was further disappointed when Churchill and Eden, returning to power in 1951, increasingly set their face against federalist ideas. Accordingly, by November 1951, both Spaak in Europe and ACUE in the United States, had started to despair of the elite route to federalism and turned to mass agitation.[60]

This growing emphasis upon publicity and propaganda began in 1950 with the overt work that ACUE conducted within the United States from its offices at 537 Fifth Avenue, New York. It tried to persuade American elite opinion to support European federalism. To this end it organised and paid for a stream of visits and lecture tours by prominent European figures, such as Churchill, Spaak and Paul van Zeeland. Robert Schuman, Paul Reynaud, Konrad Adenauer and Guy Mollet followed in their wake.[61] Spaak's visit in January and February 1951 attracted a great deal of press and radio attention and during his six-week tour he addressed audiences in thirteen cities including New York, Palm Beach, Chicago, San Francisco and Los Angeles. There was rarely a moment when ACUE did not have a major speaker in circulation around the United States and more and more it was to ACUE that student groups, colleges, radio and television in the United States turned for speakers on European issues.[62]

Congress received considerable attention during the crucial first hearings on the new Marshall Plan appropriations of February and March 1950. As we have seen, Donovan testified before the House of Representatives' Foreign Affairs Committee on the Marshall Plan in his capacity as chairman of ACUE, and Congress was continually bombarded with federalist literature. More importantly, Donovan in New York and Spaak in Brussels held simultaneous press conferences in which they released the text of pro-unity statements carefully gathered by Retinger from fifty prominent European statesmen, effectively dispelling lingering doubts about European commitment to progress and creating a very favourable atmosphere for the renewal of Marshall Plan aid by the legislature. In June of the same year the French Embassy in Washington thanked Donovan for organising an open message to Prime Minister Schuman in favour of the Schuman Plan signed by '118 American big names', including former Secretaries of State Marshall and Stimson, and released at a press conference in New York by Allen Dulles. By 1951 ACUE had produced seventeen publications and was publishing a regular fortnightly newsletter for circulation in the USA.[63] It now shifted its American focus away from elites towards a wider audience, arranging for radio broadcasts by Donovan and for his articles to be published in *Atlantic Monthly* and the *San Francisco Chronicle*. In April 1952 ACUE took out a full-page advertisement in the *New York Times* headed 'The Survival of Europe' and advocating European union.[64] This use of resources that were partly funded by the CIA for political campaigns and lobbying within the United States itself was highly unorthodox and almost certainly illegal.

ACUE also commissioned American academics to undertake research projects into the problems of federalism, begun at Harvard University in 1952.[65] This project was managed by the leading European historian and propaganda expert Carl Friedrich, who was himself deeply committed to the federalist cause. For Friedrich, European unity was a stepping stone to world federalism.[66] His work is also noteworthy because it illustrates the complex links between ACUE and liberation. Throughout the 1950s, he also worked for the Free Europe Committee as a consultant on the Soviet Zone of Germany. In 1951, he urged a forward policy upon Allen Dulles and C. D. Jackson, describing Berlin as a base from which the United States could support and expand a resistance network which he claimed was already 'effectively harassing the Soviet authorities and their German Communist stooges'.[67] Although Dulles and Jackson agreed, other US officials in Germany harboured growing doubts about the value of general troublemaking.[68]

American academics played an important part in expanding the activities of ACUE. In 1950 a Cultural Section of ACUE was launched, directed by two American historians who had served in OSS, the President of Bennington College Frederick H. Burkhardt and William L. Langer of Harvard University. The grants they distributed helped to establish the European Cultural Centre in Geneva under Denis de Rougemont and assisted the Inter-University Union of Federalists.[69] ACUE took an interest in the College of Europe at Bruges, designed to provide a training for future European officials. It also formed links with Strasbourg's Committee on Central and Eastern Europe, providing fellowships for Iron Curtain students. One of the attractions of the College was its leadership, which had played an active part in the wartime resistance. The Rector Henryk Brugman and the Director of Studies Henri Van Effentere had both been active in the resistance during the war.[70] Brugman was an important influence on the federalist ideas circulating within the wartime European resistance movements, as expressed in clandestine newspapers such as the Dutch *Het Parool* and the French *Combat* and *Résistance*.[71] In June 1951, ACUE offered scholarships for American students to attend the College.[72] American cultural leaders and academics, they asserted, could offer a federalising Europe the benefit of 'our experience – good and bad – in the fields of mass communication and intercultural assimilation'.[73]

Inside Britain, ACUE also moved away from a focus on individual figures, like Mackay, towards a wider publicity campaign. A key objective was to encourage a stronger British commercial and business interest in a federal Europe. Throughout the 1950s ACUE commissioned studies by the Economist Intelligence Unit of economic relations between Britain and Europe, hoping to persuade British industrialists to take what it called a more 'realistic' view. In 1959 alone, the Economist Intelligence Unit studies commissioned cost ACUE $11,200.[74] In 1960, when ACUE was wound up, staff from the *Economist* wrote to ACUE thanking it for its support. As others have shown, the *Economist,* Britain's most serious current affairs weekly, was the staunchest critic of the British opposition to federalism and one of the originators of the idea of Britain's 'missed opportunities' in Europe.

ACUE use of the Economist Intelligence Unit is a good example of how it homed in on those already enthusiastic for federalism. Each issue of the *Economist* has traditionally opened with a proud statement of its independence. However, on the European issue the newspaper was committed to a staunchly federalist line. Its staff in the 1950s – especially in the Intelligence Unit – was a haven for dedicated federalists and those prominent in European organisations, for example its Deputy Editor Barbara Ward. Another was Christopher Layton, who served in the Intelligence Corps in the late 1940s. After a year with ICI in 1952 he joined the Economist Intelligence Unit. In 1954 he transferred to the main staff of the *Economist* and served as 'Editorial writer – European Affairs'. Here in the paper's foreign department he met another 'crusader for Europe', François Duchêne, who had worked closely with Jean Monnet. Layton wrote memorable pieces surveying the events which had split Britain from Europe and was active in promoting the idea of Britain's 'missed opportunities' in Europe.[75] Throughout the 1950s, in the face of a British climate characterised by underlying hostility towards Europe, the *Economist* persistently urged Britain to demonstrate that it had undergone 'a real and lasting change of heart'.[76]

European unity was a Layton family business. Lord Layton, Christopher's father, was Editor of the *Economist* from 1923 until 1939. Always a committed European federalist, Lord Layton was vice president of the Consultative Committee of the European Assembly at Strasbourg between 1949 and 1957. 'In addition', as his biographer has observed, 'he was chairman, vice-chairman or treasurer of all the more important UK bodies of the European Movement which sprang up in such numbers from 1946 onwards.' He also remained influential on the *Economist.* Lord Layton was not only a member of various European federalist groups but was also a crucial link between the British section of the European Movement and ACUE, the CIA's parent American funding body for European unity organisations.[77]

One of Lord Layton's first actions was to encourage a relationship between key staff on the *Economist* and ACUE. On 5 October 1949, George S. Franklin, Secretary of ACUE, had written thanking him for briefing Barbara Ward, the Assistant Editor, about the organisation.[78]

In the same month, Layton's close friend the diplomat Sir Harold Butler had warned him that ACUE thought European Movement activities were currently 'in the doldrums' and that it 'will not part with any money unless it is convinced that the European Movement is an active body with a popular programme'. Layton responded energetically and by February 1950 had embarked on a mission to Washington with Paul Reynaud, a former French prime minister, to talk to ACUE. Thereafter they were accompanied on a speaking tour of the United States by Donovan and Braden. They were introduced to many American luminaries, and Braden assured Layton that his mission had done a great deal to 'swell the coffers of the European Movement'. Layton visited Washington again at Braden's request in the summer of 1951.[79] After Braden's departure from the post of ACUE executive director, Layton continued to work closely with his successor, Allan Hovey. In 1954, during a period of concern about growing anti-Americanism in Europe, he set up and then chaired the European–Atlantic Group, a council of the good and great, designed to improve transatlantic co-operation.[80]

As in the United States and Britain, ACUE's work in continental Europe during the early 1950s also focused increasingly upon propaganda and mass action. While the European Movement was being reorganised in 1950–1, as Frank Wisner had suggested, it turned to the European Movement's member organisations to promote federalism, including the French-dominated European Union of Federalists. The French proposed to stir Strasbourg into action by launching a grass-roots populist movement, the European Council of Vigilance, under the wartime French resistance leader Henri Frenay, which would meet in a building adjacent to the Council of Europe and shower it with local petitions supporting federalism. ACUE gave the Council of Vigilance project an initial grant of $42,000.[81]

By the spring of 1951, with Spaak's new leadership, the European Movement had been reorganised into an effective body. ACUE together with Spaak and Frenay threw themselves into an optimistic attempt to generate mass support for federalism. In the short term they hoped to create backing for the Schuman Plan, for more authority for the Council of Europe and for the idea of a European Army. After 'extensive talks' in the Spring of 1951 between Donovan and General Eisenhower, who was now NATO Supreme Commander, ACUE also asked for increasing emphasis on integrating Germany into Western Europe, to quieten fears over rearmament and US worries about a German drift towards neutrality.[82]

Mass propaganda was the key to expanded American covert funding in the 1950s. It coincided neatly with deep American concerns about the success of Eastern bloc propaganda efforts in the area of youth movements and international organisations generally. In the summer of 1951 a growing crescendo of organised communist youth activity was highlighted by a gigantic youth rally in East Berlin organised by the Freie Deutsche Jugend and attended by about two million youth representatives from all over the world. This single rally was estimated to have cost the Soviets over £20,000,000. British intelligence obtained film of the rally and its scale alarmed senior Western policy-makers including, John J. McCloy, the American High Commissioner for Germany. McCloy, already heavily involved in American psychological and covert warfare, immediately decided that counter-action was imperative. Shepard Stone, a member of his staff, contacted Joseph Retinger, the Secretary General of the European Movement, and asked if it would be willing to organise a similar demonstration in Western Europe. Considerable additional funds would be provided by the American government, again funnelled through ACUE, provided they were used specifically for youth work. Retinger readily accepted and together with Spaak and André Philip, they formed a special committee to map out what became the European Youth Campaign.[83]

Accordingly, from 1951, the majority of ACUE funds for Europe were employed on a new venture, a unity campaign among European youth. Between 1951 and 1956 the European Movement organised over 2,000 rallies and festivals on the continent, particularly in Germany, where it received the help of the US Army. One of the additional advantages of deploying American funds on the large youth programmes was that it helped to disguise the extent to which the European Movement was dependent on American funds. In May 1952 Spaak decided that funds from American sources that had previously been used in the Ordinary Budget of the European Movement would now be diverted for use in the Special Budgets used to support its growing range of new programmes. This disguised the source and avoided any accusations of American dependency. Again, in November 1953, Baron Böel, the Treasurer of the European Movement, explained that it was essential to avoid a situation where opponents of European unity could accuse the organisation of being an American creation. For this reason, 'American money, quite acceptable for the European Youth Campaign and certain restricted activities, could not be used for the normal running of the Movement'. Through the use of Special Budgets, the Ordinary Budget of the European Movement, which was employed for mundane administrative costs, revealed nothing unusual.[84]

By the end of 1951, an International Youth Secretariat had been established in Paris, with smaller offices throughout Western Europe and a campaign youth newspaper in five languages. The following year, representatives were elected to a European Parliament of Youth which was to help the European Movement 'to inform the masses of European youth of their obligations to themselves and the free world'. By the end of 1953, the campaign was costing ACUE $200,000 a year.[85] Although it is difficult to identify the extent to which these activities had an impact on mass opinion, senior Europeans, eager for more funds, attributed their recent successes to the mass campaign. Jean Monnet's letter to Donovan in October 1952 was typical: 'Your continued support, now more crucial then ever, will help us greatly toward the full realisation of our plans.'[86]

Hidden-hand funding of fronts and foundations is always a complex matter. Most of ACUE's funds came from the CIA, but it also attracted substantial private donations. Equally, not all covert American assistance to European federalist groups was distributed by the ACUE. ECA and US Information Service (USIS) were running parallel programmes of hidden funding to a myriad of European unity groups. To take another example, in Italy a senior official of the Vatican, Luigi Gedda, created an organisation of Catholic activists which helped to defeat the communists in the elections of 1948. Gedda was supported by officials in the US Embassy in Rome and in the CIA, and the support increased when he began to promote the idea of 'Western Union', explaining that the Pope had now agreed that 'the Church should carry the banner for a federation of western European states'. After the US Embassy in Rome had concluded that Gedda needed about $500,000, American officials debated whether the funding should be channelled through the Marshall Plan publicity fund or the CIA.[87] Funds from the Mutual Security Agency, the successor to the Marshall Plan, were also used to support the European Movement; indeed the Mutual Security Act of 1951 explicitly stated that its resources were to be used 'to further encourage the economic and political federation of Europe'.[88] Great use was made of counterpart funds – European currencies transferred from Marshall Plan governments to the American government to cover US administrative costs in Europe – for political purposes.[89]

CIA efforts also moved in parallel with work by USIS officers in embassies. USIS made use of counterpart funds too and, when they began to dry up in late 1953, it was anxious about the future of support to various federalist groups, which it saw as 'extremely important'. USIS officers in Paris were especially keen to continue offering money to the United European Federalists (UEF) and lobbied for an allocation of State Department funds to keep up the flow. One of the UEF's more attractive proposals for 1953–4 was 'a special programme of activities for Great Britain'. UEF's British partner, the Federal Union, had 'drawn up an extensive plan for education and propaganda in Great Britain'. This included 25,000 pamphlets on subjects such as the value to Britain of joining the Schuman Plan and the European Army. The Federal Union in Britain needed money for an Economic Research Committee to carry out comparative studies of the situation in Britain as compared to the six countries which had joined the Schuman Plan. The Federal Union also wanted to launch a special magazine for British MPs, senior officials and trade unions. For its overall European programme, UEF could put up only 48 million francs and needed 314 million francs of external support.[90]

American diplomats and USIS were also doing covert work that involved the direct supply of cash. Many USIS officers had served in OSS or the Office of War Information during the war and were adept at this sort of activity. In April 1955, Leslie Brady, the Public Affairs Officer in Paris, was busy arranging funds for Denis de Rougemont, who as we have seen was the Director of the European Cultural Centre at Geneva and a leading figure in the field of European cultural and intellectual co-operation. He too had previously worked for the Office of War Information towards the end of the Second World War and, in 1951 he had become the president of the Executive Committee of the Congress for Cultural Freedom after Arthur Koestler, the previous incumbent, suffered a minor nervous breakdown.[91] De Rougemont had put up schemes for promoting European unity to USIS for secret funding, and Brady now reported to Washington on progress:

> I have got off a letter to de Rougemont telling him that we buy two-thirds of his plan now, with a kind of option on the rest of it in a new financial year ... I have talked over the financing problem. I believe that, for security's sake and all the rest, it would be much simpler to repeat the process we went through for the payment of funds to Radoux. In other words, if you transfer the money to us here, that permits us to set up our own voucher on the entire project. When we transfer the money to Geneva for payment to de Rougemont, we need refer to the voucher here only by number. That permits us to limit the number of people who get in on the act – and in this case I think it quite essential.

Thus, while the funds that the CIA steered to the European Movement via ACUE reached more than $4 million, wider American covert funding of European unity groups was considerably greater. The complex nature of the whole European Movement, with dozens of sub-sections and splinter groups, local and national bodies, was ideal for this. Nevertheless, the United States always remained nervous of an exposé. On 20 March 1956, Washington wrote to the USIS office in Rome approving another tranche of unity projects which were 'considered excellent'. But it added anxiously, 'You are, of course, fully aware of the need for discreet handling.' It reminded Rome of the 'general guidance' for the wider programme which stated that 'efforts should be so designed to avoid impression that the United States ... is the principal driving force behind the European Movement'.[92]

During 1953 and 1954, ACUE strengthened its ties with the US government. Allen Dulles, one of its co-founders, replaced Walter Bedell Smith as director of the CIA. Meanwhile the State Department concluded that open attempts at propelling European states into the EDC during 1953–4 had backfired badly, being seen as 'undue US interven-tion' and arousing 'more public antagonism than support'. The wisdom of less direct methods seemed to be confirmed.[93] The biggest problem now facing the United States in Europe was the German question. However, ACUE efforts to assist in this area had run into trouble. For some time it had being trying to associate Strasbourg with the liberation efforts of the Free Europe Committee and the Assembly of Captive European Nations. The European Movement had even been encouraged to develop its own special Commission dealing with Central and East European affairs, led by Harold Macmillan, and designed to maintain contact between Strasbourg and the 'captive nations' of the East.

Harold Macmillan had set this up together with Joseph Retinger, the European Movement's first Secretary General. It included exiles from Bulgaria, Czechoslovakia, Hungary, Poland, Rumania and Yugoslavia. The British members were Julian Amery, Arthur Greenwood and Clement Davies representing the three political parties; they were joined by two former French Prime Ministers, Paul Ramadier and Paul Reynaud. Macmillan was chairman and Edward Beddington-Behrens, Treasurer of the European Movement, was rapporteur. The Commission worked out of offices owned by Beddington-Behrens in Park Lane. Its secretaries were John Pomian and George Morton, an ex-SOE operative. Macmillan referred to his Iron Curtain protégés as 'the bandits'. Periodically he and Beddington-Behrens would head off to Strasbourg for a conference with their East European protégés, or to press the case of the 'Enslaved Countries' in the councils of Strasbourg.[94]

But exile politics was always a volatile area. As early as 1953, German and East European groups were making conflicting claims against each other's territory. ACEN and Radio Free Europe were attracting adher-ents in the East by spinning a line that was not only anti-Soviet but also anti-German. Published documents and maps revealed ambitions against the territory of post-war Germany and areas inhabited by Germans. The German government repeatedly pressed the US High Commission 'to stop the dissemination of such anti-German Propaganda'.[95] These ten-sions threatened to disrupt relations between ACEN and the various West European delegations at Strasbourg which it had nurtured so care-fully. Efforts to improve co-ordination between Strasbourg and the Free Europe Committee led, in early 1957, to an extensive study of Radio Free Europe's activities by the Special Political Committee of the Council of Europe. After a three-day visit to its Munich headquarters, the commit-tee concluded that RFE was 'performing an extremely useful political task' and recommended greater European participation in what was still a largely American-managed programme. In 1959 the Free Europe Committee responded by forming a West European Advisory Group.[96]

Two further developments characterised ACUE strategy in the mid-1950s. First, there was revived interest in elite politics, focused on Jean Monnet's Action Committee for a United States of Europe.[97] Monnet stressed small meetings and serious publications 'rather than large manifestations and polemics'.[98] Although his activities are specifically identified in ACUE reports on supported programmes, the documentation linking him, ACUE and the CIA is very limited. This is not surprising since Monnet was even more cautious than the European Movement concerning the potential political damage that might be caused by revelations about American funding. The only precisely quantifiable American funds passed to Monnet during this period came through the Ford Foundation to support his immediate secretariat.[99]

The case of Monnet and the Ford Foundation usefully highlights the extreme difficulties that confront anyone attempting to disentangle covert American government funding from the overt funding provided by American private organisations and public foundations which worked closely with the American government. As early as 1949, at the behest of Allen Dulles, the Ford Foundation was co-operating with the CIA on a number of European programmes.[100] By 1950, ACUE and the Ford Foundation were co-ordinating their efforts to support federalism.[101] By 1953 both John J. McCloy and Shepard Stone, who had been instrumental in arranging for substantial covert government funds for the European Youth Campaign, were both on the board of trustees of the Ford Foundation. He was also a director of the Rockefeller Foundation. In 1955 he had become chairman of the Ford Foundation, while serving as chairman of the Council on Foreign Relations. Simultaneously, the same circle, including Retinger, McCloy, Allen Dulles, Harriman, David Rockefeller, Jackson and Bedell Smith were busy creating the Bilderberg Group, yet another organisation that bridged the narrowing gaps between government and private and public organisations and between overt and covert on both sides of the Atlantic.[102]

In the late 1950s ACUE gave more attention to NATO, which was developing its own programme of political warfare, and to Atlanticist ideas.[103] Finally, in May 1960, ACUE voted itself out of existence. Its Directors argued that, while European unity was an 'unfinished business', continued ACUE activity could be justified only by a 'serious reversal of present trends' towards integration. Moreover, with the recovery of European economies, European federalists were able to find their own funds. Thus, during the spring of 1960 ACUE was gradually wound down, as the Executive Director administered the last eight European grants, totalling $105,000. With many African states sweeping towards independence, ACUE toyed briefly with a Europe–Africa programme designed to tie the two continents together, but residual ACUE funds were transferred to the American Committee on NATO. It then 'deactivated', rather than dissolved, itself at the specific request of Monnet and Schuman, who wished to ensure that it was capable of 'coming back into the picture if and when necessary'.[104]

ACUE, more than any other American front organisation of the Cold War period, was a direct creation of the leading lights of the CIA. Indeed it was so replete with famous CIA figures that its 'front' was very thin. Its early years seemed to have formed something of a laboratory for figures such as Donovan, Dulles, Bedell Smith and Braden, before they moved on to other projects in the mid-1950s. Over its first three years of operations, 1949–51 ACUE received $384,650, the majority being dispersed to Europe. This was a large sum, but from 1952 ACUE began to spend such sums *annually*. The total budget for the period 1949–60 amounted to approximately $4 million.[105] As the quantity of money flowing across the Atlantic began to increase, ACUE opened a local Paris office to monitor more closely groups that had received grants. By 1956 the flood of increased funding was prompting fears among the Directors of ACUE that its work would be publically exposed, arousing criticism of the European groups it supported. Although its European representative, William Fuggit, explained that ACUE was 'able to avoid embarrassing our friends by staying in the background', he conceded that the danger of discovery 'was real'.[106]

The source of growing ACUE funds was clearly US government subventions managed by the CIA. As other historians have shown, in 1948 the US government attempted to run these sorts of projects on the basis of private donations only, but this approach was soon abandoned.[107] As late as 1951, ACUE was still soliciting donations from private American citizens, but thereafter, its accounts show that it ceased to employ a professional fundraiser.[108] He was no longer needed. This shift coincides with John McCloy's intervention, funnelled via ACUE, to boost campaigns among European youth and a tripling of resources available to ACUE. Tom Braden, in an interview given in the 1980s, specifically asserted that ACUE funds originated with the CIA; and Retinger, the Secretary General of the European Movement, recounted in his posthumous memoirs the receipt of American government funds and having to live with periodic accusations that he was working for American intelligence. As the remarkable work of F. X. Rebattet, with his unparalleled access to European Movement archives and leaders, concluded:

> There were no less than four members of the Central Intelligence Agency among the Officers and Directors of ACUE ... The vast majority of the American funds devoted to the campaign for European unity, and practically all the money received for the European Youth Campaign, came from State Department secret funds. This was of course kept very secret. ACUE thus

played the part of a legal covering organisation. Donations from business made up a maximum of one sixth of the total sums during the period under study.[109]

As already noted, there were other US programmes of hidden funding to European unity groups. It is unlikely that historians will ever trace it all.[110]

Nevertheless ACUE can be compared with contemporaneous programmes mounted by the CIA. It clearly cost less than was spent to ensure the defeat of the communists in the Italian elections of 1948, probably the CIA's biggest operation in this period and thought by Christopher Simpson to have cost approximately $10 million.[111] At the same time, ACUE received more than the $3 million spent by the CIA during the Chilean elections of 1964, and more than the $3.3 million channelled to the American National Student Association between 1952 and 1967. Spending on ACUE was broadly typical of one of the larger OPC/CIA covert operations in this period.[112] Certainly the CIA itself thought that this activity was big. In July 1953 it surveyed all its work in Western Europe in the field of political–psychological operations and covert action. It was clear about its major achievements, which fell into two categories: 'The major accomplishments of political action and propaganda operations in Western Europe have been in the area of European unification, and in reducing the power and influence of Communism. Covert operations have been chiefly in support of overt U.S. Government actions to achieve greater military, economic and political cooperation.' In the summer of 1953, the CIA judged the acceleration of European unity and co-operation to be its most successful area of covert operations in Western Europe.[113]

It is hard to reach a balanced assessment of what ACUE's covert operations in Europe actually achieved between 1949 and 1960. Plainly, appropriate funding was not available within the countries of Western Europe for the sorts of initiatives that the European Movement wished to pursue. Indeed much of the scarce overt funds available prior to American involvement came from Swiss industrialists, notably the firm of Nestlés.[114] There can be no doubt that, between 1949 and 1951, ACUE funds propped up a European Movement that seemed terminally split and was approaching bankruptcy. One-third of the European Movement's office staff had been laid off, the publication programme had been halted and bills were not being paid.[115] Once Spaak had taken the helm, and the core of the European Movement had been stabilised, its expensive public campaigns of the 1950s relied almost entirely on ACUE funds. When a French delegate from the European Union of Federalists arrived in New York in 1950 to deliver a presentation to ACUE on plans for the European Council of Vigilance, he conceded that 'it is simply impossible for us to carry out the enterprise without your help'.[116] Federalists had outlined the mass European Youth Campaign on paper as early as 1947, but the means were not at hand and the project had been 'indefinitely postponed'.[117]

The impact of ACUE upon the European Movement is undeniable. But the impact of ACUE-supported activities upon wider European populations is difficult to determine, partly because the existence of popular European federalism in post-war Europe has itself become a controversial question. Although the work of the various federalist organisations, which coalesced under the umbrella of the European Movement by 1947, is massively documented, they had little influence on the negotiations that led to the Schuman Plan or to any other landmark event in the process of unification.[118] Spaak, Count Sforza, the Italian Foreign Minister, and other European leaders who all advocated popularism expected this to create indirect pressure upon officials and Ministers, but they overestimated the influence of public opinion. Outside France, Europeans were not roused to enthusiasm by the federalist cause. Even the European Youth Campaign, which had held many youth meetings across Europe by 1956, was dependent on the participation of *organised* European youth groups, like scout and church youth groups, through the affiliation of their leadership. Their well-attended meetings may offer little more evidence of 'popular sentiment' than contemporaneous rallies of 'democratic' youth held in Eastern Europe, which they were expressly designed to counter.[119]

All this activity did create enough semblance of public pressure, however, to bother federalism's most implacable opponents, the British. As early as April 1950, Labour Party leaders complained of 'a lot of pressure from European and US public opinion'. At the same time, seemingly convinced that popular sentiment had no place in the making of foreign policy, they were adamant that they should ignore it. In November 1950, the British Labour Party delegation returned from Strasbourg and reported with satisfaction that the federalist agitators had been defeated, 'and their attempts to upset the Assembly's work through Committees of Vigilance, proved a lamentable failure'.[120]

The faith of ACUE in the United States in the role of public pressure is not difficult to understand, given the more populist traditions of American foreign policy-making. ACUE's misplaced confidence in the ease with which Europe could be propelled down the road to federalism mirrors the expectations of US officials running the Marshall Plan, who would find European institutions and society less permeable to American ideas and practices than they had hoped.[121] But the firm faith in the role of populism expressed by Spaak, Sforza and periodically

Monnet is harder to explain. The idea that a few million dollars of covert US funds might release a wave of irresistible mass pressure for federalism in Europe was misconceived and, with hindsight, faintly ludicrous. However, the fact that a number of prominent figures on both sides of the Atlantic believed it to be possible is significant in itself.

Viewed from Europe, the most striking aspect of the ACUE's work is the extent to which officials working for European reconstruction and unification shared the experience of wartime intelligence, special operations and resistance. European unity had taken root in wartime resistance movements.[122] These links with clandestine organisations continued into the post-war period. The emerging European Economic Community (EEC) and the growing Western intelligence community overlapped to a considerable degree. This is underlined by the creation of the Bilderberg Group, an informal and secretive transatlantic council of key decision-makers. Bilderberg was founded by Joseph Retinger and Prince Bernhard of the Netherlands in 1952 in response to the rise of anti-Americanism in Western Europe. It grew out of the same overlapping networks of the EEC and the Western intelligence community, and was designed to define some sort of Atlantic consensus amid diverging European and American outlooks over issues such as atomic weapons. It brought leading European and American personalities together once a year for an informal discussion of their differences. Retinger secured support from Averell Harriman, David Rockefeller and Walter Bedell Smith. The formation of the American wing of Bilderberg was entrusted to Eisenhower's psychological warfare chief, C. D. Jackson, and the funding for the first meeting, held at the Hôtel de Bilderberg in Holland in 1954, was provided by the CIA. Thereafter much of its funding came from the Ford Foundation. By 1958, those attending Bilderberg included McCloy, Dean Acheson, Paul Nitze and George Ball, the senior State Department official most concerned with Europe during the 1950s and 1960s. It is striking that the important transnational elite groups emerging in the 1950s shared the same origins and sources of support.[123]

Although Bilderberg and ACUE–European Movement shared broadly the same founders, members and objectives, arguably Bilderberg constituted the more effective mechanism of transatlantic dialogue, developing into what some have regarded as the most significant of the discreet fora for Western elites. Unlike ACUE and the European Movement, it was not constrained by subject, nor was it divided into separate European and American bodies, linked by the activities of scurrying envoys. It is clear that the Rome Treaty was nurtured by discussions at Bilderberg in the preceding year. In the mid-1950s the European delegates were most concerned to use Bilderberg to underline the damage being done to the standing of the United States by McCarthyism in general and the trial and execution of Julius and Ethel Rosenberg in particular. In 1954 C. D. Jackson went out of his way to assure the European delegates that McCarthy would be gone by the time of the next meeting – and he was. In the 1960s the focus shifted to the Third World. Again, the value of Bilderberg is impossible to assess, but there has been consistent top-level attendance, including every British Prime Minister over three decades. Its eventual development in the 1970s into the Trilateral Commission, with the incorporation of Japan, suggests that the participants have considered it worth while.[124]

Seen from the United States, ACUE's history reveals the style of early OPC/CIA covert action, not least the reliance on private networks. Allen Dulles, Thomas Braden and Walter Bedell Smith all played a prominent role in ACUE before moving to formal positions within the CIA in the early 1950s. The precise nature of the linkage between groups like ACUE and the CIA will not be known until the full records of the CIA's International Organisations Division are released, and that may not be for some considerable time.[125] Nevertheless, the work of Allen Dulles and Braden with ACUE and the Free Europe Committee clearly prompted the two men to set up the Division in 1951. From the point of view of the development of CIA doctrine and structure this was an important, even fateful, moment.

The most interesting links between ACUE and the International Organisations Division relate not to the work it conducted in Europe, but instead to the work conducted by ACUE inside the United States, which, though limited, may well have been illegal. It was the International Organisations Division that continued this domestic theme in the work of the CIA through the 1950s, typified by the funding of the American National Student Association from 1952. This controversial penchant for international operations which took place inside the United States as well as overseas would have long-term significance for the American intelligence community. It was, above all, revelations in 1960s about these activities *inside* the United States that initiated the wave of enquiries and restrictions that would descend upon the CIA by the mid-1970s. In the 1960s, the reverberations of the CIA's work in these areas were felt as strongly in Washington as they were in Europe, and would signal the end of the golden era of unrestricted covert action and special operations.[126]

17

Atomic Deception and Atomic Intelligence

Since we are, in fact, deceiving both the Soviets and our Allies with regard to
our nuclear capability, it is essential that any questions on deception plans ...
be handled with great reserve.

British Joint Planning Staff on 'Sensitive Subjects', 18 January 1956[1]

Alongside the controversies of special operations and covert action in
both Eastern and Western Europe, the business of collecting secret
intelligence on the Soviet Union went on. Atomic weapons remained the
top-priority intelligence target for both East and West. The link between
atomic weapons and deception activities was identified at an early stage,
and Britain's specific need for atomic deception was recognised as early
as July 1946. The British Chiefs of Staff had called for an updated version
of the famous Tizard Report on Future War, taking into account the
lessons of Hiroshima and Nagasaki. This report made grim reading and
concluded that as few as thirty atomic bombs might bring about the collapse of Britain. By contrast several hundred atomic bombs might be
required to inflict similar damage on the Soviets, who enjoyed great geographical dispersal. In the short term the outcome of all this was an
obsession with developing guided anti-aircraft weapons, the importance
of which anxious British planners felt 'cannot be over-emphasised'. But
in the longer term it was clear that if total war was ever to return Britain
was probably finished. Accordingly deterrence, not defence, was now the
critical field. Atomic power was important, but even more important
would be perceptions of atomic power. In this field, Britain's military
planners insisted, no one really knew how far each country was ahead.
Appearances would be as important as reality:

The uncertainty surrounding the effect of atomic and biological weapons,
together with the difficulties in precise assessment of chances of success,
should be a deterrent to aggression. Deception would have an important part

to play in maintaining this uncertainty ... uncertainty as to the degree of retaliation will be a deterrent to an aggressor, and much might be done by first-class high level deception about the character, numbers and effects of new technical developments in weapons.[2]

Britain did not test its own atomic weapon until 1952 and did not have operational atomic weapons in service with the RAF until 1955, and even then there were very few of them. But Britain did have a first-class deception organisation; indeed it was arguably the world leader in this field. Moreover, atomic weapons were instruments of political as well as military power, and here again perception was all important. This lesson was not lost on Whitehall and, in the first post-war decade, atomic deception was developed against the Soviet Union, against the United States and also against Britain's minor allies.

The hub of Britain's deception wheel, the London Controlling Section (LCS), was carefully preserved on a care-and-maintenance basis in 1945. General Leslie Hollis worked together with Dudley Clarke to create the Hollis Committee, which preserved the core of specialist LCS personnel and techniques. The services also kept shadow deception units going. In the Royal Navy permanent reserve commissions were given to 'a key nucleus of officers' who had run naval wireless deception during the war. They were recalled regularly to hone their skills with 'special equipment'. Others maintained 'certain wireless equipment specially constructed for deception work and mounted in vehicles'. There was talk of reviving deception operationally as early as 1947, under the pressure of the Palestine Campaign. But it was the Korean War in 1950 that induced the rebirth of British deception in an operational form as the Department of Forward Plans under the leadership of John Drew.[3]

Initially its main focus was the looming danger of atomic weapons and other kinds of mass destruction. Atomic deception against the Soviets took two forms. The first was the effort to shore up deterrence by exaggerating British capabilities. As early as 9 July 1947 the Hollis Committee had drawn up a deception plan dealing with 'Atomic Scientific Research and Production'. But this was a supremely tricky area since deception had triumphed in the last war because of success in detecting, catching and then turning enemy agents. This had been helped by Ultra, which then revealed to the Allies whether subsequent deceptions had been successfully accepted by Berlin. But in 1947 the Hollis Committee was working in the dark. What it did know was that the Americans had strong suspicions of pro-Soviet espionage within the atomic programme even during the war. By 1946 Gouzenkou and others had confirmed that it was widespread, but its full extent was unknown. Set against this growing suspicion that the Soviets were rather well informed, the Hollis Committee warned that deception might have been ineffective and, still worse, the Soviets might detect that active deception was under way. It stated, 'It is already well known that Communist activities have penetrated many of our industrial concerns, and there is every reason to presume that the conduct of our atomic research has also been penetrated. Until the extent of this is known to us, it would be unwise to exploit our knowledge, except where we are certain this is unique.' It was unlikely that the extent of Soviet intelligence on atomic, biological and chemical weapons in the West would be revealed in the foreseeable future, and this was bound to hamper any elaborate deception effort.[4]

The British and American atomic programmes, potentially swarming with Soviet agents, were thus an unattractive area for deception. Exaggerating the scale of British air defence was also a nightmare as this might only persuade the Soviets to devote more atom bombs to British targets at the outset of a future war. Instead the British deception planners suggested exaggerating the survivability of the British war potential by developing a cover-story about dispersal of population and industry throughout the Commonwealth. This included the capacity to retaliate from a range of colonial territories with air weapons. Numerous improbable plans on the subject of transfers of population and industry to the Commonwealth to avoid atomic attack were developed in the late 1940s, probably as part of this elaborate deception activity with the intention that it should enhance deterrence.[5]

Unsure of where the Soviets were with their atomic bomb programme, the Hollis Committee began to talk of scientific misdirection. British deception policy was now exploring the idea of hindering the Russians' research and development of new weapons by misleading them technically. There would also be a general building up of the British order of battle, especially of new types of weapons in production. Nevertheless there were also dangers here as the effects would be quite unknown and might even be counter-productive. It was thought that the Soviets underestimated the value of nerve gas, and the committee worried that the wrong sort of deception in the area of weapons of mass destruction might 'arouse the dormant Soviet interest in the potentialities of this weapon'.[6] By January 1949 British deception planners and the Ministry of Supply, which oversaw weapons production, were meeting with their American equivalents, known as Orange Team, to work on biological warfare deception, in terms of both misleading the Soviets and exaggerating their own performance. The British planners received permission to begin drawing up plans to mislead the Russians' research and development by suggesting the development of 'new weapons' that were in fact 'white elephants' and just wasted their time. This allowed the minds of the deception staffs to run riot. They briefly resurrected the wartime idea of vast ice-ships or 'Habbakuks', which had been much beloved of Admiral Lord Louis Mountbatten, though they knew that the practical difficulties in construction were insurmountable.[7]

Beyond trying to reinforce deterrence, deception was also part of atomic planning for war. The RAF realised that even when it acquired atomic weapons it would not have many of them, and some key targets would be out of range. Bizarre ideas helped them to overcome these problems. Deception could offer critical protection to the limited stock of atomic weapons available. British defence scientists had already concluded that in any future atomic attack 'The bomb is so much more valuable than the bomber or crew that they will be regarded as expendable ... It must be remembered that the actual bomber at least need not return and so will only have petrol for the out journey. There will be an "escort" of dummy bombers carrying armament and return petrol in place of a bomb.'[8] The Avro Lincoln, Britain's state-of-the-art bomber immediately after the war, had a range to target of only 1,000 miles. But by ordering the crew to bail out, perhaps fifty miles beyond the target, this attack range could be doubled to 2,000 miles. In the late 1940s, RAF bomber pilots would often joke about what life would be like if they made it into hiding in some Siberian forest.[9] US Air Force officers were thinking about operational deception in similar terms. In December 1948, General S. E. Anderson explained the importance of 'deceptive missions' to his US Strategic Air Command colleagues: 'Everything possible must and will be done to make the enemy believe that every airplane over their territory is a potential atom bomb carrier so that they may not concentrate their defensive action on atom carriers alone.'[10]

Dr Vannevar Bush, the presidential scientific adviser, had already travelled to London to 'discuss deception with Lord Portal', the head of the British atomic programme. More general discussions on deception were being developed, and Washington was encouraged to open talks with Air Commodore Jack Easton, senior London SIS officer who had overall responsibility for Anglo-American liaison and who visited Washington regularly.[11] British high-level strategic deception was complemented by tactical deception on the ground. A joint centre for deception techniques – the Visual Inter-Services Training and Research Establishment or VISTRE – was set up in Britain at Netheravon on the edge of Salisbury Plain. Its work included dummy lighting and false radio transmissions. These formed a last-ditch deception effort to lead an atomic attack off course if such a thing were ever to be launched against Britain.[12]

All the while there were worries about what the Soviets knew about deception. The Soviets had co-operated in implementing the vast deception that covered D-Day – Plan Bodyguard. Colonel Bevan, who was then running London Controlling Section, had flown to Moscow and had a 'series of talks with the Russians', who had then participated in the 'biggest deception plans ever undertaken' by enhancing their threat to the Balkans. By 1948 London was confident to the point of arrogance about its own superior capabilities in this field and, as with atomic energy, it refused to accept that Moscow was capable of excellence. It noted, 'We must expect that at first, at least, Russian deception will be clumsy by comparison with our own technique. Implementation is likely to take a rather cruder form ... in regard to their secret reports, which are not likely to be so widespread as our own, or to have the same subtlety of content.' These were extraordinary comments on a country whose secret service had run dozens of successful deception operations against émigré organisations in Europe in the 1920s and 1930s.[13]

In 1952, the Department of Forward Plans used deception to screen Britain's first atomic test from the intelligence-collection efforts of Soviet agents. The intrinsic problem had long been recognised. Measurements and debris taken from the vicinity of an atomic test site could tell an opponent a great deal about an atomic weapons programme. The United States had gone to considerable lengths to protect its own tests in the late 1940s. Every possible measure had been taken to prevent Soviet agents from gathering samples. Prior to a test counter-intelligence teams from the US Army Intelligence and Security Command would sweep every inch of neighbouring Pacific atolls while L5 spotter planes buzzed overhead. It was not unusual for them to sight unidentified submarines which 'disappeared' once they were aware of being observed.[14] At the first British test – Operation Hurricane – carried out at Montebello off the west coast of Australia on 3 October 1952, the British were equally anxious to prevent the Soviets from gaining samples. Eric Welsh, Britain's Atomic Intelligence supremo, warned that even some time after the explosion 'there will still be radio active evidence of intelligence interest available on the site for a possible collector'. For this reason HMAS *Hawkesbury* was designated to mount a 'counter-intelligence guard' on the test site until mid-January 1953.[15]

In May and June 1952 Churchill reluctantly approved deception measures by the Department of Forward Plans to hoodwink the Soviets about the date of the test. This included deliberately deceptive material published in the British press with misleading speculation about the likely date. One conduit was the *Sunday Express*, which was used with the witting co-operation of the Chief Editor and the Features Editor. However, Churchill was worried by this new phase of the Cold War. To distribute false information to cover D-Day was one thing, but to give material to newspapers in a manner that was deliberately 'deceptive' of the public had not been 'hitherto entertained in time of peace'. He asked the Minister of Defence, Earl Alexander of Tunis, if it was justified.

Alexander replied firmly that Britain was under constant attack from a hostile intelligence organisation, and he believed that in the field of deception the 'Russians are attempting the same kind of activity'. He assured Churchill that this scheme was unusual and that most of John Drew's work was the planning of deception for war.[16]

As the Hollis Committee had surmised, the Soviets knew a great deal about the British and American atomic programmes. But only in 1950, with the revelations about Klaus Fuchs' atomic espionage, were its worries confirmed. Fuchs would have blown any misguided efforts at deception over the date of the first British bomb. However, Soviet espionage could not undermine all the value of British atomic deception effort, for much of it was directed against the Allies. Arguably, it was here, both against minor Allies like Turkey and Iran and against major Allies like the United States, that John Drew and the Department of Forward Plans really secured advantage. In the Middle East the main purpose of deception was to bolster the flagging form of British military power. The co-operation of Turkey, Iran and other partners in a British-led defence agreement – the Baghdad Pact – could not have been secured if they had realised how thinly spread British forces were in reality. By January 1956, when Britain prepared for major Baghdad Pact military planning talks, the British agenda was drawn up together with John Drew and was largely dominated by deception. The plans put forward by the British to their allies were so close to the fictitious deception plans designed to fool their enemies that 'very little shading was necessary'. Plans for the Middle East, they ventured delicately, were 'necessarily somewhat optimistic' and so 'optimism is also the theme of our deception plan'. Their key objective was that, by the end of the staff talks, the United Kingdom concept was not to 'have been uncovered as a deceit' by other members of the Baghdad Pact. The nub of the matter was that London was trying 'not to disclose H.M.G.'s reluctance to become financially involved' in the defence of the region.

Atomic weapons were the crucial element in this Middle East deception. The British deception plan was 'designed to give the impression that nuclear weapons will be available in quantity at H-Hour' in the region, which was patently untrue. It was important to hide the fact that in reality no nuclear weapons would be available in the region before 1959 since, the planners observed, if this truth were uncovered 'even our interim concept could not be substantiated'. 'The present lack of nuclear capability must therefore on no account be revealed.' They also had to cover up the fact that it was not planned to reinforce the Middle East conventionally from outside the theatre in the event of war. There was political as well as military deception, for they also sought to hide from most participants the existence of parallel tripartite talks with the United

States and Turkey. The complexities involved here were mind-boggling, for all the military planning was based on false intelligence estimates of Soviet forces through a Middle East campaign that had been depleted by 'the effect of our nuclear counter-attack'. These false estimates were then used to inform Baghdad Pact planning papers. They also had to develop strategies to reassure the Iranians about the use of these fictitious nuclear weapons against the Soviets when they entered Iranian territory. It is hard to escape the conclusion that the whole Baghdad Pact itself was a huge exercise in deception.[17]

Atomic deception also had a more direct bearing on Anglo-American intelligence and information exchange. As we shall see, the restoration of American atomic co-operation, which had been broken off in 1946, depended crucially on proving to the Americans that London was catching up and that the levels of atomic expertise were broadly equal. Some have even gone so far as to suggest that the first British hydrogen bomb test in 1957, codenamed Operation Grapple, was a deliberate deception to demonstrate a thermonuclear capability to the Americans which Britain did not yet have – although the facts of this matter have been hotly disputed.[18] What is clear is that the British were seeking to mislead the Americans about the extent of their knowledge in the field of nuclear weapons. This was an awkward business, as London wished to be invited to observe American atomic tests and finally secured this privilege in the mid-1950s, but was worried about returning the favour. Washington's improving attitude on atomic exchange was driven by an impression that London knew a good deal about hydrogen bombs. But part of this 'knowledge' was clearly a pretence, for in September 1956 Frederick Brundrett, the Chairman of Britain's Atomic Intelligence Committee, together with Dr William Penney, head of the British bomb programme, strongly opposed inviting American observers to attend Operation Grapple, scheduled for the following spring. They were clear about their reasons. They stated that they were concerned about 'the danger that the Americans might discover the limitations of our knowledge. We knew that they were anxious to find out the extent of our knowledge and we should lose a strong bargaining counter if they were to do so.'[19]

It was not only in the field of atomic deception, but also in the field of atomic espionage that the boundaries between ally and adversary were becoming curiously blurred. Again, the possibility of such espionage – ally against ally – had been anticipated as early as 1945 and, again, the starting point was the seminal Tizard Report on Future Weapons. On 16 July 1945, having read its primary version, John Slessor remarked on the supreme importance of a proper scientific intelligence service, and he urged scientific, technical and intelligence co-operation between Britain and the United States. However, he then added:

If this proves impracticable – and for commercial reasons the Americans may make it so ... then our Secret Intelligence organisation must be extended to cover the United States. The Americans are insecure people, and I do not believe we should have any serious difficulty in finding out all they are doing if we were prepared to spend the money to do so. Conversely their Secret Intelligence is amateur to a degree and I do not think we should have much to fear from them.[20]

Slessor's words proved to be prophetic, particularly given that the McMahon Act of 1946 severing atomic co-operation was driven primarily by commercial concerns in Congress.

On 2 February 1950, Klaus Fuchs, a British government scientist, was arrested. Fuchs was in fact a German communist who had fled Nazi Germany in the 1930s and came to Britain. He was important because he was one of the first major Soviet agents to be arrested and imprisoned as a result of the Venona programme. He made a full confession, and a month later at the Old Bailey he pleaded guilty to atomic espionage for the Soviets and received fourteen years' imprisonment. The name of Klaus Fuchs is well known, and he was certainly the most significant of the atom bomb spies who worked at Los Alamos, the main location of the Manhattan Project. But the extent of his importance came to light only in the 1990s. At the time of his exposure, shortly after the surprise detonation of the first Soviet atomic test, he was thought to have played a crucial role in the Soviet atomic programme. Indeed he was presented by some as 'the man who gave the Soviets the atom bomb'. However, it is now clear that the most important information the Soviets received from espionage arrived as early as 1941 – simply the knowledge of the existence of the American programme during the war – prompting the Soviets to give more attention to their own competing programme. Thereafter, espionage was less important. American and Soviet atomic historians are now in broad agreement that the information passed to Moscow by Allan Nunn May was of limited use. The information passed by Fuchs, although more valuable, at best saved the Soviets between a year and eighteen months of scientific work.[21]

Not everyone accepts the idea that Fuchs' espionage brought the Soviets real benefits. Richard Rhodes, the Pulitzer Prize-winning historian of the American atomic and hydrogen bomb programmes, has argued that, paradoxically, scientists working at Los Alamos 'delayed rather than accelerated the Soviet weapons program' when they offered Soviet intelligence detailed information on the construction of the American Fat Man plutonium implosion bomb. Soviet scientists had, in his view, independently designed 'a weapon twice as powerful and half as large as Fat Man'. But they were compelled to abandon this better bomb in favour of the cruder, but proven, American design on the orders of

Stalin and the project director Lavrenti Beria. This new route proved to be slower and less productive.[22] In any case, Klaus Fuchs was not the only source. Although he gathered material of great sensitivity, Los Alamos was swarming with Soviet spies. A young physicist called Alvin Theodore Hall, codenamed Mlad, gave his Soviet handlers intelligence on the critical implosion method of detonating the bomb even earlier than Fuchs.[23]

Fuchs remains a deeply ambiguous character and ironically he may have spied for Britain more ably than he did for the Soviet Union. The real significance of his work can only be understood within the context of the British role in the Los Alamos atomic programme. Britain's contribution was considerable, but it was largely scientific and theoretical. It had taken little part in the extremely demanding technical process of producing the components of the bomb or in its assembly. The matter of producing the curious-shaped charges, funnels of high explosive crafted to produce pressure waves of minutely calculated precision, in order to detonate the core, was one of the most difficult aspects of the work. In 1946 the McMahon Act ensured that the British were cut off from their source of knowledge about this difficult technical work, and it was this which presented the real barrier to building a British bomb. Accordingly, in 1946, when Dr William Penney set out to construct, or reconstruct, Britain's independent version of the Fat Man plutonium implosion bomb, the road ahead was difficult and largely unknown. One of the hardest tasks was focusing a uniform wave of energy travelling inwards from the conventional explosive 'jacket' which was designed to trigger the plutonium core. The waves of energy had to be focused using 'lenses' of explosive of different types, but all of a very high standard, so that they arrived at the centre at exactly the same time. There was also a need for very sophisticated electronics to ensure simultaneous detonation of all the facets of the bomb.

Travelling this road was made much easier by Klaus Fuchs, who had served as liaison between the scientific and technical sections at Los Alamos and was thus uniquely well informed about the practical problems confronting Harwell, Britain's Atomic Energy Research Establishment, in the late 1940s. Precisely because of his espionage work for the Soviets, he had maintained extremely detailed notebooks, and these notebooks also guided the British bomb on its path to completion. His notebooks were Harwell's only real record of the technical dimension of the Los Alamos programme. Fuchs also had an 'outstanding' memory which amazed his colleagues. Remarkably, because of the collapse of Anglo-American atomic relations in 1946 and the passage of the McMahon Act, he effectively 'spied' for both Britain and the Soviet Union. He continued to meet his Soviet contacts during this period, making six meetings between 1947 and 1949, often outside Kew Gardens Underground station. It is unclear what he told Moscow about the progress of the British bomb, to which he was central. Even in 1950, after he had been incarcerated in Wormwood Scrubs Prison, it was essentially Fuchs' design for the atom bomb core that was incorporated into the British bomb tested by Operation Hurricane at Montebello in 1952. After his arrest, his safe at Harwell was opened and the enormous amount of detail that he had accumulated about work at Los Alamos continued to be used.[24]

The impact of the espionage of Fuchs upon the development of the British atomic weapons programme was highly beneficial. However, the psychological impact of his espionage upon Whitehall was undoubtedly catastrophic. In the days following his arrest, the British military, for the first and only time, considered giving up the idea of the British development of atomic weapons altogether. Fuchs had, they considered, completely destroyed any hope of restoring Anglo-American co-operation in this field. Despite having worked on the Manhattan Project with the Americans and the Canadians, they had been overtaken by the Soviets, whom they regarded as technically backward, despite the fact that Moscow had gone from what they thought was a standing start in 1945. Should Britain not give up its costly and unproductive solo effort to achieve a bomb and instead set to work on weapons projects more suited to its abilities?

On 10 February 1950, eight days after the arrest of Fuchs, Sir William Elliott, Senior Staff Officer at the Ministry of Defence, and previously head of the British Joint Services Mission in Washington, put a most serious question to the Chiefs of Staff: 'How does it come about that, knowing all that we did in 1945, we are still without the atom bomb, by contrast with the Russians who, starting from scratch, have apparently passed us – this, moreover, despite the fact that a special organisation was set up specifically to deal with the problems?' The Fuchs case seemed to provide him with some answers but also raised 'other issues'. Hitherto the Chiefs of Staff had given 'overriding priority' to developing a British bomb, a priority recently extended to include all means for its accurate delivery. This reflected a belief that Britain was ahead of the Soviets. Then came the surprise Soviet bomb in the autumn of 1949. This had prompted the Chiefs to seek renewed Anglo-American co-operation. 'Good progress ... was being made in our conversations with the Americans in Washington, when the news of Dr Fuchs burst.'

Elliot asked if they should not now abandon their atomic programme. The Chiefs of Staff met to discuss this three days later. The strength of the conventional wisdom was obvious. It was not certain that the Americans would completely abandon co-operation and more importantly they felt that Britain could not abandon efforts to possess 'incomparably the most powerful weapon in the world'. It was not just of military importance but also of 'immense political and economic significance'. It was being acquired 'so that we could exert the proper influence of a Great Power in world affairs, both in peace and in any future war'. There was also fear of American abandonment conjured up by memories of 1939–41, and they added that 'for all we know we might one day again find ourselves fighting alone'.

But Fuchs had prompted the Chiefs of Staff to think afresh about this conventional wisdom and they conceded that the Americans would be hostile now 'that Dr Fuchs had given away so much valuable information to the Russians'. More importantly, if the British contribution to the Western 'pool' of bombs was going to be insignificant in the next few years, would an alliance-minded country not be better concentrating on vital projects to which Britain was more suited, such as guided weapons, which would provide better air defence against bomber attack? These questions could not be answered without good intelligence. But the military did not have enough information on how many bombs Britain might produce before 1957, how many the Americans might produce, or how many the Soviets might produce. If Britain reduced its emphasis on atomic weapons and focused on other areas, what might be achieved, they asked? What was clear was that a possible change of direction was not an idea which the Chiefs of Staff dismissed out of hand. There were further, highly secret discussions with Portal, head of the atomic programme, and Sir Henry Tizard, the Chief Defence Scientist. Meanwhile 'knowledge of the fact that this matter was being considered at all' was 'confined to the minimum essential number of persons'. In the event the British Chiefs of Staff decided it was best to soldier on with the beleaguered British atomic programme.[25]

The revelation of Fuchs' espionage had some beneficial effects for the West. It forced a realistic appreciation of what the Soviet atomic programme had achieved. In September 1952 the US Air Force Intelligence Special Study Group emphasised 'the espionage help of Fuchs' in allowing the Soviets to move to the blueprint phase for hydrogen bomb facilities in February 1950. It predicted development of a Soviet hydrogen bomb as early as January 1953.[26] Fuchs was also a shock to the British military scientists working on the atomic project itself. Michael Perrin felt personally responsible for the atom spies, but Lord Cherwell, who was Paymaster General and also effectively Churchill's scientific adviser, was of the opposite opinion, arguing, 'we were unfairly blamed about the Fuchs case by the Americans. For his most dangerous work was done in America and the mere fact that our people thought that he seemed all right when we took him on is no excuse for their failing to watch him and prevent his activities several years later.' Cherwell also blamed British government penny-pinching, insisting that MI5 was handicapped by the 'foolish decision' to put atomic energy in the Ministry of Supply. This allowed the government to pay low salaries but also resulted in a slack security regime that would not have prevailed had atomic energy been a separate specialist organisation.[27] The FBI Chief J. Edgar Hoover in Washington certainly blamed the British. It appears that on 10 December 1943 W. A. Akers from British Security Co-ordination in New York wrote to the American authorities assuring them that all members of the British Mission to the Manhattan District had been given proper security clearance.[28]

Even after Fuchs, British security procedures did not fill Washington with confidence. On 3 March 1950 Attlee ordered the Secretary of State for War, John Strachey, to conduct a sweeping investigation into how Fuchs was able to keep a job in atomic research even though he was a known communist. Strachey was announced as one of those 'called on to carry out the purge in the overhauling of the Secret Service of Great Britain as a result of the breakdown in security screening in the Fuchs case'. But J. Edgar Hoover set out in a memorandum of six close-typed pages the evidence that he felt proved that Strachey was himself a communist. Having served on the Executive Committee of the British Communist Party in 1938 he had been denied permission to enter the United States on these grounds on 10 October 1938 and sent home. Although in 1944 Strachey broke with the Communist Party, his wife remained a Party member and their divergent views, the FBI noted, 'caused considerable marital unrest'. Understandably, the FBI was intensely unhappy about such a person presiding over the Fuchs case. Charles Donnelly, the senior American representative at NATO, considered Emanuel Shinwell, the British Minister of Defence, to be in the same category.[29]

The arrest of Fuchs less than six months after the surprise detonation of the Soviet bomb had important effects and accelerated a growing paranoia about communist subversion in the United States. It was no coincidence that Senator Joe McCarthy gave his first major speech on the dangers of communist penetration days after the arrest of Fuchs. McCarthy's activities unleashed an extraordinary reign of terror on the substantial liberal elements in all the government departments in Washington, even those working within the FBI and the CIA. In this state of torment, Truman and Acheson were anxious to avoid anything else which might lend further ammunition to McCarthy. Alliance mechanisms transmitted this pressure directly to London. Such was the intensity of the pressure that even Clement Attlee, one of the most radical and tough-minded British Prime Ministers of the post-war era, eventually folded.

Western defence co-operation was Klaus Fuchs' principal victim. As already noted, the McMahon Act, which had terminated American atomic co-operation with other powers, had been prompted by commercial concerns, especially about the domestic production of electricity. London had been trying to reverse these restrictions and to expand co-operation in key areas such as guided missiles. But the Fuchs case put a complete freeze on such developments. The United States would open negotiations only if Britain adopted 'positive vetting', a rigorous programme of active investigation of the background of those engaged on sensitive work that was already in place in the United States and Canada. Attlee's Cabinet Committee on Subversion now began to look at such an apparatus.[30]

The seriousness of the security problems confronting London was underlined by the fact that Attlee himself chose to take the chair. Sir Percy Sillitoe reported to him that MI5 was not coping with the weaker process of 'negative vetting', which meant checking lists of employees against lists of known communists and sympathisers. The growth in the importance of atomic weapons meant that increasing numbers of service personnel were being classified as engaged on this secret work. MI5 was negative vetting 2,500 staff per week, but was slipping behind. The services were asking for many of their staffs to be vetted, amounting to more than a third of a million people. So far MI5 was only 'checking names against lists', namely the 250,000 files that it held on subversives in the late 1940s. If it moved to positive vetting, then the numbers of enquiries dealt with would be much reduced. It would investigate only the elite, and miss out the 'cypher clerks and typists, who would have great opportunities of acquiring and disclosing information'. This was a hard lesson that the British had learned from the Herbert King case a decade earlier.

There were other problems. J. Chuter Ede, the Home Secretary, was worried that there were not the skilled staff to deal with a rapid expansion. This would lead to clumsy work, and 'the fact that enquiries were being made on a large scale was bound to come out'. Sir Norman Brook, the Cabinet Secretary, was worried about the ticklish problems of investigating university staff. He knew of a 'high proportion of scientists, often of the greatest distinction, who were members of the Communist party or sympathised with Communism'. The best MI5 could do was to draw up a very tight list of 200 top staff for positive vetting. In April 1950, a new committee on positive vetting was created, chaired by John Winnifrith of the Treasury and including Roger Hollis and Graham Mitchell of MI5.[31]

All manner of alliance pressures were now at work. In June 1950, the United States decided to convene a tripartite conference on security standards, together with Canada. Britain was extremely anxious to remain in the inner circle of Western defence powers and to avoid relegation to the second division with the French and the Italians. It had only recently secured control of security procedures for the new SHAPE and NATO organisations in Europe. Now responsible for purging the continentals, Britain could not afford to appear behindhand in these matters.

By November 1950, Attlee's new committee on small-scale positive vetting recommended its introduction. There was, the committee advised, 'an inner circle of special secret posts' that was worth extra protection. But its list was now five times longer and stood at 1,000 persons, requiring about a hundred 'special investigations' a year. It stated that the American positive vetting system, run by the FBI, was 'extremely elaborate' and involved intensive overt police enquiries based on detailed interviews and questionnaires. Any such procedure 'would be repugnant to British thinking'. But the committee conceded that even positive vetting of the sort it contemplated was unlikely to reveal the dedicated infiltrator and crypto-communist. Whether the trade-off in terms of security and liberty of the individual was acceptable was a matter for Ministers and MPs.[32]

Attlee judged the price to be too high. Revolted by the McCarthyite rampage in the United States, he judged negative vetting, merely checking names against existing records, to be more than enough. He continued to stand firm despite the defection of one of Klaus Fuchs' colleagues, Dr Bruno Pontecorvo, in October 1950. On 13 November, the Cabinet Committee on Subversion, with Attlee in the chair, ruled against any widespread use of positive vetting. Positive enquiries into an individual's background could be permitted only under circumstances that were 'quite exceptional' and then only with the approval of a Minister.[33] American pressure for positive vetting in Britain increased further after the dramatic defection of Guy Burgess and Donald Maclean in May 1951. Maclean, it soon became clear, had sat on key Anglo-American atomic committees. Attlee still held out, only accepting the advent of widespread positive vetting as virtually the last act of his departing Labour government in November 1951. He had a dry sense of humour and, given Churchill's unwarranted remarks in 1945 about the likelihood of socialism imposing a nasty security apparatus on the British people, he doubtless thought there was a certain justice in the fact that Churchill's incoming peacetime administration should be left to implement the first large-scale intrusive security investigations in Britain.[34]

What was the impact of Fuchs, followed by Burgess and Maclean, upon atomic intelligence co-operation with Washington? In the spring of 1950 London despatched the energetic Major-General Gerald Templer, Vice Chief of the Imperial General Staff, to Washington to try and resolve the general problem of technical information exchange on military projects between Britain, the United States and the Commonwealth. Templer's journey was not auspicious. On his way to the airport to fly out to the United States, he noticed the news stand at the train station. This announced the shocking revelation of a new spy-case and named Klaus Fuchs as the most important spy within the Manhattan Project. The news broke only days before Templer's first meetings in Washington. His American hosts were a model of politeness and delicately avoided any reference to Fuchs for the entire visit. Templer did surprisingly well in the circumstances, negotiating permission for the UK to pass on to Commonwealth countries, such as Australia, specific information on a 'project by project basis' in recognition of the ongoing defence science co-operation. But, equally, the resulting Templer–Burns Agreement was not all that London had hoped for.[35]

In the atomic field the bottom line was that there was a certain level of Allied co-operation that Washington dare not abandon. In 1951, when Harry Truman authorised a new set of American atomic tests at the Toponah test range in Nevada, Washington gave London precise details. This was to avoid British intelligence collecting the increased debris in the atmosphere and concluding from the data that new Soviet tests had taken place. At best that would lead to faulty British estimates of the Soviet stockpile of atomic bombs. At worst it could lead to widespread false press reporting of a large Soviet test programme with 'unfortunate international repercussions'. The fact that Britain was running an independent air-sampling operation therefore forced the United States to maintain some contact with it.[36] At the level of basic data gathering and exchange, co-operation continued. The RAF and the USAF continued to agree a careful division of labour in the painstaking business of flying round the Soviet Union, constantly sieving the air for atomic particles.[37] But Fuchs did have a serious impact on co-operation over analysing the results of this joint intelligence collection. Although the McMahon Act was amended in 1951 to allow some easing in the area of intelligence, it still banned any exchange on the matter of the design and fabrication of weapons, and this ruled out detailed discussion of Soviet bomb production.[38]

In July 1951, Lord Portal came to the conclusion that he would soon be departing as head of UK Atomic Energy. He took the opportunity to send a final missive to his old friend Walter Bedell Smith, who had been director of the CIA for less than a year. In spite of the McMahon Act Portal and Bedell Smith had been gradually increasing the atomic intelligence partnership, with the CIA expert Dr Chadwell making regular trips to London. Portal explained that for the foreseeable future Atomic Intelligence was going to remain separated from other British intelligence bodies and located in the Atomic Energy Division of the Ministry of Supply. This odd organisational arrangement had not been a problem, but leadership had. Eric Welsh had been repeatedly ill with heart problems. Portal had finally managed to get 'new blood' for British atomic intelligence, and younger more able officers were coming in.[39]

During his visit to Washington in early January 1952, Churchill had followed this up and believed he had won Truman over on the subject of more atomic intelligence co-operation. But after he departed the US Department of Defense effectively vetoed the agreement they had reached. Cherwell later told Churchill that the sole practical outcome was a conference on one particular aspect of atomic intelligence. Washington also wanted to send over its Atomic Security adviser together with FBI personnel to look over British security arrangements. Many in London were opposed to this, suggesting that Britain would be criticised because its systems were not defective but different. But Cherwell told Churchill that London should say yes because any other answer would create an even worse impression.[40]

Operation Hurricane, the testing of the first British atomic bomb, restored Britain's confidence. By early 1953, its general policy on Anglo-American atomic co-operation was becoming tougher and more sophisticated. The Ministry of Defence had begun to explore a different policy and now prepared a paper for its political masters: 'Very briefly what is proposed is that we shall cease to chase the will-o'-the wisp of American co-operation, as Lord Cherwell puts it, and instead build up a strong Commonwealth connection. There are very good reasons for doing this.' In a separate section of their report the officials set out what they called the 'mournful history of our attempts to collaborate in this field with the United States'. The British were convinced that they now had little to learn from the Americans on bomb production. The very limited links they enjoyed with the Americans on atomic matters, such as committees to control uranium supplies, only hindered their relationship with Commonwealth countries, such as Australia, but delivered no benefits. London had to have testing ranges in Australia and found it 'intolerable to have limitations on the degree to which we can take the Australians into our confidence'. Lurking beneath this was the feeling that Britain 'ought to begin thinking about our commercial interests' in industrial development of atomic energy; there were also worries about where American strategic thinking was going. The Chiefs of Staff agreed that it would be unwise 'to continue *blindly* to support the United States in their apparently unlimited programme'. In April 1953 London began 'gently [to] disassociate ourselves' from certain joint activities under the gradual implementation of a radical new policy of disengagement.[41]

The new policy was a slippery one of partial disengagement. There were American items that Britain still wanted, and London's shopping list included information on weapons effects from the very extensive series of American atomic tests, and also full intelligence co-operation on the Soviet atomic programme. From 1953, Cherwell led a concerted British effort to restore full atomic intelligence co-operation. It was a frustrating business. Churchill drew fresh assurances from Eisenhower on this subject at their first meeting in Bermuda in December 1953. But in the event the promised joint conferences on atomic intelligence were cancelled by the Americans. The problem was an old one, namely that Washington feared that by talking to London about possible Soviet weapon design it would reveal too much about American weapons design. Cherwell explained to Churchill, 'I endeavoured to convince them in Washington that we had independently discovered most of the vital secrets, just as apparently the Russians have done. It would therefore be a great pity to jeopardise the prospects we might have of discovering what the Russians were doing for fear we should tell one another what we both already knew. I hope, in talking to [Admiral] Strauss, to drive home this argument ...'[42] Admiral Strauss, the head of the American Atomic Energy programme, was sympathetic, but as yet real results remained elusive.

In October 1954 there were further irritations. Harold Macmillan, then Minister of Defence, told Churchill that over a number of weeks the British Atomic Energy Intelligence Unit and the CIA had been jointly watching a series of Soviet atomic explosions. An agreement had been reached not to make public statements on the subject, to avoid revealing to the Soviets the extent of Western capacity to detect explosions. But the State Department overruled the CIA and insisted on a quick statement 'without consultation'. London found out by reading the newspapers. Churchill had to be 'warned' by his officials about the likely barrage of questions from the press and the need to work hard not to disclose the British detection programme. The sensitive element was a network of seismic detection stations in the UK and Commonwealth countries.[43]

By January 1955 Anglo-American atomic intelligence co-operation had reached a crisis. At this point Lord Cherwell, Sir William Penney and Frederick Brundrett, together with Sir John Cockcroft, the Scientific Adviser to the Ministry of Defence, began to rethink US–UK relations in the atomic intelligence field. Sitting as the Scientific Sub-Committee of the Atomic Energy Intelligence Committee, they noted that there had been 'periodic discussions' with US experts to look at joint problems and to tune the collection process. But current US restrictions meant the Americans had 'never been able to discuss freely with us comparative data on Russian and U.S. explosions'. The British had hoped for a conference at Harwell on the Music programme, the elaborate intelligence operation which involved (as we have seen) assessing Soviet uranium production by discerning the amounts of radioactive gas in the atmosphere, a by-product of plutonium production. New US legislation had caused 'confusion' and the Americans had asked for a postponement of the conference. Sir John Cockroft had travelled to Washington and extracted an assurance that it would take place at Harwell in January 1955. This new conference would look not only at Music but at all intelligence methods for detecting and measuring Soviet atomic activities. But in early January Washington again pulled out. Brundrett exclaimed, 'This is a sorry tale.' Urgent decisions had to be taken in London. Many regarded the Music programme as expensive, inaccurate and indeed near useless and wanted to scrap it. More broadly the British yearned for 'free and frank discussions on the recent series of Russian explosions'. In the light of Eisenhower's repeated assurances, Britain's atomic energy experts regarded this US withdrawal as a form of betrayal. Eden and Macmillan together decided it was time for Churchill to 'protest' to Eisenhower. Cherwell also wrote privately to Churchill to add pressure for action.[44]

By February 1955 Churchill's protests to Eisenhower had hit their mark. Brundrett gained access to the new series of American atomic tests and Cherwell gave Churchill the full story:

> You will be delighted to learn that Admiral Strauss has played up very well about our being allowed to monitor the series of highly interesting American explosions which are to take place in the next month or two. I must confess I never thought the authorities in Washington would approve his having agreed to this in Bermuda. But everything is now in train and we are sending our aircraft to take part with the Americans in collecting debris so as to be able to extract the maximum value from the data about Russian bombs which we collected last year.

Cherwell added that co-operation in intelligence, 'on which I set the greatest store', was at last making 'definite progress'. This was underpinned by a growing conviction in Washington that both London and Moscow knew a great deal about hydrogen bomb production and so little now needed to be hidden in this area. Strauss was rewarded with an honorary degree from the University of Oxford.[45]

But Anglo-American co-operation always remained awkward in the atomic field and, when the Soviets began a new series of atomic tests in late August 1956, Antony Head, the Secretary of State for War, wrote to Eden, who was now Prime Minister, to complain about American reactions. Again the problem was public 'disclosure'. The formal arrangement was that there should be simultaneous announcements. But this had proved 'impossible' for 'internal political reasons in the United States'. Again London was unhappy and feared that this would give the game away about its new means of seismic and acoustic detection. In the press the British were emphasising air sampling of radioactive clouds, but it did not take a genius to realise that this process took some time. If the announcements were made too quickly this pointed unmistakably to new methods. Allen Dulles, during a recent visit to Britain, conceded that American policy had been adopted 'entirely against his advice' and was due to a conviction on the part of politicians that 'it is the right way to convince the American public how iniquitous the Russians reality are'. Seismic detection was the way forward, and by 1962 Britain would be spending considerable sums on a new station at Eskdalemuir which housed the Atomic Weapons Research Establishment Seismic Array and a team of three atomic intelligence specialists.[46]

The overall record on US–UK joint collection of intelligence and the exchange of raw secret intelligence on atomic weapons was quite good, given the obstacle of the McMahon Act. But the record on joint estimates was dismal. Estimates at the lower levels were hampered by the secrecy of one ally from one another. The British wanted to engage in more co-operation but only so far as would not endanger their efforts actively to deceive the Americans about their capabilities and achievements. Meanwhile, at the higher levels, the political and bureaucratic pressures were simply too intense to allow honest estimating. The United States, and especially the US Air Force, wanted estimates that would support a relatively aggressive policy and the idea that war was close. London could not countenance anything that threatened the philosophy of 'wait and see'. Eisenhower was an old hand at this game and captured the experience of Anglo-American efforts on joint estimates perfectly. On 26 April 1954 he remarked to Churchill that their two countries always 'seem to reach drastically different answers to problems involving the same set of basic facts'.[47]

Atomic intelligence was sometimes required to look at allies as well as enemies. Divergent thinking on atomic weapons, beginning in the late 1940s, rendered this increasingly essential. From the American point of view, growing British anxiety about the first use of nuclear weapons was a matter of interest. Towards the end of his administration, Attlee had begun to make it clear to the RAF that its strategic planning should not assume that permission for the use of atomic weapons was automatic; indeed it was likely that they would be used only in retaliation. Cabinet reservations reflected a conviction that first use of atomic weapons would be 'condemned by a proportion of the population as morally wrong and inhumane'. But it was bolstered by a conviction that even on practical military grounds, if the first strike was not a winning strike, then the level of retaliation could be very great. It did not take US Air Force Intelligence long to realise the wider implications of these British discussions. They threw grave doubts on the reliability 'of British bases for atom bomb attacks'. This was very serious, for by the early 1950s over half the weight of US SAC airpower would be based in Britain. Even if the British government was sincere in its promises of base availability, this could be withdrawn. Charles Cabell had already warned that 'The British people will be conscious of the fact that the Russians would hold the British responsible for American atomic bombs lifted from British bases. Public pressure under these circumstances might well, at the last minute, prevent British governmental acquiescence to such use of their bases and so effectively negate the initial phase of current U.S. Air Force planning.' In the short term there was a need for back-up bases. In the long term British public opinion on American airpower had been marked up for careful observation.[48] In December 1951 these issues were looked at with renewed anxiety. Winston Churchill, taking office for a second time, was due to visit Washington and it became known that one of his purposes was 'written formalization' of 'US–UK verbal agreements which established the SAC program in the UK' when bombers arrived in July 1948 during the Berlin Crisis. General John Samford, who had succeeded Cabell as the USAF Director of Intelligence, wrote to the Director of the CIA, Walter Bedell Smith, urging the preparation of a Special Intelligence Estimate on the subject of the availability of British bases to Strategic Air Command for atomic attacks on the Soviet Union. He wanted the CIA to give special attention to 'A survey of British groups, particularly the Bevan school, which oppose to varying degrees the basing of US bombers in the UK to determine their strength and likely effect on preventing or obstructing a formalized agreement.' He was also worried about the whole Churchill approach and whether the Prime Minister would 'insist on participation in decisions to employ the bases as SAC launching points for atomic attacks on Soviet Russia'. Churchill, he warned, during recent Parliamentary debates had publicly blamed the previous Attlee government for taking the 'formidable step' of allowing 'the great and ever-growing American air bases' in Britain. Attlee had protested that the bombers had arrived for European defence, not for atomic strikes against Moscow. Against the background of this growing cross-party unease, Bevanites, such as Sidney Silverman, had been pressing Churchill on the decision-making process for use of bases in war. Samford warned the CIA that Churchill was now insisting that the use of these bases 'would be a matter of joint decision'.[49]

US Air Force commanders increasingly associated worries about US SAC bases in Britain with the wider phenomenon of anti-Americanism. In February 1953 General Millard C. Young, serving in the Plans Division of the US Joint Chiefs of Staff, suggested that what they needed was a psychological programme to deal with the problem. British complaints about bases, he explained, were all of a piece with 'resentment' about American leadership, 'fear of U.S. inexperience in world affairs' and irritation over American activities in regions such as the Near East 'hitherto thought to be British spheres of influence'. The British, he added, were miserable about being mired in austerity, and needed something or someone on whom to vent their spleen. He argued that 'new targets' for this expression of British irritation 'need to be found and exploited', otherwise the United States would bear the brunt of British vexation with the general state of the world. In any case, he went on, 'an outlet is needed' and he proposed that 'our propaganda, by subtle indirection, should arrange to draw British attention to some outlet other than us'. This, he said, seemed a worthwhile project for US Psychological Warfare units that were now on their way to the UK, including a US Air Force Psywar Wing, currently earmarked for deployment to RAF Molesworth in Cambridgeshire.[50]

18

At the Coal Face: Intelligence-Gathering

[C]onstant friction and crossing of wires ...
Commander Courtney, Chief of British Naval Intelligence Staff Germany,
22 March 1949[1]

Personal friendships and associations between London and Washington could not prevent the emergence of a situation of intense mistrust and alarm in the early 1950s, most notably over atomic weapons. However, these human associations became important in mitigating some of the resulting tensions caused. When serious issues arose it was often someone with happy wartime associations who was sent on a mission to repair the damage. Eisenhower's wartime SHAEF HQ, which had superintended D-Day and the advance into Germany, had been an especially important generator of these friendships. In September 1950, when a tired and disgruntled Ernest Bevin attended the United Nations in New York for sessions relating to Korea, he was charmed that Walter Bedell Smith, whom he knew well and who had just become director of the CIA, offered him the use of his yacht for sailing around Long Island. A month later, another of Bedell Smith's British friends, Douglas Dodds-Parker, wrote to congratulate him on his appointment and recalled handing him the wireless message indicating that the Italians had accepted surrender terms in 1943. John Sinclair, who had been Director of Military Intelligence at the end of the Second World War and who was now Menzies' deputy at SIS, sent Bedell Smith a recent book on Rommel with Christmas greetings for December 1950.[2]

By the early 1950s the secret weapon of Anglo-American friendship was not wartime reminiscence, but fishing. Bedell Smith was a fanatic, while Portal and Tedder were similarly obsessed. In August 1951, Portal was being tempted over to Washington more frequently with the possibility that 'some fishing might be arranged'.[3] Bedell Smith used Portal as a purchasing agent for rare flies from Veniard's catalogue, which he could not obtain in the United States. On 25 April 1951 Bedell Smith wrote him a typical letter:

> My dear Peter,
> I felt very guilty when I received the Blue Dun hackle necks without a bill. Please let me pay you for these because if you don't I will have to inflict a ham or a side of bacon addressed to you on the British customs. Possibly there is something else you would like, austerity being what it is.
>
> I saw Arthur Tedder off last week with great regret. The old ties are very strong and, in addition, it was a great comfort to have him close at hand. During the years of association, the former members of SHAEF grew to speak a polyglot Anglo-American dialect which is completely intelligible to themselves and which provides a measure of confidence that can hardly be beat anywhere.
>
> I hope to be in England this fall and look forward to the possibility of seeing you.
> Faithfully
> Bedell Smith

Eisenhower was obviously the most important member of this transatlantic network. The following year it was the turn of Kenneth Strong of JIB to act as purchasing agent. Bedell Smith returned from a brief fishing trip to find Strong's 'package' of fishing materials and chided him that he 'certainly did not buy all this for five dollars'. Bedell Smith insisted on reimbursing Strong, as he wanted to use him 'as my purchasing agent again'.[4] Anglo-American intelligence relations continued to be close, at least in the area of intelligence-collection, for many reasons. Wartime bonhomie, which could sometimes be a little artificial, and fishing were helpful, but the most important factor was the tough nature of the target. Faced with secure police states like the Soviet Union and China, any information was valuable. Moreover, there were special assets available to some allies that were simply not available to others.

Spy-flights over the Soviet Union were a perfect example. In 1948 the State Department had told the USAF that they were forbidden. Five months into the Korean War, in October 1950, the same stern American diplomatic ban on overflights remained. Charles Cabell, the USAF Intelligence chief, mulled over 'certain reconnaissance requirements' with William Adams, US Strategic Air Command's intelligence chief. Adams badly wanted to risk four overflights by the fastest American reconnaissance aircraft. Three would be launched from Germany and one from Japan, and he did not think these powerful aircraft would be caught. Adams had argued that the captured Operation Dick Tracy material was now eight years old and increasingly unreliable on new Soviet targets. Cabell agreed on the 'desirability' of such flights but knew the chances that the proposals would get by State Department, the Pentagon or even the Air Force 'front office' were 'zero'. He advised Adams to bide his time.[5] Similar State Department restrictions also forbade the CIA's clandestine service from representation at the American Embassy in Moscow until 1953. Even then, the American Ambassador, George Kennan, would not permit risky operations. The CIA had recruited a middle-ranking MVD officer in Vienna, but once he returned to Moscow Kennan forbade contact with him there. His cautious approach contrasted strongly with his enthusiasm for covert action in 1949. In Beijing, the United States had no diplomatic facilities at all. Allies could fill the gap.[6]

In the same month that Cabell and Adams were containing their frustrations over spy-flights, the British held a conference on strategic photo-reconnaissance at RAF Benson, Oxfordshire. The conference logo was a delightfully irreverent cartoon of two RAF aircraft with cameras pulling back the Iron Curtain somewhere over the Caspian Sea. The British were willing to risk overflights, but British aircraft did not have the range or speed to improve much upon the current stock of captured German photography. Even in 1952 the British were still using the ageing wartime Mosquito.[7] The answer was obvious. To fill the gap the Americans transferred a number of high-performance RB-45C aircraft to the RAF. Training began in August 1951 and the first mission was flown the following March. Clearance was given by Churchill himself. Prior to the mission the Air Ministry actually sent one of the pilots across to 10 Downing Street to discuss it with Churchill. This reflected a full understanding of the Prime Minister's temperament as someone who, despite his anxieties about Cold War tensions, adored any escapade that smacked of melodrama. The young officer told him that the Soviets would know of the mission's presence. Churchill quipped back, 'The Russians already know, just don't let the MPs in the House of Commons find out.' Although Churchill was told, it appears that the USAF did not inform Truman of this proxy operation.

The RB-45C was vulnerable to the high-performance Soviet MiG-15 during the day, but without radar the Soviet pilots could not find their quarry by night. Therefore all these British missions were nighttime radar photography missions. There were no further RB-45C flights in 1953. Several more flights, considered to be highly productive, were undertaken in 1954. That year the information gathered by GCHQ on the responses of the Soviet air defence system to the flights were as important as the photography they gathered, and on at least one mission Wing Commander Rex Sanders encountered serious anti-aircraft fire over Kiev which lit up the night sky.[8] The RB-45C flights were valuable in a narrow sense. The numbers of flights were very few and their missions specific.

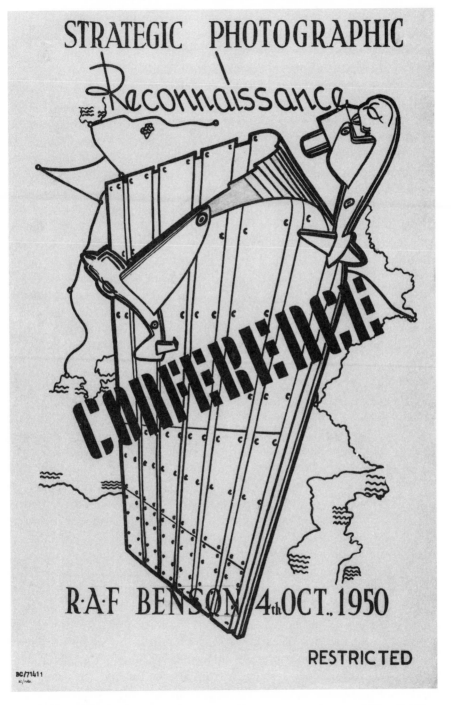

The programme for the British strategic aerial reconnaissance conference held at RAF Benson in 1950 showing aircraft with cameras peeping behind the Iron Curtain near the Caspian Sea.

Their task had been to gather radar photograph images of key targets inside the Soviet Union. Although these aircraft could fly high and fast, up to 38,000 feet, they were not invulnerable, hence their nighttime flights. In 1953 the Canberra came on stream and set a new world altitude record of 63,668 feet. Not only was this above the ceiling of the Soviet MiG-15 (50,000 feet), it was also above the level at which condensation trails might give away the position of the aircraft. The prize target was the main Soviet missile test centre at Kaputsin Yar on the Volga. As soon as the Canberra was ready, a PR7 variant was sent on a one-off flight from Germany down over the Volga, landing in Iran. The Canberra obtained some fine pictures of the missile site. However it suffered a beating at the hands of Soviet air defence artillery and rockets, limping home with the whole of the Soviet air defence network alerted. Robert Amory, a senior intelligence official, recalled Washington's delight at receiving the pictures but he added that the British themselves exclaimed, 'God, never again.' In fact the RAF risked further occasional flights during the day, bringing invaluable photography of a wider range of targets, and at the 1956 Moscow airshow Khrushchev warned that if these airspace violations continued he would turn the Canberras into 'flying coffins'.[9]

A strong atomic counter-force emphasis lurked under the activities of the new Canberra photo-reconnaissance squadrons. As early as 15 August 1950, shortly after the outbreak of the Korean War, Air Marshal H. P. Lloyd explained to the Vice Chief of the Air Staff, Ralph Cochrane, that it had already been agreed that 'the most important and most urgent task' was to expedite photo-reconnaissance work on airfields in Western Europe that might be available to Soviet bombers after a Soviet advance. A European Strategic Targets Committee had been set up for this purpose and had already held it first meeting. This focus was sustained as the Canberra PR aircraft entered service and, by May 1953, the Chief of the Air Staff was expressing a particular interest in a 'special' exercise called Operation Dragonfly. This was designed to try out the machinery for controlling photographic reconnaissance operations at the outbreak of war when it would be essential 'to cover at once all those airfields which are likely to be used to the greatest extent by the Soviet Air Force'. The main priority for the RAF would always be blunting the potentially devastating air attack against Britain in a future war.[10] Commanders worried about the lack of early warning of a strike by Soviet bombers. Senior officials hoped for some advanced warning either from the Scandinavian air defence system, or from Special Intelligence – meaning GCHQ. But reliable warning from Scandinavia awaited a new cable system, and even then there was no guarantee that aircraft would pass through Scandinavian airspace. London toyed with the idea of a system of agents watching possible airfields from which such an attack might be launched. SIS had taken some 'modest steps' in this direction, but there were simply too many airfields scattered over too large an area.[11]

AI5, the target section of British Air Intelligence, had been given priorities for the preparation of strategic target material. Again, its top priority was not Moscow or Kiev but instead 'counter atomic', which meant the Soviet TU-4 atomic-capable bomber, and specifically:

(a) Airfields in the U.S.S.R. within 1,500 n.m. of U.K. on which TU-4's are known to be based.
(b) Other airfields in the U.S.S.R. within 1,500 n.m. of U.K. which could be suitable bases for TU-4 operations.

Secondary targets were tactical objectives in support of defence forces in Europe. Remarkably, strategic objectives inside the Soviet Union in support of the Americans were only 'tertiary' targets. AI5 was given a clear priority list of fifteen types of target in ranking order, of which the first seven were types of bomber airfield.[12] The main British consumer of this intelligence was the Committee for the Co-ordination of Strategic Targets Programme, known as TAB, and its lead programme was the 'Target Study on Counter Atomic Operations'. Radar intelligence and radar photography were of growing importance in this curious area of intelligence, which combined the strategic with the very tactical and on which some thought the survival of Britain in war might depend.[13]

By the early 1950s a curious contradiction was emerging in British policy. Some of Whitehall's elite were voicing increasing anxiety about the possibility of Washington precipitating a nuclear exchange. Yet London was bending over backwards to supply strategic and tactical target intelligence to the Americans which in some cases they could not get themselves. As with liberation operations, some of the reasoning was about getting on the inside track. Without a joint strategic planning process, nothing could be done about aspects of American policy that seemed unattractive to London, and intelligence seemed to offer a way in. Moreover, in the last analysis, in the unhappy eventuality of war, London would still prefer a successful American attack to an unsuccessful attack, hoping to limit the degree of Soviet retaliation.

Some of this was apparent in early November 1953 when Sir William Dickson, the new Chief of the Air Staff, was briefed for talks with Admiral Radford, the Chairman of the US Joint Chiefs of Staff, in Washington. The Assistant Chief of the Air Staff, Intelligence suggested that Dickson should bear in mind that 'there is at present, and has been for some time, complete exchange and co-ordination with the Americans of tactical and strategic target material, in which field intelligence liaison has probably been better than any other'. It was then suggested that Dickson might 'wish to use this point to argue that, as we have gone so far to forge an essential aid to bombing, the next logical step is to co-ordinate our plans for its use'. But it was a tricky business. Dickson was also advised to do all this 'without revealing the full extent of our co-operation with the CIA'. The CIA's National Estimates team and British Air Intelligence saw eye to eye on most matters and together shared the view that the US Joint Chiefs of Staff had been guilty of 'military lapses'. But it was important that Radford did not sense this.[14]

Alongside the land overflights there was also photo-reconnaissance at sea, monitoring the growth of the Soviet Navy. Again, the United States found allies useful. In October 1952 RAF Intelligence was passing to the Americans photographic intelligence of Soviet naval forces in Spitzbergen taken by the Norwegian Air Force. But the Norwegians were unwilling to release some intelligence material directly to the Americans. In the same year, Rear Admiral Anthony Buzzard, Britain's Director of Naval Intelligence, paid a secretive visit to Norway. His list of requests was 'so sensitive' that only handwritten notes were taken. Buzzard asked for special reconnaissance flights from Norway into the Soviet Union using the new Canberra aircraft and also for elint flights conducted within Norwegian airspace. Only permission for the latter was granted.[15]

The 1950s saw the increasing development of spheres of influence in the north. The UKUSA signals intelligence agreement of 1948 had designated relations with Norway an American responsibility, while relations with the Swedes belonged to GCHQ. In June 1952 the CIA was involved in a programme which involved transferring US Air Force officers to temporary civilian duty and then assigning them to Swissair, for the purpose of intelligence-gathering over the Soviet Union. Although the project was funded, it appears the Swiss developed cold feet at the last moment.[16] By the mid-1950s the Norwegian Defence Intelligence Staff was beginning to experiment with the use of 'trawlers' for intelligence-gathering in the Barents Sea. Initially these were used for photographic reconnaissance, but were gradually expanded to involve sigint monitoring. A special 'cover' shipping company Egerfangst was established to run these operations and its first vessel, the *Eger*, was in operation by 1956. Sigint systems for these vessels were supplied by the American National Security Agency (NSA).[17]

Even flights over the open sea were sensitive and risky. On 8 April 1950 a US Navy elint aircraft, a PBY-42 Privateer, launched from Britain, was shot down while trying to identify new Soviet missile bases along the Baltic coast. The Soviets later salvaged the Privateer's elint equipment from the waters of the Baltic and were in no doubt about the nature of the aircraft's mission. Further missions were postponed.[18] Within a month of the shoot-down of the Privateer, Omar Bradley, then Chairman of the US Joint Chiefs of Staff, set out the case for resuming the flights, insisting that the intelligence was of the 'utmost importance'. Truman agreed to a resumption when told that aircraft close to Soviet-controlled territory would be armed 'and instructed to shoot in self-defense'. Truman minuted, 'Good sense, it seems to me.' His green light was received on 6 June 1950. But almost immediately the Korean War prompted second thoughts and the flights were suspended for another few weeks due to 'current hyper-tension and fear of further shoot-downs'. By the end of 1950 operations had been resumed again and by 1952 much of this Baltic work was carried out by RB-50Gs operating out of Lakenheath airbase in Britain.[19]

The Korean War triggered a massive expansion of elint work, which was closely related to planning for a hot war that many now thought to be very close. Some signals in Europe could be monitored from Germany or the UK using ground sites employed by GCHQ or by NSA and its composite arms. In 1952 the 47th Radio Squadron of the US Air Force Security Service arrived at Kirknewton airbase in Scotland from which it could monitor shipping off the Kola Peninsula. But a great deal of traffic was of a second type, short-range transmissions which required the monitors to employ ships and aircraft. By October 1952 elint had become so large that liaison arrangements had to be expanded. Squadron Leader J. R. Mitchell became the first 'liaison officer for GCHQ' on elint in Washington. Two American elint officers took up equivalent roles in the UK.[20]

The RAF also suffered casualties. On 12/13 March 1953 a British Lincoln on a training flight was destroyed by Soviet fighters after straying over the border into East Germany. The wreckage was strewn across the frontier with some of the dead in the East and some in the West. The aircraft was not trying to penetrate East Germany, but its progress was probably being monitored by British ground sigint stations. Churchill was advised that henceforth all training flights in this area would be armed.[21] Many of the RAF's elint aircraft had near misses. For example, 192 Squadron was equipped with Washingtons and also with elint versions of the Canberra and flew out of Wünsdorff in Germany or Habbaniya in Iraq. In 1955, one of the crews from 192 Squadron identified the first MiG-15 with airborne radar by running at the border near the Caspian Sea, but its slow-flying Washington aircraft only narrowly escaped being shot down. The Squadron Commander, Group Captain Norman Hoad, was awarded an Air Force Cross for this discovery.[22] Much of this sigint work was directed at the operational and tactical level, looking at issues of military deployment, tactics and morale. By 1952 the sort of air intelligence derived from sigint included the Soviet Union's air order of battle, air defence activities, production capabilities and trends, fuel storage and other indications of Soviet strength and planning not available from other sources. This reflected work against communications at divisional level and below.[23]

From the American point of view, the most valuable GCHQ operations were not in Europe but in Asia. Sigint allowed Britain to derive substantial yet discreet advantage from what Washington called 'the value of residual empire'. GCHQ joined with what became the American NSA or the equivalent Australian organisation, DSD, to develop its facilities in Hong Kong, Singapore, Ceylon, the Indian Ocean, the Persian Gulf and on the east coast of Africa. Britain's access to colonial territories, and its ability to negotiate residual base agreements during independence settlements, proved especially valuable. By contrast, in the 1950s, the United States was refused permission to construct a signals intelligence collection site in Thailand, close to Chinese territory, despite a US–Thai defence treaty concluded in 1954. Facilities in Hong Kong offered particularly good coverage of southern China and Vietnam, an area of immense importance to the United States as the Vietnam War escalated.

Washington received the full intercept output of Hong Kong, which did 'not duplicate US effort'. But with the onset of the Korean War demands went up sharply and Washington considered that combined US–UK intercept facilities in the Far East were 'far short of requirements'.[24] In July 1952, the US Communications Intelligence Board persuaded its British opposite numbers, the London Signals Intelligence Board, of the 'urgent need' to send an additional 800-strong US Air Force sigint unit to Hong Kong to join the hard-pressed British and Australians. This formed part of a vast worldwide expansion of US sigint activities in the early 1950s, with new bases being opened in locations as disparate as Germany, Turkey, Crete and Taiwan, which confirmed America's growing pre-eminence in the field.[25] The capture of Hong Kong in the event of an all-out war with China was always a possibility. GCHQ negotiated emergency facilities in Japan for the 236 British and Australian sigint personnel working there as early as 1951, and a pre-prepared emergency site was allocated on Okinawa. The Americans noted that this was 'in part quid pro quo arrangement in return for accommodation our units by British on UK or UK controlled territory plus others now in Europe'. Similar American emergency sigint plans for war in Europe provided for 'relocating 7 such US COMINT Units to UK or UK controlled territory in event emergency relocation becomes necessary'.[26]

The Hong Kong sigint site was also enhanced by the fact that Washington had neglected sigint in Asia prior to Korea and was now building up from a low base. In 1955, the United States was still negotiating to develop new sigint sites in Asia. In the 1950s, sigint sites were not small and discreet but ideally included huge 'aerial farms'. In Taiwan, American officials had run into trouble securing a 335-acre site near

Nan-Szu-Pu airfield where they had plans to locate 300 personnel from the Army Security Agency.[27]

Britain operated a clear hierarchy in its sigint alliance, and Washington was the senior partner. The old Commonwealth were partners of a lower order, while still lower were the new Commonwealth, which simply provided bases, often as unwitting hosts to GCHQ collection sites. One of these was Ceylon, which became independent in 1948. Britain was allowed to retain what it called a communications relay station at a base called HMS Anderson, close to the town of Colombo. In practice this was a large GCHQ site covering most of the Indian Ocean. Matters became more complicated in 1949 when the Ceylonese government wanted to develop the area where the aerial farm was located and so asked the British to move sites. But British officials were convinced that even at the new site 'the real purpose could be easily disguised'.[28]

By October 1951 the new station that would replace Anderson was being planned, and Dr John Burrough, a senior GCHQ official, was attending meetings at the Admiralty to discuss the technical problems. It was hard to find a site which was not too remote and yet did not suffer from interference either from town or from naval transmissions. Even the ignition systems of cars on a busy highway up to 500 yards away could cause unacceptable interference. Moreover, the required capabilities had been upgraded since the base now had to monitor signals traffic from 'all bearings' and would need a facility that covered more than 400 acres. By 1952 GCHQ had decided on a site at Perkar, about two miles away, and Anderson then gave up ten acres to urban development in July 1954. The scale of development was not important, but the type of development was. Until GCHQ shifted to its new site at Perkar it was important to discourage new power lines, high buildings, garages and car-repair facilities. All these might interfere with the collection of precious electronic signals. The Perkar site was maintained until 1964.[29] Ceylon was a classic example of residual Empire offsetting the imbalance between British and American capabilities. In January 1951 the US National Security Council noted that the Pentagon and the CIA had been keen to construct in Ceylon 'elaborate radio facilities to be operated by US personnel'. But Ceylon had resisted the idea of even a 'modest' US Navy radio station. The Americans had accepted that they were very unlikely to establish a foothold here and that only the British would have access.[30]

After 1952, Anglo-American relations were made easier in the comint field by the arrival of the National Security Agency. Washington had been shamed by the service infighting over sigint during the Korean War, a repeat of events during the war against Japan. The Brownell Report now recommended to Truman the creation of a strong centralising force to look after American sigint. The US Air Force, which had secured its own sigint arm only in 1948, fought a desperate rearguard action. General Samford of US Air Force Intelligence denounced the idea that 'strong central control of the national COMINT effort is desirable' and condemned the whole scheme as a 'major error'. He also warned darkly about comint slipping away from the control of the US Joint Chiefs of Staff towards the civilians under the Secretary of Defense.[31] On 1 November 1952, the weak AFSA, which had bumbled ineffectually during the Korean War, was replaced by the strong National Security Agency. A sign of NSA strength was rapid expansion. In 1954 it was decided to move to a new site at Fort Meade in Maryland. The new NSA headquarters was built in 1955 and occupied in 1957. General Ralph Canine, the AFSA chief, remained at the helm, but with greater authority. The most visible evidence of Canine's new status was a new NSA Pacific Headquarters in Tokyo, prompted by the débâcle during the Korean War and the steep learning curve that followed. Elint, however, remained a service battleground for many years to come.[32]

Relations between GCHQ and NSA were determined to a large extent by money. Despite the fact that GCHQ had secured a growing proportion of British resources, British dependency was clear by the early 1950s. Resource problems could be disguised in the field of sigint collection, but in other areas the threadbare nature of the British effort was glaringly obvious. This was nowhere more evident than in the area of communications security or comsec, designed to protect Western signals from unfriendly eavesdropping. By the 1950s, Britain was increasingly aware that many of the machines that it used for enciphering communications, which were of Second World War vintage, no longer offered adequate security. These included the old British Typex machine and also the Combined Cypher Machine. Financial constraints prevented the UK or indeed other NATO countries from replacing these machines rapidly. The United States therefore stepped in, allowing some of its cryptographic principles to be adopted by Britain, and paying for the new machines carrying communications between the US, UK and NATO. However, a separate system – the superior CSP 2900 machine – was reserved 'for exclusive U.S. use'.[33]

Sigint infrastructure costs also began to tell in the relay circuits sending quantities of intelligence between GCHQ and NSA. By the mid-1950s a vast network of Comint Communication Relay Centers was under construction, including one in Britain, superintended by the US Air Force Security Service. The burden fell primarily on the United States, including extra land and sea cables, to provide better security against jamming and interception. The new sigint cables were being laid across the North Atlantic by the American Cable and Radio Corporation to deal with the growing volume of traffic. But the NSA also wanted to modify the control agreement for this network, dating back to 1943, 'so that the United States would have control of both terminals of the GCHQ–NSA communications'. Predictably London resisted the idea and a conference on the Centralised Comint Communications Center (CCCC) was scheduled for June 1954 to iron out the problems.[34]

Although to British eyes the new NSA seemed to have unlimited resources, these had to balanced against seemingly unlimited demands. The US Air Force also ran four other relay centres at Klemendorf in Alaska, Karamürsel in Turkey, Onna on Okinawa and Nan-Szu-Pu on Taiwan. But funds were tight. In 1957 the Navy wanted to begin work on relay centres in North Africa and on the Hawaian island of Wahiawa, but no money was available. The Army had similar problems in Europe, Japan and the Philippines 'due to fund and personnel limitations'. Sigint was an enormously expensive business.[35] The bigger stations were built on island locations, including Britain, Japan and Cyprus, because of their security from immediate overrun in war, and one of the most important sites was Menwith Hill in Yorkshire, which began life as an outpost of the US Army cryptanalysts, the 13th US Army Security Agency Field Station, in 1956. Ten years later it was taken over and run directly by the NSA.[36]

A growing problem for London and Washington was the need to supply comint to multinational centres such as NATO. Where would these centres with their multinational groups of staff officers come in the hierarchical order of sigint? Even at Eisenhower's SHAPE HQ, where British and American officers mingled only with the French, security was considered a major problem. Yet efficacy in war would depend on a strong flow of sigint to support the direction of operations. In early December 1952 London hosted an Anglo-American conference with the Intelligence Chief at SHAPE to work out a solution to this tricky problem. The US Army agreed to place a liaison officer at GCHQ to co-ordinate the flow of comint to SHAPE, while NSA was to supply advanced cipher machines for the purpose. Remarkably, the whole system was to remain 'informal' to allow the material to stay in British and American hands only. In 1954 the presiding Chief of Intelligence at SHAPE, General Robert Schow, was replaced by another American officer.[37]

The American effort to upgrade the comsec of its NATO partners was not misplaced. By the early 1950s, the Soviet Union had launched a vigorous 'listening' offensive, using not only sigint but also the widespread 'bugging' of embassies and headquarters, a Soviet trademark. This was a growth area, for bugging could offer a way of circumventing the increasingly secure communications traffic of major states – and it was gradually becoming easier with the advent of smaller bugs, facilitated by the arrival of the transistor, which was invented in 1948 and was used widely from the mid-1950s. Even so, one of Moscow's most valuable sigint assets in post-war Europe was not small or hidden, but instead there for all to see. One of the most curious legacies of the Second World War was a major Soviet sigint monitoring station on the outskirts of London at Whetstone in Middlesex. During the war permission had been given for the Soviet Tass News Agency to construct a 'radio monitoring station'. But the permission was not time-limited and the monitoring station, with its substantial aerial farm, was still in operation in July 1951, and as a Tass Agency site it enjoyed full diplomatic immunity.

John Slessor, Britain's Chief of the Air Staff, was especially agitated and insisted that the station represented 'a grave military danger'. How could it be that Britain had provided the Soviets with a large sigint site from which they could conduct, with complete immunity, the illicit study of radio systems and traffic, including those connected with the air defence of London? At Whetstone, they could capture far more traffic than from a private house or the Soviet Embassy in the centre of London. An exasperated Slessor declared that here, in the midst of the Korean War, Britain was 'gratuitously presenting our potential enemy with ... information which he could not obtain from any number of spies'. He had been trying to get the station closed down for some time. But the Foreign Office and MI5 could not agree on how much evidence of spying activity they had, how much of it they wished to reveal and legally what action could be taken. RAF elint and radio warfare units were convinced that Whetstone was a hive of intelligence activity. Slessor reported that 'during a major Air Exercise last summer, we took steps to jam reception of operational messages by the Tass station and the reaction of the occupants left no room for reasonable doubt that it was being used for this illicit purpose'. He argued that the obvious way forward was to ask for reciprocal rights outside Moscow. If this was denied, the Whetstone station could be legitimately closed. 'It is absolutely fantastic that ... we should continue to present the Russians on a plate with the opportunity of learning such vital defence secrets'. Eventually Slessor's formula was applied and the station closed down.[38]

Elsewhere, bugs and bugging were a major source of Soviet intelligence in the 1950s. The bugging of Western diplomatic premises in Moscow had a long history. On 14 May 1937, the American Embassy warned Washington that it had uncovered the bugging of Spaso House, the Ambassador's Moscow residence. Fine wires penetrated the ceiling over the Ambassador's desk, where he dictated most of his despatches. In the attic technicians discovered a secret compartment with electronic equipment together with fresh cigarette butts and 'several piles of human excrement'. Wires were also found in other Embassy buildings.[39] But now new equipment allowed the Soviets to become more comprehensive and more audacious. The first diplomats to uncover the extent to which they were being watched were the Norwegians. In 1948, the young and energetic head of the Norwegian Intelligence Service, who enjoyed a scientific background, sent an officer to 'sweep' Norway's Moscow Embassy. He found no fewer than thirteen microphones hidden in the walls.[40]

The British were next. In July 1950, the Air Attaché in the British Embassy in Moscow was testing a wireless receiver. Suddenly, he heard the voice of the British Naval Attaché, who was in a nearby room, broadcasting loud and clear. Despite a painstaking search, nothing could be found in the Naval Attaché's office. The general opinion was that the Russians had installed a portable radio-controlled transmitter, which local Soviet employees of the Embassy had succeeded in removing before it could be found. Now the hunt was on, and sweepers combed the Western embassies. In January 1952 a microphone was found in the American Embassy. Then in September that year an American sweeper heard the voice of George Kennan, the American Ambassador, being transmitted. Further work with 'a special British detector' eventually found the device. The audacity and sophistication stunned Western observers, for this was a resonating instrument that required no power supply and so could remain in operation indefinitely. It consisted of a metal chamber about ten inches long with a nine-inch antenna and transmitted when bombarded with microwaves from a nearby building by the operator. It was hidden in a wooden model of the Great Seal of the United States which was on display in Kennan's office and had been presented to him by the Soviets. A small metal chamber actually inside the eagle modulated the sound. Kennan was present, pretending to dictate a telegram, when it was found. He felt 'acutely conscious of the unseen presence ... our attentive monitor'. The offending device was taken to Washington and an exact copy made for investigation in London.[41]

This discovery caused alarm at the highest levels in London. On 9 October 1952, Churchill urged MI5 and SIS to 'take all necessary action' and to keep him informed. By the 14th, he had been given a full briefing about the extent of the hazard posed by microwave devices. He told Alexander, his Defence Minister, that this was all 'most important'. 'It shows how far the Soviets have got in this complex sphere.' Churchill ordered an active programme of research into defensive security measures and also the development of offensive bugging techniques for Britain's own use. In the short term MI5 busied itself protecting certain key rooms in Whitehall. Meanwhile the JIC asked Sir Frederick Brundrett, the MoD's Deputy Chief Scientific Adviser, to co-ordinate technical investigations into bugging possibilities. Britain had not been inactive in this field. Since the original find of 1950, three different scientists in Britain had 'developed miniature devices which would transmit voices in the room in which they are. All the devices are different in principle from that discovered in Moscow.' But it was clear that they needed to move from the laboratory into the field, as Ministers in London now called for 'devices suitable for offensive action by ourselves'.[42]

As early as 25 October 1952, Anthony Eden was able to assure Churchill that the British now had two different types of detector that would find Soviet microwave bugs, whether they were passive or active. It eventually became clear that this kind of Soviet resonating device was bulky and had a short range. It could only really be a threat in Soviet-controlled territories where unlimited microwave power could be used from a nearby building. But Britain's offensive research went more slowly. By April 1953 a small inter-departmental committee had been set up under Sir Frederick Brundrett 'charged with the co-ordination of research and development of eavesdropping devices'. In July 1954 it had four prototypes ready for field trials.[43]

Bugging, and fear of bugging, was widespread by 1953. Just as Churchill was becoming anxious about the new Soviet bugs, J. Edgar Hoover was warning the White House about an operation with concealed microphones in New York. This was the outcome of an extensive FBI investigation into Israeli intelligence operations with 'wire tapping, monitoring of conversations through the use of concealed microphones' and similar methods. The first operation had been launched by the Israelis against the offices of the Arab League in New York in August 1948. The operations were alleged to be based in the offices of a New York city attorney, Nahun Bernstein, and there was anxiety that the same techniques were being used by the Israelis against the American mission at the United Nations in New York.[44]

Extensive bugging could constitute a psychological offensive as well as a means of gathering intelligence. Western diplomats in Eastern bloc embassies already endured a rather prison-like existence. Outside their embassies they were tailed remorselessly and denied normal contact with the population. Inside the embassies they were watched by local indigenous employees who were coerced into spying. Bugs added another layer of anxiety, and by 1960 more than 100 devices had been found in American diplomatic premises in the Eastern bloc. This was soon underlined by the construction of the first embassy 'clean rooms' which were supposed to be bug-proof.[45]

The cumulative pressure could be intense, and reportedly George Kennan did not cope well. Others became aware of the effect of his prolonged immersion in this corrosive environment. In June 1953, Peer de Silva, the head of the CIA's intelligence division dealing with the Soviet Union, met up with Kennan during a visit to London to discuss the expansion of CIA representation in Moscow, which Kennan had been resisting. During their long conversation at Claridge's Hotel, Kennan continued to insist that this would be imprudent. De Silva could not help noticing that the Ambassador was 'very tense and nervous'. Moreover, he 'was pale, his hands trembled and he seemed to have much on his mind'. When Kennan stood up, his 'hand was quivering' and his anxiety was obvious. Pacing back and forth he explained that he was extremely perturbed by reports from Korea about what the Soviets seemed to have achieved in the field of brainwashing.

Nineteen-fifty-three was indeed the height of the 'brainwashing scare' in the West which provoked a dubious rash of counter-experiments in the West, the full extent of which remains unknown. Kennan was transfixed by reports of Soviet experiments with drugs and treatments intended to destroy a person's natural inhibitions and control. Having endured the microwave incident, he now 'considered himself as a likely target for some effort along this line', particularly if a major confrontation between East and West broke out. He continued, 'I fear that there is a good possibility that I will wind up someday before long, on the radio. I may be forced to make statements that would be damaging to American policy. I understand that CIA has some form of pill a person could use to kill himself instantly. Is this right?' He was referring to the so-called 'L-Pill', L standing for lethal, that had been issued to agents parachuting into the Soviet Union. They would soon be issued to U-2 pilots flying over the Soviet Union and China. These were small glass vials of cyanide which could be placed in the mouth. One bite through the glass would bring death within seconds. De Silva was not sure that Kennan was serious, but the Ambassador added emphatically, 'Yes, and I think that I must have two of these.' When de Silva reported this conversation to Alan Dulles back in Washington there was 'shock' and 'a long silence' in the Director's office. But eventually, after a long discussion, the request was authorised and the items were sent out to Moscow by bag. In 1953, a public outburst by Kennan about the prison-like conditions of Western diplomats in Moscow led to his expulsion.

Not all ambassadors were mentally browbeaten, even by the crudest forms of surveillance. In 1949 the Greek Ambassador to Moscow, an extrovert and bachelor, turned the tables on a familiar 'honeytrap' encounter. His Russian housekeeper, inevitably working for the MGB, had also become his mistress. One evening, while they were together in bed, the entire plaster ceiling of the bedroom collapsed about them. Several microphones were now dangling down, together with the beady eye of a camera. Not content with this intrusion, the MGB then brazenly visited him to confirm that they had been watching his activities, and left many detailed photos by way of proof. He was told that, if he did not co-operate, all would be exposed. But the Ambassador trumped them by simply recounting the story at length at every diplomatic party over the next few weeks, and showing off the photographs as evidence of his prowess. After an initial frisson, everyone became bored with the tale, and the MGB gave up and repaired the ceiling.[46]

The real victims of this unpleasant aspect of the Cold War were the little people. Housekeepers, drivers and cleaners were terrorised into co-operation with the local security services and regularly subjected to brutal treatment. One British female diplomat recalled the extensive bugging of British diplomatic premises in Yugoslavia. At a time when flats were not available for all staff in the British Embassy compound in Belgrade, junior diplomats were often housed in buildings which also contained Yugoslav nationals. One day an elderly Yugoslav woman, her next-door neighbour, knocked at her door in floods of tears and begged for help. The woman explained that the Yugoslav security police had bugged the British diplomat's flat and that she had been instructed to turn on the tape-recorder whenever she observed the diplomat returning with company that might prompt conversation. But the elderly lady had never seen a tape-recorder before and the security police had offered her only the most rudimentary training, so she could not now figure out how to operate it. She was terrified of failure. The British diplomat calmly sat next door and, over a cup of tea, gave her Yugoslav neighbour extensive instructions in the operation of the tape-recorder.[47]

Even the elite Soviet scientists themselves who were working on the development of new Soviet bugs, microphones and secure scrambler telephones were, for the most part, inmates of the infamous *sharashka* or MGB prison research institutes. Until Stalin's death in 1953, so many of Moscow's top scientists were in jails that the laboratories had to be transferred inside the prisons to prevent Soviet scientific research grinding to a halt. Many of the Soviet Union's most famous post-war aircraft were designed by Andrei Tupolev and his team from inside what has been called Stalin's Aviation Gulag. An equally famous MGB scientist–prisoner was Alexander Solzhenitsyn. Solzhenitsyn worked in a special *sharashka* dedicated to communications security. One of his colleagues, Lev Kopelev, recalled the creation of this unusual outfit in 1949: 'New groups of imprisoned specialists kept arriving – mostly signal men, radio engineers, and technicians.' They were assembled before their commander and given their task:

> From now one you are workers of a scientific-research institute. A particularly important and particularly secret one. You and I have to develop a new system of secret telephony. We must invent and prepare a telephone so that over several thousand kilometres a connection can be maintained that is absolutely dependable and absolutely impervious to wire-tapping or interception. I stress *absolutely* ... Our institute will be directly supervised by Comrade Beria, who will report personally to Comrade Stalin.

Oddly, despite the intense security, these laboratories employed German POWs as labour, even in the offices. The *sharashka* also acquired the archives of the Berlin laboratories of the Phillips company, which the Soviets had hauled away in 1945. The camp's chief had been ordered to employ the Germans, despite his suspicions that when they returned to Germany they would give Western intelligence details of the work of their institute.

These Soviet scientist–prisoners, thankful to be given equipment, a useful task and somewhat better conditions, leaped into action in the service of their persecutors. However, the MGB was not an ideal administrator for scientists. Around 1950, Beria appointed a new commander to the unit, a hardened security type whom the scientists thought would be better employed as 'an executioner in a cellar shooting people'. Their new boss decided that it was time to tidy up and weed out 'non-inventoried apparatus and incorrectly filled out secret documents'. Security teams then burned a large proportion of the scientific research and broke up much of the equipment 'with crowbars and sledgehammers'. Kopelev recalled that all his work on telephone security, 'thousands of sound pictures', went into the flames simply because they had not yet been catalogued. Solzhenitsyn was allegedly pulled out of the *sharashka* by the MGB to help on active communications security operations against suspected spies, before being returned to incarceration. This *sharashka* was a surreal microcosm of Stalin's state – simultaneously a scientific laboratory, a prison and a police station rolled into one.[48]

The advent of bugs and bugging renders it peculiarly difficult to make any generalisations about who was reading whose communications during the 1950s. Broadly, the West had encountered great difficulties with Soviet traffic since the terrible lessons of Black Friday, the sea-change in Soviet communications security of 29 October 1948. Warned by William Weisband, a Soviet agent in the US Army Security Agency, as we have seen, the Soviets executed a quantum leap in communications security, wiping out years of work. Bugging and human espionage on both sides sometimes resulted in the temporary lifting of cryptographic secrecy. Excessive anxiety to obtain stolen material that made breaking ciphers so much easier, all the more valuable since 1948, could make intelligence agencies vulnerable. In the late spring of 1950, Gehlen's organisation in Germany informed the CIA that one of its Austrian contacts had access to a Soviet officer with the latest Soviet ciphers. The Austrian, who presented himself as Count Friedrich Coleredo-Wels, was prepared to provide this material in return for $25,000, a comfortable job and smooth relocation to the West. Even with the inflated prices that intelligence now fetched as the result of five years of American largesse in Germany and Austria, this was a hefty sum and CIA officers in Munich were rightly suspicious. Intelligence activity was increasingly a national industry for Germans and Austrians who were multilingual and well educated.

The CIA saw this as either inspired free enterprise by an individual, or an attempt by the MGB to lure the CIA into parading any number of its field officers before them for the purposes of identification. Moreover, while Vienna shared its status as an espionage capital with other cities, such as Berlin and Hong Kong, it was also unique for the frequent use of firearms, earning it the nickname the 'shooting gallery'. But the CIA in Munich knew that 'Washington would go for this lead like a hungry trout for a fly.' Officers were duly despatched to Vienna to contact the Austrian, armed with .38 revolvers and $25,000 in used currency. Their worst fears were confirmed when one officer narrowly survived five rounds loosed off during a nighttime drive-by shooting. Eventually a lie-detector test indicated that their Austrian Count was working for the Soviets and that he had no knowledge of their ciphers. The result was a routine 'burn notice' – a warning containing photos and description – issued to all Allied secret services in Europe. This practice was designed to thwart persistent fraudsters.[49]

Austria and Germany were the location of a much grander and more successful set of operations against Soviet communications. These were the famous 'tunnel' operations launched from Vienna and then Berlin against telephone communications in the East. The affair began with a routine intelligence report in Vienna that happened to alert the British to the fact that the main telephone cables running under their sector went out to a nearby airbase, which, since its investigation by Wing Commander Keat in 1945, had become a major Soviet HQ. They were soon tapped from an operation hidden in a private house. William Weisband's treachery in 1948, which damaged many Western signals intelligence operations, was the spur that pushed the Americans towards the Vienna and Berlin tunnel operations. The tapping of land-lines was a direct response to the calamitous loss of intelligence in 1948. The CIA history of the tunnel operation clearly alludes to this: 'As early as 1948 U.S. Intelligence Officers became interested in the benefits to be derived from tapping Soviet and Satellite landlines on a scale not previously considered necessary. The loss of certain sources during this period created gaps in our intelligence coverage which were particularly unfortunate during this period of Cold War escalation.'[50] The Berlin tunnel was the most complex and controversial joint SIS–CIA operation of the 1950s. Like its predecessor in Vienna, it sought to tap into Soviet land-line communications. Much of the controversy stems from the fact that, on 22 October 1953, even before its construction began, George Blake, an SIS officer working for the Soviets as a double agent, was part of a team briefed about the planned tunnel. The CIA continues to assert that, despite this leak, the tunnel was a success. This was indeed the case, for the Soviets had to allow the operation to continue uninterrupted for a period in order to protect Blake, a top 'agent in place'.

Some CIA officers have also suggested that the British initially decided not to tell the Americans about their early tunnel operation in Vienna. SIS came clean only when the Americans arrived at the idea independently, forcing the British to reveal their solo operation. Later, it has been claimed, the Americans failed to admit to the British that they could read certain types of traffic taken from Berlin, but the latter story is unverified. What is quite clear is that while data were genuine and freely shared, their sheer volume sometimes defeated analysis. Some 40,000 hours of telephone conversations were recorded and a further six million hours of teletype traffic was taken. Entire buildings full of translators battled to stay ahead of the wave, but inevitably fell behind.

Berlin was the hub of the Soviet empire in Eastern Europe, carrying communications not only between Moscow and Germany, but also between Moscow and Warsaw and Bucharest. Although the operation was complex, the underlying hope was that, once in place, the operation might go undisturbed for some time. Agents in the East Berlin Post Office provided maps of the locations of the cables and in February 1954 digging began in the West. The cover was the construction of a US Air Force radar site and the tunnel took a year to complete. The critical phase was the installation of the taps themselves. This was a tricky business which involved freezing the lines to prevent the interference being detected by operators in the East. This vital phase was carried out by British Post Office engineers flown out specially from Britain. Finally, at the end of February 1955, the Berlin tunnel was operational. Elaborate anti-humidity barriers and air conditioning had to be erected to prevent damp affecting the electronics. The CIA maintained a small local unit for on-the-spot monitoring of circuits for the protection of the project and also to provide items of 'hot' intelligence for the secret services in Berlin. But the overall 'take' far exceeded the capacity of any local monitoring.

On average twenty-eight telegraphic circuits and 121 voice circuits were being recorded at any one time. Voice traffic was recorded on 50,000 reels of magnetic tape, amounting to some twenty-five tons of material. At the peak of operation the voice-processing centre employed 317 people, and eventually 368,000 conversations were transcribed. The teletype centre employed a further 350 people. For each day of the tunnel's operation the output was 4,000 feet of teletype messages. Local teams watched especially productive circuits to take hot intelligence in real time. The material garnered was very varied, but Western intelligence services considered it to be a key source of early warning of attack.

Several hundred KGB (as the MGB had become in 1954) and GRU officers were also identified from this information. Most of its value was military order-of-battle information – plotting the size and position of Soviet forces, a kind of advanced military train-spotting. Although 'uncovered' by the Soviets on 21 April 1956, processing went on until 30 September 1958.[51]

Both CIA and KGB historians claim that the KGB kept the tap secret and did not warn those Eastern bloc officials routing communications through Berlin. This included those responsible for Soviet Army GRU operations. There were arguments within the KGB about whether the tap should be used to pass disinformation to the West; instead it was decided that the tap would be tolerated and then 'accidentally' discovered in April 1956. In the meantime the KGB passed out general security warnings to bureaucrats about using telephones, but to its dismay most officials ignored them.[52] On the night of 21/22 April 1956, engineers in the East pretended to 'bump' into the tunnel while repairing damage caused by heavy rain, and the next day the tunnel was revealed to the press. Far from causing embarrassment, its boldness astounded observers and it was soon hailed as one of the great intelligence operations of the Cold War. Clearly there were other tunnels of this sort, and CIA documents assert that in September 1953 there were other 'similar operations' (in the plural) being 'conducted elsewhere'. By the 1980s audacious operations of this kind were being carried out by the West underneath Moscow itself.[53] It would be interesting to know what the Soviets obtained from similar operations against the even more vulnerable telephone lines running from Berlin to the Western Zone. On 4 August 1949, the staff of Britain's ID were told that John Bruce Lockhart, the head of SIS in Germany, had learned 'that the Russians had undertaken 100% coverage of the telephone lines between Berlin and the Western Zones'. In the early 1950s, ID regularly complained that the German Security Service, the BfV, held injudicious conversations using these phone lines. The work of Alexander Solzhenitsyn, Lev Kopelev and their incarcerated friends in their prison–laboratory demonstrates that the Soviets were also busy in the area of telephone security and interception. As in the East, security warnings about using the telephone were circulated in West Berlin, but bureaucracies are much the same everywhere and the usual lapses occurred.[54]

Arguments about the equivalence of intelligence organisations East and West are often met with dismay. Nevertheless, KGB behaviour towards the GRU and the Soviet Army during the Berlin tunnel episode was not dissimilar to the selfish attitude of the NSA towards the US Air Force during the Vietnam War when it failed to pass on information about North Vietnamese air defences. Security of intelligence sources was paramount and wider concerns were of a lesser order. Oddly, in the Berlin tunnel episode, both sides could claim victory. The KGB successfully protected Blake until he was exposed by a Polish intelligence officer working for the Americans in 1961; meanwhile the West gained enormous quantities of data about its Eastern bloc military opponents. Both sides, either through Blake or through the tunnel, were offered some reassurance against the possibility that the other side was planning an attack. In that sense at least Cold War intelligence was neither fruitless nor a zero-sum game, and its most substantial benefits might be measured through inaction.[55]

Throughout the first decade of the Cold War, Germany and Austria remained in the front line of the intelligence war. Despite elaborate and expensive operations with aircraft and tunnels, it was the human tide of refugees and returned prisoners that remained the key source of information about the East. Processing them carefully, although often humdrum work, was still overwhelmingly the surest route to detailed information about the East. Alan Lang-Brown, head of the SIS scientific intelligence unit (TCS), explained to his colleagues, 'We all agree that the best hope of progress in a number of fields lies in obtaining a flow of the right kind of defector: it is probably the case that, to date, the output of the relatively small number of defectors we have had compares very favourably with the value of intelligence from all other sources.' It was this material that allowed the precise targeting of the more exotic methods of overflight and sigint.[56] Between 1948 and 1951, Britain had 'screened' about a quarter of a million returning German POWs just at Friedland Camp, its main interrogation centre. Between 1949 and 1955 the equivalent American Wringer operation interrogated between 300,000 and 400,000 refugees and POWs, generating over a million intelligence reports. Much of this was exchanged by the British and the Americans. In 1950 the British Liaison Officer at EUCOM in Heidelberg sometimes received as much as a hundredweight of paper a day (more than 50kg). These programmes were probably the only operations making use of human sources that rivalled signals intelligence in terms of their industrial scale.[57]

Defectors and refugees in Germany and Austria also brought issues of intelligence-gathering and security close together. Defectors posed an alarming security problem and were often in danger of being forcibly 'kidnapped' by the Soviets, or else they might themselves have been planted by Soviet intelligence. Kidnapped defectors could then be 'persuaded' to make wild allegations about their bad treatment to make propaganda to discourage other would-be deserters. Despite the importance of defectors, it had taken until the end of 1949 for the JIC in London to set out a general policy on this matter and it was still being refined in

1950. The difficult issue was the cost of their disposal (or resettlement) after interrogation, then running at between £100 and £200 a head, which no service wished to bear. This often involved travel costs to Australia, a sunny destination thought likely to encourage more defections. Army intelligence were pressing for these costs to be met from the secret service vote.[58] At present many were simply being dumped in 'unpleasant' Austrian DP camps. 'News travels fast' on the DP grapevine, they noted, and the fact that some satellite deserters were finally sent to DP camps was 'well known on the other side of the frontier'. Some defectors were having to be kept in cells during processing, rendering them 'soured and uncooperative'.[59]

American efforts were better funded, but were dogged by the slow hand-over of defector activities from American service intelligence to an expanding CIA in Germany. Even in 1954 the key element in Austria was a large US Army Special Operations Unit called D-35 which ran a vast programme for 'wringing' out refugees from the Eastern bloc. Observers remarked that 'Army Detachment D-35 is in complete control of this activity even to the extent of dominating CIA.'[60] D-35's determination to hang on to this operation underlines a wider issue. Throughout this period both the CIA and SIS were discomfited to find that Military Intelligence was pulling in more than the secret services. Its control of the 'wringing out' of human beings as they crossed to the West put them ahead, and this was reinforced by the fact that the military were allowed legal spies in East Germany in the form of touring military missions. Originally intended as liaison teams for the four occupying powers, they soon became a legalised form of intelligence-gathering for all sides. The British Mission was quickly given the designation 'Brixmis'.

The intelligence methods used by these legalised spies varied from the basic to the ingenious. In East Germany, British, French and American liaison teams were banned from visiting areas where military exercises were under way. But, when the manoeuvres were over, the area was scoured. One reason for this was that toilet paper was not issued to Soviet troops in the field. Any kind of paper, including letters from home and military documents, were used instead and the wind then blew the paper around. American G-2 officers on these tours recalled this dismal type of intelligence-collection. Nevertheless, as early as 1950, this material provided everything from ciphers to intelligence on morale levels and also on Army–Party–MGB relations in the field. The British, French and American missions enjoyed 'forwarding' to each other some of these unsavoury intelligence items for 'further analysis'. The untidy habits of the Soviet Army consistently proved to be one of the most startling sources of material. By the late 1950s Brixmis regarded all military rubbish bins as valuable targets. Combing of exercise areas and firing ranges could produce rain-sodden notebooks and schedules of newly arrived material with sources and serial numbers for the latest equipment. This was gold dust to the growing army of analysts in London and Washington. Occasionally items of kit could be 'liberated', but there was always the danger of attentive East German security detachments, which had been known to open fire. But the humble plundering of rubbish – now dignified with the title Operation Tamarisk – remained one of their most productive activities and lasted until the end of Brixmis in 1989.[61]

By comparison with the work of Military Intelligence, often lowly but vast in scale, the offensive human agent work of SIS and the CIA into the Eastern bloc often seemed futile. In the period between 1947 and 1951 the CIA intelligence sections responsible for the Soviet Union had been 'almost totally preoccupied' with a programme of parachuting Russian-speaking DPs, typically Ukrainians or Belorussians, into Soviet areas where they believed resistance groups existed. The missions were flown deep into the Soviet Union by courageous Polish aircrews, flying from the Middle East and Italy. Often dropped in groups of two, they were provided with forged documents and false cover-stories, in the optimistic hope that they would find jobs and places to live, and generally integrate themselves into the local scene. Where possible these individuals were sent back to their own local communities. Peer de Silva, who worked on these operations, recalled that by 1952 it was impossible to pretend that they were working. A review of the operational files led to the inescapable conclusion that 'every one of our parachuted agents was under Soviet control and was reporting back to us under duress'. The MGB was writing their messages and feeding the West with information that was misleading or confusing. Meanwhile West had 'no real assets in terms of agents that had genuinely penetrated the Soviet Union or the Baltic states', and these 'bankrupt efforts were going on at a real cost in lives, manpower, and money, and as an endeavour was obviously a failure, practically and philosophically'. Agents despatched to the Baltic states did not arrive by air, but their fate was the same. They were inserted using small but exceedingly fast patrol boats going up the Baltic, and the CIA eventually concluded that 'practically all of these were turning out to be tragic losses'. By the mid-1950s the CIA and SIS had both backed away from what they now recognised had been a 'wasteful and, in many ways, tragic programme of parachuting agents into the Western reaches of the USSR, with such calamitous results'.[62]

Some of the most sensitive flights carrying agents into the East were flown by the CIA's curious multinational air force, which consisted mostly of Polish, Czech and Hungarian pilots who had served with the Allies during the war. But by 1953 agent activities were fizzling out. Thereafter they had been located at Weisbaden and retrained for sigint operations on seven reconnaissance aircraft given the designation RB-69. Codenamed Operation Ostiary, these flights were designed to map Soviet power-grids and radar sites and had the advantage of crews that were non-American and were completely deniable if lost. This change of task symbolised a wider shift away from agent operations in the mid-1950s.[63] The only agent successes had been short-term shallow 'raids'. In 1952 Peer de Silva presided over one of the CIA's last successful 'forced entry' intelligence missions of the decade. Four DP agents trained in Florida were inserted by submarine on to Sakhalin, an island to the north of Japan occupied by the Soviets at the end of the war. Their purpose was to inspect the airfields to determine whether they were able to take heavy bombers, and whether they contained the tell-tale deep weapons-pits required to load atomic bombs. They returned successfully to report that neither was the case.[64]

As early as 1945 the British had begun to prepare for the gradual transfer of intelligence and security functions to the West Germans. Indeed, the need for huge numbers of personnel to counter the energetic activities of Soviet intelligence ensured that, from the outset, ID had recruited large numbers of Germans. The Allies had also quickly set about rebuilding the German police, which had political sections. By 1949, MI5 was helping to construct a German version of itself – a West German Security Service. The gradual creation of West Germany represented a drawdown for the British and American secret services and a decline in their rights and permissions. In 1952, the Western Allies began to negotiate 'intelligence treaties' with the Germans, insisting on the exclusive right to secure all Soviet and Eastern European defectors and to question former POWs and refugees. Simple matters such as the recruiting of German nationals was now legally difficult. The arrival of a US–Japanese Peace Treaty in 1952 had presented similar problems for American intelligence in Asia. As a result a 'separate ancillary bilateral United States–Japanese Administrative Agreement' had been drawn up, designed to continue 'certain vital intelligence activities and procedures'.[65]

Even after the end of occupation in 1955, Germany remained a crucial centre for all kinds of interception. Letters, telephone communications and radio transmissions were monitored with great intensity. The Allies had enjoyed powers to intercept all letters and telephone calls and had made abundant use of this. A massive operation examined most of the correspondence between East and West. In 1952, this trawling operation was providing no less than 70 per cent of the low-grade intelligence obtained in Germany, much of it about economic matters. In May that year there was some argument as the West attempted to compel Adenauer, West Germany's first post-war Chancellor, to sign an agreement permitting continued interception. He initially demurred, protesting that this was politically explosive. A month later it seems he was persuaded to sign away more specific powers that related to communications to and from the Soviet bloc only.[66] Despite these measures, by the summer of 1954 British and American intelligence chiefs in Germany were expressing 'a strong fear' that German sovereignty would bring about a 'severe curtailment' of intelligence activities. They had already encountered 'deliberate opposition to their field collection activities by Germans' and considered this 'a mild foretaste' of things to come.[67]

The SIS station in Berlin in the early 1950s was the best example of the benefits that were provided by the occupation to British intelligence, which were about money as well as geography. In the 1950s some SIS agent networks in Europe had to be 'laid off' due to budget cuts, but in Germany the 'whole SIS establishment was paid for out of occupation costs, which were borne in their entirety by the German taxpayer'. As a result the SIS station in Berlin was the largest in the world with 100 officers and endless support staff:

> The station was divided into several sub-stations, each with its own particular sphere of activity. There was a section responsible for the collecting of political intelligence and the penetration of the Soviet headquarters in Karlshorst (a suburb of East Berlin). Another had the task of collecting information on the Soviet and East German Armed Forces. A third was exclusively concerned with the collection of scientific intelligence. Finally there was the section concerned with the planning and execution of technical operations of various kinds.

This was good for SIS and good for many Germans. George Blake recalled that the plethora of intelligence organisations working in Berlin, together with the decline of the black market by 1950, meant that a surprising proportion of Berliners were working as agents for an intelligence organisation or even for several at the same time.[68]

With the gradual falling off of the black market, intelligence became, for some German citizens, an important source of alternative income. In the 1950s SIS undertook a review of the value of its intelligence to London departments and *en route* made some uncomfortable discoveries. It realised that a large network of agents reporting regularly on the movements of Russian materials on the East German railways was in fact completely fictitious and 'had been invented by a man sitting in the safety of Western Germany, but closely reading many newspapers and railway magazines'. SIS had the 'awful job' of going to Kenneth Strong's JIB in London and confessing that its secret intelligence on this subject was not very secret at all. But JIB was unruffled. It asked SIS to keep on sending the reports because it thought them 'rather good' and surmised that the German fraudster was nevertheless doing an excellent job of squeezing intelligence from an open source.[69] However, the end of the occupation of Western Germany in May 1955, with its drastic reduction in funding, prompted the entire reorganisation of the SIS station in Berlin. Armies of agents and contacts were summarily laid off. The same was true in Austria, where an agreed withdrawal of forces led to neutral status in the same year. At least in Austria, the British knew that the Americans and the Soviets were suffering equally. The staff of the CIA, SIS and KGB stations commiserated with each other as they all sold some of their office furniture when their headquarters all suffered 'the same traumatic compression'.[70]

Arguably, both British and American intelligence needed reshaping at home rather than abroad, and some of the longest battles in post-war intelligence were fought over reform and centralisation. In Washington in the 1950s this battle was being fought over the territory of sigint. In London the field of battle was in the more amorphous areas of scientific, technical and service intelligence. London's champion of centralisation was Kenneth Strong, head of JIB. Strong knew that intelligence from the communist countries, mostly via Germany, Austria and Hong Kong, was hard won and he was disturbed to know that when it reached Whitehall it was not being used efficiently. So in 1950 he launched an offensive, hoping to achieve breakthrough by exploiting Whitehall's financial stringency. Tactfully he began by emphasising the successes that the British system had achieved, compared to the labours of the CIA:

> C.I.A. has very largely failed to achieve effective centralisation far less integration even within the limits imposed upon it and the U.S. Services have relinquished few of their former intelligence responsibilities to the central authority, as they feel it is too remote from Service requirements; this in spite of the fact that the staff of the C.I.A. contains serving officers. We in the U.K. are thus far ahead of the U.S. in the concept of central intelligence.

Strong went on to recommend a radical change, the geographical centralisation of all operational intelligence in service departments, together with all joint intelligence done by the MoD in one building.[71] Emanuel Shinwell, the Minister of Defence, supported Strong and put his plans to Attlee. He hoped to cut the service intelligence budget, which stood at £3.5 million, most of which was absorbed by the Army. But the Chiefs of Staff resisted vigorously, claiming that intelligence and operations for each service had to be integrated. To pull the intelligence elements away from their parent services would slow response times and might be 'disastrous' in war. Although it was not explicitly stated, many knew that Strong's underlying plan was the complete amalgamation of service intelligence, but his proposals were defeated for the time being.[72]

Scientific and technical intelligence was also in a mess. Even the detonation of the Soviet atomic bomb had not shaken Whitehall sufficiently to get a grip on this problem. In October 1949, in the shadow of the Soviet explosion, a modest attempt at reform had been made by Dr Bertie Blount. Blount managed to abolish the most obscene aspect of P. M. S. Blackett's 1945 legacy, the Joint Scientific and Technical Intelligence Committees. These two semi-detached committees had eleven members, with no fixed chairmen, but sought to direct a staff of some twenty scientists and forty technicians. Rarely can an intelligence body have so perfectly met that compelling definition of a committee as an animal with 'four back legs'.[73]

In their place, Blount put himself as Director of Scientific Intelligence (DSI). He tried to achieve some of the inter-service aspirations of JIB. But the reform was incomplete, for the ground troops of technical and scientific intelligence remained with the three service intelligence sections and could not be prised away. To do so was politically too dangerous. Blount himself confessed that his own scheme had been 'designed to effect the minimum of disturbance to existing machinery', but disturbance was exactly what was required. Unsurprisingly, with Blount's Directorate of Scientific Intelligence there were three sections. On the surface they looked like areas of scientific expertise – 'electronics', 'chemistry' and 'hydrodynamics'. But these were in fact three thinly disguised service sections. The profusion of different service sections, duplicating each other's business, continued to annoy the collectors. Typically, SIS complained of the confusion created by having a 'number of different briefs existing on guided weapons'.[74]

Churchill was dismayed to find this area still a mess when he returned to office in 1952 and called R. V. Jones back from the University of Aberdeen to resume his wartime work. But Jones, although brilliant at scientific intelligence, was less adept at Whitehall politics and by 1954 little improvement had been made. In March that year, with the departure of Jones as DSI, Sir Frederick Brundrett, the MoD Chief Scientific Adviser, was asked to conduct a wide-ranging investigation into the future of scientific intelligence. At the same time Admiral Daniel was conducting a similar probe into atomic intelligence. Brundrett confessed that it was still 'extremely difficult' to get a sense of what was going wrong because of a mass of conflicting views about the nature of the problem. But he was certain that there *were* dire problems. A clear convert to the Kenneth Strong school of centralisation, he insisted that there was 'too much subdivision' and that this gave rise to 'jealousies'. Modern intelligence was 'essentially a matter of team-work' and what was needed was drastic change. The class-ridden divisions between scientific and technical intelligence staff had to be destroyed. The boundaries between the different service sections had to be eradicated and indeed all the scientific, technical and economic sections of both DSI and JIB rolled together into one effective new organisation 'under the control of a very carefully selected senior service officer'. This was essential, but it was also impractical. Brundrett knew that the Directors of Army, Navy and Air Intelligence would fight any attempt to liberate their scientific and technical sections. Thus, while his plan was undoubtedly the 'final solution', intelligence reformers would, he advised, have to 'let the matter grow rather than force it immediately'. The growth was slow and it would be ten years before intelligence centralisation really flowered in 1964.[75]

The twin intelligence probes of Brundrett and Daniel in 1954 scored a success in the area of atomic intelligence. The Daniel Report on atomic intelligence prompted the creation of a new British Atomic Energy Authority. Churchill approved the transfer of Eric Welsh's Atomic Energy Intelligence Unit to the military and put it under JIB. Keeping British atomic intelligence separate from other organisations had given it additional security, not an insignificant factor in the light of the access of figures like Klaus Fuchs and Donald Maclean to Western atomic secrets. But reasons of efficiency demanded that this effort be joined up with the rest of British intelligence. There would be a new Atomic Energy Intelligence Committee chaired by Sir Frederick Brundrett and attended by 'C', the Chair of the JIC, the head of JIB, the heads of Harwell and Aldermaston and the three service intelligence chiefs. But the core work on atomic intelligence would be done by its scientific intelligence sub-committee led by Brundrett with Penney, Cockroft and Cherwell. Welsh lingered on as the lacklustre head of the Atomic Energy Intelligence Unit and only with his death later that year was the transformation complete.[76]

19

Moles and Defectors: The Impact of Guy Burgess and Donald Maclean

British MI-6 has been so penetrated that it looks like a piece of Swiss cheese ... The German intelligence service has also been thoroughly penetrated ... and French intelligence is even more cheeselike than MI-6.

Stewart Alsop, *The Center*[1]

On the night of 25 May 1951, Guy Burgess and Donald Maclean, two Soviet spies in the Foreign Office, fled Britain on a Channel ferry. A month before, evidence from the Venona effort against Soviet intelligence traffic had conclusively identified Maclean as a long-sought mole who had previously worked in Britain's wartime Washington Embassy. But Venona material could not be used to bring a prosecution in court and MI5 had watched Maclean carefully, hoping for a slip that would allow it to gather more conventional evidence or to extract a confession from him. But it dallied too long and a tip-off from Kim Philby allowed him and Burgess to evade its surveillance and flee eastwards.[2] Once it was clear that the two men had fled, the klaxon sounded across Europe and the hunt was on for the 'missing diplomats'. Everyone presumed they were heading for the sanctuary of Soviet-controlled territory. Major-General John Kirkman, the head of ID in Germany, sent a flash message to the US Counter-Intelligence Corps explaining that the absconders were suspected of being in the US Zone and would try to cross into the Soviet Zone. Every American and German security unit was set to work scouring 'travel bureaus, banks, bus and railroad stations, border crossing points, hotels and other appropriate locations'. There were several reported sightings and some units became over-excited. German security detained 'all British citizens and suspicious personalities', who, given the time of year, turned out to be indignant holidaymakers. On 16 June, German security thought it had struck lucky when it detained two likely looking men in transit through Beggendorf. But this hapless pair were eventually 'identified as SIS (British intelligence) personalities' who had been caught up in the dragnet.[3]

Since the escape of Burgess and Maclean in 1951 there has followed half a century of writing about these two individuals, together with Kim Philby, who fled in 1963, and about those who stayed behind, including Anthony Blunt and John Cairncross. Some of this writing has been illuminating, but too much of it has been anecdotal biography, often mind-numbing in its detail, and belonging firmly to the *Hello!* magazine school of intelligence history. Despite a mountain of biographical detail, we have barely begun to unravel the contribution of these over-familiar figures to Moscow's perspective on the West, or indeed the place of moles and defectors in the wider Cold War.[4]

It is now clear that Moscow received the cream of British policy papers during the first decade of the Cold War. Donald Maclean alone had been well positioned to deliver such material. He had served in Paris until the arrival of the Germans in June 1940. He then worked in the General Department of the Foreign Office in London until May 1944, which brought all manner of interesting documents across his desk. Crucially he was then moved to the British Embassy in Washington, where he sat for four years attending sensitive meetings on atomic energy. From November 1948 until May 1950 he was in Cairo, where an alcoholic breakdown occurred. Finally, he returned to London and, despite his unstable condition, became head of the American Department of the Foreign Office in London in October 1950, during a crucial stage in the Korean War, until his disappearance, in May 1951. During his time in Washington, Maclean was head of Chancery and therefore responsible for Embassy security. William Clark, a press secretary and later press adviser to Eden at 10 Downing Street, recalled being given a censorious lecture on security by Maclean. As well as warning him not to tell anything sensitive to the French since 'they leak like sieves', Maclean added further advice: 'I would always disconnect the phone when talking to business men, because of course our phones are tapped by the U.S. Government, and we don't want them to get all our trade plans.' Burgess had occupied less sensitive posts in London and Washington, but had been private secretary to Hector McNeil, the Minister of State at the Foreign Office, between January 1947 and June 1948. McNeil had held a lot of intelligence-related responsibilities.[5]

From Maclean and others, Moscow received the infamously volatile PHP papers on future strategy that captured the anti-Soviet sentiments of British military planners in 1944. There was also Orme Sargent's more sober, and certainly more revealing, 'Stocktaking Paper' which surveyed the problems and prospects of British foreign policy at the end of the war. Agent meetings with controllers also allowed an important explanatory gloss to be placed on key materials or events, ensuring that the material was not received blind. Cipher material would also have aided the Soviets in reading more material beyond that which the agents purloined and gave to their controllers at monthly meetings.[6] During the Berlin Crisis of 1948, the Soviets were receiving streams of high-quality material. On 10 September that year Bevin addressed the British Cabinet on the crisis and by early October these minutes were available to Stalin. In the same month important messages sent by Bevin to the British Ambassador in Washington about Anglo-American disagreements over the Berlin Crisis were handed to the Soviets, almost certainly by Donald Maclean. This material was highly revealing. Other material described Bevin's meetings with Western leaders in Paris. When combined with similar material emanating from high-level spies in France and Germany, it is clear that the Soviet intelligence effort throughout the crisis was remarkably good. But not all this material made its way to Stalin. Important material that might have irritated him seems to have been suppressed. This includes the minutes of a British Cabinet meeting on 22 September 1948 in which Bevin pressed for a hardline attitude, on the ground that any other decision would lead to a general onset of appeasement and further retreats on other issues.

Even if the Soviets had enjoyed an effective means of integrating their impressive raw intelligence into Stalin's policy-making, there were serious obstacles. Much of what the Soviets wanted to know about the West fell into the category of 'mysteries' rather than secrets. During the Berlin Crisis, both London and Washington themselves lacked reliable information on how effective the airlift was, reflecting uncertainty even in the Western camp about whether it was going to be a success. This uncertainty may have encouraged Stalin to wait out the winter in the hope that it failed. Moreover, agent material was nearly always devalued by being up to a month late, reflecting an awkward compromise between the urgency of 'hot' information during a crisis and the dangers of exposing a valuable agent through frequent contact with a controller. Throughout the Berlin Crisis and on into the early 1950s, many secret issues in the West continued to be an open book to the Soviets, but the reports that reached Moscow were often recent history, rather than news.[7]

Agents such as Burgess and Maclean were probably valuable in terms of their ability to interpret the mindsets of London and Washington. This value increased with the outbreak of the Korean War. Maclean, then head of the North American Department in the Foreign Office, was in an ideal position to offer the Soviets an intimate picture of serious Anglo-American tensions. His Soviet handler, Yuri Modin, claims that Maclean gave Moscow a full account of the crucial Truman–Attlee summit of December 1950 when they confronted recent rumblings about the possible use of the atomic bomb. Maclean was a long-term critic of what he saw as the aggressiveness of American Cold War policy and was unlikely to have played this issue down in his reports.

But we have little idea of what Stalin really made of these remarkable windows into Western thinking. Some of the Soviet intelligence files have made their way to the West, either through the remarkable Mitrokhin Archive, or because valiant intelligence historians have bargained like rug merchants in the corridors of Moscow to obtain their release. But the papers of Stalin's own Commissariat – the only intelligence customer in Moscow that really mattered – are still closed. Despite the end of the Cold War we are still unsure whether the superb material gathered by Moscow's prize agents allowed Stalin to see more clearly, or alternatively served to feed his paranoia. The initial indications seem to suggest the latter. All governments distort the information they receive. These distortions occur either because of bureaucratic infighting, or because of fixed ideas that ensure that good information is rejected because it does not fit deep-rooted preconceptions. Stalin's government apparatus suffered from these twin pathologies to a greater degree than any other. Ideologically blinkered and shot through with vicious faction-fighting, it could not use information effectively. Its record as an intelligence machine at the outbreak of the Second World War was disastrous, and we have no reason to think that during the Cold War it fared any better. Perversely, good agents were sometimes suspected as plants and, as we have seen, Alexander Rado and Leopold Trepper, star wartime agents of the Red Orchestra, were recalled in 1945 and placed in the Gulag. Kim Philby, the Soviet agent in SIS who finally defected in 1963, also fell under suspicion. It is hard to escape the feeling that the remarkable espionage of Burgess, Maclean, Philby and many others, while seemingly impressive to observers in the West, may not have counted for quite so much in the East.[8]

The work of the moles and defectors had more impact in the West than in the East. It damaged Anglo-American relations, accelerated the onset of security screening and, most importantly, by generating public interest in espionage began to dissolve the barriers of secrecy which the British government had carefully erected to avoid public knowledge of the secret state. In late 1950, the Cabinet was still pondering a more draconian system of scrutiny screening, what we now know as positive vetting, in the wake of the Klaus Fuchs case. The United States was pressing for this to be taken up in Britain and combined with the use of the polygraph, a step recommended to the Prime Minister by British officials. The Burgess and Maclean defections persuaded Washington to increase the pressure. In July 1951 it called a further Tripartite Security Conference together with the Canadians, in London, and argued strongly for positive vetting to be introduced in Britain. Once again Attlee asked the civil servant, John Winnifrith, to lead a working party to review the recommendations of the Tripartite Security Conference in detail. It had already been decided to adopt positive vetting in the Atomic Energy Division of the Ministry of Supply, but what mattered was the pressure to extend it more widely. In 1950, Attlee and the Cabinet Subversion Committee had been anxious to limit positive vetting to ensure that its existence 'should be a jealously guarded secret'. Its extension would blow the system wide open, inviting serious public criticism. But this mattered less now because of the Burgess and Maclean affair, which had 'shaken public opinion' and reconciled the British to the need to take some steps to protect vital secrets. Britain's desire for American atomic secrets, locked away by the McMahon Act of 1946, was the critical issue. Winnifrith put the question very frankly:

> We want the American Atomic secrets and we won't get them unless they modify the McMahon Act. Officials have already offered the procedure now proposed and nothing short of that offer – and the direct question to the candidate about Communist associations is from the Americans' point of view a *sine qua non* – will secure their co-operation. It is fair to add that, even if we confirm the offer, there is no guarantee that the McMahon Act will be modified and that we will get their Atomic Secrets.

Looking at the positive vetting issue again, Attlee's officials concluded that, if adopted, it could no longer be confined to atomic issues only. All 'vital posts' in Whitehall would have to be dealt with on this basis, opening up a seemingly limitless purview for intrusive security enquiries.

The Chiefs of Staff were among the foremost in pressing for the acceleration of the domestic Cold War. In June 1951 they warned of a most insidious 'Fifth Column' in Britain using the techniques that 'rotted France before 1940'. They wanted aggressive vetting and urged that 'this involves being increasingly tough with internal Communist subversive activities' within Britain.[9] However, in August 1951, Clement Attlee balked again. Although Lord Portal, in his last days as Controller of Atomic Energy, argued that American doubts about British security would prove disastrous, others were not convinced. The Cabinet Subversion Committee recommended only a minimum adoption of positive vetting for new staff with access to atomic energy information only. It would not apply more widely in the civil service or to civilian contractors and university staff in sensitive posts. The issue was then left to full Cabinet for a final decision.[10]

On 9 October 1951, Lieutenant-General 'Freddy' Morgan, Portal's replacement, held conversations with American officials. He conceded that 'the thing which bothered him most about his set-up was the security situation'. He was desperate for the introduction of positive vetting to restore his credibility with Allied partners. Although he had personally agreed to revised security procedures at the recent Tripartite Security talks in London in July, he had to confess that Cabinet had not given approval. The changes, he explained, had 'important internal political potentialities'. He gave his private opinion that 'nothing would be done before the elections', but remained optimistic that no matter which party won, the situation would be very quickly cleared up after the elections were over.[11] Morgan was wrong. As we have seen, Attlee accepted positive vetting at one of the very last Cabinet meetings of his government. He was propelled by an additional factor, a growing personal conviction that organised communism had been behind some of the strikes and union trouble that had plagued his government in 1950.

The defection of Burgess and Maclean not only helped to introduce positive vetting, it also prompted Whitehall to consider additional security measures, including some FBI-type police powers for MI5, a major departure from British practice. The problem was how to stop suspects fleeing while the net was closing and evidence for a prosecution was being gathered. This was very much a problem related to Venona material, which could point the finger at a suspect but could not deliver a prosecution. There would always be a danger of the suspects fleeing while more conventional evidence was being gathered through surveillance or interrogation. In August 1952, the Home Secretary, David Maxwell Fyfe, secured Churchill's permission to set up a group chaired by Norman Brook and including Sir Percy Sillitoe, head of MI5, to examine this problem. It looked at new powers for MI5, especially the idea of allowing it to issue orders that a particular individual be detained if they tried to leave the country. But after due consideration the group decided that 'dangerous characters with treacherous intentions' would leave by unorthodox routes, perhaps even boarding a Soviet cargo ship in the Port of London, and would not risk being arraigned at an obvious point of exit. Meanwhile innocent persons would be held up. So the idea was dropped.[12]

Burgess and Maclean propelled positive vetting from the narrow arena of atomic weapons into all 'sensitive' occupations across Whitehall, including all senior diplomats and civil servants, and into defence-related industry. The Cabinet Subversion Committee had originally estimated that vetting would encompass no more than 1,000 people. But by the 1980s it had grown to 68,000. Despite the expansion of numbers, positive vetting never took on the ferocity of equivalent procedures in the United States. In part this reflected the determination of Whitehall to retain control of the security process and MI5's determination to avoid the tedium of carrying this process out. The declared number of persons dismissed, 124 civil servants in the period 1948–54, was low. This probably under-represents the impact in two ways. First, vetting prevented the employment of many others, and as the years passed it was at the entry point that the biggest impact of vetting was felt, although it did not show up in the figures. Secondly, there is some evidence that many others were removed in industry and peripheral areas by means of informal pressure and pretextual dismissal. MPs knew little and were told less of these matters.[13]

By 1956, arbitrary actions by security vetters had led to the Campaign for the Limitation of Secret Police Powers. This arose out of a case in 1951 when John Lang, a solicitor with ICI, was sacked because in the course of his job he handled confidential documents relating to work for the Ministry of Supply and was married to a member of the Communist Party. There were public protest marches led by figures such as Nye Bevan and Barbara Castle and the matter was raised at the Labour Party conference. One result of the uproar over the Lang case was the belated extension of the limited safeguards already enjoyed by civil servants to those working in industry if they wished to appeal. However, Ministers denied Lang permission for a retrospective appeal.[14]

How great was the impact of Burgess and Maclean in the United States? The long-term impact of the defectors upon Anglo-American relations was damaging but not devastating. Compartmentalisation meant that many co-operative transatlantic activities continued undisturbed. Moreover, Burgess and Maclean were soon joined by German, French and American spies and defectors who seemed to even the score. Indeed William Weisband, the American mole who undermined the Western sigint effort comprehensively, had only been uncovered a year before. For those who had enjoyed direct contact with Burgess and Maclean, the shock was clearly great and some American officials certainly felt 'tainted' by past association with them. For some the impact was unavoidable. Donald Maclean's sister Nancy was married to an American diplomat serving as an information officer at the US Embassy in Beirut, and he was immediately dismissed from the service as a security risk. Maclean's younger brother Alan, employed in the News Department at the Foreign Office, was urged by his superiors to resign and reluctantly did so.[15]

General Douglas MacArthur, now controversially removed from his command and politically active in the United States, chose to blame some of his reverses, notably at Inchon, upon sabotage by the British diplomatic spies, perhaps in the Washington Embassy. In retrospect this seems improbable. Sir Oliver Franks, the British Ambassador in Washington, was informed about the Inchon landings only on the eve of their launch, and news then had to filter through the Embassy. Most military information in the Washington Embassy was handled by its military wing – the British Joint Services Mission under William Elliott – and did not pass through diplomats. By comparison, information about the landings was readily available in Japan, the main rear area for the operation, and where the leader of a group of North Korean agents was captured with precisely this information a full week before the landings. Even before the Inchon landings were launched they had been dubbed 'Operation Common Knowledge' by staff officers in Japan. The most damaging accusations related to the leaks about Western reaction to Chinese intervention in the war, but in fact Maclean arrived from Cairo to take up his new position in London too late to be able to report on this. Later, however, as head of the American Department in the Foreign Office, he was able to inform Moscow about the troubled subject of Anglo-American–Commonwealth relations during the war and wrangles over atomic issues. Burgess also saw sensitive material, including intelligence reports of the extent of Soviet assistance to the Chinese Army in 1950, but it is unlikely that any of this was strategically decisive.[16]

American impressions mattered a great deal and rumours about the devastating impact of Burgess and Maclean upon American performance in the Korean War continued to circulate during the 1950s. In 1956 *The Times* claimed to have obtained a damage assessment compiled by the US State Department. This suggested that Burgess and Maclean were aware of the American determination not to advance into Manchuria, not to blockade the China coast and not to use nuclear weapons. In the 1970s this line was still being repeated by senior CIA officers. Peer de Silva, who had been CIA station chief at several locations in Asia, observed that these 'well placed agents have constituted a bleeding stomach wound to American policies and strategies. Our intentions were known to the Soviets and, emboldened by what they knew, they carried on their own strategies and actions with guaranteed impunity.'[17]

Dean Acheson, the Secretary of State, and Walter Bedell Smith, Director of the CIA, were alarmed by the British defections for several reasons. Beyond the real impact on internal security there was the wider problem of growing public paranoia, which needed no further encouragement. In the early 1950s government departments in Washington were under a veritable siege from McCarthyism. Anyone with a background in the 1930s that had liberal or social democratic aspects was in severe danger. This applied not only to the State Department but even to the front-line Cold War agencies. The CIA was full of East Coast liberals and intellectuals who had been recruited by Donovan during the campus-hunting days of the early 1940s. Indeed J. Edgar Hoover had successfully excluded the CIA from knowledge of the Venona programme until 1952, because of fears about left liberals taken into OSS during the war who were now in the CIA. Cord Meyer, who had replaced Tom Braden as head of the CIA's innovative and daring International Organisations Division, found himself dragged before the security hearings in Washington.[18]

Some CIA programmes were very vulnerable, including Cord Meyer's vast radio propaganda programmes, with their many Central and East European staff. Most broadcasters and writers for organisations like Radio Liberty and Radio Free Europe had spent their youth in Central and Eastern Europe and had belonged to social democratic parties. 'McCarthy picked on them,' recalled one senior staff member, and so it affected the programme 'very, very directly and very severely'. McCarthy and his henchman, Roy Cohn, stalked their building creating a 'poisonous atmosphere' and recruiting a 'loyal underground' within the building who informed on their colleagues. Paranoia was enhanced because of the Stalinist upbringing of many of the staff. The result was two suicides, including the chief of the VOA's Rumanian Service.[19]

Americans who had explored the possibility of co-operation between the United States and Asian communists were similarly persecuted. Among the more famous were the diplomats Owen Lattimore and John Paton Davis. The former found refuge as an academic at the University of Leeds in Britain, while the latter eventually escaped persecution by fleeing to Peru where he set up a small carpentry business. Curiously, these sorts of figures who had made contact with the communists in the 1940s became useful in maintaining the illusion of no direct contact in the 1950s. One American ambassador recalls a phase of the Geneva Conference in 1954:

> we were around the big table with the Communist groups on one side ... But an awful lot of the real negotiations didn't take place then. It took place between ourselves, and others, in the corridors, and so forth. We did not have a lot of contact with the Chinese. We had a fellow from the CIA who was on our delegation ... He was a Colonel who had been with Chou En-lai in Yenan, who maintained a certain amount of contact on a covert basis – not covert from our point of view – but covert from the press ... so we could also be sure they got the message ...[20]

Moles and defectors have tended to be seen in an Anglo-American frame, but they also had an important European dimension. European security brought problems, but it also offered a degree of mutual reassurance, since London and Washington considered each other to be penetrated, but less so than their allies on the continent. London certainly worked harder to disguise the nature of the Burgess and Maclean defection in 1951 because of its growing European security responsibilities. MI5 cornered the job of supervising NATO security arrangements. In early 1950 the British security team at NATO was haughtily declaring the Portuguese delegation to be 'completely unsatisfactory' from a security point of view when news of the Klaus Fuchs affair broke. Charles Donnelly, the American Secretary of the NATO Defence Committee, recalled that all of a sudden the British delegation was looked at in a new light. The British MI5 team did not want to repeat this uncomfortable experience.[21]

In October 1951, a major counter-intelligence conference was held at SHAPE. Its purpose was to plan for a 'civil security and counter-espionage' organisation within this tripartite command that would function in both peace and war. It would also help to direct security matters within subordinate Allied Commands working under Eisenhower and would liaise with NATO's Standing Group on security issues, including communications security. It was to be a large organisation with its own file registry within SHAPE, the hallmark of any serious security organism, and Britain was to play a leading part.[22] MI5 already had effective control of NATO security. The Council of Deputies now recommended 'a NATO Security Committee with headquarters in London'. Hitherto these functions had been carried out by the Military Committee of Standing Group. The role of MI5 remained strong because some countries, including Belgium, did not like being policed by military officers and wished for a security element with a more civilian complexion.[23]

Security problems within SHAPE and NATO were relatively simple compared to the problem of moles in Germany and Austria. By 1949, MI5 was helping to construct a German version of itself – a new West German Security Service. The key figures here were Guy Liddell of MI5, James Fulton of SIS and Major-General Charles Haydon, who was Tubby Lethbridge's successor as head of ID and later joined SIS. Setting up the new service was not just a question of relations between Britain and the emerging West Germany. Liddell explained to the Chiefs of Staff that it could not be considered in isolation from the problems of Soviet moles and penetration which abounded in Germany: 'There was a danger that the Americans might press for the new German security service to be built up around the framework of the security service already established in the American zone. This should be strongly resisted as it was clear that this American organisation had been penetrated by Soviet agents.' All this was being taken up in Germany with French and American representatives, who had an equally dim view of the security of British organisations.[24]

MI5 tried to avoid responsibility for German developments as it was overburdened by the growing requirements of vetting and by apparently boundless colonial insurgency in the Middle East, Africa and Asia. The UK High Commissioner in Germany, General Robertson, wanted Dick

White of MI5 together with staff from SIS to come out and discuss the technicalities of establishing the new security service with him, noting that White had already been out for preliminary discussions. Guy Liddell protested that MI5 was swamped with 'other commitments' and it would be difficult to find an experienced MI5 officer to oversee this process. But the JIC insisted that it was of the 'greatest importance' that both MI5 and SIS were involved and told Liddell that if necessary other MI5 projects might have to be 'retarded'. Germany was trying to wriggle free of intelligence control. London agreed that the Germans were likely to try and 'neutralise' the value of the British liaison officers with the new German service to maximise German independence. It decided that, whatever the outcome, existing security records in the British Zone would 'remain in British hands'. The problems were complex, for the British were trying to enforce the British MI5–Special Branch model on the Germans, to whom it was alien. One difficulty was deciding how many concessions to make to the Germans to prevent them setting up a clandestine service of their own of which the British might know little.[25]

Despite his protests it was a weary Guy Liddell who went to Germany for detailed discussions on the new German security service. The most awkward aspect of the problem was the relationship between the new service and the police. MI5 wanted the security service to be able to exercise strategic direction in important cases. The instrument they arrived at was called the Federal Office for the Protection of the Constitution or BfV. For the British this was a success. In the foreign intelligence field they had been losing ground to the Americans and their protégé, Reinhard Gehlen. But in the security field the British were able to put their own candidate, Otto John, in place. Although they dominated German security, they were never confident of its security or its effectiveness, complaining that, partly due to the 'German character', the BfV was 'unable to be as secure as, say, the British'. Their faith in the BfV was further undermined in 1952, when Otto John was involved in what appeared to be a brief defection to the East. While John soon fled back to the West, his credibility and indeed that of his organisation was fatally compromised.[26]

Germany and Austria were nightmare areas of potential Soviet penetration for which the senior officers of MI5 were determined to avoid responsibility at all costs. There was the added nightmare of neo-Nazi groups, which were still being rounded up in late 1953. In MI5's view the Attlee Doctrine, which limited its activities to British sovereign territories, was an invaluable protection from limitless security work in these two countries, where the danger of Soviet penetration was very high. By 1951, with the expansion of espionage activity by a range of Eastern bloc services, the numbers of communist agents on the ground in Germany and Austria was enormous. Two spy-rings, involving over 100 agents, had been uncovered in Austria, and a number of British NCOs had been sentenced for selling information. The temptations were considerable, since the sum of £4,000 had recently been offered for mundane documents relating to a training exercise.

The British Director of Military Intelligence, General Shortt, was in the front line and was feeling the pressure. He explained that his own Army Field Security teams were 'somewhat apprehensive of what they are going to uncover next' and were 'convinced that they are only on the fringe of the problem and have many leads'. There were 5,000 low-level Eastern bloc agents in their area; meanwhile British officers and other ranks in Vienna were 'overspending and gambling' and the end result was not hard to predict. A high-level mole was feared and British commanders in Austria had ordered a discreet purge of all officers with wives who had connections behind the Iron Curtain. SIS had already lent one of its officers, Captain Tilley, to conduct interrogations of the British Army personnel involved with the Czech Intelligence Service. Shortt now wrote to Sillitoe pleading for permanent MI5 representation in Austria. He warned of the 'great activity among the large number of small-time agents in that area'. He added darkly that his officers were 'strongly of the opinion' that Army Field Security, with its limited resources and lack of experienced personnel, 'had only scraped the surface of the problem'. But MI5 was not interested and was 'suffering as much as anyone from shortage of officers'. It sheltered behind the fact that its charter did not cover such countries. MI5 officers were always stationed in Gibraltar but not in hot-beds of Soviet activity like Vienna.[27]

The Americans were also feeling the pressure in Germany and Austria. Like Otto John, their own protégé, Reinhard Gehlen, who had led the reconstruction of a German offensive espionage capability against the Soviet Union, was soon undermined by Soviet penetration. Gehlen's stock with the CIA station at Munich had been falling since the late 1940s, but he remained credible in the absence of alternatives. Then in 1954 the Heinz Felfe case broke in Germany. Felfe had served as an SS Obersturmführer and Kriminalkommissar towards the end of the war. In 1946 he was released from a British POW camp and then 'worked for the British, circa 1948, against the KPD' or German Communist Party. By 1950 he was employed by the German Interior Ministry and in 1951 he transferred to the Gehlen Organisation's department III-F in Karlsruhe before moving out to Gehlen's Munich HQ. Felfe was uncovered by a security review after the comprehensive rolling up of Gehlen's largest Berlin network in 1954. East Germany boasted of its success, publishing the full organisational chart of the Gehlen service in the newspapers. This included details that only a few individuals knew and the finger soon pointed at Felfe. A careful check revealed how cases he had been working on had mysteriously 'fizzled out'. Moreover, he had recruited sub-agents and these were still being identified as late as 1961. A realisation that many key organisations in Germany were heavily penetrated by the East not only put British lapses in a better light, it also encouraged the shift towards more technical intelligence-gathering.[28]

Here, at the operational level, moles were costly in terms of lives and information. Somewhat later, a Hungarian intelligence officer defected to the Austrians and asked to be put in touch with the local CIA station in Vienna. Owing to fears of a Soviet attempt on his life, the Austrians agreed to hold him in maximum security accommodation. Only two days before he was due to be transferred to the United States, 'this man was found writhing on the floor of his room, crying out in agony and screaming that he had been poisoned'. He died quickly. Because access to this defector had been so strictly limited, the subsequent enquiry pointed inescapably to one Austrian security police official who later proved to be in the employ of the Czech intelligence services. This man had been the principal Austrian security liaison with the CIA throughout the 1950s. Burgess, Maclean and Philby fitted a much wider pattern of penetration in the West, though they were among the more famous examples.[29]

Defections by Soviet intelligence officers to the West were sometimes no more welcome than departures for the East. Those in Whitehall concerned with security certainly hoped for this sort of traffic, as it offered the best chance of uncovering further Soviet moles in their own secret services. George Blake, Moscow's top agent in SIS during the 1950s, was uncovered by the defection to the Americans in 1959 of a senior Polish intelligence officer, who provided enough information for Blake to be identified by 1961. But many in Westminster considered Soviet defectors to be unwelcome because of the attendant publicity and the damage to East–West relations that was often caused. The defector war, with its circus of press conferences designed to encourage others to follow, sat uneasily with the hopes of Churchill and Eden to reach some sort of deal on coexistence with Stalin's successors. Between the end of the Second World War and the death of Stalin in 1953 there had been no significant defection from Soviet intelligence. Suddenly, in 1954, there were five such defections. In the first months of that year Soviet intelligence officers defected to the CIA in Toyko and in Vienna. In April two more defected to the Australians. Early 1954 had also seen a Soviet intelligence officer called Nikolai Khokhlov fall into the hands of SIS in Germany.

Khokhlov had been tasked with the assassination of one of the leading Eastern bloc émigrés based in Germany called Georgi Sergeevich Okolovich. This task was designated Operation Rhine and followed a familiar pattern of Soviet efforts against émigré organisations which stretched back into the pre-war period. In the 1920s and the 1930s, the main émigré organisation in Western Europe had been penetrated, and senior members who could not be lured back to the Soviet Union were often assassinated.[30] The intended victim in Germany worked closely with SIS in Berlin. His SIS contact was the young Gervase Cowell, who found himself looking after émigré organisations on one of his first overseas postings to Germany. One day in early 1954, Okolovich telephoned Cowell and explained that a major in Soviet intelligence had just visited him and had confessed that he had been sent by Moscow to assassinate him. However, the Major, Nikolai Khokhlov, had lost heart and instead sat down to have a cup of tea with his intended victim. An SIS team was quickly despatched to pick up Khokhlov's two henchmen, who were carrying the weapons: 'We finally intercepted the weapons which were quite horrifying. They were cyanide bullets, disguised inside a cigarette packet, firing completely silently, penetrating a wooden plank of three inches at about ten feet.' Cowell was awed by the weapon when it was tested. Developed in a special KGB weapons laboratory it was state of the art and was fired by electricity. He later recalled that now 'if anyone offers me a cigarette I sway slightly backwards!'

Not to be outdone by their Soviet captives, and 'trying to keep our end up', Cowell showed to the KGB team SIS's own killing weapon, 'a massive sleeve gun'. But this proved to be a disappointment. It was a noisy antique compared to the sleek Soviet equipment and could not be used for a discreet killing. 'You could only fire if a locomotive happened to be leaving Frankfurt station at the time,' he remembered, because it 'let off this enormous clang' and threatened to dislocate the shoulder of the person who risked firing it. It was not a weapon of choice. SIS was bothered by the 'tremendous advance' the Soviets had made with 'really nasty toys'. The British had nothing like them. They were equally alarmed by the sophistication of the agents that the Soviets had sent and the persistence of their operations, since Khokhlov was an impressive and resourceful individual and no mere thug. Moreover, Moscow persevered and once it knew that he had defected to SIS it tried to kill him with a bottle of Coca-Cola containing prussic acid, and failed only by a narrow margin.[31]

Khokhlov's defection presented London with an awkward problem on the eve of the crucial Geneva Conference of 1954. By 1 May, Nikolai Khokhlov was *en route* to Britain and senior officials such as Sir John Rennie of IRD, together with junior Foreign Office Ministers like Anthony Nutting, were keen for him to give a press conference, which was bound to generate public excitement. They emphasised that this was the fifth defection of a Soviet intelligence officer in the previous two months and, although these people were 'despicable', they wanted more defections. For the first time the West was putting real pressure on the vast Soviet spy system. In a meeting with Churchill they explained that they also wanted 'to obtain information about possible traitors who might still be working in the British services' and so hoped to use the press conference to encourage further defections. Churchill did not like the idea and feared it would wreck the Geneva Conference. He argued that there was little corroboration for Khohklov's statements and to allow him to speak would be 'make a hero out of the traitor'. Moreover to parade him at such a moment 'was tantamount to arousing anti-Russian hate'. He was 'totally opposed to any press conference' and forbade it without even consulting Anthony Eden, the Foreign Secretary. All the Nutting team could extract from Churchill was his agreement to expel two Soviet intelligence officers from the London Embassy who had simultaneously been caught trying to recruit service officers with the usual clumsy mixture of bribery and blackmail.[32]

Churchill's response to the Khokhlov case underlines the fact that moles and defectors were probably more important in the public realm of propaganda and public perception than in the secret world of intelligence. In late 1954, a spy case in Australia which involved the defection of two Soviet intelligence officers, Vladimir and Evdokia Petrov, ensured that more details about Burgess and Maclean seeped into the public domain and as a result there was a furore in Britain. The outcome was a climate of revelation and an erosion of public trust in government secrecy as it became clear that much had been withheld to avoid ministerial embarrassment. Wartime attitudes that had inculcated a deep acceptance of the need for opaqueness were replaced with a growing public cynicism. There was also a transformation in the public perception of British secret service. During the inter-war years and in wartime the myth of an omnipotent and omniscient British secret service had abounded, especially in the United States, but this was now being replaced by a reputation for ineptitude and bumbling. More broadly, press and the British public began to develop a taste for revelations in this area which, by the time of Profumo Affair in 1963, would become a rip-tide.[33]

The story of Burgess and Maclean slipped out into the public domain only by degrees. In mid-1955, four years after their escape, the defection of Vladimir Petrov, a KGB officer in Australia, gave the press sensational new material on the two British diplomats. Hitherto the public had taken them to be 'missing diplomats' and dissolute homosexuals who were on the run. But now the Australian press revealed them to be long-term Soviet agents and suggested there were further traitors inside Whitehall. The new Prime Minister, Anthony Eden, was forced to make a statement in Parliament and to publish a White Paper. It was now clear to the public that Burgess and Maclean had been tipped off by a 'third man', and Kim

Philby's name was mentioned in this connection in Parliament. The era of the search for Stalin's numerical Englishmen, a third, then a fourth and finally a fifth man began to catch the public imagination. The hunt was on, and was further encouraged by the Soviets, who now presented Burgess and Maclean to the world at a spectacular press conference in Moscow.

Herbert Morrison, who had replaced Bevin as Foreign Secretary in the previous administration in March 1951 and had confronted the original defections in May that year, led the pressure in the House of Commons for a public enquiry. Macmillan, a deeply Edwardian figure who disliked public revelation, and who was now, briefly, Eden's Foreign Secretary, told the Cabinet that these sorts of open enquiries would be useless, even 'dangerous'. He feared the rapid growth of public interest in the secret services, something he would himself encounter during the Profumo Affair eight years later: 'Nothing could be worse than a lot of muckraking and innuendo. It would be like one of those immense divorce cases which there used to be when I was young, going on for days and days, every detail reported in the Press.' Instead the Cabinet opted for a closed enquiry by a judge, in the event Lord Radcliffe, followed by a carefully drafted White Paper.[34]

Understandably Morrison smelt a rat. He suspected he had not been told everything by officials at the time. Not content with pressing for a public enquiry, he also made private investigations among his friends. Anthony Blake had lunched with Donald Maclean at his club the day before he disappeared. Blake told Morrison that Maclean's whole attitude had been very relaxed and he was sure he had been tipped off some time after and at very short notice. He added that he was also sure that the White Paper was wrong about the limited nature of Maclean's communist background, as he was confident that Maclean had been a communist as a student and many knew that he had attended Party meetings. 'It always surprised me that on leaving Cambridge he suddenly decided to go into the FO, after apparently losing his Communist enthusiasms.'[35]

When Philby defected to the Soviet Union in 1963, Morrison was still agonising over the Burgess and Maclean episode. He then insisted that the Foreign Office write to him setting out what he had, and had not, been told in 1951. When he had arrived at the Foreign Office that year the work of investigating leaks to the Soviets from Washington or New York in 1944 and 1945, revealed by Venona, had been going on for more than two years. In mid-April 1951, Maclean had been identified as the most likely of a number of possible candidates and on 17 April Strang, the Permanent Under-Secretary, broke the news to Morrison and suggested that Maclean's background be delved into by MI5. But matters proceeded at a leisurely pace and on 25 May the Foreign Office proposed that Maclean should be interviewed by MI5 'between June 18 and 25'. On the same evening, 25 May, Maclean was already making his escape. Morrison was clearly not told about Venona at the time or subsequently. Knowledge of Venona had been kept to a very small circle and even President Truman seems to have been unaware of its existence. Understandably, therefore, Morrison remained puzzled as to why MI5 had watched Maclean for four weeks without making a move. He was equally incensed by the fact that it was four days before he was told that Burgess and Maclean had flown. More importantly, as the Foreign Office conceded in 1963: 'We have no indication that Mr Morrison was ever told, while Foreign Secretary, that Philby was suspected of having tipped off Maclean. Nor was the financial settlement made to Philby when he resigned in July 1951, mentioned to Mr Morrison.'[36]

Although MI5 believed that Philby had tipped off Maclean, many in SIS had protested his innocence. Although publicly cleared in 1955 by Harold Macmillan, in reality he had been forced to leave SIS under a cloud in 1951 and, after a long period of unemployment, eventually found work in his old inter-war cover-trade as a journalist. In 1956 he became the shared Beirut correspondent for the *Economist* and the *Observer*. This was encouraged by SIS and the Foreign Office, which told his new employers that Philby had had a bad time, had been treated unfairly and needed a break. The *Economist* was delighted. It had acquired an experienced foreign correspondent at a bargain price in a region that was hotting up. SIS 're-employed' Philby on a part-time basis in the hope of bringing his case to a conclusion and proving his guilt or innocence beyond doubt. He arrived in Beiruit in September 1956 just in time to provide most of the *Economist* coverage of the Suez Crisis. Surprisingly, he initially claimed to be pro-intervention. In Cairo, the *Economist* had commanded only the crumbs of a press agency stringer, who was in any case expelled along with all other foreign journalists as the crisis developed. Philby, whose father was Harry St John Philby, the famous Arabist, was 'very well connected' and was able to 'fill the breach'. The authorised history of the *Economist* asserts that 'Philby was indeed valuable and produced good material, for which *The Economist* collected some *kudos*.' However by the late 1950s he had begun to drink more heavily, becoming unreliable and 'slipshod'. His expense claims began to outrun his productivity and the London office was somewhat relieved when he headed for Moscow in 1963.[37]

Despite working together with the United States on Venona, London had still told Washington as little as possible about its problems with Soviet penetration. The press furore and the White Paper of 1955 revealed their seriousness for the first time to many in Washington. Nevertheless the reaction was remarkably muted and in October 1955, when Admiral Radford reviewed the real situation for the US Joint Chiefs of Staff, he found things largely unchanged since 1951, when little had been done. Even now he was more concerned about hostile press questions than about the reality of protecting security. Radford explained to his colleagues that Burgess and Maclean had been Soviet agents for many years prior to their defection and had been 'protected from exposure and dismissal for a long time by other highly placed officials' in Whitehall, 'particularly in the Foreign Office'. It was also apparent that 'all U.K. and possibly some U.S. diplomatic codes and ciphers in existence prior to 25 May 1951 are in possession of the Soviets' and were of no further use. Indeed, on that basis, almost any document generated before that date might well have been compromised. Radford also now realised that the circumstances surrounding the defection of Burgess and Maclean 'were known to certain U.S. officials in 1951', a discreet allusion to his predecessor General Omar Bradley. Yet, if confronted by the press or by Congress in 1955, Washington could 'show little or nothing in the way of positive action which has been taken either to correct past mistakes or prevent future repetition of these mistakes'. Recent renewal of interest in the defections raised the possibility that it might soon be faced with answering such questions. He was not sure what the answers would be.[38]

The reaction of Washington was always in London's mind when dealing with these issues. In January 1956, in the wake of the press outcry over Burgess and Maclean, senior officials in London had to consider the likely effect of the recent release of Allan Nunn May from prison. It was entirely possible that he might choose to defect to the Soviet bloc. The Atomic Energy Intelligence Committee was sure he now had no information of the remotest possible use. But the impact on American public opinion might hamper efforts to restore atomic co-operation. At the very least it felt he should be denied a passport and therefore forced to flee illegally. Encouraging his illegal departure would allow London to claim not to have aided and abetted his flight.[39] In the event he lived in Cambridge for some years before becoming professor of physics at the University of Ghana in 1962.

British information exchange with Washington was certainly becoming more difficult in 1955 and 1956, but the defectors were not directly responsible. In July 1956, the Chief of Air Intelligence, Air Vice Marshal William MacDonald, visited Washington and held off-the-record talks on information exchange. There was, he noted, a major attempt in Washington to tighten up on information given to foreign nationals. This was driven not by fear of moles, but by the fact that all military planning increasingly had an atomic dimension. Under the provisions of the McMahon Act it was simply illegal for Americans to hand over atomic-related information to foreigners on pain of prosecution. Intelligence continued to flow fairly freely, but other areas of exchange were being closed down. MacDonald's view was that this situation would improve only when the V-bombers – Britain's new generation of atomic strike aircraft – came on stream and Britain exploded its own hydrogen bomb. In the meantime he advised that London should respond equally sternly by tightening up on what was given to American officers in Britain.[40]

The British policy of admitting as little as possible about the nature of Soviet penetration, either publicly or to Britain's friends, or even to junior officials within Whitehall, was not unsuccessful, at least in the short term. It is hard to find evidence of substantial damage to Anglo-American intelligence relations before the 1960s, when an appreciation of the role of Philby genuinely shook Washington. The explanations for this policy of denial lie at several different levels. In part it was certainly instinctive, reflecting the age-old Whitehall tradition of obsessive secrecy. In the 1950s Britain maintained its reputation among its allies for stonewalling. When security issues appeared that London did not wish to talk about it would go to extraordinary lengths to avoid confronting them. This applied not only to the messy issue of moles and defectors but even to unpleasant legacies from the Second World War. Failed wartime SOE operations into Holland were a case in point. In the 1950s it was becoming clear that in Holland the SOE network had been badly penetrated by the German security services. By 1943 most radio traffic coming through the Dutch networks to London had been written by the Gestapo, and the scale of the secret service débâcle in Holland was gradually becoming apparent. Several post-war enquiries were launched in Holland and it was clear that dozens, if not hundreds, of lives had been lost to the Germans. An ugly situation, full of accusations and counter-accusations, rumbled on between the Dutch and the British for some years. Finally, in the spring of 1953, the Dutch Parliament decided to send a delegation of MPs to London to examine the archives relating to wartime underground activities. The Dutch delegation was determined upon a detailed reconstruction of SOE wartime operations into Holland. It was destined to be disappointed. The Dutch MPs were met by SIS officers, the inheritors of the SOE archive, who informed them with a straight face that, 'unfortunately, within the past few days there had been "a serious fire" in the MI6 archives'. The faces of the Dutch delegation were a picture as it was explained that 'By coincidence, all Dutch resistance records had been destroyed.' The Dutch MPs took the first flight back to the Hague, and an incensed Dutch government expelled the SIS head of station and all of his subordinates.[41]

But British behaviour over moles and defectors was the result of something more complex than compulsive denial. It was driven by a curious mixture of obsessive secrecy and a strong aversion to excessive security. Dealing effectively with the problem of moles seemed to point in the direction of American-style inquisitions and purges, which all sides viewed as expensive, distasteful and deeply 'unBritish'. No party wished to place such matters before Parliament against the background of the McCarthyism and the Rosenberg trials which had stirred up so much distaste in Europe. Moreover MI5 did not want the work of an expanded personnel security review, and the Treasury did not want to fund it. The lengthy episodes of Burgess and Maclean were rooted in a British schizophrenia which combined both a love of secrecy and a hatred of the secret state. Churchill in particular embodied a widely held attitude that the hidden hand was appropriate for use abroad against foreigners, but a more dubious instrument when deployed at home. Ministers continually hoped to keep domestic security measures so small that they could be concealed from the disapproving eyes of Parliament or civil service unions.[42]

Predictably, many who knew Philby, Burgess and Maclean maintained, with the benefit of hindsight, that it was always obvious that they were spies. In reality, Philby was a master dissembler whose mask rarely slipped, while the behaviour of Burgess was so outrageous that a stream of embarrassing misdemeanours continually obscured any assessment of him as a serious security risk. But in the case of Donald Maclean the strain certainly took its toll and periodically he felt the need to make surreal open declarations of his communist convictions, as if to reassure himself of his inviolability. Dutch diplomats recalled joining Maclean for a formal dinner at the Cairo Embassy in 1950. Conversation turned to the charges of spying for the Soviet Union that had been levelled at the American diplomat Alger Hiss. The Dutch were 'shocked and disgusted' to hear Maclean declare vigorously that if Hiss felt the way he did about communism he was quite right to betray his country. In Cairo, once inebriated, Maclean often became a violently argumentative champion of communism.[43]

Schizophrenic attitudes toward secrecy, together with antediluvian security practices, are helpful in explaining the British failure to identify these figures. But there is a great deal to explain and it has to be conceded that no substantive account convincingly fits the facts. The inner circle in Whitehall and Washington had long been aware of the mole problem. As early as 1943 Sir Stewart Menzies arrived in the office of Alexander Cadogan, the Permanent Under-Secretary, for a private chat. Menzies proceeded to warn Cadogan that 'I have Communists in my organisation.' A year later Whitehall was engaged in a small but secret purge to rid itself of those known to be communist.[44] The same situation prevailed in the United States. By 1943, US Army Intelligence had launched the highly secret DSM Project designed to investigate communist penetration of atomic projects in California, focused on the scientist Steve Nelson. The DSM Project was headed by Colonel Boris Pash, who would later direct sensitive work with atomic energy in occupied Germany and then with East European exile groups. But in 1943 his role was to lead a group of ten US Army Intelligence officers whose mission was to catch Soviets agents in the act of penetrating the Manhattan Project. The programme was jointly launched by General George V. Strong, the head of US Army Intelligence, and General Leslie Groves, who superintended the Manhattan Project. An 'undercover office' was to be set up in San Francisco with all the necessary facilities: 'Undercover agents or operatives will be established as rapidly as security permits within the Project at the Radiation Laboratory ... There will be established in San Francisco necessary mail covers, postal interceptions, and technical surveillance. Physical surveillance will be employed wherever necessary ... Complete technical surveillance and postal interception will be established at Santa Fe, New Mexico.' Rigorous security procedures were imposed to prevent communist penetration of the DSM Project itself. All those involved were to be vetted against the files of both US Army Intelligence and the FBI 'for Communist connections' and no agent was to be employed who had previously operated in the San Francisco area. The idea was for intelligence officers to join up with Communist Party agents and become part of their network. The whole operation was expected to last five or six months. The secrecy of the investigation was a matter of the 'first importance' and obtaining evidence of espionage was to be 'subordinated in every respect' to this first objective. Activation of the DSM Project was authorised by General Strong on 15 April 1943.[45]

It is likely that at some point London and Washington attempted to play back some of Moscow's agents along the lines of the wartime Doublecross operations, but came unstuck. Almost every other successful wartime tactic was emulated during the Cold War, and we now know that active deception teams continued beyond 1945 on both sides of the Atlantic. This activity was most likely focused on feeding suspected agents with deception materials about the scope and scale of the Western atomic weapons programmes, but it is highly unlikely that this was successful given that the West was unaware of the scale of Soviet penetration. Almost all the files of these post-war deception bodies remain closed and it may be decades before we are closer to the truth in this awkward area.[46]

What is quite clear is that, whether the West attempted deception or not, the East believed many of its best agents to be plants, in some cases precisely because of the high quality of the material they produced. Kim Philby, who was under suspicion in the West from 1951, certainly fell into this category. Ironically he had been under suspicion in the East even earlier; indeed in 1948 General F. N. Fitin of the MGB had conducted a full-scale loyalty investigation of Philby which remained on his file. Even Yuri Modin, Philby's sympathetic case officer, had his doubts: 'He was psychologically the complete British Secret Service officer. He looked like one. We thought he could never be anything else.' It is difficult to resist the conclusion that the extraordinary efforts of Burgess, Maclean, Philby and many other long-term agents, while individually impressive, may have been discounted in Moscow at moments when they were potentially most useful.[47] Ultimately, Moscow's agents presented more of a challenge to Britain's propagandists in the Information Research Department, who were charged with showing that the West was winning the Cold War, than they did to MI5.

Jerrold Schecter has offered one of the most penetrating commentaries on the fate of the moles and defectors. Between 1969 and 1970 Schecter was a foreign correspondent in Moscow based in an office on Kutuzovsky Prospekt close to Philby's residence:

> I never saw him, but one of the games correspondents played was Philby sightings. Was that him at the Bolshoi Ballet? Or at the House of Journalists? My wife said she saw a man in a sheepskin coat who looked like Philby on the street near our office. She stared hard at him. He noticed her, quickly averted his gaze and turned furtively in the opposite direction. My favourite Philby story quoted him as saying he had become bored with caviar.

Philby's legendary status owed much to the publication of his lugubrious memoirs in 1968, which crafted the picture of the master spy who had now departed to Moscow to enjoy living out his final years in the higher echelons of an elite service. But nothing could have been further from the truth. Philby was distrusted by Moscow and suffered permanent surveillance. Indeed, as he was believed to be a double agent, he was kept under virtual house arrest and never rose above the humble status of agent. His private life was characterised by alcoholism, self-doubt, despair and indeed attempted suicide. His fortunes rose briefly in the mid-1970s when the head of the KGB Yuri Andropov ordered his conditions to be improved, for fear that the reality of the fate of defectors was putting off others who might flee to the East. But by 1980 Philby was once again a neglected figure and his treatment during his last illness in a KGB hospital was lamentable. Only when he was safely cocooned in death did the KGB feel confident enough to promote the myth of a 'KGB general'. The truth was that Philby made it through the doors of the KGB officers' club only as a corpse to lie in state for his funeral.[48]

20

At Home and Abroad: The Information Research Department

A general report was made ... regarding the extension of anti-Communist propaganda activities by the Labour Party organisation.
Cabinet Committee meeting chaired by Attlee[1]

If MI5 was Britain's overstretched defensive shield against communist moles and subversion then the Foreign Office's Information Research Department or IRD was its offensive sword. In the 1950s IRD worked closely with its numerous American counterparts in the State Department and also the International Organisations Department of the CIA against a remarkable range of targets. Important characteristics were shared from the outset by these vast British and American information campaigns. Although they were designed to join battle with communism in the wider world, they soon found that they were required to battle communism on the home front. IRD in particular undertook some extraordinary interventions on the British domestic scene in areas such as student affairs and trade union politics, and the CIA eventually followed suit. This was a direct response to MI5's analysis of the main dangers presented by the Communist Party of Great Britain or CPGB. The communists, it insisted, would never become a mainstream political party as it had done in France and Italy. But it consistently warned the British Cabinet that CPGB had adopted an alarming strategy of entryism into the trade union movement, often flagrantly falsifying ballot papers. It had abundant evidence of malpractice. Within months of IRD's formation in January 1948, George Isaacs, the Minister of Labour, urged a select Cabinet Committee discussing anti-communism that one 'of the most urgent tasks was to organise effective opposition to the election of Communists to key positions in the Executives of the Unions'.[2]

MI5 warned the Cabinet that CPGB's aim was 'to secure control of each individual union and, through the unions, of the General Council and the Annual Assembly of the Trade Union Congress, potent forces in political life'. CPGB had already made astonishing progress towards this objective, a fact that was all the more surprising given that only 30,000 of the 8.7 million trade union members in Britain were communists. This had occurred because of the 'apathy' of the majority of non-communist trade unionists. Meanwhile each union contained an active 'Communist faction' taking orders from CPGB headquarters. MI5 referred to 'a recent ballot of the Boilermaker's Society, when out of a membership of some 80,000 only 4,000 voted and the Communists secured the revocation of a rule forbidding Party members to hold Office in the union'. There was clear evidence of CPGB contravention of the rules, with many signed blank ballot forms on which the name was later 'filled in at Party headquarters'. This sort of activity alarmed Attlee, and, although IRD had been conceived as an instrument of foreign policy, competition with CPGB for the soul of the British trade union movement was soon one of its main tasks. This required IRD to work closely with the labour movement, and Clement Attlee decided he would organise this personally with the Labour Party headquarters machine.[3]

This delicate work necessitated a curious mélange of government and private activity. As the Cold War revealed itself to be a war between societies rather than states, secret service had to follow its quarry on to a broader terrain. The main vehicle for this was the state–private network. Oddly, some of the most important secret service of this period was conducted not by government at all, but by private individuals and non-government groups. This theme was reinforced by the development of a wider remit, for although developed as a response to communist propaganda, at home and abroad, both British and American propaganda organisations quickly found non-communist targets.[4] IRD was soon battling anything that was viewed as anti-British, and in the mid-1950s one of its key opponents was Colonel Gamal Abdel Nasser's aggressive pan-Arab nationalism. IRD's Washington counterparts were widening their own activities and countering anything that appeared anti-American. As early as December 1947, the National Security Council had set out the remit for new propaganda organisations and had talked not of responding to communism, but of information measures 'designed to ... counteract effects of anti-US propaganda'. This was potentially complex, for by the 1950s significant anti-US propaganda was beginning to appear in Britain and, as we shall see, this too was identified for American counter-action.[5]

Permanent liaison between IRD and its Washington partners, of the sort enjoyed by SIS and the CIA, was agreed at the Foreign Ministers Conference in May 1950. That month and again in July, Edward Barrett from the State Department travelled to London to meet with

Christopher Warner and the heads of IRD and the Information Policy Department, which enjoyed a wide co-ordinating role, to develop co-operation. Adam Watson was appointed to Washington as the British liaison man for information warfare and Washington discussed a similar individual for 'closer liaison with the Foreign Office and the BBC'. Later London considered adding a military liaison officer on psywar, but then hesitated for fear of running across the 'internal friction' between CIA and the other American bodies.[6]

The Korean War accelerated the pace of co-operation. On 27 July 1950 American information officers across Asia received additional briefings on the British IRD apparatus in Asia and were urged to co-operate at ground level. At each location in Asia systems for exchanging material and pooling translation work were developed. The IRD chief in Singapore, they were told, was John Rayner and the main target of his operations in Asia was 'intellectuals, editors, teachers and labor groups':

> Most of the basic raw material is produced in London, processed and adapted locally. It is diffused though local channels – press, radio, organizations, key individuals, etc. The British believe that it is more effective to feed materials into the local radio and press without attribution, or to have material attributed to local organizations, than to indicate a British source. About 80 per cent of their effort goes into this indirect approach. They do not consider this a covert operation.

IRD's experience in Asia so far was that the greatest success was achieved when the material was prepared by local people. Washington was impressed by the IRD operation which, being 'grey' or 'borderline covert', avoided the taint of more official forms of propaganda without the complications of truly covert operation.[7]

In common with both SIS and GCHQ, staff from IRD found that the biggest problem in attempting to co-operate with American agencies was their multiplicity and mutual jealousies. The CIA, the State Department and the three American armed services all had pretensions in this area. By 1951 Washington itself was gradually becoming aware of this problem. The fissiparous nature of American activity was quickly identified by the consultancy arm of the Massachusetts Institute of Technology under Dr James R. Killian. Killian had been asked to look at the problem of the Soviet jamming of American radio propaganda under a research project codenamed Troy. But Project Troy discovered that Soviet jamming was only part of the problem. 'US psychological warfare, diplomatic action, military activities and the economic actions relative to the USSR are so poorly co-ordinated as to destroy the utility of some actions entirely.' One manifestation of this was that 'Western handling of Soviet defectors has been so poor' that news of this was getting back through the grapevine as discouraging new defectors from coming over. Killian was so shocked at what he found that he had persuaded Truman to set up a board for co-ordinating political warfare under Gordon Gray, which eventually became the Psychological Strategy Board or PSB, and later the Operations Co-ordinating Board.[8]

Gordon Gray was soon replaced by C. D. Jackson. Jackson was a remarkable figure and, like Frank Wisner, a sincere evangelist for liberation in its purest form. Because American propaganda was harnessed to controversial operations against the Eastern bloc, the predictable disagreements soon began to open up between London and Washington. Jackson was clear about where he stood on the issue of Cold War fighting, and in March 1952 he wrote to the senior CIA representative at SHAPE, Anthony J. Drexel Biddle, outlining his current thinking. He said that the three basic ingredients for this kind of work were 'adequate funds', 'no holds barred' and 'no questions asked'. Initially PSB and its successors had these and indeed had received orders from the top to 'get in there and do something'. But now he was disappointed for, at the last minute, it seemed that Washington had developed reservations. Jackson enthused 'we damn near did "it"', but now everybody in Washington was 'surprised and a little frightened and unprepared'. Truman had not allowed him to carry things through. For the last year he had been busy 'preparing one or more of Russia's satellite states for peeling off', but the potential was not being properly exploited because, he complained, the 'gentlemen of the Potomac' had failed to comprehend the real possibilities that were at hand. They still thought that psychological warfare amounted to a man 'in a black homburg stepping out of a Constellation at National Airport Washington DC'. Jackson explained to Biddle that he was 'steamed up' by the idea that 'World War III can literally be won without fighting it if Pyschwar is used intelligently and boldly'. But he was also 'frustrated' by the recent application of the brakes and the lack of central planning or co-ordination in American political warfare. Jackson, like Wisner, was the sort of determined Cold Warrior that London was anxious about in the early 1950s.[9]

In the wider world, Anglo-American wrangles also arose because of petty British resentment at the sheer scale of American psywar resources. Inevitably, as the large American information machine got going in the Third World there would be some erosion of areas of traditional British influence. This was even true in European countries such as Italy. Here SIS and then IRD had worked hard to establish agents of political influence in post-war Italian politics, but by the early 1950s the CIA and its overt partner, US Information Service (USIS), were the dominant players on the Italian scene, to the chagrin of SIS. In April 1953, Wisner had to write to General Gruenther at SHAPE headquarters warning him about 'current British unhappiness over certain arrangements with respect to Italy' in the field of psywar, adding, 'I still hope that our British friends will be able to contain their disappointment,' but predicting that the British would 'dress up' their complaints with 'superficially plausible argumentation'.[10]

Although American psywar activities in Europe had concentrated on Italy and France as the countries most vulnerable to communism, they also had targets in Britain. As early as 1947, USIS activities in Britain were also earmarked for expansion, boosted by the information wing of the Marshall Plan organisation, ECA. Whitehall was worried about this. The Treasury and then the Foreign Office objected that 'propaganda addressed to the British public by a friendly foreign government has no precedent' and feared that eventually all this would 'feed the "Fortyninth State" argument'. The British attitude was hypocritical, given the veritable barrage of British propaganda, both overt and covert, that had been directed at the United States over the previous decade aimed at ending American inter-war isolationism. However some objectives of USIS were certainly inimical to its British hosts. In 1950, USIS was anxious about Labour's social welfare policy in case it moved Britain beyond what Americans considered to be the 'bounds of liberty and democracy'. Accordingly it sought to trumpet a political alternative to state socialism and to 'present boldly the advantages of this modern American capitalist democracy'. Bevin was at the same time calling for more positive British information work to sell the advantages of social democracy with its welfare state. Some of these British and American information programmes were in ideological competition rather than complementary.[11]

The Korean War triggered further expansion of USIS and ECA information work in Britain, reflecting alarm at the rise in British criticism of American conduct of the Cold War. Washington detected a whiff of neutralism in Britain which it called 'a constantly growing threat'. In London, American officials explained, neutralism 'finds support in the latent fear in Britain of atomic weapons and of Britain's vulnerability to atomic weapons' as well as in the natural desire of a proud British population to be independent of any sort of outside aid. The Soviets, they concluded, were actively pushing the seductive idea of Europe as a neutral or 'third force' and steps were taken to try and counteract this. Top priority for their efforts were obvious opinion-formers, but there were also other useful avenues for American information programmes: 'The schools constitute a particularly important target for our work in Britain. The secondary schools especially offer a great opportunity to get the younger generation before their opinions and prejudices have set hard. There is an apparently insatiable demand from British secondary schools for information of all sorts about the United States.' By 1950 American information officers in London considered the most effective part of their operation was their relations with the British press and found they were able to place a high proportion of their releases in British newspapers. They now sought to move beyond this into mass information work of their own, using film, leaflets and cultural exchanges to reach out directly into the British population. They aimed at weekly magazines, produced by American officials, dealing with labour issues or women's affairs for distribution in Britain together with more film.[12]

By 1951, Washington had identified the labour movement as the top priority for information work in Britain, and local officers were instructed to cultivate contacts with labour leaders, press and educational organisations in the hope of correcting 'vague stereotypes about American social realities'. In that year the US Labor Information Officer (LIO) in London was reporting 'remarkable' examples of co-operation with the educational sub-committee of the London Labour Party 'against the Communist Party, pacifist, and neutralist elements of the British left'. USIS provided a great deal of material to support lectures and special conferences on current affairs at which the regular speakers were Denis Healey, Christopher Mayhew and Anthony Wedgwood Benn. William C. Gausmann, the ECA Information Officer in Britain, helped to found the think-tank Socialist Union, which was sympathetic to co-operation with the United States, as was its monthly journal *Socialist Commentary*.[13]

The American Embassy decided in July 1951 that, before proceeding further with work in this field, it needed more detailed information on the extent and character of the labour press in Britain. Because of the large number of labour publications and the need for local knowledge it felt that 'a professional survey and analysis [should] be undertaken, confidentially, by the Intelligence Unit of *The Economist*'. This survey was therefore required to include details of communist outlets where gathering the material would not 'compromise the confidential nature of the enquiry'. The US LIO and his staff in London also tried to use Smith-Mundt Awards intended for cultural exchanges to send key British labour figures to the United States. But this was sometimes blocked because the individuals they wished to send were often former communists and they could not persuade Washington to make exceptions. Two British figures who were blocked by Washington were Denis Healey, the Director of the International Department of the Labour Party, described as 'an important anti-Communist', and Evelyn Anderson, Associate Editor of the fortnightly magazine *Tribune*, 'who has been a useful pro-American influence on that periodical'.

By July 1951, the US LIO in London, Patrick O'Sheel, had developed three 'special projects' to address directly what he called 'general ideological stereotypes about America' and also the 'particular irritations' of a small but persistent British communist apparatus. The first was still at the planning stage and was 'a new indigenous organization designed to take the offensive in dealing with anti-American sentiment in Britain'. This was being done quietly in collaboration with existing groups like the English-Speaking Union and British American Associates. Its task was to go beyond the upper-middle classes, who were reached by the 'mildest public activities' of the existing organisations, and to address organisations like trade union groups. The scheme, he added, had 'major potentialities as a "cover" for distribution of political materials and for independent publishing and propaganda which we can assist without exposure'. All were aware that the climate had changed, that sympathy for America could not be taken for granted and that there was therefore 'a new job to be done in post war Britain'. There were other plans for expanded activity in Britain. The Embassy reported that its second 'special project' was:

> a series of three or more pamphlets on 'British Agents of the Cominform', to be published without any U.S. identification, aimed for mass sales through regular British newsstand distribution. The idea developed in discussion between the LIO, a Scottish ex-Communist and former Daily Worker correspondent, Fred Douglas, who wrote in offering his services to Voice of America (he has been put in touch with VOA). The Embassy security office ran a check on him, and his connections with the CP [Communist Party] appear to be definitely ended as of 1945, he is an excellent writer ... and is willing to set up a dummy publishing house to print the pamphlets. Besides consultation and the furnishing of our regular Cold-War materials, our only possible commitment would be in paying him an advance to work the project up.[14]

Fred Douglas had already been successful in selling similar anti-communist stories to *Picture Post*, the leading British mass-circulation magazine, and they were hopeful about this project.

A third scheme involved academics and intellectuals and was, inevitably, the most troublesome. This was to assist 'without direct involvement' in the creation of a new quarterly magazine devoted to the Atlantic Community. This idea was originated with T. R. Fyvel, who suggested it to Gausmann, the ECA Information Officer in London. Fyvel was a key British representative at the Congress for Cultural Freedom, a CIA-funded body countering Soviet work in the intellectual and cultural fields, and had spent the war working for Eisenhower's Psychological Warfare Board in Europe. The intention was that the magazine should attract contributions from 'leading intellectual and political writers on both sides of the Atlantic' and would have a general tone and character similar to *Foreign Affairs*. This eventually became the CIA-backed British monthly called *Encounter*.[15]

The Congress for Cultural Freedom (CCF) itself was also active in

Britain from 1950, presumably with the informal approval of Whitehall, since a leading light was Malcolm Muggeridge, who maintained links with his wartime service, SIS. Britain was one of the first countries to boast a national committee of the CCF, set up by Stephen Spender in 1951, which eventually became the British Society for Cultural Freedom. After some feuding of the sort that was *de rigueur* in organisations that contained intellectuals, this took hold the following year under the chairmanship of Muggeridge. The Society itself was eclipsed when the CCF decided to put most of its London effort into Fyvel's suggested magazine, which became *Encounter*.[16] *Encounter* was co-edited by Spender and was first published in October 1953. It was tremendously successful, combining political and cultural commentary and establishing itself as *the* English-language cultural periodical. Most commentators offered it a rapturous reception and only a few sensed a hidden agenda. The *Times Literary Supplement* accurately detected an obsession with the evils of communism, which resulted in a sort of 'negative liberalism', while T. S. Eliot dismissed it as American propaganda hidden under a veneer of British culture. Ironically, despite being branded by some in Britain for his pro-American anti-communism, Spender found that, like Denis Healey, he could not obtain a visa to enter the United States.[17]

Although *Encounter* was a runaway success, the British wing of the Congress for Cultural Freedom was plagued by troubles. British intellectuals were independently minded and were inclined to resist anything that smacked of strident anti-communism. Hugh Trevor-Roper and A. J. P. Taylor were two of a handful of British academics who attended the founding conference of the CCF in Berlin in 1950 and made trouble, attacking the fanaticism of leading speakers such as Arthur Koestler. Indeed it was the negative reaction of Taylor and Trevor-Roper that prompted the CCF to try to set up a British wing. Julian Amery and Malcolm Muggeridge were its leading lights, and it quickly recruited a wide range of leading figures, including Max Beloff, Richard Crossman, Victor Gollancz and Michael Oakeshott.

During 1952 Muggeridge took over the chair of the British Society for Cultural Freedom (BSCF), and the group entered its most energetic phase. One of its tasks was to gather information on the cultural activities of the Cominform which was passed on to bodies such as IRD. The Congress for Cultural Freedom strongly supported right-wing revisionists such as Rita Hinden, the Editor of *Socialist Commentary*, which vied with the *New Statesman* as the voice of the Labour left. The most dramatic association was the CCF-sponsored conference on the 'Future of Freedom' in Milan in 1955 with delegates from 140 countries. This was attended by many leading Labour MPs including Hugh Gaitskell, Denis

Healey and Roy Jenkins. Nevertheless, the CCF had doubts about its British collaborators. They rowed among themselves and proved ineffectual Cold Warriors, accepting substantial subventions but for projects that turned out to have little connection with cultural freedom or anti-communism. Eventually the CCF withdrew support from the BSCF and Muggeridge had to seek financial assistance from his wartime masters, SIS, to keep it going. Undoubtedly, some of the BSCF figures were tolerated only for fear that they might join a more socialist left. Bertrand Russell, the Society's Honorary President, was a prize example. Unhappy about his rampant anti-Americanism, the CCF nevertheless hung on to him to deny his prestige and status to rival groups.[18]

The specific problem of anti-Americanism in Britain became more serious in the 'McCarthy period' between 1952 and 1954. In 1954, during the infamous Owen Lattimore case, the Home Office, the British police and the American Embassy in London were attacked in the press for providing Washington with information on Lattimore's publications in Britain. In the same year, Dr Joseph Cort, a young American psychologist working at the University of Birmingham, was refused an extension to his work permit on the ground that he was wanted in the United States to answer questions about alleged membership of the Communist Party. Many Labour MPs urged the granting of political refugee status to Cort, but this was refused by David Maxwell Fyfe, the Home Secretary. In Cabinet he offered the argument that to accord the status would be tantamount to saying that the United States was a land of political persecution, which would give offence to Washington.[19]

Anti-Americanism was a growing trend of the British left in the early 1950s. Led by Nye Bevan, who had set his face against American leadership in the West and against its favourite projects, such as the European Defence Community, anti-Americanism was often referred to as 'Bevanism'. The trial and execution of the Rosenbergs, who were guilty of atomic espionage in the United States, attracted massive media attention. Although it is now clear from Venona material that the Rosenbergs were guilty, the verdict appeared less safe in 1953. With their children as pathetic onlookers, the damage done to the international profile of the United States was immense. British and American officials alike concluded that more should now be done to counter the growing tide of anti-Americanism. In May 1953, Walter Bedell Smith, who had recently moved from the CIA to the State Department, spoke to President Eisenhower about public opinion in Europe. American Ambassadors across Europe were warning that if the death sentences on the Rosenbergs were carried out this would have 'a most harmful long term effect' on attitudes to the US. Two members of McCarthy's staff, including the youthful and unpleasant Roy Cohn, had recently visited Paris and there Cohn had boasted that he had personally prosecuted the Rosenbergs. Nothing, the Ambassadors concluded, 'could be better calculated' to convince waverers that the Rosenbergs, when executed 'will be victims of what the European press freely terms "McCarthyism"'. But Eisenhower had already rejected an appeal for clemency and events were set to run their course.[20]

By March 1953 there had been 'a tremendous proliferation of the various US information services maintained by the US Government in Great Britain'. There were now ninety-three staff operating in London with an annual budget of $850,000. Some of their most interesting activities were in the area of radio and film distribution. The US Information Service claimed that it had begun discreetly to subsidise a BBC radio programme called *The Answer Man* into which, it claimed, it was able to insert 'planted questions', but exactly how this worked is not clear.[21] British and American information officials were also working together to launch the Committee for Education in Current Commonwealth–American Affairs, under the auspices of the English-Speaking Union. The committee was chaired by Francis Williams, who had been Attlee's press adviser, and particular efforts were made to involve trade union figures such as Vic Feather and Will Lawther. Because the considerable costs were met by an unnamed 'private American individual' they were able to set up an executive organisation called the Current Affairs Unit with a full-time staff. By 1954 there was further financial assistance from the Ford Foundation. The first Director of the Current Affairs Unit was General Sir Leslie Hollis, with staff seconded from Foreign Office information units, almost certainly IRD. Hollis had superintended the post-war deception body known as the Hollis Committee until 1950. The twin tasks of Hollis' Current Affairs Unit were to dispel specific Anglo-American 'misunderstandings' and to tackle the general impression in Britain that 'Americans were rough and rude and always chewed gum'.[22]

Meanwhile, in the wider world, the early secret work of British officials in the field of international organisations, youth movements and culture was being overtaken by the Americans by the 1950s. This was mainly a function of finance. Precocious Cold Warriors like William Montagu-Pollock of the Cultural Relations Department had recognised the importance of countering communist influence on world youth as early as 1944. But now their efforts looked puny compared to the resources that the Soviets and the Americans were able to put behind their front organisations. By 1954, important British projects, such as the World Assembly of Youth (WAY), had been largely taken over by the Americans. This was not always a voluntary decision on the part of British officials. Such public organisations had a life of their own and were prepared to shift their sponsorship to obtain resources.

The United States had also forged ahead in this area because of the sheer brilliance of practitioners like the CIA's Tom Braden. Braden was a former OSS officer and, as we have seen, had been the energetic Executive Director of the American Committee on United Europe. His experiences with ACUE had taught him a great deal about the need for co-ordinated international action. When he joined the CIA he found the reverse situation, because everything was in national and regional boxes, making it hard for the Agency to fight the Soviets on the plane of international movements. That is why he set up the CIA's International Organisations Division. In the 1950s, International Organisations Division proved fabulously successful, thwarting Soviet efforts to dominate international movements in areas as diverse as student affairs, culture and labour. Eventually, in the late 1960s, its activities began to be revealed and helped to prompt a devastating season of Congressional enquiry into the CIA that would last for ten years. Arguably, this was inevitable. For, though Braden was highly effective at getting under the skin of the Cold War, it was impossible to work in these public areas without eventual exposure.

While secrecy lasted, Braden and International Organisations Division scored some notable achievements. Perhaps the most remarkable was Braden's victory in the so-called 'painting war'. He was able to exploit the CIA's excellent contacts with the East Coast establishment, including major foundations, banks and wealthy individuals, to promote abstract art as a weapon of the Cold War. The key element in a modern art alliance constructed by the CIA was the Museum of Modern Art itself, known affectionately to most New Yorkers by its acronym MoMA. MoMA had been set up in the 1920s by several wealthy patrons, including Mrs J. D. Rockefeller, and had been presided over by Alfred H. Barr. Barr, who remained influential in the New York art establishment after his retirement as director in 1943, was the first publicly to proclaim the value of modern art as an instrument of anti-communism. In a high-profile article published in the *New York Times Magazine* on 14 December 1953 he declared that 'The modern artist's non-conformity and love of freedom cannot be tolerated within a monolithic tyranny and modern art is useless for the dictator's propaganda.' The extent to which tyrannies lived in fear of this pure form of individualism and self-expression was shown by the persecution of modern artists under both Hitler and Stalin, which confirmed that abstract art was the most dangerous of all.[23]

The flagship element in Braden's campaign was MoMA's International Circulating Exhibitions Programme. This promoted abstract art, and especially American abstract art, through touring exhibitions which travelled the world. The strong Western European dimension, both in terms of the importance of venues like Vienna and Prague, and also in terms of the overlap with the ACUE, the Marshall Plan and the CCF, underlines the dual nature of this programme of psychological warfare. On one level this was an operation designed to apply pressure to the Eastern bloc. But on another level it was an operation directed at America's European allies. It was no less important to demonstrate to the Western Europeans that the United States was not a cultural desert. This programme was intended to persuade Western intellectuals that the Americans were sensitive and cultured, not shallow moral equivalents of the Soviets. It was no accident that these programmes were launched at the height of anti-Americanism in France when the howls of protest over episodes such as the Rosenberg trial were at their loudest. This was a period when McCarthy was doing enormous damage to America's image abroad. In common with the ACUE, there was an obsession within International Organisations Division with capturing the minds of the young, and so the first major exhibition sponsored by this apparatus was 'Young Painters', focusing on those between the ages of eighteen and thirty-five.[24] This operation looked independent because those running the CIA and other covert warfare programmes were also running the foundations. Braden and his Division went a long way to strengthening an already strongly corporatist dimension to American foreign policy. In 1954 Nelson Rockefeller, who helped to fund this art programme, took over from C. D. Jackson as Eisenhower's special adviser on Cold War operations. Meanwhile John McCloy, the American High Commissioner in Germany, and his Publicity Chief, Shepard Stone, moved seamlessly from the Cold War front line to become Directors of the Ford Foundation.[25]

IRD was no less interested in British labour than the Americans. As early as 1946, at the very outset of the Cold War, Herbert Morrison had identified the British Labour Party machine as a vital conduit for anti-communist propaganda. The International Department of the Labour Party, then under the control of Denis Healey, proved ideal for passing on anonymous IRD briefing materials, ensuring that they could then travel to trade unions and other labour bodies from a neutral source. The volume of IRD material that was passing through the International Department remains unrecognised. This is partly because IRD material was purpose-designed to deny its own origins and, other than an obscure code number, there was nothing to indicate whence it had come. But to the trained eye an IRD brief is immediately recognisable and, to those who know what they are looking for, the archives of the International Department are amazing to behold. Somewhere between a third and a half of the material consists of documents generated by IRD and its sister departments. These archives are important because they capture a body of material that IRD primarily intended for a domestic audience, the British labour and trade union movements. It is clear that, although a

Foreign Office department, IRD had a leading role in counter-communism at home.[26]

Denis Healey's International Department became a kind of front-line station for IRD. Key figures in IRD such as Adam Watson and Colonel Leslie Sheridan were on first-name terms with Healey and sent him internal IRD materials for his own presentations and briefs. In November 1948, Watson passed on to Healey batches of the latest telegrams from Sofia, detailing the arrest and prosecution of Bulgarian social democrats, including the death sentence handed out to Dr Georgi Petkov. The social democrats in Bulgaria had strong connections with the Labour Party and it was suggested that a leader in the *Daily Herald* would be 'a good thing'.[27] IRD also assisted these labour bodies in the production of their own in-house material. This included a guide 'on the use of words in publicity about communism', a masterly handbook on attacking the Soviets through the careful choice of language. 'Kremlin', it advised, was a good word for general use as it conjured up the 'cruel, backward and tyrannical' aspects of the regime in most people's minds, whereas 'Stalinism' was 'more suitable for intellectual audiences'. Forced labour was quickly singled out as an area on which the Soviets were particularly vulnerable, and IRD advised the repeated use of the names of one or two well-known camps 'until they are as familiar as Dachau or Belsen'.[28] For both IRD and Healey's International Department, official Eastern bloc attacks on non-communist socialist parties, which often had fraternal relations with the Labour Party, followed in 1949 by the purging of the Eastern bloc communist parties themselves, was a propaganda gift. In the 1950s, IRD prepared country lists of prominent socialists who had been in prison. In Poland it identified seven leading members of the Polish Socialist Party 'accused of maintaining contact with their fellow socialists in Britain and carrying on espionage for Western intelligence'. IRD deluged the Labour Party with material on the purges from 1949.[29]

In the 1950s the International Department began to diversify its source of information materials. It now also circulated documents from the International Confederation of Free Trade Unions in Brussels on 'Stalin's slave camps' and similar material from Vilis Masens, the Chairman of the Assembly of Captive European Nations in New York. But IRD remained dominant, and it increasingly developed the idea of suppressed nationhood. In December 1952, it sent the Labour Party a stream of material including copies of a forty-page document entitled 'The Soviet Practice of Genocide'. IRD began by detailing the history of NKVD work in the Baltic states in the late 1930s and defended widespread collaboration with the Nazis there on the ground that the activities of the Russian secret police had 'so alienated and demoralized the population'. It went on to chronicle the mass deportations of Baltic populations to Siberia and to labour camps in the 'wastes of Kazakhstan' which continued into the 1950s. Many 'were shot before deportation' and 'large numbers died in their cattle trucks on the journey'. These deportees were replaced by an influx of 'Russian colonists' into the Baltic states. IRD dwelled on the disappearance of entire peoples and cultures which had enjoyed long entries in the *Soviet Encyclopedia* in the inter-war years but by 1950 had simply disappeared.[30]

IRD made particularly good use of defectors from the Eastern bloc security services, and one of its star performers was an officer of the Polish security service (UB), Colonel Joseph Swialto, who fled to the West in December 1953. Swialto was a valuable source of propaganda about the unpleasant nature of rule in the East and developed a long-term career commentating on the tribulations of East European security organs. He was in his element in the late 1950s, because the death of Stalin had prompted calls for many of those responsible for earlier reigns of terror to be brought to book. When Gomulka returned to power in Poland in 1955 he had been forced by public opinion to set up a special commission to look into the excesses of the UB. It reported in May 1957 and three senior officials responsible for the Ministry of Public Security were expelled from the Party. IRD enjoyed pointing out that this was an attempt to 'whitewash the old Politburo' and focused on the terrible things that had been done by the secretive Chief Investigator, Jozef Rozanski from the '10th department', which was responsible for the 'unity and purity' of the Polish Communist Party.

Joseph Swialto, himself an unsavoury character, was able to supply biographical detail on all these shadowy figures. These Polish security chiefs had been sent by the MGB to study the show trials of communists in Prague and Budapest, especially the Slansky Trial, in preparation for similar activities in Poland – which eventually resulted in the arrest and prosecution of Gomulka. Jozef Rozanski was given especially detailed treatment by IRD, even down to his pre-war service as an NKVD officer in Palestine and other Arab countries. Five key UB figures eventually stood trial and Rozanski was sentenced to five years in one of his own prisons.[31]

Ironically, while using the Labour Party as a conduit to publicise the purges of the East, IRD was also assisting the Labour Party in its own process of internal purging. Throughout the 1940s and 1950s the Labour Party National Executive Committee kept up a steady stream of expulsions, based on lists of proscribed organisations, most of which were communist or Trotskyist. It also banned Labour Party members from attending conferences and festivals with an extreme-left complexion. In some cases it employed travelling tribunals to investigate local Party activities which it considered dubious. These decisions were based, to a large degree, on detailed documentation passed to the Labour Party by IRD, which in turn drew on material provided by MI5, SIS, the FBI and a welter of friendly security agencies in Western Europe. In 1953, the Labour Party's International Sub-Committee presented the National Executive Committee with a long report on communist front organisations. The report included appendices on each organisation, identifying the leading members and the dates they had travelled to Eastern Europe or chaired meetings. The level of research was far beyond what the International Sub-Committee was capable of.

The Labour Party also worked with an IRD campaign to seal Britain off from the conferences of Moscow's front organisations. The Party banned attendance at the International Youth Festival run by WFDY in Prague as early as in 1947, although it was attended by Young Tories. The Berlin Youth Festival of 1951 and the British Festival of Youth in 1952 were also proscribed events for Labour Party members. Similar conferences held in Britain were harassed using informal measures. In 1950, Attlee's Cabinet discussed the problem of a World Peace Festival due to take place in Sheffield. Instead of banning it Ministers chose to refuse entry to any person from abroad who might be 'detrimental to internal security', including all the members of the World Peace Committee running the conference! Cabinet supported Bevin's exhortation to 'do everything possible to cripple the Conference'. On 12 November 1950, forty of the sixty-five delegates and support staff arriving at Dover were turned back by the authorities. IRD and the Labour Party were still working closely together on similar projects in the 1960s.[32]

IRD reached a wider British audience by placing material through contacts in the British press and with the BBC, regularly securing a front-page story. This was a tremendously successful tactic, often resulting in syndication around the world in as many as fifty countries. The IRD press operation was substantial and reached every country in the world. By the 1950s, IRD had grown to 500 staff, the biggest department in the Foreign Office. Arguably this effort was more effective than the American radios – Frank Wisner's so-called Mighty Wurlitzer – because it was 'grey'. Audiences tended to resist obvious radio propaganda. By contrast the anti-Soviet IRD material that was fed to the world's press through London and elsewhere was often sensational, but it was also well researched, factually accurate and free, and so was greatly appreciated by journalists. Once it appeared it had the semblance of a locally generated, independent story. IRD was organised like a mini-Foreign Office with 'country desks'. The main difference was that one of the larger country desks in IRD was 'Britain'. This reflected the fact that many left-wing international organisations operated from Britain. It underlined another fact, that British public opinion was a major IRD target.[33]

IRD also sought to influence British domestic opinion through its book-publishing activities. Some of IRD's first ventures into the world of publishing had initially been internal studies. In 1950, Robert Carew-Hunt's *Theory and Practice of Communism* was cleared for publication and eventually went through many Penguin editions. The book had been written as an in-house guide when Carew-Hunt was a member of Philby's R5 section of SIS, dealing with communism. Robert Conquest's highly respected work on Stalinist terror and the Soviet forced-labour camps soon followed, drawing heavily on IRD files. But most IRD books were commissioned from freelancers and were initially published through front companies such as Ampersand Books, set up by IRD's Leslie Sheridan. Ampersand published twenty books over three decades, but lacked real distributive power. The answer was to team up with mainstream publishers. IRD did this through its Background Books series, which were a great success and were eventually produced by The Bodley Head. The cover was at times a little thin and many of the books were written by those with a secret service past, including Robert Bruce Lockhart and Monty Woodhouse. A natural development was for Bodley Head to publish more secret service memoirs and intelligence history, with the result that the boundary between life and art became increasingly blurred.[34]

During the late 1940s and on into the 1950s, IRD worked with the CIA and Western trade unionists to develop an independent alternative to the Soviet-dominated World Federation of Trade Unions. However, although the United States footed much of the bill, their creation, the Free Trade Union Committee (FTUC), like the European Movement, was not a pliant creature and did not hesitate to tell its sponsor to keep its distance. Both British and American information warfare officers soon discovered that he who paid the piper did not always call the tune. Independence of mind in the world of labour reflected the fact that key labour activists had been in the game of anti-communism since the 1930s and considered organisations like the CIA or IRD as latecomers who had much to learn. Figures like Jay Lovestone and Irving Brown in the USA or Ernest Bevin in Britain were in this category. These labour figures began work earlier and were sometimes more radical and more abrasive in their activities than the American government wished them to be.

Both IRD and the CIA encountered trouble with unruly footsoldiers who wanted more money than was available but would not take orders. Jay Lovestone, the veteran American labour figure, regarded the CIA as tediously bureaucratic and staffed by unimaginative and insufficiently innovative figures reflecting their over-educated background. Lovestone dubbed these Ivy League products the 'Fizz Kids' or 'Fizzers' and the CIA as 'Fizzland'. He had contempt for CIA officers who had several degrees but no real-life experience of the areas of social and political life that they were attempting to influence. The Free Trade Union Committee was an important body and its activities overlapped with CIA support for the European Movement. Here Lovestone and Brown were joined by David Dubinsky and George Meany. From early 1949 CIA financial support far exceeded the money coming in from union bodies. FTUC's main work was the funding of anti-communist trade union organisations and newspapers in countries such as Italy and France. These operations spread as far as Finland, and in Germany its operations included an Ostbüro, operating into East Germany. There were FTUC offices in India and Indonesia, where they helped to battle local WFTU affiliates. A key office was run by Willard Etter in Taiwan, where they financed the Free China Labor League which trained agents for sabotage in mainland China. The China operations were elaborate, with a budget of $99,401 earmarked for 1949–52.

But Lovestone, Brown and Dubinsky were maverick collaborators. Braden recalled that it was 'always a sore point that we never got any accounting from them' despite the 'enormous sums of money' that were handed over for the overseas network. They would allude to strikes broken up in Italy or France, but there were never any details or receipts. Lovestone portrayed himself as quintessentially a man of action too busy to be troubled with what he called the 'petty-book psychology and laundry methods' of the CIA bureaucrats. There were also struggles over policy. In Italy, multiple American organisations, including ECA and USIS, showered the Italian non-communist unions with dollars. FTUC officers found it hard to get the Italians to do anything without an ample supply of dollars and complained bitterly that 'our Italian friends have been overfed'. In the early 1950s there was a fiery meeting between Bedell Smith as Director of the CIA and Lovestone, Brown and Dubinksy. The latter wanted the CIA to increase funding and leave the labour field to them, but Bedell Smith would have none of it and the meeting broke up in disarray.[35]

Money was also an issue for the footsoldiers of IRD and CRD, Britain's cultural warfare specialists, in London. One of the more successful British clandestine creations in the heady world of international organisations was the World Assembly of Youth (WAY), which had competed successfully with the Soviet youth front, the WFDY. But financial stringency in the early 1950s forced London to make hard choices. To its dismay, because American financial support seemed to be forthcoming for WAY, this favourite project moved over to working with Washington.

Problems began to loom as early as November 1950. CRD noted that WAY officials were 'touchy' about the money issue. Previously London had given 'considerable financial support both to the International

Headquarters of the World Association of Youth and to the British National Committee'. IRD and CRD had hoped that this was merely pump-priming money since the original intention was that WAY should eventually 'stand on its own feet' and be maintained by voluntary subscription from its component organisations. Like the CIA's Free Europe Committee in Washington, which was also supposed to become free standing, WAY remained stubbornly dependent on subventions. But, unlike its American equivalents, its impoverished parent could not afford to continue the subsidies. In what CRD called 'our present financial straits' officials began to cast around for possible subsidies from NATO.[36]

On 26 November 1951, John Nicholls, who superintended all the Foreign Office information departments, ordered a meeting to consider the future of British clandestine policy in the area of youth movements. It was led by figures from CRD, IRD and the Information Policy Department. They agreed that one of their main aims was to provide the youth of Western Europe as a whole with an antidote to communism. They also resolved to make 'special efforts' in the area of German youth and colonial youth. WAY remained the crucial vehicle for these British projects. But obtaining hoped-for additional Allied financial support for WAY was tricky, since both continental European and American governments were avidly pro-federalist. Optimistically, London hoped to obtain Allied funding for WAY, but at the same time to use the organisation within European youth programmes to apply a brake to federalist tendencies.

In 1952 London urged 'a maximum British participation' in European youth activities 'aimed at opposing Federal Europe propaganda'. It also worried about the fact that the French and the Americans were now backing a programme which the European Movement was preparing for the following year. WAY was working on this project together with the European Movement and the International Union of Socialist Youth, and a joint secretariat had been set up in Brussels. The WAY representatives on this Brussels Secretariat were the old CRD-sponsored stagers, including Elizabeth Welton, who had previously been secretary of the British National Committee of WAY, together with Guthrie Moir, one of the most 'energetic' members of this committee. But, given the federalist complexion of the wider programme, should their task in Brussels be supporting, reporting or undermining? British officials were perplexed and had to seek 'higher guidance of HMG's attitude to the European Movement'.[37] WAY was consistently used to try and blunt the strong federalist tendencies of American- and French-backed outfits, including the European Movement itself. By January 1955, Lord Hope, the Foreign Office junior minister, was backing WAY in its efforts to secure consultative status from the Council of Europe, in direct competition with the European Movement's European Youth Campaign. CRD complained of the 'federalist bias' of the European Youth Campaign, which was 'maintained by American funds' and 'run by men who draw their funds from the central organisation'. CRD had little doubt about who was really behind the lavishly funded organisation.[38]

CRD and IRD could never obtain enough money from the Treasury for their WAY protégé, even though major efforts were made. In January 1954 Anthony Eden as Foreign Secretary 'made a personal intervention' to try and lever more money from the Treasury to support this project. He was joined in this enterprise by the Colonial Office and the Commonwealth Relations Office. But the Chancellor, Rab Butler, refused to continue the subsidies, which had nevertheless been quite small. Since the launch of WAY in London in 1948, its international organisation had received only £700 a year and its British National Committee, the real engine room of WAY activity, £2,000 per year. There had also been further *ad hoc* subsidies to ensure the effective attendance of British delegations at international conferences. British leadership of WAY, an international body with a membership of sixty countries, was a stunning achievement and it had been secured at a bargain price. Guthrie Moir, now the International President of WAY, with whom CRD had 'very close relations', contacted Eden regularly pleading its case. The Second General Assembly of WAY was planned for Singapore in September 1954. The venue had been 'chosen with the encouragement of the Foreign Office', but there was now no money to send a British delegation. This was doubly embarrassing since many other Western European governments now gave subventions to WAY 'most generously'.[39]

In May 1954, Ian Page, the British President of WAY, tried scare tactics. Despairing of his sponsors in IRD and CRD, he wrote to the Treasury directly asking for £7,000, enclosing material generated by his communist rival, the Assembly of British Youth. The Treasury was indeed 'shaken' and had to concede that the communist competitors 'looked pretty devilish'. But in July, Rab Butler continued to refuse funds. American funding from the Ford or Carnegie Foundations remained a possibility, but this was a sore point for those in Whitehall looking after Colonial Affairs, who, no less than those looking after European affairs, saw the Americans as rivals. Oliver Lyttelton, the Colonial Secretary, warned Eden on 25 June 1954, 'I do not think either of us would want to see the controlling interest in this organisation passing ... to the United States.'[40]

By July 1954 relations between CRD and Guthrie Moir were reaching breakdown. The end of CRD/IRD money had prompted the Carnegie Commonwealth endowment to withdraw its sponsorship of Singapore, leaving WAY with a $50,000 shortfall. Moir had become 'very bad tempered' and had begun to leak material to the press about 'inter-departmental struggles' in Whitehall. Eventually, in desperation, CRD and IRD turned to 'sources not under Treasury control' to carry the Singapore Conference forward and to get a British delegation there. In practice this meant $20,000 from the Singapore government together with a private subvention from the Shell oil company. The Singapore government offered its own estimate that, without WAY, at least one-third of its member organisations would join the Moscow-directed front, the WFDY.[41]

The issue of longer-term funding beyond the 1954 conference remained. Guthrie Moir and his team, who controlled the International Secretariat of WAY, now threatened resignation unless secret British subventions continued. Ivone Kirkpatrick suggested a grant of £5,000 for 1955–6, about a third of all the Foreign Office's meagre allocation for developing 'multilateral co-operation'. This was mainly used to pay off previous debts and WAY pointed out that by late 1954 the British delegation was the only one in the world that was likely to default on its subscriptions for 1953 and 1954. In February 1955 the Treasury relented and found money for the deficit.[42]

Notwithstanding this, by the mid-1950s support for WAY was already passing to CIA fronts, including the Asia Foundation (previously the Committee for a Free Asia). When the Singapore Youth Council was chosen to host the next WAY conference in August 1954, it was primarily the Committee for Free Asia, under the local representative Robert Sheeks, who provided the money. Indeed even before the arrival of WAY, it was the Americans who were supporting much of the non-government anti-communist youth work, including sponsoring the launch of a Chinese edition of the Singapore Youth Council's *Youth World* magazine.[43] British Ministers and officials were increasingly uneasy about the way in which the Americans were surging ahead with front-organisation activity, especially in areas of the world where the British had been dominant, such as South-east Asia and the Middle East.

In 1955 the International Secretariat of WAY became a largely American-funded body, receiving subsidies from a range of groups. Guthrie Moir explained that the big change had begun when it obtained $70,000 from the Ford Foundation for a General Assembly meeting in Ithaca, New York. This had led to the setting up of the Foundation for Youth and Student Affairs in New York shortly afterwards. This American funding body had consistently 'invested large sums in WAY', including $114,000 for the Singapore Conference of 1954. The Asia Foundation also put up US $50,000 in travel grants towards delegates from Asian countries 'which were carefully selected by us in the light of the current political climate'. The Foundation for Youth and Student Affairs in New York was currently providing $48,000 per annum for WAY's International Secretariat in Paris, including a translation service for its magazine, *WAY Forum*. John Rennie, the head of IRD, continued to press for money in 1955, arguing that Britain 'cannot effectively influence the organisation and its activities ... without contributing to its funds', but the inescapable truth was that London had already lost the race.[44]

International youth activity, like labour activity, had its counterpart at home, and in the 1950s there was increasing scrutiny of students in Britain. University officials kept close contact with the Special Branch, MI5 and freelance bodies such as the Economic League, feeding them reports on the activities of student groups with which they had contact. They also gave American Embassy officials the same information, which they desired in order to deny visas to those considered 'radical'. A good example was A. G. Morkhill, a retired member of the Malay Civil Service and Secretary of the London University China Committee. Morkhill was able to keep an eye on communist influence among Chinese students in London because his committee administered scholarship funds and shared a building with the Central Union of Chinese Students in Britain and Ireland at the China Institute, 16 Gordon Square, near Senate House.

Morkhill told the Americans that he kept in 'close touch with Scotland Yard' on these matters. He had initially wanted to move his committee away from its co-located site with the union. But Special Branch officers at Scotland Yard told him to stay put in order to continue 'keeping a tab on the activities of various Chinese students and the Union'. He had tried to get what he called the British 'special service people' to deport those students he thought undesirable, but he had been told that they could only advise the Home Office. Attempts to get various student activists expelled had dissolved 'in the smog of inter-departmental committees'. Morkhill complained that the question of 'deporting or depriving of British citizenship these traitors' with British or colonial passports is 'dynamite which few politicians would dare to touch', but he pressed on in cases which he thought were a special source of 'danger'. However, he saved his greatest distaste for the 'British "fellow-travelling" University Don' since these figures, he insisted, were 'probably the worst' examples of what he called our 'enemies within the gate'.[45]

21

Defeat in the Middle East: Iran and Suez

The political significance of the Suez misadventure was that it was the last self-conscious fling of the old British style ... Julian Amery came round with news of plots and conspiracies ... Here was an enemy who could demonstrably be defeated and a sanctimonious American Secretary of State who could be exposed.

George K. Young, SIS Controller Middle East[1]

In the Middle East the British and the Americans had been uneasy partners for decades. As early as 1943, William J. Donovan had asked his Middle Eastern expert, a talented Harvard anthropologist called Carleton Coon, to look at the future of American intelligence in Saudi Arabia. Coon came back with a plan for a covert American intelligence network that would cover all Muslim areas, and its main focus was to be upon markets, oil and airbases. He explained that the main danger to this network was penetration by the British and the French. For this reason it would have to be kept quite separate from other American intelligence activities.[2]

Traditional intelligence rivalry had a dynamic of its own, but in the Middle East this was reinforced by deeper political tensions. The United States, as early as 1943, sought a new partnership with the young democratic republican and nationalist elements emergent in Arab societies, while the British preferred to back more conservative figures. During the war Churchill had supported right-wing and monarchist elements in Greece, to the dismay of the American press. After 1945, Bevin was markedly less anxious to dismantle the Empire than Attlee, a source of serious disagreement. In Egypt, Jordan and elsewhere, outdated monarchies provided the model collaborators for an increasingly informal network of British influence. By contrast the Americans often sought younger nationalist leaders committed to political reform of a kind that would complement programmes of American economic aid. King

Farouk of Egypt, favoured by the British, did not fit this American model and was identified as 'a reactionary landowner', typical of the princes and pashas who had long fascinated British policy in this part of the world.[3]

Further east, especially in the Gulf, American officials were anxious to promote the rival ambitions of the Saudis, lending a brittle edge to their simultaneous collaboration with the British to resist Soviet incursions. Occasionally Americans glimpsed the yawning abyss that lay between the British and American approaches to political management in the remoter parts of the Gulf. On 3 February 1949, a party of US Air Force officers passed through the British colony of Aden on a reconnaissance for possible new B-29 bomber bases. They met Air Vice Marshal H. T. Lydford and the local American Consul for discussions at Khormaksar RAF Station. They held a brief conversation with an RAF squadron leader about his current duties, largely tribal policing, who went on to describe a recent operation. A sheikh near Aden had declined to comply with certain British directives and refused to present himself at the British headquarters to negotiate a new treaty. He was warned smartly that failure to comply would result in the destruction of the villages of his tribe:

> The warning was repeated and then certain villages were attacked and destroyed by Tempest aircraft employing rockets and bombs. Certain villages were unsuitable objectives for Tempest aircraft because of their location in defiladed areas. For this exercise, a squadron of Lincolns was brought into Khormaksar Airfield, and a reasonably successful attack was carried out from medium altitude. This operation was said to have the usual desired results in restoring proper relations between the natives and the British.

From the British point of view the purpose of the story was innocent, merely showing that the base could happily accommodate numbers of Lincoln heavy bombers under operational conditions, but it also revealed something about the nature of the British position in the region. These methods, the Americans lamented, were 'typical of the British methods of control over native groups since World War I'. They were condemned not only for their inhumanity, but also for reflecting poorly on all Westerners in the region.

The British approach of operating an informal empire through pliant monarchies, bases and treaty relations with weak 'independent states' looked no better the next day, when the same survey team reached Fayid RAF Station in Egypt. Here an RAF wing commander conceded that the advanced decay of British influence was visible for all to see. Egyptian raiding parties had recently broken into RAF and Army bases in the Suez Canal area and had fired tommy guns into offices and quarters, creating what he described dryly as 'a feeling of uneasiness among troops and dependants'. A million pounds' worth of stores, including substantial quantities of arms and ammunition, had been stolen from depots in armed raids in the last year. Power to the airfield lights was frequently cut during night take-offs with dramatic results. It was well known that these operations against the British were secretly encouraged by the Egyptian government, 'which paid £1 a day to the saboteurs'. The stolen arms were then sold in Palestine for large sums, 'not to the Arabs alone, but also to the Jews, who are able to pay more'. It was not surprising that many American officials in the region had concluded that the British approach was badly off track and that London was failing to seize opportunities for real partnership with the local population.[4]

Egypt was an area where British influence was visibly wilting. Permitted control of internal security only for the duration of the war, local MI5 officers now complained about the onset of 'oriental slackness' as wartime controls were relinquished. Egyptians took over the police posts that had hitherto been occupied by Europeans, and the Egyptian government confronted the awkward problems of dealing with a range of secret societies, paramilitary organisations, nationalist fanatics and threats to public order. Egypt was a critical area of post-imperial influence, a country granted formal independence before the war but from which Britain refused to withdraw completely because of the Suez Canal and important bases. The hidden hand had been important here in attempting to sustain a regime which was acceptable to mainstream nationalists and yet pliant to British requirements. Now the local MI5 representative, Colonel G. J. Jenkins, was forced to sit back and watch from the sidelines.[5]

The Egyptian government had now to decide on its attitudes to the radical nationalist groups, such as the Muslim Brotherhood, and their attempts to use violence to provoke public disorder and so accelerate the British departure from Egypt. Initially the Muslim Brotherhood was seen by both the British and the Egyptian government as less dangerous than the communists, being a genuinely indigenous Egyptian phenomenon, indeed as something which might be controlled or even co-opted for use against the communists in industrial areas. However, as civil order disintegrated the government was increasingly required to use the Army and police to repress demonstrations by the Muslim Brotherhood and by other nationalist groups such as Young Egypt, whose violent protests were sometimes in danger of converging on royal residences.[6]

In November 1946 the paramilitary elements of these societies, who had acquired revolvers and hand grenades, turned them on the police during demonstrations. By 1947 the Muslim Brotherhood had begun to organise more specific forms of violence, marked by the appointment of Hassan al-Banna as head of its so-called Secret Apparatus. Despite its own unease at these developments, Cairo turned a blind eye to some of the rather theatrical attacks on British military bases and even condoned the training of these radical groups by Egyptian military officers and provided the Muslim Brotherhood with military equipment. When the police uncovered weapons dumps and explosives belonging to this group, they were returned if it was claimed that they were for use against the Jews in Palestine.

But the Muslim Brotherhood proved to be an uncontrollable element and launched a number of serious bomb attacks against Jewish targets in Cairo during 1948. The first bomb alone killed over fifty people. This triggered a breakdown in an already awkward relationship. Many members of the Muslim Brotherhood's Secret Apparatus were arrested and some of their arms dumps seized. They responded by assassinating the Egyptian Prime Minister, al-Nuqrashi, on 28 December 1948. The head of the Secret Apparatus, al-Banna, tried to dissociate himself from this act, but in vain. Ominously, the police bodyguard he had hitherto enjoyed was withdrawn and plans were reportedly drawn up by the Egyptian Prime Minister's Office and the police CID for his assassination. He died in a hail of gunfire in central Cairo on 12 February 1949. His immediate circle were arrested and charged with plotting the assassination of the Prime Minister. However, the Egyptian government in Cairo had only itself to blame, for once it began to play what some have aptly termed 'the game of civil disorder' the process became unstoppable. Groups which the government had attempted to harness against the British and against Israel now ran out of control. Serious rioting ensued in 1950, paving the way for the Free Officer coup which brought General Mohammed Neguib to power in 1952, succeeded by Colonel Gamal Abdel Nasser in February 1954. During the early 1950s, Kermit Roosevelt led CIA efforts to court the Free Officers movement in Egypt, and by the spring of 1952 was having meetings with Nasser.[7]

But in the early 1950s British and American attention was more intently focused on Iran. In July 1950, the Chiefs of Staff met with SIS to discuss reporting on Iran. SIS still had a nineteenth-century texture and was attuned to watching internal politics through a venerable system of agents, rather than observing international developments in the region. Air Commodore Jack Easton, a senior SIS officer who superintended Anglo-American relations, conceded that external developments on Iran's frontiers were hard for them to track and 'information on Soviet moves on the frontier might take between 2 and 2½ months to reach us, since wireless could not be used and reliance had to be placed on natives in the area'. He recommended air reconnaissance for this border-watching task.[8]

SIS, together with the giant Anglo-Iranian Oil Company (AIOC), which dominated oil-production in the country, was more attentive to regime politics and managing the problem of continued access to oil, which was critical to the ailing British balance of payments. AIOC was half-owned by the British government, and its state-of-the-art refinery at Abadan, recently completed at a cost of over £100 million, was the largest in the world. London had secured a favourable agreement on continued oil-production from Teheran in 1949, but in 1950 a more generous American deal with the neighbouring Saudis – the so-called fifty–fifty agreement – put the cat among the pigeons. In 1950 AIOC only paid between 10 and 12 per cent of its proceeds to the Iranian government, after it had paid tax to London. The leading nationalist politician in Iran, Dr Mohammed Mossadegh, now pressed for the complete nationalisation of AIOC. In the short term the British Embassy seemed to be holding the line by dealing with the government of Prime Minister General Ali Razmara, who was appointed by the Shah in June 1950. Razmara was no friend of the British, but an accommodation was being worked out and, despite his necessary public denunciations of AIOC, the troubled government was being discreetly subsidised by the same company while negotiations were progressing. But on 7 March 1951 Razmara was assassinated and Mossadegh became prime minister. An Iranian parliamentary bill nationalising AIOC and its new facilities at Abadan was made law on 2 May 1951.[9]

Hitherto, Washington had allowed London a free rein in Iran, but by 1951, with Anglo-Iranian diplomatic relations severed, it was clear that London had lost any sense of direction. Thereafter, Washington took on the familiar British role of searching for a leadership that was sufficiently nationalist without being excessively radical or pro-communist. Britain's truculent refusal to see its oil revenues diminished seemed to impede this process of accommodation.[10] By contrast London saw Iranian oil as a critical factor in the attempts to stabilise the economic crisis that had prevailed in Britain since the late 1940s. In 1950 alone AIOC returned a profit to Britain of over £100 million and, like rubber and tin from Malaya, was essential to the continued viability of sterling as a world currency.[11] Washington saw this die-hard attitude as unreasonable. Around the world, many American oil companies had recently accepted the bitter pill of nationalisation on the basis of fifty–fifty sharing arrangements with the host government. The Iranians expected nothing less, but AIOC would not submit. Truman had sent Averell Harriman on a reconciliation mission to Iran, but London simply would not accept the principle of nationalisation. After the failure of the Harriman Mission, Clement Attlee sought American support for a Suez-style military invasion of Iran during the dying days of his administration in September 1951, but Truman was not prepared to sanction a return to the days of gunboat diplomacy and urged a more modern solution.[12]

Behind the scenes, key American figures were already offering the British advice. C. D. Jackson, who became Eisenhower's psychological warfare co-ordinator, was anxious to steer the British away from a post-imperial disaster and to educate London about massaging American public opinion. One of Jackson's main complaints was that 'Americans don't know where Anglo-Iranian leaves off and the British Government begins in this mess.' He was bemused to find himself dealing with AIOC officials visiting New York, rather than with British government officials. He took the opportunity to warn AIOC that it needed a major public relations counter-offensive in the United States, ideally using a public relations consultant and spending 'quite a lot of money'. He stressed that avoiding general turbulence in the Middle East was hugely important to the United States. 'Therefore, whether we like it or not, Anglo-Iranian is important to us – and I might add we are very important to you.' But Jackson feared that American public opinion would become irritated and tell the White House to 'let you stew in your own oil'. The AIOC public profile in the United States was certainly disastrous. At a time when the American oil company Aramco had skilfully played up its effective partnership with the Saudis, it became public knowledge that AIOC was paying more taxes to London than to Teheran. AIOC, Jackson observed, still lived 'in the days of British colonial supremacy'. Every current press article suggested 'anachronistic stubbornness' and a British belief 'that the only way to win was to "frighten the niggers"'. He apologised for being 'pretty tough', but added, 'this is a hell of a situation that has got to be fixed up for Anglo-Iranian and for Great Britain – and for America'.[13]

Despite appeals for common sense from figures like Jackson, the British and American positions remained far apart. In January 1952, when Churchill and Eden had arrived for talks in Washington and the situation in Teheran was high on the agenda, Dean Acheson and Anthony Eden met on the afternoon of the 9th to try and hammer out an agreed position. The economy in Iran was deteriorating as the result of interrupted oil sales during the dispute and Washington feared that the political situation would lurch to the left. A mission from the World Bank was about to depart for Teheran to try and broker a deal and it was seeking guidance. Acheson was adamant that Mossadegh was not just after a more lucrative deal for the production and sale of oil. 'Mossadeq has made it fairly clear that this will not work. What Mossadeq wants is for the British to be paid off.' Acheson feared a complete breakdown and urged the British to pull out, abandoning the refinery at Abadan and giving Mossadegh what he wanted.

Oliver Franks, Britain's Ambassador in Washington, responded candidly and neatly summarised the points of conflict with the United States, adding that he feared that it would be 'impossible' for London and Washington to agree. The American position was that 'the future of Iran is very black indeed' and that a financial sacrifice is worthwhile in the common cause. To avoid instability Washington was willing to 'shade any possible solution in favour of Iran' and give quite a lot of ground. American anxieties were very much driven by Cold War concerns and the possibility that Mossadegh might turn to the Soviet Union. But London believed that they were all being manipulated by Mossadegh's brinkmanship. In Iran, Franks insisted, Britain had often encountered serious threats about imminent breakdown, 'but they never seem to go off the cliff'. He said Britain had been calm in the face of Mossadegh's 'blackmail' while Washington had been 'alarmist'. He then explained Britain's position in the bluntest terms, underlining the stark facts of its own economic bankruptcy:

> The basic British thinking upon the oil question is that they must keep their hands on all or most of Persia's oil. This is a question of hard physical assets, and the position is based upon the principle that those who have oil to dispose of have a very great facility, particularly under world conditions as they are today ... The outcome must be that the United Kingdom has its hands upon all or most of the oil produced by the Iranian oil industry.

Britain was willing to pay Iran something for the oil, but not in dollars, as this would 'impose an unbearable hardship upon the British economy'. Moreover, AIOC wanted 'a price for oil which gives them as big a profit as is reasonable'. Franks emphasised that 'the British hold on the oil is something that they are prepared to go a long way to secure'.

Washington saw Iran mostly through a Cold War prism, while London viewed it as an Empire and sterling question. Acheson responded: 'It is not as though we were dealing with a country remote from the Soviet Union. It is a bad spot.' He was worried about encroachment by the pro-communist Tudeh Party. Eden himself said very little and there was no obvious joint way forward. But London had learned a great deal about Washington's thinking, and henceforth, British policy on Iran would have to be presented more in terms of containing the Soviets than as an attempt to save the ailing British economy.[14] By July 1952, an opportunity to do this was offering itself. British officials in Teheran diagnosed an effort by the Tudeh Party to extend its grip. Tudeh agents had already engineered the removal of all portraits of the Shah from shop-windows without any obstruction by the security authorities. Tudeh pressure on the Mossadegh government was viewed as a dress rehearsal for the 'real thing', a coup in which the Shah, Mossadegh and the constitution would be removed and the communists installed. A British Embassy official warned, 'I think there is a very grave danger of the Tudeh bringing off a successful coup d'état. The stage is already set, and from now on, unless resisted, the communists will forge ahead ... In the present situation the oil problem is of less significance than the menace of communism.' The obvious answer, officials suggested, was a pro-British coup, employing the Iranian military. But they cautioned that 'a military "coup" may be a dangerous venture if, as is alleged, the army is badly communist-infested, especially in the junior officer grades'.[15]

American intelligence elements were picking up similar signals and emphasising the drift towards communism. On 12 June 1952 the Iranian Army Chief of Staff had warned his officers that a coup by Tudeh was likely but that counter-action against Tudeh was 'too dangerous'. The Shah, a weak and vacillating figure, was now 'convinced that Mossadegh must be removed but is not quite sure how and when to do it'. He had gone so far as to approach the American Ambassador Loy Henderson 'to ascertain the US attitude to his replacement of Mossadegh'. Henderson had indicated a favourable American reaction, especially if this led to 'a reasonable approach to the oil controversy'. In order to strengthen the Shah's domestic position, US intelligence pressed for the supply of prestigious jet aircraft, which were admittedly not justifiable on military grounds.[16] But observers were gloomy. US Army officers in Teheran concluded that, even if all the senior officers could be persuaded to turn against Mossadegh, they could not perform the necessary detailed planning to oust him without their plans leaking out. Moreover, against this background, London had little hope of persuading the White House to support the British in a coup that year. Mossadegh had repeatedly visited Washington and was regarded sympathetically by Truman.[17]

Although an SIS officer, Monty Woodhouse, had been charged by London with developing plans for Mossadegh's overthrow, many of his fellow officers were also pessimistic, including Robin Zaehner, Britain's longest-serving covert specialist in Iran. Although Mossadegh's coalition government appeared to be splintering, the Shah had only limited popular support and the Shah himself was fearful of British 'plotting'. Woodhouse met with Eden in the Foreign Office in early 1953 and asked for Zaehner to be present. Zaehner had left Iran some weeks before him and now seemed disillusioned with SIS plans for a coup. To Woodhouse's dismay, Zaehner gave an extremely defeatist account of the capabilities of the pro-Western faction in Iran. Woodhouse recalled that this seemed 'to terminate the whole project'. Foreign Office officials present were visibly relieved. Pierson Dixon, who chaired PUSC's 'C' Committee which dealt with SIS, was especially keen to stop this proposed operation, because he expected it to end in embarrassing failure. But Eden was less decided and left one loophole open. He observed that the operation being contemplated would have no chance of success without CIA support. Woodhouse took his words as tantamount to permission to pursue the idea further with the Americans:

> Not wishing to be accused of trying to use the Americans to pull British chest-nuts out of the fire, I decided to emphasize the Communist threat to Iran rather than the need to recover control of the oil industry. I argued that even if a settlement of the oil dispute could be negotiated with Mussadiq, which was doubtful, he was still incapable of resisting a *coup* by the Tudah Party, if it were backed by Soviet support. Therefore he must be removed ... The plan which came with me to Washington was called, rather too obviously, Operation Boot ...[18]

Woodhouse suggested that a coup, if it succeeded, would be immediately followed by a vigorous programme of reforms. Coups are normally expensive, for many elements need to be paid off. Woodhouse estimated that half a million pounds would be needed, in addition to the £10,000 a month which was being supplied regularly to the Rashidian brothers, the main SIS agents in Iran. On 4 April 1953 Allen Dulles agreed to make $1 million available, to be used 'in any way that would bring about the fall of Mossadegh'.[19]

On 13 May Allen Dulles sent a CIA officer and Middle East specialist called Donald Wilber to meet Norman Darbyshire at the regional SIS headquarters in Nicosia. Darbyshire was one of several SIS officers who had spent the last few years in Iran. They began detailed planning, occasionally joined by the head of the Cyprus station, John Collins. Planning was an awkward business for two reasons. First, SIS and the CIA were reluctant to reveal to each other the identity of their best assets in Teheran. Second, the plan had to take the form of a treaty setting out what could be done by whom, and how much would be paid in bribes by each service. Afterward, Wilber was charged with writing a classified CIA internal history of the coup and he recorded:

> SIS was perfectly content to follow whatever lead was taken by the Agency. It seemed obvious to Wilber that the British were very pleased about having obtained the active co-operation of the Agency and were determined to do nothing which might jeopardise US participation. At the same time there was a faint note of envy expressed over the fact that the Agency was better equipped in the way of funds, personnel and facilities than was SIS.

Useful information was exchanged. SIS revealed that it had been contacting its key agents in Iran, the Rashidian brothers, by wireless three times a week, 'employing the best of British trained stay-behind operators'. The CIA then warned SIS that the US Military Assistance Mission in Iran had supplied the Iranian Army with direction-finding equipment which would allow it to locate such illicit transmitters.[20]

The arrival of the Eisenhower administration in 1953 had rendered

Washington more amenable to action. On 25 June that year, the Secretary of State John Foster Dulles gave his approval for the preparations to topple the 'madman Mossadegh' at a meeting with Allen Dulles and Kermit Roosevelt, another of the CIA's senior Middle Eastern experts who had recently been working in Cairo. SIS and the CIA had given much attention to cultivating the young Shah. After all, the Shah was a constitutional monarch with considerable powers and had simply to dismiss the objectionable Mossadegh and appoint a more pliant figure, they hoped General Fazlollah Zahedi, who had twice been chief of police. Meanwhile SIS and the CIA tried to find local fixers who could mobilise enough popular support on the streets for such a switch.[21] The Shah was the main sticking point. If possible, he was even less impressive than the figures that the CIA and SIS had tried to install in Albania, being a coward of the first order. 'To play his role the Shah requires special preparation,' the CIA noted. 'By nature a creature of indecision, beset by formless doubts and fears, he must be induced to play his role.' An endless stream of envoys was despatched to the Shah in an ineffective attempt to bolster his courage. It did not help that he was especially frightened of British secret service activity. Ultimately the plotters depended upon Princess Ashraf, 'his forceful and scheming twin sister', to get a grip upon him and to try and remove what they called 'his pathological fear of the "hidden UK hand"'. She was only partially successful, and the CIA eventually gave him the derisory nickname 'Boy Scout'.[22]

The CIA station chief in Teheran had been there for over five years and was convinced the plan would fail. Allen Dulles overcame this resistance at a stroke, placing the operation in the hands of the upbeat Kermit Roosevelt. On 11 July 1953, Eisenhower gave the final green light and Roosevelt undertook a remarkable overland drive from Damascus to Teheran carrying with him $100,000 in Iranian notes of small denominations to pay for the rent-a-crowd to throng the streets in support of a new Prime Minister. Wilber's CIA internal history of the coup reveals that Roosevelt's CIA subordinates directed a campaign of bombings by Iranians posing as members of the Iranian Communist Party and also planted articles and cartoons in newspapers. Roosevelt did not expect to succeed. The leading Iranian operatives whom he depended upon to capture the streets of Teheran were unlikely figures he had nicknamed 'Laughing Boy' and 'the Mad Musician'. Although he handpicked some royalist Iranian military officers to help with the scheme he was uncertain whether they would play their part. Because the Shah was so nervous and doubted that Roosevelt and other local men of action had the full support of their governments, further measures had to be arranged. To offer concrete proof of high-level support, Roosevelt told the Shah of specific phrases that Churchill and Eisenhower would use during the next twenty-four hours in radio broadcasts on the BBC Persian-language programme, which they did.

The coup got off to a bad start. In mid-August the Tudeh Party appeared to be backing Mossadegh and the coup stalled on the streets as the Shah hesitated to sign papers sacking his Prime Minister. The Shah fled to Baghdad and then to Rome, and his new Prime Minister-designate, who was not much more resolute, went underground. But against Roosevelt's own expectations, on 19 August, Iranians working with the CIA, quite unbidden, seized direction of a pro-Shah demonstration in Teheran and turned it on the parliament and on offices owned by Mossadegh's key supporters. Over the next few days the tide turned as factions backed by the CIA and SIS gained the upper hand in vicious street-fighting. Three hundred people were killed and the conflict culminated in a tank battle not far from the home of Mossadegh. When the fighting was over the timid Shah, who had moved from Rome back to Baghdad, returned to Teheran in triumph. The CIA immediately funnelled in $5 million to help him consolidate power.[23]

Roosevelt was flown out of Teheran on 25 August 1953 to a triumphal reception in London. He was taken to see John Sinclair, who had replaced Menzies as the head of SIS in the summer of 1952, and other senior SIS officers that very evening. From the outset SIS made plain to Roosevelt that it was grateful, not only because of the success of the operation, but also because of 'the effect its success had already had and would continue to have upon SIS's reputation and relations with its superiors'. It was clear to Roosevelt that much of the Foreign Office had retained its pre-war dislike of any kind of special activity and that SIS was having difficulty getting some of its work approved. 'SIS was glad to take advantage of any opportunity to sell themselves to this level of the Foreign Office. It appeared that their relationships, at least in this area, were neither close nor cordial at this level.'

In the next few days Roosevelt moved around Whitehall and Westminster like a travelling showman, briefing the good and the great on their success. When he came to visit Sir William Strang, the Permanent Under-Secretary at the Foreign Office, Sinclair asked if he could sit in, explaining that 'Strang was the source of his political guidance and such authorisations as were required from the Foreign Office.' Sinclair confessed that he was 'anxious to see the impact' of the Iran operation on Strang's demeanour towards SIS. Roosevelt noted that the SIS chief was not a demonstrative person, 'but there was a definite glow emanating' as Roosevelt described their success. Just as Sinclair had hoped, the effect upon the general standing of SIS in the Foreign Office, and indeed upon its specific rights and permissions, was almost immediate. Shortly afterwards, 'one of Sinclair's staff came up to him in great glee with a folder covered with red ribbons, sealing wax and other objets d'art'. Sinclair told Roosevelt that this represented approval of a project on which they had previously been turned down by the Foreign Office and this reversal by the Foreign Office was due to the success in Iran.[24]

Yet the Iran operation was not entirely cost-free for the British, since the Iranian oil agreements were now completely renegotiated. Herbert Hoover Jnr, John Foster Dulles' deputy, arrived in Teheran to assist, and the major American companies working in Saudi Arabia – Jersey, Socony, Texas and Socal – developed a substantial presence in Iran. AOIC, which was renamed British Petroleum, retained only 40 per cent of its previous share and was given £34 million in phased compensation. Set against the desperate position it faced in 1951, namely the complete loss of its assets, it could hardly complain, but some British diehards still voiced resentment and regarded this as a defeat.[25]

The return of the Shah was of dubious value to the average Iranian. In November 1958, Sherman Kent, the CIA Assistant Director who looked after National Estimates, personally reviewed Iran's development since the coup and suggested that things were still highly unstable. Allen Dulles took Kent's warning seriously and sent it on to the White House. Unexpectedly, the timid Shah had developed into a regular martinet and there was widespread discontent with the manner in which he had 'consolidated all power under his personal authority and suppressed all opposition'. There was extreme dissatisfaction with the continuance of 'near-feudal economic and social conditions and the lack of tangible results from the expenditure of oil revenues'. The CIA found it hard to monitor the opposition as it was so vigorously suppressed, but it knew it was growing. Although the CIA was now pressing the Shah down the path towards liberalisation, this was a precarious matter. Admittedly, in 1958 the Shah had begun to give press conferences, a wholly novel development. But he had also taken the opportunity to announce his own version of 'reform'. The CIA reported that 'the Shah has decided to make an example of corrupt government officials and has ordered the heads of three guilty persons be "served to him on platter" each month'. Kent could not see how even the Shah's radical approach to reform could overcome the 'massive resistance' of the privileged classes and thought it would not assuage the 'suspicious and discontented'. He concluded that a move against the Shah was likely within the next twelve months and that his position was at best 'precarious'.[26]

George Young, the SIS Controller Middle East, who detested Americans and liberals in equal amounts, captured the nature of the Shah's new regime perfectly in his memoirs. In 1955 Young met the Shah for the first time. The Shah explained that after the war, encouraged by British and American ambassadors, he had tried to be a constitutional monarch but as a consequence had ended up on the run in Rome 'with a few thousand lire and a republic declared in Teheran'. He told Young that he was done with democracy and had now resolved to 'rule myself'. From now on 'it's part of my job', he said, 'to be shot at by assassins', although he also believed in strong counter-measures and was not anxious to present his enemies with an easy target. A team of five Americans had arrived to train members of his tough new security service called Savak. The Shah's first security service chief 'was alleged to use a wild bear as a technique for interrogating troublesome students'.[27]

The successful restoration of the Shah failed to end Anglo-American bickering in Iran. In March 1954, a working group of the Operations Co-ordinating Board (OCB) was busy trying to advise on what to do about 'virtual stalemate' between British Petroleum and the American oil companies over Iranian compensation. The situation was 'so bleak' that Eisenhower had asked OCB to do some contingency planning on the problem. The working group considered making a feint towards independent action 'to shock the British' and thus provide some psychological leverage that might break the deadlock.[28] Anxieties about the growing power of the oil companies were underlined by the career of Kermit Roosevelt himself. By 1958, Roosevelt had left the CIA to spend six years as director of government affairs at Gulf Oil. Thereafter he went on to win more than a $1 billion worth of contracts for the Northrop Corporation, mostly in building up the national communications network in Iran.[29]

Nevertheless, the coup in Iran, followed by a similarly improbable coup against the socialist Arbenz in Guatemala in 1954, formed a critical turning point for both SIS and the CIA. SIS had lost interest in special operations in the Eastern bloc as early as 1949, and by 1953 even the CIA was reluctantly accepting that Iron Curtain operations paid disappointing dividends. But the events of 1953 and 1954 seemed to point the way to a new lease of life in the Third World. Although these events were dependent more on daring and luck than on the professional deployment of secret expertise, both the CIA and SIS used them to bolster the impression of their effectiveness. London and Washington would reach for this instrument in their dealings with Asian and African countries with increasing frequency.

Elsewhere in the region the hidden hand that the Shah feared so much was not only used to bring down leaders who were inconvenient to Western policy, it also served to bring on favoured protégés. Perhaps the most significant figure befriended by the CIA in the early 1950s was Colonel Gamal Abdel Nasser. In Egypt, links between the USA and the Egyptian Officers clique were developed by the local CIA station under James Eichelberger. By 1954 the CIA was offering extensive intelligence support to Nasser's internal security forces. In particular Allen Dulles made available numbers of German wartime security specialists as part of a wider package of assistance. The CIA had achieved a marked success which was even more striking when compared with the rapid decline of SIS in Egypt.[30] The key figure supplied by Dulles was former SS Obersturmbannführer Deumling (now styling himself Dr Deumling), who had served in the German security police in Yugoslavia in 1944. Taken prisoner by the Americans that year he had escaped and worked for the British in some unknown capacity in Germany between 1948 and 1951 before moving on to a new career in Egypt. Federal Germany's new security service identified at least four other former SS or Gestapo officers advising Nasser's security service. There were natural affinities, as quite a few of the Free Officers – including Anwar Sadat – had done time in British concentration camps around Cairo during the Second World War for their avowed pro-German sympathies.[31]

Allen Dulles was notably pro-Nasser, and sustained his belief that this was the figure to back in Egypt even after his controversial arms deal with the Eastern bloc. He asserted that, for all his faults, Nasser and Arab nationalists like him were the wave of the future in the Middle East. However, John Foster Dulles came to loathe the Egyptian and eventually the view of the elder brother prevailed in Washington.[32] Nasser certainly needed all the security assistance he could get. In October 1954, he finished his negotiations with the British over a new base agreement. This was signed in the Pharaonic Hall of the Egyptian parliament on the 20th of that month. The negotiations had been long and hard, and had been accompanied by many street demonstrations and even by attacks on the British Embassy. Most Egyptian groups seemed satisfied, but fringe elements were not. On 26 October, when Nasser was addressing a crowd in Alexandria, four young men from the Muslim Brotherhood made a desperate assassination attempt, firing revolver shots at close range but missing their target. In the same year there were other attempts on Nasser's life, including one launched by the French secret service.[33]

The close relations between the local CIA station and Nasser by 1955 were extraordinary and had much to do with the arrival of a new CIA officer in Cairo called Miles Copeland, an energetic individual described by some of his visiting colleagues as 'almost breathless with impatience'. The CIA had effectively taken over the diplomatic lead from the State Department in Cairo, Bangkok and a number of other capitals. When visiting CIA colleagues suggested that it might be wise for them to pay a courtesy visit to Jefferson Caffery, the American Ambassador, Copeland was dismissive. 'The old boy has already been told that this is our show. There'll be no reason for you to see him'. Copeland reportedly used an Egyptian driver nominated for him by Nasser's security service. As station chief in Syria in 1950, he had been blamed for triggering a chain of Army coups that eventually led to an increasingly pro-Soviet dictator-ship, and he had finally been moved to Cairo after a wild party during which pistols had been fired through a ceiling.[34]

A new American Ambassador was also sent to Cairo, named Henry Byroade. Copeland soon fell out with Byroade, thinking him too friendly with his British counterpart. Nasser responded by employing the CIA as his main channel of communication with Washington. Unbeknown to the Foreign Office, CIA officials in Cairo were now conducting intense day-to-day diplomacy to limit the impact of the Soviet–Egyptian arms deal, which had potentially explosive consequences for relations between Egypt on the one hand and Britain, the United States and Israel on the other. CIA officers knew that John Foster Dulles in the State Department would take the arms deal very badly and it was the CIA officers, Kermit Roosevelt and Miles Copeland, not American diplomats, who spent three and half hours with Nasser on 26 September 1955, trying to find a placatory way of publicly announcing this shocking agree-ment and trying to work into his forthcoming speech a crucial passage holding out the offer of Egyptian–Israeli détente.

This long afternoon session was interrupted by a message that the British Ambassador had requested an urgent meeting. Before departing for an adjacent room to wait out this unwelcome interruption, Roosevelt and Copeland advised Nasser to explain that the arms were from Czechoslovakia, not the Soviet Union. The meeting with the British Ambassador, Humphrey Trevelyan, was brief and unfriendly. Eventually, CIA efforts to smooth this crisis were outflanked by the decision of both John Foster Dulles and London to confront Nasser over the deal and to withdraw American financial aid for the Aswan Dam, provoking the crisis over the Suez Canal. In 1956, CIA officials and Egyptian Ministers continued to work together to draft, among other things, a letter from Nasser to Eisenhower concerning Egyptian–Israeli détente. The CIA was now encroaching on the territory of both the American military and the State Department.[35]

Britain's attitude to Nasser had been hostile from the outset. This was made clear to the Americans at a high-level dinner during Churchill's visit to Washington in June 1953. In the company of Dean Acheson, George Marshall, Walter Bedell Smith, Bill Elliott, Omar Bradley, Averell Harriman and Gladwyn Jebb, Churchill had erupted angrily when con-versation turned to Nasser. Elliott reported that Winston had told them all that he 'was damned if he was going to have Egyptian "trash" twisting the Lion's tail, and was quite prepared to occupy the country if there was any nonsense!' This confirmed the received American picture of London's backward approach to Middle East problems.[36] Eden gave Nasser an equally unmistakable message in 1955. According to Nasser, the Foreign Secretary stopped over in Cairo on the way to a SEATO conference and asked him to call at six in the evening at the British Embassy. Nasser considered this a calculated affront, as protocol required Eden to call on Nasser, but Nasser swallowed his pride and arrived promptly at the British Embassy where he was bidden to wait in the drawing room. Eden eventually entered and proceeded to walk up and down in front of the seated Nasser, lecturing him on British Middle East policy and where Egypt fitted in. Nasser recalled: 'He invited no comment or discussion, and when his near monologue was over he looked at his watch: "I am afraid I must go now. I have to change for dinner. I thought you would like to know what our policy is. It's been very nice meeting you, Colonel Nasser."' This, Nasser claimed, was the moment when he realised how little London valued Egypt's co-operation and that he would have to strike out for a new order in the Middle East.[37]

British policy did not reach a conscious break-point with Nasser until somewhat later, perhaps on 1 March 1956. The dismissal of Sir John Glubb Pasha, Commander of the Arab Legion, by the young King Hussein of Jordan tipped Eden, by now Prime Minister, over the edge. He attributed this development to Nasser and began ranting about him as a new Hitler or Mussolini. By now the effect of a worsening medical condition was beginning to take its toll on Eden's judgement. Several operations, including a failed attempt to repair a severed bile duct, left him in agonising pain. He took increasing quantities of painkillers and then benzedrine to counteract their effect. The overall effect was violent fits of rage in which he behaved unpredictably and threw things across rooms. Some of those close to him saw instances of behaviour that they considered very irrational.[38]

Anthony Nutting, the Minister of State for Foreign Affairs, encountered one of these fits of rage a few days after Glubb Pasha's removal. Nutting had put up proposals for UN peacekeeping in the region together with restrained measures for neutralising Nasser's attacks on British interests. Eden rang Nutting in the evening on an open telephone line and berated him. 'What's all this nonsense about isolating Nasser or "neutralising" him, as you call it? I want him destroyed, can't you understand? I want him murdered, and if you and the Foreign Office don't agree, then you'd better come to Cabinet and explain why.' Nutting, who revealed details of this episode only in 1985, recalled his horror, his feeling that he 'had had a nightmare, only the nightmare was real'. Ivone Kirkpatrick, the Permanent Under-Secretary, had a similar experience shortly afterwards and flatly told Eden that SIS did not have the sort of capability required to eliminate Nasser.[39]

Very few in the Foreign Office – maybe only half a dozen people – were aware of the intended collusion with France and Israel over Suez.

Eden's plan was that Israel should feign an invasion of the Canal Zone and that subsequently Britain and France should intervene on the pretext of separating the two sides, conveniently finding themselves occupying Suez. By contrast talk of liquidating Nasser as an individual was soon alarmingly widespread in Whitehall. In April 1956, the British Ambassador in Cairo, Humphrey Trevelyan, received a visit from a Treasury official, Frederic Milner, after which he complained, 'High officials in the Treasury seem to have been very free with their proposals on what to do with Nasser, which included the most extreme solutions.' He added, 'Milner has been asked to keep his mouth shut.' Officials tried to placate Eden and he was somewhat pacified by joint Anglo-American efforts to unleash a coup in Syria. But after Egypt nationalised the Suez Canal on 27 July 1956 the Prime Minister's attention returned to the business of getting rid of Nasser.[40]

The MI5 officer Peter Wright recalled being consulted on the problem of how to eliminate Nasser by John Henry and Peter Dixon, the two SIS (MI6) Technical Services Officers from the London station:

> Dixon, Henry and I all attended joint MI5/MI6 meetings to discuss technical research for intelligence services at Porton Down, the government's Chemical and Biological Weapons Research Establishment ... Their plan was to place canisters of nerve gas inside the ventilation system, but I pointed out that this would require large quantities of gas and would result in massive loss of life among Nasser's staff. It was the usual MI6 operation – hopelessly unrealistic – and it did not remotely surprise me when Henry told me later that Eden had backed away from the operation.

After the gas-canisters plan fell through, SIS looked at some new weapons. On one occasion Wright went down to Porton to see a demonstration of a cigarette packet which had been modified by the Explosives Research and Development Establishment to fire a dart tipped with poison. Here the British seemed to be emulating the sophisticated equipment they had found in the hands of Soviet assassins, such as Nikolai Khokhlov, a couple of years earlier. Not all of Wright's recollections have the ring of truth, but it is now known that both Porton Down and Aldermaston undertook technical work for the secret services in the 1950s.[41]

Adam Watson, Britain's main psywar liaison with the United States, identified some of the attendant dilemmas of an all-out offensive against Nasser's regime. The pretence of trying to find an accommodation could not be sustained alongside an aggressive policy of trying to undermine him. 'I think we realise we cannot have our cake and eat it with Nasser.' If Britain was going to preserve its 'essential position' in the Middle East and 'particularly the oil', it was going to have to 'continue and intensify our discreet operations to detach other Arab powers from Egypt' and

17. Walter Bedell Smith, Director of Central Intelligence, 1950–3, who wanted to 'beef up' CIA covert action against the Soviets late in 1951

18. Vice Admiral Longley-Cook, Britain's Director of Naval Intelligence, who warned both Attlee and Churchill in late 1951 that Washington had 'set a date' for a preventative war against Moscow in which Britain might well be destroyed

19. American training for covert action inside the Eastern bloc. Note the mixture of German and Soviet weapons

20. Allen Welsh Dulles, Director of Central Intelligence, 1953–62, who planned the new Central Intelligence Agency headquarters at Langley, Virginia, which was opened in 1962

21. Sir Percy Sillitoe, Director General of MI5, 1946–53

22. Klaus Fuchs, the atomic scientist who 'spied' for Britain and the Soviet Union, who was arrested in 1950 as the result of the Venona signals intelligence operation

23. Secret radio location techniques were used to find and bomb the command centres of Malayan Communist Party guerrillas deep in the jungle

24. The largest bombs available were dropped into the jungle in the hope of eliminating senior members of the Malayan Communist Party

25. Commander Crabb on a post-war dive. After the loss of Crabb on an SIS mission in 1956, Anthony Eden ordered a major review of the risks involved in intelligence activities and changed the rules for clearing operations

26. The British submarine HMS *Grampus* which conducted signals intelligence operations in Arctic waters near Murmansk in the early 1960s

27. American intelligence expands. The new National Security Agency headquarters at Fort George Meade, Maryland, opened in 1957

28. Sir Eric Jones, Director of Government Communications Headquarters, 1952–60

29. The Emergency in Cyprus, 1955–9, was a bloody war of bombing and assassination

30. Terrorist attacks in Cyprus prompted Downing Street to urge a tough response and a drive to liquidate the EOKA guerrilla chief, Colonel Grivas. But by the time he was located a settlement was in sight and Harold Macmillan ordered that no action be taken

31. John F. Kennedy and Harold Macmillan. Kennedy immersed himself in the details of the Profumo Affair and flew to London to support Macmillan in 1963

32. The US Army 10th Special Forces Group practise underwater infiltration operations in their 'space suits' in a lake in southern Germany during the 1960s

also to subvert Nasser. Watson was experienced and knew that hidden-hand activities designed to influence real events did not usually remain hidden for very long. It was inevitable that Nasser would become aware of Britain's operations and relations would deteriorate sharply. Watson argued that little would be lost as co-operation with Egypt was now all but impossible.[42]

Although Suez, famously, marks the nadir of Anglo-American relations in the 1950s – painfully evident in the unprecedentedly abrupt exchanges, both public and private – by 1956 British and American objectives in the Middle East were in fact converging, and many in Washington also wished to see Nasser removed. But Eden had lost patience with Washington and believed he could exploit the confusion in American policy to take control and impose his own solution. Yet policy in London was no less confused and Eden's deliberate decision to cut much of Whitehall out and to rely heavily on SIS, destroyed any possibility of success. British military planners were unaware of the scale of contacts with the Israelis. As others have observed, had American policy been more coherent, Eden might not have attempted the invasion; and, had British policy been properly co-ordinated, he might have pulled it off.

Like the CIA, SIS was busy providing 'parallel channels' of communication in the Middle East. Without consulting either the Cabinet or the Foreign Office, Eden arranged for a combination of unofficial figures well connected in Egypt, along with SIS officers, to investigate the possibility of an alternative government in the event of Nasser being brought down. Julian Amery, a Conservative MP and former wartime intelligence officer who had served in Cairo and Chungking, was better connected than either the Foreign Office or SIS with groups of rebel officers in Egypt. Amery kept both SIS and the CIA informed of aspects of his talks with Egyptian dissidents. Ivone Kirkpatrick, a confirmed special operations enthusiast, chose not to interfere with SIS plans. It is ironic that Eden had ordered Cabinet Office officials to design a much firmer regime for the clearance of SIS operations in April 1956, and then abandoned any real procedure with regard to SIS and Egypt thereafter.[43]

In the weeks before the Anglo-French attack on Egypt, Eden worried that a direct military assault might not be possible, because of the likely strength of domestic and international opposition. Instead he wished to see Nasser 'toppled' in an Iran-type operation. This was fundamentally changed, however, by the French and Israeli positions. The French wished to use military force, but the key factor proved to be Israeli–Jordanian relations, which were deteriorating after a long series of border clashes and reprisals which neither side fully controlled. London was confronted with a situation where Israel seemed to be on the point of invading either Egypt or Britain's ally, Jordan. The British Chiefs of Staff were busy preparing detailed plans for a difficult Anglo-Jordanian war against Israel. The option of an Anglo-French–Israeli collusion against Egypt was the best of an unattractive range of alternatives. Eden was also influenced in his final decision by public opinion and by the most intensely anti-Nasser figure in the British Cabinet, Harold Macmillan.[44]

At Eden's insistence, SIS made extended attempts to organise an alternative government in Egypt. Building their case upon one supposedly high-level source in Nasser's Cabinet, senior SIS officers were becoming more convinced that Nasser could not be restrained and that drastic action should be taken. They were also convinced that Nasser was working to overthrow various Arab monarchies around the region upon whose collaboration Britain based its position. A variety of anti-Nasser proposals were discussed at conferences between SIS and CIA representatives in mid-1956, some of which envisaged the additional use of Israeli special forces. Washington decided to resist SIS ideas in Egypt, and compromised on simultaneous Anglo-American planning for an Iraqi-backed coup in Syria – Operation Straggle – designed to unseat the pro-Nasser regime in Damascus.[45]

SIS conducted a fraught search for credible figures who might form an alternative Egyptian government. There was no Egyptian khedive or king available now. A diplomat from the Embassy in Cairo made a flying trip to London with a list of names. The Egyptian Deputy Chief of Air Force Intelligence, Squadron Leader Khalil, was recruited into the plot and received valuable intelligence on Israel from SIS in order to justify to his masters his frequent trips to meet his controllers in Rome and Beirut. It appears that this operation was abandoned at the end of August when part of the SIS network in Egypt was rounded up. This scheme, known as the Restoration Plot, was revived after the Suez Crisis, only to be exposed at the end of 1957, when Khalil himself proved to be a double agent working for the Egyptian security service. These were not the only anti-Nasser plots, for there were clearly other efforts that were wholly domestic in inspiration.[46]

SIS made use of one of IRD's important operations, the Arab News Agency, which was widely respected and whose news service was taken by every newspaper in the region, sometimes without charge. Although the information programme was successful, its other activities were more vulnerable. The Arab News Agency building in Cairo was transparently a cover for SIS operations; indeed it provided hardly any cover at all. In 1956 temporary additions to its staff included Sefton Delmer the wartime black propaganda expert, and William Stephenson, the secret service biographer of 'Intrepid', the head of the wartime SIS station in

New York. The Egyptian secret police rounded up much of this network in August 1956. Those identified included James Swinburn, the business manager of the Arab News Agency, Charles Pittuck, who was his stand-in and also assistant manager of the Marconi office in Cairo, James Zarb, a Maltese businessman who had served in SOE, and John Stanley from Prudential Insurance, together with twelve Egyptians. Mustapha el Hebawi, the Egyptian head of State Security, fairly gloated over his haul and enjoyed telling the British Ambassador that three Israeli spies caught earlier had already been dealt with. Two had been executed and one had committed suicide. London was forced to conclude that its own people would be 'faced with a capital indictment' and would soon be shot. In the event, Cairo was very restrained, and only Egyptians who had become entangled in the plots were executed.[47]

SIS had lost its network in Egypt and failed to bring the Americans on board. During August 1956, it had opened long meandering talks with the CIA about what might be done to topple Nasser. Several strategies were identified, and there was some discussion of assassinating Nasser, but John Foster Dulles got cold feet at the last minute and decided to withdraw his backing. On 30 August, he called Frank Wisner on the telephone to discuss this issue:

TELEPHONE CALL TO FRANK WISNER – CIA
The Secretary [Foster Dulles] asked if AWD [Allen Dulles] had had the proposed talks in London last Monday. Wisner said yes, although he had not yet received any detailed account. The Sec. said he gathered he hadn't put his point across. The Sec. said that 'they' were more determined than ever to proceed along a certain line. The Sec. said what he had heard seemed to conflict with the views he himself had expressed to Eden and [Selwyn] Lloyd [the Foreign Secretary]. Wisner said it was clear to them they were still pulling the throttle wide open . . .

The British were exasperated by the attitude of John Foster Dulles on Nasser. Having held back in August, during the post-Suez remonstrations Dulles berated them for having gone so far as to invade Egypt without dealing with the Nasser problem.[48]

Running alongside abortive attempts to eliminate Nasser were extensive 'black radio' programmes designed to destabilise his regime. These were a direct response to the Egyptian leader's own inflammatory broadcasts to various colonial territories in Africa urging rebellion against the British and the French. One station based in southern France came on the air within forty-eight hours of the nationalisation of the Suez Canal, attacking Nasser's record on social reform and taking a pro-Iraqi line. It pulled no punches, proclaiming: 'Gamal Abdel Nasser is the foremost traitor of Egypt and the Arab east. Egyptians want to get rid very soon of this madman.' But the British psywar campaign soon ran into difficulties and its attempts to represent Nasser as an agent of Zionism produced a stream of complaints from Golda Meir, the Israeli Foreign Secretary.[49]

Eden was in no mood to hold back and encouraged Selwyn Lloyd to take resources away from propaganda directed at the Soviets and deploy it against Nasser. In April 1956 he called for a 'review' of attitudes to the Soviets. 'I do not believe the Russians have any plans at present for military aggression in the West,' he asserted, noting that the Soviets had stressed that they wished to improve relations and increase contacts. How should Britain reciprocate? He asked, 'is there anything that I.R.D. is doing which ought to be discontinued? ... Might there not be a need for some adjustment of the directive on which I.R.D. is working?'[50] By contrast Eden had long urged an expansion of the IRD effort in the Middle East. In 1954 he had visited Baghdad and had identified British propaganda in the region, both overt and covert, as especially important. A new broadcasting station in Aden covering Iraq and Syria was to receive 'first priority'. By 1956, as the confrontation with Egypt developed, Eden asked Selwyn Lloyd pointedly why the station was not yet operating: 'Meanwhile the Voice of Egypt continued unchecked and pours out its propaganda in the area of our oilfields. We have simply got to take action as quickly as possible to establish a broadcasting station of our own to compete with the Egyptians.' The SIS-owned station in Cyprus, Sharq al-Adna, he complained, could not 'penetrate to Kuwait', and these further British stations were required urgently to counter Nasser's efforts.[51]

Sharq al-Adna was the arabic name for the Near Eastern Arab Broadcasting Station. Although Sharq was an SIS-owned station, most British day-to-day broadcasting in the Middle East was directed by IRD. Eden was fixated with building this up and in late May 1956 urged that 'we must keep pressing all concerned'. John Rennie, the head of IRD, was also responsible for other stations in the Persian Gulf and Aden. Eden ordered the acceleration of four other radio projects in the Middle East, in addition to Sharq, including co-operation with Baghdad Radio and a 'Black Station', that was being developed at two other sites on Cyprus with military assistance, using a transmitter that could reach as far as Aden. Getting Arab staff to work for such British projects was 'still the problem'.[52]

Sharq had originated as a wartime British propaganda radio station that had been taken over by SIS in 1948 and had been evacuated from Palestine to the safety of Cyprus. Here the radio station was resurrected near Limassol outside a small village with the improbably apt name of Polymedia in a series of Nissen huts. One of its crucial assets was a good transmitter, and by 1949 it was thought to be the most popular station in the region. By 1951 the BBC services had edged ahead in the ratings, but

Sharq remained very widely listened to. Its local chief was Ralph Poston, former editor of the Chatham House magazine *World Today*. The core of its success were strong music and drama programmes provided by 150 hard-working and very professional staff, mostly Palestinians.[53]

In 1956, Hugh Carleton Greene, who had left the information services in Malaya to become controller of the BBC Overseas Service, joined Whitehall's secret Egypt Committee chaired by the Cabinet Secretary Norman Brook which had been formed to steer anti-Nasser propaganda. As the BBC archives show, the Foreign Office Minister and former SOE official Douglas Dodds-Parker outlined the committee's objectives in no uncertain terms. In the short term its task was to put a victorious spin on recent negotiations with Egypt. 'In the long term, we aim to get rid of Colonel Nasser.'[54]

British attempts to overturn Nasser and his regime were repaid with the same coin. As London made its final preparations for Operation Musketeer, the Anglo-French invasion of the Canal Zone in October, this uncomfortable truth began to dawn. Gerald Templer warned his fellow Chiefs of Staff that the Egyptians were building up an extensive sabotage organisation in Libya, and Sir Dick White, the new head of SIS, urged that the regional MI5 office known as SIME be heavily reinforced with officers from London over this period. SIME had uncovered a plan to assassinate the King of Libya, whom Nasser regarded as a pro-Western collaborator. London concluded there would be 'political advantage in exposing the plot' to the public and the press because it would highlight how Nasser dealt with his Arab neighbours. Such revelations would, it felt, 'point the moral to King Saud and others' about the dangers of dealing with Nasser.[55]

The invasion of Suez on 29 October 1956 – Operation Musketeer – was a complex and ambitious surprise attack. It not only required precise co-operation between the colluding British, French and Israelis, it also involved attempts to hide preparations from the Egyptians and the Americans. Eisenhower and John Foster Dulles were astonished by Anglo-French-Israeli collusion, despite a degree of warning. 'Background noise' was a key factor in inflicting this surprise, for at the highest level officials in Washington were distracted by the simultaneous uprising in Hungary, which began a few days earlier. In the Middle East, attention had shifted to the possible break-up of Jordan and the likelihood of both Israeli and Arab attempts to divide the spoils. American U-2 flights out of Turkey detected Israeli mobilisation, but this was interpreted by some as part of Israeli ambitions on the West Bank. Meanwhile Allen Dulles was distracted by reports of an imminent coup in Syria.

Revealing indicators were undoubtedly there. Most dramatically, on 24 October, the American Ambassador in London flashed to Washington that he had picked up reliable inside information that Walter Monckton, the British Minister of Defence, had resigned in protest against the Cabinet's decision to use force against Egypt. Four days later, the CIA reported on the concentration of British and French bombers in Cyprus and on an increase in Israeli–French activity, prompting some American officials to speculate about Israeli raids upon Egypt. Yet Eisenhower and Dulles placed great faith in the Israeli leader David Ben-Gurion's repeated assurances that he would avoid war and believed that Britain and France would restrain themselves until after the impending American presidential election. Paris and London mounted a deliberate information blackout against the United States. Most obviously the new British Ambassador, Sir Harold Caccia, was sent to his new post in Washington by sea, arriving a week after the invasion. During the Suez invasion there was no British ambassador in Washington.

The successful cloaking of Operation Musketeer from the Americans remains mysterious. Substantial numbers of American officers were stationed in some of the most sensitive areas of Whitehall, especially in Air Intelligence centres. Indeed, during the Suez invasion there was a simultaneous US Sixth Fleet exercise off Crete, directed from the US naval headquarters in London. Nevertheless, American Naval Intelligence conceded frankly that it had 'no warning of British intentions'.[56] The best American shot at predicting Operation Musketeer was provided by the U-2 aircraft which had been flying from Wiesbaden in Germany (Detachment A) since June 1956 and from Incirlik near Adana in Turkey since September (Detachment B). With regional tensions growing Wiesbaden aircraft reinforced overflights of the Mediterranean and the Middle East in late August, revealing large numbers of British troops in Malta and Cyprus. On 7 September, Washington, still unaware of British plans, authorised the hand-over of some of these U-2 photos to the British. James Reber and Arthur Lundahl, two senior CIA officers, flew to London with film taken on 30 August. These, they later claimed, were the last U-2 photos of the region handed over to the British during the rest of that year.

By 12 September, Robert Amory, the Deputy Director for Intelligence at the CIA, had become sufficiently worried about the region to establish the PARAMOUNT Committee, a joint group from CIA, NSA, State Department and the armed services to watch the Middle East twenty-four hours a day. This was an all-source effort using agents, sigint and U-2 aerial photography. Special new agreements were negotiated between the US Air Force and the CIA over photo-reconnaissance, never an easy relationship, to ensure an expansion of the Wiesbaden U-2 operation covering the Middle East crisis. A CIA official history claims that 'This unit's timely and accurate information enabled the PARAMOUNT

Committee to predict the joint Israeli–British–French attack on Egypt three days before it took place.'[57]

The general successes of the U-2 aircraft have been somewhat exaggerated by the CIA, and this particular claim is also somewhat misleading. Photo-reconnaissance has limitations as well as strengths. It can capture the dispositions of forces on the ground but it cannot always see into the minds of decision-makers. The U-2 evidence was not compelling enough to sway opinions in Washington or to transcend the background noise of other events in the region. On 26 October Allen Dulles briefed a National Security Council meeting and countered rumours 'flying around' that day that the King of Jordan had been assassinated. This helped to focus attention more closely on Jordan, and two days later John Foster Dulles in fact told Eisenhower that he believed what was really going on was that the Israelis were about to attack Jordan. He added in parenthesis that there might be some sideshow in which the British and the French used the confusion to occupy the Suez Canal. Washington was preoccupied by the fixed idea of the war that most had expected in 1956, a conflict between Israel and Jordan. Eisenhower knew that was something was going on and attached special significance to NSA reports of an increase in signals traffic between Tel Aviv and Paris. But Selwyn Lloyd in London deliberately deceived American diplomats by rubbishing the idea of an attack on Egypt and talking up an Israeli attack on Jordan as his 'major concern'.[58]

Later, in front of a hostile Senate, Allen Dulles claimed to have offered forewarning of Suez. The Intelligence Advisory Committee had indeed warned in September, and also at several moments during late October, of a possible *solo* Israeli attack on Egypt, but all this was clouded by a conviction that this constituted an Israeli diversion associated with a main thrust into Jordan. Allen Dulles himself took this line in his presentations to the NSC. When Eisenhower was briefed about the build-up of British forces in Cyprus he personally dismissed its significance, refusing to believe that Britain would 'be stupid enough to be dragged into this'. The British deception had been so good that six weeks after the invasion of Suez the CIA was still uncertain whether the British had colluded directly with the Israelis, though it was sure the French had.[59]

With hindsight the high-point of American efforts was a National Intelligence Estimate produced under the auspices of the CIA on 19 September, more than a month before the attack, which considered the likelihood of a British–French resort to military action against Egypt during the next few weeks. This concluded, 'The majority of the British cabinet, especially Prime Minister Eden, and virtually all the members of the French cabinet, are convinced that the elimination of Nasser is essential to the preservation of vital Western interests in the Middle East and

North Africa ... They are now in a high state of military readiness and can initiate military action at any time.' But the estimate insisted the British Cabinet would be deterred by the level of public criticism across the world and that the moment for the use of force had almost passed. The temptation for London and Paris to use force would 'occur only in the event of some new and violent provocation' by Nasser, and they argued that he knew this and would make every effort to prevent it from occurring.[60]

Deliberate surprise was not the only aspect of Suez that made Eisenhower very angry. Circumstances conspired to create a busy week for the White House in early November. On Tuesday, 30 October news broke of the British and French attacks. On Friday, 2 November, John Foster Dulles was suddenly rushed to the Walter Reed Hospital in Washington with severe abdominal pains. He was discovered to have cancer of the colon and underwent a five-hour operation. On Sunday, 4 November, with the Secretary of State incapacitated, the Soviets invaded Hungary. On Tuesday, 6 November, the United States went to the polls in the presidential election. The conjunction of Suez and Hungary made it difficult for Washington to criticise the Soviet use of force in Eastern Europe while its allies were doing the same in the Middle East. An exasperated Eisenhower decided to call Eden and let him have it with both barrels. William Clark, Eden's Press Secretary, picked up the telephone. Eisenhower asked, 'Is that you Anthony?' Clark responded, 'No' in a low voice. Eisenhower did not hear the reply and launched straight in with 'Well, this is President Eisenhower, and I can only presume that you have gone out of your mind.'[61]

American lobby groups supporting East European exiles were especially furious with the British, French and Israelis. The American Friends of the Captive Nations complained that the State Department 'gave the Suez Crisis priority' and did nothing to help Hungary. The arrival on 3 November of Herbert Hoover Jnr as the Acting Secretary of State during the absence of John Foster Dulles reinforced this idea, as Hoover was a leading figure in the oil industry and a Middle East expert. Eisenhower now sat down with his Cabinet to decide how to rein the British in and decided to put pressure on sterling, which quickly brought Operation Musketeer to a standstill.[62]

Intelligence played an important role during the Suez campaign itself. Signals intelligence was probably the most important and remains the most mysterious – few studies of Suez refer to sigint even briefly. On the eve of the Suez Crisis, Selwyn Lloyd, the Foreign Secretary, wrote to Eric Jones, the Director of GCHQ, congratulating him on the volume of material relating to the Middle East that GCHQ had provided, particularly subsequent to the seizure of the canal: 'I have observed the volume of material which has been produced by G.C.H.Q. relating to all the countries in the Middle East area'. This suggests that the traffic of many countries was being read. Lloyd added, 'I am writing to let you know how valuable we have found this material and how much I appreciate the hard work and skill involved in its production.' Jones passed on these congratulations to units such as the Army's 2 Wireless Regiment and the RAF's 192 Squadron. There had also been shipborne signals interception by the Royal Navy. During the invasion itself a small tactical sigint unit accompanied the fleet from Cyprus to Egypt. The RAF signals element was especially important and Washington aircraft from 192 Squadron, despatched to Cyprus prior to the operation, had mapped the characteristics of Egyptian anti-aircraft defence. These included the habit of shutting down air defence radar routinely just after midday – a priceless piece of information.[63]

RAF photo-reconnaissance was also critical. During the Suez operation this effort was controlled by the Joint Air Reconnaissance Intelligence Committee, Middle East. The work was mostly conducted by Canberra aircraft of 13 Squadron and by French RF-84s. The latter were simpler with fewer cameras, and so achieved a film development and initial interpretation time that was twice as fast as their more sophisticated British counterparts, which initially used all their seven cameras over the target area. The British eventually reduced this to two cameras for speed of interpretation and processing. Some of the British equipment reached Cyprus only a day before the commencement of hostilities and at H-hour the French photo-interpretation teams had still not arrived. The average processing time from landing to finished intelligence was two and quarter hours. Daily reconnaissance was flown over Egyptian airfields, military targets, roads, railways and canals, while designated 'special targets' were the Cairo Radio transmitters, radar sites and parachute-dropping zones. Two Canberras were shot at by fighters using ammunition with proximity fuses which was presumed to have been fired from the 37mm cannon in an Egyptian MiG-15, but escaped unscathed. Between 30 October and 6 November, when the campaign ended, 137 missions were flown. Syrian airfields were covered from 31 October and proved to be a more dangerous target.[64]

The CIA's U-2 aircraft of Detachment A at Wiesbaden continued to provide excellent intelligence to the PARAMOUNT Committee in Washington throughout a dangerous period which lasted until the ceasefire on 6 November. Bulganin, the Soviet Foreign Minister, had sent threatening messages to London, Paris and Tel Aviv warning of Soviet intervention to punish the aggressors. Accordingly, the skies over Syria and Lebanon were thick with British and American spy-planes searching for Soviet aircraft that might have been deployed there from the north ready for a Soviet foray into the Middle East. The high-flying U-2s remained untouchable, but one British Canberra was shot at by Meteors of the Syrian Air Force on 5 November. Later that day another was brought down by the Syrians, crashing in nearby Lebanon. The pilot and navigator ended up in a Beirut hospital, but the third member of the crew was killed. The Canberra crash set off a panic in London. In Beirut, a bemused young British air attaché received a flash telegram ordering him to head for the crash-site carrying a pot of paint. His orders were to blot out the serial number on the tail identifying it as an intelligence-gathering PR-7 aircraft. The Air Attaché confirmed that he had painted out the serial number, but added that the nature of the aircraft could be guessed by the vast camera protruding from the wreckage and the hundreds of feet of film spewed around the crash-site. By 6 November all Canberras were escorted by Hunter aircraft when withdrawing from photo-targets over Syria, and two RF-84Fs were sent on each French mission. By 8 November all work over Syria had been stopped.[65]

Despite Eden's personal exhortations British psywar was a disaster. Brigadier Bernard Fergusson had been made director of psychological warfare for the Suez campaign at very short notice but had no experience of propaganda. On 8 August 1956 the Directorate of Forward Plans had conceded that the French and the Americans had active psychological warfare units but the British 'only have plans'. Scratch units were pulled together, but the very basic nature of the efforts was revealed by a memo requiring all documents referring to 'Psychological Warfare Unit' to be changed to read 'No.1 Loudspeaker Troop'. Fergusson spoke hopefully of inducing both the military and the civil population 'to co-operate in the overthrow of Nasser' and of exploiting irritations about the failure to implement land reform, but this did not carry the ring of conviction. Without an overt political opposition in Egypt it was difficult to know exactly how to direct civilian broadcasting. In the end, British broadcasting became a military psywar project, focused on Egyptian front-line troops ready for the invasion.[66]

Fergusson's encounter with Britain's civilian radio assets on Cyprus was no less disastrous. Just before the invasion he was given authority over Sharq. It was decided to turn the station from a subtle 'grey' operation into a hardline hectoring outfit, similar to Nasser's Voice of Egypt. The station was renamed Voice of Britain and the tone changed dramatically, broadcasting obvious threats such as 'How would you like to feel the cold steel of a British bayonet in your back?' Ralph Poston, the liberal Director of the Station, summoned his staff to denounce Eden's Suez policy and the 'disastrous situation' it had caused. Poston also went on air to warn his listeners against British plots and was promptly arrested by Fergusson and brought back to Britain. Most Arab staff resigned and several were so incensed that they defected to Nasser's radios in Cairo. British Arabic speakers had to be brought in. A few Arab staff soldiered on and eventually joined a further project run jointly by IRD and major oil companies in the Persian Gulf in 1964 called the Voice of the Coast, which broadcast from facilities in the compound of the Trucial Oman Scouts in Dubai. Poston, however, abandoned broadcasting to become an Anglican vicar and eventually converted to Islam.[67]

Between the Korean War and the Suez Crisis, Attlee, Churchill and then Eden presided over a spiralling decline in Anglo-American relations. The main issue, lurking beneath myriad sources of discontent, was fear of atomic war. After 1949 Britain felt its vulnerability keenly, while many in the United States saw the logic of resolving the 'Soviet problem' before the US became vulnerable to Soviet attack, a moment heralded by the arrival of Sputnik in 1957. For almost a decade this 'vulnerability gap' between London and Washington created profound distrust. This was exacerbated by events in China and the Middle East. Sometimes the tensions became very personal. The British relationship with Eisenhower was increasingly distant, while Churchill and Eden both hated John Foster Dulles with a passion. Eden considered him to be 'bitterly anti-British', while Churchill remarked in May 1954 that Dulles was 'a dull, unimaginative, uncomprehending, insensitive man; so clumsy'. He added, 'I hope he will disappear'.[68]

But in the eyes of Washington it was Churchill and Eden who often seemed about to disappear. Their physical, and sometimes mental, decrepitude served as anthropomorphic symbols of the corroded state of the British Empire. Although the CIA and SIS had worked together in Iran, and by 1957 would be working together again against Nasser and his allies in Syria, the CIA nevertheless saw the British as a failing force. London lacked the positive vision that would allow it to co-operate with the emerging nationalist forces in the Third World. This was never more apparent than when Kermit Roosevelt returned from his success in Iran and was ushered in to see Churchill in August 1953. When he arrived at 10 Downing Street at two o'clock in the afternoon he found Churchill ill and in bed. This was 'a most touching occasion', for the Prime Minister was 'in bad shape physically'. A pathetic figure, he had difficulty hearing, occasional difficulty in speaking and difficulty seeing to his left. Nevertheless, he was able to summon up some rhetoric, expressing a wish that if he had been 'some years younger' he might have served under Roosevelt's command in this great adventure. If the Shah now stayed in power, he asserted, it would be 'the finest operation since the end of the war'. He conceded that Anglo-Iranian Oil had really 'fouled things up' and he assured Roosevelt that they would not be allowed 'to foul things up any further'.

Churchill was already suffering from a series of strokes that would leave him gravely incapacitated by 1954. His Foreign Secretary Eden was conspicuous by his absence, having embarked on a number of operations, including emergency surgery in Boston to save his life, that would leave him very ill, increasingly dependent on drugs and vulnerable to fevers and violent mood swings. The air of decrepitude was unmistakable and, standing in Churchill's bedroom at 10 Downing Street, Kermit Roosevelt might have been forgiven for wondering who was really at the helm. In the words of a CIA internal history: 'The Prime Minister made several references, which indicated that he regarded SIS as *his* service, and that it was very close to his heart. Perhaps due to his physical condition at the time, however, he was a bit hazy ... The initials CIA meant nothing to him, but he had a vague idea that Roosevelt must be connected in some way to his old friend Bedell Smith.'[69] Events in the Middle East had not only exacerbated growing tensions in the Anglo-American intelligence relationship. They had also exposed dysfunctions in the British and American policy machines. In London, SIS was plunged back into a status of distrust and dislike vis-à-vis the Foreign Office following its role in Suez, compounded by an ongoing enquiry into its command and control that had been ordered by Eden. Meanwhile in American diplomatic outposts across the Middle East, from Iran to Egypt, disgruntled ambassadors increasingly played second fiddle to the representatives of the hidden-hand services located in their own embassy, sometimes pursuing different policies. American ambassadors in Burma and Egypt had already experienced this, and would soon be joined by their colleagues in India and Indonesia.

Iran, taken *together* with Suez, also reveals a great deal about developing American attitudes to intervention. American historians have asked why Washington became so incensed about the Suez episode when, in some respects, its objectives closely mirrored those of US intervention in Iran and Guatemala during the 1950s, or even the failed operation against Cuba in 1961. Seen alongside American intervention in Iran in 1953, Eisenhower's public remarks throughout the Suez Crisis seem permeated with 'moral righteousness and hypocrisy'. But the Eisenhower administration would have argued that covert operations were *qualitatively* different from overt military intervention, a distinction that was multiplied when anti-communism was involved. Oil also loomed large in Eisenhower's thinking and helps to explain the dramatic American *volte face* on the question of action against Iran. Truman resisted intervention in 1952, but Eisenhower approved the toppling of Mossadegh a year later. British and French policy-makers failed to understand these distinctions. For Eisenhower, intervention against radical nationalists was acceptable, even desirable, if it could be hidden. But overt intervention could not be squared with Washington's public foreign policy, a country with its own anti-colonial heritage which had tried hard to befriend the new nationalist leaders. Nevertheless, hidden-hand coercion was increasingly important for the United States in resolving a deeper dilemma. What was Washington to do when the free countries of the world used their freedom to choose neutralism, or even degrees of co-operation with the Soviet Union?

Either way, after 1956, Anglo-American relations had entered a new era. Eisenhower would work hard to restore co-operation with Eden's successor, Harold Macmillan, but on a more calculating basis, stripped of any cloying sentimentality. Macmillan would promote this co-operation, one SIS officer recalled, partly by sending round an order banning 'frank discussion of American factors' within Whitehall. In November 1956, during the immediate backwash of the Suez Crisis, two former JIC chairmen wrote to one another about recent events. Sir Harold Caccia suggested to Sir Patrick Reilly that they should henceforth regard the Anglo-American relationship unsentimentally as a business relationship. He continued, 'I personally am quite glad that the post-war period of "old-boyism" is at an end. It was getting phoney and maybe the end has to be sharp.'[70]

22

Victory in Malaya

H.E. the High Commissioner has directed that the planning of operations to eliminate the members of the Central Politbureau and other high-ranking members of the MCP should start as soon as possible.
General Sir Robert Lockhart, Director of Ops, 6 February 1953[1]

After the demoralising pattern of events at Suez, the British victory in Malaya was of enormous psychological importance. Like the guerrilla conflicts in Palestine and, later, Cyprus, the Malayan Campaign was primarily an intelligence war. Success here raised Britain's standing in the eyes of the Americans, for whom these sorts of struggles in the Third World were becoming more important. The Malayan Emergency began in 1948 as a struggle with 8,000 ethnically Chinese guerrillas controlled by the Malayan Communist Party or MCP. This soon developed into a gruelling jungle war of twelve years' duration. Most appreciated that the Emergency featured elements of both colonial revolt and the containment of communism. But few understood that this struggle had its direct origins in the 1920s, when Britain's security services in Asia had penetrated many of the indigenous communist parties. In the inter-war years, the British had recruited an ethnically Vietnamese communist known as Lai Tek, offered to them by the French Sûreté in Indochina. Working as an informer for the police in Singapore, he joined the MCP, and rose through the ranks to become its secretary general. Britain's inter-war network of police surveillance was so good in 1931 that it even caught Ho Chi Minh and forced him to spend some time incarcerated in Hong Kong. Unsurprisingly, in the 1930s, the British did not consider Asian communism to be a threat. However, the arrival of the Japanese in 1941 broke this elaborate network of surveillance. The MCP headed into the jungle to set up a guerrilla army of its own, and Lai Tek slipped away from British control.[2]

When SOE in India began to establish significant links with the secretive guerrillas in 1943, it concluded that the senior MCP leaders were moderates and that the British did not have 'much to fear from them'. Instead it was the junior, more 'fanatical' local leaders who were 'dangerous'. The key was to try to ensure that the Central Committee stayed in control of its followers. This also went for Lai Tek, whom SOE reported to be the Central Committee's 'most secret and revered personality'. Lai Tek, it added, was a 'shrewd and clever man but no fanatic', although SOE never established really close contact.[3]

As in Burma, there had been volatile argument in London about SOE support for the MCP guerrillas long before the war had even ended. Here, too, an alliance of SOE and Admiral Lord Louis Mountbatten, Supreme Allied Commander South East Asia, won the argument and support continued. In the summer of 1945, London finally authorised as much assistance to the MCP guerrilla forces as was necessary to achieve control. Building up continued, but SOE's central purpose was now retardation of its own guerrilla forces which it barely controlled.[4] SOE was soon very busy in Malaya. The near-complete absence of the Japanese Air Force allowed substantial deliveries of stores by RAF Special Duties aircraft to the six main guerrilla groups, including 2,000 weapons. By 15 August 1945 there were at least 308 SOE personnel, five Gurkha Support Groups and forty-six W/T sets in the field. Nevertheless, Mountbatten's efforts to control the guerrillas were only partly successful. Their strength was first thought to be 3,000–4,000 but it was soon recalculated at 6,000–7,000. The appearance of so many guerrillas of whom SOE had no knowledge raised suspicions that they were part of an MCP 'secret army' formed from the Party's most experienced fighters in April 1945, using newly supplied weapons. These were the longest-serving members and they were given the task of storing as many weapons as possible in case the new British settlement was not to their liking.[5]

During August and September 1945 SOE liaison officers could not prevent a wave of murderous reprisals against the Japanese and against civilian collaborators and informers. Nevertheless, Mountbatten's friendly attitude encouraged the MCP Politburo to entertain hopes of a negotiated place in the post-war government, forcing its members to tread water and lose momentum. Mountbatten kept up the charade, allowing the guerrillas to conduct a victory parade through Singapore, where he decorated its leaders. Chin Peng, who would become the key MCP leader during the Emergency, personally received the OBE from Mountbatten on the steps of the Municipal Building there. Final demobilisation of the guerrillas proved difficult. An enormous sum of $350 per head was offered on disbandment, with a further payment later, but the core forces and the best weapons stayed in the jungle. By April 1946 Mountbatten and the military administration had gone. The new civil government in Singapore, Britain's restored regional power centre, was less friendly and the younger elements in the MCP pressed for armed struggle. Soon the photographs taken during Mountbatten's victory parade were being employed by the security forces in their search for the MCP leaders.[6]

The uneasy peace that characterised the winter of 1945–6 also denoted a struggle between the MCP leadership, who advocated a semi-constitutional path, and the younger militants. The MCP leadership were gradually giving way, while rice shortages and labour troubles offered ready issues for the militants to exploit. Lai Tek had also been a restraining factor. But by March 1947 other MCP leaders had uncovered his wartime contacts with the Japanese and he escaped into Thailand with most of the Party funds, only to be eliminated in Bangkok within a short period of time. Younger and more radical leaders now came to the fore.[7]

SOE had done a creditable job in winding down many of the guerrilla formations. But this good work was undermined by intelligence failure on the part of both MI5 and the separate Malayan Security Service, the security intelligence element of the local Malayan government. Intelligence in Malaya after the war was simultaneously decrepit and self-satisfied. In June 1947 the senior MI5 officer in the region gave his views on communism in South-east Asia. His office, known as Security Intelligence Far East (SIFE), also worked closely with SIS officers tasked with counter-intelligence in neighbouring countries. SIFE was somewhat complacent and regarded communism as a limited problem fomented from outside by Moscow, not as an indigenous matter. In the short term SIFE saw no problem. The war, it felt, had left communist parties in the region out of touch or disorganised and Moscow was not yet interested in South-east Asia. For the time being there was 'a certain lack of direction', although it expected them once reorganised to employ nationalism as a tool, as well as exploiting labour unrest.[8]

The Malayan Security Service (MSS) under Colonel John Dalley took the same complacent view. Lulled into a false sense of security by its pre-war success in containing what was then a small MCP, it dismissed the remaining guerrillas as a few isolated bandits. The period 1945–7 had been marked by organised labour unrest promoted by the MCP, but the main strike-organiser had been arrested and Dalley expected only more of the same. The advent of Emergency in 1948 with its massacres of European planters and miners was not only a rude shock, but represented only the first of a series of disasters in Malaya. On the first day of the declared Emergency, leaders of the MCP front organisation were arrested in a police raid led by the Special Branch. But its most talented leader, Chin Peng, escaped, leaping over a wall and fleeing into the jungle to take up the leadership of a twelve-year guerrilla war with British forces. As in Palestine, the war with the MCP in Malaya quickly became an intelligence-driven conflict which the British appeared to be losing.[9]

Matters were not improved by a new high commissioner of Malaya, Sir Henry Gurney, plucked from Palestine, and the arrival, in his wake, of a new commissioner of police, Colonel Nicol Gray, also from Palestine, with large numbers of ex-Palestine police. Arthur Creech Jones, the Colonial Secretary, thought this Palestine element was a good idea but it proved to be a major mistake. Already brutalised, but completely ignorant of local conditions, the newly introduced police proved to be a liability and on a number of occasions they resorted to arbitrary behaviour. In the early stages of the Malayan conflict one role for British propaganda was to draw a veil over some of the unpleasant 'Palestinian' incidents.[10]

Malaya now joined an excessively long list of security problems that were piling up on the desks of MI5. Intelligence there was a mess and would remain so until the arrival of General Sir Gerald Templer in early 1952. The various intelligence and security services in Malaya and Singapore had never been team players. They had indulged in backbiting in the 1930s and had discovered co-operation only on the eve of the Japanese invasion of 1941. After the war they returned to their old ways. It was symptomatic of local feuding over intelligence that the Director of the Malayan Security Services, John Dalley, was not permitted to sit on the regional JIC Far East, despite requests for his attendance by the Governors of Singapore and Malaya.[11]

In mid-1948, when the Malayan Emergency erupted with full force, the first reaction of civilians in the Malayan government was not to upgrade intelligence, but to launch special operations. They created Ferret Force, consisting of six special units with a high proportion of ex-SOE personnel from Malaya and Burma 'with intimate knowledge of both the country and the enemy'. The object was to penetrate their headquarters or attack training camps and supply routes. Now two SOE-inspired groups, the MCP guerrillas and Ferret Force, were engaged on opposing sides of this new conflict.

But almost as soon as they were formed the familiar political problems of commanding special operations reared their head. Ferret Force was hardly a military unit, for its officers were all civilians and held local commissions. Ferret Force was even paid for by the federal government. Within months of the outbreak of the Emergency, regular Army commanders were intensely resentful of this 'Private Army'. General Sir Neil Ritchie saw it as nothing less than 'the thin end of the wedge for certain civilian officials to feel it was within their province to direct its operation', and he added with satisfaction that its 'disbandment put an end to this'. The SOE veterans' Ferret Force had lasted less than a year.[12]

This was hardly surprising. Ferret Force was an intense distillation of irregular types and unconventional thinking. It not only contained many civilians who had served with SOE in Malaya alongside the MCP, including Richard Broome and John Davis, it also harboured, from the point of view of the orderly military mind, a more dangerous element. These were senior adherents of the famous Colonel Orde Wingate, who had led the Chindits in raids deep behind enemy lines in Burma. They were regarded as dangerous because Wingate, a charismatic leader, had instilled his followers with his revolutionary military philosophy which involved breaking up the established chain of command. One Wingate disciple was Robert Thompson, who after serving with the Chindits fought on as a colonel in Ferret Force in 1948 and then became a senior official directing the Emergency. Eventually he headed the British Advisory Mission to Vietnam in the 1960s which enjoyed a significant intelligence role. 'Wingate was the person who had dominated my life and thinking for the last three years of the war and who had a profound influence on me for the rest of my life,' wrote Thompson. For many, Wingate was a demigod: 'Mediocrity was stripped bare in his presence ... petty bureaucracy was thrust aside.' Regular Army officers were bound to find this sort of thing quite intolerable.[13]

Although Ferret Force was disbanded, the SAS arrived by 1952. The SAS had deliberately maintained itself as a regular force in waiting. In 1948, the Commander of 21 SAS, a territorial unit, noted that he was aiming not only at establishing a unit ready to undertake a variety of SAS tasks at short notice, but also at laying 'the foundations for expansion without delay'. A high proportion of his recruits were ex-officers and potential officers, who served for the time being in the ranks. He was also working with the SAS Association to keep an up-to-date register of ex-SAS who would volunteer in the event of mobilisation. He maintained regular contact with the secret services to ensure ready access to adequate quantities of special equipment, including 'small wireless sets, silent pistols' and 'S-phones', which were an early form of walkie-talkie.[14]

The primary problem in Malaya was not special operations but intelligence. By July 1948 the extent of British vulnerability was becoming clear. The Malayan Security Service was alarmed by a raid that month on the Batu Arang coalmine – the only one in Malaya – which supplied much of the fuel for railroads and power stations. The attack was thought to have been led by the former leader of the coalmine's labour union who had recently fled 'into the bush'. At this point many Criminal Investigation Department (CID) and MSS officers concluded, quite wrongly, that the campaign was being run from outside Malaya, pointing to Bangkok as the central HQ of the guerrillas.[15] Lurking beneath this conclusion was an equally eccentric view among many British intelligence officers that their task would have been easier if they had acquired a sizeable slice of southern Thailand, known as the Kra Isthmus, at the end of the war. On 12 November 1948 the American Ambassador in Bangkok met with Colonel Graysbrook, Director of Intelligence at Britain's Far East Land Forces HQ in Kuala Lumpur, at a cocktail party in Singapore. On several occasions he expressed 'regret that the British failed to take the entire Kra Isthmus upon their return to Malaya'. He also expressed 'deep concern for the "down-trodden" Malayan minorities' in southern Thailand. But this had little to do with the MCP problem in Malaya.[16]

Intelligence in both London and Singapore eventually decided that the escalation of violence had been orchestrated from outside. But the location they settled on was not Bangkok but the joint conference of the World Federation of Democratic Youth and the International Union of Students, both Moscow-controlled outfits, which was held in Calcutta in February 1948. This was also a red herring. Malaya was now seen as an extension of a worldwide campaign launched with the creation of the Cominform by the Soviet Union in late 1947 and spearheaded by the Kremlin's struggle against the Western powers. It seemed more politic to associate it with Moscow rather than Beijing, which London was about to recognise. In practice the intelligence to support claims of external support or direction of the MCP was practically nil: in fact, the decision to launch the Emergency had been a local one taken by the MCP's Central Committee in March 1948.[17]

By November that year, London was engaged in a surreal discussion about 'Soviet intrigues in Malaya'. It busied itself with the business of preventing the Soviet diplomatic courier service stopping off at Singapore, *en route* to Australia. MI5 considered that Soviet intelligence was supporting the MCP campaign, and added, 'it is obviously quite easy for them to contact local Communists ... pass to them documents, money etc.'. All this reflected a firm belief that the Malaya problem could not have its genesis in the British colony itself, but instead was Moscow-exported communist mischief, accelerated by 'Moscow gold'. A similar view was held by the French Colonial Sûreté in Indochina. Moscow had certainly engaged in such intrigues in the region in the 1930s, and this template was reinforced in the British mind by the uncovering of various agents in Canada and Australia during the late 1940s. But the unrest in Malaya was in fact largely indigenous.[18]

Malcolm MacDonald, Britain's Commissioner General in South-east Asia, spouted the same line to the Commonwealth Prime Ministers in October 1948. Until recently the communists had pursued a strategy of infiltrating the trade unions and at one point controlled the leadership of half of them. But in 1948 they had begun to lose ground. This, together with the Calcutta Conference, had prompted a dramatic change of tactics. So far 178 people had been killed in the Emergency, and MacDonald believed that 'we were faced with what was, in part, an overflow of the civil war in China between the Communists and the Kuomintang'. He pointed out that, of the 343 terrorists killed or captured since June, 332 were Chinese and the majority had not been born in Malaya and were 'comparatively new immigrants'. Again the anxiety was to locate the trouble outside the realm of British colonial territory, and MacDonald concluded that the 'Communist movement was largely alien and had little support from the country'.[19]

Events in Malaya had a profound impact on intelligence and security matters right across the Empire, and the Colonial Office was reluctantly persuaded to join the higher-level intelligence and security committees in Whitehall, including the JIC and the Russia Committee. Whitehall was not initially impressed by the Colonial Office contribution, and in March 1950 Gladwyn Jebb complained that the Russia Committee had been sent 'an incompetent imbecile who ought not to be allowed to go near any departmental committee of any nature'. It was also decided that it was time to stiffen anti-communist defences in all colonies, especially in Africa, and Bevin warned Attlee that sooner or later they would confront a 'major drive against our position in Africa' by a 'really serious Soviet-inspired Communist movement'. What Malaya had shown was that the British needed to have in place 'an intelligence organisation that will enable the police to forestall trouble' before things got out of hand. A 'special adviser' was being found to advise governors on strengthening intelligence and security, but the inevitable fight had broken out between the Colonial Office and the Ministry of Defence over who should own this role. Bevin ordered them to get this 'settled rapidly'.[20]

Arguably the MCP guerrillas were under pressure from the start of the Malayan Emergency and made early strategic errors. The biggest problem for the security forces was tactical intelligence, for it was nearly impossible to find a small but dangerous enemy in a very large area. But in June 1949 the security forces were heartened by a change in tactics by the guerrillas. Harry Fischer, the Chief Intelligence Officer, Malaya District, explained that a new MCP directive had been seized in a raid in Negri Sembilan. This revealed that the guerrillas were going to concentrate two-thirds of their forces in three areas in the north, while allowing a third of their forces to roam the south 'as killer squads' of about ten men each. This concentration was going to make life easier for the security forces.[21]

On 3 April 1950 the talented General Sir Harold Briggs became the Army director of operations. The major problem was spotted immediately: 'Unfortunately our Intelligence organisation is our "Achilles

Heel" ... when it should be our first line of attack.' Briggs went on, 'We have not got an organisation capable of sifting and distributing important information quickly.' But the action taken to deal with this was inadequate. Although a Joint Intelligence Advisory Committee was set up at the federal level to make recommendations and a new director of intelligence was appointed, it was over a year before their practical recommendations took effect and a flow of new Special Branch officers began to arrive. Briggs did not have the power to impose deep reform, and intelligence remained lacklustre.[22] Attempts at reforming the intelligence structure quickly ran into political problems. There was still no real Special Branch as such within police CID, and meanwhile Dalley's Malayan Security Service had operated as a 'private army', refusing to accept police authority. Dalley's outfit was forcibly disbanded under pressure from MI5, which then proposed to send out its colonial expert, Alex Kellar, to head SIFE with Colonel Hugh Winterborn, who had served in SEAC under Mountbatten, as his deputy. But Malcolm MacDonald loathed Kellar and demanded someone with local knowledge. He complained that 'Sillitoe's effort to force on us proposals which he knows that we shall object to makes an extremely unpleasant impression on me,' an effort which struck him as calculated to destroy confidence between himself and SIFE. A compromise was eventually reached in the shape of Jack Morton, a former Indian police officer who took over SIFE and was given the task of building a proper Special Branch. But, although talented, he always felt that Nicol Gray, the Commissioner of Police from Palestine, did not appreciate the critical importance of intelligence work. Intelligence was still not at the centre of the counter-insurgency effort in Malaya.[23]

In 1950, Jack Morton persuaded the authorities to bring in his former chief from the Intelligence Bureau in India as a 'consultant'. This was Sir William Jenkin, who soon became an ill-defined director of intelligence with authority over Morton but no clear relationship with Gray or Briggs. All three were soon battling it out. While Gray was away on leave, Jenkin and Morton tried to set up the Special Branch as a unit completely divorced from the main police force, and on Gray's return there was a predictable row. Jenkin departed swiftly after further clashes with the military. Briggs was now extremely ill and exhausted after his battles with Gray. He too departed in November 1951 for retirement on Cyprus but died within a year. More than three years into the Emergency, intelligence was not yet organised in a rational way and would remain a mess until the arrival of Sir Gerald Templer in 1952.[24]

Nevertheless, Harold Briggs left a valuable legacy. This was the so-called Briggs Plan, which provided the basic blueprint for success in the Emergency. Hitherto, the British forces had simply engaged in a policy of 'counter-action' which involved large-scale security force operations, detention without trial, deportation and the burning of villages. The new Briggs approach was more subtle and integrated intelligence thoughtfully into a cycle of victory by linking it to propaganda, resettlement, surrenders and food denial. The Briggs Plan moved about half a million Chinese squatters off land recovered from the jungle fringes, where some were giving aid and comfort to the guerrillas, and relocated them behind the fortified fences of 'New Villages'. The Chinese occupants were effectively retained by bribing them with entitlement to land. The MCP guerrillas were now removed from their most critical resource, the ethnically Chinese population, who had supplied them with recruits, intelligence and above all food. By controlling the population and ensuring they were secure, Briggs achieved a better flow of information and also ensured that the guerrillas would have to come out of the jungle to obtain supplies. His intention was that the guerrillas, already weakened, could then be destroyed at a time and place of his own choosing.[25]

Treating the population well would increase the flow of intelligence about the guerrillas. In turn this would allow the minimum use of force, rather than 'search and sweep' or the employment of heavy support weapons, which would alienate the locals. Precise targeting of the guerrillas, together with effective propaganda, would demoralise the enemy, leading to more surrenders and more intelligence. In theory this cycle of success would pick up momentum until victory was achieved. The Briggs Plan, although imperfectly implemented, was already pushing the guerrillas into a position of uncomfortable stalemate as early as 1951.

Chin Peng, the MCP guerrilla leader, observed half a century later that as early as 1949 one of his colleagues had asked him what they would do if confronted with this sort of strategy. The question was prompted by successful use of this approach by the Japanese against communist guerrillas in Manchuria in the 1930s. Chin Peng confidently asserted that he did not believe the British to be capable of adopting it. In any case, he argued, Malaya was a tropical area, and in the last analysis their guerrilla forces could live off the jungle. But he was mistaken. Food-denial weakened the guerrillas and forced them on to a demoralising defensive. The British had begun to embark on a cycle of victory in which intelligence played a crucial part. However, in the short term, things would become worse before they became better.[26]

Sir Henry Gurney, the High Commissioner of Malaya, was killed in an MCP guerrilla ambush on 7 October 1951. Gurney, a veteran of the Palestine Campaign, was a bold figure and often travelled about with a light escort riding in a staff car with a Union Jack flying. So he was an obvious, even tempting, target. Travelling in the hills north of Kuala Lumpur, part of his inadequate escort broke down, but he decided to push on unprotected. Slowing to round a bend at Fraser's Hill, his car came under fire. All the escorting policemen in the preceding vehicle were wounded and so was his driver. Lady Gurney and his private secretary sensibly took cover on the floor of the car, but Gurney decided to head for the bank at the side of the road and was shot as soon as he left his car. The group of thirty guerrillas that carried out the attack were pursued and five were eventually captured with incriminating documents. The nearby village of Tras had offered them support, so the population was detained and the village incinerated as a punishment.

This was the low-point of the Malayan Emergency. Intelligence was still in a mess and Sir William Jenkin had left in despair. The respected Briggs was worn out and about to depart, and now Gurney was dead. When Churchill's government was swept into power a month later, his new Colonial Secretary, Oliver Lyttelton, set out for Malaya. He was horrified by what he found. The civil administration still moved at a peacetime pace and the police force itself was in 'utter disorder', being 'divided by a great schism between the Commissioner of Police and the Special Branch'. Lyttelton warned the Cabinet that 'urgent and drastic action is called for'. Everywhere, he told it, he found a general sense of 'despair'.[27] London had two solutions, one very public and one more secret. The first was the appointment of General Sir Gerald Templer, a protégé of Montgomery. An effective and intelligent commander with a reputation as a fire-eater, he had served as director of military intelligence in the late 1940s and 'knew his onions' in that crucial area. He arrived in Malaya on 7 February 1952 after a personal briefing from Churchill and was collected from the airport and driven to his residence in Gurney's official car, which still bore the scars of the deadly ambush. Templer was made both civil and military supremo, being simultaneously High Commissioner and Director of Operations. He was given absolute power to weld all elements of the administration into a single effective machine.[28]

The second solution was a strategy of reprisal against the MCP leadership. Following the loss of Gurney, the British desire to make the struggle personal and to eliminate the MCP Politburo was overwhelming. The legacy of Palestine and Fergusson's hit squads could be detected. Covert operations against the MCP leadership were being planned even before Gurney had been killed. But after his assassination, eliminating Chin Peng became a constant obsession for the British authorities. Lyttelton told the Cabinet that what was needed were 'special' teams 'aimed at certain individuals – that is to hunt down individual men from Communist higher formations through their families, properties, sweethearts etc.'. This mission, he assured Cabinet, 'will be undertaken shortly'.[29]

Pressure for some sort of 'special' action had already come from the Australian Prime Minister, Robert Menzies, who was increasingly anxious about trouble spreading down the peninsula from Malaya to Indonesia and on towards Australia. On 26 May 1950, Menzies had written personally to London expressing his anxiety about the 'ill-success' of the current tactics. He pressed specifically for the revival of SOE techniques and also suggested that deception measures could be used in Malaya. In July, he developed his ideas in detail with Bill Slim, the Chief of the Imperial General Staff. Menzies was told that the Commander in Chief Far East did not like using unorthodox organisations on any scale. Nevertheless, they accepted his argument that there was some 'scope' and as a result a 'Special Operations expert' was sent out from Britain and 'attached to the head of Special Branch as an Adviser'. Menzies was also told that small 'special units' of the sort that the Army had enjoyed disbanding in 1948 were being re-formed and that deception was being looked at too.[30]

Deception had already been considered as a weapon against illegal immigrants heading for Palestine in 1947. The Hollis Committee had also come up with a scheme for using agents in Egypt to discredit the Communist Party there in the eyes of Arab nationalists. This was risky but the chances of such an operation been traced back to the British were, in the committee's view, 'negligible'. As we have seen, in 1950, with the advent of the Korean War, the Hollis Committee was fully remobilised as the Department of Forward Plans under a wartime MI5 officer called John Drew.[31] Malaya was a godsend to Drew, who had been looking for an opportunity for his new Department to cut its teeth. Although it was primarily a deception body, he also had ambitions to encroach on the work of both SIS and IRD. A senior forward planning officer was sent out to SIFE headquarters at Kuala Lumpur and also liaised with GHQ Far Eastern Land Forces. The deception staff he despatched to Malaya also included a locally focused 'federal deception officer' whose task was specifically 'to undertake covert action against the Malayan Communist Party' and who was located at Special Branch headquarters in Kuala Lumpur. By 1951 a nexus of expertise for special action against the MCP was building up around the Kuala Lumpur Special Branch.[32]

The first task was to find the MCP guerrilla HQs. In 1950 an electronic reconnaissance-equipped Lancaster from RAF 90 Group was sent out to Malaya to help hunt for the insurgents by tracking their radio communications. Later agents planted batteries with very high power on the guerrillas to ensure their radios were damaged. When they were brought into the towns for repair they were modified by agents to give out a stronger signal. This was used to achieve a direction-finding fix on the main guerrilla bases. RAF and RAAF bombers were standing by and lightning raids were carried out on the deemed location of the signals.

Lincoln bombers dropped thousands of tons of bombs into the dense jungle on likely HQ locations. Pilots were always impressed by the resilience of the jungle. Their largest bombs vanished into the triple-canopied green foliage below them and, from the aircraft, no impact was visible. It is not known how successful these operations were, but Chin Peng was still alive at the turn of the century to testify that the most important prize eluded them.[33]

The new British military Commander stepped up the tempo of these operations against the leadership of the MCP. In February 1953, on special orders of Templer, the authorities developed an elaborate scheme to try and liquidate Chin Peng and his followers entitled 'Planning of Operations to Eliminate the High-Ranking Members of the M.C.P.' A committee was set up under GSO 1 Ops, the senior operational planner, to carry out investigation and research into the best method of 'operating against the members of the Central Politbureau of the MCP', and to be ready to mount operations at short notice. An additional Special Intelligence Staff was being set up under Jack Morton to 'locate targets for the operations' that included one Special Branch officer and one Military Intelligence officer. Security was very tight. Both were to work from a 'special room' known as the Planning Room which had already been set aside for the purpose in 'the Keep' at Kuala Lumpur and staff were forbidden to take papers out of this room. The scheme was given the codename Operation Rattle and later renamed Operation Profit.[34]

However, after six months of intense activity little had been achieved. Templer demanded a progress report and on 7 July 1953 a high-level meeting was convened, including the head of the Special Branch Guy Madoc, the Director of Intelligence Jack Morton, the Chief of Staff and several others. After repeatedly sifting all available sources of intelligence the team had given up on the main MCP Headquarters and instead ordered Operation Matador, which sought to find one of the MCP's major propaganda organs, the *Battle News Press*. But even this lesser operation failed. The team concluded that the Profit Special Intelligence staff was so secret and compartmentalised that it was not getting enough general feed from Special Branch. The decision was taken to integrate the special intelligence component of Profit into the terrorist section of the federal Special Branch organisation, while keeping it tasked 'for PROFIT targets only'. However, it appears that no operations launched against high-profile targets were successful.[35]

Templer possessed the authority and charisma necessary to create a unified machine to implement the Briggs Plan. He also sorted out intelligence. Within weeks of his arrival he was able to offer a physical demonstration of his approach which combined a search for popular co-operation with a steely toughness. On 25 March 1952 a serious ambush occurred at the small town of Tanjong Malim, some fifty miles from Kuala Lumpur. The water supplies had been cut by the guerrillas and the repair party had then been ambushed. Twelve had been killed and another five injured. The town had a long history of incidents and poor co-operation with the security forces. Templer arrived and imposed a twenty-two-hour curfew. Addressing the population he explained that as citizens it was their duty to inform on the guerrillas. At the end of the curfew sealed boxes were taken from house to house and the inhabitants were encouraged to inform anonymously. As a result forty arrests were made.[36]

Late 1951 had represented a low point not only for the British administration but also for the guerrillas, who were already on the run. On 1 October, even before Templer arrived, the MCP Central Committee issued a new directive which contained a rethink of its strategy. One of its leaders had recently defected and was working for the government as a broadcaster, another had led a breakaway faction and had been executed for his pains. The Central Committee conceded that its forces had been attacking civilian targets and alienating those they depended upon for supplies. So it would now move to a more selective policy of targeting the security forces and British officials only. The guerrillas would be withdrawn for rest and retraining and would start to grow their own food. Most importantly, the MCP would now engage in a psychological battle with Templer for the hearts and minds of the masses. Puzzlingly, Chin Peng considered his forces to have been on the defensive from early 1950, yet the British perspective was very different. The guerrillas inflicted the highest number of casualties and achieved the highest number of incidents in 1951. The most dramatic fall-off in these grim indicators only came with arrival of Templer in February 1952.[37]

As the MCP guerrillas withdrew into the jungle hinterland to retrain and regroup they became more elusive. Intelligence, as Templer recognised, was going to be the absolute top priority. Some of the required elements were bequeathed by Briggs, including a Special Branch Training Centre and a new Interrogation Unit. But what the system also needed was an intelligence supremo who would pull together the police, military and civilian elements. Templer wanted Dick White, whom he knew well from his days as DMI in London, but White was about to take over from Sillitoe as head of MI5. Instead the task fell to Jack Morton, head of SIFE and the local MI5 representative. Morton was made director of all intelligence in Malaya and given authority over all its elements.[38]

Morton had no executive function but instead worked as a leading member of Templer's staff. His job was made a lot easier by the disappearance of Nicol Gray as police commissioner and his replacement by a London policeman, Arthur Young. Morton was served by a Combined

Intelligence Staff that was, as its name suggested, all embracing, including all the three services, the police and civilians. There was also the Federal Intelligence Committee, which was similarly holistic in its approach, encompassing not only Military, Special Branch and SIFE but also the Department of Information, the Labour Department and the Secretariat for Chinese Affairs. At the working level the police Special Branch was the lead element, while Special Military Intelligence Officers worked under the Special Branch at all levels, passing on relevant information to the Army. Only the Special Branch could run agents, and the military concentrated on combat intelligence.[39] Morton's right-hand man was Dick Noone, an anthropologist who had taken a degree at Cambridge in the 1930s and had also served with SOE in Malaya during the war. In October 1952 Noone left the service of the Australian Security Intelligence Organisation and, partly to escape an unhappy divorce, returned to Malaya to serve under Templer. Working for Morton he also helped to lead the aboriginal forces recruited for a special SAS unit called the Malayan Scouts. In 1961 anxiety about events in Vietnam led to a SEATO Counter Subversion Expert Study Group, tasked with drawing up plans for counter-subversion in Vietnam and Laos. ASIO secured the post of special adviser to the new group for Dick Noone.[40]

Meanwhile SIFE, the local MI5 office, was very small and not much involved in the day-to-day Emergency. Instead its main task was to offer strategic advice and to liaise with other security services in the area. This was valuable and in 1952 the authorities in Malaya noted that recently 'SIFE have trained considerable numbers of Thai police officers.' This was partly with a view to encouraging Thai operations against communists in the border areas. However, the real engine room of security intelligence was the new head of the Special Branch, Guy Madoc, who had previously been in charge of the Special Branch communist section. Special Branch was separated once more and Madoc revamped its Training School under Claude Fenner to try and produce professional, skilled intelligence officers who could run agents inside the MCP.[41]

Running agents inside the MCP was very difficult and Oliver Lyttelton had identified this as the core of the intelligence issue during his crisis visit of November 1951 which had led to appointment of Templer. He told the Cabinet that the importance of the intelligence in the Malayan campaign 'cannot be exaggerated'. Every police operation was in large measure an intelligence task and the whole campaign was primarily a police operation. In a country covered with dense jungle intelligence was always the starting point, for without it contact with an elusive enemy was impossible. Agents were crucial to this task. As he explained, 'it is essential that intelligence should be gained from the Communist forces without their knowing. Intelligence, therefore, to use semi-technical language, must be "live" as well as "blown" or "dead". It must come from sources whose "pumping" is unknown to the Communists.' At present, he added, the opposite occurred. Most intelligence came not from agents and contacts but from 'corpses, prisoners of war and captured documents'. This would be useful to troops fighting a regular battle, but it was of little value against a mobile and intelligent guerrilla force. What was needed was 'deep penetration of the enemy', and this was the challenge for the new intelligence machine.[42]

Templer's approach to the Malayan Emergency, and British counter-insurgency in general in the 1950s, has become indelibly associated with 'hearts and minds', with civil aid, with clever propaganda and with a sort of killing with excessive kindness. But the Malayan Emergency involved both carrot and stick, and the stick was frequently severe. Under the Emergency Regulations the authorities had the power to surround an area, arrest every Chinese within it and deport them to China without any right of appeal. This was a severe measure and was employed only a few times, but the possibility of this action hung over the heads of every community. Anyone illegally carrying arms, ammunition or explosives without a licence could be hanged. Those in possession of communist propaganda could be sentenced to ten years' imprisonment. These severe penalties were used skilfully, but illegally, to extract information from suspects. If suspects were too wily and could not be caught in the act of supporting the guerrillas, they would be set up. At dawn, communist literature would be pushed through their letter box. Five minutes later a Special Branch search party would burst through the door and 'find' incriminating communist literature in the house. The suspects would then be faced with the choice of telling all or enduring ten years in prison. They usually talked.[43]

Templer had agreed to stay only two years and was insistent that this agreement was kept. His health was already suffering from the climate, including bouts of amoebic dysentery, and he was anxious to leave. By the time of his departure in May 1954 he had made extraordinary inroads, and large areas of Malaya were essentially free of guerrilla activity, over and above small amounts of nuisance activity such as the cutting of telephone wires. Templer had exploited this by dividing Malaya into Black, Grey and White areas, the latter being relatively free from guerrilla activity. The reward for being denoted White was tangible, with a lifting of curfews and the restoration of a degree of normality. The inhabitants then had an incentive to keep their area White and informed on guerrillas more readily. In one of his last letters to Oliver Lyttelton, Templer sketched out his new strategy. There would now be a shift of deployment, with most of his forces moving to the Black areas. But the White and Grey areas where the troops would be thinner would not be left unprotected. Here, he explained, 'I propose to use special squads of experienced jungle fighters (either Special Constables, Iban trackers, soldiers or our ex-SEPs [ex-surrendered enemy personnel] now in the Special Operations Volunteer Force). They will really be 'killer squads' (though I promise you that I won't call them that, with a view to questions you might have to answer in the House).' These 'killer squads' were to be at the disposal of the Special Branch as a quick reaction force responding to any good information that came in. Templer was keen to reach out to hearts and minds and to turn guerrillas, but ultimately he preferred dead guerrillas to live ones.[44]

Planting agents inside the MCP guerrilla force, typically by sending back surrendered enemy personnel or SEPs to gather information, had always been very dangerous. Spencer Chapman, an SOE officer who had worked alongside the guerrillas during the war, had been morbidly impressed by the MCP internal security units called 'traitor-killing camps'. Suspects were tortured before death and the women guerrillas, he reported, seemed to enjoy the grisly spectacle more than the men. Vigorous internal security activity continued after the war, and in 1950 the large numbers of Chinese deaths, running at about a hundred a month, were mostly attributed to this.[45] Using SEPs as broadcasters, interrogators and agents required great sophistication. The surrender itself was never mentioned over the radio or telephone, and police officers were forbidden to mention a surrender even to friends or family. The Special Branch soon found that it could conceal the fact that a senior guerrilla had surrendered for as long as six months. Once in custody, fear of being released under suspicious circumstances, and therefore exposed to the merciless MCP traitor-killers, was often enough to ensure co-operation, but bribes were widely used. The hope was always that the SEP could be persuaded to return as an agent.[46]

The Chinese population as a whole had been neglected by the intelligence services in Malaya. So there was now an intense focus on social intelligence, which sought to find out 'what the ordinary Chinese man or woman is thinking'. This was quite different to the sort of hard-nosed intelligence that was required 'to liquidate the terrorists'. Far fewer of the Malayan civil service spoke Chinese than spoke Malay, though the Chinese and Malay communities were approximately equivalent in size. Moreover, the Chinese community was 'traditionally, almost notoriously, difficult to get in among'. This was remedied only in 1951 after a series of meetings with Chinese community leaders. The response was to strengthen the Chinese Affairs Department and to try and get Chinese into the police, which was almost entirely Malay.[47] A crucial element here was the work of figures such as Brian Stewart in the reconstructed Chinese Affairs Department of the Malayan civil service. Chinese Affairs also ran activities such as Operation Letter-Box, which involved arriving in the early morning just after curfew at a Chinese 'New Village' and interviewing every person on a one-to-one basis. This was a refinement of Templer's operation against Tanjong Malim following the unpleasant attack of March 1952. Cash was always a useful inducement for those who developed from informants into agents, but this was also potentially dangerous. Stewart recalled:

> One case I remember well was of a highly productive agent who insisted, against all advice, on taking a large cash advance against the credit which was building up in his secret account. The agent was murdered shortly thereafter by the Communist terrorists, who rightly assumed that the man's sudden wealth was in some way connected with a series of successful ambushes which had been mounted against them along their lines of communication and supply in the jungle.

Nevertheless, every SEP who surrendered was not only a loss to the guerrillas but raised the constant spectre of treachery.[48]

The MCP made its first peace offer in June 1955. London recognised that this was the clearest indicator yet that the guerrillas knew they were 'losing the shooting war'. But the Colonial Office was also placed in a quandary by this development. Peace would mean some sort of amnesty and it was not sure how much to offer. In the event London opted for a policy of rejecting the MCP offer, insisting that liberal surrender terms were already available. This was not the end of the matter, for talks were arranged between a team led by the Chief Minister of the Malayan Federation, Tunku Abdul Rahman, and an MCP delegation led by Chin Peng at Baling on 28 and 29 December 1955. John Davis, one of the SOE officers who had worked with Chin Peng during the war, and who was now a senior police officer, was sent to bring him out of the jungle. The Malayan government was adamant that it was not involved in negotiations but was there simply to explain the terms of the amnesty offer. The talks were extensive but broke down over the MCP's insistence on its recognition and legalisation and also over complete amnesty.[49]

By 1957, with victory looming, intelligence became more critical then ever. Security forces were searching for a shrinking number of guerrillas in a vast area of dense jungle. In this difficult struggle they had four main weapons. First, agents who remained in touch with the guerrillas and who were 'willing to give advanced information ... enabling ambushes to be laid'. Guerrillas were forced to contact their supporters in order to obtain food and other supplies and this made them vulnerable to being sold out. Secondly, 'informers' who were not communists but who reported guerrillas as soon as they saw them in their area for fear of the turbulence they would create. Thirdly, reconnaissance, especially air reconnaissance. Fourthly, and most importantly, growing numbers of SEPs who now proved 'surprisingly willing' to lead British patrols back to the camps from which they had just deserted. Some were even placed in a Special Operations Volunteer Force (SOVF) and went back into the jungle to attack their former comrades. The 'cycle of victory' proved to be critical, for SEPs would continue to flow only if they perceived themselves to be joining the winning side. Psychological warfare was critical in demoralising the guerrillas and their supporters and swaying the mass of the population into siding with the British. As the Director of Operations put it, 'Success breeds information and information breeds more success.'[50]

Propaganda hit the guerrillas hard. From 1955 voice broadcasting from the air was 'an important weapon' and its volume was more than doubled, using three speaker-equipped Dakotas and two Austers. 'About 70% of surrendered terrorists who have heard the broadcasts state that the Voice aircraft influenced their decision to surrender: in some cases it has been a major influence.' In 1956 alone special speaker-equipped Voice aircraft flew over 2,000 sorties, and over 100 million leaflets were dropped. Guerrillas vouched for the effectiveness of this in inducing surrenders and came forward holding the leaflets.[51] By 1957, with the flow of SEPs increasing, many expected that Chin Peng would soon vanish into the jungle of southern Thailand with a hard core of 500 guerrillas and continue hit-and-run raids from there.[52]

By 1957 increasing numbers of American officials visited Malaya, including military planners, diplomats, CIA officers and all kinds of consultants. Charles T. Cross, an information officer who went on to serve in Vietnam, recalled watching the delicate SEP work of the Special Branch at close hand. English and ethnic Chinese officers infiltrated the outside cells of the MCP, arranged defections and turnings, and planted false information about future rendezvous that later led to the ambushing of armed units. Most of the turning of MCP guerrillas was achieved by persuasion and bribery against fatigued individuals who had begun to realise their struggle was hopeless. But the Special Branch could always fall back on harsh Emergency Regulations. As Cross remembered, these Regulations 'permitted holding suspects for long periods without formal trial', and he added that the 'threat of the death penalty was often used to exact information'.

Cross admired the Special Branch officers not only for their courage, for this was 'often remarkably dangerous work', but also for their patience. Officers took time to acquaint themselves with the individual motivation of each guerrilla, exploring their homelife, schooling and their prospects for the future, recognising that the reasons for their recruitment were rarely ideological. 'I thought of the comprehensive dossiers the Special Branch was able to compile on individual CTs [Communist Terrorists] when we were trying to organise the same kind of information for the Phoenix Program ten years later in Vietnam.' In the late 1950s, Cross was escorted by the head of the Special Branch in Johore, one of the last Black areas, to a midnight rendezvous with an SEP unit. They set out in an improbable convoy at dusk, the police Morris Minor leading, the American's Chevrolet following on. After waiting what seemed an interminable period in the deep jungle:

> Suddenly in seconds, as if from a mist, a bunch of armed Chinese in nonde-script uniforms stood silently at the jungle's edge. I saw little red stars on several of their caps and ducked behind the car when the Special Branch officers began to grin. I realized I was being shown one of the most secret of their operations – one in which ex-CTs and hardened young Chinese Special Branch agents who pretended to be CTs lived in the jungle like regular CT units.

These units were normally led by a British police officer, often an ex-Army NCO who stayed in the jungle for about a month, which was as long as the British could survive in those dire conditions. They were all jumpy. Cross was told that some of these operations had 'gone sour and British officers and loyal ex-CTs had been killed'.[53]

The real collapse in guerrilla strength came in 1958. Although the campaign had swung in the government's favour as early as 1954, over 2,000 hard-core guerrillas stayed in the jungle and were still waiting it out in 1957. The endpoint came with the controversial and extremely liberal Merdeka amnesty terms offered in 1958. These, together with growing government credibility bolstered by elections and a refined propaganda strategy, prompted guerrilla collapse. In late 1958 Chin Peng was forced to demobilise the MCP, signalling the end of the shooting war. Intelligence and population control had broken the guerrilla offensive but it was psychological warfare that had brought the campaign to a successful close.[54]

The basis of the British propaganda policy for attracting surrenders had been created by Hugh Carlton Greene when he arrived to reorganise the information services in Malaya in 1950. Greene sent out teams of SEPs on lecture tours to show that they were well treated and properly rehabilitated. But both Templer and Greene had always avoided the idea of full amnesty, promising only 'fair treatment'. Guerrillas who surrendered could still be hanged or jailed for 'particularly dastardly crimes'. Both men agreed that the psychological moment for full amnesty was not yet at hand. But by 1955 the harder-core guerrillas were resistant to surrender and many feared that they would be arrested, jailed, poisoned or even 'disappeared'. Chin Peng bargained hard for complete amnesty at Baling in 1955 but failed. A qualified amnesty offered by the government in 1956 was ineffective and had ceased to produce significant surrenders. In 1957 the Tunku decided to capitalise on independence by offering a more generous, but time-limited, amnesty. It was accompanied by massive leaflet drops codenamed Operation Greenland. The number of SEPs 'sky-rocketed' to forty a month. On 5 April 1958, Hor Lung, the first member of the Central Committee to defect, arrived. Hor Lung returned to the jungle and four months later brought out 28 officials and 132 rank-and-file guerrillas. He received a reward of £55,000 for his dangerous work. By the end of 1958 only 868 guerrillas remained at large, the majority of whom were over the border in Thailand.[55]

Malayan independence had been declared on 31 August 1957, but the Emergency was not ended until 1960. The MCP had killed 1,438 people, including 353 British security personnel, and had itself lost 3,149 dead. A small hardened core of the MCP fought on, and Chin Peng remained in the jungles of northern Malaya and southern Thailand for decades. In 1960 sophisticated SEP operations were still in progress, trying to snare the last elusive guerrillas. These involved staging contacts between troops and SEPs pretending to be guerrillas in the hope of arousing interest from the local guerrilla support organisation. These were cat-and-mouse games requiring infinite patience, but the guerrilla campaign was to all intents and purposes over.[56]

The Malayan Emergency had a substantial Anglo-American dimension. British propaganda experts were quick to identify the importance of presenting this struggle correctly to the outside world. Would Washington perceive London as waging a valiant struggle against communism or as fighting a dirty colonial war designed to hang on to sterling balances and the remnants of imperial pretensions? Within weeks of the outbreak of the Emergency, Colonial Office officials were becoming anxious about 'presentation'. 'The danger we fear is that ... men who were at the start no more than a band of thugs ... may attract to themselves some of the glamour of national heroes.' Soviet propaganda, they warned, was already working to bring this change about. 'The dividing line between the terrorist and the fighter for freedom is not always so clear in the minds of the outside world.' Adam Watson, Britain's psywar liaison man in Washington, reiterated this point again in 1950:

It seems very dangerous to pretend that the troubles in Malaya are not caused by Communists but only by a kind of local banditry. As we saw in Greece, when the Greek Government were for long anxious to describe the Communists only as banditry, international public opinion in the United States ... and elsewhere is inclined to take the line that when wholesale military operations are required to suppress mere internal unrest, it is in some way due to bad government. This is especially so in a colony; and instead of receiving sympathy and support from American public opinion in our praiseworthy struggle to combat the well-known international Communist menace, we shall merely be regarded as a bad colonial power coping with rebellions.

Accordingly, the 'bandits' that were identified in Malaya in 1948 had by the 1950s become Communist Terrorists – a suitable Cold War epithet. However, IRD would confront a bigger challenge when trying to find communists during the Mau Mau rebellion in Kenya and during the war in Cyprus from 1956. Indeed, the main opponent in Cyprus, Colonel Grivas, was a neo-fascist, but he had somehow to be presented as sympathetic to Moscow![57]

The guerrilla war in Malaya was of particular interest to the growing CIA station in Thailand under Vernon Gresham, since Thailand was the main American centre for covert warfare against communism in Southeast Asia during the 1950s. In August 1953, William J. Donovan, the wartime head of the OSS and originator of the American Committee on United Europe, arrived as ambassador to Thailand with a brief to assist the Thais in developing 'special warfare' against the threat of communist insurgency. He brought with him many ex-OSS figures, including Carlton Coon and Gordon Browne, and created 'a miniature OSS'. He made frequent visits to see Templer in Malaya, anxious to study the new and successful politico-military methods of counter-insurgency that were being developed to the south. Donovan in turn pressed the Thai government to introduce initiatives he had seen in Malaya from fortified villages and health programmes to land reform.[58]

Washington had its own local window on the Malayan Emergency provided by a sizeable CIA station in Singapore. Officially the Agency was not allowed to run operations there without British approval. In the 1950s this problem was circumvented by limiting unilateral activities to a scale which, if uncovered, could be plausibly explained as 'exploratory work' which had not yet reached the operational stage. Washington demanded some independent operations by the Far Eastern Division of the CIA, as it suspected that the British were offering over-optimistic assessments of their progress against the communists in Malaya. A few journalists were also recruited on Chinese newspapers to write stories sympathetic to American policy in the region. Confusing diversity characterised liaison with the British at Singapore. SIS increasingly shared work with its co-located Australian protégé, the Australian Secret Intelligence Service or ASIS. MI5 worked alongside rival police and Army security units. IRD worked in parallel with several colonial lookalikes. The Americans always enjoyed smoother relations with the cosmopolitan SIS officers than with some of the longer-resident colonial 'types' in the police. The CIA's Joseph Buckholder Smith recalled a reception in Singapore at the house of the deputy SIS head of station in 1952. The evening, in Smith's opinion, ended on a positive note when a choleric major from the Special Branch with pronounced anti-American views suffered a nasty bite delivered by the host's pet otter.

But the CIA in South-east Asia was also a confusing animal for the British to work with. Most CIA officers assigned to the small Singapore station came from FE/5, the branch of the CIA's Far Eastern Division which looked after Singapore, Malaya, Indonesia and co-operation with ASIS. But the Far Eastern Division had no control over CIA-sponsored front organisations in the region, such as the Asia Foundation. These were the domain of the CIA's International Organizations Division run by Tom Braden and later Cord Meyer. A fortuitous combination of personalities ensured good CIA–SIS relations. James Fulton, who had been working with Paul Falla in OPS in London, became an effective regional head of SIS in the mid-1950s, and his deputy Maurice Oldfield was also well liked. The CIA station in Singapore contained Bob Jantzen and his deputy Joseph Buckholder Smith. Smith was fascinated by the divergent American views of SIS, filtered through the medium of British training offered to American wartime OSS officers. By the 1950s, he argued, there were two CIA views of liaison with the British: 'One was that it was a rare and beautiful thing to be nurtured with every care, because the British were the most sagacious spies in the business, with a long and remarkable tradition of success. The other was that it was a waste of time, the British officers were a bunch of supercilious snobs toward whom we should show an equivalent disdain.' Having been briefed by senior officers from both schools, Smith's own formula was: 'our liaison with the British is one of our greatest assets; don't tell the bastards anything important'. This liaison formula was subscribed to by most Western intelligence officers to some degree. But Smith regarded his boss, Bob Jantzen, as a master of the art of liaison, and as someone who could find his way through the maze of intelligence diplomacy. Jantzen's special talent for building close relations was severely tested in his subsequent posting as head of station in Bangkok, where he developed a special friendship with the Premier General Sarit. Working with his British counterpart, Michael Wrigley, he sought to restrain Sarit from his ardent desire to invade Prince Sihanouk's neutral Cambodia.[59]

Worries about the possibility of a communist victory in Indochina, where the French had been battling the Viet Minh between 1945 and 1954, and the additional pressures this might place on Malaya, prompted Britain actively to sell its counter-insurgency techniques elsewhere in South-east Asia. By May 1955, London had decided on 'special measures' to support Sihanouk in Cambodia against his communist opponents. These concentrated on the use of propaganda materials that would boost the standing of Sihanouk during forthcoming elections. Roger Makins, the British Ambassador in Washington, co-ordinated the campaign with the Americans, but he was instructed that 'the French authorities were to have no account of the special operations with which it was concerned'. This involved building support for Sihanouk in the outlying areas of Cambodia through radio propaganda and sending Cambodians for British training on internal security matters. This paved the way for Robert Thompson's advisory mission to Vietnam in the early 1960s.[60]

London's wariness of the French was hardly surprising. In 1953, the French Commander in Indochina, General Jean de Lattre de Tassigny, had thrown the colourful local SIS man, Arthur Trevor-Wilson, out of Hanoi. De Lattre was well within his rights for Trevor-Wilson was an undeclared 'stringer' for James Fulton, the regional SIS chief at Singapore. Trevor-Wilson was a natural intelligence officer and much-admired by his literary-minded SIS colleagues Malcolm Muggeridge and Graham Greene, with whom he had served during the war. In 1945 he had been selected for a special mission to Hanoi, serving as liaison to the French and more particularly to Ho Chi Minh. He established a close friendship with Ho, accompanying him during his abortive talks with the French in Paris in 1946. He then became the British consul in Hanoi and also worked on the side for James Fulton. Fulton had tried to keep him on full time, but having failed to do this asked that he should at least 'maintain informal contact', adding that 'we very much value the opportunity to consult you'.[61]

The CIA head of station at the time recalled that Trevor-Wilson was always busy with intelligence work in Hanoi in the early 1950s. He secured the services of a British girl as his office manager who was married to a French Foreign Legion officer, another useful source. But Trevor-Wilson also seems to have gone out of his way to provoke de Lattre, making frequent open comparisons between the British decision to leave India and the French decision to stay on in Indochina. The anglophobe de Lattre was continually in receipt of reports from the French Sûreté about 'spying activities' by Trevor-Wilson and his friend Graham Greene. But the last straw was probably the stream of insults poured out by a well-lubricated Trevor-Wilson at one of de Lattre's dinner parties. Denouncing the French as 'mercenaries' destined for defeat, he was promptly declared *persona non grata*. He left the war in Vietnam for employment in the information services in Malaya, which, as we have seen, were run by Graham Greene's brother (until 1956). After Malaya he moved on to work in Vientiane and on retirement was awarded the Order of the Million Elephants by the King of Laos.[62]

Winning in Malaya was critically important for the British in the 1950s. It restored morale in the wake of Palestine and Suez and afforded London improved status in the eyes of Washington as a leader in the fashionable new field of 'special' counter-insurgency and counter-subversion. There has been considerable debate over whether it was the Briggs Plan of 1950 with its 'population control' or the arrival of

Templer, who reformed intelligence and restored confidence, that finally allowed the British to turn the corner. But what really mattered to London was avoiding similar situations in the future in which more corners might have to be turned. What policy-makers now demanded was the sort of advanced political intelligence enjoyed by the British Raj in India that had allowed them to identify pre-insurgencies and nip them in the bud.[63] Malaya thus had a profound impact on British secret service, remaking Britain's intelligence and security effort in the wider world. Returning from Malaya, Templer was given a new brief to investigate the management of Britain's colonial security on a global scale. By April 1955, he had completed a mammoth investigation for the Cabinet, visiting locations from Cyprus to Uganda and talking to MI5. His report remains secret, partly because of its extreme frankness. But Eden's private secretary declared his picture of decrepit security intelligence in the colonies to be 'frightening'. The result was a cutback on regular military forces in favour of a mobile 'strategic reserve'. Meanwhile Templer secured a redeployment of these resources to allow a simultaneous expansion of hidden-hand activity, including new Special Branches and IRD-led counter-subversion. He also reformed the handling in Whitehall of intelligence on under-developed areas of the world.[64]

In 1954, a senior MI5 officer, A. N. MacDonald, had been seconded to the Colonial Office as security intelligence adviser to begin developing a strong corps of Special Branch sections in each colonial territory to provide 'early warning' of any recurrence of events in Malaya. The impact of the Templer Report was to accelerate this. MacDonald was given two deputies and formed the Intelligence and Security Department of the Colonial Office. He and his team acted as roving consultants, setting up Special Branches and local intelligence committees and advising on specialist training and equipment. Over three years they made fifty-seven visits to twenty-seven colonial territories. MI5 presided over an unparalleled security training scheme which resulted in 1,866 police officers employed on intelligence duties by 1957, not including those in Malaya. Further expansion was scheduled for 1958. MI5 training officers had visited almost every colonial territory. Some 637 police officers had undertaken courses run in the colonial territories and 284 had attended courses in London. These ranged from basic courses for new officers to senior courses for heads of Special Branches. There was also what was described as a 'technical training course'. Templer put in place a vast glacis plate of MI5 and Special Branch activity that would protect the colonies as they moved towards independence. There was also a deliberate effort to build up links that were 'capable of surviving the transition to independence' with the despatch of security liaison officers to new Commonwealth countries.

This would be the blueprint for Britain's secret service after 1956 as the Cold War widened to embrace all of the Third World. British intelligence was now preparing for rapid decolonisation, what Harold Macmillan would call the 'wind of change'. Gerald Templer's most important contribution was to ensure that the British intelligence and security services were prepared for this change and had refocused their attentions on the wider world. Security intelligence would continue to ensure the post-independence stability of these territories after hand-over, and guarantee a kind of British influence thereafter that was immune to erosion. As the JIC observed in 1957, 'An experienced and efficient intelligence organisation ... with close ties to the Security Service, is a legacy of particular value to Colonies moving into independent status with the Commonwealth, as well as a safeguard of H.M.G.'s long-term intelligence interests.'[65]

PART IV

The Cold War Widens
1957–1963

23

Submarines, Spy-flights and Shoot-downs: Intelligence after Suez

> Intelligence is approaching a $1 billion a year operation.
> Dr James R. Killian, 17 January 1957[1]

In 1956 a series of calamities overtook the secret services in London. During April and May the Commander Crabb Affair attracted the fixed attention of the British public. Commander Crabb was a naval diver employed by SIS to investigate the hull of a Soviet cruiser in Portsmouth Harbour during a state visit by Nikita Khrushchev, the Soviet head of state. After entering the water he disappeared, but his body was then found, without its head or hands. Anthony Eden did not enjoy the experience and chose to remove Sir John Sinclair as chief of SIS, replacing him with Dick White. Eden had then broken off a number of Anglo-American sigint and photo-reconnaissance operations as being 'too risky'. Associated with these events were several enquiries and reviews of intelligence which radically revised political clearance for operations and seriously constrained such activities. Shortly after the untimely departure of Sinclair, the Hungary and Suez Crises, which had damaged Anglo-American relations badly, resulted in the departure of Eden himself.

The dramatic events of 1956 also prompted reflection and reconsideration of intelligence matters in Washington. Before the year was out President Eisenhower had briefed Dr James R. Killian, head of the President's Board of Consultants on Foreign Intelligence Activities, to carry out a thoroughgoing investigation of American intelligence. At nine o'clock on the morning of 17 January 1957, Killian presented the board's findings to Eisenhower and the National Security Council. He pointed to the huge expenditure on intelligence, coming close to a billion dollars a year, and insisted that more effective mechanisms for co-ordinating this sprawling apparatus were essential. The board had read many previous studies, including the famous Doolittle Report of 1954 which had recommended to Eisenhower more vigorous covert action, and had conducted its own studies. It was no coincidence that it had decided to embark on an intensive case study of intelligence activities in Egypt.

Eisenhower listened patiently to a stream of recommendations on control and management, including some very technical issues relating to how to examine and assess the vast expenditure on the NSA which was moving into its new headquarters at Fort Meade. Eisenhower then revealed his instinctive command of the subject of intelligence and asked one tough question. The Director of the CIA was supposed to be the Director of Central Intelligence (DCI), he said, fulfilling exactly the co-ordinating function that all now agreed was lacking. Why was the DCI – Allen Dulles – not taking charge? There was a terse exchange: 'Allen Dulles told the President he was thinking of trying to get General Truscott to join his staff and take over the co-ordination duty. The President said he understood the proposal to be the other way around … that Mr Dulles must perform the co-ordination, and that he should get a man who could manage the operations of the CIA.' A Director of Central Intelligence was certainly what was needed, but the American system did not have one, and indeed arguably would never tolerate one. Eisenhower knew this, although this did not prevent him from venting his frustration at this intractable problem upon Allen Dulles.[2]

The late 1950s were now marked by an accelerated effort to investigate the capabilities of the Soviet armed forces. Prior to the Korean War, British concerns about the Soviet armed forces were offset by a general conviction on the part of the JIC that it would be ten years before Moscow was ready to contemplate another war. The devastation of the Second World War seemed to have retarded the Soviet economy and hence its ability to produce advanced technological systems. This misconception evaporated in the heat of the first Soviet atomic bomb. Less than a year later, the Ministry of Defence was again shocked by the appearance of the MiG-15 fighter in Korea, which displayed a performance superior to new RAF jet fighters that had not yet entered service. Soviet missile developments in the 1950s added to this anxiety. Intelligence on the pace of technical development within the Soviet armed forces was now a matter of the highest priority. This had led to an expansion of the budget of GCHQ and also an expansion of photo-reconnaissance, not only overland but also at sea, against the rapidly expanding and modernising Soviet Navy.[3]

Although detailed British aerial photography of Soviet naval vessels had become regular by the 1950s, these operations were never routine. They were a sensitive matter and each operation required the approval of the Prime Minister. How close British reconnaissance aircraft could safely approach Soviet naval vessels became a matter of increasing concern at a high level.[4] During the mid-1950s British Naval Intelligence argued that the game was worth the risk and pressed for more aggressive intelligence-gathering. In February 1953, Anthony Buzzard, the Director of Naval Intelligence, warned that although the Soviet Navy was not comparable to Western navies it was 'rapidly gaining in size, experience and efficiency'. It was engaged in extensive warship-building and experimenting with new types of submarines. But British intelligence did not know exactly how large or effective this new Soviet naval effort was. Buzzard explained that in the face of 'intense security arrangements it is becoming progressively more difficult to gather intelligence on the Soviet Navy'. He was keen to find new ways and means. Confronted with anxieties about the dangers of monitoring the Soviet Navy from British aircraft or British naval vessels, he looked for alternative platforms. One answer was to employ the innocent platforms provided by British Arctic trawlers. Moving through the seas around Norway and the Soviet Union at all times of the year they were innocent bystanders, and yet travelled to within a few miles of the major Soviet naval bases such as Murmansk.[5]

Buzzard joined with Patrick Dean, the Chairman of the JIC, to press a reluctant Ministry of Agriculture and Fisheries into finding trawlers from which to observe Soviet naval exercises and thus to gather 'valuable intelligence'. As early as September 1953 there had already been five incidents. The Soviet Navy had been 'very aggressive' and had sent out boarding parties which 'threatened jail and sudden death if the trawlers misbehaved again'. Officials complained that 'Admiral Buzzard seems prepared to sacrifice our trawlers, for the sake of a chance of a small amount of intelligence. Not a very fair bargain?' However Buzzard insisted that trawlers should take their place in the front line of the intelligence war and the operations increased in volume during the late 1950s and early 1960s with more incidents.[6] In the late 1950s the Norwegian Intelligence Service was receiving an average of 250 reports and 150 films per year from Norwegian, German and British trawler crews. Britain even stationed SIS officers in fishing ports as liaison officers. Much of the work involved photography, but they were also joined by sigint specialists from the Navy's radio establishment at HMS Mercury.[7]

However, the dangers of bungled maritime surveillance operations only became clear after the infamous death of Commander Lionel 'Buster' Crabb in April 1956. During the visit of Khrushchev and his Foreign Minister, Nikolai Bulganin, to Britain on the cruiser *Ordjonikidze,* Crabb was despatched to Portsmouth Harbour by SIS to explore the electronic fit of this new warship. Crabb was a veteran naval diver with a distinguished war record. He was briefed to look for elaborate sonar equipment and devices to ensure quieter running and also to measure the propellers. A state visit by Khrushchev carried some political risks for

Eden, but offered a chance to improve East–West understanding in a way that had not been possible under Stalin. Eden was certainly convinced that a thaw was possible and was no less anxious than Churchill had been to rein back on provocative Cold War activities directed towards the Eastern bloc. Despite some robust exchanges the visit went well and the Soviet delegation left on 27 April 1956.

Even as Khrushchev and Bulganin departed, the press had begun to speculate about the mysterious disappearance of a British naval diver in the vicinity of the visiting Soviet warships. On 4 May the Soviets sent the British government a formal note stating that a frogman had been seen in the water near the Soviet ships and demanding an explanation. His body was later recovered from the sea and the resulting furore cast a pall over a successful visit and there were pointed questions in the House of Commons. What should have been a diplomatic coup for Eden was dominated by the 'frogman' affair. The Prime Minister, now suffering considerably from his prolonged illness, reacted with anger. He had explicitly forbidden this sort of activity. But, during a previous British official visit to Leningrad, Soviet frogmen had been busy around the hulls of British ships and Naval Intelligence was keen to repay the compliment. At a higher level the risks had clearly been judged to outweigh the benefits and Eden had issued a minute forbidding any underwater spying. However, when SIS asked for clearance the request travelled no further than the Foreign Office adviser to SIS, Michael Williams, whose father had died that day. In his state of distress the paperwork was overlooked, so SIS heard no more and presumed it had authority to go ahead.[8]

Eden was enraged, not only by the incompetence and disobedience, but also by the tardy way in which he was informed. Lord Cilcennin, the First Lord of the Admiralty, arrived to brief him about it only on 4 May. By contrast Eden acted swiftly and chose Sir Edward Bridges, the senior official at the Treasury, and one of Whitehall's most experienced operators, to conduct the enquiry. Eden wrote:

> I wish you to carry out on my behalf an enquiry into the circumstances in which Commander Crabb undertook an intelligence operation against the Russian warship in Portsmouth harbour on April 19.
>   Your enquiry should include the following points:–
>   (a) what authority was given for the operation, and
>   (b) why its failure was not reported to Ministers until May 4.
>   My objective is to establish, by independent enquiry, what the facts are and where responsibility lies.

Eden wanted culprits to be found and warned Bridges that he intended to use the report to take 'disciplinary action'. He instructed Ministers concerned to order their staff to co-operate fully with the enquiry. It soon transpired that the Crabb Affair was not an isolated incident but part of a rolling programme. Contemporaneously, the Norwegian Navy was partaking in an exchange with the Soviet Navy, and had been supplied with special sigint-gathering equipment by the British and Americans for its forthcoming visit to Murmansk. Plans were afoot to use teams of frogmen to explore the underside of the Soviet ships when they repaid the courtesy visit and arrived in Oslo harbour. But by then Crabb had been lost and the Norwegian diving programme was cancelled.[9]

Predictably, the Bridges investigation into the Crabb Affair cleared Ministers and senior officials, so Eden chose to sack John Sinclair, the head of SIS. Most presumed that he would be succeeded by the energetic Jack Easton, a highly intelligent RAF officer who had been with SIS for many years. But he was replaced by Sir Dick White, head of MI5. White was an extremely well-regarded intelligence officer and this was not intended as a calculated insult to the service, although many treated it as such. Bridges undertook a typically thorough job, employing the JIC to help him ferret out all aspects of the Crabb Affair. He rightly identified 'certain questions' arising out of the affair. Such intelligence operations clearly had the capacity to cause terrible international repercussion, especially when they coincided with summits, and yet the systems for their authorisation were not clear. Bridges recommended a new enquiry of the broadest sort, reviewing all of Britain's strategic intelligence and surveillance activities. It would assess 'the balance between military intelligence on the one hand, and civil intelligence and political risks on the other'. Eden gave this job to Sir Norman Brook, the Cabinet Secretary, working with Patrick Dean, Chairman of the JIC.[10]

Norman Brook and Patrick Dean soon directed their attention on a Whitehall intelligence 'treaty' of the first importance. This was an agreement negotiated between the chiefs of Naval and Air Intelligence and the diplomats in July 1955. Entitled 'Political Approval for Certain Service Intelligence Operations', it set out a generous scheme of 'blanket approval' for various types of activities against opportunity targets to gather communications intelligence, electronic intelligence and photographic intelligence or to do underwater noise-listening. The main restrictions were that the aircraft or vessels should not enter territorial waters of another country and that they should take 'reasonable precautions to avoid incidents'. The justification for blanket approval was that certain Soviet naval vessels of extreme interest emerged into international waters only on 'rare occasions'. The Foreign Office required advanced notice from the intelligence services only of 'other operations'. Border flights and oversea flights for sigint purposes were set out broadly in six-month outline programmes with only 'approximate dates' and the 'general area' to be covered for approval by the Foreign Secretary. By contrast, penetration flights over the Soviet Union were handled carefully and individually by the chief of Air Intelligence and the Chairman of the JIC. Brook and Dean decided that this needed tightening up. More individual approvals would be needed at a higher level and substantial safety distances were introduced for a whole range of activities. Some activities were ended altogether.[11]

The new guidelines had serious consequences for aerial photographic reconnaissance. In April 1956, simultaneous with Khrushchev's visit to Britain, the new CIA U-2 reconnaissance aircraft – essentially a high-flying rocket-powered glider – had arrived at RAF Lakenheath under the cover of the '1st Weather Reconnaissance Squadron, Provisional'. Richard M. Bissell, Director of the CIA's embryonic U-2 reconnaissance programme, recalled:

> My first trip was to the United Kingdom, where I met with Prime Minister Anthony Eden and received his permission to base a squadron of three U-2s in a segregated hangar at Lakenheath … Although we were able to initiate a few practice overflights into Eastern Europe, an unfortunate incident altered the situation and adversely affected our ability to operate out of the United Kingdom. A Soviet cruiser docked in Portsmouth harbour while making a courtesy call, and apparently a British frogman was dispatched to look at the signalling gear. A short time later his body was found floating in the bay. There was a great deal of press attention and Eden's reaction was to rescind authorization for the U-2s to fly over enemy or forbidden territory from the United Kingdom … the base was closed out rather rapidly.

The high-flying U-2s had also displayed an alarming tendency to trigger Britain's early-warning system for nuclear attack. Eisenhower apparently shared British concerns about a possible incident, though American-piloted U-2 missions continued to be flown from Germany, Turkey and Pakistan.[12] The U-2 group from Lakenheath, known as Detachment A, now found itself bundled over to Wiesbaden in June 1956, without the permission of the West German authorities. Refitted with more powerful engines, the planes began work immediately. The first operational flight took place over East Germany and Poland on 20 June. Even at this stage there had been extensive 'thoughts and preparations regarding malfunctioning' during discussion between Killian, Bissell, Goodpaster and Eisenhower. Eden already felt that his summit with Khrushchev and Bulganin had been besmirched, and he suspected, quite rightly, that the potential for another major international incident was built into the activities of these delicate craft.[13]

Even more secret than the U-2 were joint intelligence operations by the British and American navies using submarines. Eden's 1956 review of intelligence risks and rewards also had its impact here. Both navies considered these operations to be of the very greatest sensitivity. The US Navy had begun them in 1952, sneaking in close to the Soviet coast in the Pacific to photograph naval vessels and monitor their communications. Discovering the existence of these activities only by accident, British naval officers in Washington suggested reciprocal arrangements with similar British submarine operations in the North Sea. By 1956 a system of reciprocity had been worked out, with British and American officers going on attachment on each other's operations. On 14 October that year, Commander John Coote, the British Staff Officer Submarines at the British Joint Staff Mission in Washington, returned from two months of such operations with the US Navy Pacific Submarine Force. He had spent thirty-four days off the coast of Petropavlosk in USS *Stickleback*. The British were surprised at the scale of these intelligence operations, with no fewer than six submarines engaged on this work between August and October 1956. The results were so impressive that four more submarines were joining this clandestine work 'to permit a greater effort next year'. The experience of working in stressful conditions in Soviet areas was considered valuable in itself. 'Besides the intelligence value of these operations, they obviously provide unparalleled training for war in a "gloves-off" atmosphere.'

Coote's productive trip on the USS *Stickleback* was being swapped for a berth for an American officer in the forthcoming British submarine intelligence operations off the Murmansk coast codenamed Pontiac. But in the backwash from the Crabb affair Pontiac was cancelled, so the British half of the deal could not be delivered. British officers in Washington spoke of their 'embarrassment' which would persist 'until we can make good our part of the bargain'. Their underlying concern was that they would soon be eclipsed by similar operations by the American submarine commander in the Atlantic, 'so as not to be outdone by the Pacific submariners'. British naval officers wanted to keep their stake in the game and so urged that Pontiac be restored. Indeed, they called for it to be followed by 'a bigger and better operation' which, they suggested, might be called Cadillac, Bentley or even Rolls-Royce.[14]

Admiral Inglis, who had replaced Buzzard as the British Director of Naval Intelligence, supported the call for restoration and expansion. The main scoop provided by American submarine operations had been a choice range of comint and elint. 'Considerable VHF voice, IFF and radar traffic' was recorded, mostly from airborne and coastal defences. The haul of captured signals was voluminous, and full analysis of all the recordings obtained 'will take some time', Inglis noted. Moreover, while the Soviets seemed ready to deal roughly with 'unfriendly air intrusion', by contrast 'no difficulties were placed in the way of submarine visitors' and Soviet anti-submarine capability seemed low. The US Commander in Chief of the Pacific Fleet was already pressing Washington to abandon the twelve-mile restriction on operations near the Soviet coast. The US Navy felt that this was an entirely new phase in the intelligence war and urged that it was 'of the greatest importance that the knowledge that such operations are carried out is restricted to the minimum number of people'. But it seemed there were to be no further British operations.[15]

By the end of 1956 the Royal Navy felt things slipping away. Admiral Elkins at the British Joint Services Mission in Washington wrote to Admiral Mountbatten to voice his concern. As predicted, the Americans had begun independent operations off Murmansk. Initially they had decided that the British would not be informed at all. But the American Admiral Warder from the secretive Op31 section, who was tasked with this mission, decided that it would be foolish not to draw on British experience of similar operations in these waters. So Commander John Coote, who had been on the Murmansk run several times, was called in to brief the first American crew. But this was only on the understanding that he informed no one else. American intelligence operations off Murmansk had clearly been prompted by the British cancellation and Elkins lamented, 'we are no longer providing sufficient cover in an area where we have hitherto been a reliable and productive source'. Ironically, the US Navy had used the reports of prior British operations to persuade the State Department that 'the risks of detection are negligible'. Elkins accepted that the British cancellation was the result of Prime Ministerial decision, but he warned that British prestige, which had been high, would suffer 'unless we resume these activities ourselves'.[16]

American undersea intelligence now expanded fast. In Washington, the Hoover Commission Report on American Intelligence Activities, completed in 1956, recommended that the US Navy expand its collection effort. This included the highly secret SOSUS project – Sound Surveillance Stations – which involved placing undersea microphones into the Atlantic. Using high-frequency radio direction-finders, contacts could be quickly co-ordinated and plotted.[17] By the 1960s, with vast new resources authorised, the Americans were ready to launch a new wave of audacious operations. They modified the submarine USS *Halibut* for use only on special intelligence operations. USS *Halibut* was an ugly vessel designed to carry the early cruise missiles off the coast of the Soviet Union, which required the submarine to have a bulbous hatch on the forward deck that measured more than twenty-two feet across. Below this hatch was a cavernous space which was inevitably dubbed the 'bat-cave' and which was modified over the years to carry all manner of intelligence-gathering equipment. This submarine would eventually attach sigint-gathering pods to Soviet ocean-floor communication cables, resulting in the recording of quantities of traffic which the Soviets never dreamed could be intercepted.[18]

By contrast, British intelligence continued to struggle against the litany of problems bequeathed by Eden's last year in office which were multiplied by the Suez fiasco. In December 1956 GCHQ was operating a new 'secret sigint station' covering the Indian Ocean at Perkar on Ceylon, which had been recently been constructed at some cost, to free up the Ceylon government demand for access to the old site at HMS Anderson. The GCHQ site at Perkar was undeclared, requiring it to sustain what it called 'the "cover story" to be used in describing its function to the Ceylonese'. However, there was growing anxiety in London about the unwillingness of the government to stand up to left-wing pressure which pursued a policy of removing all foreign bases regardless of purpose. The problems were largely a backwash of the Suez operation. In June 1956, prior to the Suez invasion, London had persuaded Prime Minister Bandaranaike to settle for a gradual Ceylonese takeover of the British bases, while allowing the British to retain 'certain facilities for communications' in perpetuity, which suited GCHQ well. However, after Suez, the Ceylonese authorities' attitude hardened because they believed the British had refuelled ships in Ceylon bound for action in Egyptian waters. They now wanted a schedule for removal of all foreign bases and the acceptance that they could be closed at any time before the agreed date. Other facilities were being developed in Ethiopia, the Gulf, Malaysia and Australia that offered alternative coverage, so Perkar could eventually be replaced, though this represented the expensive and unnecessary loss of a newly constructed facility. London concluded that 'The GCHQ station can be given up entirely, but we should like to keep it in operation for five years.' This proved to be the agreed position and the new GCHQ site at Perkar, completed in 1957, operated only until 1962, whereupon it was closed.[19]

The Harold Macmillan era was one of recovery for intelligence operations at sea and in the air. Eden had informed his Cabinet of his decision to resign on 9 January 1957 and intelligence chiefs were not slow in attempting to claw back the privileges and blanket approvals that had been withdrawn. On 5 February, Admiral John Inglis, head of Naval Intelligence, set out the case for restoration. Back in 1955, he explained, under the Whitehall agreement on 'Political Approval', they had secured blanket permission for a whole range of operations – mostly electronic intercept flights – against the Soviet Navy on the high seas. This was given the general codename Operation Grape. But from April 1956 'the whole question of active intelligence procurement was bedevilled by the political climate and the unfortunate frogman incident'. Now, with the spring and summer of 1957 approaching, large movements of

Soviet warships were expected and they wished to renew operations in co-operation with the Americans, but the absence of blanket approval made all this difficult. Inglis played the American card, emphasising that 'Failure to carry them out discredits our capability and willingness in the eyes of the U.S. Navy.'

Harold Macmillan restored the system of blanket approvals, and by 1958 the Admiralty had sought and obtained further permissions for an expanded version of Operation Grape. Macmillan was told that Grape in fact encompassed no fewer than four separate operations: Operation Moselle was a long-range tracking operation run by aircraft of Coastal Command flying from Britain and Malta. Operation Sherry consisted of detailed photo-reconnaissance of Soviet ships conducted mostly by RAF Canberras. The absolute limit was set at two runs at no lower than 2,000 feet with no orbiting of the target. Operation Claret was a programme conducted in the Atlantic 'by a specially equipped aircraft' of No. 90 Group, for the purpose of obtaining electronic reconnaissance of signals emanating from Soviet shipping. Operation Chianti was the same sort of sigint activity but conducted in the Mediterranean.[20]

When Eisenhower and Macmillan met at Bermuda in May 1957 they reversed Eden's decision of the previous year to halt U-2 flights from the UK. These flights were codenamed Aquatone. The context of these discussions at Bermuda, which covered tripartite systems for warning of surprise attack and also strategic weapons, underlines the extent to which aerial reconnaissance over the Soviet Union and nuclear issues were closely integrated. In the same year Britain and the United States signed a formal agreement to integrate their nuclear strike plans.[21] Richard Bissell, the CIA chief of the U-2 programme, wanted UK involvement because the main limiting factor on his operations was his ability to secure the permission of Eisenhower to conduct flights. Eisenhower was also becoming increasingly wary of the possibility of an incident. By involving the RAF 'on a completely equal basis' Bissell hoped to 'contrive an arrangement whereby either the British or the U.S. Government could approve an overflight independent of the other'. The new approval system would require the signature of only one Premier to launch an overflight of the Soviet Union, depending on the nationality of the pilot. Detailed negotiations were undertaken with Sir Dick White, head of SIS and with Air Vice Marshal William MacDonald, the head of British Air Intelligence, and were concluded in the spring of 1957. RAF pilots went to the United States to join the American U-2 training programme. Remarkably, in 1957, Richard Bissell offered U-2 participation to the French on his own initiative. In Paris he spoke to de Gaulle himself, who turned him down flat. He realised he had become over-confident as a result of the successful U-2 treaties concluded with London, Bonn and then Oslo; if de Gaulle had accepted he would have had to 'face a fight back at the agency'.[22]

In July 1958 Flight Lieutenant Robert Robinson of the RAF was chosen to lead a special detachment of British pilots who would fly the U-2 aircraft. The British pilots were secretly trained at Watertown Strip, a hundred miles north of Las Vegas. Flying the delicate U-2s was perilous and one RAF officer perished during this early stage in the programme. The British hydrogen bomb had also persuaded Washington to take Britain seriously again as a nuclear partner and between 1957 and 1958 full nuclear co-operation was gradually restored with the development of the first fully integrated bombing plans. Most U-2 activity in fact occurred between 1956 and 1958, and thereafter full overflights across the Soviet Union declined. By 1959 the U-2 had been withdrawn from Europe, following scares about Soviet observation of the bases, and so the British pilots were posted to Detachment B at Incirlik Air Force Base in Turkey. They joined seven American pilots and shared four U-2 aircraft. Increasingly the U-2 was being used for high-altitude elint listening against Soviet missile tests around the Caspian Sea, which involved only limited incursions over the Soviet Union, or for photo-reconnaissance work around the volatile Middle East.[23]

The ability of the US Air Force to run its own programme of penetration flights in parallel to the CIA U-2 was also enhanced by the British. By 1956 LeMay, head of US Strategic Air Command, had at his disposal the extraordinary RB-57D reconnaissance aircraft, a version of the British Canberra that had been modified and uprated by the Martin Corporation. Martin had almost doubled its wingspan and added two Pratt and Whitney engines with hugely increased power. This aircraft had an altitude that was not far short of the U-2's 72,000 feet but it was much faster and could carry a greater payload. RB-57D flights were under the control of LeMay, who bitterly resented the CIA's control of the U-2 programme. Astonishingly, these US Strategic Air Command-controlled overflights could be authorised by a four-star theatre commander and need not even be referred back to Washington for authorisation. On 11 December 1956 LeMay put three of these aircraft over Vladivostok, provoking vigorous Soviet diplomatic protests. Recollections of the pilots suggest they were as anxious about Washington discovering their activities as about Moscow doing so. Soviet records released only in the 1990s are beginning to confirm the startling number of air incursions during the late 1950s.[24]

The US Air Force reconnaissance effort was massive, and it is unlikely that Eisenhower approved all of the flights. As Paul Lashmar has convincingly shown, at this time the 55th Strategic Reconnaissance Wing was flying missions from Thule over the Arctic Circle into the northern

Soviet Union, where radar cover was thought to be thin. They were regularly pursued on the way out by MiGs. This was reconnaissance in force and the missions often involved nine RB-47 aircraft flying together. One operational series by this Wing alone in 1956 involved no fewer than 144 penetrations of Soviet airspace. The story was much the same around the perimeter of the Soviet Union. Elint aircraft would deliberately provoke the Soviets by throwing out aluminium chaff. This persuaded Soviet radar that a whole squadron had made an incursion and really stirred up a reaction. However, senior officers banned this tactic when they discovered it.[25]

By contrast, between 1956 and 1960, only twenty CIA U-2 aircraft were involved in overflights. Many of these operations involved only slight incursions into Soviet airspace, while about twenty-five deep-penetration flights were undertaken. Most of these occurred in the period before March 1958, when Eisenhower, anxious about potential political repercussion, ordered a complete stand-down. Flights were revived in the spring of 1960 because of the desperate need for intelligence on Soviet bomber and missile capabilities. The routes of the deep-penetration U-2 flights were marked out carefully, since the perilous overflights had to hit key targets to maximise their rare ventures. The locations to be photographed had been identified by the vast intelligence-gathering programmes designed to 'wring out' Germans returning from the Soviet Union. Most of the deep-penetration flights were launched from Adana in Turkey. Because Turkey would not allow penetration directly into the Soviet Union, the U-2 flew on to Peshawar in Pakistan before crossing the Soviet border. Along the southern border of the Soviet Union, radar stations were more dispersed and a variety of attractive targets presented themselves, including a range of missile-testing centres at Kazakhstan and the Caspian Sea and at Kapustin Yar on the Volga. Sites at Sary-Shagan in Kazakhstan were of particular interest because of suspicions that the Soviets were working on anti-ballistic missiles there. Some of these flights substituted elint and sigint packages for cameras. In June 1957, a pilot indulging in a dangerous deviation from his planned course found the 'crown jewels' of Soviet space technology. At Tyura Tam in Kazakhstan he located the inter-continental ballistic missile (ICBM) test site, three months before the launch of the Sputnik rocket. Sizeable atomic installations in Siberia were also photographed, new radars were found at Lake Baikal, and the main Soviet A-bomb test site at Semipalatinsk was kept under close watch. There were even flights over China.[26]

Although the risks of the U-2 programme were great, so were the potential rewards. The CIA's own internal history of the U-2 programme, declassified with heavy deletions, asserts that the U-2 marked the end of the 'bomber gap' mystery. None of the airbases photographed by the U-2 pilots had the types and numbers of new Soviet bombers that American hawks had predicted. On the strength of this, Eisenhower was willing to exert himself to resist pressure from the US Air Force and from Capitol Hill for more American bombers and missiles. In reality the U-2 offered only a partial defence against this domestic pressure. The U-2 was not photographing enough of the Soviet Union on enough days to deal with the hardline sceptics, nor could all the sceptics be briefed with the highly secret U-2 material. Eisenhower knew he was right, but he could not prove he was right.[27]

Eisenhower was in a quandary over U-2 flights. On the one hand, they provided him with the confidence to resist escalatory calls for increases in American defence spending, not least from the presidential candidate John F. Kennedy. On the other hand, it was only a matter of time before the Soviets downed a U-2, with dire consequences. In 1958 Eisenhower had virtually suspended the U-2 programme of deep penetration over the Soviet Union, though shallow penetrations continued. The CIA assured him that U-2s were getting harder to track and might soon be radar-invisible. This reflected a highly secret programme to produce special stealth U-2s – codenamed Dirty Birds – covered in radar-absorbent material. But the material caused the U-2s to overheat and a test pilot was killed in a prototype. In the summer of 1957 operational Dirty Birds were delivered to Detachment B at Adana. But the nine flights using this aircraft proved no more stealthy than other U-2 missions. From September 1957 deep-penetration flights were wound down.[28]

The dangers involved in the expanding programme of aerial surveillance were becoming more apparent in the late 1950s. The Norwegians monitored the growing number of British ferret flights from the base at Tromsø using Washington, Comet and Canberra aircraft and discovered that 'British pilots took greater risks' and at times came close to a collision course with Soviet fighters scrambled against them. The same was true of US naval reconnaissance aircraft flying out of Thule in 1958 which occasionally intruded deliberately into Soviet airspace over the Kola Peninsula, resulting in protests from the Soviet Ambassador to Norway. In May 1958 the American Secretary of Defense complained that such flights were regularly violating their instructions and flying closer to the Soviet Union than permitted. In October 1959 an RB-57D was shot down over the Pacific, although the event was not publicised. The Norwegians now decided to deny the British and Americans permission to fly ferret flights against Soviet missile tests from northern Norway, fearing that they too would be shot down by the Soviets.[29]

Aircraft were also lost over China. On 25 November 1958 the US

Commander of the Pacific Fleet, Admiral Arleigh Burke, asked to resume spy-flights over mainland China during the Taiwan Straits Crisis in preparation for further communist attacks. Burke argued that with the high-performance version of the British Canberra, the RB-57D, 'the danger of interception is virtually nil'. These flights were resumed, but less than a year later a Taiwanese RB-57D was lost over China.[30] Ray Cline, the CIA head of station in Taipei, recalled Taiwan's own U-2 unit – with its distinctive shoulder patch, a black cat with enormous yellow eyes. All the pilots were given suicide equipment, and on the flight-line the crews were adamant that if they were intercepted they would destroy their planes. One pilot whom Cline spoke to insisted that 'he would destroy the goddamn plane' and he would 'drive it into the ground'. Cline, viewing his Taiwan allies through rose-coloured spectacles, claimed that this is just what 'they all did'. In reality the Taiwan pilots were not slow to bail out. In the 1960s the Chinese government was able to line up no fewer than four intact U-2 aircraft for display in a Beijing public park.[31]

Eisenhower continued to resist the U-2 programme, and in February 1959 he stated that nothing would make him request authority to declare war more quickly than the violation of American airspace by equivalent Soviet aircraft. In April that year, he was still reluctant, consenting to one or two flights, but setting his face against an 'extensive programme'. Already aware that an East–West summit was being planned, he insisted that the West could not afford 'the revulsion of world opinion against the United States that might occur'. By February 1960 it was clear that the Soviets had a missile that could reach the approximate altitude of the U-2, though it was not very manoeuvrable. The CIA was already working on U-2 replacements, both new aircraft and satellites, and the door seemed to be finally closing on the U-2 as a deep-penetration aircraft.

The last U-2 flight was precipitated by an improbable turn of events. Ironically, increased paranoia in the West about a possible 'missile gap' was caused by the failure of the Soviet ICBM programme. Faced with repeated disasters in testing programmes, Moscow decided to deal with this by bluffing and hoping that the excitement created by Sputnik would make its bluff plausible, and it worked. In December 1958 it told a high-level international conference on Surprise Attack at Geneva that ICBMs were in mass production. By early 1959, with the disastrous Soviet missile programme literally at a standstill, Khrushchev told the world that Soviet missiles were rolling off the production line 'like sausages from a sausage factory'. Eisenhower and the CIA guessed that technical difficulties had forced the Soviets back to the drawing board, but the US Air Force asserted that testing had stopped because the Soviets had moved to the production stage. Pressure for more intelligence on the Soviet missile programme was now impossible to resist.

Accordingly, Eisenhower approved several new U-2 flights on 10 April 1959. But he was wracked by doubt and the next day he reversed his decision. He explained that he was anxious about the 'terrible' consequences if one of the U-2s were shot down. Instead special sigint U-2s and RB-57D Canberras were used along the Iranian border to achieve the first telemetry sigint intercepts of Soviet missile testing during a first-stage flight only eighty seconds after launch. Only one U-2 flight was approved in July 1959, and Eisenhower said that he was content to wait for the results of the satellite programme, which had been underway for four years and would soon produce dividends.[32] He authorised two further flights in April and May of 1960. Francis Gary Powers piloted the last, flown on 1 May. Codenamed Operation Grand Slam, it was the longest and most daring U-2 mission yet attempted, traversing the whole of the Soviet Union from Peshawar in Pakistan to Bodø in Norway. Delays caused by the weather helped to compromise the security of the mission. The Soviet May Day holiday had been a dubious choice for this U-2 mission. There was almost no military traffic over the Soviet Union and so the U-2 was easy to track, indeed it was picked up when it was still fifteen miles south of the Soviet–Afghan border.[33]

Shooting down Gary Powers' flight had nevertheless been a desperate business for the Soviets. Determined to destroy the U-2, they had fired fourteen SAM missiles, destroying one of their own MiGs that was in hot pursuit. One missile damaged the control surfaces of the flimsy U-2. With the aircraft in a flat spin, caused by the U-2s large wingspan, Powers struggled even to get the canopy open and was unable to activate the self-destruct mechanism before bailing out. The flat spin also ensured that the Soviets retrieved the aircraft all but intact.[34] The CIA had not expected pilots to be captured alive and had issued them with cyanide L-Pills of the sort requested by George Kennan in the early 1950s. The pills were highly effective, resulting in death within fifteen seconds, but pilots were not compelled to take them on flights and many chose not to. In any case, the CIA reckoned that any missile that damaged the aircraft would probably kill the pilot.[35] L-Pills (or lethal pills) had caused a near-calamity at an early stage in the U-2 programme. In December 1956 a U-2 mission over Bulgaria was undertaken by a pilot who was notably fond of lemon drops – indeed he was known to his fellow pilots as the Lemon Drop Kid, because he sucked them inflight. He carried a supply of them in the right knee pocket of his flying suit. On the morning of his pre-flight preparations the ground crew chose to place his L-Pill in the same pocket. Halfway through the flight he popped in another lemon-drop but noticed that it was peculiarly flavourless and very smooth. After sucking it a while he opened his faceplate again and spat it into his glove for inspection. He had been sucking on the lethal L-Pill, a thin glass capsule filled with potassium cyanide. After this incident the pills were placed in a special box to prevent any further close calls.[36]

A month after Gary Powers had been shot down, an American RB-47E ferret aircraft was destroyed over the Barents Sea, north of the Kola Peninsula, while engaged in maritime surveillance which was close to, but not within, Soviet airspace. This latter aircraft had been launched from RAF Brize Norton in Britain. American and Norwegian sigint stations had tracked the aircraft but disputed its course, plotting it thirty miles and twenty-three miles respectively from the Soviet coast. The aircraft crew had received orders not to go closer than fifty miles. The Soviet coastal limit was twelve miles and the margin for error was small.[37] The U-2 and RB-47 episodes in April and May 1960 led to a public outcry in Britain and endless questions in the House of Commons. The Leader of the Opposition, Hugh Gaitskell, pressed Macmillan on the nature of the agreements covering the use of U-2 bases. Macmillan employed the usual formula, refusing to discuss intelligence matters, but agreed to have renewed discussion with Washington and to keep Gaitskell informed of their substance. American officials reporting to Eisenhower were pleasantly surprised that few MPs questioned the presence of US intelligence aircraft in Britain and, in a debate that was 'serious but not highly charged, there was constructive discussion about firming up consultation between Washington and London.[38]

Khrushchev, Eisenhower, de Gaulle and Macmillan had the opportunity to discuss the matter personally at an abortive Paris summit on 16 May 1960. As the summit opened Khrushchev rose immediately and, rather red-faced, asked de Gaulle, who was in the chair, for the opportunity to make a statement. The Soviet leader demanded an apology from Eisenhower and assurances that U-2 flights would be stopped. Eisenhower confirmed that U-2 flights would be stopped, but did not apologise and insisted that they were necessary. He explained that in future he would be asking the United Nations to undertake flights over both the United States and the Soviet Union. De Gaulle pointed out that Soviet satellites had been overflying France, but Khrushchev dismissed this as a separate matter and at this point stalked out of the conference. The next day Khrushchev and his Defence Minister, Malinovsky, ostentatiously went sightseeing in the French countryside. Most observers agreed that all parties had originally wanted the summit to succeed, not least Khrushchev, who hoped to use Eisenhower to boost his domestic prestige and to show that his policy of peaceful coexistence was succeeding. Harold Macmillan, who had worked hard to bring the summit about, was bitterly disappointed and when the collapse became evident 'he was on the verge of tears'. *Pravda* enjoyed the spectacle of divided allies, repeating Macmillan's reported assertion that 'the Pentagon is blowing up the Summit Conference' by using British bases.

Middle-ranking officials from East and West who were engaged in long-running arms-control talks at Geneva met up some days later. Robert Matteson of the CIA Office of National Estimates had been in discussions with the Soviets for several weeks beforehand. One of his Soviet associates, named Ustachev, later pointed out over dinner that May Day had been an appalling day to launch the U-2 flight. Not only was this a national holiday and therefore seemingly a calculated insult, but the military far from being off duty were showing off their strength and therefore more alert than usual. Ustachev said he thought that Eisenhower's admitting that he had personally authorised the flight made things more difficult, but Khrushchev had tried to give the President a way out so that the Summit could go on. Everything had turned on an apology.[39] However, the United States decided that the best form of defence was attack. Anxious to prove that the Soviets were no respecters of sovereignty in the cause of espionage it chose this moment to expose the Soviet microwave bugging of Kennan's Embassy in 1952, displaying at the United Nations the famous seal which hid the receiver. This was intended to shock the diplomatic community, but the effect was somewhat different. The humour of the 'resonating eagle' story was not lost on the diplomats and all sides in the United Nations Assembly struggled to avoid giggling.[40]

The Soviet Union now threatened countries such as Britain and Japan, which hosted the U-2, with rocket attacks on the bases from which any future reconnaissance flights were made over the Soviet Union or other 'socialist' countries. These threats were first made by Malinovsky on 30 May and were reiterated on 3 June to a packed press conference in Moscow by Khrushchev himself. The British JIC concluded that these threats were a 'bluff' designed to scare Washington's allies, but they nevertheless induced a new caution on the part of Harold Macmillan.[41] Although he did not repeat Eden's suspension of U-2 flights from Britain, there were urgent talks on the use of British bases for further reconnaissance. A new two-part accord was signed. The first was an USAF–RAF agreement which required an American liaison officer in London to inform his hosts in advance of flights into or around the Soviet Union launched from Britain. The second was a political agreement which required a schedule of flights to be provided to the Air Ministry and the Foreign Office on the 15th of each month. However, routine took its toll of procedure and by 1961 the Americans were asking for blanket approvals and authorisation at lower levels. At the first Anglo–American summit following the Gary Powers shoot-down,

Macmillan explained to Eisenhower that he felt that tighter regulation was not the issue. The 'real question that remains is just what we should do in this program, what places we should go to, what operations we should conduct there'. He did not want to be denied access to free airspace over international waters, but the West had to recognise that the Soviets were willing to shoot over international waters and this left the West in a weak position.[42]

Norway was also threatened by the Soviets with missile strikes on the base at Tromsø, where the Gary Powers U-2 was supposed to land. More importantly, it has now emerged that, although the Norwegians had allowed two C-130 Hercules aircraft to arrive at Tromsø to receive the U-2, they were under the impression that Powers was on a perimeter flight and were not told that he was undertaking a deep-penetration mission, in direct violation of a standing CIA agreement with Oslo. Wilhelm Evang, the veteran head of Norwegian intelligence, took the opportunity to lash out at his CIA partners during a visit to Washington in February 1961. He stated his feelings of betrayal over the pathetic cover-story and asserted that it had put back the cause of Norwegian intelligence with his political masters in Oslo by several years.[43]

The U-2 incident, together with the loss of the RB-47, served as a reprise of the Crabb Affair and cast a long shadow over other British intelligence operations. Although there was no search for culprits, operational horns were drawn in and during the summer of 1960 the impact on British surveillance of the Soviet fleet was immediate. These events crushed a British plan for increased airborne surveillance of the fleet that had been emerging in the weeks and months immediately prior to the shoot-downs. In early 1960 the First Sea Lord had held a meeting with the US Navy's Chief of Naval Operations and agreed to an 'increased accent on surveillance'.[44] Accordingly, Admiral John Inglis, working closely with RAF Coastal Command, put forward a highly classified proposal for the expansion of ocean surveillance. Two established programmes were already in existence codenamed Tiara and Long Look which covered Soviet warships exiting the Baltic and the Black Seas respectively and particular attention was being given to Soviet submarines. Opportunistic surveillance operations were also being mounted in the South Atlantic by aircraft based in South Africa, and in the Indian Ocean by aircraft based in Malaya. In April, Inglis noted that the main problem would be securing ministerial approval for a programme that had 'considerable political ramifications'.[45]

But after the shoot-downs Inglis decided not even to bother putting his plans to Ministers. There was 'no point', as the chances of securing political approval were 'remote because of the situation brought about by the U-2 and RB-47 incidents'. The Ministry of Defence bided its time and in March 1961 the situation was reviewed. But the 'political climate was no better' and it was hard to see when it might improve sufficiently to make it worth while pursuing proposals further, so British plans for increased airborne surveillance of the Soviet fleet were put 'into cold storage indefinitely'.[46] Not only were new plans aborted, but long-established British photographic reconnaissance programmes, such as Operation Tiara, were brought to a close. As one senior official in the Air Ministry explained:

> You will recall that following the U-2 and RB-47 incidents the Prime Minister imposed certain additional restrictions on aircraft taking part in the surveillance operation TIARA/GARNET. The purpose of these restrictions was to prevent a situation occurring in which an aircraft may be shot down by a Soviet vessel. Because of difficulties in identifying the target, however, this effect has been so inhibiting that the operation is hardly worth mounting, and the Admiralty has not, in fact, requested any surveillance tasks since the new restrictions have been in force.

Having moved quickly to impose these specific restrictions, Macmillan followed in Eden's footsteps and now required the JIC to prepare a more general review of all surveillance and submarine tasks so that he could reassess the value of the intelligence gained from these sorts of activities.[47]

All these incidents, enquiries and restrictions contain a certain element of irony. In the early 1950s Britain and the United States had increasingly resolved to make more use of technical means to examine the Soviet armed forces and Soviet scientific–technical developments, because human espionage inside the Soviet Union had proved more and more hazardous and, with a few exceptions, notably unproductive. Of the dozens of agents despatched into the Soviet Union and China, few ever returned. Technical platforms seemed to offer a better product and safer operations. But after the political rumpus of April–May 1960, the potential political problems, even dangers, of aerial surveillance of Soviet targets were also painfully obvious. They would become even more evident during the Cuban Missile Crisis. On 27 October 1962, the loss of an American U-2 over Cuba marked the danger point at which pressure upon President Kennedy, who succeeded Eisenhower in January 1961, to take military action was at its most intense.

Despite Macmillan's review, by 1963, British Naval Intelligence had, once more, secured renewed permission for more hazardous activities, including submarine-based sigint operations into the freezing waters off Murmansk. The main submarines used were the relatively new Porpoise class, including HMS *Walrus*, HMS *Grampus* and HMS *Sealion*. These operations 'surfaced' somewhat uncomfortably during major Anglo-Norwegian intelligence meetings in Oslo during May 1963. On successive days the Norwegians berated first Sir Clive Loehnis, Director of

GCHQ, and then Dick White, head of SIS, about the extent to which Norway was used as a collection station but received few of the dividends from the process, and was not always told about operations utilising its territory.[48] Loehnis and White took the opportunity to confess an embarrassing recent incident. A British submarine of the Porpoise class from the 1st Submarine Squadron based at HMS Dolphin at Gosport had been on a sigint-gathering mission in the Barents Sea. The Captain had found himself accidentally in the middle of a major Soviet anti-submarine warfare exercise just outside the Murmansk inlet. Identified initially by a helicopter using a dipping sonar, he was pursued relentlessly by surface vessels seeking to ram him and in the ensuing mayhem there was some sort of collision. With its batteries almost exhausted, the British submarine was forced break the surface and make a run for it, eventually finding sanctuary in Norwegian waters. Finally the submarine reached Gosport, with the damaged bows carefully concealed. Sigint duty in northern waters was a substantial aspect of the British submariners' existence in the 1960s and a Royal Navy submarine was almost permanently on station outside Murmansk. One of the principal targets was telemetry from Soviet missile tests at sea. The crew were not told about their destination until after they had left Gosport. However, the departure of these highly secret missions was attended by certain rituals which quickly alerted the crew to the nature of their duties. One submariner recalled, 'these particular patrols were very often referred to as "Dodgy's" or "Mystery Trips". In the early days the only time you knew exactly where you were going was after you had left the dockyard and a dockyard tug followed you out into the shallows to paint the pennant number out on the conning tower and to weld up the hatches apart from the conning tower. Very reassuring ...' Welding the hatches was a high-risk strategy designed to give the submarine a little more protection against ramming by Soviet surface vessels.[49]

The long-term solution to many of these collection problems was satellites. The first successful spy satellite, called Project Corona was launched only three months after the loss of Gary Powers' U-2 aircraft. This programme owed its origins to a US Navy initiative in March 1946, which sought better means of ocean surveillance. It was satellite photography of Soviet ICBM sites provided by this programme during 1961, rather than the U-2, which finally destroyed the myth of the so called 'missile gap' between the Soviets and the Americans. The drive towards surveillance that did not require dangerous platforms was now under way, but the U-2 incident had left an indelible mark on public opinion. In August 1960 the US Information Agency Office of Research and Analysis commissioned a Gallup Poll on British public reactions to an American spy-satellite programme. To its surprise, of those who had a firm opinion, the majority were against, either because it was 'looking for trouble' or because it was 'not right to spy'. The U-2 shoot-down was the first of a number of major secret-service-related fiascos and scandals in the early 1960s that contributed to a growing climate of revelation and also an enhanced public suspicion of secret service.[50]

Throughout the 1960s, British Cabinet Ministers also continued to reflect the deep caution imbued by the twin shoot-downs of 1960 and the collapse of Macmillan's longed-for Geneva Summit. When George Brown, Harold Wilson's Foreign Secretary, visited Moscow in May 1967, British and American sigint flights against the Soviets were suspended for the duration to ensure there were no incidents, a procedure which had become routine for such visits. On 15 June that year, as the Middle East crisis worsened in the wake of the Six Day War, in which Israel launched a series of highly successful surprise attacks, high-level decisions were again taken to cancel 'covert flights against Syrian and Egyptian targets'. The need for caution with intelligence-collection platforms had been underlined only a week earlier by the extraordinary Israeli attack on the American NSA sigint-collection ship, the USS *Liberty*, with the loss of forty lives.[51]

By contrast most signals intelligence-gathering during the Cold War was conducted from the ground and was not hazardous. By the late 1950s, Western signals intelligence had entered a new era. High-grade ciphers employed by the major powers remained effectively impossible to break by cryptanalysis. But cryptography was a ceaseless battle of offence and defence and a great deal of attention was directed towards 'bugging' and intercepting telephone lines. The traffic of many Third World states was still proving vulnerable and as a result a stream of signals intelligence was routinely available to those serving in the Foreign Office. Before gaining access to sigint, Foreign Office officials were required to attend a day course at the Diplomatic Wireless Service Centre during which they were lectured on the importance of security. On returning from their security course, Foreign Office staff could go on the circulation list for BJs or Blue Jackets, the colour of the special folders in which sigint material was circulated. The first rule of sigint security was that this material was never to be referred to in ordinary Foreign Office paperwork – a rule often flouted – while the decrypts should always remain in the special Blue Jackets. BJs were circulated by special messenger, originating in the Permanent Under-Secretary's Department and always returning there after use. In a small office in this Department sat the Communications Security Officer, the workaday liaison with GCHQ. By contrast the more humble files dealing with policy and correspondence lived in the routine Foreign Office registry. In the 1960s, during the negotiations over the recognition of East Germany and then during the early negotiations over the Multi-Role Combat Aircraft in the 1960s, West German communications were a favourite target.[52]

By the 1960s GCHQ was confronted with a range of problems, the greatest of which were finance and security. GCHQ found itself increasingly involved in state-of-the-art research into the making and breaking of ciphers, and its junior status alongside the NSA was never more apparent. It faced an ever expanding need for scientific and engineering resources in a field at the forefront of technology. It was now working in an area which involved 'many problems on the edge of what appears to be possible'. Perennial bids for improved resources were necessary to stay in the game. In 1960 GCHQ explained what its work involved to the Radar and Signals Advisory Board. Not only did it do the obvious work of listening, intercepting and recording signals. There was a vast problem of data-processing before cipher-breaking could begin, including obscure subjects such as wave-form analysis. Communications networks were reconstructed 'by fitting together many scraps of information'. Non-communications signals – radars, navigational aids, data transmissions and so on – were a huge new area of business and presented a range of problems very different from traditional communications. All of this experience was then used 'critically and constructively' in order to enhance the security of British communications. As a result, GCHQ was devouring an ever growing proportion of the funding available for British secret service.[53]

GCHQ needed more resources to deal with new issues in the wider world of radio and communications. Because wires inevitably crossed with the parallel worlds of electronic warfare and psywar a burgeoning network of committees and sub-committees tried to keep track of all this. It was realised that the elaborate plans that the services were developing for radio warfare – the jamming of enemy radio communications and radar – were likely to hamper the efforts of GCHQ. Efforts to disrupt Soviet broadcasts of any kind could not but help to interfere with efforts to monitor them. It was the unhappy task of Air Commodore Peter Jones, Deputy Co-ordinator of Radio Plans (War), who worked in the Cabinet Office at Great George Street, to coax the services into revealing their wartime jamming schemes to GCHQ and to permit them a veto. What was needed was an overall authority that would judge whether the value of certain types of jamming was worth 'the loss of wanted intercept'. This was not only a hypothetical hot-war problem. The services were already drawing up detailed plans for a repeat of the Berlin Airlift in some future Berlin crisis. In such an event jamming, elint and comint units would be working flat out and 'every available man will be needed for signals intelligence coverage'. But how these elements were to be reconciled at short notice no one seemed to know.[54]

Some of GCHQ's most expensive work was conducted with the RAF. The core business was Radio Proving Flights or ferret flights designed to gather intelligence on Soviet air defences to support operations by Britain's main deterrent force of nuclear-armed V-bombers coming on stream in the late 1950s. These elint flights were considered critical to maintaining the effectiveness of the nuclear deterrent and they logged the radar frequencies, including surface-to-air missile batteries, working in conjunction with a number of ground station collection efforts called Operation Viking. Some of the material was eventually made available to NATO air forces in a summarised form and with its source removed.[55] The backbone of these ferret flights were Comet airliners that were expensively re-equipped. In 1958 the RAF's 192 Squadron was renumbered 51 Squadron and its parent organisation – 90 Group – became RAF Signals Command. Ageing Washingtons were replaced by three Comet Mk 2s specially modified with a great deal of electronic equipment. They could carry an expanded crew, often as many as ten operators including three comint linguists and ground crew if the aircraft was deploying overseas. The three Comets of 51 Squadron were effectively the eyes and ears of the British nuclear deterrent. However, in 1959 one aircraft was burned out in an accident. The answer was to convert another transport version of the Comet to replace the lost aircraft. But even though most of the equipment to be installed was American, of which there was sufficient stock, the cost of converting the airframe alone was over £300,000, which was resisted by the Treasury.[56]

Clive Loehnis, the Director of GCHQ, wheeled out one of his senior managers, Joe Hooper, who had worked with the Treasury down the years on 'cost of sigint' statements and knew how to make a financial case. Hooper accepted that these flights were 'an expensive form of Sigint operation' both in relation to the results obtained and in comparison with ground-based units. But the 'unique' results were necessary for planning nuclear attacks on the Soviet Union by Britain's new V-bomber force. Such flights had been chewed over at length in 1959 on cost grounds by the Director of GCHQ and the RAF, and again in 1960 by the JIC after the RB-47 and U-2 incidents. But Ministers had finally agreed that they should be continued with each flight receiving high-level approval. Three aircraft was the minimum necessary for this operation, which was largely based in the Mediterranean. The Treasury eventually relented and another Comet was fitted out.[57]

Until 1960 both British and American airborne operations had made much use of airbases in Turkey, but by April 1961 Ankara was having second thoughts. In 1958 an American C-130 Hercules aircraft converted into a sigint-collector had been destroyed by Soviet fighters on the border. Nervousness had been heightened by the Gary Powers shoot-down. On

27 March 1961 the Turkish General Staff placed severe restrictions on overflights, including a ban on approaching the border within 100 kilometres and a height ceiling of 40,000 feet. These rendered Western ferret flights almost inoperable and the Turks knew it. The result was a high-level meeting with the Chief of the Turkish General Staff, General Sunay, attended by Mounbatten, who was now Chief of the Defence Staff (a new post occupied by Britain's senior serviceman), the Chairman of the US Joint Chiefs of Staff, General Lemnitzer, and a British signals specialist, Captain W. D. Hodgkinson. It was over an hour and a half before they could bring the Turks to discuss the issue of airborne sigint-collection, whereupon they emphasised that it was of 'vital importance to the maintenance of the deterrent'. After prolonged bargaining General Sunay agreed to remove the height restriction and allow flights closer to the border. The local British Air Attaché explained that what the Turks were really after was more resources, including expensive American equipment for their own sigint service and for their own jamming units.[58]

Throughout the mid-1960s, RAF sigint flights by 51 Squadron followed a fairly consistent pattern. Approximately fourteen flights a month were mounted into the Baltic, no closer than twenty-six miles from the Soviet coast, using mostly Canberras. Seven flights a month were mounted against Indonesia, using mostly Comets. Comet sorties were also being flown 'against targets in East Germany ... at short notice, i.e. with approximately 30 minutes warning, against opportunity targets'. These were separate from more routine East German border flights. There were also routine sorties against Soviet naval shipping in the Mediterranean, especially in the Aegean, where the neighbouring airspace was friendly. There were more irregular flights against Middle Eastern countries. Schedules of these flights were provided monthly by the Minister of Defence personally to the Foreign Secretary for approval, as they had been since the advent of new rules in 1960, with some discretion being allowed for the less risky flights along borders and over international waters.[59]

Alongside the ever present problem of money for elaborate airborne sigint-collection, was the grimy problem of security. There were problems of physical security and also of personnel security, and both were hard to solve. In April 1956, Washington was rocked by the news that the Soviets had successfully bugged the EUCOM headquarters building in Paris. Clandestine listening devices had been discovered in the EUCOM conference room there and similar devices had also been found in 'certain key diplomatic offices', including 'the Offices of the U.S. Ambassadors in Belgrade and Tel Aviv'. The EUCOM revelations prompted a thorough sweep, and Admiral Radford, who was then Chairman of the US Joint Chiefs of Staff, told the Secretary of Defense that 'as a result of further examination of the EUCOM area, it was reported that the first 14 telephones examined were found to be equipped with jumper circuits which kept the telephones alive when the receivers remained in their cradles. Thus, what was formerly a suspicion of compromise is now a discomforting reality.' Bugging was now understood to be a 'major threat to national security'. Radford lamented that many years after the discovery of bugs in Kennan's Moscow Embassy there was still no US agency with central responsibility for countering this problem. Moreover, as early as November 1952 there had been warnings that EUCOM was a security disaster waiting to happen. Officers had cautioned that war plans, US Joint Chiefs of Staff papers and cryptographic systems were all 'horribly and inexcusably exposed', but no action had been taken.[60]

London was also discomfited by the growth of hostile Soviet listening. In the early 1960s, shadowing Soviet vessels became more important with the increasing appearance of Soviet comint-collection vessels, usually 'trawlers'. In September 1964, Peter Thorneycroft, the Minister of Defence, asked the Prime Minister for permission to shadow these sorts of craft more vigorously. Three were moving round the British coast at this time. During the last NATO exercise the number of flying hours devoted to this problem had been enormous and the Ministry of Defence now sought permission to go back to shadowing with ships. Safer guidelines for the Royal Navy in shadowing Soviet sigint-collection vessels known as the Sampan rules had just appeared.[61] Despite shadowing, by 1963 the attentions of Soviet sigint trawlers around the shores of Britain were becoming tiresome. Their presence frequently disrupted trials of new equipment or sensitive exercises involving strategic procedures. Some Soviet vessels visibly bristled with aerials, but it was thought that 'other ELINT-equipped vessels might be able to conceal their equipment'. Soviet ships regularly visited Preston and were suspected of watching the development of the TSR-2 aircraft, Britain's planned strike aircraft for the late 1960s, especially its electronics fit. Parts of this were being developed on a Buccaneer being flown by Ferranti at Turnhouse and more sensitive equipment in a Canberra being flown from Pershore. RAF signals units were therefore assigned to 'shadow monitor' communications to ensure their security due to the constant presence of the sigint trawlers.[62]

Personnel security within GCHQ itself was considered to be a huge problem. In the mid-1950s there was a failed attempt to reduce civilian components in the sigint programme and instead to militarise them. Anxiety had been expressed about civilians as early as February 1948 during integration between systems run by the services and by Cable and Wireless. Hirtherto the RAF had handled 'all Sigint traffic as an interservice agreement'. The RAF talked up the threat of union action and did not hesitate to point out that 'a threatened GPO strike of mechanics and operators would have paralysed communications', adding that Cable and Wireless had many non-British personnel. The RAF was adamant about resisting any economies that involved integration with civilian workers.[63]

Following what officials called 'an embarrassing domestic security case' involving trade union representation at GCHQ in the spring of 1954, the decision was taken to terminate the civilian monitoring units which contributed to GCHQ's collection effort. Elements of the Army, Navy, RAF and Foreign Office radio services were brought together into something called the Composite Signals Organisation. The process of shifting away from civilian monitors was slow. The Admiralty Director of Signals warned about the 'fundamental security problem' of a collection service 'which is civilian manned in a democratic country, and therefore with Trade Union affinities which no-one can guarantee cannot be communist (vide the E.T.U.)'. This reflected ongoing concerns in MI5 and elsewhere about communist elements in the ETU or Electrical Trades Union. Fears about union activity were the main driver, but there were other issues. The London Signals Intelligence Board had been told that there was an 'increasing need to have "Y" stations close to the "Iron Curtain" and to increase the number of Special Operations'. These requirements could be met only by uniformed personnel.[64] In March 1955 the Cabinet Security Committee agreed there was a security risk involved in trade union membership and hoped for a slow drift to decivilianisation, accepting that it 'would take many years to achieve'.[65]

In the late 1950s the ETU issue came in for concerted attention. MI5 decided that the communists had adopted a central strategy of capturing the leadership of trade unions by fair means or foul. Electoral tampering and fraud were certainly widespread. The Cabinet Secretary Norman Brook told Eden that it was time for counter-action as early as May 1956. Officials in the Ministry of Labour, he complained, were 'frightened to death' of intervention, but the communist strategy had very nearly succeeded and it was time to offer anti-communist trade union leaders unobtrusive help 'in this struggle'. In July discreet meetings were held with union leaders, Sir Vincent Tewson and Sir Tom Williamson, who were briefed with MI5 material. Recent efforts to expose the problem by the MP and journalist Woodrow Wyatt in a television documentary had swung the latest elections away from the communists. However, Eden was alarmed by the thought of intervention and stressed 'we shall have to go very carefully'.[66]

The ETU issue was of additional importance because of persistent American interest in the problem of communist entryism within British unions. When the CIA compiled a survey of communist activity in Britain, noting that its strength was small but growing, it warned that in the early 1950s the communists had achieved a strong position through ballot-rigging, although this was being exposed later in the decade by campaigning journalists. Eventually in June 1961 the communist General Secretary of the ETU was turfed out by a court judgement that declared his election fraudulent, and Jock Byrne was installed in his place. The battle was a prolonged one with some communist officials only removed in 1963. In 1965 communists were banned from holding office in the ETU. The moderate Frank Chapple went on to occupy the post of general secretary until 1984.[67] Wyatt presented himself as an interested independent who had happened on the story of communist penetration of the unions by accident. In fact he had longstanding associations with IRD and formed the lead element in an organised attack. He was an obvious candidate for this role as he had links to IRD as a shareholder in the Arab News Agency and a book of his had been published by Leslie Sheridan through a front company.[68]

Union issue distracted from the main security problem at GCHQ, which was the scale of positive vetting required. Targets for vetting certain groups of personnel had been set by secretive Cabinet sub-committees on personnel security. But vetting was not effective in the 1950s and resources to improve matters were not available. Arthur de la Mare recalled the lamentable state of British vetting when he became head of the Foreign Office Security Department in 1955. The whole business of security vetting was still looked upon as somehow 'unBritish' or distasteful and many diplomats regarded it with 'contempt and derision'. Several of his colleagues wondered what he could have done to deserve such a 'degrading' post. All those being vetted had to nominate two outsiders as referees, and these were interviewed by members of the Security Department. The interviewers then delivered a report on each case, but as the Treasury would allow only five staff for this task they delivered at best only ten reports a week, often fewer. Vetting all the members of the Diplomatic Service was going to take years. The system was also flawed in that those being vetted could nominate their own referees. 'Many of the referees protested to us and their MPs at being interrogated by "snarks" on the background and integrity of their friends.' De la Mare concluded that positive vetting 'was in many cases a farce', and he eventually went to see the Permanent Under-Secretary, Sir Ivone Kirkpatrick, fearing that there would be adverse criticism in Parliament 'when our very slow rate of positive vetting' became known. Kirkpatrick accepted that they needed many more staff on positive vetting, but the Treasury would not pay for any more. He refused to allow measures to 'try to speed up', arguing that if as a result 'someone got through the net' everybody would blame the Foreign Office. 'I do not want us to have to accept blame which rightly falls upon the Treasury.'

Far from making any inroads into the huge backlog, 'the number not yet vetted went on increasing'.[69]

The problem for GCHQ was even greater. GCHQ and its out-stations was as big as the Foreign Office, but everyone was involved in very sensitive work, with large numbers of persons doing tours overseas. In April 1957 this issue made its way up to the Cabinet Personnel Security Committee. Quite a lot of people in GCHQ were turning out to be a 'security risk', not because of communist or fascist affiliations but because of aspects of their private lives which were thought to make them vulnerable to manipulation. Some examples they identified included recovered schizophrenics, those in financial difficulty because of 'matrimonial entanglements', 'suspected homosexuals about whom there is no direct evidence' and, they added rather coyly, 'instances where a man is living a very shady existence but has not been brought to Court'. Security officials were also keen to remove from GCHQ anyone with religious convictions 'which require him to owe no allegiance to the Crown', giving the example of Jehovah's Witnesses. Elsewhere in Whitehall the solution was to transfer the civil servant to non-secret work. But in GCHQ there were not enough of these posts and they were all low grade. Moreover, GCHQ staff were specialists and were 'unsuitable' to be moved to other parts of Whitehall, so there was 'no alternative to dismissal'. But in the majority of cases nothing had been proved against the individual concerned other than vague 'character defects' and they worried about appeals and possible court action.[70]

By the mid-1960s the problem had become worse rather than better. The scope and scale of security measures in government departments was gradually increased with ever more categories of personnel being subjected to positive vetting. Faced with a continuing stream of embarrassing revelations about security lapses and mindful of the damage inflicted on Macmillan by the Profumo Affair in 1963, Prime Minister Harold Wilson gave the Paymaster General, George Wigg, the special brief of looking after government security matters. Wigg was asked to conduct a review of security in the Diplomatic Service, GCHQ and the Ministry of Defence. Although GCHQ was a department of the Foreign Office it was 'autonomous to a considerable extent' and its size was now vast. There were 11,500 people working on sigint – 8,000 with GCHQ directly – and 3,500 as services personnel in the Composite Signals Organisation, working on collection. This was several times the size of MI5 and SIS combined. Of those working for GCHQ, half were in Cheltenham and half scattered around listening stations at home and abroad. With the exception of a very few ancillary staff, just over 600, everyone had to be positively vetted. GCHQ had a large team of twenty-one investigating officers, many of whom were retired Cheltenham police officers. This was 'advantageous' as many of the GCHQ staff at Cheltenham were recruited locally and the ex-police had acquired 'considerable knowledge' of their background and circumstances. Despite increasing the investigating officers to twenty-five, Wigg conceded that 'a backlog of positive vetting has built up'.

There was also the problem of document security. GCHQ's product was tightly controlled. It was circulated in the form of top-secret documents with special procedures laid down by the UKUSA agreement and watched over by communications intelligence security officers in each Whitehall department receiving the material. GCHQ policy documents were also closely controlled. But, uniquely to GCHQ, the basic 'working material' of breaking ciphers was also highly secret and was not catalogued in registries. Indeed this material, often scraps of paper, 'is not known to exist except among those officers who generate or work on it'. In other words it was easy for cryptanalysts to smuggle out papers that their own specialist branches were working on.[71]

In short, vetting was a horrific problem which expanded yearly and which no-one wanted to touch. In October 1962 Sir Roger Hollis, who had replaced Dick White as the head of MI5, had a long meeting with the Chiefs of Staff about the subject. Hollis was there to repel suggestions that vetting for all of Whitehall should become an MI5 responsibility. In theory, it was mostly done by in-house vetting squads from each department. But in practice much of it was pooled and done by the Ministry of Supply, which had experience because of its past atomic work. Hollis rightly described vetting as thankless and endless and could not be persuaded to take it on.[72] Revelations about the treachery of George Blake, a Soviet agent inside SIS, who was first identified in 1961 by the Americans, had made London doubly nervous on the subject of security and a repeat of the British mole escapades of the early 1950s was feared. However, the early 1960s proved to be marked by the defection of American sigint specialists from the NSA rather than GCHQ. William Martin and Bernon Mitchell defected to the Soviets and a 'massive investigation' was launched by a team of fifteen NSA investigators. What they discovered was that American vetting had also proved weak and ineffective. Martin and Mitchell had been taken on by NSA despite the fact that during their security vetting one of them had spoken freely of a range of disconcerting private practices and idiosyncrasies, including a penchant for bestiality. The NSA informed GCHQ and the now familiar 'damage assessments' were set in train.[73]

24

Missiles and Mergers: Strategic Intelligence

It is only with the advent of missiles that working difficulties have arisen ...
Air Chief Marshal Sir Thomas Pike (CAS), 'Missile Intelligence',
March 1961[1]

In the late 1950s and early 1960s the highest priority target for GCHQ and NSA remained atomic weapons and their delivery systems, such as missiles. Macmillan had made a major effort to improve Anglo-American relations in the intelligence field which coincided with the restoration of Anglo-American atomic exchanges during 1957 and 1958. The British JIC concluded that the new British hydrogen bomb had helped to persuade Washington to take London seriously again, assisted by the new British V-bomber force which, because of its geographical location, would 'lead the attack on Russia by some 6 hours'.[2] Achieving hydrogen-bomb status had tested British technical capabilities to their very limits. The first British hydrogen bombs, deployed with the RAF in February 1958 and codenamed Violet Club, were alarmingly unstable. Cobbled together using some components from earlier atomic bombs, this weapon became live as soon as the safety device was removed and it was clear that even a small accident might trigger 'a full yield nuclear explosion'. The Controller of Armaments at the Ministry of Supply protested its premature deployment, insisting that it broke the 1953 Cabinet ruling on nuclear custody. By 1959 it had to be withdrawn because of serious corrosion of some of its component parts. As Len Scott and Stephen Twigge have conclusively shown, there is good evidence that, in order to join the nuclear elite, Britain was 'prepared to both compromise safety and sanction *ad hoc* custodial arrangements for nuclear weapons'. However, if the aim of this gamble was to convince the Americans that the British were worth taking seriously and co-operating with, then it proved effective.[3]

Intelligence on strategic weapons was certainly a live issue on which

London wished to engage fully with Washington. The late 1950s saw a gradual lessening of British worries about an American preventative war or provocative liberation activities. Instead they were overshadowed by the arrival of the Soviet Sputnik and American alarms over Khrushchev's claims about Soviet missile production. However, London and Washington could not agree on the meaning of the intelligence they had jointly collected and became adversaries in the famous 'bomber gap' and 'missile gap' debates of the late 1950s.

They came close to consensus regarding intelligence on the Eastern bloc only in their conclusion that liberation efforts were now quite fruitless, though there was confusion about what should be put in their place. The senior PUSD officials confessed that they had 'no bright ideas', but seem to have reached an accommodation with Washington on covert action in the East just before the Hungarian rising in 1956. 'Before our attack on Egypt the C.I.A. party which came here were in full agreement with our own attitude towards the satellites, including the need for caution in encouraging too violently revolutionary tendencies there.' But PUSD faced the perennial British problem of the hydra-headed nature of American policy. Patrick Dean lamented that 'on the covert and semi-covert side, the multiplicity of American organisations concerned with their large staffs and ample funds is liable to cause great confusion'.[4]

After Hungary, almost all had agreed that the idea of prising away a satellite was not a good one. But American ideological commitment to liberation had been strong and some, especially those working in the area of propaganda, found it hard to let go. C. D. Jackson, Frank Wisner's long-term partner in the assault on the ramparts of the Soviet empire, was one such figure. Following a renewed crisis over Berlin in 1958, Jackson hoped for an opportunity to revive liberation. But the tide of events was against him as the administration in Washington searched for a less aggressive solution to a Berlin crisis in which Khrushchev had proved a resilient and wily operator. Jackson rightly suspected that a deal might be struck by Washington that would trade accommodation over Berlin in return for informal assurances of less Western pressure on Eastern Europe. Although the military backed his tough line on Berlin, he suspected that a policy of drift was setting in. Allen Dulles agreed with Jackson in principle that the United States should not go on to the defensive and 'not let K[hrushchev]. and Company feel they can push us around without stirring up some trouble in their own backyard', but Dulles knew he was in a minority. Jackson spent 1959 exhorting his colleagues about the need to 'contain Communist psychological aggression' by resuming covert activities against Eastern Europe. Christian Herter, the new Secretary of State, touched a raw nerve when he made a television speech on 12 May 1959 about Eastern Europe that suggested a softening of the American position. If the United States was not going to conduct active political warfare against the East, Jackson said, then it should say so and the Free Europe Committee and Radio Free Europe should 'go out of business forthwith'. A wistful Jackson reminded Allen Dulles that he had once made him the 'unofficial "uncle" to the oppressed countries of the East', for which he had developed a 'forlorn affection'. But his arguments were not prompted by sentiment alone and he had a point to make. In an era of greater strategic parity, he said, only psychological warfare could apply pressure to the Kremlin. In the post-Sputnik era, 'there is one gimmick that is not a gimmick – it is a real nightmare for Kruschev – and that is the thought of trouble simultaneously within the satellite belt'. Jackson's suspicion that Eisenhower had given up on creating trouble in the East was confirmed by Khrushchev's arrival on a tour of the United States in May 1959. John Foster Dulles, one of the sternest opponents of talking to the Soviets, was already in hospital with terminal cancer and died shortly after Khrushchev's departure.[5]

Harold Macmillan's anxiety to build a programme of summitry with the Soviets was especially distasteful to cold warriors like C. D Jackson. Macmillan had already embarked on a successful tour of the Soviet Union in February 1959 which had softened the Soviet line somewhat. Jackson suspected that Macmillan was a major factor in propelling Washington towards détente and he complained to Allen Dulles of 'Handsome Harold' and the 'customary ambiguities' that descended on American foreign policy after any discussions with the British. Instead, he suggested, the right approach was to relaunch Eisenhower's Volunteer Freedom Corps idea of 1953. He couched his arguments for the revival of liberation in terms of pragmatism. He no longer saw real liberation as a practical project, but argued that it should be a tactical instrument of pressure, representing it as a 'counter-brush-fire' that could be lit to prevent the possibility of a retreat from Berlin without equivalent concessions from Moscow. He conceded that 'we suffered a terrible set-back in Hungary' and that liberation was always 'tricky and risky', but with retreat over Berlin a possibility, he asked, 'shouldn't the word and the concept be very skilfully revived now?' 'Were we really smart in abandoning the policy of liberation and carefully never mentioning the word again?'

Sputnik, together with Khrushchev's skilful exaggeration of Soviet capabilities, had done its work and stable deterrence was setting in. Raw military power and US Strategic Air Command (SAC) bomber alerts, Jackson argued, no longer held any terrors for the Kremlin. 'Even getting a third or a half of SAC in the air no longer has the bite it once had.' The Americans now had to face the fact that they had entered the era of strategic parity. But, more fundamentally, Jackson was also driven by ideological as well as practical concerns. Liberation was not only about exerting tactical pressure on Moscow, it was also about self-expression. Liberation was the most tangible aspect of America's ideological crusade against the Soviet Union and to let it go was symbolically troubling. Jackson put this very clearly: "'Liberation" is not an ugly word; it is a good word; it is an American word; it is an unambiguous word. It is the one word the Kremlin fears."[6] Here Jackson conveyed the essence of American policy on this difficult issue. Peeling away states from Soviet control had never been the primary goal of liberation and, instead, it had served other functions. At the practical level it had been part of the war of nerves in which Moscow and Washington pressurised each other. Meanwhile, at the ideological level, it was the perfect expression of the wider American purpose in the Cold War. It represented the concept of freedom in action and the reality of America as an 'idea nation'. However, it is difficult to see Jackson's ideas of 1959 as anything but very cynical, since the revival of this pressure on Moscow meant massacres for resistance groups on the ground in Eastern Europe. Emotionally, Allen Dulles felt some personal commitment to Jackson and his protégés at Radio Free Europe. But he was also smarter and, like Khrushchev, realised that the focus of liberation was now shifting to the Third World.

London's worries about American impetuosity in this area faded only slowly. In 1957 the British JIC was still warning that attempts to liberate one of the satellites 'would give rise to extreme tension' and identified an American effort in this area as being one of only three plausible scenarios which could create 'the risk of Global War'.[7] In 1958, key British liaison officers in psychological warfare and covert activities, like Adam Watson, were briefed to track the changing American attitudes to liberation, and during the Berlin Crisis Watson worked closely with his opposite numbers, including Jackson, on 'the Problem', which he formulated as 'after Containment, what?.'[8]

Although Macmillan had stabilised relations with the Americans over issues of Cold War fighting, the difficult calculation was how much restraint to apply. This was underlined during the Taiwan Straits Crisis of 1958. Taiwan, more than any other American ally, was a dedicated practitioner of calculated provocation and 'raiding'. Macmillan resolved to deal with this dangerous crisis by tacitly supporting the Americans and ordering British officials to avoid criticism at all costs. But privately his thoughts were very different, as he believed that the communists had 'an unanswerable case to the possession of these islands'. Sir Frank Roberts, British Ambassador in Paris, put the options for Britain with unpalatable clarity. On the one hand there was 'a policy of silence with its connotations of unwilling satellitism' and on the other hand there was 'one of leading the allies against the Americans'. Macmillan and his Foreign Secretary Selwyn Lloyd chose the former. Ultimately they could do this because they were fairly confident that Eisenhower himself was not keen on brinkmanship and was doing everything possible to avoid all-out war with China. In retrospect, Lloyd explained to Macmillan that they had got the handling of the Americans about right. Had they tried to lecture Washington this would have made it 'extremely resentful and less liable to take our advice'. 'Indeed I think it would have changed the whole nature of our present relationship.' Macmillan agreed, pointing out that it was the fact that the Americans were isolated on this issue that had made them value British support. But ultimately his objective was no different from that of other British premiers since 1949. Above all, he wished to maintain close relations with the Americans so that he could apply the handbrake.[9]

In 1960 and again in mid-1961 the liberation issue was still being pondered by a high-level Foreign Office group called the Steering Committee. This was run by Philip Ziegler (later to become a well-known biographer), who had previously worked with Paul Falla in OPS. Steering Committee set out a new strategy. Although the tragic events in Hungary in 1956 had now receded further into the past, it argued that the result was that Soviet control had been further consolidated and the communist regimes in the Eastern bloc had become even more firmly entrenched. The populations had become more acquiescent, their discontent having been appeased to some extent by an improvement in living conditions. More alarmingly, the pattern of post-Stalinist satellite–Soviet relations had been developing towards that of a 'Socialist Commonwealth' in which there was now much more mutual consultation and, perhaps, more scope for the pursuit of national interests by individual satellites.

'The West cannot at present achieve the liberation of the Satellites, and serious unrest will lead, not to the establishment of independent regimes, but to Soviet repression,' the committee asserted in April 1960. All the West could do was seek 'inconspicuously' to maintain the spirit of free thinking and to try and persuade the Soviets that their current policies were not beneficial. Hungary and Czechoslovakia seemed to be the most promising targets for this low-key approach. The shadow of Hungary in 1956 had reinforced British reluctance to attempt anything creative. Officials conceded in retrospect that 'we had a hand in provoking the Budapest uprising', albeit only a minor one, through 'the general effect of our broadcasts'. This had rendered them doubly cautious and they were keen to condemn 'a policy of stimulating revolts, only to stand by when they are crushed, as wickedly irresponsible'.[10]

If there was eventually to be any weakening of the Soviet hold over the satellites, they argued, 'it will come about through evolution rather than revolution'. The West should do more to encourage evolutionary trends, particularly by fostering a spirit of nationalism in the Eastern bloc states and 'playing up to their sense of national identity'. This meant developing closer relations with the regimes and intensifying efforts to keep in touch with the populations. It also implied a much more subtle approach in which détente would be used as a weapon, and in which the Cold War would be fought to an even greater degree at the informational, cultural and societal levels. The emphasis was slipping away from covert operations, which were too noisy, and away from the hectoring propaganda of the early 1950s, with its references to 'jackals and wolves'. The stealthiest of all activities, they had now decided, were in fact gentle overt operations typified by the British Council and the US Information Agency.

Accordingly, Ziegler's group now called for 'more attention to information work' and stressed that '[we] should increase our cultural activities substantially'. Both London and Washington had vast experience of information activities and of propaganda shaded from white through grey to black. But the practitioners of the gentler variants of these arts, who had hitherto been neglected, were now increasingly centre stage. Tensions remained, exacerbated by the arrival of new players, not least the Germans. Ziegler's Steering Committee knew that its doctrine appealed more strongly to Britain's European partners than to Washington. There were lengthy arguments about how far this doctrine needed to be agreed with the Americans before it was presented to NATO. All this underlined a more complex climate of Allied relations in the field of unconventional warfare in the 1960s.[11]

The futility of liberation was one of the few strategic assessment issues on which London and Washington agreed in the late 1950s. Co-operation on estimates and analysis of the Eastern bloc had always been awkward. While great volumes of finished estimates were exchanged, and attention was paid to improvements in each other's intelligence assessment machinery, nevertheless the whole process of exchange was characterised by justified suspicions. Fears were expressed that refined intelligence might be used to manipulate policy, or that requests for comments on estimates might be a device to draw policy-makers into discussions on subjects which they did not wish to address in an Allied context. Attempts to produce so-called Agreed British–American Intelligence estimates or, later, agreed NATO estimates failed or else resulted in compromise papers that were ignored by policy-makers.

Estimates with a bearing on atomic issues were an area of perennial disagreement because of their profound policy implications. As we have seen, British JIC teams despatched on liaison visits to Washington usually had to extend their stay, becoming enmeshed in interminable debates over the most likely date of a future Soviet attack. Such speculative subjects often revealed more about the mindset of the participants than about that of the Soviet Union. There were multiple points of disagreement. Throughout the 1950s, analysts working under the US Joint Chiefs of Staff tended to take a much more optimistic line than the British on the results of any air offensive against the Soviet Union, especially a counterforce strike against Soviet strategic weapons. Washington also held a more optimistic view of the extent of the damage that might be inflicted by any Soviet strategic air offensive against Britain, at least during discussions with the British. Both eventually accepted that this disparity of view stemmed more from their different geo-strategic perspectives than from differing information.[12] Missiles were the major issue and, commonly, the British found that they agreed with CIA estimates, but not with the estimates produced by those working close to operational planners under the US Joint Chiefs of Staff.[13]

The advent of Sputnik in 1957, which seemed to herald the arrival of Soviet ballistic missiles, provoked a stream of intelligence queries from 10 Downing Street. Macmillan specifically asked the JIC, 'What is the capacity of the Russians to make missiles to reach the United Kingdom?' The JIC was quite upbeat, insisting that successful Soviet tests had been limited to 650 nautical miles, which put Britain out of range. The Soviets could use bases in Eastern Europe but none had been detected. However, by 1961 the Soviets would have missiles with a range of up to 1,600 miles, bringing the UK comfortably within reach. Macmillan also asked awkward questions regarding 'Soviet intentions for the missiles', and predictably this produced a more elusive answer. The JIC conceded that in a worst case it could not rule out a Soviet search for a first-strike missile capability that would prevent serious American retaliation.[14]

This affected the British by removing the luxuries of warning time. In the early 1950s, the JIC had expected a reasonable warning of attack. It thought it unlikely that the Soviets would launch an atomic attack without a follow-up conventional attack and advance rapidly into Western Europe. This build-up would be unmistakable, and it concluded Britain was likely to get some warning. But after Sputnik the certainty about warning – perhaps as much as seven days – ebbed away to a day or two, and then to almost nothing.[15] Warning times were an awkward political issue. British units pledged to NATO suffered from a 'lack of readiness and low strength' and Whitehall worried about how they would meet a sudden attack. Seven days' notice would not be enough to remedy this. The problem was complicated by the fact that, at a time of crisis, Ministers might be reluctant to mobilise for fear of provoking the crisis further or creating 'alarm and despondency' in the domestic population.[16]

Sputnik also generated repeated Anglo-American efforts to negotiate agreed high-level estimates, but the result was a superficial compromise which was of little practical value to policy-makers. In late 1957 Britain was adamant that there was no 'missile gap' and that the United States was not being outpaced by the Soviets in this area, while Washington argued the reverse. At first glance, the procedures adopted as a result of this clash appear to constitute a model of alliance co-operation over intelligence estimates. Patrick Dean, Chairman of the British JIC, was invited to Washington to attend talks with the CIA on Sputnik:

> In Washington we held discussions with Mr Allen Dulles, Mr Amory, General Cabell and Mr Cumming (State Department). The basis for discussion was a memorandum prepared by the C.I.A. Sir Patrick Dean suggested certain amendments to their memorandum to bring it into line with British thinking, these amendments were accepted by the American representatives and the resultant document is attached ... Finally, the agreed views in the memorandum at Annex were reported by Mr Allen Dulles to a plenary meeting of the recent Anglo-American Conference in Washington, and were approved by both President Eisenhower and the Prime Minister.

However, appearances were deceptive. Robert Amory of the CIA informed Dean privately that, in reality, American intelligence agencies in Washington could not accept the essence of the British view that there would be at least a three-year gap between Sputnik and the arrival of a real threat from Soviet inter-continental ballistic missiles (ICBMs). Instead, the Americans believed that 'appreciable quantities' of ICBMs could be deployed 'in the next one to two years'. Accordingly, Amory warned Dean that the estimate which incorporated British views would cut little ice in Washington, despite formal approval at the very highest level.[17]

The British were no less guilty of rushing to jettison the intelligence agreements achieved by British and American analysts. Somewhat earlier, 'a compromise between the U.K. and U.S. views' on the progress of the Soviet ICBM programme had been incorporated into a major Cabinet Defence Committee paper. But this did not prevent Sir Frederick Brundrett, Chief of Defence Science and Chairman of the Defence Research Policy Committee, urging senior figures, including the Minister of Defence, to disregard it, precisely because it was a compromise with the Americans:

> although the Russians have carried out a very long series of trials ... we think that they will not be able to solve the problems involved in the very long range missiles for them to attack the Americans before 1965 and will be unlikely to be able to mount a very serious threat against North America until some years later, possibly even 1970.
>
> The Americans, however, take a much more pessimistic view ... The evidence on which the American views are based is known to us and is considered, in my opinion absolutely rightly, to be totally unacceptable.

Brundrett warned that all this derived from an excessive American 'fear of under-estimating the enemy' which in turn stemmed from the surprises delivered by the Soviet atomic bomb in 1949 and the MiG-15 in 1950. All this gave Brundrett a sense of reassurance. He believed 'very firmly indeed' that the Soviets would not attack Britain until they could mount a convincing attack on the United States at the same time. This meant substantial numbers of effective ICBMs which, he was sure, were 'at least 10 years away and may be longer'.[18]

Matters were complicated by the many levels of intelligence estimate circulating in the United States. Officials in both London and Washington understood the extent to which American policy-makers, particularly the US Joint Chiefs of Staff, took only limited notice of the agreed American high-level National Intelligence Estimates (NIEs), because of the compromises involved in their production, and instead preferred estimates prepared by their own departments. Therefore one of the main tasks of British intelligence liaison officers in Washington was to disperse plenty of copies of British JIC papers through the decentralised American policy-making machine, often to quite a low level, as well as trying to influence high-level or centrally agreed American NIE papers during the drafting process.[19]

Much the same situation was to be found in London. Mid-level planners continued to give close attention to intelligence estimates, but when senior policy-makers did not like a British JIC report they chose to disregard it, justifying their action with reference to their vast operational experience which, they claimed, gave them a superior ability to 'draw the strategic or tactical deductions from the facts'. Air Chief Marshal Sir John Slessor remarked that he simply refused to accept the pessimistic JIC estimates of Soviet military capabilities vis-à-vis Western Europe. 'I just do not believe these estimates that the Russians could be at the Rhine in a few days ... I don't believe the Intelligence people are the best qualified to do this sort of appreciation.' Intelligence people, he suggested, were in the business of offering the worst possible case.[20]

Senior figures in London and Washington did not hesitate to bend or disregard estimates where they proved inconvenient, whatever their source. General Matthew Ridgeway, returning to Washington from a period at SHAPE, noticed that US National Intelligence Estimates seemed to carry little weight. 'During Friday's JCS [US Joint Chiefs of Staff] meeting I was struck with the manner in which National Security Council approved Intelligence Estimates appear to have been brushed aside or at least the existing Soviet capabilities were ignored, and decisions taken in the meeting based on off-hand estimates of intentions.' This was, he added, 'but one of several recent instances of which I have personal knowledge.'[21] But Europe was no better, and those assigned to

SHAPE intelligence during the 1950s, with the task of producing agreed intelligence estimates in support of NATO, summed up the experience of Allied co-operation in tones of cynicism. '[We] felt that we had nations who wanted to plant intelligence to support their national aim as opposed to having intelligence speak to the issue as it really was.' London and Washington were therefore ever alert to attempts to influence policy through intelligence estimates.[22]

There were other reasons why estimates were distrusted. The British JIC regularly produced a number of 'standard' intelligence reviews on important strategic subjects which, although revised annually, tended to reiterate the same basic assumptions about the nature of Soviet thinking. Major-General Kenneth Strong, whose star was rising with the growth of the JIB (dealing with inter-service intelligence matters), and who was now taking over atomic energy intelligence, was alive to the dangers of this. In February 1958 he warned British defence chiefs that the scenarios the JIC envisaged were, in reality, unlikely to capture the real situation:

> J.I.C.'s efforts and expenditure produce much intelligence on the U.S.S.R., but there is scarcely any evidence as to how their leaders think or would act in given circumstances. For this reason, hypotheses are made which are repeated from year to year and, like advertisements, take root. This is inevitable, but we should not forget the lack of evidence and should keep open minds. Paragraph 3, for example, says that the Russian Leaders are reasonably certain that the West will not deliberately start war on them. Although I agree with this argument, it is equally possible that, imbued as they are with Marxist doctrine, they do not reject the possibility of some desperate American reaction during the next few years to the growing military and economic strength and widening political influence of the U.S.S.R. That the capitalist world might come to think that it is being overtaken by Communism and react desperately is a danger that they may feel they cannot discount. While, therefore, the West should maintain a firm and unambiguous position, we should remember how sensitive they are in this direction.[23]

Strong's absorption of atomic energy intelligence into his growing domain brought with it some demanding tasks. He found himself increasingly beset by ministerial requests to assess Khrushchev's cheery and literally bombastic remarks about Soviet weapons production. Every mischievous off-the-cuff remark about missile production had Western analysts scurrying back to their calculations. Khrushchev was mostly bluffing, but he kept up a first-class performance. At the Kremlin New Year's Eve party at the end of 1959 he declared triumphantly that 'the Soviet Union had 50 bombs ready for Britain, 30 for West Germany and perhaps as many for France. He would not say how many he had for the USA.' In February 1960 Strong asserted that Khrushchev was boasting because of a genuine fear of the West. This fear, he believed, had three separate strands. First, fear of an irrationally inspired attack from the West – 'he has harped for years on "capitalist madmen" and "crazy US generals and admirals"'. Second, fear of accidental nuclear war. Third, fear of a small war escalating into a larger one. Strong did not feel it necessary to add the observation that all these were fears that had long been shared by the British JIC.[24]

The much vaunted achievements of the U-2 photo-reconnaissance aircraft, which were available to both Britain and the United States, still failed to resolve Anglo-American differences over the 'missile gap' controversy. From 1955, a curious alignment emerged in the United States between weapons manufacturers, defence officials in the Pentagon, Air Force officers and the opposition Democrats in Congress. They projected an alarmist vision of Soviet strategic weapons programme as a stick with which to beat the Republican administration and also as a means to inflate America's own strategic programmes. No 'bomber gap' or 'missile gap' existed and throughout this period the United States enjoyed massive strategic superiority. Khrushchev, however, countered by bragging about the scale of the Soviet Union advanced strategic weapons programme. This represented the skilful deployment of the Soviet Union's strongest card, the secrecy it enjoyed as a closed society. It was impossible to disprove Khrushchev's assertions, and unintentionally Congress, the US Air Force and the Democrats were working to assist him in his programme of deception.

The U-2 was not a war-winning weapon in these intelligence struggles and too much has been claimed for its limited number of missions. The CIA history programme has tended to use the U-2 to advertise the wider virtues of intelligence as something which can liberate policy-makers from dangerous misperceptions. There can be no doubt that the U-2 reduced the vastly inflated estimates that officials in Washington had developed of Soviet bomber and missile forces. By 1957 estimates of the size of the Soviet bomber force had already fallen dramatically. The U-2 also began to make some headway against the 'missile gap', but here it was up against some serious obstacles. It could not offer blanket coverage, and so could not prove the non-existence of a well-hidden Soviet programme. The U-2 was simultaneously chasing many targets, not only missiles but also bombers, air defence sites, submarines and atomic energy production sites. Just when missile intelligence was becoming more important, the number of flights were being tailed off. Moreover, Eisenhower had decided that raw U-2 intelligence could not be used in the public forum where the 'missile gap' debates were being played out, not least the electoral hustings of 1959 and 1960. Senator Stuart Symington was Eisenhower's key opponent in the public missile debate.

Previously a Secretary of the Air Force, he chose to confront Eisenhower directly on the issue of the quality of strategic intelligence and Eisenhower treated him in an offhand manner which was probably a political mistake. Although Allen Dulles was regularly despatched to Capitol Hill to brief senators, most remained in the dark about sources. As a result, the U-2 strengthened Eisenhower's backbone in resisting demands for increased American arms spending, but it could not be used to silence all his opponents.[25]

By 1960 there had been enough U-2 flights to lower the estimated number of ICBMs that would be available to the Soviets by 1963. But US Air Force Intelligence had lowered their number to 700, the CIA to 400, the Army and Navy Intelligence to 200. As Raymond Garthoff, who worked on the NIEs, has recalled, the evidence from the U-2 was 'indicative and substantial, but not conclusive'. There was no pretence at agreement and, in fact, all these lowered estimates were still substantial overshoots. The real end of missile inflation only came with the launch of the first successful satellite in the Corona programme in August 1960. In a single day this provided photo-coverage of one million square miles of the Soviet Union, more than all the thirty U-2 overflights put together. Satellites, together with seismic detection, were the wonder-weapons of strategic intelligence and gave Eisenhower and Macmillan the confidence to move towards substantial arms limitation.[26]

Macmillan called the disaster of the U-2 shoot-down and the cancelled Paris Summit in May 1960 'the most tragic moment of my life'. This episode had not made Anglo-American co-operation in this area any easier. Nevertheless important low-key work was going on in the background. On 29 March that year, Macmillan and Eisenhower had met with a group of officials including Sir William Penney, head of research at the UK Atomic Energy Authority, and John McCone, Chairman of the US Atomic Energy Commission, to consider the problem of detecting underground atomic tests. Fully reassured that anyone who tried to carry out 'clandestine explosions' faced 'a real risk of getting caught', they decided that mutual monitoring was in everyone's interests. Accordingly, on 11 May, a group of British, American and Soviet scientists skilled in the detection of nuclear explosions through seismic techniques met to exchange information with a view to improving mutual verification. Constant efforts in this area would produce real results with the Mutual Test Ban Treaty signed in 1963.[27]

Agreement in Anglo-American discussions over missile estimates was duly reached in the early 1960s assisted by the arrival of the first satellite photographs. Other Anglo-American estimates were also coming together. By 1961, British and American intelligence on Soviet plutonium and uranium production was 'really identical', reflecting an improved exchange of data. In the past the CIA had come up with estimates 'considerably greater' than the British ones. Despite the growing closeness, the British and Americans were still guessing about each other's own real nuclear stockpiles, with the JIB nuclear specialists suggesting that American capacity in this area was two and a half to three times that of the Soviet Union.[28] By now Britain and the United States were working together on the Ballistic Missile Early Warning System at Fylingdales in Yorkshire, but the days of proper war warning were gone. When this system was completed at a total cost of over $1,328,000,000, it was expected to offer Britain only twelve minutes' warning, and the United States only thirty minutes' warning, of the arrival of Soviet missiles. Alerts were critical to the dispersal of Britain's V-bomber force, but there was never enough warning. The RAF required not twelve minutes, but twelve hours, to get 75 per cent of its V-bomber force dispersed and ready for action.[29]

Washington was aware of the value of its superior satellite collection capabilities and increasingly handled them gracefully, to some advantage. In 1964 John McCone, who had replaced Allen Dulles as director of the CIA, toured Europe to brief heads of state, taking with him news of the imminent first Chinese nuclear test. 'I went to Europe,' McCone recalled, 'and said they'd explode a bomb within thirty to sixty days, and the thirty-first day they exploded the bomb.' As he put it, 'they made a prophet out of me'. British intelligence had anticipated as early as June 1960 that China was close to a nuclear test. Archie Potts, who was in charge of atomic energy intelligence, pointed to four straws in the wind which were all blowing the same way: a special ministry running a large programme; substantial procurement of uranium ore; withdrawal of all anti-nuclear-weapon propaganda; and policy statements indicating an intention to have a nuclear weapon. Chou En-lai had recently told Montgomery something of Chinese efforts in this area.[30] Collection of raw intelligence data remained the most important level of Anglo-American co-operation. Following McCone's tip-off about the Chinese test, Whitehall sprang into action. London was convinced that 'our chances of getting the fullest available information from the Americans would be very much helped if we took a hand in the information-collecting effort'. So the JIC offered to cover air-sampling of the Chinese test in the area between Hong Kong and Singapore, deploying for the task a specially equipped Canberra from the UK and two locally based Canberras.[31]

The restoration of Anglo-American atomic intelligence co-operation during 1957 and 1958 was important in prompting some reshaping of the British intelligence machine at the centre. New British weapons and new delivery systems had encouraged the Americans to take London more seriously. But there was also personal goodwill in Washington. The key figure in restoring Anglo-American collaboration on atomic intelligence was Lewis L. Strauss, Chairman of the Atomic Energy Commission. As early as November 1957 Strauss was steering the subject through the US–UK Technical Committee of Experts, which he had deliberately given a remit that was 'quite broad' to circumvent some of the earlier tiresome restrictions. He used this forum to press for increased collaboration together with other members including Donald Quarles, Sir Edwin Plowden and Sir Richard Powell. High-level meetings with Sir William Penney and Sir Frederick Brundrett on intelligence were already scheduled by December 1957.[32]

A new American Atomic Energy Act that lifted all barriers to full Anglo-American co-operation was passed in 1958. This also owed something to a personal effort by Eisenhower. On the morning of 21 August, just before eleven o'clock, the President met with officials from the Atomic Energy Commission. His purpose was to explain what he called 'his philosophy regarding exchange of atomic information with the British'. The 'essence' of his view, he said, was that it should be full and generous:

> any attempt to do otherwise with true allies is bound to alienate them. The President cited the British assistance to us in World War II through making their intelligence available to us (when we had no intelligence of our own, not having maintained intelligence sections between the wars); he further cited their assistance to us in getting work started on atomic weapons, in providing us information about radar, and information about the design and development of jet engines.

Eisenhower's discourse indicated several things. It underlined the importance of individuals with a sense of history in maintaining the intelligence relationship, even though some were fast fading. It also revealed a remarkably accurate catalogue of the fundamentals of Anglo-American exchange in key areas, which suggested a degree of cost-accounting, as well as sentimentality. US Atomic Energy Commission officials noted that Congress was now ready to 'go all the way' and added that on the British side there was information on atomic matters of 'commercial significance' to which they wished to have access.[33]

At the same time, avuncular figures such as Eisenhower who knew London well were gradually disappearing from the Washington scene. A new generation of senior American commanders was appearing that had less experience of the British. In September 1958, the senior British naval officer in Washington, Admiral Robert Elkins, warned Mountbatten about the new American Chief of Naval Operations, Admiral Rickover, explaining that it was difficult to convey in writing 'exactly *how* difficult he is to deal with'. The new American naval chief was, he complained, 'like a spoilt American child who needs disciplining. When he doesn't get exactly what he wants, he either sulks or screams the roof off and indulges in all kinds of rudeness.' Admiral Rickover would also make his presence felt in the realm of Anglo-American atomic relations over the next few years.[34]

The gradual restoration of Anglo-American atomic intelligence links was accompanied by a shake-up of the British system in this area which favoured Strong's growing JIB empire. The current arrangements, set out after a review by Admiral Sir Charles Daniel in 1954, had always been regarded as interim. The small and specialist Technical Research Unit which looked at the Soviet production of fissile materials was now to be placed physically alongside Strong's JIB. A new Nuclear Division of the JIB would absorb its product and undertake the 'subsequent collation of all atomic intelligence'. Archie Potts headed up this new section and also chaired a new JIC sub-committee on Intelligence on Nuclear Weapons.[35]

A shake-up in the area of atomic energy intelligence was followed by a more troublesome attempt to reshape British intelligence on missiles. This raised the old and thorny problem of how to integrate intelligence from the three services on scientific and technical subjects which even Frederick Brundrett had backed away from in 1953 and 1954. This had been considered again and then postponed in 1958 and 1959. Only the toughest of figures could tackle this nasty problem, and finally in 1960 just such a figure was wheeled out in the form of Gerald Templer. Templer, a known advocate of centralisation, recommended that all aspects of guided missile intelligence, including the Soviet missile order of battle, should be transferred from the service intelligence departments to committees under the JIB. The arguments were heated and involved accusations that the RAF intelligence effort in this area was biased or 'slanted'. There were strong implications that the RAF had been playing down the role of the rocket in the hope of prolonging the life of manned combat aircraft.[36] The Air Ministry responded by raising what it called the 'Issue of Principle' – that of ministerial responsibility – and resistance on this basis continued into 1961. But it also had practical points to make. It could point to the uselessness of the comparable American committee-based National Intelligence Estimates for policy purposes. The head of British Air Intelligence, Air Vice Marshal Sydney Bufton, was also perceptive enough to realise that, even if this was not an issue of principle, it was an issue of precedent. Efforts to transfer missile intelligence to the JIB were a stalking horse for a fully centralised Defence Intelligence Staff that would be created under the expanded MoD in 1964.

Bufton rooted his defence in the responsibilities of the Chief of the Air Staff. He identified these as meeting the strategic air threat from bombers and missiles; maintaining the validity of the British nuclear deterrent; and undertaking preparations to penetrate the Russian defences and retaliate should Britain be attacked. All this rested on a detailed intelligence analysis of Soviet capabilities. This meant having an Air Intelligence Staff 'in which he has full confidence' and being able to appoint personnel of the right calibre and qualifications. The nub of it was that it would be quite unacceptable to any Chief of the Air Staff to base his policy and advice on a joint committee intelligence estimate on which his own staff might have registered a dissenting minority opinion. Bufton had a point, given that the US Joint Chiefs of Staff, the US Air Force and US Strategic Air Command all regularly ignored agreed American compromise NIEs. He continued, 'I am certain no C.A.S. would willingly launch his bomber forces against Russia unless the defences which they had to penetrate had been analysed and estimated with all the technical and professional skill available to the Royal Air Force. A "committee" estimate with which the Air Force did not agree would never be acceptable as a basis for either preparation or operations.' Templer, he complained, proposed a 'committee' system of threat assessment similar to the American system under which the CIA heard the views of all departments and then tried to persuade them to amalgamate into an NIE. Bufton was adamant that the 'divergences of views are such that this Committee estimate is of little or no use for policy decisions', and so recourse had to be made to the American method of Congressional committees and lobbying. He warned that, by introducing the principle of 'centralisation' in intelligence, Templer would create a most undesirable precedent. The ultimate principle that he was defending was that 'all assessments of the military threat to this country should be the responsibility of the Service Department concerned since it must provide the men and the weapons to meet the threat'.[37]

Although there is no direct evidence of a connection, it is hard to escape the conclusion that the ferocity of this dispute over missile intelligence was provoked, in part, by the intelligence controversy surrounding the cancellation of the British independent air-launched nuclear missile, Blue Streak, intended for service with the RAF in the 1960s. During the late 1950s, intelligence estimates of the vulnerability of this weapon to attack by Soviet missiles while on the ground had been in the hands of RAF intelligence officers, who alone had the expertise to make this assessment. But in 1959 the business of considering this issue slipped away to joint Whitehall committees, which felt compelled to look at it on the basis of a worst-case analysis. Partly on these grounds, Blue Streak was cancelled and the Royal Navy felt that this had enhanced its chances of taking over the main provision of the British nuclear deterrent, with hopes of securing the more survivable submarine-based Polaris missile system from the United States.[38]

Bufton was never going to get very far in an age of increasingly elaborate intelligence bureaucracies. Strong's JIB had already established the principle that all types of intelligence of interest to more than one service should be handled by JIB committees, including atomic and scientific intelligence. This process seemed unstoppable, although the JIC conceded that it had been 'a running sore over the last five years'. There was also no dodging the fact that Air Intelligence was the key interpreter of the intelligence on missiles, which came largely from GCHQ work on the signals emitted during test-firings: 'The bulk of intelligence on Soviet scientific research and development on missiles comes from G.C.H.Q. intercepts which is processed by A.I.(Tech) as well as the J.I.B. and must be as it is "hot" intelligence, and in the past from air reconnaissance (U-2).' The assessment of this intelligence was done by 'R.A.F. experts' who had been trained in missiles and who had 'a close and continuous collaboration with U.S.A.F. missile intelligence experts'. By contrast 'the J.I.B. contribution is not large'.[39] But, in spite of the fact that analysing missile intelligence was a mainstream RAF business, the tide was against it, with the civilianisation and centralisation of MoD now imminent. Mountbatten, Chief of the Defence Staff, was a committed advocate of centralisation and had the task of steering prickly service intelligence interests towards a central MoD structure. He declared the judgement of the Templer Committee to be 'sound', and the fate of missile intelligence was to become the product of inter-service committees.[40] British efforts to turn the JIB into a fully fledged Defence Intelligence Staff were spurred on by the knowledge that the Americans were doing something similar. In 1961 Washington began the work of creating a Defence Intelligence Agency to serve the Department of Defense.[41]

The creation of Britain's Defence Intelligence Staff represented the closure of one of the longest-running battles in British intelligence. Since the late 1940s Kenneth Strong had been fighting the battle for more joint intelligence centres, urging the Attlee government that a 'separation of staff brings separation of minds'. He had always wanted an effective inter-service intelligence system with functional specialism in areas of common interest, such as the Soviet economy or Chinese electronics. In 1964, a tough triumvirate formed by Strong, Mountbatten and a new Minister of Defence, Denis Healey, forced the plan through. Over the next decade, staff fell from 1,100 to 800 and costs fell by 25 per cent, but the quality of intelligence improved. Intelligence led the way to a newly centralised MoD.[42]

25

Cyprus: The Last Foothold

Cyprus ... an indispensable and irreplaceable centre for providing 'Y' service
intelligence ...

Air Vice Marshal Peter Philpott to VCAS, 27 April 1959[1]

The most remarkable aspect of the British Empire in the Middle East
by the 1950s was its absence of real colonies. Certainly there were
base agreements, many of dubious value, there were commercial treaties
and some local rulers accepted advisers and residents. But territory
which was 'coloured red' on the map was now almost non-existent. It
was partly for this reason that the British Chiefs of Staff had been
anxious to hang on to Palestine and to military base rights in Egypt. After
the ignominious departure from Palestine in 1948, and later from the
Canal Zone, the only significant bases on British-controlled soil in this
region were in Cyprus. After the ejection of bases from Iraq in 1958, little
was available by way of a British military foothold all the way from Libya
in the Western Mediterranean to Kenya in East Africa. By default,
Cyprus became an unsinkable aircraft carrier of growing importance to
both Britain and the United States. London considered that the
Americans would base atomic weapons here which they would hesitate
to place at more vulnerable sites and was soon locating its own atomic
weapons in Cyprus.

Strategic airpower enjoyed an obvious high-profile presence.
However, Cyprus also hosted a panoply of covert facilities and elaborate
listening stations. This island was excellent for listening to signals from
the main missile test sites in the southern Soviet Union, and there were
regular visits by Britain's strategic fleet of elint-equipped Comet aircraft,
together with large British and American ground sigint sites that monitored the Middle East. Britain's overt and covert broadcasting capability,
which Eden had been so keen to build up, continued to operate from
Cyprus after Suez. In the early 1950s, when the decision was taken to
move the regional SIS headquarters away from the Canal Zone, it was

also relocated on Cyprus at Nicosia. And in July 1954 London announced the move of the British Middle East Headquarters from Egypt to Episkopi on Cyprus. Having suffered endless evictions since 1945, this was an outpost that neither London nor Washington was prepared to lose.[2]

As early as April 1948, Cyprus had been identified as a site for a Very Heavy Bomber (VHB) base that would eventually project British airpower into the Middle East and beyond. The Chiefs of Staff concluded that there were 'great strategic advantages' in having a VHB base in Cyprus because it 'will permit us to penetrate further into Russia than is possible from any other likely base in the Middle East'. Cyprus was almost 1,000 miles closer to targets in the Soviet Union than comparable bases in Libya. Moreover, an island like Cyprus would be more easily defended in war than mainland bases, at least in the early stages of a war. Even before Britain had acquired its own atomic bomb, the bomber airbase at Famagusta had been earmarked by the RAF to received 'special cargoes' in time of war. However, in practice Britain did not have enough nuclear weapons to allow such deployment until the late 1950s.[3]

The sigint effort located on Cyprus was immense. The British had between 800 and 900 RAF personnel running a large sigint site at Ayios Nikolaos. This number increased in 1958 when the revolution in Iraq led to the loss of the GCHQ site there at RAF Habbaniya. There was also a substantial presence by 9 Signals Regiment, which, like the RAF unit, served as a collection organisation for GCHQ. Curious radar sites and additional monitoring facilities had begun to sprout elsewhere in the Troodos Mountains.[4] The Americans also had several sites. In January 1952, Major-General Ralph Canine, Director of the Armed Forces Security Agency, and soon to become director of the new NSA, described the American sigint facilities on Cyprus:

> The Central Intelligence Agency maintains, with the knowledge of the United States Communications Intelligence Board and the consent of the British, a radio intercept station near Nicosia on the Island of Cyprus. The station, USF-61 (covername: APPLESAUCE), is operationally controlled by the Director, Armed Forces Security Agency, who receives all of the traffic intercepted. The personnel employed at USF-61, for cover purposes, have been integrated into the Foreign Service of the Department of State.

It appears that a big American sigint operation was hidden at Yerolakkos and Karavas outside Nicosia under the cover of the Foreign Broadcast Information Service. Canine's major worry in 1952 was the rapid evacuation of these staff in the event of a general war. Their duties were 'of such a highly sensitive nature' that if they were captured there would be 'serious damage to the communications intelligence effort of the United

States'. But where should they be evacuated to? An agreement was reached to take them to a site which would also be occupied by 'a British intercept station'. But there were few other safe British- or American-controlled sites in the Eastern Mediterranean, and the likely path of evacuation was west to Malta, Gibraltar or Libya.[5]

Cyprus was also a centre for the Western intelligence effort against Soviet missiles, which, as we have seen, was an area of intense political controversy. A curious phenomenon in the ionosphere dictated that signals from the crucial Soviet testing sites in the southern Soviet Union bounced plentifully over the Aegean, where they could be intercepted. Together with American missile-watching installations at Samsun in Turkey, Cyprus became a key centre for listening into the Soviet missile centre at Kapustin Yar. Piecing together a picture of Soviet missile technology was a complex business. German scientists who were being released by the Soviet Union and were now returning to Germany offered reports on some parts of the programme. The RAF and US Air Force also had to operate elint flights to pick up missile telemetry during the first phases of missile take-off which could not be intercepted from the ground. The same missile bases were the target of the U-2 photo-reconnaissance flights by both British and American pilots in the late 1950s. Cyprus and Turkey together offered an important window on the hottest questions of the day, the 'bomber gap' and the 'missile gap'. Cyprus also intercepted an astonishing range of sigint traffic across the Mediterranean and the Middle East.[6]

After the outbreak of the Korean War in 1950, increased defence funding meant that American sigint sites in the region were expanding fast. Late the following year the United States had made a preliminary request to base US Air Force sigint units on Cyprus – the 14th Radio Squadron (Mobile) – tasked with 'conducting communication intercept activities' across the Middle East, and this had been agreed in principle by London. Another US Air Force sigint site on Crete had just been authorised, while others in Greece and Iran were being investigated. However, during April 1953 the London Signals Intelligence Board reconsidered permission for the new American sigint unit on Cyprus because space for such activities was 'at a premium' and it wished to establish an RAF sigint unit on the same site. It now hoped to persuade the Americans to divert their unit to Turkey.[7]

As already noted, Cyprus was also the home of British overt and covert broadcasting in the region. This information effort continued to grow even after the disastrous farce of the Voice of Britain during the Suez campaign. Indeed this failure helped inspire a major review of British broadcasting in the Middle East during February 1957, led by C. B. Stewart of the Information Policy Department. Stewart and his colleagues were determined to rebuild the operation with a new Arab staff, reproducing the familiar Sharq recipe for a mass audience, a light programme of popular music and drama. There would also be 'comment' on current events and a general subliminal 'projection of Britain in the Middle East' for commercial purposes. A new and powerful 100 kilowatt medium-wave transmitter had already been purchased and was being installed on the Sharq site at Polymedia owned by the Near East Arab Broadcasting Station (NEABS), but control would remain 'with the Government'. London was anxious to 'compete with Radio Cairo', observing, quite rightly, that radio was the principal way by which Arab populations learned about the rest of the world and 'virtually the only means open to the illiterate majority outside the principal towns'. This new transmitter would reach Lebanon, Syria, Jordan, Iran, northern Egypt and even parts of Saudi Arabia. It was intended to complement the efforts in the Gulf of the British-controlled Aden Radio, which was joined in the 1960s by a new British project, the Voice of the Gulf.[8]

Planners in London and Washington were wrong to think they had at last found a trouble-free outpost for strategic installations. From 1954 the island was swept by a violent revolt organised by Greek Cypriots who sought political union – or *enosis* – with the Greek mainland. The Cyprus Emergency, as it became known, was small and personal. It was generated by the determination of two men, Colonel George Grivas, an Army officer who had studied and fought against Greek communist guerrilla activity in the 1940s, and Archbishop Makarios III, the leader of the Greek Orthodox Church in Cyprus. Their preparations moved slowly, building from initial decisions taken as early as 1950. By 1953 the Greek government in Athens had swung behind them and was covertly assisting with arms. Grivas was in total control of the military effort by his EOKA guerrillas and there were very few immediate subordinates in what was quite a compact organisation. Although his operational teams were organised into secure cells, a ruse copied from the Greek communists, there was little command structure. This simply consisted of Grivas sending out handwritten notes by courier and, once this became known, he enjoyed the dubious status of being the number-one target for British intelligence on Cyprus.[9]

Arguably London had missed its chance in the early 1950s when it was offered a generous '*enosis* for bases' deal by Athens, but had turned it down. Some SIS officers who had been very close to the Greek government, including Monty Woodhouse, the veteran of the Iran operation in 1953, pressed for *enosis* as the happiest solution and also urged the CIA to recommend this solution to London. But Harold Macmillan was adamantly opposed and preferred a policy of stirring up the Turks against the Greeks and trying to maintain Cyprus as a long-term British colony.

Lack of trust prevented a compromise before the fighting started and made it even harder once it was in progress. Although EOKA was right wing and had no dealings with the communists, London feared that any transition might offer opportunities to the communists on Cyprus, whom it considered '100% Kremlin controlled'. Holding the bases there was not only about their intrinsic value but also about their denial to others.[10]

As in Malaya, there was little advanced warning of the coming troubles. The Cyprus Special Branch had been set up only in 1954 as the result of efforts by Alex MacDonald, the first MI5 officer seconded to the Colonial Office as security adviser. In 1954 it had little by way of a registry with files on personalities and was slow to penetrate EOKA, being engaged on vetting rather than the active gathering of political intelligence. Indeed, during the early stages of the campaign it was probably Grivas who enjoyed more infiltration and more inside information than the security forces. Grivas even claimed that in 1956, as the result of planting agents in the Special Branch, he was able to obtain tape-recordings of high-level security conferences. Certainly the Army did not always trust the police, perhaps advisedly, for prisoners escaped from detention camps with impressive ease. One of the key functions of the Special Branch was to try and identify those who had penetrated police ranks. Conversely, like the Malayan Communist Party (MCP), Grivas operated a ruthless policy against potential informers in EOKA. During the entire campaign EOKA killed 203 Greeks against only 156 members of the security forces, a measure of its obsessive internal security.[11]

The first intelligence break came not from the inexperienced Special Branch, but from SIS in Athens. In November 1954 an intelligence tip-off had allowed the Royal Navy to intercept an arms shipment bound for Cyprus, but the offending vessel had dumped its cargo at sea before being stopped. The following January, information about another shipment of supplies to EOKA allowed a more considered approach. HMS *Comet* intercepted the gun-running vessel, the *Ayios Georghios*, close to shore, with 10,000 sticks of dynamite. Divers soon recovered guns and ammunition from the water where they had been thrown overboard shortly before the arrest. The reception party were also picked up by the Special Branch and thirteen people were arrested, including a prominent EOKA activist, Socrates Loizides, who was sentenced to twelve years' imprisonment. Documents recovered from Loizides were the first substantial indication of an organised underground group plotting to overthrow the government of Cyprus by armed force. However, this success also gave British officials a sense that this conspiracy had been effectively strangled at birth. This would be the first of many false dawns in the long-running Cyprus troubles.[12]

EOKA responded by attempting to prove that this setback had not hampered its effectiveness. In 1955 the EOKA campaign began as it meant to go on, consisting mostly of waves of bombings. With so many strategic facilities withdrawn from the Middle East to Cyprus, the island was a target-rich area covered in expensive installations and teeming with sensitive personnel. On 16 March, sixteen bombs went off across the island. Targets included power plants, police stations and even a building close to 9 Signals Regiment at Ayios Nikolaos, the main British sigint site. London responded with a familiar solution, appointing Field Marshal Sir John Harding, who had fought in Malaya, as governor of Cyprus and extending to him Templer-like powers in both the military and civilian domains. Centralisation was intensified with joint committees bringing together civilians, the military and the police, including a Cyprus Intelligence Committee and a new information organisation. A price of £5,000 was put on Grivas' head, and disguised informers, who quickly earned the soubriquet the 'hooded toads', were used to try and identify the EOKA guerrillas among the suspects who were being rounded up.[13]

Cyprus was very different terrain to Malaya. Equipped with helicopters and sniffer dogs, the British made real headway against Grivas' mountain guerrillas, forcing him to concentrate his activity in the towns where his teams could hide among the population. Early in the campaign, he recognised that while the idea of mountain guerrillas was a useful symbolic activity it was always likely to be a romantic fiction rather than reality. Malaya loomed large in British thinking and, despite capturing significant quantities of EOKA documents, including parts of Grivas' diary, the island authorities persisted in thinking of EOKA as a communist-type organisation with complex politburo and commissars. It was not until the end of 1956 that the weight of evidence began to overcome these stereotypes. Gradually they realised that in fact Grivas was extremely right wing and enjoyed poor relations with the Cypriot Communist Party (AKEL).[14]

Mountain operations were dealt a decisive blow in December 1955 by Operation Foxhunter. This involved a search of all Greek Orthodox monasteries on Cyprus for arms. Although the operation was undermined by tip-offs from EOKA's men in the police it almost succeeded in capturing Grivas. At one point he hid behind a tree with British soldiers close enough to reach out and touch him. Documents and for the first time part of his diary were recovered. He had several further close shaves during the first six months of 1956. In June that year he was almost captured by Operation Lucky Alphonse. Although seven EOKA men in his group were captured in the operation, Grivas was alerted by a barking patrol dog and fled, leaving his favourite Sam Browne belt and a further section of his diary. This was recovered from a field near the village of Lyssi in a screw-top glass jar. This 'fragment' alone was more than 250,000 words (almost the size of this book). As Grivas fled through a host of security cordons, a forest fire spread through the Troodos foothills, started, allegedly, by the Army. But this fire changed direction, killing nineteen soldiers, and in the ensuing commotion Grivas made his escape.[15]

Guerrilla leaders should not be compulsive diarists. The maintenance of this diary, filled with extraordinary detail, was a supreme blunder on the part of the otherwise cautious Grivas. It probably stemmed from a desire to keep a detailed record of his dealings with Makarios, whom he distrusted. This intelligence coup was so great that many believed it a forgery and a graphologist had to be sent out from London to check its authenticity. The diary was flown to London and translated, and sections were then read out at a press conference. Ivone Kirkpatrick, the Permanent Under-Secretary at the Foreign Office, visited the American Ambassador with the material to give him the 'full works'. Together with arms and guerrilla finds around various monasteries, it provided damning evidence of links between EOKA and Archbishop Makarios, and as a result the British decided to publish extensive sections of the diary. It provided London with welcome additional evidence to justify its refusal to negotiate with Makarios and instead to banish him from Cyprus earlier that year. On 9 March 1956, Makarios had been due to fly to Athens for discussions with the Greek government. When he reached the airport at Nicosia he was politely shepherded on to an RAF transport aircraft and only then served with a deportation order. He was flown to Kenya and then taken by Royal Navy frigate to Mahé, the most remote island in the Seychelles.[16]

Moving into the towns had made EOKA more vulnerable to the activities of the Special Branch, and Grivas knew that this was now his main enemy. As early as August 1955 he ordered the assassination of one particular officer who was proving to be effective at running agent networks in Nicosia; the man was finally killed at the third attempt. Partly because of fears about the Special Branch, Grivas tried to limit the size of urban groups to four or six men to counter the risk of penetration. He also continued his extensive efforts to infiltrate the police. Nevertheless, by the summer of 1956, Harding believed that he was slowly winning. More infiltration of small parties and more ambushes were being used by the security forces. Finding the enemy was the key, as British intelligence estimated EOKA to consist of no more than sixty terrorists operating in seven gangs in the Troodos Mountains and another thirty in the Kyrenia area.[17]

Harding's gradual path to victory was reversed by the Suez Crisis. Cyprus was the main staging post for Operation Musketeer and this simply served to present EOKA with a fantastic number of targets of opportunity. It was quick to exploit its good fortune. Between 1 April 1955 and 30 November 1956 Cyprus suffered 638 major explosions and 517 minor explosions, together with a further 488 unexploded bombs. Over the same period EOKA accounted for the deaths of seventy-one British servicemen, nine British policemen and eleven British civilians. The violence was dramatic and included the blowing up of aircraft, the shooting of off-duty personnel while they were bathing, the murder of picnicking civilians and the mining of a drinking fountain used by British soldiers after their customary Sunday game of soccer. In April 1956, an employee of Government House even left a bomb at Harding's bedside. It failed to explode and the Field Marshal slept soundly alongside the device all night, discovering it only in the morning. London was anxious about the graphic stories and photographs appearing in the British newspapers. There were some extremely lurid accounts, such as one about British servicemen killed by bombs thrown from a car in a funeral cortège. Harding was bitter and felt that the Suez operation had given EOKA a boost. It had not only supplied an ample range of targets, it also heightened anti-British feeling in Cyprus and throughout the region. It was only after the Suez Crisis in November 1956 that a formal emergency was declared on the island.[18]

At the end of November 1956 Harding responded with another offensive and a renewed focus on intelligence-led operations designed to bring the conflict to an end. The influence of Malaya revealed itself again with the increased use of 'pseudo' operations using surrendered guerrillas and lookalikes. The Special Branch recruited selected Army officers to help it run groups of false guerrillas. Grivas claimed that they consisted of 150 Turkish Cypriots imported from the gangs of London's East End, but it is now clear that they were mostly turned EOKA or collaborating Greeks. These groups were given the designation Q-Patrols, taking their name from the disguised British armed merchant ships which had sunk U-boats during the First World War. Unlike in Palestine, they were used not so much as hit squads as for gathering intelligence. They would arrive in a village looking like guerrillas fleeing from pursuit and asking to be put in touch with those who might shelter them. Q-Patrols were effective and over a six-month period they were able to obtain intelligence that led to the death or capture of thirty-five further EOKA personnel and the uncovering of sixty hidden weapons. Among those arrested were twenty priests and six policemen who were deemed to be collaborating with EOKA. The Special Branch also had many casual 'peasant' informers who made their way through the villages by donkey picking up snippets of gossip.[19]

The increased flow of intelligence from Q-Patrols and from Special

Branch agents was now proving effective. In one swoop alone in Limassol in December 1956, forty-four members of EOKA were rounded up. On 19 January 1957, Makros Drakos, third in command of EOKA, was killed. On 3 March, the second in command of EOKA, Gregory Afxentiou, was also killed after a spectacular fire-fight that lasted over eight hours. That month, thirty EOKA bases were uncovered and twenty-two senior guerrillas killed or captured. The security forces were elated and, rather rashly, announced that EOKA had been defeated. Grivas was inclined to agree and offered a ceasefire in return for the release of Archbishop Makarios, who flew back from the Seychelles to engage in tortuous negotiations. The ceasefire lasted until October 1957, but attempts to negotiate with Grivas and Makarios were clumsy and unsuccessful.[20]

October 1957 also reflected a change of policy by London. Harold Macmillan, who had earlier urged a policy of divide and rule to maintain permanent British ownership of Cyprus, now reversed his position and sought a path to independence. Harding was relieved as governor and replaced by Sir Hugh Foot, who was a brother of the MP Michael Foot and enjoyed a reputation as a left-winger. There was now a clear divide in the British camp. Hardliners felt that they were finally getting a grip on the security situation as the numbers of EOKA guerrillas at large decreased. Those who preferred a new initiative to find a negotiated political solution pointed out that there were still a great many incidents. The struggle was also becoming much more complicated since Foot's new policies unleashed a spate of violence between the Greek and Turkish communities. Meanwhile Grivas had decided to turn against AKEL, the Cypriot Greek Communist Party, underlined by some particularly bloody murders of trade unionists.[21]

The guerrilla war was accompanied by an increasingly intricate propaganda war. Athens Radio continually broadcast propaganda on behalf of Grivas, and Britain attempted to jam these efforts. EOKA also ran an effective campaign accusing British security forces of brutality and of running 'concentration camps' in which torture was routinely used to extract information. Meanwhile IRD had been working hard to twist EOKA's cell-like structure into evidence of communist connections, with an eye to American audiences.[22] London's largest information problem was left-wing Labour MPs who were suspicious of government policy. Barbara Castle had been an outspoken advocate of early independence for Cyprus since 1957. In 1958 she travelled to the island with several other MPs, including Jennie Lee and Fenner Brockway, to investigate EOKA accusations of British torture and atrocity against the background of London's resistance to the idea of a public enquiry. She also met with Archbishop Makarios and was given one of the first serious indications of his emerging flexibility on a solution to the Cyprus question. She and her colleagues intended to return and present their finding to the press and at public meetings. Cyprus had been a nasty conflict with a degree of brutality and excesses on all sides, so the security forces were alarmed by this visit. Reportedly, towards its end, a sensitive operation was organised to secure details of what the delegation had uncovered in Cyprus, involving a 'black bag' operation against Mrs Castle and other MPs. Accommodation and luggage were rifled and documents photographed. This material was then telegraphed to London ahead of the delegation's return so that the authorities were forearmed against press releases and questions asked in the House of Commons.[23]

Curiously, radical reform of intelligence was not undertaken until 1958, arguably very late in the campaign. At this point, the newly arrived head of the Special Branch, John Prendergast, who had held a similar position in Kenya during Mau Mau, became overall director of intelligence. A wave of additional MI5 and SIS officers was also sent out. Special Branch remained the lead element, but the overall control of intelligence was becoming more militarised, a departure from the Malayan approach.[24] Structural changes disguised a continuity of objectives. Since 1956, when the central role of Grivas had become plain to the authorities, their main objective had been to kill or capture him. Prendergast now oversaw a more concerted effort to locate and eliminate Grivas which was given the codename Operation Sunshine. As in Malaya and Egypt, the British authorities had come to the conclusion that 'getting' their opponent, although crude, was the approach most likely to produce satisfaction, if not dramatic success. The Director of Operations, General Sir Kenneth Darling (brother to Douglas Darling of OPS), recalled that Prendergast had been sent to Cyprus with instructions to 'set his sights firmly on Grivas'. But there was 'no easy route to Grivas', as EOKA's chain of command was so exiguous. Prendergast and his agents moved around Cyprus on Grivas' trail and through 'well chosen agents we got closer and closer'.[25]

However, despite the increasingly successful recruitment of individuals close to Makarios, the possibility of negotiations in the autumn of 1958 prompted the Foreign Office to press for the suspension of any action to eliminate Grivas. Sir Hugh Foot also intervened to commute executions of guerrillas who had been sentenced by courts, for fear that this might upset the delicate political process. This reflected the opening of secret negotiations at the United Nations between the Greek and Turkish delegations, though these soon reached an impasse and dragged on for months. The focus of intelligence operations now broadened from mostly military activities towards intelligence support for ever more convoluted sets of negotiations.[26]

Hardliners in London were still pressing for security activities to be beefed up. On 27 November 1958, the Minister of Defence Duncan Sandys asked the Chief of Defence Staff whether the full panoply of secret service measures was being energetically deployed in Cyprus. 'Have we', he asked, deployed 'an efficient organisation for obtaining information from Cypriot prisoners by tape-recording overheard conversations, by means of stool-pigeons and by other methods which proved effective in the last war?' These measures were indeed already in place. A few days later Alan Lennox-Boyd, the Colonial Secretary, wrote to Sir Hugh Foot to press for the resumption of more risky techniques. Is this, he queried, 'the right moment at which to reinstate the special operations which were suspended some time ago?' There had, he said, been objections from the Foreign Office on political grounds because of the possibility of a negotiated solution. But Lennox-Boyd argued that things on the diplomatic front were going through a lull and the possible dividends justified the resumption of these activities. This almost certainly referred to the possibility of reviving efforts to eliminate Grivas.[27]

But Foot was not getting on with Prendergast and did not trust him; indeed he wanted him replaced. The Governor was surrounded by tough figures who had fought in Palestine, Malaya and Kenya and was not convinced of their methods. He told London that in the intelligence field the 'overriding need' was for a first-class figure to organise and co-ordinate. 'We have always been weakest on the intelligence side and our effort against EOKA cannot be fully effective until all intelligence work is pulled together and given better central direction.' He wanted someone of the 'highest calibre' to take charge of the intelligence organisation with the least possible delay – but that person was not, in his view, Prendergast. The specialists from Malaya and Kenya, he lamented, had 'not been able to give us much practical assistance in our unique circumstances here'.[28]

In February 1959 news came through that Operation Sunshine had finally located the exact whereabouts of Grivas. Grivas had been hard to find because his organisation was so small. His HQ had been moved at an early stage from a monastery to a series of secret rooms in a former British Army billet in Limassol which were occupied only by himself. Here Grivas, the formidable EOKA commander, slept in a cell constructed beneath the kitchen sink. His communications were handled by two dedicated female couriers who were the only persons who knew his whereabouts. But he had now moved from Limassol to Nicosia, drawn out by the negotiations, which increasingly required him to be above ground.[29]

The news that the intelligence services had found Grivas and were ready to pounce was rather awkward, for a full conference on Cyprus was now in progress at Lancaster House. Those involved in the negotiations urged Selwyn Lloyd that it would be disastrous if Grivas were captured or killed – and it was unlikely that he would be taken alive. But the security forces had been after Grivas for four years, and agencies on the ground wanted to send in a snatch squad and finish their work. Prendergast was ordered to contact London to discover 'whether Grivas's head was required on a charger or whether he should be allowed to stew in his own juice'. He flew to London to consult with Macmillan. Macmillan's approach required the full deployment of his favourite stage persona, the slightly bored Edwardian patrician. Over conversation at dinner in the early evening of 16 February 1959, he put a question to Angelos Averoff, the Greek Foreign Minister, which was seemingly prompted by idle speculation. What would be the consequences if the security forces happened to succeed in the taking of Grivas at this point? Averoff advised him that if this was to occur it would cause the negotiations to collapse and lead to the resumption of the 'bloodbath'. Late that evening Macmillan met with Prendergast and instructed him that Grivas would have to be left alone and should not be killed.[30]

The end of the Emergency was declared in 1959. This reflected concessions on the part of Makarios, who had realised that *enosis* would mean war with Turkey and therefore almost certain defeat. It also reflected American pressure in Athens, notably through the CIA station, to help bring the conflict to an end, which was in turn prompted by the growing recognition in Washington of the importance of the Cyprus bases to Western policy in the Middle East. Cyprus would become independent but would not secure *enosis*. There would be a guaranteed place for the Turkish Cypriot community in the constitution and the British would retain control over large sovereign base areas, while leasing others. In August 1960, on these terms, Cyprus became an independent republic. Grivas emerged from hiding with a promise of safe conduct away from the island and was received as a hero in the streets of Athens. This was a matter of profound irritation to those who had been working day and night for years to find him.[31]

For good or ill, Cyprus formed a crucial link in the learning curve of British counter-insurgency intelligence. Active efforts had been made to incorporate the experiences of Palestine, Malaya and Kenya. There was also concerted effort to draft in personnel with specialist knowledge. John Prendergast, who had headed up the Special Branch in Kenya and who had alarmed Sir Hugh Foot in Cyprus, now moved on to head the Special Branch first in Hong Kong and then in Aden. There were many other examples, including Ian Henderson, who had been prominent in intelligence in Kenya and who moved on to Rhodesia before becoming a security adviser in the Gulf. As the Cold War took a firmer grip on the

Third World, a body of counter-insurgency intelligence doctrine was emerging, accompanied by a travelling band of specialists who could implement it. Portable doctrine brought both advantages and problems. Initially, EOKA had been seen by some British intelligence officers in Cyprus as bearded mountain-dwelling variants of Chin Peng's MCP guerrillas, which they most certainly were not.

Both London and Washington were greatly relieved by the success that flowed from the Lancaster House talks. In November 1959, when the outcome was becoming clear, the National Security Council Planning Board reviewed American policy on Cyprus. In discussion it gave 'special consideration' to the United States' direct interests in the island 'because of the communications facilities located there', and the Secretary of Defense expanded further on the importance of 'the communications facilities on Cyprus'. In the short term no immediate troubles were anticipated, but the long-term future looked more complex. The local population were becoming more alert to the value of their real estate. 'Cypriot leaders already have indicated they will seek some form of *quid pro quo* for continued availability of these facilities.' The National Security Council agreed that continued unhampered use of these facilities was an affirmed objective, so attention turned to what the cost might be. With a political settlement emerging, London had informed Washington that it was happy for the United States to supply military equipment to the various Cypriot forces permitted under the settlement, which seemed to form an unspoken additional rental for the bases. The discussions in the NSC related to the supply of $2–2.5 million worth of arms to keep the Makarios element on side. This was set against about $2.5 million a year being spent on US facilities on Cyprus.[32] American interest in Cyprus was continuing to grow. In the same year, GCHQ noted that the United States wanted to expand the number of sigint personnel on Cyprus dramatically by enlarging a resident US Naval Security Group unit stationed in the Nicosia area. Washington wished to acquire a further 800–1,000 acres to construct its own aerial farm for the more satisfactory capture of distant signals. Naval intelligence was of mounting importance with the build-up of the US Sixth Fleet in the region, which had recently been involved in American operations in Lebanon.[33]

The shoot-down of the U-2 and the RB-47 in the spring of 1960 served only to alert Cypriot politicians and the local population still more to the utility of Cyprus as an intelligence watchtower. London became anxious when Makarios' new Foreign Minister, Spyros Kyprianou, began to ask embarrassing questions about spy-flights from Cyprus. The Commonwealth Relations Office had panicked and assured him that no spy-flights were carried out using aircraft based in Cyprus. Strictly speaking this was true, but special aircraft from RAF Signals Command made regular visits, and London doubted if the 'subtleties' of this distinction would be appreciated by Kyprianou. It was alarmed by the prospect of this subject emerging into the public arena and observed that ' "Spy flight" is an unfortunate term.' Following the U-2 and RB-47 incidents Harold Macmillan had stepped in and given clear instructions to try and limit any further public revelations: 'The line which has been taken, on the express instructions of the Prime Minister, ever since the American incidents has been that we do not discuss intelligence operations. This line has been very rigidly maintained ... once one begins to discuss even the fringes of such activities, one is compelled to discriminate between what are normal and what are special activities and the slippery slope gets steeper.' The enquiries by Cypriot politicians were a good example of how the new climate of revelation could 'inhibit future operation'. Massive press coverage of the shoot-downs had prompted awkward questions on Cyprus, so London wanted to ensure that 'no rumours started about what the Signals Command aircraft were doing' before it resumed aerial sigint operations from Cyprus, planned for November 1960. But despite Macmillan's attempted clamp-down, an era of exposure was dawning. Further dramatic revelations and fiascos were not far away, many of them in the Third World, leading to intense public interest in secret service in the early 1960s.[34]

26

Working Groups: Special Operations in the Third World

> Guerrilla warfare has … become a very fashionable subject in Washington, and its discovery is one of the more publicised achievements of the New Frontier. Everyone has views on it, and hardened jungle fighters like Professor Rostow and Professor Schlesinger talk with conviction about it.
> British Embassy in Washington to London, June 1962[1]

In March 1957, when Eisenhower and Macmillan met for the first time as heads of government at Bermuda, the odour of Suez still hung in the air. The events in Egypt the previous year had left a persisting legacy and both sides moved uneasily towards convergence on how to deal with it. The subject of what to do about Nasser as an individual came in for 'very special and searching investigation'. Macmillan's Foreign Secretary, Selwyn Lloyd, opened the batting and 'delivered a tirade against Nasser' that was worthy of Eden, asserting that he was 'not only an evil, unpredictable and untrustworthy man, but was ambitious to become a second Mussolini'. Just as Mussolini had become a stooge of Hitler, he warned, so Nasser would become 'a stooge of the Kremlin'. But Lloyd added that London now needed to obtain some satisfactory agreement from him for the continued use of the Canal and it viewed this as the 'most important' current issue. Eisenhower seized on the obvious inconsistency. He agreed that Nasser was not pleasant and asserted that the West should do 'everything in our power overtly and covertly to get rid of him'. But it was also obvious that, if this was going on, efforts to reach an early agreement on use of the Suez Canal would be 'completely futile'. Lloyd and Macmillan conceded the point that a Canal agreement would have to come first, 'while earnestly retaining the hope that Nasser would come to some bad end.'[2]

The Bermuda Conference of early 1957 had permitted the restoration of some important Anglo-American intelligence programmes, notably

U-2 flights from Britain and joint work on atomic attack warning. But it was also dogged by embarrassing incidents. All references to discussions on intelligence and 'planning', often a euphemism for covert action and psychological warfare, were carefully omitted from the final communiqué released to the press. However, this omission was somehow revealed in an American newspaper. Eisenhower wrote to Macmillan to explain that 'the part of the article that disturbs me so deeply' was a near-verbatim account of the discussions about keeping intelligence and planning out of the final communiqué, together with some offensive material about the French. These revelations threatened the 'interruption of the close communion and co-ordination that we consider so important' to continued joint business. Macmillan held his ground, insisting that his team was not responsible for the leak. He then took the opportunity to expand on his general view of the perils of the press in this sensitive area:

> I dislike publicity as much as you do. I hate newspapers and am very bad at handling them, and I remember you saying that you never read them. This modern technique of doing everything in public makes life almost intolerable. For my part, I would certainly be relieved if our meetings in future could be on a quite different basis – that they should be more personal, with a very limited number of advisers and with no publicity at all.

Macmillan added that Patrick Dean, Chairman of the JIC, had already arrived in Washington to flesh out the detail of the agreements reached at Bermuda on the U-2 and other matters and he hoped that, despite the press embarrassments, 'his programme can go ahead as planned'.[3]

Attention remained focused on the Middle East because of events in Syria, Iraq, Lebanon and Jordan. The CIA was disturbed by the wave of turbulent anti-Westernism that Suez had unleashed across the Arab world. Iraq was an obvious case in point. In late November 1956 Allen Dulles reported that the rather timid and elderly Iraqi leader, Prime Minister Nuri al-Said, 'long regarded in the Arab world as a British stooge', now found himself besieged by angry populist pro-Nasser sentiment and accused of colluding with the British, French and Israelis. He was in danger of being toppled. Forty Army officers had been arrested for plotting and senior officers thought that if they were ordered to protect Nuri al-Said their troops would not obey. The British position was now 'seriously eroded' and Dulles hoped that Iraqis who wished to work with the West would turn away from Britain to the United States. But there was also a danger that the US they would be confronted with a less discriminating anti-Westernism.[4]

In the early 1950s the CIA had been visibly the poor relation in Iraq to British intelligence, which effectively ran much of the Baghdad Pact, the alliance of countries in the region close to the Soviet border. Donald

Wilber, a CIA officer who had assisted in the Iran operation in 1953, recalled his experiences in Baghdad. The CIA station there was understaffed, and even the two CIA office secretaries had to arrange communications drops and safe-house meetings with agents. There were a few CIA officers working under 'deep cover', mostly Americans in educational or archaeological roles who maintained contact with agents. The CIA head of station was inclined to accept the view that Iraq would always remain a British client state. Unsurprisingly he obtained this view from liaison with a large number of British intelligence officers, some overt, some covert, working throughout Iraq. The CIA was keen to develop a GLADIO-type network in Iraq and to 'plant communications and demolitions to be used by stay-behind agents' in case the Russians made an advance into the area. But, almost invariably, potential Iraqi agents 'had been pre-empted by British intelligence'. Indeed, he lamented, 'the CIA reported little about Iraq that did not have a British source'.

However, after Suez, Allen Dulles decided to send out a new CIA chief to Iraq called Dick Kerin, who was less in awe of the British network. Kerin favoured the younger generation of Iraqis who were critical of Prime Minister Nuri al-Said's 'blind allegiance to British policies' and pointed out that it alienated other Arab states and would lead to uprisings by pro-Nasser elements, pan-Arabists and students. Many regarded Kerin's warnings as 'bordering on heresy', but they proved to be wholly accurate. In 1958 Nuri al-Said was toppled in a coup and as a consequence British informal influence, British bases and the Baghdad Pact were sent packing. In the eyes of Washington, events in Iraq seemed to underline everything it feared about London's unreconstructed attitude to Western influence in the Third World.[5]

Unlike Iraq, which had induced profound British self-satisfaction, Syria aroused in both Dick White and Allen Dulles a disturbing anxiety. Indeed in early 1956 the CIA had agreed on a joint operation with SIS in Syria, codenamed Operation Straggle, in the hope of distracting the British from their obsession with bringing down Nasser. The operation had been launched, but then aborted as a result of confusion caused by the Suez invasion. Washington continued to worry about growing leftist influence in Damascus during and after the Suez Crisis. 'Syria is in a critical condition where a Communist Coup might be pulled off,' Allen Dulles declared on 10 November 1956, and he considered the neighbouring pro-British state of Jordan 'equally vulnerable'. He anticipated a chain of events that would involve the overthrow of Syria's government followed by an invitation to Moscow to send troops to protect it from Israel. Syria, he said, represented 'a second power vacuum', which was even more attractive to Moscow than Egypt.[6]

Nevertheless, Allen Dulles believed that Syria offered greater opportunities for Western action than some of its neighbours. On 26 February 1957, he reported to the White House that death sentences had been announced for twelve prominent Syrian politicians and army officers allegedly involved in plotting a rightist *coup d'état*. As a result conservative and Army groups were stirred rather than cowed and began to show stronger resistance to the left-orientated government. The army started an anti-leftist purge, removing Lieutenant-Colonel Sarraj, a pro-leftist figure from a key post as head of Army Intelligence. The CIA was delighted that 'the tide may be shifting against the leftists', but was frustrated by the natural tendency of the Syrian politicians, especially the Cabinet, to seek a harmonious solution through compromise. 'One major problem in the current behind-the scenes struggle is the lack of sufficient provocation for a decisive showdown.' Meanwhile the Syrian public at large, shielded by press censorship, was 'unaware of the real facts of the struggle'.[7]

On 5 September 1957, Secretary of State John Foster Dulles, who had recovered from surgery and had returned to his desk, had reached agreement with his brother Allen that it was time to act in Syria and relaunch the joint CIA–SIS Operation Straggle. He sent a cable to Harold Macmillan explaining his position. He was the first to concede that the road ahead would be difficult: 'there is nothing that looks particularly attractive and the choice of policy will be hard'. But he felt that further delay was dangerous and urged Macmillan, 'We must work together in this matter,' adding, 'Any positive action, once begun, must, even at great risk, be pushed through to a success. Speed and simplicity are very important elements.'[8] On 25 September the Chiefs of Staff were briefed by Sir Dick White, the head of SIS, together with Sir Patrick Dean, the long-serving Chairman of the JIC, on the situation in Syria. They 'then considered the military implications of certain proposals dealing with the situation in Syria'. Operation Straggle went ahead but came to nothing. Several CIA and SIS efforts to encourage a coup had already failed and power was consolidating itself among left-wing elements in the Syrian Army.[9]

Nevertheless, Operation Straggle in Syria paved the way for a fuller restoration of Anglo-American intelligence co-operation in the autumn of 1957. On 5 November, Eisenhower wrote to Allen Dulles to brief him on Harold Macmillan's recent visit to Washington. This had been more successful than their Bermuda meeting in the spring and was not dogged by press revelations about sensitive issues. In their final talk, Eisenhower explained, they had come up with 'certain procedural measures' to achieve maximum possible co-ordination, especially on problems of a character 'that cannot be easily dealt with through normal channels'.

These were 'working groups' of senior British and American planning officers who tracked developments together and ensured that London and Washington made joined-up policy on operational issues. A Syrian Working Group was established. Eisenhower believed this was the way forward and told Allen Dulles of his 'personal interest' in seeing that the Working Groups programme was given maximum attention and also kept secret.[10]

Working Groups were a major breakthrough for Anglo-American co-operation on the Third World and indeed other issues. For the first time since the Second World War there were permanent Anglo-American planning mechanisms functioning permanently and at a high level. They were essential to British and American joint intervention in Jordan and the Lebanon in early 1958. By June that year, when Macmillan was briefed on propaganda and counter-subversion ready for another visit to Washington, it was clear that they had been successful across a wide field of unconventional and special activities. The crucial point was to ensure that high-level people were assigned to them. Macmillan was advised that Working Groups could not eradicate all difficulties, and some of the traditional problems of dealing with Washington's hydra-headed secret bureaucracy remained. Covert propaganda was still an especially awkward area. The State Department's overt effort through the US Information Agency and the 'CIA grey and black operations are in practice conducted almost independently'. Macmillan was warned that 'Neither side trusts the other.' Officials claimed that it was this dysfunction in Washington, which London could not cure, that had 'led to failure to mount an Anglo-U.S. joint propaganda effort during the Lebanon crisis'.[11]

In the eyes of Washington, British prestige was nowhere higher than in South-east Asia. This had much to do with success in the Malayan Emergency, since by 1958 a self-declared communist revolution seemed to have been stopped in its tracks. Even more impressive was the fact that a felicitous political settlement had been found. At independence the new Malayan leader, Tunku Abdul Rahman, proved to be that rare person which every Western policy-maker sought, a leader who was at one and the same time plausibly nationalist yet moderate and pro-Western. Britain had been accused of favouring the Tunku because he was a classic British puppet – good at golf and easy to manage – but in his meetings with Chin Peng he had proved himself to be a tough and independent-minded customer.

Although Americans flocked in increasing numbers to view British achievements in Malaya, the main area of covert collaboration in the region was now Indonesia. Indonesia was plunged into violent conflict when a rebel government was declared in Padang, the capital of West

Sumatra, on 15 February 1958. The Indonesian President, Sukharno, launched an offensive operation against the rebels, who were located mostly in Sumatra and the Celebes. The campaign closed with government victory on 26 June, when Menado, the last city to be held by the rebels, fell to government forces. Some rebel leaders settled with the government, others fled into the interior. This marked the end of a major rebellion and also the end of what had in fact been an insurrection against Sukharno supported by the CIA, SIS and the new Australian Secret Intelligence Service, ASIS.

Allen Dulles had been keen to put pressure on Indonesia for over a year and, together with his brother, John Foster Dulles, detested the neutralist line taken by Sukharno. They also suspected him of drifting closer to the Indonesian Communist Party, the PKI, although they accepted that it was a long way from being in a position where it could seize power, as it was held in check by the Army.[12] Allen Dulles hoped to apply pressure to Sukharno by supporting separatists in Sumatra and Celebes who wished to break away from the main island of Java. At the very least these islands might be saved from domination by the PKI. Late 1957 seemed to offer the West an opportunity. Economic troubles had been making Sukharno's position more difficult and, in the midst of an already deteriorating situation, assassins struck. The militant wing of the Indonesian Islamic Youth Movement mounted a bomb attack and, although Sukharno escaped unharmed, members of his Cabinet and several bystanders were killed or injured. Sukharno was disturbed and depressed. On 20 December he transferred his powers to a deputy and left on a tour of India, Egypt, Yugoslavia, Burma, Thailand and Japan, only returning on 16 February the following year, the day after rebellion broke out.[13]

The British authorities had been very resistant to American ideas of a rebellion. The catalyst for change was the intervention of Sir Robert Scott, Britain's Commissioner General in South-east Asia. In December 1957 he had become concerned about the possibility of Indonesia falling to the PKI and sought to save at least some of the Indonesian archipelago from communist rule. He wrote directly to Macmillan urging 'support from outside' for important anti-communist elements in areas such as Sumatra and Celebes:

> I think that the time has come to plan secretly with the Australians and the Americans how best to give these elements the aid they need. This is a bold policy, carrying considerable risks. It assumes that for the time being we cannot cope with the central problem of Java but are resolved to help the anti-Communist elements elsewhere. I believe this assumption justified: in Java, Soekarno has irredeemably identified himself with the Communists, who are powerful and well organised, whereas the opposition are weak and disunited.

PUSD in the Foreign Office was not keen on the operation. However, Macmillan, Selwyn Lloyd and John Foster Dulles discussed the issue while attending a NATO meeting in Paris on 14 December and decided that action should be taken. Macmillan and Lloyd promised all possible support, as long as local political conditions in Singapore allowed. By 23 December a Working Group on Indonesia had been set up. This met five times during January 1958; and Frank Wisner was a regular attender.[14]

On the last day of January Allen Dulles seized his chance. He urged the White House that, with Sukharno away for a long period, the time was now ripe for action. CIA officers already with the Padang Group, which was the most substantial rebel faction, reported that an ultimatum would probably be given to central government around 5 February. Although still reluctant to break entirely with Java, the Padang Group seemed determined to secure more autonomy and to reduce communist representation at the centre. However, Allen Dulles judged that, even if it did not secure its objectives, the chances of a break with Java were better than even. A major factor in its calculation was expectations of 'Western' and 'particularly US support'. Dulles believed that the rebels could hold out against the government unless Sukharno received a 'massive' shipment of Eastern bloc weapons. He also predicted that the central government would seek to negotiate rather than crush the rebels. All of these predictions proved to be quite wrong.[15]

Macmillan gave his approval on condition that assistance to the rebels remained at the level of what he called 'disavowable help'. British airbases were crucial for the refuelling of missions flown by the CIA's Civil Air Transport aircraft, and he confirmed the availability of Singapore airbases and RAF aircraft so long as Robert Scott and the Governor of Singapore were in agreement. Singapore and Malaya were vital staging posts for supplies sent to the rebels. They were also important in acquiring intelligence on the developing battle and the United States stationed reconnaissance aircraft at Changi aerodrome in Singapore during the rebellion. Facilities in Australia and the Philippines were also used.[16]

However, as early as 24 March it was clear that the rebels were not doing well against central government forces. Macmillan lamented in his diary, 'The "rebels" are losing out in Indonesia, in spite of as much "covert" help that we and the US can give them quietly. This means, unless they can hold on and some compromise emerges, a Communist regime in Indonesia, with all that means for South East Asia.' As further fighting developed in April, London stopped short of offering open assistance. On 15 April the British Chiefs of Staff met with Sir Stanley Tomlinson, one of the senior Foreign Office officials superintending British policy in South-east Asia, to consider their developing line on support for some *coup de main* in Indonesia. This would almost certainly mean moving from covert to overt force and visibly assisting the rebels to overturn Sukharno. Templer, who was Chief of the Imperial General Staff, was keen on the idea. It had, he stressed, 'been clear for some five to six years past that we would one day be faced with the serious threat of a pro-Communist regime in Indonesia. The situation had come to a head and a most serious threat to Singapore and to our whole position in the Far East was developing.' The British were already committed to a policy of 'maximum disavowable aid' to the rebels, but this now seemed to stand 'only a slender chance of success'. They faced the choice of standing by and watching their proxies defeated or else assisting them more openly. Mountbatten, who was Chief of the Naval Staff, felt that they could boost covert support further without coming into the open by using submarines and the Special Boat Service to increase supplies, although air-drops were the preferable route. However, open intervention risked a long-drawn-out limited war and Soviet intervention. Tomlinson reminded his colleagues that while Harold Macmillan had approved the current policy he was certainly 'opposed to any overt intervention in Indonesia'.[17]

John Foster Dulles discussed the rebellion privately with Selwyn Lloyd on the evening of 6 May. Lloyd said he thought the most recent news from Indonesia was encouraging. Despite some reverses they should not give up hope of keeping up the pressure through the rebellious forces in the Celebes. He considered it possible that insurgent activity in Sumatra would revive if there were success in the Celebes. He conceded that British opinion was split. His own Ambassador in Djakarta strongly favoured a political solution and abandoning any assistance to the rebels, while Rob Scott, the British Commissioner General in the region, whose judgement Lloyd valued more highly, wanted to keep going.[18]

The end of Western support to the rebels came unexpectedly. On 18 May, one of the American black-painted B-28 bombers used by the CIA to provide air support to the rebels was shot down after a raid against the Indonesian Navy had gone wrong and a church had been bombed killing most of the congregation. A CIA contract pilot by the name of Allen Pope was captured by pro-government forces. Washington insisted that he was merely a soldier of fortune, but documentation that Pope was carrying suggested otherwise. John Foster Dulles now decided to terminate the operation, and the CIA field teams were cabled with instructions to abandon their positions and their local allies. They were then quietly evacuated by submarine.[19] In June Macmillan was briefed on the Indonesian operation and told that it had 'failed militarily'. Washington, the British noted, was working through political channels to effect changes in the regime, but the Foreign Office was not optimistic of success. The CIA and SIS, Macmillan was informed, were 'keeping our clandestine planning and assets in being' in case they were needed again. London suspected that sooner rather than later the Americans would want to try another rebellion 'before all their dissident assets are lost'. But the reality was that Washington had now accepted defeat.[20]

Covert airpower was a growing aspect of CIA activity in Asia, and Washington was keen to learn the lessons of Indonesia. A retrospective study of its use in the Indonesian uprising was organised, using the CIA field cables from the operation. It concluded that airpower had initially played 'a brilliant role in the Indonesian action' but had been hamstrung by political constraints. Limited in how many aircraft it could field the CIA could not cope with the concerted airpower used by Sukharno, who employed airborne commandos and close air support by P-51 Mustangs to break the morale of rebel units, which could not command this kind of firepower. The CIA had countered by gradually stepping up the size of the rebel air force until 15 May, when the Indonesian Air Force caught it napping and 'destroyed practically the whole rebel Air Force on the ground at Menado'. This, rather than the capture of Pope three days later, was the real turning point and the rebels never recovered. 'Although fighting continued after this, there was never again much question as to the outcome.'[21]

CIA covert airpower was always a critical factor. During March and early April 1958, heavy bombing by the CIA's black-painted B-26s had helped to stem government advances and 'virtually paralysed central government offensive operations for about a month'. The Shell oil refinery at Balikpapan was evacuated after rebel air attacks on 28 April. Cover for this level of air activity was wearing very thin, and the Indonesian government spokesman asserted that the rebels did not have sufficient resources to mount these air attacks and blamed the 'SEATO powers'. Individual press commentators were close to the mark when they identified soldiers of fortune from Taiwan, the Philippines and the United States as flying for the rebels. Once the rebel air force was destroyed, the government was able to make unopposed landings at Gonrontalo and Morotai, and the tide was soon turning. Air support for the rebels was not entirely ended by the CIA for there were further spo-radic attacks by rebel B-26s in June and July, but these were token efforts designed to cover an ignominious withdrawal.[22] Withdrawal of airpower was accompanied by reverses on the political front. The rebel leadership had fragmented and, to their surprise, the military commander of the South Sumatra district refused to join them. Former Vice President Hatta was expected to join them too and also refused. The rebels expected the oil companies to divert support quickly in return for oil concessions but this did not occur, and consequently there was little financial pressure on Djakarta. The going looked rougher than had been expected, and the Western powers decided to pull out before suffering further embarrassment.[23]

The capture of Allen Pope ensured that there would indeed be further embarrassment. Pope had flown aircraft for the CIA's Civil Air Transport on Taiwan and also held a reserve US Air Force commission. He was one of the Agency's most experienced pilots and had flown fifty-seven missions to Dien Bien Phu alone between March and May 1954. In Indonesia he was dubbed 'Hariman Hithm' (or 'Black Tiger') because his B-26 bomber was painted solid black, and he was regularly subjected to mock executions while in captivity. On 28 December 1959 he was finally brought to trial on a string of charges including assisting the enemy in time of war, conducting aerial reconnaissance for the rebels, manslaughter and illegal possession of firearms. His plea that the first charge, referring to 'time of war', entitled him to POW status and protection under the Geneva Convention was rejected and on 16 March 1960 he was sentenced to death.[24]

The CIA went into a frenzy of activity at the prospect of Pope's execution and various improbable schemes were developed to attempt a rescue. One of these involved the use of the Skyhook apparatus. This was a canvas harness from which was suspended a helium-filled balloon on a nylon rope. This could be snatched by an aircraft using a hook and an elasticated rope. The person wearing the harness could be caught and winched on board, using the elasticated rope to lessen the shock. But the plans for smuggling such an apparatus into Pope's remote prison compound were far fetched, to say the least. Pope made a series of lengthy appeals to Sukharno for clemency and by the time these were considered Eisenhower had been succeeded by John F. Kennedy. This allowed an improvement of relations, and a meeting between Kennedy and Sukharno was scheduled. Washington had begun to supply the Indonesian military with hardware, including new C-130 Hercules transport aircraft and jeeps, which were explicitly tied to Pope's eventual release. Allen Dulles personally urged Kennedy's advisers to do anything possible to 'mitigate his sentence'. Kennedy was active on Pope's behalf and pressed Sukharno about him during his visit to the US and wrote again to the Indonesian leader shortly after his departure. Pope's family streamed backwards and forwards adding their tearful entreaties. He was eventually returned in August 1962. Before his departure Sukharno admonished him personally with the words 'Hide yourself, get lost, and we'll forget the whole thing.'[25]

By 1963 the Americans were attempting to distance themselves from the developing 'Confrontation' between Indonesia on the one hand and the Malaysian Federation on the other. (The Federation, formed that year, included Malaya, Singapore and Borneo, and was supported by Britain.) On 4 November, Howard Jones, the departing American Ambassador, made his final call on Djuanda, the Indonesian Foreign Minister. Djuanda asserted that 'Brit. intelligence (he hoped not supported by CIA) was behind recent series of incidents involving time bombs ... aimed at strategic military installations in Indonesia'. Jones expressed surprise, as he had not heard of the bombings. He suggested that provocation by Moscow was much more likely and suggested 'communist forgeries' and other tactics designed to implicate the Americans and the British. But Djuanda was not convinced and explained that the memory of CIA and SIS efforts in 1958 cast a long shadow in Indonesia and would continue to do so.[26]

Success in the Malayan Emergency allowed the British entry into Vietnam. Parallels between Malaya and Vietnam were nevertheless misleading, for although the Malaya campaign had been difficult, the British had enjoyed some obvious natural advantages. Malaya had been a near-island, a feature which cut off the MCP from outside supplies. It also had a divided population over which London enjoyed absolute control. None of these advantages awaited the Americans in the altogether larger conflict of Vietnam. Instead, Eisenhower and then Kennedy were seeking to work through the corrupt and unstable regime of President Ngo Dinh Diem in a country whose border was hard to find, never mind defend.

Templer – the so-called Tiger of Malaya – had received a very favourable press and this allowed British 'experts' to make quite an impression on the increasingly fashionable area of counter-insurgency. Britain's emphasis upon insurgency as a problem requiring an integrated political, economic and social as well as military programme to bring about its successful resolution always impressed CIA officers visiting Templer's headquarters at Phoenix Park in Malaya in the 1950s. Yet it is often forgotten that prior to 1950, while Britain had been struggling to hold on, the Americans had been pursuing a successful campaign against the Huk rebellion in the Philippines. Here Ed Lansdale, the charismatic local OPC/CIA chief, had developed a policy which also emphasised the role of propaganda and economic development and stressed political rather than military solutions. Lansdale's Economic Development Corps had notably strong parallels with schemes launched in Malaya.[27]

However, it was the legendary figure of Templer who commanded the limelight and who made a visit to Saigon in October 1960 at the invitation of President Diem. He held a three-hour discussion with Diem and also met members of the US Military Aid Advisory Group. Henry Hohler, the British Ambassador, accompanied him and was awe-struck by the effect he had. President Diem, he explained, was a great talker and the difficulty of getting any idea across to him was to choose the right moment to 'interrupt the discursive monologues to which he is prone'. Templer gave him no chance to get going and seized the initiative right at the start. He described the circumstances in which he had been nominated high commissioner in Malaya after the assassination of his predecessor. Sir Winston Churchill, he said, had sent for him and looked him over for three days before deciding to appoint him. He claimed that at the end of his first fourteen days in Malaya he had alighted on three key principles, one of which was focused on intelligence. These were:

(a) By every means – social organisation, improvements, information services – seek to gain the hearts and minds of the working population.
(b) At each centre, on each level establish an intelligence set-up consisting of a military officer, a policeman and a civilian administrator under the orders of the last named. If any of them fails to co-operate, throw him out.
(c) Pay particular attention to the junior officers in the Army, Police and Home Guard. It is Captains and Lieutenants – not Generals – who are in contact with the population.

At this stage Diem took up a pad and wrote down Templer's three principles and he continued during the interview to make notes of what he said. Templer expanded on the need for a unified system of intelligence, both in the provinces and at the centre. When he arrived in Malaya, there had been two Army, one civilian and several political intelligence organisations. Such organisations should all be unified under one man who could be trusted. Diem asked who that had been in Malaya and Templer replied that it had been an MI5 man from London. It was still an Englishman, but in six months' time it would be a Malay. Templer paid particular attention to internal dissidents and asked Diem 'which sector of the population gave him the most trouble'. But Diem was reluctant to admit that sizeable sectors in Vietnam were opposed to him and could not be persuaded to offer a straight answer. Hohler was astonished by Diem's silent attentiveness. Templer's opening statement took about forty minutes, and the American Ambassador commented that Diem had never been known to take notes. Hohler added, 'The fact that it was possible to speak to M. Diem for forty minutes without being interrupted has indeed created a minor sensation among my colleagues here.'[28]

Within days of Templer's departure, Diem was nearly toppled by a serious coup attempt. PUSD in London thought there would soon be 'a new and successful coup d'état' and had learned from Australian intelligence sources that another being planned. If there was not a coup soon, it suspected that morale in the South Vietnamese Army would deteriorate to the point where it would either collapse or major outside intervention would be required. There seemed little hope that recent advice offered by Templer and others on improving counter-insurgency would be accepted by Diem. However, the really big problem, it asserted, was not Diem but his repugnant brother Nhu: 'While the President's brother Nhu remains the effective power behind the scenes, the Can Lao [Diem's semi-secret political party] continues its repressive actions and corrupt practices and Nhu's intelligence services continue to terrorise all those who express any criticisms of the regime, it is hard to see how President Diem's image can be improved in the public mind.'[29] It was in this area, schooling Nhu and his colleagues in more sophisticated approaches to security intelligence and police work, that sustained efforts were required.

In 1961 the Tunku in Malaya seems to have suggested that a British advisory mission to Vietnam would allow more sustained and detailed advice from figures like Templer, especially in the improvement of the police, security and intelligence services. Vietnamese police were already passing though intelligence training courses in Malaya, although the Malayan authorities were not keen to advertise the fact. Britain responded with the British Advisory Mission (BRIAM), in the summer of 1961, headed by Sir Robert Thompson, who had served in the Chindits and then, as we have seen, in Ferret Force in 1948 before becoming the last Secretary of Defence of the Federation of Malaya. In designing BRIAM over the summer of 1961 there had been worries about local rivalry and competition. Diem already had no fewer than thirteen advisory missions scrambling for influence. Thompson had observed that it would be essential for him to 'get inside the American machine' and he was fully prepared ' to become an American for this purpose if necessary', though in the event his mission retained purely British identity. He also warned the Foreign Office at an early stage that 'the sort of advice he gave to the Vietnamese might not always be palatable to her Majesty's Government' but wanted it understood that if he led the Mission he would have to be given 'a free hand'. Britain's Ambassador to Saigon thought that 'this was a risk which would have to be accepted'.[30]

Thompson had already visited Vietnam and submitted a preliminary report to Diem in 1960. Accompanying him were Desmond Palmer of the Malayan police, who was considered 'a first-rate intelligence officer', and Dennis Duncanson, a Colonial Office official. He also secured the services of Claude Fenner, who was just retiring from the Malayan Special Branch. Periodically he had 'one or two specialists attached', including Dick Noone, who had organised the Aboriginal Hill Tribes in Malaya and later went on to do similar work during the confrontation with Indonesia after 1963. BRIAM set up its headquarters in a large French villa at 196 Cong Ly in Saigon in the autumn of 1961.[31]

Offering British security advice to a regime as unstable and as unpleasant as that run by Diem in Vietnam was always going to be tricky. The nature of the regime, and especially the excesses of Diem's brother and security chief Nhu, were already well known to both the CIA and SIS. In late 1961, shortly after Thompson's Mission appeared in Vietnam, a new chief of the CIA station in Saigon also arrived called John Richardson. Not liking the residence occupied by his predecessor, Richardson and his family set about house-hunting. The Chief of the Vietnamese National Police insisted on helping with the search and the police eventually procured a spacious house not far from the centre of Saigon and ideal for official entertaining. However, the house suffered from 'one serious drawback':

> The house had been used as an interrogation center for Vietcong suspects and it was common knowledge among the Vietnamese that a number of them had gone to their reward under interrogation in the house. Although it had been completely renovated inside and out, no servant would work or live there because of the spirits which inhabited it. Before the Richardsons could move in, a groups of Buddhist monks had to be called in to exorcize the demons who were present, following which a household staff could be employed.

Henry Cabot Lodge, the American Ambassador in Saigon, later fired Richardson and promptly had the residence further redecorated before moving in himself.[32]

The South Vietnamese security services that Thompson was attempting to improve were operating at full stretch. The Diem regime was in trouble, emphasised by the fact that some 5,000 political opponents were being arrested each month. In early 1962 Thompson and his team were asked to undertake an extensive tour of several provinces to examine security forces in the field and thereafter 'to submit recommendations for the re-organisation of the Police Force and the Intelligence Services of Vietnam'. At the end of February, Thompson submitted his report. His line of command, significantly, was direct to Diem rather than through any government department or supporting American agencies.

Predictably, Thompson urged Diem to carry out sweeping Malaya-style reforms. The tangled network of competing security organisations should be cleared away. Instead one single department of the government should be charged with the responsibility of identifying all internal threats, both current and future, to the security of the state. This single organism, to be called the Security Intelligence Bureau, would be a civil entity and would orchestrate the counter-measures and advise on how to oppose these threats. The new Security Intelligence Bureau, or SIB, should be a specialist section of the national police. This reflected the British doctrine of police primacy and was similar to the approach 'which has been so successful in Malaya'. A key advantage here, Thompson argued, was cover. If the SIB was to be effective it was 'essential' that 'the specialist staff do not have their identities as such revealed to the public'. Listing them as ordinary police offers provided the 'most effective method of concealment over a long period'. However, in Vietnam it was also crucial to improve the status of the police vis-à-vis the armed forces and other government bodies.

Thompson was also anxious to secure some change in the core executive that handled the interaction between all intelligence services and the President. Vietnam, he urged, should adopt something like the British JIC to generate assessment in the political, economic, foreign and military fields. A small Central Intelligence Organisation, he said, should combine all the intelligence available and provide it in a collated form for the Cabinet and the Vietnamese National Security Council. Like the JIC in Britain this would have authority 'to give general direction on all intelligence requirements and targets'. It would stitch intelligence properly into policy-making at the centre of government.

Thompson did not mince his words when he offered Diem his detailed blueprint for a future SIB. He envisaged a powerful central organism which would 'eliminate every internal threat to the security of the state'. SIB would take responsibility for countering all attempts at espionage and sabotage together with threats from within or without the country with the intention of subverting the security of the state. In this broad area, Thompson insisted, the capacity for really sophisticated counter-intelligence work was the key. The 'elimination of the threat nearly always involves the arrest of the individuals concerned and this process needs to be tightly, and, at the same time, delicately controlled' to allow 'continued intelligence exploitation'. This required an integrated organisation, whereas in the current situation, with several organisations engaged on intelligence duties, 'jealousies and rivalry inevitably arise to hinder close co-operation'.

Thompson gave Diem and his officials the most detailed advice on how SIB should be organised for work in this area. There would be three main elements dealing respectively with communist terrorist armed attack, with communist political subversion and with penetration by communist agents into the South Vietnamese government. There would also be 'specialist' sections including a Research Section constituting a secretive inner element. Thompson explained that,

> since it is impossible for anyone, except those who have direct responsibility for their work, to determine what an officer in the Research Section may be doing, they can be employed for running secret penetration operations. This is an ideal 'cover' for running such operations. In the same way the number of staff employed on the work of research can be considerable and thus present an opportunity to conceal within their numbers the staff employed on the most secret work.

There would also be a Technical Section taking responsibility for interrogation, surveillance and interception and for the continual development of all forms of technical aids to intelligence investigation. This was another section behind which it was possible to conceal more secret operational activities. Many of the staff of the Technical Section were usually employed 'as a screen behind which are hidden those engaged on more secret activities'.

But Thompson's extensive reorganisation of police and security intelligence would have to be carried out against the background of a major Vietcong offensive that was already under way. He conceded that the reforms would have to be incremental so as not to 'disrupt the present intensive effort against communist terrorism', so the SIB in its final form could be achieved only gradually. Thompson argued that the critical area on which attention had to be focused immediately was at the district and province level, where the Vietcong offensive was already biting in the villages and the hamlets, 'upon which the Vietcong depend for their supplies, information and recruits'. In the event Diem dodged the issue and did not implement the plan.[33]

Thompson's message about creating an SIB with Special Branch-type primacy in intelligence-gathering did not go down well with either the new CIA head of station, William Colby, or the head of the Military Advisory Assistance Group, Lieutenant-General Lionel McGarr, who had obvious preferences for other agencies. Multiple agencies were a problem that Thompson identified at an early stage:

> It was our general view that, if everyone starts collecting intelligence and running agents (and all love to), they end up spying on each other and there is no intelligence. That was to be the history of intelligence for most of the Vietnam War. Some years later there were eighteen separate agencies gathering intelligence in the Saigon area alone. One of the American errors was to use the CIA to organize South Vietnamese internal security intelligence and train its officers. To get the right approach it should have been an FBI job.

Thompson was right about the need for centralisation but wrong about many other things. The American Public Safety Programme that trained many of the South Vietnamese police was indeed run by the CIA at the top but employed many FBI agents and indeed ordinary domestic American police to do the job on the ground. The real problem lay elsewhere. The civil infrastructure which made police primacy work in Malaya was missing in Vietnam. The South Vietnamese government had to build a civil infrastructure in which the people had confidence before they could win the war, but this objective fell at the first fence.[34]

Ed Lansdale, who had been a free-wheeling CIA officer with his own operation in Vietnam in the late 1950s, was more sympathetic to

Thompson. In November 1962 he concluded that Thompson's ideas were 'indeed sound', but his presence was inevitably resented by the American military. The Saigon government was 'lagging' in the field of political and psychological warfare and Thompson was the government's 'sole advisor' on the political warfare side. His plan did not exactly fit the situation because he was trying to cast the solution to the Vietnamese problem in the mould he had learned in Malaya. But, Lansdale added, 'it's better than no plan at all, which would be the alternative'. Thompson was counter-productive when he moved out of the area of internal security and dabbled in military tactics. But in his favour, said Lansdale, 'he doesn't do too much of that'.[35]

By October 1963 there was wide discussion in London, Washington and Saigon about the continuing effectiveness of Diem. Thompson was away on a brief visit to New Zealand when he was handed a top-secret message from London. John F. Kennedy was requesting his views on Ngo Dinh Diem and what should be done about him. Kennedy was a big fan of Thompson, who had been the first British official ever invited to partake in US National Security Council discussions in 1962. Thompson argued that Diem should stay as there were no obvious successors, but by the time he was back in Saigon on 22 October the air was thick with rumours. Speculation abounded on whether the generals would get their coup in first or whether Diem would 'strike first and execute them'. There was a lull and Thompson dismissed the generals as 'a gutless lot' who would not act until they were sure that they had at least the passive support of all the military elements around Saigon. By the afternoon of 1 November the long-awaited coup was under way. Only the Palace Guard resisted. Thompson retreated from his house just in front of the Gia-Long Palace and positioned himself on the roof of the British Embassy to 'watch the fireworks'.[36]

The Diem brothers escaped from the Gia-Long Palace to find sanctuary in a Catholic church in Cholon, the Chinese sector of the city. They surrendered shortly afterwards. Within hours they were summarily shot in the back of an armoured vehicle *en route* to Army headquarters. The officers responsible reputedly removed a large quantity of diamonds that they were carrying. Washington seems merely to have given orders not to inhibit the coup, rather than encouraging it. Dick Helms, who was in charge of CIA Far Eastern operations at the time, was adamant that the CIA had no part in the removal of Diem. 'It was the Vietnamese who got together and chopped up Diem and Nhu.' However, Peer de Silva, who was one of the 400 staff at the CIA station, observed that, although 'no-one had planned' the deaths of Diem and his brother, the murders represented the 'not altogether illogical consequences' of positions and policies taken in Washington.[37]

Thompson and his BRIAM mission remained beyond the Diem era to offer similar detailed advice to the government of his long-term successor, General Khanh. In February 1964, Thompson and Palmer also offered advice to Lodge, the American Ambassador, on the deteriorating security situation in Saigon. The 'morale' of the National Police was low as the result of the disorganisation brought on by the coup, a subsequent political purge and increasing Viet Cong penetration of their ranks, and Thompson was seriously worried about 'panic' setting in. He was still forlornly selling his one big idea, the reorganisation of all the disparate paramilitary forces, numerous police forces and 'private armies' including the intelligence service and Special Branch into one coherent force led by a Malayan-style SIB. Colonel Dong Ngoc Lam of the Civil Guard was the man he had identified as 'just the sort of ruthless rogue with an instinct for survival who could carry this out effectively'. But he failed to appreciate that the factional interests would not permit the emergence of the centralised system which had helped to deliver victory in Malaya. By 1965 Thompson had departed, although numbers of British colonial policemen continued to serve in the Public Safety Division training the South Vietnamese police.[38] William Colby considered Thompson's team 'perhaps the highest ratio of talent to numbers seen in Vietnam previously or since'. Colby was especially impressed by the British emphasis on intelligence penetration of the Viet Minh and the formation of a credible and effective civilian police force with a large intelligence element. However, he understood that the South Vietnamese Army would always vigorously resist the development of the police primacy in the counter-insurgency effort.[39]

American efforts in the Third World, especially under the Dulles brothers, concentrated much effort on drawing states away from neutralism and non-alignment. This had been the essence of the joint American, British and Australian efforts in Indonesia in 1958, which were considered by some to be an effort not to replace Sukharno but to 'hold his feet to the fire'. CIA operations in South Asia had the same purpose but were more sophisticated in their approach, seeking to draw Delhi into conflict with Beijing and thus to 'educate' it in the perils of communist expansionism. The medium of this operation continued to be a rather fruitless struggle for the liberation of Tibet.

In 1957, Washington managed to restore its relations with Pandit Nehru, inviting him for a lavish state visit and succeeding in eradicating the suspicions generated by previous US–Pakistan agreements. There followed a programme of military and intelligence assistance, worth $38 million, some of which was directed at reopening the struggle to liberate Tibet. Himalayan tensions had been building for some time. The Chinese had built a new highway from Xinjiang into the Khampa region of western Tibet and the Chinese were animated about CIA and Taiwanese support for the Khampa rebels directed from Kalimpong near Darjeeling. The CIA had been recruiting in this area in 1955 and 1956 during a period when Sino-Indian relations were still in relatively good repair and the Taiwan secret service had maintained a steady drip-feed of support to the rebels throughout the decade. The civil war was now ready to flare again.

The war in Tibet was never likely to deliver an independent country, but it did seem to Washington to offer a major antidote to neutralism and non-alignment in the region. Having achieved the co-operation of both Pakistan and India against China, the CIA launched an expanded programme. Working with both the Indian IB and the Pakistani Inter-Service Intelligence, they began the extensive military support of about 14,000 Tibetan guerrillas. The CIA brought the most senior figures to the American-administered island of Saipan in the Pacific and later to Camp Hale in Colorado for courses run by the American Special Forces. While in Colorado the Tibetans were told that they were in another region of the Himalayas and were not aware that they were inside the United States. They were taught communications, map reading and the use of modern weapons. These individuals became the leading edge of a reinvigorated NVDA, the main Tibetan guerrilla force, and five of the first batch of CIA trainees were parachuted back into Tibet in 1957, with more following in 1958. Each CIA-trained Tibetan was provided with a watch containing a cyanide pill, and there were substantial supply drops by both the Americans and the Taiwanese. The PLA replied by using airpower against Khampa and NVDA rebel strongholds, but the rebels replied with some remarkable victories over PLA units and by 1959 there were claims of as many as 75,000 Chinese casualties.

By 1959 the Cold War in the Himalayas was threatening to turn hot as China poured in more troops. The rebellion in the Khampa area spread to Lhasa and engulfed the Dalai Lama. On 12 March that year the Tibetan Cabinet denounced its previous treaty with China and declared its country fully independent. In the words of one CIA officer serving in neighbouring Nepal, 'It was a disaster. Despite our indoctrination of the Tibetan intelligence/training teams, the Tibetan freedom fighters were not inclined to conduct guerrilla warfare against the Chinese Army, but pursued conventional set-piece battles, perhaps because many of them carried amulets that they believed made them impervious to bullets. They were quickly decimated.'[40] On 17 March the Dalai Lama fled to India, escorted by Khampa guerrilla fighters, including some of those trained and dropped by the CIA in 1957. A wave of 100,000 of his followers joined him in exile. On arrival the Dalai Lama's party were destitute, but local Khampa representatives received CIA instructions to hand over 200,000 rupees to allow him to establish a base in India.

In late April Nehru and his Foreign Minister Krishna Menon tried to persuade the Dalai Lama to issue a subdued call for autonomy rather than for complete independence, but the Dalai Lama insisted on full independence, believing that anything less would be 'to betray his people'. The CIA reported that Menon's request had 'provoked' the Dalai Lama. He insisted that he had tried Delhi's recommended path of seeking gradually expanded autonomy:

> The Chinese Communists had ignored this approach, continually pressured him to denounce the resistance movement and to go to Peiping and finally endangered his life enforcing him to escape to India. He and all Tibetans were now convinced that attempts to obtain autonomy were useless, that Tibetans were fighting and dying for complete freedom and independence, and that he was determined to struggle for this goal no matter how long it took and regardless of the GOI [Government of India] attitude.

By 28 June 1959 Beijing had replaced the Tibetan government with a puppet regime and the Dalai Lama was in permanent exile.[41]

American assistance to both Indian and Pakistani special forces expanded, while Chinese operations against the rebels regularly resulted in incursions into India. Both India and Pakistan were also willing to provide bases for American photo-reconnaissance operations over the Soviet Union and China. The fighting in Tibet and the presence of growing numbers of PLA troops on the Himalayan plateau destabilised Sino-Indian relations. Indian policy towards China and Tibet had, in any case, always been confused and inconsistent, and it now lurched towards increased support for the rebels against China. After several tense campaigns Nehru increased the temperature by deploying regular forces on the border and this contributed to the Sino-Indian border war of late 1962, a war which lasted a month and in which the PLA delivered a shattering blow to the Indian Army. Despite the gradually rising crescendo of covert action, the full-scale PLA assault took India by surprise. The CIA despatched a large contingent of advisers, including experts on mountain warfare, to the American Embassy in Delhi, but to no avail. China had underlined its commitment to Tibet as a 'strictly internal matter' on which it would brook no interference. Meanwhile, the United States and China had both made inroads of sorts into South Asian security. China had scored a military victory, but Washington also had cause for self-congratulation since Nehru's public policy of non-alignment, which had proved so awkward for American diplomats during the Korean War, also lay in ruins.[42]

In contrast to South Asia, Britain remained a dominant player on the

African scene. Here a Soviet offensive had been long forecast. As early as 1948, Ernest Bevin had warned Attlee about an impending deluge of Soviet subversion on the African continent, but in fact it was a full decade before it arrived. On 24 April 1958, PUSD received reports from the CIA dealing with the recent Pan-African Congress. On 19 April, triggered by this conference, Moscow Radio had begun broadcasting in English and French across most of Africa for the first time. In London this was held to be an important event and to mark a new phase of Soviet subversion in the Third World.[43]

But tensions in these remote areas were multi-faceted and Anglo-American–European–African problems were also a growing aspect of secret service work. This was partly a manifestation of recruitment and retirement patterns. In the vast expansion of secret service between 1939 and 1945, all major countries had recruited heavily from the business world, partly in search of people with unusual languages or overseas experience, and after the war many had returned to world commerce. There were extensive links between secret service and large corporations with operations overseas, which increasingly developed their own intelligence departments. By the late 1950s SIS and the CIA were making more use of non-official cover, including journalists and commercial postings, to hide their operatives. In areas like Africa the worlds of secret service and the large corporation were knitting together and this did not always make for smooth relations between the secret services of the Western powers.

Harold Macmillan had this drawn to his attention when, in December 1959, a senior SIS officer completed a tour of Africa south of the Sudan. His purpose was 'to consider the contribution that S.I.S. might make in the area' and in his ensuing report he also offered some general impressions. Norman Brook, the Cabinet Secretary, informed Macmillan that he thought that one of the most notable parts of the report related to 'anti-American feeling in East and Central Africa' and 'local suspicion of C.I.A. agents'. The SIS officer said he was most struck by the 'very strong anti-American talk I heard in East and Central Africa'. All this was driven by the fact that there were 'a number of private American agencies operating in Black Africa, backed by a great deal of money often provided by traditionally anti-Colonial Middle Western American groups'. British diplomats and colonial administrators in locations such as Salisbury in Rhodesia found them 'infuriating', and he added that it was 'very difficult for everyone who has British interests at heart to make a distinction between the policies of the United States Government and the activities of these variously motivated private agencies'. This involved a degree of mirror-imaging, for any CIA officer touring the Middle East might have made an identical observation about SIS and its relations with the Anglo-Iranian Oil Company in the early 1950s.

Indeed, OSS, the CIA's predecessor, had arguably learned much about the importance of commercial espionage on behalf of national interests from SIS and SOE during the war. It was clear to Macmillan that the Americans were regarded only as allies of a kind by SIS in sub-Saharan Africa.

African tensions were complex, for in the French and Belgian colonies security chiefs also suspected British plots. While touring Léopoldville and Brazzaville, the Director General of the Belgian Security Service in the Congo spoke frankly to SIS of the deep suspicions held by his colleagues concerning what they called London's 'Machiavellian plan for West Africa': 'They believed that the British Government were using N'Krumah [the leader in Ghana] as their "front man". They believed that, when the dust from the present nationalist troubles in Africa had settled, the world would find the French and Belgian Empires disappeared, and the British still in position, having taken all the valuable trade concessions.' The SIS officer contested this wild conspiracy theory 'very strongly'. But the Belgian security chief 'merely smiled wanly' at his protests and said that his colleagues were somewhat myopic. In Africa, the Cold War, with its anxieties about Russian and Chinese ambitions on the African continent, was only part of an intricate picture. The British, the Americans, the French and Belgians, as well as the local settler populations and rival Commonwealth countries were all watching each other with intense distrust and this would all erupt when Rhodesia declared unilateral independence in 1965. For the time being SIS noted gloomily that 'all the germs of dislike, jealousy and rivalry are there'.[44]

Anglo-American frictions in Africa and Asia were caused primarily by substantial differences in policy or by obvious commercial rivalries. But at the service level they were exacerbated by problems of size and resource. The continual expansion of American covert and semi-covert programmes outstripped anything the British could offer and began to impinge even in areas which the British regarded as their own preserve. This was re-emphasised as Kennedy succeeded Eisenhower, with his more pronounced interest in Africa and Asia. In February 1962, Kennedy asked Cord Meyer, who ran the CIA's International Organisations Division, including its radios, to prepare a presidential talk for him to give on Radio Free Europe which would be beamed out to Eastern bloc audiences. Characteristically, the talk was not to be about Europe but instead about the way in which the Czechs and the East German were acting as the agents of the Soviets in the underdeveloped countries of Africa and Asia.[45]

In the early 1960s, British efforts in these areas were superintended at the highest level by the Cabinet Counter-Subversion Committee. This committee typified the odd collection of overt and covert agencies working in this confusing realm. Run by Sir John Nicholls, it consisted of senior SIS and MI5 officers (either the chiefs or their deputies), officials from PUSD, Information Policy and Economic Relations Departments from the Foreign Office, together with officials from the MoD, Colonial Office and Commonwealth Relations Office. Its brief was hazy and consisted of watching 'threats by subversion' to British interests overseas and co-ordinating counter-action. Its task was to co-ordinate a vast territory that ran from economic aid and technical assistance through military and security advice to matters such as information and cultural activities, sponsored visits and education. It also included 'other activities of an unattributable and covert nature'.[46]

Counter-Subversion Committee had a potentially exciting remit, but limited British resources ensured that the work was often mundane. Numerous working groups met and many country studies were completed. But the recommendations were often marginal and frequently there were not the funds to implement them. In 1961 the committee completed a review of a programme of work done on 'Sino-Soviet penetration of Black Africa'. It worried endlessly about possible reductions in the numbers of English teachers and technical advisers going to the region, which provided useful opportunities 'for British influence'. It declared, 'The Working Group agreed that the visit of a British football team to ... countries in West Africa would be desirable for counter-subversion purposes ... £3,000 would be needed for air fares, with more for hotel expenses, but so far it had been impossible to find the money.' Counter-subversion in the Third World at the level of economic, cultural, education and information programmes directed at the mass populations required massive resources and Britain could no longer afford to play in the big league.[47]

A typical British answer to this problem was to concentrate limited resources on the elites in developing countries. While MI5 was busy touring the colonies training up new Special Branches, SIS was employed on a parallel beat in non-British territories. Middle-ranking SIS officers were often sent on briefing tours around underdeveloped areas with classified material revealing the nature of plots by the Soviet Union to extend its grip into Asia and Africa. Nicholas Elliott recalled being despatched on such a mission to Ethiopia in the early 1960s and being met on arrival by Douglas Busk, the local British Ambassador. The next day they drove out to give the prepared SIS presentation on the global communist menace to the Ethiopian Foreign Minister. Although the Foreign Minister was 'a charming little man', after ten minutes of the presentation it was clear that he was becoming bored and Elliott was increasingly embarrassed. The Minister then interrupted and asked, 'Tell me, Mr Elliott, what do you think of our Ethiopian women?' Elliot found a polite way of dodging the unwelcome question, but his host was persistent. 'How do you think the breasts of your women at home compare with ours?' Any chance of engaging the Foreign Minister in serious talk about the perils of the Kremlin was fast slipping away, so they gave up and made their polite farewells. Afterwards, Elliott was despondent and thought his visit 'a failure', but the local Embassy staff assured him that by Ethiopian standards it had gone well and a 'real rapport' had been established.[48]

London officials found counter-subversion in the Third World confusing and frustrating. By the early 1960s it was clear that Britain now lacked the scale of resources required to deal with the problems arising in an effective way, and to pretend otherwise amounted to self-delusion. By contrast Washington clearly had these in abundance, together with intelligent, energetic and talented figures in charge of its programmes. Yet London despaired of the American approach, which seemed to it to lack central objectives or indeed any centre at all. In 1962, after a year in Vietnam, Robert Thompson had visited Washington and made a grand tour of the agencies including State, Pentagon, the White House, the CIA, the Rand Corporation and many others. Several individuals deeply impressed him with their perceptiveness. The Secretary of State, Dean Rusk, discussed the issue of civil–police relations with him at length and obviously understood the intrinsic unpopularity of central government on the ground in rural areas and the instinctive culture of peasant resistance. Rusk recalled his own boyhood in the rural South and remarked that back then three telephone rings on the party line had meant 'a fire, a mad dog or a Federal Officer'. But, although such individuals inspired confidence, the overall landscape of Washington did not. 'The impression left with me was of a vast machine completely unco-ordinated, rather like a large four-engined aircraft with its engines unsynchronised.'[49] Throughout the 1960s the Third World presented a growth area for American covert action, and for the CIA in particular.

On the evening of 8 January 1968, a group of luminaries from the world of American statecraft met at the Council on Foreign Relations for a closed think-tank session on the subject of the future of American intelligence and foreign policy. Two dozen individuals from senior policy-making circles were led in earnest discussion by the CIA's Richard Bissell, chief of the U-2 project and one of the architects of the Bay of Pigs (the failed insurrection against Castro using Cuban exiles in 1961). Others in attendance from the American intelligence community included Frank Altschul, Robert Amory, Allen Dulles, George S. Franklin and Henry Howe Ransom. This meeting was deemed 'especially sensitive' since its purpose was an open-ended rethink of the role of the CIA in a world in which technical collection seemed ever more dominant and indeed was thought by some to be on the verge of making human espionage operations obsolete in areas like Europe. There had also been recent public revelations about some of Tom Braden's more daring covert operations in the West, using student and cultural groups, and this area of CIA activity was also under pressure. There were now 'problems involving CIA relationships with private institutions'. Against this worrying background the discussions developed in a manner which was wide ranging and thought provoking.

All were agreed that, against the Soviet bloc or other sophisticated societies, human espionage could no longer be considered an important source of intelligence. Occasionally there were walk-ins or high-level defectors, but the CIA now had to face the fact that 'it is enormously difficult to recruit high-level agents'. Meanwhile low-level agents, though easy to recruit, simply could not tell you much of what you wanted to know, especially in a closed society like the Soviet Union or China. The role of the CIA in gathering intelligence against these targets was increasingly marginal. Equally, Bissell added, as to allies and neutrals, they could learn most of what they needed to know through overt contacts: 'We don't need espionage to learn British, or even French intentions.'

'In contrast, the underdeveloped world presents greater opportunities for covert intelligence collection.' Bissell explained that there had already been a 'shift in priorities ... toward targets in the underdeveloped world', and consequently the 'scale of classical espionage effort mounted in Europe has considerably diminished'. Espionage was now needed in the Third World, which offered real opportunities for secret intelligence. Intelligence could easily be gathered there because some of these countries were less centralised, others less security conscious. The primary purpose of the CIA in these areas was to provide timely knowledge of internal shifts in power, and occasionally the possibility of influencing those shifts. Hitherto the record had not always been good in an area in which it was felt the CIA should have excelled. Changes in the internal balance of power in these countries, he argued, were extremely difficult to learn without frequent contact with the 'power elements'. 'Again and again we have been surprised at coups within the military; often we have failed to talk to the junior officers or the non-coms who are involved in the coups. The same applies to labor leaders, and others.' Bissell argued that underdeveloped states were now the primary area for CIA activity, but not always of a strictly conventional secret service kind:

> There is real scope for action in this area: the technique is essentially that of 'penetration', including 'penetrations' of the sort which horrify the classicists of covert operations, with a disregard for the 'standards' and 'agent recruitment rules'. Many of the 'penetrations' don't take the form of 'hiring' but of establishing a close or friendly relationship (which may or may not be furthered by the provision of money from time to time).

The role of the CIA was clearly changing in the 1960s. In some countries the CIA head of station served as the close counsellor, or 'in at least one case a drinking companion', of the chief of state. Here the tasks of intelligence-collection and political action overlapped to the point of being 'almost indistinguishable'.

This curious blend of overt and covert, and the merging of the tasks of intelligence and influence, seemed puzzling to much of the audience. They asked the inevitable question – why could diplomats not do this sort of thing? Richard Bissell replied that sometimes they could. But often the head of state in an underdeveloped country did not like to be seen close to a senior American with a high profile. In some cases the head of state had asked that the American Ambassador not be informed of his meetings with the CIA. Bissell added that in one case the restriction had been 'imposed upon the specific exhortation of the Ambassador' in a certain Third World country, who had decided that he 'preferred to remain ignorant of certain activities'. In many places the CIA chief could 'maintain a more intimate and informal relationship' which could better be kept secret both in the host country and in the United States.[50]

Although the CIA was still enmeshed in the Cold War battlegrounds of Berlin, Vienna and Hong Kong, by the early 1960s it had discovered that more could be achieved in the Third World. The last decade had underlined the lesson that in countries as diverse as Iran, Thailand and Egypt, much could be learned by the local CIA officers simply through a process of hanging out with local notables, albeit in discreet venues. Ray Cline, CIA head of station in Taipei, who was especially enamoured of the Chinese Nationalist cause, cultivated such a relationship with Chiang Kai-shek's son and eventual successor Chiang Ching-kuo. Chiang Ching-kuo and his wife could often be seen with Cline in the CIA station club bar, relaxing and playing the slot machines. Certainly these sorts of 'operations' were less likely to be blown and there was less likely to be a press outcry when they were, but was this really a vision of the future role for the CIA? Setting out a blueprint for the future of secret services in the turbulent 1960s was no easy matter.[51]

27

The Hidden Hand Exposed: From the Bay of Pigs to Profumo

A sacrifice is increasingly demanded here, and the appointed lamb for the altar is the Prime Minister, who must already have appreciated the sad truth that no ingratitude surpasses that of a democracy.
David Bruce to John F. Kennedy, 15 June 1963[1]

The early 1960s marked a period of important change for Western secret service. Most obviously, the gradual shift towards high technology, including signals intelligence and satellites, was gathering pace as the effort continued to collect intelligence from secure police states such as the Soviet Union. Meanwhile agent-based secret service was shifting its focus from Europe and China away towards the struggle for the Third World. Khrushchev had explicitly stated that all-out military confrontation between East and West was unthinkable, but then added that the United States would be defeated through wars of liberation in remote regions. John F. Kennedy, who was inaugurated in January 1961, took notice. Arguably, much of the momentum for growing United States involvement in Vietnam stemmed from Kennedy's obsessive desire to find a revolution and publicly defeat it. His first attempt came to grief when a CIA-sponsored invasion force of Cuban exiles was defeated at the infamous Bay of Pigs. Thereafter, he looked for other opportunities to defeat communism, mostly in Latin America, but eventually turned to South-east Asia, a choice that was to prove fateful.[2]

The public humiliation which the CIA endured at the Bay of Pigs in 1961 underlined a significant trend in the world of secret service, namely the arrival of the era of exposure. This was unwelcome and occurred despite the very best efforts of Eisenhower and Macmillan during the late 1950s to reverse the growing tide of media interest in secret service matters. This had proved impossible against the background of high-profile fiascos beginning with the twin shoot-downs of the U-2 and the

RB-47 in the late spring of 1960, swiftly followed by the Bay of Pigs in 1961 and the capture and trial of Oleg Penkovsky in 1963. In 1963 Kennedy followed lurid reports from London of the Vassall spy-case and then of the Profumo Affair, and became convinced that Macmillan was unlikely to survive this level of scandal. By the end of 1963 the press were aggressively probing into secretive areas which they had hitherto avoided and were rewarded with front-page stories. Public curiosity about secret service matters grew exponentially and the previous readiness by newspapers to practise deliberate self-censorship was being swept aside by a new conviction that these were matters of public interest. This reached its apogee in 1967 with revelations about Tom Braden's CIA activities in the United States and about the role of Kim Philby in SIS.

The CIA-sponsored effort to overturn Castro's regime in Cuba was perhaps the most public and spectacular fiasco of the Kennedy era. Fidel Castro came to power in Cuba after his third attempt at a coup against the dictator Fulgencio Batista in 1959. Although later hailed as a triumph of revolutionary-war doctrine, Castro's ascendancy was neither very violent nor revolutionary. He was a middle-class lawyer frustrated by the absence of a democratic process and took power only because the existing regime had crumbled 'like a rotten bone'. His confrontations with the United States over oil and sugar, and his corresponding drift towards the Soviet Union, occurred some time after he had obtained power and could have been avoided by Washington.

It is difficult to escape the sense that, in the wake of the Suez Crisis, Macmillan rather enjoyed watching Eisenhower and then Kennedy struggle with the problem of an increasingly pro-Soviet dictator inside the American backyard. On 24 November 1959, the Director of Central Intelligence Allen Dulles warned the British Ambassador in Washington that Castro was 'like a Cuban Hitler' and 'was not only a bad man but had a streak of lunacy which might have incalculable results'. A month later Dulles' subordinates had recommended plans for the 'elimination of Castro', but he was uneasy about assassination and instead recommended destabilising the Castro regime through economic sabotage. Eisenhower demanded something stronger for, like so many American presidents, his impatience and his willingness to resort to tougher measures increased markedly towards the end of his period of office. During the summer of 1960, Richard Bissell, Director of Plans at the CIA, worked on a series of assassination plots. But, like the British, the CIA lacked any team of experienced hit-men. Sheffield Edwards in the CIA's Office of Security came up with the idea of contracting the job out to the Mafia, who, he argued, were seasoned in this line of work. Moreover, the Mafia had lost gambling casinos in Cuba and presumably also wished to see Castro removed. Bissell supported the plans, although he remained anxious to avoid personal contacts with the Mafia, who had somehow got hold of his office telephone number. Ultimately, the CIA and the Mafia were stylistically incompatible. The CIA supplied the Mafia with high-tech toxins in pill form, and even with deadly chocolates and lethal cigars. These items disappeared mysteriously into the hands of agents bound for Cuba but had no visible effect.[3]

In November 1960, Macmillan drew another obvious analogy when discussing Castro with Eisenhower: 'Castro is your Nasser, and of course with Cuba sitting right on your doorstep, the strategic implications are even more important than the economic. I feel sure Castro has to be got rid of, but it is a tricky operation for you to contrive, and I only hope you will succeed.'[4] Despite Macmillan's expressions of sympathy on the subject of Castro, Britain and the United States were always somewhat out of step on Latin American issues, a region of perennial 'unspecial relationship'. London had been uncomfortable about a CIA operation designed to remove Jacobo Arbenz, the leader of Guatemala in 1954.[5] In the late 1950s Britain was still in trouble with its balance of payments and resisted Eisenhower's ban on arms sales to Batista's Cuba and then the more general COCOM trade restrictions imposed upon Castro. Britain had even hoped to sell Hunter jet aircraft to Castro in early 1960 and had to be dissuaded by Washington. In the summer of 1960, Castro's decision to nationalise Western oil refineries on Cuba, including the large Shell facility, finally brought Britain into line with Washington on the matter of oil supplies and economic embargo. Nevertheless, Britain had managed to sell seventeen Sea Fury fighter aircraft equipped with air-to-ground missiles to the failing Batista regime in 1958 and these were later used to bombard the CIA's hapless insurgent forces that landed at the Bay of Pigs in 1961.[6]

By the end of November 1960, Eisenhower was holding detailed meetings with his advisers about their plans to land armed Cuban exiles with the intention of overthrowing Castro. Despite the unhappy experiences of CIA-supported rebels in Indonesia in 1958 and more recently in Tibet in 1959 and early 1960, estimates of what the insurgents could do against regular armed forces, and also about their ability to do this covertly, were hopelessly optimistic. Any operation involving large numbers of exiles was a security nightmare and was bound to be badly penetrated. But the Bay of Pigs operation achieved new heights of pre-publicity when an article about the training of anti-Castro guerrillas appeared in the *New York Times* on 10 January 1961.[7]

One week earlier, at 9.30 a.m. on Tuesday, 3 January, Eisenhower had sat down with a range of key advisers, including Allen Dulles and Richard Bissell, to discuss Cuba. Eisenhower was only eighteen days away from handing over to Kennedy. He explained that while he had no immediate

or urgent reason for calling the meeting 'he was constantly being bombarded by people outside government as to the situation in Cuba'.
Eisenhower felt inclined to take action sooner rather than later, not least
because the security surrounding their anti-Castro forces in the region
was becoming very weak. All of South America, they complained,
seemed to know what they were intending. Eisenhower also worried that
there was little way of protecting US citizens in Cuba if the invasion went
ahead. There were two or three thousand US citizens still in Cuba who
refused to leave, and he feared that once trouble started 'it would be relatively easy to take them in groups of ten or twenty into the hills and
shoot them without any public knowledge'.[8]

When John F. Kennedy was inaugurated on 21 January 1961 the
Cuban invasion, now codenamed Operation Zapata, had already built up
a considerable momentum. In early February, the new President was
briefed on preparations and was told by Allen Dulles that the prospects
were better than those for the CIA operation that had removed Arbenz
in Guatemala in 1954. Kennedy was concerned about the danger that
this would turn quickly from a covert to an overt operation. Plans were
modified to try and make them more covert. Kennedy's estimate of the
likely success of the operation may have been buoyed up by the belief
that by the time the invasion took place Castro would have been eliminated, so he approved it.[9]

The rather ramshackle invasion flotilla carrying the CIA's Cuban
brigade arrived off the coast of Cuba on 17 April 1961. Kennedy was
already having second thoughts and had reduced the available air cover
to one quick strike. Fighter cover from the escorting carrier, the USS
Boxer, was also denied for fear of discovery. A small stick of paratroops
had made their way inland to capture an airfield and their operations
seemed to be going well, with some Cuban surrenders. But the landing
ships then began to run into coral reefs that the planners had failed to
spot. The first elements of the 1,400-strong brigade who made it to the
beach immediately ran into a Cuban patrol, and Castro now ordered his
air force into action.[10]

Britain's only significant contribution to the Bay of Pigs fiasco was
entirely unintentional. The Sea Fury fighter aircraft with their air-
to-ground rockets, originally supplied to Batista against the wishes of the
Eisenhower administration in 1958, now proved to be the decisive
weapon. Castro ordered his air force to go for the main ships in the
invading flotilla and this they did, destroying two of the six elderly
freighters before they approached the shore. One had been carrying
most of the ammunition for the brigade landing on the beach, while the
other carried all the radio equipment. Defeat was setting in. The
American-trained pilots of Castro's air force did not like the Sea Fury and

found it unrefined compared with American aircraft. The automatic starters did not work and they had to be fired up by the ground crews manually using a jerry-rigged system that employed a length of rope. But there was no denying its awesome firepower. Captain Enrique Carreras, the senior Cuban Air Force officer, recalled firing at close range into the side of the vessel the *Rio Escondido* 'with all eight rockets' and watching it disappear in a tremendous explosion, taking with it the exile brigade's communications centre.[11]

The backwash of defeat was extremely damaging and Kennedy chided himself for taking the advice of the CIA at face value. Some of Allen Dulles' close friends were also very critical. Charles Willoughby, a friend who had been MacArthur's intelligence chief, wrote to him shortly afterwards. Willoughby was the first to concede that 'intelligence is the whipping boy of operations' and also 'the scape-goat of faulty command decisions'. But he was also incredulous at some of the figures involved in the Bay of Pigs operation. He could not resist asking Dulles, 'who the hell selected Jose Miro Cardona, Manuel Ray, Antonio de Varoona, Hevia, Carillo and Carbo? On what conceivable ground could ex-henchmen of Castro become the "hope of Liberation"?' Willoughby did not exactly have a sparkling record as an intelligence chief, but it was clear even to him that the operation had been deeply flawed.[12] Kennedy was unhappy about being sold a programme which had been developed under Eisenhower and which was almost ready to go when he came into office in January 1961. He now chose to replace Allen Dulles with the former atomic energy chief, John McCone. Kennedy's unhappiness at this episode was also underlined by budget cuts. Retrenchment was going on across all of Washington in 1961, but it bore particularly heavily on the CIA, with as many as one in five Agency employees being made redundant.[13]

Over-sensitive about its failure to bring down Castro's increasingly left-leaning government in Cuba, the CIA became more active elsewhere in Central America. Paranoia about the spread of Castroism around the region prompted it to launch a series of improbable operations against some of the region's more innocuous leaders. In November 1961 it conducted operations to bring down the regime of President José Velasco Ibarra of Ecuador, who had refused to follow other countries in the region in severing relations with Cuba. Velasco Ibarra's successor also proved truculent and was in turn removed after his government was destabilised by the Americans in July 1963. Events in South and Central America were not a primary concern for London. However, the CIA was also active in the Commonwealth state of British Guiana. The CIA reportedly funded a run of strikes and riots that undermined the leftist government there and led to the overthrow of Cheddi Jagan and his ruling

People's Progressive Party. A number of groups, including the American labour organisation AFL–CIO, which had a long history of working with American government, helped to place Forbes Burnham in control.[14]

Castro was engaged in his own covert activities and was training guerrillas for action in countries such as Algeria, which sensitised the CIA to developments in Africa. The arrival of Soviet technicians and supplies in the unstable Congo in 1961 caused immense excitement in Washington. Many believed that they were only months away from the creation of another Cuba. On a recent visit to Washington the ruler of the Congo, President Patrice Lumumba, had deliberately raised the possibility of inviting in Soviet troops as a clumsy exercise in brinkmanship. In August 1960, Allen Dulles attended a meeting of the Special Group, the NSC sub-committee that supervised covert action, with Eisenhower in the chair. Eisenhower gave vent to 'extremely strong feelings on the necessity for straightforward action' and the meeting concluded that planning for the Congo should 'not necessarily rule out consideration of any particular kind of activity which might contribute to getting rid of Lumumba'. Richard Bissell noted that the cable sent by Dulles to the CIA station in the Congo was couched in similar terms, requiring it to get rid of Lumumba and underlining the high-level authorisation of the order. There was some talk of using biological toxins to eliminate an unnamed 'African leader'. Assassination was now a possibility, although still the weapon of last resort. In the event Lumumba was captured by troops loyal to General Mobutu, Chief of Staff of the Congolese armed forces, and he was imprisoned. By 1961 he had been murdered by local security elements probably encouraged by former Belgian intelligence officers who were still in the country.[15]

The clandestine US Cold War apparatus was now making the Third World its top priority. By July 1961, Ed Lansdale, veteran of the successful OPC operations against the Huks, had taken charge of the Pentagon's expanding Office of Special Operations. Under the Defense Secretary, Robert McNamara, he superintended programmes for unconventional warfare, focusing particularly on Latin America and South-east Asia, notably Cuba, Laos, Vietnam and Cambodia. He sought to explain some of the United States' recent reverses in terms of the extensive advisory work of the KGB and GRU, and referred especially to visits to Cuba by 'teams of East German security, intelligence and military experts ... under a commercial cover'. With the KGB and the GRU seemingly switching their attention to underdeveloped areas, pressure for the CIA to do the same was irresistible. Kennedy had informed Lansdale that his top priority was Operation Mongoose, designed to destabilise Cuba and if possible bring down Castro, a revenge for the Bay of Pigs.[16]

These developments in the Third World reverberated powerfully and unpredictably in Western capitals. This was particularly evident in Paris, where the unwelcome publicity generated by the Bay of Pigs episode combined with the Algerian civil war to inflict considerable damage on relations between Macmillan, Kennedy and de Gaulle. In April 1961, Kennedy and Macmillan met together for the first time and established a substantial personal rapport. There were important issues to discuss not least in the atomic field, including a possible European nuclear deterrent and the status of Thor medium-range ballistic missiles (MRBMs) in Britain. French reactions were a key issue at a time when Paris was trying to enhance its nuclear programme and when Macmillan was hoping to join the European Economic Community, a goal which Kennedy supported. De Gaulle eventually rejected nuclear co-operation with NATO, just as he rejected the British application for entry into the European Economic Community in January 1963. Increased British participation in Europe threatened a complete realignment of the EEC along NATO lines, with France losing influence to London, perhaps working as a Trojan Horse for Washington. There are indications that Kennedy saw Britain's hoped-for accession to the EEC in exactly these terms. Strategic issues, such as the deal between Macmillan and Kennedy over Polaris missiles at the Nassau conference in December 1962, were important in determining de Gaulle's hostile attitude to Britain and the United States in NATO and the EEC in the early 1960s. But it is now clear that secret service matters provided an additional irritant, which increased the abiding French sense of alienation.

Macmillan and Kennedy needed to win de Gaulle over, yet their courtship would be drawn out, painful and ultimately fruitless. This was apparent from the unfortunate circumstances of Kennedy's early visit to Paris in May–June 1961. At a distance the visit offered possibilities for a rapprochement. The French were requesting American aid for their growing nuclear programme, requests supported by General Gavin, the American Ambassador in Paris, while Kennedy and Macmillan desired de Gaulle's support for the impending British request to join the EEC. But events conspired against them. The weeks before Kennedy's arrival were dominated by two failed coup attempts. The first was the attempted invasion of Cuba by the brigade of CIA-trained exiles and their calamitous defeat at the Bay of Pigs in mid-April. The second occurred a week later when elements in the French military known as OAS attempted a coup against de Gaulle aimed at perpetuating French control of Algeria and thwarting de Gaulle's search for a settlement in that troubled country.

Like an electrical charge arcing between two points, the French public mind connected these two events. The CIA was already widely exposed as the instigator of events in Cuba and so was also accused of supporting efforts to topple de Gaulle on account of his awkward policies towards

NATO. The charges seemed to carry weight because the two coup leaders in Algeria, Generals Challe and Zeller, were known to be close to the US Supreme Commander Allied Forces Europe, General Lauris Norstad, and were outspokenly pro-American and pro-NATO. They had repeatedly urged Paris to move away from its semi-independent stance towards full military integration with NATO. General Gavin, the US Ambassador in Paris, a military figure who had little diplomatic experience, became panicked by growing public suspicions of American involvement in the Algerian affair. On the night of 23 April 1961, it seemed possible that the OAS rebels might succeed in toppling de Gaulle. In a state of some anxiety, Gavin finally decided to wake de Gaulle at midnight to convey to him an offer from Kennedy of American military assistance in putting down the rebels. This was, at best, eccentric behaviour and at worst open to misinterpretation. De Gaulle disdainfully rejected this offer and within a few days it was clear that the revolt was failing to make any headway. The French populace continued to suspect CIA involvement, while de Gaulle was affronted by a seemingly patronising offer to intervene in French affairs.[17]

To what extent did the CIA enjoy contact with the military elements that were trying to destabilise de Gaulle? Historians have now uncovered what appears to be the real story, as revealed by Gavin's private papers. In 1980 Gavin confided to Henry Kissinger that, when he arrived as ambassador, he was dismayed to discover that the CIA had indeed engaged in injudicious activities and had certainly 'supported political opponents of de Gaulle'. Gavin continued, 'This took place when I was in Paris and I brought it to a stop.' Although he had managed to halt these activities the reprieve was only temporary, for he added, 'To the best of my knowledge it was resumed under Bohlen [his successor in Paris].' The French seemed to have become aware of some of these activities. Gavin also observed that 'I got the Head of the CIA to put a stop to some of his activities that would clearly have made the Kennedy visit in the spring of 1961 a very unpleasant one.'[18]

Although the CIA undertook some anti-Gaullist activity in the 1960s there is no evidence to link it with support for the Algerian rebels. It was certainly watching the OAS rebel elements very closely. Following an earlier failed revolt in January 1960, the CIA had developed contacts that had allowed it to gather some detailed intelligence on military resistance to de Gaulle's plans for Algeria. This had required tangential contact with the rebels and sparked rumours of support. Rumours concerning American support of OAS through the CIA continued to circulate as the rebels pursued their murderous campaign of terrorism into the autumn of 1961. Kennedy decided that public disclaimers would only have generated more unfortunate press speculation and instead he gave the French

Ambassador in Washington, Hervé Alphand, express personal assurances that the rumours were not true.

Kennedy and his Secretary of State, Dean Rusk, suspected that the rumours of CIA involvement had originated with both the OAS rebels, who wished to unsettle de Gaulle by exaggerating support for their cause, and the French communists, who saw this as an ideal opportunity to damage Washington. More broadly it was a lesson in the perils of close American association with widespread covert action in the public mind. March 1962 saw an Algerian settlement, but this was not respected by the OAS rebels. The State Department, anxious to distance Washington from the rebels, launched a vigorous press campaign condemning them for 'wanton murder'. OAS replied swiftly to American criticism by bombing the US Information Agency building in Algiers on 9 June 1962. The staff fled from the building with only minutes to spare.[19]

The CIA's contacts with dissident elements led it to be pessimistic about de Gaulle's chances of hanging on. It concluded that most of the Army and the Air Force were 'violently anti' his efforts to bring a settlement to Algeria, while conversely the French population were weary and wanted 'peace at almost any price'. The CIA warned, 'The army is much more hostile now than ever before. De Gaulle will certainly not last if he attempts to let Algeria go. He will be finished probably before the end of the year – either deposed or assassinated ... a pre-revolutionary atmosphere prevails in France.'[20] Although at pains to reassure de Gaulle that Americans were not engaged in acts of impropriety, Kennedy was nevertheless repeatedly infuriated by him. Walt Rostow, one of the closest presidential advisers, recalled Kennedy remarking how much he 'hated de Gaulle's having a whip hand over him – getting our protection for free; hurting us whenever he could'. Rostow agreed, explaining that de Gaulle wanted to run the continent of Western Europe without American participation but with full American subsidy and support. When he could not do this he simply wanted to make trouble.[21]

In early 1962 there were further secret service frictions between Washington and Paris. The CIA's suspicions of the French had been enhanced by the arrival of a Soviet defector, Anatoli Golitsyn, who inflated his position by exaggerating his knowledge of KGB penetration in the West to a preposterous degree. Golitsyn advised the Americans that the KGB had an operation deep within French government known as Sapphire. This espionage ring had supposedly penetrated the key French government ministries together with the NATO administrative officers there. The CIA took the decision to inform Kennedy in the spring of 1962 and the Director of the CIA, John McCone, counselled him to tell de Gaulle at once. The CIA head of station in Paris was ordered to deliver a letter from Kennedy personally to de Gaulle.

Golitsyn's exaggerated claims were well calculated, picking up on the specific security concerns about pro-communist elements in Paris that Washington and London had nurtured for more than a decade. Golitsyn's 'revelations' also fed the anxieties of zealous security officials in the West, including James Jesus Angleton, the CIA counter-intelligence officer with responsibility for the Soviet Union.[22]

James Angleton effectively recruited the French secret service (SDECE) representative in Washington, Philippe de Vosjoli, who then began to work with the Americans against the supposed Soviet penetration of his own secret service at home. De Gaulle reacted with predictable vigour, ordering the severing of relations between French intelligence and the CIA. He also ordered an intelligence counter-offensive, requiring the French secret service to acquire by stealth the nuclear information which the Americans had refused to give France openly. Kennedy had decided not only to reverse Eisenhower's policy of giving more nuclear information to the French but also to press the French to draw down their nuclear programme. Meanwhile both Britain and the United States were actively monitoring the French nuclear test programme using air-sampling aircraft.[23]

Angleton was right for the wrong reasons. Although hopelessly paranoid and open to manipulation by Golitsyn, he was also correct about Soviet penetration in France. Golitsyn did not have accurate information on the supposed Soviet infiltrators of the French service and subsequent meetings with French representatives from SDECE proved to be frustrating and unproductive. Nevertheless, French intelligence was badly penetrated by agents who had been recruited as early as 1940 by communist elements in the resistance. Indeed during the Cuban Missile Crisis, the best Soviet intelligence on Western reactions came from the KGB's 'excellent French sources'. By contrast similar sources in Britain seem to have been largely eradicated by the early 1960s, despite fears in MI5 to the contrary.[24]

Signals intelligence tried to follow these Anglo–American–French vexations on all sides. In late 1960, Britain managed to plant a series of listening devices inside the French Embassy in London which allowed GCHQ to break some of the French cable traffic that was sent to and from Paris. This activity, known as Operation Stockade, continued for three years and allowed considerable insights into the thinking of French diplomats and some windows into thinking in the Quai d'Orsay. London and Washington had worked together on French traffic since the Second World War, but Stockade provided new levels of access at a time of fraught relations.[25]

London and Washington also became aware of possible French intelligence efforts against their own communications. Back in September

1959, Eisenhower had made real efforts to repair relations with de Gaulle and, on a visit to Paris, had suggested improved communications between London, Paris and Washington. Little was accomplished at the meeting, other than the agreement to install a secure telephone hotline to the Elysée Palace which would allow the same sort of top-level discussions that occurred between the White House and 10 Downing Street. Although de Gaulle was pessimistic about these efforts to cement tripartite consultations, technicians got to work extending the hotline system to Paris. The apparatus employed was a state-of-the-art scrambler telephone known as KY9. This required some dexterity on the part of the user, and an ability to remember to press the right buttons when sending and receiving, a knack which some of the users found surprisingly hard to master. The system was installed in London and Washington by 1961, and finally extended to Paris in 1962. Macmillan's officials had recommended the installation, not least because Macmillan could speak to de Gaulle directly in French, 'and not, like Mr Kennedy, via two interpreters'. Macmillan had initially asked who would pay for the installation. Once satisfied that London was not footing the bill, he decided that the project should go ahead.[26]

However, installation of the KY9 system raised unexpected issues. In June 1963, when relations with Paris were reaching a new low, Cabinet officials were required to inform McGeorge Bundy, Kennedy's Special Assistant for National Security, that it was quite possible that the French had been able to use the KY9 system to eavesdrop on conversations between London and the British Embassy in Paris, and indeed there was evidence that they had done so. They also worried that the French had been listening into conversations between American officials in Paris and London using the KY9 system. It was even conceivable that they had been able to listen in to Macmillan and Kennedy. Doubtless any dividends that the French collected through this system were enhanced by the knowledge that the Americans had paid for the installation of the equipment.[27]

Insights into the Anglo-American relationship gained by the French in the early 1960s would have been extremely interesting. Within the nuclear partnership, as elsewhere, the Americans were very much the senior partners and Anglo-American relations were not always as smooth as they outwardly appeared. By September 1962, Macmillan was furious that the Americans were preventing London from selling nuclear technology to the French, but were willing to do it themselves. Macmillan's private secretary called this Washington's 'brutal self-interest'. Macmillan himself saw the whole American attitude to European defence as selfish and blundering. On 19 June 1962 he noted in his diary that a recent 'foolish speech' by the American Defense Secretary, Robert McNamara, had 'enraged the French' and caused London a lot of difficulty:

In NATO, all the allies are angry with the American proposal that we should buy rockets to the tune of umpteen million dollars, the warheads to be under American control. This is not a European rocket. It's a racket of the American industry. So far as the Common Market is concerned, the Americans are (with the best intentions) doing our cause great harm. The more they tell the Germans, French etc., that they (U.S.A.) want Britain to be in, the more they incline these countries to keep us out.[28]

These vexations exploded as a result of the abrupt American cancellation of the programme that was supposed to provide the British with its next-generation nuclear deterrent. Although Kennedy eventually promised the submarine-based Polaris system to Britain, the whole episode seemingly revealed a cavalier attitude in Washington to Britain's world position. More broadly, Macmillan was worried about the restless energy of the young President and his staff. These anxieties were increased during the thirteen days of the Cuban Missile Crisis in October 1962.[29]

By the early 1960s, abiding British fears that Washington might be thinking of some sort of preventative war against the Soviets had evaporated. The strategic balance between East and West was stabilising and, despite periodic confrontations, there seemed to be a growing dialogue on issues such as nuclear testing, reflecting a general consensus that nuclear confrontation was unacceptable. However, any sense of increasing security was undermined by intelligence from Moscow that the Soviets did not share the same sense of stability. On 25 September 1962, only weeks before the onset of the Cuban Missile Crisis, London considered the latest JIC review of Soviet defence policy. This was completed by a select group using available intelligence from both human sources and signals intelligence of a 'most secret nature'. The JIC pointed to an alarming change in Soviet policy. The Soviets were rapidly building up their military potential, both nuclear and conventional, especially at sea. This was prompted not only by fears of a military imbalance between East and West, but also by recent American behaviour. Sir Hugh Stephenson, Chairman of the JIC, explained that 'recent discoveries of the United States reconnaissance potential had made them think that their present deterrent might not be valid. Photographs obtained from the American U-2 aircraft, coupled with confident announcements by the United States had made them believe they might be victims of a pre-emptive attack.' Worries about a pre-emptive American strike, facilitated by accurate U-2 intelligence, were magnified by the persona of Kennedy himself. The Soviets had believed that Eisenhower, a steady figure whom they knew of old, and also a senior general, had influence over the American military and 'would be capable of controlling the apparent warlike attitude of the United States'. They did not have the same trust in the youthful Kennedy. The JIC added that Moscow was also very worried by the new American programme of building fall-out shelters in major cities, which did not seem to be 'idle gestures'.[30]

London's confident assertions about how the Soviets really felt about the U-2, about Kennedy and about the general direction of the Cold War depended upon a new intelligence source of the first importance. In August 1960, Colonel Oleg Penkovsky, an officer in Soviet military intelligence, the GRU, and with a range of high-level contacts in the Soviet command structure, offered his services to the West. In part he was motivated by his father's role in the civil war on the side of the White Russians, which was now blighting an otherwise promising career. Over the next two years he provided intelligence of extraordinary quality on Soviet war plans, missile programmes and intelligence activities, including approximately 10,000 pages of highly classified documents. Most importantly he gave new insights into Soviet decision-making and into Khrushchev's intentions towards the West. This information played a part in Western decision-making during the Berlin Crisis of 1961 and the Cuban Missile Crisis of October 1962.[31]

Some have claimed that Penkovsky's intelligence played a dominant role in the Cuban Missile Crisis, with the SIS Chief Sir Dick White reportedly insisting that it was central to the American decision not to carry out a pre-emptive nuclear strike at the height of the crisis in October 1962. But those who sat with Kennedy on the Executive Committee of the National Security Council during the dark days of late October 1962 recall that Penkovsky, or Ironbark as he was codenamed, provided only general background information. It now seems that the latter view is correct.[32] Each delivery of fresh intelligence had exposed Penkovsky to risk. During the summer of 1962 he became increasingly aware of KGB surveillance, but he could not determine what had excited their suspicions. He delivered his last minox camera film of Soviet documents to a case officer on 27 August and was arrested, according to the KGB, on 22 October. By the time the JIC was reviewing the very valuable intelligence he had provided on the new anxieties of Soviet defence policy on 25 September 1962, the KGB were closing in on him. Following his interrogation he was put through a very public trial and then shot.

During the period while Penkovsky was operative, almost eighteen months, he not only passed messages to his CIA and SIS handlers, he was also debriefed in person at a safe house in Kensington in London. A joint SIS–CIA team spent a long time with him during his three-week visit to London as part of a Soviet delegation in late July 1961. Sir Dick White attended one of these sessions and a great fuss was made of their star agent. Penkovsky revealed some eccentric traits. He wished to have an audience with the Queen so that he could swear his allegiance to the

Crown in person, a request which was not easy to meet. SIS was, however, able to arrange to have him photographed in the uniform of a British and then an American colonel. It also provided him with a prostitute selected by SIS and a supply of presents, including French Cognac.[33]

Much has been made of Penkovsky's intelligence on the Soviet missile programme. But by 1962 good information on Soviet capabilities was already coming from the American satellite programme and Penkovsky's information in this area probably did little more than confirm existing reports (although this confirmation was valuable). His real worth was his ability to offer insights, through his associates and superiors, into the texture of current Kremlin politics and Soviet decision-making. Senior Western officials and intelligence chiefs sat enthralled at the debriefings as he recounted the inner machinations of the Soviet hierarchies. Penkovsky told them, 'You should know what is going on in the leadership and how Khrushchev is promoting generals to win their loyalty.' He explained that among the leadership 'there exists a secret opposition' which remained secret because the majority were still Khrushchev's protégés 'and the others don't want to lose their jobs'. But Penkovsky also said that there could be a realignment of forces and a split as a result of the Berlin question. Some wanted a confrontation with the West now. But those who were more aware of the nature of the military balance were saying 'it is too early to go to war. We've got to wait. What's the point of heating up the situation because of a Berlin which has existed for the last sixteen years?'[34]

The exact manner in which the KGB uncovered Penkovsky remains unknown. What is clear is that the apparatus for running Penkovsky was not ideal. Human agents who remained in place, as opposed to defectors who ran when the first opportunity presented itself, were rare and the associated human tradecraft in this field had remained archaic. Also, because it was unusual to be running a penetration agent of this quality and at this level, the British procedures for circulating resulting intelligence were rather rudimentary. Although Penkovsky's real name was known to only a few, the fact that very sensitive intelligence was processed under only four code words made clear to a wider audience that the West enjoyed a single high-quality source within Soviet officialdom. In later years, new procedures were devised to avoid this problem.[35]

Photography from the U-2 was much more important during the crisis than the work of Penkovsky, yet there was also real hesitancy before launching U-2s over Cuba. A U-2 operated by Taiwan had just been shot down over mainland China and there were worries about what the consequences would be if one was lost over Cuba. Dean Rusk was especially appreciative of the risks and there were ineffectual experiments with long-range photography taken on the slant from a great distance. As one expert witness has observed, the perilous weeks of September and October 1962 were dogged by a 'litany of intelligence failures'. Indeed, as late as 19 September US National Intelligence Estimates were predicting that the Soviets were more likely to establish a submarine base in Cuba than to station missiles.[36] Over 3,500 reports were considered during the crisis, but in a retrospective review only eight of these were capable of being proper indicators of the presence of offensive missiles on the island. This suggests that many of the CIA agents on Cuba had been doubled back by the Cuban intelligence service. However, on 14 October a U-2 flight finally found clear evidence of an MRBM site at San Cristóbal.[37]

During the opening stages of the crisis in October 1962 a British intelligence team was in Washington. This included General Kenneth Strong, who had gathered responsibility for atomic and missile intelligence under his JIB organisation; Sir Hugh Stephenson, Chairman of the JIC; and the official who was about to become Cabinet Secretary, Sir Burke Trend. They assured the Americans repeatedly that the Soviets would never put missiles in Cuba. Only on 19 October, towards the end of their visit, did an amused Ray Cline, the CIA's Deputy Director for Intelligence, offer them the detailed evidence in their possession. This seems to confirm that Penkovsky, whose material was available to the British, was telling them very little about Cuba.[38]

The Director of Central Intelligence, John McCone, appears to have deduced the presence of the Soviet MRBMs partly on the basis of an obvious question. The Soviets had installed many surface-to-air missile (SAM) sites on Cuba, so what were they there to protect? During late August, McCone and Kennedy had discussed the difficulty of distinguishing SAM sites from possible MRBM sites on Cuba. In September McCone was on his honeymoon in southern France but even during this romantic interlude he remained troubled by the question and sent frequent cables to Washington. Important intelligence also came from Allied sources. The British networks were probably eliminated when the Shell refinery closed in 1960, and many American networks had been cleaned up after the Bay of Pigs in 1961. But the French had also paid a lot of attention to Cuba because Castro had been training the FLN guerrillas who had been fighting against the French in Algeria. Philippe de Vosjoli, the troubled SDECE head of station in Washington, who eventually chose to side with Angleton and Golitsyn in the row over Soviet penetration in France, has claimed to have been the first to bring back reliable agent material on the missiles. Len Scott has recorded that 'both the French and the Dutch intelligence services alerted the Americans to the presence of offensive missiles in Cuba in August and

September respectively'. Although French claims were rather hasty, for the missiles arrived only in September, nevertheless it was French intelligence that helped to pinpoint the MRBM site on Cuba at San Cristóbal, which was then photographed by a U-2 on 14 October, precipitating the crisis.[39]

The U-2 photography of the missiles was certainly important in convincing Western leaders that the threat was real, and various teams were despatched from Washington to Paris, Bonn and London with packs of photographs. Chet Cooper arrived in Britain to assist the American Ambassador, David Bruce, in presenting the material. However, reactions were not always ideal. Macmillan was not especially excited by the photos and simply observed that the Americans would have to get used to living under the shadow of Soviet missiles like everyone else. After all, long-range ICBMs were not far away from being developed. Nor was Macmillan sure that the naval blockade of Cuba that Kennedy proposed was the right course of action. More importantly, as early as 22 October it occurred to Philip de Zulueta, Macmillan's private secretary, that one of the best things the White House could do was to publish the U-2 photographs. Macmillan agreed and was soon pressing Kennedy to release the photographs through the British Ambassador in Washington, David Ormsby-Gore. Not everyone was convinced by the U-2 photography, for the same material was shown to senior opposition figures, including Denis Healey, who was already extremely irked by the Bay of Pigs and now angrily denounced the material as fraudulent.[40]

The U-2 flights over Cuba during the crisis have been described as 'one of the greatest contributions to American security ever made by the intelligence community'. The flights certainly provided the clearest evidence that Soviet MRBMs had indeed arrived, although nuclear warheads could not be detected by the U-2. We know now that the Soviets had in fact shipped over 102 nuclear warheads to Cuba. But the Cuban Missile Crisis also reveals something of the wider role of the CIA in Washington as policy-maker, as well as intelligence-provider, joining in with the other agencies and elements in making active recommendations. McCone urged that the United States should issue an ultimatum requiring the missiles to be dismantled and, if there was no response, to follow this up with a massive attack on Cuba. He acknowledged some way into the crisis that such an action was almost bound to escalate into a general invasion of the island. It is likely that this would have provoked Soviet retaliation and perhaps a general conflagration. The US Air Force was making similar recommendations and, ultimately, both based their position on other kinds of photographic intelligence. The American satellite programme had now proved beyond any doubt that there was no 'missile gap' and indeed the US Air Force was now very confident that it was ahead. Confidence in this sort of intelligence helped both McCone and the US Air Force to take forward positions, but fortunately, although Kennedy, Rusk and McNamara gave these options serious consideration, they were not in the end persuaded.[41] Macmillan had also sided with the latter in arguing they should not attack.[42]

The darkest point in the crisis was 27 October – known as 'Black Saturday' – when a U-2 was shot down by a SAM site while overflying Cuba. The FBI reported that the Soviet diplomats and KGB officers in the Soviet Embassy in Washington were destroying their codes and ciphers, a standard procedure immediately prior to the outbreak of war. American troops were already preparing for a possible invasion and Kennedy now gave consideration to aerial attacks on the SAM sites. Meanwhile the Soviets had been sent a message that was half an offer of a deal and half ultimatum. It required Soviet missiles be withdrawn, but also offered an unpublicised and secret withdrawal of equivalent American missiles from Turkey. On Sunday morning the White House received a Soviet message undertaking to remove the missiles from Cuba and the crisis was effectively over. Everyone began to ease back and Ed Lansdale's Operation Mongoose activities in Miami were also stepped down.[43]

London was kept abreast of these broader developments. But it was not told about another most dangerous U-2 episode on the same day, 27 October, which McNamara was convinced would unleash disaster. In the midst of this crisis, with both the Soviets and the Americans on a high state of alert, US Strategic Air Command had continued routine U-2 flights around the perimeter of the Soviet Union. One of these flights launched from Alaska became lost and accidentally flew into Soviet airspace over the Arctic. This was a routine daily 'sniffing mission' designed to gather high-altitude debris from Soviet atomic tests for analysis. Because these did not move closer than a hundred miles to Soviet airspace it had not occurred to anyone to postpone the flights. But this flight strayed over the Chukotsky Peninsula and Soviet MiG interceptors were scrambled to attempt to shoot it down. The U-2 pilot Major Charles Maultsby, realising his predicament, radioed a US command post and was ordered to reverse his course. Running out of fuel over Siberia, he now attempted to glide back towards Alaska. In an effort to protect the U-2, American F-102A interceptors were launched. Because Alaskan command area was at DEFCON-3 (Defence Condition 3) alert status, the aircraft were armed with nuclear-tipped Falcon air-to-air missiles in full readiness to fire. The decision whether to use these nuclear weapons against the MiGs was now in the hands of the individual pilots flying over the Bering Strait. By happy chance the US interceptors met up with the U-2 rather than the MiGs and escorted it to a landing site on the coast.

Although McNamara then ordered these U-2 flights suspended, his message did not reach Alaska quickly and, incredibly, by that time another U-2 was already in the air following the same course and had to be recalled. But the principal danger here was not from the nuclear-armed interceptors. The real problem, as both McNamara and Kennedy appreciated, was that the Soviets might presume this flight to be the final pre-strike reconnaissance as a prelude to an American pre-emptive nuclear attack.[44]

Britain was no mere military spectator during the Cuban Missile Crisis. The Americans had also deployed dual-key-controlled Thor missiles with nuclear warheads in Britain, together with Jupiter missiles in Italy and Turkey, all MRBM systems within range of the Soviet Union. Britain's Thor missiles were kept on a high state of alert throughout the Cuban Missile Crisis, and because of their short flight-time to the Soviet Union may have been a significant factor in Moscow's calculations. By 1962 the United States was also making use of the Holy Loch base in Scotland for its Polaris submarines.[45]

The Cuban Missile Crisis, and in particular the role of the U-2 over Cuba during this episode, left deep scars on the mental outlook of the British government. This was still apparent two years later in September 1964 during a visit to London by John McCone, who remained Director of Central Intelligence. McCone's mission was to brief European leaders on the forthcoming Chinese test, a mission which, as we have seen, was widely appreciated. While sharing the dividends of satellite reconnaissance over China, he also talked quite freely of other reconnaissance matters, explaining American plans for continuing U-2 flights over Cuba. Peter Thorneycroft and Rab Butler, Minister of Defence and Foreign Secretary respectively, both 'felt some unease' when they heard this. Thorneycroft was sufficiently anxious to press Sir Solly Zuckerman, the Chief Defence Scientist, to look for some alternatives to more U-2 missions. Zuckerman could offer only two suggestions. First, that the Americans limit themselves to conducting oblique long-distance surveillance of Cuban ports from outside Cuban airspace. In fact the Americans had already attempted this with little success. Secondly, and more improbably, he suggested, 'Cuba must come within the focus of the Soviet satellites whose orbit enables them to carry out photographic reconnaissance of the United States. Is it completely out of the question to contemplate a deal whereby the Russians would make available to the United States their photographs of Cuba?' Thorneycroft also sent this rather silly suggestion to the Prime Minister and to the Cabinet Secretary, Burke Trend. Their reply is not recorded and what they made of it one can only guess, but the Soviets had no satellite reconnaissance capability at that time. If they had, they would not have given photos to the

Americans, and had they done so the Americans would not have placed much faith in them. Butler knew this was improbable and asked the JIC to bring Thorneycroft gently back to earth by patiently setting out the impediments to his schemes. Nevertheless, London entertained real anxiety about the consequences of more U-2 flights over the numerous SAM SA-4 missile batteries on Cuba.[46]

We now know that it was not only the aerial reconnaissance, but also human agents, that were potentially destabilising in this crisis. Oleg Penkovsky in Moscow had been issued with a crude but effective warning system in case he came across evidence that the Soviets were about to launch a nuclear attack. Given his specific responsibilities concerning Soviet rocketry it was not unlikely that such evidence would come his way. He was given various telephone numbers in the American Embassy and was instructed to ring one of these numbers and then blows three times into the receiver. He should then wait one minute and do the same again. But he was told of the seriousness of this sort of war warning, which might lead to a high-level reaction in London or Washington. On 2 November 1960, after the crisis had passed, Penkovsky's warning message was received by the CIA in Moscow. A CIA officer was despatched to service Penkovsky's usual dead-drop letterbox, but he found himself arrested by the KGB. All parties were surprised. The KGB had expected to arrest an SIS officer and was clearly unaware that Penkovsky was being run jointly with the CIA. The CIA and SIS did not know that Penkovsky had himself been arrested. How or why the message was sent remains unclear. Most have presumed that under interrogation Penkovsky told the KGB of the signal, but not what it meant, hoping that they would use it and inadvertently bring down destruction on Moscow, and indeed himself.[47]

It is often observed that the strategic intelligence effort helped leaders to see more clearly during the various crises of the early 1960s. But newly emerging evidence suggests that intelligence was part of the problem as well as part of the solution. Information about the exact state of the military balance did not always prompt more restrained counsel, nor were the operations to gather this intelligence without considerable risk. The secret services of East and West not only offered timely warning but also contributed to the hair-trigger environment of the 1960s.

The extent of this problem was only revealed to London in 1971 when a KGB officer called Oleg Lyalin defected in London. Lyalin was a 'real' KGB special operative of the sort that the West rarely encountered. An expert in unarmed combat, a crack shot and a trained parachutist, he had belonged to the KGB's Department V. This unit prepared plans for producing mayhem through sabotage and assassination in the nerve centres of government, transport and communications at the outbreak of war and in certain crises short of war. Lyalin was recruited by MI5 and handed over detailed plans for sabotage in London, Washington, Paris, Bonn, Rome and other Western capitals that the Soviets had developed in the 1960s. Little of this fantastic information was made public but it chilled the blood of Whitehall's policy-makers. It was these unpleasant revelations that led to the spectacular expulsion of 105 Soviet intelligence officers from Moscow's London Embassy in 1971. But this also pointed to a wider problem. Each side had developed elaborate hidden-hand units that were trained to disable command and control centres on the eve of the outbreak of war, the very facilities that would be required to draw down and stabilise any emerging crisis. In West Germany too, US Special Forces had continued to prepare for activities in the Eastern bloc in the event of hostilities, and senior figures in Washington felt that a substantial ability to stir up trouble in the Soviet rear in the early stages of any conflict was a key part of 'our deterrence posture'. In West Germany, US Special Forces worked on a bizarre plan to infiltrate into Eastern Germany by swimming under the surface of the rivers and waterways that crossed the Inner German Border, allowing them to attack command centres and generally create mayhem on the eve of war. Occasionally these surreal figures could be glimpsed out for a day of infiltration-training on the lakes of southern Germany, wearing their spacemen-like wetsuits.[48]

Which secret service activities were, in hindsight, justified and which were injudicious and destabilising will offer commentators endless scope for nice argument. What is now clear is that strategic intelligence during the early 1960s was a more precarious business than was previously thought. The notorious security dilemmas that helped to escalate the arms race also applied to intelligence-gathering. The search for information that Eisenhower and then Kennedy needed to slow their own side down could simultaneously serve to convince the Soviets that they were preparing to attack. Added to this there was also the sheer human capacity for misinterpretation and accident. Intelligence power, like military power, was deeply ambiguous, and whether it appeared offensive or defensive depended on the eye of the beholder. Moreover, better intelligence did not always lead to better decisions. Although Western intelligence performed well as a machine during the Cuban Missile Crisis it is hard to dissent from the views of one participant that, had it been able to provide full intelligence on the situation, this 'could have made the resolution of the crisis much more difficult'.[49]

All these very public events had contributed to the heightened public profile of secret service, and media interest in these matters was now growing fast. Curiously, secret service itself contributed to the new climate of exposure. SIS and IRD had moved into the publishing business in the

1950s with enterprises such as Background Books. In publicising the disagreeable nature of Stalin and his successors, their work gave full attention to the Soviet secret service and its malignant activities. This process began as early as 1949 with Alexander Foote's autobiography, *Handbook for Spies*, sponsored by MI5 and ghosted by one of its officers, Courtney Young. The British left also entered the field early and in 1953 it offered an acerbic depiction of CIA covert action, written by Gordon Stewart, with the catchy title *The Cloak and Dollar War*. This depicted CIA activities in the Eastern bloc from the Soviet point of view, with a chapter entitled 'Cleaning Up after Allen Dulles'. It defended the recent purges in Eastern Europe and declared, 'The Slansky trial was a great defeat for the "liberation" policy.' This book was written at a time when many in Britain had not even heard of either liberation or the CIA. Secret service exploits were emerging as one of the most eye-catching variants of the Cold War story and each side wished to be seen as ahead in this clandestine war. Accordingly, the 1960s were peppered with authorised memoirs by veterans of secret service. Karl Anders' *Murder to Order*, the autobiography of a trained KGB assassin armed with a poison spray pistol that fired prussic acid, was published by IRD's own Ampersand imprint in 1965. Kim Philby's KGB-inspired autobiography *My Silent War* was the landmark volume in 1968 and for months after the British press seemingly talked of nothing else. Senior Ministers from Macmillan onwards complained about the boundless public appetite for stories of spies and scandals, but the secret services themselves repeatedly fanned the flames of public interest.[50]

The gradually expanding public appetite for security scandals combined with a new kind of investigative journalism to jeopardise Harold Macmillan's government in its last years. In September 1962 there had been the case of John Vassall, who had worked in Naval Intelligence and had then been a cipher clerk in the British Embassy in Moscow. Vassall was an active homosexual which gave an opportunity for the KGB to entrap him with incriminating photographs and blackmail him into handing over classified material. There were rumours of his involvement with Tom Galbraith, who had become under-secretary at the Scottish Office. Galbraith resigned, although the rumours were later found to be untrue. The main issue was not the spy-case, which was unremarkable, but the public reception. Peter Thorneycroft, the Minister of Defence, treated the manner flippantly in the House of Commons, prompting Opposition charges of negligence and incompetence. Macmillan was alarmed by the scale of public interest and set up a tribunal under Lord Radcliffe to look into 250 sensational newspaper stories about the event. Much of what had been reported had proved to be untrue, and Macmillan was left perplexed about how to respond to intense public interest in areas in which he felt they had no right to probe.[51]

Four months later, on 23 January 1963, Kim Philby disappeared from Beirut after being confronted with new evidence of his treachery by Nicholas Elliott of SIS. Philby had been employed part time by SIS since the 1950s, often under journalistic cover. In this way SIS had hoped still to catch him if he proved to be guilty, and by offering him continued employment it had also hoped to salve its conscience over his sorry treatment if he was not. But by January 1963 there could be no doubt. The story of his disappearance appears to have been spiked in an orchestrated campaign by the Information Policy Department in London. Under pressure from the *Observer*, the Foreign Office finally agreed to a statement which was made by Edward Heath, Lord Privy Seal, to the House of Commons on 20 February. Heath simply said that Philby had left the Foreign Service in 1951 and since then had had access to no official information. The Macmillan government had a narrow escape here, since some journalist colleagues presumed he had simply gone on a wild drinking session and would eventually turn up. The reality would not emerge until an investigation launched by Harold Evans of the *Sunday Times* in 1967.[52]

By the time Heath had made his statement regarding Kim Philby to the House of Commons, the Macmillan government was already preoccupied with another breaking scandal which became known as the Profumo Affair. On 4 February 1963, Macmillan arrived back in London following a visit to Italy and was warned in some detail about the nature of the potential scandal. However, he was probably unaware of the extent to which the press was already on the trail, and might have hoped it would blow over. The scandal concerned John Profumo, the Secretary of State for War. Profumo was accused of having an affair with a call girl, Christine Keeler, who had had a simultaneous relationship with the Russian Naval Attaché, Captain Yevgeny Ivanov, in London. The following day Macmillan had a meeting with Brigadier John Redmayne, the government Chief Whip, who informed Macmillan that, when interrogated about the rumours, Profumo had denied them. Redmayne assured Macmillan that he believed Profumo's denials and had advised him not to resign. Inevitably, perhaps, not only was the story true, it was also much more complicated than it appeared at first sight. Keeler's relationship with Captain Ivanov had been encouraged by a Svengali figure, Dr Stephen Ward, on behalf of MI5, in what was clearly a 'honeytrap' operation to ensnare the Soviet officer into working for British intelligence. This had a curious similarity to the scheme that was used by the KGB to entrap John Vassall in Moscow. However, Ward was eventually charged with living off immoral earnings and at this point MI5 disowned him, as

Macmillan became alarmed that Ward might name Ministers in court proceedings.[53]

Macmillan was also quite aware that the Soviet connection was complex. It has now been shown beyond any measure of doubt that Captain Ivanov was being used by the GRU during the Cuban Missile Crisis to try and open up some sort of backdoor diplomacy with the Macmillan government, either to promote a summit or to split the British from the Americans by persuading Macmillan to try and intercede. The latter was likely given that the Soviets were only too aware of Macmillan's penchant for negotiation rather than confrontation. On 26 October 1962 Ward conveyed a message from Ivanov to the Foreign Office asking for a London summit. Indeed, Ivanov had been using Ward or his immediate circle to try and pass Soviet proposals on disarmament and for the settlement of the Berlin issue to the Foreign Office since 1961. Ward seems in retrospect an unlikely GRU intermediary, but it has to be remembered that his social contacts were unrivalled. The GRU had tried to open a similar backdoor diplomacy with Robert Kennedy at the White House during the crisis, but again to little effect. All this adds weight to the view that both John Profumo and Stephen Ward had genuine reasons to be connected with Ivanov and that they were treated in a dubious manner by MI5, by Macmillan and also by Lord Denning in his subsequent enquiry. This may have reflected Whitehall's desire to avoid suggesting to the Americans that it had been talking to Moscow in a disloyal way during the crisis.[54]

But in March 1963 these deeper matters were not widely understood. Instead the Profumo Affair was simply a sex and security scandal that no newspaper would yet print without substantial confirmation. However, it was bound to come out, as Keeler had already sold the rights to her story to the *Sunday Pictorial*, the forerunner of the *Sunday Mirror,* and another of Keeler's lovers, a West Indian drug pusher called Jonny Edgecome, was about to be put on trial on suspicion of having shot at Keeler in her flat. Macmillan, a deeply Edwardian figure, instinctively attempted to stem the rising tide of public interest in these things. But Fleet Street attitudes were changing. In the 1950s newspapers had happily accepted Whitehall advice not to publish on intelligence-related matters, but the press was increasingly uncooperative. More specifically, two journalists, Brendan Mulholland and Reginald Foster of the *Daily Mail* and the *Daily Sketch* respectively, had been jailed for refusing to name their sources when required to give evidence before the Radcliffe tribunal on the reporting of the Vassall case. Mulholland received six months and Foster three. These journalists were seen in Fleet Street as martyrs to the cause of a free press.

The Macmillan government was not completely entrapped until the early hours of the morning of 22 March 1963. During a House of Commons debate on the Vassall Affair the previous evening George Wigg, supported by several other MPs including Barbara Castle, Richard Crossman and Michael Foot, gently raised the Profumo issue. Martin Redmayne and the other government whips panicked and Profumo was summoned to a meeting at the House of Commons at 2.30 a.m. to be interrogated by Redmayne and four Ministers. Profumo was groggy having taken a sleeping pill and in these extraordinary circumstance chose to answer 'No' to the charges put before him. But the scandal gradually emerged, first in private newsletters and then in the full press during June 1963, while Macmillan continued to plead ignorance about the matter. Profumo admitted the full story to the Cabinet and then resigned on 4 June. High-profile court cases followed in which Christine Keeler received a prison sentence and Jonny Edgecome was acquitted, but Keeler's unfortunate associate, Stephen Ward, committed suicide before the judge could pass sentence.[55] On 12 and 13 June, as the full nature of the scandal emerged in the press, there were recriminations in Cabinet. Ministers remonstrated with those who had interrogated the 'groggy' Profumo on the night of 22 March and insisted that they should have been tougher and less credulous. Others saw the whole Profumo Affair as a sinister extension of the work of the KGB against Vassall, believing that Ward was working with the KGB in an attempt to entrap Profumo in the same way. The Cabinet was clearly still unaware that Ward had been working with MI5 against Ivanov.[56]

Across the Atlantic John F. Kennedy was taking an intense interest in the Profumo Affair. This reflected the fact that he was due to visit Macmillan at the end of the June. It is hard to resist the observation that, because of Kennedy's aversion to monogamy, the dangers of such scandals must have rung alarm bells closer to home. To his credit, although he presumed that Macmillan was finished, he continued with his plans for the visit to London to support his friend and duly arrived at 10 Downing Street. He had been briefed by his Ambassador in London, David Bruce, who was well acquainted with the Westminster scene. The news did not seem good and on 15 June Bruce had sent an 'eyes only' message to Kennedy and Dean Rusk predicting Macmillan's impending fall.

Macmillan, he explained, was 'under heavy attack' and about to make the most difficult speech of his long career in the House of Commons and was bound to suffer a long and damning interrogation. Over the previous week Macmillan's stock had been falling fast. He was faced with alternate charges that either he had been involved 'in collusion with Profumo in the telling of a palpable lie' or else through naivety or stupidity, as well as 'because of an indolent disregard ... of the warnings of

British security services', he had accepted Profumo's denials at face value. Bruce thought that few people in government really believed that Macmillan would have connived at a clumsy attempt to avoid an almost inevitable disclosure if he had known that Profumo had lied. What was likely to do the damage was the charge of incompetence and bungling in an area that concerned national security. Everyone expected the government to try and buy Parliament off by appointing a tribunal or special committee to review the security aspects of this affair, but this seemed unlikely to satisfy. Bruce put his finger on it when he told Kennedy that the British people, 'their appetite for sensations already whetted by partial revelation', would call for some sort of sacrifice and the victim was bound to be Macmillan.

> Meanwhile, the lurid details of the involvement of degraded personalities like Dr. Ward, Miss Keeler and other nymphs, fan the popular imagination, inciting both meretricious and wholesome indignation in the public, who feel betrayed by dereliction in official circles ...
> It is ironical and sad that la Keeler, who was led by the sleazy Dr. Ward through London streets, harnessed to a dog collar, might occasion the demise of a government. Her frank predilection for her 'hairy chested Russian', her laments for her beloved Profumo, who was less fortunate than her lucky Jamaican lover, do not create the image of a sensitive individual.

No one, Bruce continued, suspected Macmillan of other than gullibility or stupidity, but as Prime Minister he was bound to bear the burden of leadership, criticism and atonement.[57]

Whitehall was naturally gripped by a fear that the twin cases of Vassall and Profumo would shake American confidence in British security further. As Bruce had predicted, a senior judge, Lord Denning, was appointed to conduct an enquiry into the affair. But London was completely unaware that Profumo had in fact sent the White House into a security panic of its own. Kennedy's brief visit at the end of the month, which was announced as a successful meeting on nuclear issues, was clearly a generous effort to boost the standing of Macmillan. It was also a brave gesture because, since the onset of the Profumo affair, FBI agents had been trying to ascertain the movements of Christine Keeler and her friend Mandy Rice-Davies when they visited New York a year earlier. At the same time Robert Kennedy was asking J. Edgar Hoover if he could discover exactly whom the two girls had met, anxious that they might have had an encounter with his brother, whose sexual appetites we now know to have been prodigious. But it appears unlikely that there was any encounter between Christine Keeler and John F. Kennedy.[58]

The crucial figures who precipitated the Profumo Affair had not been the obvious protagonists, either Macmillan, Profumo, Keeler or the curious menagerie maintained by Stephen Ward. Instead two relatively minor figures had caused the Profumo Affair to have a major political impact. The first was Martin Redmayne, the government Chief Whip, a weak character who questioned Profumo and believed his denials of sexual associations with Christine Keeler. Assured by the Chief Whip, Macmillan believed what he was told and this led him into trouble. The second was the Labour MP George Wigg, who nurtured an abiding interest in security matters and exploited this skilfully to put Macmillan's government on the rack. Wigg knew Profumo was not privy to high-grade secrets as a non-Cabinet minister and probably had not passed any of the tedious things he did know to Keeler. He was also aware of Ivanov's backdoor diplomacy. But Wigg did not let this stand in the way of a sustained and damaging attack which he had been planning as early as January 1963. One veteran Labour MP recalled, 'As the scandal developed, the vulture Wigg scented carrion.' Harold Wilson, the Labour leader, valued Wigg's expertise in this specialist area and went on to make him Cabinet security supremo. Wigg later conducted investigations of the Foreign Office, MoD and GCHQ in the late 1960s. Wilson knew how politically damaging a combination of security scandal and persistent press interest could be and was determined not to endure the same torments as Macmillan. However, Wigg's praetorian role in Wilson's first Cabinet was not popular with his ministerial colleagues.[59]

The Macmillan era was not, as many had expected, ended by the Profumo Affair. Macmillan received the final draft of the Denning report into the Profumo Affair on 16 September 1963 and was relieved to find himself largely exonerated. It was published on 23 September and queues formed to buy copies of what became a bestseller. But the report meandered and certainly did not get to the bottom of the security issues, nor did it deliver to the public the expected diet of salacious material. Instead it contented itself with a few censorious paragraphs about the 'perverted sex orgies' and 'activities of a vile and revolting nature' indulged in by Ward and his circle. On 24 September, a day after publication, Macmillan met with Iain Macleod, the Conservative Party Chairman. In the light of the general anti-climax from Denning, Macmillan had decided not resign, nor would there be an election in 1963. Everyone now presumed that he would lead the Conservatives into an election in 1964. However, two weeks later he was struck by prostate trouble and, on 8 October, underwent an operation for what he believed was cancer. The next day his resignation was announced, although in the event Macmillan soon recovered his health and could have carried on without difficulty.[60]

John F. Kennedy's end came the following month and was very different. He was brutally assassinated during a visit to Texas on Friday, 22 November 1963. In Britain there followed a spontaneous outpouring of grief on a scale unseen before or since at the time of a death of a foreign head of state. In retrospect, many have observed, perhaps unkindly, that the manner of his passing was somewhat of a piece with a period when the American presidency had itself approved a number of coups and assassination plots against foreign leaders, most obviously against Castro. It had also nodded its benign assent at similar work by others, not least the toppling of Diem and Nhu in Vietnam, only a month before. Heavily sanitised documents on these matters suggest there were other escapades which as yet remain hidden from public view. As Richard Bissell wisely observed, one of the reasons why democratic states should abstain from these sorts of activities, other than the obvious dictates of law and morality, is that their own leaders are themselves far more vulnerable than those in other sorts of states.[61]

With the Profumo Affair the era of revelation had arrived with a vengeance and some sensitive stories were beginning to emerge into the public domain. In 1963 and 1964 there were continued rumblings in the British press about secret British and American government subventions to the magazine *Encounter*. To try and deal with these charges its funding was transferred to an independent trust in 1964. The press had also begun to pick away at connections between CIA front organisations and centre and right-wing revisionist elements of the Labour Party in Britain. *Encounter* had consciously worked with the Hugh Gaitskell wing of the Labour Party. Anthony Crosland used the magazine as a key platform to develop his revisionist 'social democratic programme' which included support for NATO and British membership of the European Economic Community. When Harold Wilson formed the first Labour government for more than a decade in 1964 half a dozen of his ministers were regular *Encounter* writers.[62]

More about the extent of CIA activities inside Western democracies was revealed in 1967. At this point there were press revelations about Tom Braden's operations with labour groups and with the US National Student Association, the equivalent of the British National Union of Students. However, in January 1968 Richard Bissell believed that the damage was limited. In the United States, he noted, 'the public is not likely to be concerned by the penetration of overseas institutions, at least not nearly as much as by penetration of US institutions'. Ironically the 'blowing' of these operations had opened new opportunities; indeed there had been an increase in discreet enquiries about covert funding from public associations to an extent that had been 'embarrassing'. Formerly, foreign groups had presumed that American diplomats were short of funds, 'but now they all assume we have secret CIA money, and they ask for more help'. Meanwhile, Bissell argued, the American public had come to tolerate a degree of covert intervention as a mainstream element in foreign policy, and he added, 'We've come to accept the CIA, like sin.'[63]

Kennedy's Director of Central Intelligence, John McCone, was similarly resilient in the wake of the revelations about the CIA's National Student Association activities, insisting that the story had been somewhat distorted. He suggested that the initiative had come from the National Student Association to CIA officers who were former members of the organisation. Moreover, he insisted, it had been 'a very, very successful operation'. 'I have never been apologetic for one minute for the role,' he said, and went on to say that he felt that the government should have taken the same line. In his view the administration in Washington should have been bolder, and he asserted, 'We did it, and we'll do it again. We think it's a good idea.' The era of revelation had introduced awkward new complications and calculations, but it had not impeded the continued growth of secret service activity.[64]

More importantly, by the mid-1960s the CIA had become exactly what its name suggested, an 'Agency' alongside other agencies in Washington, rather than a mere secret service. It was no longer a subordinate service that supplied information to the institutions that made foreign policy, or that assisted at the margins with implementation. Instead it had become a policy-maker in its own right, alongside the State Department and the military. Symbolic of this change was the new seven-storey CIA headquarters building completed at a beautiful rural site at Langley in Virginia in 1962. This building had been the ambition of Allen Dulles since he had become director of central intelligence in 1953 and had taken almost a decade to realise. Prowling around the downtown Washington accommodation of the CIA in the early 1950s, Dulles had angrily pronounced it to be 'a damn pigsty'. The CIA's quarters at that time were certainly unattractive, consisting of a number of 'temporary' buildings on the Mall, including some alongside the Reflecting Pool dating back to 1917. During Washington's humid summers the malodorous effect of inadequate drains mixed with vapours from the nearby cafeteria earned the buildings the collective nickname 'Cockroach Alley'. By contrast the shiny new building at Langley delighted CIA personnel, not least because of the ample parking areas, a sought-after but almost unobtainable commodity in downtown Washington. Sadly for Allen Dulles, the Bay of Pigs fiasco had ensured his departure and in 1962 he was only able to show John F. Kennedy around the new building before making way for John McCone. Nevertheless, the headquarters was a powerful monument to the manner in which the CIA had moved alongside and was overtaking major policy-making departments in Washington. This was in striking contrast to SIS, which for all its occasional infelicities remained a 'service', subordinated to the Foreign Office.[65]

Although the CIA had become an independent player in Washington with an increasingly public persona, not everyone was comfortable with this change. In June 1961, in the wake of the Bay of Pigs, Kennedy had asked Arthur Schlesinger Jnr, his special assistant, to review the 'autonomous' position the CIA had reached in American government. Schlesinger was himself a former member of OSS and long-term CIA consultant. Although his findings conceded that on balance the CIA's record had been 'very good', he concluded that further débâcles could not be afforded. Moreover, the CIA's growing public profile was a problem, and he warned that it was beginning to be associated with unpleasant international events of which it was entirely innocent.

Schlesinger pointed the finger of blame at the State Department for missing the 'opportunity to seize firm control of CIA operations' and believed that these should have remained under the control of the Secretary of State. Instead, in 1950, the reverse had happened when Walter Bedell Smith had insisted on ending the subordination of the CIA's covert action arm to the State Department. This also reflected the fact that many ambassadors preferred not to know what was afoot. During the 1950s the CIA not only grew in size and power, it began to 'outstrip the State Department in the quality of its personnel', partly because it paid higher salaries and partly because Allen Dulles was vigorous in defending his staff against McCarthyite attacks. By the late 1950s the State Department was losing ground in traditional areas such as overt political reporting and 'even in the maintenance of overt diplomatic contacts'. This was disturbing and Schlesinger cautioned:

> For its part, CIA had developed a whole series of functions paralleling already existing functions of the State Department, and of the Defense Department as well. Today it has its own political desks and military staffs; it has in effect its own foreign service, it has (or has had) its own combat forces; it even has its own air force. Its annual budget is about [two] times that of the State Department. The contemporary CIA possesses many of the characteristics of a state within a state.

There were, he added, alarming questions which no one had yet begun to ponder. Domestically, the United States had not yet considered what sort of CIA was consistent with 'a free social order'. Meanwhile, overseas it was clear that CIA activity was stirring up 'much potential friction with friendly states'. Washington was being exposed to a multitude of embarrassments usually when the CIA was 'discovered recruiting agents or developing sources in a friendly country'. But no one had an overview of how many of these problems in friendly countries were currently being created by the CIA. Events at the Bay of Pigs, he said, showed that it was time for a fairly drastic rearrangement of the present intelligence set-up. But Schlesinger's words were not heeded.[66] Nor was he alone in his anxieties about the new role of the hidden hand as maker of, rather than servant of, American foreign policy. Clark Clifford, who served on the White House staff of four Presidents, and who knew more about the inner working of Washington than perhaps any other observer during the early Cold War, shared these anxieties. He echoed Schlesinger's words precisely when he described the CIA during this period as something which was growing into 'a government within a government'.[67]

Predictably, London was also concerned about these developments in Washington. Even the steeliest British advocates of a forward Cold War policy were unnerved by the recent work of the CIA, which they viewed as destabilising. Sir John Slessor, who together with Tedder had been one of the early advocates of using hidden-hand activities to fight the Cold War, now had reservations. Speaking about the challenges of 'Anglo-American Understanding' in the summer of 1966 he confessed to harbouring 'some genuine doubts'. These were the result of 'the Bay of Pigs and the U-2 affair, neither of which had done much to inspire confidence in American judgement', so now 'there was some mistrust of the CIA'. There was also a wider sense after the Cuban Missile Crisis that Britain was living in a world dominated by two superpowers in which its voice counted for less. This problem had been masked to some degree by the good working relationship between Macmillan and Kennedy which, while not always close, was effective and respectful. But with the assassination of Kennedy and the departure of Macmillan at the end of 1963, this vital personal link was gone and over the next decade the two countries would drift apart. Secret co-operation on nuclear weapons and intelligence, although areas of periodic anxiety and distrust, remained the hard core of an otherwise deteriorating relationship.[68]

'Behind the scenes of history'

The Automatic Waste Collection System processed 35 tons of classified paper every 24 hours and, during the first half decade, was fed a long list of unclassified but mysterious items, including a pair of ski boots, a washing machine motor, a pair of man's pants, a lady's bra and slip, a pencil sharpener and some .22 caliber bullets.

NSA internal history, September 1986[1]

The importance of hidden-hand activities during the Cold War will always be a matter of dispute, but what cannot be denied is their enormous size. Irrefutably, the secret aspects of government were also big government. A revolution in the nature of secret service, especially intelligence-collection, beginning with the outbreak of the Second World War, accelerated over the next half-century. The end result was intelligence and security organisms on an unimaginable scale. The intensely secret NSA observed that by 1980 the American cryptologic system was 'clearly a major industry', and by this point it was employing more postgraduates in fields such as mathematics and electronics than any other body, public or private. In a single day the NSA was producing more classified documents than a historian could reasonably expect to read in a lifetime.[2]

Most of these sorts of materials pertaining to the Cold War have been destroyed or remain closed, constituting what has famously been called the 'Missing Dimension' of history.[3] Some historians have dealt with the issue of vast secret service activities during the Cold War by simply not discussing them at all. The importance of codebreaking and cryptography in the Second World War is now established beyond any doubt, yet some magisterial studies of national security policy during the Truman administration do not pause for a second to consider the impact of these things on American post-war policy. Even the CIA often secures no more than a few passing references. To some degree this is understandable. Viewing the subject as being like a distant iceberg, with the immense bulk of its matter still dangerously submerged, some commentators have decided to steer well clear.[4] Only a minority of scholars has yet attempted to integrate secret service with international history.[5]

All contemporary historians who study aspects of the state share a quite unique experience, that of being dependent upon their governments for information. Few other fields of enquiry have this problem. Those working in areas as diverse as French literature or the biological sciences are masters of their subject, but contemporary historians are often the supplicants before the state. Serious-minded journalists repeatedly suggest that interviews offer a very worthwhile alternative approach to the problem of a government near-monopoly on historical raw materials. Yet the consensus remains that it is better to say less, supported by 'real' archival evidence, than say more constructed upon the shifting sands of oral testimony. This study has attempted to make use of the latest archival releases and to 'say it with documents'. But in the field of secret service, where not everything is written down, this approach has obvious limitations.[6]

Experienced practitioners of secret service, such as Edmond Taylor, occasionally pause to offer a warning to those who are addicted to archives. Taylor began his career as an American journalist covering the Middle East in the 1930s, frequently complaining about the manipulation of news and other hidden-hand activities by the 'professional scoundrels' of the British secret service. But by 1941 he had become a member of Donovan's fledgling secret service, which would become OSS, and found himself being trained in Britain as an 'apprentice scoundrel'. After a wartime OSS career and a spell doing propaganda in post-war Germany, he found himself working for C. D. Jackson on the Psychological Strategy Board or PSB in 1953. Taylor recalled what he termed the 'chronic Washington affliction' – crash planning sessions that went on into the night, which usually followed some new development on the world scene, such as the death of Stalin or the East Berlin riots. Initially he believed that these all-night sessions contained a reward of sorts, a feeling of being on the inside track of events and, in his words, the 'sense of initiation into the algebra of crisis'. But after a while the truth of the matter dawned on him:

> I gradually came to realise ... the feeling that one had at last got behind the scenes of history was to a large extent illusory. The staff of PSB ranked fairly highly in the Washington hierarchy of documentary security clearance, but, I soon discovered, above the nominal aristocracy of Top Secret, Cosmic or Q-Clearance holders there was an inner super-elite contemptuous of all classificatory ritualism, whose thoughts were so arcane that they were seldom committed to paper at all, at least not in any official form. As one of these Great Initiates revealed to me in a rare moment of confidence ... the US, like many other nations, has two levels of national policy, the exoteric and the

esoteric. The former found its expression in the papers of the NSC ... As to the esoteric policy my informant's lips were naturally sealed.

This is a dismal message for those who are convinced that the truth resides in the once highly classified National Security Council papers and in National Intelligence Estimates. There is much to suggest that even these top-secret papers are exactly in Taylor's former category, being rather predictable and designed for wide circulation among officials or even trusted political journalists and not always the inner stuff of a secret history.[7]

It will be a long time before we can achieve a confident summation of the importance of secret services during the Cold War. Stalin's foreign policy remains one of the most enduring puzzles. Many different interpretations of Soviet intentions were explored by the West during the Cold War, and George Kennan sometimes managed to express three contradictory and unresolved interpretations of Stalin's foreign policy in the space of a single paragraph. Was Stalin paranoid and defensive, a ruthless expansionist or simply a pragmatic Russian statesman in the old style? Which intelligence analysts successfully captured the reality of Stalin's foreign policy-making in their endless appreciations and estimates? Beatrice Heuser has argued that we will be able to pass a verdict on the success or failure of intelligence services in the West only when we know exactly what Stalin's intentions were: 'yet to this day it is still extraordinarily difficult to surmise Stalin's intentions at any time after the Second World War. Despite *glasnost*, and in spite of the Soviet campaign to till this virgin soil and to fill in the white spots of Soviet history, Soviet foreign policy and military archives have remained curiously impenetrable.' The situation remains little changed and the files of Stalin's Secretariat are still closed. Stalin, apparently, never permitted minutes to be taken during meetings with Ministers; but, even had minutes been taken, would they offer much in the way of extensive rationalisation or honest argument? It is entirely possible that an objective yardstick of Western intelligence on Stalin during the Cold War will always elude us.[8]

Soviet agents themselves have expressed views on these matters. George Blake, a Soviet agent inside SIS, has suggested that spying by both sides may have been a positive and helpful activity rather than a destabilising factor. Unlike Kim Philby, who offers little justification for his espionage, other than his impish aside that one does not look twice at an offer of recruitment from a first-class service, Blake advances a more substantial rationale. The intelligence effort of both sides was neither pointless nor wasteful. Instead of being a zero-sum game in which spies, and spying on spies, cancelled each other out, the collective intelligence effort by all sides may have lent a degree of mutual transparency at a time when international tensions were sometimes dangerously high. At a minimum, the intelligence services of East and West provided constant reassurance that neither side wanted all-out war as an objective, and that neither side was actively preparing for war. Arguably these were re-assurances which, if offered openly, would not have been believed. Curiously, Blake's argument has a resonance with the observations of George K. Young, with whom he served in SIS but whose political values he did not share. Young also insisted that, in an age when many had aban-doned their respect for honest dealing, the spy remained the last guardian of intellectual integrity. In their separate ways each argued that secret service offered the only hope of truth in the Cold War.[9]

Similar claims have been made for technical intelligence-gathering, especially for the U-2 spy-flight programme. In the 1950s eager politi-cians on the electoral hustings and arms-racing bureaucracies had com-bined to exploit the mythical 'bomber gap' and 'missile gap' for their own purposes. Secret service flying at 70,000 feet, it is often suggested, offered the accurate answers needed to counter these volatile lobbyists. The U-2 has been deliberately portrayed as the instrument which not only helped to detect the Soviet missiles in Cuba, but also gave Eisenhower the inner confidence to resist the worst arms-racing zealots. Had Khrushchev himself candidly asserted that the Soviet Union had no ICBMs in 1959, and that its missile programme was in deep trouble, no one would have believed him. Eisenhower's contemporaneous 'open skies' proposal for unrestricted photo-reconnaissance by all sides was the logical extension of the argument that the truth would set the policy-makers free from fear and mutual suspicion.[10]

In 1959 there was a flurry of high-level exchanges and visits between East and West. Macmillan visited Khrushchev in Moscow. Richard Nixon, the Vice President, followed and famously exchanged ideological banter with Khrushchev in a model kitchen at an exhibition of American consumerism. Then in September 1959 Khrushchev repaid the visit and came to the United States. There, Allen Dulles also engaged in some quips, suggesting to Khrushchev that he might already have seen some of his reports from time to time. Khrushchev responded brightly, 'I believe that we get the same reports, and probably from the same people'. Dulles pressed this to its logical conclusion, suggesting, 'Maybe we should pool our efforts.' Khrushchev enjoyed the joke, adding, 'We should buy our intelligence data together and save money – we'd have to pay the same people only once!'[11]

But neither aerial espionage nor human espionage was cost free, and serious damage could be done. Khrushchev's visits were building towards Macmillan's longed-for summit in Geneva scheduled for May 1960. But the vexed exchanges between Eisenhower and Khrushchev after the Gary Powers U-2 shoot-down led directly to the collapse of what most regarded as a promising meeting. This was not an isolated mishap, for the Buster Crabb Affair had cast a shadow over the Eden–Khrushchev meeting in 1956 and only Churchill's determination prevented the Khokhlov defection casting a shadow over the Geneva Conference of 1955. Espionage could create strategic as well as diplomatic crises. In 1962, during the Cuban Missile Crisis, two U-2 flights would bring the United States and the Soviet Union closer to the nuclear abyss than at any other moment in the twentieth century. More broadly, the British JIC feared that U-2 flights had combined with bellicose American statements about US superiority in arms to convince the Kremlin that the Soviet Union might soon be the victim of a pre-emptive American strike. If collection was hazardous, so were the potential purposes to which the resulting intelligence could be put. During the Cuban Missile Crisis the US Air Force used precisely this sort of information to argue that the United States was ahead and could carry out an attack on Cuba with impunity. Accurate intelligence could render the policy-maker free, but free to undertake what?

The Cold War encouraged not only an intelligence-gathering revolution, but also a remarkable expansion in special operations or covert action, including clandestine propaganda, that sought to change events in the world by means of the hidden hand. For both Britain and the United States these measures represented an attempt to escape restrictions. For the United States they were a way of eluding the problem of a muscle-bound superpower hemmed in by the restriction of increasingly stable deterrence and unable to make its vast military power pertinent. For Britain they often helped to fill the gap when there was simply not enough power, and were conjured into existence, more often than not, during awkward end-of-Empire struggles. In their different contexts, both London and Washington required these covert measures to maintain the liberal fiction that democratic states did not commit aggression against other democratic or popular regimes, especially ones that were small and weak.

More importantly, during the Cold War the secret services of the West were required to tunnel their way into the fabric of everyday domestic society and begin a process which emulated what their communist counterparts had been about for a long time. Willi Münzenberg had pioneered this very successfully for the Comintern in the 1920 and 1930s, persuading all manner of unwitting Western intellectuals to parade themselves on behalf of front organisations supporting Moscow's foreign policy. The Germans soon picked up on the act, employing the 1936 Olympics as a showcase not only for Germany, but also for fascism as a creed and a way of life. William Montagu-Pollock began the British effort in this area with the Cultural Relations Department in the 1940s, followed by IRD. In the 1950s Thomas Braden followed suit with the CIA's International Organisations Division. Some neophyte intellectuals, like André Malraux, assisted Münzenberg in the 1930s and then favoured Braden's activities in the 1950s. Once London and Washington had accepted that the Cold War was a competition between two ways of life, played out on every level of human activity, then arguably they had little choice but to follow the Soviet example and to use the hidden hand to address quite mundane domestic areas of Western existence. Secret services increasingly became managers of diverse and uneasy coalitions, using state–private networks in the hope of harnessing the power of civil society.[12]

Secret services therefore accelerated the transformation of the Cold War from an old-fashioned conflict between states into a subversive competition *between societies*. As Miles Copeland, one-time head of the CIA's London station, explained, by the 1950s the secret services of both the West and the Soviet bloc were covertly funding political parties, trade unions, student groups, writers, painters and even orchestras and ballet troupes, in an attempt to triumph in the competition between two different ways of life. This, in turn, required the secret services to address their own domestic populations as well as those overseas. Co-operation between right-wing British trade union leaders, MI5, the CIA and IRD to defeat the influence of the extreme left in labour politics is also now a matter of public record.[13] Most British officials, however, remained uncomfortable about intervention in domestic affairs, whether through the mundane issue of positive vetting or through the elaborate schemes of IRD. Only the British military were out of step with the rest of Whitehall on this subject and throughout the 1950s pressed for a more acerbic domestic Cold War to deal with what they saw as troublesome elements, including the problem of 'communism among teachers' in British schools.[14]

Operations with front organisations and foundations that traversed the international and the domestic scenes constituted some of the most innovative activities of the Cold War. Figures such as George Kennan are often revered as the intellectual giants of this conflict, but in time it may be Tom Braden who will prove to have offered the clearest vision of what the Cold War really meant. But hidden-hand activity on any scale within open societies was unlikely to remain hidden for very long and an era of revelations was bound to follow. Those international operations which stretched back into their own countries inevitably contained the seeds of their own destruction. In the decade between Profumo and Watergate, many of these activities were revealed, changing the landscape of Western secret service and helping to unleash a season of enquiry that culminated in the Church Committee hearings into the CIA in the mid-1970s.[15]

Throughout the early Cold War, Britain's contribution to the Anglo-American secret service partnership loomed larger in the field of intelligence-collection than in special operations or covert action. While the Cold War increasingly assumed many different forms, the eyes of policy-makers remained transfixed by the problem of weapons of mass destruction. Britain skilfully exploited its abilities in this realm, deploying a kind of 'intelligence power' that outlasted its military capability or commercial competitiveness. In the field of secret intelligence, perhaps more than any other, Britain was able to retain its place in the premier league. Intelligence co-operation, together with atomic co-operation, was the engine room that sustained London's desired close relationship with the United States.[16] It is unlikely that 'agreed estimates', even when they were approved jointly by Macmillan and Eisenhower, did much to encourage convergent policies. Privately, those making policy regarded these agreed estimates as a flawed compromise contrived for political reasons. Nevertheless, British premiers were pleased to discover that on a workaday basis intelligence power allowed them to 'punch above their weight' in international affairs. By the mid-1960s, with Britain hard pressed to sustain its defence commitments and, in Washington's eyes, 'making every possible effort' to avoid appearing to choose between its imperial and European roles, intelligence helped to redress the balance and allow it to be taken seriously in the corridors of Washington.[17]

Britain's use of secret service to extend and protect its relationship with the United States was at times an ambiguous process. During the 1950s, while Washington was beset by argument over the mythical 'bomber gap' and 'missile gap', London was arguably fixated with what might in retrospect be termed the 'vulnerability gap' that existed between the United States and Britain. American planners knew that if a military confrontation was going to occur between the United States and the Soviet Union then it would be better if it occurred soon, before American cities became vulnerable. There was little doubt in some minds in London that, if the Cold War was going to turn into a hot war, it might well result from some action in Washington, provoked by some unpredictable incident or accident. During the period before 1958, when atomic co-operation was limited, it was strategic intelligence discussions at the JIC level that offered London the clearest window on this alarming problem.

Liaison was valued by the United States for different reasons. Walter Bedell Smith had worried in the early 1950s about the preference of the CIA for covert action, rather than intelligence-gathering. After 1953 he was succeeded by Allen Dulles, a figure who, rather than worrying about this disturbing trend, embodied it. In the human intelligence field, liaison with its allies, principally Britain but also the revitalised German and Japanese services, freed the CIA to play other roles and gave it spare capacity for other activities. Prior to 1963, asserts one retired CIA officer, most CIA intelligence-gathering was 'carried out through liaison arrangements with foreign governments'. Moreover, 'maintenance of liaison became an end in itself against which independent collection operations were judged'.[18]

Intelligence played a vital role in cementing the Anglo-American alliance as a whole during the Cold War, a period when Britain was continually shifting towards a more subordinate position vis-à-vis the United States. Britain's intelligence contribution was important, helping to offset the growing post-war imbalance of the 'special relationship'. While Britain's intelligence-gathering capabilities declined relative to those of the United States after 1945, the rate of their relative decline was slower than that of other British capabilities.[19] This was certainly the view taken by Washington. In February 1968, on the eve of Prime Minister Harold Wilson's visit to Washington, Dean Rusk, the American Secretary of State, called for a review of the 'nature and worth of the "special relationship"'. The resulting report, produced by the Bureau of Intelligence and Research, was entitled 'What Now for Britain?' It stated bluntly that Wilson's visit came at a time when Britain had 'never cut a less impressive figure in Washington's eyes'. The Prime Minister's popularity was judged to be 'at an abysmal low', and the report added that 'his country has few friends and no future course that promises future success'. In the previous three months the Wilson government had been forced into currency devaluation through the failure of its economic policies, its attempts to enter Europe had received a brutal French rebuff, and it had announced a wholesale retreat from defence commitments East of Suez. President Lyndon Johnson had tried without success to persuade London to reverse these defence cuts on account of American burdens in Vietnam, prompting Washington to conclude that Britain had finally conceded 'its inability to remain a world power'. One recent acerbic press critic, it noted, had described the Anglo-American relationship as special now only in the sense that the relationship between a master and an old family retainer was special, 'with all that this implies about inequality, loyalty, permanence, and toleration of eccentricities'.

Surprisingly, and notwithstanding this catalogue of disasters and disappointments, the State Department dismissed these gloomy predictions, insisting that Britain remained a valued partner. There were still, it asserted, certain important features of alliance co-operation that remained genuinely 'quite special':

> At bottom the most concrete proof that the United States and the United Kingdom are each other's favoured partner is found in the fields of nuclear weaponry and intelligence. Each government provides the other with material and information that it makes available to no-one else . . .

There is a division of labor in certain geographic and functional fields, and on some areas and subjects, each nation is dependent for its intelligence mainly on the other ...

As Washington peered ahead into the 1970s, the British contribution remained valuable because of the related fields of intelligence and strategic weaponry. In both these fields, much of the British contribution was derived from its overseas territories, from its 'residual Empire', which provided not only invaluable political contacts but also a vast panoply of key airbases, naval installations and suitable sites for technical collection. Britain's far-flung dependencies and Commonwealth affiliates, American officials stated, provided 'an unrivalled network of ... facilities that served US foreign policy interests'. Around the globe, they continued, 'these installations provide valuable – in some cases indispensable – contributions to US security arrangements'.[20]

The reasons for the persistence of the Anglo–American intelligence relationship ran deeper than the mere availability of valuable real estate, convenient though that was. In the mid-twentieth century Britain and the United States alone shared the experience of managing genuinely global networks of power and influence. In the game of world dominance, whether formal or informal, whether expanding or contracting, both discovered that the role of the hidden hand was indispensable. Secret intelligence, clandestine operations, deception, black propaganda and domestic security activities were all central to this business. For Britain, these techniques were often a substitute for real power and part of the 'fancy footwork' of sustaining a world role with diminishing resources. Meanwhile, for the United States they provided some answers to curiously intractable problems of Third World management, especially among neutral countries. Additionally, and sometimes unintentionally, these techniques provided London and Washington with a mutual window upon each other's inner purposes, including what Edmond Taylor called the 'esoteric' policies which were rarely committed to paper. Accordingly, the hidden hand constituted a large part of what made the relationship between Britain and the United States not only special, but also quite unique.

Appendix

Note by John Drew for Chiefs of Staff and SIS, 24 Nov. 1949, DEFE 28/43

TOP SECRET
FUTURE DECEPTION POLICY

Conclusion

It appears that little thought has yet been given by the Governments of the Western powers to the political sabotage and destruction of Stalinism, but this it is suggested should become, without further delay, the main aim of Western policy.

In achieving this aim it is suggested a Deception organisation would have a very considerable part to play. More and more is gradually becoming known of organised opposition movements, not only in the recently Communised countries, but also in the Soviet Union itself. Recent purges of leading Communists in the satellite countries, and the prolonged postponement of the overdue congress of the Communist party of the Soviet Union (Bolshevik) must have forcibly reminded many prominent Soviet Communists of the bloody purges of the nineteen thirties. It may therefore be assumed that very few amongst the members of the Politbureau and amongst the high officials of the Soviet government will not be taking at this time very careful stock of their personal positions, and be considering means of ensuring their own survival should a grand purge start once more in Russia.

There is no doubt that the Soviet leaders are aware of factions within their own ranks, and of serious opposition to the Regime among the Soviet peoples. Their mutual distrusts, their anxiety for personal survival, and their essential capacity for cynical disloyalty towards their colleagues, make them vulnerable to 'planted' as well as to real suspicions concerning each other.

If used with great subtlety, and having access to all available information, it is strongly suggested that a Deception organisation could link, both directly and indirectly, various prominent Soviet Communists with various opposition movements and deviationists doctrines, and thereby provoke in due course such purges and oppressive measures in the Soviet Union as might lead to complete disruption of the Soviet governmental system and eventually to effective anti-Stalinist counter revolution.

24.11.49

Notes

ADDITIONAL ABBREVIATIONS USED IN REFERENCES

ACFE	Air Command Far East [British]
ADM	Admiralty
AFHQ	Allied Forces Headquarters
AIOC	Anglo-Iranian Oil Company
AIR	Air Ministry
AS/SS	Alphabetical Subseries, Subject Series at DDEL
AVIA	Ministry of Aviation
BAFB	Bollings Air Force Base, Washington DC
BDEE	*British Documents on End of Empire*
BJSM	British Joint Staff Mission in Washington
BL	British Library
BLPES	British Library of Political and Economic Science
BNS	Briefing Notes Subseries (NSC)
BOD	Bodleian Library
BRO	Brotherton Library
BT	Board of Trade
BUL	Birmingham University Library
CAB	Cabinet
CAFH	Center for Air Force History, Bollings Air Force Base
CCC	Churchill College, Cambridge
CDJP	C. D. Jackson Papers, DDEL
CDS	Chief of the Defence Staff [British]
CO	Colonial Office
COI	Central Office of Information
COIS	Commanding Officer Intelligence Staff Singapore
CWIHP	Cold War International History Project
DDEL	Dwight D. Eisenhower Library, Abilene, Kansas
DDRS	Declassified Document Reference System
DEFE	Ministry of Defence
DH	*Diplomatic History*
DMO	Director of Military Operations
DO	Dominions Office
D of I records	USAF Director of Intelligence records
DSD	Defence Signals Directorate [Australian]
ESI	*Espionage, Security and Intelligence in Britain*
FAOHP	Foreign Affairs Oral History Programme
FO	Foreign Office
FOIA	document obtained by Freedom of Information Act
FPS/FE	Forward Plans Section/Far East
FRUS	*Foreign Relations of the United States*
GAF	German Air Force
GEN	General Cabinet Committee
HIWRP	Hoover Institute on War, Revolution and Peace, Stanford

HL	Hartley Library, University of Southampton
HoC	House of Commons
HS	SOE records
HSTL	Harry S. Truman Library, Independence, Missouri
HUA	Harvard University Archives
ICCDS	Informal Commonwealth Conference of Defence Science
ID/LP	International Department of the Labour Party, NMLH
IJICI	*International Journal of Intelligence and Counter-Intelligence*
I&NS	*Intelligence and National Security*
INSCOM	Intelligence and Security Command [American]
IOLR	India Office Library and Records, Blackfriars, London
IWM	Imperial War Museum
J	*Journal*
JAIEC	Joint Atomic Energy Intelligence Committee [American]
JFKL	John F. Kennedy Library, Boston
LAB	Ministry of Labour
LC	Library of Congress
LHCMA	Liddell Hart Centre for Military Archives, King's College, London
LL	Lauinger Library, Georgetown University
MA	Military Attaché
MAF	Ministry of Agriculture and Fisheries
MEDC	Middle East Defence Committee [British]
MEF	Middle East Forces [British]
MI3	Military Intelligence section dealing with the Soviet Union
MI4	Military Intelligence section dealing with the Middle East
MI8	Military Intelligence section dealing with signals intelligence
MI16	Military Intelligence section dealing with science and technology
MML	MacArthur Memorial Library, Norfolk, Virginia
MoS	Ministry of Supply
NA	National Archives, Washington DC
NAM	National Army Museum, London
NC	Nuffield College
NMLH	National Museum of Labour History, Manchester
NY	New York
OAB, WNY	Operational Archives Branch, Washington Navy Yard
OR	Office of Intelligence and Research in the State Department
OSANA	Office of the Special Assistant for National Affairs
PM	Prime Minister
POF	President's Official File
PREM	Prime Minister's Office
PRO	Public Record Office, Kew, Surrey
PS	Private Secretary
PSF	President's Secretaries File
PSO	Principal Staff Officer
PS/SAS	Presidential Subseries, Special Assistant Series, DDEL
RG	Record Group of the US National Archives
SAC	US Air Force Strategic Air Command
SACMED	Supreme Allied Commander Mediterranean
SPDR	Strategic Plans Division Records
SRO	Scottish Records Office
TLHA	Tidewater Local History Archive
UEF	United European Federalists
UP	University Press
USIA	US Information Agency
USIS	US Information Service
USMHI	US Military History Institute, Carlisle Barracks
USNOA	US Navy Operational Archive, Navy Yard, Washington DC
WBS	Walter Bedell Smith Papers, DDEL
WHO	White House Office
WO	War Office

Historians of Secret Service and their Enemies

1. COS (45) 187th mtg, Confidential Annexe, 31 Jul. 1945, discussing JIC (45) 223 (0) Final, 'Use of Special Intelligence by Official Historians', CAB 76/36.
2. Cavendish-Bentinck min. on 3rd mtg of Combined Intelligence Priorities Committee, 15 Jul. 1944, C9682/9386/18, FO 371/39171.
3. Central Office Note 195, 27 Apr. 1945, HW 3/29; Special Order by Sir Edward Travis (GCHQ), 7 May 1945, ibid.
4. LSIB Meetings Summary No. 13, 18 Jul. 1945, WO 208/5126.
5. Guy Liddell (MI5) to FO, 27 Apr. 1945, N4806/346/G42, FO 371/48032; Sir David Petrie (MI5) to Sargent, 9 Jun. 1945, N6745/346/42G, ibid.
6. Now published as Hesketh, *Fortitude*.
7. COS (45) 187th mtg, Confidential Annexe, 31 Jul. 1945, discussing JIC (45) 223 (0) Final, 'Use of Special Intelligence by Official Historians', CAB 76/36; Conference between Adm. Rushbrooke and Adm. Thebaud in NID, 20 Jul. 1945, Records of the CNO, Box 4, RG 38.
8. Cornwall-Jones to Wingate (LCS), 13 Mar. 1946, DEFE 28/28; Dickenson (DFP) to Oak-Rhind (FPS/FE), 7 Nov. 1952, ibid.
9. Bower, *Perfect English Spy*, 366–7.
10. Butterfield, *History*, 196.
11. See the persuasive article by Gill, 'Re-asserting Control'.
12. See for example 'MI5 Thrills Historians by Opening Up its Files', *Sunday Times*, 19 May 1997.
13. Dean, 'Assault on the Mountain'; DoD 1998 report at http://www.fas.org/sgp/other-gov/dod_opsec.html. I am indebted to Stephen Aftergood for this reference.
14. Knight, 'Russian Archives', 325–37. For the best achievements see Andrew and Gordievsky, *KGB*; Andrew and Mitrokhin, *The Sword*.
15. Andrew, 'Whitehall, and Washington', 404; Rimmington, 'Secrecy and Democracy', 5.
16. Stafford, *Camp X*, 87–8.
17. Jakub, *Spies and Saboteurs*, 197.
18. See in particular Grose, *Operation Roll-Back*; Lucas, *Freedom's War*; Mitrovich, *Undermining the Kremlin*.
19. Lucas and Morris, 'Very British Crusade', 85–111.
20. Twigge and Scott, *Planning Armageddon*, 249.
21. Eisenhower to Swede, in Griffith, *Ike's Letters to a Friend*, 125. I am indebted to Saveria Mezzana for drawing this reference to my attention.
22. Kennan was responding to a document entitled 'OPC Projects Fiscal 1949–1950'. Kennan to Wisner, 6 Jan. 1949, Box 12, Records of the PPS, 1947–53, Lot Files 64 D 563, RG 59.
23. Lovett to Kennan, 29 Oct. 1948, Box 12, Records of the PPS, 1947–53, Lot Files 64 D 563, RG 59.
24. Geo L. King (OPC) to Bedell Smith, 25 Aug. 1950, Box 14, WBS, DDEL. On tangled CIA–OPC relations Darling, *Central Intelligence Agency*, 273–81, 303–11. CIA planning during the 1950s is described in Phillips, *Night Watch*, 56–60.
25. The manner in which this persisted in the 1970s is memorably surveyed in Dunn, *Politics of Threat*.
26. Entry for 26 Jun.–19 Aug. 1946, Montgomery diary, 175/1, IWM.
27. Deighton, 'Say It with Documents', 393–402; Mitrovich, *Undermining the Kremlin*, 177.

Chapter 1 *Fighting with the Russians*

1. Keat to MEF, 1 Oct. 1945, N15322/3955/38, FO 371/47954.
2. MA Warsaw to Ambassador, 1 Oct. 1945, N13520/3935/38, FO 371/47954; Ryan, 'Royal Navy,' PhD, 103.
3. Hopkirk, *Setting the East Ablaze*, 12–66.
4. Steveni, 'From Empire to Welfare State', TSS memoir, LHCMA.
5. Duncannson, 'Ho Chi Minh', 92–6.
6. Dorwart, *Conflict of Duty*; Jensen, *Army Surveillance*; Talbert, *Negative Intelligence*.
7. Smith, *Sharing Secrets*, 4–5.
8. Hauner, *India*, 23–86; Waddington, 'Ribbentrop', 7–34.
9. Thurlow, *Secret State*, 107–72; Kitchen, *British Policy*, 270–4.
10. Osborn, *Operation Pike*, 143–5; entry for 14 Jun. 1940, Cadogan diary, 1/9, CCC; Folly, 'British Government Attitudes', PhD, 23.
11. Rothwell, *Britain*, 79; Hinsley, *British Intelligence*, vol. 1, 433–5; Hinsley, 'British Intelligence and Barbarossa', 43–75; entry for 31 May 1941, Dilks (ed.), *Cadogan*.
12. Andrew and Gordievsky, *KGB*, 190–2.
13. Ibid., 211.
14. Ibid., 209–11; Hinsley, 'British Intelligence and Barbarossa', 43–76; Whaley, *Barbarossa*, 129; Rothwell, *Britain*, 80–1.

15. Smith, *Sharing Secrets*, 13–15

16. Bennett, *Behind the Battle*, 277–80; Boyd, *Hitler's Japanese Confidant*, 97–106.

17. Hinsley, *British Intelligence*, vol. 1, 199; Aldrich, *Intelligence and the War against Japan*, 250; Croft, 'Reminscences', 133–43. Some of the product, the Iscott traffic, can be seen in HW 17 in the PRO.

18. Smith, *Sharing Secrets*, 18–19, Aldrich, *Intelligence and the War against Japan*, 248–50.

19. Smith, *Sharing Secrets*, 42–4, 52.

20. Butler, *Mason-Mac*, 131–4; Kitchen, *British Policy*, 58–9.

21. Hill, *Go Spy the Land*, 125–9; HS 4/332, 351, 355.

22. Hazelton, 'Soviet Foreign Policy', PhD, 246.

23. Kitchen, *British Policy*, 98–9.

24. C in C Far East to WO, 11 Sept. 1941, WO 193/603; WO to COIS Singapore, 9 Dec. 1941, WO 193/607; C in C Far East to WO, 25 Dec. 1941, ibid.

25. Kitchen, *British Policy*, 58–62; Mandelstam, *From the Red Army*, 147–8.

26. Memo, 1942, enclosed in TSS, 'Reminiscences of Four Years with the NKVD', Sept. 1941–May 1945', p. 145, File 1, Hill papers, HIWRP.

27. SOE Russian Section War Diary, 1942–4, HS 7/278; Mandelstam, *From the Red Army*, 121–35, 145; private information.

28. Erickson, *Road to Stalingrad*, 374.

29. Ryan, 'Royal Navy', PhD, 95–7.

30. MI8 War Diary, 1940–42, WO 165/38; Smith, *Sharing Secrets*, 37, 51, 57, 81, 100–1, 111.

31. Smith, *Sharing Secrets*, 31–5.

32. Aldrich, *Intelligence and the War against Japan*, 142–4, 178–84.

33. Smith, *Sharing Secrets*, 140–1; Cave Brown, *Wild Bill*, 418–25.

34. Warner min., 9 Apr. 1942, N18233/343/38, FO 371/32955; Wilson min. 11 Sept. 1942, N4666/343/38, ibid.

35. Smith, *Sharing Secrets*, 144–5.

36. Hinsley, *British Intelligence*, vol. 2, 624–5; Mulligan, 'Spies', 235–60; Smith, *Sharing Secrets*, 154–5. The conspiratorial version of these events, and others, is offered in Read and Fisher, *Operation Lucy*, 162.

37. Kitchen, *British Policy*, 171–3; Smith, *Sharing Secrets*, 166–7, 180–1, 207.

38. COS (44) 49th mtg (9), 16 Feb. 1944, N1829/26/38, FO 371/43284; Warner min., 17 Feb. 1944, ibid.; Cavendish-Bentinck min., 23 Feb. 1944, ibid.

39. Clark-Kerr to FO, 25 Sept. 1944, PREM 3/398/1.

40. Thorne, *Allies of a Kind*, 7–11, 167; Thorne, *Issue of War*, 27–32, 33, 124, 144, 169–72.

41. Folly, 'British Government Attitudes', PhD, 98.

42. Smith, *Sharing Secrets*, 201.

43. 'German Naval "Y" Service Reports on Russian Units in Northern Waters, 1/12–26/12/44', ADM 223/6. I am indebted to Joseph P. Ryan for this reference.

44. See the intercept – C in C GAF Ops IA to C in C Armed Forces SE Luft., 11. Jun. 1942, AIR 40/1989; AI3(F) 1946, 'German Intelligence Work on the Russian AF OB', AIR 40/2597.

45. Chapter VIII, 'The Russian Liaison', HW 3/101.

46. MI3 min., 29 Jun. 1945, WO 208/1862.

47. 'PWE Summaries of Russian Propaganda on Europe' and Allen min., 7 Jun. 1944, C7278/7278/62, FO 371/39037.

48. I am indebted to Christopher Hazelton for this information.

49. Gusev to Eden, 8 Jun. 1944, N3523/1737/38, FO 371/43399; Andrew and Gordievsky, *KGB*, 247–9, 253–4.

50. Smith, *Sharing Secrets*, 211.

51. Cave Brown, *Wild Bill*, 674–7; Smith, *Shadow Warriors*, 380–2.

52. Ryan, 'Royal Navy', PhD, 175; Smith, *Sharing Secrets*, 238–9, 243.

53. I am most grateful to Peter Hennessy for sight of GEN 183/1, 29 May 1947 and appendix 'Russian and Communist Espionage'. Watt, 'King'.

54. Petrie to Maxwell, 6 Jul. 1942, and Hollis to Petrie, 15 Jun. 1942, reproduced in Kerr, 'Roger Hollis'. Masters, *The Man Who Was 'M'*, 169–84; Hinsley and Simkins, *British Intelligence*, vol. 4, 283–94.

55. Clark-Kerr presentation to High Commissioners, 3 Dec.1942, DO 121/12.

56. Clark-Kerr to Eden, 12 Nov. 1943, N6739/22/38, FO 371/36926.

Chapter 2 *A Cold War in Whitehall*

1. Eden mins. 23 Aug. 1944, N5126/36/38, FO 371/43306.

2. Kitchen, *British Policy*, 135–7; Alanbrooke diary in Bryant, *Triumph*, 242.

3. Smith, *Sharing Secrets*, 178–9.
4. Cadogan quoted in Folly, 'British Government Attitudes', PhD, 32.
5. Hauner, *India*, 324–51; entry for 13 Nov. 1940, Dilks (ed.), *Cadogan*.
6. Hinsley, *British Intelligence*, vol. 1, 481–3.
7. Hyde, *I Believed*, 126. For a superb account of the development of the co-operation school see Folly, 'British Government Attitudes', PhD, 6 ff.
8. Warner min., 4 Nov. 1942, 1742/70 FO 371/31595.
9. Boyle, *American–Soviet Relations*, 37.
10. ARAGS min., 27 Jul. 1943, N4253/22/38, FO 371/36925; mins by Warner, 28 Jul. 1943, Sargent, 28 Jul. 1943, Eden, 28 Jul. 1943, ibid.; entry for 6 Oct. 1943, Dilks (ed.), *Cadogan*.
11. Tolstoy, *Victims of Yalta*, 428–31; Charmley, *Churchill: End of Glory*, 467–73; de Mowbray, 'Soviet Deception', 16–24; Lewis, *Changing Direction*, 127–43, 359–69.
12. 'Annual Report, Soviet Union', 1944, N4455/4455/38, FO 371/56883.
13. Rothwell, *Britain*, 1–20; Ross, *Foreign Office*, 3–17.
14. Cadogan min., 20 Feb. 1942, N939/5/38, FO 371/32876.
15. Kitchen, *British Policy*, 65.
16. Warner min., 3 Dec. 1941, N7081/3/38, FO 371/29501; Cavendish-Bentinck min., 4 Dec. 1941, ibid., quoted in Folly, 'British Government Attitudes', PhD, 75.
17. Aldrich, *Intelligence and the War against Japan*, 94.
18. Beddington, 'My Life', TSS memoir, 244, LHCMA.
19. Philby, *Silent War*, 68.
20. Ross, 'Foreign Office Attitudes', 525.
21. WP (42) 480, 'Post War Atlantic Bases', 22 Oct. 1942, CAB 66/30; MSC (42) 3, PHHP/MSC/3, 'Post War Strategic Requirements in the Middle East', 11 Dec. 1942, L/WS/1/1341, IOLR; Jebb to Cadogan, 12 May 1943, U2235/2231/70, FO 371/35449.
22. Lewis, *Changing Direction*, 44–54.
23. Jebb min., 19 Feb. 1944, U1731/748/70, FO 371/40740.
24. O'Malley to FO, 30 Apr. 1943, U2011/58/72, FO 371/35261; mins. by Jebb, 10 May, Strang, 29 May, and Cadogan, 4 Jun. 1943, ibid.
25. PHP (44) 13 (0) Final, 'Effect of Soviet Policy on British Strategic Interests', 6 Jun. 1944, CAB 81/45, which underwent many revisions. See also Gorst, 'British Military Planning', 91–108.
26. JIC (44) 105 (0) Final, 'Soviet Policy after the War', 20 Mar. 1944, CAB 81/121.
27. Lewis, *Changing Direction*, 98–125.
28. Jebb min., 15 Jun. 1944, U6804/748/70, FO 371/40741A; Jebb min. 18 Jul. 1944, ibid.
29. Cavendish-Bentinck min., U6254/748/70, FO 371/40741A.
30. Cavendish-Bentinck mins, 16 and 18 Jun. 1944, U6804/748/70, FO 371/40741A.
31. PHP (44) 17 (0) (Final), 'Security in Western Europe and the North Atlantic', 20 Jul. 1944, U6792/748/70, FO 371/40741A; Folly, 'British Government Attitudes', PhD, 238.
32. Warner min., 24 Jul. 1944, U6793/748/70, FO 371/40741A.
33. Jebb min., 28 Jul. 1944, U6792/748/70, FO 371/40741A.
34. Ward, Warner and Eden mins, 28–29 Aug. 1944, C11955/146/18, FO 371/39080; Rothwell, *Britain*, 120–2.
35. Min. on PHPS, n.d., U6770/573/70, FO 371/40736.
36. Ward min., 15 Aug. 1944, N5792/748/70, FO 371/43306. See also Gorst, 'British Military Planning', 91–108.
37. Sargent to Eden, 18 Aug. 1944, N5126/36/38, FO 371/43306; Eden mins, 23 and 25 Aug. 1944, ibid.
38. Cavendish-Bentinck min., 31 Jul. 1944, U6793/748/70, FO 371/40741A.
39. JIC (44) 366 (0) (Final), 22 Aug. 1944, CAB 81/124; Sloan min., 15 Aug. 1944, U6875/748/70, FO 371/40741A; Davies to Cornwall Jones, 30 Aug. 1944, CAB 122/1566.
40. Lewis, *Changing Direction*, 124–5; Hinsley, *British Intelligence*, vol. 1, 296–7; Wark, 'Failure of FOES', 499–512.
41. Smith, *Sharing Secrets*, 206; Sargent to Eden, 30 Aug. 1944, N5126, FO 371/43306; Wilson min., 1 Sept. 1944, N6214, ibid.
42. Wilson min., 24 Sept. 1944, N6214/36/38, FO 371/43306; Eden min., 26 Sept. 1944, ibid.
43. Eden meeting with COS, 4 Oct. 1944, N6177/183/38, FO 371/43336; COS (44) 346th mtg (13) Confidential Annexe, 24 Oct. 1944, CAB 79/82. Davies to Cornwall Jones, 17 Oct. and 25 Nov. 1944, CAB 122/1566, and FO 371/39080, passim.
44. Lewis, *Changing Direction*, 135; Manne, *Petrov*, 180–2; Oleg Tsarev presentation on the KGB and the early Cold War, Sept. 1999, University of Oxford.
45. Smith, *Sharing Secrets*, 187.

46. JIC (44) 467 (0), 'Russia's Strategic Interest and Intentions from the Point of View of her Security', N678/20/38, FO 371/47860; JIC (45) 163 (0) Revised Final, 'Relations with the Russians', 23 May 1946, CAB 81/129.

47. A careful account is offered in the second edition of Lewis, *Changing Direction*, ch. 1.

48. *Guardian*, 2 Oct. 1998. I am indebted to Gary Rawnsley for this reference. Operation Unthinkable, 22 May 1945 (Final), CAB 120/691.

49. PM to Ismay, 10 Jun. 1945, CAB 120/691; Bryant, *Triumph*, 469–70; Lewis, *Changing Direction*, 242–3. For Churchill and Truman on this see Bryden, *Best Kept Secret*, 262–4.

50. Ryan, *Bridge Too Far*, 80–5, 137–40.

51. Entry for 23 Aug. 1950, Bright-Holmes (ed.), *Like It Was*; Deighton, *Impossible Peace*, 14–35; Sharp, *Zonal Division*, 146.

52. Rose min., 30 Dec. 1942, R8820/216/G, FO 371/33154.

53. Rothwell, *Britain*, 163, 177.

54. Cavendish-Bentinck min., 7 Aug. 1944, Pol/44/144, FO 954; Greenwood to Eden, 26 Aug. 1944, Pol/44/180, FO 954.

55. O'Malley to Sargent, 22 May 1945, N6645/165/G, FO 371/47882.

56. JIC (45) 167 (0), 19 May 1945, CAB 79/34.

57. O'Malley to Sargent, 22 May 1945, N6645/165/G, FO 371/47882; Eden, *Reckoning*, 527.

58. Entries for 17 and 22 Jul. 1945, Dilks (ed.), *Cadogan*.

59. Entry for 24 Jul. 1945, TSS memoir, Box 2, Donnelly papers, MHI.

60. Heuser, 'Stalin', 18–20.

61. Folly, 'British Government Attitudes', PhD, 175; entry for 13 Jan. 1942, Pimlott (ed.), *Dalton Diary*. Arthur Tedder had similar experiences when he accompanied Churchill to Moscow in Aug. 1942. At an interminable dinner on the second evening he managed to get 'on hugging terms with no. 1 Gestapo Chief Beria, who was very drunk', Kitchen, *British Policy*, 135–7.

62. Churchill to Eden, 18 Mar. 1943, FO 954/26A, microfilm copy, BRO.

63. Bullock, *Bevin*, 493; E. A. Lightner, Oral History, 15–26, HSTL; Deighton, *Impossible Peace*, 47–8, 277.

Chapter 3 *Secret Service at the War's End: SIS and the CIA*

1. Entry for 24 Nov. 1944, Dilks (ed.), *Cadogan*.

2. Smith, *Sharing Secrets*, ix.

3. Dening to FO, 12 Feb. 1945, F746/127/61, FO 371/46325. See also Boyle, 'Reversion to Isolationism', 179–83.

4. Admiral Rushbrooke (DNI 1942–6) in ADM 223/297.

5. Stafford, *Churchill*, 302–11.

6. Lewis, *Changing Direction*, 178–241.

7. Slessor min., 16 Jul. 1945, AIR 2/12027.

8. JIC (45) 265 (0) Final, 'Post-War Organisation of Intelligence', 7 Sept. 1945, CAB 81/130; DO (47) 44, 22 May 1947, CAB 21/1800; Aldrich, 'Secret Intelligence for a Post-War World', 15–16.

9. Entries for 29 Nov. 1939 and 25 May 1940, Dilks (ed.), *Cadogan*; Andrew, *Secret Service*, 477; Cecil, 'Cambridge Comintern', 179.

10. Steveni, 'From Empire to Welfare State', TSS memoir, LHCMA.

11. Reilly's recollections reproduced in Andrew and Aldrich (eds), 'Intelligence Services in World War II', 133; and private information. For contrasting views of wartime SIS, see Cecil, '"C"'s War', and Harrison, 'More Thoughts'. Harrison is more convincing.

12. Hinsley and Simkins, *British Intelligence*, vol. 4, 134–48.

13. Philby, *Silent War*, 68. Also Ferris, 'Broadway', 442.

14. Cecil, 'Cambridge Comintern', 180–1.

15. Davies, 'SIS', 86–8; Cavendish, *Inside Intelligence*, 39–40.

16. Entry for 26 Aug. 1948, Bright-Holmes (ed.), *Like It Was*. On Steptoe, see Aldrich, *Intelligence and the War against Japan*, 29–30; Wasserstein, *Secret War*, 198, 213.

17. M.I.6/203/1353, 'Minutes of M.I.6 Liaison Meeting No. 22 Held at the War Office Room 218, at 1500 Hrs, 4 Dec. 1947', *ESI*, 1.3.

18. Appendix A to MI6 Liaisons Meeting 19, 4 Sept. 1947, MI6/206/1138, WO 208/4749.

19. Entry for 18 Jul. 1948, Bright-Holmes (ed.), *Like It Was*.

20. MEDC to COS, CCL/52, 23 Aug. 1945, E6566/1630/65, FO 371/45272; JIC (48) 60 (Revised Final), 'Review of Intelligence Organisation in the Middle East', 12 Nov. 1948, L/WS/1/1051, IOLR.

21. Stafford, *Britain and the European Resistance*, 56–7; Harrison, 'British Subversion', 340.

22. Dorril, *MI6*, 27–8; Cecil, '"C"'s War', 179–89.

23. Andrew, *Secret Service*, 476–7; Thompson, *War behind Enemy Lines*, 417; Aldrich, *Intelligence and the War against Japan*, 184.

24. Entry for 24 Nov. 1944, Dilks (ed.), *Cadogan*.

25. I am most grateful to Jim Siddeley for drawing my attention to this episode.

26. Eden to Churchill, PM 44/716, 23 Nov. 1944, AP20/11/726, Avon Papers, BUL; Churchill to Eden, 25 Nov. 1944, Char 20/153, CCC; Stafford, *Churchill*, 308.

27. CD to Cadogan, 19 Jun. 1945, and Sargent to CD, 3 Feb. 1945, R1628/1628/21G, FO 371/48496; Kitchen, *British Policy*, 62

28. Killearn to Cavendish-Bentinck, 8 Jun. 1945, E4569/1630/G65, FO 371/45272; Cavendish-Bentinck min., 12 Jun. 1945, ibid.; SOE Middle East Report, 1946, p. 3, HS 7/285; Aldrich, 'Unquiet', 201.

29. Aldrich, 'Unquiet', 200; Davies, 'Special Operations', 55–76.

30. McCreevy to Cabinet Office, 26 Oct. 1945, and Hankey min., 28 Oct. 1945, C7716/72/G3, FO 371/46604; Mack to Troutbeck, 13 Dec. 1945, C9727/72/G3, ibid.

31. Starbird to Hull, 'Intelligence Foray into Czechoslovakia', 20 Feb. 1946, 350.05.TS, Box 75, P&O files, RG 319; ACIGS (O) to DNI, 2 Oct. 1945, WO 193/637A; SOE Germany Section History, 1946, HS 7/147.

32. Wilson (for Warner) to Sporborg, 14 May 1945, N4771/265/G, FO 371/47710.

33. COS (45) 304, 'Evaluation of lessons learned', memo by Gubbins, 2 May 1945, AIR 20/7958; COS (45) 123rd mtg, 10 May 1945, ibid.; COS (45) 106, 'Value of SOE Operations', memo by SHAEF, 18 Jul. 1945, ibid.; COS (45) 665 (0), 'Value of SOE Operations', memo by SACMED, 18 Nov. 1945, ibid.; COS (45) 664 (0), 'Report on SOE Operations', C in Cs ME, 17 Nov. 1945, ibid.

34. Slessor to Grigg, 13 Mar. 1945, AIR 23/874.

35. Mountbatten to Ismay, 20 Aug. 1945, CAB 127/25.

36. Ismay to Attlee, 14 and 27 Aug. 1945, CAB 120/827; Attlee min., 27 Aug. 1945, ibid.; Foot, *SOE, 1940–6*, 245.

37. Bevin to Attlee, PM/45/8, 21 Aug. 1945, PREM 8/107; Rowan min., 23 Aug. 1945, ibid.; Foot, *SOE in France*, 443.

38. COS (46) 9th mtg (6), 17 Jan. 1946, L/WS/1/970, IOLR; entry for 23 Jan. 1946, Alanbrooke diary, LHCMA.

39. COS (46) 12th mtg (1), 23 Jan. 1946, AIR 19/816.

40. Davies, 'From Special Operations', 55–76; Smiley, *Irregular Regular*, 188–9; private information. By 1947 SIS also had a War Plans section, which had acquired some SOE officers such as David Smiley, who liaised with Brian Franks, the Adjutant of the now territorialised SAS.

41. Appendix B, 'Draft Charter of the JIC (Far East)', 5 Jan. 1948, L/WS/1/1050, IOLR.

42. Greene, 'Security in Room 51', *Sunday Times*, 14 Jul. 1963, quoted in Sherry, *Greene*, vol. 2, 490.

43. *OSS*, starring Alan Ladd, Paramount 1946; Andrew, *President's Eyes Only*, 159–61.

44. Hoover to Clark, 29 Aug. 1945, *FRUS, 1945–50, Emergence*, 24–5; Tam to Hoover, ibid., 27–30.

45. Meeting between Byrnes, Patterson and Forrestal, 16 Oct. 1945 *FRUS, 1945–50, Emergence*, 63–5 (see also 109); Andrew, *Secret Service*, 491–2.

46. Summary of SSU Activities during Nov. 1945, File 2814, Box 201, Entry 146, RG 226; Covering Report for SSU Mission to Great Britain by Col. John A. Bross, 7 Dec. 1945, ibid.

47. Magruder to Quesada (head of A-2), 7 Dec. 1945, 'Special Reports from British Intelligence', USAF D of I records, File 1-200, Box 37, RG 341.

48. SSU Mission to Great Britain, Progress Report, 1–31 Dec. 1945, File 2814, Box 201, Entry 146, RG 226.

49. Philby to Scott (X-2), 29 Apr. 1946, File 779, Box 63, Entry 171A, RG 226.

50. US JIC memo, 'Exchange of Intelligence Estimates and Evaluation Thereof between the US and the British JICs', 25 Sept. 1946, Reel 7, Entry 190 (M1642), RG 226.

51. JIC (47) 42 (0) Final and JIC (48) 26 (0) Final, 091 Russia TS, Box 12, RG 319.

52. JIC memo 224, 12 Jul. 1946, Reel 7, Entry 190 (M1642), RG 226; British JIC Washington, Paper 77, 'Short Term Intentions of the Soviet Union in Palestine', 13 Feb. 1948, 21000, Box 40, D of I records, RG 341.

53. JIC 77th mtg, 13 Jan. 1949, CCS 334 JIC (5–27–48), RG 218.

54. JIC 183rd mtg, 14 Apr. 1949, CCS 334 JIC (5–27–48), RG 218.

55. In the autumn of 1947, Vilhelm Evang, the young Chief of the fledgling Norwegian service, travelled to Germany and Britain to conclude agreements with the British JIB and also SIS. Then in Nov. 1947 he travelled to Washington for agreements with the newly established CIA. Riste, *Norwegian Intelligence Service*, 11.

56. Survey Group, 'Interim Report No. 2: Relations between Secret Operations and Secret Intelligence', 13 May 1948, *FRUS, 1945–50, Emergence,* 683.

57. Kennan to Lovett and Marshall, 19 May 1948, *FRUS 1945–50, Emergence,* 684. See also Miscamble, *Kennan*, 203–5.

58. Cf. pp. 635.

59. Pforzheimer interview, quoted in Berger, AFSC Study, 'Use of Covert Paramilitary Activity', 16.

60. Howe to Armstrong, 8 Sept. 1949, *FRUS, 1945–50, Emergence,* 1010; Andrew, *President's Eyes Only,* 183–4.

Chapter 4 *MI5: Defectors, Spy-trials and Subversion*

1. Hollis to Tizard, 19 Feb. 1948, DEFE 11/50.

2. Entry for 6.00 p.m., 13 Aug, 1943, Cadogan diary, 1/12, CCC; Bower, *Perfect English Spy,* 66–7. On Venona see the important essay by Andrew, 'Venona Secret', 203–25.

3. WP (43) 109, 'Communist Party of Great Britain', 13 Mar. 1943, CAB 65/37; WP (44) 202, 'The Trotskyist Movement in Great Britain', memo by the Home Secretary, 13 Apr. 1944, N2417/2417/38, FO 371/43410.

4. Entry for 25 Apr. 1942, MSS 59398, Harvey diary, BL; entry for 30 Sept. 1942, Alanbrooke diary, 5, LHCMA.

5. Driberg to Eden and PostMaster General, 9 Jul. 1944, C8021/8021/55, FO 371/39526; Eden to Driberg, ibid.

6. Eden to Churchill, 6 Feb. 1944, PM 44/45, AP20/11/45, Avon Papers, BUL.

7. Entries for 19 and 22 Nov. 1944, Alanbrooke diary, 9, LHCMA; 24 Oct. 1944, Cadogan diary, 1/13, CCC; Tangye, *Way to Minack,* 142–3.

8. *The Times,* 5 June 1945, quoted in Morgan, *Labour in Power,* 38, and Gilbert, *Never Despair,* 32–5; Colville, *Fringes of Power,* 612.

9. Sir Edward Bridges reviewed the salaries of the heads of the secret services in the summer of 1951 and his salary then went up to £4,000, Padmore (WO) to Turner (T), 8 Jun. 1951, Sillitoe's Personal File, WO 335/6.

10. Entries for 8, 9, 14, 19 Nov. 1945, Cadogan diary, CCC; Browning to Penney, 19 Nov. 1945, Penney Papers, 5/33, LHCMA.

11. Jones, *Reflections,* 21; Sillitoe, *Cloak without Dagger,* xiv.

12. Andrew, *Secret Service,* 489.

13. Aldrich, 'Secret Intelligence for a Post-War World', 32–3.

14. Sir David Petrie (MI5) to Sargent, 9 Jun. 1945, N6745/346/42G, FO 371/48032.

15. 'The Soviet campaign against Britain in Germany', 27 Jul. 1946, N10929/5769/, FO 371/56885.

16. Mins by Lotte, 2 Apr. 1944, and Russell, 5 Apr. 1944, N2672/2093/38, FO 371/43407.

17. Bly, *Communism,* 124–5.

18. Trepper, *Great Game,* 322–6; Deacon, *C,* 58–9.

19. SIME Report No. 12, 'Alexander Rado', 13 Jan. 1945, N16622/16622/38, FO 371/48006. Also Aldrich, 'Soviet Intelligence', 196–217. I am indebted to Hugh Dovey for some SIME details.

20. This is meticulously reconstructed in Bryden, *Best Kept Secret,* 270–7.

21. Ibid.; Whitaker and Marcuse, *Cold War,* 30–2.

22. Whitaker and Marcuse, *Cold War,* 43–8; Boyle, *Climate,* 287–90; Hyde, *Atom Bomb Spies,* 36.

23. Whitaker and Marcuse, *Cold War,* 43–8.

24. Herken, *Winning Weapon,* 130–3, 137–9; Whitaker and Marcuse, *Cold War,* 58–9.

25. Dixon mins, 22 Aug. and 18 Sept. 1946, N1221G/10772/38, FO 371/56912; Warner to Lockhart, 2 Sept. 1946, ibid.

26. Petersen to FO, 4 Aug. 1946, N10036/71/38, FO 371/56750: Tass Bulletin No. 7556, 'The Gouzenkou Case in Canada: The Poison Which Did Not Work', N10057/71/38, ibid.

27. Whitaker and Marcuse, *Cold War,* 93–9.

28. Ward min., 6 Jun. 1946, N7080/605/38, FO 371/56833; Hankey min., 30 Jun. 1946, N10049/605/38, ibid.

29. JIC (46) 70 (0) (Final), 'The Spread of Communism throughout the World and the Extent of its Direction from Moscow', 23 Sept. 1946, CAB 81/133; JIC (46) 110 (0) (Final), 'Organisation of the Soviet Intelligence Services', 26 Mar. 1947, CAB 81/134.

30. Morrison to Attlee, 28 Nov. 1946, N12572/10772/38, FO 371/59913; Hankey min., 13 Aug. 1946, N9460/605/38, FO 371/56834; JIC (47) 13 (0), which became DO 47 (25), 'Acquisition of Technical Information by a Certain Power', CAB 131/4.

31. Entry for 26 Jun.–19 Aug. 1946, Montgomery diary, 175/1, IWM; Tedder to Montgomery, 10 Sept. 1946, 175/31, ibid.

32. Aronsen, 'Peace, Order and Good Government', 360–1; MI5 Report, 'Security in the Dominions', Appendix to JIC (48) 127 (Final) Guard, 17 Dec. 1948, L/WS/1/1074, IOLR.

33. McKnight, *Australia's Spies,* 10–11.

34. CCW (45) 66 Final, 'Chemical Warfare Research in the Tropics', 7 Nov. 1945, L/WS/1/989, IOLR; ICCDS 17 (Final), 'Informal Commonwealth Conference of Defence Science', 4 Jul. 1946, L/WS/1/992, IOLR.

35. Sillitoe (MI5) to JIC, 11 Jan. 1945, CAB 176/14.

36. Entry for 8 Jul. 1947, Montgomery diary, 180/34, IWM.

37. Andrew, 'Venona Secret', 209–13.

38. Hillenkoetter, 'Memorandum for the President', 27 Jan. 1948, HSTL, quoted in Cain, 'Missiles and Mistrust', 13; Manne, *Petrov*, 180–1.

39. Entry for 25 Apr. 1946, Alanbrooke diary, LHCMA.

40. Andrew, 'Australian Intelligence Community', 127–9; Sillitoe, *Cloak without Dagger*, 112; McKnight, *Australia's Spies*, 10–11; MI5 Report, 'Security in the Dominions', Appendix to JIC (48) 127 (Final) Guard, 17 Dec. 1948, L/WS/1/1074, IOLR.

41. McKnight, *Australia's Spies*, 19–22.

42. Andrew, 'Venona Secret', 217; McKnight, *Australia's Spies*, 30–1, 49–50.

43. Attlee to Truman, 4 Apr. 1949, Box 170, PSF Subject File, HSTL.

44. COS (49) 130th mtg, 17 Sept. 1949, DEFE 4/24.

45. 'Note on possible measures to be taken with India and Pakistan', 29 Oct. 1948, L/WS/1/1214, IOLR. The Secretary's Standard Files are now DEFE 32.

46. JIC (47) 63rd mtg (3) and Annexe, 19 Sept. 1947, L/WS/1/1046, IOLR.

47. JIC (49) 70th mtg, 14 Jul. 1949, L/WS/1/1051, IOLR.

48. MI5 Report, 'Security in the Dominions', Appendix to JIC (48) 127 (Final) Guard, 17 Dec. 1948, L/WS/1/1074, IOLR

49. Bevin to Attlee, 9 Nov 1946, PM 46/173, CAB 21/1920; Attlee to Bevin, 11 Nov. 1946, ibid.

50. DO (47) 25, 'Acquisition of Technical Information by a Certain Power', 13 Mar. 1947 (based on JIC (47) 30 (0) Final), CAB 131/4.

51. DO (47) 9th (2), Confidential Annexe, 26 Mar. 1947, discussing DO (47) 25, CAB 21/2554.

52. Hennessy and Brownfeld, 'Security Purge', 965–7.

53. Hansard, HC Debs., 15 Mar. 1948, 1703–8.

54. GEN 183/1, 29 May 1947 and appendix 'Russian and Communist Espionage'; GEN 183/1st mtg, 16 Jun. 1947. I am indebted to Peter Hennessy for sight of this material.

55. MI5 report, 'The Communist Party – Its Strengths and Activities: Its Penetration of Government Organisations and of the Trade Unions', Annexe 1 to GEN 226/1, 26 May 1948, CAB 130/37.

56. Hennessy and Brownfeld, 'Security Purge', 968.

57. Memo for DNI by Op-321E/jhn, 'Subversive Trends of Current Interest', 27 Sept. 1949, Box 249, SPDR, OAB, WNY.

58. Anderson, 'Blackett in India', 355–60.

59. Grantham, 'Labour Party', PhD, 159.

60. Memo from Cabell [USAF D of I] to Spaatz [US SAC], 26 Mar. 1948, 'Security Aspects of Possible Staff Talks with France (TAB A), Belgium, Holland and Luxembourg (TAB B)', D of I records, File 2-1200-1299, Box 40, RG 341.

61. 'Statement of the American Military Attaché in Paris', 24 Aug. 1948, Exec Office C. W. Clark folder, G-2, 1943–7, RG 165.

Chapter 5 *The Counter-Offensive: From CRD to IRD*

1. Bevin min., 23 May 1946, FO 930/488.

2. Clark-Kerr to FO, 26 Nov. 1945, N16816/989/38, FO 371/47935; Clark-Kerr to FO, 15 Dec. 1945, LC6031/1406/452, FO 924/206.

3. Owen to FO, 20 Jun. 1945, LC2454/1406/45, FO 924/205; Hookham to Bevin, 23 Oct. 1945, LC5033/1406/452, FO 924/206; Kotek, *Students*, 81.

4. Montagu-Pollock min., 19 Feb. 1946, W6865/524/50, FO 371/54787; Aitken min., 23 Apr. 1946, W6861/524/G, ibid.

5. Brimelow min., 10 Mar. 1946, W6861/524/G, FO 371/54787.

6. Cowell min., 4 Jun. 1946, W6864/524/50, FO 371/54787; Kotek, *Students*, 128.

7. Brimelow min., 12 June 1946, W6864/524/50, FO 371/54787.

8. Cowell min., 6 Jun. 1946, LC2675/21/452, FO 924/383.

9. Montagu-Pollock min., 27 May 1946, and Lambert min., 30 May 1946, 6784/524/50, FO 371/54787. See also Kotek, *Students*, 39.

10. Cowell min., 31 May 1946, 6784/524/50, FO 371/54787.

11. CRD memo, 'British Participation in an International Student Congress', 28 Jul. 1946, W8195/524/50, FO 371/54788.

12. Kim Philby (R5A) to FO, CX.94999/96, 17 Jul. 1946, W7377/524/50, FO 371/54787.

13. Cowell min., 5 Jul. 1946, LC3185/21/452, FO 924/384.

14. Lambert min., 3 Jul. 1946, W8195/524/50, FO 371/54788. Also Bowen min., 2 Aug. 1946, ibid.

15. CRD memo, 'British Participation in an International Student Congress', 28 Jul. 1946, W8195/524/50, FO 371/54788.

16. Nicholls to FO, 14 Jun. 1946, ibid.

17. Hector McNeil min., 10 Jan. 1947, W8186/540/50, FO 371/54788. Also Haynes to Montagu-Pollock, 'Consultation between International Youth Organisations', 3 Dec. 1946, ibid.

18. Kotek, *Students*, 110–11.

19. Hookham to Cripps, 27 Jul. 1948, File 524, Cripps papers, NC.

20. Powell min., 2 Jan. 1948, LC20/20/452, FO 924/670; Mason min., 7 Jan. 1948, LC253/20/452, ibid. On grants see MacDermot to COI, 24 Feb. 1948, LC804/20/452, FO 924/672.

21. Powell min., 16 Jan. 1948, LC159/20/452, FO 924/670; mins of the International Youth Conference chaired by Professor D. Hughes Parry, LC404/20/452, FO 924/670.

22. JIC (46) 1 (Final Revise), 22 Feb. 1946; Smith, 'Climate of Opinion', 635–7; Merrick, 'Russia Committee', 454–5. Lashmar and Oliver suggest that Philby was the SIS liaison for Russia Committee, *Britain's Secret Propaganda War*, 58.

23. Aldrich, 'Secret Intelligence for a Post-war World', 18–19; Lewis, *Changing Direction*, 98–178. Thomas, *Armed Truce*, 550–1, mistakenly attributes Russia Committee to the JIC.

24. Warner to Jebb, 22 Nov. 1946, N12649/765/38, FO 371/71687; Hayter, *Double Life*, 82–3.

25. Warner, 'The Soviet Campaign against This Country and Our Response to It', 2 Apr. 1946, N5169/5169/38, FO 371/56885. Bullock argues that this was Bevin's 'own view', but it was the work of his officials, *Bevin*, 234.

26. Memo by Kirkpatrick, 'The Soviet Campaign against This Country', 22 May 1946, P449/1/9, FO 930/488; Sargent min., 23 May 1946, ibid. Mins by Bevin, undated, ibid. Lashmar and Oliver, *Britain's Secret Propaganda War*, 59.

27. E.g. Healey to Mayhew, 23 Dec. 1946, C201/37, FO 371/67252B.

28. Bullock, *Bevin*, 262, 282, 694; Rothwell, *Britain*, 233–4.

29. Howard, 'Forgotten Dimensions', 975–87; Lashmar and Oliver, *Britain's Secret Propaganda War*, 25–9; Dorril, *MI6*, 72–3.

30. PMM (48) 8th mtg, 16 Oct. 1948, L/WS/1/1211, IOLR.

31. Lucas and Morris, 'A Very British Crusade', 90–4; private information.

32. Rothwell, *Britain*, 364–88; Conquest, *Kolyma*, 104–25; Lashmar and Oliver, *Britain's Secret Propaganda War*, 29–30. Robert Conquest pointed out to me that the problem was not finding negative material about the Soviet police state but that the real facts were often too awful to be credible to those who came to the subject afresh.

33. Entries for 9–11, 12 Apr. 1948, 21 Jul. 1949, 2–16 Aug. 1950, Bright-Holmes (ed.), *Like It Was*. Muggeridge had also joined the TA remnant of the SAS.

34. Entries for 9 Jul., 16–19 Nov. 1945, 19–20, 23 Mar. 1949, ibid.

35. Deery, 'Orwell'; Lashmar and Oliver, *Britain's Secret Propaganda War*, 96–7.

36. Stephenson min., 23 Feb. 1955, FO 1110/738; EA min., 25 Jan. 1955, FO 1110/740; Saigon to IRD, 9 Mar. 1955, FO 1110/740.

37. Acheson to US Embassy London, 26 Jun. 1951, 511.4121/6–2651, RG 59.

38. Kirby, *Church*, 165–6.

39. Ibid., 33, 46, 114.

40. Kuniholm, *Origins*, 383–99.

41. L'Estrange Fawcett, 'Struggle for Persia', PhD, 314–17, 352–5, 381–3.

42. 'Future of S.O.E. in the Middle East', 16 Jun. 1945, and Cavendish-Bentinck min., 17 Jun. 1945, E4569/1630/G65, FO 45272; SOE Middle East Report, 1946, pp. 47–8, HS7/285. Note the redaction of three following pages in this Iran section, pp. 48–51

43. Mtg on Propaganda to Persia, 30 Aug. 1946, N10616/10616/38, FO 371/56911.

44. L'Estrange Fawcett, 'Struggle for Persia', PhD, 314–17, 352–5, 381–3.

45. US Milt. Mission Teheran to Maddocks, 24 Nov. 1948, 381 TS, Box 115, P&O Files, RG 319. This was also drawn up in accordance with London's JP 48 (69) Final 'Doublequick', also in this file.

46. Filipelli, *American Labor*, 11–36, 96–8; Miller, *U.S. and Italy*, 217–19, 235; Romero, *European Trade Union Movement*, 92–8.

47. Karabell, *Architects*, 46–7; Miller, 'Taking Off the Gloves', 34–7.

48. Wall, *US and the Making of Postwar France*, 103.

49. Devinat to Donovan, 26 Apr. 1948, enclosed in Donovan to Gruenther (JCS), 18 May 1948, Box 6, Gen Corresp., Gruenther Papers, DDEL.

50. Wall, *US and the Making of Postwar France*, 151.

51. Douglas to SoS, 30 Apr. 1949, 841.20200/4–3049, RG 59.

52. 'Checklist of French Government Anti-Communist Activities since 1950 Aimed at Reducing

Communist Strength and Influence', 22 Oct. 1953, Box 12, PSB Central Files Series, NSC Staff Papers, WHO, DDEL. See also Wall, *US and the Making of Postwar France*, 150–3.

53. Wisner to Gruenther, 3 Aug. 1951, Box 20, General Corresp., Gruenther papers, DDEL.

54. Wood to Davidson (SHAPE Liaison Office), 11 Sept. 1952, enclosing Gruenther from Smith, Box 1, Gruenther papers, DDEL.

55. Hankey min., 28 Mar. 1947, N2797/271/38, FO 371/66365; Cadogan to FO, 13 Oct. 1949, FO 1110/756.

56. Prior memorandum, 'Assignment of Codeword', 28 Feb. 1950, 21700, Box 48, D of I records, RG 341.

57. Kennan to Souers, 'The Position of the US with Respect to Iceland in the Event of an Internal Communist Coup d'Etat or Threat Thereof', 23 Jun. 1949, 091 Iceland, 1949–50, Box 158, RG 319; Memo on JCS 1950/12, 'Planning for the Security of Iceland', 4 Aug. 1949, ibid.

Chapter 6 *The Fifth Column of Freedom: Britain Embraces Liberation*

1. Slessor to Liddell Hart, 6 Sept. 1947, 1/644, Liddell Hart papers, LHCMA.

2. Report by Theodore Grayson, American Naval Attaché, 20 Dec. 1946, to Chief of Naval Intelligence, 'Underground and Guerrilla Activities in Ukraine and Belorussia', Odessa File, RG 38.

3. SSU Washington Intelligence Brief 13, 15 Oct. 1946, enclosing 'The Ukrainian Nationalist Movement', 72 pp, File 775, Box 63, Entry 171A, RG 226; also private information.

4. Bower, *Perfect English Spy*, 205–6, 350; private information.

5. Foot, *SOE: The Special Operations Executive*, 221.

6. Aldrich, 'Unquiet', 198–9; COS (46) 12th mtg (1), 23 Jan. 1946, AIR 19/816.

7. Memo by Kirkpatrick, 22 May 1946, P449/1/907, FO 930/488. I am indebted to Philip Taylor for observations on this subject.

8. Slessor to Liddell Hart, 6 Sept. 1947, 1/644, Liddell Hart papers, LHCMA; Liddell Hart to Slessor, 8 Jan. 1948, ibid.

9. By 1950 he would question resistance work as carrying with it an erosion of civil morality and law and order, which was permanent and irreversible, Liddell Hart, *Defence of the West*, 54–8.

10. Slessor to Donovan, 16 Oct. 1947, AIR 75/116; Slessor to Liddell Hart, 22 Jan. 1948, Liddell Hart papers, 1/644, LHCMA.

11. Slessor to VCAS, JCS.37, 21 Jan. 1948, AIR 75/116.

12. COS 128 (48) 1, 'World Strategic Review', 11 Sept. 1948, DEFE 4/16.

13. Walter Pforzheimer, former CIA legislative counsel, interviewed in Berger, AFCS Study, 'Use of Covert Paramilitary Activity', 13.

14. Warner, *CIA under Harry Truman*, 174–5.

15. Ibid., 234–8.

16. Montgomery diary, ch. 67, BLM1/184 (Germany 3–7 Apr. 1948), IWM. I am grateful to Donald Cameron Watt for his recollections of being repeatedly 'stood to' in Austria in this period.

17. Mitrovich, *Undermining the Kremlin*, 28–34.

18. NSC 20/1, 'US Objectives with Respect to Russia', 18 Aug. 1948, in Etzold and Gaddis (eds), *Containment*, 173, 223

19. Kennan to Hillenkoetter, 23 Dec. 1948, Box 12, Records of PPS 1947–53, Lot Files 64 D 563, RG 59.

20. Notes on the First Meeting between Messrs. Christopher Warner and Edward Barrett, at London, Secret, Saturday May 20, 1950, *FRUS* 1950, vol. 3, *Western Europe*, 1641–4.

21. Entries for 22–26 Sept. 1948, Bright-Holmes (ed.), *Like It Was*.

22. Montgomery's diary records the date as 29 Jun., but this is clearly an error.

23. Montgomery diary, Sept.–Oct. 1948, 'SECTION D – The Cold War', Montgomery papers, BLM 186/1, Reel 18, IWM.

24. CP (48) 8, memo by the Foreign Secretary, Ernest Bevin, 'Future Foreign Publicity Policy', 4 Jan. 1948, CAB 129/23.

25. Montgomery diary, Sept.–Oct. 1948, 'SECTION D – The Cold War', Montgomery papers, BLM 186/1, Reel 18, IWM.

26. 'Statement by C.A.S. at Meeting of Commonwealth Prime Ministers on Defence, 20 Oct. 1948', AIR 75/116.

27. RC (48) 16 (2), Russia Committee mins, 25 Nov. 1948, N3016/765/38, FO 371/71687.

28. NSC 10/2. 'National Security Directive on the Office of Special Projects', 18 Jun. 1948, Etzold and Gaddis (eds) *Containment*, 125–8; Mitrovich, *Undermining the Kremlin*, 8–34.

29. 'Scope of Possible Special Operations in the Event of Hostilities in the Middle East before Jul., 1949', Appendix 'H', British War Plan SANDOWN, Aug. 1948, AIR 8/1605; also private information.

30. JP (48) 135 (Final), 'Destruction of Persian Communications and Neutralisation of Middle Eastern Oil

Installations', 4 Nov. 1948, DEFE 6/7; TX-S-49, 22 Sept. 1949, 091 Turkey, Box 167, P&O Files 1949–50 TS, RG 319; Coleridge (BJSM) to Glover RDC 5/106, 5 Aug. 1949, 381 ME TS, Box 243, P&O Files 1948–50, RG 319.

31. Reilly to COS, 3 Apr. 1952, DEFE 11/433.

32. Sterndale Bennett to Pumphrey, N3357/1051/38, FO 371/77616; Imperial Defence College (1949 Course), Problem No. 3, 'Cold War' (8 Feb.– 4 Mar.), ibid.; Alexander to Attlee, 7 Mar. 1949, ibid.

33. London to Washington, 'British FO Experimenting with Equivalent of Department's Policy Planning Staff', 20 Apr. 1949, Box 17, PPS Lot Files 64 D 563, RG 59.

34. Warner to Price, 1 Mar. 1949, DEFE 11/275; COS (49) 90th mtg, 17 Jun. 1949, DEFE 4/22.

35. Entry for 15 Jun. 1949, Bright-Holmes (ed.), *Like It Was*.

36. Hillgarth to Churchill, 12 Sept. 1949, Church 2/36, Churchill papers, CCC.

Chapter 7 *Liberation or Provocation? Special Operations in the Eastern Bloc*

1. NSC 58, in Etzold and Gaddis (eds.) *Containment*, 220–1.

2. British JIC paper sent to US JCS, 'Russian Short-term Intentions in Greece', 4 Feb. 1948, 091, Box 14, P&O Files 1946–8, RG 319; ORE 67–48, 'Continuing Satellite Aid to the Greek Guerrillas', CIA, 8 Oct. 1948, CIA microfilm, Europe, Reel 3, LL.

3. Entry for 3 Oct. 1949, Bright-Holmes (ed.), *Like It Was*.

4. Private information.

5. Macarger interview, cited in Berger, AFSC Study, 'Use of Covert Paramilitary Activity', 17; Powers, *Man Who Kept the Secrets*, 44–5.

6. OIR Report No. 5112, 'Albanian Political Exiles', 28 Nov. 1949, RG 59.

7. Prados, *Presidents' Secret Wars*, 48.

8. Based on the remarkable account in Heuser, *Western 'Containment'*, 44–7.

9. 'Conversation between Bevin and Acheson on Albania', 14 Sept. 1949, Box 312, Records of Post CFM mtgs, RG 49.

10. Owen, 'Britain and Decolonization', 3; Bullock, *Bevin*, 508–9; Wilson, *King Abdullah*, 96.

11. Acheson–Bevin–Schuman mtgs, 13–15 Sept. 1949, PSF General File, A-Ato (112), HSTL.

12. Smiley, *Irregular Regular,* 192; private information.

13. See for example Bethell, *Great Betrayal*.

14. FO to Athens, 23 Dec. 1946, R18485/67, FO 371/58665.

15. Memo of a meeting with CIA and SIS by the Chief of the USAF Psychological Warfare Division, Colonel O. L. Grover, 17 Nov. 1949, *ESI*, 10.4 (I am indebted to Len Scott and Stephen Twigge for drawing this document to my attention); JCEC 933/1, 'CIA Circuit Requirements from the Department of Defense', 30 Mar. 1954, Strategic Issues, Series 2, Reel 1, US JCS microfilm, BRO.

16. INSCOM/CIC Report YR-231687, 'Anders', 26 Jan. 1961, FOIA.

17. Rositzke, *CIA*, 168–9.

18. Andrew, *President's Eyes Only*, 183.

19. Grose, *Gentleman Spy*, 355–6.

20. 'Ukrainian Nationalist Movements', FORD report, 13 Dec. 1945, N17195/4356/38, FO 371/47957. For an alternative view on the scale of SIS efforts in the East see Dorril, *MI6*, 161–299.

21. Kuromiya, *Freedom and Terror*, 266–7, 288.

22. Armstrong, *Ukrainian Nationalism*, 171, 208–10; Czubatyi, 'Ukrainian Underground', 154–66.

23. Kuromiya, *Freedom and Terror*, 295.

24. Memo by Asst US Naval Attaché, 30 Dec. 1946, 'Underground and Guerrilla Activities in Ukraine and Belorussia', Odessa File 45–7, Box 5, Planning Branch, RG 38.

25. Memo by Asst. US Naval Attaché, 5 Dec. 1946, 'Underground and Guerrilla Activities in Ukraine and Belorussia', ibid.

26. Cavendish, *Inside Intelligence*, 50–1.

27. Berger, AFSC Study, 'Use of Covert Paramilitary Activity', 3.

28. Memo to Colonel Sleeper (AFOAI-SV), 29 Dec. 1948, 25700, Box 43, D of I records, RG 341.

29. Rositzke, *CIA*, 166–7.

30. Kennan to Wisner, 6 Jan. 1949, Box 12, PPS Lot Files 64 D 563, RG 59; 'List of D of S and FS Personnel Having Knowledge of Political Warfare Operations', 11–17/8, Box 11A, ibid.; Kennan to Lovett, 29 Oct. 1948, Box 12, ibid.

31. Kennan quoted in Rudgers, 'Origins', 260.

32. Miscamble, *Kennan*, 203–6; Mitrovich, *Undermining the Kremlin*, 29–34.

33. Lucas, *Freedom's War*, 1–15.

34. Mastny, *Cold War*, 84, 128; Stueck, *Korean War*, 32–4.

35. Hodos, *Show Trials*, 5, 26–8.

36. OIR Report No. 6102, 'The Purges in the Communist Party of Czechoslovakia (KSC)', 20 Oct. 1953, RG 59. See also OIR Report No. 6297.2, 'Czechoslovakian Public Order', 20 May 1955, ibid.

37. Childs and Popperwell, *Stasi*, 39–55; Fricke, *Die DDR-Staatssicherheit*, 24–6; Major, 'German Communist Party', PhD, 99–108.

38. Steven, *Splinter Factor*, 97–100; Andrew and Gordievsky, *KGB*, 413–16.

39. Steven, *Splinter Factor*, 97–108

40. Kovrig, *Walls and Bridges*, 42; Dorril, *MI6*, 255–6, 484; Bower, *Perfect English Spy*, 205–6; Mastny, *Cold War*, 131–2.

41. Bower, *Red Web*, 28–48; Hazard, *Cold War*, 150–81.

42. RC (16) 48, Appendix A, T of R for 'Cold War' Sub-Committee, 24 Nov. 1948, N13016/765/38, FO 371/71687; RC (27) 48, mins., 16 Dec. 1948, N13677/765/38, ibid.

43. NSC 58, in Etzold and Gaddis (eds), *Containment*, 220–1.

44. Drew, memo, 'Future Deception Policy', 24 November 1949, DEFE 28/43 (see Appendix 1); Drew, memo, 'A Policy for Deception', draft, July 1950, ibid.; mins. of mtg. at the FO, 28 July 1950, ibid.

45. PUSC (51) 16 (Final), 'Future Policy towards Soviet Russia', and Annexe B, 'Liberation of the Satellites', 17 Jan. 1952, ZP10/4, FO 371/25002.

46. Major, 'German Communist Party', PhD, 96; B.282, 'Political Prisoners in the Satellites', 1956, File: E. Europe, 1956, Political Prisoners, IDLP, NMLH; Hodos, *Show Trials*, xv; Kovrig, *Walls and Bridges*, 43.

Chapter 8 *The Front Line: Intelligence in Germany and Austria*

1. Entry 22 Sept. 1948, Bright-Holmes (ed.), *Like It Was*.

2. 15 Schleswig-Holstein Intelligence Office Monthly Summary, Dec. 1947, Part II, FO 371/70613A; Biddiscombe, *Werwolf*, 53–4; Biddiscombe, 'Problem with Glass Houses', 131–45.

3. Entry for 15 March 1946, Ziegler, *Personal Diary*.

4. JIC (44) 48th mtg (1), 15 Sept. 1944, CAB 81/92; Goode (MoD) to author, 1 Feb. 1994; Gimbel, *Science, Technology and Reparations*, xiii.

5. Ryan, *Bridge Too Far*, 128–9; Whiting, *Werewolf*, 175.

6. Press File: Operation Selection Board, Lethbridge Papers, now at LHCMA.

7. Cesarini, *Justice Delayed*, 82–3, 102–4, 130–6. In the 1970s I encountered some of these (by then) rather ancient figures still serving in BAOR Germany.

8. Mins on 'Combined Intelligence Priorities Committee' by Cavendish-Bentinck, 5 Jul. 1944, and Harrison, 4 Jul. 1944, C9386/9386/18, FO 371/39171.

9. Dean min., 18 Jun. 1946, U5804/5488/73, FO 371/57671 quoted in Jones, 'British Policy', PhD, 1989. See also Bower, *Blind Eye to Murder*, 225, 227–9.

10. Kirkpatrick to FO, 8 Jul. 1945, and Galsworthy min. 21 Aug., 1945, N641/3936/38, FO 371/47955.

11. See especially the thoughtful discussion in Kitchen, *British Policy*, 262–6.

12. Rothwell, *Britain*, 18–20.

13. Watt, 'Austria as a Special Case', 260–97.

14. Gimbel, *Science, Technology and Reparations*, ix.

15. Ibid., 41.

16. Ibid., 3–20.

17. ACAO/P (44) 78, 'Obtaining of Technical Intelligence from Germany and Occupied Europe', 12 Jun. 1944, U5586/5586/70, FO 371/40825; min. for DNI, 9 Mar. 1946, ADM 116/5571.

18. JIC (46) 79 (0), 'Russian Enticement of German Scientists and Technicians', 21 Aug. 1946, L/WS/1/992, IOLR.

19. TS/33/B, memo, 6 Sept. 1946, EIS/CCG, BT 211/33; JIC/1000/46, 26 Jul. 1946, BT 211/60. The MI5 officers were Colonel T. H. Adams and Captain G. C. Byrde.

20. FIAT EP 092.76/10, 'German Scientists and Technicians with Special Knowledge', 22 Aug. 1946, FO 1031/65; Liddell (MI5) to Drew, 24 Dec. 1946, DEFE 7/1975; Liddell (MI5) to Powell, 9 Jan. 1947, DEFE 7/1975. Also Maddrell, 'Britain's Exploitation', PhD, 44; Hunt, *Secret Agenda*, 12–14.

21. Gimbel, *Science, Technology and Reparations*; Gimbel, 'American Exploitation'; Kramer, 'British Dismantling Politics'. This section draws on Farquharson's excellent piece, 'Governed or Exploited'. I am also indebted to two senior British industrialists for their views.

22. Bower, *Paperclip*, 96–106.

23. Memo to Chief, Air Int. Requirements, AC/AS-2, 'Lowrie Campaign against the Exploitation Programme', 8 Aug. 1947, Microfilm Reel 1035, CAFH. On war criminals see: Bower, *Blind Eye to Murder*; Bower, *Paperclip*; Cesarini, *Justice Delayed*; Hunt, *Secret Agenda*; Loftus, *Belarus*; Simpson, *Blowback*.

24. SR 25, 'United Kingdom, CIA, 7 Dec. 1949, CIA microfilm, Europe, Reel 4, LL; Montgomery, address to MoS scientists, 10 Apr. 1947, WO 216/206.

25. Strong to JIC London and CIC Washington, 2 Jun. 1945, C2795/2795/G18, FO 371/46927;

Brimelow min., 14 Jun. 1945, ibid.; e.g. JIC (45) 318 (0), 'Potentialities of the Soviet Air Force', 26 Nov. 1946?, N16448/16448/G38, FO 371/48005.

26. Trudeau (G-2) to Gruenther, 6 Jan. 1955, Box 4, Gruenther papers, DDEL.

27. Persuasively argued in Maddrell, 'Britain's Exploitation', PhD, 6–8, 21.

28. Evans to Turner, 8 May 1953, DEFE 41/124.

29. Director, STIB to Chief, ID CCG, 'Operation "Dragon Return" – Brief for Chief', 4 Dec. 1950, *ESI,* 4.3.

30. MI16, 'The Soviet Air Force Engineering Academy', 1 Mar. 1948, DEFE 40/25; MI16, 'USSR Guided Weapons Research', 6 Aug. 1948, ibid.

31. JIC (48) 124 (Final), 'Procedure for Handling Defectors Arriving in the British Zone of Occupation', 8 Dec. 1948, CAB 158/5; Ambassador Horace G. Torbert transcript, 31 Aug. 1988, FAOHP, 6–7.

32. The JIC paper was JIC (49) 107 (Final) discussed in Shortt (DMI) to Sec. JIC, 5 Jun. 1950, *ESI,* 4.2. See also Wark, 'Red Army Defectors'.

33. Ambassador William C. Trueheart transcript, FAOHP, 17 Mar. 1989, 6.

34. Memo by Schow (CIA), 'The NSC Approval of the Dulles Report', 26 Aug. 1949, *FRUS, 1949–50,* 1008–9.

35. Murphy, Kondrashev and Bailey, *Battleground Berlin,* 15.

36. CIA Chief of Station Berlin, Report for Jan. 1946–Mar. 1948, in Steury, *Front Lines,* 31.

37. Watt, 'Austria as a Special Case', 260–97.

38. I interviewed Major-General Lethbridge's widow, Mrs Katy Lethbridge, in 1993, who kindly allowed me to inspect private papers. These have now been deposited at LHCMA.

39. Monthly Int. Summary, Jan. 1947, BAFO, *ESI,* 6.3.

40. See the excellent thesis by Major, 'German Communist Party', PhD, 202.

41. Schaller, *American Occupation,* 134–6.

42. Major, 'German Communist Party', PhD, 209–10; Cesarini, *Justice Delayed,* 149–56; Andrew and Gordievsky, *KGB,* 451–3; John, *Twice through the Lines,* 231–83.

43. Major, 'German Communist Party,' PhD, 211–12, 216, 222.

44. HICOG to SD, 10 Aug. 1954, quoted in Major, 'German Communist Party', PhD, 234.

45. Dept of Justice, *Barbie: Report,* xviii, 5–7. See also Bower, *Barbie,* 95–9.

46. CIC Special Interrogation Report 62, CI-SIR/62, TAB 27, Dept of Justice, *Barbie: Report.*

47. CIC memo, Operation Selection Board, 9 February 1947, TAB 1, Dept of Justice, *Barbie: Report.*

48. Bower, *Barbie,* 126–7.

49. Dept of Justice, *Barbie: Report,* 10–11; interviews with Robert Frazier.

50. British Special Interrogation Report No. 55, DIC, CCG (BE), 23 Jun. 1947, 'Operation Dry Martini', discussed at TAB 29, Dept of Justice, *Barbie: Report.*

51. Dept of Justice, *Barbie: Report,* 13–14.

52. CS IR/66, 'BARBIE, Klaus', CIC memo, 28 Jun. 1948, TAB 29, Dept of Justice, *Barbie: Report.*

53. Major, 'German Communists Party', PhD, 218.

54. Bower, *Barbie,* 153.

55. D-153204, Memo by Vidal, CIC, 3 May 1950, TAB 57, Dept of Justice, *Barbie: Report.*

56. Lieutenant-Colonel Golden memo, CIC Region IV, 'Klaus Barbie', 1 Dec. 1947, TAB 18, Dept of Justice, *Barbie: Report.*

57. Dept of Justice, *Barbie: Report,* 20–2, 30–42, 59.

58. On this general area see particularly Westerfield, 'America and the World of Liaison'.

59. Stewart (IS Chief – SSU Germany) to Hans Tofte and Whitney Shepardon, 'Meeting[s] with Brigadier Robin Brooke and Brigadier General Sibert', 8 Feb. 1946, Reel 73, Entry 190 (M1642), RG 226.

60. Dodderidge to Washington, 3 May 1946, Reel 73, Entry 190 (M1642), RG 226.

61. Murphy to Pace, 26 Dec. 1950, Box 90, Murphy papers, HIWRP; CC (M) (49) 16, 4 Aug. 1949, DEFE 41/78.

62. Ambassador Horace G. Torbert transcript, 31 Aug. 1988, FAOHP, 6–7.

Chapter 9 *Operation Dick Tracy: Air Intelligence in London and Washington*

1. Paine, 'Berchtesgaden to Brampton: The History of German Air Intelligence Photography', Nov. 1960, AIR 14/4104.

2. Entry for 11 Feb. 1943, Barnes and Nicholson (eds), *Amery Diaries.*

3. General Charles P. Cabell, 'Memoirs of an Unidentified Aide', ch. 31, TSS, Reel 33080, IRIS 1025177, 168.2026.33080, CAFH.

4. Campbell, *Unsinkable Aircraft Carrier,* 28; Duke, *US Defence Bases in the UK,* 20–1; Tamnes, *High North,* 47; Scott and Twigge, *Planning Armageddon,* 35–6.

5. Walker, 'GX Photography – History', 4 Oct. 1965, AIR 14/4104; Paine, 'Berchtesgaden to Brampton: The History of German Air Intelligence Photography', Nov. 1960, ibid.

6. Quesada (Chief G-2) to McDonald (Chief A-2), 6 Aug. 1945, 22459, Box 37, D of I records, RG 341; Moss to Quesada, 5 Aug. 1945, ibid.

7. As note 4 above. Also private information. In July 1946, US Naval Intelligence joined the exploitation teams looking at the photographs of Soviets ports and harbours, McDonald (chief A-2) to DNI, 24 Jul. 1946, 22284, Box 37, D of I records, RG 341; memo for Air Staff by Harbold DACAS-2, 24 Jul. 1947, Microfilm Reel 1030, CAFH.

8. As note 4 above.

9. Parsons memo for OP4, 8 Nov. 1948, Box 243, SPDR (Series XVI), OAB, WNY; Twigge and Scott, *Planning Armageddon*, 233–4.

10. Putney (ed.), *Ultra*, 60–2.

11. Quesada (head G-2) to McDonald (head A-2), 7 Aug. 1945, 23609A, Box 37, D of I records, RG 341.

12. McDonald (chief A-2) to Pendred (ACAS(I)), 25 Jun. 1947, 21400, Box 41, D of I records, RG 341.

13. CINCEUR to War Dept, re Wright Field, 4 Apr. 1947, Box 95, ACS, G-2 Entry 58, TS Incoming and Outgoing Cables, RG 319.

14. AI3(F) 1946, 'German Intelligence Work on the Russian AF OB', AIR 40/2597.

15. Military Attaché to DMI, 16 Jul. 1946, N9263/639/42, FO 371/56951; Air Attaché to ACAS (I), 27 Jul. 1946, ibid.

16. Elmhirst to BJSM for McDonald, 4 Sept. 1946, 22459, Box 37, D of I records, RG 341.

17. Elmhirst (ACAS(I)) to McDonald (chief A-2), 13 Aug. 1946, 22284, Box 37, D of I records, RG 341.

18. Selko (JIB) to Watson (A-2), 26 May 1948, enclosing JIB 3/30 June 1947, 'The Characteristics of Russian Towns as Targets for Air Attack', 2–20001, Box 42, D of I records, RG 341.

19. Semi-Annual History, D Director for Targets, D of I, 1 Jul.–31 Dec. 1952, Tab 98, Box 71, D of I records, RG 341.

20. Pendred (ACAS(I)) to Cabell (D of I, USAF), 12 Jul. 1948, 23003, Box 42, D of I records, RG 341; memo for the record, 2 Sept. 1948, ibid; Pendred (ACAS(I)) to Cabell (D of I, USAF), 13 Sept. 1948, 23600, Box 43, ibid.

21. General Charles P. Cabell, 'Memoirs of an Unidentified Aide', ch. 33, TSS, Reel 33080, IRIS 1025177, 168.2026.33080, CAFH.

22. 'Presentation Made by Rear Admiral Inglis in the Office of the Secretary', 22 Oct. 1947, Records of the CNO, Box 5, RG 38.

23. Packard, *Century*, 432–3.

24. January Informal Letter, 1954, Box 22, Planning Branch, RG 38.

25. McDonald (head of A-2) memo to Vandenburg, 'Documents Captured at Goering's Headquarters', 27 Feb. 1946, 22710, Box 37, D of I records, RG 341.

26. Washington to Harvey-Brown (London), 'New Photo Cover', 16 Dec. 1948, 25400, Box 43, D of I records, RG 341.

27. Nesbit, *Eyes of the RAF*, 238–44.

28. Memo for CNO by DDNI, 'Soviet Interception of Swedish Photo Plane', 23 Nov. 1948, Box 249, SPDR (Series XVI) OAB, WNY.

29. A-2 to COS, USAF, Apr. 1948, Box 41, D of I records, RG 341.

30. Fuller (Reconnaissance Branch A-2) to Mallory, 'British Provocation of Immediate', 29 Sept. 1948 (Top Secret – Air Force Eyes Only), 25000, Box 43, D of I records, RG 341. On the arrival of American atomic weapons in Britain see Twigge and Scott, *Planning Armageddon*, 35.

Chapter 10 *The Failure of Atomic Intelligence*

1. Welsh, 'Atomic Energy Intelligence', briefing, 9–19 Jun. 1952, DEFE 41/126.

2. Annexe to JS/TIC (49) 55, 22 Jun. 1949, DEFE 41/150, and quoted and discussed in Maddrell, 'Britain's Exploitation', 99, 107.

3. JP (48) 7 (Final), 'Mounting of an Air Offensive in 1957 Use of Naval Carriers', 11 Mar. 1948, DEFE 4/11; Holloway, *Stalin*, 301–2.

4. COS (45) 402 (0), 'Future Developments in Weapons and Methods of War', 16 June 1945, Air 20/12027; Jones min., 14 Aug. 1945, and Slessor min., 16 Jul. 1945, ibid.; Lewis, *Changing Direction*, 178–242; Aldrich, 'Secret Intelligence for a Post-war World', 27–30.

5. Jones memo, 'An improved Scientific Intelligence Service', 2 May 1945, Air 20/1714; JIC (45) 35th mtg (1), 23 May 1945, CAB 81/93; JIC (45) 229, 26 Jul. 1945, ADM 1/20088.

6. Jones, *Reflections*, 497.

7. Mins of JIC mtg, 11 Sept. 1945, Annexe to JIC (45) 272 (0), 'Intelligence on Atomic Energy', 12 Sept. 1945, CAB 81/130; Jones, *Reflections*, 6–8, 12, 16–17.

8. JIB (46) 1st mtg, 20 Sept. 1946, L/WS/1/1088, IOLR; Aldrich, 'Secret Intelligence for a Post-war World', 17.

9. Kramer, *Griffin*, 90–7.

10. Ibid., 242–3.

11. Chief STIB to John Bruce Lockhart (SIS) – copy No. 1, 'Special Surveillance of Certain Nuclear Physicists (Operation SCRUM Half)', 14 May 1948, DEFE 41/26.

12. DSTIB to Chief, 'Visit of Dr. Perrin and Cdr. Welsh', 22 Apr. 1948, DEFE 41/26.

13. Blount to Haydon (chief ID), 20 Aug. 1948, DEFE 41/26; Haydon to Blount, 29 Aug. 1948, ibid.

14. Schow to British Liaison Officer EUCOM, 'Security of Certain Special Scientists', 4 Feb. 1948, DEFE 41/26; memo by Wedemeyer for the COS, USA, 'Employment of German and Austrian Nuclear Physicists', 10 Oct. 1948, 000.9, Box 1, P&O series, RG 319.

15. Murphy, Kondrashev and Bailey, *Battleground Berlin*, 13–15; Maddrell, 'Britain's Exploitation', PhD, 173.

16. Mtg of JAEIC, 30 Mar. 1950, A-90, Box 35, D of I records, RG 341.

17. Ziegler and Jacobson. *Spying*, 193–5; Dorril, *MI6*, 152–3.

18. Memo of CG, AAF, 18 Mar. 1947, Microfilm 1030, CAFH.

19. JCS 1942/8, Annexe, CIA memo to NSC, 'Atomic Energy Program of the USSR', 30 Apr. 1949, 091 SU, Box 165, 1949–50 TS, P&O Files, RG 319.

20. JIC (46) 95 (0) Final, 'Future Scale of Air Attack against the United Kingdom', 12 Nov. 1946, AIR 20/2740.

21. COS (47) 227 (0) (2nd Revise), 'World Strategic Summary', CAB 21/1800.

22. Memo, 'Target Date for the Re-equipment of the Fleet', 16 Mar. 1948, ADM 116/5966.

23. JIC (48) 9 (0) Final, 'Russian Interests, Intentions and Capabilities', 23 Jul. 48, L/WS/1/1173, IOLR.

24. JICM-2A, 'Agreed Statement on Russian Atom Bomb Production', 29 Mar. 1948, Series 1, Reel 1, Strategic Issues, US JCS Microfilm, BRO.

25. JIC (46) 95 (0) Final, Future Scale of Air Attack against the United Kingdom', 12 Nov. 1946, AIR 20/2740.

26. Lang-Brown to Neville, 'TCS/441', 6 Sept. 1949, DEFE 40/26.

27. TWC (45) 42, 'Potentialities of Weapons of War during the Next Few Years', 12 Nov. 1945, DEFE 2/1252; 'Elimination of Bacteriological Warfare', annexe to JP (46) 36 (Final), 'Control of Atomic Energy, 27 Feb. 1946, ibid.

28. JIG 297/2, 'Soviet Capabilities for Employing Biological and Chemical Weapons', 2 Dec. 1948, 360 (12-9-42) Sec. 8, RG 218.

29. Ministry of Supply to CO, 28 Oct. 1948, CO 537/2702. See Paxman and Harris, *Higher Form*, 179–81 and Maddrell, 'Britain's Exploitation', PhD, 30.

30. Ziegler and Jacobson, *Spying*, 4–6.

31. Hillenkoetter to SoS for War, 'Long Range Detection of Atomic Explosions', 30 Jun. 1947, 000.9, Box 1, P&O series, RG 319; Lema memo, 1 Aug., ibid.

32. Ziegler and Jacobson, *Spying*, 194–6; Tracerlab memo, 'Special Filter Paper Analysis', 18 Sept. 1949, HSTL microfilm, Pt. 3, Reel 41, HUL; Memo, 'An Interim Report of British Work on Joe', 22 Sept. 1949, HSTL microfilm, Pt 3, Reel 41, HUL.

33. Morgan to Slessor (CAS), 9 Oct. 1951, AIR 75/92; Slessor to Morgan, 12 Oct. 1951, ibid.

34. Turney, ADNI (Sc), 'The Organisation of Scientific and Technical Intelligence', 21 Oct. 1947, DEFE 40/26.

35. ADNI (Sc), 'Scope and Sources of Scientific Intelligence', 10 Oct. 1949, DEFE 40/26.

36. Kramer, *Griffin*, 191.

37. Welsh, 'Atomic Energy Intelligence', briefing, 9–19 Jun. 1952, DEFE 41/126. See also 'Talk on Atomic Energy by A. Cowman', DEFE 41/125.

38. Maddrell, 'Britain's Exploitation', PhD, 83.

39. Welsh, 'Atomic Energy Intelligence', briefing, 9–19 Jun. 1952, DEFE 41/126; Dorril, *MI6*, 150–1.

40. Transcript of USAF Commanders Conference on Operation Dualism, Maxwell Air Force Base, 6–8 Dec. 1948, OPD 337 Sec. 2, RG 341.

41. JIS 161/8, 'Estimate of British Post-War Capabilities and Intentions', 28 Dec. 1945, RG 218.

Chapter 11 *GCHQ: Signals Intelligence Looks East*

1. Welchman, Hinsley and Crankshaw to Travis, 'A Note on the Future of G.C. & C.S.', 17 Sept. 1944, HW 3/169.

2. Davies, *British Secret Service*.

3. Wigg to Wilson enclosing 'The Organisation of Security in the Diplomatic Service and Government Communications Headquarters', 17 Aug. 1966, reproduced in Young, 'GCHQ'.

4. LSIB Mtgs Summary No. 13, 18 Jul. 1945, WO 203/5126.

5. Welchman, Hinsley and Crankshaw to Travis, 'A Note on the Future of G.C. & C.S.', 17 Sept. 1944, HW 3/169. On Slim, see Aldrich, *Intelligence and the War against Japan*, 316–17.

6. Part 1, 'The General Problem of Intelligence and Security in Peace' (personal for Director), Preliminary Draft, Sept. 1944, HW 3/169.

7. Bamford, *Puzzle Palace*, 317, 335.

8. Clarke, 'Post War Organisation', HW3/30 (I am indebted to Ralph Erskine for this reference).

9. Erskine, 'Anglo-US Cryptological Co-operation'; conversation with John Croft.

10. Aldrich and Coleman, 'The Cold War, the JIC and British Signals Intelligence', 538–40; Hinsley et al., *British Intelligence*, vol. 2, 618–19.

11. Whitaker and Kruh, 'From Bletchley Park to the Berchtesgaden', 129–30.

12. Col. Kurt Goitschling, 'The Radio Intercept Service of the German Air Force', vol. 2, KL13.107–191, 8–115–21, (E)K10262, CAFH.

13. 'The German G-2 Service in the Russian Campaign', 22 Jul. 1945, WO 208/4343; van der Meulen, 'Cryptologic Services of the Federal Republic'; and private information.

14. Jenkins, *Life*, 57. (I am indebted to Ralph Erskine for this reference.) Parrish, *Ultra Americans*, 283–4 (I am indebted to Matthew Aid for this reference).

15. Penney min. to SAC, 22 Sept. 1945, WO 203/5051; Russell, *Sheridan's Story;* Donini, 'The Cryptographic Services of the Royal (British) and Italian Navies', 97–127.

16. Russell, *Sheridan's Story*, 112–15.

17. AFHQ to MI8 London, 10 Jul. 1945, 'SID Cryptographic Documents', WO 208/5073. Also AFHQ to MI8 London, 'Diplomatic Interception in Northern Italy', 16 May 1945, and Annexe, 'SIM Success on British and US Diplo', ibid.

18. Churchill to Eden, 25 Nov. 1944, U7917/180/70, FO 371/40720; Brown, 'Interplay of Information'; Schlesinger, 'Cryptanalysis for Peacetime'; private information.

19. Clark-Kerr to Eden, 12 Nov. 1943, N6739/22/38, FO 371/36926; Thomas, 'France in British Signals Intelligence', 64–6.

20. McKane to DDY, 'Italian Sigint Service', 15 May 1946, WO 208/5073.

21. McKane to Director LSIC (for head of TA Group), 31 May 1946, enclosing 'Further Notes on Italian Cover', ibid.; McKane to K. H. Sachse (LSIC), 'Italian Intercept Organisation', 4 Jun. 1946, ibid.

22. Y Services Summary, Dec. 1945 and Mar. 1946, WO 212/228.

23. Lewin, *Ultra Goes to War*, 129–33; Jones, *Reflections,*15.

24. JIC (48) (0) (second revised draft), 'Sigint intelligence requirements', 11 May 1948, *ESI*, 2.3.

25. Stripp, *Codebreaker in the Far East,* 50–60; Jones, *Reflections*, 14–16.

26. Ball, 'Over and Out', 32–44; Thomas, 'France in British Signals Intelligence', 103–7; Sawatsky, *For Services Rendered*, 23–6.

27. Eubank (COS) to Rowlands (MoS), 31 Jan. 1952, DEFE 11/350; Eubank to DRPC, 31 Jan. 1952, ibid.

28. COS (52) 152nd mtg (1), Confidential Annexe, 4 Nov. 1952, DEFE 11/350.

29. Entry for 21 Nov. 1945, Cunningham diary, MSS 52578, BL; Wark, 'Cryptographic Innocence', 558–9; Andrew, *President's Eyes Only*, 161.

30. Hughes to Hodges (Asst CoAS A-2), 26 Feb. 1945, File 1945, Box 77, Vandenberg Papers, LC; 'Condensed Analysis of the Ninth Air Force in the European Theatre of Operations', 1984, 120, CAFH.

31. Meilinger, *Vandenberg*, 71.

32. Andrew, 'Australian Intelligence Community', 223–5; Bamford, *Puzzle Palace*, 314–17; Richelson and Ball, *Ties That Bind*, 141–5.

33. Wark, 'Cryptographic Innocence', 639–65; Sawatsky, *For Services Rendered*, 29. I am much indebted to the guidance of Matthew Aid on these matters.

34. Brigadier-General USAF, Acting D of I, Walter R. Agee, to US Coordinator of Joint Operations, 7 Jun. 1948, 'Proposed U.S.–Canadian Agreement', USAF D of I records, File 2-1200/2-1299, Box 40, RG 341.

35. Memo by the Cypher Policy Board, 'Disclosure of Information on Cypher Systems and Cryptographic Information to Commonwealth Countries', Annexe to JIC (48) 127 (Final) Guard, 5 Feb. 1949, L/WS/1/1074, IOLR; 18 Oct. 1949 Replacement, RG 319.

36. Aldrich, *Intelligence and the War against Japan,* 82–3; Croft, 'Reminiscences', 133–44; Bowen, Socony Vacuum Oil, NY, to Barry, Socony Vacuum Oil, London, intercepted by tel. censorship, 12 Apr. 1944, U3271/3271/70, FO 371/40776.

37. 'Instructions for the Use of Guard', 1948, AIR 20/2794; Notice (Limited Circulation) N11/49, 7 Jul. 1949, ibid.

38. MoD to Forward, 31 Aug. 1956, DEFE 13/414.

39. Aid, 'US Humint and Comint', part 1, 15–50.

40. 'On Watch: Profiles from the National Security Agency's Past 40 Years', 17, declassified by NSA under FOIA.

41. A-2 to Naval Communications Annexe, 'Request for British Comintsum Publications', 19 Mar. 1948, 21450, Box 41, USAF D of I records, RG 341.

42. Cabell to Air Police Division, 28 Apr. 1948, 21200, Box 40, D of I records, RG 341.

43. Paige to Espe (Op. 23-Y), 'American Codes Held by Stella Polaris', 8 May 1946, Box 64, Entry 171A, RG 226.

44. Cain, 'Venona in Australia', 244–7; presentation by Oleg Tsarev, Oxford Conference, Sept. 1999.

45. CIA document, Appendix B, 'Recapitulation of the Intelligence Derived', in Steury (ed.), *Front Lines*, 401; The National Cryptological School, *On Watch: Profiles from the National Security Agency's Past 40 Years*, ch. 3, 'Treachery and Triumph: Black Friday', 19–22, FOIA.

46. Andrew and Gordievsky, *KGB*, 308–9.

47. Kahn, 'Soviet Comint', 7; Andrew and Mitrokhin, *The Sword*, 143–5.

48. Jones, *Most Secret War*, 92.

49. SEAC Noise Investigation Bureau report for May 1945, WO 203/4089.

50. Captain Wenger, U.S. Navy Coordinator of Joint Operations, to Colonel R. P. Klocko, USAF, CJO 0001922, 12 Mar. 1948, memo, 'British proposal for liaison on "noise investigation"', File 2-1100/2-1199, Box 40, D of I records, RG 341.

51. Dunlop memo, 'CSE and Radio Warfare', AIR 20/9660.

52. McMurtie (JSM) to Moore (Pentagon), 20 Nov. 1948, File 2-8300–2-8399, D of I records, RG 341; presentation given by Wing Commander B. Paton, 51 Sqdn, at 'Cold War Intelligence Gathering', Hendon, 18 Apr. 2000.

53. Partridge memo, 'Northern European Ferret Flights', 20 Aug. 1947, File 2-800–2-899, USAF D of I records, RG 341.

54. I am indebted to Matthew Aid's forthcoming study of US sigint for this point.

55. Memo for Chief AI Div., 3 July 1946, Microfilm Reel 1035, CAFH.

56. Memo for D of I and CNI, 17 Nov. 1948, Microfilm Reel 1031, CAFH.

57. Sontag and Drew, *Blind Man's Buff*, 7–24.

58. Air Technical Center, Air Technical Intelligence Study No. 102-EL-23/51-54: Radio Frequency Transmissions, Jul.-Sept. 1950, File 2-20944, D of I records, RG 341.

59. Tamnes, *High North*, 77.

60. Ibid., 50–2; Air Technical Intelligence Study, 'Soviet Electronic Countermeasures', 10 Jun. 1951, 20034, Box 149, D of I records, RG 341; Air Technical Intelligence Study, 'Soviet Air Communications', 12 Jul. 1951, 20032, Box 149, D of I records, RG 341.

61. Tamnes, *High North*, 116–17; D of I USAF to US Air Attaché London, 'Liaison with GCHQ', 26 Oct. 1952, 235700, Box 68, D of I records, RG 341.

62. AFOIN-T to D of I USAF, 16 Apr. 1952, 223200, Box 64, D of I records, RG 341.

Chapter 12 *Defeat in Palestine*

1. JIC (47) 52 (0) Final, 'Possible Future of Palestine', 9 Sept. 1947, L/WS/1/1162, IOLR.

2. LCS (47) 5, 'Illegal Immigration into Palestine', 9 Jul. 1947, CAB 81/80. I am indebted to Julian Lewis for this reference.

3. Hoffman, *Failure*, 9–10.

4. JIC (47) 52 (0) Final, 'Possible Future of Palestine', 9 Sept. 1947, L/WS/1/1162, IOLR.

5. Kumamoto, *International Terrorism*, 17.

6. Bowyer Bell, *Terror Out of Zion*, 23–51; Kumamoto, *International Terrorism*, 13–15.

7. Smith, 'Two Revolts', PhD, 113, 205; Charters, 'British Intelligence', 124–5.

8. Smith, 'Two Revolts', PhD, 204.

9. Charters, 'British Intelligence', 115–141; Heather, 'Intelligence and Counter-Insurgency', 57.

10. Aldrich and Zametica, 'Rise and Fall'.

11. SIME Security Summary No. 236, 21 Dec. 1945, Folder 81, Box 19, Entry 120, RG 226.

12. Smith, 'Two Revolts', PhD, 207.

13. Clark, 'Colonial Police', PhD, 215; Hoffman, *Failure*, 21–4; Kumamoto, *International Terrorism*, 30–4.

14. Cunningham to CO, 23 Nov. 1946, in Montgomery papers, 211/18, IWM.

15. Hoffman, *Failure*, 32–3; Clark, 'Colonial Police', PhD, 238.

16. Fergusson to Parl. Sec., CO, 12 Feb. 1947, CO 537/2270.

17. Farran, *Winged Dagger*, 348; Fergusson, *Trumpet*, 226.

18. Charters, 'Farran Case', 56–61; Smith, 'Two Revolts', PhD, 281. The present author has interviewed a member of Farran's squad.

19. High Comm. Palestine to SoS for Colonies, 12 Oct. 1946, F10453/10453/31, FO 371/52655.

20. Nesbit, *Eyes of the RAF*, 267–8.

21. McNeil to Attlee, PM/MH/47/61, 31 Mar. 1947, PREM 8/624; Attlee to McNeil, M189/47, 23 Apr. 1947, ibid.; Marseilles to FO, 29 Jul. 1947, ibid.

22. West, *Friends*, 33, 35.

23. Sherr (MI5) and Maude (MI5) at mtg at WO, 22 Sept. 1948, CO 537/5299.

24. Kumamoto, *International Terrorism*, 59.

25. Hillenkoetter (CIA) to Truman, 'Clandestine Air Transport Operations in Europe', 12 Apr. 1948, CIA docs, Europe, Reel 1, LL.

26. Mins by Alexander, 23 Dec., Bevin, 28 Dec., Attlee, 30 Dec. 1948, PREM 8/1051.

27. Alexander to Attlee, 1 Jan. 1949, PREM 8/1051.

28. Draft Statement by the SoS for Air, Jan. 1949, PREM 8/1051.

Chapter 13 *The Korean War*

1. Kleffens min., NS 1052/6/G, FO 371/100840.

2. Ford, *Estimative Intelligence*, 60–5; Singlaub, *Hazardous Duty*, 165–7.

3. Malcolm, *White Tigers*, 14.

4. Alexander, *Strange Connection*, 112–13.

5. Convers. memo, 11 Dec. 1947, 'ESD 44 Operations', Box 12, Office of Chinese Affairs, Lot Files 110, RG 59; Darling, *Central Intelligence Agency*, 119–20; Maochun, *OSS in China*, 262; Singlaub, *Hazardous Duty*, 150–3.

6. Aldrich, *Intelligence and the War against Japan*, 232, 277; Singlaub, *Hazardous Duty*, 145, 166.

7. Aid, 'US Humint and Comint', 17–63; Schaller, *MacArthur*, 121.

8. See the excellent account in Aldous, *Police*, 166–7.

9. Aid, 'US Humint and Comint', 17–63.

10. Willoughby to Wedemeyer (DCOS P&O), 10 Feb. 1949, Willougby papers, File: Wedemeyer, RG 23, MML.

11. General Charles P. Cabell, 'Memoirs of an Unidentified Aide', ch. 34, TSS, Reel 33080, IRIS 1025177, 168.2026.33080, CAFH.

12. Farrar-Hockley, *Korean War*, vol. 1, 49.

13. Blake, *No Other Choice*, 120–4.

14. COS (50) 107th mtg (with Directors of Intelligence), 11 Jul. 1950, DEFE 11/349.

15. Farrar-Hockley, *Korean War*, vol. 2, 163–4, 169.

16. I am indebted to Anthony Farrar-Hockley for this information.

17. Aid, 'US Humint and Comint', 17–63.

18. Ibid.

19. Ibid.; Evanhoe, *Darkmoon*, 11–12.

20. Aid, 'US Humint and Comint', 17–63.

21. Private information.

22. Singlaub, *Hazardous Duty*, 182–3.

23. Almond (FECOM) to Wisner (CIA), 30 Jul. 1950, Box 1, Gruenther Papers, DDEL; Aid, 'US Humint and Comint', 17–63.

24. James, *Years of MacArthur*, 416.

25. Ranelagh, *Agency*, 217–19; private information from four interviews in Washington, 1992–3.

26. Singlaub, *Hazardous Duty*, 182. British forces were not privy to JACK reports but received 200–300 unevaluated CCRAK agent reports per day, the reliability of which they thought 'doubtful', 'Experience in Korean Operations: Intelligence, Part III – Section VII', ADM 116/6231.

27. Malcolm, *White Tigers*, 128.

28. JCS 1969/33, 'Command Relationship between CINCFE with CIA after Ceasefire and Armistice in Korea', 13 Oct. 1952, Strategic Issues, Series 2, Reel 1, US JCS microfilm, BRO; PM-2541–53, 'Designation of a Central Intelligence Agency Commander, FECOM', 20 Apr. 1953, ibid.

29. Carruthers, 'Not Just Washed', 47–66; Singlaub, *Hazardous Duty*, 183. Apparently SIS conducted a study of claims in the field of communist brainwashing during the Korean War and concluded that the fears were greatly exaggerated.

30. Hall to Attlee, 18 Aug. 1950, DEFE 11/293; Bouchier to COS, 15 Sept. 1950, ibid.; Inter-Service Committee on Raiding Operations, 3 Dec. 1952, attended by 'SOE rep' Lieutenant-Colonel P. J. Dixon, DEFE 2/1848.

31. CINCFE Tokyo to Washington, 23 Sept. 1950, WARCX D4, RG 9, MML.

32. Farrar-Hockley, *Korean War*, vol. 1, 326–8; 'Korea Report: Part II – Command, Staff and Control of Operations', ADM 116/6231.

33. Connor, *Ghost Force*, 22; Anderson, *Banner*, 35–6.

34. Malcolm, *White Tigers*, 121–40.

35. Ibid. These issues are also confirmed by Farrar-Hockley, *Korean War*, vol. 2, 302–3.

36. Anderson, *Banner*, 34–5, 90–2, 160, 179–87, 199–201. Aspects of Anderson's account are challenged by Evanhoe, *Darkmoon*, 103–34.

37. Malcolm, *White Tigers*, 136–7; Clark to CSUSA Washington, 13 Dec. 1952, ACS (G-2 Army Intelligence) Files, TS Incoming and Outgoing Cables, Box 189, Entry 58, RG 319.

38. Schaller, *MacArthur*, 157–8.

39. Nichol, *How Many Times*, 187; Futrell, 'Case Study', 280–2; interview with a British Field Security officer.

40. Highlights of Conference HK EUSAK (item 3), 8 Jan. 1951, Korea Special File Dec. 1950–Mar. 1951, Box 20, Ridgway papers, USMHI.

41. Halliday and Cumings, *Korea*, 92, 136–7.

42. See especially Shaw, 'IRD', 269–70.

43. The Blake issue is explored in Halliday and Cumings, *Korea*, 69, 134–5.

44. Aid, 'US Humint and Comint', 17–63.

45. Ibid.

46. Ibid.

47. COS (50) 107th mtg, 12 Jul. 1950, DEFE 32/1. See also document no. 71, CWIHP Bulletin No. 5.

48. COS to Tedder (BJSM), 28 Jul. 1950, DEFE 32/1.

49. Shuckburgh to Franks, 25 Nov. 1952, AP20/15/18A, Avon papers, BUL. See also Lowe, *Containing*, 254–5.

50. John Talhoudin speaking in the television documentary *Reputations: Anthony Eden*, BBC2, 6 May 2000.

51. Ruane, 'Containing America', 142–62; Lowe, *Containing*, 215–18.

Chapter 14 *Cold War Fighting in Asia*

1. SD–JCS 11th mtg, 4 Apr. 1951, Box 77, PPS Lot Files 64 D 563, RG 59.

2. Directorate of Intelligence and Research to Dean Rusk, 'What Now for Britain? Wilson's Visit and Britain's Future', REU-11, 7 Feb. 1968, Kaiser papers, Box 8, HSTL.

3. Ruane, 'Containing America', 142–62.

4. Foot, *Practice of Power*, 76–84; Schaller, *United States and China*, 126–56; Zhai, *Dragon*, 84–96; Singlaub, *Hazardous Duty*, 180–1

5. Mtg of Attlee and Truman, 7 Dec. 1950, Box 17, PPS Lot Files 64 D 563, RG 59.

6. Strong memo, 'Support of China Mainland Resistance and Use of Nationalist Forces on Formosa', 24 Jan. 1951, Box 29, Records of the Office of Chinese Affairs, Lots 56 D 625, 57 D 633, 58 D 395, RG 59.

7. *China Handbook*, 1953–4, 'Coastal Raids', 197–9. I am indebted to Gary Rawnsley for this reference.

8. Holober, *Raiders*, 58–9, 87.

9. McGehee, *Deadly Deceits*, 25; Holber, *Raiders*, 3, 182; 'Instructions to U.S. Ambassador to the National Government of the Republic of China', 14 Jul. 1952, Box 11, Records of PPS 1947–53, Lot Files 64 D 563, RG 59.

10. Lecture at the Naval War College, 7 May 1953, File: Donovan: 53–6, Allman papers, HIWRP.

11. JCS 1735/224, 'Coastal Raiding and Maritime Interdiction Operations (China)', 5 Apr. 1954, CCS 385 (6–4–46), Sec. 81, RG 218.

12. Halpern interview in Weber, *Spymasters*, 119.

13. McGehee, *Deadly Deceits*, 26–7.

14. JCS-SD 15th mtg, 8 Jun. 1951, Box 77, PPS Lot Files 64 D 563, RG 59; JCS 1992/154, 'Tripartite Intelligence Conference held at Singapore, 21–23 Feb. 1952', 5 May 1952 092.Asia (6–25–48), Sec. 28 RG 218.

15. Convers. memo, 31 Jul. 1951, Box 29, Records of the Office of Chinese Affairs Lot Files 56 D 625, 57 D 633, 58 D 395, RG 59.

16. Halpern interview in Weber, *Spymasters*, 123. See also Powers, *Man Who Kept the Secrets*, 50.

17. Burma: Monthly Summary, 16 Jan. 1954, DEFE 7/369.

18. Entries for 16 Jan., 5 Feb., 16 Nov. 1953, Sebald diary, HIWRP.

19. Mins Joint Committee on Evac., 22, 26 and 28 Oct. 1953, PSA: Office i/c Burma Affairs, Lot Files 58 D 321, RG 59.

20. U Nu to Eisenhower, 15 Mar. 1954, Box 5, Ann Whitman Int. Series, DDEL.

21. Ambassador Arthur W. Hummel Jnr transcript, 13 Jul. 1989, FAOHP, 25; Cline, *Chiang Ching-kuo*, 62–79.

22. Convers. memo, 23 Sept. 1953, INPOLCO, Box 4, Bureau of FE Affairs, Lot Files 33 D 388, RG 59.

23. Convers. memo, 'Arms Aid for Tibet', 24 Jul. 1950, Box 18, Office of Chinese Affairs, Lot Files 110, RG 59. See also Shakya, *Dragon*, 19, 75–6; Smith, *Tibetan Nation*, 507.

24. Acheson to Henderson, 27 Oct. 1950, *FRUS*, 1950, vol. 6, 545–6.
25. Ali, 'South Asia', 259–68. Ali dates American assistance to 1950, somewhat earlier than Shakya.
26. Ibid. On British attitudes see Zhai, *Dragon*, 50–1.
27. Marchetti and Marks, *CIA*, 128–3; Robbins, *Invisible Air Force*, 96–100; Singlaub, *Hazardous Duty*, 154; Smith, *Unknown CIA*, 86–71; Schaller, *MacArthur*, 179; Lowe, *Origins*, 53.
28. Strong memo, 'Support of China Mainland Resistance and Use of Nationalist Forces on Formosa', 24 Jan. 1951, Box 39, Records of the Office of Chinese Affairs Lots 56 D 625, 57 D 633, 58 D 395, RG 59; Convers. with General Li Tsing-jen, 26 Jan. 1951, ibid.; Jessup memo, 'CIA Appraisal of Chinese Nationalists', 22 Jan. 1951, ibid. See also Holober, *Raids*, 182.
29. Philby, *Silent War*, 117.
30. Smith, *Portrait*, 147–8.
31. Aldrich, *Intelligence and the Far Eastern War*, 269, 281, 288; 'Chinese Communists', appendix to CP (49) 39, 4 Mar. 1949, CAB 129/32.
32. Colby, *Honorable Men*, 103. Also Richard E. Johnson transcript, 30 Jan. 1991, FAOHP, 7.
33. US Army LO, Hong Kong, to G-2 Washington, 13 May and 6 Jun. 1952, ACS (G-2 Army Intelligence) Files, TS Incoming and Outgoing Cables, Box 189, Entry 58, RG 319; de Silva, *Sub Rosa*, 194.
34. Colby, *Honorable Men*, 103: McGehee, *Deadly Deceits*, 21–2.
35. JCS 2118/17, 'Courses of Action Relative to Communist China and Korea – Anti-Communist Chinese', 7 Mar. 1951 (3-14-57), RG 218.
36. CIA Report 00-B-14066, 'Prediction and Causes of Unrest in Kwantung Province', 27 Mar. 1950, Frame. 32, Reel I, *CIA Research Reports on China*, BRO.
37. JIC 551, 'Estimate of Effectiveness of Anti-Communist Guerrillas Operating in China', 12 Feb. 1951 (3-14-57), RG 218, estimated numbers of c.622,000; CIA Report RSS No. 0035/69, 'The Political Security Apparatus', 20 Feb. 1969, Frame 186, Reel IV, *CIA Research on China*, BRO.
38. NSC 6007/1, cited in Lombardo, 'American Consulate', 51; Ambassador Edwin W. Martin transcript 3, 17 Mar. 1988, FAOHP, 1–5.
39. Ball, 'Over and Out', 74–96.
40. Richard E. Johnson transcript, 30 Jan. 1991, FAOHP, 7–8; de Silva, *Sub Rosa*, 192.
41. Martin memo, 'Use of Hong Kong USIS as Cover for Covert Operations', 17 Dec. 1952, Box 38, Office of Chinese Affairs, P Files, 1953–5, Lot 56 D 625, RG 59; (draft) NSC 48/2, 9 Feb. 1950, Box 17, Office of Chinese Affairs, Lot Files 110, RG 59.
42. Ambassador Arthur W. Hummel Jnr, transcript, 31 Jul. 1989, FAOHP, 15–16.
43. Press Summary, Thurs., 20 Nov. 1958, F1695/1, FO 371/13337.
44. Lombardo, 'American Consulate', 64–81.
45. Graham to Lennox-Boyd, 20 May 1955, PREM 11/1309.
46. Peking to FO, 14 Aug. 1955, PREM 11/1309.
47. PM (55) 72, Lennox-Boyd to Eden, 'Air India Crash', and Eden min., n.d., PREM 11/1309; PM (56) 4, 'Air India Crash', Lennox-Boyd to Eden, 7 Jan. 1956, PREM 11/1309. See also Lombardo, 'American Consulate', 72–3; Tucker, *Taiwan*, 206–7.
48. de Silva, *Sub Rosa*, 194–5.
49. Foot, *Wrong War*, 77–84.
50. Zhai, *Dragon*, 114.
51. 18 Feb. 1955, Dulles–Herter convers. microfilm, Reel 3, LL.
52. Zhai, *Dragon*, 162. On the role of ideology in American policy see Lucas, *Freedom's War*, 1–15, 184–7.

Chapter 15 *The Struggle to Contain Liberation*

1. NID 7956, Longley-Cook (DNI) memo, 'Where Are We Going?', 6 July 1951, PREM 11/159.
2. Rudgers, 'Origins', 257.
3. Entries for 6 Jul. and 6–8 Dec. 1950, Bright-Holmes (ed.), *Like It Was*.
4. RC/19/50, 7 Feb. 1950, NS1053/5/G, FO 371/86762.
5. 'Ukrainian and Baltic Language Broadcasts', 9 May 1950, NS1052/47/G, FO 371/86754.
6. NSC68, 'United States Objectives and Programs for National Security', 14 Apr. 1950, *FRUS*, 1950, vol. 1, 237–92.
7. MDM (51) 2, 'Defence Policy and Global Strategy', Jun. 1951, CAB 21/1787.
8. Roberts to Strang, 19 Nov. 1951, ZS/19/60, FO 371/124980; 'Russia Committee Re-organisation', 13 Nov. 1952, RC/62/52, FO 371/125005; interviews with former members of OPS, 1998.
9. COS (51) 97th mtg, 13 Jun. 1951, DEFE 11/275. The place of these committees including the elusive OPS sketched in Appendix B 'Position of IRD in the Foreign Office', Oct. 1951, DEFE 11/275.
10. Note by ACAS (P), Chairman, (PSW) 3 (Final), 'Psywar – Policy for Provision of Psychological Warfare', AIR 20/9599.

11. I am indebted to Gulnur Aybet for guidance on abandonment–entrapment.
12. Ross, *Interests of Peace*, 52.
13. Chester H. Opal transcript, 10 Jan. 1989, FAOHP.
14. Annexe No. 5 to NSC 68/3 in Nitze et al., 'Newly Declassified Annexes'. I am indebted to Erik Jones for this reference.
15. Edward Alexander transcript, n.d., FAOHP, 8. See also Roosevelt, *For Lust*, 300–11.
16. Harrison min., 1 Jul. 1951, ZP 27/18/9, FO 371/124970; WTN/Brief/6, 3 Sept. 1951, ZP 27/2/G, ibid.
17. Falla min., head of OPS, 3 Apr. 1951, NSI052/30/G, FO371/100842.
18. Kovrig, *Myth of Liberation*, 65–78.
19. Berger, AFSC Staff Study, 'Use of Covert Paramilitary Activity', 16.
20. Simpson, *Blowback*, 210–21; Colby, *Honorable Men*, 84–109; Tamnes, *High North*, 76.
21. Intell. and Evaluation Branch, Psy War, 'Planning and Effective Use of Soviet Prisoners of War', 6 Dec. 1951, 091 Rs. Case 46, Box 43, G-3 TS 1950–1, RG 319.
22. Staff Conference, 22 Oct. 1951, in Warner (ed.), *CIA under Harry Truman*, 434–6.
23. Mins of the JCS–SD Co-ordinating Committee, 12 Mar. 1952, Box 77, PPS Records, Lot Files 64 D 563, RG 59; also private information.
24. Young, *Winston Churchill's Last Campaign*, 107–8.
25. PUSC (51) 16 (Final), 'Future Policy towards Soviet Russia', and Annexe B, 'Liberation of the Satellites', 17 Jan. 1952, ZP10/4, FO 371/25002. This is reproduced in full and discussed by John Young, who secured its declassification, in 'Cold War Fighting'.
26. JCS–SD mtg, 12 Mar. 1952, Box 77, PPS Lot Files 64 D 563, RG 59. Throughout the 1950s the United States produced a stream of high-level estimates on this subject, see for example NIE 10–58, 'Anti-Communist Resistance Potential in the Sino-Soviet Bloc', 4 Mar. 1958, *FRUS 1958–60*, vol. 10, part 1, pp. 7–11.
27. NID 7956, Longley-Cook (DNI) memo, 'Where Are We Going?', 6 Jul. 1951, PREM 11/159.
28. Churchill to First Lord of the Admiralty, 9 Jan. 1952, PREM 11/159; Churchill to Private Office, 12 Apr. 1952, ibid. On the visit to Washington see Young, *Winston Churchill's Last Campaign*, 84–5.
29. Young, *Winston Churchill's Last Campaign*, 78–81.
30. Slessor min. to VCAS, 1 Oct. 1951, AIR 75/107.
31. Garrod to Tedder, 24/4/AIR, 18 Mar. 1948, AIR 75/116.
32. Kenney to Vandenberg, 29 Apr. 1950, 212900, Box 49, D of I records, RG 341.
33. 'The Chairman said the JIC team had not yet come back from the US', RC mtg, 12 Sept. 1950, NS1053/26/G, FO 371/86762; AI2, 'An Estimate of the Period in Which Hostilities Are Most Likely to Commence between the USSR and the Western Powers', 28 Aug. 1950, CCS 337 (8–16–49), Sec. 3, RG 218. Washington tabled an alternative paper to London's JIC (50) 77.
34. Landon memo, 'U.S.–U.K. Conversations on the Present World Situation', 7 Aug. 1950, 21890, Box 56, D of I records, RG 341.
35. General Charles P. Cabell, 'Memoirs of an Unidentified Aide', ch. 32, TSS, Reel 33080, IRIS 1025177, 168.2026.33080, CAFH.
36. FORD paper, 'Internal Stability of the Soviet Regime', NS 1030/50/G, FO 371/100842.
37. Memo by R.P.2 to OPS, 29 Feb. 1952, NS 1053/29/G, FO 371/100842.
38. Holher memo, 'Soviet Internal Stability', 1 Jul. 1952, NS 1052/27/G, FO 100842.
39. OPS memo, 'Criticisms by M.I.6 – FORD paper on the Internal Stability of the Soviet Regime', Jul. 1952, NS1052/30/G, FO 371/100842; interviews with former OPS members, 1998.
40. SD–JCS 7th mtg, 15 Mar. 1951, PPS Records, Box 77, Lot 64 D 563, RG 59.
41. JCS–SD 16th mtg, 27 Jun. 1951, Box 77, PPS Lot Files, 64 D 563, RG 59.
42. Slim, 'Address to SHAPE Staff', 22 Aug. 1952, Box 24, Ridgway papers, USMHI. Newly opened Czech archives reveal 'sharply rising foreign infiltration' into Czechoslovakia during 1951–3, Mastny, *Cold War*, 118.
43. Larres, 'Preserving Law and Order', 320–50; Marchio, 'Resistance Potential and Rollback', 219–41; Osterman, 'United States', 7–15.
44. Bank, *OSS*, 188; 'Use of Soviet Troops in Aid of the Civil Power', Berlin, 16 Jun.–10 Jul. 1953, Brigadier Meadmore, BRIXMIS, WO 208/5002.
45. CIA OCI No. 4491, 'Comment on East Berlin Uprising', 17 Jun. 1953, Box 3, C. D. Jackson records, DDEL.
46. Dr Robert R. Bowie transcript, 15 Mar. 1988, FAOHP, 22–4. See also Kovrig, *Walls and Bridges*, 66–9.
47. Kennan to Jackson, 15 Sept. 1953, Box 4, C. D. Jackson records, DDEL.
48. 'Concept and ideas for psychological warfare in Europe developed by the Chief of Mission meeting at Luxembourg on Sept. 18–19, 1953', Box 14, PSB Central Files Series, NSC Staff Papers, WHO, DDEL.

49. Entries for 7 and 10 Dec. 1953, Moran, *Winston Churchill*. See also Seldon, *Indian Summer*, 390–1, and Kovrig, *Walls and Bridges*, 52–5.

50. Entries for 12 Apr. and 4 May 1954, Moran, *Winston Churchill*. See also Young, *Winston Churchill's Last Campaign*, 306–8.

51. Crittenberger memo to OCB, 'Timing of the Implementation of the VFC', 11 May 1954, Box 8, OCB Secretariat Series, National Security Staff, WHO, DDEL; OCB, 'Report on Activation of a VFC (NSC 143/2), 3 Aug. 1955, ibid.

52. Kovrig, *Walls and Bridges*, 101.

53. De Silva, *Sub Rosa*, 87–96.

54. Private information; Anderson, *Banner*, 204–5.

55. Deletant, *Communist Terror*, 267.

56. Chester H. Opal transcript, 10 Jan. 1989, FAOHP, 22.

57. Dulles to Goodpaster, enclosing 'Radio Free Europe', 20 Nov. 1956, Box 7, AS/SS Office of Staff Sec., WHO, DDEL. See also Kovrig, *Walls and Bridges*, 93; Rawnsley, 'Cold War Radio in Crisis', 197–217.

58. Peter Mod, Hungarian Permanent Representative UN, 'Memo. on the Question of Hungary in Connection with the Events on 23 Oct. 1956 and After', NH10110/150, FO 371/128670.

59. Crittenberger to Jackson, 29 May 1958, Box 44, CDJP, DDEL; Crittenberger to Jackson, 5 Nov. 1956, enclosing 'Report on Free Europe Press Operations', 3 Oct. 1956, ibid.

60. Kovrig, *Walls and Bridges*, 93; Ranelagh, *Agency*, 306–7.

61. Jackson to Allen Dulles, 2 Jul. 1958, Box 40, CDJP, DDEL.

Chapter 16 *The CIA's Federalist Operation: ACUE and the European Movement*

1. Action Items, 19 Oct. 1953, File: OCB Special Staff, Box 1, C. D. Jackson records, DDEL.

2. Braden,, 'Birth of the CIA', 13.

3. Gillingham, *Coal*, 148–78; Milward, *Reconstruction*, 56–84; Pisani, *CIA*, 34–58; Warner, 'Eisenhower', 320.

4. Brief references to this have surfaced over the years: Barnes, 'Secret Cold War', 666–7; Eringer, *Global Manipulators*, 19–20; Fletcher, *Who Were They Travelling With?*, 71; Melandri, *Les Etats Unis face à l'unification de l'Europe*, 320, 354–5; Thompson, 'Bilderberg and the West', 184; Zurcher, *Struggle to Unite Europe*, 71. There is now a useful and extended account in Dorril, *MI6*, 455–82.

5. Rebattet, 'European Movement', PhD.

6. On AFL-CIO efforts see Wall, *United States*, 99–104, 151–3, 211–15; Pisani, *CIA*, 99–100, 119, 145; Romero, *United States*, 12–17, 88–95.

7. Coleman, *Liberal Conspiracy*, xi. See also, Colby, *Honorable Men*, 51–107.

8. Thorne, 'American Political Culture', 316–20; Hogan, *Marshall Plan*, 213–14, 332–3.

9. Meyer, *Facing Reality*, 110–39; Ranelagh, *Agency*, 133–8; Simpson, *Blowback*, 138–56; Bank, *OSS*, 138–89. On stay-behind see Colby, *Honorable Men*, 51–107.

10. Miller, 'Taking Off the Gloves', 35–46; Ellwood, '1948 Elections in Italy', 19–35.

11. Romero argues that, while operations to support non-communist unions in Italy and France 'were financed in large measure by the CIA', the role of intelligence agencies should not be exaggerated, *United States*, 94–6.

12. Coleman, *Liberal Conspiracy*, passim; Meyer, *Facing Reality*, 66–7.

13. Braden's own recollections are recounted in Barnes, 'Secret Cold War', 666–7, and in Braden, 'Birth of the CIA', 4–13. See also Copeland, *Real Spy World*, 230.

14. Zurcher, *Struggle to Unite Europe*, 24; Rebattet, 'European Movement', PhD, 294–6.

15. Sandys to Beddington-Behrens, 11 Oct. 1948, and 'Report by Chairman of Finance Sub-Committee', 8 Dec. 1948, EX/P/53, European Movement Archives, cited in Rebattet, 'European Movement', PhD, 195. Retinger had undertaken a previous unsuccessful trip to the United States in Nov. 1946, ibid., 299.

16. Coudenhove-Kalergi to Donovan, 24 Nov. 1949, Box 38, Allen W. Dulles papers, Mudd Library, Princeton University; mins of the Second Mtg of the Executive Committee, 1 Jul. 1949, Folder 90, ACUE records, LL; Churchill to Donovan, private, 4 Jun. 1949, folder 90, ACUE records, LL.

17. Churchill, *War Speeches*, vol. 2, 427–8.

18. Young, *France*, 210–14; Young, *Britain and European Unity*, 4–6, 22–3.

19. NSC 5430, 'Status of US Program for National Security as of 30 Jun. 1954, Part 7, USIA Program', 18 Aug. 1954, *FRUS, 1952–4*, vol. 2, 1780; Bank, *OSS*, 186–7.

20. Darling, *CIA*, 267–8, 301–45. Thomas W. Braden appears to have ceased to be executive director in the spring of 1951. He was succeeded by William P. Durkee and then by Alan Hovey in 1953. Durkee had served in OSS with Braden and later became vice president of Free Europe Inc. with special responsibility for Radio Free Europe. On Braden's departure see Braden to Sandys, 30 Mar. 1951, and Sandys to Braden, 17 Apr. 1951, 9/1/10, Duncan Sandys papers, CCC.

21. List of ACUE Directors attached to details of a visit by Robert Schuman, 20 Sept. 1950, Folder 5, ACUE records, LL; Filipelli, *American Labor*, 112, 134–5, 211.
22. 'Report to the Executive Directors of the American Committee on United Europe' by William P. Durkee, May 1952, WBS, DDEL.
23. Churchill to Donovan, private, 4 Jun. 1949, Folder 90, ACUE records, LL.
24. Meyer, *Facing Reality*, 63–6; Pomian (ed.), *Joseph Retinger*, 237; Aldrich, 'European Integration', 163–4.
25. Churchill to Donovan, private, 4 Jun. 1949, Folder 90, ACUE records, LL.
26. Address by Churchill to the ACUE, New York, 29 Mar. 1949, Folder 2, ACUE records, LL.
27. Mins of a discussion between Kennan and Hayter (JIC Chairman), 26 Jul. 1949, W627/2/500G, FO 371/76383.
28. Braden to Bedell Smith, 28 Dec. 1949, WBS, DDEL. Some initial funding in 1949 appears to have come from private sources, 'Report to the Directors of the ACUE' by William P. Durkee, May 1952, 7–8, WBS, DDEL.
29. Confidential memo enclosed in Braden to Bedell Smith, 27 Jun. 1950, WBS, DDEL.
30. 'Report to the Directors of the ACUE', by William P. Durkee, May 1952, 7–8, WBS, DDEL; Rebattet, 'European Movement', PhD, 49, 186; Aldrich, 'European Integration', 165. On Sandys in 1945 see Young, *Britain and European Unity*, 19–20.
31. Wisner (CIA) to Harriman (ECA), 'Western European Political Integration', 15 Feb. 1950, CIA, FOIA.
32. Report by Braden, 'Activities of ACUE, Part V, Summary Program for the Future', Apr. 1950, File 20, Box 1, ACUE records, LL.
33. 'Report to the Directors of the ACUE' by William P. Durkee, May 1952, 9–10, WBS, DDEL.
34. Memo enclosed in Braden to Bedell Smith, 27 Jun. 1950, WBS, DDEL.
35. Retinger to Sandys, 31 Mar. 1950, European Movement Archives, quoted in Rebattet, 'European Movement', PhD, 408.
36. Rebattet, 'European Movement', PhD, 198–9. Hitherto the ACUE had offered little specific direction as to precise use of the funds, remarking in January 1950, 'up to now all funds have been sent to the European Movement to use as it sees fit', mins of the mtg of the Executive Committee, ACUE, 20 Jan. 1950, WBS, DDEL.
37. 'Report to the Directors of the ACUE', by William P. Durkee, May 1952, 7–8, WBS, DDEL. Braden, confidential memo on ACUE to Bedell Smith, 6 Jul. 1950, WBS, DDEL.
38. Gillingham, *Coal*, 147. Another historian has identified a 'long American intrigue to make him "director-general" of the OEEC', Milward, *European Rescue*, 324.
39. Memo enclosed in Braden to Bedell Smith, 27 Jun. 1950, WBS, DDEL.
40. Memo of the tripartite preliminary meetings on Items 5 and 8, MIN/TR/P/4, 9 May 1950, *FRUS, 1950*, vol. 3, 1081; Elsey to Lloyd, 16 May 1951, enclosing Special Guidance memo by Policy Advisory Staff, 'The Concept of Europe', 8 May 1951, *DDRS (1975)*, 1, 3, p. 176D. Lloyd noted, 'I agree, it sounds very good.'
41. Miscamble, *Kennan*, 284–5; mins of a discussion between Kennan and Hayter, 26 Jul. 1949, W627/2/500G, FO 371/76383.
42. Memo of a convers. between Acheson, Kennan, Spaak and Silvercruys, 19 Jan. 1950, *FRUS, 1950*, vol. 3, 613–14; mins of the 7th mtg of the PPS, ibid., 617–20. See also Gillingham, *Coal*, 134–7, 147–8.
43. Statement of Donovan on ERP, 3 Mar. 1950, and subsequent discussions in the House Foreign Affairs Committee between Donovan, Congressman Richards and Chairman Kee, Folder 20, Box 1, ACUE records, LL.
44. Acting SoS to Donovan, 29 Sept. 1950, Exhibit 6, Appendix IV, May 1952, WBS, DDEL.
45. Mtgs of US Ambassadors in Paris, 21 Oct. 1949, *FRUS, 1949*, vol. 4, 490–3; memo of a conversation between Harriman, Bruce and McCloy, 20 Jan. 1950, *FRUS, 1950*, vol. 3, 1608–9; mtgs of US Ambassadors in Rome, 22–24 Mar. 1950, *FRUS, 1950*, vol. 3, 809.
46. Braden confidential memo on the ACUE to Bedell Smith, 6 Jul. 1950, WBS, DDEL.
47. Ibid.
48. 'Report to the Directors of the ACUE', by William P. Durkee, May 1952, 6–7, WBS, DDEL; Aldrich, 'European Integration', 168–9.
49. Braden to Bedell Smith, 28 Dec. 1949, WBS, DDEL. On Britain's 'obstructionism' at Strasbourg in the summer of 1950 see Anderson to State Department, 31 Jul. 1950, *FRUS, 1950*, vol. 3, 777–80.
50. N.E.C. mins. (E.C.6.1946–47), 22 Jan. 1947, in Grantham, 'Labour Party', PhD, 168–9.
51. A copy of the Mackay Plan is available at File 2, Group 7, Mackay Papers, BLPES; 'Report to the Directors of the ACUE, by William P. Durkee, May 1952, 6–7, 10–11, 14–15, WBS, DDEL; mins of the mtg of the Executive Committee, ACUE, 20 Jan. 1950, WBS, DDEL; entry for 11 Sept. 1948, Pimlott (ed.), *Dalton Diary*.
52. Mackay, 'Memo on the ERP and European Political Union', New York, 1 Feb. 1949, fol. 8, File 2, Group 7, Mackay Papers, BLPES.

53. Report by Braden, 'Activities of ACUE', Apr. 1950, Folder 20, Box 1, ACUE records, LL.

54. Mackay to Allen Dulles, 21 Jan. 1950, Folder 20, Box 1, ACUE records, LL. See also Mackay to Braden, 29 Mar. and 8 Apr. 1950, ibid.

55. Report by Braden, 'Activities of ACUE', Apr. 1950, Folder 20, Box 1, ACUE records, LL. See also Mackay to Allen Dulles, 21 Jan. 1950, Folder 20, Box 1, ACUE records, LL.

56. Report to Attlee, Mar. 1950, Subject Files 'Council of Europe', Dalton papers, BLPES, cited in Grantham, 'Labour Party', PhD, 254.

57. Aldrich, 'European Integration', 168–78. Mins of Annual Mtg, 24 Apr. 1951, WBS, DDEL.

58. Presentation by Braden, 18 Jan. 1951, Folder 6, Box 1, ACUE records, LL.

59. Retinger to Cripps, 7 Feb. 1950, UP3117/2, FO 371/88643; Hooper mins, 8 and 10 Feb. 1950, Makins and Jebb mins, 9 Feb. 1950, ibid. See also Curtins to Retinger, 1 Jan. 1950, 9/1/10, Duncan Sandys papers, CCC.

60. Donovan report from Strasbourg, 5 Dec. 1951, Folder 58, ACUE records, LL; 'Report to the Directors of the ACUE' by William P. Durkee, May 1952, 6–7, 14–15, WBS, DDEL.

61. E.g. address by Paul-Henri Spaak, 1 Apr. 1952, New York, Folder 9, ACUE records, LL.

62. Rebattet, 'European Movement', PhD, 308.

63. 'Statement of General William J. Donovan, ACUE to Committee on Foreign Affairs, House of Representatives', 3 Mar. 1950, Folder 56, ACUE records, LL; Bonnet to Donovan, 26 Jun. 1950, and attached note to Bedell Smith, WBS, DDEL; ACUE newsletter, nos 1–20, Folder 64, ACUE records, LL.

64. 'Report to the Directors of the ACUE' by William P. Durkee, May 1952, 19, WBS, DDEL; Appendix IV, exhibit 4, 'material published by the ACUE and Publications Distributed', ibid.

65. Braden, 'Activities of the ACUE', p. 13, Apr. 1950, Folder 20, ACUE records, LL; 'Report to the Directors of the ACUE' by William P. Durkee, May 1952, 19, WBS, DDEL. The ACUE planned to allocate $62,500 to research on federalism at Harvard Law School in 1952.

66. See for example Friedrich's studies, *Federalism: Trends in Theory and Practice* and *Europe: An Emergent Nation?*. On his ideas see Tormey, *Making Sense of Tyranny*.

67. 'The Soviet Zone of Germany', ed. Carl Friedrich (Subcontractor's monograph, HRAF-34, Harvard-1, 1956); Friedrich to Altschud, 1 Jan. 1951, NCFE File, Box 28, Friedrich papers, HUG (FP) – 17, 12, HUA.

68. Allen Dulles to Friedrich, 11 Jan. 1951, NCFE File, Box 28, Friedrich papers, HUG (FP) – 17, 12, HUA; Clay to Friedrich, 15 Jan. 1951, ibid.; Jackson to Friedrich, 31 Jan. 1951, ibid.

69. Braden to Langer, 12 Jan. 1950, File: ACUE, Box 9, Langer papers, HUA; Langer to Braden, 20 Jan. 1950, ibid.; Burkhardt to Langer, 24 Jul. 1950, File: B-General, Box 9, Langer papers, HUA. On Langer's career in OSS and subsequently CIA see Winks, *Cloak and Gown*, 79–82, 495–6.

70. 'Report on the College of Europe' by P. C. Dodd, Jun. 1951, Folder 1, Box 1, ACUE records, LL.

71. Rebattet, 'European Movement', PhD, 34.

72. 'Report on the College of Europe' by P. C. Dodd, Jun. 1951, Folder 1, Box 1, ACUE records, LL.

73. 'Program and Budget for 1950', 6, WBS, DDEL.

74. White (American Committee on NATO) to Karp, 17 Sept. 1959, Folder 89, ACUE records, LL; the cost of the Economist Intelligence Unit studies for 1959 is given in 'Report to the Directors' by Foster, 13, Oct. 1959, Folder 100, ACUE records, LL.

75. In 1962 Christopher Layton moved on to a number of advisory roles for the EEC; he became an honorary director general of the EEC and later became its special adviser on technology, *Who's Who 1986*, 1018; Edwards, *Pursuit of Reason*, 923–5.

76. See Daddow's path-breaking thesis, 'Rhetoric and Reality', PhD, 9–12, 111–77, discussing Pinder and Mayne, *Federal Union*, 168. See also Daddow, *Harold Wilson and European Unity*, 1–15.

77. Hubback, *No Ordinary Press Baron*, 205–6; *Who's Who 1959*, 1765.

78. Franklin to Layton, 9 Oct. 1949, Box 82, Layton Papers, Trinity College, Cambridge.

79. Butler to Layton, 19 Apr. 1950, Box 142, Layton Papers, Trinity College, Cambridge; Braden to Layton, 4 Feb. 1950, ibid; Braden to Layton, 24 Feb. 1950, ibid; See also Allen Dulles to Layton, 2 Feb. 1950, ibid.; Braden to Rebattet, 15 Jan. 1950, ibid.; Braden to Layton, 6 Jun. 1951, Box 136, ibid.

80. Hovey to Layton, 6 Apr. 1953, Box 135, Layton Papers, Trinity College, Cambridge. The records of the European–Atlantic Group are at Box 144, ibid.

81. Mins of the mtg of the Executive Committee, ACUE, 11 Oct. 1950, WBS, DDEL; memo concerning the International Campaign for the Creation of a European Council of Vigilance, 1950, ibid.; mins of the mtg of the Executive Committee, ACUE, 11 Oct. 1950, ibid.; 'Report to the Directors of the ACUE' by William P. Durkee, May 1952, 11–12, ibid.

82. Donovan to Bedell Smith, 25 Jul. 1951, WBS, DDEL. German activities included an ACUE-sponsored German–Europe conference at Hamburg in Nov. 1951, mins of the mtg of the Executive Committee, ACUE, 11 Oct. 1950, 12, 17–18, WBS, DDEL. On worries over Germany see Leffler, *Preponderance*, 318–19, 323.

83. 'Report by M. Moreau, Secretary General of the European Youth Campaign, to the International Executive Bureau of the European Movement', BE/P/60, European Movement Archives and interview with G. Rebattet, cited in Rebattet, 'European Movement', PhD, 449–50. On McCloy's interest in covert activities see Bird, *Chairman*, 345–58.

84. BE/M/8, Luxemburg, 21 May 1948, 2, European Movement Archives, and BE/M/14, Paris, 23 Nov. 1953, 3, ibid., quoted in Rebattet, 'European Movement', PhD, 201.

85. European Youth Campaign, 1953, CCS/P/2, box 1, ACUE collection, HIWRP. Much of the youth campaign material has survived in the archives at Stanford, see for example, *Bulletin d'Information des Jeunesses Européenes Fédéralistes*, Dec. 1951, Box 2, ibid. Monnet to Donovan, 3 Oct. 1952, Folder 61, ACUE records, LL.

86. 'Reports to the Directors of ACUE' by William P. Durkee, Jul. 1951 and May 1952, WBS, DDEL. Rebattet suggest that all the resources for the European Youth Campaign came from the ACUE, which acted as 'a covering organisation' for the United States government, and that £444,080 was transferred for this purpose between 1 May 1951 and 31 May 1953. On this see FIN/P/6, 'European Movement: European Youth Campaign, Treasurer's Report', 1 Sept. 1953, European Movement Archives, cited in Rebattet, 'European Movement', PhD, 206–7.

87. Page to Kennan, 11 Oct. 1948, 865.00/10/1148, RG 59; American Ambassador to Lovett, 11 Oct. 1948, 865.00/10/1148, RG 59; both quoted in Filipelli, *American Labor*, 150–1. Nevertheless, Gedda also appears to have had ACUE associations; see for example *The Union of Europe: Declarations of European Statesmen*, p. 57, 9/1/10, Duncan Sandys papers, CCC.

88. Rebattet reports that European Movement's international review, *Europe Today and Tomorrow*, was 'almost completely financed by subscriptions from the Mutual Security Agency and ACUE', 'European Movement', PhD, 201, 302.

89. Pomian (ed.), *Joseph Retinger*, 237; retired American official in correspondence with the author, 15 Jul. 1993.

90. USIA memo, Caldwell, and Hulley, 'United European Federalists', 17 Dec. 1953, USIA, FOIA; UEF memo, 'Plan of Action, B) External Activities, b) Great Britain', USIA, FOIA; UEF memo, 'Plan of Action: III Financing of the UEF's Activities', USIA, FOIA; memo of a convers. with Altiero Spinelli, 'American Interest in European Federalist Union', 31 May 1955, USIA, FOIA. I am indebted to Xiomara George of the USIA Office of the General Counsel for processing my very extensive FOIA requests with speed and good humour.

91. Coleman, *Liberal Conspiracy*, 38.

92. Brady (Paris) to Clark, 2 Apr. 1955, USIA, FOIA; Washburn to USIS Rome, 'Projects in Support of Atlantic Community and European Unity', 20 Mar. 1956, USIA, FOIA.

93. Warner, 'Eisenhower', 320–3. Allen Dulles succeeded Bedell Smith on 26 Feb. 1953.

94. Beddington-Behrens, *Look Back*, 184. Also Beddington-Behrens to Jackson, 13 Aug. 1955, Box 25, CDJP, DDEL.

95. Chipman (HICOG) to State Department, 'Eastern Propaganda of the National Committee for a Free Europe', 15 Jan. 1953, 540.40/1–1953, RG 59.

96. Vilis Mosens (Chairman ACEN) to Philips, 13 Mar. 1956, File: Eastern Europe/Nationalism in Europe, Labour Party International Department records (post-1947), NMLH; 'Proposed West European Advisory Committee', 1 Feb. 1959, Box 44, CDJP, DDEL.

97. For an example of associated publicity materials see, *L'Action Fédéraliste européenne*, Jun. 1957, Box 6, ACUE collection, HIWRP.

98. Mins of a mtg of the Board of Directors, 6 Jun. 1956, Folder 91, ACUE records, LL.

99. One of his closest assistants, his principal private secretary, recalls that 'He made it plain on many occasions that CIA or quasi-CIA funds must be avoided because of the political risks to his prestige,' correspondence from François Duchêne to the author, 3 Feb. 1995. I am most grateful to François Duchêne for sharing his recollections with me.

100. Pisani, *CIA*, 47–52.

101. Rebattet, 'European Movement', PhD, 315.

102. Bird, *Chairman*, 416–17; 471–2; Duchêne, *Jean Monnet*, 339.

103. Kuhn memo, 'Non-military activities of NATO', 9 Jul. 1950, Box 4, Records of the Office of European Regional Affairs (1946–53), J. Graham Parsons, Lot Files 55 D 115, RG 59.

104. 'Memo. to the Board of Directors' by Alex Hovey, 6 Apr. 1960, Folder 94, ACUE records, LL.

105. ACUE statement of Receipts and Disbursements, 16 Feb. 1949 through 31 Jan. 1952, WBS, DDEL. ACUE's budget for 1952 was $400,000. Appendix IV, Exhibit 1, 'Report to the Directors of the ACUE' by William P. Durkee, May 1952, WBS, DDEL; Bedell Smith to Donovan, 12 Jan. 1953, ibid. See also Alex Hovey memo to the Board of Directors, 6 Apr. 1960, Folder 94, ACUE records, LL.

106. Mins of Annual Mtg, 24 Apr. 1951, WBS, DDEL; mins of a mtg of the Board of Directors, 6 Jun. 1956, Folder 91, ACUE records, LL.

107. Barnes, 'Secret Cold War', 666–7; Pomian (ed.), *Joseph Retinger*, 216, 228, 237; Miscamble, *Kennan*, 204.

108. Connely to Bedell Smith, 16 Feb. 1952, WBS, DDEL; mins of a mtg of the Board of Directors, 6 Jun. 1956, Folder 91, ACUE records, LL.

109. Rebattet, 'European Movement', PhD, 314–15. Rebattet's review of documentation in the European Movement's archives shows that these contain the minutes of the ACUE Board of Directors meetings discussing funding.

110. On propaganda see 'Psychological Action to Counter Totalitarian Propaganda', in record of a mtg between Acheson and De Gasperi, 24 Sept. 1951, *FRUS*, 1951, vol. 4, part 1, 685–6.

111. The figure of $10 million is given in Simpson, *Blowback*, 92. The most authoritative account of the elections by Miller, 'Taking Off the Gloves', 36, merely refers to 'millions of dollars'. Colby, in his memoir *Honorable Men*, 108–40, asserts that the 1948 elections constituted the largest OPC operation.

112. On Chile see Treverton, *Covert Action*, 14, 18, 41. On the American National Student Association, see Ransom, 'Secret Intelligence in the United States', 212.

113. CIA Report to the Psychological Strategy Board, PSB D-47, 29 Jul. 1953, Annexe D – Western Europe, FOIA.

114. Rebattet, 'European Movement', PhD, 48.

115. Braden to Bedell Smith, 28 Dec. 1949, WBS, DDEL.

116. Mins of the mtg of the Executive Committee, ACUE, 11 Oct. 1950, WBS, DDEL.

117. 'European Youth Campaign', CCS/P/2 1953, Box 1, ACUE collection, HIWRP.

118. Lipgens, *History of European Integration, 1945–1947,* vol. 1; Lipgens and Loth (eds), *Documents on the History of European Integration*, vol. 3; Milward, *European Rescue*, 14–17.

119. Miller, 'Approaches to European Institution Building of Carlo Sforza', 55–70; mins of a mtg of the Board of Directors, 6 Jun. 1956, Folder 91, ACUE records, LL.

120. Ernest Davies memo, 'The Labour Party and European Co-operation', 25 Apr. 1950, fol. 31, 9/9, Hugh Dalton papers, BLPES; 'Supplementary Report on the Second Session of the Consultative Assembly, Strasbourg', 18–24 Nov. 1950, 20, File: United Europe 1950, Box: European Unity, Labour Party International Department records, NMLH.

121. Romero, *United States*, 221–2; Hogan, *Marshall Plan*, 436.

122. Delzell, 'European Federalist Movement in Italy', 241–50; Bosco, 'Federal Union, Chatham House and the Anglo-French Union', 237–62.

123. Bird, *Chairman*, 471–2; Gill, *American Hegemony*, 125, 129, 151. Gill remarks upon 'the strong connections' between Bilderberg and the European Movement.

124. Eringer, *Global Manipulators*, 22–54; Pomian (ed.), *Joseph Retinger,* 250–9; Gill, *Trilateral Commission*, 151–5; Williams (ed.), *Diary of Hugh Gaitskell*, 542, 585. Bilderberg members in the 1950s included Victor Cavendish-Bentinck, Christopher Foster, Hugh Gaitskell, Sir Colin Gubbins and H. Montgomery Hyde.

125. In a response to a request by the author the CIA's Centre for the Study of Intelligence searched its archives for further material and replied that it had 'nothing unclassified available', David D. Gries, Director CSI, to author, 2 Mar. 1994.

126. Questions about operations inside the United States were initially raised by Stern, 'NSA and the CIA', 29–38. See also Treverton, *Covert Action*, 237–8; Jeffreys-Jones, *CIA*, 156–63; Johnson, *America's Secret Power*, 102–3. On legality see Ranelagh, *Agency*, 270–1.

Chapter 17 *Atomic Deception and Atomic Intelligence*

1. JP (56) 10 (Final), Annexe to 'The Baghdad Pact: background brief', 18 Jan. 1956, in Kent (ed.), *BDEE, Middle East*, B, 4, part III, 482.

2. TWC (46) 15 (Revise), 'Future Developments in Weapons and Methods of War', Limited Circ., 1 Jul. 1946, DEFE 2/1252.

3. Mins by Frith (DSD), 12 Sept. and 9 Oct. 1945, Rushbrooke (DNI), 14 Sept. 1945, ADM 1/26905. The path-breaking work here is Lewis, *Changing Direction* (2nd edn), ch. 1.

4. LCS (47) 3 (Prelim. Draft), 'Atomic Scientific Research and Production', 9 Jun. 1947, CAB 81/80. See also LCS (47) 7, 17 Sept. 1947, ibid.

5. Lewis, *Changing Direction* (2nd edn), ch. 1; Zametica, 'British Defence Planning', PhD, 156–74.

6. HC (48) 1, 'Outline Deception Plan', 18 May 1948, CAB 81/80.

7. LCS (49) 1, 'Review of Overall Deception Policy', 7 Jan. 1949, CAB 81/80.

8. TWC (45) 38, 'Effect of Atomic Bombs on Warfare in the Next Few Years', 24 Oct. 1945, DEFE 2/1252.

9. Aldrich and Coleman, 'Strategic Air Offensive', 405; private information.

10. Transcript of USAF Commanders Conference on Operation Dualism, Maxwell Air Force Base, 6–8 Dec. 1948, OPD 337, Sec. 2, RG 341.

11. Hollins (BJSM) to A1, 11 Apr. 1948, Box 8, Leahy papers, OAB, WNY.

12. A paper on Air Defence Deception by Assistant Commandant VISTRE, Netheravon, 11 Nov. 1948, 25971, Box 96, D of I records, RG 341.

13. LCS (48) 3, 'Russian Knowledge of Deception', 30 Jul. 1948, CAB 81/80.

14. COMGENUSARPAC to Wedemeyer, 'Operation SANDPIPER', 22 Feb. 1948, CM-IN 3746, RG 319.

15. Welsh to Lloyd, 9942/E14, 31 Oct. 1952, DEFE 16/188; Gene to Penney, 31 Dec. 1952, ibid.

16. Brook to Churchill, 18 Aug. 1952, PREM 11/257; Churchill to Alexander, 26 Aug. 1952, ibid.; Alexander to Churchill, 2 Sept. 1952, ibid. See for example entry for 1 Sept. 1954, 11.00 a.m., 'Mr J. A. Drew UK Deception Planning Briefing', Diary, Book No. 2, 1 Jul–31 Dec. 54, Box 5, SACEUR DIARY, Gruenther papers, DDEL.

17. JP (56) 10 (Final), Annexe to 'The Baghdad Pact: background brief', 18 Jan. 1956, in Kent (ed.), *BDEE, Middle East*, B, 4, part III, 482.

18. The prevailing opinion appears to be that the British hydrogen bomb test in 1957 was genuine, though it led to a volatile interim weapon called Violet Club with a yield of 0.5 megatons, Baylis, 'Myth or Reality', 159–74.

19. COS (56) 94th mtg, 18 Sept. 1956, DEFE 32/5.

20. Slessor min., 16 Jul.1945, on COS (45) 402 (0), AIR 2/12027.

21. Andrew and Gordievsky, *KGB*, 254–7.

22. Rhodes, 'Myth of Perfect Nuclear Security', *NY Times*, 24 July 2000.

23. Maddrell, 'Britain's Exploitation', PhD, 39; Andrew, 'Venona Secret', 215–17.

24. Cathcart, *Test*, 54, 104–7; Szasz, *British Scientists*, 87–95, 98–90. I am also indebted to the remarks of Brian Cathcart and Lorna Arnold at the AWE–University of Luton Conference on the atomic programme in 1998.

25. Elliot memo to COS, 10 Feb. 1950, DEFE 32/1; COS (50) 26th mtg, Special Circ., 13 Feb. 1950, ibid.

26. D of I USAF, Special Study Group, 'Notes on the Timing of the Soviet Hydrogen Bomb', 16 Sept. 1952, 2235100, Box 68, D of I records, RG 341.

27. Cherwell to Skinner, Jun. 1951, J117/12, Cherwell papers, NC.

28. Hoover to Souers, 6 Feb. 1950, HSTL microfilm, Pt 3, Reel 21, HUL.

29. Hoover to Souers, 'John Strachey', 10 Mar. 1950, HSTL microfilm, Pt 3, Reel 22, HUL; entries for 4 Feb., 1 Mar., 10 Mar. 1950, TSS memoir, Box 2, Donnelly papers, MHI.

30. Hennessy and Brownfeld, 'Security Purge', 969.

31. GEN 183/5th mtg, 5 Apr. 1950. I am indebted to Peter Hennessy for sight of this document.

32. GEN 183/8, 'Positive Vetting', 3 Nov. 1950.

33. GEN 183/6th mtg, 13 Nov. 1950; Hennessy and Brownfeld, 'Security Purge', 969.

34. Aldrich, 'Secret Intelligence for a Post-war World', 34.

35. DO (50) 5th mtg (2), 5 Apr. 1950, CAB 131/8; ANZUS Council Mtg, 2 Sept. 1953 – Exchange of Classified Information, Bureau of FE Affairs 1953, Box 3, Lot 55 D 388, RG 59; Cloake, *Templer*, 180.

36. Twinning to Marshall, 24 Jan. 1951, 20659, Box 36, D of I records, RG 341.

37. Lebanon to D of I USAF, 'Proposed US–UK Agreement for Cooperative AEDS Surveillance Operations in the Near and Middle East', 3 Aug. 1951, 220400, Box 59, D of I records, RG 341.

38. Acheson to Truman, 'Your Meeting with Prime Minister Churchill', 7 Jan. 1953, HST microfilm, Pt 2, Reel 4, HUL.

39. Portal to Bedell Smith, 2 July 1951, Box 18, Bedell Smith papers, DDEL.

40. Cherwell to Churchill, 1 May 1952, PREM 11/267; Cherwell to Churchill, 29 Dec. 1952, J122/12, Cherwell papers, NC.

41. C (53) 129 and 130, 'Atomic Energy: Future External Policy', brief for MoD by Wheeler, 29 Apr. 1953, DEFE 13/60.

42. Cherwell to PM, 1 Dec. 1953, J138/5, Cherwell papers, NC.

43. Wright to Macmillan, 28 Oct. 1954, DEFE 13/60; Macmillan to Churchill, 28 Oct. 1954, ibid.

44. Brundrett to Macmillan, 'Atomic Energy Intelligence Discussions with the U.S.', 17 Jan. 1955, DEFE 13/60; Macmillan to Eden, 'Atomic Energy Intelligence', 19 Jan. 1955, ibid.; Eden to Macmillan, 20 Jan. 1955, ibid.; Macmillan to Churchill, 21 and 28 Jan. 1955, ibid.; Cherwell to PM, 19 Jan. 1955, J146/31, Cherwell papers, NC.

45. Brundrett to Macmillan, 5 Feb. 1955, DEFE 13/60; Cherwell to PM, n.d. [late 1955], J146/1, Cherwell papers, NC.

46. Head to Eden, 23 Aug. 1956, DEFE 13/414; RP/522/62, 30 Nov. 1962, DEFE 19/12.

47. Gilbert, *Never Despair*, 973.

48. Cabell (Chief A-2) to Director P&O, 27 May 1948, 21600, Box 41, D of I records, RG 341.

49. Samford (D of I USAF) to Bedell Smith (DCI), 13 Dec. 1951, 221952, Box 61, D of I records, RG 341.

50. SPDM-82–53, Memo for the Chief, Psychological Warfare Division, 'The Problem of Analyzing and Re-orienting Present Sources of British Discontent and Misunderstanding', 12 Feb. 1953, CCS 385 (6–4–46) Sec. 58, RG 218.

Chapter 18 *At the Coal Face: Intelligence-Gathering*

1. Courtney, CONIS(G), 'Naval Technical Intelligence in Germany', 22 Mar. 1949, DEFE 40/26.

2. Bevin to Bedell Smith, 24 Sept. 1950, Box 13, Bedell Smith papers, DDEL; Dodds-Parker to Bedell Smith, 6 Oct. 1950, Box 13, ibid.; Bedell Smith to Dodds-Parker, 20 Nov. 1950, ibid.; Bedell Smith to Sinclair, 12 Dec. 1950, Box 14, ibid.

3. Bedell Smith to Portal, 8 Aug. 1951, Box 18, Bedell Smith papers, DDEL.

4. Bedell Smith to Portal, 25 Apr. 1951, Box 18, Bedell Smith papers, DDEL; Bedell Smith to Strong, 16 Apr. 1952, Box 20, ibid.

5. Cabell to Vandenberg, 5 Oct. 1950, 215600, Box 52, D of I records, RG 341.

6. De Silva, *Sub Rosa*, 17, 73.

7. Strategic Photographic Reconnaissance Conference, RAF Benson, 4 Oct. 1950, AIR 14/3879.

8. Testimony given by Wing Commander Rex Sanders and also by Air Historical Branch at 'Cold War Intelligence Gathering', RAF Hendon, 18 Apr. 2000. A superb account of the RB-45C episode is given in Lashmar, *Spy-Flights*, 62–75.

9. Robert Amory, Oral History, 113, JFKL; Maddrell, 'Britain's Exploitation', PhD, 313; Lashmar, 'Canberras', 32–5.

10. Lloyd to Cochrane, 15 Aug. 1950, AC 71/9/144, Robb papers, RAF Museum, Hendon; CAS to Sec. of State, 11 May 1953, AIR 19/675.

11. Cochrane (VCAS) to U. Sec. of State, 14 Jan. 1952, AIR 19/745.

12. 'Priorities for the Preparation of Strategic Target Material by A.I.5', attached to agenda for 7th ESTC, 17 Jul.1952, AIR 40/2547. All this sits awkwardly alongside the assertions of a 'counter-city' targeting policy in some of the literature on British strategic planning.

13. TAB/9/5, mins of 5th mtg, 16 Apr. 1953, AIR 40/2547. There was also a European Strategic Targets Committee.

14. Brief for CAS for talks with Radford, 2 Nov. 1953, AIR 8/1852. See also Twigge and Scott, *Planning Armageddon*, 29.

15. Tamnes, *High North*, 79; Riste, *Norwegian Intelligence*, 62–3.

16. Tamnes, *High North*, 76–7; Ackerman to MATS, 25 Jun. 1952, 223400, Box 64, D of I records, RG 341.

17. Tamnes, *High North*, 122–3.

18. Packard, *Century*, 195–7; Tamnes, *High North*, 77.

19. Bradley memos, 'Special Electronic Airborne Search Operations', 5 May and 22 Jul. 1950, and Truman min., 19 May 1950, HST microfilm, Pt 2, Reel 3, HUL.

20. Tamnes, *High North*, 116–17; D of I USAF to US Air Attaché London, 'Liaison with GCHQ', 26 Oct. 1952, 235700, Box 68, D of I records, RG 341.

21. HQ 2nd TAF to Air Min., 13 Mar. 1953, AIR 19/675; Sec. of State to Churchill, 23 Sept. 1953, ibid.

22. Lashmar, *Spy-Flights*, 124–5.

23. Ackerman memo, 19 Sept. 1952, 2-35000 to 2-35099, D of I records, RG 341.

24. JCS to CINCFE Tokyo, JCS 86211, 20 Mar. 1951, FECOM records, RG 4, Box 43, DMM. I am indebted to Matthew Aid for a copy of this document.

25. Young (USAF) to Coordinator USCIB, 'Site Requirement', 15 Jul. 1952, 224100, Box 66, D of I records, RG 341.

26. JCS to CINCFE Tokyo, JCS 86211, 20 Mar. 1951, FECOM records, RG 9, Box 43, DMM. I am greatly indebted to Matthew Aid for a copy of this document.

27. Counter-draft, 'Formosa–US Government on Radio Communications Units', 8 Mar. 1955, Box 55, Records of the Office of Chinese Affairs, Lot 56 D 625, RG 59.

28. UKHC Ceylon to Defence Dept, 21 Apr. 1950, DO 35/2418.

29. Mtg at the Admiralty, 26 Oct. 1951, DO 35/2418; L62/370A, 'Ceylon, Anderson WT Station', 6 Jul. 1954, ADM 1/25489; Milt Branch to C in C EI, 23 Mar. 1955, ADM 1/24680.

30. Mtg No. 80, 17 Jan. 1951, PSF–NSC mtgs, Box 211, HSTL.

31. Samford (D of I USAF) to Twining, 6 Aug. 1952, 224400, Box 66, D of I records, RG 341.

32. 'On Watch: Profiles from the National Security Agency's Past 40 Years', 23–4, FOIA, NSA.

33. US JCS decision on JCS 2074/14, Report by Chairman, US AFSA Council on 'Security of the Combined Cipher Machine', 19 May 1952, 1951–3 CCS 311 (1–10–42), Sec.14, RG 218.

34. Memo from US Dir. Communications-Electronics (Corput), to Director NSA (Canine), 15 Jun. 1954, DCEM 878, 'Trans-Oceanic Cables', CCS 334 NSA (7–24–48), Sec.12, RG 218; Goulett (USN) for US

Director Communications-Electronics to Director NSA (Canine), 1 Jun. 1954, DCEM 865, 'Interim Outline Plan for Handling NSA and Individual Security Services Traffic', ibid.

35. Wenger to Director NSA, 23 May 1957, DDCEM 1425, 'Plan for Telecommunications in Support of the National Security Agency', CCS 334 CIA (12–6–42), Sec.16, RG 218.

36. *Menwith Sentimental*, 13th USASA Field Station Assoc. newsletter, Nov. 1997, http://www.sninet/menwith/news/9711pres.htm.

37. 'Results of US–UK Conference in London on Comint Service to SHAPE and its Subordinate Commands', 23 Dec. 1952, 3–1, Box 70, D of I records, RG 341; Gruenther to Brownjohn, 15 Apr. 1954, Box 3, Gruenther papers, DDEL.

38. Slessor to Sec. of State, enclosing 'TASS Agency Monitoring Station', 13 Jul. 1951, AIR 75/92.

39. Kahn, 'Soviet Comint', 17.

40. Riste, *Norwegian Intelligence*, 11.

41. Kennan, *Memoirs, 1950–1963*, 157.

42. Colville to Morrison, 9 Oct. 1952, DEFE 13/16; MoD memo, 'Russian Eavesdropping', enclosed in Morrison (MoD) to Colville, 13 Oct. 1952, *ESI*, 11.3.

43. Eden to Churchill, 25 Oct. 1952, PREM 11/760; Alexander to Churchill, 'Russian Eavesdropping', 15 Jul. 1954, ibid.

44. Hoover to Cutler, 12 Mar. 1953, DDRS 1995/1676.

45. Kahn, 'Soviet Comint', 17; private information.

46. De Silva, *Sub Rosa*, 35, 74. On brainwashing see Carruthers, 'Not Only Brainwashed'.

47. Private information.

48. Kopelev, *Ease my Sorrows*, 35, 54, 73, 89, 155. See also Kerber, *Stalin's Aviation Gulag*.

49. De Silva, *Sub Rosa*, 50–7.

50. Clandestine Services History, 'The Berlin Tunnel Operation', 25 Aug. 1967, CIA microfilm, Europe, Reel 2, LL. See also Andrew and Mitrokhin, *The Sword*, 398–400.

51. CIA internal histories reproduced in Steury, *Front Lines*, 328–405; Clandestine Services History, 'The Berlin Tunnel Operation', 25 Aug. 1967, CIA microfilm, Europe, Reel 2, LL.

52. *Cold War: Espionage* (Ted Turner Productions), BBC2, 18 Apr. 1999.

53. Private information; CIA internal histories produced in Steury, *Front Lines*, 328–405.

54. CC (M) (49) 16, 4 Aug. 1949, DEFE 41/78; JIC (52) 73, 'German Security', 21 Nov. 1952, CAB 158/74.

55. Leary, 'George Blake and the Berlin Tunnel'; Smith, *New Cloak*, 115–17.

56. Lang-Brown (TCS) to Chairman of JS/TIC, 6 Sept. 1949, enclosing 'TCS/441', DEFE 40/26; Maddrell, 'British–American Scientific Collaboration', 83.

57. 'Talk on Tech (Int) BAOR' by Birch, DEFE 41/125; Maddrell, 'Britain's Exploitation', PhD, 159.

58. DMI (Shortt) to JIC, 'Soviet and Satellite Defectors and Refugees', 5 Jun. 1950, WO 208/5015.

59. Colonel Whiteoord, Int Org, Allied Commission Austria, to MI1, 20 Apr. 1950, WO 208/5015; report on visit by Mr Roy Tod, US Operational Consultant, 15 Mar. 1950, ibid.

60. Report of Air Intell. Team Visit to Europe, 22 Jun.–30 Jul. 1954, 41912, Box 76, D of I records, RG 341.

61. TSS memoir (G-2 Germany), 118–19, Schance papers, MHI. Also Brixmis presentations at RAF 'Cold War Intelligence Gathering', RAF Hendon, 18 Apr. 2000. Private information. Brixmis is chronicled in Gerraghty, *Beyond the Front Line*.

62. De Silva, *Sub Rosa*, 56–7, 84.

63. Conboy and Morrison, *Feet*, 71; Miller, *Lockheed*, 57.

64. De Silva, *Sub Rosa*, 59; JCEC 933/1, 'CIA Circuit Requirements from the Department of Defense', 30 Mar. 1954, Strategic Issues, Series 2, Reel 1, US JCS microfilm, BRO.

65. JCS 2124/60, 'Intelligence Problems Incident to Proposed Contractual Relations with Germany', 4 Sept. 1951, NATO Reel 1, US JCS Microfilm, BRO; JIC 586/2, 'Effect on US Intelligence of the Japanese Peace Treaty', 31 Aug. 1951, Series 2, Reel Far East 6, ibid.

66. Maddrell, 'Britain's Exploitation', PhD, 99, 142–50; note by Chief of ID, 'Intelligence and the Future German Government', Appendix A, 'Powers under the Occupation Statute Which It Is Wished to Retain', Jun. 1952, DEFE 41/119.

67. Report of Air Intelligence Team Visit to Europe, 22 Jun.–30 Jul. 1954, 41912, Box 76, D of I records, RG 341.

68. Blake, *No Other Choice*, 166–8. See also JIC (51) 27, 'Future of Intelligence in Germany', 16 Mar. 1951, CAB 158/12.

69. Gervase Cowell, reminiscences in Andrew and Aldrich (eds), 'Intelligence Services', 164.

70. De Silva, *Sub Rosa*, 87.

71. Strong memo, 17 May 1950, DEFE 11/349.

72. Shinwell to Attlee, 22 Jun. 1950, MoD Chief Staff Officer, Elliot to Shinwell, 'Organisation of Intelligence Services', COS 1403/23/10/50, Top Secret, 21 Oct. 1950, DEFE 11/349.

73. Le Carré, *Tinker Tailor*, 315.
74. Blount, 'Organisation of Scientific Intelligence: Deficiencies of the Present Organisation', Oct. 1949, DEFE 40/26; JSTIC (49) 20th mtg (2), DEFE 41/72.
75. COS (54) 70, 'Directorate of Scientific Intelligence', 2 Mar. 1954, DEFE 32/4.
76. Alexander to Churchill, 30 Apr. 1954, PREM 11/787. Welsh was replaced by Archie Potts.

Chapter 19 *Moles and Defectors: The Impact of Guy Burgess and Donald Maclean*
1. Alsop, *Center*, 251,
2. The limitations of Venona as evidence are illuminated by Andrew, 'Venona Secret', 203–19.
3. INSCOM/CIC Report, 'Missing British Diplomats', V-10335, 21 Jun. 1951, INSCOM, FOIA: 66th CIC Det EUCOM to HQ, 'BURGESS & MACLEAN', 15 Jun. 1951, ibid.
4. The two landmark studies are Andrew and Gordievsky, *KGB,* and Andrew and Mitrokhin, *Mitrokhin Archive.* See also West and Tsarev, *Crown Jewels,* and Costello and Tsarev, *Deadly Illusions.*
5. Hennessy and Townsend, 'Documentary Spoor', 293.
6. I am especially indebted to Oleg Tsarev's illuminating presentation on the KGB and the early Cold War given in Oxford in September 1999.
7. Kerr, 'The Secret Hotline to Moscow', 71–87.
8. Modin, *My Five Cambridge Friends*, 183; Andrew and Mitrokhin, *The Sword*, 120–1.
9. MDM (51) 2, 'Defence Policy and Global Strategy', Jun. 1951, CAB 21/1787.
10. GEN 183/12, 'Atomic Energy Security', 15 Aug. 1951; GEN 183/7th mtg, 17 Aug. 1951.
11. Memo of a conversation with Morgan, 9 Oct. 1951, *ESI*, 11.2.
12. Brook memo, Committee on Restriction of Travel of Security Suspects, 2 Apr. 1955, PREM 11/999.
13. Hennessy and Brownfeld, 'Security Purge'; 970, Williams, *Not in the Public Interest*, 171–7.
14. Malvoney, 'Civil Liberties', PhD, 170–1.
15. Thomas C. Sorensen, transcript, 25 Jul. 1990, FAOHP, 5–6; Maclean, *No, I Tell a Lie*, 106–7.
16. Cecil, *Divided Life*, 122–5; Costello, *Mask of Treachery*, 534; Farrar-Hockley, *Korean War*, 97, 148–9; Hennessy and Townsend, 'Documentary Spoor', 296–7.
17. De Silva, *Sub Rosa*, 80.
18. Meyer, *Facing Reality*, 60–85.
19. Edward Alexander transcript, n.d., FAOHP, 10–12.
20. Ambassador Robert O. Blake transcript, 7 May 1990, FAOHP, 20.
21. Entries for 4 Feb., 1 Mar., 10 Mar. 1950, TSS memoir, Box 2, Donnelly papers, MHI.
22. JIC 566/5, 'Guidance for the US Military Delegation at the SHAPE Counter Intelligence Conference', 2 Oct. 1951, Strategic Issues, Series 2, Reel 1, US JCS Microfilm, BRO.
23. JCS 2080/7, 'Nato Security Committee, Europe', 9 Jan. 1952, Series 2, NATO Reel 7, US JCS Microfilm, BRO. See also Edwards, *Anglo-American Relations*, 238–9.
24. COS (49) 66th mtg, 6 May 1949, DEFE 11/285. See also JIC (50) 56, 'Security in a Certain Country', 17 Jun. 1950, CAB 158/10.
25. UKHC to FO, 12 Oct. 1949, DEFE 11/285; COS (49) 156th mtg, 24 Oct. 1949, ibid.; JIC (49) 168th mtg, 14 Nov. 1949, ibid.; JIC (49) 100, 'Establishment of Security Services in Germany', 12 Nov. 1949, ibid.
26. Gilchrist to O'Neill, 11 Jan. 1950, discussing JIC (49) 100, C168/168/18, FO 371/85192; INT DIV/S/15333/1, 17 Jan. 1950, ibid.; JIC (52) 73, 'German Security', 21 Nov. 1952, CAB 158/74.
27. Shortt (DMI) to Director of MI5, Sillitoe, MI1(E)/1884/3, Secret, Oct. 1951, WO 216/951. Also Shortt to VCIGS, 4 Oct. 1951, ibid.; min to DDMI, 22 Sept. 1951, ibid.
28. AMSO-OSG, 'Soviet penetration of BND and ASBW (S)', 12 Jan. 1967, FOIA; INSCOM/CIC Report, 'FELFE, Heinz', III-35714, 10 Jun. 1954, FOIA.
29. De Silva, *Sub Rosa*, 144.
30. The best account is Andrew and Gordievsky, *KGB*, 352–3.
31. Cowell reminiscences in Andrew and Aldrich (ed.), 'Intelligence Services', 163–4. See also Khokhlov, *In the Name of Conscience.*
32. Mins of mtg between Churchill, Rennie, Kirkpatrick and Nutting, 1 May 1954, PREM 11/773; Churchill to Kirkpatrick, 14 May 1954, ibid.; Selwyn Lloyd to Churchill, 15 May 1954, ibid.
33. Kerr, 'NATO's First Spies', 304.
34. Hennessy and Townsend, 'Documentary Spoor', 296–7.
35. Blake to Morrison, 5 Oct. 1955, Burgess and Maclean File, 8/5, Morrison papers, BLPES.
36. Andrew, 'Venona Secret', 203–20; FO to Morrison, 19 Jul. 1963, Burgess and Maclean File, 8/5, Morrison papers, BLPES.
37. Edwards, *Pursuit of Reason*, 779–81; Cave Brown, *Treason*, 463.
38. Memo by Radford, 26 Oct. 1955, CM-221-55, 'National Security Implications Resulting from the Defection of British Diplomats, Donald Duart McLean [sic] and Guy DeMoncy Burgess,' *ESI*, 10.5.

39. Powell through Brundrett, 16 Jan. 1956, DEFE 7/2259.

40. ACAS (I) to VCAS, 16 Jul. 1956, DEFE 7/292.

41. De Silva, *Sub Rosa*, 78–9.

42. This is very well captured by Stafford, *Churchill*, 256–8.

43. Balfour, *Not Too Correct an Aureole*, 114; Cecil, *Divided Life*, 90–107.

44. Entry for 23 Aug. 1943, Cadogan diaries, ACAD, CCC; Stafford, *Churchill*, 253; Bower, *Perfect English Spy*, 66. The possible identities Menzies was referring to were many, including Michael Lindsay, who was usefully close to Mao Tse-tung and Chou En-lai in China.

45. Lansdale to Strong, 'DSM Project-Communist Espionage', 5 Apr. 1943, File: DSM Project, Pash papers, HIWRP; Strong to CG Western Defense Command, 15 Apr. 1943, ibid.

46. The records of the Department of Forward Plans are almost entirely closed at DEFE 28.

47. Modin interview quoted in Brown, *Treason*, 512; Andrew and Mitrokhin, *The Sword*, 159–61.

48. Jerrold Schecter, review of Rufina Philby, *Private Life*, in *I&NS*, 166–8.

Chapter 20 *At Home and Abroad: The Information Research Department*

1. GEN 226, 2nd mtg, 1 Jun. 1948, CAB 130/37.

2. Ibid.

3. Ibid.; MI5 report, 'The Communist Party: Its Strengths and Activities: Its Penetration of Government Organisations and of the Trade Unions', Annexe to GEN 226/1, 26 May 1948, CAB 130/37.

4. Lucas, *Freedom's War*, 1–15.

5. NSC 4, 'Report by the National Security Council on Co-ordination of Foreign Information Measures', 17 Dec. 1947, *FRUS, 1945–50*, 640. On IRD as 'anti-anti-British' see especially Lucas and Morris, 'Very British Crusade'.

6. *FRUS*, 1950, vol. 3, 1641–8; HICOG to DoS, 18 Jul. 1950, 741.5200/7–1850, RG 59; COS (51) 410, 11 Jul. 1951, DEFE 11/275; Ewbank to Barry (BJSM), 23 Oct. 1951, DEFE 11/275.

7. DoS to Certain Diplomatic and Consular Officers, 27 Jul. 1950, 511.41/7–2750, RG 59.

8. Sleeper (USAF Psywar) to Samford (USAF D of I), 12 Oct. 1951, 221316, Box 60, D of I records, RG 341.

9. Jackson to Biddle, 17 Mar. 1952, Box 28, CDJP, DDEL.

10. Wisner to Gruenther, 13 Apr. 1953, Box 1, Gruenther papers, DDEL.

11. On British propaganda in the United States see Cull, *Selling War*; Goodman, 'Who Is Anti-American?', PhD, 111–12.

12. Browne (London) to DoS, 17 Jul. 1950, 'USIE Country Paper – Britain', 511.41/7–1750, RG 59.

13. Goodman, 'Who Is Anti-American?', PhD, 170.

14. O'Sheel (LIO) to DoS, 'Progress Report on Labor Information Activities – Britain', 25 Jul. 1951, 511.41/7–2651, RG 59.

15. O'Sheel (LIO) to DoS, 'Progress Report on Labor Information Activities – Britain', 25 Jul. 1951, 511.41/7–2651, RG 59.

16. Coleman, *Liberal Conspiracy*, 146.

17. Goodman, 'Who Is Anti-American?', PhD. 301; Caute, *Great Fear*, 252–3; Meyer, *Facing Reality*, 60–84.

18. See the excellent article by Wilford, 'Unwitting Assets', 42–60.

19. Goodman, 'Who Is Anti-American?', PhD, 251.

20. Smith to Eisenhower, 20 May 1953, enclosing, Dillon to Washington, 15 May 1953; Smith to Dillon, 20 May 1953, Box 5, C. D. Jackson records, DDEL.

21. Report of the Mutual Security Program Evaluation Team, Mar. 1953, Strategic Issues, Series 1, Reel 12, US JCS Microfilm, BRO.

22. Goodman, 'Who Is Anti-American?', PhD, 299–300.

23. Lindey, *Art in the Cold War*, 112–14, 122–7; Matthews, 'Art and Politics in Cold War America', 762–87; Saunders, *Who Paid the Piper?*, 252; Cockcroft, 'Abstract Expression'.

24. Cockcroft, 'Abstract Expression'.

25. Schapiro, *Socialist Realism*, p. 76.

26. See for example Box: Malaya, IDLP, NMLH.

27. Watson to Healey, 12 Nov. 1948, Sofia to FO, 11 and 12 Nov. 1948, File: Anti-Communist Propaganda, 1948, IDLP, NMLH.

28. PR.704/G, 'Memorandum on the Use of Words About Communism', 1949, IDLP, NMLH.

29. B.282, 'Political Prisoners in the Satellites', 1956, File: E. Europe, 1956, Political Prisoners, IDLP, NMLH; Sheridan to Healey, 'General Bor's Appeal to World's Conscience', 22 Nov. 1948, File: Arrests in Eastern Europe, Box: Eastern Europe, IDLP, NMLH.

30. 'The Soviet Practice of Genocide', Dec. 1952, File: 1950–53, Box: USSR memoranda 1946–53, IDLP, NMLH.

31. B.458, 'Polish Police Reform', Jun. 1957, File: Poland 1957, Box: Poland Correspondence, 1955–63, IDLP, NMLH; B.466, 'Polish Security Chiefs Stand Trial', Jul. 1957, ibid.
32. CAB 130/64, GEN 341, quoted in Malvoney, 'Civil Liberties', PhD, 52–8, 115–21; B.618, 'Soviet Double Standards', Apr. 1961, Box: Anti-Communist Propaganda, IDLP, NMLH.
33. Lashmar and Oliver, *Britain's Secret Propaganda War*, 29.
34. Ibid., 95–105.
35. This passage draws on Carew's article, 'American Labor Movement'. See also Grose, *Gentleman Spy*, 305–8; Dubinsky, *Life with Labor*, 261–2. Over the period 1948–58 the FTUC received $464,167, about 10 per cent of what the US gave the European Movement.
36. Mayall min., 22 Nov. 1950, L317/48, FO 924/871.
37. Mtg, 26 Nov. 1951, CRL20017/2, FO 924/919; mtg, 1 Dec. 1951, ibid.
38. Hope (FO) to Hollis (HoC), 27 Jan. 1955, CRL2006/6, FO 924/1100.
39. Moir to Eden, 10 Feb. 1954, CRL20014/4, FO 924/1039; Grant min., 1 Mar. 1954, ibid.; Haigh min., 1 Apr. 1954, L20012/17, ibid.
40. Page to Butler, 8 May 1954, L20014/27, FO 924/1039; Grant min., 19 May 1954, L20014/30, ibid.; Lyttelton to Eden, 25 Jun. 1954, L20014/43, FO 924/1040.
41. De Zulueta min., 29 Jul. 1954, L20014/55, FO 924/1040; Walsh min., 12 Aug. 1954, L20014/62, ibid.; Nicholls (Singapore) to FO, 14 Aug. 1954, L20014/68, ibid.; Haigh min., 16 Sept. 1954, CRL20004/70, FO 924/1041.
42. Page (WAY) to Haigh, 4 Dec. 1954, CRL20014/85, FO 924/1041; Haigh min., 13 Dec. 1954, ibid.; Brooke to Hope, 1 Feb. 1955, CRL20014/10, FO 924/1100.
43. Blum (President CFA) to Staats (OCB), 22 Apr. 1954, Box 86, OCB records, DDEL.
44. Moir to Hope, 17 Mar. 1955, CRL2004/25, FO 924/1101; Rennie min., 20 May 1955, FO 1110/756.
45. Memo for John Baker-White of the Economic League by Morkhill, 'Communism and Chinese Students', enclosed in Zimmerman to DoS, 2 Apr. 1954, 741.001/4–254, RG 59. When these practices were uncovered at another university in Britain in the 1960s the university registry was attacked and burned by outraged students.

Chapter 21 *Defeat in the Middle East: Iran and Suez*
1. Young, *Who Is My Liege?*, 80–1.
2. Aldrich, *Intelligence and the War against Japan*, 307–8.
3. Lucas, *Divided We Stand*, 5–17; Smith and Zametica, 'Cold Warrior', 237–42; Louis, *British Empire in the Middle East*, 13–77.
4. Report of Operation Girdle, Jan.–Feb. 1949, 413002, Box 157, D of I records, RG 341.
5. E.g. DSO report (Jenkins), 9 Mar. 1946, J1565/53/16, FO 371/53315; Thistlethwaite (MI5 London) to FO, 10 Feb. 1947, enclosing DSO Cairo report for Dec. 1946, J722/13/16, FO 371/62961, discussed in Tripp, 'Egypt, 1945–52', 139.
6. LCS (47) 6, 'Deception, The Spead of Communism – Middle East Outline Plan', 17 Sept. 1947, CAB 81/80.
7. Tripp, 'Egypt, 1945–52', 113–29; Lucas and Morey, 'Hidden "Alliance"', 98.
8. COS (50) 107th mtg (with Directors of Intelligence), 11 Jul. 1950, DEFE 11/349.
9. A full account with much useful detail on personalities is offered in Dorril, *MI6*, 559–62. See also Lapping, *End*, 206–8; Stafford, *Churchill*, 338–9.
10. Bamberg, *History*, vol. 2, 436–8; Karabell, *Architects*, 55.
11. Ferrier, 'Anglo-American Oil Dispute', 164–92.
12. Bamberg, *History*, vol. 2, 439–43; Karabell, *Architects*, 60–1.
13. Jackson to Keating (AIOC), 6 Aug. 1951, Box 52, CDJP, DDEL.
14. Memo of a convers. on Iran, 9 Jan. 1952, Box 17, PPS Lot Files, 64 D 563, RG 59.
15. Teheran to Greenhough, 28 Jul. 1952, LAB 13/1069.
16. D of I to DCoS Ops, 'Iran – Political Situation Now in Combustible Stage', 13 Jun. 1952, 223805, Box 146, D of I records, RG 341.
17. Daily Briefs, D of I USAF, 'Iran – Probability of an Early Military Coup Considered Remote', 6 Oct. 1952, 235399, Box 151, D of I records, RG 341.
18. Woodhouse, *Something Ventured*, 117–18; Dorril, *MI6*, 583.
19. CIA Clandestine Service History: Overthrow of Premier Mossadegh of Iran, Nov. 1952–Aug. 1953, by Donald Wilber, March 1954, 6, http://www.nytimes.com/library/world/mideast/041600iran-cia-intro.html (hereafter Clandestine Service History–Iran). See also Karabell, *Architects*, 51.
20. CIA Clandestine Service History–Iran, 30–4.
21. Dorril, *MI6*, 575.
22. CIA Clandestine Service History–Iran, 3.

23. Ibid., 30–8, 54–63; Berry (Baghdad) to SoS, 92, 17 Aug. 1953, Box 29, Ann Whitman Int. Series, DDEL. See also obituary of Kermit Roosevelt, *Washington Post*, 10 Jun. 2000; Grose, *Gentleman Spy*, 366–8.

24. CIA Clandestine Service History–Iran, 79–81.

25. Bamberg, *History*, vol. 2, 489–96; Dorril, *MI6*, 595; Stafford, *Churchill*, 342.

26. Kent (ONE) to Allen Dulles, 'Prospects in Iran', 10 Nov. 1958, enclosed in Dulles to Gray, 12 Nov. 1958, Box 11, Briefing Notes Subseries, NSC Series, OSANA, WHO, DDEL.

27. Young, *Who Is my Liege?*, 9.

28. OCB Working Group on NSC 5402 (Iran), 18 Mar. 1954, OCB 091 Iran: File #1, Box 42, OCB Central File Series, NSC Staff Papers, WHO, DDEL.

29. Obituary of Kermit Roosevelt, *Washington Post*, 10 Jun. 2000.

30. Lucas and Morey, 'Hidden "Alliance"', 102.

31. MI4 memo, 'German in Egyptian Service', 30 Nov. 1956, JE1194/11, FO 371/118975; Wilkinson to Garvey, 6 Apr. 1956, ibid.

32. Grose, *Gentleman Spy*, 433; Lucas, *Divided We Stand*, 13–17, 38.

33. Murray to FO, 1 Nov. 1956, Kent (ed.), *BDEE, Middle East*, B, 4, part III, 329.

34. TSS, 'Ropes of Sand', 178–9, Box 1, Eveland papers, HIWRP.

35. Lucas, *Divided We Stand*, 58–64. On Yugoslavia see the efforts of Frank Wisner detailed at *FRUS, 1948*, vol. 4, 1048, 1095 and also *FRUS, 1951*, vol. 4, part II, 1951, 1741–7, 1792.

36. Elliot to Brook, 10 Jun. 1953, 5/1/55a, Elliot papers, LHCMA.

37. Wyatt, *Confessions*, 241.

38. Charmley, *Grand Alliance*, 315; Dorril, *MI6*, 612–13; James, *Eden*, 368–8; Kyle, *Suez*, 69; Lapping, *End*, 261–2.

39. Stephen Dorril reviews the evidence carefully in *MI6*, 612–13. Nutting's revelations were covered in the *Daily Telegraph*, 24 May 1985. See also Bower, *Perfect English Spy*, 195; Louis, 'Dulles, Suez and the British', 145; Lucas and Morey, 'UK–US Intelligence', 104.

40. Andrew, *President's Eyes Only*, 225–7; Kyle, *Suez*, 101.

41. Wright, *Spycatcher*, 160–2.

42. Watson to Trevelyan, 12 May 1956, Kent (ed.), *BDEE, Middle East*, B, 4, part III, 329.

43. Lucas, *Divided We Stand*, 99–103. The subject of command and control is especially perplexing; see for example the suggestion that the Chiefs of Staff had 'approved' a special operation at COS (53) 123rd (9), 2 Nov. 1953, DEFE 32/3.

44. Lucas, *Divided We Stand*, 228–35, 250–1; Kyle, *Suez*, 95, 208, 299, 328–9.

45. Andrew, *President's Eyes Only*, 225–33; Kyle, *Suez*, 102–3; Gorst and Lucas, 'Straggle'.

46. Kyle, *Suez*, 148–50.

47. Trevelyan (Cairo) to FO, 1 Sept. 1956, JE1693/55, FO 371/119306; Blackham min., 26 Sept. 1956, JE1693/57, ibid.; Mrs Swinburne to FO, 11 Nov. 1956, JE1963/53, ibid. See also Lashmar and Oliver, *Britain's Secret Propaganda War*, 70–3.

48. 30 Aug. 1956, Dulles–Herter convers. microfilm, Reel 5, LL. Also private information. For discussion of the Allen Dulles visit see Lucas and Morey, 'Hidden "Alliance"', 109.

49. Kyle, *Suez*, 151–2, 238–9.

50. Eden to Selwyn Lloyd, 30 Apr. 1956, M 86/56, AP 20/21/84, Avon papers, BUL.

51. Eden to Selwyn Lloyd, 4 May 1956, M 95/56, AP20/21/94, Avon papers, BUL.

52. De Zulueta to Millard, 25 May 1956, PREM 11/1450; Eden min., 26 May 1956, ibid.

53. Lashmar and Oliver, *Britain's Secret Propaganda War*, 69.

54. Ibid., 64.

55. COS (56) 100th mtg, 12 Oct. 1956, DEFE 32/5.

56. Packard, *Century*, 432–3.

57. Pedlow and Welzenbach, *CIA and the U-2*, 115–17.

58. DDE diary, 28 Oct. 1956, DDEL. On American reactions see especially Andrew, *President's Eyes Only*, 230–2.

59. Hahn, *United States, Great Britain and Egypt*, 224–30; Dorril, *MI6*, 642–3.

60. Special NIE 30–5–56, 'Likelihood of a British–French Resort to Military Action against Egypt in the Suez Crisis', 19 Sept. 1956, CIA Microfilm, Middle East, Reel 2, LL.

61. Grose, *Gentleman Spy*, 441; Dimbleby and Reynolds, *Ocean Apart*, 214.

62. AFCN press release, Box 7, Emmet Papers, HIWRP.

63. Selwyn Lloyd to Director of GCHQ, E. M. Jones, 20 Sept. 1956, AIR 20/10621 (I am indebted to Scott Lucas for drawing this document to my attention); GHQ ME to MoD, 17 August 1956, AIR 20/9228; presentation given by Wing Commander B. Paton, 51 Sqdn, at 'Cold War Intelligence Gathering', RAF Hendon, 18 Apr. 2000.

64. Dixon memo, 'General Report on Reconnaissance Operations and Organisation leading up to and during Operation Musketeer', ATF/TS.26/36, 13 Nov. 1956, *ESI*, 7.4.

65. Ibid.; Gorst and Lucas, 'Secrets of Suez', 1–2.

66. DAP (PAW) c/7/8/56, 8 Aug. 1956, AIR 20/9570; PAW (56) 4 (Final), 'Psychological Warfare Arrangements for Operation Musketeer', 16 Aug. 1956, ibid.; Fergusson memo, 'Psychological Warfare Campaign', 2 Oct. 1956, ibid.; Fergusson memo, 'Nomenclature of Units', 5 Oct. 1956, ibid.

67. Murray (AFHQ) to Rennie, 1 Dec. 1956, AIR 20/10369; Drew (DFP) to Hobbs, 5 Dec. 1956, ibid.; Lashmar and Oliver, *Britain's Secret Propaganda War*, 73–8; Rawnsley, 'Overt and Covert', 497–522; Richard Beeston, 'My Part in Britain's Secret War', *The Times*, 16 Sept. 1994. I am indebted to Andrew Defty for this last reference.

68. Charmley, *Grand Alliance*, 317; entry for 4 May 1954, Moran, *Winston Churchill*.

69. CIA Clandestine Service History–Iran, 79–81.

70. Young, *Who Is my Liege?*, 81; Kunz, *Economic Diplomacy*, 32–3, 87, 155, 189.

Chapter 22 *Victory in Malaya*

1. Memo by Lockhart, D of Ops, DEF.T.S.25/29, 'Planning of Operations to Eliminate the High-Ranking Members of the M.C.P.', 6 Feb. 1953, AIR 23/8559.

2. Aldrich, *Intelligence and the War against Japan*, 20–3.

3. Memo by the head of the SOE Malaya Country Section, 15 Aug. 1945, WO 203/4403.

4. Cruickshank, *SOE*, 208–9.

5. Draft brief for SAC, 'Malaya Resistance Movement', Jul. 1945, WO 203/4404; memo by the head of the SOE Malaya Country Section, 15 Aug. 1945, WO 203/4403. See also Cruickshank, *SOE*, 209; Cheah Boon Kheng, *Red Star*, 62–3, 75.

6. Cheah Boon Kheng, *Red Star*, 258–9; Miller, *Menace in Malaya*, 60–2; Short, *Communist Insurrection*, 35–7.

7. Cheah Boon Kheng, *Red Star*, 242, 246; Short, *Communist Insurrection*, 39, 54–62; Thorne, *Allies*, 606–7; McLane, *Soviet Strategies*, 310–11.

8. SIFE report, 'Communism in South East Asia', summarised in Killearn to FO, 15 Jul. 1947, F9979/90/61, FO 371/63520.

9. Dalley, MSS memo, 'Internal Security in Malaya', 14 Jun. 1948, CO 537/6006; MSS Political Intelligence Journal no. 15/48, supplement no. 11, 'Effect of Action by Governments in Malaya to Counteract Malayan Communist Party Plans', 15 Aug. 1948, Stockwell (ed.), *BDEE, Malaya*, B, 3, part II, 53; *Observer*, 14 Jun. 1998.

10. CP (48) 171, 'The Situation in Malaya', 1 Jul. 1948, Stockwell (ed.), *BDEE, Malaya*, B, 3, part II, 41; private information.

11. BDCC FE 2nd mtg (6), Appendix C to JIC (48) 10, 'T of R: Composition and Functions of the JIC' (Far East), 29 Jan. 1948, L/WS/1/1050, IOLR; Short, *Communist Insurrection*, 15, 155, 229–30, 275, 335, 358.

12. Ritchie, 'Report on Operations in Malaya', Jun. 1948–Jul. 1949, WO 106/5884.

13. Thompson, *Make for the Hills*, 71–99.

14. Annual Report, 21 SAS Regt, 31 Oct. 1948, McLeod Papers, LHCMA; memo on SAS organisation, 1948, ibid.

15. Blue to DoS, 16 July 1948, 846E.00/7–1648, RG 59.

16. Stanton to SoS, 16 Nov. 1948, 846E.00/11–1248, RG 59.

17. Carruthers, *Hearts and Minds*, 74–5, 81.

18. Annexe II, 'Coordination of Communist Party Policy', Hamlin to DoS, 'Mtg. of the British Far East Defense Subcommittee in Singapore', 9 Nov. 1948, 841.20/11–948, RG 59; Lambert to Cade, 8 Nov. 1948, CO 537/2648.

19. PMM (48) 4th mtg, 12 Oct. 1948, L/WS/1/1211, IOLR.

20. Jebb min., 27 Mar. 1950, FO 371/86761; Bevin to Attlee, PM 48/88, 6 Nov. 1948, N12163/51/38, FO 371/71660.

21. Blue to DoS, 3 Jun. 1949, 846E.00/6–349, RG 59. See also McHugh (Director of Public Relations, Malaya), 'The Anatomy of Bandit Propaganda, Jul.–Dec. 1948', Jan. 1949, 846E.00/6–749, RG 59.

22. Bower (D/Ops), 'Review of the Emergency in Malaya from Jun. 1948 to Aug. 1957', WO 106/5990.

23. Defty, 'Organising Security and Intelligence', 2–5; Sunderland, *Antiguerrilla Intelligence*, 20. Dalley had only been in post a year, his predecessor was N. G. Morris.

24. BDCC FE 2nd mtg (6), Appendix C to JIC (48) 10, 'T of R: Composition and Functions of the JIC' (Far East), 29 Jan. 1948, L/WS/1/1050, IOLR; Short, *Communist Insurrection*, 15, 155, 229–30, 275, 335, 358.

25. Hack, 'British Intelligence', 126–7; Cloake, *Templer*, 196–7.

26. *Observer*, 14 Jun. 1998.

27. C (51) 59, 'Malaya', 21 Dec. 1951, Stockwell (ed.), *BDEE, Malaya*, B, 3, part II, 66; Chandos, *Memoirs*, 366.

28. Cloake, *Templer*, 199. For a sophisticated dissection of the historiography surrounding the achievements of Briggs and Templer see Hack, 'British Intelligence', 125–55.

29. C (51) 59, 'Malaya', 21 Dec. 1951, Stockwell (ed.), *BDEE, Malaya*, B, 3, part II, 344–5.

30. Memo, 'Malaya Committee and Australian Prime Minister', 13 Jul. 1950, CAB 21/1795.

31. Lewis, *Changing Direction* (2nd edn), ch. 1.

32. COS (50) 548, 'Deception Staff in the Far East', Special Circ., 29 Dec. 1950, DEFE 11/377.

33. Presentation given by Wing Commander B. Paton, 51 Sqdn, at 'Cold War Intelligence Gathering', RAF Hendon, 18 Apr. 2000. I am grateful to Anthony Short for information about radios.

34. Memo by Lockhart, D of Ops, DEF.T.S.25/29, 'Planning of Operations to Eliminate the High-Ranking Members of the M.C.P.', 6 Feb. 1953, AIR 23/8559.

35. Oliver (PSO) to Templer, DEF.TS.25/29, 'Future of "Profit" Planning Committee and Intelligence Staff', 14 Jul. 1953, AIR 23/8559; Oliver (PSO) memo, 'Operation Profit', 17 Jul. 1953, ibid.

36. Cloake, *Templer*, 224–6.

37. Hack, too scholarly to avoid awkward evidence, sets out all the figures in 'Corpses', 224–5.

38. Cloake, *Templer*, 228–9.

39. Bower (D/Ops), 'Review of the Emergency in Malaya from June 1948 to August 1957', WO 106/5990; Sunderland, *Antiguerrilla Intelligence*, 26–7.

40. McKnight, *Australia's Spies*, 225.

41. Presentation on SIFE by Morton, 21–23 Mar. 1950, WO 208/4835; 'Note on the reciprocated arrangements between the Thai Government and the Federal Government', 8 Oct. 1952, 8310–154–115, File J, Lockhart papers, NAM; Hack, 'British Intelligence', 130–1.

42. C (51) 59, 'Malaya', 21 Dec. 1951, Stockwell (ed.), *BDEE, Malaya*, B, 3, part II, 344.

43. I only have this information from an interview with an retired MI5 officer who served in Malaya and Borneo, conducted in August 1986. On other draconian measures see Thompson, *Make for the Hills*, 93.

44. Cloake, *Templer*, 260–1.

45. Memo to Garnons-Williams, 1 Sept. 1945, G3/10/1/4821, enclosing 'The AJUF in Malaya' and 'The History of British Left Behind Parties in Malaya, Dec. 1941–May 1945', vol. 2, Garnons-Williams papers, IWM. Hack, 'Corpses', 217.

46. Sunderland, *Antiguerrilla Intelligence*, 44–6.

47. Lloyd to Gimson and Newboult, 23 Aug. 1948, Stockwell (ed.), *BDEE, Malaya*, B, 3, part II, 66–7; del Tufo to Lyttelton, 30 Oct. 1951, ibid., 302–3.

48. Stewart, 'Winning in Malaya', 275–7.

49. PM (55) 36, Lennox-Boyd to Eden, 'Malaya', 23 Jun. 1955, Stockwell (ed.), *BDEE, Malaya*, B, 3, part III, 124; 'Report by the chief minister of the Federation of Malaya on the Baling talks', 29 Dec. 1955, ibid., 213–26.

50. Bower (D/Ops), 'Review of the Emergency in Malaya from June 1948 to August 1957', WO 106/5990.

51. Ibid.; Def Y40/19/A, 'Review of the Enemy Situation at the End of 1955' by D Ops Malaya, 31 Jan. 1956, para. 55, AIR 20/10375.

52. Bower (D/Ops), 'Review of the Emergency in Malaya from June 1948 to August 1957', WO 106/5990.

53. Cross, *Born a Foreigner*, 118–23.

54. This is persuasively argued in Ramakrishna, 'Content', 243–66.

55. Ibid., 258–60.

56. West, *Friends*, 49. See the description of Operation Jaya in Sunderland, *Antiguerrilla Intelligence*, 52–5, 68–70.

57. Lloyd to Gimson and Newboult, 23 Aug. 1948, Stockwell (ed.), *BDEE, Malaya*, B, 3, part II, 65; Lashmar and Oliver, *Britain's Secret Propaganda War*, 86; Carruthers, *Hearts and Minds*, 80–1.

58. Cave Brown, *Last Hero*, 825.

59. Smith, *Portrait*, 148–9; Powers, *Man Who Kept the Secrets*, 98–9; Bitar, 'Bombs Plots and Allies', 149–80.

60. FO to Washington, 20 May 1955, DF1019/52/G, FO 371/117125; SEAD memo: 'Cambodia', top-secret annexe 'Special measures which might be taken to strengthen the Cambodian government and administration', May 1955, ibid. These are discussed in Selby, 'British Policy', PhD, 220–3, 228.

61. Aldrich, *Intelligence and the Far Eastern War*, 349–51; Ho Chi Minh to Trevor-Wilson, 29 Jul. 1947, 9007-235-24, Trevor-Wilson papers, NAM; Fulton to Trevor-Wilson, 22 Mar. 1954, 9007-235-45, Trevor-Wilson papers, NAM.

62. De Lattre to Trevor-Wilson, 14 Oct. 1951, 9007-235-34, Trevor-Wilson papers, NAM; Shelden, *Greene*, 392–3; Sherry, *Greene*, vol. 2, 481–3; interview with William Colby, Georgetown, Apr. 1992; private information.

63. Hack, 'British Intelligence', champions Briggs, while Short, *Communist Insurrection*, and Stubbs, *Hearts and Minds*, lean towards Templer. Cloake, *Templer*, interestingly is agnostic. On the Indian system see particularly Popplewell, 'Lacking Intelligence', 336–52.

64. De Zulueta to Eden, 13 May 1955, PREM 11/2247.

65. JIC (57) 115, 'Intelligence Organisation in the Colonial Territories', 8 Nov. 1957, CAB 158/30.

Chapter 23 *Submarines, Spy-flights and Shoot-downs: Intelligence after Suez*

1. Goodpaster, 'Memorandum of Conference with the President', 21 Aug. 1958, Box 6, Office of Staff Sec., WHO, DDEL.

2. Ibid.

3. JIC (48) 9 (0), 'Russian Interests, Intentions and Capabilities', 23 Jul. 1948, L/WS/1/1173, IOLR; Aldrich, 'Anglo-American Intelligence'.

4. See for example a minute to Attlee from the Air Ministry requesting permission 'to fly a special reconnaissance' of two Soviet submarines in Valona Bay, 17 Mar. 1950, AIR 19/1107. Hockaday to PS to Eden, quoting message by Churchill to First Sea Lord, 24 Dec. 1951, ibid.

5. Buzzard, GC Report, Jan. 1953, DEFE 13/352.

6. Buzzard to Dean, 2 Sept. 1953, MAF 209/1482; Dean to Buzzard, n.d., ibid.; Leach min., 4 Sept. 1953, ibid.

7. Riste, *Norwegian Intelligence*, 75–6. Network First Documentary, *The Riddle of the Gaul*, ITV, 12 Oct. 1996. It has been suggested that by the 1970s they were involved in operations to try and recover Soviet missiles from the Barents Sea. I am indebted to Mason Redfearn and Jonathan Davies for guidance on these matters.

8. James, *Eden*, 436–7; Smith, *New Cloak*, 120–1.

9. Eden to Bridges, M.104.56, 9 May 1956, AP20/32/78, Avon papers, BUL; Riste, *Norwegian Intelligence*, 77.

10. Eden to Head, 22 Dec. 1956, AP20/21/228, Avon papers, BUL; private information.

11. ZY/268, 'Political Approval for Certain Service Intelligence Operations', 4 Jul. 1955, ADM 1/29320.

12. Bissell, *Reflections*, 115–16.

13. Goodpaster memo, 21 Jun. 1956, Box 14, Alph. Subseries, Subject Series, WHO, DDEL; Pedlow and Welzenbach, *CIA and the U-2*, 94–5.

14. Elkins (BJSM) to Mountbatten, 16 Oct. 1956, ADM 205/110.

15. Inglis (DNI) to Flag Officer, Submarines, 19 Oct. 1956, ADM 205/110; Coote, USS *Stickleback* report, ibid.

16. Elkins (BJSM) to Mountbatten, 31 Dec. 1956, ADM 205/110.

17. Packard, *Century*, 51.

18. Sontag and Drew, *Blind Man's Buff*, 169–83.

19. Hailsham to Eden, 17 Oct. 1956, DEFE 13/230; Draft Brief, 1 Dec. 1956, ibid.; D (57) 3, 'Defence Facilities in Ceylon', 21 Jan. 1957, ibid.

20. DNI memo, 5 Feb. 1957, ADM 1/29320; G. R. W. to Macmillan, 26 Jun. 1958, ibid.

21. Macmillan to Eisenhower, 22 Mar. 1957, *ESI*, 7.6; Twigge and Scott, *Planning Armageddon*, 237.

22. Bissell, *Reflections*, 114–17.

23. Andrew, *President's Eyes Only*, 243; Lashmar, *Spy-Flights*, 146–57; Nesbit, *Eyes of the RAF*, 258–9.

24. Lashmar, *Spy-Flights*, 158–61; Mikesh, *B-57: Canberra*, 122–30.

25. Lashmar, *Spy-Flights*, 93–4, 119. Lashmar's identification of the discrepancies in the oral and written record is illuminating.

26. Maddrell, 'Britain's Exploitation', PhD, 323; Tamnes, *High North*, 128–9, Nesbitt, *Eyes of the RAF*, 258; Bissell, *Reflections*, 119.

27. Pedlow and Welzenbach, *CIA and the U-2*, 110–11; Roman, *Eisenhower and the Missile Gap*, 194–208.

28. Andrew, *President's Eyes Only*, 243; Pedlow and Welzenbach, *CIA and the U-2*, 130–3.

29. Riste, *Norwegian Intelligence*, 65; Tamnes, *High North*, 123–5.

30. CINCPAC to JCS, 'Resumption of Photographic Reconnaissance Flights', 25 Nov. 1958, Op-60IC5, Box 14, AS/SS, Office of the Staff Secretary, WHO, DDEL; CIA, Current Intelligence Memorandum, 'Apparent Loss of Chinese Nationalist Aircraft over Chinese Mainland', 8 Oct. 1959, Box 15, ibid.

31. Cline interview in Weber, *Spymasters*, 195. A photo of the aircraft can be seen in Rich and Janos, *Skunk Works*.

32. Beschloss, *Mayday*, 176–7; Freedman, *US Intelligence*, 69–72; Pedlow and Welzenbach, *CIA and the U-2*, 161–4.

33. Bissell, *Reflections*, 121–9; Pedlow and Welzenbach, *CIA and the U-2*, 177–8.

34. Andrew, *President's Eyes Only*, 246.

35. Beschloss, *Mayday*, 41–61; Pedlow and Welzenbach, *CIA and the U-2*, 66.

36. Pedlow and Welzenbach, *CIA and the U-2*, 125.

37. Ambrose, *Eisenhower, 1953–69*, 584; Riste, *Norwegian Intelligence*, 74.

38. Calhoun to Goodpaster, enclosing US Embassy (London) to SoS, 12 July 1960, File: UK (2) Feb.–Aug. 1960, Box 13, Office of the Staff Sec. Int Series, WHO, DDEL.

39. Reilly (Moscow) to FO, 14 Jun. 1960, NS1381/82, FO 371/152002; Matteson, 'A Search for Adventure and Service' (memoir), IV, 254–7, Box 1, Matteson papers, DDEL.

40. Kahn, 'Soviet Comint', 17.

41. The JIC paper was JIC (60) 43 (Final), 'Soviet Threats against Reconnaissance Flight Bases Following the U-2 Incident', and is summarised in DEFE 13/342.

42. Twigge and Scott, *Planning Armageddon*, 235–6; memo of a conference with the President, 22 Sept. 1960, *ESI*, 7.10.

43. Riste, *Norwegian Intelligence*, 73

44. Mins, 'Surveillance Meeting', 26 Apr. 1960, 16/W/160, ADM 1/27680.

45. Memo by DNI, 7 Apr. 1960 and attached paper 'The Need to Extend Surveillance Operations', (Top Secret – Not to be passed through any registry), ADM 1/27680.

46. Min. by head of Military Branch II, 10 Mar. 1961, ADM 1/27680.

47. Memo from PS to VCAS to PS to S of S, 'Aircraft Approach Restrictions – Operation TIARA/GARNET', Oct. 1960, AIR 20/12222. The JIC paper prepared for Macmillan was JIC (60) 62 (Revised), 1 Sept. 1960.

48. Riste, *Norwegian Intelligence*, 229.

49. Ibid., and private information.

50. Bissell, *Reflections*, 133; Tamnes, *High North*, 135–6; ORS/USIA, 'British Reactions to the Idea of a Reconnaissance Satellite', 506, DDRS 1993.

51. Brown memo, 'Suspension of RAF and USAF Radio Proving Flights during the Foreign Secretary's Visit to Moscow', 24 Apr. 1967; AIR 20/12133; Thomson memo, 'RAF Proving Flights over the Mediterranean', 15 Jun. 1967, ibid.

52. Private information; entry for 14 Oct. 1968, Benn, *Office without Power*.

53. Memo to the RSB, 'Government Communications Headquarters' (GCHQ Ref. M/8087/100/1), 11 Feb. 1960, *ESI*, 2.13. I am indebted to Rob Evans for drawing this document to my attention.

54. Jones to S(1), Air Ministry, 14 Apr. 1956, DEFE 26/5; GCHQ to BJCEB, 4 Sept. 1956, ibid.; Morgan memo., 'Berlin Airlift – Possible Soviet ECM Opposition', 9 Feb. 1959, ibid.; CCC (EW) (65) 5, 9 Sept. 1964, CAB 134/1458.

55. Aide-mémoire, 'Radio Proving Flights', Apr. 1961, DEFE 25/11.

56. Humphrey-Davies to Peck, 21 Mar. 1961, DEFE 25/11.

57. Hooper (GCHQ) to Peck (Treasury), 10 Apr. 1961, DEFE 25/11.

58. Mtg with Chief of Turkish Gen. Staff, 25 Apr. 1961, recorded by Captain Hodgkinson, DEFE 25/11.

59. Healey to Brown, MO/15/2/1, 19 Apr. 1967, AIR 20/12133.

60. Radford to Secretary of Defense, 'Clandestine Listening Devices', 6 Apr. 1956, CCS 371.2 (1–31–56), Sec. 1, RG 218; Phillips to JCS, 'Clandestine Listening Devices', 6 Apr. 1956, ibid.; Rudge memo, 'Security of US EUCOM', 14 Nov. 1952, Box 273, SPRD, OAB, WNY.

61. Thorneycroft to Douglas-Home, 12 Sept. 1964, DEFE 13/403; Jellicoe to Butler, 11 Sept. 1964, ibid.

62. Vanse to Hockaday, 16 Apr. 1963, DEFE 13/16; 591 Signals Unit, Monitor Report, 27/63, 3 Sept.–15 Oct. 1963, AIR 29/3545.

63. Jones (VCAS) to Lloyd (HQ ACFE), 6 Feb. 1948, AIR 20/2794.

64. Lenox-Conygham min., 19 Nov. 1954, ADM 1/26478; head of CE Branch IV, 15 Feb. 1955, ADM 1/26478; Lenox-Conygham (DSD), 25 Feb. 1955, ibid.

65. Head of CE Branch IV min., 2 Apr. 1955, ADM 1/26478.

66. Brook to Eden, 'Communism and the Trade Unions', 30 May 1956, PREM 11/1238; Macleod to Eden, 'Communism and the Trade Unions', 5 Jul. 1956, and Eden mins, ibid.

67. CIA Special Report, 'The British Communist Party', 12 Apr. 1963, OCI 0275/63B, Box 171, NSF, JFKL; Wyatt, *Confessions*, 252–64.

68. Lashmar and Oliver, *Britain's Secret Propaganda War*, 111.

69. De la Mare, *Perverse and Foolish*, 99–100.

70. S (PS) (57) (23), 'Civil Servants as security risks on other than Communist or fascist grounds', 26 Apr. 1957, CAB 21/4530.

71. Wigg to Wilson, Aug. 1966, PREM 13/1203, reproduced in full in Young, 'GCHQ'.

72. 'Meeting with Sir Roger Hollis', COS (62) 68th mtg (1), 30 Oct. 1962, DEFE 32/7.

73. Douglas memo to Gray, 21 Nov. 1960, Box 5, PS/SAS, OSANA, DDEL; Strong to Watkinson, 29 Aug. 1960, DEFE 13/9. See also Andrew and Mitrokhin, *The Sword*, 178–80.

Chapter 24 *Missiles and Mergers: Strategic Intelligence*

1. 'Missile Intelligence: Air Ministry Comments on the Templer Report', note by CAS, Mar. 1961, AIR 8/1953.

2. JIC 57 (30), quoted in 'The Air Defence of the UK', Sept. 1957, DEFE 7/970.

3. Twigge and Scott, *Planning Armageddon*, 52, 60. This important study is essential reading.

4. Mins by Reilly, 17 Nov. 1956; Dean, 19 Nov. 1956; Grey, 19 Nov. 1956, on 'Relations with the Soviet Union and the Satellites', N1052/10/G, FO 371/122081.

5. Jackson to Allen Dulles, 30 Mar. 1959, Box 40, CDJP, DDEL; Dulles to Jackson, 31 Mar. 1959, ibid.; Jackson to Dulles, 12 May 1959, ibid.

6. Jackson to Allen Dulles, 25 Mar. 1959, Box 40, CDJP, DDEL; Dulles to Jackson, 16 Mar. 1959, ibid.; Jackson to Dulles, 24 Feb. 1959, ibid. For an excellent account of the Volunteer Freedom Corps idea see Dockrill, *Eisenhower's New Look*, 154–6.

7. JIC (57) 30, quoted in 'Air Defence of the UK, Annexe E: The Likelihood of Attack on the British Isles in Each Year between Now and 1965', Sept. 1957, DEFE 7/970.

8. Watson to Jackson, 18 Apr. 1958, Box 91, CDJP, DDEL.

9. See especially Steele, 'Allied and Interdependent', 230–47; Lamb, *Macmillan*, 296–404.

10. SC (58) 46 Revised, 'UK Policy toward the East European Satellites', Apr. 1960, ZP24/3/G, FO 371/52129; Brimelow min., 27 Mar. 1960, ibid.

11. Ziegler note on SC (61) 25, 'United Kingdom Policy towards the Satellites', 27 Jun. 1961, FO 371/177821.

12. Mins of a Russia Committee meeting, 12 Sept. 1950, RC/133/50, N1053/26/G, FO 371/86762; JIC (52) 30 (Final) discussed at COS (52) 102nd mtg, 15 Jul. 1952, DEFE 32/2; DNI memo, 6 Jul. 1953, ADM 205/89; Brownjohn to Minister of Defence, 26 Jun. 1953, DEFE 13/352. See also Clark and Wheeler, *British Origins*, 186–9.

13. Brownjohn to Minister of Defence, NCDB/M/4, 10 Feb. 1953, DEFE 13/352. For American sanitisation of material destined for London, see mins of JIC 177th mtg, 13 Jan. 1949, CCS 334 JIC (5–27–48), RG 218.

14. 'Replies to Questions Asked by the PM of the JIC in the Course of his Minute to the MoD No 630/57', 24 Jan. 1958, DEFE 7/970.

15. Alexander to Churchill, 10 Feb. 1954, DEFE 13/352.

16. Brief for Watkinson, 'Warning and Timing of Soviet Attack on the West in Global War up to 1965', 22 Nov. 1960, DEFE 13/342; Scott and Twigge, *Planning Armageddon*, 254–5.

17. JIC Sec. to Chairman COS, 'Comments on Various Military Factors Affecting Soviet Capabilities and Intentions over the Next Five Years', JIC/2291/57, Limited Circ., 31 Oct. 1957, and Annexe, CIA Memo No. 1416446, 22 Oct. 1957, DEFE 13/342.

18. Brundrett to Minister of Defence, FB/483/55, 'Note on Military Potential Section of Annexe to DC (55) 46', 28 Oct. 1955, DEFE 13/342. See also Scott and Twigge, *Planning Armageddon*, 245.

19. Ridgway to JCS, 18 Jul. 1953, Box 28, Ridgway papers, USMHI.

20. Slessor to VCAS, JCS 37/1, 20 Sept. 1949, AIR 75/92. For American examples see Mescall, 'Triumph of Parochialism', 127–34.

21. Ridgway to JCS, 18 July 1953, File: COS Jul.–Dec. 53, Box 28, Ridgway papers, USMHI.

22. Oral history of Colonel Herron W. Maples, SHAPE Intelligence and DIA, Box 1, Oral History Collection, USMHI. The classic realist statement on intelligence is McGarvey, 'DIA: Intelligence to Please', 318–28.

23. Note for Dickson by Strong (JIB), summarising JIC (58) 4 (Final), 'Soviet Strategy in Global War up to the End of 1962', 6 Feb. 1958, *ESI*, 5.9. See the thorough discussion of this issue in Twigge and Scott, *Planning Armageddon*, 256–8.

24. Strong (JIB) to Watkinson, 8 Feb. 1960, DEFE 13/342.

25. Roman, *Eisenhower*, 40–6. See also Andrew, *For the President's Eyes*, 223–4; Freedman, *US Intelligence*, 67, 82; Prados, *Soviet Estimate*, 49–50.

26. Roman, *Eisenhower*, 44–5.

27. Lamb, *Macmillan*, 340; memo of a convers., 29 Mar. 1960, DDE–Macmillan mtg 1, Box 5, McCone papers, DDEL.

28. Strong (JIB) to Watkinson, 'The Soviet Atomic Energy Programme', 25 Jan. 1961, UK Eyes Only, DEFE 13/342.

29. JIC/1713/60, 21 Oct. 1960, DEFE 13/342; Twigge and Scott, *Planning Armageddon*, 52.

30. Potts min., 'Chinese Interest in Nuclear Weapons', 1 Jun. 1960, IAE410/8G, FO 371/149546, and discussion of JIC (AUST) (60) 21 Final, Apr. 1960, ibid.

31. McCone, Oral History, 19, JFKL; CAS memo, 'Chinese Nuclear Test', 15 Oct. 1964, DEFE 13/403.

32. Strauss to SoS and Secretary of Defense, 13 Nov. 1957, 'Sharing of Atomic Energy Information with Certain Allies', Box 16, BNS, NSC Series, OSANA, WHO, DDEL. See also Twigge and Scott, *Planning Armageddon*, 237.

33. Goodpaster, 'Memorandum of Conference with the President', 21 Aug. 1958, 10.50 a.m., File AEC vol. II (4) Aug.–Sept. 58, Box 3, AS/SS, Office of the Staff Sec., WHO, DDEL.

34. Elkins (JSM) to Mountbatten, 24 Sept. 1958, I/478, Mountbatten papers, HL.

35. Morgan to Brownjohn, 21 Sept. 1953, DEFE 7/2105; 'C' to Parker, 8 Oct. 1953, ibid.; COS (54) 101, 'Atomic Energy Intelligence', 31 Mar. 1954, ibid.; COS (57) 7th mtg, 22 Jan. 1957, ibid.; Dean to Powell, 31 May 1957, ibid.

36. Memo by CAS, 'Missile Intelligence', 7 Mar. 1961, AIR 8/1953.

37. Memo by ACAS (I), Bufton, to CAS, 'Templer Report: The issue of "principle"', 20 Mar. 1961, AIR 8/1953.

38. Cole, 'British Technical Intelligence', 83–91.

39. Hunt (JIC) to Bufton (ACAS (I)), 9 Sept. 1960, JIC/1482/60, AIR 8/1953.

40. Mountbatten memo, 'Missile Intelligence', 15 Mar. 1961, AIR 8/1953.

41. Memo on JCS 2031/166, 'Establishment of a Defence Intelligence Agency', 11 Apr. 1961, CCS 2010, RG 218.

42. Twigge and Scott, *Planning Armageddon,* 25–7; Ziegler, *Mountbatten*, 633.

Chapter 25 *Cyprus: The Last Foothold*

1. Philpott to VCAS, 'RAF Requirements in Cyprus', 27 Apr. 1959, AIR 20/10328, quoted in Kyriakides, 'British Cold War Strategy', PhD, 285.

2. COS 70 (55) 7, 'Cyprus – military arguments against a leased base', 30 Aug. 1955, Kent (ed.), *BDEE, Middle East*, B, 4, Part II, 329.

3. COS (48) 70 (0), 'Cyprus – Strategic Requirement for Development of a Very Heavy Bomber Airfield', 2 Apr. 1948, DEFE 2/1654; JAP/P (48) 16 Final, 'Cyprus – Administrative Implications of Development of VHB Airfield', ibid.

4. Kyriakides, 'British Cold War Strategy', PhD, 285; Richelson and Ball, *Ties That Bind*, 335.

5. Canine (AFSA) to CNO, 'Evacuation of APPLESAUCE Personnel in an Emergency', 9 Jan. 1952, Box 270, SPDR (Series XVI), OAB, WNY.

6. Maddrell, 'Britain's Exploitation', PhD, 315, citing Mathams, *Sub-Rosa*, 27–8; Bamford, *Puzzle Palace*, 158–9.

7. Ackerman to D of I, 21 Sept. 1951, 219900, Box 58, D of I records, RG 341; MoD to GCHQ Middle East Land Forces, 15 Apr. 1953, AIR 20/7028.

8. 'Report of Working Party on Broadcasting in the Middle East', Mar. 1957, and mins of 1st mtg, 22 Feb. 1957, DO 35/9645.

9. Grivas, *Memoirs*, 13–14; Melshen, 'Pseudo Operations', PhD, 115.

10. Woodhouse, *Something Ventured*, 133–5; Kyriakides, 'British Cold War Strategy', PhD, 135.

11. Clark, 'Colonial Police', PhD, 370–1.

12. Dorril, *MI6*, 550–1; Durrell, *Bitter Lemons*, 196–7; Holland, *Britain and the Revolt in Cyprus*, 49–50; West, *Friends*, 70–1.

13. Carver, *Harding*, 203–5; Clark, 'Colonial Police', PhD, 311; West, *Friends*, 72–3.

14. Melshen, 'Pseudo Operations', PhD, 116–17.

15. Grivas, *Memoirs*, 57–8; Holland, *Britain and the Revolt in Cyprus*, 151; Craig and O'Malley, *Cyprus Conspiracy*, 35.

16. Holland, *Britain and the Revolt in Cyprus*, 151–3; Lapping, *End of Empire*, 336–7.

17. Melshen, 'Pseudo Operations', PhD, 121–2; Kyriakides, 'British Cold War Strategy', PhD, 214–16.

18. Carruthers, *Hearts and Minds*, 198–9; Holland, *Britain and the Revolt in Cyprus*, 133; Kyriakides, 'British Cold War Strategy', PhD, 214–16.

19. Melshen, 'Pseudo Operations', PhD, 125; Clark, 'Colonial Police', PhD, 328.

20. Clark, 'Colonial Police', PhD, 326.

21. Lapping, *End of Empire*, 338–9.

22. Carruthers, *Hearts and Minds*, 210–11.

23. There is no documentary evidence for this assertion, which is based on private information. On resistance to a public enquiry see Carruthers, *Hearts and Minds*, 238–9.

24. Melshen, 'Pseudo Operations', PhD, 114.

25. The most reliable account of Operation Sunshine has been beautifully reconstructed from Darling's papers by Holland in *Britain and the Revolt in Cyprus*, 312–13.

26. Dorril, *MI6*, 555–7; McDermott, *Eden Legacy*, 174–7; West, *Friends*, 76–7; Lapping, *End of Empire*, 343.

27. Sandys to CDS, 27 Nov. 1958, DEFE 13/6; Sandys to Foot, 5 Nov. 1958, DEFE 13/97.

28. Foot to Lennox-Boyd, 9 Nov. 1958, *ESI*, 12.5.

29. Lapping, *End of Empire*, 334–5.

30. The definitive account is Holland, *Britain and the Revolt in Cyprus*, 312–13.

31. Lapping, *End of Empire*, 349.

32. Briefing Note for NSC Meeting, 1 Dec. 1959, 'US Policy toward Cyprus' (S. E. Belk), Box 6, Briefing Notes Subseries, NSC Series, OSANA, WHO, DDEL; Belk (NSC) to Gray, 10 Nov. 1959, ibid.

33. Middle East Defence Secretariat memo, 30 Apr. 1959, CO 926/978, cited in Craig and O'Malley, *Cyprus Conspiracy*, 82–3.

34. Grandy to MacDonald, 9 Sept. 1960, AIR 20/12222.

Chapter 26 *Working Groups: Special Operations in the Third World*

1. COS (62) 304, 21 Aug. 1962, DEFE 11/158.

2. Eisenhower's Record of the Bermuda Conference, 21 Mar. 1957, DDRS 456/1992.

3. Eisenhower to Macmillan, 26 Mar. 1957 and Macmillan to Eisenhower, 29 Mar. 1957, Eyes Only, DDRS, 1997/518 and 1997/745.

4. Allen Dulles to Gray, 22 Nov. 1956, Box 7, AS/SS, Office of the Staff Sec., WHO, DDEL.

5. TSS, 'Ropes of Sand', 66–7, Box 1, Eveland papers, HIWRP.

6. Andrew, *President's Eyes Only*, 225–33; Dulles (CIA) to SoS, 10 Nov. 1956, Box 7, AS/SS, Office of Staff Sec., WHO, DDEL.

7. Allen Dulles to Goodpaster, 22 Mar. 1957, enclosing, 'Situation Report on Syria', Intel. Matters (2), Nov. 1956–Mar. 1957, AS/SS, Office of Staff Sec., WHO, DDEL.

8. John Foster Dulles to Macmillan, 5 Sept. 1957, File Syria (3), Box 43, Ann Whitman Int. Series, DDEL.

9. COS (57) 74th mtg, 25 Sept. 1957, DEFE 32/5.

10. Eisenhower to Allen Dulles, 5 Nov. 1957, File: Allen Dulles (2), Box 13, Admin Series, Ann Whitman File, DDEL.

11. Note for the Prime Minister, 'Propaganda/Counter-Subversion', 8 Jun. 1958, PREM 11/2324. See also Jones, 'Maximum Disavowable Aid', 1196.

12. OIR Report No. 7527, 'The Subversive Threat to Indonesia', 13 Jun. 1957, RG 59.

13. OIR No. 7902, 'Rebellion in Indonesia', 18 Dec. 1958, RG 59.

14. See especially Jones, 'Maximum Disavowable Aid', 1189–93.

15. Allen Dulles to White House (Cutler), 31 Jan. 1958, Box 11, Briefing Notes Subseries, NSC Series, OSANA, WHO, DDEL.

16. Macmillan min. to Bishop, 'Points discussed with Foreign Secretary last night', 4 Mar. 1958, *ESI*, 16.3; HQ FEAF to ACAS (P), 26 Apr. 1958, AIR 8/1954.

17. Jones, 'Maximum Disavowable Aid', 1200–1; COS (58) 34th mtg, 15 Apr. 1958, DEFE 32/6.

18. Copenhagen to Washington (signed Dulles), Dulte 15, 7 May 1958, *ESI*, 16.4.

19. Grose, *Gentleman Spy*, 454; Halpern interview in Weber, *Spymasters*, 127.

20. Note for Macmillan, 'Indonesia', 8 Jun. 1958, PREM 11/2324.

21. Donnelly to CoS USAF, 'The Role of Air Power in the Indonesian Civil War', 4 Jun. 1959, Box 29, White Papers, LC.

22. OIR No. 7902, 'Rebellion in Indonesia', 18 Dec. 1958, RG 59.

23. Higgins and Higgins, 'Indonesia', 156–65.

24. 'Brief History of the Allen Pope Case', 14 Mar. 1961, Box 114, PSF Files, JFKL. Also Andrew, *President's Eyes Only*, 250–1; Phillips, *Devil's Bodyguard*, 306–9.

25. Elder (CIA) to Bundy, 8 Apr. 1961, Box 114, PSF Files, JFKL; Kennedy to Sukharno, 21 Jun. 1961, ibid.; Pope to Kennedy, 11 Jul. 1962, ibid. See also Conboy and Morrison, *Feet to the Fire*, 160–5.

26. Jones to SoS, 4 Nov. 1963, Box 114, NSF, JFKL.

27. Smith, *Unknown CIA*, 90–1; Smith, *Cold Warrior*, 104–15, Landsdale, *Midst of Wars*, 35–120; *FRUS*, 1951, Asia Pacific, 1566–7.

28. Hohler (Saigon) to Lord Home, 5 Nov. 1960, ZP14/40, FO 371/159673. All of para. 11 of this document is sanitised.

29. Brief for talks between Caccia and Rusk in Washington, Nov. 1960, ZP14/40, FO 371/159673.

30. UK Assistance to South Vietnam, mins of mtgs on 13 and 15 Jun. 1961, DO 169/109.

31. Ibid.; Beckett, 'Robert Thompson', 49–51; Thompson, *Make for the Hills*, 123–5.

32. De Silva, *Sub Rosa*, 210–11.

33. Thompson to Ngo Dinh Diem, 28 Feb. 1962, Landsdale papers, Box 60, File 1570, HIWRP; BRIAM memo, 'Identification of Individual Communists', 2 May 1963, ibid.

34. Thompson, *Make for the Hills*, 128; Colby, *Honorable Men*, 148, 175–8; Beckett, 'Robert Thompson', 52–3; Freedman, *Kennedy's Wars*, 85–93.

35. Landsdale to Wally, 30 Nov. 1962, File 1373, Box 49, Landsdale papers, HIWRP.

36. Thompson, *Make for the Hills*, 140–1.

37. Ibid.; Helms interview in Weber, *Spymasters*, 307; de Silva, *Sub Rosa*, 205, 215. The most cogent review of the evidence is Short, *Origins*, 263–71.

38. Thompson to Lodge, 26 Feb. 1964, 76951/64, FO 371/175536; Beckett, 'Robert Thompson', 50–2.

39. Colby, *Honorable Men*, 148, 175–8, 276; Spector, *Advice and Support*, 240–1.
40. Clarridge, *Spy for All Seasons*, 67.
41. CIA Report, 23 Apr. 1959, 'Desire of the Dalai Lama to Continue the Struggle for the Freedom and Independence of Tibet', Box 44, Ann Whitman Int. Series, DDEL. See also Alexander, *Strange Connection*, 181–2; Shakya, *Dragon*, 170–3, 207.
42. Ali, 'South Asia', 259–68; Shakya, *Dragon*, 286; Smith, *Tibetan Nation*, 506–10.
43. Watson min., copy for IRD, 9 May 1958, J1431/1, FO 371/131226.
44. Brook to Macmillan, Top Secret and Personal, 16 Dec. 1959, enclosing SIS memo, 'Notes on a Visit to Africa', 11 Dec. 1959, PREM 11/2585. I am indebted to Keith Kyle for drawing this document to my attention.
45. Meyer to Bundy, 5 Feb. 1962, Box 106, POF, JFKL
46. SV (65) 4, 'Progress Report – Terms of Reference', 1 Mar. 1965', CAB 134/2544; SV (65), 'Revised Composition and T. of R.', 17 Mar. 1965, ibid.
47. SV (65) 9, 'Report on the Activities of Working Groups', 18 May 1965, CAB 134/2544.
48. Elliott, *With my Little Eye*, 56.
49. Thompson, *Make for the Hills*, 134–5.
50. CFR, 'Intelligence and Foreign Policy', 3rd mtg, 8 Jan. 1968, in Freney, *Australian Connection*, 81–91.
51. McGehee, *Deadly Deceits*, 50–1.

Chapter 27 *The Hidden Hand Exposed: From the Bay of Pigs to Profumo*

1. Bruce to Kennedy and SoS, 15 Jun. 1963, *ESI*, 11.6.
2. Short, *Origins*, 240–2; Rabe, *Most Dangerous Area*, 3–15.
3. Andrew, *President's Eyes Only*, 251; Bissell, *Reflections*, 157–8; Freedman, *Kennedy's Wars*, 151–2.
4. Andrew, *President's Eyes Only*, 255; Horne, *Macmillan, 1957–1986*, 298.
5. Meers, 'British Connection', 425–9; Young, 'Great Britain's Latin American Dilemma', 584–92.
6. Scott, *Macmillan*, 17–18.
7. Andrew, *President's Eyes Only*, 255.
8. Gray, memo of mtg with the President, 3 Jan. 1961, Box 4, PS/SAS, OSANA, DDEL.
9. Andrew, *President's Eyes Only*, 263–5.
10. Phillips, *Night Watch*, 107–10; Wyden, *Bay of Pigs*, 173–288.
11. Wyden, *Bay of Pigs*, 251–6; Freedman, *Kennedy's Wars*, 141–5.
12. Willoughby to Allen Dulles, 2 Jun. 1961, Willoughby papers, Series 1, CIA corresp. 1951–67, MML.
13. McGehee, *Deadly Deceits*, 54–5.
14. Ibid., 58–9.
15. Andrew, *President's Eyes Only*, 253; Bissell, *Reflections*, 140–5, 253.
16. Secretary of Defense Staff Meeting, 17 Jul. 1961, Box 46, Lansdale papers, HIWRP. See also Andrew, *President's Eyes Only*, 275.
17. See the excellent account in Pagedas, *Anglo-American Strategic Relations*, 151–4.
18. Gavin papers quoted in ibid., 172.
19. Horne, *Savage War*, 484–5; Kumamoto, *International Terrorism*, 104–9.
20. Van Houten, 'British and American Policy', PhD, 154.
21. Ibid., 146.
22. Mangold, *Cold Warrior*, 95–104.
23. Van Houten, 'British and American Policy', PhD, 186–9; Twigge and Scott, *Planning Armageddon*, 235.
24. Fursenko and Naftali, 'Soviet Intelligence', 73–5.
25. Van Houten, 'British and American Policy', PhD, 198–9; private information.
26. De Salute to Macmillan, 29 Aug. 1961, PREM 11/5084; Rogers (LCESA) to de Salute, 2 Jan. 1962, ibid.; de Salute to Macmillan, 25 Feb. 1962, ibid.
27. De Zulueta to Bundy, 14 Jun. 1963, PREM 11/4460.
28. Macmillan, *At the End*, 335, quoted in Van Houten, 'British and American Policy', PhD, 203.
29. Nunnerley, *President Kennedy*, 127–61.
30. JIC (62) 81 discussed at COS (62) 58th mtg, 25 Sept. 1962, DEFE 32/7.
31. Scott, 'Espionage and the Cold War', 26–30.
32. May and Zelikov, *Kennedy Tapes*, 2–13; Schecter and Deriabin, *Spy*, 3, 420–1. The state-of-the-art assessment is Scott, 'Espionage and the Cold War', 29–36, which confirms Freedman's earlier observations in *US Intelligence*, 73–5.
33. Schecter and Deriabin, *Spy*, 115–272.
34. Meeting No. 23, London, 28 Jul. 1961, para. 31, quoted in Schecter and Deriabin, *Spy*, 212–13.
35. De Silva, *Sub Rosa*, 61.
36. Garthoff, 'US Intelligence', 24.

37. PFIAB memo for the President, 4 Feb. 1963, McAuliffe (ed.), *Cuban Missile Crisis*, 365–9; McCone memo for the President, 28 Feb. 1963, ibid., 373.
38. Scott, 'Espionage and the Cold War', 30.
39. McCone memo of a mtg with the President, 22 Aug. 1962, in McAuliffe (ed.), *Cuban Missile Crisis*, 27–9. The value of French intelligence is questioned by Porch, *French Secret Services*, 409–11, but convincingly asserted by Scott, *Macmillan*, 33.
40. Scott, *Macmillan*, 50–1, 81–3, 117–18.
41. There are arguments that it would have been disastrous in Johnson, *Secret Agencies*, 183–5, or that McCone's judgement was 'sound' and there would have been no major reaction, Garthoff, 'US Intelligence', 32.
42. Scott, *Macmillan*, 8, 184–5; Nunnerley, *President Kennedy*, 71–90.
43. Kennedy, *Thirteen Days*, 91–100; Freedman, *Kennedy's Wars*, 180–1.
44. The outstanding account, from which this information is drawn, is Sagan, *Limits of Safety*, 135–41.
45. Underlined by Scott, 'The Other Other Missiles', 2–11.
46. Thorneycroft to Butler, 22 Sept. 1964, DEFE 13/403.
47. Schecter and Deriabin, *Spy*, 261–4, 336–50. The KGB surveillance film of the CIA officer servicing of the dead-drop has been released. Earlier in his career as a Western agent, Penkovsky had asked his handlers for miniature atomic bombs, so that he could lead a devastating surprise attack on Moscow.
48. Twigge and Scott, *Planning Armageddon*, 87–8; Andrew and Gordievsky, *KGB*, 433–6; Lansdale to Riley, 'Special Forces, West Germany', 18 Jul. 1963, File: DoD/OSO, Lansdale papers, HIWRP; private information.
49. Garthoff, 'US Intelligence', 53, 55.
50. Foote, *Handbook for Spies*; Stewart, *Cloak and Dollar War*; Anders, *Murder to Order*; Philby, *Silent War*.
51. This point is well made in Lamb, *Macmillan*, 452–3.
52. The IPD file on Philby's disappearance is at FO 953/2165; Knightley, *Master Spy*, 215–18; Evans, *Good Times*, 19–83.
53. First revealed in West, *Matter of Trust*, 91–8; Lamb, *Macmillan*, 457–8.
54. Denning Report, Cmnd 2512, Sept. 1963, dissected in Scott, *Macmillan*, 100–7.
55. Knightley and Kennedy, *Affair of State*, 144–5; Lamb, *Macmillan*, 453–64.
56. CC (63), concs, 12 Jun. 1963, CAB 128/113; CC (63), concs, 13 Jun. 1963, CAB 128/114.
57. Bruce to Kennedy and SoS, 15 Jun. 1963, *ESI*, 11.6.
58. Knightley and Kennedy, *Affair of State*, 206.
59. Wyatt, *Confessions*, 286–7.
60. Horne, *Macmillan, 1957–1986*, 564–5; Lamb, *Macmillan*, 490–1.
61. Nunnerley, *President Kennedy*, 219–21; Bissell, *Reflections*, 157, 215. Bissell is adamant that the United States did not itself act against Diem.
62. Coleman, *Liberal Conspiracy*, 185.
63. CFR, 'Intelligence and Foreign Policy', 3rd mtg, 8 Jan. 1968, in Freney, *Australian Connection*, 81–91.
64. McCone, Oral History, 24, JFKL.
65. Phillips, *Night Watch*, 58, 137.
66. Memo. by Schlesinger for the President, 'CIA Reorganisation', 30 Jun. 1961, Box 273, NSF, JFKL. The budgetary multiplier is still classified but knowledgeable commentators suggest that the CIA had twice the resources of State.
67. Clifford, *Counsel*, 170–1.
68. Slessor, Introductory Address, 'Anglo-American Understanding', 1st ESU Summer School, Oxford, July 1966, AIR 75/146.

'Behind the scenes of history'

1. 'On Watch: Profiles from the National Security Agency's Past 40 Years', 91, declassified by NSA under FOIA.
2. Ibid.
3. Andrew and Dilks (eds), *Missing Dimension*, 1–16: Andrew, 'Intelligence and International Relations', 321–30; Andrew, *President's Eyes Only*, 1–6.
4. Leffler, *Preponderance*. Similar examples of ignoring include Crockatt, *Fifty Years*, and Hogan, *Cross of Iron*. For an extended discussion of integrating intelligence into Cold War history see Gaddis, 'Intelligence'.
5. Impressive examples include Andrew, *President's Eyes Only*; Lucas, *Divided We Stand*; Fursenko and Naftali, *One Hell of a Gamble*; Twigge and Scott, *Planning Armageddon*; Kahin and Kahin, *Subversion as Foreign Policy*.
6. Deighton, 'Say It with Documents'.
7. Scott and Smith, 'Cuban Missile Crisis' 659–84; Ball, 'Harold Macmillan', 99–103.

8. Heuser, 'Stalin', 18–19.

9. Blake, *No Other Choice*, 168; Young, *Who Is my Liege?*, 32, 35; Dorril, *M16*, 609.

10. Leary, 'George Blake and the Berlin Tunnel'.

11. Grose, *Gentleman Spy*, 467–8, citing *Time* magazine, 28 Sept. 1959.

12. Koch, *Double Lives*, 181–205; Lucas, *Freedom's War*, 1–15; Wilford, 'Information Research Department', 359–67.

13. Wilford, 'Information Research Department', 359–63.

14. Mountbatten to Stirling, 9 Jan. 1956, I/400, Mountbatten papers, HL.

15. Meyer, *Facing Reality*, 60–84.

16. Herman, *Intelligence Power*, 2–3.

17. CIA/RR 65–64, Intelligence Brief, 'UK Defense Review: Problems and Prospects', DDRS 1997/1213.

18. McGehee, *Deadly Deceits*, 29.

19. A rigorous analysis of the generic issues of intelligence alliance is Westerfield, 'America and the World of Liaison'.

20. Memo from the Directorate of Intelligence and Research, DoS, to Rusk, 'What Now for Britain? Wilson's Visit and Britain's Future', REU-11, 7 Feb. 1968, Philip M. Kaiser papers, Box 8, HSTL.

Bibliography

All archival references in the endnotes are to the Public Record Office, Kew, unless they carry an alternate designation, for example 'RG' for United States National Archives Record Groups, or LC for the Library of Congress. In the case of books listed in the Bibliography the place of publication is London unless otherwise stated.

Major Repositories of Unpublished Government Documents

Public Record Office, Kew Gardens, Surrey, England
India Office, Blackfriars Road, London
National Museum of Labour History
US National Archives, Washington, DC
US Naval Operational Archives Branch, Navy Yard, Washington, DC

Freedom of Information Act Requests

Additional documentation was secured via FOIA from: Central Intelligence Agency; National Security Agency/Central Security Service; State Department; US Air Force Intelligence Command; US Army Intelligence and Security Command; US Information Agency.

Microforms

Declassified Document Reference System
Records of the Joint Chiefs of Staff, 1946–53, BRO
The papers of John Foster Dulles and Christian A. Herter, LL
The Office Files of Harry S. Truman, HUL

Private Papers

I. Great Britain
Field Marshal Lord Alanbrooke (LHCMA)
Lord Avon, Foreign Secretary (PRO and BUL)
Lord Beaverbrook (House of Lords)
Brigadier Sir Edward Beddington (LHCMA)
Sir Frederick Brundrett (CCC)
Lord Butler (Trinity College, Cambridge)
Sir Alexander Cadogan (CCC)
Lord Chandos (CCC)
Lord Cherwell (NC)
Sir Winston Churchill (CCC)
William Clark (BOD)
Sir Stafford Cripps (NC)
Sir Andrew Cunningham (BL)
Hugh Dalton (BLPES)
General F. Davidson (LHCMA)
Ernest Davies (BLPES)

Admiral Edelsten (CCC)
Air Vice Marshal Sir William Elliott (LHCMA)
Air Vice Marshal Elmhirst (CCC)
Brigadier Leonard Field (IWM)
David Footman (St Antony's College, Oxford)
Sir Basil Liddell Hart (LHCMA)
Sir Oliver Harvey (BL)
General Sir Leslie Hollis (IWM)
Lord Ismay (LHCMA)
Lord Killearn (Middle East Centre, St Antony's College, Oxford)
Lieutenant-General Sidney Kirkman (LHCMA)
Werner Klatt (St Antony's College, Oxford)
Lord Layton (Trinity College, Cambridge)
Selwyn Lloyd (CCC)
Major-General Robert Lockhart (NAM)
Colonel McLeod (LHCMA)
Richard McKay (BLPES)
Lieutenant-Colonel W. J. Martin (IWM)
Viscount Monckton (BOD)
Field Marshal Lord Montgomery of Alamein (IWM)
Baron Morrison (BLPES)
Admiral Lord Mountbatten (HL)
Admiral William Parry (IWM)
Major-General Sir William Penney (LHCMA)
Air Chief Marshal Pirie (LHCMA)
Brigadier Pyman (LHCMA)
Air Chief Marshal Sir James Robb (RAF Museum, Hendon)
Vice Admiral Gerard Rushbrooke (IWM)
Duncan Sandys (CCC)
Sir Robert Scott (SRO)
General Frank Simpson (IWM)
Lieutenant-Colonel David Smiley (IWM)
Lord Strang (CCC)
Sir Roger Stevens (CCC)
Lord Swinton (CCC)
Lieutenant-Colonel Arthur G. Trevor-Wilson (NAM)
Lieutenant-Colonel Gerald Wilkinson (CCC)
Lord Woolton (BOD)

II. United States
Norwood F. Allman (HIWRP)
American Committee on United Europe (HIWRP and LL)
Adolf Berle (HSTL)
Russell J. Bowen Collection (LL)
General Charles Cabell (BAFB)
General Claire Chennault (HIWRP)
Charles Donnelly (MHI)
General William J. Donovan, OSS (USMHI and CCC)
Frank Dorn (HIWRP)
President Dwight D. Eisenhower (DDEL)
C. E. Emmet (HIWRP)
Wilbur Eveland (HIWRP)
Foreign Affairs Oral History Program (LL)
General A. M. Gruenther (DDEL)
Admiral Thomas B. Inglis (HIWRP)
C. D. Jackson (DDEL)
Philip M. Kaiser (HSTL)
General Edward Lansdale (HIWRP)
Admiral William D. Leahy (OAB, WNY)
Paul Linebarger (HIWRP)

General Douglas MacArthur (MML)
John McCone (DDEL)
Herron W. Maples (USMHI)
Robert Elliot Matteson (DDEL)
Robert Murphy (HIWRP)
Boris Pash (HIWRP)
Brigadier-General W. W. Quinn, (USMHI)
General Matthew B. Ridgway (MHI)
A. E. Schance (USMHI)
William J. Sebald (HIWRP)
General Walter Bedell Smith (DDEL)
General Joseph Stilwell (HIWRP)
President Harry S. Truman (HSTL)
General Hoyt Vandenberg (LC)
Colonel Thomas D. White (LC)
General Charles A. Willoughby (MML and HIWRP)

Published Documents, Reports, Diaries, Memoirs and Autobiography

Ackerman, E. C., *Street Man* (Miami: privately published, 1976).
Alsop, S., *The Center: People and Power in Political Washington* (NY: Harper & Row, 1968).
Amery, J., *Approach March: A Venture in Autobiography* (Hutchinson, 1973).
Amery, L. S., *My Political Life,* vol. 3 (Hutchinson, 1955).
Anders, K., *Murder to Order* (Ampersand, 1965).
Andersen, H., *The Dark City* (Cresset Press, 1954).
Anderson, E., *Banner over Pusan* (Evans, 1960).
Annan, N., *Changing Enemies: The Defeat and Regeneration of Germany* (HarperCollins, 1995).
Balfour, J., *Not Too Correct an Aureole: The Recollections of a Diplomat* (Michael Russell, 1983).
Bank, A., *From OSS to the Green Berets: The Birth of the Special Forces* (Novato, CA: Presidio, 1986).
Barnes, J. and Nicholson, D. (eds), *The Empire at Bay: The Leo Amery Diaries, 1929–45* (Hutchinson, 1988).
Beddington-Behrens, E., *Look Back, Look Forward* (Macmillan, 1963).
Beeston, R., *Looking for Trouble* (Brassey's, 1997).
Bell Smith, T., *The Essential CIA* (self-published, 1976).
Benn, T., *Office without Power, Diaries 1968–72* (Hutchinson, 1988).
Benson, R. L. and Warner, R., *Venona: Soviet Espionage and the American Response, 1939–57* (Menlo Park: Aegean Park Press, 1997).
Bissell, R. M., *Reflections of a Cold Warrior from Yalta to the Bay of Pigs* (New Haven: Yale UP, 1996).
Blake, G., *No Other Choice* (Cape, 1990).
Bly, H. O., *Communism, the Cold War and the FBI Connection* (NY: Huntingdon House, 1998).
Boyle, P. G., *The Churchill–Eisenhower Correspondence, 1953–55* (Chapel Hill: Uni. of North Carolina Press, 1990).
Breckenridge, S. D., *The CIA and the Cold War: A Memoir* (NY: Praeger, 1993).
Bright-Holmes, J. (ed.), *Like It Was: The Diaries of Malcolm Muggeridge* (Collins, 1981).
Bristow, D. and Bristow, B., *A Game of Moles: The Deceptions of an MI6 Officer* (Little, Brown, 1993).
Bryant, A., *The Alanbrooke Diaries: Triumph in the West, 1943–1946* (Collins, 1959).
Burke, M., *Outrageous Good Fortune* (Boston: Little, Brown, 1984).
Cavendish, A., *Inside Intelligence* (Collins, 1990).
Chandos, Lord, *The Memoirs of Lord Chandos* (The Bodley Head, 1962).
Chapman, F. S., *The Jungle Is Neutral* (Chatto & Windus, 1963).
Chester, E. T., *Covert Network: Progressives, IRC and the CIA* (NY: M. E. Sharpe, 1995).
Churchill, W. S., *War Speeches*, vol. 2 (Cassell, 1951).
Clark, R., *The Man Who Broke Purple* (Boston: Little, Brown, 1977).
Clarridge, D. R., *A Spy for All Seasons: My Life in the CIA* (NY: Scribner, 1997).
Clifford, C., *Counsel to the President: A Memoir* (NY: Random House, 1991)
Colby, W., *Honorable Men* (NY: Simon & Schuster, 1978).
Colville, J., *The Fringes of Power* (Hodder & Stoughton, 1985).
Colvin, J., *Twice around the World* (Pen & Sword, 1990).
Cooper, J., *One of the Originals: The Story of a Founder Member of the SAS* (Pan, 1991).
Copeland, M., *The Game Player: Confessions of the CIA's Original Political Operative* (Aurum Press, 1989).

Copeland, M., *The Real Spy World* (Weidenfeld & Nicolson, 1974).

Cross, C. T., *Born a Foreigner: A Memoir of the American Presence in Asia* (Lanham, MA: Rowman & Littlefield, 1999).

Cross, J., *Red Jungle* (Robert Hale, 1957).

Crozier, B., *Free Agent: The Unseen War, 1941–1991* (HarperCollins, 1993).

de la Mare, A., *Perverse and Foolish: A Jersey Farmer's Son in the Diplomatic Service* (Jersey: La Haule Books, 1994).

de Silva, P., *Sub Rosa: The CIA and the Use of Intelligence* (NY: Times Books, 1978).

Dept of Justice, *Klaus Barbie and the United States Government: A Report with Documentary Appendix to the Attorney General of the United States* (Frederick, MD: UP of America, 1984).

Dilks, D. (ed.), *The Diaries of Sir Alexander Cadogan, 1938–1945* (Cassell, 1971).

Driberg, T., *Ruling Passions: Autobiography* (Quartet, 1991).

Dubinsky, D., *David Dubinsky: A Life with Labor* (NY: Simon & Schuster, 1977).

Durrell, L., *Bitter Lemons* (Faber, 1959).

Eden, A., *The Reckoning* (Cassell, 1965).

Elliott, N., *Never Judge a Man by his Umbrella* (Michael Russell, 1992).

——, *With my Little Eye: Observations along the Way* (Michael Russell, 1994).

Etzold, T. and Gaddis, J. L. (eds), *Containment: Documents on American Policy and Strategy, 1945–50* (NY: Columbia UP, 1978).

Evans, H., *Downing Street Diary: The Macmillan Years, 1957–63* (Hodder & Stoughton, 1981).

——, *Good Times, Bad Times* (Weidenfeld & Nicolson, 1983).

Eveland, W., *Ropes of Sand: America's Failure in the Middle East* (NY: W. W. Norton, 1980).

Farran, R., *Winged Dagger: Adventures on Special Service* (Collins, 1988).

Fergusson, B., *The Trumpet in the Hall, 1930–58* (Collins, 1970).

Flicke, W. F., *War Secrets of the Ether* (Laguna Hills, CA: Aegean Park Press, 1994).

Foote, A., *A Handbook for Spies* (Museum Press, 1949).

Foreign Relations of the United States (Washington, DC: Government Printing Office, 1952–99).

Freney, D., *The CIA's Australian Connection* (Sydney: Freney, 1977).

Gladwyn, Lord, *Memoirs* (Weidenfeld & Nicolson, 1972).

Glass, L., *The Changing of Kings: Memoirs of Burma, 1937–49* (Peter Owen, 1985).

Glees, A., *War Crimes Enquiry Report* (HMSO, 1989).

Goldsmith, J. (ed.), *Stephen Spender: Journals, 1939–83* (NY: Random House, 1986).

Granatstein, J. L. and Bothwell, R., *The Gouzenkou Transcripts* (Ottawa: Deneau, 1982).

Grivas, G., *Memoirs* (Longmans, 1964).

Griffith, R. (ed.), *Ike's Letters to a Friend* (Lawrence: Uni. of Kansas Press, 1984).

Hackworth, D. H., *About Face* (Sidgwick & Jackson, 1989).

Han Suyin, *The Wind in the Tower* (Boston: Little, Brown, 1976).

Harvey-Jones, J., *Getting It Together* (Heinemann, 1991).

Havaszti-Taylor, E. (ed.), *The Hungarian Revolution of 1956: A Collection of Documents from the British Foreign Office* (Nottingham: Astra Press, 1995).

Hayter, W., *A Double Life* (Hamish Hamilton, 1974).

Hill, G., *Go Spy the Land* (Cassell, 1932).

Holober, F., *Raiders of the China Coast: CIA Covert Operations during the Korean War* (Annapolis MD: Naval Institute Press, 1999).

Hussein, King of Jordan, *Uneasy Lies the Head* (privately published, 1974).

Hyde, D., *I Believed: The Autobiography of a former British Communist* (Heinemann, 1951).

Ismay, Lord, *Memoirs* (NY: Viking Press, 1960).

John, O., *Twice through the Lines* (Macmillan, 1972).

Johnson, C. L., *More Than my Share of It All* (Washington, DC: Smithsonian Press, 1985).

Johnson, W. R., *Thwarting Enemies at Home and Abroad: How to be a Counter-Intelligence Officer* (Bethesda, MD: Stone Trail Press, 1987).

Jones, R. V., *Most Secret War* (Hamish Hamilton, 1978).

——, *Reflections on Intelligence* (Heinemann, 1989).

Kalugin, O. and Montaigne, F., *The First Directorate: My First 32 Years in Intelligence and Espionage Against the West – The Ultimate Memoirs of a Master Spy* (NY: St Martin's Press, 1994).

Kemp, P., *Arms for Oblivion* (Cassell, 1961).

——, *The Thorns of Memory* (Sinclair-Stevenson, 1990).

Kennan, G., *Memoirs, 1950–1963* (Hutchinson, 1973).

Kennedy, R., *Thirteen Days* (Macmillan, 1969).

Kent, J. (ed.), *British Documents on the End of Empire: Egypt and the Defence of the Middle East*, B, 4, part III (HMSO, 1998).

Kerber, L. L., *Stalin's Aviation Gulag: A Memoir of Andrei Tupolev and the Purge Era* (Washington, DC: Smithsonian Institute, 1996).

Khokhlov, N., *In the Name of Conscience* (Muller, 1960).

Kitson, F., *Low Intensity Operations: Subversion, Insurgency, Peacekeeping* (Faber, 1971).

Kopelev, L., *Ease my Sorrows: A Memoir* (NY: Random House, 1983).

Kot, S., *Conversations with the Kremlin and Dispatches from Russia* (Oxford: Oxford UP, 1963).

Kuhns, W. J. (ed.), *Assessing the Soviet Threat: The Early Cold War Years* (Washington, DC: CIA/CSI, 1997).

Langer, W. L., *In and Out of the Ivory Tower: The Autobiography of William L. Langer* (NY: Neale Watson Academic Publications, 1977).

Lansdale, E., *In the Midst of Wars: An American's Mission to Southeast Asia* (NY: Fordham UP, 1991).

Lilienthal, D. E., *The Journals of David E. Lilienthal*, vols. 1–7 (NY: Harper & Row, 1964–83).

Lipgens, W. and Loth, W. (eds), *Documents on the History of European Integration*, vol. 3: *The Struggle for European Integration by Political Parties and Pressure Groups in Western European Countries, 1945–50* (Berlin: Verlag, 1988).

McAuliffe, M. (ed.), *CIA Documents on the Cuban Missile Crisis* (Washington, DC: CIA, 1992).

McDermott, G., *The Eden Legacy* (Frewin, 1969).

MacDonald, E. P., *Undercover Girl* (NY: Macmillan, 1947).

McGehee, R. W., *Deadly Deceits: My 25 Years in the CIA* (NY: Sheridan Square, 1983).

Maclean, A., *No, I Tell a Lie, It was the Tuesday . . .* (Kyle Cathie, 1997).

Macmillan, H., *At the End of the Day* (Macmillan, 1973).

Malcolm, B. S., *White Tigers: My Secret War in North Korea* (Washington, DC: Brassey's, 1996).

Mandelstam, L. M., *From the Red Army to SOE* (William Kimber, 1985).

Mathams, R. H., *Sub-Rosa; Memoirs of an Australian Intelligence Analyst* (Sydney: George Allen & Unwin, 1982).

May, E. and Zelikov, P., *The Kennedy Tapes* (Cambridge, MA: Harvard UP, 1997).

Meyer, C., *Facing Reality: From World Federalism to the CIA* (Lanham, MA: UP of America, 1982).

Millar, T. B., *Australian Foreign Minister: The Diaries of R. G. Casey* (Collins, 1972).

Modin, Y., *My Five Cambridge Friends: Burgess, Maclean, Philby, Blunt and Cairncross – By their KGB Controller* (Headline, 1994).

Montague-Brown, A., *Long Sunset: Memoirs of Winston Churchill's Last Private Secretary* (Cassell, 1995).

Moon, P. (ed.), *Wavell: The Viceroy's Journal* (Oxford UP, 1973).

Moran, Lord, *Winston Churchill: The Struggle for Survival, 1940–1965* (Granada, 1966).

Mountbatten, Lord, *Report to the Combined Chiefs of Staff* (HMSO, 1951).

Nichol, D., *How Many Times Can I Die?* (Brooksville, FL: Vanity Press, 1981).

O'Brien, T., *The Moonlight War: The Story of Clandestine Operations in South-East Asia, 1944–5* (Collins, 1987).

Pavlov, V., *Memoirs of a Spymaster: My Fifty Years in the KGB* (NY: Carroll & Graf, 1994).

Philby, K., *My Silent War* (MacGibbon & Kee, 1968).

Philby, R., *The Private Life of Kim Philby* (MacGibbon & Kee, 1968).

Phillips, D., *The Night Watch: 25 Years inside the CIA* (Robert Hale, 1977).

Phillips, J., *The Devil's Bodyguard* (Williamstown: Phillips Publications, 1976, 1986).

Pimlott, B. (ed.), *The Second World War Diary of Hugh Dalton, 1940–45* (Cape, 1986).

——, (ed.) *The Political Diary of Hugh Dalton, 1918–40, 1945–60* (Cape, 1986).

Pomian, J., (ed.), *Joseph Retinger: The Memoirs of an Eminence Grise* (Brighton: Sussex UP, 1972).

Prouty, L. F., *The Secret Team* (NY: Prentice Hall, 1973).

Putney, D. (ed.), *Ultra and the Army Air Forces in World War II: An Interview with Associate Justice of the U.S. Supreme Court Lewis F. Powell Jr.* (Washington, DC: Office of Air Force History, 1987).

Quinn, W. W., *Buffalo Bill Remembers* (Fowlerville, MI: Wilderness Adventure Books, 1991).

Rich, B. R. and Janos, L., *Skunk Works: A Personal Memoir of my Years at Lockheed* (NY: Little, Brown, 1994).

Roosevelt, A., *For Lust of Knowing* (Weidenfeld & Nicolson, 1988).

Ross, G., *The Foreign Office and the Kremlin: British Documents on Anglo-Soviet Relations* (Cambridge: Cambridge UP, 1984).

Russell S., *Sheridan's Story: Sheridan Russell, 1900–1991* (privately published, 1993).

Samuelli, A., *Woman behind Bars in Roumania* (Frank Cass, 1997).

Sawatsky, M., *For Services Rendered* (Markham, Ontario: Penguin Books, 1983).

Sheymov, V., *Tower of Secrets: The Inside Story of the Intelligence Coup of the Cold War* (Annapolis, MD: Naval Institute Press, 1993).

Sillitoe, P., *Cloak without Dagger* (Cassell, 1995).

Simpson, J. with Adkin, M., *The Quiet Operator* (Leo Cooper, 1993).

Singlaub, J. K., *Hazardous Duty: An American Soldier in the Twentieth Century* (NY: Summit Books, 1991).

Smith, J. B., *Portrait of a Cold Warrior* (NY: Putnam's, 1976).

Smith, R. J., *The Unknown CIA: My Three Decades with the Agency* (NY: Pergamon-Brassey's, 1989).
Smith, W., *Covert Warrior* (Novato, CA: Presidio, 1996).
Steury, D. P. (ed.), *On the Front Lines of the Cold War: Documents on the Intelligence War in Berlin, 1946 to 1961* (Washington: CIA Center for the Study of Intelligence, 1999).
Stockwell, A., *Documents on the British End of Empire,* Series B, vol. 3, parts II and III: *Malaya,* (HMSO, 1995).
Stripp, A. J., *Codebreaker in the Far East* (Frank Cass, 1989).
Sudoplatov, P., *Special Tasks: The Memoirs of an Unwanted Witness – A Soviet Spymaster* (Little, Brown, 1994).
Sweet-Escott, B., *Baker Street Irregular* (Methuen, 1965).
Tangye, D., *The Way to Minack* (Michael Joseph, 1968).
Thompson, R., *Make for the Hills: Memories of Far Eastern Wars* (Leo Cooper, 1989).
Trepper, L., *The Great Game: The Story of the Red Orchestra* (Michael Joseph, 1979).
Tumanov, O., *Tumanov: Confessions of a KGB Agent* (Chicago: Editions Q, 1993).
Verrier, A., *Through the Looking Glass: British Foreign Policy in the Age of Illusions* (Cape, 1983).
Warner, M. (ed.), *CIA Cold War Records: The CIA under Harry Truman* (Washington, DC: CIA Center for the Study of Intelligence, 1994).
Weber, R. E., *Spymasters: Ten CIA Officers in their own Words* (Wilmington, DE: Scholarly Resources, 1999).
White, W., *The Little Toy Dog* (NY: Dutton, 1962).
Wilber, D. L., *Adventures in the Middle East: Excursions and Incursions* (Princeton, NJ: Darwin, 1986).
Williams, P. (ed.), *The Diaries of Hugh Gaitskell, 1945–56* (Cape, 1983).
Willoughby, C. A. and Chamberlain, J., *MacArthur, 1941–51* (NY: McGraw-Hill, 1954).
Woodhouse, C. M., *Something Ventured* (Granada, 1986).
Wright, P., *Spycatcher: The Candid Autobiography of a Senior Intelligence Officer* (NY: Viking, 1987).
Wyatt, W., *Confessions of an Optimist* (Collins, 1985).
Young, G. K., *Who Is my Liege?* (Gentry Books, 1972).
——, *Subversion and the British People* (Glasgow: Ossian, 1985).
Young, K., *The Diaries of Sir Robert Bruce Lockhart, 1919–1965*, vol. 2 (Macmillan, 1980).
Ziegler, P., *The Personal Diary of Admiral Lord Louis Mountbatten: Supreme Commander South East Asia, 1943–6* (Collins, 1988).

Secondary Works: Books and Theses

Aarons, M., *Sanctuary: Nazi Fugitives in Australia* (Victoria: Mandarin Publishers, 1990).
Aarons, M. and Loftus, J., *Ratlines: How the Vatican's Nazi Network Betrayed Western Intelligence to the Soviets* (Heinemann, 1991).
Accinelli, R., *Crisis and Commitment: US Policy towards Taiwan, 1950–55* (Chapel Hill: Uni. of North Carolina Press, 1996).
Agee, P. and Wolf, L. (eds), *Dirty Work: The CIA in Europe* (NY: Dorset Press, 1987).
Aldous, C., *The Police in Occupation Japan: Control, Corruption and Resistance to Reform* (Routledge, 1999).
Aldous, R. and Lee, S., *Harold Macmillan and Britain's World Role* (Macmillan, 1995).
Aldrich, R. J. (ed.), *British Intelligence, Strategy and the Cold War, 1945–51* (Routledge, 1992).
——, (ed.), *Espionage, Security and Intelligence in Britain, 1945–70* (Manchester: Manchester UP, 1998).
——, *Intelligence and the War against Japan: Britain, America and the Politics of Secret Service* (Cambridge: Cambridge UP, 2000).
Aldrich, R. J. and Hopkins, M. F. (eds), *Intelligence, Defence and Diplomacy: British Policy in the Post War World* (Frank Cass, 1994).
Aldrich, R. J., Rawnsley, G. and Rawnsley, M. Y. (eds), *The Clandestine Cold War in Asia, 1945–65* (London: Frank Cass, 1999).
Alexander, B., *The Strange Connection: US Intervention in China, 1944–72* (Westport, CT: Greenwood Press, 1992).
Alin, E. G., *The United States and the 1958 Lebanon Crisis: American Intervention in the Middle East* (Lanham, MA: UP of America, 1994).
Ambrose, S., *Eisenhower: The President, 1953–69* (George Allen & Unwin, 1984).
Anderson, D. and Killingray, D. (eds), *Policing and Decolonization: Nationalism, Politics and the Police, 1917–65* (Manchester: Manchester UP, 1991).
Andrew, C. M., *Secret Service: The Making of the British Intelligence Community* (Heinemann, 1985).
——, *For the President's Eyes Only: Secret Intelligence and the American Presidency from Washington to Bush* (HarperCollins, 1995).
Andrew, C. M. and Dilks, D. (eds) *The Missing Dimension: Governments and Intelligence Communities in the Twentieth Century* (Macmillan, 1982).
Andrew, C. M. and Gordievsky, O., *KGB: The Inside Story* (Hodder & Stoughton, 1990).

Andrew, C. M. and Mitrokhin, V., *The Sword and the Shield: The Mitrokhin Archive and the Secret History of the KGB* (NY: Basic Books, 1999).

Andreyev, C., *Vlasov and the Russian Liberation Movement* (Cambridge: Cambridge UP, 1996).

Armistead, E. L., *Grease Pencils and Flying Bananas: The History of American AEW Aircraft* (E. L. Armistead, 1998).

Armstrong, J. A., *Ukrainian Nationalism* (NY: Columbia UP, 1963).

Ashton, N. J., *Eisenhower, Macmillan and the Problem of Nasser: Anglo-American Relations and Arab Nationalism, 1955–9* (Macmillan, 1996).

Atz, R. J., 'The British Colonial Police Service: A Study of its Organization and its Operations in Six Different British African Colonies, 1937–1966', Ph.D, Temple, 1988.

Bamberg, J. H., *The History of the British Petroleum Company*, vol. 2: *The Anglo-Iranian Years, 1928–54* (Cambridge: Cambridge UP, 1994).

Bamford, J., *The Puzzle Palace: America's National Security Agency and its Special Relationship with GCHQ* (Sidgwick & Jackson, 1983).

Bance, A. (ed.), *The Cultural Legacy of the British Occupation of Germany* (Stuttgart: Verlag Hans Dieter Heinz, 1997).

Baylis, J., *Ambiguity and Deterrence: British Nuclear Strategy, 1945–64* (Oxford: Clarendon Press, 1995).

Beckett, F., *The Rise and Fall of the British Communist Party, 1917–1992* (Michael Joseph, 1995).

Bennett, R., *Behind the Battle: Intelligence in the War with Germany* (Sinclair-Stevenson, 1994).

Berdal, M., *The US, Norway and the Cold War, 1954–60* (Macmillan, 1996).

Beschloss, M. R., *Mayday: Eisenhower, Khrushchev and the U-2 Affair* (NY: Harper & Row, 1986).

Bethell, N., *The Great Betrayal: The Untold Story of Kim Philby's Biggest Coup* (Hodder & Stoughton, 1984).

Biddescombe, P., *Werwolf: The History of the National Socialist Guerrilla Movement, 1944–46* (Cardiff: Uni. of Wales Press, 1997).

Bill, J. A. and Louis, W. R. (eds), *Mussadiq, Iranian Nationalism and Oil* (Austin: Uni. of Texas Press, 1988).

Bills, S. L., *Empire and Cold War: The Roots of US–Third World Antagonism, 1945–7* (Macmillan, 1990).

Bird, K., *The Chairman: John J. McCloy and the Making of the American Establishment* (NY: Simon & Schuster, 1992).

Blum, W., *Killing Hope: US Military and CIA Intervention since World War II* (Common Courage Press, 1995).

Bookmiller, K. N., 'The War of Words without War: The RM, the BBC World Service, and the Voice of America in the Old and the New World Order', PhD, Uni. of Virginia, 1992.

Borovik, G., *The Philby Files* (Little, Brown, 1994).

Botti, T. J., *The Long Wait: The Forging of the Anglo-American Nuclear Alliance, 1945–58* (Westport, CT: Greenwood Press, 1988).

——, *Ace in the Hole: Why the United States Did Not Use Nuclear Weapons in the Cold War* (Westport, CT: Greenwood Press, 1996).

Bowen, R., *Innocence Is Not Enough* (Vancouver: Douglas McIntyre, 1986).

Bower, T., *Klaus Barbie: The Butcher of Lyon* (NY: Pantheon, 1984).

——, *The Paperclip Conspiracy: The Battle for the Spoils and Secrets of Nazi Germany* (Michael Joseph, 1987).

——, *Blind Eye to Murder* (Warner Books, 3rd edn, 1997).

——, *The Red Web* (Aurum Press, 1989).

——, *A Perfect English Spy* (Heinemann, 1995).

Bowyer Bell, J., *Terror Out of Zion* (NY: St Martin's Press, 1977).

Boyd, C., *Hitler's Japanese Confidant: General Oshima Hiroshi and MAGIC Intelligence, 1941–45* (Kansas: Uni. of Kansas Press, 1993).

Boyle, A., *The Climate of Treason: Five Who Spied for Russia* (Hutchinson, 1979).

Boyle, P. G., *American-Soviet Relations* (Routledge, 1993).

Brands, H. W., *Cold Warriors* (NY: Columbia UP, 1988).

Breindel, E. and Romerstein, H., *The Venona Secrets: The Soviet Union's World War II Espionage Campaign against the United States and How America Fought Back* (NY: Basic Books, 2000).

Broad, W. J., *The Universe Below: Discovery of the Secrets of the Deep* (NY: Simon & Schuster, 1997).

Bryden, J., *Best Kept Secret: Canadian Intelligence in the Second World War* (Toronto: Lester Publishing, 1993).

Bulkeley, R., *The Sputniks Crisis and Early US Space Policy* (Macmillan, 1991).

Bull, H. and Louis, W. R. (eds), *The Special Relationship* (Oxford: Oxford UP, 1986).

Bullock, A., *Ernest Bevin: Foreign Secretary, 1945–51* (NY: W. W. Norton, 1982).

Burke, C. J., *Information and Secrecy: Vannevar Bush, Ultra, and the Other Memex* (Metuchen, NJ: Scarecrow Press, 1994).

Buscher, F. M., *The U.S. War Crimes Trial Program in Germany, 1946–1955* (Westport, CT: Greenwood Press, 1989).

Butler, E., *Mason-Mac: A Life of Lieutenant General Sir Noel Mason-MacFarlane* (Macmillan, 1972).

Butterfield, H., *History and Human Relations* (Collins, 1951).

Cain, F., *The Australian Security and Intelligence Organization: An Unofficial History* (Frank Cass, 1994).

Cain, P. J. and Hopkins, A. G., *British Imperialism: Crisis and Deconstruction* (Longmans, 1993).

Calhoun, D. F., *Hungary and Suez: An Exploration of Who Makes History* (Lanham, MA: UP of America, 1991).

Calvocoressi, P., *Threading my Way* (Duckworth, 1994).

Campbell, D., *The Unsinkable Aircraft Carrier* (Michael Joseph, 1984).

Cannadine, D., *Pleasures of the Past* (Collins, 1989).

Carruthers, S. L., *Winning Hearts and Minds: British Government, the Media and Colonial Counter-Insurgency, 1944–60* (Leicester: Leicester UP, 1995).

Carver, M., *Harding of Petherington* (Weidenfeld & Nicolson, 1978).

Castle, T. N., *At War in the Shadow of Vietnam: U.S. Military Aid to the Royal Lao Government* (NY: Columbia UP, 1993).

Cathcart, B., *Test of Greatness: Britain's Struggle for the Atom Bomb* (John Murray, 1994).

Caute, D., *The Great Fear: The Anti-Communist Purge under Truman and Eisenhower* (Secker & Warburg, 1978).

Cave Brown, A., *The Last Hero: Wild Bill Donovan* (NY: Times Books, 1982).

——, *'C': The Secret Life of Sir Stewart Menzies* (NY: Macmillan 1987).

——, *Treason in the Blood: H. St John Philby, Kim Philby and the Spy Case of the Century* (Robert Hale, 1994).

Cawthorne, N., *The Iron Cage: Are British Prisoners of War Abandoned in Soviet Hands Still in Siberia?* (Fourth Estate, 1993).

Cecil, R., *A Divided Life: Donald Maclean* (The Bodley Head, 1988).

Cesarini, D., *Justice Delayed: How Britain Became a Refuge for Nazi War Criminals* (Heinemann, 1992).

Chalou, G. C. (ed.), *The Secrets War: The Office of Strategic Services in World War II* (Washington, DC: NARA, 1992).

Chang, G. H., *Friends and Enemies: The United States, China and the Soviet Union, 1948–72* (Stanford: Stanford UP, 1990).

Charmley, J., *Churchill: The End of Glory* (NY: Harcourt & Brace, 1993).

——, *Churchill's Grand Alliance* (NY: Harcourt & Brace, 1995).

Charters, D. A., *The British Army and the Jewish Insurgency in Palestine, 1945–1947* (Macmillan, 1989).

Cheah Boon Kheng, *Red Star over Malaya: Resistance and Social Conflict during and after the Japanese Occupation, 1941–6* (Singapore: Singapore UP, 1987).

Chester, E. T., *Covert Network: Progressives, the International Rescue Committee and the CIA* (NY: M. E. Sharpe, 1995).

Childs, D. and Popperwell, R., *The Stasi* (Macmillan, 1996).

Clark, D. J., 'The Colonial Police and Anti-Terrorism: Bengal 1930–6, Palestine 1937–47, Cyprus 1955–9', DPhil, St Antony's College, Oxford 1978.

Clark, I., *Nuclear Diplomacy and the Special Relationship: Britain's Deterrent and America, 1957–62* (Oxford: Clarendon Press, 1994).

Clark, I. and Wheeler, N., *The British Origins of Nuclear Strategy, 1945–1955* (Oxford: Oxford UP, 1989).

Clarke, T., *By Blood and Fire* (NY: Putnam's, 1981).

Clayton, A., *Counter-Insurgency in Kenya, 1952–60* (Manhattan KS: Sunflower UP, 1984).

——, *Forearmed: A History of the Intelligence Corps* (Brassey's, 1993).

Clayton, J. D., *The Years of MacArthur* (Boston: Houghton Mifflin, 1985).

Clegg, H. A., *A History of British Trade Unions since 1899*, vol. 3: 1934–51 (Oxford: Clarendon Press, 1994).

Cline, R., *Chiang Ching-kuo Remembered: The Man and his Legacy* (Washington, DC: United States Global Strategy Council, 1983).

Clinton, A., *Post Office Workers: A Trade Union and Social History* (George Allen & Unwin, 1984).

Cloake, J., *Templer: Tiger of Malaya* (Harrap, 1985).

Close, D. H., *The Greek Civil War: Studies in Polarisation* (Routledge, 1993).

Coates, J., *Suppressing Insurgency: An Analysis of the Malayan Emergency, 1948–54* (Boulder, CO: Westview, 1992).

Cockrill, A. W., *Sir P. Sillitoe* (W. H. Allen, 1975).

Cohen, M. J. and Kolinsky, M. (eds), *Demise of the British Empire in the Middle East: Britain's Response to Nationalist Movements, 1943–55* (Frank Cass, 1999).

Cole, D. J., *Geoffrey Prime: The Imperfect Spy* (Robert Hale, 1998).

Coleman, P., *The Liberal Conspiracy: The Congress for Cultural Freedom and the Struggle for the Mind of Europe* (NY: The Free Press, 1989).

Conboy, K. and Morrison, J., *Feet to the Fire: CIA Covert Operations in Indonesia, 1957–1958* (Annapolis, MD: US Naval Institute Press, 1999).

Connell, J., *Most Important Country* (Cassell, 1957).

Connor, K., *Ghost Force: The Secret History of the SAS* (Weidenfeld & Nicolson, 1998).

Conquest, R., *Kolyma: The Artic Death Camps* (Macmillan, 1978).

Cook, B. W., *The Declassified Eisenhower* (NY: Doubleday, 1981).

Corley, T. A. B., *A History of the Burmah Oil Company, 1886–1996*, vol. 2 (London, 1988).

Corn, D., *Blond Ghost: Ted Shackley and the CIA's Crusades* (NY: Simon & Schuster, 1994).

Costello, J., *Mask of Treachery* (Collins, 1988).

——, *Ten Days to Destiny: The Secret Story of the Hess Peace Initiative and British Efforts to Strike a Deal with Hitler* (NY: William Morrow, 1991).

Costello, J. and Tsarev, O., *Deadly Illusions* (Century, 1993).

Craig, A., 'The Joint Intelligence Committee and Britain's Intelligence Assessment, 1945–56', PhD, Uni. of Cambridge, 1999.

Craig I. and O'Malley, B., *The Cyprus Conspiracy: America, Espionage and the Turkish Invasion* (I. B. Tauris, 1999).

Cram, C., *Of Moles and Molehunters: A Review of Counter-Intelligence Literature* (Washington, DC: CIA Center for the Study of Intelligence, 1993).

Crockatt, R., *The Fifty Years War: The United States, and the Soviet Union in World Politics, 1941–1991* (Routledge, 1995).

Cruickshank, C., *SOE in the Far East: The Official History* (Oxford: Oxford UP, 1983).

Cull, N. J., *Selling War: The British Propaganda Campaign against American 'Neutrality' in World War II* (NY: Oxford UP, 1995).

Currey, C. B., *Edward Lansdale: The Unquiet American* (NY: Houghton Mifflin, 1988).

Curtis, M., *The Ambiguities of Power: British Foreign Policy since 1945* (Zed, 1995).

Daddow, O., 'Rhetoric and Reality: The Historiography of British European Policy, 1945–73', PhD, Uni. of Nottingham, 2000.

——, (ed.), *Harold Wilson and European Unity: Britain's Second Attempt to Join the EEC* (Frank Cass, 2001).

Danchev, A., *On Specialness* (Macmillan, 1998).

Darling, A. B., *The Central Intelligence Agency: An Instrument of Government to 1950* (Uni. Park, PA: Pennsylvania State UP, 1990).

Davies, P. H. P. *The British Secret Service: A Bibliography* (Oxford: Clio, 1996).

Davis, J. K., *Spying on America: The FBI's Domestic Counter-Intelligence Programme* (NY: Praeger, 1993).

Deacon, R., *The British Connection: Russian Manipulation of British Individuals and Institutions* (Hamish Hamilton, 1979).

——, '*C': A Biography of Sir Maurice Oldfield* (Macdonald, 1984).

——, *The Silent War: A History of Western Naval Intelligence* (Grafton, 2nd edn, 1988).

Deighton, A., *The Impossible Peace: Germany* (Oxford: Clarendon Press, 1988).

——, (ed.), *Britain and the First Cold War* (Macmillan, 1990).

——, (ed.), *Building Postwar Europe: National Decision Makers and European Institutions, 1948–63* (Macmillan, 1995).

Deletant, D., *Communist Terror in Romania: Gheorghiu-Dej and the Police State, 1948–65* (Hurst, 1999).

Dell, E., *The Schuman Plan and the British Abdication of Leadership in Europe* (Oxford: Clarendon Press, 1995).

Delve, K., Green, P. and Clemons, J., *The English Electric Canberra* (Earl Shilton, Leics: Midland Counties Publications, 1992).

Diamond, S., *The Compromised Campus: The Collaboration of Universities with the Intelligence Community, 1945–1955* (NY: Oxford UP, 1992).

Diba, F., *Mossadegh: A Political Biography* (Croom Helm, 1986).

Dimbleby, D. and Reynolds, D., *An Ocean Apart: The Relationship between Britain and America in the Twentieth Century* (Hodder & Stoughton, 1988).

Dockrill, S., *Eisenhower's New Look National Security Policy, 1953–61* (Macmillan, 1996).

Dorril, S., *MI6: Fifty Years of Special Operations* (Fourth Estate, 2000).

Dorwart, J., *Conflict of Duty: US Naval Intelligence, 1917–41* (Annapolis, MD: US Naval Institute Press, 1987).

Drummond, S. H., 'Britain's Involvement in Indonesia, 1945–63', PhD, Uni. of Southampton, 1979.

Duchêne, F., *Jean Monnet: First Statesman of Interdependence* (NY: W. W. Norton, 1994).

Duke, S., *US Defence Bases in the United Kingdom* (Macmillan, 1987).

Duke, S. W. and Krieger, W., *US Military Forces in Europe: The Early Years, 1945–70* (Boulder, CO: Westview, 1993).

Dunn, D., *The Politics of Threat: Minuteman Vulnerability in American National Security Policy* (Macmillan, 1998).

Dutton, D., *Eden: A Life and Reputation* (Arnold, 1997).

Edwards, J., *Anglo-American Relations and the Franco Question* (Oxford: Oxford UP, 1999).

Edwards, R. D., *The Pursuit of Reason: The Economist 1943–1993* (Hamish Hamilton, 1993).

Elm, M., *Oil, Power and Principle: Iran's Oil Nationalization and its Aftermath* (NY: Syracuse UP, 1994).

Erickson, J., *The Road to Stalingrad* (Grafton, 1985).

Erickson, J. and Dilks, D. (eds), *Barbarossa: The Axis and the Allies* (Edinburgh: Edinburgh UP, 1994).

Eringer, R., *The Global Manipulators: The Bilderberg Group, the Trilateral Commission, Covert Power Groups of the West* (Bristol: Pentacle Press, 1980).

Eshed, H., *Reuven Shiloah: The Man behind the Mossad* (Frank Cass, 1997).

Esposito, C., *America's Feeble Weapon: Funding the Marshall Plan in France and Italy, 1948–50* (Westport, CT: Greenwood Press, 1994).

L'Estrange Fawcett, L., 'The Struggle for Persia: The Azerbaijan Crisis of 1946', PhD, Uni. of Oxford, 1988.

Evanhoe, E., *Darkmoon: Eighth Army Special Operations during the Korean War* (Annapolis, MD: Naval Institute Press, 1995).

Faligot, R. and Krop, P., *La Piscine: French Secret Service since 1914* (Oxford: Blackwell, 1989).

Farquar, J. T., 'The Need to Know: The Role of the Air Force in Reconnaissance in War Planning, 1945–53', PhD, Ohio State Uni., 1991.

Farrar-Hockley, A., *The British Part in the Korean War*, 2 vols (HMSO, 1990, 1995).

Faughan, S. A., 'The Politics of Influence: Churchill, Eden and Soviet Communism, 1951–7', PhD, Uni. of Cambridge, 1997.

Filipelli, R., *American Labor and Postwar Italy, 1943–1953* (Stanford: Stanford UP, 1989).

Finnegan, J. P., *Military Intelligence: A Picture History* (Fort Belvoir, VA: History Office of US Army INSCOM, 2nd edn, 1993).

Fitzgerald, P. and Leopold, M., *Strangers on the Line: A History of Phone-tapping* (The Bodley Head, 1987).

Fitzgibbon, C., *Secret Intelligence in the Twentieth Century* (NY: Stein & Day, 1976).

Fletcher, R., *Who Were They Travelling With?* (Nottingham: Spokesman Books, 1977).

Follows, R. and Popham, H., *The Jungle Beat: Fighting Terrorists in Malaya, 1952–61* (Blandford Press, 1990).

Folly, M., 'British Government Attitudes to the USSR, 1940–1945', PhD, Uni. of London, 1997.

Foot, M. R. D., *SOE in France* (HMSO, 1966).

——, *Resistance* (Eyre Methuen, 1976).

——, *SOE: The Special Operations Executive, 1940–1946* (BBC, 1984).

Foot, R., *The Wrong War: American Policy and the Dimensions of the Korean Conflict, 1950–3* (Ithaca: Cornell UP, 1985).

——, *The Practice of Power: American Relations with China since 1949* (Oxford: Oxford UP, 1995).

Ford, H., *Estimative Intelligence* (Lanham, MD: UP of America, 1992).

Fowells, G., *From the Dogs of War to a Brave New World and Back Again – Burma, 1947* (privately published, 1997).

Fraser, C., *Ambivalent Anti-Colonialism: Funding the Marshall Plan in France and Italy, 1948–50* (Westport, CT: Greenwood Press, 1994).

Freedman, L., *US Intelligence and the Soviet Strategic Threat* (Macmillan, 1976)

——, *Kennedy's Wars: Berlin, Cuba, Laos, Vietnam* (Oxford: Oxford UP, 2001).

Freeman, I., *Lord Denning: A Life* (Hutchinson, 1994).

Freiberger, S. Z., *Dawn over Suez: The Rise of American Power in the Middle East, 1953–7* (Chicago: Ivan R. Dee, 1992).

Freyberg, P., *Bernard Freyberg VC: Soldier of Two Nations* (Hodder & Stoughton, 1991).

Fricke, W., *Die DDR-Staatssicherheit. Entwicklung, Strukturen, Aktionsfelde* (Köln: Wiss. U. Politik, 1982).

Friedrich, C., *Federalism: Trends in Theory and Practice* (Pall Mall, 1968).

——, *Europe: An Emergent Nation* (NY: Harper & Row, 1969).

Furedi, F., *The Mau Mau War in Perspective* (J. Currey, 1989).

Fursenko, A. and Naftali, T., *One Hell of a Gamble: Khrushchev, Castro, Kennedy and the Cuban Missile Crisis, 1958–1964* (John Murray, 1997).

Gaddis, J. L., *What We Know Now: Rethinking Cold War History* (Oxford: Oxford UP, 1997).

Garbett, M. and Goulding, B., *The Lincoln at War, 1944–1966* (Ian Allen, 1979).

Garson, R., *The United States and China since 1949* (Cassell, 1995).

Garthoff, R. L., *Assessing the Adversary: Estimates by the Eisenhower Administration of Soviet Intentions and Capabilities* (Washington, DC: Brookings Institution, 1991).

Gasiorowski, M. J., *US Foreign Policy and the Shah: Building a Client State in Iran* (Ithaca: Cornell UP, 1991).

Gerraghty, T., *Beyond the Front Line: The Untold Exploits of Britain's Most Daring Spy Mission* (HarperCollins, 1996).

Gilbert, M., *Winston Churchill: 'Never Despair', 1945–1965* (Boston: Houghton Mifflin, 1988).

Gill, S., *American Hegemony and the Trilateral Commission* (Cambridge: Cambridge UP, 1990).

Gillingham, J., *Coal, Steel and the Rebirth of Europe, 1945–1955* (Cambridge: Cambridge UP, 1992).

Gimbel, J., *Science, Technology and Reparations: Exploitation and Plunder in Post War Germany* (Stanford: Stanford UP, 1990).

Goncharov, S. N., Lewis, J. W. and Xue Litai, *Uncertain Partners: Stalin, Mao and the Korean War* (Stanford: Stanford UP, 1995).

Goode, J. F., *The United States and Iran: In the Shadow of Mussadiq* (Macmillan, 1997).

Goodman, G., 'Who Is Anti-American? The British Left and the United States, 1945–56', PhD, Uni. of London, 1996.

Gorodetsky, G., *Stafford Cripps' Mission to Moscow, 1940–2* (Cambridge: Cambridge UP, 1984).

——, *Grand Delusion: Stalin and the German Invasion of Russia* (New Haven: Yale UP, 1999).

Gowland, D. and Turner, A., *Reluctant Europeans: Britain and European Integration, 1945–96* (Longmans, 1999).

Grantham, J. T., 'The Labour Party and European Unity, 1939–1951', PhD, Uni. of Cambridge, 1977.

Grayson, W. C., *Chicksands: A Millennium of History* (Shefford: Shefford Press, 1992).

Grémion, P., *Intelligence de l'Anticommunisme: Le Congrès pour la liberté de la culture à Paris, 1950–1975* (Paris: Fayard, 1995).

Grose, P., *Gentleman Spy: The Life of Allen Dulles* (Boston: Houghton Mifflin, 1994).

——, *Operation Rollback: America's Secret War behind the Iron Curtain* (Boston: Houghton & Mifflin, 2000).

Hahn, P. L., *The United States, Great Britain and Egypt, 1945–1956* (Chapel Hill: Uni. of North Carolina Press, 1991).

Hall, R., *The Rhodes Scholar Spy* (Sydney: Random House, 1991).

Halliday, J. and Cumings, B., *Korea: The Unknown War* (Viking, 1988).

Hannant, L., *The Infernal Machine: Investigating the Loyalty of Canada's Citizens* (Toronto: Uni. of Toronto Press, 1994).

Harrison, D., *These Men Are Dangerous* (Grafton, 1990).

Hathaway, R. M., *Ambiguous Partnership: Britain and America, 1944–7* (NY: Columbia UP, 1981).

Hauner, M., *India in Axis Strategy: Germany, Japan and Indian Nationalists in the Second World War* (Stuttgart: Klett-Cotta, 1981).

Hazard, E., *Cold War Crucible: United States Foreign Policy and the Conflict in Romania, 1943–1953* (NY: Columbia UP, 1996).

Hazelton, C. S. R., 'Soviet Foreign Policy during the Initial Phase of the War with Germany: June–December 1941', PhD, LSE, 1989.

Heale, M. J., *McCarthy's Americans: Red Scare Politics in State and Nation, 1935–65* (Macmillan, 1998).

Healey, D. (ed.), *The Curtain Falls: The Story of Socialism in Eastern Europe* (NY: Lincolns-Praeger, 1951).

Heclo, H. and Wildavsky, A., *The Private Government of Public Money* (Macmillan, 1981).

Heikel, M., *Iran: The Untold Story* (NY: Random House, 1982).

Heller, J., *The Stern Gang: Ideology, Politics and Terror, 1940–9* (Frank Cass, 1994).

Hennessy, P., *Whitehall* (NY: The Free Press, 1989).

——, *Never Again: Britain, 1945–51* (Vintage, 1993).

——, *The Prime Minister* (Allen Lane, 2000).

Herken, G., *The Winning Weapon: The Atomic Bomb in the Cold War, 1945–50* (NY: Vintage, 1982).

Herman, M., *Intelligence Power in Peace and War* (Cambridge: Cambridge UP, 1992).

Hersh, B., *The Old Boys: The American Elite and the Origins of the CIA* (NY: Scribner, 1992).

Hesketh, R., *Fortitude: The D-Day Deception Campaign* (Little, Brown, 1999).

Heuser, B., *Western 'Containment' Policies in the Cold War: The Yugoslav Case, 1948–53* (Routledge, 1989).

Heuser, B. and O'Neill, R. (eds), *Securing Peace in Europe, 1945–62* (Macmillan, 1991).

Hibbert, R., *Albania's National Liberation Struggle* (Pinter, 1991).

Hinsley, F. H., *British Intelligence in the Second World War*, vols 1–3 (HMSO, 1979–83).

Hinsley, F. H. and Simkins, C. A. G., *British Intelligence in the Second World War*, vol. 4 (HMSO, 1990).

Hinsley, F. H. and Stripp, A. (eds), *Codebreakers: The Inside Story of Bletchley Park* (Oxford: Oxford UP, 1993).

Hirsh, F. and Fletcher, R., *The CIA and the Labour Movement* (Nottingham: Spokesman Books, 1977).

Hitchcock, W. T. (ed.), *The Intelligence Revolution in Historical Perspective* (Washington, DC: US Air Force Academy, 1991).

Hodos, G. H., *Show Trials: Stalinist Purges in Eastern Europe, 1948–54* (NY: Praeger, 1987).

Hoe, A. and Morris, E., *Re-enter the SAS: The SAS and the Malayan Emergency* (Leo Cooper, 1994).

Hoffman, B. R., 'Jewish Terror Activities and the British Government in Palestine, 1939–47', DPhil, St Antony's College, Oxford, 1985.

——, *The Failure of British Military Strategy within Palestine, 1939–1947* (Jerusalem: Bar-Ilan UP, 1983).

Hogan, M. J., *The Marshall Plan: America, Britain and the Reconstruction of Europe, 1947–52* (Cambridge: Cambridge UP, 1987).

——, *Cross of Iron: Harry S. Truman and the Origins of the National Security State* (Cambridge: Cambridge UP, 1999).

Holland, R., *Emergencies and Disorder in the European Empires after 1945* (Frank Cass, 1994).

——, *Britain and the Revolt in Cyprus* (Oxford: Oxford UP, 1998).

Holloway, D., *The Soviet Union and the Arms Race* (New Haven: Yale UP, 1984).

——, *Stalin and the Bomb: The Soviet Union and Atomic Energy, 1939–56* (New Haven: Yale UP, 1994).

Hong, Yong-Pyo, *State Security and Regime Security: President Syngman Rhee and the Insecurity Dilemma in South Korea, 1953–60* (Macmillan, 1999).

Hood, W., *Myths Surrounding James Angleton* (Washington, DC: Consortium for the Study of Intelligence, 1993).

Hopkirk, P., *Setting the East Ablaze: Lenin's Dream of an Empire in Asia* (Oxford: Oxford UP, 1984).

Horne, A., *A Savage War of Peace* (Macmillan, 1974).

——, *Macmillan,* vol. 1: *1894–1956* (Macmillan, 1988).

——, *Macmillan,* vol. 2: *1957–86* (Macmillan, 1989).

Horner, D. M., *SAS Phantoms of the Jungle: A History of the Australian Special Air Service Regiment* (Greenhill Books, 1991).

Howarth, P., *Intelligence Chief Extraordinary* (The Bodley Head, 1986).

Hubback, D., *No Ordinary Press Baron: A Life of Walter Layton* (Weidenfeld & Nicolson, 1985).

Hui, Lee Ting, *The Open United Front: The Communist Struggle in Singapore, 1954–66* (Singapore: The South Seas Press, 1997).

Humphreys, P. J., *Media and Media Policy in West Germany* (Oxford: Berg, 1990).

Hunt, L., *Secret Agenda: The US Government, Nazi Scientists and Project Paperclip, 1944–1990* (NY: St Martin's Press, 1991).

Hyde, H. M., *The Atom Bomb Spies* (Hamish Hamilton, 1980).

Jackson, R., *Canberra: The Operational Record* (Shrewsbury: Airlife Publishing, 1988).

——, *The Malayan Emergency* (Routledge, 1990).

——, *High Cold War: Strategic Air Reconnaissance and Electronic Intelligence War* (Patrick Stephens, 1998).

Jakub, J., *Spies and Saboteurs: Anglo-American Collaboration and Rivalry in Human Intelligence Collection and Special Operations, 1940–45* (Macmillan, 1999).

James, J. D., *Years of MacArthur,* vol. 3 (Boston: Houghton Mifflin, 1983).

James, R. R., *Anthony Eden* (Weidenfeld & Nicolson, 1986).

Jeffreys-Jones, R., *The CIA and American Democracy* (New Haven: Yale UP, 1991).

Jeffreys-Jones, R. and Lownie, A., *North American Spies: New Revisionist Essays* (Edinburgh: Edinburgh UP, 1991).

Jensen, J. M., *Army Surveillance in America, 1775–1980* (New Haven: Yale UP, 1991).

Johnson, L., *America's Secret Power: The CIA in a Democratic Society* (NY: Oxford UP, 1989).

——, *Secret Agencies: US Intelligence in a Hostile World* (New Haven: Yale UP, 1996).

Jones, G. E., 'The Allied Reconstruction of the Berlin Police, 1945–8', PhD, Uni. of California, San Diego, 1986.

Jones, H., *A New Kind of War: America's Global Strategy and the Truman Doctrine* (NY: Oxford UP, 1997).

Jones, P., *America and the British Labour Party: The Special Relationship at Work* (I. B. Tauris, 1997).

Jones, P. D., 'British Policy towards 'Minor' Nazi War Criminals, 1939–1958', PhD, Uni. of Cambridge, 1989.

Jones, T., 'The Development of British Counter-Insurgency Policies and Doctrine, 1945–52', PhD, Uni. of London, 1992.

Kahin, A. R. and Kahin, G. McT., *Subversion as Foreign Policy: The Secret Eisenhower and Dulles Debacle in Indonesia* (I. B. Tauris, 1995).

Kahn, D., *The Codebreakers* (NY: Scribner, 2nd edn, 1996).

Karabell, Z., *Architects of Intervention: The United States and the Third World and the Cold War, 1946–1962* (Baton Rouge: Louisiana State UP, 1999).

Katouzian, H., *Mussadiq and the Struggle for Power* (I. B. Tauris, 1990).

Katz, B. M., *Foreign Intelligence: Research and Analysis on the Office of Strategic Services, 1942–1945* (Cambridge, MA: Harvard UP, 1989).

Keeley, E., *The Salonica Bay Murder* (Princeton: Princeton UP, 1989).

Kelling, G. H., *Countdown to Rebellion: British Policy in Cyprus, 1939–55* (Westport, CT: Greenwood Press, 1990).

Kemp, A., *The SAS: Savage Wars of Peace* (John Murray, 1994).

Kennedy-Pipe, C., *Stalin's Cold War: Soviet Strategies in Europe* (Manchester: Manchester UP, 1995).

Kent, J., *British Imperial Strategy and the Origins of the Cold War* (Leicester: Leicester UP, 1993).

Kirby, D., *Church, State and Propaganda: The Archbishop of York and International Relations: A Political Study of Cyril Forster Garbett, 1942–1955* (Hull: Uni. of Hull Press, 1999).

Kitchen, M., *British Policy towards the Soviet Union during the Second World War* (Macmillan, 1986).

Knight, A. W., *Beria: Stalin's First Lieutenant* (Princeton: Princeton UP, 1993).

Knightley, P., *The Master Spy: The Story of Kim Philby* (André Deutsch, 1988).

Knightley, P. and Kennedy, C., *An Affair of State: The Profumo Case and the Framing of Stephen Ward* (Cape, 1987).

Koch, S., *Double Lives: Spies and Writers in the Secret Soviet War of Ideas against the West* (NY: The Free Press, 1993).

Kotek, J., *Students and the Cold War* (Macmillan, 1996).

Kovrig, B., *The Myth of Liberation* (Baltimore: Johns Hopkins UP, 1973).

——, *Of Walls and Bridges: The United States and Eastern Europe* (NY: New York UP, 1991).

Kramer, A., *The Griffin* (Boston: Houghton Mifflin, 1986).

Krop, P., *Les Secrets de l'espionnage français de 1870 à nos jours* (Paris: J. Clattes, 1994).

Kumamoto, R., *International Terrorism and American Foreign Relations* (Boston: Northeastern UP, 1999).

Kuniholm, B. R., *The Origins of the Cold War in the Near East* (Princeton: Princeton UP, 1980).

Kunz, D., *The Economic Diplomacy of the Suez Crisis* (Chapel Hill: Uni. of North Carolina Press, 1991).

——, *The Diplomacy of the Crucial Decade* (NY: Columbia UP, 1994).

Kuromiya, H., *Freedom and Terror in the Donbas: The Ukraine-Russian Borderlands, 1870s-1990s* (Cambridge: Cambridge UP, 1998).

Kyle, K., *Suez* (Weidenfeld & Nicolson, 1991).

Kyriakides, K. A., 'British Cold War Strategy and the Struggle to Maintain Military Bases in Cyprus', PhD, Uni. of Cambridge, 1997.

Lamb, R., *The Macmillan Years: The Emerging Truth* (John Murray, 1995).

Lane, A., *Britain, the Cold War and Yugoslav Unity, 1941–9* (Brighton: Sussex Academic Press, 1997).

Lapping, B., *End of Empire* (Granada, 1985).

Lasby, C., *Project Paperclip* (NY: Athenaeum, 1975).

Lashmar, P., *Spy-Flights of the Cold War* (Sutton, 1996).

Lashmar, P. and Oliver, J., *Britain's Secret Propaganda War: The Foreign Office and the Cold War, 1948–1977* (Sutton, 1998).

Leary, J., 'The SAS in Malaya', PhD, Monash Uni., 1991.

Le Carré, J., *Tinker, Tailor, Soldier, Spy* (Coronet, 2000).

Leffler, M., *A Preponderance of Power: National Security, the Truman Administration and the Cold War* (Stanford: Stanford UP, 1992).

Leigh-Phippard, H., *Congress, and US Military Aid to Britain, 1949–56* (Macmillan, 1995).

Leitch, D., *Guy Burgess* (Lennard, 1989).

Levenberg, H., *Military Preparations of the Arab Community in Palestine, 1945–8* (Frank Cass, 1993).

Lewin, R., *Ultra Goes to War: The Secret Story* (Hutchinson, 1978).

Lewis, J., *Changing Direction: British Military Planning for Post-War Strategic Defence, 1942–7* (Sherwood Press, 1988, 2nd edn, Frank Cass, forthcoming).

Liddell Hart, B., *Defence of the West: Some Riddles of War and Peace* (Cassell, 1950).

Lindey, C., *Art in the Cold War: From Vladivostock to Kalamazoo* (Herbert, 1990).

Lintner, B., *Burma in Revolt: Opium and Insurgency since 1948* (Boulder, CO: Westview 1994).

Lipgens, W., *A History of European Integration, 1945–47,* vol. 1: *The Formation of the European Unity Movement* (Oxford, 1982).

Litvan, G. (ed.), *The Hungarian Revolution of 1956* (Longmans, 1996).

Loftus, J., *The Belarus Secret* (NY: Knopf, 1982).

Louis, W. R., *The British Empire in the Middle East, 1945–51: Arab Nationalism, the United States and Post War Imperialism* (Oxford: Oxford UP, 1984).

Low, D. A., *Lion Rampant: Essays in the Study of British Imperialism* (Frank Cass, 1973).

——, *Eclipse of Empire* (Cambridge: Cambridge UP, 1991).

Lowe, P., *The Origins of the Korean War* (Longmans, 1986).

——, *Containing the Cold War in East Asia: British Policies towards Japan, China and Korea, 1948–54* (Manchester: Manchester UP, 1997).

Lucas, W. S., *Divided We Stand: Britain, the US and the Suez Crisis* (Hodder & Stoughton, 1991).

——, *The Lion's Last Roar* (Manchester: Manchester UP, 1997).

——, *Freedom's War: The US Crusade against the Soviet Union, 1945–56* (Manchester: Manchester UP, 1999).

Lundestad, G., *'Empire' by Integration: The US and European Integration, 1945–1997* (Oxford: Oxford UP, 1998).

Lustgarten L. and Leigh, I., *In from the Cold: National Security and Democracy* (Oxford: Oxford UP, 1994).

Lytle, M. H., *The Origins of the Iranian-American Alliance, 1941–53* (NY: Holmes & Meier, 1987).

MacDonald, P., *SAS in Action* (Sidgwick & Jackson, 1990).

McKnight, D., *Australia's Spies and their Secrets* (Uni. College London Press, 1994).

McLane, C. B., *Soviet Strategies in Southeast Asia: An Exploration of Eastern Policy under Lenin and Stalin* (Princeton: Princeton UP, 1966).

McLynn, F., *Fitzroy Maclean* (John Murray, 1992).

MacMahon, R. J., *Cold War on the Periphery: The United States, India and Pakistan* (Columbia: Columbia UP, 1994).

MacShane, D., *International Labour and the Origins of the Cold War* (Oxford: Oxford UP, 1992).

Maddrell, P., 'Britain's Exploitation of Occupied Germany for Scientific and Technical Intelligence on the Soviet Union', PhD, Uni. of Cambridge, 1998.

Major, P., 'The German Communist Party (KPD) in the Western Zones, 1945–56', DPhil, Uni. of Oxford, 1993.

Mallet, M. A., 'Images of the Soviet Threat: Complexity and Change in the Beliefs of Four American Presidents', PhD, American Uni., 1993.

Malvoney, J., 'Civil Liberties in Britain during the Cold War', PhD, Uni. of Cambridge, 1990.

Mangold, T., *Cold Warrior: James Jesus Angleton, the CIA's Master Spy Hunter* (NY: Simon & Schuster, 1991).

Manne, R., *The Petrov Affair: Politics and Espionage* (NY: Pergamon, 1987).

Maochun Yu, *OSS in China: Prelude to the Cold War* (New Haven: Yale UP, 1997).

Marchetti, V. and Marks, J. D., *The CIA and the Cult of Intelligence* (NY: Knopf, 1974).

Marks, F. W., *Power and Peace: The Diplomacy of John Foster Dulles* (NY: Praeger, 1993).

Markus, U., 'A Case Study of Soviet Counter-Insurgency: The Guerrilla War in Lithuania and the Ukraine, 1944–1953', PhD, Uni. of London, 1992.

Marrus, M. R., *DP: Europe's Displaced Persons, 1945–51* (Philadelphia: Associated UP, 1989).

Marton, K., *The Polk Conspiracy: Murder and Cover Up in the Case of CBS Correspondent George Polk* (NY: Farrar, Straus & Giroux, 1990).

Masters, A., *The Man who was 'M': The Life of Maxwell Knight* (Oxford: Blackwell, 1984).

Mastny, V., *The Cold War and Soviet Insecurity: The Stalin Years* (NY: Oxford UP, 1996).

Meilinger, P. S., *Hoyt S. Vandenberg* (Bloomington: Indiana UP, 1989).

Melandri, P., *Les Etats Unis à face à l'unification d'Europe* (Paris: Plon, 1980).

Melissen, J., *The Struggle for Nuclear Partnership: Britain, the United States and the Making of the Ambiguous Alliance, 1952–9* (Groningen: Styx, 1993).

Melshen, P., 'Pseudo Operations: The Use by British and American Armed Forces of Deception in Counter-Insurgency, 1945–73', PhD, Uni. of Cambridge, 1996.

Mikesh, R. C., *B-57: Canberra at War* (Ian Allan, 1980).

Milano, J. and Brogan, P., *The Rat Line* (NY: Brassey's, 1995).

Miller, H., *Menace in Malaya* (Harrap, 1954).

Miller, J., *Lockheed's Skunk Works: The First Fifty Years* (Arlington: Aerofax, 1993).

Miller, J. E., *The United States and Italy, 1945–50* (Chapel Hill: Uni. of North Carolina Press, 1984).

Milward, A., *The Reconstruction of Western Europe, 1945–51* (Berkeley: Uni. of California Press, 1984).

——, *The European Rescue of the Nation State* (Routledge, 1994).

Miscamble, W. D., *G. F. Kennan and the Making of American Foreign Policy, 1947–50* (Princeton: Princeton UP, 1992).

Mitrovich, G., *Undermining the Kremlin: America's Strategy to Subvert the Soviet Bloc, 1947–56* (Ithaca: Cornell UP, 2000).

Montague, L. L., *General Walter Bedell Smith as Director of Central Intelligence, October 1950 – February 1953* (Uni. Park, PA: Pennsylvania State UP, 1991).

Morgan, P., *Labour in Power* (Oxford: Oxford UP, 1985).

Morris, G., *CIA and American Labour: The Subversion of the AFL-CIO's Foreign Policy* (NY: International Publishers, 1967).

Mount, G. S, *Canada's Enemies: Spies and Spying in the Peaceable Kingdom* (Ontario: Dundurn Press, 1993).

Murphy, D. E., Kondrashev, S. A. and Bailey, G., *Battleground Berlin: CIA vs KGB in the Cold War* (New Haven: Yale UP, 1997).

Naimark, N., *The Russians in Germany* (Cambridge, MA: Harvard UP, 1995).

Nasser, H. G. A., *Britain and the Egyptian Nationalist Movement, 1939–1952* (Reading: Ithaca Press, 1994).

Navias, M., *Nuclear Weapons and British Strategic Planning, 1955–8* (Oxford: Clarendon Press, 1991).

Neff, D., *Warriors at Suez* (NY: Simon & Schuster, 1981).

Nesbit, R. C., *Eyes of the RAF: A History of Photo Reconnaissance* (Alan Sutton, 1996).

Neville, J. F., *The Press, the Rosenbergs and the Cold War* (NY: Praeger, 1995).

Newton, V., *The Cambridge Spies: The Untold Story of Maclean, Philby and Burgess in America* (NY: Madison Books, 1991).

Nunnerley, D., *President Kennedy and Britain* (The Bodley Head, 1972).

Oliver, K., *Kennedy, Macmillan and the Nuclear Test Ban Debate, 1961–6* (Macmillan, 1997).

Oren, M. B., *The Origins of the Second Arab-Israeli War and the Great Powers, 1952–6* (Frank Cass, 1992).

Osborn, P. R., *Operation Pike: Britain Versus the Soviet Union, 1939–1941* (Westport, CT: Greenwood Press, 2000).

Ovendale, R., *Britain, the United States and the Transfer of Power in the Middle East, 1945–62* (Cassell, 1996).

Packard, W., *A Century of U.S. Naval Intelligence* (Washington, DC: Office of Naval Intelligence, 1996).

Pagedas, C. S., *Anglo-American Strategic Relations and the French Problem, 1960–63* (Frank Cass, 1999).

Painter, D., *The Cold War as International History* (Routledge, 1999).

Parrish, M., *The Lesser Terror: Soviet State Security, 1939–1953* (NY: Praeger, 1996).

Parrish, T., *The Ultra Americans: The US Role in Breaking Nazi Codes* (NY: Stein & Day, 1986).

Parry-Giles, S. J., 'Exporting America's Cold War Message: The Debate over America's First Peacetime Propaganda Programme, 1947–57', PhD, Indiana Uni., 1992.

Pash, B., *The Alsos Missions* (NY: Award House, 1969).

Paxman, J. and Harris, R., *A Higher Form of Killing: The Secret Story of Gas and Germ Warfare* (Paladin, 1983).

Paxton, R. O. and Wahl, N., (eds), *De Gaulle and the United States: A Centennial Reappraisal* (Oxford: Berg, 1994).

Peake, H. and Halpern, S. (eds), *In the Name of Intelligence: Essays in Honor of Louis Pforzheimer* (Washington, DC: NIBC Press, 1994).

Pedlow, G. W. and Welzenbach, D. E., *The CIA and the U-2 Program, 1954–1974* (Washington, DC: Central Intelligence Agency, 1998).

Phillips. J., *The Great Alliance: Economic Recovery and the Problems of Power, 1945–51* (Pluto, 1996).

Pinder, J. and Mayne, R., *Federal Union: the Pioneers* (Macmillan, 1990).

Pisani, S., *The CIA and the Marshall Plan* (Edinburgh: Edinburgh UP, 1991).

Porch, D., *The French Intelligence Services from the Dreyfus Affair to the Gulf War* (Macmillan, 1995).

Powers, T., *The Man Who Kept the Secrets: Richard Helms and the CIA* (Weidenfeld & Nicolson, 1979).

Prados, J., *The Soviet Estimate: US Military Intelligence and Soviet Strategic Strength* (NY: Dial Press, 1982).

——, *Presidents' Secret Wars: The CIA and the Pentagon Covert Operations since 1945* (NY: William Morrow, 1984).

Price, A., *Instruments of Darkness* (Los Altos: Peninsula Publishing, 1987).

——, *The History of US Electronic Warfare*, vol. 2: *1946–64* (The Association of Old Crows, 1989).

Raak, R. C., *Stalin's Drive to the West: The Origins of the Cold War* (Stanford: Stanford UP, 1996).

Rabe, S. G., *The Most Dangerous Area in the World: John F. Kennedy Confronts Communist Revolution in Latin America* (Chapel Hill: Uni. of North Carolina Press, 1999).

Ranelagh, J., *The Agency: The Rise and Decline of the CIA* (NY: Simon & Schuster, 1986).

Rathmell, A., *Secret War in the Middle East: The Covert Struggle for Syria, 1949–61* (I. B. Tauris, 1995).

Rawnsley, G., *Radio Diplomacy and Propaganda: The BBC and VOA in International Politics, 1956–64* (Macmillan, 1996).

—— (ed.), *Cold War Propaganda in the 1950s* (Macmillan, 1999).

Read, A. and Fisher, D., *Operation Lucy* (Hodder & Stoughton, 1980).

Rebattet, F. X., 'The European Movement, 1945–53: A Study in National and International Non-Governmental Organisations Working for European Unity', DPhil, Oxford, St Antony's College, Oxford, 1962.

Rees, G. W., *Anglo-American Approaches to Alliance Security, 1955–60* (Macmillan, 1996).

Reese, M. E., *General Reinhard Gehlen: The CIA Connection* (Washington, DC: George Mason UP, 1990).

Republic of China, *The China Handbook, 1953–4* (Taipei: ROC Press, 1954).

Rhodes, A., *The Vatican in the Age of the Cold War, 1945–92* (LA Russel, 1992).

Rhodes, F., 'The National Union of Students, 1922–67', MEd, Uni. of Manchester, 1968.

Rhodes, R., *The Making of the Atomic Bomb* (NY: Simon & Schuster, 1986).

——, *Dark Sun: The Making of the Hydrogen Bomb* (NY: Simon & Schuster, 1995).

Richards, P. S., *Scientific Information in Wartime: The Allied-German Rivalry, 1939–45* (Westport, CT: Greenwood Press, 1995).

Richelson, J., *A Century of Spies: Intelligence in the Twentieth Century* (NY: Oxford UP, 1995).

Richelson J. and Ball, D., *Ties That Bind: Intelligence Co-operation between the UKUSA Countries* (Boston: George Allen & Unwin, 1985).

Riley, M., *Philby: The Hidden Years* (Penzance: United Writers Publications, Ailsa, 1990).

Riste, O., *The Norwegian Intelligence Service, 1945–70* (Frank Cass, 1999).

Robbins, C., *The Invisible Air Force: The Story of the CIA's Secret Airlines* (Macmillan 1975).

Robertson, K. G. (ed.), *War, Resistance and Intelligence* (Macmillan, 1999).

Rogers, D. E., *Politics after Hitler: The Western Allies and the German Party System* (Macmillan, 1995).

Roman, P. J., *Eisenhower and the Missile Gap* (Ithaca: Cornell UP, 1995).

Romero, F., *The United States and the European Trade Union Movement* (Chapel Hill: Uni. of North Carolina Press, 1993).

Rositzke, H., *The CIA's Secret Operations* (Boulder, CO: Westview Encore, 1988).

Ross, D. A., *In the Interests of Peace: Canada and Vietnam, 1954–73* (Toronto: Uni. of Toronto Press, 1984).

Rothwell, V., *Britain and the Cold War, 1941–7* (Cape, 1982).

Ryan, C., *A Bridge Too Far* (Hamish Hamilton, 1974).

Ryan, J. F., 'The Royal Navy and Soviet Seapower, 1930–50: Intelligence, Naval Co-operation and Antagonism', PhD, Uni. of Hull, 1996.

Sagan, S. D., *The Limits of Safety: Organisations, Accidents and Nuclear Weapons* (Princeton: Princeton UP, 1993).

Saunders, F. S., *Who Paid the Piper? The CIA and the Cultural Cold War* (Granta, 1999).

Schaller, M., *The United States and China in the Twentieth Century* (New York: Oxford UP, 1984).

——, *The American Occupation of Japan: The Origins of the Cold War in Asia* (NY: Oxford UP, 1985).

——, *Douglas MacArthur: The Far Eastern General* (NY: Oxford UP, 1989).

Schapiro, D., *Art as a Weapon* (NY: Frederick Ungar, 1973).

Schecter, J. L. and Deriabin, P. S., *The Spy Who Saved the World* (NY: Charles Scribner's, 1992).

Schneer, J., *Labour's Conscience: The Labour Left, 1945–51* (Boston: Unwin Hyman, 1988).

Schwartz, T. A., *America's Germany: John J. McCloy and the Federal Republic of Germany* (Cambridge, MA: Harvard UP, 1991).

Schwepcke, B., 'The British High Commissioners in Germany: Some Aspects of their Role in Anglo-German Relations, 1949–1955', PhD, LSE, 1991.

Scott, L. V., *Macmillan, Kennedy and the Cuban Missile Crisis: Political, Military and Intelligence Aspects* (London: Macmillan, 1999).

Seldon, A., *Churchill's Indian Summer: The Conservative Government, 1951–1955* (Hodder & Stoughton, 1981).

Shakya, T., *A Dragon in the Land of Snows: A History of Tibet* (Pimlico, 1999).

Sharp, T., *The Wartime Alliance and the Zonal Division of Germany* (Oxford: Oxford UP, 1975).

Shaw, T., *Eden, Suez and the Mass Media: Propaganda and Persuasion during the Suez Crisis* (I. B. Tauris, 1995).

Shelden, M., *Graham Greene: The Man Within* (Heinemann, 1994).

Sherry, N., *The Life of Graham Greene*, vol. 2: *1939–55* (Cape, 1994).

Shipley, P., *Hostile Action: The KGB and Secret Operations in Britain* (Leicester: Leicester UP, 1989).

Short, A., 'British Policy towards a European Union, 1945–51', PhD, St Antony's College, Oxford, 1963.

——, *The Communist Insurrection in Malaya, 1948–1960* (Muller, 1975).

——, *The Origins of the Vietnam War* (Longmans, 1989).

Shurmacker, E. C., *Our Secret War against Red China* (NY: Paperback Library, 1962).

Simpson, C., *Blowback: American Recruitment of Nazis and its Effect on the Cold War* (Weidenfeld & Nicolson, 1988).

——, *Science of Coercion: Communication Research and Psychological Warfare, 1945–1960* (NY: Oxford UP, 1994).

Skogmar, G., *Nuclear Triangle: Relations between the United States, Great Britain and France in the Atomic Energy Field, 1939–50* (Copenhagen: Political Studies Press, 1993).

Smith, B. F., *The Shadow Warriors: OSS and the Origins of the CIA* (André Deutsch, 1983).

——, *The Ultra-Magic Deals and the Most Secret Special Relationship, 1940–1946* (Shrewsbury: Airlife Publishing, 1993).

——, *Sharing Secrets with Stalin: How the Allies Traded Intelligence, 1941–5* (Kansas: Uni. of Kansas Press, 1996).

Smith, C., 'Two Revolts: An Examination of the British Response to Arab and Jewish Rebellion 1936 to 1948', PhD, Uni. of Cambridge, 1991.

Smith, J. D., *The Attlee and Churchill Administrations and Industrial Unrest, 1945–55: A Study in Consensus* (Pinter, 1994).

Smith, M., *New Cloak, Old Dagger: How Britain's Spies Came in from the Cold* (Victor Gollancz, 1996).

Smith, R. B. and Stockwell, A. J., *British Policy and the Transfer of Power in Asia* (SOAS, 1988).

Smith, R. H., *OSS: The Secret History of America's First Intelligence Agency* (Berkeley: Uni. of California Press, 1972).

Smith, W., *Tibetan Nation: A History of Tibetan Nationalism and Sino-Tibetan Relations* (Boulder, CO: Westview, 1996).

Sontag, S. and Drew, C., *Blind Man's Buff: The Untold Story of American Submarine Espionage* (NY: Public Affairs, 1998).

Stafford, D., *Britain and the European Resistance, 1940–1945: A Survey of the Special Operations Executive, with Documents* (St Antony's/Macmillan, 1980).

——, *Camp X: SOE and the American Connection* (Viking, 1987).

——, *Churchill and Secret Service* (John Murray, 1997).

Stebenne, D. L., *Arthur J. Goldberg: New Deal Liberal* (Oxford: Oxford UP, 1996).

Stefanidis, I., 'United States, Great Britain and Greece, 1949–1952: The Problem of Greek Security and Internal Stability', PhD, LSE, 1989.

Steven, S., *Operation Splinter Factor* (Hodder & Stoughton, 1974).

Stewart, G., *The Cloak and Dollar War* (Lawrence & Wishart 1953).

Stubbs, R., *Hearts and Minds in Guerrilla Warfare: The Malayan Emergency, 1948–60* (Oxford: Oxford UP, 1989).

Stueck, W., *The Korean War: An International History* (Princeton: Princeton UP, 1995).

Sunderland, R., *Antiguerrilla Intelligence in Malaya, 1948–60* (Rand Corporation RM-4172–ISA, Sept. 1964).

Sword, K., *Deportation and Exile: Poles in the Soviet Union, 1939–48* (Macmillan, 1994).

Szasz, F. M., *British Scientists and the Manhattan Project: The Los Alamos Years* (Macmillan, 1992).

Talbert, R., *Negative Intelligence: The Army and the American Left, 1917–41* (Jackson: Uni. of Mississippi Press, 1991).

Tamnes, R., *The United States and the Cold War in the High North* (Aldershot: Dartmouth, 1991).

Tantin, K., *Revolt in Paradise* (Heinemann, 1960).

Taylor, J. G., *Indonesia: Forgotten War* (Zed, 1995).

Thomas, E., *The Very Best Men: Four Who Dared – The Early Years of the CIA* (NY: Simon & Schuster, 1995).

Thomas, H., *Armed Truce: The Beginnings of the Cold War, 1945–6* (Hamish Hamilton, 1986).

Thompson, J., *The Imperial War Museum Book of War behind Enemy Lines* (Sidgwick & Jackson, 1998).

Thorne, C., *Allies of a Kind: The United States, Britain and the War against Japan, 1941–1945* (Hamish Hamilton, 1978).

——, *The Issue of War: States, Societies and the Far Eastern Conflict of 1941–1945* (Hamish Hamilton, 1985).

Thurlow, R., *The Secret State: British Internal Security in the Twentieth Century* (Oxford: Blackwell, 1994).

Tolstoy, N., *Victims of Yalta* (Hodder & Stoughton, 1974).

Toohey, B. and Pinwill, B., *Oyster: The Story of the Australian Intelligence Service* (Sydney: Heinemann, 1989).

Tormey, S., *Making Sense of Tyranny* (Manchester: Manchester UP, 1995).

Townshend, C., *Britain's Civil Wars: Counter-Insurgency in the Twentieth Century* (Faber, 1988).

Treverton, G., *Covert Action: The Limits of Intervention in the Postwar World* (NY: Basic Books, 1987).

Tucker, N. B., *Taiwan, Hong Kong and the United States, 1945–1992: Uncertain Friendships* (NY: Twayne, 1994).

Twigge, S., and Scott, L. V., *Planning Armageddon: Britain, the United States and the Command and Control of Western Nuclear Forces, 1945–64* (Harwood, 2000).

Van Houten, C. S., 'British and American Policy towards France, 1958–63', PhD, Uni. of Cambridge, 1996.

Wall, I. M., *The United States and the Making of Postwar France, 1945–54* (Cambridge: Cambridge UP, 1991).

Wardinski, M. L., 'Truman and Eisenhower's Perceptions of the Soviet Military Threat: A Learning Process', PhD, The Catholic Uni. of America, 1993.

Warshaw, S. A. and Galambos, L. (eds), *Re-examining the Eisenhower Presidency* (Westport, CT: Greenwood Press, 1993).

Wasserstein, B., *Secret War in Shanghai* (Profile, 1998).

Watt, D. C., *Succeeding John Bull: America in Britain's Place, 1900–1975* (Cambridge: Cambridge UP, 1984).

Wehl, D., *The Birth of Indonesia* (George Allen & Unwin, 1948).

Weiler, P., *British Labour and the Cold War* (Stanford: Stanford UP, 1988).

Welham, M. G. and Welham, J. A., *Frogman Spy: The Mysterious Disappearance of Commander Buster Crabb* (Allen, 1990).

West, N., *A Matter of Trust: MI5, 1945–72* (Weidenfeld & Nicolson, 1982).

——, *GCHQ: The Secret Wireless War, 1900–86* (Weidenfeld & Nicolson, 1986).

——, *The Friends: Britain's Secret Intelligence Operations* (Weidenfeld & Nicolson, 1988).

——, *Venona* (HarperCollins, 1999).

West, N. and Tsarev, O., *The Crown Jewels: The British Secrets Exposed by the KGB Archives* (HarperCollins, 1997).

Westerfield, H. B., *Inside the CIA's Private World: Declassified Articles from the Agency's Internal Journal, 1955–92* (New Haven: Yale UP, 1995).

Whaley, B., *Codeword Barbarossa* (Boston: MIT Press, 1973).

Whitaker, R. and Marcuse, G., *Cold War Canada: The Making of a National Insecurity State, 1945–1957* (Toronto: Uni. of Toronto Press, 1994).

Whiting, C., *Werewolf: The Nazi Resistance Movement, 1944–1945* (Leo Cooper, 1996).

Whitney, C. R., *Spy Trader: The Darkest Secrets of the Cold War* (NY: Times Books, 1994).

Wilkinson, P. and Astley, J. B., *Gubbins and SOE* (Leo Cooper, 1993).

Williams, D. G. T., *Not in the Public Interest* (Hutchinson, 1965).

Williams, R. C., *Klaus Fuchs: Atom Bomb Spy* (Cambridge, MA: Harvard UP, 1987).

Wilson, M. C., *King Abdullah, Britain and the Making of Jordan* (Cambridge: Cambridge UP, 1990).

Winks, R. W., *Cloak and Gown: Scholars in the Secret War, 1939–61* (NY: William Morrow, 1987).

Winterbotham, F. W., *The Ultra Secret* (Weidenfeld & Nicolson, 1974).

Wittner, L. S., *US Intervention in Greece, 1943–1949* (NY: Columbia UP, 1982).

——, *One World or None: A History of the World Nuclear Disarmament Movement* (Stanford: Stanford UP, 1993).

Woodhouse, R., *British Policy towards France, 1945–51* (Macmillan, 1995).

Woods, R. B., *The Changing of the Guard: Anglo-American Relations, 1941–6* (Chapel Hill: Uni. of North Carolina Press, 1990).

——, *Fulbright: A Biography* (Cambridge: Cambridge UP, 1996).

Wyden, P., *Bay of Pigs* (Cape, 1979).

Wynn, H., *The RAF Nuclear Deterrent Forces, their Origins, Roles and Deployment, 1946–69: A Documentary History* (HMSO, 1994).

Xiang, Lanxin, *Recasting the Imperial Far East: Britain, America and China, 1945–50* (NY: M. E. Sharpe, 1995).

Young, H., *This Blessed Plot: Britain and Europe from Churchill to Blair* (Macmillan, 1998).

Young, J. W. *France, the Cold War and the Western Alliance, 1944–49: French Foreign Policy and Postwar Europe* (Leicester: Leicester UP, 1990).

——, *Britain and European Unity, 1945–92* (Macmillan, 1993).

——, *Winston Churchill's Last Campaign: Britain and the Cold War, 1951–55* (Oxford: Clarendon Press, 1996).

Zabihr, S., *The Mossadegh Era: Roots of the Iranian Revolution* (Chicago: Lakeview Press, 1982).

Zadka, S., *Blood in Zion: How the Jewish Guerrillas Drove the British Out of Palestine* (NY: Brassey's, 1995).

Zaloga, S. J., *Target America: The Soviet Union and the Strategic Arms Race, 1945–54* (Novato, CA: Presidio, 1993).

Zametica, O., 'British Strategic Planning for the Eastern Mediterranean and the Middle East, 1944–1947', PhD, Uni. of Cambridge, 1986.

Zhai, Qiang, *The Dragon, the Lion and the Eagle: China, Britain and the United States, 1949–58* (Kent, OH: Kent State UP, 1994).

Ziegler, C. A. and Jacobson, D., *Spying without Spies: The Origins of America's Secret Nuclear Surveillance System* (NY: Praeger, 1995).

Ziegler, P., *Mountbatten* (Collins, 1985).

Zubok, V. and Pleshakov, C., *Inside the Kremlin's Cold War from Stalin to Kruschev* (Cambridge: Harvard UP, 1997).

Zuckerman, Lord, *6 Men Out of the Ordinary* (Peter Owen, 1992).

Zurcher, A., *The Struggle to Unite Europe, 1940–1958* ((NY: New York UP 1977).

Secondary Works: Articles and Papers

Aid, M., 'Relations With Allies', unpublished paper.

——, 'US Humint and Comint in the Korean War: From the Approach of War to the Chinese Intervention', *I&NS* 14, 4 (1999): 17–63.

——, 'US Comint in the Korean War (Part II): From the Chinese Intervention to the Armistice', *I&NS*, 15, 1 (2000): 14–49.

Aldrich, R. J., 'Imperial Rivalry: British and American Intelligence in Asia, 1942–46', *I&NS*, 3, 1 (1988): 5–55.

——, 'Unquiet in Death: The Survival of the Special Operations Executive, 1945–51', in Gorst, A., Jonman, L. and Lucas, W. S. (eds), *Contemporary British History: Politics and the Limits of Policy, 1931–61* (Pinter, 1991), 193–217.

——, 'Soviet Intelligence, British Security and the End of the Red Orchestra: The Case of Alexander Rado', *I&NS*, 6, 1 (1991): 196–217.

——, 'Secret Intelligence for a Post War World', in Aldrich, *British Intelligence, Strategy and the Cold War*, 15–49.

——, 'Conspiracy or Confusion: Churchill, Roosevelt and Pearl Harbor', *I&NS*, 7, 3 (1992): 335–47.

——, 'The Foreign Affairs Oral History Program', *Diplomacy and Statecraft*, 4, 2 (1993): 210–17.

——, 'Never Never Land and Wonderland? British and American Policy on Intelligence Archives', *Contemporary Record*, 8, 1 (1994): 133–52.

——, 'The Waldegrave Initiative and Secret Service Archives: New Materials and New Policies, *I&NS*, 10, 1 (1995): 192–7.

——, 'European Integration: An American Intelligence Connection', in Deighton (ed.), *Building Postwar Europe*, 141–58.

Aldrich, R. J. and Coleman, M., 'The Cold War, the JIC and British Signals Intelligence, 1948', *I&NS* 4, 3 (1989): 535–49.

——, 'Britain and the Strategic Air Offensive against the Soviet Union, 1945–9', *History*, 74, 242 (1989): 400–26.

Aldrich, R. J. and Zametica, J., 'The Rise and Decline of a Strategic Concept: The Middle East, 1945–51', in Aldrich, *British Intelligence, Strategy and the Cold War*, 236–74.

Ali, S., 'South Asia: The Perils of Covert Coercion', in Freedman, L. (ed.), *Strategic Coercion: Concepts and Cases* (Oxford: Oxford UP, 1998), 249–76.

Allen, L., 'Burmese Puzzles: Two Deaths That Never Were', *I&NS*, 5, 1 (1990): 193–9.

——, 'The Escape of Captain Vivian: A Footnote to Burmese Independence', *J. of Imperial and Commonwealth History*, 19, 1 (1991): 65–70.

Anderson, R. S., 'Patrick Blackett in India: Military Consultant and Scientific Intervenor, 1947–1972', *Notes and Records of the Royal Society of London*, 53, 3 (1989): 345–60.

Anderson, S., '"With Friends Like These..." The OSS and the British in Yugoslavia', *I&NS*, 8, 2 (1993): 140–72.

Andrew, C. M., 'Whitehall, Washington and the Intelligence Services', *International Affairs*, 53, 3 (1977): 390–404.

——, 'The Growth of Intelligence Collaboration in the English Speaking World', *Wilson Center Working Paper*, 83 (November 1987).

——, 'Churchill and Intelligence', *I&NS*, 3, 3 (1988): 181–94.

——, 'More Unreliable Memoirs from General Philby', *Daily Telegraph*, 15 Apr. 1988.

——, 'The Growth of the Australian Intelligence Community and the Anglo-American Connection', *I&NS*, 4, 2 (1989): 213–57.

——, 'Intelligence Collaboration between Britain and the United States during the Second World War', in Hitchcock, W. T. (ed.), *The Intelligence Revolution: A Historical Perspective* (Washington, DC: US Air Force Academy, 1991), 111–23.

——, 'The Making of the Anglo-American SIGINT Alliance', in Peake and Halpern, *In the Name of Intelligence*, 95–109.

——, 'The Venona Secret', in Robertson, (ed.), *War*, 203–25.

——, 'Intelligence and International Relations in the Early Cold War', *Review of International Studies*, 24, 3 (1998): 321–30.

Andrew, C. M., and Aldrich, R. J. (ed.), 'Intelligence Services in the Second World War', *Contemporary British History*, 13, 4 (1999): 130–69.

Annan, N., 'The Spy with No Excuses', *Independent*, 13 May 1988.

Anstey, C., 'The Projection of British Socialism: Foreign Office Publicity and American Opinion, 1945–50', *J. of Contemporary History*, 19 (1984): 435–54.

Aronsen, L. R., 'Some Aspects of Surveillance – 'Peace, Order and Good Government' during the Cold War – The Origins and Organization of Canada's Internal Security Program', *I&NS*, 1, 3 (1986): 357–80.

Ball, Desmond J., 'Allied Intelligence Co-operation Involving Australia during World War II', *Australian Outlook*, 32 (1978) 299–309.

——, 'Over and Out: Signals Intelligence (Sigint) in Hong Kong', *I&NS*, 11, 3 (1996): 474–96.

Ball, S. J., 'Harold Macmillan and the Politics of Defence: The Market for Strategic Ideas during the Sandys Era Revisited', *Twentieth Century British History*, 6, 1 (1995): 99–100.

Barnes, T., 'The Secret Cold War: The CIA and American Foreign Policy in Europe, 1946–56', Part II, *Historical J.*, 25, 3 (1982): 649–70.

Barros, A., 'Prying Loose the Spoils: The Soviet Intelligence Archives', *European Review of History*, 11 (1993): 196–200.

Baylis, J., 'The Development of Britain's Thermonuclear Capability, 1954–61: Myth or Reality', *Contemporary Record*, 8, 1 (1994): 159–74.

Beckett, I. F. W., 'Robert Thompson and the British Advisory Mission to South Vietnam, 1961–1965', *Small Wars and Insurgencies,* 8, 3 (1997): 41–63.

Berger, D. H., AFSC Study, 'The Use of Covert Paramilitary Activity as a Policy Tool: An Analysis of Operations Conducted by the United States Central Intelligence Agency', http://www.fas.org/irp/eprint/berger.htm.

Bessell, R., 'Police of a "New Type"? Police and Society in East Germany after 1945', *German History*, 10, 3 (1992): 290–302.

Biddiscombe, P., 'Prodding the Russian Bear: Pro-German Resistance in Romania, 1944–5', *European History Quarterly*, 23, 2 (1993): 193–232.

——, 'The Problem with Glass Houses: Soviet Recruitment and Deployment of SS Men as Spies and Saboteurs', *I&NS*, 15, 3 (2000): 131–45.

Bitar, M., 'Bombs Plots and Allies: Cambodia and the Western Powers, 1958–9', *I&NS*, 14, 4 (1999): 181–94.

Bosco, A., 'Federal Union, Chatham House and the Anglo-French Union', in Bosco, A. (ed.), *The Federal Idea: The History of Enlightenment to 1945* (Lothian Trust: 1991), 237–62.

Boyle, P., 'Reversion to Isolationism: British Foreign Office Views of US Isolationism and Internationalism in World War II', *Diplomacy and Statecraft*, 8, 1 (1997): 168–83.

Braden, T., 'I'm Glad the CIA Is Immoral', *Saturday Evening Post*, 240 (20 May 1967): 10–14.

——, 'The Birth of the CIA', *American Heritage*, 28 (1977): 4–13.

Brands, H. W., 'The Limits of Manipulation: How the United States Didn't Topple Sukarno', *J. of American History* 76, 3 (1989): 785–809.

Brook, R., 'The London Operation: The British View', in Chalou (ed.), *Secrets War*, 69–77.

Brown, K., 'Churchill's Golden Eggs – British Interception of US and French Communications', unpublished paper given in London, 3 October 1994.

——, 'The Interplay of Information and Mind in Decision-Making: Signals Intelligence and Franklin D. Roosevelt's Policy-Shift on Indochina', *I&NS*, 13, 1 (1998): 109–31.

Burridge, T. D., 'A Postscript to Potsdam: The Churchill–Attlee Electoral Clash, June 1945', *J. of Contemporary History* 12, 4 (1977): 725–39.

Cain, F., 'An Aspect of Postwar Relations with the UK and the US: Missiles, Spies and Disharmony', *Australian Historical Studies*, 23, 92 (1989): 186–203.

——, 'Venona in Australia and its Long-term Ramifications', *J. of Contemporary History*, 35, 2 (2000): 211–48.

Calvert, R. J., '39 Steps', *Aircraft Illustrated*, 29, 5 (1996): 76–81.

Carew, A., 'The American Labor Movement in Fizzland: The Free Trade Union Committee and the CIA', *Labor History*, 39, 1 (1998): 25–42.

Carruthers, S., 'Two Faces of 1950s Terrorism: The Film Presentation of Mau Mau and the Malayan Emergency', *Small Wars and Insurgencies*, 6, 1 (1995): 17–43.

——, 'A Red under Every Bed? Anti-Communist Propaganda and Britain's Response to Colonial Insurgency', *Contemporary Record*, 9, 2 (1995): 294–319.

——, '"Not Just Washed But Dry Cleaned": Korea and the "Brainwashing" Scare of the 1950s', in Rawnsley (ed.), *Cold War Propaganda*, 47–66.

Cecil, R., 'Legends Spies Tell', *Encounter*, 50, 4 (1978): 9–17.

——, '"C"'s War', *I&NS*, 1, 2 (1986): 170–89.

——, 'The Cambridge Comintern', in Andrew and Dilks (eds), *Missing Dimension*, 169–98.

Charters, D., 'Special Operations in Counterinsurgency: The Farran Case, Palestine, 1947', *J. of the Royal United Services Institute*, 124, 2 (1979): 56–61.

——, 'British Intelligence and the Palestine Campaign', *I&NS*, 6, 1 (1991): 115–41.

Clark, I. and Angell, D., 'Britain, the USA and the Control of Nuclear Weapons: Diplomacy of the Thor Deployment, 1956–8', *Diplomacy and Statecraft*, 2, 3 (1991): 153–78.

Clarke, W. F., 'Post War Organisation', *Cryptologia*, XIII, 2 (1989): 118–22.

Clutterbuck, R. L., 'Bertrand Stewart Essay Prize, 1960', *Army Quarterly and Defence J.*, 91 (1960): 167–8.

Cockroft, E., 'Abstract Expression: Weapon of the Cold War', *Artforum*, 12, 10 (June 1974): 39–41.

Cole, B., 'British Technical Intelligence and the Soviet Intermediate Ballistic Missile Threat', *I&NS*, 14, 2 (1999): 70–92.

Corke, S. J., 'Bridging the Gap: Containment: Covert Action and the Search for the Missing Link in American Cold War Policy, 1948–53', *J. of Strategic Studies*, 20, 4 (1997): 45–65.

Cox, M., 'Western Intelligence, the Soviet Threat and NSC-68: A Reply to Beatrice Heuser', *Review of International Studies*, 18, 1 (1992): 75–85.

Croft, J., 'Reminiscences of GCHQ and GCB, 1942–5', *I&NS*, 13, 4 (1998): 133–43.

Cromwell, V., 'The FCO', in Steiner, Z. (ed.), *The Times Survey of Foreign Ministries of the World* (Times Books, 1982), 542–72.

Crossman, R. H. S., 'Psychological Warfare', *J. of the Royal United Services Institute* (Feb.–Nov. 1952): 319–32.

Czubatyi, N. D., 'The Ukrainian Underground', *Ukrainian Quarterly*, II, 2 (1946): 154–66.

Davies, P. J., 'Organizational Politics and the Development of British Intelligence Producer/Consumer Interfaces', *I&NS*, 10, 4 (1995): 113–32.

——, 'From Special Operations to Special Political Action: The "Rump SOE" and SIS Post-war Covert Action Capability, 1945–1977', *I&NS*, 15, 3 (2000): 55–76.

——, 'The SIS Singapore Station and the SIS Far Eastern Controller', *I&NS*, 14, 4 (1999): 105–29.

Deakin, A., 'The International Trade Union Movement', *International Affairs*, 26, 2 (1950): 167–71.

Dean, J., 'Assault on the Mountain', July 2000, http://www.govexec.com.

Deery, P., 'Confronting the Cominform: George Orwell and the Cold War Offensive of the Information Research Department, 1948–50', *Labour History*, 73 (1997): 219–25.

Defty, A., 'Organising Security and Intelligence in the Far East: Further Fruits of the Waldegrave Initiative', *SGI Newsletter*, 16 (1997/8): 2–5.

De Graff, B., 'Hot Intelligence in the Tropics: Dutch Intelligence Operations in the Netherlands East Indies during the Second World War', *J. of Contemporary History*, 22, 4 (1987): 563–84.

Deighton, A., 'Say It with Documents: British Policy Overseas, 1945–52', *Review of International Studies,* 18, 2 (1992): 393–402.

Delzell, C. F., 'The European Federalist Movement in Italy: The First Phase, 1918–1947', *J. of Modern History* (1960): 241–50.

de Mowbray, S., 'Soviet Deception and the Onset of the Cold War: British Documents for 1943–A Lesson in Manipulation', *Encounter*, 63, 2 (1984): 16–24.

Denham, H., 'Bedford–Bletchley–Kilindi–Colombo', in Hinsley and Stripp (eds), *Codebreakers*, 265–81.

Denniston, A. G., 'The Government Code and Cypher School between the Wars', *I&NS*, 1, 1 (1986): 48–70.

Devereux, D., 'British Planning for Post War Civil Aviation, 1942–5', *Twentieth Century British History*, 2, 1 (1991): 26–47.

Dockrill, M., 'British Attitudes to France as a Military Ally', *Diplomacy and Statecraft*, 1, 1 (1990): 49–70.

Doherty, P. O., 'The GDR in the Context of Stalinist Show Trials and Anti-Semitism in Eastern Europe, 1948–54', *German History,* 10, 3 (1992): 302–17.

Donini, L., 'The Cryptographic Services of the Royal (British) and Italian Navies: A Comparative Analysis of their Activities in World War II', *Cryptologia*, XIV, 3 (1990): 97–127.

Duncannon, D., 'Ho Chi Minh in Hong Kong, 1931–2', *China Quarterly*, 57, 1 (1974): 84–101.

Ellwood, D. W., 'The 1948 Elections in Italy: A Cold War Propaganda Battle', *Historical J. of Film, Radio and Television*, 13, 1 (1993): 19–35.

Erskine, R., 'Anglo-US Cryptological Co-operation', paper to the Fifth Annual Meeting of the International Intelligence History Study Group, Tutzing, Bavaria, June 1999.

Evangelista, M. A., 'Stalin's Postwar Army Re-appraised', *International Security,* 7, 1 (Winter 1982–3): 110–38.

Farquharson, J., 'Governed or Exploited: The British Acquisition of German Technology, 1945–8', *J. of Contemporary History*, 32, 1 (1997): 23–42.

Ferris, J., 'From Broadway House to Bletchley Park: The Diary of Captain Malcolm Kennedy, 1934–46', *I&NS*, 4, 3 (1989): 421–51.

——, 'Coming in from the Cold: The Historiography of American Intelligence, 1945–1990', *DH,* 10, 1 (1995): 87–116.

Fish, M. S., 'After Stalin's Death: The Anglo-American Debate over a New Cold War', *DH*, 10, 1 (1986): 333–55.

Fletcher, R., 'British Propaganda since World War II – A Case Study', *Media, Culture and Society*, 4 (1982): 96–109.

Foot, M. R. D., 'Was SOE Any Good?', *J. of Contemporary History*, 16, 1 (1981): 167–83.

——, 'OSS and SOE: An Equal Partnership?', in Chalou (ed.), *The Secrets War*, 295–301.

Foot, R. J., Anglo-American Relations and the Korean Crisis: The British Effort to Avoid an Expanded War Effort, December 1950–January 1951', *DH*, 10, 1 (1986): 43–59.

Forster, A., 'No Entry: Britain and the EEC in the 1960s?', *Contemporary British History*, 12, 3 (1998): 139–46.

Fraser, C., 'Understanding American Policy towards the Decolonization of European Empires, 1945–64', *Diplomacy and Statecraft*, 3, 1 (1992): 105–26.

Furedi, F., 'Decolonisation through Counter-Insurgency: Kenya and the Mau Mau, 1953–5', in Gorst, A. *et al.* (eds), *Contemporary British History, 1931–61* (Pinter, 1991), 141–69.

Fursenko, A. and Naftali, T., 'Soviet Intelligence and the Cuban Missile Crisis', *I&NS*, 13, 3 (1998): 64–87.

Futrell, R. W., 'A Case Study: USAF Intelligence in the Korean War', in Hitchcock, W. T. (ed.), *The Intelligence Revolution: A Historical Perspective*, Proceedings of the Thirteenth Military History Symposium, US Air Force Academy (Washington DC: Office of Air Force History, 1991).

Gaddis, J. L., 'The Insecurities of Victory: The US and the Perception of the Soviet Threat after World War II', in Gaddis, J. L., *The Long Peace* (NY: Oxford UP, 1987), 20–47.

——, 'Intelligence, Espionage and Cold War Origins', *DH,* 13, 2 (1989): 191–213.

Garthoff, R. L., 'Estimating Soviet Military Force: Some Light from the Past', *International Security*, 14, 4 (1990): 93–116.

——, 'The KGB Reports to Gorbachev', *I&NS*, 11, 2 (1996): 223–44.

——, 'US Intelligence in the Cuban Missile Crisis', *I&NS*, 13, 3 (1998): 18–63.

Gasiorowski, M. J., 'The 1953 Coup d'Etat in Iran', *International J. of Middle East Studies*, 19 (1987): 261–86.

Gelber, Y., 'Reuven Shiloah's Contribution to the Development of Israeli Intelligence', in Carmel, H., *Intelligence for Peace: The Role of Intelligence in Times of Peace* (Frank Cass, 1999), 16–29.

Gill, P., 'Reasserting Control: Recent Changes in the Oversight of the UK Intelligence Community', *Intelligence and National Security* 11, 2 (1996): 313–331.

Gimbel, J., 'US Foreign Policy, German Scientists and the Early Cold War', *Political Science Quarterly*, 101, 3 (1986): 433–51.

——, 'The American Exploitation of German Technical Know-How after World War II', *Political Science Quarterly,* 105, 1 (1990): 295–309.

——, 'Project Paperclip: German Scientists, American Policy and the Cold War', *DH,* 14, 3 (1990): 343–67.

Gorst, A., 'British Military Planning for Post-War Defence', in Deighton (ed.), *Britain and the First Cold War,* 91–100.

Gorst, A. and Lucas, W. S., 'Secrets of Suez', *Contemporary Record,* 1, 4 (1986): 1–2.

Gorst, A. and Lucas, W. S., 'The Other "Collusion": Operation STRAGGLE and Anglo-American Intervention in Syria, 1955–6', *I&NS,* 4, 1 (1989): 576–96.

Grosbois, T., 'L'Action de Jósef Retinger en faveur de l'idée européene, 1940–46', *European Review of History,* 6, 1 (1999): 59–82.

Grunbaum, W. F., 'The British Security Programme, 1948–58', *Western Political Quarterly,* XIII (1960): 764–79.

Guy, S., 'High Treason (1951): Britain's Cold War Fifth Column', *Historical J. of Film, Radio and Television,* 13, 1 (1993): 35–98.

Hack, K., 'British Intelligence and Counter-Insurgency in the Era of Decolonisation: The Example of Malaya', *I&NS,* 14, 2 (1999): 124–55.

——, 'Corpses, Prisoners of War and Captured Documents: British and Communist Narratives of the Malayan Emergency and the Dynamics of Intelligence Transformation', *I&NS,* 14, 4 (1999): 211–41.

Handel, M., 'The Politics of Intelligence', *I&NS,* 2, 4 (1987): 5–47.

Hanhimaki, Y., 'The United States and Finland, 1948–9', *DH,* 18, 3 (1994): 353–72.

Harrison, E. D. R., 'Some Reflections on Kim Philby's *My Silent War* as a Historical Source', in Aldrich and Hopkins (eds), *Intelligence, Defence and Diplomacy,* 205–25.

——, 'More Thoughts on Kim Philby's *My Silent War*', *I&NS,* 10, 3 (1995): 514–26.

——, 'British Subversion in French East Africa, 1941–42: SOE's Todd Mission', *English Historical Review,* CXIV, 456 (1999): 339–70.

——, ' "Something Beautiful for 'C' ": Malcolm Muggeridge in Lourenço Marques', in Robertson (ed.), *War,* 187–201.

Hathaway, R. M., 'Present at the Creation: The Birth of the CIA and America's Post War Intelligence Community', *DH,* 18, 3 (1994): 425–31.

Heather, R., 'Intelligence and Counter-Insurgency in Kenya, 1952–56', *I&NS,* 5, 3 (1990): 57–84.

Hedman, E. E., 'Late Imperial Romance: Magsaysay, Lansdale and the Philippine–American "Special Relationship" ', *I&NS,* 14, 4 (1999): 181–94.

Hennessy, P. and Brownfeld, G., 'Britain's Cold War Security Purge: The Origins of Positive Vetting', *Historical J.,* 25, 4 (1982): 965–73.

Hennessy, P. and Townsend, K., 'The Documentary Spoor of Burgess and Maclean', *I&NS,* 2, 2 (1987): 291–301.

Heuser, B., 'Covert Action within British and American Concepts of Containment, 1948–51', in Aldrich (ed.), *British Intelligence, Strategy and the Cold War,* 65–84.

——, 'NSC-68 and the Soviet Threat: A New Perspective on Western Threat Perception and Policy-Making', *Review of International Studies,* 17, 1 (1991): 17–41.

——, 'Stalin as Hitler's Successor: Western Interpretations of the Soviet Threat', in Heuser and O'Neill (eds), *Securing Peace,* 17–40.

Higgins, B. and Higgins, J., 'Indonesia: Now or Never', *Foreign Affairs,* 37, 1 (1958): 156–65.

Hinsley, F. H., 'British Intelligence and Barbarossa', in Erickson and Dilks (eds), *Barbarossa,* 43–75.

Howard, M., 'The Forgotten Dimensions of Strategy', *Foreign Affairs,* 54, 5 (1979): 975–87.

Huntington, T., 'The Berlin Spy Tunnel', *American Heritage of Invention and Technology,* 10 (1995): 44–52.

Jeffery, K., 'Intelligence and Counter-Insurgency Operations: Some Reflections on the British Experience', *I&NS,* 2, 1 (1987): 118–50.

Jones, J., 'Eradicating Nazism from the British Zone of Germany: Early Policy and Practice', *German History,* 8, 2 (1990): 145–63.

Jones, M., 'Maximum Disavowable Aid: Britain, the United States and the Indonesian Rebellion, 1957–58', *English Historical Review,* CXIV, 459 (1999): 1179–1215.

Jones, R. V., 'Science, Intelligence and Policy', *J. of the Royal United Services Institute,* 124, 2 (1979): 9–17.

Jones, T., 'The British Army and Counter-Guerrilla Warfare in Transition, 1944–1952', *Small Wars and Insurgencies,* 3, 2 (1996): 265–307.

Kahn, D., 'Soviet Comint in the Cold War', *Cryptologia,* XXII, 1 (1998): 1–24.

Karabell, Z. and Naftali, T., 'History Declassified: The Perils and Promise', *DH,* 18, 4 (1994): 615–27.

Kerr, S., 'The Secret Hotline to Moscow: Donald Maclean and the Berlin Crisis of 1948', in Deighton (ed.), *Britain and the First Cold War,* 71–87.

——, 'British Cold War Defectors: The Versatile, Durable Toys of Propagandists', in Aldrich (ed.), *British Intelligence, Strategy and the Cold War*, 111–42.

——, 'NATO's First Spies: The Case of the Disappearing Diplomats – Guy Burgess and Donald Maclean', in Heuser and O'Neill (eds), *Securing Peace*, 293–309.

——, 'Roger Hollis and the Dangers of the Anglo-Soviet Treaty of 1942', *I&NS*, 5, 3 (1990): 148–57.

——, 'The Secret Hotline to Moscow: Donald Maclean and the Berlin Crisis of 1948', in Deighton (ed.), *Britain and the First Cold War*, 71–87.

Kitchen, M., 'SOE's Man in Moscow', *I&NS*, 12, 2 (1991): 93–109.

Knight, A., 'Russian Archives: Opportunities and Obstacles', *IJIC*, 12, 3 (1999): 325–38.

Knight, W., 'Labourite Britain: America's Sure Friend?', *DH*, 7, 4 (1985): 267–82.

Kramer, A., 'British Dismantling Politics, 1945–9: A Reassessment', in Turner, I. D. (ed.), *Reconstruction in Post-War Germany: British Occupation Policy and the Western Zones, 1945–55* (Oxford: Berg, 1989), 125–54.

Larres, K., 'Preserving Law and Order: Britain, the United States and the East Berlin Uprising of 1953', *Twentieth Century British History*, 5, 3 (1994): 320–56.

Lashmar, P., 'Canberras over the USSR', *Aeroplane Monthly*, 23, 2 (1995): 32–5.

Laurie, C. D., 'The "Sauerkrauts": German POWs as OSS Agents, 1944–5', *Prologue*, 26 (1994): 49–60.

Leary, B., 'George Blake and the Berlin Tunnel: Success or Failure?', paper to the Fifth Annual Meeting of the International Intelligence History Study Group, Tutzing, Bavaria, June 1999.

Little, D., 'The Cold War and Covert Action: The United States and Syria, 1945–58', *Middle Eastern J.*, 44, 1 (1990): 51–76.

Lombardo, J. R., 'American Consulate in Hong Kong, 1949–1964: A Mission of Espionage, Intelligence Gathering and Psychological Operations', *I&NS*, 14, 4 (1999): 64–81.

Loow, H., 'Swedish Policy towards Suspected War Criminals, 1945–87', *Scandinavian J. of History*, 14, 2 (1989): 135–55.

Louis, W. R., 'American Anti-Colonialism and the Dissolution of the British Empire', *International Affairs*, 61, 3 (1985): 395–420.

——, 'Dulles, Suez and the British', in Immerman, R. (ed.), *John Foster Dulles and the Diplomacy of the Cold War* (Princeton: Princeton UP, 1990), 133–58.

Lucas, W. S., 'Campaigns of Truth: The Psychological Strategy Board and American Ideology, 1951–53', *International History Review*, XVIII, 2 (1996): 253–304.

Lucas, W. S. and Morey, A., 'The Hidden "Alliance": The CIA and MI6 before and after Suez', *I&NS*, 15, 2 (2000): 95–121.

Lucas, W. S. and Morris, C., 'A Very British Crusade: The Information Research Department and the Beginning of the Cold War', in Aldrich (ed.), *British Intelligence, Strategy and the Cold War*, 85–111.

McDonald, J. K., 'Commentary on 'History Declassified'', *DH*, 18, 4 (1994): 627–30.

McGarvey, P. J., 'DIA: Intelligence to Please', in Halperin, M. and Kanter, A. (eds), *Readings in American Foreign Policy: A Bureaucratic Perspective* (Boston: Little, Brown, 1973), 318–28.

McKay, C. G., 'British SIGINT and the Bear, 1919–41: Some Discoveries in the GC&CS Archive', *Kungl Krigsvetenskapsakademiens Handlingar Och Tidskrift* (2 Haftet 1997), 81–96.

MacMahon, R. J., 'Eisenhower and Third World Nationalism: A Critique of the Revisionists', *Political Science Quarterly* 101, 3 (1986): 453–73.

Maddrell, P., 'British-American Scientific Intelligence Co-operation during the Occupation of Germany', *I&NS*, 15, 2 (2000): 74–94.

Malvoney, J., 'Civil Liberties in Britain during the Cold War: The Role of Central Government', *American J. of Legal History*, 33, 1 (1989): 53–100.

Marchio, J., 'Resistance Potential and Rollback: US Intelligence and the Eisenhower Administration's Policies Towards Eastern Europe, 1953–56', *I&NS*, 10, 2 (1995): 219–41.

Mark, E., 'The War Scare of 1946 and its Consequences', *DH*, 21, 3 (1997): 383–416.

Markus, U., 'Conciliation and Repression: Soviet Policy in the Western Republics, 1945–51', *Slovo*, 4, 2 (1992): 6–21.

Mastny, V., 'Stalin and the Militarization of the Cold War', *International Security*, 9, 3 (1984/5): 109–29.

——, 'Europe in US–USSR Relations: A Topical Legacy', *Problems of Communism*, XXXVII (1988): 19–29.

Matthews, J. D. H., 'Art and Politics in Cold War America', *American Historical Review*, 81, 4 (1976): 762–87.

Mayers, D., 'After Stalin: The Ambassadors and America's Soviet Policy, 1953–62', *Diplomacy and Statecraft*, 5, 2 (1994): 213–48.

Meers, S. I., 'The British Connection: How the United States Covered its Tracks in the 1954 Coup in Guatemala', *DH*, 16, 3 (1992): 409–28.

Mellisen, J., 'The Restoration of the Nuclear Alliance: Great Britain and Atomic Negotiations with the United States, 1957–8', *Contemporary Record*, 6, 1 (1992): 72–106.

Merrick, R., 'The Russia Committee of the British Foreign Office and the Cold War, 1946–7', *J. of Contemporary History*, 20, 3 (1985): 453–68.

Merrill, D., 'Indo-American Relations, 1947–50: A Missed Opportunity in Asia', *DH*, 11, 3 (1987): 203–26.

Miller, J. E., 'Taking Off the Gloves: The United States and the Italian Elections of 1948', *DH*, 7, 1 (1983): 35–55.

Miller, M., 'Approaches to the European Institution Planning of Carlo Sforza, Italian Foreign Minister, 1947–51', in Deighton, *Building Postwar Europe*, 55–70.

Millman, B., 'Toward War with Russia: British Naval and Air Planning in the Near East, 1939–40, *J. of Contemporary History*, 29, 2 (1994): 261–83.

Muggeridge, M., 'Books, CIA Cultural Penetration', *Esquire,* 68 (1967): 12–16.

Mulligan, T. P., 'Spies, Ciphers and Zitadelle: Intelligence and the Battle of Kursk, 1943', *J. of Contemporary History* 22, 2 (1987): 235–60.

Naftali, T., 'Intrepid's Last Deception: Documenting the Career of Sir William Stephenson', *I&NS*, 8, 3 (1993): 72–100.

Nitze, P., 'Newly Declassified Annexes of NSC 68', *SAIS Review*, XIX, 1 (1999): 13–33.

O'Doherty, P., 'The GDR in the Context of Stalinist Show Trials: Anti-Semitism in Eastern Europe, 1948–54', *German History*, 10, 3 (1992): 302–17.

Osterman, C., 'The United States, the East German Uprising of 1953, and the Limits of Rollback', *CWIHP Working Paper,* no. 11 (Dec. 1994).

Owen, N., 'Britain and Decolonization: The Labour Government and the Middle East, 1945–51', in Cohen and Kolinsky (eds), *Demise*, 3–22.

Parry-Giles, S., 'The Eisenhower Administration's Conceptualization of the USIA: The Development of Overt and Covert Propaganda Stratagems', *Presidential Studies Quarterly*, XXIX, 2 (1994): 263–77.

Paschall, R., 'Special Operations in Korea', *Conflict*, 7, 2 (1987): 155–78.

Pikart, E., 'The Military Situation and the Assessment of the Threat', in Foester, R. G. and Wiggerhaus, N., *The Western Security Community, 1948–50* (Oxford: Berg, 1993).

Popplewell, R. J., 'Lacking in Intelligence: Some Reflections on Recent Approaches to British Counterinsurgency, 1900–1960', *I&NS*, 12, 2, (1995): 336–52.

Potter, K., 'British McCarthyism', in Jeffreys-Jones, R. and Lownie, A. (eds), *North American Spies* (Edinburgh: Edinburgh UP, 1991).

Ramakrishna, K., 'Content, Credibility and Context: Propaganda, Government Surrender Policy and the Malayan Communist Terrorist Mass Surrenders of 1958', *I&NS*, 14, 4 (1999): 242–66.

Ransom, H. H., 'Secret Intelligence in the United States, 1947–1982: The CIA's Search for Legitimacy', in Andrew and Dilks (eds), *Missing Dimension*, 199–227.

Rawnsley, G. D., 'Cold War Radio in Crisis: The BBC Overseas Service, the Suez Crisis and the Hungarian Uprising, 1956', *Historical J. of Film, Radio and Television*, 15, 2/3 (1995): 197–217.

——, 'Overt and Covert: The Voice of Britain and Black Radio Broadcasting in the Suez Crisis, 1956', *I&NS*, 11, 3 (1996): 497–22.

Reynolds, D., 'Competitive Co-operation: Anglo-American Relations in World War II', *Historical J.*, 23, 1 (1980): 233–45.

——, 'A "Special Relationship"?: America, Britain and the International Order since the Second World War', *International Affairs*, 62, 1 (1985/6): 1–20.

——, 'Re-thinking Anglo-American Relations', *International Affairs*, 65, 1 (1989): 89–111.

Rhodes, R., 'The Myth of Perfect Nuclear Security', *New York Times*, 24 July 2000.

Rimmington, S., 'Security and Democracy – Is There a Conflict?', transcript of the Richard Dimbleby Lecture, BBC1, 12 June 1994 (BBC Educational Developments, 1994).

Ross, G., 'Foreign Office Attitudes to the Soviet Union, 1941–1943', *J. of Contemporary History*, 16, 3 (1981): 521–40.

Roth, K. H., 'The Nazi Pillage of West European Trade Union Archives, 1940–1944', *International Review of Social History,* 34 (1989): 273–86.

Ruane, K., 'Containing America: Aspects of British Foreign Policy and the Cold War in South East Asia, 1951–4', *Diplomacy and Statecraft*, 7, 1 (1996): 142–62.

Rudgers, D. F., 'The Origins of Covert Action', *J. of Contemporary History,* 35, 2 (2000): 249–62.

Ruehsen, M. de M., 'Operation "Ajax" Revisited: Iran 1953', *Middle Eastern Studies*, XXIX (1993): 467–86.

Schlesinger, S., 'Cryptanalysis for Peacetime and the Birth of the Structure of the United Nations', *Cryptologia*, XIX, 2 (1995): 217–35.

Scott, L., 'The Other Other Missiles of October: The Thor IRBMs and the Cuban Missile Crisis', http://www.ihrinfo.ac.uk/publications/ejihmnu.html.

——, 'Espionage and the Cold War: Oleg Penkovsky and the Cuban Missile Crisis', *I&NS*, 14, 4 (1999): 23–48.

Scott, L., and Smith, S., 'Lessons of October: Historians, Political Scientists, Policy-makers and the Cuban Missile Crisis', *International Affairs*, 40, 4 (1994): 659–84.

Shaw, T., 'The Information Research Department and the Korean War', *J. of Contemporary History*, 34, 2 (1998): 263–81.

Sillitoe, P., 'My Answer to Critics of MI5', *Sunday Times*, 22 Nov. 1953.

Smith, B. F., 'A Note on the OSS, Ultra and World War II's Intelligence Legacy for America', *Defense Analysis*, 3, 2 (1987) 184–9.

——, 'Sharing Ultra in World War II', *IJICI*, 2, 1 (1988): 59–72.

Smith, R., 'A Climate of Opinion: British Officials and the Development of Soviet Policy, 1945–7', *International Affairs*, 64, 4 (1988): 635–47.

Smith, S., 'The Special Relationship', *Political Studies*, 38, 1 (1990): 126–37.

Stafford, D., 'Intrepid: Myth and Reality', *J. of Contemporary History*, 22, 2 (1987): 304–16.

——, 'The British Foreign Office and the Intelligence Struggle in Germany during the 1960s: A Personal Perspective', paper to the Fifth Annual Meeting of the International Intelligence History Study Group, Tutzing, Bavaria, June 1999.

Steele, T. L., 'Allied and Interdependent: British Policy during the Chinese Offshore Islands Crisis of 1958', in Gorst, A., Jonman, L. and Lucas, W. S. (eds), *Contemporary British History: Politics and the Limits of Policy, 1931–61* (Pinter, 1991), 230–47.

Stern, S., 'NSA and the CIA', *Ramparts*, 5 (1967): 29–39.

Stewart, B., 'Winning in Malaya: An Intelligence Success Story', *I&NS*, 14, 4 (1999): 267–83.

Stripp, A. J., 'Breaking Japanese Codes', *I&NS*, 2, 4 (1987): 135–50.

Stueck, W., 'Western Defensive (and Offensive) Strategies in the Cold War, a Multi-archive, Multi-linguistic Approach', *DH*, 14, 4 (1990): 623–9.

Tang, J. S., 'From Empire Defence to Imperial Retreat: British Post War China Policy and the Decolonization of Hong Kong', *Modern Asian Studies*, 28, 2 (1984): 317–38.

Taylor, T., 'Anglo-American Signals Intelligence Co-operation', in Hinsley and Stripp (eds), *Codebreakers*, 71–3.

Thomas, A., 'British Signals Intelligence after the Second World War', *I&NS*, 3, 4 (1988): 103–10.

Thomas, M., 'The Dilemmas of an Ally of France: British Policy towards the Algerian Rebellion, 1954–62', *J. of Imperial and Commonwealth History*, 23, 1 (1995): 129–54.

——, 'France in British Signals Intelligence, 1939–1945', *French History*, 14, 1 (2000): 41–66.

Thompson, P., 'Bilderberg and the West', in Sklar, H. (ed.), *Trilateralism, the Trilateral Commission and Elite Planning for World Management* (Boston, 1980), 174–90.

Thorne, C., 'American Political Culture and the End of the Cold War', *J. of American Studies*, 26, 4 (1992): 316–30.

Thorpe, A., 'Comintern Control of the Communist Party of Great Britain, 1920–43', *English Historical Review*, CXII, 452 (1998): 637–62.

Trevor-Roper, H., 'The Philby Affair: Espionage, Treason and Secret Services', *Encounter*, 30, 4 (1968): 3–26.

Tripp, C., 'Egypt, 1945–52: The Uses of Disorder', in Cohen and Kolinsky (eds), *Demise*, 112–41.

Tsang, S., 'Strategy for Survival: The Cold War and Hong Kong's Policy towards the Kuomintang and Chinese Communist Activities in the 1950s', *J. of Imperial and Commonwealth History*, 25, 2 (1997): 294–317.

van der Meulen, M., 'Cryptologic Services of the Federal Republic after 1945', paper to the Fifth Annual Meeting of the International Intelligence History Study Group, Tutzing, Bavaria, June 1999.

Varsori, A., 'Il Congresso dell'Europa dell'Aja (7–10 maggio 1948)', *Storia Contemporanea*, XXI, 3 (Jun. 1990): 364–80.

Voltaggio, F., 'Out in the Cold: Early ELINT Activities of Strategic Air Command', *J. of Electronic Defence*, 10, 2 (1984): 127–40.

Waddington, G., 'Ribbentrop and the Soviet Union, 1937–1941', in Erickson and Dilks (eds), *Barbarossa*, 7–33.

Wark, W. K., 'Great Investigations: The Public Debate on Intelligence in the United States after 1945', *Defense Analysis*, 3, 2 (1987): 119–32.

——, 'Coming in from the Cold: British Propaganda and the Red Army Defector', *International History Review*, IX, 1 (1987): 48–73.

——, 'In Never Never Land? The British Archives on Intelligence', *Historical J.*, 35, 1 (1992): 196–203.

——, 'British Intelligence and Operation Barbarossa, 1941: The Failure of FOES', in Peake, H. D. and Halpern, S., *In the Name of Intelligence: Essays in Honor of William Pforzheimer* (Washington: NIBC Press, 1994), 499–512.

——, 'Cryptographic Innocence: The Origins of Signals Intelligence in Canada in the Second World War', *J. of Contemporary History*, 22, 3 (1997): 639–65.

Warner, G., 'Eisenhower, Dulles and the Unity of Western Europe, 1955–1957', *International Affairs*, 69, 3 (1993): 318–24.

Watt, D. C., 'Francis Herbert King: A Soviet Source in the Foreign Office', *I&NS* 3, 4 (1988): 62–82.

——, 'Intelligence and the Historian', *DH*, 14, 2 (1990): 199–205.

——, 'Austria as a Special Case in Cold War Europe', in Ableitner, A., Beer, S. and Stavenger W.G. (eds), *Östereich unter alliester Bratzung, 1945–1955* (Vienna: Boulen, 1998), 260–97.

Weightman, J., 'The Best Kind of Conspiracy', *Sunday Telegraph*, 18 Jul. 1999, 13.

Weiler, P., 'The United States, International Labour and the Cold War: The Breaking of the World Federation of Trade Unions', *DH*, 5, 1(1981): 1–22.

——, 'British Labour and the Cold War: The London Dock Strike of 1949', in Cronin, J. E. and Schneer J. (eds), *Social Conflict and the Political Order in Modern Britain* (London, 1982), 146–78.

Weingartner, J., 'War against Subhumans: Comparisons between the German War against the Soviet Union and the American War against Japan', *Historian,* 58 (1996): 557–74.

Welch, D., 'Political Re-education and the Use of Radio in Germany after 1945', *Historical J. of Film, Radio and Television,* 13, 1 (1993): 75–82.

Westerfield, H. B., 'America and the World of Intelligence Liaison', *I&NS,* 11, 3 (1996): 523–60.

Whitaker, P. and Kruh, L., 'From Bletchley Park to the Berchtesgaden', *Cryptologia*, XI, 3 (1987): 129–41.

Whitaker, R., 'The Origins of the Canadian Government's Internal Security System, 1946–52', *Canadian Historical Review,* LXV, 2 (1984): 154–83.

Wiebes, C. and Zeeman, B., 'United States Big Stick Diplomacy: The Netherlands between Decolonisation and Alignment, 1945–9', *International History Review*, XIV, 1 (1992): 47–51.

Wilford, H., 'The Information Research Department: Britain's Secret Cold War Weapon Revealed', *Review of International Studies* 24, 3 (1998): 353–70.

——, '"Unwitting Assets?": British Intellectuals and the Congress for Cultural Freedom', *Twentieth Century British History,* 11, 1 (2000): 42–60.

Yemelyanov, V. S., 'The Making of the Soviet Bomb', *Bulletin of Atomic Scientists,* 43, 10 (1987): 39–41.

Young, J. W., 'Great Britain's Latin American Dilemma: The Foreign Office and the Overthrow of Communist Guatemala, 1954', *International History Review*, VIII, 3 (1986): 573–92.

——, 'George Wigg, the Wilson Government and the 1966 Report into Security in the Diplomatic Service and GCHQ', *I&NS,* 14, 3 (1999): 198–209.

——, 'The British Foreign Office and Cold War Fighting in the Early 1950s', P95/2 (April 1995), *Discussion Papers in Politics*, University of Leicester.

Acknowledgements

Many have given generously of their time to assist me in understanding the workaday life of those engaged in secret service during the Cold War. Over the last decade I have been privileged to speak to many who were engaged on intelligence operations, or who were in regular receipt of their dividends. Sadly, not all of those individuals have survived to see the completion of this project and most would perhaps prefer not to be named here. Their insights, sometimes breathtaking, have changed the way I think about not only the history of secret service, but also the practice of history. I should like to acknowledge this debt first and foremost.

Many other individuals and institutions have offered kind support or commentary on early findings. I would particularly like to thank Matthew Aid, Sue Carruthers, Ian Clark, Michael Coleman, Michael Cox, Oliver Daddow, Philip Davies, Andrew Defty, Anne Deighton, Saki Dockrill, Stephen Dorril, David Easter, Paul Elston, Ralph Erskine, Rob Evans, M. R. D. Foot, Anthony Gorst, Michael Handel, E. D. R. Harrison, Peter Hennessy, Michael Herman, Michael Hopkins, Rhodri Jeffreys-Jones, Matthew Jones, Sheila Kerr, Dianne Kirby, Paul Lashmar, Julian Lewis, W. Scott Lucas, Paul Mercer, Kate Morris, James Oliver, David Painter, Tilman Remme, E. Bruce Reynolds, Len Scott, Anthony Short, Bradley F. Smith, Michael Smith, David Stafford, Stephen Twigge, Wesley K. Wark, Donald Cameron Watt, Hugh Wilford, Neville Wylie and John W. Young. Responsibility for interpretation and errors, however, remains with the author.

Armies of archivists, librarians and departmental record officers – tireless in their efforts – have extended their kindness and cannot all be named here. Pat Andrews, Richard Bone, Duncan Stewart and Heather Yasamee in London deserve a special mention, as does John E. Taylor in Washington. Above all it is the staff of the Public Record Office, overworked and often confronted with an irascible researcher, but unfailingly courteous and helpful, who have facilitated this book. The School of Politics at the University of Nottingham has provided a wonderfully friendly environment during the decade over which this study was written. Georgetown University offered a happy home for a visiting research fellow and I would like to thank Rosamund Llewellyn, David Painter, Nancy Berkoff Tucker and Aviel Roshwald for all their kindness.

Permission to quote from private papers was given by the Liddell Hart Centre for Military Archives and by Lady Avon. Parts of Chapters 11 and 17 appeared in an earlier form in the journal *Diplomacy and Statecraft* and I acknowledge its placet here. Early research was begun under the auspices of an ESRC project in 1992–3. The American dimension was made possible by an American Studies Fellowship supported by the American Council of Learned Societies, the British American Studies Association and the Fulbright programme. Most importantly, a year of study leave supported by the British Academy allowed its completion.

There are a few individuals to whom I owe a particularly heavy debt of gratitude. Andrew Lownie offered crucial encouragement at the outset. Grant McIntyre and his colleagues have been especially supportive and forbearing during a process that has taken longer than we had hoped. C.W. Haigh offered remarkably generous and painstaking advice at a later stage. Christopher Andrew and Wesley Wark have offered continuous encouragement and inspiration. I owe an enormous debt to my family for their forbearance over the years. My children, Nicholas and Harriet, deserve special thanks for their patience when they discovered that their father was again spending the weekend tapping away in the study. As ever my wife Libby offered boundless love, support and sound advice on a project that seemed to have no end.

Index

Combined Command for Reconnaissance
Activities, Korea, 281–6
Combined Intelligence Objectives Sub-
committees, 187
Combined Intelligence Priorities Committee,
237
Cominform, 131
Comint Communications Relay Centres, 403
Comintern , 21–2, 28, 130; traffic, 237
Common Market, 618
Commonwealth, 11; Informal
Commonwealth Conference on Defence
Science 1946, 109; Commonwealth
Investigation Service, 109
Communications Branch of the National
Research Council, Canada, 246
communications security, 246–8, 402
Communist Parties: Australia, 112; France,
121; Great Britain, 24, 92–121, 443–4;
India, 112; Germany, 176; Spain, 40
compartmentalisation, 15
Conferences: Bermuda, 387; Geneva, 429;
London Foreign Ministers 1945, 83;
London Foreign Ministers Conference
1950, 352; Paris 1946, 131; Potsdam
1945, 61; Yalta 1945, 102
Congo, 612
Congress for Cultural Freedom, 139, 449
Congress of Industrial Organisations, 137
containment: of the Soviet Union, 19–21; of
the United States, 10; of a hot war,
10–11; as coercion, 317
control of secret service, 73
Coon, Carleton, 464
Cooper, Chet, 622
Cooper, Gary, 81
Coote, Commander John, 527–8
Copeland, Miles, 477
Cort, Dr Joseph, 451
Cotton, P. F., 241
counter-force targeting, 254
covert air power, 589–91
Cowgill, Colonel Felix, 69
Cox, Al, 301
Crabb, Commander Lionel 'Buster', 521,
523–4
Crankshaw, Edward, 34, 234
Creech Jones, Arthur, 497
Crick, Francis, 220
Cripps, Sir Stafford, 25–6, 31, 34, 47, 127,
214
Croft, John, 237
Crosland, Anthony, 633
Cross, Charles T., 511
Crossman, Richard, 630

Cuba, 607–13; Cuban missile crisis 1962,
539, 618–25; and French intelligence,
621; U-2 flights over, 620
Cultural Relations Department, 122–8
Cunningham, Admiral Andrew, 244
Cunningham, General, 261
Current Affairs Unit, 452
Curries, Sam, 49, 69
cyanide bullets, 434
Cyprus, 567–80
Cyprus Special Branch, 574
Czechoslovakia, 77; coup 1948, 153

Daily Express, 229
Daily Herald, 455
Daily Mail, 183
Daily Telegraph, 133
Daily Worker, 287
Dalai Lama, 134, 599–600
Dalley, Colonel John, 496–8
Dalton, Hugh, 29, 63, 72, 150, 356
Daniel, Admiral Charles: review of atomic
intelligence 419, 564
Darkness at Noon, 133
Darling, Colonel Douglas, 319
Darling, General Sir Kenneth, 576
Davis, John, 498
D-Day, 2, 81, 95, 221, 374
de Gaulle, General Charles, 120, 613–18
de Rougemont, Denis: payments to, 358, 363
De Silva, Peer, 407, 416, 597
de Tassigny, General Jean de Lattre, 298, 516
Dean, Patrick, 523, 537, 551, 557, 582
Deane, Major-General John, 35
deception: and provoking purges, 178; of
Americans, 485–7
defectors, 91–121, 122–42, 194, 413
Defence Intelligence Staff, 221; creation,
564–6
Defence Research Policy Committee, 557–80
Defence Signals Bureau, Australia, 245
Defense Intelligence Agency, 13
Delestraint, General, 198
Dening, Esler, 153
Denmark, 124
Denning, Lord, 631
Department of Forward Plans, 504
Depuy, Colonel Bill, 294
Derbyshire, Norman, 472–3
Deumling, Dr, 477
Director of Central Intelligence, 522
Director of Naval Intelligence: American, 84;
British, 188
'Dirty Bird' programme, 533
Dixon, Major, 71